subject to annual unannounced inspections. Inspectors assess patient care and quality of life. The process includes interviewing a sample of residents (usually 10 percent), reviewing residents' medical records, interviewing staff members, touring the facility, observing interaction between residents and staff, checking to see that medicine is properly administered, and observing dining areas to see if adequate meals are served. Once the report is issued, the facility must take steps to remedy any deficiencies or face loss of certification or even closure.

The disadvantage of inspection reports is that they assess only whether the facility meets the minimal federal standards for nursing homes. The home that provides high-quality care will not be distinguishable from the home that merely meets the minimum standards. Also, the report refers only to a period of a few days when the inspectors were actually on the premises. There is no guarantee that a week or a month later new problems will not develop.

Inspection reports are available to the public. Some states require that reports be posted on bulletin boards in the nursing home; in other states, the state licensing authority for nursing homes will make a copy of the report available on request.

Staffing is another factor to consider in selecting a nursing home. It is a good idea to find out how many hours the medical director is on duty at the home. Sometimes this can be as few as four hours a week, which may be less than ideal. A guideline adopted by some experts in the field is that if a facility has 100 residents, the medical director should be in the home for 10 to 20 hours a week.

The ratio of nursing staff to residents, and the correct mix of nurses, are also important. One recommendation (which is above the state minimum) is that there should be three hours of nursing time available per day for each resident, although not all nursing homes will reach this figure. The nursing staff should comprise registered nurses (RNs), who are licensed to perform a wide range of medical services; licensed practical nurses (LPNs), who provide personal care and may perform some other medical procedures under the supervision of an RN; and nursing assistants or aides, who assist in personal care, with supervision. Ask the nursing home administrators what level of nursing staff is on duty 24 hours a day. How experienced are the nurses? Generally speaking, not-for-profit nursing homes and government-run homes have the highest staff-to-resident ratios, and that includes staff available for therapeutic services as well as nurses.

For Further Information

Bua, Robert N. *The Inside Guide to America's Nursing Homes: Rankings & Ratings for Every Nursing Home in the U.S., 1998–1999.* New York: Warner, 1997. This 850-page volume is an invaluable guide to choosing a dependable, high-quality nursing home. Bua provides up-to-date information and gives readers the tools they need to make the best choices.

Cleveland, Joan. *Everything You Need to Know About Retirement Housing*. New York: Penguin, 1996. Informative and upbeat in tone, this contains well-researched material and some good, commonsense advice about all the available options.

The Consumers' Directory of Continuing Care Retirement Communities. Washington, D.C.: AAHSA Publications, 1997. Lists more than 500 CCRCs, describing fees, services available, con-

tract type, and entrance fee refund options offered. In addition, the directory provides helpful information for the senior evaluating the CCRC concept.

Fox, Richard L., ed. *America's Best Places to Retire*. Houston: Vacation Publications, 1995. Sixty-six places rated, with information about population, climate, cost of living, taxes, housing costs, crime rates, health care, housing options, as well as articles that capture the flavor of each place.

Friedman, Jack P., and Jack C. Harris. *Keys to Buying a Retirement Home*. New York: Barrons, 1991. Two real estate professionals give sound advice on how to select retirement housing that best suits your needs, from independent living to skilled care. Also includes financial advice, as well as a glossary, checklist, and list of state agencies on aging.

Goldsmith, Seth B. *Choosing a Nursing Home*. New York: Prentice-Hall, 1990. Some facts and figures may now be out of date, but this remains an authoritative guide for what to look for in a nursing home, whom to talk to, and how to make the final decision.

Savageau, David. *Retirement Places Rated,* 4th ed. New York: Macmillan, 1995. Ranks and compares more than 180 top retirement areas. Criteria include cost of living, housing, climate, personal safety, service, work opportunities, and leisure living.

Stern, Ken. *50 Fabulous Places to Retire in America,* 2nd ed. Franklin Lakes: Career Press, 1996. Examines factors such as climate, housing, recreation, and health care in 50 popular retirement communities. Easy-to-use format.

tuart, Lettice. *Making the Move: A Practical Guide to Senior Residential Communities*. New York: Avon Books, 1997. One of the most useful books for those who plan to move to a CCRC, ALF, or nursing home. Includes checklists, glossary, and appendices listing useful organizations, including state regulatory bodies and state agencies on aging.

Young, Heather M., and Rheba de Tornyay. *Choices: Making a Good Move to a Retirement Community*. Thorofare, New Jersey: SLACK, 1996. Contains helpful advice on how to make the decision to move, where to move, and the actual process of moving, as well as tips on settling in at a new home and adjusting to the new situation.

Internet Resources

Many retirement facilities have their own sites on the World Wide Web. If you do not know the name of a particular facility, or want to look at a number of communities, select an Internet search engine, such as Yahoo or Infoseek, and search under "retirement housing," "retirement communities," "continuing care retirement facilities," etc.

Useful Web sites include:

Retirement Living Information Center

www.retirementliving.com

Contains many useful pages and links to other sites.

AgeNet Eldercare Network

www.assistedliving.com

Run by a financial services and marketing company specializing in senior care, this site offers a search engine to locate a suitable ALF or other retirement home, tips on how to select one, financial information, and more.

American Association of Homes and Services for the Aging

2519 Connecticut Avenue NW
Washington, D.C. 20008-1520

Phone (202) 783-2242
Fax (202) 783-2255

www.aahsa.org

The Web site of the American Association of Homes and Services for the Aging, a nonprofit organization representing 5,000 not-for-profit nursing homes, continuing care retirement communities, and assisted living facilities. This site includes useful consumer tips on how to select a suitable retirement home. Contains a searchable database of homes and services (for example, you can search for all CCRCs in a certain state, etc.). Also has a list of all accredited CCRCs in the United States. Offers links to related Web sites.

Health Care

By Kate McGahan, CSW, CMC*

Most people think long-term health care means nursing home care, a prospect many seniors regard with some dread. The fact is, only about 5 percent of the current elderly population is receiving nursing home care. The rest are living reasonably healthy, active lives in their own homes, or they're receiving care in the homes of relatives, in assisted living programs, at day care centers or other options. Long-term care really means a wide range of services provided in a variety of settings to assist seniors with their ongoing daily needs.

For some people, it takes a medical crisis to make them realize they should have started to plan much earlier. Have you planned ahead? Who will provide your long-term care and how will you pay for it? Where will you go for help? What if you are unable to express your needs? How will your caregivers know what you want? What steps can you take right now to ensure that everything will be in place when you need it?

The questions can seem overwhelming, but this chapter will help you find the answers. Fortunately, new government regulations have improved the quality of health care delivery under Medicare and Medicaid and sparked innovative private and group health insurance programs. You stand to benefit from these, but the first step is to become fully informed.

Let's begin with where you are today. You may already have a health plan that will meet your needs. If you're shopping around for one, there are more choices for you in health insurance than ever before. As with everything else, the health insurance industry has been growing and changing dramatically to meet the needs of the aging.

Managing Health Care Costs

The process of choosing and using health insurance can be complicated and at times frustrating. Review this chapter, then talk to friends and coworkers about their health plans. Ask your doctor and other professionals which health plans they recommend and why. Then choose a plan that is most relevant to your own situation and your potential health care needs.

You may be able to secure group health insurance through your employer, trade or professional association, labor union, credit union, or another organization. Health insurance is extended to individuals in the group through a master contract, usually without evidence of insurability. With a group of members the insurer can provide more benefits at lower rates than in individual plans. As the policy owner, your employer or association is responsible for premium payments. Your employer may pay the entire premium, or may require some contribution to help cover the cost. The

* Kate McGahan, CSW,CMC, President of Elderplanning Inc., has more than 15 years of experience as a geriatric care manager in Central New York, providing planning and resource services for older people. She is a New York State certified social worker, a nationally certified care manager, and a New York State licensed health and life insurance agent specializing in long term care insurance.

policy covers you and can cover your spouse and your dependent children as well.

If you have to purchase individual health insurance, many companies require that you provide evidence of insurability. Look for a policy that can't be canceled or is guaranteed renewable as long as you keep paying the monthly premiums. That way the insurance company can't disqualify you on the basis of age or medical condition. Though all companies have standard policies for the coverages they offer, most will allow you to select various options or benefits (for example, dental or chiropractic coverage) to create a plan that best meets your needs. In general, this type of plan doesn't cover prescription drugs or preventive care.

Both individual and group insurance policies can be delivered under a fee-for-service or managed care plan.

Fee-for-Service Plans

A fee-for-service plan is exactly what it sounds like: Your policy is based on set fees for services rendered, according to the contractual agreement between the provider and the insurance company. Although this type of insurance is typically the most expensive to buy, it has several advantages:

1. You can choose whatever doctor and health care setting you want.
2. You have easier access to a wide range of specialists.
3. You have a wider range of services and no restrictions on either the number or the length of the visits.

You usually pay your health care provider at the time of your office visit, and your insurer reimburses you if the particular service you received is covered in your policy. You must pay an annual deductible before insurance will cover any costs, and you also pay some portion of the fees (usually 20 percent). You can apply for a fee-for-service (or "indemnity") plan through commercial or casualty insurance companies that specialize in medical and disability insurance.

Even fee-for-service plans, however, may include a certain amount of managed care. You may need to be preapproved for elective admission to a hospital or surgical center. And your doctor's proposed treatment plan may need to be reviewed by the insurance company in a process known as utilization review. Preventive services may not be included, so be sure to check the extent of coverage for such services as annual physicals.

Managed Care Plans

Most Americans are enrolled in some form of managed care program. Alternately praised and criticized, the concept of managed care arose from the need to control costs in the health care system. Managed care programs attempt to control these costs by systematically determining if the treatments, procedures, and hospitalizations ordered for you by health care professionals are necessary and appropriate, and what fees should be charged for those services.

Managed care plans are usually based on a "capitation" system, which may be loosely defined as a system of figuring costs for the plan per "head"—that is, by the number of people covered in the plan. The capitation system allows your insurer to pay your service provider a set fee for your care rather than paying individual fees for services as you use them. It sets a limit on the amount of health care services and coverage that you can receive based on your diagnosis. For

each particular diagnosis, you are allowed a certain treatment protocol. A case manager/reviewer will scrutinize your doctor's requests for tests and treatments, approving or disapproving procedures on the basis of actual need. This scrutiny reduces the number of unnecessary tests and treatments and at the same time prevents fraudulent claims and duplication of services. It also prevents unnecessary hospitalization and reduces the length of hospital stays. The plan works with you and your doctor to coordinate your care, home care, hospice care, or cost-effective alternative treatment that may enhance your quality of life.

The main concerns about managed care have to do with the ease of access to providers, the continuity and coordination of services given the various providers you may have to work with, and the flexibility of the programs.

Health Maintenance Organizations (HMOs)

A health maintenance organization (HMO) is a type of managed care plan. Like an insurance company, an HMO provides coverage for your personal medical care. But besides financing health care services for their subscribers, it organizes and delivers the actual health care services. The plan contracts with independent doctors, hospitals, and clinics—"providers"—to furnish health care services to its members at a lower price than the standard costs for such services. Members are required to seek medical care from this network of contracted providers. They must use only those doctors and facilities associated with their plan.

Your monthly fee allows you to access the specific providers in the HMO network. You also pay a fixed amount (a "copayment") for each office visit. Typically there are no deductibles, and the provider handles the paperwork for you. The plan usually includes preventive care and pays for most other covered services, including prescription drugs. Coverage is extensive, so with a managed care plan you should have no need for supplemental insurance. Be careful, however. If you sign up for a managed care plan and decide to cancel your policy in exchange for a traditional fee-for-service plan, your age and/or physical condition may limit your choice in health insurance policies.

Preferred Provider Organizations (PPOs)

A preferred provider organization (PPO) combines the features of a traditional health insurance plan with the features of an HMO. A PPO also contracts with a network of providers who offer their services at prearranged prices. PPO providers are typically in private practice. They have agreed to offer their services to members of the group at fees that are typically less than what they normally charge. The organization usually takes care of the paperwork for you if you use one of their network providers. Alternately, you can choose a provider from outside the network, but if you do, you'll pay a higher fee. And you'll probably be expected to pay for services at the time of the visit, then submit a claim for reimbursement. Some people choose a PPO because it allows them their choice of physicians and hospitals; it also usually offers low copayments and broader benefits as well.

Getting the Most from Your Managed Care Plan

To find your way through the managed care system, it helps to understand the benefits and claims procedures. Read your entire insurance manual to learn the details of your coverage. Your policy should tell you whether you have a deductible and what it is, and whether there is a lifetime limit on your benefits. You should also know the plan's policy on second opinions and preauthorizations. Many plans require that you get a

second opinion or be pre-approved before treatment can take place, except in an emergency. Know what your policy requires before you enter the doors of a hospital, or your treatment may not be covered. Check also whether your plan covers home nursing care and related services and, if so, exactly what is covered.

Be proactive, not reactive, in matters of health insurance. If you ever need to file a complaint or appeal a decision regarding coverage, you must have the documentation you need to support your case. Maintain accurate records and keep copies of all bills and correspondence filed for easy review. If you make a telephone call related to your insurance coverage, write down the date, the name of the person you spoke with, and the details of the conversation. If your inquiry or appeal is not moving forward, talk to your state insurance commissioner's office to learn how to file a complaint. If necessary, contact your representative in Congress. All senators and House members have staff people who help constituents with health insurance problems.

Other Health Care Support Programs

Medicare

The federally and primarily tax-funded program called Medicare took effect in 1965 as a response to our nation's commitment to provide a national insurance program for the elderly and disabled. Medicare is directed by the Health Care Financing Administration (HCFA) with the help of the Social Security Administration. Under Medicare, health insurance protection is extended to individuals age 65 and over and to certain disabled persons under 65. This includes people who are blind, those who have received Social Security disability benefits for at least 24 months, and those who suffer from chronic kidney disease.

Eligibility for Medicare

If you are 65 (or under 65 and disabled) and eligible for Social Security, you're entitled to hospital and medical insurance coverage under Medicare. Medicare begins automatically, regardless of income, as long as you have been employed or are married to or widowed from someone who was employed.

Coverage starts when you apply for your Social Security (or Railroad Retirement) benefits. Everyone who receives Social Security payments automatically gets a Medicare card at age 65. If you don't qualify for Social Security, you still could qualify for Medicare and should apply for coverage three months before your 65th birthday. You may be able to enter the program by paying a monthly premium or by meeting certain income limits. If you don't receive Social Security benefits because you are still employed, you may continue to use your employer group health plan as your primary insurance for hospital care.

Medicare consists of two portions: Part A, Hospital Insurance, and Part B, Supplementary Medical Insurance.

Medicare Part A (Hospital Insurance)

When you qualify for Social Security benefits, you automatically get Medicare Part A at no cost. Part A provides coverage for inpatient hospital care, post-hospital care in a skilled nursing facility, some home health care, and hospice care for terminally ill patients. In all cases, Part A covers only those services that are medically necessary and only up to an amount deemed "reasonable" by Medicare.

For the first 60 days of hospitalization during any one benefit period, Medicare pays for all of your covered hospital care services, except for an initial deductible. Covered services in a hospital include blood transfusions, lab tests, X-rays,

operating room and recovery room costs, and rehabilitation services. For the 61st through the 90th day of hospitalization, Medicare pays a reduced amount of the covered services. During this time, you are responsible for a daily copayment. Often this copayment may be covered by your supplemental insurance plan, if you have one. This 90-day hospitalization coverage is renewed with each benefit period. A benefit period starts when you enter the hospital and ends when you have been out of the hospital for 60 days.

If you reenter the hospital before the end of a benefit period, the deductible is not reapplied, but the 90-day hospital coverage period is not renewed. However, if you reenter a hospital after a benefit period ends, a new deductible is required and the 90-day hospital coverage period is renewed. You also have a lifetime reserve of 60 days of hospital coverage. If you are hospitalized longer than 90 days in a benefit period, you can tap into the 60-day reserve. The lifetime reserve is a one-time benefit; it does not renew with a new benefit period. If you are hospitalized and need to access your reserve days, you will be required to pay a higher copayment. If hospitalized beyond the 60th lifetime reserve day, you exhaust the reserve and are responsible for all hospital charges.

Part A covers the costs of your care in a skilled nursing facility (for example, a nursing home or rehabilitation facility), as long as you were hospitalized for three consecutive days (not including the day of discharge). You must also meet Medicare's strict criteria for needing true "skilled nursing care." If you do qualify for treatment in a skilled nursing facility under Medicare, you will be covered in full for the first 20 days. From the 21st to the 100th day, you (or your supplemental insurance plan) must pay the daily copayment. Medicare does not cover treatment in a skilled nursing facility beyond 100 days.

To qualify for Medicare's home health services, you must be "homebound" and need part-time skilled nursing services (care that can be carried out only by, or under the supervision of, licensed nursing personnel) on an "intermittent" basis. The home health care agency providing the service must also be Medicare-certified. Home health care is typically allowed for a limited period of time, usually when you are recovering from a hospital or nursing home stay. A prior hospitalization is not necessary to qualify for home care coverage. However, if you order home health services without a doctor's order, you will be responsible for all charges. Keep in mind also that the insurance does not cover nonmedical homemaker and companion services; only those services provided by a trained nursing professional are included.

Medicare Part B (Supplemental Medical Insurance)

Part B insurance covers physician services, diagnostic tests, durable medical equipment (walkers, wheelchairs), health clinic and outpatient services, and ambulance services. Part B is optional and can only be obtained by paying a monthly premium. After you pay an annual deductible, Part B will pay 80 percent of "approved" charges, subject to Medicare's standards.

Unless you specify otherwise, if you receive Social Security benefits, your monthly Medicare premium is automatically deducted from your Social Security check. If you are fully covered under another plan, you can elect to cancel Part B coverage and the Part B premium through your local Social Security office. Otherwise, you may enroll in Part B between January 1 and March 31 of any year after you turn 65, although you may have to pay a penalty for the post-enrollment. If you do not receive Social Security benefits, you can opt to pay quarterly premiums for Part B coverage.

Medicare tries to keep expenses under control by deciding on a reasonable fee for each medical procedure, office visit, and so on. Under Part B, when your doc-

tor accepts Medicare's assigned fee as full payment for a given service (called "accepting assignment"), you pay only the 20 percent copayment. Most providers accept assignment. If your doctor does not accept assignment, you must pay the 20 percent copayment plus the difference between your doctor's fee and Medicare's approved fee.

Medicare covers most reasonable and necessary medical and hospital services but does not cover most preventive care, dental services, long-term care, experimental procedures, prescription drugs outside the hospital setting, or most care received outside the United States.

The Limits of Coverage

Obviously, you must meet a number of strict requirements to qualify for Medicare coverage, so be aware of the criteria. The basic requirements for coverage stipulate that the care that you receive (1) must be reasonable and necessary, (2) must require skilled care, and (3) must be provided by a Medicare-certified agency or facility.

Despite extensive coverage provided by Part A and Part B, Medicare is an insufficient safeguard against the problems of financing ongoing long-term care. The usual expenses associated with long-term care are the less skilled services such as assistance with bathing, eating, dressing, and other daily activities. These services, while expensive, can be performed by someone far less skilled than a doctor or a nurse. Consequently, Medicare doesn't solve all your long-term health care problems.

To compound matters, private insurance plans often base their coverage on Medicare's determination. A person can be admitted to a skilled nursing facility and not need skilled nursing care—only custodial care. If Medicare doesn't pick up these costs, private supplemental insurance companies may also refuse coverage.

The Appeals Process

If you do not agree with a Medicare decision, there is an effective Medicare appeals process in place. Many people do challenge Medicare decisions, and about 70 percent of those who file an appeal do recover some benefits.

Conflicts can emerge especially when hospitals discharge patients earlier than the patients want. To protect patients from early discharge, Congress created the Medicare Peer Review Organization (PRO), a national network of physicians contracted by the federal government to review hospital decisions to ensure that all patients receive proper care.

All Medicare patients receive *An Important Message from Medicare* in their hospital admission information, which explains exactly how the process works. Rarely do we take the time to read these documents until it is absolutely necessary, but it is smart to have a basic knowledge of the appeals process. Medicare requires that hospitals inform patients at least 48 hours in advance of a scheduled discharge. Be wary of physicians or hospitals that want to discharge you prematurely. If you are a Medicare patient and feel that you are not ready for discharge when the hospital says it's time to leave, you have the right to appeal that decision.

During the appeals process, you can remain in the hospital. The PRO is required to review your case and arrive at a decision within three working days after you appeal. If the PRO denies your request, you become liable for all hospital costs starting the third day after you received the hospital's original written notice of your pending discharge.

You may wish to appeal other decisions, such as when a nursing home or home care provider tells you that you do not qualify for Medicare benefits for services provided. Written notice is required in such circumstances. If an institution or health care provider says that Medicare will not cover a specific service or procedure, ask the provider to

submit a claim anyway. This will initiate an official decision from Medicare. You always have the right to appeal any decision that has to do with Medicare.

How Managed Care Fits in with Medicare

Not all managed care companies have contracts with Medicare, but those HMOs that do have contracts receive premiums directly from the government. If you are a member of such a plan, you never have to fill out any Medicare claim forms, you never pay the 20-percent copayment for doctor bills, and you never pay deductibles. You just need to pay your regular monthly Medicare Part B premium, which changes yearly. No matter how ill or disabled you become, your HMO cannot cancel your benefits. One disadvantage of HMO membership is that your choice of doctors is limited to those who participate in the plan.

The Balanced Budget Act of 1997 created an additional Medicare program called the Medicare Plus Choice Program. This pilot program, implemented in December 1998, provides Medicare beneficiaries with a variety of supplemental insurance alternatives, each of which must complement existing Medicare services. These choices include various managed care organizations as well as some creative financial options such as Medical Savings Accounts (see Chapter 3 for more information on these). If you return to a traditional program within 12 months of your first enrollment in a Medicare Plus Choice Plan, or if you move out of the health plan's service area, you are guaranteed the right to obtain Medigap insurance, explained below.

If you are soon turning 65, close to retirement, and currently enrolled in your employer's health plan, you should begin reviewing your coverage. Some retirees have coverage through a previous employer's group health plan and do not need additional coverage. But group health insurance coverage may end upon retirement. If that's the case, under COBRA you have the option to continue in your employer's health plan for a period of 18 to 36 months. COBRA stands for Comprehensive Omnibus Budget Reconciliation Act and is a federal law that gives you the right to continue health insurance coverage if you lose or leave your job. Under COBRA you may have to pay the full premium for your coverage, but you will be charged the group rate, which is considerably less than an individual policy.

Your employer's obligation to provide continuing coverage ceases when you become eligible for Medicare. You will therefore need to investigate new coverages, including Medigap policies. These policies, also referred to as Medicare supplements, are private insurance policies designed specifically to fill some, but not all, of the "gaps" in Medicare coverage.

Medigap Insurance

Medigap is a supplemental insurance plan that pays the cost of premiums, copayments, deductibles, and physicians' bills that exceed Medicare's approved charges. The Omnibus Budget and Reconciliation Act of 1990 (OBRA 1990—not to be confused with COBRA) was a federal law that standardized Medigap policies on a national basis. Regulations established rules for selling Medigap coverage and provided for standardized benefits. Thus, there is essentially no difference between what one company offers and what another offers, so find an insurance agent and company you trust.

When shopping for Medicare supplement insurance, look for a policy that covers as many major gaps in Medicare coverage as possible. These gaps include: (1) Medicare deductibles and copayments, (2) items and services not covered by Medicare, and (3) costs exceeding Medicare's "approved charges." States limit Medigap to 10 standard plans ranging from A to J, although not all insur-

ance companies offer every plan. All 10 plans begin with a core package of Medigap benefits. "A" plans offer basic coverage. The rest of the plans increase in coverage and cost, with "J" plans being the costliest and most comprehensive. Not everyone needs a J plan; be sure to choose a plan that best meets your needs.

If you are not covered by a former employer's health insurance plan and you can afford supplemental insurance, be sure to enroll in a Medigap plan *within six months of enrolling in Medicare Part B*. During this period, you cannot be denied coverage for health reasons. At the end of this six-month enrollment period, insurance companies can increase the price of the policy, refuse to cover you, or attach conditions to the policy.

Medigap policies are an important option, but they are not for everyone. They may not be a good choice if you are nearing the financial eligibility limits for Medicaid, if you are enrolled in an HMO or other managed-care plan, or if your group health plan provides ample coverage.

Low-Income Assistance with Medicare

Many states have developed programs to provide Medicare coverage for those with limited incomes and assets. The Qualified Medicare Beneficiary Program (QMB), also known as the Medicare Buy-In Program, is for people with limited assets and incomes at or below the national poverty level. In this plan the state pays Medicare premiums, deductibles, and copayments.

The Specified Low-Income Medicare Beneficiary Program (SLMB) is for people whose incomes are up to 10 percent above the national poverty level. Under this program, the state pays the Medicare Part B premium only. To qualify for these assistance programs, you generally need to complete an entire Medicaid application. In the process, you may find out about other programs for which you qualify.

Medicaid

Medicaid offers medical assistance to persons of all ages whose income and resources are insufficient to meet the costs of necessary medical care. Since the program was launched in 1965 under Title XIX of the Social Security Act, Medicaid has become the primary source of public funding for nursing home care. The program operates under federal mandates, but each state administers its own program and sets statewide eligibility and coverage standards.

Many people confuse Medicaid with Medicare. Medicaid is not an insurance program. Once you are approved for Medicaid, most medical costs—whether at home or in a nursing home—are covered. The program pays almost all home care costs for part-time skilled nursing care, home health services, and medical supplies and equipment. Custodial and home care coverage may include adult day care, respite care, a transportation plan for medical appointments, and an emergency response system.

Medicaid patients often have limited choice regarding where they can receive care. Most residential care facilities and providers prefer to admit and treat private pay patients. Not all doctors and facilities accept patients who are on Medicaid, although legally they are not allowed to discriminate based on the source of payment. Medicaid pays only for facilities and providers that are Medicaid-approved.

Medicaid Eligibility

There are strict guidelines for eligibility, and the rules vary from state to state. If your income, resources, and expenses fall within your state guidelines, you will be eligible for assistance. Calculating your ongoing medical and health care expenses in relation to your income level is a very important aspect

of the Medicaid application process. After all, the reason you are applying for Medicaid is because your medical expenses exceed your ability to pay for them. You will need to verify your medical expenses and account for your income and assets.

If your income is too high, you may still be eligible for assistance if your medical bills, when subtracted from your income, bring you within the eligibility guidelines. This process of subtracting your medical bills from your income is called a "spend down."

If you require care in a nursing home or residential care facility, Medicaid will come up with a budget for you that sets aside a significant portion of your monthly income to cover the cost of your monthly care at the facility. The program allows you to keep enough of your income to continue paying your health insurance premiums and to provide you with a monthly personal allowance for special expenses such as cable TV, hairdresser services, and the newspaper. If you need Medicaid assistance and you currently reside in your home or apartment, Medicaid will set up a budget for you based on your income and medical expenses. There are laws that protect you so that you should always be able to live within the budget that is designed for you.

Many people are afraid that they will lose their home in the process of qualifying for Medicaid. However, your home will be protected so long as you reside there or have the potential to return there after your period of rehabilitation in a residential care facility. Your home may also be exempt if your spouse or your minor, blind, or disabled child is living in the home, or if an adult child, sibling, or other relative was living with you for an extended period prior to your application for Medicaid and has established residency at that address. In such circumstances, Medicaid will give you an allowance to cover home maintenance costs during your stay at the facility.

Your spouse is the only person whose income and assets are included in the calculation of your eligibility for Medicaid. In general, your combined income and assets are totaled and then divided equally to determine eligibility. However, the Medicare Catastrophic Coverage Act of 1989 introduced the "spousal impoverishment rule," a provision that allows your spouse to keep his or her own income and usually some portion of your income to go toward maintaining his or her standard of living. The "at home" spouse can also keep the home, car, personal belongings, and half of the assets up to a set amount (usually around $75,000). Your spouse has the right to appeal if he or she believes that the resource allowance is so low it will cause a hardship. Some states have a "Spousal Refusal" law which gives your spouse the right to refuse to pay towards your cost of care.

If your health care needs are extensive, regardless of income, you may be eligible for a Medicaid waiver. With a waiver, certain regulations regarding income are suspended to allow you to qualify for Medicaid coverage for those specific health care needs.

Applying for Medicaid Benefits

You apply for Medicaid assistance through your county department of social services. You must prove that you do not have the ability or means to pay for your own medical care. The Medicaid application process has been likened to the IRS's auditing process. First you complete a lengthy questionnaire, disclosing all assets and income, and providing verification and documentation of your assets, income, and personal affairs. Then you are interviewed by a Medicaid caseworker whose goal is to get a "snapshot" of your current situation based on income, resources, and expenses. After all this information is gathered, a decision is made on your eligibility for Medicaid benefits.

Once you are approved for benefits, you'll participate in a Medicaid recertification process at least annually. Recertification determines your continuing eligibility based on a review of your income, resources, and expenses. Your budget is also updated.

Currently Medicaid has a three-year lookback period. This means the agency can research your total financial history three years prior to the date of application. If you have established a trust or changed a deed, the lookback period is five years.

Because of this time frame, advance planning is imperative if you think you may need Medicaid in the future. Proper planning takes time, so start as soon as you can to put your estate plan in place-and before you have a health crisis.

Because the Medicaid application process is complicated, it's a good idea to seek advice from an attorney, geriatric care manager, or agency adviser. Be sure to work with a professional familiar with Medicaid eligibility, the limitations of transfers, and the right to retain income and assets.

Long-Term Care Insurance

Long-term health care is expensive by any standard. One year in a nursing home costs $30,000 to $80,000 per year, depending on your geographic area. Home care can cost twice that much for round-the-clock care. Given these figures, private insurance companies have finally expanded their coverage to close the last remaining gap between standard health insurance and Medicare coverage: long-term care insurance. (See a full discussion of this in Chapter 3).

The marketplace for long-term care insurance is highly competitive, with more comprehensive policies being introduced all the time. Compare several policies to find the one that best suits your needs, preferences, and budget.

Legislation drafted in 1996 states that all long-term care insurance policies must now contain certain provisions in order that their benefits qualify for tax-exempt treatment.

The amounts you receive to cover care are not counted as income, and the premiums you pay on a policy are now tax-deductible up to certain limits.

Minimizing Taxes

Certain of your annual expenditures can be subtracted from your adjusted gross income to reduce the amount of income that is subject to taxation. Medical and dental expenses fall into this category and are allowed as itemized deductions. You may include expenses for yourself, your spouse, and your dependent. Expenses are deductible to the extent that they exceed 7.5 percent of your adjusted gross income. These expenses include: nursing home costs, home health care services, diagnostic and treatment-related expenses for disease, prescription drugs, and certain home improvements made to accommodate people with disabilities. You may deduct the costs of almost any travel for medical purposes, including the cost of having a nurse or companion travel with you to assist with your care during the course of the trip. If your doctor advises you to do something or buy something for your overall health, it's probably deductible.

Keep good records of all your medical and dental expenses. Save all receipts and bills for treatments, medications, eyeglasses and hearing aids, health insurance premiums, and more. Premiums are also deductible and include not only health, Medicare, and Medigap

Shopping for Long-Term Care Insurance: A Dozen Things to Look For

When choosing a long-term care insurance policy, remember that the price of the premium is based on a number of factors: your age, your health, and the type and level of benefits you want covered. Any extra feature will add substantially to the cost. Here are some things to look for:

- *Broad coverage.* Be sure a policy covers a range of services such as home health care, day care, and residential options such as assisted living and nursing home care. Some policies will even allow you to pay a friend or relative to care for you at home.
- *Few restrictions.* A policy should not have prerequisites for coverage, such as specifying that nursing home care be preceded by hospitalization or that coverage is based only on "medical necessity." Your policy should cover you as soon as you have personal care needs that affect your ability to care for yourself independently.
- *Adequate reimbursement.* Most policies pay a fixed dollar amount for each day of covered service that you require, regardless of the cost of that care. The broader the daily coverage, the higher the premium. Compare the daily benefit with the daily costs of nursing homes in your area. There are also policies that offer a "pool" of money rather than a straight daily rate. Borrowing from this fund makes it possible for you to stretch the policy, as you draw on the fund to cover only the specific services you use.
- *Inflation protection.* This is one of the most important features in a long-term care policy. It will dramatically affect the price of the premium, but will allow for long-term rises in inflation, such as what happens when the same nursing home bed that cost $45 per day in 1982 now costs more than $225 per day in 2001.
- *A reasonable waiting period.* Many policies have a waiting period before the policy starts paying. This period may be 30, 60, or 90 days—or more. Buy a policy with the longest waiting period that you can comfortably afford.
- *Waiver of premium.* A policy should include a waiver that frees you from paying premiums while you are receiving long-term care services.
- *Special care coverage.* Be sure there is coverage for dementia and other cognitive diseases such as Alzheimer's disease. Also make sure coverage will be available based on a physician's diagnosis of cognitive impairment rather than on "demonstrable evidence," which generally means "based on a biopsy," which is generally not performed on the brain while a person is alive.
- *Guaranteed renewals.* Almost all long-term care policies are now guaranteed renewable. This means that a company can't cancel your policy unless the premiums aren't paid.
- *Nonforfeiture protection.* If you forget to pay your premium, your policy could lapse. A nonforfeiture benefit would prevent your policy from being terminated for nonpayment. (For example, the policy might stipulate that the insurance company would send the bill to a second party for collection prior to canceling your policy.)
- *Fixed premiums.* Because you're likely to be living on a fixed income, find a policy that has fixed premiums.
- *Potential upgrades.* Upgrades give you the choice to purchase a greater daily benefit or to add a feature that didn't exist at the time you purchased your original policy.
- *A solid company.* Buying from a strong company is essential. Check rating directories such as *AM Best, The Insurance Rating Guide* (Standard and Poor's), *Moody's Investor Services,* and *Duff & Phelps* to make sure the company has one of the highest ratings.

insurance and copayments, but also a portion of your long-term care insurance premium.

Did you know that you can also claim your parent as a dependent on your income tax? In order to take this deduction, you must contribute more than half of his or her total support. If you covered your parent's expenses during the year for drugs, health care, insurance premiums, and the like, check with your tax adviser to see if you're entitled to a dependent deduction.

Medical Savings Accounts

Another creative approach to the high cost of health care is the tax-free medical savings account (MSA). An MSA is like a savings account for medical expenses, but you don't pay taxes on the interest you earn. You then supplement this account with a health insurance policy that has a high deductible to protect you in case of a catastrophic illness or accident. When you need medical care, you use the funds and tax-free earnings from this account to pay the costs of any care not covered by your insurance plan.

Contributions to MSAs may be deducted from income when calculating federal income taxes. Also, you can deduct from your taxable income up to 65 percent of your annual deductible if you are single, or 75 percent if you have a family.

In summary, when researching health care insurance, your goal is to get the best possible coverage based on what is right for you. To get the most from your insurance, know your policies and what they do and do not cover. If you don't follow the rules of your plan, you could be without coverage, even for necessary and qualified care.

As health care costs continue to climb, insurance companies of all types are struggling to keep pace. Some companies are merging and consolidating, while others are increasing or reducing their plan benefits and changing their health care providers. Managed care in particular is attempting to change the health care system as a whole by driving down costs to a "manageable" level.

How to Be a Smart Health Care Consumer

To be a smart health care consumer, you not only need to understand your health insurance alternatives, but also how the health care system operates, and who will be providing services to you.

Three Levels of Medical Care

The concept of a three-tiered medical system has arisen out of managed care. Here's how the three levels differ:

- ***Primary care*** refers to your point of first contact with a health care system, through a provider who oversees all of your medical care. This is usually your family physician, now known as your "primary care provider." While primary care physicians are sometimes in private practice, more frequently you will find them working in group practices or in community health centers or clinics. Primary care may also be provided by physician's assistants and nurse practitioners. The primary care team may also include a nurse or a care manager, nutritionist, or other related professional. More recently, some nontraditional health providers, such as naturopaths and chiropractors, have also offered primary care.

Your primary care provider is concerned not only with your current symptoms and health. Your family history, mental health, work issues,

Who's Who Among Health Care Providers

Here's a brief recap of various health care players and what they do:

Primary Care

- ***Family physicians*** receive the broadest training in primary care. They're concerned with all the medical and psychosocial factors that affect overall health, and their strengths lie in understanding medicine from the broadest perspective. They can treat the entire family and recognize problems that arise from family interactions.
- ***Internists*** can serve as primary care physicians or as specialists. Internists who specialize in fields such as cardiology or oncology often serve as primary care providers for their patients. They have more training and experience than family physicians in dealing with certain types of medical conditions, such as heart disease or cancer.
- ***Osteopathic physicians (DOs)*** provide comprehensive medical care, on the theory that the entire body must be considered when treating disease. They focus on preventive medicine and a holistic approach to diagnosis and treatment, emphasizing the body's ability to heal itself.
- ***Physician assistants (PAs)*** provide diagnostic and therapeutic medical services, always under the direction and supervision of a physician. Most PAs have three or more years of college, with additional specialized schooling and on-the-job training. They can take health histories, perform physical exams and minor surgery, develop treatment plans, and facilitate referrals to health care agencies. In some states, they can prescribe medications. PAs may specialize in specific fields.
- ***Nurse practitioners*** **(NPs)** are advanced practice nurses with education who provide a full range of comprehensive services. Much like PAs, they can assess, diagnose, and treat your general condition as well as educate you and coordinate your care.

Secondary Care Specialists

If you have a debilitating disease or medical condition, your primary care physician will refer you to the appropriate medical or surgical specialist or subspecialist. A subspecialist has completed additional medical training and focuses in a very specific area. The American Medical Association regulates specialty boards that set standards for specialists and subspecialists and confirm a physician's competence in the field. It is becoming increasingly common for physicians to become "board certified" in a particular specialty. Some of the specialists you might encounter include:

- ***Cardiologist***—heart disease
- ***Endocrinologist***—functions of the endocrine glands (including pituitary, thyroid, and others)
- ***Gastroenterologist***—problems of the digestive system (for example, the intestinal tract)
- ***Geriatrician***—diseases of the elderly and problems associated with aging
- ***Gynecologist***—functions associated with the female reproductive organs
- ***Nephrologist***—diseases of the kidney
- ***Neurologist***—disorders of the nervous system
- ***Oncologist***—cancers and tumors
- ***Ophthalmologist***—diseases of the eye
- ***Orthopedist***—damage to the musculoskeletal system; bone, muscle, joint, and ligament problems
- ***Proctologist***—diseases of the anus and colon
- ***Psychiatrist***—mental illness (not to be confused with a clinical psychologist who is a PhD but not an MD)
- ***Radiologist***—radiation and the use of X-rays in the diagnosis and treatment of disease
- ***Rheumatologist***—arthritis and other joint-related issues
- ***Urologist***—diseases of the urinary system and reproductive organs in men, such as the prostate

There are probably many more specialists and subspecialists in your community. Check your Yellow Pages for a complete listing.

and personal circumstances are all part of the picture. Basic primary care may include physicals, immunizations and flu shots, counseling, and screening tests such as mammograms. Your team should ensure that you receive timely, quality care from all pertinent agencies in the health system.

Under managed care, your primary care provider is required to make a referral to any other provider in the plan. You can't go anywhere else in the system (and be covered by insurance) without his or her recommendation.

- ***Secondary care*** is provided by medical professionals with expert training, or specialists. A primary physician will refer you to secondary care providers and specialists when your illness is beyond his or her level of expertise. For example, your family doctor may refer you to a cardiologist for heart care or to an orthopedist to set a broken bone. Secondary care is often provided in hospitals and long-term care facilities.
- ***Tertiary care*** is the most highly specialized level of health care. It is designed for patients who need the highest levels of care, such as intensive care or coronary care. Either a primary or secondary provider may refer you on to this level of care if your medical condition requires a complete team of specialists with advanced diagnostic capabilities. There is often a case manager on the team, because now you probably need ongoing, long-term intervention. The case manager, usually a nurse, coordinates and arranges services for you and ensures that the services you do receive are the most appropriate and cost-effective.

Choosing Your Primary Care Physician

Choosing the right primary care physician is one of the most important decisions you can make for yourself and your family. Remember, you're seeking a "partner" in health care, someone who will help you feel in control, respect your individual needs and preferences, and support your future health care decisions.

In selecting your doctor, consider his or her training and field of expertise. Take a look at the doctor's professional credentials—medical school, residency training, and board certifications. "Board certified" doctors have additional years of training in their specialty. All health care providers are licensed by an agency of the state government, usually called a licensing board or board of registration. If a health care provider has acted negligently or unethically, you can find out through the licensing board.

The doctor's reputation and experience is just as important as his or her official credentials. Talk to other health care professionals. Gather recommendations from family, friends, and colleagues. Gender and temperament may be determining factors for you. You may want a doctor who specializes in geriatrics or who devotes a significant percentage of his or her practice to older patients. Look for a conveniently located office.

A good doctor will schedule time for you to come in and get acquainted. There may be a fee for this visit, but given the fact that good communication is essential to the doctor-patient relationship, such an initial visit can be an excellent investment in your long-term well-being. Come prepared with a list of questions, such as:

- Will you always be available to see me, or will I be assigned to whoever is available on the day I come in?

- What are your professional affiliations?
- Who are some of the specialists you refer to most often?
- At which hospitals do you have admitting privileges?
- Are you available on an emergency basis?
- Who covers your practice during vacations?
- What are the fees for standard treatments?
- Do you accept Medicare assignment?

Making Sure You Receive Only the Care You Want

Now that advancements in medical technology have made it possible to sustain life even when death is imminent, many individuals fear the possibility of being kept alive by artificial means when there is no chance of recovery. The Patient Self-Determination Act of 1991 requires that all hospitals, nursing homes, diagnostic and treatment centers, home health agencies, hospices, and HMOs advise patients of their right to refuse life-sustaining treatment and to establish advance directives. An advance directive is a written document that states your choices for health care and/or designates someone to make those choices for you if you become unable to make your own decisions.

Decisions regarding medical treatment are deeply personal and should reflect your values, personality, and beliefs. You have the right to refuse medical treatment even though that treatment may be necessary to preserve your life. In many states, the only way to maintain control over your treatment is to put your wishes in writing. A description of your wishes or any evidence of planning on your part can provide much needed guidance.

There are several common advance directives. They include:

- *The Do Not Resuscitate Order* (DNR): Although not a legal document, the DNR is a doctor's written order that instructs medical personnel that you do not want heroic measures taken in the event that you go into respiratory or cardiac arrest. Doctors address this issue with their patients during routine visits and update the order on a regular basis.
- *The Health Care Proxy* (also known as a *Durable Power of Attorney for Health Care*) is a document that permits you to designate another adult to make health care decisions on your behalf if you are unable to make your own decisions. This document guarantees your right to self-determination and to express this right through another chosen adult.
- *A Living Will* is a document that allows you to indicate the kind and extent of life-prolonging medical care you would or would not want if you were dying or in an irreversible condition and could not communicate. It's particularly important to document your specific wishes regarding artificial nutrition and hydration, because if there is no documentation, or if your wishes cannot be reasonably determined, your agent may not have the authority to make decisions regarding these particular extra measures.

The rules for living wills and health care proxies vary from state to state, so again, it pays to consult a local attorney. You can't legally sign these documents if you are incompetent. That is why you need to plan ahead, discuss your preferences with your relatives and doctors, and sign these forms while you are clearly competent. Discuss your preferences and your decisions with your family and physicians and provide them with copies of any documents you've

signed. An advance directive will do you no good if no one knows you've signed one.

Where to Get Help and Information

The rules regarding health insurance and Medicaid can vary from state to state. The advice and professional services of your primary care physician, a geriatric care manager, an attorney who specializes in Medicaid and estate planning, and a trusted insurance professional can help you create the best possible long-term health care plan for yourself and your family.

Here's a list of organizations that can help you get the assistance you need:

AARP (American Association of Retired Persons)

(800) 424-3410 or (202) 434-2277

www.aarp.org

An educational and lobbying organization with local chapters and many membership benefits; a good source for printed materials.

Partnership for Dying

(800) 989-WILL

www.partnershipforcaring.org

Counseling and information on advance directives.

ELDERCARE Locator

National Association of Area Agencies on Aging

(800) 677-1116

www.n4a.org/locator.cfm

A resource that can put you in touch with virtually every state and county office on aging and a wealth of useable local information.

Medicare Hotline

Health Care Financing Administration

(800) 633-4227

www.Medicare.gov or *www.hcfa.gov*

Information on Medicare, Medigap, state insurance, and the reporting of Medicare fraud.

National Association of Professional Geriatric Care Managers

(520) 881-8008

www.caremanager.org

Referrals to regional geriatric care managers.

National Council on Aging

(202) 479-1200

www.ncoa.org

Information and referral to local services; training programs and research.

National Insurance Consumer Helpline

(800) 942-4242

Information on health, home, life, and government insurance.

National Library of Medicine at the National Institutes of Health

(888) 346-3656

www.nlm.nih.gov

Health-related information.

People's Medical Society

(610) 770-1670

www.peoplesmed.org

Monitors the practice of doctors, nurses, and hospitals; provides information on patients' rights and how to file a complaint.

Other important Web sites:

www.hmopage.org
Information on HMOs and managed care.

www.asaging.org
American Society on Aging.

www.aoa.gov
Administration on Aging.

Retirement Income and Finances

by Kate McGahan, CSW, CMC*

Retirement is no longer a brief period between an active, working lifestyle and death. Indeed, many Baby Boomers will spend as much time in retirement as they did in their careers. It's an ideal time to start a business, further your education, or pursue activities that you've always wanted to do. But none of these goals can be realized if you don't have the financial wherewithal to pay for them.

It's never too early to start saving for retirement and to create a sound financial plan to help you reach your goals in later life. As a first step, you need to develop a retirement budget that includes your cost of living, with inflation and the ever-rising cost of long-term health and disability care factored in. You also need to know what you can expect from Social Security, your employee pension, any individual retirement accounts, and your savings and investments. To complete the picture, you have to understand the role of insurance, how you can make the best use of your assets to create a diverse portfolio, and how you can pay as little tax as possible.

This chapter discusses all the most popular retirement income options and provides basic information that can point you in helpful directions. It doesn't go into great detail, however, because the laws on personal financial planning vary from state to state. Your personal circumstances will also dictate the right combination of options for you. Use the information you find here as a starting point, and consult a qualified financial planner to help you with your financial strategy. The resource list at the end of this chapter will help you locate appropriate planning professionals.

Government Programs

Social Security, Supplemental Security Income (SSI), and veterans' benefits are all designed for use in retirement. Here's what you should know about them.

Social Security

The Social Security Act was passed in 1935, following the financial hardships of the Great Depression. The idea behind the Social Security system is that, in exchange for paying federal taxes during your working years, you and members of your family are eligible to receive monthly benefits when you retire or become disabled. Social Security payments are intended to *supplement* your savings and pensions, not to be your sole source of income.

Over 90 percent of seniors receive Social Security benefits. Those who are not covered include federal employees covered by their own Civil Service Retirement System, employees of state and local governments that have retained their own retirement programs, railroad workers covered by railroad retirement programs, household workers, farmworkers, self-employed people who may not earn enough to be covered,

---

* Kate McGahan, CSW,CMC, president of Elderplanning Inc., has more than 15 years of experience as a geriatric care manager in central New York, providing planning and resource services for older people. She is a New York State certified social worker, a nationally certified care manager, and a New York State licensed health and life insurance agent specializing in long-term care insurance.

and a very small number of individuals whose work (for example, family employment) does not meet the requirements established by Social Security law.

Qualifying for Benefits

To qualify for benefits, your wages must have been earned over a period of time when you were simultaneously paying into the Social Security system. The higher your earnings were, the higher your benefit amount. Benefits usually are adjusted yearly to allow for cost-of-living increases.

To get an official statement of your approximate retirement benefits based on your earnings thus far, contact your local Social Security office and request Form SSA-7004. This form tells you how much you can expect when you retire and provides an estimate of the amount of benefits you and your family would be entitled to should you die or become disabled. As of 1999, the Social Security Administration sends annual benefit reports to every worker age 25 and older.

Applying for Benefits

According to the latest *Guide to Social Security and Medicare* (29th edition), the official retirement age has been adjusted according to your year of birth. The minimum age is 65 (for those born before 1937), and the maximum age is now 67 (for those born after 1960), according to the following table:

Year of Birth	Full Retirement Age
1937 or earlier	65
1938	65 and 2 months
1939	65 and 4 months
1940	65 and 6 months
1941	65 and 8 months
1942	65 and 10 months
1943–1954	66
1955	66 and 2 months
1956	66 and 4 months
1957	66 and 6 months
1958	66 and 8 months
1959	66 and 10 months
1960 and after	67

Social Security benefits do not come to you automatically at full retirement age. You must apply for them at your local Social Security office. Apply at least three months before you reach retirement age. In 2001, the maximum monthly benefit for retirees age 65 was $1,536.

You may choose, however, to retire early, at age 62, with reduced benefits, or you may delay your retirement past your official retirement age. If you don't collect Social Security benefits until you're beyond retirement age, you'll receive significantly larger monthly checks when you do start collecting. (For each month you postpone collecting benefits, your retirement benefit increases by a certain percentage based on your age.) And if you keep working beyond retirement age, the wage base on which your benefits are calculated will continue to increase, giving you an even larger benefit.

As you weigh the decision whether to start collecting benefits at age 65, consider your health, your level of job satisfaction, and your tax liability. Remember also that your earnings may reduce your benefits if you choose to collect Social Security while continuing to work.

Effects of Other Income

Generally income that is not "earned" income will not affect your Social Security benefits. Income that doesn't affect earnings may come from stock dividends, interest, retirement pensions, veteran benefits, annuities, capital gains, gifts, and rental income. If you are receiving, or expect to receive, Social Security benefits, your earned income could reduce your benefits. Earned income sources include wages, commissions, tips, and other forms of payment in exchange for services. In 2001, the maximum allowable earned income under age 65 was $10,680. Be sure to investigate how pursuing income-related activities will affect your benefits.

When you work, you must repay Social Security some or all of the benefits you receive if your earnings exceed the allowable limit (which changes annually). For example, you will have to pay approximately $1 for every $3 of "excess earnings" in the form of taxes. If you are under 65, you will pay approximately $1 for every $2 you earn.

Family

Social Security will cover certain dependent family members of a retired worker. Your spouse may be eligible if he or she is (1) age 62 or older or (2) under 62 and caring for a child who is either 16 years of age or younger or disabled. Your unmarried children are eligible if they are still in high school and are 18 years of age or younger. A traditional married couple of retirement age receives two Social Security checks. A wage earner and a homemaker spouse receive benefits based on the wage earner's earnings history, plus an additional 50 percent for the spouse.

Survivor Benefits

A husband and wife will both receive Social Security benefits each month. In the case of spousal death, the benefit check received in the month of death for the deceased spouse must be returned to the Social Security Administration, along with a copy of the death certificate. This will initiate coverage for the surviving spouse, who will receive one check equal to the deceased's or the survivor's standard amount—whichever was higher. This means that if the husband was the primary breadwinner with the higher Social Security monthly benefit and he dies, his wife will forfeit her benefits and receive his monthly benefits for the remainder of her life. The survivor will also receive a small one-time lump sum death payment.

Survivor benefits can be paid to the following people if you die:

- your spouse if 60 years of age or older (full benefits at age 65) or if between 50 and 60 years of age and disabled;
- your spouse of any age if caring for your child, who is disabled or is 16 years of age or younger;
- your unmarried children under the age of 18 if they are enrolled in an elementary or secondary school full-time;
- your children over 18 if disabled or still in high school;
- your dependent parents, age 62 or older, if they depended on you for half of their support at the time you died or became disabled.

Taxes on Social Security Income

Most people who collect Social Security do not pay taxes on their benefits. However, as mentioned above, the effects of other income in addition to your Social Security income can mean up to 85 percent of your benefits being subjected to federal income tax. A portion of your benefits may be taxable in any year in which your adjusted gross income plus your nontaxable interest income and one half of your Social Security benefits exceeds a specific amount. The IRS can provide you with a form to help you determine how much, if any, of your benefits are taxable.

Disability Benefits

Most people think that the federal Social Security program is just a retirement program. Social Security actually offers other protections as well.

In addition to the disability-related benefits available through Medicare, the federal government also provides disability assistance to eligible Social Security beneficiaries. Disability benefits paid through Social Security are designed to replace your earnings if you can no longer pursue "substantial and gainful employment" due to a medical impairment.

If you become disabled, file for disability benefits as soon as possible. If your application is approved, you'll receive monthly assistance beginning in the sixth month of your disability. The amount of your monthly payment takes into consideration other benefits or compensations you may be receiving (for example, worker's compensation). Your benefits will continue until your condition improves or until you return to work. In some cases, after receiving these benefits for a period of two years, you may be eligible for Medicare Part A, even if you are not yet 65.

If you qualify for Social Security disability benefits, your spouse will also be entitled to benefits based on your earnings record. In order to qualify, your spouse must be (1) 62 years of age or older or (2) under 62 years of age and caring for a child who is either age 16 or younger or disabled. Your children who are still in elementary or high school can receive benefits until they reach age 18, or until any age if disabled before age 22.

Supplemental Security Income

Supplemental Security Income (SSI) is provided under a federal program that guarantees a minimum monthly income to individuals who are 65 and over, blind, or disabled and who lack the income and resources to provide for their own needs. SSI was enacted by Congress in 1972 as the first federal program to ensure the economic security of America's neediest individuals. The program is administered by the Social Security Administration, and benefits are paid out in the form of an additional monthly check. If you don't qualify for Social Security benefits, or if your benefits are very low, you may qualify for Supplemental Security Income. SSI supplements your income to raise it to the poverty level. Benefits can vary from state to state based on added funding. If you meet the eligibility requirements, you may also automatically qualify for Medicaid coverage and for food stamps benefits. Although the program makes monthly payments to people who have few resources and little or no income, it is possible to own a home, a car, and personal belongings of reasonable value and still receive SSI benefits. An individual may have assets of up to $2,000 ($3,000 for a couple), a home where the applicant lives, a car worth $4,500 or less (or a car of greater value if required for employment or medical treatment), and a burial fund/life insurance policy (with a face value of up to $1,500.)

Veterans' Benefits

The Department of Veterans' Affairs (VA) was established in 1930 to create and administer the many government programs for veterans who have had honorable or general discharges from military service. There are three types of benefits available to every older American who has ever served in the armed forces, or to his or her spouse and dependents:

- health care that includes a variety of programs such as comprehensive dental and medical care in outpatient clinics, medical centers, and nursing homes around the country;
- disability compensation and pensions provided to any veteran whose disability was caused by or aggravated during his or her military service;

- burial entitlements including cemetery plots, markers, flags, and financial compensation at time of death.

If you are the surviving spouse of a veteran, you may also be entitled to a pension.

Military veterans are entitled to retirement pay after 20 years of service. The formula used to compute benefits varies, depending on when you entered the military, your length of service, and your age at retirement. Full benefits begin immediately upon retirement and continue until your death. If you are a military retiree, the Military Survivor Benefit Plan allows you to have a portion of your retirement pay withheld to provide a benefit to your survivors. Any veteran who has had 90 days or more of active miliary service and is permanently and totally disabled for reasons unrelated to the military may also be eligible for support, if he or she has limited income and is unable to defray the cost of care elsewhere.

Employer-Employee Programs

Pensions

Many people rely on Social Security and their company pension as their major sources of retirement income. Traditional pension plans base your retirement benefits on your salary and your length of service with the company. In this type of pension, your employer makes the contributions and manages the plan. Most pension plan funds are invested with mutual fund companies or managed by professional money managers. Typically, you have to work until age 65 to qualify for the maximum pension benefit, although your employer may allow you early retirement with reduced benefits.

If you do have a pension plan through your employer, find out what your benefit is worth. By law, in accordance with the requirements of ERISA (Employee Retirement Income Security Act of 1974), your employer should provide you with a summary description of any ERISA-qualified pension or profit-sharing plan and update that summary from time to time. (Note that government pension plans are not covered by ERISA; they are managed by their plan administrator.) Your employer should also provide a pension benefit statement indicating the amount and type of deferred vested benefit to which you are entitled. These pension documents outline the policies governing your pension and will be helpful to you in planning for your retirement.

Unfortunately, pension plans are no longer as secure as they used to be. We live in an age when corporations merge, dissolve, go bankrupt, or get taken over by competitors. Some companies in financial straits are forced to modify existing plans, reducing pensions previously promised to employees. In short, there are no absolute guarantees that your pension will be there for you when you need it.

If a company pension plan is a key element in your retirement income strategy, be sure to research your plan and, if necessary, seek professional guidance.

The Costs of Early Retirement

Many companies offer middle-aged staff members attractive incentives to retire early. Early retirement has many advantages and one very obvious drawback: the loss of income generated by your employment. Consider, of course, what will make you happy, but keep in mind that if you take early retirement:

- *You will probably need to pay your health insurance premiums* at the employer group rate until you turn 65 and are covered by Medicare.
- *You will decrease your overall retirement pension benefits.*
- If you take an early lump sum distribution from a pension or profit-sharing plan, *your withdrawal will be subject to a 20% withholding tax* unless you roll over the funds into a qualified plan or IRA.

And if you didn't feel the pinch of rising inflation while you were working, you certainly will feel it once you are retired and living on a fixed income. In short, unless you plan to take on a new job, start a new business, or somehow continue to build your cash reserves, you are probably better off working longer, accumulating more resources for your future.

If you are considering an early retirement package, first create a budget that reflects what it will cost you to live the way you want to in retirement. Then enlist the help of your financial and legal advisers, your employee benefits office, and your local Social Security office to help you understand the offer and determine whether you can afford to accept it.

Claiming Your Pension

If you participate in a qualified pension plan, payment generally begins no later than 60 days following the close of the plan year in which the *last* of the three following events takes place: (1) you reach retirement age 65, or earlier if the plan specifies a normal "retirement age"; (2) you have completed 10 years of participation in the plan; (3) you separate from service with your employer.

You can start drawing your pension at age 55 (or younger in some plans), but you can't receive a lump sum payment until age 59½ without rolling it over to an IRA unless you accept a substantial tax penalty. If your plan allows you to roll over the funds to another qualified plan, you may want to consider doing so.

Pensions can be claimed in one of two ways. Many plans allow you to take a lump sum distribution of the value of your retirement benefit and roll over these funds into an individual retirement account (IRA) within 60 days to avoid taxes and/or penalties that may apply if you have not reached age 59½. (This 60-day limit only applies if you actually take possession of the money. You can leave money in a 401(k) for as long as you want after you leave a job.)

Your other choice is to take a payout option that will guarantee you monthly payments at retirement age. These monthly payments can be spread out over your lifetime, or you may choose to receive a smaller monthly payment in order to allow the payments to continue after your death to cover the life of your surviving spouse. Once you make this decision, you can't change it.

Taking Your Pension Before Standard Retirement Age

Some companies, particularly those that are downsizing, offer employees attractive severance packages as retirement incentives. These packages may allow employees to retire as early as age

55 with lesser benefits, perhaps reduced by only 20 to 30 percent, or at age 55 with a certain number of years of service with no reduction in benefits. Some people choose to take this reduced benefit while supplementing it with another job or self-employment. If your pension plan offers early retirement benefits, be sure to determine whether those benefits are full or reduced benefits. You may want to delay your retirement until you reach normal retirement age to receive the full amount.

Many people use a company pension plan as a tool to save for retirement. If you have been making your own contributions into any qualified pension plan on a regular basis, you've seen your investment grow. When you collect your pension early, however, substantial income taxes may also be due, biting into your earnings. You can postpone paying those taxes until you may be in a lower tax bracket by rolling over the distributed funds into an individual retirement account (IRA).

Before accepting a severance package, review the figures and terms of the offer with your accountant. Talk to a financial planner, especially when you're making a career transition. If you mishandle your employee retirement account, the resulting taxes and penalties could seriously affect your lifetime savings.

Individual Retirement Accounts (IRAs)

Whether or not you are covered by an employee pension, you may want to establish an individual retirement account (IRA). These are popular tax-deferred retirement plans that can be established under the age of $70^1/_2$. Created by the federal government in 1981, IRAs granted a special tax-deferred status to encourage people to save for retirement. If you qualify under current tax law and meet certain income requirements, the money you set aside each year to fund your IRA ($2,000 maximum) is deducted from your gross income on your federal income tax return. What's more, while your money is growing, you don't have to pay taxes on the accumulating investment. Your tax payments are deferred or postponed until you withdraw the money at retirement. With a deductible IRA, every dollar coming out at retirement is subject to tax—not just on the interest growth, but on the total amount. However, with a nondeductible IRA, only the interest, growth, or earnings on your contributions are subject to tax.

Once you invest in your IRA, these funds are essentially locked up until you reach age $59^1/_2$. Retirement income benefits may be withdrawn *without penalty* anytime between age $59^1/_2$ and $70^1/_2$. There are stiff penalties for both the premature and the delayed withdrawal of funds from your IRA. If you withdraw funds prior to age $59^1/_2$, these funds are taxed as ordinary income, *plus* you may also be subjected to a 10 percent penalty tax, unless you are taking systematic equal periodic payments. These eliminate penalties on distributions before age $59^1/_2$ (specific rules apply). At age $70^1/_2$, you must start to withdraw funds from your IRA to avoid the risk of a 50 percent tax on those funds.

There are two exceptions to these restrictions. The Kennedy-Kassebaum Health Insurance Portability Law of 1996 makes it possible for you to avoid the penalty on premature withdrawals if the money you withdraw is used to pay medical expenses that exceed 7.5 percent of your adjusted gross income. If you are not employed or if you are self-employed, you can also take money out of your IRA to buy health insurance and to purchase a home for the first time. There's a $10,000 limit on that withdrawal.

As part of your overall financial plan, try to determine your future IRA benefits. Remember that there are contribution limits if you're covered by a retirement plan at work (single, $31,000 to $41,000; married, $51,000 to $61,000). There's no limit if you're not covered under a retirement plan.

The Roth IRA

The Roth IRA, created by the Taxpayer Relief Act of 1997, is a tax-deferred, non-tax-deductible individual retirement account. You can invest up to $2,000 a year in a Roth IRA only if you have earned income, but there are income restrictions. Not everyone qualifies for a Roth IRA.

Even though you pay taxes on the income you contribute to the Roth, you are not taxed on the accumulated interest, dividends, or capital gains. Qualified distributions are not taxed in certain states. A qualified distribution is one that is made:

- after you reach age 59$^1/_2$;
- upon your death to your beneficiary;
- after you have become disabled, or
- if you need the funds to buy your first home or pay educational costs.

Paying taxes up front may be difficult, but worth it if you prefer greater after-tax income in the future.

Many people appreciate the flexibility of the Roth IRA. There is no mandatory withdrawal at age 70$^1/_2$ as there is with traditional IRAs. But you must take distributions from a Roth IRA you inherit if it's not from your spouse. Your contributions, being made with after-tax dollars, can come out any time. But earnings in less than five years and withdrawn before age 59$^1/_2$ are taxed and penalized. Earnings in less than five years and withdrawn after age 59$^1/_2$ are taxable at the regular federal income tax rate, but are not penalized. Some exceptions apply.

Other IRAs

You should also know about some other specific types of IRAs:

- *Rollover IRAs* allow individuals who have received a distribution from a qualified plan to reinvest the funds in a new tax-deferred account and continue to shelter those funds and their earnings from current taxes. You can name anyone as your beneficiary and, with some restrictions, that person can receive the disbursement tax-free.
- *Educational IRAs* can be useful for grandparents, for example, who wish to set up funds for their grandchildren's college education.
- *Spousal IRAs* (both traditional and Roth IRAs) are possible for nonworking spouses with the same $2,000-a-year limit.

Keogh Accounts

Keogh accounts, created in 1962 under the Self Employed Individuals Retirement Act, allow unincorporated business owners to participate in and benefit from a qualified retirement plan, just as their employees are able to do. You must be self-employed with earned income to participate.

The money you contribute to your Keogh plan is deducted from your gross income, and the taxes on this money are deferred until you withdraw funds from the plan, presumably in retirement. If you have employees, you must provide the plan to them as well, and you must contribute the same percent to their plan as you contribute to your own. There is a penalty of 10 percent if you take withdrawals before age 59$^1/_2$, or before age 55 if you leave or close your business. When you reach age 59$^1/_2$, you can withdraw funds without penalty and the Keogh is treated much like an IRA. Unlike the IRA, however, you can continue making tax-deductible contributions so long as you continue to have income from your self-employment.

Simplified Employee Pensions (SEPs)

A Simplified Employee Pension (SEP) is an IRA designed for small businesses of 25 or fewer employees. SEPs were introduced in 1978 specifically for the purpose of facilitating retirement accounts for small business owners and their employees. If you are self-employed or work part-time, you as an "employer" can contribute to your own SEP, but there are limitations to plan contributions. "Employer" contributions are not included in the "employee's" gross income.

401(k) Plans

A 401(k) plan is a tax-deferred qualified employer retirement plan set up by an employer for the benefit of his or her employees. Under this plan, you, as an employee, can elect to take a reduction in your current salary and contribute that portion to a retirement plan. The amount is deducted from your taxable income. Your employer can opt to contribute to this fund on your behalf as well. Many companies contribute their company stock to 401(k) plans.

The 401(k) is designed for your retirement, so there is a stiff penalty if you choose to withdraw funds before age of $59^1/_2$. Funds can sometimes be accessed due to hardship (for example, death, disability, separation from service, or termination of the plan) but must be redeposited within a certain time frame. You must take distributions by April 1 following the year you turn $70^1/_2$. When you withdraw money from this account after you retire, you will be taxed on both the principal and the interest/investment earning gained.

If you change jobs, arrange for your former employer to transfer the balance in your retirement plan directly to your new employer's plan or to a rollover IRA. When you roll funds over and then take income as needed, you are much further ahead than if you withdraw a lump sum. If you leave your workplace and receive a lump sum distribution, you have 60 days after receipt of the funds to roll over the amount from one 401(k) plan to another, or to an IRA. Be careful whom you name as beneficiary; there are legal, tax, and personal considerations if you name someone other than your spouse.

Alternate plans for teachers and not-for-profit employees are annuity plans called 403(b)s. These plans offer similar features, but are simply administered differently because of the specialized characteristics and tax implications of the particular business entity.

Annuities

An annuity can serve as a flexible tax-deferred retirement plan to help you meet your long-term goals. You may be able to choose a qualified annuity or an individual annuity, which is also known as a nonqualified annuity. *Qualified annuities* are funded with pretax dollars and have contribution limits. They can only be funded with earned income and they have required withdrawal rules. *Nonqualified annuities* are funded with posttax dollars. They have no contribution limits and can be funded with income from any source.

Annuities allow you to choose when you want to receive income. *Immediate annuities* will allow you to start receiving income right away, while *deferred annuities* let you build the account for years to provide income in the future. Immediate annuities require a single lump sum payment, and then you can begin to draw on the funds within 13 months. The time period for when you receive funds and the dollar amount is specified in the contract. Deferred annuities give you the opportunity to build savings over a period of years and draw on those funds during retirement. You also have choices regarding the type of earnings you want. *Fixed annuities* produce level payments. *Variable annuities* provide a variable payout based on the investment risk you want to take.

Earnings in all types of annuities compound tax-deferred until you take money out. If your annuity has been purchased through a salary reduction plan, or is a qualified annuity, you will usually have to take withdrawals beginning at age $70^1/_2$. Non-qualified annuities can allow for tax deferral for a longer period of time, but each insurance company has its own required distribution age, so read the contract carefully. With most annuities, the principal is guaranteed if you die before you begin regular withdrawals. This is referred to as the guaranteed death benefit. If you annuitize your withdrawals, you are guaranteed lifetime income.

Qualified plans offered by employers must have the same eligibility rules for all employees. Most firms have a one-year waiting period before you can begin to contribute.

Individual Assets

Personal Savings

Do you have enough money in the bank for emergencies? Ideally, you should have ready cash that will cover your personal expenses for at least three to six months. Familiarity and predictability motivate people to keep their liquid assets in guaranteed bank accounts. Be careful, however, not to leave too much money in a checking account or in a day-to-day savings account with no opportunity to earn interest. If you keep your money in the bank, divide your assets, perhaps using a three-tiered approach, keeping just the minimal amount of money in your savings and checking accounts (perhaps two to four weeks' coverage), dividing the rest first into a money market account, then moving about half of that into certificates of all types.

As you know, banks and savings and loan companies offer different types of savings plans. These plans offer depositors a number of short-term investment opportunities that provide liquidity and flexibility. Money market funds offer attractive interest rates and keep your funds accessible to you whenever you need them, but they may have annual fees. Compare the net annual yield to the alternatives. Certificates of deposit (CDs) carry penalties for early withdrawal, but the bank guarantees the rate of return and your principal is guaranteed by the FDIC. If you do not need your money for a couple of months, look into a no-risk CD or a U.S. Treasury Bill, both of which can earn you a higher rate of interest than a traditional savings account.

Another type of certificate that's being used more these days is the stock market certificate. Unlike other certificates, your interest rate isn't locked in—it's tied to the performance of the S&P 500 and your specified percentage of participation in market gains. Your principal is guaranteed, and the term is 12 months. This type of certificate has the potential to yield greater returns over the long term.

Many older individuals prefer to put their savings into institutions which provide full guarantees, even if these insti-

tutions offer a lower return on investments. You have to do what is most comfortable for you, but be knowledgeable about your investment decisions.

Beware of losing money "safely." Low bank returns *minus* inflation and taxes can actually mean a loss for you. If you're getting only 2 percent interest, but facing, for example, 2 percent inflation and a tax bracket of 28 percent, you're certainly not getting ahead.

There are countless ways to invest your personal savings. You can keep money in the bank, you can invest in stocks and mutual funds, real estate, corporate, municipal, and Treasury bonds, life insurance, and more. Once you have secured funds to meet your basic living needs (housing, insurance, and an emergency cash fund), you can think about investment planning.

Investments

Inflation is the biggest enemy we face. If your investments are a significant factor in your retirement income and if earnings on those investments do not surpass the rate of inflation, you may not have enough income to support yourself adequately in retirement.

Many people in their 60s, 70s, and 80s are highly conservative in their investment portfolio. They are afraid of stocks and growth funds because of their volatility. These seniors aren't thinking "growth," but they should be. According to the U.S. Census Bureau, 50 percent of those turning 50 in 1997 can expect to live to 100. Since we are living longer, we have to adjust to the possibilities that go with it.

Do what you can to keep your money growing for you. Keep a diverse portfolio. This means you should spread your investments among different classes of assets (for example, stocks, bonds, and cash equivalents), so that they work together to help balance your risk, build your capital, protect you from inflation, and weather market downturns.

Get a new perspective on investing by meeting with a financial adviser. This professional will review your age, health, and lifestyle to help you develop an investment strategy that meets your cash flow needs and reflects your personal degree of risk tolerance.

Mutual Funds

Mutual funds can provide you with a type of diversity by spreading your money out over a number of stocks or bonds at once. Certain funds are made up of just stocks or just bonds, but most represent an assortment of stocks, bonds, and other securities that are owned by a group of investors and managed by a professional firm. What appeals most to people who buy mutual funds is the professional management of the funds, plus the diversification of investments that they might not otherwise be able to afford. Mutual funds are not risk free, but they at least diversify the risk. You avoid the specific risk associated with owning individual stocks and bonds, namely, sharp declines in the price of the particular stock or default of the individual bond without the benefit of counterbalancing securities.

Your financial adviser can help you choose the proper mutual funds for your portfolio, and you can do some research on your own by reviewing any number of publications, such as *The Morningstar Report, Investor's Business Daily, The Wall Street Journal, Money, Kiplinger's, Fortune,* and *Forbes*. It's wise to invest in fund managers that have been around for a while and have a proven track record.

Some mutual funds will let you make investments by arranging to have money transferred automatically from your bank account on a regular basis; some funds can arrange payroll deductions to establish an automatic savings plan. You can choose to have dividends and capital gains from the fund directly reinvested or take the dividends and capital gains as income. Note that if you reinvest your

Choosing Your Team of Advisers

Financial planning for retirement is not an event; it is a process. It requires solid knowledge about law, financial forecasting, insurance, taxes, and long-term care options. It is unlikely that any one person has all the knowledge, skills, and experience to handle the job alone. Therefore, it makes sense to assemble a carefully chosen team of advisers. Where do you start?

Ask friends, relatives, and associates—as well as lawyers, accountants, and insurance agents—to suggest a good financial adviser. If you're assisting your aging parents, try to sit down with an objective professional whose only goal is to meet their long-term needs. Get the entire family together to talk. Once you have the outlines of a possible long-term plan, you should consult a few specialized professionals to examine the strength of each aspect of the plan. Talk to a geriatric care manager for advice on long-term care and care providers and how to finance these options. A conference with your parents' insurance or pension advisers will give you a better understanding of assets available through their life insurance policies, IRA, and pension funds. Check with an accountant to minimize the tax bite of any financial decisions.

Before you enlist the services of a financial planner, ask questions about his or her investment policy. What are the charges, and what services do these charges cover? Be wary of advisers who have particular affiliations that may bias their investment advice. Check their credentials and look for integrity, reputation, competency, and experience with Medicaid and with long-term care options and planning issues. Various professionals may be qualified to advise you, including the following:

- A ***certified public accountant*** (CPA) has extensive training, has passed rigorous professional exams, is licensed by the state, and can help you anticipate the tax consequences of your financial decisions.
- An ***attorney (J.D.)*** well versed in estate, elder law, and tax-planning issues can help you in any of these areas.
- A ***personal finance specialist*** (PFS) is a CPA who has passed a personal finance planning exam.
- A ***certified financial planner*** (CFP) has completed a two-year course in financial planning and has passed a 10-hour exam to prove competency. A CFP can help you select investments that will maximize your income and can manage your assets in a way that will help you achieve your personal goals.
- A ***chartered financial consultant*** (ChFC) is usually an insurance professional who has focused on financial planning issues and has passed a series of exams.
- A ***chartered retirement planning counselor*** (CRPC) has passed an exam focusing on helping individuals plan for retirement. The designation, issued by the College for Financial Planning, is generally sought by financial service professionals, though others will benefit from the course work.
- A ***certified retirement counselor*** (CRC) has also passed an exam focusing on helping individuals plan for retirement. This designation, issued by the International Foundation for Retirement Education (InFRE), is generally sought by human resource/employee benefits professionals, though others will benefit from the course work.

dividends and capital gains, you will still be taxed on them, even though you don't actually receive any money in your hands. It will increase your tax basis in your investment, so you need to keep track of all reinvested amounts. Watch out when buying funds close to the end of the year. If you invest just before the year-end dividends and capital gains are paid, you will be taxed on them as if you had been in the fund for a long time. Your fund value may not change, but you will have a taxable event for which you must pay taxes, even if you just invested in the fund.

Making the Most of Your Assets

In most states there are equity-based financing options for home-owning seniors who are "house rich" but "cash poor." If your home is paid off, but you don't have much money in the bank, you may be able to take advantage of programs that offer various home loan plans, sales plans, and deferred payment plans. Consult your financial adviser and attorney before taking out any type of loan.

Home Equity Loans

Almost all states have a home equity loan or conversion mortgage program that allows you to borrow against the equity you have built up in your home. A home equity loan can free up cash for home improvements, health care costs, or other living expenses. You can arrange for monthly guaranteed payments or draw on the equity amount as a line of credit. Most home equity loans allow you to borrow up to 75 percent of the value of your home and deduct the interest you pay on your loan from your taxes. (Some allow you to borrow up to 100 percent.)

Home equity loans make sense if you really need to have the money, but be sure your loan is federally insured. The HUD home equity conversion program guarantees that you may continue to live in your home until you relocate, sell your home, or die. You cannot be forced to sell your home to pay off the mortgage. If you do not specifically have a HUD conversion loan, you could lose your home completely if you fail to pay off your equity loan.

Reverse Mortgages

Reverse mortgages are mortgage loans that work in "reverse." Under a standard mortgage, the borrower sends the lender a check every month to pay interest and reduce debt. With a reverse mortgage, the lender (or bank) sends the borrower (you) a check every month. You are basically getting cash payments "borrowed" or drawn from your equity in the home, which is decreased as payments are made. You gain cash income as your equity is put to work for you. In most cases, a reverse mortgage can be paid either as a lump sum or in monthly installments. Some reverse mortgages will defer "repayment" of the loan until your death or until you sell the house. Again, avoid any reverse mortgage that is not insured by the federal government.

Sale-Leasebacks

A leaseback is another option that will convert your home equity into cash. A sale-leaseback allows you to sell your house to a third party and enter into a lease that states that you may rent the house for as long as you wish, usually for life. You go from owning your home to renting your home, without moving. Be sure to consult an experienced real estate lawyer before entering into a leaseback agreement.

Life Estates

Life estates have been referred to as "the poor man's trust." If you have real property, the deed for that property can be put in the names of your children (or other chosen individuals), yet allow you to retain use of the property during your lifetime. In effect, your property has two concurrent owners. You get life use of the property, which automatically goes to the other owner(s) when you die. Life estates can be used for purposes of Medicaid and estate planning.

Charitable Remainder Trusts

This option is for those who are charitably inclined and who have sufficient assets. A charitable remainder trust, created as a result of the 1969 Tax Reform Act, allows you to convert highly appreciated assets with a low cost basis into a more productive income-producing arrangement, all without incurring capital gains tax on the appreciation. You place the asset into a trust that provides income during your lifetime; upon your death, the capital that remains in the trust goes to a charity tax-free. You are literally giving away your assets to avoid capital gains and to gain a tax benefit. A charitable remainder trust can eliminate capital gains tax, estate tax, and gift tax. The trust also qualifies the giver for an income tax deduction.

An estate-planning attorney can help you structure the trust properly.

Insurance Coverage

Life Insurance

The primary reasons for having a life insurance policy in your retirement years is to help provide for your dependents in the event of your death, pay your estate taxes, and generate liquidity to pay off your debts. Life insurance can be a creative and important financial tool in the overall estate planning process due to its unique financial and tax advantages.

There is a vast array of life insurance plans designed to serve various functions and meet different needs.

Term insurance, the least expensive and simplest type of plan, insures you only for a specified period, or "term." At the end of the term, the protection expires and you can extend the coverage if you wish. As you get older, term insurance gets more expensive and eventually is not a choice available to you when you become elderly.

Whole life insurance combines insurance protection with a savings or accumulation element. Your policy retains a cash value ("surrender" value) which builds over the life of the policy. Interest is credited to the policy on a regular basis and grows over time, tax-deferred. If you have a whole life policy and live to age 100, the full-maturity cash value of the policy (in lieu of the death benefit) is paid to you tax-free and the policy terminates. If you are buying whole life insurance for estate planning purposes, you need to realize that you may have only the cash value, not the full amount of insurance, for your estate. (Some policies, however, do have extended maturities beyond age 100.)

In most cases, however, life insurance benefits pass directly on to your beneficiary income-tax-free. However, depending on how the policy is structured, the proceeds paid at death may be included in your estate for federal estate tax purposes.

Life insurance is protected from creditors. You can use the accumulated cash value of your life insurance policy to purchase an annuity or fund a loan. You can also take a loan from the value of your policy or use it to help pay your estate taxes.

Universal life insurance allows for decreasing annual premiums and changes in death benefits.

Variable life insurance lets you choose which investments (such as stocks) you want, rather than being limited to a fixed account. This type of policy has the potential for a tax-deferred savings vehicle.

Survivor insurance, also known as "second-to-die" insurance, insures two lives, paying benefits after the second death. The death benefit is income tax–free, and heirs can use the benefit to pay estate taxes. The policy may actually have lower premiums than two individual policies on each spouse.

Take time to review your life insurance coverage. Many people have a number of life insurance policies purchased years ago, some fully paid up, others still on a premium-paying basis. If the total death benefits exceed what you might reasonably need, you may wish to discuss the possibility of surrendering policies that are no longer needed. Before you take this step, read the conditions carefully. Consider your reasons for cashing in any insurance policy, and find out if the benefit will be taxed or if the infusion of capital will affect your potential Medicaid eligibility. Unless you have a life insurance agent who is proficient in estate planning, don't purchase life insurance without checking with your estate planner.

Disability Insurance

While life insurance is necessary for those with dependents to protect, disability insurance is an option for almost anyone who relies on earned income to survive and provide for their family. Statistics prove you are more likely to suffer a disability during your working years than to die. If you become disabled by an illness or accident and are unable to work, you will need some form of income to cover your living expenses and to pay for extra expenses related to your disability (doctor visits, in-home care, and so on).

Disability income insurance is designed to provide you with a guaranteed flow of income while you are disabled. The benefits are usually paid monthly. Of course, the higher the monthly benefit you desire, the higher your premium will be. Premiums are based on your age, overall health status, occupation, and the special provisions of your policy. These provisions will specify the elimination period (the number of days that must elapse after you become disabled and before you can begin to collect benefits) and the duration of the benefit (how long you can collect benefits). Make sure you understand all the provisions of your policy. For example, some policies will pay if you can't perform the duties of your own occupation, while others will deny benefits if you can perform the duties of any occupation, even if you will earn much less than what you were trained for and had been doing prior to your disability.

With few exceptions, your disability benefit will be less than your regular income. If you work for a moderate-to-large-sized employer, you probably also have group long-term disability insurance that replaces more than 50 percent of your income. Remember that if your employer pays the disability premium, your benefits are taxable, but if you pay the premium with dollars that haven't been tax-sheltered, they're tax-free. If you are unable to work because of a disability, your financial and insurance plans should work together to help you get the care and rehabilitation services you need to regain your independence.

To purchase private disability insurance, you need to contact an insurance company and agent whom you trust to determine the scope of income benefits that will be best suited to you. Policies will often exclude preexisting conditions related to conditions such as war-related disabilities or self-inflicted injuries. The company will gather complete historical medical information and arrange for you to have a complete physical and interview to determine whether or not it will cover you and, if so, what your status and premium will be based on your risk for disability.

Long-Term Care Insurance

Long-term care (LTC) insurance can help you meet the staggering costs associated with chronic disability or catastrophic illness. When physical or mental illness, whether acute or chronic, impairs your ability to perform the basic activities of daily living—such as eating, toileting, bathing, dressing, and walking—LTC insurance may help cover the ongoing costs of home health care, care

in a skilled nursing facility, day care, and assisted living programs. While some policies offer a resource "fund," most policies pay an indemnity that provides a set amount per day for home care, nursing care, or other care options.

Long-term care insurance has been available for over two decades, but only recently became a trusted and accepted way of providing for long-term care needs. The Health Insurance Portability Act of 1996 introduced new industry regulations and provided incentives designed to encourage seniors to purchase private insurance of this type. One incentive is a provision that allows you to deduct a portion of your premiums from your federal taxes as a health care expense. Certain limitations exist.

LTC coverage could be described as a cross between health insurance and disability insurance. It supplements the limited long-term care benefits paid by traditional health care insurance (if any) and the very restricted long-term care benefits paid by Medicare. Policies are more reasonably priced and more flexible than ever before. Prices vary, depending on the type of plan, the age of the buyer, and any preexisting health conditions that might increase the chance of a claim. An 80-year-old person in good health will pay more than twice the premium of a 65-year-old in similar health. If you are too old or too sick, you may be unable to qualify for LTC coverage at all.

If your present health and your family history lead you to believe you may one day be a candidate for long-term care, and you can't depend on a network of informal caregivers, think about investing in long-term care insurance. Premiums can be expensive, but even the most expensive premium is nominal compared to the cost of the services and care provided under the plan. At younger qualifying ages, the average annual premium for LTC policy is often less than the cost of one month of care in a skilled nursing facility. Nevertheless, because this insurance has a substantial cost, only those with adequate income should invest in LTC policy. A good rule of thumb is that LTC insurance should not cost more than 5 percent of your total income.

See Chapter 2 for a list of factors to consider when shopping for an LTC policy. The sooner you investigate your options, the better.

Some states offer "partnership policies" that bring together the public and private sectors in an attempt to meet long-term care needs. These partnership policies are intended to help you maintain your financial independence by allowing you to share the responsibility for your long-term care needs with your "partner," the state system. These policies can be good for people who have many assets but lower incomes. Under such a plan, once you exhaust the benefits of your policy (usually three years of coverage in a nursing home, six years of home care), you are automatically eligible for Medicaid without regard to your assets.

If partnership policies are available in your state, you can obtain one through any local LTC insurer. Of course, this is an area where you will want a professional to advise you and help you determine whether a partnership policy is a good option for you. You may want to consider rearranging your assets and income to get the most from your income before you need long-term care.

Tax Breaks for Older People

Most states offer exemptions to individuals age 55 to 65. People over 65 are entitled to a tax credit, as well as a higher standard deduction, and may qualify for tax-relief programs which vary from state to state. These state and local tax-relief provisions can include exemptions for disability retired pay,

military retired pay, and utilities taxes. Some states have additional exemptions for real property taxes. If you are 65 or older and on a limited income, taxes may exclude up to 50 percent of the assessed value of your residence. You must apply for these exemptions; they will not be automatic.

The government gives us tax incentives to encourage us to care for our aging parents. If you are supplying financial support for an aging parent or other relative, or caring for a dependent family member in your home, you are entitled to an exemption as well as a dependent care credit. This dependent might be a child, a spouse, or a parent who looks to you for caregiving and financial support. If you contribute to your aging parent's medical expenses, you can deduct this amount on your income tax if you itemize your deductions.

Until 1999, tax law stated that if you sold your primary residence, you were required to buy a new home of equal or greater value, or pay tax on the difference. For those over age 55 the IRS provided a one-time capital gains exclusion of up to $125,000 for the sale of the home. New tax law allows a tax-free capital gains exclusion of $250,000 for a single person, or $500,000 for a married couple if they have lived in the home as their primary residence for two out of five years, regardless of age.

If you are considering relocating to a new state for your retirement, investigate your options from a cost-of-living and tax standpoint. Look into state income taxes, property taxes, sales tax, and estate taxes. Some states have no income tax but will tax you in other ways, such as on the amount you have in stocks and bonds ("intangible assets"). Don't lose sight of the fact that relocating to a new state is a major decision. Make your choice based on how you want to live your life as well as on your potential net worth.

Handling the Finances of an Aging Parent

Many middle-aged people find themselves in the position of needing to deal with many financial responsibilities—adapting to employment transitions and downsizing, planning for their own retirement, paying for their children's education and wedding expenses—and possibly also assuming the cost of long-term care for their aging parents. It has been said that some Baby Boomers may end up spending as many years caring for their aging parents as they did caring for their own children. If you are in this situation, welcome to the Sandwich Generation.

It may be difficult for you to bring up the subject of long-term care with your parents, but it's important for you to know in advance whether they expect to be able to take care of themselves or whether they will need your help or assistance from government programs. If they haven't done much planning, it may not be too late for them to make some important decisions that can significantly improve their situation. At the very least, they should address the issues of financial and estate planning and put the following in place: advance directives, a new or revised will and testament, and a power-of-attorney document. Discuss these matters with them and know where the relevant documents (all the above, plus insurance policies and financial statements) are filed. You may be the one who has to make decisions for them one day; you'll want to know their wishes to make informed decisions.

Tread gently when you raise the subject of money with your parents. Families can be complicated by nature, and a frank discussion about finances is almost certain to make some members of the family uncomfortable. Older people in particular perceive money as deeply con-

nected to issues of control, independence, and dignity. It may help if you explain that planning in advance will actually give them *more control* over their future, because they will be making the financial and personal decisions that will shape their retirement.

Try to encourage your parents to take every step to maximize their financial security, but in the end, you must respect their decisions. Understand that they may be coming from an entirely different perspective. If your parents grew up in the Depression, for example, their view of saving and spending money may be vastly different from yours.

For Further Information

American Bar Association

(800) 285-2221; (312) 988-5522
www.abanet.org
Information and referral to local bar associations.

American Institute of Certified Public Accountants

(888) 777-7077; (212) 596-6200
www.AICPA.org
Information, referrals, and publications related to financial planning.

Certified Financial Planner Board of Standards

(303) 830-7543
www.cfp-board.org
The agency that licenses certified financial planners.

Department of Veterans' Affairs

(800) 827-1000
www.va.gov
General information about veterans' benefits and eligibility; regional referrals.

Financial Planning Association

(800) 322-4237; (404) 845-0011
www.fpanet.org
Information and referrals.

Institute of Certified Financial Planners

(800) 282-7526
www.fpanet.org
Information and referrals to certified financial planners in your area.

Internal Revenue Service

(800) 829-1040 for tax information; (800) 829-3676 for publications and tax forms
www.IRS.gov

Association for Financial Counseling and Planning Education

(614) 485-9650
www.afcpe.com
Information and links to other sites.

National Academy of Elder Law Attorneys

(520) 881-4005
www.naela.org
Information and listings of certified elder law attorneys.

National Foundation for Credit Counseling

(800) 388-2227
www.nfcc.org
Information on home equity loans, reverse mortgages, other financing options.

Pension Rights Center

(202) 296-3776
www.pensionrights.com
Legal guidance and information.

Securities and Exchange Commission

(202) 942-8088
www.SEC.gov
To get background information on a financial adviser or to file a complaint.

Social Security Administration

(800) 772-1213

www.SSA.gov
For general information, to check benefits, to change your address.

The Society of Financial Service Professionals (formerly American Society of Chartered Life Underwriters and Chartered Financial Consultants)

(800) 392-6900

www.financialpro.org
Information on how to select an adviser, plus referrals to professionals in your area.

Legal Concerns

By Charles M. Sprock Jr., Esq., with contributions from Benjamin D. Levine, Esq.*

If you're retired or just thinking about retiring, you have unique legal concerns. At this time of your life, you need the law not only to protect your assets, but also to ensure your rights.

If you've worked hard and saved wisely all of your life, you may have accumulated some wealth. Your estate needs management and protection, so you need to be familiar with laws governing estate planning, estate administration, estate taxes, and powers of attorney.

You also have to be vigilant in other areas. As grossly unfair as it is, older Americans are very likely to experience age and disability discrimination, consumer fraud and other scams, loss of control over health care and financial decisions, loss of their estate assets due to poor planning or lack of planning, and even a loss of control over funeral arrangements.

The good news is that there are protections in place for Americans who are in or approaching retirement. There are laws that protect your assets for the next generation, and laws that ensure that your health care wishes will be carried out by the person of your choice. Other protections can save you from fraud, discrimination, and loss of rights.

The bad news is that too many people don't take full advantage of these protections. Why?

- **They don't set forth their business and health care directives in the right way**—that is, in the way recognized under the law. You have the right to manage your own affairs (personal, business, and health matters), and to appoint others to carry these wishes out for you. But your wishes won't be carried out unless you set them forth, along with the name of the person you wish to fulfill them, in the proper legal document.
- **They don't structure their taxable estates in the best way to minimize taxes**. Although you can leave your assets to whomever you choose, this right has no value if everything you own is consumed by estate taxes and administrative fees.
- **They don't know exactly what to do if they've been "taken."** Most people realize when they're victims of discrimination or fraud, but they do not know how to bring an action to seek a remedy.

This chapter discusses these legal issues facing retired Americans, including estate planning, age and disability discrimination, and consumer fraud. It also defines and

---

* Charles M. Sprock Jr., Esq., is an associate with Rifken, Frankel & Greenman, P.C., Syracuse, New York, where he practices in the areas of asset protection planning, probate, estate administration, domestic partnership, and real property. He also writes on issues related to estate and tax planning for older Americans.
Benjamin D. Levine, Esq., a partner in Rifken, Frankel & Greenman, P.C., is an expert in asset protection planning, elder law, probate, trusts, and estate administration. He has lectured extensively on issues related to long-term care planning and Medicaid law.

analyzes estate planning tools such as wills, revocable trusts, and irrevocable trusts in plain language. Finally, it tells you how you can use the law to meet your goals and protect your legal rights.

Remember, however, that this chapter is a description of options, not legal advice. It's not a substitute for legal counsel. Since everyone's situation is different, and laws differ from state to state (and are always changing), you need to seek legal counsel for your own unique situation.

Estate Planning

This section will cover two major topics: asset management planning (making decisions about the distribution of your estate upon your death, as well as the use and management of your assets while you're alive) and asset protection and health care planning (setting forth your wishes for your medical treatment and care in the event that you can't make these decisions at the time of your injury or illness). In the event that you do not make your own estate plan, your state laws will most likely direct how your assets and health care will be managed. But be aware—many people find that their state's plans for their asset distribution and health care are not the plans that they would have made for themselves.

Asset Management Planning and Protection

A successful asset protection plan is one that reaches the goals you set and meets both your needs and the needs of those you love. With this in mind, you should know what your goals are, and what assets you have available with which to reach these goals.

A successful plan also involves teamwork. Your team should include a financial planner and an estate planning attorney. Your financial planner can help you select various financial products such as mutual funds, annuities, life insurance, and long-term care insurance that you will use to accomplish your goals. The estate planning attorney can guide you through the selection process of various estate planning tools that will protect your assets for the goals that you've set. Your financial planner and attorney should have experience in estate planning for older Americans, and be able to provide solid references. You should feel you can trust them, because you'll be sharing all of your personal and financial business with them. Chapter 3 lists several organizations that you can consult for references on financial planners and estate planning attorneys.

Goal Setting

Your goals should drive the entire asset planning process, so first try to draft them in a format that will be clear for you, your financial planner, and your attorney. Write down exactly what your wishes are and the beneficiaries of those wishes. For example, everyone should have as one of his or her goals "maximizing the enjoyment of my assets for my benefit during my lifetime." A goal like this lets your attorney and/or financial planner know what your goal is and who benefits from it. Some other goals that many people in or approaching retirement have are:

- providing a comfortable life for my spouse/life partner;
- helping my disabled child lead a comfortable life;
- giving a gift to my church or some other charity at my death;
- paying as little as possible in estate taxes;
- leaving my grandchildren money for their education;

- protecting the family business, so that it doesn't have to be sold when I die;
- making sure that the person I live with is able to keep our house;
- saving enough money to cover home medical care if I ever need it;
- buying a condominium on a golf course in the South where I can spend the winters;
- traveling the world with my life partner while we are both young and healthy.

When sharing these goals with your financial planner and attorney, give them background on the beneficiaries of your goals. This will help them choose the tools that will maximize the recipient's gift. For example, if a disabled child is receiving government benefits, a direct distribution from you or your estate could jeopardize the child's benefits. A child with substantial income or assets already may not want a direct bequest because of the tax consequences to his or her estate. Someone with a credit problem or someone who is experiencing marital turmoil will need protections that other beneficiaries may not. If your attorney and financial planner know these situations, they can help you accomplish your distribution goals by planning around the circumstances of your beneficiaries.

Since most married couples hold their assets jointly, have similar goals, and have a desire to provide for each other, they should do their goal setting and the rest of their estate planning together. Joint planning can also reduce estate taxes. For similar reasons, if you have a life partner or other individual with whom you share these goals and desires, you should set your goals and make your plans with him or her.

As you write down these goals, you may appear to have competing objectives. Don't let this stop you. Write down all of your goals and put them in order of importance to you and your spouse/life partner. You, your planner, and your attorney can work together to balance these objectives, and to determine which of these goals you can accomplish with the resources available to you.

Who Will Carry Out Your Plan?

While setting the goals for your asset protection plan, keep in mind that you will have to choose someone to carry out this plan. In most estate planning instruments, this person is known as a "fiduciary." Your spouse/life partner is a likely choice to carry out your plan, since he or she is most likely the beneficiary of that plan. Along with a fiduciary, you should choose an alternate fiduciary. This protects your estate in the event that:

- your fiduciary dies before you, and you die before you have a chance to amend your asset protection plan;
- your fiduciary suffers an injury or illness and isn't able to act on your behalf;
- your fiduciary dies on or about the same time that you do.

Your fiduciary and alternate fiduciary should be comfortable with financial matters, able to work with the members of your financial team, and trustworthy.

Identifying Your Assets and Liabilities

After you set your goals, identify what assets you can use to meet these goals and what liabilities may prevent you from reaching these goals. On the following page is a sample worksheet that will help you list those assets and liabilities.

When you're completing this worksheet, use today's fair market values for the assets rather than the amount for which you purchased them. These present-day values will be useful to you and your planners when calculating how your assets will help you meet your goals. It's also important to identify the name in which you took title to the asset.

Total Net Estate

ASSETS	
Residence	$
Vacation Home	$
Furnishings	$
Automobiles	$
Jewelry and Art	$
Real Estate	$
Stocks	$
Mutual Funds	$
Life Insurance w/Cash Value	$
IRA, SEP, or 401(k) Accounts	$
Business Interests	$
Face Amount Certificates	$
Annuities	$
Bank/Credit Union Accounts	$
Certificates of Deposit	$
Other	$
TOTAL ASSETS	$

LIABILITIES	
Home Mortgage	$
Other Mortgage(s)	$
Auto Loans	$
Other Loans	$
Charge & Credit Card Accounts	$
Other Debts	$
TOTAL LIABILITIES	$
NET WORTH	
Total Assets	$
Less Total Liabilities	$
TOTAL NET WORTH	$
NET ESTATE	
Net Worth (from above)	$
Life Insurance Death Benefits	$
TOTAL NET ESTATE	$

Monthly Budget

INCOME	
Salary	$
Pension Benefits	$
Social Security	$
Dividends	$
Interest	$
Rents	$
Bank/Credit Union Accounts	$
Certificates of Deposit	$
Investments	$
TOTAL INCOME	$

EXPENSES	
Rent/Mortgage	$
Insurance Premiums	$
Taxes	$
Loan Payments	$
Credit Card/Installment Payments	$
Utilities	$
Food/Clothes	$
Medications	$
Auto Repair/Transportation	$
Misc. Expenses	$
TOTAL EXPENSES	$

TOTAL MONTHLY INCOME	$
TOTAL MONTHLY EXPENSES	$
TOTAL MONTHLY SURPLUS/DEFICIT	$

This will help you and your team members determine how assets will be distributed at your death, and what the estate tax consequences of the distribution will be. On a separate page, you may wish to list a description of your individual assets in one column and the names in which you took title to the asset in another. You should also list any tenancy language or other restrictions on the property. Here are a few examples of some assets and the ways they are titled:

Property	Title	Fair Market Value
2-unit house, 123 Main St. Our Town, USA	John Doe & Mary Doe, tenants by the entirety	$100,000.00
100 shares of common stock ABC Corp	John Doe and Mary Doe joint tenants	$56.50/ share; $5,650.00 total
LifeCo Term Life Insurance Policy #987654321	Life Insured: Mary Doe; Owner: Mary Doe; Beneficiary: John Doe	coverage: $50,000; cash value: $10,000
1996 Acme Sedan	Mary Doe	$7,000.00

If you're unsure as to the title or vesting of the asset, or its value, list the asset and let your planner and attorney know what further information you need. They may be able to find the answers.

This information on your existing assets is very basic and preliminary. Don't be surprised if after you create this list, your financial planner and attorney request even more information. Try to keep in mind that they are not "prying," but rather trying to be as thorough as possible to make sure that they're protecting your goals and assets. The information that you and your estate planning team compile will be a great help to your future fiduciary. Make sure this financial information is stored with your estate planning documents.

Estate Taxes

Once you, or you and your partner, have identified your assets and liabilities and reviewed the information with your estate planning team, you'll have a rough idea of your estate value. If you're like most older Americans, you'll probably be surprised that you've accumulated such a large estate. Your estate value is the important number that your estate planning team will use in determining whether your estate will be subject to estate taxes.

The federal government and several states impose estate taxes. These taxes are usually based on the value of the decedent's estate and are charged against the estate before any distributions are made. Under the changes in the Taxpayer Relief Act of 1997, the value of estates exempt from federal estate tax increases through 2006. Many states that impose estate taxes have decided to increase their estate exemption amounts as well. The table below sets forth the new exemption amounts.

1997	$600,000	2002	$ 700,000
1998	$625,000	2003	$ 700,000
1999	$650,000	2004	$ 850,000
2000	$675,000	2005	$ 950,000
2001	$675,000	2006	$1,000,000

These changes are a great help to many Americans. A person whose house is paid for, who has saved for his or her retirement, and who has other assets is likely to have a $600,000 estate, so this new legislation has saved many estates from paying any estate tax. By 2006, you will have to have a million-dollar estate to incur any estate tax.

Estate taxes cut into the available assets for surviving partners and other beneficiaries of your estate. Your attorney and financial planner will work with you to determine if your estate will be subject to estate tax and, if so, how to reduce the tax as much as possible. If you're married, they also help you determine if a part of the tax should be paid when one of you dies and a part when the other dies.

Setting your goals, choosing your fiduciaries, and gathering your financial information are the first steps in the asset protection process. The next step is sharing this information with the rest of your team. Once your financial planner and attorney know your goals and assets, they'll be able to help you select from the various financial products and estate planning instruments that will best work for you.

Financial Products

We'll be discussing the use of financial products in estate planning here. If you're unclear on the definition of any of these products, consult Chapter 3, "Retirement Income and Finances," which discusses these products in detail. The emphasis here is on how these products are taxed, how they are used during your lifetime, and how they will pass to your beneficiaries at your death.

The following list of products and their benefits is not intended to be exhaustive-it's merely a sampling of some financial products that you may already own or want to discuss with your financial planner and attorney.

Tax-Deferred Retirement Investment Vehicles

These products, which include 401(k)s, 403(b)s, traditional IRAs, Keogh accounts, and SEPs, serve two purposes:

1. *They give you a specific account in which to invest for your retirement.* They often yield great returns given the length of your investment, the reinvestment of dividends earned, and the growth in value of the stocks in these funds. With 401(k)s and 403(b)s, some employers even match your contribution in whole or in part, which sweetens the incentive to contribute.
2. *The money you contribute and the income generated from this investment are not taxed until they're withdrawn.* Since most people generate less income in their retirement years than in their working years, retirees are likely to be in a lower tax bracket than they were while they were employed. So when they draw their tax-deferred earnings from these accounts, they pay less tax than they would have had the tax been paid at the time the money was earned.

Most 401(k)s and 403(b)s allow you to designate an account beneficiary who will receive the balance of the fund at your death. If that beneficiary is your lawful spouse, then he or she does not pay any tax on the money until he or she draws on it. If the beneficiary is anyone other than your spouse, the tax consequences can be very severe. Unlike a spouse, the nonspouse may be required to withdraw the money within five years after your death. How the withdrawals are made will depend upon various factors such as the rules of the company managing the account, the choices you have made for the account, and your age. Your financial adviser and/or attorney can review with you the specifics of your retirement account to help you maximize the benefit of the account for your beneficiaries.

Without careful planning, needless taxation may occur. For example, Mary designates her son as the beneficiary to her 401(k) account valued at $200,000 at her time of death. If he must withdraw all of this money in five years, the son has $40,000 of taxable income for the next five years on top of his regular income (and this is assuming no more growth in the fund). This increase is likely to move

the son up a tax bracket (maybe two), and the son could lose as much as 40 percent of the IRA, or $80,000, to income taxes. Also keep in mind that the money in these funds is subject to estate tax. Because of this double taxation, these assets are best consumed during your and your spouse's lifetimes.

However, if you and your spouse have a favorite charity, the unused portion of your tax-deferred retirement account may be used to make a charitable gift. Qualified not-for-profit organizations and corporations do not pay income tax. If the IRA in the example above had gone to a not-for-profit organization or a church, that organization could have received the full $200,000.

Non–Tax-Deferred Retirement Accounts (Roth IRAs)

Unlike the other retirement account contributions, Roth IRA contributions are not tax deferred. You make your contributions out of your after-tax income. Although you do not get a tax-deferral break, you do get two other advantages if you qualify under the current tax law: (1) you pay no tax when you withdraw your contributions, and (2) the income and growth that your contributions generate are tax-free—you will never pay income tax on these earnings.

Your Roth IRA can be a valuable estate planning tool to reach such goals as traveling the world or buying a vacation home. As long as you've met the withdrawal requirements (which are discussed in Chapter 3), you can use these funds income-tax–free to make that trip or to buy that property. Of course, you will want to check with your attorney and financial adviser before making a withdrawal to assure that the rules at that point in time will allow for such a withdrawal without penalties. A Roth IRA is also a good tool for after-death transfers to non-spouses. If you leave the balance of it to your life partner, he or she pays no income tax on the money received. You paid the tax on the money you invested when you earned it, and the dividends and gains that were generated are tax free. The Roth IRA is, however, subject to estate tax.

Most people approaching retirement have traditional IRAs rather than Roth IRAs since the Roth has only been available since 1998. But you do have the option of converting your traditional IRA into a Roth IRA. The downside to this option is that you must pay income tax on the conversion amount. Your team can calculate the tax the transfer would create and advise you whether this option is right for you. If conversion doesn't work for you, your advisers may suggest that you start a Roth IRA in addition to your existing traditional IRA. The law allows you to maintain both Roth and traditional IRAs.

Nonretirement Investments

Mutual funds, stocks, and real property can all be purchased without any legal relationship to your retirement. They can be purchased and sold without relation to your age or working status. They can also be used as collateral to secure loans (for example, a home equity line of credit or a reverse mortgage). However, they don't receive the tax benefits that most retirement vehicles do. The dividends, rents, and/or capital gains these products generate are taxed to you as income, and if you own these assets at the time of your death they will be subject to estate tax.

These products can be great assets to pass on to loved ones. Through the use of trusts, you may use them to generate income during your lifetime and then have them pass on to loved ones at your death. In many cases the assets will pass to beneficiaries within weeks after death.

Annuities

In simplest terms, an annuity is the right to receive fixed periodic payments, either for life or for a term of years. Annuities come in many forms and are

created in different ways. They may be part of an employer's retirement plan, or purchased out of your personal funds. Some are created by converting existing retirement savings plans. Some may pay funds to your estate upon your death, and others may not. Your financial planner and attorney can help you determine what the estate planning benefits and drawbacks are for your particular annuity, or one that you're considering buying.

Life Insurance

If used properly, life insurance allows money to pass to your loved ones within weeks after your death. This money may allow them to hold on to assets that might otherwise have to be sold to pay funeral bills, estate taxes, estate administration costs, and existing debt.

Some pitfalls to life insurance include the problems of missed premiums and certain clauses that can make collecting on life insurance difficult. If a policyholder misses premiums, the insurance may lapse and the beneficiary may be left with an amount equal to premiums paid, or nothing at all. The same may happen if the insurance company concludes that the insured died of a condition that he or she failed to disclose to the insurer, or that the cause of death was suicide.

With term insurance, you are covered for a certain period of time and when that term expires you have no coverage. Your beneficiaries will receive nothing unless you die during the term of the coverage. Even with its pitfalls, this can be a good, low-cost estate planning product if you are using it to pay off a liability, such as a home mortgage. Term insurance works best if the debt that it is supposed to cover (e.g. a 15-year mortgage with 10 years of payments left) will be paid off before the end of the term of the insurance.

Whole life coverage, although more expensive, is not limited to a fixed term. As long as the premiums are paid regularly, and the insurer raises no questions as to medical condition or cause of death, your beneficiary will receive the benefits. Whole life coverage, however, can be harder to obtain than term insurance. Because the insurer is taking a bigger risk, it often requires a more stringent physical examination, and it may deny you coverage if you have certain medical conditions. Your financial planner can best advise you as to what those conditions are for various insurance companies. As the coverage amount increases, so does the scrutiny of your medical condition and the cost of your premiums. Premiums also increase with age. Some people, due to age and/or medical condition, are just not insurable. With these concerns in mind, the best time to obtain insurance is while you are healthy and as soon as possible.

Another benefit to whole life is that you may be able to borrow against it. If you borrow against your policy, be aware that this will reduce the benefits received by your beneficiaries. Accordingly, you will want to consult with your financial adviser and attorney before borrowing against your whole life policy to make sure that this loan will not interfere with the rest of your estate plan.

In most circumstances insurance proceeds are not subject to income tax, but they may be subject to estate tax. You will want to work carefully with your asset planning team to be sure that the "beneficiary" and the "owner" of your policy are selected in the way that best minimizes estate tax.

Long-Term Care Insurance

This is a relatively new financial tool that may enable you (1) to protect assets for your survivors by providing income to offset medical care expenses if you require long-term care at home or at a nursing home, and (2) to make sure you have enough money for quality care, particularly if you and your planning team don't think you'll qualify for Medicaid.

This money is paid to you during your lifetime to pay for your care and it's not taxed as income. This coverage frees you from having to liquidate the assets that you've planned to use for other purposes.

Like life insurance, long-term care insurance is available in various coverage amounts, and obtaining coverage depends on your medical condition at the time of your application. Discuss the topic early on with your estate planning team.

Asset Planning and Management Instruments

There are various legal instruments, or tools, to assist you in the management and disposition of your assets. Some are very complicated and expensive to prepare and maintain. Others are simple and free. The abundance of options available shows that the law has something for everyone of every economic background with every kind of estate planning goal.

You and your attorney may want to consider some of the tools listed below for your asset management plan. You also need to know the consequences of having no plan in place. There are state laws and procedures that dictate how a person's funds are managed if he or she can no longer do so. But as you will see, the results may not be what you would choose.

Power of Attorney

With this instrument, you as the "principal" designate an "agent" or an "attorney-in-fact" to make personal (but nonmedical) business and financial decisions for you, to act on your behalf, or in your place, if you are unable to do so yourself. This agent is usually another individual, but for people with substantial assets, it may be a bank or other financial institution. Most important, it's a person or institution of your choice, one you know and trust. Along with a primary agent, you may designate an alternative agent. Illness, vacations, business trips, and simply not being able to be in two places at one time all are good reasons to have a power of attorney. And it's typically an inexpensive asset management tool.

As the principal, you designate what powers your agent will have. You can restrict your agent's powers so that he or she has a very limited scope, or you can give your agent very broad powers. For example, you may give a very limited power of attorney to an escrow company so it can complete a transfer of a particular parcel of land because you can't attend the closing. You may choose to give your spouse, life partner, or child a very broad power of attorney that allows him or her to manage any personal or business matter. You also have the right to revoke the power of attorney, usually at any time. Your agent's powers will automatically terminate at your death.

You should advise your agent what your feelings and wishes are regarding the various personal and business matters you have appointed him or her to manage on your behalf. Remember, that person will have control over whatever assets you empower him or her to manage. It is certainly in your best interest to give your agent as much direction as possible.

Even a very broad power of attorney can be ineffective if you become incapacitated, unless you executed either a durable power of attorney or a springing power of attorney. A *durable power of attorney* is one that becomes effective upon its execution by the principal, and it stays in effect if the principal becomes incapacitated. A *springing power of attorney* does not take effect until the disability or incapacity of the principal occurs. Without one of these instruments in place, your agent will have no authority to act on your behalf if you are incapacitated.

A properly executed power of attorney is recognized by banks, creditors, and the court system. The signature of the agent has the same value as the signature of the principal. However, if the document is not properly executed, or if it is

not the correct power of attorney form, then it is useless. This is why it's important to consult with an attorney before executing a power of attorney. Don't rely on a supply store form as your power of attorney instrument, particularly if you are dealing with a bank. Banks tend to be very particular about the form and execution of powers of attorney. You and your attorney should make sure that the form you use is acceptable to your bank *before* you execute it.

Guardianship

If you fail to execute a durable or springing power of attorney and you become incapacitated, the courts may have to appoint an agent to manage your personal and business affairs. In many states, this involves a guardianship proceeding.

A guardianship proceeding is brought in the courts, usually by a family member. It can be a costly process in terms of time, money, and emotional drain. Lawyers for the person bringing the action, lawyers for the "alleged incapacitated person" (AIP), and the judge may review testimony from care providers, family members, and sometimes the AIP. If the court finds that the AIP is indeed incapacitated, then a guardian is appointed. This guardian will be given powers over the person's assets and/or his or her health care decision making. In some cases, the guardian is someone whom the incapacitated person did not know before the disability struck. This can be avoided with a properly executed power of attorney.

Inter Vivos Gifts

This term refers to gifts made during your lifetime. If part of your estate plan involves leaving money, personal property, or real estate to loved ones, it may be in your best interest to make these gifts while you're living. You can make gifts up to $10,000 per year to any individual with no gift tax consequence to you or the recipient. In fact, by making this transfer, you are reducing your ultimate estate value, which will result in lower estate taxes. You can also receive an income tax deduction if the recipient of your gift is a qualified not-for-profit corporation. Gifts to charities are particularly good tax planning tools if the gift is in the form of property that has appreciated in value since you purchased it. By giving this appreciated asset to charity, you escape the capital gains tax that you would incur by selling the asset, and the charity will have no income tax liability on its sale of the asset.

Life Estates or Life Interests

These are devices by which you relinquish ownership of your real property while maintaining the right to live on the premises for the rest of your life, or until *you* choose to relinquish the life use. This may allow you to reduce your estate assets while protecting your right to stay in your home. In many cases the life tenant agrees to pay the taxes and other maintenance charges on the property during his or her lifetime. In some states it may be necessary to include this tax and maintenance agreement in the deed to protect a senior citizen's or a veteran's property tax exemption on the real property. The new owner of the property is likely to be a family member who shares the house with the life tenant, or another individual who would like to own the property someday. Your attorney and financial adviser can work with you to make certain that the transfer is made in the best way to maximize your tax basis for gift and estate tax purposes.

Tenancies

When you purchase real property, open a bank account, or purchase a security such as stocks or mutual funds, you're making an estate planning decision when taking title. If you put the property in your name alone, then the distribution will go through your will or estate administration. If you put it in the name

of your trust, then your trustee will administer the asset under the terms of the trust.

You also have the option of using tenancy language. The following tenancy language will determine how these assets are managed during the life of the owners and how the property will pass on the death of the owners:

- **Tenants-in-common** is the tenancy to use when your intent is to own property with one or more individuals; and upon the death of an owner, his or her share will pass to his or her estate. You can establish this tenancy on a deed by adding the language "tenants-in-common," or by adding no language at all. Tenants-in-common is the "default tenancy" in some states when no other tenancy is specified.
- **Joint tenants with rights of survivorship** is the tenancy to use if you want the survivor to take the decedent's share when one owner dies. This tenancy must be established with clear language. It's particularly important to make sure this language is in place when unmarried people purchase real property subject to a mortgage. If a coborrower dies, the surviving coborrower is liable for the full debt. Since the survivor is liable for the full debt, he or she should at least receive the decedent's share of the property. While most financial institutions recognize these rules on establishing joint tenancy or tenancy in common, not all do. Check with the financial institution and your estate planning team when opening accounts or purchasing securities with another person.
- **Tenants-by-the-entirety** is used by married couples. It means that they take title to the whole property, that neither spouse has his or her own share, but they share equally in the whole property. It is very similar to "joint tenants with rights of survivorship" because the surviving tenant-by-the-entirety takes the decedent's share.

Trusts

A trust is a legal arrangement under which you, as the grantor (or "settler" as the term is sometimes used), transfer assets to another individual or financial institution, known as the trustee. The trustee serves as the manager of the trust assets for the benefit of the beneficiaries named in the trust. Trusts can be broadly categorized as either testamentary trusts or living (inter vivos) trusts.

The testamentary trust is created by your last will and testament. A living trust is created by an agreement between the grantor and the trustee. In either case the trust instrument (will or agreement) names the person or institution who will serve as the trustee to manage the trust. It will also contain your specific instructions on how you want the trust to be managed and distributed.

A living trust can be either revocable or irrevocable. With a revocable living trust you retain the right and power to alter, amend, or revoke the trust during your lifetime. With an irrevocable living trust, you give up that right, although under some circumstances you may still be able to make limited amendments to an irrevocable trust. With both the revocable and the irrevocable trust, you can still receive benefits from both the income and the principal, depending on the purpose and intent of the trust.

Revocable Living Trust

The most common reasons for establishing a revocable living trust are estate management and avoidance of probate. Such a trust doesn't usually provide income tax or estate tax savings, nor does it protect your assets against the expenses of long-term illness or against the claims of creditors. But it does allow you to manage your own estate during your lifetime, without losing any control or independence. You can serve as your

own trustee (in some states) as well as the lifetime beneficiary of the income. Since it is revocable, you also have full access to the principal of the trust during your lifetime.

The revocable living trust usually provides for the grantor, or lifetime beneficiary, to receive the trust income during the grantor's or the beneficiary's lifetime. The trust usually terminates upon the death of the lifetime beneficiary. The trust assets are then distributed to the remainder beneficiaries whom you name in the trust. Or, the trust can continue after the lifetime beneficiary's death to provide for a minor or an adult disabled child.

The trust is a valuable tool for allowing your estate to be administered for you or your family during your lifetime if illness or disability makes you incapable of managing your affairs. Without a living trust or some other legal tool for property management, such as a power of attorney, your family would have to bring a guardianship proceeding to have a guardian appointed for you. The use of the revocable trust allows you to decide (1) who will handle your affairs if you become disabled (the successor or cotrustee) and (2) how he/she will manage it during your incapacity. When your disability ends, you can go right back to handling your own affairs without first having to prove to a court or anyone else that you have the ability to do so.

Your successor trustee can also wind up the affairs of the trust and distribute its assets after you die, or manage the trust after your death. As in a will, you can provide in your living trust what will happen to your assets after you die. You can provide for any portion of your estate that passes through your will to "pour over" into the trust and to be administered with the other trust assets. You can provide for them to be distributed immediately to your heirs, or other remainder beneficiaries. You can also provide in your trust agreement that the trust will continue for a period of time after your death and be administered by the successor trustee in a manner which you specify. Unlike a will, however, the assets in your trust can be distributed to the remainder beneficiaries, or continue to be managed by the successor trustee, without probate, that is, without having to file anything in court. That keeps the affairs of your trust private and avoids the costs and delays of court proceedings.

Irrevocable Living Trust

The irrevocable living trust is most often used when the grantor wants to divest himself of ownership and control over certain assets, but doesn't want the beneficiary to receive the assets outright or immediately. Unlike the revocable trust, you do not have absolute authority to amend or modify the trust, and you have no right to revoke the trust or invade it for your own benefit. Some of the reasons for establishing an irrevocable trust include asset protection, charitable giving, estate tax avoidance, the funding of a grandchild's education, and asset management. Like the revocable trust, however, the grantor can reserve the right to receive the income during his lifetime, but that may affect the estate tax obligations of the grantor's estate at death.

The irrevocable trust can sometimes be used to protect assets against the high cost of a catastrophic illness, long-term medical costs, or nursing home care. But be aware that the federal and state Medicaid rules are very strict and difficult to follow. Improper or untimely use of an irrevocable trust for Medicaid purposes can result in penalties. However, in some situations, a properly drafted irrevocable trust can allow the grantor or the beneficiaries of the trust to qualify for government benefits for the payment of nursing home and long-term home care expenses without depleting the family's savings. Because of the complexity of the federal and state Medicaid regulations, an asset protection trust should be prepared by

an attorney with expertise in the area of Medicaid law and long-term care planning.

The irrevocable trust is also often used to protect one's estate from invasion by third parties, such as creditors of the beneficiary or an estranged spouse. A properly prepared irrevocable trust will enable you to set aside a portion of your estate for the benefit of a child or other family member who is a poor money manager, or who may have other financial problems, without risking the loss of those assets to his or her creditors, or others who would attempt to take the assets away. This type of trust, however, may not protect your assets against your own creditors.

This type of trust is an excellent tool for helping your grandchildren meet their college expenses. By setting the fund aside in an irrevocable trust, you control the management and use of the funds for your grandchildren's education, while reducing your own estate for estate tax purposes. This trust can also reduce the federal and state income tax liability on the income earned by the trust's assets by shifting the income tax liability to the lower income tax bracket of the grandchildren.

The irrevocable trust is also suited for other special needs. You can use it to set aside a fund for a disabled individual without causing the disabled person to lose valuable government benefits, such as Medicaid and supplemental Social Security benefits. The trust fund can be used to supplement the government benefits and provide the disabled individual with personal items and services not usually covered by government benefits. Such items and services can include companion care, travel to visit relatives, special vans, and other similar items and services intended to enrich the quality of the disabled person's life. This popular estate planning tool must comply strictly with the complex federal Medicaid regulations. Accordingly, it should be prepared by an attorney with expertise in such matters.

The *irrevocable charitable remainder trust* is a valuable and widely used estate planning tool that can provide you with significant income tax and estate tax benefits. If you have one or more qualified charities that you want to benefit and you are willing to make the irrevocable commitment, you can establish this trust now. With the irrevocable charitable remainder trust, you can reserve the income benefits for your lifetime, or the joint lifetime of yourself, your spouse, and even your children. (Estate planners often fund these trusts with assets that have a low tax basis because the transfer into the trust will not result in a capital gains tax, which would occur if the assets were sold.) The remainder, or principal balance, of the trust passes to the charities after the death of the lifetime beneficiaries. You will receive an immediate income tax deduction for a portion of the gift, and an estate tax deduction at your death.

Totten Trusts

A Totten trust is usually a savings account or other banking instrument that you hold in your name "in trust for" someone else. You maintain control and use of the account during your lifetime, and the person for whom you are holding it in trust receives whatever money is in the account at the time of your death. You pay income tax on any interest or dividends the account generates during your lifetime because you have the use and benefit of it. It is part of your taxable estate for estate tax purposes, but the account balance passes to the beneficiary. In some cases the beneficiary may have to pay some of the estate tax attributed to the value of the Totten trust.

Wills

A will is a written document that directs how your assets are to be distributed when you die. It designates an executor or representative who is responsible for administering your estate, paying your final debts, and then distributing

the balance of your estate to your beneficiaries. It is not a tool for managing your assets during your lifetime. The will controls the distribution of assets that are not otherwise directed for distribution by tenancy arrangement, Totten trust, beneficiary designation, or revocable/irrevocable trust.

Your will is filed with the court and interested parties are given notice of its filing. If the court finds that the will is genuine and was properly signed, the executor is appointed by the court in accordance with your will. The court then takes jurisdiction over your probate assets, which are those assets you owned in your own name at the time of your death.

The probate process can be costly and time-consuming, particularly for larger or more complicated estates. There are court filing fees involved as well as a minimum waiting period before your estate can be distributed. Also, probate is an open process that allows any member of the public to examine your will and to see what you owned when you died and where it went. There are advantages to probate, however. The court oversees the administration and distribution of your estate, so you have some assurance that it will go where you want.

State Intestacy Laws

If you die without a will or trust, and your property does not automatically pass to another individual as a surviving tenant or as the beneficiary of your retirement account or life insurance, then the distribution of your estate will take place under the intestacy laws of your state. Your estate will not necessarily go to the people you want or in the percentages that you want. Some of your estate may even go to the state. Without a will or trust,

- your estate may be subjected to higher estate taxes than necessary;
- the court may appoint someone not of your own choosing to look after your estate;
- you are leaving important estate decisions up to somebody else who may make those decisions without any regard to your own preferences.

As an example of what can happen if you do not have an asset protection plan, the following table shows how your assets would pass under New York law without a will or trust. *Issue* refers to children, or grandchildren of the deceased if his or her children have died. *By representation* means that members in this class will share equally the share that their parent would have received. For example, your will leaves everything to your three children. At the time of your death one of your children has passed away, but is survived by two children (i.e., your grandchildren). If the will distributes "by representation," then the two children of your deceased child each receive one-half of their deceased parent's share, or one-sixth of your estate. *Per capita* means that all people in a class will share equally regardless of what their respective parents would have received. For example, if your first child has four children, the second has one, and the third has two, and your will leaves everything to your grandchildren "per capita," then each grandchild receives one-seventh of your estate.

New York Intestate Distribution for Decedents Dying on or after September 1, 1992:

Persons Surviving	Distribution Share
Spouse and no issue	**Spouse takes all.**
Spouse and issue	**Spouse takes $50,000 plus one-half of residue. Issue take rest** by representation.
Issue and no spouse	**Issue take all** by representation.
Both parents and no spouse	Parents take one-half each.
Brothers and sisters or their issue, and no spouse or issue or parent	**Brothers and sisters take all** by representation.
Maternal and paternal grandparent or grandparents or their issue and no spouse, issue, parents, brothers, sisters, or their issue	**Maternal grandparents take one-half** (or issue by representation). **Paternal grandparents take one-half** (or issue by representation).
Only maternal or only paternal grandparents or their issue and no spouse, issue, parents, brothers, sisters, or their issue	**The grandparents or their issue take all** by representation.

Persons Surviving	Distribution Share
Great-grandchildren of grandparents and no spouse, issue, parents, brothers, sisters or their issue	**Maternal great-grandchildren take one-half** per capita. **Paternal great-grandchildren take one-half** per capita. **If only maternal or only paternal great-grandchildren survive, they take the whole** per capita.

Health Care Planning

You have the right to make your own decisions relative to your health care matters. You also have the right to appoint an agent to make health care decisions for you.

The best way to protect your right to control your health care is to execute a *living will* and/or *health care proxy* (sometimes referred to as a *health care advance directive* or a *durable power of attorneys for health care*) that is legally recognized in your state. If you don't set forth your directions clearly and in legal form, your health care can become a matter for the courts.

A living will sets forth your wishes concerning the treatments you wish to receive or have withheld in the event that you can't communicate these wishes. In addition to the living will, some states require a health care proxy. A health care proxy is a document in which you designate an individual to carry out your wishes.

The requirements for living wills and health care proxies vary from state to state. Consult with a legal or medical professional before executing them. Since more and more hospitals and physicians are requesting that a health care proxy and living will be completed, you may find that your own family doctor has a currently acceptable form available.

If you don't have a living will and/or health care proxy in place, you have no certainty as to who will make your health care decisions or what those decisions may be. In emergency situations, health care providers will consult family members if they are available. Otherwise, they may rely on established hospital policy. If the family is available, the hospital may make a recommendation to them based on the hospital's policy. Keep in mind that if you would rather have your best friend, significant other, or another individual who is not part of your immediate family make your health care decisions, the only way a health care provider will recognize that person's authority is by the designation of that person in your health care proxy and/or living will. (It is also a good idea to designate in the instrument who may *not* be your agent.)

If your illness or injury is not an immediate emergency, your health care provider or your family will have to bring a guardianship proceeding to have someone appointed to make your health care decisions.

Five Wishes Living Will

In an effort to make the living will a more widely accepted document, a gentleman named Jim Towey, a full-time volunteer with Mother Teresa and the founder of Aging with Dignity, developed an instrument called "Five Wishes," with the help of the Robert Wood Johnson Foundation. This instrument

- designates the person you want to make your health care decisions in the event you can't;
- describes the medical treatment you want or do not want;
- describes how comfortable you wish to be;
- describes how you want to be treated;
- sets forth what you want your loved ones to know.

Unlike most standard health care proxies/living wills, this instrument walks you through various questions that will help you create a directive specifically tailored to your needs and desires. For example, under the section, "How You Wish to Be Treated," you are asked if you want people from your church or synagogue to be told that you are sick and if you want to ask that you are prayed for and visited. You can even have the instrument tell your family and friends that you wish them to make peace with each other before your death, if they can.

Presently, 33 states and the District of Columbia recognize the Five Wishes as a health care proxy/living will. More information on this document may be obtained by visiting Aging with Dignity's Web site at *www.agingwithdignity.org*, or by writing to Aging with Dignity, Post Box 1661, Tallahassee, Florida 32302.

Employment Discrimination

Many corporations have been "downsizing" or "laying off" large numbers of employees. They believe that by reducing labor costs (usually their costliest expenses), they will increase profits and better the fiscal condition of the business. The victims of downsizing are often older employees, who are discriminated against because factors related to their age or disabilities create high business costs. To protect older employees from unfair hiring, firing, and treatment related to age and disability, Congress has enacted laws such as the Age Discrimination in Employment Act (ADEA), the Older Workers Benefit Protection Act (OWBPA), and the Americans with Disabilities Act (ADA).

Age Discrimination in Employment Act (ADEA), 1967

This Act has three goals: (1) to promote the employment of older persons based on their abilities rather than their age, (2) to prohibit arbitrary age discrimination in employment, and (3) to assist employers and workers in finding ways of addressing problems resulting from the impact of a worker's age on employment.

The ADEA seeks to reach these goals by (1) prohibiting employers from discriminating against employees who are age 40 and older, (2) prohibiting the use of age preference language in public notices and advertisements for employment, and (3) prohibiting employers from punishing employees for filing complaints related to age discrimination or for assisting the government with investigations related to age discrimination. Specific activities that the ADEA prohibits include:

- basing a layoff plan on employee age;
- making hiring decisions based on age;
- requiring that workers of a certain age accept mandatory retirement;
- denying older employees benefits afforded to younger employees;
- denying older employees training, promotions, and enticing job assignments afforded to younger employees;
- age-based harassment;
- age-based advertising.

As long as age is one factor in the employer's discriminatory practice, the discrimination will violate the provisions of the ADEA, unless the employer meets one of a few narrow exceptions, such as using an age requirement as a bona fide occupational qualification. This is more common in public safety fields such as police work, fire fighting, and airline piloting. In reality, there may be other factors in the employer's decision-making (such as economic factors), but if you believe your employer has taken action against you in an unfair way based on your age, you may very well have a valid claim under the ADEA.

This federal law does not apply to every employment situation but it does apply to government employers, employment agencies, private employers with 20 or more employees, and labor organizations with 25 or more members.

Taking Action

The Equal Employment Opportunity Commission (EEOC) is the federal agency that investigates, mediates, and

files lawsuits on behalf of older Americans to end age discrimination. You should also consult your state's department of labor or your state department of human rights to determine whether your state has laws prohibiting age discrimination as well. You will also want to ask these agencies about the correct procedures for filing charges or complaints for your specific situation. If you elect to bring a private lawsuit, you should, of course, consult an attorney with expertise in this area before taking any action.

Older Workers Benefit Protection Act (OWBPA), 1990

The ADEA was amended in 1990 by the Older Workers Benefit Protection Act (OWBPA). This Act was designed to protect older workers who decide to leave their employment in exchange for severance pay and other benefits, but as part of this agreement must release their employers from any claim of age discrimination. OWBPA allows an employee to release an employer from a federal age discrimination claim if the following conditions are met:

- The employer and the employee must sign a written agreement that explicitly states that the employee has foregone his or her rights to bring a federal age discrimination claim. The agreement must be written in clear, easy-to-understand language.
- The employee must have at least 21 days to consider the release in a situation where a layoff or other reduction in workforce is not in place, and at least 45 days if there is a planned reduction of workforce.
- After an employee signs such a release, he or she must have 7 days to revoke the release.

The rules under OWBPA are strictly enforced to ensure that older workers are treated fairly. In fact, the courts have held that in cases in which employees have received their severance pay and then elected to pursue a federal age discrimination claim, they do not have to return the severance money if the employer did not meet all of the requirements of OWBPA (See *Oubre v. Entergy Operations, Inc.*, 118 S.Ct. 838, 1998). So, if you signed a release but still feel you have a discrimination claim because these guidelines were not followed, consult an employment attorney regarding your protections under OWBPA.

Americans with Disabilities Act (ADA), 1990

Many retired Americans face physical disabilities. This reality is one reason why disability insurance premiums are so high and why they increase with age. Nevertheless, while disabilities pose challenges to workers, they are not necessarily insurmountable. If employers can make reasonable accommodations to the working conditions of the disabled worker, that employee may be able to successfully complete the tasks he performed prior to his disability.

The Americans with Disabilities Act (ADA) protects employees from discrimination in the workplace. The clearest and most obvious way that the ADA protects employees is by requiring employers to make reasonable accommodations for qualified workers who are challenged with a disability. The ADA protects employees in the following workplaces:

- state and local government offices;
- any private employer with more than 15 workers.

Some states go beyond the ADA requirements and require that employers with fewer than 15 employees not discriminate based on disability as well.

If you feel that you have been discriminated against due to disability and your employer falls into one of the two categories above, then your employer may be required to make reasonable accommo-

dations to allow you to continue your work. Your employer may have to make these accommodations if, with your disability, you are still able to perform the essential functions of your job. Be aware that these accommodations may not be made immediately. In instances where the employer can show that the accommodations cause financial hardship, they may not be made at all. Some examples of these reasonable accommodations include:

- getting wheelchair ramps and other features that make your workplace more accessible to you;
- changing your work schedule to allow for doctors' appointments and physical therapy;
- allowing your seeing eye dog to join you at the office;
- providing you with assistance in the form of equipment or human assistance if your sight, hearing, or physical ability is impaired.

If you feel that your employer should accommodate your disability under the ADA, speak to your employer about the situation. You and your employer may be able to work out accommodations on your own. If that's not successful, you can contact the Office of the ADA, Civil Rights Division, Department of Justice; the EEOC; or your state department of human rights. Since some actions must be taken quickly, you should consult an employment attorney to ensure that your claim is filed promptly and correctly.

Age, Disability, and Driving

The operation of a motor vehicle is not a "right"—it is a privilege. Each state is authorized to determine who will receive this privilege. These privileges or "licenses" may be suspended or revoked by the issuer. While age or disability alone will not result in your license being revoked or suspended, your impaired ability to operate a vehicle, which may be influenced by your age or disability, can result in your license being taken away.

When you first obtained your license, you had to prove to a state examiner that you were able to operate a vehicle and that you had a working knowledge of the laws of the road. Some states may require you to take these tests again when you reach a certain age. Because driving is a privilege rather than a right, states can force older drivers to be retested without being guilty of discrimination.

If you are disabled, certain accommodations may be made to your vehicle that will allow you to operate it safely. However, all drivers, regardless of disabilities, are required to operate vehicles safely under the same laws as all other drivers.

Some points to remember about the driving privilege are:

- Like any other driver, if you are convicted of too many moving violations or you have had several accidents or a conviction for driving while intoxicated (DWI), you may lose your license.
- If you fail a road test or a written test, you may lose your license.
- If someone reports you as an unsafe driver, you may lose your license.
- If the license issuer determines that you are not capable of operating a motor vehicle under all conditions, the issuer may restrict your license. Restricted licenses include limits such as operating the vehicle only during daytime hours, operating a motor vehicle with glasses or contact lenses, or operating a vehicle only at certain speeds.

Although you may be able to appeal a revocation of your license, keep in mind that you must be able to show that you have the ability to operate the vehicle under the existing laws and conditions. Information on the procedures for appealing the restriction or revocation of your license can be obtained at your local department of motor vehicles.

Consumer Fraud

While technology has tremendously improved the way that we communicate, it has also made it easier for less than honest solicitors to prey upon the public. Although some vendors have legitimate products and services to offer, many do not. Here are a few examples of consumer fraud schemes commonly targeted at retired Americans:

Health care/medical sales. Solicitors will offer you miracle cures that they claim are covered by Medicare. Do not purchase or try any treatment without first speaking with your doctor. Remember, no one knows your medical condition and how to treat it better than your own physician.

Financial scams. Do not agree to donate to a charity, create a living trust or make any investments based on a telephone or mail solicitation. Estate planning, funeral arrangements, investing, and charitable giving, like your health care, should be addressed with the professionals with whom you work on a regular basis. Discuss with your planners what investments, charities, and plans are right for you.

Prizes with no contests. Remember some basic rules for dealing with any solicitation involving a "prize."

- You can't win a contest you did not enter.
- You haven't won anything if you have to pay to have it shipped.
- If someone asks you for your credit card number, you know you are being charged for something.

Your state attorney general or your Better Business Bureau can help you if you have been the victim of a prize scam.

- ***Unsolicited contractors.*** Home improvements should be made at your initiation. Beware of individuals who come to your door saying they are doing work in your area and ask you to enlist their services. Never hire a contractor without solid recommendations, a written estimate, and payment terms that you feel are reasonable. Especially beware of any contractor who works for cash only. Always ask a contractor for a clear written estimate of the work to be done.
- ***Telephone sales.*** High-pressured salespeople will call to sell you services and products that you have not requested. They may encourage you to act quickly and to pay with a credit card. Avoid making any purchases in this manner. You are essentially purchasing goods sight unseen, and running the risk of hidden costs and further use of your credit card and credit information by other telemarketers.

Your Rights and Remedies

As a consumer, you have certain rights:

- You may have the right to cancel some contracts you enter into within three business days.
- You have the right to receive what you bargained for. In other words, if you enter into an agreement to provide a payment in exchange for specific goods, you have the right to receive those specific goods.
- You can't be charged more than the legal allowable rate of interest for any remaining payment balance related to a purchase.

- You have the right not to be bothered before 8:00 A.M. and after 9:00 P.M. by telemarketers and other solicitors.
- You have the right to have your name removed from solicitation lists (see upcoming discussion, "Getting Off the Solicitation Lists," later in this chapter.)

If your rights are violated, you have remedies under the law. Here are some you can take:

- Go to a small claims court. This forum is less formal than other state courts and usually only deals with claims under a certain dollar amount (for example, $3,000 or less).
- Stop payment on your check.
- Call your credit card company, report the fraud, and ask them to reverse the charge.
- File a complaint with the Better Business Bureau.
- File a complaint with your state attorney general.
- Enlist the services of an attorney familiar with consumer fraud.

While these remedies are certainly available to you as a victim of fraud, it's better to prevent the fraud from occurring.

10 Ways to Avoid Being Scammed

Here are some basic ideas and practices that can reduce the likelihood that you will be scammed:

1. If it seems too good to be true, than it probably is. No one sells you something for nothing. Don't fall for it.
2. Do not hire anyone to work for you unless he or she has reliable references.
3. You do not have to talk to anyone that you do not want to talk to. If a telemarketer/solicitor is bothering you, hang up.
4. Any phone numbers you call with an area code of 900 or 976 is a call for which you will pay a heavy charge. Avoid them.
5. Although a call whose exchange begins with 800 or 888 may be a free call, don't be surprised if you are asked for your credit card number. Make sure you have a good reason to provide it.
6. If salespeople are honest and have nothing to hide, they will have no problem giving you their names and phone numbers. If they can't give you this information, they have something to hide, so dismiss them.
7. Be leery of anyone who accepts cash only. In today's business world, most companies will accept credit cards and/or checks, and from a business standpoint, these terms are usually preferred over cash.
8. Portable phones are like "walkie talkies" because they are easily picked up by scanners and other listening devices. Therefore, don't ever give out your credit card number and expiration date over a portable phone.
9. Don't ever give your credit card number and expiration date to someone *who calls* or *solicits* your business. You may discover that the person calling does not have a product or service to sell, and that the caller just wanted your credit card information to make his/her own purchases on your account.
10. If something is marked "Urgent—Time dated material, must be opened immediately," check to see how the letter was delivered. If this "vital" information was delivered via bulk mail, it is not as important as the sender would like you to believe. Don't be taken in by this marketing technique.

Your Credit Card Can Protect You

Credit cards are often considered the bad guys in the consumer world. They're known for their high interest rates and huge credit limits that put consumers into unmanageable debt. However, credit cards can protect consumers from the damages caused by fraud. If you feel you have been scammed by a less than credible vendor, and you have paid for this scam with your credit card, your credit card issuer may be able to help you. For example, if you have taken the appropriate action with your vendor to cancel the services or delivery of the product within the allowable right-to-cancel time frame and the vendor still refuses to cancel the charges, call your credit card company. They may be willing to cancel the charges on your account and charge back the vendor for any funds that have been advanced.

Credit card companies will also help you if someone has fraudulently used your credit card number and expiration date. Some common consumer purchases that require only an account number and expiration date are airline tickets, telephone chat/sex lines, and Internet services. Make sure you check your statement every month for unfamiliar purchases. If you find that someone has used your credit card number, call your credit card company immediately. They'll cancel your card and issue you a new one. They want to stop credit card fraud too.

Getting off the Solicitation Lists

One of the best ways to minimize the chances of experiencing consumer fraud is to reduce your junk mail and phone solicitations. You have the right to request that your name be removed from mailing lists, phone solicitation lists, and fax advertising lists. Here are some places that can help you take control over consumer solicitation:

To take your name and address off mailing lists, write to:

Mail Preference Service Direct Marketing Association
PO Box 9008
Farmingdale, NY 11735-9008

To take your name and phone number off telemarketing lists, write to:

Telephone Preference Service Direct Marketing Association
PO Box 9014
Farmingdale, NY 11735-9014

To take your name off a fax solicitation list,

1. Contact the sender (the name, phone number, and/or address should be on the fax) and direct them to remove your name and phone number from their list.
2. If the fax advertisement does not have a name and phone number, report this to:

Federal Communications Commission
Consumer Information Bureau Complaints
445 12th St. SW
Washington, DC 20554

These organizations can help you with nationally based consumer lists. For problems and questions regarding solicitations in your local area, contact your local Better Business Bureau.

You have the right not to be contacted by telemarketers if you have asked them not to call. You should notify your state's attorney general's office if a telemarketer continues to call after you have been taken off their list. These persistent telemarketers not only are annoying you, they are breaking the law.

The Personal Side of Retirement

By PricewaterhouseCoopers LLP and Helen Dennis*

Some people might think having enough money is the key to a successful retirement. But bank accounts and investment portfolios are only part of the story. In fact, if you only consider your finances, you may find your retirement experience missing something: having a reason to get up in the morning, having something to do, and feeling good about yourself and the world around you.

Coming to grips with the various psychological and social changes that often are part of the experience of retirement is just as important as financial planning. As you enter this new phase of life, you'll need to learn what leaving a full-time job and having more time on your hands will actually mean for you and your spouse or partner.

Knowing about these changes—and why they occur—can help prepare you to deal with them. Remember, although change is often difficult, it presents opportunities for you to develop into what you want to become.

Perhaps the single most important idea in this chapter is that *you* are in charge. A positive attitude, greater self-awareness, and self-knowledge can combine to create the retirement experience you want.

Change as Part of the Process

Years ago, our picture of a retiree was someone passively watching the world go by. Today we know this simply isn't true.

Change is part of every major life phase—retirement is no exception. Noted sociologist Robert Atchley put forth the theory that there are four predictable phases or changes that people go through during retirement. Think of yourself in any one of these phases:

- *The honeymoon phase:* You love the new freedom of retirement. You're doing all the things you never had time to do while working. You're very busy with family, friends, activities, travel, and more. In fact, it's the most exciting time in your life.
- *Disenchantment:* You're in a period of letdown and disappointment. You may have few alternatives because of little money or poor health. If your honeymoon phase was unrealistic, you might come crashing into the disenchantment phase.
- *Reorientation:* You are pulling yourself together, with realistic goals and alternatives that are meaningful and achievable.
- *Stability:* You've mastered the retirement role. You know what's important and how to achieve it and do it. You have learned to manage change and make it work for you.

Actually, you may experience all of these phases. You may stay in the honeymoon phase for the next 30 years, or you may move from honeymoon to disenchantment, back to honeymoon, and end

* This chapter has been adapted with permission from *Secure Your Future*, © PricewaterhouseCoopers LLP. Irwin Professional Publishing: Burr Ridge, Ill., and New York, 1996. Special thanks to the Financial Planning Solutions practice of PricewaterhouseCoopers LLP for their cooperation and to Helen Dennis, specialist and frequently published author in the areas of aging, employment, and retirement, for her contributions to this chapter.

up in stability. The point is that retirement, like all other life stages before it, is a highly dynamic period of life in which change is likely to occur.

Transitioning from Work to Retirement

Work currently may play a central role in your life, providing a number of the following benefits:

- *Financial stability:* Work is probably the major source of your income.
- *Time management:* Work provides structure so that your life has some order.
- *Sense of purpose:* Work provides meaning and direction.
- *Social life:* Work brings you in contact with people.
- *Status:* Work often provides status in the community. People may identify who you are by what you do.
- *Source of power and influence:* Work provides the environment for you to create and influence policies, programs, products, and people.

How Important Is Work in Your Life?

To get an idea, check which of the following statements best describes you:

- ❑ I place great importance on my work, particularly during the time I spend working.
- ❑ I think about my work most of my waking hours, even when I am home.
- ❑ I feel I am indispensable to my company.
- ❑ I place my work before my family, friends, and leisure time.

If you answered yes to most of these questions, you may have high work identification. In fact, work may be one of your strongest sources of joy and gratification.

Consider what has kept you at your company. Here is a list of what well over 6,000 preretirees said kept them at their jobs for the past two to three years. Some motives may be familiar to you:

- feeling challenged by my work;
- liking the people I work with;
- having the opportunity to learn;
- traveling for the company;
- working as a team member;
- helping the company grow;
- being part of a respected company;
- receiving the income and benefits;
- influencing the company's direction and success.

If work is central to your life, use that information as a planning tool. Use your present work values to help identify what you want to do in retirement. Remember, people generally do not go through major personality change in retirement. In fact, their values remain rather consistent. Examine the list, decide which of these you will *miss most* when you retire, and begin to think about what you will do to replace them.

Even if you're already aware of the important role work plays in your life, you may find the transition to retirement unexpectedly difficult. Why? Here are four possible reasons:

1. *Retirement is a new experience.* As a working adult, the standards and expectations are set for you by your boss, your peers, and your environment. Success is easily measured. You know when you're doing a good job and when you're not. You also know when you're on the right track and what to expect. There are *external factors* that determine your expecta-

tions, accomplishments, and effectiveness.

By contrast, the retirement experience is *motivated from within.* You must develop your own mission, goals, and objectives. You develop your own strategies and meaningful activities. You become the judge and the jury. There are few external reference points or guideposts. In a sense, you are the CEO of your own retirement.

2. *Retirement may move you to the "unknown."* You've never done this before, you've had no practice, coaching, mentoring, or trial run in this area. You may not have identified what you're retiring to. You may have been too busy working to think about it.
3. *You may feel a sense of loss.* You may be concerned about losing friends from work, suddenly lacking a sense of purpose, or not being a part of something larger than yourself. Many retirees find the potential loss of power, influence, and prestige difficult to acknowledge and even more difficult to discuss. You may find the retirement transition particularly complex if you are unaware of the possible losses and have no plan to compensate for them.
4. *You may be surprised with an early retirement offer.* The thought of retirement may be a shock. You may never have thought of yourself as old enough to retire. In fact, you may have envisioned yourself working for your company for another three to ten years. In making the early retirement decision, the first step is to understand whether you can afford to retire. After that, consider additional questions. For example, do you *want* to retire? What will you do with this newly found time? If you really don't want to retire, what are the consequences of turning down the retirement offer? Will your department be phased out? Will your job change? Will you be demoted? Will your position be eliminated in the next round of downsizings? Will the next early retirement package offer you less? Unfortunately, the answers to these questions may be based on your best guess at the moment, not on a column of figures that easily add up to the right answer.

Your New Identity in Retirement

You may have met people who've been retired for years but continue to identify exclusively with their former profession or job: "I'm a retired engineer." "I'm a retired salesperson." This response is understandable. However, the question remains: What additional roles or activities are important to these people now in retirement?

American society has been criticized throughout the world because we do not have clear roles for retirees. This may be a curse or a blessing. Because of our loosely defined roles in retirement, you have choices. There is no typical U.S. retiree. You truly have the opportunity to choose or create the role you want in retirement.

Here are four roles that you might relate to. Consider some or all of them.

- *Consider work.* Why would you want to work in retirement? Isn't work what you wanted to get away from? Or was it just *full-time* work you wanted to avoid? Part-time work in particular has become the choice of many retirees. Many employers seek part-time employees because they don't need to provide benefits and can gain a great deal from the experience and skills of seasoned workers.Working for someone else is not

the only approach. Becoming a self-employed entrepreneur is immensely popular. You might turn a hobby into a money-making venture, do consulting, or enter into something completely new.

- *Become a student.* It's never too late to learn. In fact, retirees are moving into classrooms in large numbers, pursuing degrees or just taking courses out of personal interest. Elderhostel, a successful Boston-based organization, has signed up close to 250,000 students age 60 and up in classes ranging from "Japanese Brush Painting" to "Prehistoric Art of Southwest New Mexico." Colleges and cultural institutions in 52 countries host these weeklong classes, even while regular classes are still in session. (For more information, call (877) 426-8056 or write to Elderhostel, 11 Avenue de Lafayette, Boston, MA 02111-1746.)
- *Become a volunteer.* There are ways to apply what you love to do as a volunteer. Approximately 25 percent of men and women 55 years and older volunteer. Their combined efforts are equivalent to 500,000 full-time workers. To be part of this growing, vibrant segment of our society, you will have to reach out to create that volunteer opportunity. The need for effective volunteers is greater than ever. Contact your local Volunteer Action Center for a list of positions available in your community. Remember, volunteering can be part-time, on your own terms, and give additional meaning to your retirement years.
- *Don't forget leisure.* The list of leisure activities is endless. What do you enjoy? What new leisure activities do you want to try? White-water rafting? Going on an archaeological dig? Gardening? This is your opportunity for fun and enjoyment. Go for it!

But do it with a bit of thought. Do you want to spend 100 percent of your time in one or two leisure activities? If you think of retirement as a week full of Saturdays, your retirement experience may turn shallow or boring. So think about how much time you'll be allocating to leisure and the types of activities that bring meaning and pleasure to your life. Also, decide how much of your leisure time you want to spend in solo activities and how much time with someone else.

Relationships in Retirement

Oddly enough, marital relationships aren't usually addressed in corporate-sponsored retirement planning programs—for many reasons. First, there never seems to be enough time to discuss this issue. Second, marriage is a personal subject, and having an outsider discussing your relationship appears intrusive. Third, couples who have been doing fine for the past 30 to 40 years may see no reason to discuss their relationships. Still, retirement is a time of change, and that includes changes in your marital relationship.

Where do you begin in this reexamination? Look at your need for privacy and your current work environment. Do you leave your home daily to go to work in a cubicle, office, suite, or desk—a space that's yours? When you retire, you give up that space.

In moving home, many retirees take over their house as though it belonged to them exclusively, just like the office. You've heard about the husband who retires and takes over his wife's kitchen. He reorganizes all the shelves, cuts coupons, writes a daily grocery list (whether it's needed or not), buys in large quantities to save money, and even alphabetizes the items in the refrigerator! He cannot believe that his wife has managed all these years without him. What

he may not realize is that he and his wife have a need for some private physical space.

Ask yourself, Do I need some area that is just for me? Look at your home and determine what space can be allocated as yours. Perhaps an area can be converted into a den, computer room, wood shop, library, or art studio.

Men, let's not forget about your wife. She has privacy needs, too. So wives, assess the space you need and speak up. Yes, you need to talk this over with each.

Aside from physical space, ask yourself if you need some private "mental space." Do you need to do some things alone without accounting for every minute of your time?

Casey Stengel summed it up well when he said to his wife, "I married you for better or worse, but not for lunch." The point is, examine your own needs for private time, independence, and time away from the home. This applies to both husbands and wives.

Togetherness Too

Also try to remember why you married each other. In the first few years of marriage, you never had enough time to be together. Well, here's your chance. Rediscover your spouse, but remember that having a splendid marital relationship in retirement doesn't require spending 100 percent of your time together. Each of you is an individual, so give each other the "space" that is needed to be a whole person. The more complete you are as an individual, the more there is to share with your spouse. In retirement, think of this relationship as a wonderful new merger, not a takeover!

For the Unattached

Although most people retire as one-half of a couple, a large segment of retirees are single, divorced, or widowed. Those individuals in particular should plan how to create new relationships, keep up with old ones, and stay connected to compensate for possible social losses in the workplace. Specialized retirement programs have been developed for single people, specifically women. For the helpful pamphlet *Retirement Planning for Women,* email *info@agingfocus.com* or call the National Center for Women, (631) 287-2888.

Healthy Behaviors

No matter how good your financial plan, you need a healthy, physically fit body and mentally active mind to enjoy your retirement. Your overall health and wellness is a combination of many factors, both physical and mental. For our purposes, let's define health as being the best you can be or functioning at your highest level during your retirement years.

Aging itself is an inevitable process for all of us, and it's one of those "bad news good news" stories. The bad news is that aging is a process of decline. The good news is that there is much we can do to slow it down. Researchers in the field of aging have found that

- We are living longer and healthier lives than ever before.
- Healthy behaviors have been proven to slow down the normal aging process.
- You can have fitness and vigor, intellectual growth, and mental sharpness in your 70s and 80s.

Genetics and Lifestyle

We all age differently—at different rates—because of our unique genetic makeup and lifestyles. Recent research by John Rowe and Robert Kahn in their book *Successful Aging* indicates that 70 percent of our physical aging is genetic and 30 percent is due to lifestyle. While we can't do much about our genes, we do have some influence over our lifestyles.

What Can You Expect from the Normal Aging Process?

As you age, many of the following changes can occur, but if you practice healthy behaviors, you can significantly slow the aging process.

- *Change in the ratio of lean (muscle) tissue and fat tissue.* As you age, your fat tissue increases and your muscle tissue decreases. One reason for this is that your metabolism slows down with age.
  Here's the bad news. If you don't change your caloric intake or activity level, on the average you may gain about one pound a year between ages 35 and 65. That is a possible 30-pound weight gain, depending on your height, frame, and so on.
  More bad news. Fat tissue redistributes with age. For example, it often seems to disappear from just under the skin in your face and "mysteriously" appears in other areas such as your hips and waist. Yes, this is part of normal aging. The good news is that you can also slow down this process.
  Action: To decrease your fat tissue and increase your lean muscle tissue, as well as maintain your body weight, decrease your calories and increase your level of activity through exercise. (Of course, before adopting any exercise program you should consult your physician.)
- *Skin changes.* We also know that skin becomes less elastic with age. You may recall your first recognition of aging when you looked in the mirror and saw a little wrinkle. The wrinkle was caused by two factors: the protective lining of fat under the skin decreased and your skin was less elastic. Since the skin does not shrink, a wrinkle formed. Too much sunlight over a period of years causes the skin to become even less elastic.
  Action: To maintain skin elasticity, stay out of the sun and/or use sunscreen. Some people also choose cosmetic surgery, which of course isn't for everyone.
- *Changes in bone or musculoskeletal system.* Bones tend to lose calcium with age. The common result is loss of bone mass and height. An abnormally large loss of calcium can indicate osteoporosis, a bone disease characterized by an increased risk of fractures. This is a particular problem for women, but more and more men are being diagnosed with it also.
  Action: To retain bone mass, eat foods that are rich in calcium, take a calcium supplement (after consulting with your physician), and adopt an exercise program that creates impact, such as walking or jogging. The recommended daily calcium supplement is 1,000 mg. for premenopausal women and 1,500 mg. for postmenopausal women. Estrogen supplementation has also been effective in maintaining bone mass in women, although it may also increase cancer risk. Consult your physician.
- *Changes in vision.* Changes in vision typically begin during the 40s. The pupil decreases in size, allowing less light to reach the retina. Also, the lens of the eye becomes less elastic, causing farsightedness, so that it's hard to focus on things that are

close. You may already be reading the newspaper with an outstretched arm!
Action: As you guessed—glasses.

- *Changes in hearing.* Hearing typically begins to change in the 50s. The loss is so gradual that many people don't notice it. High-pitched sounds and consonant sounds of *z, s, g, f,* and *t* often become hard to hear. Also, with age, background noise seems to interfere more with hearing.
Action: You guessed it again. Get a hearing aid if needed—and select a more quiet restaurant.
- *Changes in reaction time.* Reaction time slows with age. This begins in the 20s and continues gradually. Reaction time is related to many of our daily activities such as driving, playing tennis, typing, and even dodging a car or falling object.
Action: To improve your reaction time, engage in activities that require a quick response, and then practice. Reaction time can be improved at almost any age, which is very good news.
- *Changes in the digestive system.* With age, there are lower secretions of acid in the small intestines. This means that nutrients are not absorbed as well as when we were younger.
Action: Eat well! Have a nutritious diet that is low in fat and high in complex carbohydrates. The latter refers to anything that grows in the ground such as fruits, vegetables, and whole grains. At 21, you could get by with Twinkies, a soda, and chips—but not in your 50s.
- *Changes in the connective tissues.* With age, cells in the connective tissue tend to lose water. The problem is dehydration. Connective tissue is located around every joint in the body, and is vital for flexibility and mobility.
Action: If the problem is dehydration, what do you think is the solution? Most people say drink more water. Good answer, but not the complete one. Exercise, particularly exercises that increase flexibility and range of motion, helps the cells retain water. And yes, with exercise we'll still be able to play the piano, enter data in our computers, pick up a screw from under our RV, and cross the street with some agility before the light turns red.
- *Changes in bone growth.* With age, bones tend to calcify. For example, hips tend to "grow" a bit, the bone at the top of the spine gets larger, and here's the best—the tip of the nose (which is cartilage) tends to grow a bit.
Action: None known.

Here's a familiar picture of aging: someone with wrinkles, a long nose, large hips, short neck, and possibly a hearing device and glasses! But even if you experience these changes, do they affect your productivity, creativity, or what you want to do with your life? The answer is, *only if you let them.* These changes have no impact on intellectual capacity, creativity, performance, or abilities.

The Value of Exercise

A few decades ago, experts believed that physical conditioning after 40 had little effect. And they assumed that exercise after 60 produced no observable improvement in functioning. In 1967, Dr. Herbert A. deVries, professor emeritus of exercise sciences at the University of Southern California, challenged these notions. Studying men and women in the Leisure World community in Laguna Hills, California, deVries found that healthy older people who engaged in appropriate physical exercise benefited

as much as younger people. His results have been corroborated by investigators all over the world.

More recent studies show that men in their 80s can still build muscle mass and get stronger. Frail older people have been found to benefit from training designed to increase their strength. With strength training programs, a selected group of nursing home residents averaging age 87 increased their walking speed and ability to climb stairs. Some no longer needed walkers and used canes instead.

Master senior athletes continue to perform well between ages 40 and 65. And athletes who continue to train are competitive in their 70s, 80s, and even 90s.

Exercise is valuable at any age, but it's probably more important the older you get. Different kinds of exercise have different purposes. For example, range-of-motion exercises help to maintain a joint's complete movement. Strengthening exercises help muscles contract and do work, and endurance or aerobic exercises improve the body's capacity to use oxygen.

Overall, however, exercise can decrease body fat, improve circulation, and lower your blood pressure. It improves endurance, increases strength and flexibility, and builds muscle. Some studies show that exercise can even decrease certain kinds of depression, particularly if the individual exercises with someone.

But not everyone likes to exercise. You may be one of them, much like James Thurber, who said, "Oh, exercise! When I feel like exercising, I lie down until the feeling goes away."

In general, people don't continue a particular physical activity that they don't like. The key is finding an exercise that you enjoy. It can be as simple as walking only twenty minutes a day. The most important thing is to *do it.*

Nutrition

Research has long confirmed the link between nutrition and health. The following are Dietary Guidelines for Americans published by the U.S. Department of Agriculture and the U.S. Department of Health and Human Services:

- Eat a well-balanced diet.
- Maintain healthy weight.
- Choose a diet that's low in fat, saturated fat, and cholesterol. It's recommended that 30 percent or less of your calories per day come from fat.
- Choose a diet with plenty of vegetables, fruits, and grain products.
- Use salt in moderation.
- If you drink alcoholic beverages, do it in moderation.

Obstacles to Good Health Behaviors

The information in this chapter probably isn't new to you. Most of us have been bombarded with health data in newspapers, magazines, and on TV. Perhaps the real issue is not lack of information, but rather the obstacles preventing each of us from adopting a healthy lifestyle.

In studies of over 6,000 preretirees, these were typical responses to the question of what keeps them from exercising and eating a nutritious diet:

- There is no time to exercise.
- I feel fine and look good. Why change?
- This information is not relevant to my life.
- Rich food tastes great.
- I'm exhausted after work. The last thing I want to do is exercise.
- It's hard to break a habit and change.
- My husband (or wife) isn't very supportive of a change.

- I'll have more time in retirement for this healthy behavior business.

The Message for You

There are actually two messages: You are in charge and it's never too late to change. George Burns said, "If I had known I was going to live this long, I would have taken better care of myself."

Elevate your health plan to an equal level of importance as your financial plan. You need both for a happy, healthy retirement!

Part II: State-By-State Retirement Housing Options

Introduction

The names of facilities listed in this section were gleaned from numerous sources. For licensed facilities providing health care or personal living assistance, we drew on information from the individual state departments and from such organizations as the American Association of Homes and Services for the Aging (AAHSA) and their state affiliates, the Assisted Living Federation of America (ALFA), Health Care Financing Administration (HCFA), Joint Commission on the Accreditation of Health Care Organizations (JCAHO), the Continuing Care Accreditation Commission, and other reliable sources.

As space was limited in this edition, we established certain additional criteria beyond licensing for the selections. Where possible, accredited facilities were given preference over nonaccredited facilities. However, since accreditation standards vary from state to state, this is not always a definitive indicator. Readers should be sure to see the specific information about each state's own licensing and accreditation requirements at the beginning of each state's listings. Preference was also given to nonprofit facilities and to facilities with the broadest admission requirements.

For all housing categories, we tried to represent a balance of facilities in low, medium, and high price ranges as far as possible.

For facilities or developments that do not provide health care or personal assistance, we consulted numerous national and regional publications, as well as such organizations as the Association of Retirement Resorts International (ARRI), and we secured additional information by direct contact. Most facilities were contacted by phone to update and expand their profiles because we required information that was not easily available.

Important: The inclusion of a facility or development in no way constitutes an endorsement of it, and the producer and publisher accepts no liability for any problems experienced with any of the facilities or developments.

Since the information provided here is subject to change, we recommend that you call any facility of interest to you directly to get exact costs and answers to any other questions you might have. It is a good idea to visit the facility and talk with both the management and the residents themselves to form your opinion. Do not make any commitments without complete information and/or professional advice.

General State Information

At the beginning of each state, you will find helpful general information about the state itself, including climate, transportation (major airports and highways, plus bus, rail, and ground transportation), cultural attractions (theater, music, museums, and so forth), and organizations (advocacy groups and volunteer programs). Cost-of-living information is included as well, featuring:

- Cost-of-living ranking for each state, 1 having the highest cost of living and 51 having the lowest, based on the ranking system of the John F. Kennedy School of Government at Harvard University. For an explanation of their cost-of-living formula, go to *http://www.ksg.harvard.edu/fisc99*
- State/local taxes as percent of income, current as of 2000, from the Tax Foundation (*http://www.taxfoundation.org*).
- State sales tax rates and prescription tax reductions or exemptions, current as of January 1, 2001, from the Federation of Tax Administrators (*http://www.taxadmin.org*).

How to Read the Listings

The information for each listing is organized in a standard format, using the following abbreviations in the interest of space:

AC Adult Care
ACH Adult Care Home
ACQ ENT Acquisition Entrance Fee
ADC Adult Day Care
ADL Activity of Daily Living (same as PC or AL)
ADMN Admission
AIG Aging in Place
AL Assisted Living (same as personal care)
ALZ/MEM IMP Alzheimer's/Memory Impaired
APPL Application Fee
ASSOC Association
BC Basic Care
CCRC Continuing Care Retirement Community
CC Continuing Care
COMM Commons Fee
CONG Congregate Housing (provides extended assisted living care)
DEP Deposit
ENT Entrance Fee
HCC Health Care Center
HHC Home Health Care
HSP Hospice
ICF Intermediate Care Facility
IND Independent Living
IND CL Independent Congregate Living
IND COM Independent Community Investment
LC Life Care
LCF Life Care Facility
LL Life Lease
LTC Long-Term Care
MO Monthly
NC Nursing Care
NH Nursing Home
PC Personal Care (assistance with one or more of the following: bathing, dressing, grooming, and eating)
PCC Personal Care Community
PROC Processing Fee
RAF Resident Agreement Fee
RC Residential Care
REHAB Rehabilitative Care
REQ Requirements
RH Residential Housing
RL Residential Living
RLUF Refundable Life Use Fee
RSP Respite Care
RSV AGR Reservation Agreement
RSVF Reservation Fee
SA Subacute
SC Skilled Care
SNF Skilled Nursing Facility

Here's a sample listing showing how to locate specific information in each listing:

Llanfair Retirement Community, CCAC, JCAHO

1701 Llanfair Ave
Cincinnati, OH 45224

Ph: (513) 681-4230
Fax: (513) 681-0417

E-mail: *Kgoetzel@Llanfair.OPRS.ORG*

IND: Yes. AL: Yes. SNF: 75. ALZ: Yes

Nonprofit; nondenominational; Ohio Presbyterian Retirement Services. Homes, apartments, studios, and suites. Skilled nursing care; staff medical director on call 24 hours; dentist, podiatrist, and optician on-site; licensed social worker; physical, speech, and occupational therapies; respite care; restorative/rehabilitative services; personal care; medication administration; Medicare/Medicaid-approved; security; transportation; up to 3 daily meals; housekeeping and laundry services; inhome care; postal and banking services; residence councils and committees; barber/beauty shop.

IND ENT: $12,000–$102,000. IND MO: $723–$1,765; (no ENT option), $1,458–$2,400. AL ENT: $8,500–$30,500. AL MO: $2,036–$3,492; (No AL ENT option), $2,213–$4,127. SNF ENT: $8,200. SNF Daily: $150, $172, $184; (no ENT option), $164, $185, $198. ALZ ENT: $8,200. ALZ/MEM IMP Daily: $154 and $165; (no ENT option), $168, $178, and $189.

Alabama

http://www.state.al.us

General Information

Climate

Mild. January average between 46° F and 52° F; July average about 80° F.

Cost of Living

Ranks 40th in the nation.

Taxes

State/Local as % of Income: 9.0%

Property Tax Reduction: Residents 65+ may be eligible for state and county homestead exemptions.

Sales: 4%.

Prescription Exemptions: Drugs and medicines sold on prescription are exempt from sales tax.

Transportation, Travel, and Tourism

General

Alabama Bureau of Tourism and Travel, (800) ALABAMA.

Major Airports

- Birmingham International Airport, 5900 Airport Highway, (205) 595-0533.
- Huntsville International Airport, 1000 Glenn Hern Blvd., SW, (205) 772-9395.
- Mobile Downtown Airport, 1981 9th St., (334) 438-7334
- Mobile Regional Airport, 8400 Airport Blvd., (334) 438-7334

Railways

- Amtrak, 11 Government St., Mobile, AL, (334) 432-4052.
- Amtrak, 1819 Morris Ave., Birmingham, AL, (205) 324-3033.

Bus Tours

- Greyhound Bus, (800) 231-2222.

State Highways

- Interstate 65 runs north-south.
- Interstate 20 runs east-west.

Theater and Music

North

- Back Street Opry, PO Box 740, Vernon, AL 35592, (205) 695-7029. Fax: (205) 695-9501 (music groups every Saturday night).

South

- Dothan Opera House, PO Box 2128, Dothan, AL 36302, (334) 793-0127.

Central

- Performing Arts Centre, PO Box 137, Selma, AL 36702, (334) 874-2145 (260-seat auditorium and art gallery).
- Alabama Shakespeare Festival, 1 Festival Drive, Montgomery, AL, 36117-4605, (334) 271-5353 or (800) 841-4ASF. Fax: (334) 271-5348 (open all year).

Museums, Crafts, Historical, Recreational

North

- Alabama Music Hall of Fame, PO Box 709, Tuscumbia, AL 35674, (204) 381-4417 or (800) 239-AMHF (exhibits of Alabama's musical achievers).
- Weeden House Museum, 300 Gates Ave., Huntsville, AL 35801, (205) 536-7718 (furniture and art displayed).

- Huntsville Museum of Art, 700 Monroe St., NW, Huntsville, AL 35801, (205) 535-4350 (leading visual arts center in No. AL).
- Looney's Tavern Amphitheater and Park, PO Box 70, Double Springs, AL 35553, (205) 489-5000, *http://bham.net/looneys* (historical Civil War drama replayed).
- Alabama Constitution Village, 404 Madison St., Huntsville, AL 35801, (205) 535-6565 or (800) 678-1819 (reconstructed buildings from 1819).

South

- Mobile Museum of Art, 4850 Museum Drive, Mobile, AL 36608, (334) 343-2667, Fax: (334) 343-2680 (collection includes more than 4,000 works, spanning 2,000 years of history).
- Gulf Beaches, Gulf Shores, Alabama Gulf Coast Convention and Visitors Bureau, PO Box 3388, Gulf Shores, AL 36547, (334) 968-4600.

Central

- Montgomery Museum of Fine Arts, One Museum Drive, Montgomery, AL 36117, (334) 244-5700 (19th- and 20th-century paintings and regional art).
- Birmingham Museum of Art, 2000 Eighth Ave., N., Birmingham, AL 35203, (205) 245-2565 (collection of over 17,000 works of art).
- Ruffner Mountain Nature, 1214 81st St., S, Birmingham, AL 35206, (205) 833-8264 or 8112. Fax: (205) 836-3960 (hiking trails; recreational areas).
- Magnolia Grove, 1002 Hobson St., Greensboro, AL 36744, (334) 624-8618 (Greek Revival structure).

Organizations

Advocacy Groups

- Alabama Commission on Aging, 770 Washington Ave., RSA Plaza, Suite 470, Montgomery, AL 36130, (334) 242-5743, Fax: (334) 242-5594.

Volunteer Programs

- Literacy Volunteers of America, AL Liaison, (843) 681-5024.
- Volunteers of America, North Alabama, (205) 830-2155; South Alabama, (334) 666-2836.

Housing

Long-Term Care Facilities

In the state of Alabama, these facilities are called ***Continuing Care/Long-Term Care/Nursing Care Facilities****.*

These facilities provide residential living and/or various levels of nursing and medical services to seniors for an extended period of time.

Types of Authorization

Licensing and/or Certification

These facilities must be licensed by the Department of Public Health, Licensure and Certification Division.

Memberships

- American Association of Homes and Services for the Aging (AAHSA) represents not-for-profit organizations committed to providing high-quality health care, housing, and services to the elderly. AAHSA, 901 E St. NW, Suite 500, Washington, DC 20004-2011. Ph: (202) 783-2242. Fax: (202) 783-2285. *http://www.aahsa.org*
- Alabama Association of Homes and Services for the Aging (ALAHSA) is an AAHSA Affiliated State Association. ALAHSA, PO Box 830605, Birmingham, AL 35283. Ph: (205) 715-7529.
- National Association of Senior Living Industries (NASLI).

- Alzheimer's Association (AA).

Accreditations

- Continuing Care Accreditation Commission (CCAC) accredits facilities that offer seniors a contract or contracts that provide residential living and health care services for the remainder of the person's lifetime and meet CCAC's accreditation standards.
- Joint Commission on the Accreditation of Healthcare Organizations (JCAHO) is an independent, not-for-profit organization, and the nation's oldest and largest standards-setting and health care accrediting institution.

Southwest

Westminster Village

500 Spanish Fort Boulevard
Spanish Fort, AL 36527

Ph: (334) 626-2900 or in AL, (800) 225-8461, or nationwide, (800) 843-3740

IND: Yes. AL: Yes. HCC: Yes

Nonprofit; nondenominational; managed by Life Care Services Corporation. Garden homes, apartments, and private and semiprivate rooms. Skilled nursing care; 24-hour nursing care; resident health services program; doctors clinic; physical, speech, and occupational therapies; wellness center; pharmacy; personal care; medication administration; security; emergency response system; maintenance; transportation; up to 3 daily meals; housekeeping and laundry services; swimming pool; exercise program; chapel; library; bank services; activities directors; recreational and social activities; woodworking shop; arts and crafts; travel club; walking paths; picnic areas; convenience store.

IND ENT: (ref.), $90,000–$225,000; 2nd person, $2,750. IND MO: $1,300–$2,000; 2nd person, $625.

Central

Kirkwood by the River

3605 Ratliff Road
Birmingham, AL 35210

Ph: (205) 956-2184

IND: Yes. AL: Yes. SNF: Yes

Nonprofit; nondenominational; affiliated with the Independent Presbyterian Church. Apartments and private and semiprivate rooms. 24-hour nursing care; skilled nursing care; medical director; blood pressure monitoring; immunizations; health maintenance; personal care; medication administration; security; emergency response system; maintenance; transportation; up to 3 daily meals; housekeeping and laundry services; exercise programs; chapel; weekly Bible study; swimming pool; delivery of prescription drugs; weekly shopping cart; social and recreational activities; library and reading rooms; gardening; walking paths; barber/beauty shop.

IND ENT: (two ref. plans) $28,000–$154,000. IND MO: $1,100–$3,600. AL MO: $2,400–$4,300. SNF MO: $3,400–$5,100.

St. Martins-in-the-Pines

4941 Montevallo Rd.
Birmingham, AL 35210

Ph: (205) 956-9440
Fax: (205) 951-1547

http://www.stmartinsinthepines.org

IND: 95. AL: 102. HCC: 138

Nonprofit; Episcopal Church affiliation; nondenominational. Apartments and private rooms. Comprehensive, long-term care; 24-hour skilled nursing care; physical, occupational, and speech therapies; personal care; medication administration; Medicare/Medicaid-approved; security; emergency response system; maintenance; transportation; up to 3 daily meals; housekeeping and laundry

services; chapel; mail and banking services; arts and crafts area; library; gardening; activity rooms; recreational and spiritual activities; barber/beauty shop.

APPL: $100. IND ENT: $2,200–$4,100. IND MO: $1,700–$2,500. AL ENT: $600. AL MO: $2,000. HCC Daily: $115–$130. Investment plan available for IND.

Assisted Living and Residential Care Facilities

These facilities provide room and board for ambulatory and independent adults who need minimum support.

Types of Authorization

Licensing and/or Certification

These facilities must be licensed by the Department of Public Health, Licensure and Certification Division.

Memberships

- Assisted Living Federation of America (ALFA) is a national nonprofit membership organization whose mission is to enhance the quality of life in assisted living facilities and promote the interests of the assisted living industry. ALFA, 10300 Eaton Place, Suite 400, Fairfax, VA 22030. Ph: (703) 691-8100. Fax: (703) 691-8106. *http://www.alfa.org*
- Assisted Living Homes Association of Alabama (ALHAA) is a state affiliate of ALFA. ALHAA, PO Box 3099, Montgomery, AL 36109. Ph: (334) 273-0201. Fax: (334) 273-0218.

North

Pine Crest Estate, ALHAA, ALFA

582 Shields Road
Huntsville, AL 35811

Ph: (256) 851-9161

AL: Yes. ALZ/MEM IMP: Yes

Nondenominational. Limited to older adults in the early stages of adult dementia. Personal care; medication administration; CNA certified staff. Bed checks; vital signs recorded regularly; security; emergency response system; maintenance; transportation; 3 daily meals; housekeeping and laundry services; daily activities; secured garden/lawn area.

Contact facility for fees.

South

Wesley Gardens

1555 Taylor Road
Montgomery, AL 36117

Ph: (334) 272-7917
Fax: (334) 272-5774

AL: Yes

Owned and operated by Methodist Homes for the Aging Corp.; non-denominational. Personal care; medication administration; 24-hour supervision; security; emergency response system; maintenance; transportation; 3 daily meals (tray service when needed); housekeeping and laundry services; chapel; exercise room; recreational and social activities; putting green; gardening area; shuffleboard court; porches; gift shop barber/beauty shop.

APPL: (no ref.), $100. AL MO: $1,900–$3,000. AL Daily: (short-term stays), $85 and $105.

Central

The Adams House

5017 King Drive
Adamsville, AL 35005

Ph: (205) 674-0100
Fax: (205) 744-4677
E-mail: *AALInc@aol.com*

AL: Yes

Locally owned and operated by Adamsville Assisted Living, Inc.; nondenominational. Semiprivate apartments. Personal care; medication administration; individualized health services; security; emergency response system; maintenance; transportation; up to 3 daily meals; housekeeping and laundry services; close to major hospitals; all utilities (except phone and cable); television rooms with VCR; living room with piano; screened porch; recreational, religious, and social activities; barber/beauty shop.

APPL: $100. RSV: (no ref.), $200. AL MO: $1,500.

Galleria Oaks Guest Home

570 Southland Drive
Birmingham, AL 35226

Ph: (205) 823-2393
Fax: (205) 823-2304

AL: Yes. ADC: Yes

For-profit; nondenominational; Marriott residence. Suites and private and semiprivate rooms. 24-hour staffing; personal care; medication administration; pharmacy services; security; emergency response system; maintenance; transportation; 3 daily meals; housekeeping and laundry services; exercise program; living room with entertainment center; library; activities director; off-site activities; games; cooking/baking; whirlpool bath; barber/beauty shop.

AL MO: $1,700–$2,900. RSP Daily: $80–$100. ADC Daily: $35–$60.

Independent Living

Independent housing (primarily rentals) for seniors that may offer security features, meal service, and activities.

North

Presbyterian Towers

1824 Presbyterian Dr., SW
Decatur, AL 35603

Ph: (256) 350-3323
Fax: (256) 350-3329

ND: 101

Age 62+. Nonprofit; nondenominational; nonsectarian. Apartments. 24-hour emergency system; maintenance; pets allowed.

Low-income housing for seniors; rent includes electric and water. DEP: one mo. rent. IND MO: 30% of income.

Southwest

Baptist Oaks Apartments

800 Conti St.
Mobile, AL 36602

Ph: (334) 432-2312
Fax: (334) 432-2314

IND: 52

Age 62+. Nonprofit; nondenominational. Apartments. Emergency response system; maintenance; transportation; laundry facilities; pets allowed; planned social activities.

IND MO: Maximum is 30% of income. Guidelines established by HUD.

Central

Episcopal Place

1112 26th Street, South
Birmingham, AL 35205

Ph: (205) 939-0085
Fax: (205) 939-0101

IND: 141

Age 62+. Nondenominational; nonprofit; operated by Episcopal Housing Foundation and Episcopal Housing of Birmingham. Apartments. Some supportive services; health screenings; security; maintenance; transportation; midday meal program; some laundry and housekeeping services; worship and clergy services; hospital and shopping nearby; social and educational activities; crafts; volunteer opportunities; barber/beauty shop.

HUD residence. IND MO: 30% of adjusted income. Income must not exceed $15,400 (Episcopal Place I) or $24,650 (Episcopal Place II).

South Central

Epworth House

2500 Franklin Street
Selma, AL 36703

Ph: (334) 875-6450

IND: 48

Age 62+. Nondenominational; affiliated with the United Methodist Church. Apartments. Security; emergency response system; laundry services; recreational room; planned activities; nearby shopping.

HUD residence. IND MO: 30% of adjusted income.

Seton Haven Apartment Complex

3821 Wares Ferry Rd.
Montgomery, AL 36109-2802

Ph: (334) 272-4000
Fax: (334) 272-1788

E-mail: *sh36109@aol.com*

IND: 100

Age 62+. Nonprofit facility. Apartments. Security; emergency response system; maintenance; 1 daily meal (not included in MO); planned activities; lobby; park and picnic area; gardening; walking paths; barber/beauty shop.

DEP: 30% of income. IND MO: 30% of income.

Adult/Resort Communities

Communities for active adults (not all are age-restricted; primarily ownership).

North

Canebrake at Piney Creek

PO Box 410
Athens, AL 35612

Ph: (888) 895-2520 or (256) 230-6622
Fax: (256) 230-6442

Individual homes, patio homes, courtyard homes, estate homes, homesites. Golf course; clubhouse; pro shop; tennis; swimming pool; fitness center.

PURCHASE: Homes, $193,000–$660,000+; homesites, $27,500–$115,500.

South

Craft Farms

100 Cotton Creek Drive
Gulf Shores, AL 36542

Ph: (800) 327-2657 or (334) 968-7528

http://www.craftfarms.com

Individual homes, condominiums, homesites. Golf course; tennis; swimming pool; hiking/biking; fishing; social clubs.

PURCHASE: Homes, from $204,000; homesites, from $38,500.

Kiva Dunes

815 Plantation Drive
Gulf Shores, AL 36542

Ph: (334) 540-7100
Fax: (334) 540-7003

http://www.kivadunes-golf.com

Individual homes, homesites. Golf course; swimming pool; hiking trails; fishing; beach.

PURCHASE: Homesites, $55,000–$412,500.

Lake Forest Yacht and Country Club

1 Golf Terrace
Daphne, AL 36526

Ph: (800) 486-6232 or (334) 626-0788
Fax: (334) 626-4502

Individual homes, condominiums. Golf course; tennis; swimming pool; fishing; riding stables; boating/waterskiing; social clubs; yacht club.

PURCHASE: Homes, $82,500–$275,000.

Marriott's Lakewood Golf Club

1 Grand Blvd.
Point Clear, AL 36564

Ph: (334) 990-6312 or (334) 990-6353

Individual homes, condominiums, homesites. Golf course; tennis; swimming pool; hiking trails; fishing; boating/sailing; riding stables; fitness center; beach; social clubs.

PURCHASE: Homesites, $55,000–$192,500.

Peninsula

10 Peninsula Blvd.
Gulf Shores, AL 36542

Ph: (800) 646-5554 or (334) 968-8008
Fax: (334) 968-8007

Individual homes, condominiums, villas, homesites. Golf course; tennis; swimming pool; hiking; fishing; fitness center; private beach.

PURCHASE: Homes, from $220,000.

Central

Greystone Golf Club

4000 Greystone Drive
Birmingham, AL 35242

Ph: (205) 980-5210 or (205) 443-4700
Fax: (205) 443-4832

http://www.greystonecommunity.com

Individual homes, garden homes, homesites. Golf course; tennis; swimming pool; hiking/biking; fishing; social clubs.

PURCHASE: Homes, $385,000–$2.2 million.

Heatherwood Golf Club

400 St. Annes Drive
Birmingham, AL 35244

Ph: (205) 991-7474
Fax: (205) 995-8691

Individual homes, homesites. Golf course; tennis; swimming pool; fishing; dining; social clubs.

PURCHASE: Homes, $247,500–$550,000.

Inverness

1 Country Club Drive
Birmingham, AL 35242

Ph: (205) 991-8608
Fax: (205) 980-5284

Individual homes, condominiums, homesites, rental apartments. Golf course; tennis; racquetball; swimming pool; hiking trails; fishing; boating/waterskiing; social clubs.

PURCHASE: Homes, $154,000–$1.32 million; homesites, $44,000–$230,000.

North River Yacht Club

New Watermelon Rd.
Tuscaloosa, AL 35404

Ph: (205) 345-0202
Fax: (205) 343-4013

Individual homes, condominiums, homesites. Golf course; tennis; swimming pool; fishing; hunting; boating/waterskiing; fitness center; social clubs.

PURCHASE: Homes, $275,000–$1.32 million; homesites, $60,500–$137,500.

StillWaters

1816 Still Water Drive
Dadeville, AL 36853

Ph: (888) 797-3767 or (256) 825-4945

http://www.stillwaters.com

Individual homes, condominiums, cooperative units, homesites. Golf course; tennis; swimming pool; hiking trails; fishing; boating/waterskiing; marina; fitness center; library; social clubs.

PURCHASE: Homes, $143,000–$715,000; homesites, from $22,000.

Alaska

http://www.state.ak.us

General Information

Climate

Wide range. Anchorage: January average, 8.4° F, July average 65° F; average yearly snowfall, 69.5 inches. Fairbanks: January average, -18° F, July average 72° F; average yearly snowfall, 70 inches.

Cost of Living

Ranks 6th in nation.

Taxes

General: No statewide sales tax; no personal state income tax; some municipalities levy property and sales taxes.

State/Local as % of Income: 6.8%.

Property Tax Reduction: Citizens 65 and over are exempt from property taxes on the first $150,000 of assessed value, and senior renters receive a rebate for that portion of their yearly rent on their permanent residence that goes toward payment of property taxes.

Sales: No state sales tax; however, 98 of about 162 municipalities levy a sales tax of from 2% to 7%.

Prescription Exemptions: Check with individual municipalities.

Transportation, Travel, and Tourism

General

Alaska Division of Tourism, PO Box 110801, Juneau, AK 99811, (907) 465-2012.

Major Airports

- Anchorage International Airport, PO Box 196960, Anchorage, AK 99519, (907) 266-2525.
- Fairbanks International Airport, 6450 Airport Way, Suite 1, Fairbanks, AK 99709, (907) 474-2500.

Railways

- Alaska Railroad Corp., PO Box 107500, Anchorage, AK 99510, (800) 544-0552.

Bus Tours

- Alaskon Express, 745 W 4th Ave. #200, Anchorage, AK 99501, (907) 277-5581.
- Capital Transit, 10099 Bentwood Pl., Juneau, AK 99801, (907) 789-6901.
- Gray Line, P O Box 5097, Ketchikan, AK 99901, (907) 225-5930.
- Laidlaw Transit Inc., 2014 Mill Bay Rd., Kodiak, AK 99615, (907) 486-3600.
- Princess Tours, 3045 Davis Rd., Fairbanks, AK 99709, (907) 479-9640.
- Seward Bus Line, 1915 N. Seward Hwy., Seward, AK 99664, (907) 224-3608.

Cruise Lines

- Alaska Sightseeing/Cruise West, 4th at Battery Bldg., #700, Seattle, WA 98121, (800) 426-7702 (six ships). (Also offers bus tours. Offices at: 513 W 4th Ave., Anchorage, AK 99501, (907) 276-1305.)
- Glacier Bay Tours & Cruises, 520 Pike St., Suite 1400, Seattle WA 98101, (206) 623-7110 (four ships).
- Holland American Line Westours, 300 Elliot Ave. West, Seattle, WA 98119, (800) 426-0327 or -0329 (six ships).
- Princess Cruises, 2815 Second Ave., #400, Seattle, WA 98121, (800) 421-1700 (for cruise only) and (800) 426-0442 (for cruise tours) (six ships).

State Highways

- The Alaska Highway runs southeast from Fairbanks to Delta Junction, with an extension continuing to Dawsons Creek, B.C.
- Rte. 1 runs northeast from Anchorage to Tok, where it meet the Alaska Highway.
- Rte. 3 runs north from Anchorage to Fairbanks.

Theater and Music

Far North

- Midnight Sun Festival, celebrations on the weekend closest to June 21 (summer solstice), Nome, (907) 443-5535.

Interior

- Ester Gold Camp, PO Box 109, Ester, AK 99725, (907) 479-2500.

Southeast

- Chilkat Center for the Arts (Tlingit dancers each summer), Box 271, Haines, AK 99827, (907) 766-2160.
- Sitka Music Festival (June), Sitka. (Sitka Visitors Bureau, (907) 747-3739.)
- Juneau Jazz and Classics Festival (May), Juneau. (Juneau Visitors Bureau, (907) 586-2201 or (888) 581-2201.)

Southwest

- Alutiiq Museum, 215 Mission Rd., Suite 101, Kodiak, AK 99615, (907) 486-7004.

Museums, Crafts, Historical, Recreational

Far North

- Carrie McLain Memorial Museum, 200 E. Front St., Nome, AK 99762, (907) 443-2566.
- Inupiat Heritage Museum, (Temporary Address) Ilisagcik College, Barrow, AK 99723, (800) 478-7337.
- National Association of Native Alaskans (NANA) Museum, 100 Shore Ave., Kotzebue, AK 99752, (907) 442-3304.
- Bering Land Bridge National Preserve (visitors center, cabins), PO Box 220, Nome, AK 99762, (907) 443-2522.
- Northwest Alaska Areas (Cape Krusenstern National Monument, Kobuk Valley National Park, and Noatak National Preserve) (no facilities in parks), PO Box 1029, Kotzebue, AK 99752, (907) 442-3890.

Interior

- Dog Mushing Museum, 250 Cushman St., Courthouse Square, Suite 2B, Fairbanks, AK 99708, (907) 456-6874.
- Fairbanks Gold Co. Mining Museum and Gold Works, near Railroad Depot, Fairbanks, AK 99709, (907) 457-6058.
- University of Alaska Museum, 907 Yukon Drive, Fairbanks, AK 99775, (907) 474-7505.
- Denali National Park (visitors center, hotel, camping), PO Box 9, Denali Park, AK 99755, (907) 683-2294. (For camp reservations, (800) 622-7275).
- Gates of the Arctic National Park (visitors center, camping outside park), PO Box 74680, Fairbanks, AK 99707, (907) 456-0281.
- Matanuska Glacier, near Glenn Hwy., north of Palmer.
- Yukon-Charley Rivers National Preserve (visitors center, 4 cabins), PO Box 167, Eagle, AK 99738, (907) 547-2234.

South Central

- Anchorage Museum of History and Art, 121 W. 7th St., Anchorage, AK 99501, (907) 343-4326.
- Eklutha Historical Park, Spirit Houses, and Russian Orthodox Churches, 16515 Centerfield Drive, Suite 201, Eagle River, AK 99577, (907) 696-2828.

- Alaska Museum of Natural History, 11723 Old Glenn Hwy., Eagle River, AK 99577, (907) 696-8513
- Alaska SeaLife Center, 301 Railway Ave., PO Box 1329, Seward, AK 99664, (800) 224-2525.
- Iditarod Sled Dog Race, Anchorage to Nome, starts first Sat. each March, (907) 476-5155.
- Talkeetna Historical Society, PO Box 76, Talkeetna, AK 99676, (907) 733-2487.
- Ahtna Heritage Foundation Museum, Mile 115 Richardson Hwy, Glennallen, AK 99588, (907) 822-5778.
- Kenai Fjords National Park (visitors center, cabins, camping), PO Box 1727, Seward, AK 99664, (907) 224-3175.
- Lake Clark National Park (visitors center, cabins, camping), 4230 University Drive, Suite 311, Anchorage, AK 99508, (907) 271-3751.
- Portage Glacier, Seward Hwy., SE of Anchorage.
- Anchorage Golf Course, 3651 Omalley Rd., Anchorage, AK 99516, (907) 522-3363
- Full Swing Golf of Alaska, 9360 Old Seward Hwy, Anchorage, AK 99515 (907) 344-4653.

Southeast

- Klondike Gold Rush National Historical Park (visitors center, camping), 2nd and Broadway, Box 517, Skagway, AK 99840, (907) 983-2921.
- Sitka National Historic Park (visitors center, no camping), 106 Metlakatla St., Box 738, Sitka, AK 99835, (907) 747-6281.
- Tongass Historical Museum, 629 Dock St., Ketchikan, AK 99901, (907) 225-5600.
- Sheldon Museum & Cultural Center, Corner of Main and First streets, Haines, AK 99827, (907) 766-2366.
- Alaska State Museum, 395 Whittier St., Juneau, AK 99801, (907) 465-2901.
- Sheldon Jackson Museum, 104 College Dr., Sitka, AK 99835, (907) 747-8981.
- Glacier Bay National Park (visitors center, hotel, camping), PO Box 140, Gustavus, AK 99826, (907) 697-2230.
- Misty Fjords National Monument Wilderness and Tongass National Forest, 3031 Tongass Ave., Ketchikan, AK 99901, (907) 225-2148.
- Wrangell St. Elias National Park (visitors center, no campgrounds), PO Box 439, Copper Center, AK 99573, (907) 822-5234.
- Mendenhall Glacier, 13 miles from Juneau, (907) 789-0097.

Southwest

- Aniakchak National Monument and Preserve (no facilities), and Katmai National Park (visitors center, camping), PO Box 7, King Salmon, AK 99613, (907) 246-3305.
- Kodiak National Wildlife Refuge, 1390 Buskin River Rd., Kodiak, AK 99615, (907) 487-2600.

Organizations

Advocacy Groups

- Division of Senior Services, Information and Referral Service, 3601 C Street, Suite 310, Anchorage, AK 99053, (907) 269-3666 or (800) 478-9996.

Volunteer Programs

- Volunteers in Parks, 3601 C St., Suite 2100, Anchorage, AK 99503, (907) 762-2612.

Housing

Long-Term Care Facilities

*In the state of Alaska, these facilities are called **Continuing Care/Long-Term Care/Nursing Care Facilities.***

These facilities provide residential living and/or various levels of nursing and medical services to seniors for an extended period of time.

Types of Authorization

Licensing and / or Certification

Nursing homes are licensed and certified by the Department of Health and Social Services, Division of Medical Assistance (Health Facilities Licensing and Certification).

Memberships

- American Association of Homes and Services for the Aging (AAHSA) represents not-for-profit organizations committed to providing high-quality health care, housing, and services to the elderly. AAHSA, 901 E St. NW, Suite 500, Washington, DC 20004-2011. Ph: (202) 783-2242 Fax: (202) 783-2285. *http: / / www.aahsa.org*

South

Alaska Pioneer's Home

c/o Division of Alaska Longevity Programs
PO Box 110211
Juneau, AK 99811-0211

Ph: (907) 465-4400
Fax: (907) 465-4108

IND: Yes. AL: Yes. NH: Yes. ALZ/MEM IMP: Yes

Age 65+. Alaska Pioneer Homes are located in Anchorage, Fairbanks, Juneau, Ketchikan, Palmer, and Sitka. Applicants are eligible if they have a cognitive or other disability, making them unable to live without assistance. Government sponsored. Private and semiprivate rooms. Nursing care; medical services; personal care; medication administration; security; emergency response system; maintenance; transportation; up to 3 daily meals; housekeeping and laundry services; social and recreational activities.

IND MO: $1,500. AL MO: $2,400–$3,000. ALZ/MEM IMP MO: $3,000. NH MO: $3,800. Payment assistance available.

St. Ann's Care Center

415 Sixth Street
Juneau, AK 99801

Ph: (907) 586-3883

NH: 45

Nonprofit; nondenominational. Rooms. 24-hour nursing care; medical director; rehabilitative therapies; lab services; respiratory services; IV therapy; dental and podiatry care; social worker; emergency response system; Medicare/Medicaid-approved; maintenance; transportation; up to 3 daily meals; housekeeping and laundry services; social and recreational activities.

DEP: $11,000 (private pay). NH Daily: $350. Therapies and lab and other services are at additional costs.

Assisted Living and Residential Care Facilities

*In the state of Alaska, these facilities are called **Assisted Living Homes.***

These facilities offer housing with personalized support services and health care services.

Types of Authorization

Licensing and / or Certification

These facilities are regulated by the Department of Administration, Division of Senior Services. Assisted living facilities provide a homelike environment for those persons who need assistance with the activities of daily living. Assisted living homes may provide nursing services to residents who do not need 24-hour nursing care on a long-term basis.

Memberships

- Assisted Living Federation of America (ALFA) is a national nonprofit membership organization whose mission is to enhance the quality of life in assisted living facilities and promote the interests of the assisted living industry. ALFA, 10300 Eaton Place, Suite 400, Fairfax, VA 22030. Ph: (703) 691-8100. Fax: (703) 691-8106. *http://www.alfa.org*
- Northwest Assisted Living Facilities Association (NOR-ALFA) is a regional affiliate of ALFA. NOR-ALFA, 34004 16th Avenue South, Suite 201, Federal Way WA 98003. Ph: (253) 874-5211. Fax: (253) 874-5350. *http://www.noralfa.org*

Northwest

Kotzebue Senior Citizens Cultural Center

PO Box 1073, 5th and Bison Street
Kotzebue, AK 99752

Ph: (907) 442-3590
Fax: (907) 442-2195

AL: 20

Age 60+. Nonprofit. Apartments. Nursing care; medical services; rehabilitative therapies; personal care; medication administration; security; emergency response system; maintenance; transportation; up to 3 daily meals; housekeeping and laundry services; social and recreational activities.

AL MO: $700.

South

Homer Assisted Living Kachemak Bay Senior Housing

250 Herndon Drive
Homer, AK 99603

Ph: (907) 235-6727
Fax: (907) 235-0586

E-mail: *hscc@ptialaska.net*

IND: 24. AL: 40. ALZ/MEM IMP: Yes

Age 55+. Nonprofit; nondenominational. Apartments. Respite care; personal care; medication administration; security; emergency response system; maintenance; transportation; up to 3 daily meals; housekeeping and laundry services; exercise program; social and recreational activities; card and board games; arts and crafts; gardening; fishing.

DEP: (ref.), $450. IND MO: $450–$650. AL MO: $700 plus $230 for meal plan and $900–$2,700 for AL services.

Horizon House

4140 Folker Street
Anchorage, AK 99508

Ph: (907) 261-4140
Fax: (907) 261-4160

AL: Yes

Nonprofit; nondenominational; owned by Providence Health System. Studio apartments. Wellness programs; personal care; medication administration; security; emergency response system; maintenance; transportation; up to 3 daily meals; housekeeping and laundry services; social and recreational activities; bingo; card and board games; courtyard; parlor; convenience store; barber/beauty shop.

DEP: $1,100. AL Daily: $120.

The Source

PO Box 772623
Eagle River, AK 99577

Ph: (907) 688-6222
Fax: (907) 688-2004

AL: Yes. ALZ/MEM IMP: 14

Nonprofit. Private and shared rooms. Nursing care; home health services; personal care; medication administration; security; emergency response system; maintenance; transportation; up to 3 daily meals; housekeeping and laundry services; social and recreational activities.

MO: $2,200–$2,400.

Independent Living

Independent housing (primarily rentals) for seniors that may offer security features, meal service, and activities.

South

Chester Park Cooperative

2020 Muldoon
Anchorage, AK 99504

Ph: (907) 333-8844
Fax: (907) 333-7094

IND: 142

Age 55+. Condos. Home health care services; some medical services; security; emergency response system; maintenance; transportation; meal plan; housekeeping and laundry services; fitness center; library; woodworking shop; craft room; gardening.

CONDOS: $97,000–$247,500. IND MO: $500–$625.

Cook Inlet Housing Complex

9131 Centennial Circle
Anchorage, AK 99504

Ph: (907) 338-2211
Fax: (907) 333-8597

IND: 215

Age 62+. Nonprofit; Cook Inlet Housing Authority (CIHA), 2600 Cordova St, Suite 201, Anchorage, AK 99503, Ph: (907) 276-8822 Fax: (907) 258-4957. CIHA owns and operates low rent apartments in Anchorage, Kenai, Ninilchik, and Seldovia. CIHA provides affordable housing for low-income Alaska Natives, American Indians, and the elderly. Apartments. Security; maintenance; transportation; pets allowed; library; sewing room; pottery and ceramics; common areas; social and recreational activities.

DEP: $275; with pet, $550. IND MO: 25% of income. HUD-subsidized housing.

Glacier View

200 Lowell Canyon Rd
PO Box 1475
Seward, AK 99664

Ph: (907) 224-3737
Fax: (907) 224-5527

http://www.ahfc.state.ak.us
E-mail: *mholvort@ahfc.state.ak.us*

IND: 30

Age 62+. Managed by Alaska Housing Finance Corp. (AHFC manages several hundred facilities in 11 locations throughout Alaska). Apartments. Security, emergency response system; maintenance; pets allowed.

DEP: 1 mo. rent. MO: 30% of income; HUD-subsidized.

Vintage Point Manor

381 Senior Court
Kenai, AK 99611

Ph: (907) 283-4156
Fax: (907) 283-3200
E-mail: *senior@kenai.ci.ak.us*

IND: 40

Age 62+. Nonprofit. Apartments. Security; emergency response system; maintenance; fitness center; media room; common areas; adjacent to Senior Center; flower gardens; ocean nearby; solarium.

DEP: nonsmoker, $500; smoker, $1,000.
IND MO: $525–$675.

Central

Golden Towers

330 3rd
Fairbanks, AK 99701

Golden Ages

1271 9th
Fairbanks, AK 99701

Southall Manor

401 7th
Fairbanks, AK 99701

Ph: (907) 456-1855
Fax: (907) 456-1855

IND: 96 (Golden Towers), 20 (Golden Ages), 40 (Southall Manor)

Age 62+. Nonprofit; nondenominational. Apartments. Home health care services; monthly blood pressure checks; annual flu shots; security; emergency response system; maintenance; pets allowed; resident councils; social and recreational activities.

IND MO: $275–$1,250.

Arizona

http://azportal.clearlake.ibm.com/webapp/portal

General Information

Climate

Average desert lows from 37° F to 73° F; highs from 66° F to 100° F. Average mountain lows from 21° F to 48° F; highs from 50° F to 89° F.

Cost of Living

Ranks 17th in nation.

Taxes

State/Local as % of Income: 9.3%.

Property Tax Reduction: Property tax credit up to $502 for full-year residents 65 or older with lower incomes.

Sales: About 5%.

Prescription Exemptions: Prescription medication and other prescribed devices, e.g., eyeglasses, hearing aids, prosthetics, are exempt from sales tax.

Transportation, Travel, and Tourism

General

Arizona Office of Tourism, 2702 N. 3rd St., Suite 4015, Phoenix, AZ 85004-4608, (602) 230-7733.

Major Airports

- Phoenix Sky Harbor International Airport, 3400 Sky Harbor Blvd., Phoenix, AZ 85034, (602) 273-3300.
- Tucson International Airport, Tucson, AZ 85706, (520) 573-8000.
- Flagstaff Pulliam Airport, (520) 556-1234.

Railways

- Amtrak, (800) USA-RAIL.

Bus Tours

- Arrow Stage Lines, (800) 777-3484.

State Highways

- Interstate 40, east-west (northern).
- Interstates 8 and 10, east-west (southern).
- Interstate 17, north-south (central).

Theater and Music

Flagstaff

- Northern Arizona University, P.O. Box 4084, Flagstaff, AZ 86011-4048, (520) 523-5511. Arizona only: (800) 345-1987. Home to a variety of cultural events, including the Grand Canyon Shakespeare Festival and Flagstaff Symphony performances.
- Flagstaff Symphony Orchestra, 113A E. Aspen Ave., P.O. Box 122, Flagstaff, AZ 86002-0122. (520) 774-5107. Fax: (520) 774-5109. 85-member orchestra.

Tucson

- Tucson Convention Center 260 South Church, Tucson, AZ, (520) 791-4101. Conventions, concerts, sports and more.
- Valley of the Sun (drama, dance, and musical productions in

Tempe and Phoenix

- Northwest Valley Chamber of Commerce, (602) 583-0692.
- Sundome Center for the Performing Arts, Tempe Chamber of Commerce, (602) 967-7891.

Museums, Crafts, Historical, Recreational

Canyon Country (Grand Canyon, skiing, campgrounds, national forests, outdoor activities)

- Flagstaff Visitor Center, (520) 774-9541.
- Grand Canyon Chamber of Commerce, (928) 527-0359.

High Country

- Alpine Chamber of Commerce, (520) 619-2722.
- Pinetop-Lakeside Chamber of Commerce, (520) 367-4290.
- Springerville Eagar Round Valley Chamber of Commerce, (520) 333-2123.

Valley of the Sun (including Champlin Fighter Museum, winter home of Chicago Cubs, and Arizona Mormon Temple)

- Phoenix & Valley of the Sun Convention & Visitors Bureau, (602) 254-6500.
- Carefree/Cave Creek Chamber of Commerce, (602) 488-3381. (Outdoor activities, shopping, dining.)
- Gilbert Chamber of Commerce, (602) 892-0056, (Old Western flavor).
- Mesa Convention & Visitors Bureau, (602) 827-4700.
- Native American Tourism Center, (602) 945-0264.

Central (including river tours, Verde Valley, dude ranches, mines)

- Black Canyon City Chamber of Commerce, (520) 374-9797.
- Cottonwood/Verde Valley Chamber of Commerce, (520) 634-7593.
- Wickenburg Chamber of Commerce, (800) WICKCHAMBER.

River Country (including water sports, wildlife refuges, original London Bridge)

- Lake Havasu City Visitor & Convention Bureau, (520) 855-4115.
- Yuma Convention & Visitors Bureau & Chamber of Commerce, (520) 783-0071.

Indian Country (including monument valley, natural rock formations, Petrified Forest, Painted Desert)

- Holbrook/Petrified Chamber of Commerce, (800) 524-2459.
- Navajo Nation Tourism Office, (520) 871-6659.

Organizations

Advocacy Groups (area agencies on aging, by county)

- AAA Region I, Phoenix, (602) 264-2255.
- Pima Council on Aging, Tucson, (520) 790-7262.
- Northern Arizona Council of Governments, Flagstaff, (520) 774-1895.
- Western Arizona Council of Governments,Yuma, (520) 782-1886.
- Pinal/Gila Council for Senior Citizens, Casa Grande, (520) 836-2758.
- South Eastern Arizona Governments Organization, Bisbee, (520) 432-5301.
- Navajo AAA, Window Rock, (520) 871-6797 or -6783.
- Intertribal Council Arizona, Inc., Phoenix, (602) 248-0071.
- ElderVention, (888) 783-7500.
- Senior Help Line, (602) 264-HELP (4357).

State Volunteer Programs

- Senior Volunteer Programs of Northern Arizona, (520) 523-3560. Fax: (520) 523-6395.
- Volunteer Center of Maricopa County, (602) 263-9736. Fax: (602) 631-4865. E-mail: volunteerctr@cirs.org
- ElderVention Program, Maricopa County, (888) 783-7500. Volunteer outreach program.

Housing

Long-Term Care Facilities

In the state of Arizona, these facilities are called ***Continuing Care/Long-Term Care/Nursing Care Facilities.***

These facilities provide residential living and/or various levels of nursing and medical services to seniors for an extended period of time.

Types of Authorization

Licensing and/or Certification

Required by the Department of Health for facilities that offer assisted/intermediate living and nursing care services.

Memberships

- American Association of Homes and Services for the Aging (AAHSA) represents not-for-profit organizations committed to providing high-quality health care, housing, and services to the elderly. AAHSA, 901 E St. NW, Suite 500, Washington, DC 20004-2011. Ph: (202) 783-2242. Fax: (202) 783-2285. *http://www.aahsa.org*
- The Arizona Association of Homes and Housing for the Aging (AAHHA) is an AAHSA Affiliated State Association. AAHHA, 3839 North 3rd St, Suite 201, Phoenix, AZ, 85012-2069. Ph: (602) 230-0026. Fax: (602) 230-0563.

Central

Arizona Eastern Star Retirement Center

4602 North 24th St.
Phoenix, AZ 85016

Ph: (602) 954-9178 Fax: (602) 553-8344

IND: Yes. AL: Yes. SNF: Yes

Nonprofit; nondenominational; nonsectarian. Apartments, studios, private and semiprivate rooms. Hand feeding; 24-hour nursing care; restorative nursing; therapeutic recreational activities; medical services include: physician, podiatrist, and dentist; personal care; medication administration; security; emergency response system; maintenance; transportation; up to 3 daily meals; housekeeping and laundry services; planned activities; barber/beauty shop.

IND MO: $475–$675. AL MO: Semiprivate, $1,200; private, $1,800. SNF Daily: Semiprivate, $130, private, $185, Medicare semiprivate: $140.

Ancillary services (housekeeping, laundry, meal delivery, and professional consultations) are charged separately.

REQ: Independent living applicants must be able to care for themselves without assistance and be mentally stable; personal interview and financial records.

Baptist Village Youngstown, AAHSA

11315 West Peoria Ave.
Youngstown, AZ 85363

Ph: (602) 933-4683 Fax: (602) 972-4993

IND: Yes. AL: Yes. HCC: 128. ALZ/MEM IMP: Yes

Age 55+. A not-for-profit, nondenominational facility. Homes, duplexes, apartments, efficiency and studios, private and semiprivate rooms. 24-hour licensed nursing staff; social services; physical, speech, and occupational therapies; on-site pharmacy; subacute and special care (Alzheimer's and related memory disorders); personal care; medication assistance; emergency call system; transportation; up to 3 daily meals; small pets allowed; housekeeping and laundry services; social and recreational programs.

IND ENT: Homes/duplex, $75,500; Studio/efficiencies, $29,000; Apt., $35,000–$75,500. IND MO: Homes, $370 (does not include utilities); Duplex, $525–$575 (utilities included); Studio/efficiencies: single, $400–$800; double, $450–$1,000;

Apt.: single, $430–$1,200; double, $500–$1,200. AL Daily and MO: semiprivate, $45/day or $1,300/mo.; private, $60–$70/day or $1,700–$2,100/mo. HCC Daily: semiprivate, $105–$200; private, $130–$240.

The Beatitudes Campus of Care, AAHA, The Council for Health and Human Services Ministries, and United Church of Christ memberships

1616 West Glendale Ave.
Phoenix, AZ 85021

Ph: (602) 995-2611

IND: 337. AL: Yes. SNF: Yes

United Church of Christ; nonprofit; nondenominational. Studios, apartments, private and semiprivate rooms. Nursing care and supervision; respite care; optical, dental, and podiatry services; 24-hour assistance; personal care; medication administration; Medicare-approved; security; emergency response system; maintenance; transportation; up to 3 daily meals; housekeeping and laundry services; pastoral care; activity program; vespers; wellness check; theme dinners; bingo; swimming pool; guest apartments; intergenerational program; Men's Club; library; pharmacy; bank; mini-mart; barber/beauty shop.

IND ACC: $6,600. DEP: single, $440; double, $550. IND MO: $600–$1,200; 2nd person, $110. AL MO: $2,250–$2,550 plus deposit (half of mo. rent). HCC Daily: $125–$275.

Fellowship Square

2002 W. Sunnyside Drive
Phoenix, AZ 85029

Ph: (800) 628-1232

IND: Yes. AL: Yes. SNF: Yes

Christian Care Company; nonprofit. Garden homes, apartments, private and semiprivate rooms. Complete supervisory care; personal care; medication reminders; Medicare-approved; security; emergency response system; maintenance; transportation; up to 3 daily meals; housekeeping and laundry services; pool and spa; exercise room; library; walking paths; gift shop; putting green; barber/beauty shop.

IND MO: $1,150–$2,200; 2nd person, $300. AL MO: $1,700–$2,300; 2nd person, $550. SNF Daily: semiprivate, $110; private, $125; semiprivate/intermediate care, $103.

Freedom Plaza/Plaza del Rio Health Care Center, ARRI, AAHSA

13373 Plaza del Rio Blvd.
Peoria, AZ 85381

Ph: (602) 876-2415
Fax: (602) 933-1901

IND: 349. AL: 32. HCC: 128. ALZ/MEM IMP: 34

Age 62+. For-profit; nondenominational; owned by Freedom Group and Sun Health; managed by American Retirement Corporation. Apartments and private and semiprivate rooms. 24-hour nursing care; medical care; rehabilitative therapies; dental and podiatry services; pharmacy; wellness program; blood pressure and weight checks; personal care; medication administration; security; emergency response system; maintenance; transportation; up to 3 daily meals; housekeeping and laundry services; exercise room with walking track; pool; library; banking and postal services; social and recreational activities; ham radio room; lapidary room; woodworking shop; card/game room; gift shop and snack bar; barber/beauty shop.

IND ENT: $54,000–$229,000. IND MO: $1,200–$2,400. AL MO: $2,500–$6,000. HCC and ALZ/MEM IMP Daily: $130–$250. (AL and HCC/ALZ/MEM IMP fees are private pay; life care residents' fees are discounted.)

Friendship Village, AAHSA

2645 East Southern Ave.
Tempe, AZ 85282

Ph: (800) 824-2225 (AZ) or (800) 824-1112 (national)
Fax: (602) 413-0285

IND: Yes. AL: 38. HCC: 128 (about 700 residents total)

Age 62+. Managed by the Life Care Services Corp. Garden homes, apartments, and private and semiprivate rooms. Emergency medical care; nursing care; personal care; medication administration; security; emergency response system; maintenance; transportation; up to 3 daily meals (1/day included in mo. fee); housekeeping and laundry services; pool; library; scheduled activities; recreation center.

IND ENT: Garden home: standard plan, $96,000–$150,000; return-of-capital plan, $177,000–$277,000; 2nd person, $6,600; Apt: standard plan, $45,000–$148,000; return-of-capital plan, $83,000–$273,000; 2nd person, $6,600. IND MO: Garden home: $1,500–$1,700; 2nd person, $750. Apt: $1,100–$1,800; 2nd person, $700. HCC: Inclusive/unlimited usage.

Glencroft Retirement Community

8611 North 67th Ave.
Glendale, AZ 85302

Ph: (602) 847-3013

IND: Yes. AL: 20. HCC: 225. ALZ/MEM IMP: Yes

Nondenominational. Condos, garden apartments, and private and semiprivate rooms. 24-hour nursing care; short- and long- term care; physical, occupational, and speech therapies; respiratory therapy; IV therapy; social worker; medical services; hospice services; clinic with dental, podiatry, chiropractic, and hearing services; home health care services; Medicare-approved; personal care; medication administration; security; emergency response system; maintenance; transportation; up to 3 daily meals; housekeeping and laundry services; fitness center; exercise program; nondenominational church services; Bible study; woodworking shop; ceramics studio; computer center; quilting room; on- and off-site activities; musical programs; educational opportunities; bank; flower and gift shop; barber/beauty shop.

Apartments are available on a 70/30 refund plan. Residents who leave may receive 70% of ENT fee upon reoccupation of unit. Contact facility for ENT fees. IND MO: $350–$1,100. AL MO: Single, $1,800; double, $3,100. HCC Daily: $125–$350.

Some units are HUD-subsidized.

Good Shepherd Retirement Center

10323 West Olive Ave.
Peoria, AZ 85345

Ph: (602) 875-0100
Fax: (602) 875-0110

IND: 72 HCC: 220

Age 62+. Evangelical Lutheran Good Samaritan Society, a Christian, nonprofit organization. Apartments and private and semiprivate rooms. Physical, speech, and occupational therapies; 24-hour health care when needed to provide support services; personal care; medication administration; security; emergency response system; maintenance; transportation; up to 3 daily meals; housekeeping and laundry services; pool; specialized activities; clubhouse; chapel; meditation garden; Bible study; barber/beauty shop.

IND ENT: $27,500–$88,000 (refund 90% to 50% depending upon mo. of termination) IND MO: $340–$2,200 (2nd person $35). HCC Daily: Basic: semiprivate, $110 and $150; private, $200. Activities of daily living: semiprivate, $115 and $150; private, $200. Moderate: semiprivate, $130 and $165; private, $210. Special: semiprivate, $140 and $180; private, $220. Complex: semiprivate, $150 and $190; private, $240. Maximum: semiprivate, $370 and $400; private, $440.

Life Care Center of Scottsdale, JCAHO

9499 E. Becker Lane
Scottsdale, AZ 85260

Ph: (602) 860-6396
Fax: (602) 391-9699
http://www.lifecarecenter.com

SNF: 141. ALZ/MEM IMP: 22

For-profit; nondenominational; operated by Life Care Centers of America. Suites and private and semiprivate rooms. 24-hour skilled nursing care; physical, occupational, and speech therapies; dental and podiatry services; wound care; IV and respiratory therapies; pharmacy; X-ray and lab services; Medicare-approved; security; emergency response system; maintenance; transportation; up to 3 daily meals; pets allowed; housekeeping and laundry services; chapel; exercise classes; pet therapy; social and recreational activities; bingo; arts and crafts; outdoor courtyards; ice cream parlor; barber/beauty shop.

SNF: $130–$185.

Orangewood

7550 North 16th St.
Phoenix, AZ 85020

Ph: (602) 944-4455

http://www.retirementlife.com/orange.html

IND: Yes. AL: Yes. HCC: Yes

American Baptist Homes of the West; nonprofit; non- denominational. Apartments and private and semiprivate rooms. Specialized nursing care; therapies; personal care; medication administration; housekeeping; security; emergency response system; maintenance; transportation; up to 3 daily meals; housekeeping and laundry services; social activities; health services; heated pool; recreation center; gift shop; work shop; crafts; residents council; volunteer programs; barber/beauty shop.

IND ENT: $53,000–$117,000. IND MO: $1,200–$2,000. AL ENT: $15,500–$44,000. AL MO: $1,700–$2,700. Double occupancy, add 10% to entrance fee and $335 per month to IND and $440 per month for AL.

Royal Oaks, AAHSA

150015 W. Royal Oak Rd.
Sun City, AZ 85351

Ph: (602) 933-2807

IND: 249. HCC: 100. ADC: Yes. ALZ/MEM IMP: Yes

Age 62+. People of Faith, Inc; nonprofit; nondenominational. Garden homes, apartments, and private and semiprivate rooms. Skilled nursing; residential aide and social services; Adult Day Care; recuperation, rehabilitation, respite, and long- and short-term care; security; emergency response system; maintenance; transportation; up to 3 daily meals (1 meal/day included in IND MO fee); housekeeping and laundry services; chaplain; all utilities (excluding air conditioning, cable, and phone); planned activities; resident association; barber/beauty shop.

DEP: $550 (no ref.). Entrance fee part. ref. upon termination, good up to 7 yrs. IND ENT: $51,000–$176,000; 2nd person, $7,000. IND MO: $925–$1,900; 2nd person, $575. SNF Daily: Semiprivate, $125; private, $160; Medicare, $185; private conversion, $225. ALZ/MEM IMP Daily: $125.

Sierra Winds Lifecare

17300 North 88th Ave.
Peoria, AZ 85382

Ph: (602) 977-0807

IND: 240. AL: 30. SNF: 40

For-profit; nondenominational; managed by Life Care Services Corp. Apartments. Skilled nursing care; personal care; medication administration; Medicare-approved; security; emergency response system; maintenance; transportation; up to 3 daily meals; housekeeping and laundry services; fitness center; swimming pool; Jacuzzi; cultural, educational, and social activities; off-site activities; board and game room; woodworking shop; arts and crafts studio; shuffleboard courts; greenhouse; ice

cream parlor; gift shop; covered patio; nearby restaurants and shopping; barber/beauty shop.

IND ENT: Traditional plan, $55,000–$139,000; 905 return-of-capital plan, $85,000–$208,000. IND MO: $1,200–$2,200; 2nd person, $700. AL and SNF fees inclusive.

Sun Valley Lodge

12415 North 103rd Ave.
Sun city, AZ 85351-3597

Ph: (623) 933-0137
Fax: (602) 933-5846

IND: Yes. AL: Yes. HCC: Yes

Nondenominational facility. Apartments and private and semiprivate rooms. 24-hour skilled nursing care; physical, occupational, and speech therapies; psychological services; audiology, optometry, podiatrist, dental and physician services; lab and X-ray services; pharmacy; hospice care; personal care; medication administration; security; emergency response system; maintenance; transportation; up to 3 daily meals; housekeeping and laundry services; recreational and social activities; barber/beauty shop.

IND ENT: (garden apts.), $623,000. IND MO: $1,200–$1,800; 2nd person, $440. AL MO: up to $550 (in addition to IND MO). HCC: $120–$220.

Westchester Villa, AAHSA

6150 S. Rural Rd.
Tempe, AZ 85283

Ph: (480) 897-9130
Fax: (602) 820-7663

IND: 90. AL: 24. HCC: 94. ALZ/MEM IMP: 17

Age 55+. Nonprofit; nondenominational; Volunteers of America. Apartments. Emergency nursing care; rehabilitative services; podiatry care; Medicare/Medicaid-approved; personal care; medication administration; security; emergency response system; maintenance; transportation; up to 3 daily meals; housekeeping and laundry services; exercise classes; swimming pool; Jacuzzi; volunteer opportunities; grocery delivery service; social, spiritual, educational, and recreational activities.

DEP: $440–$500. IND MO: $750–$1,350. SNF MO: $3,300–$6,600.

Westminster Village

12000 N. 90th St.
Scottsdale, AZ 85260

Ph: (800) 955-8455
Fax: (480) 451-2000

IND: 249. SNF: Yes. ALZ: Yes

Age 62+. A nonprofit, nondenominational facility. Suites and apartments, private and semiprivate rooms. Intermediate and skilled nursing care; 24-hour professional care; Alzheimer's program; Medicare-approved; security; emergency response system; maintenance; transportation; up to 3 daily meals; housekeeping and laundry services; scheduled activities; recreational programs; heated pool; bank and postal service; library; wood shop; greenhouse; barber/beauty shop.

IND ENT: $78,000–$139,000; 2nd person, $7,000. IND MO: $1,400–$2,400; 2nd person, $800.

South

La Posada, AAHSA

501 South La Posada Circle
Green Valley, AZ 85614

Ph: (520) 648-8131
Fax: (520) 648-8397

IND: Yes. AL: Yes. SNF: Yes. ALZ/MEM IMP: Yes

Nonprofit, full-service senior living community. Garden homes, apartments, suites, private and semiprivate rooms. Therapy and Alzheimer's program; routine nursing care; care management; 24-hour supervision; wellness clinic; in-house therapy programs; respite care;

care management; personal care; medication administration; Medicare-approved; open to various HMOs and hospice providers; security; emergency response system; maintenance; transportation; up to 3 daily meals; housekeeping and laundry services; fitness center; spa; scheduled activities; game room; special outings; library; putting greens; barber/beauty shop.

IND: Homes APPL: (no ref.) $11,000–$15,300. Homes ENT: (ref.) $109,000–$153,000. Homes MO: $1,800–$2,400; 2nd person, $370. APT APPL: (no ref.) single, $5,000; double, $8,250. APT ENT: (ref.) $35,000–$90,000. APT MO: $1,400–$3,100; 2nd person, $550. AL APPL: (no ref.) single, $3,850; double, $5,500. AL MO: $2,500–$4,325. RSP Daily: $100. HCC Daily: $105–$215. ALZ/MEM IMP Daily: $155–$170.

Quiburi Mission Samaritan Center

850 So. Hwy. 80
Benson, AZ 85602

Ph: (520) 586-2372
Fax: (520) 586-7003

SNF: 60

Evangelical Lutheran Good Samaritan Society; nonprofit; nondenominational; nursing home. Private and semiprivate rooms. 24-hour nursing care; physical, occupational, and speech therapies; temporary and long-term care; individual care plans; security; emergency response system; maintenance; transportation; up to 3 daily meals; housekeeping and laundry services; weekly worship services; crafts; games; music; reading; discussion groups; planned activities; barber/beauty shop.

SNF Daily: Level I: Private, $130; semiprivate, $115. Level II: Private, $140; semiprivate, $127. Level III: Private, $150; semiprivate, $135. Medicare: $135. Therapies (per hour): Physical, $60; occupational, $70; speech, $70; restorative, $100.

Santa Catalina Villas

7500 N. Calle Sin Envidia
Tucson, AZ 85718

Ph: (520) 742-6242

IND: Yes. AL: 70. SNF: 42. MEM IMP: 15

American Retirement Corp.; nondenominational. Apartments, private and semiprivate rooms. Social worker consultation and rehabilitation services; health care services; short- or long-term care; 24-hour care; personal care; administration; security; emergency response system; maintenance; transportation; up to 3 daily meals; housekeeping and laundry services; exercise room; clergy visits; activities; pool; library; walking paths; barber/beauty shop.

IND MO: $1,300–$3,600; 2nd person, $400. AL MO: $2,200–$3,400 ($450 for 2nd person and $350 for each additional level of care). SNF Daily: Semiprivate, $130; private, $150. ALZ/MEM IMP MO: $3,300.

North

Atria Kachina Point Retirement Community, ARRI

405 Jacks Canyon Rd.
Sedona, AZ 86351

Ph: (520) 284-1021
Fax: (520) 284-2834
E-mail: *Kpoint@sedona.net*

IND: 102. AL: 42. ALZ/MEM IMP: 42. SNF: 120

Age 55+. For-profit; nondenominational. Skilled nursing care; wellness clinic; personal care; medication administration; security; emergency response system; maintenance; transportation; up to 3 daily meals; housekeeping and laundry services; exercise program; Bible study; library; nondenominational religious services; pool; off-site activities; social and recreational activities; arts

and crafts room; book club; game/card room; walking trails; barber/beauty shop.

DEP: $550 (ref.). IND ENT: $550. IND MO: $1,400–$3,100. AL ENT: $1,650. AL MO: $2,300–$3,500.

West

Lake Hills Inn

2781 Osborn Drive
Lake Havasu City, AZ 86406

Ph: (928) 505-5552
Fax: (520) 505-2660

NH: 80. ALZ/MEM IMP: 22

For-profit facility. Private and semiprivate rooms. 24-hour skilled nursing care; physical, occupational, and speech therapies; IV and nutritional therapies; dental and podiatry services; pharmacy; social services; Medicare/Medicaid-approved; maintenance; transportation; 3 daily meals; pets allowed; housekeeping and laundry services; exercise program; recreational activities; crafts, music, and cooking classes; barber/beauty shop.

NH Daily: $115–$170. ALZ/MEM IMP Daily: $120.

Assisted Living and Residential Care Facilities

In the state of Arizona, these facilities are called ***Residential Care and Assisted Living****.*

These facilities offer housing with personalized support services and health care services and are licensed by the Arizona Department of Health.

Types of Authorization

Licensing and/or Certification

Department of Health. Requirements require the facility to provide: supervisory care, personal care, or directed care services, a written service plan for each resident, daily activities, medication monitoring if needed, and 3 daily meals.

Memberships

- Assisted Living Federation of America (ALFA) is a national nonprofit membership organization whose mission is to enhance the quality of life in assisted living facilities and promote the interests of the assisted living industry. ALFA, 10300 Eaton Place, Suite 400, Fairfax, VA 22030. Ph: (703) 691-8100. Fax: (703) 691-8106. *http://www.alfa.org*
- Arizona Assisted Living Federation of America (Arizona-ALFA) is a state affiliate of ALFA. Arizona-ALFA, 1913 E Libra Drive, Tempe AZ 85283. Ph: (888) 520-2532 or (602) 831-6123. Fax: (602) 831-6123. *http://www.azalfa.org*

Central

Baptist Village Thunderbird

13617 N. 55th Ave.
Glendale, AZ 85304

Ph: (602) 938-5500
Fax: (602) 843-9530

IND: Yes. AL: Yes (total units, 207)

Nondenominational; owned and operated by Arizona Baptist Retirement Centers. One- and two-bedroom apartments. Respite care; blood pressure monitoring; pharmacy services; personal care; medication administration; escort services; security; emergency response system; maintenance; transportation; up to 3 daily meals; pets allowed; housekeeping and laundry services; exercise classes; swimming pool; religious services and Bible study; library; social and recreational activities; board and card games; convenience store; gift shop; community room; restaurant; barber/beauty shop.

DEP: $330. IND MO: $740–$1,500. AL MO: $1,000–$2,300.

Brighton Gardens

6001 E. Thomas Rd.
Scottsdale, AZ 85251

Ph: (480) 941-2222
Fax: (602) 941-2741

AL: Yes. HCC: Yes

Marriott Senior Living Service community; nondenominational; nonsectarian. Rooms with private kitchenettes and baths. Licensed nurse on staff; reality orientation and other behavioral therapies; daily safety checks; regular health and wellness assessments; personal care; medication administration; security; emergency response system; maintenance; transportation; 3 daily meals; housekeeping and laundry services; resident activities director; library; activities and crafts studio; large common areas; barber/beauty shop.

AL MO: $2,100–$3,100; 2nd person, $550. HCC Daily: $180–$260.

Chris Ridge Village

6250 N. 19th Ave.
Phoenix, AZ 85015

Ph: (602) 433-6464

IND: Yes. AL: Yes. ADC: Yes. ALZ: Yes. HHC: Yes

Baptist Hospitals and Health Systems; nondenominational. Apartments, private and semiprivate rooms. Inpatient/outpatient rehabilitation services; wellness programs; personal care; medication administration; scheduled transportation; up to 3 daily meals (1 meal per day included in mo. fee); laundry facilities; heated pool; scheduled daily activities; Bible study; library; barber/beauty shop.

IND MO: One bedroom, $1,250–$1,900; two bedroom, $2,000–$2,400. AL MO: $825. Or, á la carte 1 to 4 daily services (per month): 1 service, $130; 2 services, $250; 3 services, $360; 4 services, $460.

La Villita, Participant Arizona Model program (developed by Greater Phoenix Chapter of Alzheimer's Association and approved by Arizona Legislature)

2935 North 18th Place
Phoenix, AZ 85016

Ph: (602) 265-9813
Fax: (602) 277-9420

AL: Yes. ALZ/MEM IMP: Yes

Assisted Living and Secured Alzheimer's and Memory Loss Residence. Studios, apartments, private and semiprivate rooms. 24-hour staff and programming; medication assistance; incontinence care and management; personal care; medication administration; transportation to medical appointments; 3 daily meals; laundry service; exercise; escort to meals and activities; cooking; arts and crafts; nature walks; entertainment; outings; games.

AL MO: $1,320–$1,800 plus flexible (4 levels) assistance charges ($440–$1,650) when needed. ALZ/MEM IMP MO: Semiprivate, $2,500; private, $3,600. RSP Daily: $110.

SunGrove Resort Village

10134 West Mohawk Lane
Peoria, AZ 85282

Ph: (602) 566-1563
Fax: (602) 566-1563

IND: Yes. AL: Yes

Apartments. Personal care; medication administration; daily visits; emergency call system; 2 daily meals; some housekeeping; spa and swimming pool; activities program; ice cream parlor; barber/beauty shop.

IND MO: $1,500–$2,100. Home health care program and assistance are additional monthly fee.

SunPointe

10045 Royal Oaks Drive
Sun City, AZ 85351

Ph: (602) 977-8385
Fax: (602) 977-8393

http://www.sunh.com

IND: 77. AL: waiting for licensing

Age 55+. Sun Healthcare Group. Studios and apartments. Wellness center; home health services; physical, occupational, and speech therapies; personal care; medication administration; emergency response system; scheduled transportation; up to 3 daily meals (1 meal included in mo. fee); housekeeping and laundry services; all utilities; library; ice cream parlor.

ADM: $550. MO: Studio, $1,300; one-bedroom, $1,650; two-bedroom; $2,150–$2,250; 2nd person, $360. Medicare-approved for home health visits.

South

Atria Campana del Rio

1550 East River Rd.
Tucson, AZ 85718

Ph: (800) 804-7137
Fax: (520) 529-2572

IND: Yes. AL: 65. ALZ/MEM IMP: 10

A nondenominational facility. Villas and apartments (some semiprivate). 24-hour professional care; wellness center; chronic incontinence management; personal care; medication administration; security; emergency response system; maintenance; transportation; up to 3 daily meals; housekeeping and laundry services; structured, intensive resident activities program; chapel; library; game and card room; barber/beauty salon.

IND MO: Villas, $2,150–$2,550; 2nd person, $275. Suites, $1,200–$1,300; one-bedroom, $1,500–$1,750; two-bedroom, $1,800–$2,100; 2nd person, $330. AL MO: $2,200–$3,300; 2nd person, $550.

The Cascades of Tucson, ALFAA

201 N. Jessica
Tucson, AZ 85710

Ph: (520) 886-3171

http://www.cascadestucson.com/

IND: 190. AL: 48

Nondenominational. Apartments and studios. Personal care; medication administration; security; emergency response system; maintenance; transportation; up to 3 daily meals; housekeeping and laundry services; pets allowed for additional fee; spa; scheduled activities; pool; barber/beauty shop.

IND MO: $1,350–$1,700. AL MO: $1,900–$2,500. $370 additional monthly fee for extra person.

Devon Gables Health Care Center

6150 East Grant Rd.
Tucson, AZ 85712

Ph: (520) 296-6181
Fax: (520) 298-0997

IND: Yes. AL: Yes

Efficiency and one-bedroom apartments. 3 service packages: Package I: Medication administration; laundry; daily personal visit; 24-hour nursing staff on call; weekly blood pressure checks; monthly housekeeping. Package II: Includes all of Package I plus shower assistance 3 times per week. Package III: Includes all of Package I services plus shower assistance 3 times a week, daily assistance with dressing, and a minimum of 3 daily personal visits.

Included in all: security; maintenance services; transportation for food shopping and doctor appointments; up to 3 daily meals; laundry facilities; planned activities; pool; barber/beauty shop.

IND MO: $525–$575. AL MO: Package I: $440; Package II: $550; Package III: $660. Additional service fees for housekeeping and meal delivery.

The Fountains at La Cholla, ARRI

2001 W. Rudasill Rd.
Tucson, AZ 85704

Ph: (520) 797-2001
Fax: (520) 531-8219

IND: 276. AL: 62. ALZ/MEM IMP: 34. ADC: Yes

Age 62+. For-profit; nondenominational. Apartments. Wellness center; home health care; nursing consultations; assurance checks; personal care; medication administration; security; emergency response system; maintenance; transportation; up to 3 daily meals; pets allowed; housekeeping and laundry services; fitness center; swimming pool; chapel; banking services; library; computer classes; intergenerational program; cultural, social, and spiritual activities; game room; crafts; media room; clubs; concierge services; dry cleaning services; convenience store; coffee shop; gardening; golf course and riding stable nearby; barber/beauty shop.

DEP: (ref.) $400. IND MO: $1,200–$2,750. AL MO: $2,200–$4,200.

Handmaker Jewish Services for the Aging

5100 E. Grant Rd.
Tucson, AZ 85712

Ph: (520) 881-2323
Fax: (520) 322-3620

http://www.azstarnet.com/~handmkr/

ACH: Yes. AL: Yes. SNF: Yes. ALZ MEM/IMP: Yes. ADC: Yes. HSP: Yes. HHC: Yes

Nonprofit facility; all faiths. Apartments and rooms. Therapeutic recreation; social services; 24-hour supervision; long-term or subacute/rehab. care; personal care; medication administration; Medicare-approved; daily reassurance; social services; up to 3 kosher meals; housekeeping and laundry services; clergy; personalized activities.

ACH Daily: $140–$200. AC MO: $2,300–$3,300. AL MO: About $1,400–$1,550. ALZ/MEM IMP MO: $2,400–$2,600.

SunBridge

5660 N. Kolb Rd.
Tucson, AZ 85715

Ph: (520) 577-6940

http://www.sunh.com
E-mail: *GailFarmer@sunh.com*

AL: 92

No age limit. A Sun HealthCare Group facility. Studios and apartments. Respite care; 24-hour registered nursing care; therapeutic massage, aromatherapy, and relaxation therapy; personal care; medication administration; security; emergency response system; maintenance; transportation; up to 3 daily meals plus snacks and teas; small pets allowed; housekeeping and laundry services; activities director; scheduled daily activities.

DEP: (ref.) $1,100. MOVE IN: $2,200. AL MO: $1,800–$4,400. RSP Daily: $125 (includes all wellness care through level 5). MO Medication Services: $200 (preparation; storage; reminders; supervision).

REQ: Complete physical including TB test.

Adult Care Homes

These are residential care facilities that provide supervisory, personal, or custodial care to not more than 10 adults.

Types of Authorization

Licensing and/or Certification

Adult care homes must be licensed by Department of Health and are inspected yearly for compliance. Requirements for facilities include: provisions for physical exercise, mental stimulation, and social interaction, daily assistance with personal care and other needs, nutritious meals served in a family setting, and medication monitoring.

Adobe Residential Care Centers, Inc.

7615 W. Wagoner Rd.
Glendale, AZ 85308

Ph: (602) 862-9355

ALZ, REHAB, IV, RSP

Up to 10 residents. Initial registered nurse assessment for care plan; in-home therapies; personal care; medication administration; 3 daily meals plus snacks; housekeeping and laundry services; interactions with children and pets; gardening; arts and crafts; reading; scheduled daily activities; barber/beauty service.

ACH MO: $2,000 $2,750.

Bethany Home Adult Care Home

2219 W. Bethany Home Rd.
Phoenix, AZ 85015

Ph: (602) 242-6930

http://www.adultcarehomes.com/beth.htm

ALZ, REHAB, IV, HSP

Up to 10 residents. 24-hour supervision; 24-hour house-call physician; therapies; personal care; medication administration; on-site management; transportation; 3 daily meals plus snacks; housekeeping and laundry services; indoor and outdoor activities; barber/beauty services.

ACH MO: $1,800 and up.

Betty's Residential Care Homes, Inc.

4719 W. Harmont Drive
Glendale, AZ 85302

Ph: (602) 486-0971 or (602) 930-6764

ALZ/MEM IMP, REHAB, HSP, RSP

Up to 10 residents. Care assessments by registered nurse; on-call/house-call physician; on-site podiatrist, certified caregivers; personal care; medication administration; 3 daily meals; planned activities; crafts; social gatherings; in-house movies.

ACH MO: $1,800 $2,200.

Elderhaven

2501 N. Soldier Trail
Tucson, AZ 85749

Ph: (520) 749-8936
Fax: (520) 760-8865

All types of care in a Christian family atmosphere.

Up to 10 residents. Singles or couples. No disability restrictions. 24-hour caregiver service; personal care; medication administration; 3 daily meals; housekeeping and laundry services; chaplain service; light exercises; bingo; planned activities; hair and nail services.

ACH MO: About $3,100 (private room/private pay).

Elder Kare of America, Inc.

DBA Home at 74th Street Scottsdale
2211 N. 74th St.
Scottsdale, AZ 85257

Ph: (602) 990-8638
Fax: (602) 874-2248

ALZ, REHAB, Parkinson's, RSP

Women only; up to 5 residents. 24-hour supervision; personal care; medication administration; 3 daily meals plus snacks; scheduled off-site trips; barber/beauty shop.

ACH MO: $2,100–$2,600.

Independent Living

Independent housing (primarily rentals) for seniors that may offer security features, meal service, and activities.

Central

CPLC Villa/Guadalupe Huerta

7235 S. 7th St.
Phoenix, AZ 85040

Ph: (602) 243-4137

Age 62+. 42 HUD-subsidized apartments.

Small pets allowed; recreation room; library; potlucks and holiday dinners. Close to public transportation for trips to senior center.

Sliding scale payment.

Adult/Resort Communities

Communities for active adults (not all are age-restricted; primarily ownership).

North

Forest Highlands

876 Forest Highlands
Flagstaff, AZ 86001

Ph: (520) 556-8606
Fax: (520) 556-3178

http://www.dmbrealty.com/fh

Individual homes, homesites. Golf courses; clubhouses; tennis; swimming pools; health and fitness center; basketball and volleyball courts; fishing; hiking trails.

PURCHASE: Homes, $195,000–$1.1 million+.

Oakcreek Country Club

690 Bell Rock Blvd.
Sedona, AZ 86351

Ph: (520) 284-1660
Fax: (520) 284-3138

Individual homes, condominiums. Golf course; tennis; community center; library; social clubs.

PURCHASE: Homes, $110,000–$385,000; homesites: $35,500–$165,000.

Central

Apache Wells Country Club

5601 E. Hermosa Vista
Mesa, AZ 85215

Ph: (480) 830-4725
Fax: (480) 854-8938

Age 55+. Golf course; swimming pool; hiking/biking trails; community center; dining; fitness center; library; social clubs.

PURCHASE: Homes, $93,500 $220,000.

The Boulders

34631 N. Tom Darlington Drive
Carefree, AZ 85377

Ph: (480) 488-9009
Fax: (480) 488-4118

http://www.grandbay.com

Individual homes, townhomes, homesites. Golf course; tennis; swimming pool; hiking/biking trails; community center; dining; fitness center; social clubs

PURCHASE: Homes, from $385,000.

Chaparral Pines

500 N. Chaparral Pines Drive
Payson, AZ 85541

Ph: (800) 889-8016 or (928) 474-1222
Fax: (928) 472-8900

Individual homes, homesites. Golf course; tennis; swimming pools; volleyball; softball; basketball; boating; fishing; hiking/biking trails; fitness center.

PURCHASE: Homes, from $275,000; homesites, from $55,000.

Coyote Lakes Golf Club

18800 N. Coyote Lakes Parkway
Surprise, AZ 85374

Ph: (623) 566-2323
Fax: (523) 566-8336

Individual homes. Golf course; tennis; swimming pool; community center; dining; social clubs.

PURCHASE: Homes, $93,500–$143,000.

DC Ranch

9255 E. Desert Camp Drive
Scottsdale, AZ 85255

Ph: (480) 502-2725

http://www.dcranch.com

Individual homes, attached villas. Golf course; tennis; swimming pool; hiking/biking; fitness center; community center; dining; telecommunity.

PURCHASE: Homes, from low $242,000; villas, from $407,000.

Desert Highlands Golf Club

10040 E. Happy Valley Rd.
Scottsdale, AZ 85255

Ph: (480) 585-8510
Fax: (480) 585-7333

http://www.azdeserthighlands.com

Individual homes. Golf course; tennis; swimming pool; hiking trails; fitness center; social clubs.

PURCHASE: Homes, $660,000–$3.3 million.

Desert Mountain

38621 N. Cave Creek Rd.
Scottsdale, AZ 85262

Ph: (800) 322-0044 or (480) 595-4045

http://www.desertmountain.com

Individual homes, homesites. Championship golf courses; clubhouses; pro shops; tennis complex; swimming pools; fitness center; spa; dining.

PURCHASE: Homes, $935,000–$1.76 million; homesites, $440,000–$2.75 million.

Eagle Mountain Community

14915 Eagle Mountain Parkway
Fountain Hills, AZ 85268

Ph: (480) 816-0800

http://www.eaglemtn.com

Individual homes, townhomes, homesites. Golf course; pro shop; clubhouse; dining.

PURCHASE: Homes, $187,000–$440,000; homesites, $99,000–$220,000.

Florence Gardens Mobile Homes

3830 Florence Blvd.
Florence, AZ 85232

Ph: (520) 868-4770
Fax: (520) 868-1040

Age 55+. Manufactured housing. Golf course; swimming pool; hiking/biking trails; hunting; community center; dining; library; social clubs.

PURCHASE: Homes, $49,500–$132,000.

Gainey Ranch Golf Club Community

7720 Gainey Ranch Rd.
Scottsdale, AZ 85258

Ph: (480) 951-0321
Fax: (480) 951-0923

Individual homes. Golf course; tennis club; swimming pool; walking paths; community center; fitness center; social clubs.

PURCHASE: Homes, $275,000–$1.1 million.

Grayhawk

8623 E. Thompson Peak Parkway
Scottsdale, AZ 85255

Ph: (800) GRAYHAWK or (480) 502-1547
Fax: (480) 502-4654

http://www.grayhawk.com

Individual homes, townhomes, patio homes, condominiums, homesites. Golf course; tennis; swimming pool; hiking/biking; dining; social clubs.

PURCHASE: Homes, $165,000–$770,000+.

Happy Trails Golf Resort

17200 W. Bell Rd.
Surprise, AZ 85374

Ph: (800) 872-4579 or (623) 584-6645
Fax: (623) 584-6293

http://www.happytrailsresort.com

Age 55+. Manufactured housing, homesites. Golf course; tennis; swimming pool; community center; fitness center; library social clubs.

PURCHASE: Homes, $65,000–$110,000+.

Leisure World

908 S. Power Rd.
Mesa, AZ 85206

Ph: (480) 832-7451
Fax: (480) 832-0832

http://www.leisureworldarizona.com

Age 55+. Individual homes, condominiums. Golf courses; tennis; swimming pool; two community centers; fitness center; library; social clubs.

PURCHASE: Homes, $88,000–$325,000.

Palmbrook Country Club

9350 W. Greenway Rd.
Sun City, AZ 85351

Ph: (623) 977-8383
Fax: (623) 815-9738

http://www.usagolfgreens.com/arizona/arizona/palmbrookcc.htm

Age 40+. Individual homes, condominiums, high-rise complex. Golf course; tennis; dining; social clubs; trips.

PURCHASE: Homes, $66,000–$435,000.

Pebble Creek Golf Resort

3639 Clubhouse Drive
Goodyear, AZ 85338

Ph: (800) 795-4663 or (602) 935-6700

http://www.robson.com

Age 55+. Individual homes. Golf course; clubhouse; tennis; swimming; fitness center; clubs.

PURCHASE: Homes, $110,000–$440,000.

Pointe Hilton on South Mountain

7777 S. Pointe Parkway
Phoenix, AZ 85044

Ph: (602) 431-6480 or (602) 431-1280
Fax: (602) 431-1840

http://www.pointerealestate.com

Individual homes, patio homes, condominiums, rental apartments. Golf course; tennis; racquetball; swimming pool; hiking trails; riding stables; dining; fitness center; sand volleyball.

PURCHASE: Homes, $110,000–$330,000.

Rancho de los Caballeros Resort

1551 S. Vulture Mine Rd.
Wickenburg, AZ 85390

Ph: (520) 684-5484
Fax: (520) 684-2267

http://www.SunC.com

Individual homes. Golf course; tennis; swimming pool; hiking trails; riding stables; dining; social clubs.

PURCHASE: Homes, $220,000–$550,000.

Sun City West

13950 Meeker Blvd.
Sun City West, AZ 85375

Ph: (800) 341-6121 or (623) 546-5000

http://www.delwebb.com

Age 55+. Golf courses; tennis; racquetball; swimming pool; hiking trails; community center; dining; fitness center; library; social clubs.

PURCHASE: Homes, $99,000–$275,000.

SunRidge Canyon

13100 N. Sunridge Drive
Fountain Hills, AZ 85268

Ph: (800) 822-2885 or (480) 837-2300

http://www.sunridgecanyongolfaz.com

Individual homes, homesites. Golf course; tennis; swimming pool; fitness center; bowling; basketball; soccer; community center; social clubs.

PURCHASE: Homes, from $165,000; homesites, from $91,000.

Superstition Mountain

8000 E. Club Village Drive
Superstition Mountain, AZ 85219

Ph: (480) 983-3300
Fax: (480) 983-3500

http://www.superstitionmountain.com

Individual homes, villas, homesites. Golf courses; pro shop; tennis; swimming pool; fitness center; dining.

PURCHASE: Homesites, from $192,500.

Troon Golf and Country Club

25000 N. Windy Walk Drive
Scottsdale, AZ 85255

Ph: (480) 585-4310
Fax: (480) 563-5233

http://www.trooncc.com

Custom homes. Golf course; tennis; swimming pool; dining; fitness center; library.

PURCHASE: Homes, from $550,000.

The Wigwam Resort

451 N. Litchfield Rd.
Litchfield Park, AZ 85340

Ph: (800) 909-4224 or (623) 922-7458
Fax: (623) 856-1059

http://www.wigwamresort.com

Individual homes, condominiums, homesites. Golf course; tennis; swimming pool; hiking trails; dining.

PURCHASE: Homes, from $110,000.

South

Fairfield Homes

P0 Box 587
Green Valley, AZ 85622

Ph: (800) 528-4930 or (520) 625-4441
Fax: (520) 648-2145

http;//www.retireaz.com

Age 55+. Golf course; tennis; swimming pool; hiking/biking trails; fishing; dining; community center; fitness center; library; social clubs.

PURCHASE: Homes, $132,000–$440,000.

Heritage Highlands

4949 W. Heritage Club Blvd.
Marana, AZ 85653

Ph: (888) 386-2344 or (520) 579-2000

http://www.ushome.com/retire

Age 55+. Individual homes, attached homes. Golf course; pro shop; tennis; swimming pool; spa; fitness center; library; billiards, dining.

PURCHASE: Homes, from $121,000.

Sabina Springs

9945 E. Snyder Rd.
Tucson, AZ 85749

Ph: (520) 760-1253
Fax: (520) 760-0073

Individual homes; homesites. Golf course, dining.

PURCHASE: Homes, $176,000–$330,000; homesites: $105,000–$143,000.

Starr Pass

3645 W. Starr Pass Blvd.
Tucson, AZ 85745

Ph: (800) 503-2898 or (520) 670-0400

http://www.starrpasstucson.com/

Age 55+. Individual homes, condominiums. Golf course; Olympic pool; tennis; fitness center; hiking/biking trails; dining.

PURCHASE: Builder-designed homes, from $165,000; Custom homes, from $330,000.

Sun City Tucson

1565 E. Rancho Vistoso Blvd.
Tucson, AZ 85737

Ph: (800) 422-8483 or (520) 825-5900

http://www.delwebb.com

Age 55+. Golf course; tennis; racquetball; swimming pool; hiking/biking trails; community center; dining; fitness center; library; social clubs.

PURCHASE: Homes, $148,000–$256,500.

Tucson National Golf Resort

2727 W. Club Dr.
Tucson, AZ 85743

Ph: (800) 528-4856 or (520) 297-2271
Fax: (520) 742-2452

http://www.tucsonnational.com

Age 55+. Individual homes, condominiums. Golf course; tennis; swimming pool; hiking/biking trails; dining; fitness center.

PURCHASE: Homes, from $154,000.

Ventana Canyon

6200 N. Clubhouse Lane
Tucson, AZ 85750

Ph: (520) 577-1400 or (520) 529-9199
Fax: (520) 529-9168

Individual homes, condominiums, homesites. Golf course; tennis; swimming pool; hiking trails; dining; fitness center; social clubs.

PURCHASE: Homesites, $87,000–$240,000.

West

London Bridge Golf Club

2400 Clubhouse Dr.
Lake Havasu City, AZ 86406

Ph: (520) 855-9096
Fax: (520) 855-3877

Individual homes, condominiums, high-rise complex, rental apartments. Golf course; tennis; swimming; boating; hiking; fitness center; dining; social clubs.

PURCHASE: Homes, $77,000–$385,000; homesites, $11,000–$110,000.

Arkansas

http://www.state.ar.us

General Information

Climate

Mild winters, hot summers. In Little Rock, generally between 51°F and 29°F in January; between 93°F and 71°F in July. Summers are dry.

Cost of Living

Ranks 47th in the nation.

Taxes

State/Local as % of Income: 10.0 %.

Property Tax Reduction: Residents age 62 or older and with incomes of $15,000 or less who own and reside in their home may receive a refund for part or all of their real estate taxes paid up to $250.

Sales: 5.125%. Counties and municipalities may levy additional sales taxes.

Prescription Exemptions: Prescription medicines and medical supplies are exempt from sales tax.

Transportation, Travel, and Tourism

General

Arkansas Department of Parks and Tourism, One Capitol Mall, Little Rock, AR 72201, (800) NATURAL.

Major Airports

- Little Rock National Airport, One Airport Dr., Little Rock, AR 72202, (501) 372-3439.
- Arkansas International Airport, PO Box 166, Blytheville, AR 72316, (501) 532-2100. For airport manager, (870) 532-5628.

Railways

- Amtrak, stations in Little Rock and throughout the state, (800) USA-RAIL.

Bus Tours

- Greyhound Bus, stations throughout the state, (800) 231- 2222.
- 4-State Coaches, 1004 N. State Line Ave., Texarkana, AR 71854, (870) 772-7078.
- Arrow Coach Lines, PO Box 251704, Little Rock, AR 72225, (501) 663-6002.

State Highways

- Interstate 40 runs east-west from West Memphis to Fort Smith.
- Interstate 30 runs northeast-southwest from Little Rock to Texarkana.
- Interstate 55 runs north-south from Blytheville to West Memphis.

Theater and Music

North

- North Arkansas Symphony Society, PO Box 1243, Fayetteville, AR 72702, (501) 521-4166.

South

- South Arkansas Arts Center, 101 E. 5th St., El Dorado, AR 71370, (870) 862-5474.

Central

- Arkansas Repertory Theatre, PO Box 110, Little Rock, AR 72203, (501) 378-0445.
- Robinson Center Music Hall, Statehouse Plaza, Little Rock, AR 72201 (501) 376-1500.

- Community Theater of Little Rock, 5821 Cantrell Rd., Little Rock, AR72207, (501) 663-9494.
- University of Arkansas at Little Rock Fine Arts Galleries & Theatre (art, concerts, theater), 2801 S. University, Little Rock, AR 72204, (gallery) (501) 569-3183, (theatre) (501) 569-3291.
- Wildwood Park for the Performing Arts (opera, jazz, cabaret), 20919 Denny Road, Little Rock, AR 72211, (501) 821-7275.
- Riverfest Amphitheatre, Riverfront Park, Little Rock, (administrative) (501) 371-4517, (concert line) (501) 371-4444.
- SoHo Autumn Festival of Music and Art (every September), Quapaw Quarter Area, Little Rock, (501) 374-5200.

East

- Youth Repertory Theatre Co., The Forum, 115 E. Matthews, Jonesboro, AR 72401-3127, (870) 935-2726.
- Collins Theatre, PO Box 904, Emerson and 2nd Sts., Paragould, AR 72451, (501) 236-6252.
- Blues Fest, every Labor Day weekend, Craighead Forest Park, Jonesboro, (870) 933-7070 (or contact Jonesboro Parks and Recreation, 1212 S. Church St., Jonesboro, AR 72401-4125, (870) 933-4604).

West

- Fort Smith Little Theatre, 401 N. 6th Street, Fort Smith, AR 72901-2003, (501) 783-2966

Museums, Crafts, Historical, Recreational

North

- Mammoth Spring State Park (state's largest spring, museum, boats), PO Box 36, Mammoth Spring, AR 72554, (870) 625-7364.
- Razorback Park Golf Course (public), 2514 West Lori Drive Fayetteville, AR 72704, (501) 362-3131.
- Pea Ridge National Military Park (Civil War battlefield, visitors center, no facilities), PO Box 700, Pea Ridge, AR 72751, (501) 451-8122.
- Ozark Folk Center State (lodging, festivals, crafts April Nov.), PO Box 500, Mountain View, AR 72560, (park): (870) 269-3851 (lodge): (800) 264-3655.
- Arkansas Air Museum (air craft), PO Box 1911, Drake Field, Fayetteville, AR 72703, (501) 521-4947.
- Buffalo National River (95,000-acre park), PO Box 1173, Harrison, AR 72601, (501) 741-5443.

South

- Arkansas Museum of Natural Resources (oil-drilling machinery), 3853 Smackover Hwy., Smackover, AR 71762, (870) 725-2877.
- Lions Club Golf Course (public), E. 19th & N. Quaker, El Dorado, AR 71730, (501) 664-1531.

Central

- Toltec Mounds Archeological State Park (visitors center, tours), 490 Toltec Mounds Rd., Scott, AR 72142, (501) 961-9442.
- Hot Springs National Park (visitors center, lodging, camping, hot springs), PO Box 1860, Hot Springs, AR 71902, (501) 624-3383, ext. 640.
- Plantation Agriculture Museum, PO Box 87, Scott, AR 72142, (501) 961-1409.
- Lake Ouachita State Park (water activities, fishing, camping), 5451 Mountain Pine Rd., Mountain Pine, AR 71956, (park/campsite): (501) 767-9366, (cabins): (800) 264-2441.
- Burns Park Golf Course (public), Burns Park, Little Rock, AR 72118, (520) 776-7888.
- Rebsamen Park Golf Course (public), 4500 Rebsamen Park Rd., Little Rock, AR 72202, (602) 253-3963.

- War Memorial Golf Course (public), 5511 W Markham St., Little Rock, AR 72205, (501) 565-5830.
- Arkansas Museum of Discovery, 500 E. Markham, Suite 150, Little Rock, AR 72201, (501) 396-7050.
- Mid America Museum, 500 Mid America Blvd., Hot Springs, AR (501) 767-3461.
- Arkansas Arts Center, MacArthur Park, 9th & Commerce Sts, Little Rock, AR, Mailing Address: PO Box 2137, Little Rock, AR 72203, (501) 372-4000.
- Arkansas Territorial Restoration Museum, 200 East 3rd St., Little Rock, AR 72201-1694, (501) 324-9351.
- DeGray Lake Resort State Park (visitors center, camping, lodging, golf, marina), Rt. 3, Box 490, Bismarck, AR 71929, (501) 865-2801.
- River Market, Riverfront Park (adjacent to Riverfest Amphitheater), 400 E. Markham, Little Rock, AR 72201, (501) 375-2552.
- Little Rock Zoo, 1 Jonesboro Dr., Little Rock, AR 72205-5401, (501) 664-2406.

East

- Arkansas Post Museum, 55301 Hwy. 165 South, Gillett, AR 72055, (870) 548-2634.
- Arkansas State University Fine Arts Gallery, Fine Arts Center, Caraway Road, Jonesboro, AR 72401, (501) 972-3050.
- Arkansas State University Museum, Dean B. Ellis Library, Marshall St., Jonesboro, AR 72401, (870) 972-2074.
- Hampson Museum State Park (artifacts from 1350 to 1700), PO Box 156, Wilson, AR 72395, (870) 655-8622.
- White River National Wildlife Refuge (hardwood forest), PO Box 308, De Witt, AR 72042, (501) 946-1468.

West

- Crater of Diamonds State Park (dig your own, camping), Rte. 1, PO Box 364, Murfreesboro, AR 71958, (870) 285-3113.
- Fort Smith National Historic Site, PO Box 1406, Fort Smith, AR 72902, (501) 783-3961.

Organizations

Advocacy Groups

- Division of Aging and Adult Services, Dept of Human Services, PO Box 1437, Slot 1412, 7th and Main Sts., Little Rock, AR 72201, (501) 682-2441.
- Eldercare Locator (nationwide service to help older persons and caregivers locate support resources), (800) 677-1116.

Volunteer Programs

- Beautification Commission (Keep America Beautiful program), 659 Ouachita Ave., Hot Springs, AR 71901, (501) 623-7871.
- Jacksonville Senior Center, Inc. (recreation, meals on wheels, transportation, social activities), 100 Victory Circle, Jacksonville, AR 72076, (501) 982-7531.
- The Lane House (education and recreation for young people), 34 Prospect St., Eureka Springs, AR 72632, (501) 253-8060.

Housing

Long-Term Care Facilities

*In the state of Arkansas, these facilities are called **Continuing Care/Long-Term Care Nursing Care Facilities**.*

These facilities provide residential living and/or various levels of nursing and medical services to seniors for an extended period of time.

Types of Authorization

Licensing and/or Certification

Facilities are licensed by the Office of Long Term Care. These facilities include nursing facilities, skilled nursing facilities, and intermediate care facilities.

Memberships

- American Association of Homes and Services for the Aging (AAHSA) represents not-for-profit organizations committed to providing high-quality health care, housing, and services to the elderly. AAHSA, 901 E St. NW, Suite 500, Washington, DC 20004-2011. Ph: (202) 783-2242. Fax: (202) 783-2285. *http://www.aahsa.org*

Accreditations:

- Continuing Care Accreditation Commission (CCAC) accredits facilities that offer seniors a contract or contracts that provide residential living and health care services for the remainder of the persons lifetime and meet CCAC's accreditation standards.
- Joint Commission on the Accreditation of Healthcare Organizations (JCAHO) is an independent, not-for-profit organization and the nation's oldest and largest standards-setting and health care accrediting institution.

Central

Good Samaritan Campus

121 Cortez Rd.
Hot Springs Village, AR 71909

Ph: (501) 922-2000 or 623-8889
Fax: (501) 922-4068

IND: 82. AL: 25. RH: 18. SNF: 40

Age 62+. Nonprofit; nondenominational; Evangelical Lutheran church affiliation. Townhomes, apartments, and private and semiprivate rooms. 24-hour skilled nursing care; medical services; rehabilitative therapies; dental and podiatry care; pharmacy services; Medicare/Medicaid-approved; personal care; medication administration; security; emergency response system; maintenance; transportation; up to 3 daily meals; housekeeping and laundry services; exercise room; swimming pool; chapel; library; billiards room; woodworking shop; arts and crafts; social and recreational activities; golf courses; lakes; barber/beauty shop.

DEP: $550–$2,750. IND ENT: (partial ref.) $55,000–$85,000. IND MO: $900–$1,400 AL MO: $2,100–$2,700. RH ENT: (partial ref.) $203,500–$247,500. RH MO: $895. SNF Daily: $125–$135.

Parkway Village

14300 Chenal Parkway
Little Rock, AR 72211

Ph: (501) 202-1626 or (800) 262-0054
Fax: (501) 202-1685

http://www.baptist-health.com

E-mail: *DMJones@baptist-health.org*

IND: 286. AL: 34. HCC: 105

Age 60+. Nonprofit; nondenominational; Baptist Church affiliation. Cottages, apartments, and private rooms. 24-hour nursing care; medical services; rehabilitative therapies; pharmacy ser-

vices; Medicare-approved; personal care; medication administration; security; emergency response system; maintenance; transportation; up to 3 daily meals; housekeeping and laundry services; fitness center; swimming pool; religious services; chapel; library; social and recreational activities; on- and off-site activities; media room; concerts; guest speakers; crafts; ATM; convenience store; barber/beauty shop.

DEP: (ref.) IND, $1,100; AL, $880. IND ENT: (partial ref.), $48,000–$247,500. IND MO: $840–$2,200. AL MO: $2,000–$3,600. HCC MO: $2,000–$3,300.

Trinity Village, AAHSA

6400 Trinity Drive
Pine Bluff, AR 71603

Ph: (870) 879-3113
Fax: (870) 879-2246

IND: 125. AL: 33. SNF: 80

Age 62+. Nonprofit; nondenominational; sponsored by 5 local churches. Lodges, condos, and private and semiprivate rooms. Nursing care; rehabilitative therapies; medical services; dental and podiatry care; pharmacy services; infirmary; personal care; medication administration; security; emergency response system; maintenance; transportation; up to 3 daily meals; pets allowed; housekeeping and laundry services; fitness center (includes arthritis program); swimming pool; chapel; library; social and recreational activities; on- and off-site activities; game room; barber/beauty shop.

APPL: $175. IND LL: (ref.) Yes. IND MO: $400–$1,400. AL MO: $1,500. HCC Daily: $70–$85.

Northwest

Concordia of Bella Vista

1 Concordia Drive
Bella Vista, AR 72714

Ph: (501) 855-3714
Fax: (501) 855-6688

IND: 151. AL: 36. HCC: 99. ALZ/MEM IMP: 16

Age 65+. For-profit; Extendicare Facility. Townhomes, apartments, and private rooms. Nursing care; medical services; dental care; rehabilitative therapies; outpatient therapies; IV therapy; wound care; hospice care; pharmacy services; blood pressure checks; Medicare/Medicaid-approved; personal care; medication administration; security; emergency response system; maintenance; transportation; up to 3 daily meals; pets allowed; housekeeping and laundry services; exercise program; swimming pool; library; religious services; social and recreational activities; on- and off-site activities; woodworking shop; lounge; meeting room; lakes; clubhouse; parks; tennis courts; barber/beauty shop.

IND MO: $1,200–$2,400; 2nd person, $220. AL MO: $2,000. HCC Daily: $105–$125.

Assisted Living and Residential Care Facilities

These facilities provide housing, food service, and one or more personal services.

Types of Authorization

Licensing and/or Certification

Facilities are licensed by the Office of Long Term Care. These facilities include residential care facilities and adult day care facilities.

Memberships

- Assisted Living Federation of America (ALFA) is a national nonprofit membership organization whose mission is to enhance the quality of life in assisted living facilities and promote the interests of the assisted living industry. ALFA, 10300 Eaton Place, Suite 400, Fairfax, VA 22030. Ph: (703) 691-8100. Fax: (703) 691-8106. *http://www.alfa.org*

Northwest

Homestyle Assisted Living

2175 Orchard St.
Springdale, AR 72762

AL: Yes

Nondenominational. Private rooms. 24-hour professional staff; personal care; medication administration; security; emergency response system; maintenance; transportation; up to 3 daily meals; housekeeping and laundry services; social and recreational activities; walking paths; barber/beauty shop.

Contact facility for fees.

Mercy Crest

1300 Strozier Lane
Barling, AR 72923

Ph: (501) 478-3000

AL: Yes

Nonprofit; nondenominational; operated by the Religious Sisters of Mercy. Studios, one- and two-bedroom apartments. 24-hour staffing; respite services; personal care; medication administration; security; emergency response system; maintenance; transportation; up to 3 daily meals plus snacks (tray service available); housekeeping and laundry services; chapel and religious services; social and recreational activities; on- and off-site activities; atrium; sun rooms; walking paths; gift shop; barber/beauty shop.

AL MO: $1,500–$2,200. RSP Daily: $45.

Oak Ridge Retirement Community

103 Wade Lane
Pea Ridge, AR 72751

Ph: (501) 451-1800

IND: Yes. RH/AL: 40

Nondenominational; division of LDG, Inc. Apartments and private rooms. Personal care; medication administration; security; emergency response system; maintenance; transportation; up to 3 daily meals; pets allowed; housekeeping and laundry services; social and recreational activities; card and board games; patios; barber/beauty shop.

DEP: (no ref.), nonsmokers/no pets, $220; smokers/pets, $550.

IND: $1,500–$1,800. RH/AL: $1,250–$1,850.

Sunset Lodge

1200 W. Center
Greenwood, AR 72936

Ph: (501) 996-7878

AL: Yes

Nondenominational. Suites and private and semiprivate rooms. 24-hour staffing; emergency care; personal care; medication administration; security; emergency response system; maintenance; transportation; up to 3 daily meals; housekeeping and laundry services; exercise area; whirlpool; social and recreational activities; lounges; barber/beauty shop services.

MO: Fees based on income; HUD-subsidized.

Willow Brook Retirement Community

5501 Duncan Rd.
Fort Smith, AR 72903

Ph: (501) 484-5556

IND: 91. AL: Yes

Nondenominational; owned by Health Resources. Suites and one- and two-bedroom apartments. 24-hour staffing; personal care; medication administration; security; emergency response system; maintenance; transportation; up to 3 daily meals; pets allowed; housekeeping and laundry services; social and recreational activities.

IND MO: $1,300–$2,000; 2nd person, $330. AL MO: $1,700–$2,000; 2nd person with assistance, $575; 2nd person without assistance, $330.

Central

Pleasant Hills

800 Napa Valley Rd.
Little Rock, AR 72211

Ph: (501) 225-9405
Fax: (501) 225-6863

IND: 150. AL: 19

Age 55+. For-profit; nondenominational; a Marriott Senior Living Community. Studios and cottage apartments. Personal care; medication administration; security; emergency response system; maintenance; transportation; up to 3 daily meals; pets allowed; housekeeping and laundry services; exercise classes; library; social and recreational activities; on- and off-site activities; arts and crafts room; speakers and seminars; music room; gift shop; barber/beauty shop.

APPL: $275. IND MO: $1,250–$2,100

Outlook Pointe

9880 Brockington Rd.
Sherwood, AR 72120

Ph: (501) 835-6000
Fax: (501) 835-6509
http://www.balancedcare.com

AL: Yes

For-profit; nondenominational; managed by Balanced Care Corporation. Studios and private rooms. 24-hour staffing; respite care; outpatient rehabilitation services; preventative and curative therapies and services; health screenings; personal care; medication administration; security; emergency response system; maintenance; transportation; up to 3 daily meals; housekeeping and laundry services; exercise programs; spa; religious services; library and computer center; social and recreational activities; game and card room; patio; barbecue area; barber/beauty shop.

Contact facility for fees.

Retirement Center of Arkansas

8900 Sylvan Hills Hwy.
Sherwood, AR 72120

Ph: (501) 835-5931
Fax: (501) 835-4120

RH: 65

For-profit; nondenominational. Private rooms. Pharmacy services; medication administration; security; maintenance; transportation; up to 3 daily meals; housekeeping and laundry services; social and recreational activities; lounge.

RH MO: $950–$1,400.

West Markham Retirement Care, ARALA

10905 W. Markham St.
Little Rock, AR 72211-2898

Ph: (501) 228-9519
Fax: (501) 227-7292
E-mail: *ramaloft@aristotle.net*

AL: 49

For-profit; nondenominational. Private rooms. Nursing care; rehabilitative therapies; medical services; dental and podiatry care; pharmacy services; personal care; medication administration; security; emergency response system; maintenance; transportation; up to 3 daily meals; pets allowed; housekeeping and laundry services; social and recreational activities; close to shopping.

AL MO: $440–$1,650.

Northeast

Rosehaven Retirement Home

1400 Stone St.
Jonesboro, AR 72401

Ph: (870) 932-0761

Rosehaven Villa Retirement Home

3009 Hill Drive
Jonesboro, AR 72401

Ph: (870) 935-5961

PC: Yes

For-profit; nondenominational. Apartments. 24-hour staffing; Medicaid-approved; personal care; medication administration; security; emergency response system; maintenance; transportation; up to 3 daily meals; housekeeping and laundry services; church services; social and recreational activities; lounge with TV; nearby shopping and medical facilities; barber/beauty shop.

Contact facility for fees.

Independent Living

Independent housing (primarily rentals) for seniors that may offer security features, meal service, and activities.

Central

Andover Place

2601 Andover Court
Little Rock, AR 72227

Ph: (501) 224-0441
Fax: (501) 224-3239

IND: Yes

For-profit; nondenominational; Holiday Retirement Corp. Studios and one- and two-bedroom apartments. 24-hour staffing; independent home health services; security; emergency response system; maintenance; transportation; up to 3 daily meals; housekeeping and laundry services; exercise program; religious services; game room; media room; social and recreational activities; on- and off-site activities; movies; bingo; barber/beauty shop.

IND MO: $1,200–$2,200; 2nd person, $400.

Audubon Pointe

Audubon Drive
Maumelle, AR 72113

Ph: (501) 851-1821
Fax: (501) 851-2488

IND: Yes

Age 62+. Nondenominational; managed by TESCO Properties. One- and two-bedroom apartments. Blood pressure checks; security; emergency response system; maintenance; transportation; laundry services; close to doctor/dentist offices and pharmacy; social and recreational activities; religious services; game room; gardening; lake on property; patio with barbecue; barber/beauty shop.

IND MO: 30% of income; HUD-subsidized.

REQ: Yearly incomes must not exceed—1 person, $16,050; 2 persons, $18,350.

Country Club Village

1925 Malvern Ave.
Hot Springs, AR 71901

Ph: (501) 624-6435
Fax: (501) 624-2925

IND: 165

For-profit; nondenominational. Security; emergency response system; resident manager; maintenance; transportation; up to 3 daily meals; pets allowed; housekeeping and laundry services; library; exercise equipment room; social and recreational activities; game room; billiard room; media room; barber/beauty shop.

APPL: (ref.) $100. DEP: (partial ref.) 1 mo. rent. IND MO: $1,300–$1,900; 2nd person, $330.

Parkstone Place

One Parkstone Circle
North Little Rock, AR 72116

Ph: (501) 771-1228

IND: 84

Age 55+. Nondenominational; North Little Rock Residential Housing Board. One- and two-bedroom apartments. Security; emergency response system; maintenance; transportation; up to 2 daily meals (tray service available); pets allowed; housekeeping and laundry services; exercise room; whirlpool; religious

services; chapel; library; social and recreational activities; craft room; barber/ beauty shop.

IND MO: $1,200–$2,100.

Retired Teachers Housing

1200 Commerce
Little Rock, AR 72202

Ph: (501) 372-3610

IND: 128

Age 62+. Nondenominational. Apartments. Security system; maintenance; pets allowed.

IND MO: $275–$475.

East

Ecumenical Village

217 W. Jackson Ave.
West Memphis, AR 72301

Ph: (870) 735-1115
Fax: (870) 732-2190
http://www.ncr.org

IND: 67

Age 62. Nonprofit; church affiliation. Emergency response system; maintenance; transportation; pets allowed; laundry services; community room; social and recreational activities.

HUD-subsidized.

Northwest

Chateau of Rogers

1151 West New Hope
Rogers, AR 72756

Ph: (501) 636-6285
Fax: (501) 636-4174

IND: 16

For-profit; nondenominational; part of Beverly Healthcare. Private suites. 24-hour staffing; some medication administration; security; emergency response system; maintenance; transportation; up to 3 daily meals; housekeeping and laundry services; social and recreational activities; outdoor patios.

IND MO: $1,600.

Gardens at Arkanshire

5000 Arkanshire Circle
Springdale, AR 72764

Ph: (501) 750-1134
Fax: (501) 750-1161

IND: 130

For-profit. Apartments. Security; emergency response system; maintenance; transportation; up to 3 daily meals; pets allowed; housekeeping and laundry services; fitness center; social and recreational activities.

DEP: 1 mo. rent. IND MO: $1,100–$2,200.

Peachtree Village

17 S. Fresno
Fort Smith, AR 72901

Ph: (501) 785-5578

IND: Yes

Nondenominational. One- and two-bedroom apartments. Home health care services; 24-hour staffing; security; emergency response system; maintenance; transportation; up to 3 daily meals; housekeeping and laundry services; social and recreational activities.

Contact facility for fees.

Adult/Resort Communities

Communities for active adults (not all are age-restricted; primarily ownership).

North

Bella Vista Village

210 Town Center S.E.
Bella Vista, AR 72714

Ph: (800) 553-6687 or (501) 855-3036
Fax: (501) 855-6634
www.cooper-land.com/bellavista

Individual homes, condominiums, homesites. Golf courses; tennis; racquetball; swimming pool; hiking; lakes; fishing; boating/waterskiing; fitness center; library; social clubs; skeet/trap range.

PURCHASE: Homes, $61,000–$550,000.

Cherokee Village

PO Box 250
Cherokee Village, AR 72525

Ph: (888) 261-2167 or (870) 257-3241
Fax: (870) 257-3404
http://www.king-rhodes.com

Individual homes, condominiums, homesites. Golf courses; tennis; swimming pool; hiking; lakes; fishing; boating/waterskiing; social clubs.

PURCHASE: Homes, $38,500–$220,000; homesites: $550–$44,000.

Fairfield Bay

PO Box 1159
Fairfield Bay, AR 72088

Ph: (888) 244-4FUN or (501) 884-3324
Fax: (501) 884-5205
http://www.ffbchamber.org

Individual homes, condominiums, homesites. Golf courses; tennis; swimming pools; hiking trails; fishing; riding stables; boating/water skiing; clubs.

PURCHASE: Homes, $49,500–$550,000+.

The Links at Harrison

1919 Club Circle
Harrison, AR 72601

Ph: (870) 365-3621
Fax: (870) 365-0244

Rental apartments. Golf course; tennis; swimming pool; hiking trails; fitness center; clubs; basketball; sand volleyball.

RENTALS: $350–$450.

Central

Chenal Valley

7 Chenal Club Blvd.
Little Rock, AR 72223

Ph: (800) 848-9559 or (501) 821-5555
Fax: (501) 821-5656
http://www.chenal.com

Individual homes, homesites. Golf course; tennis; swimming pool; hiking trails.

PURCHASE: Homes, $176,000–$1.1 million+.

Diamante

2000 Country Club Drive
Hot Springs Village, AR 71909

Ph: (501) 922-1114
Fax: (501) 922-4353
http://www.diamantecountryclub.com

Individual homes, homesites. Golf course; swimming pool; tennis; hiking/biking; fishing; hunting; riding stables; boating/waterskiing; fitness center; clubs.

PURCHASE: Homes, $192,500–$660,000; homesites, $38,500–$110,000.

Diamondhead Country Club

245 Independence Dr.
Hot Springs, AR 71913

Ph: (501) 262-4470
Fax: (501) 262-3044

Individual homes, condominiums. Golf course; tennis; swimming pool; hiking trails; fishing; boating/waterskiing; social clubs.

PURCHASE: Homes, $82,000–$264,000.

Holiday Island Country Club

1 Country Club Dr.
Holiday Island, AR 72631

Ph: (501) 253-9700
Fax: (501) 253-5829
http://www.holidayisland.com

Individual homes, condominiums, homesites. Golf courses; tennis; swimming pool; hiking; fishing; boating/waterskiing; fitness center; social clubs.

PURCHASE: Homes, $82,500–$330,000+.

Hot Springs Village

895 DeSoto Blvd.
Hot Springs Village, AR 71909

Ph: (501) 922-0200
Fax: (501) 922-5968

http://www.hsvvoice.com

Individual homes, townhomes, homesites. Golf course; tennis; swimming pool; hiking/biking; boating/waterskiing; fishing; fitness center; library; lawn bowling, bocce; social clubs.

PURCHASE: Homes, $55,000–$1.1 million.

Red Apple Inn & Country Club on Eden Isle

317 Club Rd.
Heber Springs, AR 72543

Ph: (800) RED-APPL or (501) 362-5025
Fax: (501) 362-5048

http://www.redappleinn.com

Individual homes, condominiums, homesites. Golf course; tennis; swimming pool; fishing; bicycle paths; boating/waterskiing; fitness center; social clubs.

PURCHASE: Condos, $88,000–$198,000; homes, $198,000–$825,000; homesites, $11,000–$220,000.

California

http://www.state.ca.us

General Information

Climate

Widely varied. Coast: mild winters, cool summers, very dry in south. Central Valley: hot summers. Northeast: cold winters. Southeast: Extremely hot summers.

Cost of Living

Ranks 14th in the nation.

Taxes

State/Local as % of Income: 10.6%.

Property Tax Reduction: Assistance for low-income homeowners or renters 62 and older and/or disabled. Call (800) 852-5711 for information.

Sales: 7 %; some special districts levy additional taxes, from 7.35% to 8.5% total.

Prescription Exemptions: Prescriptions by physician or dentist and many medical devices are tax exempt.

Transportation, Travel, and Tourism

General

California Travel and Tourism Authority, (800) GOCALIF. For publications, write to 19600 Fairchild Rd., Suite 260, Irvine, CA 92715, (714) 833-9002.

Major Airports

- Los Angeles International Airport, 1 World Way, Los Angeles, CA 90045, (213) 646-5252 or (818) AIRPORT.
- Palm Springs Airport, 3400 E. Tahquitz Canyon Way, Palm Springs, CA 92262, (619) 323-8163.
- Oakland International Airport, 1 Airport Dr., Oakland, CA 94621, (510) 577-4000.
- Ontario International Airport, Airport Drive & Vineyard Ave., Ontario, CA 91761, (909) 988-2700.
- Sacramento International Airport, 6900 Airport Blvd., Sacramento, CA 95837, (916) 929-5411.
- San Diego International Airport, San Diego, CA 92101, (617) 231-5220 or (619) 291-2087.
- San Francisco International Airport, Rt. 101, San Francisco, CA, (415) 876-2217.
- San Jose International Airport, 1661 Airport Blvd. #205, San Jose, CA 95110, (408) 998-0707.

Railways

- Amtrak, stations throughout the state, (800) USA-RAIL.

Bus Tours

- Bay Area Rapid Transit, stations in the San Francisco area, (510) 465-BART.
- Greyhound Bus Lines, stations throughout the state, (800) 231-2222.
- Los Angeles Transportation Authority, Bus and Rail, 1-800-COMMUTE.

State Highways

- Interstate 5 runs north-south, Oregon to San Diego.
- Interstate 80 runs east-west, from Reno through Sacramento to San Francisco.
- Interstate 15 runs south-north from San Diego to Barstow, then northeast to Las Vegas.
- Interstate 10 runs east-west from Arizona to Santa Monica.
- Interstate 8 runs east-west from Yuma, AZ, to San Diego.

Theater and Music

North

- Napa Valley Symphony, 2407 California Blvd., Napa, CA 94558, (707) 22MUSIC (226-6872).
- San Francisco Opera, 301 Van Ness Ave., San Francisco, CA 94102, (415) 864-3330.
- San Jose Symphony, 495 Almaden Blvd., San Jose, CA 95110, (408) 287-7383 or for tickets, (408) 288-2828.
- Theatre on the Square, 450 Post St., San Francisco, CA 94102, (415) 433-9500.

South

- Mark Taper Forum/Ahmanson Theatre, Center Theatre Group, 135 N. Grand Ave., Los Angeles, CA 90012, Forum (213) 972-7355, Ahmanson (213) 972-7289.
- Los Angeles Philharmonic, Dorothy Chandler Pavilion, Music Center of Los Angeles County, 135 N. Grand Ave., Los Angeles, CA 90012-3013.
- Old Globe Theater, Balboa Park, San Diego, (619) 239-2255.
- Orange County Performing Arts Center, 600 Town Center Drive, Costa Mesa, CA 92626, (714) 556-2787.
- Sierra Madre Playhouse, 87 W. Sierra Madre Blvd., Sierra Madre, CA 90124, (626) 355-4318.
- Wilshire Theatre Box Office, 8440 Wilshire Blvd., Beverly Hills, CA 90211 (no phone sales) .

Museums, Crafts, Historical, Recreational

North

- Ahwahnee Resort & Country Club (golf), 46516 Opah Dr., Ahwahnee, CA 93601, (209) 683-6620.
- Alpine Mountains (skiing), North Lake Tahoe, (800) 441-4423 or (530) 583-4232.
- Chardonnay Club Vineyard Course (public golf), 2555 Jameson Canyon Rd., Napa, CA 94559, (707) 257-1900.
- Crystal Springs Golf Course (public), 6650 Golf Course Drive, Burlingame, CA 94010, (650) 342-0603.
- M. H. de Young Memorial Museum, 75 Tea Garden Drive, San Francisco, CA 94118; (415) 750-3600.
- Eureka Municipal Golf Course (public), 4750 Fairway Drive, Eureka, CA 95501, (707) 443-4808.
- Golden Gate National Recreation Area (Fort Point Site, Muir Woods Monument, Alcatraz Island, Presidio), (visitors center, lodging, golf, camping, beaches), Fort Mason, Bldg. 201, San Francisco, CA 94123, (415) 556-0560.
- Golden State Museum, 1020 O Street, Sacramento, CA 95814 (916) 653-7524.
- Hearst Castle, 750 Hearst Castle Rd., San Simeon, CA 93452, (805) 927-2000 or (800) 444-4445.
- Lake Tahoe Golf Course (public), Hwy 50, Meadowvale Rd., S. Lake Tahoe, CA 96158, (916) 577-0788.
- Lassen Volcanic National Park (visitors center, lodging), PO Box 100, Mineral, CA 96063, (530) 595-4444.
- Monterey Bay Aquarium, 886 Cannery Row, Monterey, CA 93940, (408) 648-4888.
- Redwood National Park (visitors center, camping), 1111 2nd St., Crescent City, CA 95531, (707) 464-6101.
- San Francisco Maritime National Historical Park (ships, museum), Bldg. E, Fort Mason Center, San Francisco, CA 94123, (415) 556-3002.
- San Jose Museum of Art, 110 S. Market St., San Jose, CA 95119, (408) 294-2787.
- Squaw Valley (skiing), North Lake Tahoe, (530) 583-6985.
- USS Hornet Aircraft Carrier National Historic Landmark, Pier 3, PO Box 460, Alameda, CA 94501, (510) 521-8448 or (888) 865-2812.
- Whiskeytown-Shasta-Trinity National Recreation Area (visitors center, boating, camping), PO Box

188, Whiskeytown, CA 96095, (530) 241-6584.
- Yosemite National Park (visitors center, camping), PO Box 577, Yosemite, CA 95389, (209) 372-0200.

South

- Anaheim Dad Miller Golf Course (public), 430 N. Gilbert, Anaheim, CA 92801, (714) 774-8055.
- Big Bear Mountain Resort (skiing), 43101 Goldmine Drive, PO Box 6812, Big Bear Lake, CA 92315, (800) BEAR-MTN, (lodging) (800) 4-BIG-BEAR.
- Canyon South Golf Course (public), 1097 Murray Canyon Drive, Palm Springs, CA 92264, (619) 327-2019.
- Channel Islands National Park (visitors center, hiking, camping), 1901 Spinnaker Drive, Ventura, CA 93001-4354, (805) 658-5730.
- Death Valley National Park (visitors center, lodging, camping), PO Box 579, Death Valley, CA 92328, (760) 786-2331.
- The Getty Center, 1200 Getty Center Dr., Suite 400, Los Angeles, CA 90049, (310) 440-7300.
- The Huntington Library, Art Collections, and Botanical Gardens, 1151 Oxford Rd., San Marino, CA 91108, (626) 405-2100.
- Mission San Juan Capistrano, PO Box 697, San Juan Capistrano, CA 92693, (949) 248-2048.
- Newport Beach Golf Course (public), 3100 Irvine Ave., Newport Beach, CA 92660, (714) 852-8689.
- Palm Desert Country Club (public), 77200 California Ave., Palm Desert, CA 92260, (619) 345-2525.
- The Queen Mary, 1126 Queens Hwy., Long Beach, CA 90802, (562) 435-3511.
- San Diego Zoo, 2920 Zoo Drive, San Diego, CA 92112, (619) 234-3153.
- Santa Monica Mountains National Recreation Area (visitors center, hiking, lodging, camping), 401 W. Hillcrest Dr., Thousand Oaks, CA 91360, (805) 370-2301.
- Sequoia and Kings Canyon National Parks (visitors centers, lodging, camping), Three Rivers, CA 93271, (209) 565-3341.
- Snow Valley (skiing), Running Springs, CA 92382, (800) 680-7669.

Organizations

Advocacy Groups

- California Department of Aging, 1600 K St., Sacramento, CA 95814, (916) 322-4989.
- Health Insurance Counseling and Advocacy Program, California Department of Aging, (800) 510-2020.
- Long-Term Care Ombudsman Program, California Department of Aging, (916) 323-6681.
- Taxpayers' Rights Advocate, MIC:70, State Board of Equalization, PO Box 942879, Sacramento, CA 94279, (916) 324-2798 or (888) 324-2798.

Volunteer Programs

- Friends of the Los Angeles Philharmonic, Los Angeles Philharmonic Development Department, 135 N. Grand Ave., Los Angeles, CA 90012, (213) 972-7557.
- Senior Companion Program, California Department of Aging, (916) 323-7514.
- Volunteers in Parks (VIP), Golden Gate National Recreation Area, Fort Mason, Bldg. 201, San Francisco, CA 94123, (415) 561-4325.

Housing

Long-Term Care Facilities

*In the state of California, these facilities are called **Continuing Care/Long-Term Care/Nursing Care Facilities**.*

These facilities provide residential living and/or various levels of nursing and medical services to seniors for an extended period of time.

Types of Authorization

Licensing and / or Certification

These facilities are regulated by the Department of Health Services, Licensing and Certification. CCRCs provide one or more elements of care. Payment includes an entrance fee, monthly fee, and fees for medical services. Long-term care facilities provide all levels of care on-site. Payment includes entrance fee and monthly fee with medical services inclusive.

Memberships

- American Association of Homes and Services for the Aging (AAHSA) represents not-for-profit organizations committed to providing high-quality health care, housing, and services to the elderly. AAHSA, 901 E St. NW, Suite 500, Washington, DC 20004-2011. Ph: (202) 783-2242. Fax: (202) 783-2285. *http: / / www.aahsa.org*
- California Association of Homes and Services for the Aging, 7311 Greenhaven Drive, Suite 175, Sacramento, CA, 95831-3572. Ph: (916) 392-5111. Fax: (916) 428-4250.

Accreditations

- Continuing Care Accreditation Commission (CCAC) accredits facilities that offer seniors a contract or contracts that provide residential living and health care services for the remainder of the person's lifetime and meet CCAC's accreditation standards.
- Joint Commission on the Accreditation of Healthcare Organizations (JCAHO) is an independent, not-for-profit organization, and the nation's oldest and largest standards-setting and health care accrediting institution.

Southwest

Fredericka Manor, AAHSA, CAHSA

111 Third Ave.
Chula Vista, CA 91910

Ph: (619) 427-2777

SNF: 174. ALZ/MEM IMP: Yes

Nonprofit; nondenominational; owned and managed by Pacific Homes. Private rooms. Skilled nursing care; physical, occupational, and speech therapies; lab and radiology services; dental and podiatry care; hospice; pharmacy services; respite care; Medicare/Medicaid-approved; personal care; medication administration; security; emergency response system; maintenance; transportation; 3 daily meals; housekeeping and laundry services; religious services; crafts, music, movies; social and recreational activities.

Contact facility for fees.

HillCrest, CCAC, AASHA, CAHSA

2705 Mountain View Drive
La Verne, CA 91750-4398

Ph: (909) 593-4917 or (800) 566-4373
Fax: (909) 392-439

RH: 191. CONG: Yes. AL: 45. HCC: 78. ALZ/MEM IMP: 22

Age 62+. Nonprofit; affiliated with the Church of the Brethren. Homes, apartments, and private and semiprivate rooms. 24-hour nursing care; skilled nursing care; physical, occupational, and speech therapies; social services; medical services; dental and podiatry care; phar-

macy services; wellness program; respite care; home health care services; Medicare/Medicaid-approved; personal care; medication administration; security; emergency response system; maintenance; transportation; up to 3 daily meals; housekeeping and laundry services; exercise program; chaplain; nondenominational religious services; Bible study; social and recreational activities; computer lab; library; woodworking shop; arts and crafts; aviary; gardening; shuffleboard; book shop; lounge; barber/beauty shop.

DEP: (ref.) $1,100. RH ENT: $97,000–$157,000. RH MO: $1,000–$1,600. CONG ENT: $41,000–$70,000. CONG MO: with ENT, $1,400–$3,300; without ENT, $2,100–$4,800+. AL MO: $2,700–$5,400. HCC Daily: Semiprivate, $150; private, $185. ALZ/MEM IMP MO: $3,300 and $4,700.

Mt. San Antonio Gardens, CCAC

900 E. Harrison Ave.
Pomona, CA 91767

Ph: (909) 624-5061
Fax: (909) 621-3327

E-mail: *njoylife@gte.com*

IND: 271. AL: 60. HCC: 64. ALZ/MEM IMP: Yes. ADC: Yes

Age 60+. Nonprofit; nondenominational; nonsectarian. Cottages, apartments, and private and semiprivate rooms. Skilled nursing care; rehabilitative services; medical services; dental and podiatry care; pharmacy services; home health services; visual aid room; Medicare-approved; personal care; medication administration; security; emergency response system; maintenance; transportation; up to 3 daily meals; pets allowed; housekeeping and laundry services; fitness center; swimming pool; library; banking services; social and recreational activities; resident committees and clubs; volunteer opportunities; educational program; boutique; gift shop; gardens; barber/beauty shop.

APPL: (no ref.): $275. DEP: (ref.), $1,100. IND ENT: $100,000–$285,000. IND MO: $1,700. AL and HCC services inclusive.

Pacific Regent

3890 Nobet Drive
San Diego, CA 92122

Ph: (619) 597-8000
Fax: (619) 623-2839

http://www.thefountains.com

IND: 148. SNF: 59

Age 62+. For-profit; nondenominational. Condos and private and semiprivate rooms. Skilled nursing care; rehabilitative therapies; medical services; dental and podiatry care; pharmacy services; personal care; medication administration; security; emergency response system; maintenance; transportation; up to 3 daily meals; housekeeping and laundry services; fitness center; swimming pool; social and recreational activities; computer center.

IND ENT: $242,000–$1.1 million. IND MO: $1,500–$1,900. SNF Daily: Semiprivate, $165; private, $220–$275.

Redwood Terrace

710 W. Thirteenth Ave.
Escondido, CA 92025-5599

Ph: (760) 747-7751 or (800) 842-6775
Fax: (760) 747-1625

IND: Yes. AL: Yes. HCC: Yes

Nonprofit; nondenominational; affiliated with Southern California Presbyterian Homes. Studios and one- and two-bedroom apartments. Nursing care; rehabilitative therapies; medical services; dental and podiatry care; pharmacy services; personal care; medication administration; security; emergency response system; maintenance; transportation; up to 3 daily meals; housekeeping and laundry services; exercise classes; swimming pool; library; workshop; craft room; social and recreational activities; resident council; lounges; gift shop; barber/beauty salon.

IND ENT: $53,000–$222,000. IND MO: $2,100–$3,600.

Regents Point, CCAC

19191 Harvard Ave.
Irvine, CA 92612-4670

Ph: (714) 8554-9500 or (800) 278-8898

IND: 238. AL: 64. SNF: 59

Nonprofit; nondenominational; affiliated with Southern California Presbyterian Homes. Suites, apartments, and private and semiprivate rooms. 24-hour skilled nursing care; long- and short-term care; rehabilitative therapies; physician services; dental care; pharmacy services; pain management; IV therapy; eye care; wound care management; lab and X-ray services; personal care; medication administration; security; emergency response system; maintenance; transportation; up to 3 daily meals; pets allowed; housekeeping and laundry services; exercise classes; swimming pool; library; social and educational activities; volunteer program; residents association; woodworking shop; arts and crafts; caf; putting green; gardens; barber/beauty shop.

IND ENT: $47,000–$352,000. IND MO: $1,300–$3,000. AL ENT: $38,000–$65,000. AL MO: with ENT, $3,000–$3,200; without ENT, $3,500–$4,000. SNF Daily: Nonresidents, $190 and $375; residents, $150, $220, $300.

Royal Oaks Manor/Bradbury Oaks, CCAC

1763 Royal Oaks Drive N.
Bradbury, CA 91010

Ph: (626) 305-2433
Fax: (626) 357-9723

IND: Yes. AL: Yes. HCC: 48

Age 62+. Nonprofit; nondenominational; affiliated with Southern California Presbyterian Homes. Cottages, apartments, and private and semiprivate rooms. Skilled nursing care; physical, occupational, and speech therapies; medical services; podiatry and dental care; short- and long-term care; pharmacy services; clinic; personal care; medication administration; security; emergency response system; maintenance; transportation; up to 3 daily meals; housekeeping and laundry services; exercise classes; library; media room; lectures; arts and crafts; business center; residents association; volunteer program; convenience store; on- and off-site activities; walking paths; outdoor patio; putting green; pond; gardens; barber/beauty shop.

IND ENT: (amortized ref.) $49,500–$335,500. IND MO: $1,300–$3,600. AL and HCC services at reduced rates for members.

Valle Verde Retirement Community, CCAC

900 Calle de los Amigos
Santa Barbara, CA 93105

Ph: (805) 687-1571
Fax: (805) 687-5540

E-mail: *valleverde@aol.com*

IND: 232. AL: 54. HCC: 77

Nonprofit; nondenominational. Apartments and private and semiprivate rooms. 24-hour nursing care; physical, occupational, and speech therapies; podiatry, audiology, ophthalmology, dentistry, and psychology services; pharmacy services; physician services; respite care; postoperative care; personal care; medication administration; security; emergency response system; maintenance; transportation; up to 3 daily meals; housekeeping and laundry services; exercise classes; swimming pool and Jacuzzi; educational and cultural activities; woodworking shop; crafts; media room; putting green; gift and convenience store; bed and breakfast; garden patios; barber/beauty shop.

IND ENT: (amortized ref.) $44,000–$247,500. IND MO: $1,600–$3,000; 2nd person, $600. AL ENT: (amortized ref.) $38,500–$77,000. AL MO: $2,600–$5,100; 2nd person, $900, $1,000, $1,600.

HCC Daily: 4-bedroom, $140; semiprivate, $165; private, $235.

The White Sands of La Jolla, CCAC

7450 Olivetas Ave.
La Jolla, CA 92037

Ph: (619) 450-5102 or 454-4201
Fax: (619) 450-5298

IND: Yes. AL: Yes. SNF: Yes

Nonprofit; nondenominational; affiliated with Southern California Presbyterian Homes. Studios, one- and two-bedroom apartments, and private and semiprivate rooms. 24-hour skilled nursing care; rehabilitative therapies; medical services; dental care; pharmacy services; personal care; medication administration; security; emergency response system; maintenance; transportation; up to 3 daily meals; housekeeping and laundry services; exercise classes; swimming pool; library; crafts; woodworking shop; shuffleboard; multimedia room; lawn bowling; gardens; located on the ocean; barber/beauty shop.

IND ENT: $41,000–$528,000. IND MO: $1,400–$3,400. AL MO: About $2,800. HCC Daily: $120.

Windsor Manor, CCAC

1230 E. Windsor Rd.
Glendale, CA 91205

Ph: (818) 244-7219
Fax: (818) 240-3887

IND: Yes. AL: Yes

Age 62+. Nonprofit; nondenominational; affiliated with Southern California Presbyterian Homes. Suites, apartments, and private and semiprivate rooms. 24-hour skilled nursing care; physician services; rehabilitative therapies; short- and long-term care; medical services; wellness seminars; outpatient clinic; personal care; medication administration; security; emergency response system; maintenance; transportation; up to 3 daily meals; housekeeping and laundry services; exercise program; social and recreational activities; conference room; community room; volunteer opportunities; residents association; billiard room; arts and crafts; convenience store; gardens; courtyard; barber/beauty shop.

IND ENT: $49,500–$110,000. IND MO: $1,300–$2,600. AL MO: About $2,700. HCC Daily: About $125.

South Central

The Fountains at the Carlotta

41-505 Carlotta Drive
Palm Desert, CA 92211

Ph: (760) 346-5420
Fax: (760) 341-9815

http://www.thefountains.com/

IND: 109. AL: 22. HCC: 59

Age 62+. For-profit; nondenominational. Apartments and private and semiprivate rooms. Skilled nursing care; rehabilitative therapies; medical services; dental and podiatry care; pharmacy services; personal care; medication administration; security; emergency response system; maintenance; transportation; up to 3 daily meals; housekeeping and laundry services; fitness center; swimming pool; social and recreational activities.

DEP: $2,750. IND ENT: Starts at $65,000. IND MO: Starts at $1,100. AL Daily: $105. HCC Daily: Starts at $120.

Rosewood, CCAC

1301 New Stine Rd.
Bakersfield, CA 93309-3515

Ph: (805) 834-0620, ext. 106 or (877) 843-5433
Fax: (805) 834-0280

E-mail: *Cmofield@abhow.com*

IND: 129. AL: 22. HCC: 79

Age 62+. Nonprofit; nondenominational; affiliated with the American Baptist Homes of the West. Lodges, apartments, and private and semiprivate rooms. 24-hour nursing care; reha-

bilitative therapies; medical services; podiatry and dental care; pharmacy services; Medicare-approved; personal care; medication administration; security; emergency response system; maintenance; transportation; up to 3 daily meals; housekeeping and laundry services; social and recreational activities; crafts; barber/beauty shop.

IND ENT: $22,000–$105,000. IND MO: $1,400–$2,800. AL ENT: $12,000–$37,000. AL MO: $2,300–$3,900. HCC MO: $4,700–$6,500.

Central West

Canterbury Woods

651 Sinex Ave.
Pacific Grove, CA 93950

Ph: (831) 657-4193 or (800) 211-5558
Fax: (831) 372-2850

IND: Yes. AL: Yes. SNF: Yes

Age 65+. Nonprofit; nondenominational; affiliated with Episcopal Homes Foundation. Cottages, alcoves, studios, apartments, and private and semiprivate rooms. Skilled nursing care; physician visits; lab and X-ray services; emergency care; rehabilitative therapies; short- and long-term care; psychiatric services; dental and podiatry care; pharmacy services; personal care; medication administration; security; emergency response system; maintenance; transportation; up to 3 daily meals; pets allowed; housekeeping and laundry services; exercise classes; chapel; libraries; arts and crafts room; media room; billiards room; social, recreational, and cultural activities; volunteer program; auditorium; lounges; gardening; walking paths.

LCF: $67,000–$302,000; 2nd person, $22,000. IND MO: $1,800–$3,000. AL and SNF fees inclusive.

Forest Hill Manor

551 Gibson Ave.
Pacific Grove, CA 93950

Ph: (831) 657-5200
Fax: (408) 649-1695

IND: 95. AL: 12. SNF: 51

Age 62+. Nonprofit; nondenominational; affiliated with the United Methodist Church. Apartments. Skilled nursing care; 24-hour nursing staff; medical services; medical director; pharmacy services; medical clinic; Medicare/Medicaid-approved; personal care; medication administration; security; emergency response system; maintenance; transportation; up to 3 daily meals; housekeeping and laundry services; exercise classes; library; banking services; social and recreational activities; lounges; arts and crafts room; woodworking shop; community kitchen; grocery and dry-cleaning delivery services; gardening areas; ocean views; barber/beauty shop.

DEP: $1,100. APPL: (no ref.), $275. IND ENT: (ref.), $24,000–$255,000. IND MO: $1,800–$4,000.

AL and SNF fees inclusive.

Northwest

Friends House

684 Benicia Drive
Santa Rosa, CA 95409-3058

Ph: (707) 573-0152 TDD: (707) 573-4518
http://www.friendshouse.org

IND: 60. AL: Yes. SNF: 34. ADC: Yes

Nonprofit; nondenominational; owned and operated by the Friends Association of Services for the Elderly; Quaker-sponsored. Garden apartments and private and semiprivate rooms. 24-hour skilled nursing care; rehabilitative therapies; short- and long-term care; medical services; pharmacy services; social work services; personal care; medication

administration; security; emergency response system; maintenance; transportation; up to 3 daily meals; pets allowed; housekeeping and laundry services; exercise classes; social and recreational activities; arts and crafts; on- and off-site activities.

IND ENT: $81,000–$147,000. IND MO: $325–$475. AL MO: $3,500. SNF Daily: Semiprivate, $165; private, $215. ADC Daily: $55–$80.

Lake Park Retirement Residence, AAHA, CAHA

1850 Alice St.
Oakland, CA 94612

Ph: (510) 835-5511
Fax: (510) 273-0529

IND: 160+. AL: Yes. SNF: Yes

Nonprofit; nondenominational; nonsectarian; affiliated with Life Care of California–Nevada Methodist Homes. Studios, alcoves, apartments, and private and semiprivate rooms. Skilled nursing care; 24-hour nursing care; physical, occupational, and speech therapies; medical services; dental and podiatry care; pharmacy services; social services; wellness program; home health care; personal care; medication administration; security; emergency response system; maintenance; transportation; up to 3 daily meals; housekeeping and laundry services; religious services; Bible study; exercise program; library; social and recreational activities; educational program; woodworking room; sewing room; crafts; music groups; board and card games; coffee shop; gardening; barber/beauty shop.

IND LC: $33,000–$203,000. IND MO: $1,900–$4,500. AL and SNF fees inclusive.

The Meadows

1800 Atrium Parkway
Napa, CA 94559

Ph: (707) 257-7885

IND: Yes. AL: Yes. HCC: 69

Nonprofit; nondenominational; affiliated with the Odd Fellows and Rebekahs. Apartments and private and semiprivate rooms. 24-hour nursing care; holistic health care; physical, occupational, and speech therapies; respiratory therapy; IV therapy; X-ray and lab services; dental and podiatry services; pain management; social services; audiology services; blood-pressure checks; personal care; medication administration; Medicare-approved; security; emergency response system; maintenance; transportation; up to 3 daily meals; housekeeping and laundry services; exercise room; swimming pool; chapel; library; social and recreational activities; craft and woodshop; billiards and game room; media room; gift shop; koi pond; gardens; barber/beauty shop.

IND MO: $1,400–$2,800; 2nd person, $325. AL MO: $1,600–$3,000; 2nd person, $550. HCC Daily: Semiprivate, $150; private, $175.

Mercy Retirement and Care Center

3431 Foothill Blvd.
Oakland, CA 94601

Ph: (510) 534-8540
Fax: (510) 261 7551

RH: 71. AL: 24. HCC: 59. ALZ/MEM IMP: 22

Age 60+. Nonprofit; nondenominational; sponsored by the Sisters of Mercy, Burlingame. Private rooms. Nursing care; medical services; wellness clinic; rehabilitative therapies; dental and podiatry care; pharmacy services; respite care; social services; Medicare/Medicaid-approved; personal care; medication administration; security; emergency response system; maintenance; transportation; up to 3 daily meals; housekeeping and laundry services; chapel; religious services; social and recreational activities; educational and cultural programs; game room; courtyards; walking paths; store; barber/beauty shop.

RH/AL ENT: $10,000–$11,000. RH/AL MO: $2,000–$3,800. HCC Daily: $200–$250.

Salem Lutheran Home, CCAC

2361 East 29th St.
Oakland, CA 94606

Ph: (510) 534-3637
Fax: (510) 534-0851

IND/RH: 43. AL: 71. SNF: 47. ALZ/MEM IMP: 30

Age 60+. Nonprofit; nondenominational; sponsored by Sierra Pacific Synod. Cottages, studios, apartments, and private rooms. 24-hour nursing care; medical services; physical, occupational, and speech therapies; social services; dental, podiatry, and audiology care; respite care; pharmacy services; Medicare/Medicaid-approved; personal care; medication administration; security; emergency response system; maintenance; transportation; up to 3 daily meals (tray service available); pets allowed; housekeeping and laundry services; chapel; religious services; library; social and recreational activities; educational and cultural programs; lounges; walking paths; barber/beauty shop.

APPL: $220. ENT: $11,000–$126,500. IND MO: $1,400–$4,000. RH MO: $1,100–$4,000. AL MO: $475–$2,000 (does not include rent). ALZ/MEM IMP ENT: $16,500 ALZ/MEM IMP: $4,100–$4,400 SNF Daily: $175–$235.

The Sequoias, CCAC

1400 Geary Blvd.
San Francisco, CA 94109-6569

Ph: (415) 922-9700
Fax: (415) 567-2576

IND: 292. AL: 18. SNF: 50. ADC: Yes

Age 65+. Nonprofit; nondenominational; affiliated with Northern California Presbyterian Homes and Services. Apartments and private and semiprivate rooms. 24-hour nursing care; skilled nursing care; rehabilitative therapies; medical services; dental and podiatry care; physician services; Medicare-approved; personal care; medication administration; security; emergency response system; maintenance; transportation; up to 3 daily meals; housekeeping and laundry services; exercise program; gym; banking and postal services; social and recreational activities; educational opportunities; resident council; library; art room and gallery; billiards; workshop; gift shop; barber/beauty shop.

IND ENT: $47,000–$360,500. IND MO: $1,700–$4,000. AL and SNF fees are inclusive.

Sunny View Manor, CCAC

22445 Cupertino Rd.
Cupertino, CA 95014

Ph: (408) 253-4300
Fax: (408) 255-6015

http://www.sunny-view.org

IND: 79. AL: 40. HCC: 45. ALZ/MEM IMP: 12

Age 62+. Nonprofit; nondenominational; Lutheran church affiliation. Apartments, villas, and private and semiprivate rooms. 24-hour nursing care; skilled nursing care; physician visits; rehabilitative therapies; medical services; dental and podiatry services; pharmacy services; health screenings; on-site clinic; social services; resident assistance program; Medicare/Medicaid-approved; personal care; medication administration; security; emergency response system; maintenance; transportation; up to 3 daily meals; pets allowed; housekeeping and laundry services; fitness center; chaplain and religious services; Bible study; educational seminars; social, recreational, and spiritual activities; woodworking shop; craft room; convenience store; gardens; barber/beauty shop.

APPL: $330. IND ENT: $44,000–$105,000. IND MO: $1,400–$2,700. AL ENT: $27,500–$49,500. AL MO: $2,300–$3,500. HCC Daily: $130–$150.

Assisted Living and Residential Care Facilities

These facilities provide housing, food service, and one or more personal services.

Types of Authorization

Licensing and/or Certification

Facilities are licensed by the Department of Health Services.

Memberships

- Assisted Living Federation of America (ALFA) is a national nonprofit membership organization whose mission is to enhance the quality of life in assisted living facilities and promote the interests of the assisted living industry. ALFA, 10300 Eaton Place, Suite 400, Fairfax, VA 22030. Ph: (703) 691-8100. Fax: (703) 691-8106. *http://www.alfa.org*
- California Assisted Living Facilities Association (CALFA) is a state affiliate of ALFA. CALFA, 455 Capitol Mall Suite 330, Sacramento CA 95814. Ph: (916) 448-1900. Fax: (916) 448-1659. *http://www.calfa.org*

North

Kirkwood

395 Hilltop Drive
Redding, CA 96003

Ph: (530) 241-2900

AL: Yes. ALZ/MEM IMP: Yes

Nonprofit; nondenominational; affiliated with Southern California Presbyterian Homes. Private and semiprivate rooms. Licensed nurse on staff; reassurance checks; health and wellness care; personal care; medication administration; security; emergency response system; maintenance; transportation; up to 3 daily meals; housekeeping and laundry services; social and recreational activities; library; educational programs; barber/beauty shop.

Contact facility for fees.

South

Grey Gables of Ojai

Montgomery at Grand
Ojai, CA 93023

Ph: (805) 646-1446

IND: 63. AL: Yes

Nondenominational. Studios and one- and two-bedroom apartments. Nursing services; respite care; personal care; medication administration; security; emergency response system; maintenance; transportation; up to 3 daily meals; pets allowed; housekeeping and laundry services; swimming pool; social and recreational activities; volunteer opportunities; Jacuzzi; hobby room; table games; lounge; walking and bicycle paths; gardens; barber/beauty shop.

APPL: $220. Contact facility for monthly fees.

Keiro Retirement Home

325 S. Boyle Ave.
Los Angeles, CA 90033

Ph: (323) 263-9651

IND: Yes. AL: Yes (total of 154 residents)

Age 60+. Nonprofit; nondenominational; operated by Keiro Services. Studios and one-bedroom apartments. Social services; personal care; medication administration; security; emergency response system; maintenance; transportation; up to 3 daily meals (Western and Japanese-style); housekeeping and laundry services; exercise classes; religious services; library; social and recreational activities; on- and off-site activities; tea ceremonies; flower arrangement; karaoke; sewing; cooking; gift shop; ball field; barber/beauty shop.

Contact facility for fees.

Redwood Town Court

500 E. Valley Parkway
Escondido, CA 92025-3006

Ph: (760) 737-2437 or (800) 321-7101
Fax: (760) 737-2439

IND: Yes. AL: Yes

Nonprofit; nondenominational; affiliated with Southern California Presbyterian Homes. Studios, one- and two-bedroom apartments. Personal care; medication administration; 24-hour staffing; security; emergency response system; maintenance; transportation; up to 3 daily meals; housekeeping and laundry services; exercise program; swimming pool; clergy services; social and recreational activities; library; lounge; craft room; convenience store; barber/beauty shop.

IND MO: $1,200–2,400; 2nd person, $600. AL MO: $2,300–3,000; 2nd person with AL, $1,100; 2nd person without AL, $600.

Note: Adult day care and rehabilitative services available at off-site facility, Redwood Elderlink, 1151 S. Redwood St, Escondido, CA 92025, (619) 480-1030.

Independent Living

Independent housing (primarily rentals) for seniors that may offer security features, meal service, and activities.

South

Casa de la Paloma

133 S. Kenwood St.
Glendale, CA 91205

Ph: (818) 243-0337

IND: 167

Nonprofit; nondenominational; affiliated with Southern California Presbyterian Homes. Studios and one-bedroom apartments. Security; emergency response system; maintenance; transportation; staff trained in human services; social services; social and recreational activities; resident council; volunteer opportunities.

IND MO: 30% of adjusted monthly income. HUD-subsidized.

Castle Argyle

1919 N. Argyle Ave.
Los Angeles, CA 90068

Ph: (213) 465-2082

IND: 98

Nonprofit; nondenominational; affiliated with Southern California Presbyterian Homes. Studios and one-bedroom apartments. Security; emergency response system; maintenance; transportation; staff trained in Human Services; social services; social and recreational activities; resident council; volunteer opportunities.

IND MO: 30% of adjusted monthly income. HUD-subsidized.

Covenant Manor

600 E. Fourth St.
Long Beach, CA 90802

Ph: (562) 435-1804

IND: 100

Nonprofit; nondenominational; affiliated with Southern California Presbyterian Homes. Studios and one-bedroom apartments. Security; emergency response system; maintenance; transportation; staff trained in human services; social services; social and recreational activities; resident council; volunteer opportunities.

IND MO: 30% of adjusted monthly income. HUD-subsidized.

Central

The Meadows

3900 W. Tulare Ave.
Visalia, CA 93277

Ph: (209) 734-3275

IND: 100

Age 62+. Nonprofit; nondenominational; multi-church affiliated. Apartments. Security; emergency response system; maintenance; close to public transportation; meal program; pets allowed; laundry services; social and recreational activities; bingo; residents club; potluck dinners.

HUD-subsidized; monthly fee is 30% of income.

Pacific Meadows

5315 Carmel Valley Rd.
Carmel, CA 93923

Ph: (831) 624-9355
Fax: (831) 624-9179
http://www.retirementlife.com

IND: Yes

Age 62+. Nonprofit; nondenominational; nonsectarian; managed by American Baptist Homes of the West. Studios and one- and two-bedroom apartments. Personal care; medication administration; security; emergency response system; maintenance; transportation; meal program available; pets allowed; laundry services; exercise program; library; movies; social and recreational activities.

IND MO: $275–$1,000. HUD-subsidized; maximum incomes, single, $17,300–$41,520; couple, $19,750–$47,400.

Adult/Resort Communities

Communities for active adults (not all are age-restricted; primarily ownership).

North

Brookside

PO Box 7576
Stockton, CA 95267

Ph: (209) 956-LAKE or (209) 473-6262
Fax: (209) 956-8450

Individual homes, homesites. Golf course; clubhouse; recreation center; biking; boating/waterskiing; fishing; lakes; wildlife preserve.

PURCHASE: Homes, $132,000–$1.1million+; homesites, from $77,000.

Clover Springs

200 Hot Springs Rd.
Cloverdale, CA 95425

Ph: (888) 6-DELWEBB or (707) 894-7100
http://company.occ.com/delwebb/sacramento.htm

Age 55+. Individual homes. Recreational facility; tennis; swimming pool; fitness center; walking/biking trails; billiards; arts and crafts; bocce; social clubs.

PURCHASE: Homes, $187,000–$330,000.

Heritage Lakeside

Harbour Pointe Drive
Elk Grove, CA 95758

Ph: (916) 683-4747

Age 55+. Individual homes. Lake; boat dock; wildlife preserve; clubhouse; tennis; swimming pool; spa; walking trails; billiards; fitness center; library.

PURCHASE: Homes, $168,000–$220,000+.

Kelly Ridge Golf Course

5131 Royal Oaks Dr.
Oroville, CA 95966

Ph: (530) 589-0777
Fax: (530) 589-3572

Individual homes. Golf course; tennis; swimming pool; hiking/biking; fishing; hunting; boating/waterskiing; social clubs.

PURCHASE: Homes, $77,000–$330,000.

La Contenta

1653 Hwy. 26
Valley Springs, CA 95252

Ph: (800) 446-5321 or (209) 772-1081
Fax: (209) 772-1085

http://www.empiregolf.com

Individual homes, condominiums, homesites. Golf course; swimming pool; hiking trails; fishing; hunting; boating/waterskiing; fitness center; social clubs.

PURCHASE: Homes, $165,000–$385,000.

Oakmont Village

310 White Oak Drive
Santa Rosa, CA 95409

Ph: (888) 625-6668

http://www.oakmontvillage.com

Age 55+. Individual homes. Golf courses; pro shops; clubhouse; tennis; swimming pools; lawn bowling; bocce; shuffleboard; petanque; computer center; social clubs.

PURCHASE: Homes, from $165,000–$550,000+.

Rossmoor

PO Box 2070
Walnut Creek, CA 94595

Ph: (800) 980-SOLD or (925) 932-1162

http://www.rossmoorrealty.com

Age 55+. Garden homes, condominiums, cooperatives. Golf courses; clubhouses; tennis; swimming pools; exercise facility; lawn bowling; hiking trails; library; social clubs; outpatient medical center; bus transportation.

PURCHASE: Homes, $44,000–$550,000+.

Ruby Hill

2001 Ruby Hill Blvd.
Pleasanton, CA 94566

Ph: (800) 887-RUBY or (925) 417-2250
Fax: (925) 417-8586

http://www.sigprop.com

Individual homes, homesites. Golf course; sports park; tennis; swimming pool; softball; soccer; volleyball; basketball; community center.

PURCHASE: Homes, $676,500–$2,615,000+; homesites, $313,500–$698,500.

Serrano El Dorado

4525 Serrano Parkway
El Dorado Hills, CA 95762

Ph: (800) 866-8786 or (916) 939-3333

http://www.serranoeldorado.com

Individual homes, homesites. Golf courses; clubhouse; tennis; swimming pool; hiking/biking; fitness room; dining; village green.

PURCHASE: Homes, from $242,000; homesites, from $132,000.

Silverado Country Club and Resort

1600 Atlas Peak Rd.
Napa, CA 94558

Ph: (707) 257-5459

http://www.silveradoresort.com

Individual homes, condominiums, homesites. Golf courses; clubhouse; pro shop; tennis; swimming pools; biking/jogging/walking trails; health spa and fitness center; dining.

PURCHASE: Condos, from $308,000; villa homes, from $528,000; estate homes, from $715,000; homesites, from $424,000.

Sonora Hills

19601 Greenley Rd.
Sonora, CA 95370

Ph: (800) 223-2346 or (209) 532-3600

Age 55+. Individual homes. Clubhouse; swimming pool; spa; walking trails; billiards; social clubs.

PURCHASE: Homes, $116,000–$148,000.

Whitney Oaks

4308 Live Oak Lane
Rocklin, CA 95765

Ph: (916) 632-1177
Fax: (916) 632-1280

http://www.whitneyoaks.com

Some age-restricted areas. Individual homes, homesites. Golf course; clubhouse; pro shop; recreation center; swimming pools; fitness center; hiking/biking.

PURCHASE: Homes, from $198,000; homesites, from $72,000.

South

Big Horn Golf Club

100 Tamit Place
Palm Desert, CA 92260

Ph: (800) 551-5578 or (760) 773-5300
Fax: (760) 779-1983

http://www.bighorngolf.com

Individual homes, villas, estate homes, homesites. Golf courses; clubhouse; tennis; swimming pool; health and fitness center; spa; hiking.

PURCHASE: Homes, from $770,000; homesites, $550,000–$3.85 million.

The Club

27801 Invitation Drive
Sun City, CA 92585

Ph: (800) CLUB-888 or (909) 672-7360
Fax: (909) 672 8490

http://www.seniorresource.com/club.htm

Age 55+. Individual homes. Clubhouse; tennis; swimming pool; spa; exercise equipment; library; crafts studio; recreation staff.

PURCHASE: Homes, from $118,000.

Desert Horizons

75-486 Augusta Drive
Indian Wells, CA 92210

Ph: (760)568-0207
Fax: (760) 341-5641

http://www.deserthorizons.com

Individual homes. Championship golf course; tennis; swimming pools; spas; lakes; social director; dining.

PURCHASE: Homes, $307,000–$484,000.

Heritage Palms

44-291 Heritage Palms Drive South
Indio, CA 92201

Ph: (800) 893-8439 or (760) 772-7333

http://www.ushome.com/retire/CAHeritagePalms

Age 55+. Individual homes, villas. Golf course; pro shop; clubhouse; tennis; swimming pools; fitness center; bocce; billiards; library; dining.

PURCHASE: Homes, $176,000–$275,000; villas, from $160,000.

Huntington Village

16171 Springdale
Huntington Beach, CA 92649-2700

Ph: (714) 840-1203

http://www.huntingtonvillage.com

Age 62+. Rental apartments. Recreation room; pool; Jacuzzi; library; arts and crafts; exercise classes; social activities. Parking available.

Studio: $700–$725. One bedroom: $825–$900. Two bedrooms: $975–$1,050. Monthly rent includes utility charges.

Jess Ranch

11000 Apple Valley Rd.
Apple Valley, CA 92308

Ph: (888) 240-JESS or (760) 247-6460
Fax: (760) 240-3609

http://www.jessranch.com

Age 55+. Individual homes, duplexes, condominiums, patio homes, townhomes. Golf course; tennis; swimming pool; biking; health club; billiards; lakes; social clubs.

PURCHA0SE: Homes, from $137,500; duplexes, from $95,000; patio homes, from $110,000.

Leisure World

PO Box 2220
Laguna Hills, CA 92654

Ph: (800) 711-9273 or (714) 597-4360

Age 55+. Individual homes, condominiums, high-rise complex, cooperative units. Golf course, tennis; swimming pool; hiking/biking; fishing; boating/waterskiing; community center; fitness center; dining.

PURCHASE: Homes, $44,000–$330,000.

Ocean Walk at San Pacifico

567 Dew Point Ave.
Carlsbad, CA 92009

Ph: (760) 931-9370

Individual homes. Private recreation center; tennis; swimming pool; Jacuzzi; basketball; beach.

PURCHASE: Homes, from $385,000.

Palmia

Santa Margarita Parkway
Mission Viejo, CA 92692

Ph: (949) 580-5728

http://www.palmia.com

Age 55+. Individual homes, condominiums. Recreation center; tennis; swimming pool; spa; fitness center; trails; golf; lake; boating; billiards; library; social clubs.

PURCHASE: Homes, $275,000–$385,000; attached homes, $198,000–$275,000.

PGA West

55-955 PGA Blvd.
La Quinta, CA 92253

Ph: (800) PGA-WEST or (760) 564-7111
Fax: (760) 771-2823

http://www.pgawest.com

Individual homes. PGA golf courses; clubhouses; tennis; swimming pools; hiking; fitness center.

PURCHASE: Homes, from $308,000.

Rams Hill

PO Box 2294
Borrego Springs, CA 92004

Ph: (800) 732-9200 or (800) 524-2800 (in CA)

http://www.golfsd.com/rams_hill.html

Individual homes, duplexes, homesites. Golf course; tennis; swimming pools; spas; hiking/biking; shuffleboard.

PURCHASE: Homes, $121,000–$440,000.

Rancho La Quinta

48500 Washington St.
La Quinta, CA 92253

Ph: (800) 779-3376 or (760) 777-7755

http://www.rancholaquinta.com

Individual Homes, patio homes, courtyard homes. Championship golf course; pro shop; racquet club; tennis; swimming pool; fitness center.

PURCHASE: Homes, $275,000–$770,000.

Stonecrest Village

3110 W. Canyon Ave.
San Diego, CA 92123

Ph: (619) 565-8220

http://www.uniontribune.com/marketplace/new

Individual homes, townhomes, condominiums. Park; recreational facilities; tennis; swimming pool; exercise room; walking paths; jogging/biking; home theater. K. Hovnanian community.

PURCHASE: Homes, $330,000–$396,000; townhomes and condos, from $198,000.

Summerset at Brentwood

190 Summerset Dr.
Brentwood, CA 94513-6426

Ph: (888) 786-7738

http://www.summersetlife.com

Age 55+. Individual homes. Golf course; clubhouse; pro shop; tennis; swimming pool; fitness center; dining; social clubs.

PURCHASE: Homes, from $162,000.

Sun City Palm Desert

78257 Rainbow Drive
Palm Desert, CA 92211

Ph: (800) 847-0754 or (760) 772-5400

http://www.suncity.com

Age 55+. Individual homes. Golf course; clubhouse and recreation center; tennis; swimming pools; spas; fitness center; walking/jogging; biking; bocce; billiards; library; dining.

PURCHASE: Homes, $165,000–$550,000.

Sun Lakes

6350 W. Ramsey, Suite N
Banning, CA 92220

Ph: (800) 720-7378 or (909) 845-7378

http://www.sunlakesrealty.com

Age 55+. Individual homes, condominiums. Golf courses; clubhouse; tennis; swimming pools; fitness center; shuffleboard; billiards; library; arts and crafts.

PURCHASE: Homes, $112,000–$153,000; condos, $110,000–$167,000.

Colorado

http://www.state.co.us

General Information

Climate

Semiarid climate; cold winters. July average 73°F; January average 30°F. Average snowfall in Boulder/Denver: 10 inches in January, 14 inches in March.

Cost of Living

Ranks 15th in the nation.

Taxes

State/Local as % of Income: 8.7%.

Property Tax Reduction: Residents 65 years and over with a surviving spouse at least 58 years old, or disabled for all of the year, regardless of age but with specified income requirements, may qualify for a state property tax, rent, or heat rebate.

Sales: 2.9%; some municipalities also levy sales tax.

Prescription Exemptions: Prescription drugs, insulin and insulin supplies, and doctor-prescribed prosthetic and medical supplies are exempt from state sales tax.

Transportation, Travel, and Tourism

General

Colorado Travel and Tourism Authority, (800) COLORADO.

Major Airports

- Denver International Airport, Peña Blvd., Denver, CO 80249, (303) 342-2200 or (800) 247-2336 (AIR DENVER).
- Colorado Springs Airport, 7770 Drennan Rd., Colorado Springs, CO 80916, (719) 550-1900 or (800) 462-6774.

Railways

- Amtrak, Denver, (800) USA-RAIL.

Bus Tours

- Grace Coach Lines, Inc., P.O. Box 309, Lafayette, CO 80026, (303) 661-0732.
- Greyhound Bus Lines, 2450 Curtis St., Denver, CO 80205, (303) 293-6590.
- Peoples Choice Transportation, Inc., 5455 E. 52nd Ave., Commerce City, CO 80403, (303) 289-2222
- Pikes Peak Tours & Charters Inc., 3704 W. Colorado Ave., Colorado Springs, CO, (719) 633-1181.
- Ramblin' Express, Inc., 4360 Buckingham Dr., Suite 100, Colorado Springs, CO 80907, (719) 590-8687.

State Highways

- Interstate 25 runs north-south;
- Interstate 70 runs east-west, both through Denver.
- Interstate 76 runs diagonally northeast-southwest from Nebraska to Denver.

Theater and Music

Central

- Boulder Philharmonic Orchestra, Dairy Center for the Arts, 2590 Walnut St., Suite 6, Boulder, CO 80302, (303) 449-1343.
- Breckenridge Music Festival (seasonal, jazz, classical, pop), 111 S. Main, 2nd Floor, PO Box 1254, Breckenridge, CO 80424, (970) 453-9142 or 547-3100.
- Central City Opera (seasonal), Central City, CO, (800) 851- 8175.
- Denver Center Theatre Company, Denver Performing Arts Complex,

Speer and Arapahoe, Denver, CO, box office (303) 893-4100 or (800) 641-1222.
- Vail Jazz Festival (August), Vail, CO, (800) 525-3875.

East

- Glenn Miller Festival (June), Fort Morgan, CO, (800) 354-8660.

West

- Aspen Music Festival, (seasonal), Aspen, CO, (970) 925-3254.

Museums, Crafts, Historical, Recreational

Central

- Arvada Center for the Arts and Humanities, 6901 Wadsworth Blvd., Arvada, CO 80003, (303) 431-3939.
- Denver Art Museum, 100 W. 14th Ave. Parkway, Denver, CO 80204, (303) 640-4433.
- Denver Museum of Natural History, 2001 Colorado Blvd., Denver, CO 80209, (303) 285-4380 or (800) 925-2250.
- Denver Zoo, 2300 Steele St., Denver, CO 80205, (303) 376-4800.
- Denver Botanic Garden, 909 York St., Denver, CO 80206, (303) 331-4000.
- Hudson Gardens, 6303 S. Santa Fe Drive, Littleton, CO 80120, (303) 797-8565.
- Wings Over the Rockies Air and Space Museum, 7711 E. Academy Pkwy, Denver, CO 80220, (303) 360-5360.
- Museum of Outdoor Arts, 7600 E. Orchard Rd., Suite 160N, Englewood, CO 80111, (303) 741-3609.
- Mira Vista Golf Course (public), 10110 E. Golfers Way, Aurora, CO 80010, (303) 340-1520.
- Colorado Springs Country Club, 3333 Templeton Gap Rd., Colorado Springs, CO 80907, (719) 473-1782.
- Boulder Country Club, 7350 Club House Rd., Boulder, CO 80301, (303) 530-2226.
- Vail Golf Course (public), 1778 Vail Valley Dr., Vail, CO 81657, (970) 479-2260.
- Arapaho Basin Skiing, PO Box 8787, Arapahoe Basin Resort, CO 80435, (970) 468-0718 or (888) ARAPAHO.
- Breckenridge, PO Box 1058, Breckenridge, CO 80424, (970) 453-5000 or (800) 221-1091.
- Copper Mountain Skiing, PO Box 3001, Copper Mountain, CO 80443, (970) 968-2882 or (800) 458-8386.
- Crested Butte Skiing, PO Box A, Mt. Crested Butte, CO 81225, (970) 349-2333 or (800) 544-8448.
- Keystone Skiing, PO Box 38, Keystone, CO 80435, (970) 496-2316 or (800) 427-8216.
- Silver Creek Skiing, PO Box 1110, Granby, CO 80446, (970) 887- 3384.
- Snowmass Skiing, PO Box 5566, Snowmass Village, CO 81615, (970) 923-2000 or (800) 598-2004.

East

- Koshare Indian Museum, 115 W. 18th St., La Junta, CO 81050, (719) 384-4411 or (800) 693-5482.

West

- Aspen Art Museum, 590 N. Mill St., Aspen, CO 81611-1510, (970) 925-8050.
- Anasazi Heritage Center, 27501 Hwy. 184, Dolores, CO 81323, (970) 882-4811.
- Mancos Valley Visitor Center and Pioneer Museum, 171 Railroad, PO Box 494, Mancos, CO 81328, (970) 533-7434 or (800) 873-3310.
- The Museum of Western Colorado, 248 South 4th St., PO Box 20,000, Grand Junction, CO 81502-5020, (970) 242-0971 or (888) 488- DINO.
- Adobe Creek Golf Course, 1853 I Rd., Fruita, CO 81521, (303) 858- 0521.
- Mesa Verde National Park (visitors center, lodging, camping), PO Box 8, Mesa Verde National Park, CO 81330, (970) 529-4465.
- Toh-Atin Gallery, 145 W. 9th St., Box 2329, Durango, CO 81301, (800) 525-0384.

North

- Steamboat Skiing, 2305 Mt. Werner Circle, Steamboat Springs, CO 80487, (970) 879-6111 or (800) 922-2722.
- Rocky Mountain National Park (visitors center, lodging, camping), Estes Park, CO 80517, (970) 586-1206.

Organizations

Advocacy Groups

- Division of Aging and Adult Services, 110 16th St., Suite 200, Denver, CO 80202, (303) 620-4127.
- Adult Income and Medical Support Services, (303) 620-4138.
- Adult Protection and Elder Rights Services, (303) 620-4137.
- Colorado Long-Term Care Ombudsman, The Legal Center, 455 Sherman St., Suite 130, Denver, CO 80203, (303) 722-0300.
- Department of Human Services, 1575 Sherman St., Denver, CO 80203, (303) 866-5096.

Volunteer Programs

- Volunteers of America, Colorado Branch, Denver, (303) 297- 0408.
- Heartbeat of Evergreen, PO Box 4266, Evergreen, CO 80437, (303) 647-8489.

Housing

Long-Term Care Facilities

In the state of Colorado, these facilities are called ***Continuing Care/Long-Term Care/Nursing Care Facilities****.*

These facilities provide residential living and/or various levels of nursing and medical services to seniors for an extended period of time.

Types of Authorization

Licensing and / or Certification

These facilities are licensed by the Department of Health. A long-term care facility provides supportive, restorative, and preventive services to persons who require continuous or regular inpatient care. This includes nursing homes, nursing care facilities, and intermediate care facilities.

Memberships:

- American Association of Homes and Services for the Aging (AAHSA) represents not-for-profit organizations committed to providing high-quality health care, housing, and services to the elderly. AAHSA, 901 E St. NW, Suite 500, Washington, DC 20004-2011. Ph: (202) 783-2242. Fax: (202) 783-2285. *http: / / www.aahsa.org*
- Colorado Association of Homes and Services for the Aging, 1888 Sherman St., Suite 610, Denver CO, 80203-1160. Ph: (303) 837-8834. Fax: (303) 837-8836.

North Central

The Argyle

4115 W. 38th Ave.
Denver, CO 80212

Ph: (303) 455-9513
Fax: (303) 433-7127

IND: 50. AL: 109. HCC: 57

Nonprofit; nondenominational. One-bedroom apartments, and private and semiprivate rooms. 24-hour nursing care; medical director; rehabilitative therapies; medical services; pharmacy services; physician visits; social services; personal care; medication administration; security; emergency response system; maintenance; transportation; up to 3 daily meals; housekeeping and laundry services; fitness program; social and

recreational activities; wake-up service; craft room; entertainment room; barber/ beauty shop.

IND MO: HUD-subsidized. AL Daily: Base rate starts at $1,200. HCC Daily: Semiprivate, $110; private, $120.

Exempla Colorado Lutheran Home

7991 West 71st Ave.
Arvada, CO 80004

Ph: (303) 403-3100

IND: Yes. AL: 27. SNF: 120. ALZ/MEM IMP: Yes

Nonprofit; nondenominational; affiliated with the Lutheran church. Apartments, studios, and private and semiprivate rooms. Skilled nursing care; subacute care; long-term care; rehabilitative therapies; medical services; dental and podiatry care; pharmacy services; personal care; medication administration; security; emergency response system; maintenance; transportation; up to 3 daily meals; housekeeping and laundry services; exercise program; religious services; Bible study; on- and off-site activities; social and recreational activities; patios; barber/beauty shop.

IND MO: $330–$600 (meals not included). AL MO: $1,300 (meals included). SNF Daily: Semiprivate, $140; private and ALZ, $150.

Kenton Manor Health Care Center, JCAHO

850 27th Ave.
Greeley, CO 80631

Ph: (970) 353-1018
Fax: (970) 352-5648

E-mail: *jlr@riesberg.com*

NH: 113

For-profit; nondenominational. Private and semiprivate rooms. 24-hour nursing care; medical services; rehabilitative therapies; dental and podiatry care; hospice care; pharmacy services; Medicare/ Medicaid-approved; personal care; medication administration; security; emergency response system; maintenance; transportation; up to 3 daily meals; pets allowed; housekeeping and laundry services; exercise program; gym; social and recreational activities; intergenerational program; ice cream parlor; barber/ beauty shop.

NH Daily: Private, $130–$140; semiprivate, $115–$130.

Park Manor

1801 E. 19th Ave.
Denver, CO 80218

Ph: (303) 839-7000
Fax: (303) 839-7036

IND: Yes. AL: Yes. SNF: Yes

Nondenominational; affiliated with Presbyterian/St. Luke's Medical Center. One- and two-bedroom apartments and semiprivate rooms. 24-hour nursing care; skilled nursing care; rehabilitative therapies; dental and podiatry care; respite care; medical services; pharmacy services; personal care; medication administration; security; emergency response system; maintenance; transportation; up to 3 daily meals; housekeeping and laundry services; exercise class; Bible study; library; social and recreational activities; on- and off-site activities; bingo; music; solarium; gift shop; barber/beauty shop.

IND MO: $1,200–$1,300. AL MO: $1,500–$1,650. SNF Daily: Semiprivate, $135.

The Villas at Sunny Acres

2501 E. 104th Ave.
Thornton, CO 80233

Ph: (303) 255-4151 or (800) 447-2092

http://www.centura.org

IND: Yes. AL: Yes. HCC: 118

Nondenominational; sponsored by PorterCare Adventist Health System and Catholic Health Initiatives. Cottages, studios, apartments, and private and semiprivate rooms. 24-hour nursing care; skilled nursing care; geriatric care specialists; primary care clinic; physician services; eye, foot, and dental care;

hospice care; rehabilitative therapies; social services and counseling; pharmacy services; home health care; Medicare/ Medicaid-approved; personal care; medication administration; security; emergency response system; maintenance; transportation; up to 3 daily meals; housekeeping and laundry services; exercise program; fitness center; library; chaplain; interdenominational religious services; social and recreational activities; general store; lakes; gardens; gazebo; walking paths; barber/beauty shop.

IND ENT: (80% ref.), $61,000–$174,000. IND MO: (with ENT fee), $850–$2,600; (without ENT fee), $1,100–$2,300. AL MO: $1,900–$4,000. HCC Daily: $130. AL and HCC fees are inclusive with the IND ENT; IND monthly rentals can earn 1 free day of nursing care/month, up to 30 free days. After free days, the rate is private pay.

South Central

Liberty Heights and Liberty Manor

12105 Ambassador Drive
Colorado Springs, CO 80921-3640

Ph: (719) 481-9494 or (800) 635-7438
Fax: (719) 481-5008

IND: Yes. AL: Yes. SNF: Yes

Nondenominational. Townhomes, apartments, suites, and private rooms. 24-hour nursing care; skilled nursing care; physical, occupational, and speech therapies; respiratory therapy; medical services; pharmacy services; personal care; medication administration; security; emergency response system; maintenance; transportation; up to 3 daily meals; housekeeping and laundry services; fitness center; tennis court; swimming pool and spa; Bible study; library; social and recreational activities; resident council; arts and crafts; movies; billiard room; lounges; barber/beauty shop.

IND MO: $2,350–$3,250; 2nd person, $440. AL MO: $2,400. SNF Daily: Private room, $140; private suite, $170.

The Bridge Assisted Living Life Care Center of Colorado Springs and

2494 International Circle
Colorado Springs, CO 80910

Ph: (719) 630-3330
Fax: (719) 633-7730

AL: 53. SNF: Yes

Nondenominational; operated by Life Care Centers of America. Apartments and private and semiprivate rooms. Skilled nursing care; 24-hour nursing assistance; physical, occupational, speech, and respiratory therapies; medical services; dental and podiatry care; pharmacy services; wellness clinic; health promotion programs; personal care; medication administration; security; emergency response system; maintenance; transportation; 3 daily meals; housekeeping and laundry services; exercise classes; library; social and recreational activities; lounges; craft room; ice cream parlor; gift shop; gazebo and picnic area; barber/beauty shop.

Contact facility for fees.

Medallion East

1719 E. Bnou
Colorado Springs, CO 80909

Ph: (719) 471-9812
Fax: (719) 381-4978

IND: 76. AL: 23. HCC: 48

Age 62+. Nondenominational. Apartments. Nursing care; rehabilitative therapies; medical services; pharmacy services; Medicare-approved; personal care; medication administration; security; emergency response system; maintenance; transportation; up to 3 daily meals; housekeeping and laundry services; swimming pool; chapel; activities director; social and recreational activities.

IND MO: $700–$800. AL MO: $50–$80.

Medallion West

417 E. Kiowa
Colorado Springs, CO 80909

Ph: (719) 471-9812
Fax: (719) 381-4978

IND: 89. AL: 31. HCC: Yes

Age 62+. Nondenominational. Apartments. Nursing care; rehabilitative therapies; medical services; pharmacy services; Medicare/Medicaid-approved; personal care; medication administration; security; emergency response system; maintenance; transportation; up to 3 daily meals; housekeeping and laundry services; swimming pool; chapel; activities director; social and recreational activities.

IND MO: $1,400–$2,750. AL MO: $50–$70. HCC Daily: $125–$130.

Assisted Living and Residential Care Facilities

*In the state of Colorado, these facilities are called **Residential Care and Assisted Living**.*

These facilities offer housing with personalized support services and health care services.

Types of Authorization

Licensing and/or Certification

These facilities are licensed by the Department of Health. They provide room and board, personal care services, security, and social care to persons who are unable to live independently but do not need 24-hour medical or nursing care.

Memberships:

- Assisted Living Federation of America (ALFA) is a national nonprofit membership organization whose mission is to enhance the quality of life in assisted living facilities and promote the interests of the assisted living industry. ALFA, 10300 Eaton Place, Suite 400, Fairfax, VA 22030. Ph: (703) 691-8100. Fax: (703) 691-8106. *http://www.alfa.org*
- Colorado Association of Homes and Services for the Aging (CAHSA) is a state affiliate of ALFA. CAHSA, 1888 Sherman St., #610, Denver CO 80203. Ph: (303) 837-8834. Fax: (303) 837-8836.

North Central

Allied Jewish Apartments

22 S. Adams St.
Denver, CO 80209

Ph: (303) 399-1146
Fax: (303) 394-4149
E-mail: *ALL1146@AOL.com*

IND: 362. AL: 26

Age 62+. Nonprofit; nondenominational; Jewish faith affiliation. Apartments. Home health care; medical services; rehabilitative therapies; pharmacy services; Medicaid-approved; personal care; medication administration; emergency response system; maintenance; transportation: up to 3 daily (kosher) meals; pets allowed; laundry services; exercise classes; volunteer opportunities; social and recreational activities; on- and off-site activities; bingo; movies; ice cream parlor; convenience store; barber/beauty shop.

DEP: 1 mo. rent. IND MO: $510–$620; HUD-subsidized. AL MO: $1,100–$1,650.

Bee Hive Homes of Colorado

920 54th Ave., Suite 200
Greeley, CO 80634

Ph: (970) 590-1997
Fax: (970) 284-9198

AL: 11 units/facility (8 facilities throughout Colorado)

For-profit; nondenominational. Private rooms. Nursing care; medical services; home health care services; Medicaid-approved; personal care; medication

administration; security; emergency response system; maintenance; transportation; up to 3 daily meals; housekeeping and laundry services; social and recreational activities; barber/beauty shop.

DEP: $330. AL MO: $2,100–$2,500.

Eaton Terrace

333 S. Eaton St.
Lakewood, CO 80226

Ph: (303) 937-5074
Fax: (303) 937-3090

IND: 234. AL/RH: 66

Age 62+. Nonprofit; affiliated with the West Alameda Community Baptist Church. Case management; social services; wellness care; home health care; Medicaid-approved; personal care; medication administration; security; emergency response system; maintenance; transportation; up to 3 daily meals; housekeeping and laundry services; nondenominational religious services; educational program; activities director; social and recreational activities.

AL APPL: $50. DEP: 1 mo. rent. IND MO: 30% of income; HUD-subsidized. AL MO: $1,700–$2,550. RH MO: $270–$650.

Francis Heights, Inc.

2626 Osceola St.
Denver, CO 80220

Ph: (303) 433-6268
Fax: (303) 455-5359

IND: 383. AL: Yes

Age 62+. Nonprofit; nondenominational; church affiliated. Efficiencies and one- and two-bedroom apartments. Visiting nurse service; wellness clinic; mobile eye clinic; personal care; medication administration; security; maintenance; close to public transportation; up to 3 daily meals; meals on wheels services; pets allowed; housekeeping and laundry services; religious services; library; swimming pool; social, recreational, educational, and spiritual programs; postal services; resident council; bookmobile; thrift shop; food co-op; barber/beauty shop.

IND MO: 30% of income; HUD-subsidized. AL MO: $275–$575.

Garden Square at Westlake

3151 W. 20th St.
Greeley, CO 80631

Ph: (970) 346-1222
Fax: (970) 346-1228
E-mail: *jlr@riesberg.com*

AL: 48

For-profit; nondenominational. Private rooms; personal care; medication administration; security; emergency response system; maintenance; transportation; up to 3 daily meals; pets allowed; housekeeping and laundry services; social and recreational activities; community areas; parks and lake nearby; shopping nearby; barber/beauty shop.

AL MO: $2,500–$3,600.

Golden West A Senior Residence

1055 Adams Circle
Boulder, CO 80303

Ph: (303) 444-3967
Fax: (303) 939-0808

IND: 255. AL: 56

Age 62+. Nonprofit; nondenominational; First Christian Church–Disciples of Christ affiliation. Efficiencies, apartments, and private rooms. Medical services; rehabilitative therapies; pharmacy services; wellness center; Medicaid-approved; personal care; medication administration; security; emergency response system; maintenance; close to public transportation; up to 3 daily meals; pets allowed; housekeeping and laundry services; exercise classes; religious services; computer center; recreation room; meeting rooms; social and recreational activities; educational program; barber/beauty shop.

DEP: 1 mo. rent plus $40. IND MO: $385–$550; meals, $180. AL MO: $1,550–$2,300; meals included.

Harvard Square Retirement Community, ALFA

10200 E. Harvard Ave.
Denver, CO 80231

Ph: (303) 696-0622

IND: Yes. AL: Yes

Nondenominational; managed by Leisure Care. Studios, one- and two-bedroom apartments. Short-term care; physician services; daily health monitoring; personal care; medication administration; security; emergency response system; maintenance; transportation; up to 3 daily meals; housekeeping and laundry services; exercise areas; library; billiards room; media room; social and recreational activities; pet visits; full time program supervisor; resident council; outdoor deck; gift and convenience store; walking paths; nearby golfing; banks, shopping, and medical facilities; barber/beauty shop.

APPL: (no ref.), $25. DEP: $275. IND MO: $1,500–$2,100; 2nd person, $330. Additional charges for AL care.

The Legacy at Lowry

150 Quebec Court
Denver, CO 80220

Ph: (303) 364-7149
Fax: (303) 365-1510

IND: 76. AL: 89

Age 62+. Nonprofit; nondenominational. Studios and one- and two-bedroom apartments. Medicaid-approved; personal care; medication administration; security; emergency response system; maintenance; transportation; up to 3 daily meals; pets allowed; housekeeping and laundry services; social and recreational activities; on- and off-site activities.

DEP: 1 mo. rent. IND MO: $1,000–$2,800. AL MO: $1,800–$2,100.

Libby Bortz Assisted Living Center

5844 S. Curtice St.
Littleton, CO 80120

Ph: (303) 347-9755
Fax: (303) 347-9642

AL: 111

Age: 62+. Apartments. Nursing care; foot clinic; personal care; medication administration; security; emergency response system; maintenance; transportation; up to 3 daily meals; housekeeping and laundry services; library; social and recreational activities; whirlpool tub; convenience store.

DEP: 1 mo. rent. AL MO: $1,200.

REQ: Income maximums, single, $27,500; couple, $31,000.

Springwood Retirement Community

6550 Yank Way
Arvada, CO 80004

Ph: (303) 424-6550

IND: 124. AL: 53. ALZ/MEM IMP: 28

Age 65+. For-profit. Nondenominational. Cottages and apartments. Health and wellness programs; ear, hearing, and foot care clinics; on-site nurses; 24-hour staffing; personal care; medication administration; security; emergency response system; maintenance; transportation; up to 3 daily meals; housekeeping and laundry services; exercise classes; fitness center; interfaith religious services; library; social and recreational activities; close to hospitals, banking, and shopping services; media room; billiards room; ceramics; visiting entertainers; convenience store; ice cream parlor; barber/beauty shop.

ADMN: (no ref.), $660. IND MO: $1,600–$2,300; 2nd person, $275. AL MO: $1,900–$2,600.

South Central

Village at Skyline

2365 Patriot Heights
Colorado Springs, CO 80904

Ph: (719) 473-1976

IND: 270. RH: 61. AL: 41. ALZ/MEM IMP: 13

Age 55+. Nonprofit; nondenominational; First Christian Church (Disciples of Christ) affiliation. Homes and apartments. Wellness center; Medicaid-approved; home health care; personal care; medication administration; security; emergency response system; maintenance; transportation; 1 daily meal; pets allowed; housekeeping and laundry services; fitness center; library; social, recreational, and spiritual activities; outdoor patios.

ENT: $1,100. MO: $925–$2,500.

Independent Living

Independent housing (primarily rentals) for seniors that may offer security features, meal service, and activities.

North Central

Cathedral Plaza

1575 Pennsylvania
Denver, CO 80205

IND: 154

Nonprofit; nondenominational; affiliated with Archdiocesan Housing Committee, Inc. One- and two-bedroom apartments. Security; emergency response system; maintenance; close to public transportation; up to 2 daily meals; exercise room; library; social, cultural and spiritual activities; crafts; lounge; game room; greenhouse; barber/beauty shop.

IND MO: 30% of income. HUD-subsidized.

Kentucky Circle Village

4901 E. Kentucky Circle
Denver, CO 80246

Ph: (303) 756-5218

IND: 120

Nonprofit; nondenominational; affiliated with three church denominations. Security; maintenance; close to public transportation; meal service available; pets allowed; laundry services; residents council; social and recreational activities; gardens.

APPL: (ref.), $50; pet deposit, $100. IND ENT: $770–$1,100. IND MO: $250–$525; 2nd person, $25.

Metro Manor

1523 Quitman St.
Denver, CO 80204

Ph: (303) 572-7716
Fax: (303) 623-6208

IND: 192

Age 55+. Nonprofit; nondenominational. Apartments. Security; maintenance; 1 daily meal; pets allowed; library; exercise room; close to public transportation.

DEP: 1 month's rent; pet deposit, $350.

IND MO: $300–$475.

RiverPointe

5225 S. Prince St.
Littleton, CO 80123

Ph: (303) 797-0600
Fax: (303) 794-3490

http://www.seniorresource.com/riverp.htm

IND: 171

Age 55+. For-profit; nondenominational. Apartments. Wellness program; blood-pressure checks; health classes; foot care; security; emergency response system; maintenance; transportation; up to 2 daily meals; housekeeping and laundry services; exercise classes; banking services; library; educational program; social and recreational activities; on-and off-site activities; woodshop; arts and crafts; hobby room; billiards room; spa; barber/beauty shop.

DEP: (ref.), $550. IND MO: $1,100–$1,950; 2nd person, $90; 3rd person, $165.

Adult/Resort Communities

Communities for active adults (not all are age-restricted; primarily ownership).

North

Aspen Glen
9929 State Highway 82
Carbondale, CO 81623
Ph: (800) 277-4536 or (970) 963-4536
http://www.aspenglen.com/

Individual homes, townhomes, homesites. Golf course; clubhouse; golf and tennis pro shops; tennis; swimming pool; fitness center; spa; dining; fly-fishing tackle shop.

PURCHASE: Homes, $797,000–$2.2 million+; townhomes, $589,000–$715,000; homesites, $181,000–$825,000.

Beaver Creek Golf Club
103 Offerson
Beaver Creek, CO 81620
Ph: (970) 845-5775
Fax: (970) 845-6223
http://www.slifer.net

Individual homes, condominiums, high-rise complex, homesites. Golf course; tennis; racquetball; hiking/biking; swimming pool; fishing; hunting; snow skiing; social clubs.

PURCHASE: Homes, $440,000–$2.2 million+.

Castle Pines Village
482 Happy Canyon Rd.
Castle Rock, CO 80104
Ph: (800) 213-1999 or (303) 688-6100
http://www.castlepines.com

Individual homes. Golf courses; canyon club; swimming pool; tennis.

PURCHASE: Homes, $500,000–$1.26 million.

Fox Acres
PO Box 10
Red Feather Lakes, CO 80545
Ph: (800) 577-6610 or (970) 881-2191
http://www.foxacres.com

Individual homes, patio homes, townhomes, condominiums, homesites. Golf course; clubhouse; pro shop; tennis; fishing; fitness trail; lakes; dining.

PURCHASE: Homes, $275,000; homesites, $76,000–$131,000.

Heather Gardens Golf Club
2888 S. Heather Gardens Way
Aurora, CO 80014
Ph: (303) 755-0652
Fax: (303) 745-5253
http://www.heathergardens.org

Age 39+. Individual homes, condominiums, high-rise complex. Golf course; tennis; swimming pool; fitness center; library; social clubs.

PURCHASE: Homes, $93,500–$330,000.

Heritage at Eagle Bend
22801 E. Ridge Trail Drive
Aurora, CO 80016
Ph: (303) 693-9977
http://www.heritageeaglebend.com/

Age 55+. Individual homes, patio homes, townhomes. Golf course; clubhouse; tennis; swimming pools; amphitheater; trails.

PURCHASE: Homes, $137,500–$286,000.

Pinehurst Country Club
6255 W. Quincy
Denver, CO 80235
Ph: (303) 985-1551
Fax: (303) 969-0849

Individual homes, townhomes. Golf course; tennis; swimming pool; clubhouse; dining; social clubs.

PURCHASE: Homes, $330,000–$1.1 million+.

Plum Creek Golf & Country Club

331 Players Club Drive
Castle Rock, CO 80104

Ph: (800) 488-2612 or (303) 688-2611
Fax: (303) 660-2100

Individual homes, condominiums, cooperative units, homesites. Golf course; tennis; swimming pool; hiking/biking; social clubs.

PURCHASE: Homes, $154,000–$550,000+.

Riverwalk

2751 W. Riverwalk Circle
Littleton, CO 80123

Ph: (303) 798-1130 or (303) 738-8124

http://www.golfcoursecommunities.com/riverwalk

Condominiums, golf homes. Golf course; clubhouse; tennis; swimming pool; spa; fitness center; billiards; walking/jogging/biking path.

PURCHASE: Centennial Condo (55+), $142,000–$191,000; golf homes, $164,000–$211,000; ranch and townhomes, $274,000–$307,000.

Sonnenalp Golf Club

1265 Berry Creek Rd.
Edwards, CO 81632

Ph: (800) 654-8312 or (970) 926-3533

http://www.vail.net/sonnenalp

Individual homes, condominiums, homesites. Golf course; tennis; hiking trails; fitness center.

PURCHASE: Homes, $220,000–$1.1 million; homesites, $66,000–$220,000.

The Village at Cotton Ranch

530 Cotton Ranch Drive
Gypsum, CO 81637

Ph: (800) 404-3542 or (970) 524-6100

http://www.cottonranch.com

Individual homes, townhomes, homesites. Golf course; clubhouse; pro shop; tennis; swimming pool; health and fitness center; dining.

PURCHASE: Homes, from $493,000; townhomes, from $344,500; homesites, from $90,000.

South

Crested Butte Country Club

385 Country Club Drive
Crested Butte, CO 81224

Ph: (800) 628-5496 or (970) 349-6869
Fax: (970) 349-6134

http://www.toski.com/crestedbutte/real.html

Individual homes, condominiums, homesites. Golf course; tennis; racquetball; swimming pool; hiking; biking; fishing; hunting; snow skiing; fitness center.

PURCHASE: Homes, from $516,000.

Dalton Ranch & Golf Club

589 C.R, 252
Durango, CO 81301

Ph: (970) 247-7921
Fax: (970) 247-2958

http://www.daltonranch.com

Individual homes, townhomes, homesites. Golf course; tennis; swimming pool; hiking; fishing; snow skiing; future fitness center.

PURCHASE: Homes, from $25,000.

Deer Creek Village

500 SE Jay Ave.
Cedaredge, CO 81413

Ph: (970) 856-7781
Fax: (970) 856-5011

http://www.golfcolorado.com/deercreek

Individual homes, townhomes. Golf course; fishing; bicycle paths.

PURCHASE: Homes, $143,000–$264,000.

Fairway Pines Village & Golf Club

117 Ponderosa Drive
Ridgway, CO 81432

Ph: (800) 433-7760 or (970) 626-5271
Fax: (970) 626-5052

http://www.fairwaypines.com

Individual homes. Golf course; tennis; racquetball; swimming pool; fitness center; aerobics; billiards; dining; social clubs.

PURCHASE: Homesites, $54,000–$143,000.

Gleneagle Golf Club

345 Mission Hills Way
Colorado Springs, CO 80921

Ph: (719) 488-0900
Fax: (719) 488-0276

Individual homes, condominiums. Golf course; tennis; swimming pool; fitness center.

PURCHASE: Homes, $200,000–$396,000.

Connecticut

http://www.state.ct.us

General Information

Climate

Warm summers and cold winters.

Cost of Living

Ranks 5th in the nation.

Taxes

General: Department of Revenue Services, (in state) (800) 382-9463; TDD (860) 297-4911.

State/Local as % of Income: About 10.8%.

Property Tax Reduction: Eligible elderly homeowners may qualify for a credit on a portion of their local property taxes. Renters may also receive grants.

Sales: 6%.

Prescription Exemptions: Exemptions include over-the-counter drugs, e.g., vitamins and cold medicines, as well as prescription drugs, eyeglasses, dentures, hearing aids and batteries, repairs to crutches, walkers, wheelchairs, and other vital life support equipment. Also, eligible seniors 65 and older may get additional financial support for prescription drugs through the ConnPACE program.

Transportation, Travel, and Tourism

General

Connecticut Office of Tourism, 505 Hudson St., Hartford, CT 06106, (860) 270-8080 or (800) CT-BOUND.

Major Airport

- Bradley International Airport, 2800 Berlin Turnpike, PO Box 317546, Newington, CT 06131-7546, (860) 292-2000

Railways

- Amtrak, (800) USA-RAIL.

Bus Tours

- Arrow Line, Inc., 19 George St., PO Box 280807, East Hartford, CT 06128-0807, (800) 243-9560 or (860) 289-1531, Fax: (860) 289-1535.
- Country Squire Tours, (800) 966-9445.
- Greyhound Bus, (800) 231-2222.

State Highways

- Interstate 84 runs east-west.
- Interstate 395 runs south-north.
- Interstate 95 runs east-west.
- Interstate 91 runs south-north.

Theater and Music

Hartford Area

- Hartford Civic Center, 1 Civic Center Plaza, Hartford, CT 06103, (860) 727-8010 (sporting events, performances, entertainment).
- Theaterworks, 233 Pearl St., Hartford, CT 06103, (860) 527-7838 (Off-Broadway-style productions Oct. Aug.).
- Lincoln Theater, 200 Bloomfield Ave., West Hartford, CT 06117, (800) 274-8587 (year-round drama, dance, lectures, concerts).

Litchfield Area

- Litchfield Performing Arts, Litchfield, CT 06759, (860) 567-4162 (music, theater, dance Sept. Aug.).
- Norfolk Chamber Music, Rtes. 44 & 272, Norfolk, CT 06058, (860) 542-3000 (seasonal).

Waterbury Area

- Thomaston Opera House, 158 Main St., Thomaston, CT 06787, (860) 283-8558 (year-round).
- Seven Angels Theater, Plank Rd., Waterbury, CT; Mailing address: P.O. Box 3358, Waterbury, CT 06705, (203) 757-4676.

New Haven

- Lyman Center for the Performing Arts, Southern Connecticut State Univ., 501 Crescent St., New Haven, CT 06515, (203) 392- 6154.
- Shubert Performing Arts, 247 College St., New Haven, CT 06501, (203) 562-5666 or (800) 228-6622.

Coastal Fairfield County

- Downtown Cabaret Theatre, 263 Golden Hill St., Bridgeport, CT 06604, (203) 576-1636.
- Westport Arts Center, 17 Morningside Drive S., Westport, CT 06880, (203) 222-7070 (seasonal).

Connecticut River Valley

- National Theatre of the Deaf, 5 W. Main St., Chester, CT 06412, (860) 526-4971 or TTY-(860) 526-4974.
- Opera Theater of CT, Main St., Clinton, CT 06413, (860) 669-8999 (summer series).
- Goodspeed Opera House, Rte 82, East Haddam, CT 06423, (860) 873-8668 (seasonal).

Museums, Crafts, Historical, Recreational

Hartford Area

- Hillstead Museum, 35 Mountain Rd., Farmington, CT 06032, (860) 677-9064 (collections include French impressionist paintings).
- CT Audubon Center at Glastonbury, 1361 Main St., Glastonbury, CT 06033, (860) 633-8402.
- Elizabeth Park Rose Gardens, Prospect Ave., Hartford, CT 06106, (860) 722-6514 or 6511 (nature walks, rose garden).
- Wadsworth Atheneum, 600 Main St., Hartford CT 06103, (860) 247-9111 or 278-2670 (nation's oldest public art museum).

Litchfield Area

- White Memorial Conservation Center Museum, Rte. 202, Litchfield, CT; Mailing address: PO Box 3358, Litchfield, CT 06759, (860) 567-0857.

Greater New Haven

- Whitney Museum, 915 Whitney Ave., New Haven, CT 06517, (203) 777-1833.
- Peabody Museum of Natural History, 170 Whitney Ave., New Haven, CT 06511, (203) 432-5050 (Yale Univ.).
- Yale University Art Gallery, 1111 Chapel St. at York St., New Haven, CT 06520, (203) 432-0600.

Coastal Fairfield County

- Beardsley Zoological Gardens, 1875 Noble Ave., Bridgeport, CT 06610, (203) 576-8082 (36 acres of exhibits).
- The Maritime Aquarium of Norwalk, 10 N. Water St., Norwalk, CT 06854, (203) 852-0700.
- Stamford Museum and Nature Center, 39 Scofieldtown Rd., Stamford, CT 06903, (203) 322-1646 (nature trails, picnic areas, and fine art galleries).

Connecticut River Valley

- Nathan Hale Schoolhouse, Main St., East Haddam, CT 06423, (860) 873-9547.
- Connecticut River Museum, 67 Main St., Essex, CT 06426, (860) 767-0681.
- Henry Whitfield State Museum, 248 Whitfield St., Guilford, CT 06437, (203) 453-2457 or (860) 566-3005 (Connecticut's oldest house).

Organizations

Advocacy Groups

- Connecticut Coalition on Aging, PO Box 370585, West Hartford, CT 06137- 0585, (203) 497-8378.
- Connecticut Commission on Aging, 25 Sigourney St., 12th Fl., Hartford, CT 06106, (860) 424-5360. Fax: (860) 424-4985.
- Long-Term Care Ombudsman, 25 Sigourney St., Hartford, CT 06106, (860) 424-5200.
- Connecticut Partnership, (800) 547-3443 (long-term care financial information).

Volunteer Programs

- Foster Grandparents and Senior Companion Program, CT chapters. Corp. for National and Community Service, 1 Commercial Plaza, 21st Fl., Hartford, CT 06103-3510, (860) 240- 3240.

Housing

Long-Term Care Facilities

In the state of Connecticut, these facilities are called ***Long-Term Care/Nursing Home Facilities.***

These facilities provide residential living and/or various levels of nursing and medical services to seniors for an extended period of time.

Types of Authorization

Licensing and / or Certification

These facilities are not licensed by the state. However, specific areas of the CCRC health care package, such as assisted living or skilled nursing, are licensed as health services. A CCRC must be registered with the Department of Social Services and meet certain disclosure requirements. Provisions include, through contractual agreements, lifetime housing and a range of services including long-term health care. Residents pay a substantial entrance fee and monthly fees in exchange for housing and services. Levels of care may include independent living, assistance with daily activities, and nursing home care.

Memberships:

- American Association of Homes and Services for the Aging (AAHSA) represents not-for-profit organizations committed to providing high-quality health care, housing, and services to the elderly. AAHSA, 901 E St. NW, Suite 500, Washington, DC 20004-2011. Ph: (202) 783-2242. Fax: (202) 783-2285. *http: / / www.aahsa.org*
- Connecticut Association of Non-Profit Homes and Services for the Aging (CANPFA) is an AAHSA Affiliated State Association. CANPFA, 300 Research Parkway, Meriden, CT 06450-7137, (203) 237-4556. Fax: (203) 237-4908, *http: / / www.health-connect.com / canpfa /*
- Connecticut Hospital Association (CHA), 110 Barnes Rd., PO Box 90, Wallingford, CT 06492-0090, (203) 265-7611.

Accreditations:

- Continuing Care Accreditation Commission (CCAC) accredits facilities that offer seniors a contract or contracts that provide residential living and health care services for the remainder of the person's lifetime and meet CCAC's accreditation standards.
- Joint Commission on the Accreditation of Healthcare Organizations (JCAHO) is an independent, not-for-profit organization, and the nation's oldest and largest standards-setting and health care accrediting institution.

Central

Ashlar Village, CCAC, JCAHO

Cheshire Rd.
Wallingford, CT 06492

Ph: (203) 949-4425 or (800) 382-2244

IND: 244. HCC: 548

Age 55+. Nonprofit; affiliate of Masonicare. Cottages, apartments, and private and semiprivate rooms. Skilled nursing care; short- and long-term care; home care; full-time physicians; wellness program; Medicaid and Medicare-approved; emergency response system; security; maintenance; up to 3 daily meals; housekeeping and laundry services; recreational, social, and cultural programs; religious services; lounges; game room; library; bank services; village store; stocked fish pond; walking paths; darkroom; barber/beauty shop.

IND ENT: (ref.) $99,000–$229,000. IND MO: $1,250–$2,300. 2nd person, $150–$330.

Avery Heights

705 New Britain Ave.
Hartford, CT 06106

Ph: (860) 527-9126
Fax: (860) 525-2090

IND: Yes. AL: Yes. ICF: Yes. HCC: Yes. ADC: Yes

Nondenominational; nonprofit; Church Homes, Inc. Cottages, apartments, and private and semiprivate rooms. Skilled nursing care; IV therapy; respiratory and inhalation therapy; continuous ambulatory peritoneal dialysis; wound therapy; physical, occupational, and speech therapies; rehabilitative care; social work; home care aides; respite care; health clinic; personal care; medication monitoring; security; emergency response system; maintenance; transportation; up to 3 daily meals; housekeeping and laundry services; libraries; educational and cultural programs; gift shop; barber/beauty shop.

IND MO: $600–$1,700. AL Daily: $90–$145. ICF Daily: $160–$200. HCC Daily: $250–$325.

Bradley Home

320 Colony St., PO Box 886
Meriden, CT 06450

Ph: (203) 235-5716
Fax: (203) 634-6851

IND: 30. AL: 74. SNF: 30

Nonprofit; nondenominational. Private and semiprivate rooms. Skilled nursing care; long- and short-term care; doctor visits; physical, occupational, and speech therapies; pharmacy; personal care; medication administration; security; emergency response system; maintenance; transportation; up to 3 daily meals; housekeeping and laundry services; scheduled activities; barber/beauty shop.

IND Daily: $90. SNF Daily: $175. RSP and EXTENDED Daily: $175

Connecticut Baptist Homes

292 Thorpe Ave.
Meriden, CT 06450

Ph: (203) 237-1206

IND: 38. ICF: Yes. SNF: 30. AL/RES: Yes. ALZ/MEM IMP: Yes

Age 62+. Nonprofit; nondenominational; affiliated with the American Baptist Church. Apartments private and semiprivate rooms and 24-hour skilled nursing care; personal care; medication administration; social services; security; emergency response system; maintenance; transportation; up to 3 daily meals; housekeeping and laundry services; activities.

IND MO: $800 RES MO: $1,600. ICF Daily: $190. SNF Daily: $205.

Covenant Village of Cromwell, CCAC

52 Missionary Rd.
Cromwell, CT 06416-2143

Ph: (860) 635-2690
Fax: (860) 635-2407

http://www.covenantretirement.com

IND: Yes. AL: Yes. ICF: Yes. SNF: Yes

Nonprofit; Evangelical Covenant Church; a Christian facility. Cottages, studios, apartments, and private and semiprivate rooms. Skilled nursing care; long- and short-term care; 24-hour emergency health care; rehabilitative care; personal care; physical, occupational, and speech therapies; personal care; medication administration; Medicare-approved; security; emergency response system; maintenance; transportation; up to 3 daily meals; housekeeping and laundry services; health club; craft and hobby rooms; woodworking and refinishing shop; gardening; gift shop; village store; barber/beauty shop.

APPL: $400. DEP: $1,100. IND ENT: $70,000–$121,000; 2nd person, $9,400–$12,000. IND MO: $1,000–$1,600; 2nd person, $360. ENT fee covers 60 days of additional services, i.e., assisted living, intermediate care, skilled nursing care. After 60 days, the daily rate is discounted.

Duncaster

40 Loeffler Rd.
Bloomfield, CT 06002

Ph: (860) 726-2000 or (800) 545-5065
Fax: (860) 242-8004

www.duncaster.org

IND: Yes. AL: Yes. HCC: 60

Age 65+. Nonprofit; nondenominational; Lifecare Retirement Community. Studios, apartments, and private and semiprivate rooms. 24-hour nursing care; outpatient medical clinic; physical, occupational, and speech therapies; Apartcare program; personal care; medication administration; security; emergency response system; maintenance; transportation; up to 3 daily meals; housekeeping and laundry services; grocery service; lobby; meeting rooms; activities and educational programs; Gentlemen's Club and hospitality room; workshop; greenhouse; library; gardens; walking paths.

APPL: ($200 no ref.) single, $2,000; double, $2,500. IND ENT: Plan I, $130,000–$300,000; Plan II, $98,000–$202,000; Plan III, $68,000–$106,000. 2nd person, $22,000. IND MO: Plan I, $1,700–$2,900; Plan II, $1,500–$2,500; Plan III, $1,900–$3,500. 2nd person, $825. HCC included in ENT fees.

Elim Park Place, CCAC, JCAHO,CAIC

140 Cook Hill Rd.
Cheshire, CT 06410

Ph: (203) 272-7550 or (800) 994-1776
Fax: (203) 271-7753

www.elimpark.com

ICF: 137. AL: Yes. HCC: 90. RC: 42.
ALZ/MEM IMP: Yes

Age 60+. Nonprofit; nondenominational; owned and operated by the Elim Park Baptist Home, Inc. Apartments and private and semiprivate rooms. Long- and short-term care; rehabilitative care; skilled nursing care; 24-hour care; IV therapy; hospice care; hydrotherapy treatments; social services; physical, occupational, and speech therapies; personal care; medication monitoring; security; emergency response system; maintenance; transportation; up to 3 daily meals; pets allowed; housekeeping and laundry services; chaplain; scheduled activities; banking and postal services; gym; woodworking shop; library; gardening; barber/beauty shop.

ENT: $136,000–$237,000; MO: $1,100–$1,600. RC Daily: $115 and $135. SNF Daily: $275–$315.

Jefferson House

One John H. Stewart Drive
Newington, CT 06111

Ph: (860) 667-4453

Fax: (860) 667-4459

SNF: Yes. ICF: Yes. ADC: Yes. ALZ/ MEN IMP: Yes

Affiliated with Hartford Hospital; nondenominational. Private and semiprivate rooms with baths. 24-hour nursing care; medical consultants, e.g., dentistry, optometry, podiatry, psychiatry, audiology; pharmacy; physical, occupational, and speech therapies; social services personal care; medication administration; emergency response system; 3 daily meals; housekeeping and laundry services; chaplain; activities.

SNF Daily: Semiprivate, $260; private, $270. ICF Daily: Semiprivate, $210; private, $230.

The McAuley

275 Steele Rd.
West Hartford, CT 06117

Ph: (860) 236-6300
Fax: (860) 232-4077

IND: Yes. AL: Yes. HCC: Yes

Nondenominational; owned by Hyatt. Apartments, studios, and private and semiprivate rooms. Skilled nursing care; in- home care; wellness services; physician referrals; meal service; 24-hour licensed health care personnel; podiatrist services; personal care; medication administration; security; emergency response system; maintenance; transportation; up to 3 daily meals; housekeeping and laundry services; exercise classes; activities program; educational programs; gardening; knitting; woodworking; resident committees; barber/beauty shop.

IND ENT: (ref. declines at 2%/mo. for 50 mos.; reduced MO), $103,000–$200,000; (ref. declines at 2%/mo. for 50 mos.; standard MO), $64,000–$130,000; ($^2/_3$ of ENT is ref.; standard MO), $103,000–$195,000. IND MO: $1,700–$4,200. AL MO: $3,000–$4,900; 2nd person, $770. HCC included in ENT fees.

St. Mary's Home, JCAHO

2021 Albany Ave.
West Hartford, CT 06117

Ph: (860) 236-1924
Fax: (860) 236-0695

RH: 100. ICF: 40. SNF: 177. ADC: Yes

Nonprofit; nondenominational; nonsectarian; sponsored by Sisters of Mercy. Apartments and private and semiprivate rooms. 24-hour skilled nursing care; long- and short-term care; IV therapy; pain management; wound care; podiatry, dental, eye, and psychiatric services; rehabilitative services; hospice; respite care; social services; security; emergency response system; maintenance; transportation; up to 3 daily meals; housekeeping and laundry services; ecumenical services and daily Mass; social, recreational, and cultural activities; library; coffee shop and gift store; barber/beauty shop.

RH Daily: $45–$105. SNF Daily: $265 and $315. ADC Daily: $75.

Seabury, AAHSA, CCAC

200 Seabury Drive
Bloomfield, CT 06002-2650

Ph: (860) 286-0243 or (800) 340-4709
Fax: (860) 242-4552

http://www.seaburyretirement.com

IND: Yes. AL: Yes. HCC: Yes

Nonprofit; nondenominational; sponsored by the Church Home of Hartford. Apartments, cottages, and private and semiprivate rooms. Skilled nursing care; 24-hour nursing assistance; geriatric physician; blood pressure and glaucoma checks; rehabilitative services; prescription delivery; personal care; medication administration; security; emergency response system; maintenance; transportation; up to 3 daily meals; housekeeping and laundry services; wellness clinic; fitness center; chapel; postal and banking services; hobby room; activities coordinator; lounge; library with computer cen-

ter; game room; caf; photo lab; greenhouse; gardens; convenience store; barber/beauty shop.

DEP: 10% of ENT fee. IND ENT: Plan A, $82,500–$231,000; Plan B, $60,500–$138,000; Plan C, $111,000–$302,500. IND MO: Plan A, $1,600–$3,800; Plan B, $2,100–$5,200; Plan C, $1,600–$3,750. Plans A and B ref. minus 2%/mo. up to 50 mos. Plan C 67% ref. any time. AL and HCC included in IND fees.

North

McLean Home, JCAHO, CHA, CAHC, CANFA

75 Great Pond Rd.
Simsbury, CT 06070

Ph: (860) 658-3901
Fax: (860) 658-7672

IND: Yes. RC: Yes. RSP: Yes. SNF: Yes. ADC: Yes

Nonprofit; nondenominational health care facility. Suites and private and semiprivate rooms. Skilled nursing care; rehabilitation services; health monitoring; home health care; personal care; medication monitoring; transportation; warm water therapeutic pool; meals-on-wheels; groceries-on-wheels; caregivers; 3 daily meals; housekeeping and laundry services; library; gift shop; barber/beauty shop.

IND MO: $850–$4,150. ICF Daily: $210–$235. SNF Daily: $285–$300; hospice, $350. ADC Daily: $75.

Noble Horizons, JCAHO, AAAHSA, CALTC

17 Cobble Rd.
Salisbury, CT 06008

Ph: (860) 435-9851
Fax: (860) 435-0636

IND: Yes. AL: Yes. SNF: Yes

Nondenominational; nonprofit; Church Homes, Inc. Cottages, apartments, private rooms with baths, and private and semiprivate rooms. 24-hour nursing care; rehabilitative services; intermediate care; personal care; medication monitoring; security; emergency response system; maintenance; transportation; up to 3 daily meals; pets allowed; housekeeping and laundry services; staff chaplain; chapel; gardening; volunteer programs; library; computer room; educational activities; nature programs.

IND MO: Cottages, $950–$1,500. Daily: Private rooms with baths, $150/person and $160/person. ICF Daily: $240/person. SNF Daily: $250–$280.

West

East Hill Woods

611 E. Hill Rd.
Southbury, CT 06488

Ph: (203) 262-6161 or (800) 435-4249

IND: 173. AL: 20. HCC: 30

Age 65+. Governed by a board of trustees that includes residents; nonprofit. Skilled nursing care; access to medical services; long- and short-term care; in-home health care; 24-hour staffing; personal care; medication administration; security; emergency response system; maintenance; transportation; up to 3 daily meals; pets allowed; housekeeping and laundry services; exercise center; social worker; activities director; library and computer center; games; gardening; outdoor sports arena; walking paths; barber/beauty shop.

IND ENT: (85% ref.), $159,000–$347,000; (traditional), $135,000–$295,000. IND MO: $1,850–$3,100; 2nd person, $1,100.

Pomperaug Woods

80 Heritage Rd.
Southbury, CT 06488

Ph: (203) 262-6555
Fax: (203) 264-2155

IND: Yes. HCC: Yes

Age 65+. Managed by Life Care Services Corp.; nondenominational. Apartments and private and semiprivate rooms. Skilled nursing care; emergency care; long- and short-term care; therapies; personal care; medication administration; security; emergency response system; maintenance; transportation; up to 3 daily meals (1 meal included in mo. fee for IND); community facilities, activities.

IND ENT: Return of capital plan (part. ref.), $122,000–$320,000; traditional plan (no ref.), $98,000–$255,000. IND MO: $1,800–$2,500; 2nd person, $1,200.

South

Saint Regis

1354 Chapel St.
New Haven, CT 06511

Ph: (203) 867-8300

SNF: Yes

Affiliated with Saint Raphael Healthcare System; nondenominational. Private and semiprivate rooms. Long- and short-term care; board-certified geriatricians; licensed nurses; X-rays; IV therapy; physical, occupational, and speech therapies; dietitians; social services; pastoral care; 3 daily meals; laundry and housekeeping services; activities; barber/beauty shop.

SNF Daily: Extended care: semiprivate, $210 and $230; private, $270; Restorative care: semiprivate, $235 and $255; private, $300.

3030 Park, CCAC

3030 Park Ave.
Bridgeport, CT 06604

Ph: (203) 373-6282 or (800) 930-3072
Fax: (203) 374-2871
http://www.3030park.com

IND: Yes. AL: Yes. HCC: Yes

Age 62+. Volunteer board of directors; nondenominational. Efficiencies, apartments, and private and semiprivate rooms. Skilled nursing care; clinic; medical, nursing, podiatry, dentistry, and rehabilitative services; pharmacy; personal care; medication administration; 24-hour health assessments; security; emergency response system; maintenance; transportation; up to 3 daily meals; housekeeping and laundry services; chapel; weekly volunteer programs.

IND ENT: (ref.) $38,500–$192,500. MO: $1,400–$3,100.

Wesley Village, JCAHO

580 Long Hill Ave.
Shelton, CT 06484

Ph: (203) 944-1999
Fax: (203) 929-2067

IND: 182. AL: 67. HCC: 80. AL/MEM IMP: 30

Age 62+. Nonprofit; nonsectarian; United Methodist Homes; church affiliated. Apartments, cottages, and private rooms. 24-hour nursing care; rehabilitative therapies; IV therapy; respiratory care; hospice; dental and podiatry services; pharmacy; Medicare/Medicaid-approved; personal care; medication administration; security; emergency response system; maintenance; transportation; up to 3 daily meals; pets allowed; housekeeping and laundry services; religious services; intergenerational program; activities; library; solarium; barber/beauty shop.

IND MO: $1,300–$1,500. AL DEP: $550. AL MO: $2,550–$3,000. HCC Daily: Semiprivate, $240; private, $270.

Whitney Center, CCAC

200 Leeder Hill Drive
Hamden, CT 06517-2749

Ph: (203) 281-6745 or (800) 237-3847
http://www.whitneycenter.com

IND: Yes. AL: Yes. HCC: 59 (total residents, 250)

Nonprofit; nondenominational; 24-hour emergency nursing care; long- or short-term care; rehabilitative care; physical, occupational, and speech therapies; personal care; medication administration; security; emergency response system; maintenance; transportation; up to 3 daily meals; housekeeping and laundry services; ecumenical chaplain; bank services; lecture series; concerts; coffee and gift shop; corner store; barber/beauty shop.

ENT: (basic), \$63,000–\$231,000; (50% ref.), \$82,000–\$301,000; (90% ref.), \$135,000–\$491,000; 2nd person, \$11,000. MO: \$1,500–\$2,400; 2nd person, \$910. HCC included in ENT fees.

Assisted Living and Residential Care Facilities

In the state of Connecticut, these facilities are called ***Assisted Living, Congregate and Residential Care Facilities****.*

Managed residential communities that provide supportive services.

Types of Authorization

Licensing and/or Certification

Must be licensed by the Department of Health as an Assisted-Living Services Agency (ALSA). Facilities must provide the following: meals, laundry and housekeeping, transportation, maintenance and activities, security, emergency call systems, sufficient community space for the residents.

Memberships

- Assisted Living Federation of America (ALFAA) is a national nonprofit membership organization whose mission is to enhance the quality of life in assisted living facilities and promote the interests of the assisted living industry. ALFA, 10300 Eaton Place, Suite 400, Fairfax, VA 22030. Ph: (703) 691-8100. Fax: (703) 691-8106. *http://www.alfa.org*

West

Ogden House

100 River Rd.
Wilton, CT 06897

Ph: (203) 762-8035
Fax: (203) 762-0607

RC: 84

Age 62+, and/or handicapped. Nonprofit; nondenominational; HUD program. One- and two-bedroom apartments. Direct emergency alarm; medical suite; access to common areas; laundry facilities; arts and crafts; gardens; lobby and management office; mail room; kitchen facilities.

Rent (30% of actual mo. income) is determined on the basis of a person's income and assets.

REQ: residents must have an annual adjusted income not more than \$34,500 (one person) or \$39,500 (two persons).

South

Laurel Gardens of Hamden

2323 Whitney Ave.
Hamden, CT 06518

Ph: (203) 248-1864 or (888) 748-9722

IND: Yes. AL: Yes

Nondenominational; owned by David Reis and Senior Care Development; managed by CareMatrix Corp. One- and two-bedroom apartments and studios. Wellness center; personal care; medication administration; security; maintenance; transportation; up to 3 daily meals; housekeeping and laundry services; library and computer center; media room; social, cultural, and recre-

ational activities; caf and lounge; enclosed courtyard; walking paths; barber/beauty shop.

Contact facility for fees.

Silverbrook Estates

100 Red Cedar Rd.
Orange, CT 06477

Ph: (203) 891-8265
Fax: (203) 891-8050

IND: 45

Age 62+ who meet Connecticut income guidelines. Sponsored by the town of Orange; nondenominational; nonsectarian. Apartments. Emergency response system; maintenance; up to 3 daily meals; housekeeping and laundry services; library; community room and activities.

MO: Rent, $350; congregate: $600. State subsidized. Income limits: single, $35,000; double, $38,500.

Central

Laurel Gardens of Avon

101 Bickford Drive Extension
Avon, CT 06001

Ph: (860) 677-2155 or (888) 748-9747

IND: 108. AL: Yes

Age 62+. For-profit; nondenominational; operated by CareMatrix Corp. Apartments. Personal care; medication administration; security; emergency response system; maintenance; transportation; up to 3 daily meals; housekeeping and laundry services; wellness/fitness center; daily activities; library; computer center; caf; country store; walking paths; courtyard; barber/beauty shop.

IND MO: From $2,500.

Southwick at Cheshire

1356 S. Main St.
Cheshire, CT 06410

Ph: (203) 271-0255

IND: Yes. AL: Yes

Nondenominational. Cottages and apartments. Wellness center; personal care; medication administration; security; maintenance; transportation; up to 3 daily meals; tray service when necessary; housekeeping and laundry services; health club; exercise program; swimming pool; library and computer center; banking services; creative arts area; auditorium and theater; concierge service; convenience store; barber/beauty shop.

PURCHASE: (Cottages), starting at $167,500; (apartments), $121,000.

Independent Living

Independent housing (primarily rentals) for seniors that may offer security features, meal service, and activities.

South

Parish Court

175 Warde Terrace
Fairfield, CT 06432

Ph: (203) 333-4912
Fax: (203) 333-2310

IND: 100

Nonprofit; nondenominational; owned by Church Housing for Fairfield. Efficiency apartments and one-bedroom units. On-site administrator and resident superintendent; community room; craft room; housekeeping and laundry services; office; maintenance area; small pets allowed.

HUD-subsidized. Resident annual income maximum: single, $35,000; double, $40,000. IND MO: 30% of income.

Saye Brooke Village East and West

55 Sheffield St.
Old Saybrook, CT 06475

Ph: (860) 388-5915
Fax: (860) 388-6359

IND: 50

Age 62+. Nonprofit; nondenominational. Apartments. Maintenance; pets welcome; close to town and community services; Senior Center and lunch program next door.

IND MO: HUD-subsidized. East max. income: single, $24,000; double, $27,000; 30% of income. West max. income: single, $48,000; double, $55,000; $675 and $800.

Central

Rose Commons

540 Hartford Tpke
Vernon, CT 06066

Ph: (860) 870-9636
Fax: (860) 870-9636

E-mail: *rosecommons@snet.net*

RH: 31

Age 62+. Nonprofit facility. Apartments. Security; emergency response system; maintenance; transportation; on-site administrator and resident security person; pets allowed; community room; social areas; shopping nearby; group activities.

DEP: 1 mo. rent. IND MO: 30% of adjusted income. HUD-subsidized.

Adult/Resort Communities

Communities for active adults (not all are age-restricted; primarily ownership).

Candlewood Lake Club

919 Candlewood Lake Rd.
Brookfield, CT 06804

Ph: (860) 354-4004

Individual homes. Golf course; tennis; hiking/biking trails; fishing; boating/waterskiing; community center; dining; library; social clubs.

PURCHASE: Homes, $154,000–$880,000.

Heritage Village

Heritage Rd.
Southbury, CT 06488

Ph: (800) 724-1698 or (203) 264-0888
Fax: (203) 264-0166

http://www.villagers.com

Age 50+. Condominiums. Golf course; tennis; swimming pool; hiking/biking trails; fishing; snow skiing; community center, dining, fitness center; library, social clubs; ambulance service.

PURCHASE: Homes, $71,500–$275,000.

Oronoque Village

600 North Trail
Stratford, CT 06614

Ph: (203) 377-5313
Fax: (203) 380-6156

Age 55+. Condominiums. Golf course; tennis; swimming; community center; fitness center; library.

PURCHASE: Homes, $127,000–$275,000.

The River Highlands

5 Highland Crossing
Cromwell, CT 06416

Ph: (860) 635-7111

http://www.river-highlands.com

Individual homes, attached homes. Golf course; clubhouse; tennis; swimming pool; dining; maintenance free.

PURCHASE: Homes, $286,000–$633,000.

Spring Lake Village

761 Kettle Path
Southington, CT 06489

Ph: (860) 621-8989 (in CT) or (800) 922-8988

http://www.spring-lake-village.com/

Age 55+. Condominiums. Clubhouse; swimming pool; tennis; gardens; lake; walking paths; billiards.

PURCHASE: Condos, from $149,000.

Delaware

http://www.state.de.us

General Information

Climate

Moderate. Average monthly temperatures range from 76° F to 32° F.

Cost of Living

Ranks 13th in the nation.

Taxes

State/Local as % of Income: About 9.6%.

Property Tax Reduction: None.

Sales: None.

Prescription Exemptions: None.

Transportation, Travel, and Tourism

General

Department of Transportation, (302) 739-3264.

Delaware Tourism Office, (800) 441-8846 or (302) 739-4271.

Major Airport

- New Castle County Airport, (302) 571-6300.

Railways

- Amtrak, (800) USA-RAIL.
- DART, (800) 652-DART or (302) 652-DART.

Bus Tours

- Trailways; Wilmington, (302) 652-7391; Dover, (302) 734-1417.

Waterways

- Cape May Lewes Ferry (302) 645-6346. Water shuttle connecting Lewes, DE, and Cape May, NJ.
- Rehoboth Bay Shuttle, (302) 645-9380. Connects the beach areas.

State Highways

- Route 13 runs north-south.

Theater and Music

North

- Candlelight music dinner theater, 2208 Millers Rd., Ardentown, Wilmington, DE 19810, (302) 368-2248 (open year-round).
- Delaware Theater Company, 200 Water St., Wilmington, DE 19801-5048, (302) 594-1100.
- Chapel Street Players, 27 N. Chapel St., Newark, DE 19711, (302) 368-2248.
- Delaware Ballet, 177 Old Camden Rd., Camden, DE 19934, (302) 697-8116. Performances at Delaware State University.

Central

- Delaware Symphony Orchestra, PO Box 163, Dover, DE 19903, (302) 734-1701.
- Russian Ballet Theater of Delaware, Box 263, Rockland, DE 19732, (302) 656-4401.

Museums, Crafts, Historical, Recreational

- Delaware Art Museum, 2301 Kentmere Parkway, Wilmington, DE 19806, (302) 571-9590.
- Delaware Center for Contemporary Arts, 103 East 16th St., Wilmington, DE 19801, (302) 656-6466 (includes four galleries with a total of 27 yearly exhibitions).
- Delaware Museum of Natural History, 4840 Kennett Pike, PO Box 3937, Wilmington, DE 19807, (302) 658-9111 (senior discounts).

- Winterthur, (800) 448-3883 or (302) 888-4600 or TTY (302) 888-4907. Public gardens owned by DuPont family.
- Delaware's 13 state parks, (302) 739-4702. Hiking, camping, swimming, fishing, nature programs, and historic sites.

Organizations

Advocacy Groups

- Adult Protective Services: New Castle County, (800) 223-9074. Kent and Sussex Counties, (800) 292-1515.
- Delaware Medicare Hotline: (800) 422-8804.

Volunteer Programs

- Arthritis Foundation Delaware Chapter: (800) 292-9599 or (302) 777-1212 (clerical, program, and fund-raising activities).
- Stewardship and Volunteer Program: (302) 645-4253 (must live by inland bays; water samples).

Housing

Long-Term Care Facilities

*In the state of Delaware, these facilities are called **Long-Term Care/ Nursing Home Facilities**.*

These facilities provide residential living and/or various levels of nursing and medical services to seniors for an extended period of time.

Types of Authorization

Licensing and / or Certification

These facilities must be licensed by the Department of Health. Regulations require: a definition of the admissions agreement or entrance contract (includes costs, services, and legal responsibilities of the resident); the basic daily rate to cover room, meals, housekeeping, linen, general nursing care, medical records and services, and recreation and personal care; that a security deposit (if requested) can be no more than three months' prepayment and must be deposited into an interest-bearing account; and that upon a resident's leaving or death, any amount paid over the cost of services already provided must be refunded.

Memberships

- American Association of Homes and Services for the Aging (AAHSA) represents not-for-profit organizations committed to providing high-quality health care, housing and services to the elderly. AAHSA, 901 E St. NW, Suite 500, Washington, DC 20004-2011. Ph: (202) 783-2242. Fax: (202) 783-2285. *http: / / www.aahsa.org*
- Delaware Association of Homes and Services for the Aging (DAHSA) is an AAHSA Affiliated State Association. DAHSA, Ingleside Homes, 1010 N. Broom St., Wilmington, DE 19806-4514. Ph: (302) 777-0130. Fax: (301) 777-0131.

Accreditations:

- Continuing Care Accreditation Commission (CCAC) accredits facilities that offer seniors a contract or contracts that provide residential living and health care services for the remainder of the person's lifetime and meet CCAC's accreditation standards.
- Joint Commission on the Accreditation of Healthcare Organizations (JCAHO) is an independent, not-for-profit organization, and the nation's oldest and largest standards-setting

and health care accrediting institution.

North

Arbors at New Castle, Nursing Center, JCAHO

32 Buena Vista Drive
New Castle, DE 19720

Ph: (302) 328-2580
Fax: (302) 328-6262

SNF: Yes

Arbor Health Care Co.; nondenominational; nonsectarian. Private and semiprivate rooms. Respite care, medical rehabilitation program for those recovering from strokes, orthopedic problems, arthritis, trauma, and neuromuscular disorders; 24-hour comprehensive nursing care; social services; special diets; physical, occupational, speech/language therapies; subacute rehabilitative services; wound care; infusion and respiratory therapies; medication administration; 3 daily meals plus snacks; housekeeping and laundry services; clergy visits; recreational and entertainment activities; barber/beauty services.

ICF Daily: $130 and $125. SNF Daily: $140 and $180.

Brandywine Nursing and Rehabilitation Center

505 Greenbank Rd.
Wilmington, DE 19808

Ph: (302) 998-0101
Fax: (302) 998-2922

SNF: 106. RC: Yes. ICF: Yes

Private and semiprivate rooms with bath. Respite care; physician on call; 24-hour nursing care; pharmacy; physical, occupational, and speech therapies; dental, optometry, and podiatry services; IV therapy; tracheotomy care; nasogastric and gastrostomy feedings; personal care; medication administration; transportation; 3 daily meals; housekeeping and laundry services; exercise; clergy; lounge; game; crafts; ceramics; special occasion celebrations.

SNF Daily: $125–$145.

Churchman Village

4949 Ogletown-Stanton Rd.
Newark, DE 19713

Ph: (302) 998-6900

IND: Yes. HCC: Yes

Age 55+. Genesis ElderCare Network; nondenominational. Apartments and private and semiprivate rooms. 24-hour nursing care; short- and long-term care; personal care; medication administration; Medicare-approved; security; emergency response system; transportation; up to 3 daily meals; housekeeping and laundry services; recreational and social activities; chapel; lounges; activity programs; barber/beauty shop.

IND MO: $2,000 $3,200; additional supportive services, $140/mo. HCC: $130 and $150.

Cokesbury Village, CCAC

726 Loveville Rd.
Hockessin, DE 19701

Ph: (800) 530-2377 or (302) 234-4444.

IND: Yes. HCC: Yes. MEM IMP: Yes

Age 60+; spouse may be younger. Nonprofit; Peninsula United Methodist Homes, Inc.; affiliated with Peninsula-Delaware Annual Conference of the United Methodist Church. Studios, apartments, and cottages, private and semiprivate rooms. Nursing care; personal care; medication administration; maintenance; up to 3 daily meals; housekeeping and laundry services; bank; gift shop; barber/beauty salon; grocery store; clergy services; on-campus shuttle; resident committees; resident council; volunteer programs; lectures; concert performers; walking paths.

IND ENT: (Traditional ref. less 2% for each mo. of occupancy), $48,000–$54,000; (50% refundable), $69,000–

$391,000; 2nd person, $13,000. IND MO: $1,900–$4,400. HCC: Complete service plan includes all services and unlimited health care days. Monthly credits if no housekeeping/linen service. Meal credits also available.

Forwood Manor

1912 Marsh Rd.
Wilmington, DE 19810

Ph: (302) 529-1600
Fax: (302) 529-1689

IND: 140. AL: 37. HCC: 66

Age 60+. For-profit; nondenominational; owned by Marriott. Apartments, suites, and private and semiprivate rooms. Short- and long-term care; skilled nursing care; hospice care; medical director; visiting podiatrist; dental services; 24-hour care; IV therapy; physical, occupational, and speech therapies; personal care; medication administration; Medicare-approved; security; emergency response system; maintenance; transportation; up to 3 daily meals; pets allowed (IND and AL); housekeeping and laundry services; wanderguard personal accountability system; exercise room; clergy visits; banking services; activities; off-site activities; barber/beauty shop.

IND ADM: $1,100. IND MO: $2,000–$3,900; 2nd person, $600. AL Daily: $135–$150. HCC Daily: $155–$200.

Franciscan Health System, Care Center at Wilmington

801 N. Broom St.
Wilmington, DE 19806

Ph: (302) 652-3861

SNF: Yes

Ministry of the Sisters of St. Francis of Philadelphia. Private and semiprivate rooms. Skilled nursing care; physical, occupational, and speech therapies; personal care; medication administration; 3 daily meals; social, intellectual, and spiritual activities; off-site trips; community interaction; individual and group activities.

SNF Daily: $140–$160.

Gilpin Hall, 1998 Excellence in Wound Care Award by Christiana Wound Care Center

1101 Gilpin Ave.
Wilmington, DE 19806

Ph: (302) 654-4486
Fax (302) 655-8601

NH: 96. AL: 18. ADC: Yes. ALZ/MEM IMP: Yes

Nonprofit; nondenominational. Suites and private and semiprivate rooms. Nursing care; rehabilitative therapies; dental and podiatry care; pharmacy; Medicare/Medicaid-approved; personal care; medication administration; emergency response system; maintenance; transportation; 3 daily meals; housekeeping and laundry services; activities; horticulture area and programs; screened decks; gardens; barber/beauty shop.

AL Daily: $80–$140. NH Daily: $150–$160.

Methodist Country House, CCAC, JCAHO

4830 Kennett Pike
Wilmington, DE 19807

Ph: (302) 571-9662

IND: Yes. HCC: Yes

Age 60+; spouse may be younger. Nonprofit; Peninsula United Methodist Homes, Inc.; affiliated with the Peninsula Delaware Conference of the United Methodist Church. Studios, apartments, and private and semiprivate rooms. 24-hour nursing care; short-term care; personal care; medication; security; emergency response system; maintenance; transportation; up to 3 daily meals; housekeeping and laundry service; chapel services; walking and biking paths; lounge; game room; woodworking shop; gardens; gift shop; postal and banking services; conference room; barber/beauty shop.

IND ENT: (Traditional return of entry fee, less 2% per month, within first 50 mos., or death), $39,000–$181,000; (Refundable return of the entry fee upon withdrawal or death within 12 mos., less 4% per mo., after this time, estate guaranteed return of half the entry fee), $53,000–$256,000. 2nd person, $13,000. IND MO: $1,900–$3,600. 2nd person, $725. HCC: Mo. fee includes short- and long-term care in the health care center. Routine medical care not covered by Medicare or supplementary insurance is covered by monthly fee.

Millcroft

255 Possum Park Rd.
Newark, DE 19711

Ph: (302) 366-0160
Fax: (302) 366-7634

IND: 62. AL: 26. HCC: 110

For-profit; nondenominational; affiliated with Marriott Senior Living Communities. Apartments, and private and semiprivate rooms. Skilled nursing care; rehabilitative services; physical, occupational, and speech therapies; personal care; medication administration; Medicare-approved; security; emergency response system; maintenance; transportation; up to 3 daily meals; housekeeping and laundry services; fitness center; library; arts and crafts room; educational, social, and recreational activities; lounge; barber/beauty shop.

IND: $2,100–$3,000; 2nd person, $575. AL Daily: $105–$125. HCC Daily: $135–$155.

South

Capitol HealthCare Services Nursing and Rehabilitation

1225 Walker Rd.
Dover, DE 19904

Ph: (302) 734-1199
Fax: (302) 734-5845

SNF: 90. ALZ/MEM IMP: 30. HSP: Yes

Private and semiprivate rooms. Physical, occupational, speech respiratory, restorative nursing, and recreational therapies; all levels of nursing care; IV therapy; wound and head injury care; pain management; Alzheimer's program; Medicare/Medicaid-approved; 3 daily meals; housekeeping and laundry services; activities program.

ICF Daily: $110 and $130. SNF Daily: $170. ALZ/MEM IMP Daily: $115 and $135.

Harrison House of Georgetown

110 W. North St.
Georgetown, DE 19947

Ph: (302) 856-4574

SNF: 57

Privately owned. Private and semiprivate rooms with adjoining baths. Intermediate nursing care; 24-hour skilled nursing care; recreational therapy; personal care; Medicare/Medicaid-approved; Veterans Administration Programs; special diets; 3 daily meals and snacks; housekeeping and laundry services; religious services; social events; crafts; games; barber/beauty.

SNF Daily: $115–$130.

Lewes Convalescent Center, JCAHO

440 Market St.
Lewes, DE 19958

Ph: (302) 645-6606

NH: Yes. RSP: Yes

Transitional care affiliated with Beebe Medical Center; nondenominational. Short-term, rehabilitative care; physical, occupational, and speech therapies; home health care; social services; physician services; personal care; medication administration; Medicare/Medicaid-approved; 3 daily meals; activities director; family and resident council meetings; religious programs; barber/beauty shop.

Daily: Semiprivate, $115; private, $125.

Silver Lake Center, JCAHO, AHCA, DHCFA

1080 Silver Lake Blvd.
Dover, DE 19904

Ph: (302) 734-5990
Fax: (302) 734-8008

NH: Yes

For-profit; nondenominational; Genesis ElderCare Network. Private and semiprivate rooms. 24-hour nursing care (skilled and intermediate); medical director; short- and long-term care; physical, occupational, and speech therapies; lab and X-ray services; wound care; IV therapy; oxygen therapy; respiration therapy; individual care plans; Medicare/Medicaid-approved; security; emergency response system; maintenance; transportation; up to 3 daily meals; housekeeping and laundry services; religious services; exercise program; mail and newspaper delivery; planned activities; off-site activities; barber/beauty shop.

NH Daily: Semiprivate, $120 and $130; private, $135 and $145.

Stone Gates Retirement Community

4031 Kennett Pike
Greenville, DE 19807

Ph: (302) 658-6200
Fax: 302: 658-1510

IND: 162. HCC: 39

Condominium community. Cottages, apartments, and private and semiprivate rooms. 24-hour skilled nursing care; long- and short-term care; physical therapy; medication administration; security; emergency response system; maintenance; transportation; up to 3 daily meals; housekeeping and laundry services; social directors; planned activities; lectures; concerts; barber/beauty shop.

DEP: (ref. within 30 days) $1,100. CONDO: $96,000–$363,000. MO: Single, $1,900–$2,900; double, $2,700–$3,500. HCC: $150–$190.

Residents are entitled to 60 free days at HCC. Permanent HCC residents can opt to have their condo bought back.

Westminster Village, Dover, CCAC

1175 McKee Rd.
Dover, DE 19904

Ph: (302) 674-8030
Fax: (302) 674-8656

IND: 121. AL: 59. ALZ: 17. SNF: 110

Nonprofit, nondenominational; Presbyterian Homes, Inc. Apartments, cottages, private and semiprivate rooms. Rehabilitative services; respite care; hospice care; short- and long-term nursing care; physical, occupational, and speech therapies; 24-hour skilled nursing care; post-therapy care providing counseling for patients and family; social services; personal care; medication administration; Medicare/Medicaid-approved; security; emergency response system; maintenance; transportation; nutrition counseling; up to 3 daily meals (IND includes 1 meal/day in mo. fee); chaplain services; housekeeping and laundry services; lounges; recreation center; crafts; library; flower and vegetable gardens; residents council; recreational and social activities; barber/beauty shop.

IND: Preliminary Application and Financial form. DEP: (ref.) $1,100. ENT Plan I: (Accommodation and communities fees reduced by 2% per mo. for 50 mos., after which no refund.) ENT Plan II: (Accommodation fee reduced 2% per mo. for 12 mo., then 1% per mo. for 6 mo. after which ref. is at 70% of orig. fee. Community fee reduced by 2% per mo. until completed.) IND ACC: $47,500–$190,000. IND COM: $6,600/person. IND MO: $1,000–$1,900. AL Daily: About $80–$170. HCC Daily: Private, $135; semi-private, $115–$125; Alzheimer's Unit, $120.

Southwest

LifeCare at Lofland Park

715 King St.
Seaford, DE 19973

Ph: (302) 628-3000

SNF: 117

Affiliate of Nanticoke Memorial Hospital. Private and semiprivate rooms. Skilled nursing care; specialty subacute care; audiology services; dental and podiatry care; pharmacy services; lab; physical, occupational, speech, and respiratory therapies; pain management; hospice; respite care; social services; Medicare/Medicaid-approved; security; emergency response system; maintenance; transportation; up to 3 daily meals; housekeeping and laundry services; activities; walking trails.

SNF Daily: $120 and $130. Specialized Care Unit Daily: $380. RSP Daily: $130.

Methodist Manor House, CCAC

1001 Middleford Rd.
Seaford, DE 19973

Ph: (302) 629-4593
Fax: (302) 629-6520

http://www.pumh.org

IND: Yes. HCC: Yes. ALZ/MEM IMP: Yes

Age 60+; spouse may be younger. Nonprofit; nondenominational; Peninsula United Methodist Homes; affiliated with Peninsula-Delaware Conference of the United Methodist Church. Studios, apartments, cottages, and rooms. Long- and short-term care; emergency medical assistance; annual physical exam; pharmacy; wellness center; personal care; medication administration; security; emergency response system; maintenance, transportation; up to 3 daily meals; housekeeping and laundry services; priority admission to health center; indoor swimming; exercise room; walking paths; gardening; boardwalk; putting green; gift shop; library; woodworking shop; arts and crafts; resident council and committees.

IND ENT: (Traditional partial ref. within the first 50 mos.), $38,500–$157,000; (50% refund of the original fee upon withdrawal or death): $54,000–$218,000. 2nd person, $6,000. IND MO: $1,100–$2,000. MO Meal Plan: Breakfast, $70; lunch, $120; dinner, $200. HCC Daily: Respite/Personal Care private room: $95. Semiprivate, $125 and $135; private, $140. Alzheimer's Care, $150. IND residents get discount of $10 per day for health center stay, up to a $5,000 discount.

Seaford Center, JCAHO

1100 Norman Eskridge Hwy.
Seaford, DE 19973

Ph: (302) 629-3575

IND: 16. NH: 124

Age 55+. For-profit; nondenominational. Apartments with private baths, suites, and private and semiprivate rooms. 24-hour skilled and intermediate nursing care; medical director; dental and podiatry services; physical, speech, and respiratory therapies; Medicare/Medicaid-approved; security; emergency response system; maintenance; transportation; 3 daily meals; housekeeping and laundry services; exercise program; banking and postal services; religious services; daily activities; off-site activities; barber/beauty salon.

Monthly rental; contact facility for fees.

Assisted Living and Residential Care Facilities

These facilities provide room and board for ambulatory and independent adults who need minimum support.

Types of Authorization

Licensing and / or Certification

Requires licensing by the Department of Health. Must provide long-term residential care, room, board, housekeeping, personal care, and supervision to five or more adults. Adult Homes, or any adult care facilities, are not licensed to provide any nursing or medical care.

Memberships

- Assisted Living Federation of America (ALFA) is a national nonprofit membership organization whose mission is to enhance the quality of life in assisted living facilities and promote the interests of the assisted living industry. ALFA, 10300 Eaton Place, Suite 400, Fairfax, VA 22030. Ph: (703) 691-8100. Fax: (703) 691-8106. *http: / / www.alfa.org*

North

Captain's Deck

7807 Governor Printz Blvd.
Claymont, DE 19703

Ph: (302) 798-3500 or (800) 432-6630
Fax: (302) 798-7662

IND: Yes. AL: Yes

A nondenominational facility. Apartments. 24-hour nursing staff; wellness center; personal care; medication administration; security; emergency response system; maintenance; transportation; up to 3 daily meals; housekeeping and laundry services; fitness room and exercise program; reading room and library; lounge; media room; on- and off-site activities; convenience store; ice cream parlor; barber/beauty shop.

IND MO: $2,100–$3,100; 2nd person, $550. AL Daily: $115; $85 for 2nd related person not needing AL.

Foulk Manor South

407 Foulk Rd.
Wilmington, DE 19803-3899

Ph: (302) 655-6249
Fax: (302) 655-5451.

AL: Yes. AL/MEM IMP: Yes. ICF: Yes

Owned and operated by Marriott; nondenominational. Private and semiprivate rooms. Nursing care; respite care; music therapy; reality orientation; podiatry services; physical, occupational, and speech therapies; personal care; medication administration; 3 daily meals; housekeeping and laundry services; social programs; exercise classes; arts and crafts; barber/beauty shop.

AL Daily: $90–$180. ICF Daily: $130–$160.

Ingleside Assisted Living

2210 Swiss Lane
Wilmington, DE 19810

Ph: (302) 475-9580

IND: Yes. AL: Yes

Age 62+. Nonprofit; Ingleside Homes, Inc. Private and semiprivate rooms. 24-hour health care; respite care; wellness program; home health care; personal care; medication administration; security; emergency response system; maintenance; transportation; 3 daily meals; resident cat; birds; housekeeping and laundry services; interdenominational religious services; intergenerational programs; banking services; crafts; flower and vegetable gardens; scheduled educational and musical activities; daily activities; walking paths; barber/beauty shop.

APP: (no ref.) $85. DEP: (ref.) Semiprivate, $1,200; private, $1,700. MO: Semiprivate room, $2,1000–$2,350; private room, $3,100–$3,500. RC Daily: Semiprivate, $85–$90; private, $115–$120. Some financial assistance available for eligible residents.

The Layton Home

300 E. Eighth St.
Wilmington, DE 19801

Ph: (302) 656-6413

AL: 108

Nondenominational; nonsectarian; Peninsula United Methodist Homes. Private and semiprivate rooms. 24-hour nursing care; physicians on call 24 hours; physical, occupational, speech, and recreational therapies; 3 daily meals; lounge; community room; movies; gift shop; craft room; classes; barber/beauty shop.

SNF Daily: $130 and $140.

The Lorelton

2200 W. Fourth St.
Wilmington, DE 19805

Ph: (302) 573-3580
Fax: (302) 573-3590

IND: Yes. AL: Yes

Apartments and shared suites. 24-hour nursing supervision; personal care; medication administration; security; emergency response system; maintenance; transportation; up to 3 daily meals (1 meal with IND mo. fee); housekeeping and laundry services; exercise programs; speakers and entertainment; wellness programs; trips; activities.

IND ENT: (min. ref. ent. deposit) $2,200; (max. ref. ent. deposit) $66,000–$149,000. IND MO: $1,400–$3,100; 2nd person $470. AL Daily: Deluxe suite, $85; Apt., $95–$112. 2nd person $10/day. AL DEP: (ref.) $2,200. RC Daily: $110. Includes 3 meals per day.

Montchanin at Carillon Crossing

1519 Rockland Rd.
Wilmington, DE 19803

AL: 92. ALZ/MEM IMP: Yes

Age 65+. Senior Life Choice Community; privately owned. Private apartment living. 24-hour licensed caregivers; emergency call system; home health care; physical, occupational, speech therapies; physician services; companion services; personal care; medication administration; transportation; 3 daily meals plus snacks; housekeeping and laundry services; wellness program; activities; barber/beauty shop.

AL Daily: $135, $150, and $165; 2nd person, $550/mo. (independent); $1,100/mo. (assistance).

South Park Terrace

1605 N. Broom St.
Wilmington, DE 19806

Ph: (302) 655-2909
Fax: (302) 655-2907

AL: 54. ADC: Yes

For-profit; nondenominational. Private rooms. Nursing care; psychological consultations; podiatry and dental services; therapies; pharmacy services; respite care; personal care; medication administration; security; emergency response system; maintenance; transportation; up to 3 daily meals; housekeeping and laundry services; intergenerational program; social and recreational activities.

APP: $330. DEP: (ref.) daily rate + 14 days. AL MO: $1,800–$3,750.

Independent Living

Independent housing (primarily rentals) for seniors that may offer security features, meal service, and activities.

North

B'nai B'rith House

8000 Society Drive
Claymont, DE 19703

Ph: (302) 798-6846

IND: 208

Age 62+ or physically mobility handicapped. Nonprofit; nondenominational. One-bedroom apartments. Security; emergency response system; maintenance; transportation; noon meal; laundry services; library; resident organizations; off-site activities; commu-

nity room; coffee room; nearby shopping, banks, restaurants, and public transportation; barber/beauty shop.

IND MO: 30% of adjusted monthly income. HUD residence.

South

Luther Towers of Dover

430 Kings Highway
Dover, DE 19901

Ph: (302) 674-1408

IND: 258 apt.; 33 efficiencies.

Age 62+; must be on fixed limited income. Owned and operated by Lutheran Senior Services of Dover, Inc. All home maintenance; all utilities; 24-hour security; fitness room; beauty parlor; coin-operated laundries; library; transportation to all medical appointments.

Rents are subsidized by the Delaware State Housing Authority or HUD.

Adult/Resort Communities

Communities for active adults (not all are age-restricted; primarily ownership).

Kings Creek Country Club

1 Kings Creek Circle
Rehoboth Beach, DE 19971

Ph: (302) 227-7172
Fax: (302) 227-7015

http://www.mygolf.com/golf/courses/2296

Individual homes, homesites. Golf course; tennis; swimming pool; clubhouse; fitness center; clubs.

PURCHASE: Homes, $385,000–$770,000.

Magnolia Meadows

PO Box 1680
Millsboro, DE 19966

Ph: (800) 270-1619 or (302) 934-1082

Duplexes. Private picnic area; walking path; nearby river, ocean beach, dining, shopping, and senior center.

PURCHASE: Homes, from $77,000.

Pot-Nets Communities

RD 1, Box 291
Long Neck, DE 19966

Ph: (800) 647-7500 or (302) 945-4032

http://www.potnets.com

Manufactured homes. Six separate communities. Overall amenities include: marinas, swimming pools; tennis; basketball; volleyball; shuffleboard; private beaches; dining.

PURCHASE: Homes, $53,000–$109,000; resale homes, $11,000–$136,000.

Florida

http://www.state.fl.us

General Information

Climate

Temperate in the north to subtropical in the south. Average winter temperature from 51° F in the north to 70° F in the south. Average summer temperature is in the low 80s.

Cost of Living

Ranks 33rd in the nation.

Taxes

General: Tax Information and Assistance, (800) 352-3671. TDD, (800) 367-8331.

State/Local as % of Income: About 9.7%.

Property Tax Reduction: $25,000 Homestead Exemption for any resident. Owners 65 or older may defer that portion of the tax that exceeds 3% of the yearly household income. Property taxes also deferred entirely for those 65 through 69 whose household income is less than $10,000. Taxes deferred for those 70 or older whose yearly household income is less than $12,000.

Sales: 6%.

Prescription Exemptions: Prescription drugs are exempt from sales tax.

Transportation, Travel, and Tourism

General

Florida Division of Tourism, (904) 487-1462.

Major Airports

- Jacksonville Int'l, (904) 741-2000.
- Daytona Beach Int'l, (904) 248-8030.
- Orlando Int'l, (407) 825-2001.
- Tampa Int'l, (813) 870-8700.
- Southwest Fla. Int'l, (904) 768-1000.
- Palm Beach Int'l, (561) 471-7400.
- Fort Lauderdale/Hollywood Int'l, (954) 359-6100.
- Miami Int'l, (305) 876-7077.
- Key West Int'l, (305) 296-7223.

Railways

- Amtrak, (800) USA RAIL.

Bus Tours

- Greyhound Bus, (800) 231-2222.
- Parnell Worldwide Bus Charter, (800) 472-7125.

State Highways

- Florida's Turnpike, (800) 749-7453.
- Interstate 10 runs east-west.
- Interstates 75 and 95 run north-south.

Theater and Music

Central West

- Clearwater: Outdoor concerts, orchestra performances at Ruth Eckerd Hall, Jazz Holiday and festivals. Clearwater Chamber of Commerce, (888) 799-3199 or (727) 447-7600.
- Tampa: Tampa Bay Performing Arts Center. Tampa visitor information, (800) 44-TAMPA or (813) 223-2752.

Northeast

- Jacksonville: Riverwalk entertainment pavilion. Bradford County Chamber of Commerce, (904) 964-5378.

Southeast

- Ft. Lauderdale: Performance Arts Center. Ft. Lauderdale Convention and Visitors Bureau, (954) 765-4467.

- Miami Beach: Colony Theater, 1040 Lincoln Rd., Miami Beach, FL 33131, (305) 674-1040.

Museums, Crafts, Historical, Recreational

Central West

- Clearwater: Pinellas County Recreational Trail, Clearwater Marine Aquarium, Boatyard Village (1890s-period fishing village). Clearwater Chamber of Commerce, (888) 799-3199 or (727) 447- 7600.
- Tampa: Tampa visitor information, (800) 44-TAMPA or (813) 223-2752.

Southwest

- Fort Myers: Historical Museum, Lee County Nature Center and Planetarium, public golf courses, beaches. Lee Island Coast, (800) 533-4753, ext. 700, for free vacationer's guide.
- Sanibel Island: J. N. "Ding" Darling National Wildlife Refuge, Pine Island Sound. Sanibel Chamber of Commerce, (942) 472- 1080.

Southeast

- Historical Museum of Southern Florida, 101 W. Flagler St., Miami, FL 33130-1504, (305) 375-1492.
- Miami Museum of Science and Space Transit Planetarium, 3280 S. Miami Ave., Miami, FL 33129-2899, (305) 854-4247.
- Vizcaya Museum and Gardens (Italian Renaissance-style villa and formal gardens on more than 10 acres), 3251 S. Miami Ave., Miami, FL 33129-2897, (305) 250-9133.
- Oleta River State Recreation Area, 3400 NE 163rd St., Miami, FL 33160, (305) 919-1846.
- Miami Beach Convention Center, 1901 Convention Center Drive, Miami Beach, FL 33139, (305) 673-7311.

Central East

- Cape Canaveral: Kennedy Space Center, (407) 452-2121; U.S. Astronaut Hall of Fame, (407) 269-6100
- Merritt Island National Wildlife Refuge, Valiant Air Command (flying museum), Merritt Island, (321) 268-1941.
- Memorial Space Science Center and Planetarium, 1519 Clearlake Rd., Coco, FL 32922, (407) 634-3732.

Northwest

- Panama City: award-winning golf courses, Zoo World Zoological and Botanical Park, St. Andrews State Recreational Area beaches. (800) PC-BEACH.
- Tallahassee: Museum of Florida History, State Capitol. Chamber of Commerce, (850) 224-0152.
- Pensacola: Historic District (museums, shops, restored homes, galleries), beaches, Civil War Fort Pickens, Old Pensacola Lighthouse. Chamber of Commerce, (850) 438-4081.

Organizations

Advocacy Groups

- Agency for Health Care Administration, (904) 414-7209.
- Elder Helpline, (800) 963-5337.
- Legal Hotline for Older Floridians, (305) 576-5997; (800) 252-5997; (outside FL).
- Medicaid Choice Counseling hotline, (888) 367-6554.
- Department of Insurance, (800) 342-2762.

Volunteer Programs

- Serving Health Insurance Needs of Elders Program (SHINE). Volunteers provide information on Medicare, Medicaid, long-term care insurance, managed care programs, and related health insurance issues to needy individuals, (904) 414-2060.
- Office of Volunteer Community Services, 4040 Esplanade Way, Suite

260 B, Tallahassee, FL 32399-7000, (904) 414-2060.

Housing

Long-Term Care Facilities

*In the state of Florida, these facilities are called **Continuing Care/Long Term Care/Nursing Home Facilities**.*

These facilities provide residential living and/or various levels of nursing and medical services to seniors for an extended period of time.

Types of Authorization

Licensing and / or Certification

The Agency for Health Care Administration regulates the quality of care and medical facilities of continuing care and nursing homes. Financial security of continuing care facilities is regulated by the Department of Insurance. These retirement facilities furnish shelter, food, and health care in return for an entrance fee and monthly fees.

Memberships:

- American Association of Homes and Services for the Aging (AAHSA) represents not-for-profit organizations committed to providing high-quality health care, housing, and services to the elderly. AAHSA, 901 E St. NW, Suite 500, Washington, DC 20004-2011. Ph: (202) 783-2242. Fax: (202) 783-2285. *http: / / www.aahsa.org*
- Florida Association of Homes for the Aging (FAHA) is an AAHSA Affiliated State Association. FAHA, 1812 Riggins Rd., Tallahassee, FL 32308-4885, Ph: (850) 671-3700. Fax: (850) 671-3790. *http: / / www.faha.org*

Accreditations:

- Continuing Care Accreditation Commission (CCAC) accredits facilities that offer seniors a contract or contracts that provide residential living and health care services for the remainder of the person's lifetime and meet CCAC's accreditation standards.
- Joint Commission on the Accreditation of Healthcare Organizations (JCAHO) is an independent, not-for-profit organization, and the nation's oldest and largest standards-setting and health care accrediting institution.
- American Society on Aging (ASA).
- Association of Retirement Resorts International (ARRI).

Central West

Calusa Harbour

2525 E. First St.
Fort Myers, FL 33901

Ph: (941) 332-3333

IND: 223. AL: 147. HCC: 100

For-profit; nondenominational; a Marriott Living Community. Apartments, studios, and private and semiprivate rooms. Skilled nursing care; rehabilitative services; restorative long-term care; physical, occupational, and speech therapies; consultative services; respiratory therapy; counseling and social services; pharmacy and lab services; Medicare/Medicaid-approved; personal care; medication administration; security; emergency response system; maintenance; transportation; up to 3 daily meals (IND includes 1 daily meal); housekeeping and laundry services; pool; cultural and recreational activities; banking services; country store; barber/beauty shop.

PROC: $550. IND MO: $1,200–$3,400. AL MO: $1,600–$3,100. HCC Daily: $125–$185.

The Fountains at Boca Ciega Bay

1255 Pasadena Ave. South
St. Petersburg, FL 33707

Ph: (727) 347-2169
Fax: (727) 343-3023

http://www.thefountains.com/boca

IND: 404. AL: 80. SNF: 120. ALZ/MEM IMP: Yes. ADC: Yes

Age 65+. For-profit; nondenominational facility. Apartments and private and semiprivate rooms. 24-hour skilled nursing care; rehabilitative services and therapies; wellness center; Medicare/Medicaid-approved; home health care; personal care; medication administration; security; emergency response system; maintenance; transportation; up to 3 daily meals; pets allowed; housekeeping and laundry services; chapel; exercise room; pool; fishing pier; banking services; educational; cultural, and social activities; computer center; library; intergenerational program; craft workshops; clubs and organizations; country store; off-site excursions; gardens and nature trails; barber/beauty shop.

DEP: $550. IND MO: $1,200. AL MO: $1,850. SNF Daily: $125.

The Fountains at Lake Pointe Woods, ASA

7979 S. Tamiami Trail
Sarasota, FL 34231

Ph: (941) 923-4944
Fax: (941) 922-9374

http://www.thefountains.com/lake

IND: 184. AL: 95. HCC: 119

Age 62+. For-profit; nondenominational. Apartments, suites, studios, and private and semiprivate rooms. Nursing care; rehabilitative therapies; podiatry care; health and wellness services; Medicare/Medicaid-approved; personal care; medication administration; security; emergency response system; maintenance; transportation; up to 3 daily meals; some pets allowed; housekeeping and laundry services; fitness center; pool; activities.

IND ENT: $99,000–$330,000. IND MO: $1,500–$3,000. AL MO: $2,500–$4,100. HCC Daily: $140–$185.

Palm Shores

830 North Shore Drive, NE
St. Petersburg, FL 33701

Ph: (727) 894-2102 or 894-2819
Fax: (727) 822-1234

IND: Yes. AL: Yes. SNF: 42

Owned by American Baptist Homes of the Midwest; nonprofit; nondenominational. Apartments and private and semiprivate rooms. Skilled nursing care; physical, occupational, and speech therapies; clinic and wellness program; security; emergency response system and daily check-in; maintenance; transportation; up to 3 daily meals; tray service when needed; housekeeping and laundry services; exercise classes; fitness center; libraries; bank services; planned daily activities; common lounges; barber/beauty salon.

IND ENT: (% ref.), $32,000–$83,000; 2nd person, $3,850. IND MO: $1,200–$2,600; 2nd person, $310. (Rental only), $1,450–$3,300; 2nd person, $330. AL Daily: $75 and $125. SNF Daily: Semiprivate, $110; private, $125.

Northwest

Westminster Oaks, CCAC

4449 Meandering Way
Tallahassee, FL 32308

Ph: (850) 878-1136
Fax: (850) 942-4924

IND: Yes. AL: Yes. ALZ/MEM IMP: Yes. SNF: 120

Non-profit; church-affiliated; member of Presbyterian Retirement Communities. Apartments, private and semi-private rooms. Long-term skilled nursing care; short-term rehabilitative care; 24-hour nursing care; social workers; personal care; medication monitoring; well-

ness center; security; emergency response system; maintenance; transportation; up to 3 daily meals; housekeeping and laundry services; clergy service; exercise programs; clinic; bank services; theater/recreation room; arts and crafts; swimming pool; clubhouse; library; computer room; woodworking shop; daily activities; country store.

DEP: (ref.), $1,100/person. IND ENT: (ref.), $44,000–$115,500. IND MO: $975–$1,350. AL ENT: $38,500 and $57,500; 2nd person, $13,500. AL MO: $1,900–$3,200. ALZ/MEM IMP ENT: $38,500; MO: $2,200. SNF Daily: $95–$135.

Northeast

Vicar's Landing

1000 Vicar's Landing Way
Ponte Vedra Beach, FL 32082

Ph: (904) 285-1055
Fax: (904) 285-1384

IND: 226. AL: 38. HCC: 60

Nonprofit; nondenominational facility. Apartments and private and semiprivate rooms. 24-hour nursing care; medical/physician services; therapies; dental and podiatry services; pharmacy; wellness clinic; regular blood pressure and hearing checks; Medicare-approved; personal care; medication administration; security; emergency response system; maintenance; transportation; up to 3 daily meals; tray service when needed; housekeeping and laundry services; exercise room and program; chapel; banking, postal, and travel services; pool; lounge; arts and crafts room; off-site activities; sandwich shop; gift shop; barber/beauty shop.

APPL: $385. DEP: $2,750. IND ENT: (75% ref.), $163,000–$482,000. IND MO: $1,650–$3,200. AL ENT: $55,000. AL MO: $3,200. HCC Daily: $145.

Southwest

Shell Point Retirement Community, CCAC, ARRI

15000 Shell Point Blvd.
Fort Myers, FL 33908

Ph: (941) 466-1131
Fax: (941) 454-2217

http://www.shellpoint.org

IND: 750. AL: 120. HCC: 180 .ALZ/MEM IMP: 64

Age 65+. Nonprofit; nondenominational; affiliated with the Christian and Missionary Alliance. Apartments and private and semiprivate rooms. Nursing care; medical services; rehabilitative therapies; dental and podiatry services; pharmacy services; Medicare-approved; personal care; medication administration; security; emergency response system; maintenance; transportation; up to 3 daily meals; housekeeping and laundry services; exercise program; religious services; library with computers; banking services; social and recreational activities; educational and cultural programs; art studio; woodworking shop; photography studio with darkroom; pottery; billiards; convenience store; deli; travel agency; putting green; tennis courts; orchid house; walking paths; barber/beauty shop.

IND ENT: $62,000–$387,000. IND MO: $850–$3,700. AL ENT: $81,000–$136,000. AL MO: $2,400–$4,900. HCC Daily: $135–$350.

Central

Orlando Lutheran Towers

300 E. Church St.
Orlando FL 32801

Ph: (407) 425-1033
Fax: (407) 839-5033

http://www.faha.org/community/lutherantowers.htm

IND: 202. AL: 62. HCC: 126. ALZ/MEM IMP: 42

Age 62+. Nonprofit; nondenominational; Lutheran church affiliation. Apartments and private and semiprivate rooms. Nursing care; medical services; physical, occupational, and speech therapies; podiatry services; pharmacy; home health care; personal care; medication administration; security; emergency response system; maintenance; transportation; up to 3 daily meals; housekeeping and laundry services; exercise programs; church; social and recreational activities.

DEP: 10% of ENT fees. IND ENT: From $40,000. IND MO: $1,200. AL ENT: From $26,000.

Southeast

Abbey Delray

Delray Beach, FL 33445

Ph: (561) 278-3249 or (800) 936-7397
Fax: (561) 278-8956

IND: 358. AL: Yes. HCC: 100

Age 62+. Nonprofit; nondenominational; owned by Life Care Retirement communities; managed by Life Care Services Corporation. Villas, apartments, and private and semiprivate rooms. Nursing care; blood pressure clinic; podiatry services; pharmacy; Medicare/Medicaid-approved; personal care; medication administration; security; emergency response system; maintenance; transportation; up to 3 daily meals; housekeeping and laundry services; exercise programs; interdenominational church services; banking services; swimming pool; social, cultural, and recreational activities; activities director; recreation rooms; woodworking shop; arts and craft studio; clubs; gift shop; assembly hall; billiards room; barber/beauty shop.

IND ENT: $70,000–$177,000. IND MO: $1,000–$1,650; 2nd person, $725.

REQ: Medicare parts A & B, and supplemental insurance.

Bishop Gray Inn

4445 Pine Forest Drive
Lake Worth, FL 33463

Ph: (561) 965-5954
Fax: (561) 433-9161

IND: 66. AL: Yes. HCC: 60

Nonprofit; nondenominational; owned by the Episcopal Church; managed by Life Care Services. Apartments and private and semiprivate rooms. Skilled nursing care; long- and short-term care; personal care; medication administration; security; emergency response system; maintenance; transportation; up to 3 daily meals (tray service when necessary); housekeeping and laundry services; exercise programs; chapel; cultural and social activities; volunteer opportunities; lounges; library; gift shop; walking paths; barber/beauty shop.

DEP: 1st mo. rent. IND MO: $1,500–$2,300; 2nd person, $450. HCC Daily: $150.

Covenant Village of Florida, CCAC

9201 W. Broward Blvd.
Plantation, FL 33324-2452

Ph: (954) 472-2860 or 472-3007

IND: Yes. AL: Yes. HCC: Yes

Age 62+. Nondenominational (Christian faith oriented); affiliated with the Evangelical Covenant Church. Studios, apartments, and private and semiprivate rooms. Short- and long-term nursing care; skilled nursing care; personal health monitoring; blood pressure checks; personal care; medication administration; security; emergency response system; maintenance; transportation; up to 3 daily meals; housekeeping and laundry services; exercise room; fitness classes; religious services; lounges;

library; game and craft room; hike and bike paths; cultural and social activities; gardening; barber/beauty shop.

IND ENT: $52,000–93,000; 2nd person, $6,900 and $9,300. IND MO: $1,000–1,400; 2nd person, $385.

East Ridge

19301 SW 87th Ave.
Miami, FL 33157

Ph: (305) 256-3564 or (800) 605-7778
Fax: (305) 256-1911

IND: 246. AL: 51. HCC: 60

Age 62+. Nonprofit; nondenominational facility. Apartments, villas, and private and semiprivate rooms. 24-hour skilled nursing care; short- and long-term care; personal; medication administration; home health care; security; emergency response system; maintenance; transportation; up to 3 daily meals; housekeeping and laundry services; exercise programs; inter-denominational chapel; appliance repair; yoga; swimming pool; bowling; bicycling; line dancing; clubs; off-site activities; social and recreational activities; arts and crafts; putting green; barber/beauty shop.

IND ENT: (traditional plan), $60,000–$125,000; 2nd person, $5,300; (founder's fee plan), $104,000–$219,000; 2nd person, $9,300. IND MO: $1,350–$2,200; 2nd person, $700.

The Hebrew Homes

North Miami Beach Hebrew Home

1800 NE 168th St.
North Miami Beach, FL 33162

Ph: (305) 947-3445
Fax: (305) 949-1970

South Miami Beach Hebrew Home

320 Collins Ave.
Miami Beach, FL 33139

Ph: (305) 672-6464
Fax: (305) 672-6423

CONG: Yes. SNF: Yes. NH: Yes. ALZ/MEM IMP: Yes

Nonprofit; nondenominational; nonsectarian. Private and semiprivate rooms. 24-hour nursing care; physical, occupational, speech, and respiratory therapies; IV therapy; respite care; hospice care; personal care; medication administration; Medicare/Medicaid-approved; security; emergency response system; maintenance; transportation; 3 daily (kosher) meals plus snacks; housekeeping and laundry services; daily activities; off- site excursions.

AL MO: (semiprivate), $1,100; (private), $2,000. NH Daily: $210. SNF Daily: $110.

John Knox Village, CCAC

651 S.W. 6th St.
Pompano Beach, FL 33060

Ph: 783-4040 or (800) 998-5669
Fax: (954) 783-4044

IND: 630. AL: 62. HCC: 177. ALZ/MEM IMP: Yes

Nonprofit; nondenominational facility. Low-, mid-, and high-rise apartments, cottage-style villas, and private and semiprivate rooms. 24-hour nursing care; visiting nurses; skilled and custodial nursing care; blood pressure and weight monitoring; wound care; recreation therapy; restorative nursing; physician services; home health care services; daily reassurance check; personal care; medication administration; security; emergency response system; maintenance; transportation; up to 3 daily meals; housekeeping and laundry services; exercise programs; swimming pool; pool tables; social, cultural, and recreational activities; bank and notary services; library areas; on-site rare bird habitat; botanical gardens; lakes; workshop; arts and crafts room; auditorium; garden plots; gift shop; barber/barber shop.

IND ENT: $64,000–$151,800. IND MO: $975–$1,250; 2nd person, $450–$530.

Oak Harbor

4755 S. Harbor Drive
Vero Beach, FL 32967

Ph: (561) 562-3808 or (800) 801-7770
Fax: (561) 978-4399

http://www.oakharborfl.com

IND: Yes. AL: Yes. HCC: Yes

Nondenominational; for profit; owned by Legend Properties; managed by Life Care Services. Villas, cottages, condos, and private and semiprivate rooms. 24-hour skilled nursing care; long- and short-term care; visiting nurse service; personal care; medication administration; security; emergency response system; maintenance; transportation; up to 3 daily meals; housekeeping and laundry services; health club; clubhouse; activities; crafts and hobby rooms; library with computers and Internet connection; lounges; walking and biking paths; golf course; tennis; wildlife preserve and estuary; pool.

PURCHASE: $275,000–479,000+. Country Club: (with service agreement), single, $1,900; double, $2,500. ASSOC. MO: $475–$650. HCC services are separate.

St. Andrews Estates North, CCAC

6152 N. Verde Trail
Boca Raton, FL 33433-2430

Ph: (561) 487-4728 or (800) 850-2287
Fax: (561) 883-3823

http://www.acts-retirement.org

IND: Yes. AL: Yes. HCC: Yes

Nonprofit; nondenominational; church-affiliated; an ACTS Retirement-Life Community. Apartments, studios, and private and semiprivate rooms. On-site medical center; skilled nursing care; 24-hour nursing care; personalized health care services; regular doctor's hours; wellness program; personal care; medication administration; security; emergency response system; maintenance; transportation; up to 3 daily meals; small pets allowed; housekeeping and laundry services; exercise room and programs; pool; chaplain; banking services library; caf; arts and crafts; woodworking shop; social, recreational, and cultural activities; shuffleboard courts; walking paths; auditorium; stocked fishing lake; barber/beauty shop.

IND ENT: (traditional), $65,000–$181,000; (50% ref.), $98,000–$286,000. IND MO: (traditional), $1,650–$2,500; (50% ref.), $1,300–$2,800.

Assisted Living and Residential Care Facilities

In the state of Florida, these facilities are called ***Assisted Living/Adult Living and Residential Care Facilities****.*

These facilities provide room and board for ambulatory and independent adults who need minimum support.

Types of Authorization

Licensing and/or Certification

Requires compliance of regulations set by the Division of Health Quality Assurance. An assisted living facility must provide housing, meals, and one or more personal services for an extended period of time. Congregate living provides extended assisted living services.

Memberships:

- Assisted Living Federation of America (ALFA) is a national nonprofit membership organization whose mission is to enhance the quality of life in assisted living facilities and promote the interests of the assisted living industry. ALFA, 10300 Eaton Place, Suite 400, Fairfax, VA 22030. Ph: (703) 691-8100. Fax: (703) 691-8106. *http://www.alfa.org*
- Florida Assisted Living Association (FALA) is a state affiliate of ALFA. FALA, PO Box 7, Tallahassee, FL 32302. Ph: (850) 425-2699. Fax: (850) 224-2336. *http://www.fala.com*

South

Baywinds Retirement Center

12221 W. Dixie Highway
North Miami, FL 33161

Ph: (305) 893-2634
Fax: (305) 893-0930

AL: Yes

Nondenominational. Private and semiprivate rooms. 24-hour nursing supervision; respite care; personal care; medication administration; security; 3 daily meals; housekeeping and laundry services; exercise classes; arts and crafts; library; scheduled daily activities; common areas; hair care.

AL MO: Semiprivate room and bath, $1050; private room and shared bath, $1,800; private room and bath, $2,000.

Brighton Gardens

6341 Via de Sonrisa del Sur
Boca Raton, FL 33433

Ph: (561) 392-2772
Fax: (561) 392-5154

AL: Yes. ALZ/MEM IMP: Yes

A Marriott Senior Living facility; nondenominational; nonsectarian. Suites and apartments. Licensed nurse on staff; personal care; medication administration; security; emergency response system; maintenance; transportation; 3 daily meals; housekeeping and laundry services; social, cultural, and educational programs; beauty/barber shop.

AL MO: $2,800–$3,900.

Carlyle on the Bay

1900 N. Bayshore Drive
Miami, FL 33132

Ph: (305) 371-3035

IND: Yes. AL: Yes

For-profit; nondenominational; owned and managed by Congregate Associates, Ltd. Apartments and private and semiprivate rooms. Wellness clinic; nurse on duty 24 hours; private nurse services; personal care; medication administration; security; emergency response system; maintenance; transportation; up to 3 daily meals; housekeeping and laundry services; exercise classes; nondenominational chapel; library; banking services; social and recreational activities; educational programs; media center; arts and crafts; board and card games; barber/beauty shop.

IND MO: $1,350–$2,100; 2nd person, $550. AL MO: $900–$2,750.

Hidden Palms

2675 N. Andrews Ave.
Fort Lauderdale, FL 33311

Ph: (954) 563-2288
Fax: (954) 564-4860

AL: Yes

Nondenominational; Extendicare facility. Private and semiprivate suites. Wellness program; personal care; medication administration; security; emergency response system; maintenance; transportation; up to 3 daily meals; housekeeping and laundry services; social and recreational activities; arts and crafts; media room; barber/beauty shop services.

AL MO: Semiprivate, $1,750; private, $2,350.

Towers Retirement Home

824 SE 2nd St.
Fort Lauderdale, FL 33301

Ph: (954) 463-4973
Fax: (954) 463-7025

AL: 80

For-profit; nondenominational; family owned and operated. Private rooms. Some nursing care; physical therapy; personal care; medication administration; security; emergency response system; maintenance; transportation; up to 3 daily meals; housekeeping and laundry services; activities.

DEP: 1 mo. rent. AL MO: $825–$2,000.

Central

Bethesda Baptist Retirement Home

2800 Fordham Rd. NE
Palm Bay, FL 32905

Ph: (407) 723-3288

AL: 72. RSP: Yes

Church related; nondenominational. Apartments and private rooms. 24-hour personal care; medication administration; security; emergency response system; maintenance; transportation; 3 daily meals; small pets allowed; housekeeping and laundry services; planned daily activities; beauty/barber shop.

AL ENT: (no ref.), $550. AL MO: $1,250–$1,850. RSP ADM: $220. RSP Daily: $50.

Oak Meadow

112980 SW Hwy. 484
Dunnellon, FL 34432

Ph: (352) 465-0300

IND: Yes. AL: Yes. RSP: Yes. ADC: Yes

Nondenominational. Private and semiprivate rooms. Personal care; medication administration; maintenance; transportation; up to 3 daily meals; housekeeping and laundry services; activities program; resident council; hair care.

IND MO: Semiprivate, $1,100; private, $1,650. AL MO: Semiprivate, $1,200; private, $1,800; extra care, $1,350. ADC Daily: $35. RSP Daily: $50.

Spring Haven

1225 Havendale Blvd., NW
Winter Haven, FL 33881

Ph: (941) 293-0072
Fax: (941) 294-4935

IND: Yes. AL/PC: Yes. ALZ/MEM IMP: Yes

Family-owned; nondenominational. Apartments and rooms. 24-hour supervision; nurse on staff; personal care; medication administration; wellness program; security; emergency response system; maintenance; transportation; up to 3 daily meals; housekeeping and laundry services; exercise programs; swimming pool; chapel; daily activities; educational program; off-site excursions; arts and crafts; ice cream parlor; country store; library; common lounge; beauty/barber salon.

IND MO: $1,150–$1,850; 2nd person, $440. AL/PC MO: $1,700–$2,500. ALZ/MEM IMP MO: $1,800–$2,800. RSP Daily: $80; $90; $100.

West

Bayview Gardens

2855 Gulf to Bay Blvd.
Clearwater, FL 33759

Ph: (727) 797-7400
Fax: (727) 726-7357

IND: Yes. AL/CONG: Yes

Affiliated with Morton Plant Mease Health Care; nondenominational. Apartments. Personal care; medication administration; on-site nursing personnel; visiting physician; clinic; security; emergency response system plus daily check-ins; maintenance; transportation; up to 3 daily meals; housekeeping and laundry services; library; social and cultural events; lounge; recreation room; activities.

IND MO: (basic), $875–$1,800; 2nd person, $300; (deluxe), $1,350–$2,500; 2nd person, $425. AL MO: (basic), $1,900; (4 additional services), $2,000; (5 additional services), $2,100; 2nd person, $525.

Lakeshore Villas

16002 Lakeshore Villa Drive
Tampa, FL 33613

Ph: (813) 968-5093

IND: Yes. AL: Yes. SNF: 179. ADC: Yes (800+ residents)

For-profit; nondenominational; nonsectarian. Apartments and private and semiprivate rooms. Skilled nursing care; physician's visits; physical, occupational, speech, and respiratory therapies; mental health care; pharmacy services; personal care; medication administration; podiatry services; security; emergency call system and daily check-ins; transportation; up to 3 daily meals; housekeeping and laundry services; all utilities; fitness center; daily activities; resident lounge; entertainment center; fishing; coffee lounge; beauty/barber salon.

IND MO: $1,300–$2,600; 2nd person, $500. AL MO: (additional to the IND MO rate), $400; $475; $550; 2nd person, $625. HCC Daily: Semiprivate, $130; private, $150. ADC: (weekly), $185.

Palma Ceia Adult Community

3011 W. DeLeon St.
Tampa, FL 33609

Ph: (813) 876-5235

IND: 4. AL: 86. ADC: Yes

For-profit; nondenominational; a division of Homestead Health Services. Studios, apartments, and private and semiprivate rooms. Nursing care; orthopedic program; neurological program; pain management; ear care; rehabilitative therapies; 24-hour home health care; Medicare-approved; personal care; medication administration; security; emergency response system; maintenance; transportation; up to 3 daily meals; housekeeping and laundry services; exercise classes; pet visits; social and recreational activities; card and board games; bingo; arts and crafts; walking paths; porches.

APPL: $110. IND MO: $1,000–$1,650.

Sunshine State Christian Home

5250 Whippoorwill Drive
Holiday, FL 34690

Ph: (813) 934-8092

IND: 86. AL/CONG: 142

Nonprofit; affiliated with Christian Churches/Churches of Christ; nondenominational. Apartments and private and semi-private rooms. Personal care; medication administration; security; emergency response system; maintenance; transportation; up to 3 daily meals; housekeeping and laundry services; visiting areas; library; chapel; activities; boutique; beauty/barber salon.

IND ENT: $19,500 and $30,500. IND MO: $125 and $130. AL MO: $750–$1,250.

Northwest

The Grand Court

1706 Olive Rd.
Pensacola, FL 32514

Ph: (904) 477-4929
Fax: (904) 477-5471

AL: Yes. RSP: Yes. ADC: Yes

Nondenominational. Private and semiprivate rooms. Personal care; medication administration; physical, occupational, and speech therapies; respite care; security; emergency response system; maintenance; transportation; 3 daily meals; housekeeping and laundry services; utilities; scheduled activities; hair care.

AL MO: (pkg. 1 basic), $1,250–$2,300; (pkg. 2 includes basic + 1–5 AL services), $1,500–$2,500; (pkg. 3 includes basic + 6–11 AL services), $1,600–$2,700. RSP Daily: $50–$85.

Northeast

Riverside Presbyterian Residences

Nonprofit; managed by Presbyterian Retirement Communities; nondenominational.

Presbyterian Apartments

1045 Oak St.
Jacksonville, FL 32204

Ph: (904) 353-6111

IND: 204

Age 62+ or physical handicap. Studios and apartments. 24-hour desk services; emergency call system; utilities; transportation for food shopping; planned educational and recreational activities; library; lounge; crafts; country store; beauty/barber salon.

IND MO: (income must not exceed $28,000, single; $32,000, couple), $450–$600.

Presbyterian House

2020 Park St.
Jacksonville, FL 32204

Ph: (904) 388-9376

AL: 188

Age 62+. Hotel-style furnished private rooms. Personal care; medication monitoring; security; emergency response system; maintenance; transportation; 3 daily meals; housekeeping and laundry services; planned educational and recreational activities; beauty/barber salon.

AL MO: (income must not exceed $28,000, single; $32,000, couple), $1,350.

Independent Living

Independent housing (primarily rentals) for seniors that may offer security features, meal service, and activities.

West Central

Belleair Towers

110 Ponce de Leon Blvd.
Clearwater, FL 33756

Ph: (727) 581-6540
Fax: (727) 585-7874

IND: 56

Age 55+. For-profit. Apartments. Podiatry care; emergency response system; maintenance; transportation; up to 2 daily meals; pets allowed; housekeeping and laundry services; fitness activities; swimming pool and spa; library; social and recreational activities; community rooms; billiards room; gardens; close to shopping and banks; barber/beauty shop.

IND MO: $2,100–$2,400; 2nd person, $400.

Regency Residence

6711 Embassy Blvd.
Port Richey, FL 34668

Ph: (727) 849-9335

IND: 133

Age 55+. For-profit. One- and two-bedroom apartments. Security; emergency response system; maintenance; transportation; up to 3 daily meals; pets allowed; housekeeping and laundry services; exercise room; Jacuzzi; swimming pool; library; social and recreational activities; billiards room; arts and crafts room; lounges; close to shopping and medical facilities; barber/beauty shop.

DEP: (ref), $110. IND MO: $1,450–$1,800; 2nd person, $375.

Adult/Resort Communities

Communities for active adults (not all are age-restricted; primarily ownership).

North

Carillon Beach

23313 Front Beach Rd.
Panama City Beach, FL 32413

Ph: (850) 234-5600
Fax: (850) 234-0123

http://www.Carillon-Beach.com

Individual homes, homesites. Beach club; swimming pool; tennis; meeting house; beach pavilions; shops; dining; nearby golf courses.

PURCHASE: Homes, $385,000–$2.2 million; homesites, $88,000–$495,000.

Oak Run Country Club

6028 SW Hwy 200
Ocala, FL 34481

Ph: (800) 874-0898 or (352) 873-2442

Individual homes. Golf course; clubhouse; swimming pool; sports club; island club.

PURCHASE: Homes, $77,000–$330,000.

Sandestin

9300 Highway 98 East
Destin, FL 32541

Ph: (800) 277-0801 or (904) 267-8100

http://www.sandestin.com

Individual homes, condominiums, homesites. Golf courses; tennis; swimming pool; health club and spa; boating/waterskiing; marina; deep sea fishing; dining.

PURCHASE: Homes, $220,000–$2.2 million; condos, $165,000–$2.2 million; homesites, $55,000–$935,000.

Savanna Pointe

4095 SW Williston Rd.
Gainesville, FL 32608

Ph: (352) 376-8033
Fax: (352) 378-8888

http://www.savannapointe.com

Individual homes, attached villas, estate homes, homesites. Golf course; clubhouse; swimming pool; walking/jogging trails.

PURCHASE: Homes, $220,000–$880,000.

The Residences at World Golf Village

500 Royal Pines Parkway
St. Augustine, FL 32092

Ph: (800) 279-1743

http://www.wgvresidences.com

Condominiums. Golf course; tennis; swimming pools; fitness facility; beachfront club.

PURCHASE: Condos, $275,000–$605,000.

Central

Citrus Hills

2468 N. Essex
Hernando, FL 34442

Ph: (800) 817-9009 or (352) 746-1468
Fax: (352) 746-1017

http://www.citrushills.com/

Individual homes, patio homes, villas, condominiums, homesites. Golf courses; tennis; swimming pool; exercise facility; horseback riding; fishing; dining; social clubs; trips.

PURCHASE: Homes, $91,000–$330,000.

The Country Club of Mount Dora

1400 Country Club Blvd.
Mount Dora, FL 32757

Ph: (800) 213-6132 or (904) 735-0115

Individual homes, villas. Golf course; pro shop; tennis; swimming pool; spa; fitness center; community center; biking; dining; social clubs.

PURCHASE: Homes, $110,000–$550,000+.

Crescent Oaks

1017 Kings Way Lane
Tarpon Springs, FL 34689

Ph: (727)937-7661

http://www.internest.com/costanzahomes/costanzahomes859.asp

Individual homes, villas. Golf course; clubhouse; pro shop; tennis; swimming pool; spa.

PURCHASE: Homes, from $220,000; villas, from $165,000.

DeBary Golf and Country Club

100 DeBary Plantation Blvd.
DeBary, FL 32713

Ph: (800) 246-5344 or (407) 668-7054

http://debary-cc.com

Individual homes, estate homes. Golf course; clubhouse; dining; social activities.

PURCHASE: Homes, from $102,000; homesites, from $31,000; estate homes, $440,000–$1.1 million; homesites, from $110,000.

Fairways Country Club

14205 E. Colonial Drive
Orlando, FL 32826

Ph: (800) 453-8005

Age 55+. Manufactured homes. Golf course; pro shop; clubhouses; tennis; swimming pools; bocce; shuffleboard; horseshoes; community activities.

PURCHASE: Homes, $22,000–$77,000.

Four Lakes Golf Club

990 LaQuinta Blvd.
Winter Haven, FL 33881

Ph: (800) 826-7076 or (941) 299-4777
http://www.retirenet.com/fourlakes

Age 40+. Manufactured homes. Golf course; clubhouse; tennis; swimming pool; boating; fishing; sailing; marina; jogging/hiking; lakes; bocce; billiards; shuffleboard; activities director.

PURCHASE: Homes, from $44,000.

Heathrow

1275 Lake Heathrow Lane
Heathrow, FL 32746

Ph: (800) 443-1485 or (407) 333-1400
Fax: 333-2945
http://www.heathrowland.com

Individual homes. Golf course; clubhouse; racquet and swim club; tennis; swimming pool; fitness center; fishing; biking/jogging.

PURCHASE: Homes, from $154,000; custom homes, from $308,000; estate homes, $825,000–$1.1 million.

Heritage Pines

11612 Vista Royal Drive
Hudson, FL 34667

Ph: (800) 541-3111 or (727) 819-0901
Fax: (727) 869-8882
http://www.realviews.com/realsite/pgs/hp.html

Age 55+. Individual homes, villas. Golf course; clubhouse; tennis; swimming pool; spa; fitness center; personal trainer; arts and crafts; billiards; computer internet room; dining.

PURCHASE: Homes: from $132,000. Villas: from $99,000. Luxury homes, from $176,000.

Heritage Springs

11509 Hidden Cove Court
New Port Richey, FL 34655

Ph: (888) 398-2233

Age 55+. Individual homes, villas. Golf course; clubhouse; tennis; swimming pool; spa; fitness center; personal trainer; arts and crafts; billiards; computer Internet room; dining.

PURCHASE: Homes, from $132,000; villas, from $99,000; luxury homes, from $187,000.

Indian River Club

2055 South U.S. 1
Vero Beach, FL 32962

Ph: (800) 575-0005 or (561) 569-9495
Fax: (561) 569-9470
http://www.indianriverclub.com

Golf cottages, courtyard homes, estate homes, homesites. Golf course; clubhouse; swim center; fitness center.

PURCHASE: Homes, $231,000–$495,000; homesites: $80,000–$158,000.

Kings Ridge

1900 Kings Ridge Blvd.
Clermont, FL 34711

Ph: (800) 311-7434 or (352) 242-1192
Fax: (352) 242-0769
http://www.kingsridge.com

Individual homes. Golf course; clubhouse; health club; fitness center; tennis; swimming pool; bocce; billiards; shuffleboard; social clubs.

PURCHASE: Homes, $86,000–$330,000.

Kissimmee Bay Country Club

1700 Lee Janzen Drive
Kissimmee, FL 34744

Ph: (800) 523-6286 or (407) 348-6222

http://www.kissimmeebay.com

Individual custom homes. Golf course; clubhouse; tennis; swimming pool; fitness center; boating; fishing; basketball court.

PURCHASE: Homes, $275,000–$660,000.

Lake Hammock Village

1300 U.S. Hwy. 27 North
Haines City, FL 33844

Ph: (800) 833-4536 or (941) 421-1286
Fax: (941) 421-1935

http://www.floridahousing.net/lake-hammock

Age 55+. Manufactured homes. Clubhouse; swimming pool; spa; lake; fishing; boating; shuffleboard; trips.

PURCHASE: Homes, $44,000–$88,000.

Lake St. Charles

10001 Remington Drive
Riverview, FL 33569

Ph: 813-910-7044
Fax: (813) 677-2836

Individual homes. Clubhouse; tennis; swimming pool; hiking/biking; basketball; soccer; beach volleyball; lake; boating.

PURCHASE: Homes, from $128,000.

Oakbridge

3604 Harden Blvd.
Lakeland, FL 33803

Ph: (800) 677-1301 or (941) 647-1100
Fax: (941) 648-4998

http://www.oakbridge.com

Individual homes, villas, courtyard homes, condominiums, homesites. Golf course; clubhouse; swim and tennis club; clinic; stores.

PURCHASE: Homes, $157,000–$484,000; villas and courtyard homes, $187,000–$330,000; condominiums, $130,000–$162,000; homesites, $59,000–$197,000.

PGA Village

9700 Reserve Blvd.
Port St. Lucie, FL 34986

Ph: (800) 682-5551 or (561) 467-1299

http://www.pgavillage.com

Individual homes, townhomes. Four PGA golf courses; clubhouse; golf pro shop.

PURCHASE: Golf and estate homes, from $154,000–$550,000+.

Pipers Landing

6160 SW Thistle Terrace
Palm City, FL 34990

Ph: (877) 774-7377 or (561) 283-7000
Fax: (561) 287-1282

http://www.piperslanding.com

Individual homes, condominiums, homesites. Golf course; clubhouse; pro shop; tennis; swimming; yacht club; marina; boating; fishing; beach; dining.

PURCHASE: Homes, $165,000–$1.1 million; condos, from $132,000; homesites, from $110,000.

Rose Lake Estates

201 Palm Drive
Tampa, FL 33613

Ph: (800) 962-6404 or (813) 961-6404
Fax: (813) 961-3303

Age 55+. Manufactured homes. Clubhouse; swimming pool; recreation hall; shuffleboard; horseshoes; bocce; bowling.

PURCHASE: Homes, $43,000.

Sea Oaks

1235 Winding Oak Circle E.
Vero Beach, FL 32963

Ph: (800) 223-6227 or (561) 231-5656

http://www.seaoaks.com

Individual homes, courtyard homes, villas. Tennis club; clubhouse; yacht club.

PURCHASE: Homes, from $291,000; villas, from $164,000.

Spring Lake Village

3797 Boggy Creek Rd.
Kissimmee, FL 34744

Ph: 800-969-8901 or (407) 344-8900
Fax: (407) 344-8955

Individual homes. Clubhouse; tennis; swimming pool; boating; fishing; fitness center; dining.

PURCHASE: Homes, $109,000–$154,000.

The Villages of Highlands Ridge

PO Box 768
Sebring, FL 33871

Ph: (800) 922-8099 or (941) 471-1171
Fax: (941) 471-1743

http://www.highlandsridge.com

Individual homes. Golf course; lake; lakefront clubhouse; dining; tennis; swimming; fishing; full-time activities director.

PURCHASE: Homes with homesites, from $88,000.

South

Ballen Isles Country Club

100 Ballen Isles Drive
Palm Beach Gardens, FL 33418

Ph: (800) 577-8419 or (561) 694-1600

http://www.ballenisles.com

Individual luxury homes. Three golf courses; clubhouse; swimming pool; tennis and fitness centers.

PURCHASE: Homes, $248,000–$2.75 million+.

Bonita Bay

26911 S. Bay Drive
Bonita Springs, FL 34134

Ph: (888) 875-5263 or (941) 495-1105

Individual homes, villas, patio homes, condominiums, homesites. Golf courses; clubhouses; beach club; tennis, fitness, and swim center; marina; dining.

PURCHASE: Homes, $220,000–$3.3 million+; condos, $440,000–$2.2 million+; homesites: $275,000–$550,000+.

Deering Bay Yacht and Country Club

13605 Old Cutter Rd.
Miami, FL 33158

Ph: (800) 395-2288 or (305) 254-2100

http://www.wcicommunities.com

Villas, condominiums, homesites. Golf course; clubhouse; tennis center; swimming pool; fitness center; water marinas; dining.

PURCHASE: Homes, $550,000–$1.1 million+.

Del Tura Country Club

18621 N. Tamiami Trail
North Fort Myers, FL 33903

Ph: (800) 734-3433

Age: 55+. Manufactured homes. Golf course; pro shop; clubhouse; fitness and exercise room; tennis; swimming pools; spas; shuffleboard; horseshoes; bocce; social clubs.

PURCHASE: Homes, $27,500–$85,000.

Eagle Creek

625 Eagle Creek Drive
Naples, FL 34113

Ph: (800) 552-4452 or (941) 774-4452

http://www.eaglecreeknaples.com

Individual homes, condominiums, homesites. Golf course; pro shop; clubhouse; tennis; swimming pool; spa; exercise rooms; dining.

PURCHASE: Homes, $282,000–$770,000+; condos, $178,000–$252,000; homesites, $93,000–$217,000.

Fiddler's Creek

8152 Fiddler's Creek Parkway
Naples, FL 34114

Ph: (800) 434-6660 or (941) 732-9300
Fax: (941) 732-9311

http://www.fiddlerscreek.com

Attached carriage, coach, and villa homes. Individual patio and estate homes. Golf course; clubhouse; tennis; swimming pool; spa; hiking/biking; fitness trainers; yacht club; beach.

PURCHASE: Attached homes, from $1.452 million; homes, $242,000–$1.1 million+.

Herons Glen

2250 Avenida del Vera
Fort Myers, FL 33917

Ph: (800) 521-9557

http://www.heronsglen.com

Villa, patio, and custom homes. Golf course; tennis; swimming pool; clubhouse; spa; dining; recreational facility.

PURCHASE: Homes, $132,000–$286,000; homesites, $32,000–$99,000.

Ironhorse Country Club

8000 Ironhorse Blvd.
West Palm Beach, FL 33412

Ph: (800) 896-7969 or (561) 624-7900
Fax: (561) 694-1185

http://www.ironhorse-cc.com

Individual homes. Golf course; clubhouse; fitness center; swim and tennis club; dining.

PURCHASE: Homes, $242,000–$880,000+.

Pelican Pointe Golf and Country Club

1805 San Trovaso Way
Venice, FL 34292

Ph: (941) 496-8338
Fax: (941) 496-8227

http://www.westfieldhomes.com/pelican.html

Attached villas. Golf course; conservation area; clubhouse; swimming pool.

PURCHASE: Villas, from $146,000.

Georgia

http: / / www.state.ga.us

General Information

Climate

Temperate. Summer temperatures average in the 80s and winter temperatures average above freezing.

Cost of Living

Ranks 46th in the nation

Taxes

General: Taxpayer Assistance, (404) 656-4071.

State/Local as % of Income: About 10.0%

Property Tax Reduction: $4,000 exemption for residents 65 years of age or older whose total income does not exceed $10,000. Residents 62 and older may also qualify for property tax deferral.

Sales: 4%.

Prescription Exemptions: Sales tax exemptions on durable medical devices and prosthetics when paid for by Medicaid or Medicare.

Transportation, Travel, and Tourism

General

Georgia Tourist Division, (404) 656-3590.

Major Airports

- Savannah International Airport, (912) 964-0514.
- Hartsfield-Atlanta International Airport, (404) 486-8834.

Railways

- Amtrak, (800) USA-RAIL.

Bus Tours

- Metropolitan Atlanta Rapid Transit Authority (MARTA) bus and rail system, (404) 848-4711.
- Greyhound Bus, (800) 231-2222.

State Highways

- Interstate 75 runs north-south.
- Interstate 20 runs east-west.

Theater and Music

- Atlanta Symphony Orchestra, (404) 733-4900 (performances in the Woodruff Arts Center).
- Georgia Ballet Studio and Company, (770) 425-0258.

Museums, Crafts, Historical, Recreational

Piedmont Region

- Sweetwater Creek State Park, Lithia Springs, (770) 732-5871 (hiking, picnicking, educational programs).
- Robert Toombs House, Washington, (706) 678-2226 (historic site; tour of grounds and house).

Highlands Region

- Dahlonega Gold Museum, Dahlonega, (706) 864-2257 (mining history).
- Travelers Rest State Historic Site, Toccoa, (706) 886-2256 (plantation home).

Coastal Region

- Little Ocmulgee State Park and Lodge, McRae, (912) 868-7474 (camping, cottages, lake with beach, golf course, tennis, lodge.)

- Sapelo Island, (912) 485-2251 (guided tours, wildlife, lighthouse, lodging.)
- Plains Region George T. Bagby State Park and Lodge, Ft. Gaines, (912) 768-2571 (lake, lodge, golfing, fishing, picnic sites.)

Organizations

Advocacy Groups

- Division of Aging Services, (404) 657-5258.
- Medicaid Fraud and Abuse Hotlines, (404) 656-4445 or (800) 533-0686.
- Georgia Nursing Home Association, 3735 Memorial Dr., Decatur, GA 30032-2202, Ph: (404) 284-8700. Fax: (404) 286-07522. *http://www.gnha.org*

Volunteer Programs

- National Kidney Foundation of Georgia, (404) 248-1315 or (800) 633-2339 (volunteers assist at health fairs, serve as counselors for Camp Independence, serve on committees).
- Hands On Atlanta, (404) 872-2252 (nonprofit volunteer organization partners with community-based agencies).

Housing

Long-Term Care Facilities

In the state of Georgia, these facilities are called ***Long-Term Care/Intermediate and Skilled Nursing Home Facilities****.*

These facilities provide residential living and/or various levels of nursing and medical services to seniors for an extended period of time.

Types of Authorization

Licensing and/or Certification

These facilities must be licensed or registered by the Department of Human Resources, Office of Regulatory Services. Intermediate nursing care facilities provide food, shelter, laundry, and personal care services. Skilled nursing facilities provide continuous medical supervision for skilled nursing and rehabilitative care.

Memberships:

- American Association of Homes and Services for the Aging (AAHSA) represents not-for-profit organizations committed to providing high-quality health care, housing and services to the elderly. AAHSA, 901 E St. NW, Suite 500, Washington, DC 20004-2011. Ph: (202) 783-2242. Fax: (202) 783-2285. *http://www.aahsa.org*
- Georgia Association of Homes and Services for the Aging (GAHSA) is an AAHSA Affiliated State Association. GAHSA, 1655 Tullie Circle, NE, Suite 108, Atlanta, GA 30329-2316.
- Ph: (404) 728-0223. Fax: (404) 636-6753.

Accreditations:

- Continuing Care Accreditation Commission (CCAC) accredits facilities that offer seniors a contract or contracts that provide residential living and health care services for the remainder of the person's lifetime and meet CCAC's accreditation standards.
- Joint Commission on the Accreditation of Healthcare Organizations (JCAHO) is an independent, not-for-profit organization, and the nation's oldest and largest standards-setting and health care accrediting institution.

South

Magnolia Manor

2001 S. Lee St.
Americus, GA 31709-4797

Ph: (912) 924-9352

IND: 94. AL: 176. SNF: 238. ALZ/MEM IMP: Yes

Age 62+. Affiliated with the United Methodist Church; nondenominational. Cottages, apartments, villas, and private and semiprivate rooms. Medical professionals; 24-hour skilled nursing care; IV treatment; pain management; diabetic care; hospice care; rehabilitative care; physical, occupational, and speech therapies; dietitians; social workers; pharmacy; personal care; medication administration; Medicare-approved; security; emergency response system; maintenance; transportation; up to 3 daily meals; housekeeping and laundry services; chaplain services; social services; library; activities; barber/beauty shop.

IND VILLA ENT: $18,000; MO: $8,000. IND APT MO: (maximum income limit) $500. IND APT MO: $950. IND COTTAGES MO: (for retired ministers) $200. AL MO: $1,750 and $2,100 (2nd person, $500). SNF Daily: $75, $90, $95, $110, $110.

St. Mary's Convalescent Center

805 Dilworth St.
St. Marys, GA 31558

Ph: (912) 882-4282

NH: 78

Private and semiprivate rooms. 24-hour nursing care; physical, occupational, and speech therapies; oxygen therapy; pharmacy; dental and podiatry consultation; social services; Medicaid-approved; 3 daily meals plus snacks; housekeeping and laundry services; daily activities.

NH Daily: (semiprivate) $80, (private) $90.

Central

Muscogee Manor and Rehabilitation Center

3800 Schatulga Rd
Columbus, GA 31907-3118

Ph: (706) 561-3218

NH: Yes. PC: Yes. REHAB: Yes

Owned and operated by the Hospital Authority of Columbus; nondenominational. Private and semiprivate rooms. Skilled and intermediate nursing care; physical, occupational, and speech therapies; long- and short-term care; IV treatment; personal care; medication administration; security; maintenance; transportation; up to 3 daily meals; housekeeping and laundry services; recreational activities; lounges; chapel; games; movies; off-site activities; library; gift shop.

PC Daily: $90–$100. SNF Daily: $15–$350.

East

Tara at Thunderbolt

3223 Falligant Ave.
Thunderbolt, GA 31404

Ph: (912) 691-2512
Fax: (912) 354-1267

NH: 134

For-profit; nondenominational. Private and semiprivate rooms. 24-hour nursing care; skilled and intermediate nursing care; physical, occupational, speech, and hearing therapies; lab and X-ray services; podiatry and vision services; psychological and social services; respite care; security; emergency response system; maintenance; transportation; 3

daily meals plus snacks; housekeeping and laundry services; exercise classes; religious services; activity director; recreational and therapeutic activities; resident council; ice cream parlor; barber/beauty services.

NH Daily: (private), $130 and $275; (semiprivate), $110 and $275.

North

Brandon Wilde

4275 Owens Rd.
Evans, GA 30809

Ph: (706) 868-9800
Fax: (706) 868-3525

http://www.brandonwilde.com

E-mail: *info@brandonwilde.com*

IND: 250. AL: 40. HCC: 65. ALZ/MEM IMP: 15

Age 62+. Nonprofit Life Care community sponsored by St. Joseph Center for Life, Inc., and University Health Services, Inc.; nondenominational. Apartments, cottages, and private rooms. Skilled nursing care; respite care; rehabilitative services and restorative nursing; dental and podiatry services; therapies; pharmacy; personal care; medication administration; Medicare-approved; security; 24-hour emergency call system; maintenance; transportation; up to 3 daily meals (1 daily meal included in IND mo. fee); pets allowed; housekeeping and laundry services; exercise classes; pool; putting greens; croquet courts; gardens; fishing pond; clubhouse; activities; card parlor; walking trails.

DEP: 10% of ENT fee. IND ENT: (2 ref. plans; % refund up to 47 mos. and 90% refund at exit), $51,000–$338,000. IND MO: $1,300–$3,000. AL MO: (Life Care residents' AL fees are inclusive; direct admission fees only), $2,600 and $3,000. HCC Daily: (Life Care residents' HCC fees are inclusive; direct admission fees only), (semiprivate), $135; (private), $165; (ALZ/MEM IMP), $145.

Canterbury Court

3750 Peachtree Rd. NE
Atlanta, GA 30319-1399

Ph: (404) 261-6611
Fax (404) 2331-9119

IND: 130. AL: 11. ICF: 36

Age 62+. Nonprofit; church-affiliated; Episcopal. Apartments and private and semiprivate rooms. Intermediate nursing care; rehabilitative therapies; dental and podiatry services; pharmacy; security; emergency response system; maintenance; transportation; up to 3 daily meals; small pets allowed (no dogs); housekeeping and laundry services; fitness center; religious services; hobby and craft room; woodworking shop; activities; gardens; greenhouse.

IND ENT: (ref. and nonref. plans) starts at $36,000. IND MO: starts at $1,350. AL MO: starts at $2,000. ICF Daily: (private), $115; (semiprivate), $90.

REQ: Minimum yearly income, $41,000.

Lenbrook Square, CCAC

3747 Peachtree Rd. NE
Atlanta, GA 30319

Ph: (404) 233-3000
Fax: (404) 264-3380

IND: Yes. AL: Yes. HCC: Yes

Nonprofit; nondenominational facility. Apartments and rooms. 24-hour nursing care; physical and occupational therapies; pharmacy and lab services; long- and short-term care; podiatry services; social worker; personal care; medication administration; security; emergency call system; maintenance; transportation; up to 3 daily meals; housekeeping, laundry, and linen services; social, recreational, and educational activities; off-site excursions; banking services; library; game room; putting green; greenhouse; convenience store; beauty/barber shop.

IND ENT: (ref.) $107,000–$277,000. IND MO: $2,050–$4,500 (includes up to 60

days in HCC). AL fees additional to the mo. fee.

Life Care Center of Gwinnett

3850 Safehaven Drive
Lawrenceville, GA 30044

Ph: (770) 923-0005
Fax: (770) 279-7067

SNF: Yes

Private and semiprivate rooms. 24-hour nursing care; long- and short-term care; physical, occupational, and speech therapies; respiratory therapy; personal care; medication administration; 3 daily meals; housekeeping and laundry services; activities director; planned daily activities; intergenerational program; arts and crafts; special occasion celebrations; socials; games; barber/beauty shop.

SNF Daily: $145–$330.

Magnolia Hill of Augusta

PO Box 3409
Augusta, GA 30914

Ph: (706) 737-8258
Fax: (706) 733-6203

SNF: 126

For-profit; nondenominational; nonsectarian. Private, semiprivate, and 3-bed rooms. Skilled and intermediate nursing care; 24-hour nursing care; rehabilitative therapies; pharmacy; Medicare/Medicaid-approved; security; emergency response system; maintenance; transportation; up to 3 daily meals; housekeeping and laundry services.

NH Daily: (private), $90; (semiprivate), $80; (3-bedroom), $70.

Presbyterian Village, PAHA

2000 East-West Connector
Austell, GA 30106-1123

Ph: (770) 819-7014
Fax: (770) 819-7070

IND: 170+. AL: 24. HCC: 107. ALZ/MEM IMP: 30

Ministry of the Presbyterian Church. Apartments, cottages, and private and semiprivate rooms. Long- and short-term care; nursing care; physical, occupational, and speech therapies; rehabilitative and restorative programs; social worker; pharmacy; personal care; medication administration; 24-hour security; emergency response system; transportation; up to 3 daily meals; housekeeping and laundry services; library; indoor pool; fitness center; chapel; educational programs; learning center; lounges; banking and postal services; volunteer programs; biking and walking paths; gardening; barber/beauty shop.

IND Homes/Cottages ENT: (ref. up to 50%) $141,000–$193,000. IND MO: $925 and $1050; 2nd person, $425. IND APT MO: $1,500–$2,500; 2nd person, $625. AL MO: $3,000; 2nd person, $2,500. Nursing Daily: $150 and $175. HCC Daily: $145 and $165.

Rosemont at Stone Mountain

5160 Springview Ave.
Stone Mountain, GA 30083

Ph: (770) 498-4144

NH: 149. ALZ/MEM IMP: 22

Nondenominational. 24-hour nursing care; medical director; physical, occupational, and speech therapies; podiatry, dental, and eye care; security; emergency response system; maintenance; transportation; 3 daily meals; housekeeping and laundry services; exercise program; full activities program; resident council; barber/beauty shop.

NH Daily: (semiprivate), $115; (private), $130.

Starcrest of McDonough

198 Hampton St.
McDonough, GA 30253

Ph: (770) 957-9081

SNF: 210. REHAB: Yes

For profit facility; nondenominational. Private, semiprivate, and 3-bed, semiprivate rooms. Skilled nursing care; restor-

ative nursing; physical, occupational, and speech therapies, audiology program; recreation therapy; short- and long-term care; hospice; 3 daily meals; activities; barber/beauty shop.

SNF Daily: (3-bed), $90; (semiprivate), $95; (private), $100 and $105.

Sunrise Nursing and Rehabilitation

315 Upper Riverdale Rd.
Riverdale, GA 30274

Ph: (770) 991-1050
Fax (770) 991-1008

NH: 152

No age requirement. For-profit; nondenominational. Private and semiprivate rooms. Nursing care; rehabilitative therapies; pharmacy; Medicare/Medicaid-approved; dental and podiatry care; security system; emergency call system; maintenance; 3 daily meals; housekeeping and laundry services; activities.

NH Daily: (semiprivate), $105; (private), $115.

Northwest

Royal Oaks

1220 Broadrick Drive
Dalton, GA 30720

Ph: (706) 275-8899 or (800) 275-8969

IND: 72. AL: 42. HCC: 100

Age 62+. Nonprofit; nondenominational; hospital affiliated. Apartments and private and semiprivate rooms. 24-hour nursing care; medical director; podiatry and dental services; individualized care plans; restorative therapies; personal care; medication administration; security; emergency response system; maintenance; transportation; up to 3 daily meals; pets allowed; housekeeping and laundry services; exercise program; scheduled daily activities; bank and postal services; resident council; walking paths; barber/beauty salon. Health Care Center opening in March 1999. Resident deposit and rental payment plans available. Contact facility for fees.

Assisted Living and Residential Care Facilities

*In the state of Georgia, these facilities are called **Assisted Living and Personal Care Facilities**.*

These facilities provide housing, food service, and one or more personal services.

Types of Authorization:

Licensing and/or Certification

These facilities must be licensed or registered by the Department of Human Resources, Office of Regulatory Services.

Memberships:

- Assisted Living Federation of America (ALFA) is a national non-profit membership organization whose mission is to enhance the quality of life in assisted living facilities and promote the interests of the assisted living industry. ALFA, 10300 Eaton Place, Suite 400, Fairfax, VA 22030. Ph: (703) 691-8100. Fax: (703) 691-8106. *http://www.alfa.org*
- Georgia-ALFA is a state affiliate of ALFA. Georgia-ALFA, PO Box 15495, Atlanta, GA 30333-9998. Ph: (404) 378-2747. Fax: (404) 378- 9318.

North

Arbor Terrace

425 Winn Way
Decatur, GA 30030

Ph: (404) 292-5910
Fax: (404) 292-3096

AL: Yes

Affiliate of the Wesley Woods Geriatric Center at Emory University. Apartments. 24-hour supervision; personal care; medication administration; emergency call system; transportation; meal escort; 3 daily meals; housekeeping and laundry services; activities director; lecture programs; exercise programs; arts and crafts; spiritual programs; pet therapy; games; gardening.

AL Daily: $75, $95, and $105. Additional personal care services, $35.

Ashley Glen

441 Prime Point
Peachtree City, GA 30269

Ph: (770) 631-0205

AL: Yes. ALZ/MEM IMP: Yes. ADC: Yes

Grace Management, Inc. Private suites. Medical appointment scheduling; health monitoring; personal care; medical administration, emergency call system; scheduled transportation; 3 daily meals plus snacks; housekeeping and laundry services; activities center; social programs; garden and walking paths.

AL MO: $2,050 and $2,750; 2nd person, $550. ALZ/MEM IMP MO: $3,100. RSP Daily: $95. ADC Daily: $50.

Autumn Breeze

2215 Old Hamilton Place
Gainesville, GA 30507

Ph: (770) 297-1100

AL: Yes. ALZ/MEM IMP: Yes. RSP: Yes

Managed by ServiceMaster Senior Living Services. Private and semiprivate rooms. Licensed nursing care; 24-hour supervision; personal care; medication administration; emergency response call system; transportation; 3 daily meals with snacks; laundry and housekeeping services; activity programs; library; lounges; barber/beauty shop.

AL Reservation: $330. DEP: $880. AL MO: $2,700, $2,000, and $1,375 per person. ALZ/MEM IMP MO: $2,500 and $1,900 per person. Additional personal care, $220 and $330. RSP Daily: $85 and $110.

Grace Assisted Living

5455 Glenridge Drive, NE
Atlanta, GA 30342

Ph: (404) 252-6271
Fax: (404) 252-6508

IND: Yes. AL: Yes. ALZ/MEM IMP: Yes

Apartments and private and semiprivate rooms. Staff physician; podiatrist; on-site rehab center with staff nurse; personal care; medication administration; 24-hour security; scheduled transportation; 3 daily meals; housekeeping and laundry services; gardening; daily activities; snack bar and ice cream parlor; sun rooms.

IND MO: $1,600. AL Daily: $75–$90. ALZ/MEM IMP Daily: $95.

Morningside of Loganville

580 Tommy Lee Fuller Drive
Loganville, GA 30052

Ph: (770) 466-CARE

IND: Yes. AL: Yes

Affiliated with the Georgia Baptist Health System and LifeTrust America. Cottages and private suites. Personal care; licensed nurse on staff; wellness program; respite care; personal care; medication administration; 24-hour emergency call system; transportation; up to 3 daily meals and snacks; housekeeping and laundry services; exercise program; chapel services; arts and crafts; games; gardening; banking; resident council.

IND MO: $1,375. AL MO: $1,600–$2,650; 2nd person, $550. Additional personal care monthly charges: $165, $330, $660, $90 (depending upon level of care).

Sunrise Assisted Living

920 Clairemont Ave.
Decatur, GA 30030

Ph: (404) 371-9362

AL: 77. ALZ/MEM IMP: 30

For-profit; nondenominational. Private and companion suites. Nursing care; respite care; hospice care; personal care; medication administration; security; emergency response system; maintenance; transportation; 3 daily meals; housekeeping and laundry services; recreational activities; pet therapy; concierge service; cultural and religious programs; educational program.

AL Daily: $70–$150. ALZ/MEM IMP Daily: $105–$180.

South

Fairhaven

1950 Glynco Parkway
Brunswick, GA 31525

Ph: (912) 280-0078

AL: Yes. ADC: Yes. ALZ: Yes

Family-owned; limited partnership; nondenominational. Private rooms (ALZ unit has semiprivate rooms). Personal care; medication administration; 24-hour security; emergency call system; 3 daily meals; pets allowed; housekeeping and laundry services; appointment setups; social and recreational activities; religious activities; volunteer program; library; crafts; game room; barber/beauty shop.

AL MO: $2,050; $2,300; $2,600. ALZ MO: $2,200.

Independent Living

Independent housing (primarily rentals) for seniors that may offer security features, meal service, and activities.

North

Foster Place

E. Foster Ave.
Dallas, GA 30132

Ph: (770) 445-6515

IND: 64

Age 55+. Managed by Rental Property Management. Townhouse. Security; maintenance; pets allowed; within short distance to shopping; picnic area; walking trails; no association fees.

IND MO: $625 (1-year leases).

Saint Anne's Terrace

3100 Nourished Parkway NW
Atlanta, GA 30327

Ph: (404) 238-9200

IND: Yes

One- and two-bedroom apartments. Nursing care; wellness checks; security; emergency response system; maintenance; transportation; up to 3 daily meals; pets allowed; housekeeping and laundry services; exercise room; library; banking services; scheduled activities; close proximity to social and recreational opportunities; woodworking shop; walking paths; barber/beauty shop.

IND MO: $1,600–$2,800.

East

River's Edge

6206 Waters Ave.
Savannah, GA 31406

Ph: (912) 354-6146

IND: 114

Owned by Holiday Retirement Corp. Apartments and cottages. Security; emergency response system; maintenance; transportation; up to 3 daily meals (apartments, 3 meals; cottages, 1 meal); housekeeping and laundry services; group activities and classes; centrally located in Savannah; near hospitals and shopping; barber/beauty shop.

APT MO: $1,250–$2,200. COTTAGE MO: $2,500.

Adult/Resort Communities

Communities for active adults (not all are age-restricted; primarily ownership).

North

Big Canoe

591 Big Canoe
Big Canoe, GA 30143

Ph: (888) 49-CANOE or (706) 268-3333

Individual homes, homesites. Golf courses; tennis; swim club; lake; beach; hiking trails; boating.

PURCHASE: Homes, $110,000–$880,000; homesites, $22,000–$192,500.

Bridge Mill

3440 Sixes Rd.
Canton, GA 30114

Ph: (770) 345-1888

http://www.bridgemill.com

Individual homes. Golf course; clubhouse; sports and recreation club; tennis center; aquatic center.

PURCHASE: Homes, $121,000–$440,000+.

Country Club of the South

4230 Old Alabama Rd.
Alpharetta, GA 30022

Ph: (800) 966-5002 or (770) 442-3838

http://38.240.220.10/ccos

Individual homes, homesites. Golf course; pro shop; clubhouse; exercise room; tennis center; swimming pool; recreation centers; football/soccer; basketball.

PURCHASE: Homes, $462,000–$3.3 million+; homesites $105,000–$825,000.

Horseshoe Bend Country Club

2100 Steeplechase Lane
Roswell, GA 30076

Ph: (770) 992-2310
Fax: (770) 518-2192

Individual homes. Golf course; clubhouse; pro shop; tennis complex; swim complex.

PURCHASE: Homes, $468,000–$765,000.

Laurel Springs

5360 Laurel Oak Drive
Suwanee, GA 30024

Ph: (800) 324-8369 or (770) 886-7274
Fax: (770) 886-7046

http://www.laurel-springs.com

Individual homes. Golf course; clubhouse; golf shop; swim and tennis complex; exercise room; dining.

PURCHASE: Homes, $308,000–$1.1 million+.

The Orchard Golf and Country Club

PO Box 1270
Clarkesville, GA 30523

Ph: (800) 522-1768 or (706) 754-8733

http://www.web1812.com/The_Orchard.htm

Individual homes, cottages, homesites. Golf course; pro shop; clubhouse; tennis; swim center; lakes; fly-fishing streams; hiking/biking; dining.

PURCHASE: Homes, $220,000–$550,000+; cottages, from $209,000; homesites, $35,500–$165,000+.

Sugarloaf Country Club

2798 Sugarloaf Club Drive
Duluth, GA 30097

Ph: (770) 495-7660

http://www.sugarloafcc.com

Individual homes, homesites. Golf course; 10-acre natural area; tennis; swimming; trails; clubhouse; sports center.

PURCHASE: Homes, from $550,000; homesites, from $88,000.

Central

Arbor Springs Plantation

250 Arbor Springs Plantation Drive
Newnan, GA 30265

Ph: (770) 463-0000
Fax: (770) 463-8833

http://www.arborsprings.com

Individual homes. Golf course; clubhouse; tennis; swimming pool; lakes; nature trails; dining.

PURCHASE: Homes, $363,000–$550,000.

Butler Creek

1850 Phinizy Rd.
Augusta, GA 30906

Ph: (706) 790-4666

http://www.chateaucomm.com

Manufactured homes. Clubhouse; swimming pool; fishing; activities.

PURCHASE: Homes, $22,000–$44,000+.

Reynolds Plantation

100 Linger Longer Rd.
Greensboro, GA 30642

Ph: (800) 733-LAKE or (706) 467-3151
Fax: (706) 467-3078

http://www.reynoldsgolf.com

Individual homes, cottages, homesites. Golf courses; clubhouse; tennis; swimming pools; lake; marina; fishing; boating/waterskiing; trails.

PURCHASE: Homes, $264,000–$1.1 million; golf cottages, $202,000–$274,000; club cottages, $184,000–$209,000; homesites, $82,500–$825,000.

SummerGrove

333 SummerGrove Parkway
Newnan, GA 30265

Ph: (770) 252-9000 or (770) 252-4524

http://www.summergrove.com

Individual homes, homesites. Golf course; clubhouse; tennis; swimming pools; lake; community park; canoeing; trails; social clubs; telecommunity.

PURCHASE: Homes, from $176,000.

South

The Landings on Skidaway Island

PO Box 13727
Savannah, GA 31416

Ph: (800) 841-7011 or (912) 598-0500
Fax: (912) 598-3233

http://www.thelandings.com

Individual homes, homesites. Golf courses; pro shops; clubhouses; tennis; stadium court; fitness center; swimming pools; nature trails; marina; dining.

PURCHASE: Homes, $275,000–$990,000; homesites, $55,000–$132,000.

Maple Ridge

4700 Maple Ridge Trail
Columbus, GA 31909

Ph: (706) 563-1102

http://www.mapleridgemagazine.com

Individual homes, patio homes, estate homes, condominiums, homesites. Golf course; clubhouse; tennis; pool and swimming center; dining.

PURCHASE: Homes, from $252,000; condos, $204,000–$330,000; homesites, from $52,500.

Misty Harbor

PO Box 679
Kingsland, GA 31548

Ph: (888) 534-8409 or (912) 729-6769

http://www.registryone.com

Individual homes, homesites. Community boat launch and dock; playgrounds; nearby golf course; pro shop; dining.

PURCHASE: Homesites, $22,000–$165,000.

Osprey Cove

123 Osprey Drive
St. Mary's, GA 31558

Ph: (888) 871-9555 or (912) 882-5555

http://www.ospreycove.com

Individual homes, homesites. Golf course; tennis complex; swimming complex; river; nearby ocean access; beaches; boating; fishing.

PURCHASE: Homes, $176,000–$495,000; homesites, $38,500–$132,000.

Hawaii

http://www.state.hi.us

General Information

Climate

The average temperature in Honolulu is 72° F in winter and 78° F in summer. Average water temperatures off Waikiki Beach range from 75° F in February to 79° F in September. Mountain regions are cooler.

Cost of Living

Ranks 1st in the nation.

Taxes

State/Local as % of Income: 12.5%.

Property Tax Reduction: Property taxes are set by counties, and reductions for senior citizens vary by location and by citizen age.

Sales: No sales tax, but a general excise tax is levied on gross income from most business activities, including sales and services, and may be passed on to consumer. Rates vary; from 0.15% to 4% on most consumer activities.

Prescription Exemptions: Sales of prescriptions and prosthetic devices are exempt from the general excise tax.

Transportation, Travel, and Tourism

General

Hawaii Tourism Office, PO Box 2359, Honolulu, HI 96804, (808) 586-2550.

Hawaii Visitors and Convention Bureau, (800) GO-HAWAII.

Major Airports

- Hilo International Airport, Hilo, HI 96720, (808) 934-5801.
- Honolulu International Airport, 300 Rodgers Blvd., #12, Honolulu, HI 96819, (808) 836-6411.
- Keahole-Kona International Airport, PO Box 1660, Kailua Kona, HI 96745, (808) 329-2484.

Railways

- Hawaiian Railroad (scenic), Oahu, (808) 681-5461.
- Lahaina-Kaanapali and Pacific Railroad (reconstruction of narrow-gauge sugar cane trains), 975 Limahana Plaza, Suite #203, Lahaina, HI 96767, (808) 667-6851.

Bus Tours

- Gray Line Hawaii, (800) 472-GRAY(4729).
- Oahu Transit Services, The Bus, (808) 848-5555.
- Polynesian Adventure Tours, (800) 622-3011.
- Trans Hawaiian Services (shuttles and tours), (808) 566-7420 or (800) 533-8765.

Cruise Lines

- American Hawaii Cruises (cruises and shore trips to Oahu, Kauai, Maui, and Kona), 800-513-5022.
- Royal Princess Cruises, 808-847-4800.
- Windjammer Cruises Maui, (808) 661-8600 or (800) SEA-HULA.
- Voyager Submarine tours, (808) 592-7850 or (800) 767-7551.

State Highway

- On Oahu Island, Hawaii Rte. H1 (Lunalilo Freeway) runs southeast-northwest from Waikiki Beach Park through Honolulu to Makakilo City, where it joins Rte. 93 (Farrington Hwy.), running along the west coast.

Near Pearl City, it junctions with Hawaii Rte. H2, which runs north through the center of the island to Wahiawa, where it joins Rte. 80, which becomes Rte. 99-83 (Kamehameha Hwy.), and then circles most of the north and east coasts.
- Hawaii Island is circled by Rtes. 11 and 19, in one continuous road.
- Kauai Island is circled by Rtes. 50 and 56, except for the northwest coast.

Theater and Music

Oahu

- Diamond Head Theatre, 520 Makapuu Ave., Honolulu, HI 96816, (808) 734-0274.
- Hawaii Opera Theatre, 987 Waimanu St., Honolulu, HI 96814, (808) 596-7372.
- Honolulu Academy of Arts, 900 S. Beretania St., Honolulu, HI 96814, (808) 532-8700.
- Manoa Valley Theatre, 2833 E. Manoa Rd., Honolulu, HI 96822, (808) 988-6131.
- Nu'uanu Nights (street festival, music, food), end of April, Nu'uanu Ave. from Pauahi St. to King St., Honolulu, (808) 732-9575.

Maui

- Maui Arts Cultural Center, Maui Central Park, PO Box 338, Kahului, HI 96733, (808) 242-2787.
- Maui Community Theatre, 68 N. Market St., Wailuku, HI 96793, (808) 242-6969.
- Hawaii Experience Theater, 824 Front St., Lahaina, HI 96761, (808) 661-7111.
- Kapalua Celebration of the Arts (dance, art, food), every April, (808) 669-6200.
- Maui Agricultural Show (food, florals, demos), end of April, Ulupalakua Ranch & Tedeschi Winery, (808) 875- 0457.
- Maui Music Festival (jazz), last weekend in May, (800) MAUI-SOS.

Hawaii

- Hilo Community Players, 141 Kalakaua St., Hilo, HI 96720, (808) 935-9155.
- Akebono Theatre, PO Box 710, Pahoa, HI 96778, (808) 965-9943.
- Aloha Community Players, Kealakekua, HI 96750, (808) 322-9924.
- Kahei Theatre, PO Box 117, Hawi, HI 96719, (808) 889-6831.

Museums, Crafts, Historical, Recreational

Kauai

- Koke'e Natural History Museum, PO Box 100, Kekaha, HI 96752, (808) 335-9975.
- Koke's State Park (camping, lodging, hiking), Koke's Rd. (Hwy 550), Kekaha (adjoins Waimea Canyon State Park) (for information, call Kauai District Park Office, (808) 274-3444).

Oahu

- The Bishop Museum (State Museum of Natural and Cultural History), 1525 Bernice St., Honolulu, HI 96817, (808) 847-3511.
- Waikiki Aquarium (founded 1904), 2777 Kalakaua Ave., Honolulu, HI 96815, (808) 923-9741.
- USS Bowfin Submarine Museum & Park, 11 Arizona Memorial Drive, Honolulu, HI 96818, (808) 423-1341.
- USS Missouri Memorial (commemorates Pearl Harbor attack), PO Box 6339, Honolulu, HI 96818, (808) 423-2263 or (888) USS-MISSOURI.
- USS Arizona Memorial (commemorates Pearl Harbor attack), 1 Arizona Memorial Pl., Honolulu, HI 96818, (808) 422-0561.
- Ala Wai Golf Course (public), 404 Kapahulu Ave., Honolulu, HI 96815, (808) 682-1911.
- `Iolani Palace (residence of King Kalakaua and Queen Liliuokalani), PO Box 2259, Honolulu, HI 96804,

corner of King and Richards streets, (808) 522-0832.
- Honolulu Zoo, 151 Kapahulu Ave., Honolulu, HI 96815-4096, (808) 971-7171.
- Diamond Head State Monument, off Diamond Head Rd., Honolulu (for information, call Oahu District Park Office, (808) 587-0300).
- Hawaii State Fair (food, games, rides), end of May June, Aloha Stadium, Oahu, (808) 486-9300.
- Aloha Festivals Downtown Ho'olaule'a (food, parades, music), mid-Sept., Bishop St., Honolulu, (808) 589-1771 or (800) 852-7690.

Molokai

- Kalaupapa National Historical Park (visitors center, no camping or facilities), north shore of Molokai, PO Box 2222, Kalaupapa, HI 96742, (808) 567-6802.

Maui

- Haleakala National Park (visitors center, museum, camping), PO Box 369, Makawao, HI 96768, (808) 572-9306.
- Hui No'eau Visual Arts Center, 2841 Baldwin Ave., Makawao, HI 96768, (808) 572-6560.
- Maui Ocean Center (aquarium), 192 Maalaea Rd., Wailuku, Maui, HI 96793, (808) 270-7000.
- Polipoli Spring State Recreation Area (camping, hiking), Waipoli Road off Kekaulike Ave., Kula. For information, call Maui District Park Office, (808) 984-8109.

Hawaii

- Hawaii Volcanoes National Park (visitor center; museum, trails, camping), PO Box 52, Hawaii National Park, HI 96718, (808) 967-7184.
- Hawaii Botanical Garden, 27-717 Old Mamalahoa Hwy., PO Box 80, Papaikou, HI 96781, (808) 964-5233.
- Kaloko-Honokhau National Historic Park (hiking, few facilities, petroglyphs), Kona coast, 73-4786 Kanalani St. #14, Kailua-Kona, HI 96740, (808) 329-6881.
- Panaewa Rain Forest Zoo, Stainback Highway, Hilo, (808) 959-7224.
- Pu'uhonua o Honaunau National Historical Park (visitors center, fishing), PO Box 129, Honaunau, Kona, HI 96726, (808) 328-2326.
- Pu'ukohola Heiau National Historic Site (hiking, camping), PO Box 44340, Kawaihae, HI 96743, (808) 882-7218.
- Akaka Falls State Park (hiking, 2 falls), Akaka Falls Rd., Honomu. For information, call Hawaii District Park Office, (808) 974-6200.

Organizations

Advocacy Groups

- Hawaii Executive Office on Aging, 250 S. Hotel St., Suite 107, Honolulu, HI 96813, (808) 586-0100.

Volunteer Programs

- Department of Land and Natural Resources, Community Services, 1151 Punchbowl St., Rm. 130, Honolulu, HI 96813, (808) 587-0393.
- Ka`ala Farm, Inc. (cultural center), PO Box 630, Waianae, HI 96792, (808) 696-4954.
- Flotilla 3-25 U.S. Coast Guard Auxiliary (promotes boat safety), Molokai Yacht club, Kaunakakai, HI 96748, (808) 553-5503.

Housing

Long-Term Care Facilities

*In the state of Hawaii, these facilities are called **Long-Term/ Intermediate and Skilled Nursing Care Facilities**.*

These facilities provide residential living and/or various levels of nursing and medical services to seniors for an extended period of time.

Types of Authorization

Licensing and/or Certification

These facilities are licensed by the Department of Health. Intermediate care facilities provide skilled nursing care 8 hours a day along with other personal and supportive care on a 24-hour basis. Skilled nursing facilities offer all-day nursing care, health, and social services.

Memberships

- American Association of Homes and Services for the Aging (AAHSA) represents not-for-profit organizations committed to providing high-quality health care, housing, and services to the elderly. AAHSA, 901 E St. NW, Suite 500, Washington, DC 20004-2011. Ph: (202) 783-2242. Fax: (202) 783-2285. *http://www.aahsa.org*

Accreditations:

- Continuing Care Accreditation Commission (CCAC) accredits facilities that offer seniors a contract or contracts that provide residential living and health care services for the remainder of the person's lifetime and meet CCAC's accreditation standards.
- Joint Commission on the Accreditation of Healthcare Organizations (JCAHO) is an independent, not-for-profit organization, and the nation's oldest and largest standards-setting and health care accrediting institution.

Honolulu

Arcadia Retirement Residence

1434 Punahou St.
Honolulu, HI 96822

Ph: (808) 941-0941
Fax: (808) 949-4965
http://www.arcadia-hi.org
E-mail: *jwelch@arcadia-hi.org*

IND: 250. AL: 12. HCC and ALZ/MEM IMP: 60

Age: 62+. Nondenominational. Apartments. Nursing care; medical services; rehabilitative therapies; personal care; medication administration; 24-hour security system; 24-hour emergency response system; maintenance; transportation; up to 3 daily meals; housekeeping and laundry services; library; computers with Internet connection; social and recreational activities.

APPL: ($1,000 ref.), $1,400. IND ENT: $99,000–$330,000. IND MO: $1,500–$2,900.

One Kalakaua Senior Living

1314 Kalakaua Ave.
Honolulu, HI 96826

Ph: (808) 949-1111

IND: 100. AL: Yes. SNF: Yes

Nondenominational; managed by Life Care Services Corporation. Condominium apartments. Nursing care; medical services; Medicare-approved; personal care; medication administration; 24-hour security; 24-hour emergency response system; maintenance; up to 3 daily meals; housekeeping and laundry services; exercise classes; library; social and recreational activities; game room; arts and crafts facility; barber/beauty shop.

IND MO: $1,200–$1,700; 2nd person, $440. Condos: $440,000–$589,000.

Kaneohe

Pohai Nani Good Samaritan Retirement Community

45-090 Namoku St.
Kaneohe, HI 96744

Ph: (808) 247-6211
Fax: (808) 247-9312

http://www.assistguide.com/pohainani

E-mail: *gsscenter147@worldnet.att.net*

IND: 202. AL: 10. SNF: 42

Age 62+. Nonprofit, owned and operated by the Evangelical Good Samaritan Society. Apartments, cottages, and private rooms. Skilled nursing care; medical services; rehabilitative therapies; wellness clinic; Medicare/Medicaid-approved; personal care; medication administration; 24-hour security; 24-hour emergency response system; maintenance; transportation; up to 3 daily meals (cottages not included); housekeeping and laundry services; swimming pool; religious services; library; social and recreational activities; Jacuzzi; club rooms; artists' studios; auditorium; lounges; barber/beauty shop.

APPL: $100. IND ENT: $3,300–$4,400. IND MO: $1,800–$4,200. Apartments: $1,800–$4,200; cottages: $1,500–$2,700. SNF MO: $4,400–$5,500. SNF Daily: private room: $220; semiprivate room: $200.

Assisted Living and Residential Care Facilities

*In the state of Hawaii, these facilities are called **Adult Residential Care Homes (ARCH)**.*

These facilities provide housing, food service, and one or more personal services.

Types of Authorization

Licensing and/or Certification

These facilities are licensed by the Department of Health. There are two types of ARCHs: Type I home for five or fewer residents; and Type II home for six or more residents. All ARCHs provide 24-hour living arrangements for a fee to individuals who require minimal assistance in daily living activities, but who do not need the services of an intermediate care facility.

Memberships

- Assisted Living Federation of America (ALFA) is a national nonprofit membership organization whose mission is to enhance the quality of life in assisted living facilities and promote the interests of the assisted living industry. ALFA, 10300 Eaton Place, Suite 400, Fairfax, VA 22030. Ph: (703) 691-8100. Fax: (703) 691-8106. *http://www.alfa.org*

Ewa Beach

Aiea Heights Rest Home

99-1657 Aiea Heights Drive
Ewa Beach, HI 96701

Ph: (808) 488-5521
Fax: (808) 488-5521

E-mail: *Angeleester@aol.com*

RH: 23. ALZ/MEM IMP: 4

Age 50. Nondenominational. Private rooms in large house. Nursing care; medical services; personal care; medication administration; 24-hour security; 24-hour emergency response system; maintenance; transportation; up to 3 daily meals; pet visitations; housekeeping and laundry services; social and recreational activities; located one block from state park; panoramic view of Pacific Ocean, view of Pearl Harbor; active community volunteer program.

DEP: (nonref. if not admitted; applies to first month's rent), $220–$550. RH MO: $2,000–$3,000. ALZ/MEM IMP MO: $2,000.

Honolulu

Hawaii Kai Retirement Community

428 Kawaihae St.
Honolulu, HI 96825

Ph: (808) 394-9599 or (800) 324-1295
Fax: (808) 395-0071

IND: 150. AL: 43 (2 levels)

Age 55+. For-profit. Apartments, studios, garden cottages. Personal care; medication administration; 24-hour staff; 24-hour emergency response system; maintenance; transportation; up to 3 daily meals; pets allowed; housekeeping and laundry services; exercise room; Jacuzzi; religious services; library; social and recreational activities; several lounge areas; close to hospitals and clinics.

DEP: (ref.), $100. IND MO: $2,000–$5,000; 2nd person, $440. AL MO: $2,000–$3,000.

Palolo Chinese Home, Inc.

2459 Tenth Ave.
Honolulu, HI 96816-3098

Ph: (808) 737-2555
Fax: (808) 735-1754

http://www.palolohome.com/

E-mail: *palolochinesehome@worldnet.att.net*

RH: 60. ADC: Yes. ALZ/MEM IMP: Yes. RSP: Yes

Nonprofit; nondenominational. Private rooms. Nursing care; personal care; medication administration; security system; 24-hour emergency response system; maintenance; scheduled transportation; up to 3 daily meals; housekeeping and laundry services; social and recreational activities.

APPL: $55. RH MO: $2,000–$2,600. RSP Daily: $100 (minimum stay of two nights).

Kaneohe

Holy Family Care Home

47-410 Ahuimanu Rd.
Kaneohe, HI 96744

Ph: (808) 239-7993
Fax: (808) 239-9868

AL: 30. ALZ/MEM IMP: 10. RH: 5

Age 50+. For-profit; nondenominational. Private and semiprivate rooms. Nursing care; medical services; personal care; medication administration; 24-hour security; 24-hour emergency response system; maintenance; transportation; up to 3 daily meals; pets allowed; daily housekeeping and linen services; exercise program; social and recreational activities; daily reality orientation.

AL MO: $2,000–$2,200. RH MO: Private room, $2,200; semiprivate room, $2,000; ward, $1,650.

Independent Living

Independent housing (primarily rentals) for seniors that may offer security features, meal service, and activities.

Honolulu

Kapuna I Elderly

1015 N. School St.
Honolulu, HI 96817

Ph: (808) 845-2130
Fax: (808) 845-6684

IND: 161

Age 62+. Apartments. 24-hour security; 24-hour emergency response system; maintenance; pets allowed; activity center with TV and some exercise equipment.

IND MO: HUD-subsidized.

One Kalakaua Senior Living

1314 Kalakaua Ave.
Honolulu, HI 96826

Ph: (808) 949-1111

IND: Yes

Condominiums. Wellness program; 24-hour reception and security desk; night patrol; maintenance; meal plan; housekeeping and laundry services; library; game room; social and recreational activities; arts and crafts room.

PURCHASE: $302,500–$660,000. IND MO: $1,200–$1,700. 2nd person: $440.

Adult/Resort Communities

Communities for active adults (not all are age-restricted; primarily ownership).

Hawaii

Mauna Kea Resort

62-100 Mauna Kea Beach Drive
Kamuela, HI 96743

Ph: (808) 882-5600
Fax: (808) 882-5350

http://www.maunakearesort.com

Individual homes, villas. Golf course; tennis; swimming pool; hiking; riding stables; fitness center.

PURCHASE: Condos, from $550,000; homes, from $660,000.

Mauna Lani Resort

68-1050 Makaiwa Place
Kohala Coast, HI 96743

Ph: (800) 367-5100
Fax: (808) 885-5536

http://www.maunalanirealty.com

Individual homes, condominiums, homesites. Golf course; tennis; swimming pool; hiking/biking; fishing; community center; fitness center; social clubs.

PURCHASE: Homes, $825,000–$27.5 million.

Waikoloa Village and Beach Resort

PO Box 383609
Waikoloa, HI 96738

Ph: (808) 886-7874, ext. 41
Fax: (808) 883-9951

Individual homes, condominiums, homesites. Golf course; tennis; swimming pool; hiking; riding stable; community center; fitness center; social clubs; dining; shops.

PURCHASE: Condos, $55,000–$660,000; homes, $165,000–$660,000; homesites, $49,500–$143,000.

Kauai

Princeville Resort

5-4280 Kuhio Hwy.
Princeville, HI 96722

Ph: (800) 826-4400 or (808) 826-3400
Fax: (808) 826-9884

http://www.garden-isle.com/kauaivr/

Individual homes, condominiums, homesites. Golf course; tennis; swimming pool; hiking/biking; fishing; riding stables; boating/waterskiing; fitness center.

PURCHASE: Homes, $220,000–$1.1 million.

Maui

The Kapalua Resort

300 Kapalua Drive
Kapalua, HI 96761

Ph: (800) 545-8439 or (808) 669-0210

http://www.kapaluamaui.com

Individual homes, condominiums, homesites. Golf courses; tennis; swimming pool; hiking; fitness center; beaches; shops; dining; shuttle service.

PURCHASE: Condos, $352,000–$1.65 million; homes, $1.265 million–$7.15 million; homesites, $357,500–$4.125 million.

Wailea Resort

161 Wailea Ike Place
Wailea, HI 96753

Ph: (800) 332-1614 or (808) 879-1911
Fax: (808) 879-6481

http://www.waileagolf.com

Individual homes, condominiums, homesites. Golf course; tennis club; swimming pool; beaches; dining.

PURCHASE: Homes, $220,000–$2.75 million+.

Oahu

The Estates at Turtle Bay

PO Box 366
Kahuku, HI 96731

Ph: (888) 200-4202 or (808) 293-0600
Fax: (808) 293-0471

http://www.ivacation.com/p5565.htm

Condominiums. Golf course; tennis; swimming pools; hiking/biking; fishing; riding stables; boating; public access beach.

PURCHASE: Condos, from $165,000.

Idaho

http://www.state.id.us

General Information

Climate

Extremely diverse. January averages from 17° F at Deadwood Dam to 31° F at Orofino. July averages from 60° F at Deadwood Dam to 77° F at Grand View.

Cost of Living

Ranks 29th in the nation.

Taxes

State/Local as % of Income: 10.9%.

Property Tax Reduction: Owner-occupied residences qualify for a homeowner's exemption, which exempts 50% or $50,000 (whichever is less) of the taxable value of the home (excluding land). Additional property tax reduction of up to $1,100 available to citizens 65 and older, or widowed or disabled persons meeting requirements.

Sales: 5%.

Prescription Exemptions: Prescription drugs are exempt from sales tax.

Transportation, Travel, and Tourism

General

Idaho Division of Tourism Development, (800) VISIT-ID.

Major Airports

- Boise Municipal Airport, 3201 Airport Way, Boise, ID 83705, (208) 383-3110.
- Coeur d'Alene Airport, 11401 N. Airport Rd., Hayden Lake, ID 83835, (208) 772-7838.
- Joslin Field Magic Valley, 492 Airport Loop, Twin Falls, ID 83301, (208) 733-5215.
- Lewiston Nez Perce County Airport, 406 Burrell Ave., Lewiston, ID 83501, (208) 746-7962

Railways

- Amtrak station in Idaho Falls, (800) USA-RAIL

Bus Tours

- Greyhound Bus, stations throughout the state, (800) 231-2222.
- Sun Valley Stages, Inc., 119 S. Park Ave., West, Twin Falls, ID 83301, (208) 733-3921.
- Teton Stage Lines, PO Box 51455, Idaho Falls, ID 83405, (208) 529-8036.

State Highways

- Interstate 84 runs southeast-northwest from Utah to Rupert, then to Oregon border.
- Interstate 86 runs west-east from Rupert to Pocatello.
- Interstate 15 runs south-north from Utah to the Montana border.
- Interstate 90 runs east-west from Mullan to Post Falls and Washington.

Theater and Music

North

- Lake City Playhouse, corner of 14th & Garden, Coeur d'Alene, (208) 667-1323.

Central

- Evergreen Theater, 55 Deinhard Lane, McCall, ID 83638, (208) 634-4133.
- Sun Valley Center for the Arts (music, dance, theater), 191 5th St. East, Ketchum, ID 83340 (write to:

PO Box 656, Sun Valley, ID 83353), (208) 726-9491.

East

- Roxy Community Center Theatre, 116 N. Bridge St., St. Anthony, ID 83445, (208) 624-3044.

West

- Idaho Shakespeare Festival (performances in summer), PO Box 9365, Boise, ID 83707, (208) 336-9221.
- Boise River Festival (music, food, children's events), last weekend in June, 7032 S. Eisenman Rd., Boise, ID 83705, (208) 338-8887.
- Gene Harris Jazz Festival, every April, Boise State University, 1910 University Drive, Boise, ID 83725, (208) 426- 1203, or for tickets, (208) 426-1766.
- Boise Little Theatre, 100 E. Fort St., Boise, ID 83712, (208) 342-5104.
- Opera Idaho, 501 S. 8th St., Boise, ID 83702, (208) 345-3531.
- The Morrison Center (Boise State University), 1910 University Drive, Boise, ID 83725, (208) 385-1609.

Museums, Crafts, Historical, Recreational

North

- Highlands Golf and Country Club (public), N. 701 Inverness Drive, Post Falls, ID 83854, (208) 343-1769.
- Schweitzer Mountain Resort (skiing), 10000 Schweitzer Mountain Rd., Sandpoint, ID 83864, (208) 263-9555.
- Museum of North Idaho, 115 Northwest Blvd., Coeur d'Alene ID 83816, (208) 664-3448.
- Spragpole Museum, PO Box 425, Murray, ID 83874, (208) 682-3901.
- Silver Mountain Ski and Summer Resort, 610 Bunker Ave, Kellogg, ID 83837, (208) 783-1111.
- Crystal Gold Mine (1880s gold mine), PO Box 510, 51931 Silver Valley Rd., Kellogg, ID 83837, (208) 783-4653.
- Kootenai National Wildlife Refuge (3,000 acres), HC 60 Box 283, Bonners Ferry, ID 83805, (208) 267-3888.

South

- City of Rocks National Reserve (primitive camping, hiking), PO Box 169, Almo, ID 83312, (208) 824-5519.
- Massacre Rocks State Park (visitor center, displays of Oregon Trail), 3592 N. Park Lane, American Falls, ID 83211, (208) 548-2672.
- Lava Hot Springs (public hot spring pools, open in summer), 430 E. Main, Lava Hot Springs, ID 83246, (800) 423-8597.
- Twin Falls County Fair and Rodeo (annual fair), PO Box 257, Filer, ID 83329, (208) 326-4396.
- Hagerman Fossil Beds National Monument (hiking, no facilities), PO Box 570, Hagerman, ID 83332, (208) 837-4793.
- Cassia County Historical Museum, PO Box 331, E. Main St. & Highland, Burley, ID 83318, (208) 678-7172.
- Idaho Heritage Museum, Rte. 1, Box 2390, Hwy. 93 South, Twin Falls, ID 83301, (208) 655-4444.
- Twin Falls Municipal Golf Course (public), Grandview Drive, Twin Falls, ID 83301, (208) 687-1311.
- Herrett Center for Arts and Science and Faulkner Planetarium, College of Southern Idaho, PO Box 1238, Twin Falls, ID 83303, (208) 733-9554.

Central

- Sun Valley Arts and Crafts Festival (every August), PO Box 656, Sun Valley, ID 83353, (208) 726-9491.
- Lemhi County Historical Museum, PO Box 645, 210 Main St., Salmon, ID 83467, (208) 756-3342.
- Sawtooth National Recreation Area, Star Route Hwy. 75, Ketchum, ID 83340, (208) 726-7672.
- Sun Valley Ski Resort, Sun Valley, ID 83353, (208) 726-3423 or (800) 634-3347.

- Craters of the Moon National Monument (visitor center, trails, camping), PO Box 29, Arco, ID 83213, (208) 527- 3257.
- Elkhorn Country Club (public), 1 Elk Horn Rd., Sun Valley, ID 83354, (208) 772-0555.

East

- Bonneville Museum, Eastern and Elm Sts., Idaho Falls, (208) 522-1400.
- Spencer Opal Mines (tour, dig your own), HC 62 Box 2062, Spencer, ID 83446, (208) 374-5476.
- Riverside Golf Course (public), 3500 Bannock Hwy., Pocatello, ID 83204, (208) 528-5535.

West

- Zoo Boise, Julia Davis Park, Capitol Blvd. at Battery St. (write to 1104 Royal Blvd.), Boise, ID 83702, (208) 384- 4260.
- Lewis/Clark Center for Arts & History, 415 Main St., Lewiston, ID 83501, (208) 799-2243.
- Hells Canyon National Recreation Area (in ID, OR, and WA), PO Box 699, 2535 Riverside Drive, Clarkston, WA 99403, (509) 758-0616.
- Nez Perce National Historical Park (visitors center), Rte. 1, Box 100, Spalding, ID 83540, (208) 843-2261.
- Snake River Stampede (rodeo, food), third week every July, PO Box 231, 109 12th Ave. S., Nampa, ID 83653, (208) 466-8497.
- Bogus Basin Ski Resort, 2405 Bogus Basin Rd., Boise, ID 83702, (208) 332-5151.
- Boise Art Museum, 670 S. Julia Davis Drive, Boise, ID 83702, (208) 345-8330.
- Idaho Botanical Garden, 2355 Old Penitentiary Rd., Boise, ID 83712, (208) 343-8649.
- Idaho Historical Museum, 610 N. Julia Davis Drive, Boise, ID 83702, (208) 334-2120.
- Purple Sage Municipal Golf Course (public), 15192 Purple Sage Rd., Caldwell, ID 83605, (208) 344-7807.
- Payette National Forest (fishing, skiing, camping), PO Box 1026, 106 W. Park St., McCall, ID 83638, (208) 634-1400.

Organizations

Advocacy Groups

- Idaho Commission on Aging, 3380 Americana Terrace, Suite 120, Boise, ID 83706, (208) 334-3833.
- State Ombudsman for the Elderly, (208) 334-4693.

Volunteer Programs

- Retired and Senior Volunteer Program, 5420 Franklin Rd., Boise, ID 83705, (208) 345-4357.
- Boise River Festival (music, sports, food), every June, 7032 S. Eisenman Rd., Boise, ID 83705, call (208) 345-8363 or 338-8887 to volunteer.

Housing

Long-Term Care Facilities

*In the state of Idaho, these facilities are called **Continuing Care/Intermediate and Skilled Nursing Facilities**.*

These facilities provide residential living and/or various levels of nursing and medical services to seniors for an extended period of time.

Types of Authorization

Licensing and / or Certification

These facilities are regulated by the Department of Health and Welfare.

Memberships

- American Association of Homes and Services for the Aging (AAHSA) represents not-for-profit organizations committed to providing high-quality

health care, housing and services to the elderly. AAHSA, 901 E St. NW, Suite 500, Washington, DC 20004-2011. Ph: (202) 783-2242. Fax: (202) 783-2285. *http://www.aahsa.org*

Accreditations

- Continuing Care Accreditation Commission (CCAC) accredits facilities that offer seniors a contract or contracts that provide residential living and health care services for the remainder of the person's lifetime and meet CCAC's accreditation standards.
- Joint Commission on the Accreditation of Healthcare Organizations (JCAHO) is an independent, not-for-profit organization, and the nation's oldest and largest standards-setting and health care accrediting institution.

North West

Good Samaritan Village

640 N. Eisenhower
Moscow, ID 83843

Ph: (208) 882-6560
Fax: (208) 882-6569

E-mail: *gsscenter160@worldnet.att.net*

IND: 83. AL: 22. HCC: 52. ALZ/MEM IMP: 12

Nonprofit; nondenominational; Lutheran church affiliation. Duplexes, apartments, and private and semiprivate rooms. 24-hour skilled nursing care; hospice services; rehabilitative therapies; medical services; dental and podiatry care; pharmacy services; Medicare/Medicaid-approved; personal care; medication administration; security; emergency response system; maintenance; transportation; up to 3 daily meals; pets allowed; housekeeping and laundry services; exercise classes; religious services; library; computer lab; recreation room; social and recreational activities; cultural and educational programs; gardening; barber/beauty shop.

IND MO: $910–2,400. AL MO $2,200–$2,800. HCC Daily: $135–$160.

Valley Vista Care Services

820 Elm St.
St. Maries, ID 83861

Ph: (208) 245-4576
Fax: (208) 245-2138

E-mail: *imichael@valleyvista.org*

AL: 42. HCC: 75

Nonprofit; locally owned; Christian affiliation. Apartments and private rooms. Nursing care; medical services; rehabilitative therapies; dental and podiatry care; pharmacy services; Medicare/Medicaid-approved; home health services; personal care; medication administration; security; emergency response system; maintenance; transportation; meal service; housekeeping and laundry services; social and recreational activities; atrium with waterfall; barber/beauty shop.

AL MO: $310–$1,450. HCC Daily: $120–$130.

South

Bridge View Estates

1828 Bridgeview Blvd.
Twin Falls, ID 83301

Ph: (208) 736) 3933
Fax: (208) 736-3941

IND: 99. AL: 47. HCC: 116. ALZ/MEM IMP: 16. ADC: Yes

Age 55+. Nondenominational. Apartments and private and semiprivate rooms. Nursing care; medical services; rehabilitative therapies; dental and podiatry care; pharmacy services; Medicare/Medicaid-approved; personal care; medication administration; security; emergency response system; mainte-

nance; transportation; up to 3 daily meals; pets allowed; housekeeping and laundry services; fitness center; social and recreational activities; educational and cultural programs.

APPL: $165. DEP: $165. IND MO: $1,450–$2,000. AL MO: $2,300–$3,500. HCC MO: $3,900–$4,400.

Assisted Living and Residential Care Facilities

In the state of Idaho, these facilities are called ***Licensed Community Homes (previously referred to as "Residential and Assisted Living Facilities and Personal Care Services Homes").***

These facilities provide housing, food service, and one or more personal services.

Types of Authorization

Licensing and/or Certification

These facilities are regulated by the Department of Health and Welfare.

Memberships

- Assisted Living Federation of America (ALFA) is a national nonprofit membership organization whose mission is to enhance the quality of life in assisted living facilities and promote the interests of the assisted living industry. ALFA, 10300 Eaton Place, Suite 400, Fairfax, VA 22030. Ph: (703) 691-8100. Fax: (703) 691-8106. *http://www.alfa.org*
- Northwest Assisted Living Facilities Association (NOR-ALFA) is a regional affiliate of ALFA. NOR-ALFA, 34004 16th Ave. South, Suite 201, Federal Way, WA 98003. Ph: (253) 874-5211. Fax: (253) 874-5350. *http://www.noralfa.org*

North

The Bridge Assisted Living

1123 N. Division
Sandpoint, ID 83864

Ph: (208) 263-1524
Fax: (208) 263-6361
E-mail: *bridge@micron.net*

AL: 43

For-profit; nondenominational. Apartments. Life care center on campus; personal care; medication administration; security; emergency response system; maintenance; transportation; up to 3 daily meals; pets allowed; housekeeping and laundry services; exercise; social and recreational activities; ice cream parlor.

DEP: $550. AL MO: $1,300–$2,200.

Juniper Meadows Retirement and Assisted Living

2975 Juniper Drive
Lewiston, ID 83501

Ph: (208) 746-8676
Fax: (208) 746-9843

IND: 20. AL: 57

Age 55+. For-profit. Apartments. Nursing care; medical services; personal care; medication administration; security; emergency response system; maintenance; transportation; up to 3 daily meals; pets allowed; housekeeping and laundry services; social and recreational activities.

DEP: (ref.) $400. IND MO: $1,450–$1,750. AL MO: $2,300–$2,750.

Loyalton

205 E. Anton
Coeur d'Alene, ID 83815

Ph: (208) 667-6490
Fax: (208) 765-4352

IND: 50. AL: 58. ADC: Yes

For-profit; nondenominational. Studios, and one- and two-bedroom apartments. Licensed nurse on staff; respiratory care; behavior management; personal care; medication administration; security; emergency response system; maintenance; transportation; up to 3 daily meals; pets allowed; housekeeping and laundry services; Bible study; social and recreational activities; cultural and educational programs; bingo; bookmobile.

APPL: (single) $350; (double) $500. IND MO: $1,000–$1,700. AL MO: (base rent) $1,250–$1,850; (additional assistance) $750–$1,500.

Wedgwood Terrace Assisted Living

2114 Vineyard Ave.
Lewiston, ID 83501

Ph: (208) 734-4545
Fax: (208) 743-2268

AL: Yes. ALZ/MEM IMP: Yes

Nondenominational; a Greenbriar Community. Studios and apartments. 24-hour staffing and supervision; respite care; blood pressure and weight checks; personal care; medication administration; security; emergency response system; maintenance; transportation; up to 3 daily meals; housekeeping and laundry services; social and recreational activities; educational programs; common areas; lounges; activity room; barber/beauty shop.

AL MO: $2,200–$2,400; 2nd person, $450. ALZ/MEM IMP MO: $3,100.

East

Lincoln Court Retirement Community

850 Lincoln Drive
Idaho Falls, ID 83401

Ph: (208) 529-3456
Fax: (208) 529-0641

IND: Yes. AL: Yes (total units, 133)

Age 55+. Nondenominational. Apartments. Nursing care; 24-hour staffing; Medicaid-approved; personal care; medication administration; security; emergency response system; maintenance; transportation; up to 3 daily meals; housekeeping and laundry services; exercise room; exercise equipment; social and recreational activities; billiard room; activity room; gift shop; barber/beauty shop.

DEP: $100. IND MO: $1,450–$2,600. AL MO: $55–$550.

Parkwood Meadows Assisted Living Community

1885 Parkwood St.
Idaho Falls, ID 83401

Ph: (208) 523-7800
Fax: (208) 523-2240

AL: 62. ALZ/MEM IMP: 17

Age 55+. For-profit; nondenominational; nonsectarian. Apartments. Nursing care; Medicaid-approved; personal care; medication administration; security; emergency response system; maintenance; transportation; up to 3 daily meals; pets allowed; housekeeping and laundry services; exercise program; library; social and recreational activities; whirlpool; resident council.

DEP: (ref.) $220. AL MO: $1,850–$3,100.

Southeast

Ridge Wind

4080 Hawthorne Rd.
Chubbuck, ID 83202

Ph: (208) 237-3000
Fax: (208) 237-6024

IND: Yes. AL: Yes

Nondenominational. Apartments. Nursing care; on-site therapy clinic; behavior management; personal care; medication administration; security; emergency response system; mainte-

nance; transportation; up to 3 daily meals; housekeeping and laundry services; social and recreational activities.

Contact facility for fees.

Southwest

Atria Hillcrest Assisted Living

1093 S. Hilton
Boise, ID 83705

Ph: (208) 345-4460
Fax: (208) 345-0178

E-mail: *hillcres@micron.net*

AL: 115

For-profit; owned by Atria. Studios and apartments. Nursing care; wellness program; personal care; medication administration; security; emergency response system; maintenance; transportation; up to 3 daily meals; pets allowed; housekeeping and laundry services; social and recreational activities; cultural and educational programs; barber/beauty shop.

AL MO: $1,900–$3,400.

Autumn Wind

200 W. Beech St.
Caldwell, ID 83605

Ph: (208) 459-3335

AL: Yes

For-profit; nondenominational; owned by Prestige Care. Studios and one-bedroom apartments. 24-hour staffing; health monitoring; ambulation assistance; behavior management; personal care; medication administration; security; emergency response system; maintenance; transportation; up to 3 daily meals; pets allowed; housekeeping and laundry services; social and recreational activities; activity room; lounges; courtyard with patio; barbecue area.

AL MO: $1,550–$1,700; 2nd person, $625. Additional levels of care: $440–$990+.

Plantation Place

3921 Kessinger Lane
Boise, ID 83706

Ph: (208) 853-7300
Fax: (208) 853-9328

http://www.assistedlvng.com

IND: Yes. AL: Yes

Age 55+. For-profit; nondenominational. Apartments. Medical services; rehabilitative therapies; personal care; medication administration; emergency response system; maintenance; transportation; up to 3 daily meals; pets allowed; housekeeping and laundry services; social and recreational activities; golf course; Jacuzzi; barber/beauty shop.

DEP: $440. IND MO: $1,750–$2,850. AL MO: $2,000–$3,600.

Regent at Willow Park

2600 N. Milwaukee Ave.
Boise, ID 83704

Ph: (208) 373-1234
Fax: (208) 375-1316

E-mail: *Willow_park@earthlink.net*

IND: 10. AL: 79. ALZ/MEM IMP: 34

For-profit; nondenominational. Apartments. Nursing care; personal care; medication administration; security; emergency response system; maintenance; transportation; up to 3 daily meals; pets allowed; housekeeping and laundry services; social and recreational activities.

MO: $1,650.

RiverPlace Retirement and Assisted Living

739 E. Parkcenter Blvd.
Boise, ID 83706

Ph: (208) 338-5600
Fax: (208) 338-6553

IND: 78. AL: 80

Age 55+. For-profit; nondenominational. Apartments. Nursing care; personal care; medication administration; security; emergency response system;

maintenance; transportation; up to 3 daily meals; pets allowed; housekeeping and laundry services; social and recreational activities; loggers creek and wildlife.

DEP: (ref.) $550. ENT: $550. IND/AL MO: $1,200–$3,100.

South Central

Crossings

1367 Locust St. North
Twin Falls, ID 83301

Ph: (208) 735-0700
Fax: (208) 735-0900

E-mail: *hbarnes@assisted.com*

AL: 70. ALZ/MEM IMP: 20

Age 50+. For-profit; nondenominational. Apartments. Nursing care; 24-hour staffing; rehabilitative therapies; respite care; personal care; medication administration; security; emergency response system; maintenance; transportation; up to 3 daily meals; pets allowed; housekeeping and laundry services; exercise room; library; game room; enclosed courtyard.

AL ENT: $770. AL MO: $2,100–$2,800.

Independent Living

Independent housing (primarily rentals) for seniors that may offer security features, meal service, and activities.

Southeast

Christensen Court

711 N. Sixth Ave.
Pocatello, ID 83201

IND: 75

Portneuf Towers

666 W. Day
Pocatello, ID 83205

IND: 72

Age 62+. Nonprofit. Efficiencies and one-bedroom apartments. Maintenance; laundry services. HUD-subsidized housing.

Southwest

Harrison Hills

2260 Harrison Blvd. #104
Boise, ID 83702

Ph: (208) 342-4716
Fax: (208) 342-4716

IND: Yes

Age 62+. Apartments. Maintenance; some transportation; exercise equipment; pets allowed.

IND MO: 30% of income; HUD-subsidized.

Oakhaven Retirement Center

115 W. Ogden Ave.
Nampa, ID 83651

Ph: (208) 465-7200
Fax: (208) 465-7200

IND: Yes

Age 62+. Nonprofit. Apartments. Transportation; pets allowed. Contact facility for fees.

Adult/Resort Communities

Communities for active adults (not all are age-restricted; primarily ownership).

North

Heatherstone

1185 W. Honeysuckle
Hayden, ID 83835

Ph: (208) 762-4083

Manufactured homes. Walking park; future clubhouse; nearby golf and lake.

PURCHASE: Homes, from low $79,500.

The Highlands

North 701 Inverness Drive
Post Falls, ID 83854

Ph: (208) 773-3673

Individual homes, homesites. Golf course; pro shop; clubhouse; dining; social clubs.

PURCHASE: Homes, $176,000–$2.2 million.

Leisure Park

1480 Leisure Drive
Hayden, ID 83835

Ph: (800) 851-8527 or (208) 772-9617

Age 40+. Individual homes, patio homes, condominiums, homesites. Clubhouse; putting green; exercise facilities; library and game rooms; RV and boat parking.

PURCHASE: Homes, from $96,000; patio homes, from $110,000; condos, from $115,500; homesites, $23,000–$37,000. Resales available.

Twin Lakes Village

East 2600 Village Blvd.
Rathdrum, ID 83858

Ph: (888) 387-6039 or (208) 687-6039
http://www.golfnorthidaho.com

Individual homes, garden homes, condominiums, homesites. Golf course; pro shop; tennis; swimming pool; hiking trails; fishing; snow skiing; basketball; private beach.

PURCHASE: Homes, $76,000–274,000.

South

The Senator Retirement Community

421 S. Curtis
Boise, ID 83705

Ph: (208) 344-2491
Fax: (208) 367-0338
E-mail: *SenatorRet@aol.com*

Age 55+. 120 homesites. Maintenance; clubhouse; library; media room; bingo; billiards; crafts; activity groups; exercise room.

PURCHASE: Homes, $77,000. MO: $310–$315.

Soldier Mountain Ranch Country Club and Resort

600 North 400 West
Fairfield, ID 83327

Ph: (208) 764-2506
Fax: (208) 764-2927

Individual homes, homesites. Golf course; pro shop; tennis; swimming pool; fishing; cross-country skiing; mountain biking; horseback riding; dining; nearby hunting and downhill skiing.

PURCHASE: Homesites, $27,500–$71,500.

Terrace Lakes Resort

101 Holiday Drive
Garden Valley, ID 83622

Ph: (208) 462-3250 or (208) 462-3200
http://www.terracelakes.com

Individual homes, homesites. Golf course; tennis; swimming pool; hiking trails; fishing; hunting; cross-country skiing; snowmobile; community center; dining.

PURCHASE: Homes, $44,000–$302,500.

Illinois

http://www.state.il.us

General Information

Climate

January mean temperature in the northern portion of the state is about 19° F; in the midsection, 25° F; and in the southern portion, 32° F. July mean temperature in the northern portion of the state is about 74° F; in the central portion, 75° F; and in the southern portion, 78° F. The annual mean temperature for the entire state ranges from the low to high 50s.

Cost of Living

Ranks 19th in the nation.

Taxes

State/Local as % of Income: 9.7%.

Property Tax Reduction: Seniors may be eligible for property tax relief through the Circuit Breaker Program, Illinois Department of Revenue, IDOR, (800) 624-2459.

Sales: 6.25%.

Prescription Exemptions: There is a 1% sales tax on prescription drugs. Seniors may be eligible for prescription drug sales exemptions through the Circuit Breaker Program, Illinois Department of Revenue, IDOR, (800) 624-2459.

Transportation, Travel, and Tourism

Major Airports

- Chicago O'Hare International Airport, 100000 O'Hare, Chicago, IL 60666-3104, (773) 686-2200.
- Bloomington-Normal Airport, RRI, Bloomington, IL 61704-9801, (309) 663-7383.
- Willard Airport, 11 Airport Rd., Savoy, IL 61874-9730, (217) 244-8600.

Railways

- Metra, (312) 322-6777 (Northeast IL).
- Amtrak, (800) USA-RAIL.

Bus Tours

- Keeshin Charter Service, (773) 245-6400 or (800) 843-3247, Chicago area.
- Greyhound Bus, (800) 231-2222.

State Highways

- Interstates 55/155 and 57 run north-south.
- Interstates 70, 64, 80, and 72 run east-west.

Theater and Music

Northeast

- Riverfront Playhouse, 11-13 S. Water St. Mall, Aurora, IL 60505-3321, (630) 896-7144.
- Shakespeare Repertory, 1016 N. Dearborn, Chicago, IL 60610-2804, (312) 642-2273.
- Apollo Theater Center, 2540 N. Lincoln, Chicago, IL 60614-2314, (773) 935-6100.
- Civic Opera House, 20 Wacker Drive Chicago, IL 60606, (773) 332-2244.
- Light Opera Works, 600 Emerson St., Evanston, IL 60201, (847) 689-6300, Fax: (847) 869-6388.
- Pheasant Run Dinner Theater, 4051 E. Main, St. Charles, IL 60174-5200, (708) 584-6342.

Museums, Crafts, Historical, Recreational

Northwest

- U. S. Grant Home, PO Box 333, Galena, IL 61036, (815) 777-0248 or 3310.
- Old Market House State Historic Site, Galena, IL (815) 777-0248 or 3310 (exhibits of the history of Galena).
- Black Hawk State Historic Site, 1510 46th Ave., Rock Island, IL 61201, (309) 788-0177 (Indian Museum, public lounge, hiking).

Northeast

- Lockport Gallery, 200 W. 8th St., Lockport, IL 60441, (815) 838-7400 Fax: (815) 838-7448 (past and current IL artists and artisans).
- The Nature Museum, 2430 N. Cannon Drive, Chicago, IL 60614, (773) 549-0606, *http://www.chias.org* (natural history of the Midwest from the Great Lakes to the prairies).

South

- Southern Illinois Artisans Shop and Visitors Center, Interstate 57, Benton, (618) 629-2220, Fax: (618) 629-2704 (a branch of the Illinois State Museum).

Central

- Illinois Amish Country, 106 E. Progress, Arthur, IL 61911-1301, (800) 722-6474, *http://www.illinois-amishcountry.com*
- The Prairie Aviation Museum, PO Box 856, Bloomington, IL 61702-0856.

Organizations

Advocacy Groups

- Senior Health Insurance Program (SHIP), (800) 548-9034.
- Illinois Comprehensive Health Insurance Plan (CHIP), (800) 367-6410 (supplements Medicare coverage).
- Office of the Ombudsperson, (800) 252-8635 (Illinois Department of Public Aid; assistance with medical costs including prescription drugs).
- Senior HelpLine, (800) 252-8966.
- Illinois Department on Aging, (312) 814-6200 (Chicago area); (217) 785-3356 (Springfield).
- Bureau of Long-term Care, 525 W. Jefferson St., Springfield, IL 62761, (217) 782-2913.

Volunteer Programs

- Volunteer services to help children in Chicago area, (312) 456-0600.
- YMCA of Metro Chicago (counseling, day care, educational programs), (312) 280-3400.
- Retired and Senior Volunteer Program of Lake County, 106 South Sheridan Rd., Waukegan, IL 60085, (847) 249-4330.

Housing

Long-Term Care Facilities

*In the state of Illinois, these facilities are called **Long-Term Care/Nursing Home Facilities**.*

These facilities provide residential living and/or various levels of nursing and medical services to seniors for an extended period of time.

Types of Authorization

Licensing and/or Certification

These facilities must be licensed by the Department of Public Health, Office of Health Care Regulation, (217) 782-2913. Hotline to register complaints against health care facilities, (800) 252-4343.

Memberships

- American Association of Homes and Services for the Aging (AAHSA) represents not-for-profit organizations committed to providing high-quality health care, housing, and services to the elderly. AAHSA, 901 E St. NW, Suite 500, Washington, DC 20004-2011. Ph: (202) 783-2242. Fax: (202) 783-2285. *http://www.aahsa.org*
- Life Services Network of Illinois, 911 N. Elm St., Suite 228, Hinsdale, IL 60521-3634, Ph: (630) 325-6170. Fax: (630) 325-0749; Springfield, Ph: (217) 789-1677. Fax: (217) 789-1778.

Accreditations

- Continuing Care Accreditation Commission (CCAC) accredits facilities that offer seniors a contract or contracts that provide residential living and health care services for the remainder of the person's lifetime and meet CCAC's accreditation standards.
- Joint Commission on the Accreditation of Healthcare Organizations (JCAHO) is an independent, not-for-profit organization, and the nation's oldest and largest standards-setting and health care accrediting institution.

North

Carroll County Good Samaritan Center

1006 N. Lowden
Mt. Carroll, IL 61053

Ph: (815) 244-7715
Fax: (815) 244-3127

NH: 75

Nonprofit; nondenominational facility. Private and semiprivate rooms. Nursing care; medical services; therapies; pharmacy; dental and podiatry services; Medicare/Medicaid-approved; personal care; medication administration; security; emergency response system; maintenance; transportation; up to 3 daily meals; housekeeping and laundry services; chapel services; daily activities.

NH Daily: $105–$125.

Northwoods Care Center, JCAHO

2250 Pearl St.
Belvidere, IL 61008

Ph: (815) 544-0358
Fax: (815) 544-5006

NH: 120

Nondenominational; for-profit facility. Private and semiprivate rooms. Nursing care; medical services; physical, occupational, and speech therapies; skin and wound care; IV therapy; pain management; hospice; respite care; dental and podiatry services; pharmacy; Medicare/Medicaid-approved; personal care; medication administration; security; emergency response system; maintenance; transportation; up to 3 daily meals; housekeeping and laundry services; activities; barber/beauty shop.

NH Daily: $115–$165.

Northeast/Chicago Area

Brighton Gardens By Marroitt

700 E. Euclid Ave.
Prospect Heights, IL 60070-3409

Ph: (847) 797-2700
Fax: (847) 797-2705

AL: 104. HCC: 30

For-profit; nondenominational. Apartments and private and semiprivate rooms. 24-hour skilled nursing care; rehabilitative therapies; dental and podiatry care; hearing and eye care; pharmacy services; Medicare/Medicaid-approved; personal care; medication administration; security; emergency response system; maintenance; transpor-

tation; up to 3 daily meals; housekeeping and laundry services; social and recreational activities; sun porch; courtyard.

ENT: $550. AL MO: $3,310–$3,900. HCC Daily: $215.

Casa San Carlo Retirement Community

420 N. Wolf Rd.
Northlake, IL 60164

Ph: (708) 562-4300
Fax: (708) 562-5677

IND: 170. AL: 12. NH: Yes

Nonprofit; nondenominational; affiliated with the Catholic Charities of the Archdiocese of Chicago. Apartments and private and semiprivate rooms. 24-hour nursing care; medical services; rehabilitative therapies; dental and podiatry care; pharmacy services; wellness program; personal care; medication administration; security; emergency response system; maintenance; transportation; up to 3 daily meals; housekeeping and laundry services; fitness center; religious services; social and recreational activities; banking services; library; arts and crafts room; billiards room; greenhouse; country store; barber/beauty shop.

DEP: (ref.) $1,100. IND ENT: (plan A 90% ref.), $57,500–$143,000; (plan B 90% ref.), $3,300. IND MO: (plan A), $1,000–$1,850; (plan B), $1,300–$2,700; 2nd person, $475. AL ENT: (90% ref.), $5,500. AL MO: $2,900; enhanced living plus is additional $425; 2nd person, $500; with enhanced living plus, $880.

The Fountains at Crystal Lake

965 N. Brighton Circle West
Crystal Lake, IL 60012

Ph: (815) 455-8400
Fax: (815) 477-6502

http: / / www.thefountains.com

E-mail: nikwilson@thefountains.com

IND: 139. AL: 80. SNF: 99. ALZ/MEM IMP: 24

Age 62+. Nonprofit; nondenominational. Apartments and private rooms. 24-hour nursing care; rehabilitative therapies; dental and podiatry services; pharmacy; home health care; Medicare-approved; personal care; medication administration; security; emergency response system; maintenance; transportation; up to 3 daily meals; pets (cats) allowed; housekeeping and laundry services; chapel; library; media room; craft room; social and recreational activities; English pub; barber/beauty shop.

DEP: $1,650. IND MO: $1,600–$2,600. AL MO: $2,400–$3,300. SNF Daily: $130–$215. ALZ/MEM IMP: $100–$185.

Friendship Village, CCAC

350 W. Schaumburg Rd.
Schaumburg, IL 60194

Ph: (847) 884-5050 or (800) 475-9092
Fax: (847) 884-5473

IND: Yes. AL: Yes. HCC: Yes

Nonprofit; owned by the Evangelical Retirement Homes of Greater Chicago. Apartments and private and semiprivate rooms. Nursing care; medical services; rehabilitative therapies; dental and podiatry care; pharmacy services; home health care services; wellness clinic; personal care; medication administration; security; emergency response system; maintenance; transportation; up to 3 daily meals; housekeeping and laundry services; exercise program; chaplain; religious services; banking services; library; computer room; social and recreational activities; arts and crafts room; gift shop; convenience store; billiards room; woodworking shop; gardens; fishing pond; barber/beauty shop.

IND ENT: (ref.), $63,000–$157,000. IND MO: (with ENT fee), $1,050–$1,800; (without ENT fee), $1,400–$1,750; 2nd person, $575. HCC Daily: $175.

Lake Forest Place, CCAC

1100 Pembridge Drive
Lake Forest, IL 60045

Ph: (847) 604-8800

Fax: (847) 604-8505
http://www.presbyterianhomes.org

IND: 262. AL: 33. HCC: 63. ALZ/MEM IMP: 13

Age 62+. Nonprofit; nondenominational, nonsectarian; affiliated with Presbyterian Homes. Cottages, apartments, and private and semiprivate rooms. Medical clinic; medical director; 24-hour medical assistance; skilled nursing care; physical, occupational, and speech therapies; dental care; hearing and eye services; blood pressure and cholesterol monitoring services; short- and long-term care; counseling and social services; Medicare-approved; personal care; medication administration; security; emergency response system; maintenance; transportation; up to 3 daily meals; pets allowed; housekeeping and laundry services; exercise programs; chapel; swimming pool; library; community hall; arts and crafts; woodworking shop; banking services; social and recreational activities; gift shop; dry cleaner; greenhouse; gardening; walking paths; lily ponds; barber/beauty shop.

DEP: (ref.), $2,750. ENT: Traditional, $141,000–$484,000; 2nd person, $19,000; 90% ref., $213,000–$726,000; 2nd person, $28,500. MO: $1,650–$3,000; 2nd person, $575.

Swedish Retirement Association

2320 Pioneer Rd.
Evanston, IL 60201

Ph: (847) 328-8700
Fax: (847) 328-8274

IND: Yes. AL: Yes. ICF/SNF: 48

Nonprofit; nondenominational. Apartments and private and semiprivate rooms. Skilled nursing care; 24-hour nursing care; social services; medical services; physical, occupational, and speech therapies; lab and X-ray services; ear and foot care; personal care; medication administration; security; emergency response system; maintenance; transportation; up to 3 daily meals; housekeeping and laundry services; exercise program; chaplain; religious services; social and recreational activities; library; lounges; game room; multipurpose room; barber/beauty shop.

APPL: $220. DEP: (ref.) $5,500. IND ENT: (life care unlimited days in AL and SNF), $91,000–$108,000; 2nd person, $55,000; (continuing care 180 days of AL or SNF plus, 10% discount off rates), $47,000–$58,000; 2nd person, $27,500. IND MO: (life care), $1,750; (continuing care), $1,550. AL MO: $2,100–$3,500. SNF Daily: (semiprivate), $150; (private), $200.

North Central

Fairhaven Christian Retirement Center

3470 N. Alpine
Rockford, IL 61114

Ph: (815) 877-1441
Fax: (815) 877-2040

IND: 114. RH: 128. AL: 28. HCC: 96

Age 62+ for IND; age 69+ for units. Nonprofit; nondenominational. Apartments and private and semiprivate rooms. Intermediate nursing care; rehabilitative therapies; social services; Medicaid-approved; personal care; medication administration; security; emergency response system; maintenance; up to 3 daily meals; housekeeping and laundry services; social, recreational, and religious activities; woodworking shop; crafts.

DEP: (ref.) $1,100. IND ENT: $9,400–$47,000; 2nd person, $6,600 and $8,300. IND MO: $1,100–$1,700; 2nd person, $825–$875. AL MO: Resident, $65–$100; nonresident, $90–$130. HCC Daily: Residents, $80 and $110; nonresidents, $130–$135.

The Lutheran Home

7019 N. Galena Rd.
Peoria, IL 61614-2294

Ph: (309) 692-4494
Fax: (309) 692-4374

IND: 41. AL: 21. HCC: 88

Age 60+. Nondenominational; Lutheran church affiliation. Homes, apartments, and private and semiprivate rooms. 24-hour nursing care; skilled nursing care; physical, occupational, and speech therapies; medical director; dental services; personal care; medication administration; security; emergency response system; maintenance; transportation; up to 3 daily meals; pets allowed; housekeeping and laundry services; exercise programs; chapel and religious services; Bible study; wellness training; off-site activities; computer/Internet training and access; arts and crafts; aviary; gift shop; barber/beauty shop.

IND MO: $1,300–$2,700. AL: (fees on per visit basis), $8–$20. HCC Daily: $80 and $125.

Meadows Mennonite Retirement Community

RR1, Box 310
Chenoa, IL 61726-9705

Ph: (309) 747-2702
Fax: 309-747-2944

IND: 44. AL: 14. SNF: 60. ALZ/MEM IMP: 59

Nondenominational; nonprofit; affiliation with Mennonite Church. Apartments and private and semiprivate rooms. Skilled and intermediate nursing care; on-staff doctor; long- and short-term care; physical, occupational, and speech therapies; social services; podiatrist; eye, ear, and dental services; personal care; medication administration; security; emergency response system; maintenance; transportation; up to 3 daily meals; housekeeping and laundry services; exercise classes; chapel and religious services; Bible study; ceramics; card club; arts and crafts; book club; scheduled activities; resident advisory board; barber/beauty shop.

APPL: $100. SNF Daily: $75–$140. Contact facility for other fees.

OSF Saint Claire Home, JCAHO

5533 N. Galena Rd.
Peoria Heights, IL 61614

Ph: (309) 682-5428
Fax: (309) 682-8478

IND: 155. HCC: 98

Hospital affiliation; nonprofit; nondenominational. Apartments, efficiencies, and private and semiprivate rooms. 24-hour skilled nursing care; dental and podiatry services; physical, occupational, and speech therapies; pain management; case management; aquatic therapy; psychology services; respite care; security; emergency response system; maintenance; transportation; up to 3 daily meals; housekeeping and laundry services; pastoral care and religious services; educational and recreational activities; barber/beauty shop.

Contact facility for fees.

P. A. Peterson Center for Health

1311 Parkview Ave.
Rockford, IL 61107

Ph: (815) 399-8342
Fax: (815) 399-8342

IND: Yes. PC/SH: Yes. SNF: Yes

Nondenominational; nonprofit; affiliated with the Evangelical Lutheran Church of America. Apartments, suites, and private and semiprivate rooms. Skilled nursing care; 24-hour nursing care; long- and short-term care; wound care; physical, occupational, and speech therapies; medical services; personal care; medication administration; security; emergency response system; maintenance; transportation; up to 3 daily meals (1 meal included in IND MO fee); housekeeping and laundry services;

exercise classes; devotionals; on- and off-site activities; movies; bingo; barber/beauty shop.

IND MO: $1,550. PC/SH Daily: $65–$150. SNF Daily: $130–$165.

St. Anne Place

4444 Brendenwood Rd.
Rockford, IL 61107

Ph: (815) 399-6167

IND: Yes. PC: Yes

Sponsored by the Catholic Diocese of Rockford. Apartments. Nursing care; wellness center and program; personal care; medication administration; security; emergency response system; maintenance; transportation; meal plan; housekeeping and laundry services; library; social and recreational activities; cultural and educational programs; billiards and game room; crafts; woodworking shop; community room; courtyard; convenience store; barber/beauty shop.

IND ENT: (partial ref.) $56,000–$146,000. IND MO: $1,350–$1,950; 2nd person, $675.

Northwest

Friendship Manor, JCAHO

1209 21st Street
Rock Island, IL 61201

Ph: (309) 786-9667
Fax: (309) 786-5611

IND: 217. AL: 34. SNF: 63

Age 62+. Nonprofit; nondenominational; affiliated with the International Order of King's Daughters and Sons. Apartments and private and semiprivate rooms. Skilled nursing care; physical therapy; occupational and speech therapy consultation; podiatry services; home health care; personal care; medication administration; blood pressure clinic; dental consultation; security; emergency response system; maintenance; transportation; up to 3 daily meals; housekeeping and laundry services; exercise program; chapel and religious services; banking, postal, and notary services; game room; arts and crafts studio; hobby and woodworking shop; coffee hour; gift shop; barber/beauty shop.

APPL: $825. IND ENT: Endowment, $44,000–$88,000; 90% ref., $44,000–$88,000; rental, $2,200–$4,400. IND MO: Endowment and 90% ref., $825–$1,800; rental, $825–$1,950. AL Daily: $90. SNF Daily: $115.

Southeast

The United Methodist Village

1616 Cedar St.
Lawrenceville, IL 62439

Ph: (618) 943-3347
Fax: (618) 943-3823

IND: Yes. AL: Yes. HCC: Yes. ALZ/MEM IMP: Yes

Nonprofit; nondenominational; affiliation with the Southern Illinois Conference of the United Methodist Church. Apartments and private and semiprivate rooms. Comprehensive 24-hour nursing care; three levels of care; physical, occupational, and speech therapies; Medicare-approved; personal care; medication administration; security; emergency response system; maintenance; transportation; up to 3 daily meals; housekeeping and laundry services; exercise program; chaplain and religious services; library; volunteer opportunities; community room; arts and crafts; game room; activities and activities staff; gardening; barber/beauty shop.

IND DEP/ENT: $66,000. IND MO: without deposit, $1,300–$1,500; with deposit, $325–$1,200. AL Daily: $40–$65. HCC Daily: $75–$105. ALZ/MEM IMP Daily: $105–$125.

Central

MapleRidge Care Centre

2202 N. Kickapoo St.
Lincoln, IL 62656

Ph: (217) 735-1538
Fax: (217) 732-4818

IND: 39. SNF: 120. ALZ/MEM IMP: Yes

Nondenominational; owned by First Health Care Associates. Apartments and private and semiprivate rooms. Skilled nursing care; physical, occupational, and speech therapies; IV therapy; respiratory therapy; skin and wound care; respite care; hospice care; dental, podiatry, and eye care services; Medicare/Medicaid-approved; personal care; medication administration; security; emergency response system; maintenance; transportation; up to 3 daily meals; housekeeping and laundry services; exercise classes; arts and crafts; cooking; bingo; community involvement; social and recreational activities; covered patio and picnic areas; barber/beauty shop.

IND ENT: $500. IND MO: $425 and $440. HCC Daily: Semiprivate, $95 and $115; private, $140.

Oak Manor Health Care Center

438 W. North St.
Decatur, IL 62522

Ph: (217) 429-7265
Fax: (217) 429-9841

ICF: 252

Nonprofit; nondenominational facility; owned by MidAmerica Care Foundation. Private and semiprivate rooms. Nursing care; 24-hour professional care; physical, occupational, and speech therapies; dental and podiatry services; pharmacy; personal care; medication administration; Medicaid-approved; security; emergency response system; maintenance; transportation; up to 3 daily meals; housekeeping and laundry services; exercise classes; religious services; social and recreational directors; holiday and birthday celebrations; crafts; reading; music.

ICF Daily: $90–$105.

East

The Carle Arbours

302 Burwash Ave.
Savoy, IL 61874-9572

Ph: (217) 383-3090
Fax: (217) 383-3194

SNF: 240. ALZ/MEM IMP: Yes

Nondenominational; affiliated with the Carle Foundation Hospital. Apartments, private and semiprivate rooms. 24-hour nursing care; skilled nursing care; geriatric nurse practitioner; respite care; short- and long-term care; hospice; physical, occupational, and speech therapies; social worker; personal care; medication administration; security; emergency response system; maintenance; transportation; 3 daily meals; housekeeping and laundry services; activities assistant.

Contact facility for fees.

Champaign County Nursing Home

1701 E. Main
Urbana, IL 61801

Ph: (217) 384-3784
Fax: (217) 337-0120

NH: 243. ALZ/MEM IMP: 15

Age 45+. Nonprofit; nondenominational; county owned. Private and semiprivate rooms. 24-hour nursing care; skilled and intermediate nursing care; physical, occupational, and speech therapies; social services; dental, eye, and podiatry care; respite care; pharmacy; Medicare/Medicaid-approved; personal care; medication administration; security; emergency response system; maintenance; transportation; 3 daily meals; housekeeping and laundry services; reli-

gious services; recreational, educational, and spiritual activities; barber/beauty shop.

Contact facility for fees.

Assisted Living and Residential Care Facilities

*In the state of Illinois, these facilities are called **Assisted Living/ Personal/Sheltered Care Facilities**.*

These facilities provide room and board for ambulatory and independent adults who need minimum support.

Types of Authorization

Licensing and/or Certification

Requires licensing by the Department of Health. These facilities provide supervision, limited nursing care, personal care, and therapies to residents who are not in the need of skilled nursing care, but who need some assistance to live independently.

Memberships

- Assisted Living Federation of America (ALFA) is a national nonprofit membership organization whose mission is to enhance the quality of life in assisted living facilities and promote the interests of the assisted living industry. ALFA, 10300 Eaton Place, Suite 400, Fairfax, VA 22030. Ph: (703) 691-8100. Fax: (703) 691-8106. *http://www.alfa.org*
- Life Services Network of Illinois (LSN) is a state affiliate of ALFA. LSN, 911 N. Elm St., #228, Hinsdale, IL 60521. Ph: (630) 325-6170. Fax: (630) 325-0749.

Northeast

Arden Courts

1940 Nerge Rd.
Elk Grove Village, IL 60007

Ph: (847) 534-8815
Fax: (847) 534-9843

AL: 56 (specifically for ALZ/MEM IMP)

For-profit. Private rooms. Nursing care; medical services; Medicare, Part B approved; personal care; medication administration; security; emergency response system; maintenance; transportation; up to 3 daily meals; housekeeping and laundry services; specialized activities; secured courtyards; barber/beauty shop.

DEP: $1,100. AL MO: $3,600–$5,200.

Bethlehem Woods Retirement Center

1571 W. Ogden Ave.
La Grange Park, IL 60526

Ph: (708) 579-3663
Fax: (708) 579-7159

IND: 270. AL: 64

Age 62+. Nonprofit; owned and sponsored by Catholic Charities Housing Development Corporation. Studios and one- and two-bedroom apartments. Health Resource Nurse; wellness clinic; health screening and monitoring; home health services; medical director; hearing specialist; massage therapy; Medicare-approved; personal care; medication administration; security; emergency response system; maintenance; transportation; up to 3 daily meals; housekeeping and laundry services; exercise program; chapel and religious services; banking services; travel services; social and recreational activities; educational program; arts and crafts room; community rooms; game room; dry cleaning delivery services; bicycle and walking paths; barber/ beauty shop.

DEP: (ref.) $1,100. ENT: (90% and 50% ref.), $2,750–$143,000; (no ref.), $40,000–$88,000. IND MO: $1,200–$2,700; 2nd person, $550. AL MO: $2,600–$3,000; 2nd person, $750; with AL, $1,400. Plus program, $350/mo.

Brighton Gardens of Hoffman Estates

2569 Golf Rd.
Hoffman Estates, IL 60194

Ph: (847) 755-0735
Fax: (847) 755-0736

IND: Yes. AL: Yes. ALZ/MEM IMP: Yes

For-profit; nondenominational. Studios, one- and two bedroom apartments, and private and semiprivate rooms. Licensed nurse on staff; wellness care; personal care; medication administration; security; emergency response system; maintenance; transportation; up to 3 daily meals; housekeeping and laundry services; library; social and recreational activities; common areas; arts and crafts room; barber/beauty shop.

AL MO: $2,700–$4,300; 2nd person, $825. ALZ/MEM IMP MO: $3,300–$4,200.

Fox Knoll

421 N. Lake St.
Aurora, IL 60506

Ph: (630) 844-0380

IND: Yes. AL: Yes. ALZ/MEM IMP: Yes

Age 62+. Part of Provena Senior Services; Catholic Church affiliation. Apartments. Respite care; wellness care; 24-hour staffing; home health care services including nursing care; personal care; medication administration; security; emergency response system; maintenance; transportation; up to 3 daily meals; housekeeping and laundry services; exercise program; pastoral care; religious services; library; social and recreational activities; cultural and educational programs; banking and postal services; convenience store; barber/beauty shop.

IND MO: $1,500–$1,900. AL MO: $220–$770 (in addition to IND MO).

Manor at Essington Park

3320 Executive Drive
Joliet, IL 60431

Ph: (815) 729-4773
Fax: (815) 729-3423

AL: Yes

Nondenominational; managed by XL Management Company, LLC. Efficiencies, alcoves, and one- and two-bedroom apartments. Wellness center; personal care; medication administration; security; emergency response system; maintenance; transportation; up to 3 daily meals; housekeeping and laundry services; exercise programs; religious services; social and recreational activities; bingo; card and board games; barber/beauty shop.

PROC: $400. DEP: (ref.), $100. AL MO: $2,200–$3,300; 2nd person (with supportive services), $1,100; (without supportive services), $440.

North Shore Hotel

1611 Chicago Ave.
Evanston, IL 60201

Ph: (847) 864-6400
Fax: (847) 864-0947

http://www.retirementhotel.com

IND: Yes. AL: Yes

Nondenominational. Apartments. Visiting nurse services; on-site registered nurse; physician services; eye care; wound care; weight and blood pressure checks; pain management; medication injections; social services; Medicare-approved; personal care; medication administration; security; emergency response system; maintenance; transportation; up to 3 daily meals; housekeeping and laundry services; fitness center; swimming pool; library; social and recreational activities; on- and off-site activities; educational programs; arts and crafts center; billiard room; ballroom; theater; gardens.

IND MO: $975–$1,750+; 2nd person, $325.

St. Andrew Home

7000 N. Newark
Niles, IL 60714

Ph: (847) 647-8332
Fax: (847) 647-7073

IND: 131. AL: 18. ICF: 52

Age 65+. For-profit. Private rooms. Nursing care; Medicare-approved; personal care; medication administration; security; emergency response system; maintenance; transportation; up to 3 daily meals; housekeeping and laundry services; social and recreational activities.

APPL: $50.00. DEP: (ref.) 1 mo. rent. IND MO: $1,350–$1,800. AL MO: $2,200–$2,250.

Independent Living

Independent housing (primarily rentals) for seniors that may offer security features, meal service, and activities.

North

Lilac Apartments

3 Lilac
Fox Lake, IL 60020

Ph: (847) 587-8830

IND: 105

Age 55+. For-profit; nondenominational. Apartments. Security; maintenance; exercise classes; library; card and board games; social and recreational activities; coffee lounge; bingo; walking trails; picnic tables; gardens; close to public transportation, medical facilities, shopping, and restaurants.

IND MO: $700–$950.

Wedgewood Manor Senior Apartments

50 Boulder Hill Pass
Montgomery, IL 60538

Ph: (630) 897-1764
Fax: (630) 897 1764

IND: 50

Age 55+. For-profit; nondenominational. Apartments. Security; emergency response system; maintenance; meal plan; pets allowed; social and recreational activities; crafts; billiards room; lounge; close to shopping, medical facilities, restaurants; barber/beauty shop.

DEP: (ref.) $825. IND MO: $725–$875.

Central

Brenden Gardens

900 Southwind Rd.
Springfield, IL 62703

Ph: (217) 529-4586
Fax: (217) 529-4625

IND: 55

Nondenominational. Apartments. Some medical services; security; emergency response system; maintenance; transportation; up to 3 daily meals; pets allowed; housekeeping and laundry services; exercise equipment; social and recreational activities.

IND MO: $1,400–$1,600.

Montvale Estates

2601 Montvale Drive
Springfield, IL 62704

Ph: (217) 546-5577

IND: Yes

For-profit. Apartments. Home health services; on-site resident manager; security; emergency response system; maintenance; transportation; up to 3 daily meals; housekeeping and laundry services; exercise room; library; social and recreational activities; cultural and educational programs; billiards room; media room; gardens; barber/beauty shop.

DEP: (ref.) $100. IND MO: $1,100–$2,100; 2nd person, $150 and $375.

Adult/Resort Communities

Communities for active adults (not all are age-restricted; primarily ownership).

North

Boulder Ridge

99 Boulder Drive
Lake in the Hills, IL 60102

Ph: (847) 854-3008

Individual homes, homesites. Golf course; pro shop; clubhouse; tennis; swimming pool; community center; dining; social clubs.

PURCHASE: Homes, $263,000–$550,000; homesites, $82,500–$237,000.

Del Webb's Sun City

12940 Del Webb Blvd.
Huntley, IL 60142

Ph: (888) 278-6248

http://www.suncity.com/suncity

Age 55+. Individual homes. Golf course; pro shop; recreation campus; exercise facilities; tennis; swimming pools; fitness center; bocce; ballroom; arts and crafts; dining; computer lab; wellness center.

PURCHASE: Homes, $174,000–$320,000.

Eagle Ridge Inn and Resort

444 Eagle Ridge Drive
Galena, IL 61036

Ph: (800) 635-0371 or (815) 777-2800
Fax: (815) 777-2803

http://www.eagleridgerealty.com

Individual homes, condominiums, homesites. Golf course; clubhouse; pro shop; tennis; swimming pool; hiking/biking trails; fishing; riding stables; boating; snow skiing; community center; fitness center; dining; library; massages; indoor golf center; social clubs.

PURCHASE: Homes, $93,500–$825,000; homesites, $8,800–$110,000.

Golf Vista Estates

25807 Firestone Drive
Monee, IL 60449

Ph: (708) 534-1950

http://www.retirenet.com/il/goviest/index.html

Age 55+. Manufactured homes. 9-hole golf course; clubhouse; pro shop; billiards.

PURCHASE: New homes, $53,000–$108,000; resale homes, $44,000–$83,000.

Heather Ridge

5900 Heather Ridge Drive
Gurnee, IL 60031

Ph: (847) 367-6010

Individual homes, condominiums, high-rise complex. Golf course; clubhouse; pro shop; tennis; swimming pool; trails; fishing; biking; cross-country skiing; community center; fitness center; social clubs.

PURCHASE: Homes, $72,000–$220,000.

Lake Barrington Shores

64 Old Barn Rd.
Barrington, IL 60010

Ph: (847) 382-1660 or (847) 381-5555

Condominiums. Golf course; tennis; swimming pool; hiking/biking trails; fishing; community center; fitness center; library; social clubs; marina.

PURCHASE: Condos, $160,000–$550,000.

The Ponds of Turnberry

8475 Watson Circle
Lakewood, IL 60014

Ph: (815) 459-2270

http://www.westfieldhomes.com/turnberry.html

Individual homes. Golf courses; clubhouse; pro shop; swimming pool; tennis; dining.

PURCHASE: Homes, from $297,000.

Willow Lake Estates

161 Tollview Rd.
Elgin, IL 60123

Ph: (847) 742-3620

http://www.retirenet.com/il/willowle/index.html

Age 55+. Manufactured homes. Clubhouse; swimming pool; river; stocked lake; row boats; shuffleboard; horseshoes.

PURCHASE: New homes, $65,000–$105,000; resale homes, from $16,500.

Wynstone

101 S. Wynstone Drive
North Barrington, IL 60010

Ph: (847) 381-7100

http://www.wynstone.com

Golf villas, village homes, estate homes, homesites. Golf course; clubhouse; pro shop; tennis; swimming pool; sauna; dining; social activities.

PURCHASE: Golf villas, from $715,000; village homes, from $495,000; estate homes, $605,000–about $3.3 million; homesites, $77,000–$506,000.

Central

Macomb Country Club

20 Hickory Grove
Macomb, IL 61455

Ph: (309) 837-2132

Individual homes, condominiums, homesites. Golf course; clubhouse; pro shop; tennis; swimming pool; hiking trails; dining; social clubs.

PURCHASE: Homes, from $149,000; condos, from $99,000; homesites, $16,500–$60,500.

Oak Run Property Owners' Association

1470 Knox Rd. 1725 North
Dahinda, IL 61428

Ph: (309) 879-2603 or (309) 879-2742

http://www.oak-run.com

Individual homes, homesites. Golf course; pro shop; clubhouse; tennis; swimming pool; fishing; boating; beaches; dining; social clubs.

PURCHASE: Homes, $69,000–$412,500; homesites, $3,600–$181,500.

South

Stonewolf Golf and Residential Community

1195 Stonewolf Trail
Fairview Heights, IL 62208

Individual homes, villas, townhomes. Golf course; clubhouse; pro shop.

PURCHASE: Homes, from $219,000; villas, from $132,000; townhomes, from $358,000.

Indiana

http://www.state.in.us

General Information

Climate

Mean temperature for January is mid-20s; mean temperature for June is high 70s.

Cost of Living

Ranks 24th in the nation.

Taxes

State/Local as % of Income: 10.3%.

Property Tax Reduction: Residents 65 or older may qualify for a property tax reduction of $1,000.

Sales: 5%.

Prescription Exemptions: Prescription drugs are exempt from sales tax, as are eyeglasses or contact lenses, hearing aids, syringes or other instruments used to administer insulin, and other medical equipment and devices.

Transportation, Travel, and Tourism

General

Indiana Tourism, (800) 291-8844.

Major Airports:

- Indianapolis International Airport, 51 S. New Jersey St., Indianapolis, IN 46204-2616, (317) 955-8652.
- Evansville Regional Airport, 7801 Bussing Drive, Evansville, IN 47711-6728, (812) 421-4400.
- Gary Regional Airport, 6001 Industrial Hwy, Gary, IN 46406-1024, (219) 949-9722.

Railways

- Amtrak, (800) USA-RAIL.

Bus Tours

- Greyhound Bus, (800) 231-2222.

State Highways

- Interstates 65 and 69 run north-south.
- Interstates 70, 64, and 74 run east-west.

Theater and Music

Central

- Carmel Symphony Orchestra, PO Box 761, Carmel, IN 46082-0761, (317) 844-9717.
- Deer Creek Music Center, Noblesville, (317) 841-8900, *http: www.concertline.com* (seasonal).

South:

- Norman Bluegrass Festival, Norman (812) 277-1705 (seasonal).
- Old Capital Traditional Music Festival, Corydon, (888) 738- 2137.

East

- Chamber Music Festival, Ball State University, Muncie, (765) 285-5501.

Northeast

- Fort Wayne Ballet, 324 Penn Ave., Fort Wayne, IN 46805-1938, (219) 484-9646.
- Fort Wayne Civic Theater, Performing Arts Center, 303 E. Main St., Fort Wayne, IN 46802-1999, (219) 422-8641.
- Embassy Theater, 121 W. Jefferson Blvd., Fort Wayne, IN 46802-3012, (219) 424-5665 (home of Fort Wayne's Philharmonic).

Museums, Crafts, Historical, Recreational

Central

- Conner Prairie, 13400 Allisonville, Rd., Fishers, IN 46038-4499, (317) 776-6006 or (800) 966-1836, *http: www.connerprairie.org* (living history museum).
- Merchant Marine Museum, 1230 Jackson St., Anderson, IN 46016-1653, (765) 643-7447, *http://www.netdirect.net/anderson/merchant.htm*
- Wetlands Nature Preserve, PO Box 2100, Anderson, IN 46018 (765) 648-6850.
- Indiana Transportation Museum, 325 Cicero Rd., Noblesville, IN 46060-1408, (317) 773-6000, *http://www.itm.org* (seasonal).
- Indiana State Museum, 202 N. Alabama St., Indianapolis, IN 46204-2185, (317) 232-1637.
- Grissom Air Museum, 6500 Hoosier Blvd., Peru, IN 46970-3647, (765) 688-2654. Fax: (765) 688-2956.

Southwest

- Angel Mound State Historic Site, 8215 Pollack Ave., Evansville, IN 47715-6231, (812) 853-3956. Fax: (812) 853-6271 (historic Indian town).

Southeast

- Pigeon Roost State Historic Site, US 31 (5 mi. south of Scottsburg), (812) 265-3526. Fax: (812) 265-3501 (battles fought here during the War of 1812).

West

- Old Soldiers Reunion/Civil War Reenactment, Hymera Grove, (812) 665-2695 (seasonal).
- Country Treasures Show, Wabash Valley Fairgrounds, Terre Haute, (618) 539-3395 (seasonal; arts and crafts).

Organizations

Advocacy Groups

- Indiana State Department of Health, 2 N. Meridian St., Indianapolis, IN 46204, (317) 233-1325.
- Indiana State Information Center, toll free for state agencies, (800) 45-STATE.
- Division of Disability, Aging, and Rehabilitative Services; Aging and In-Home Services-Advocacy Unit, (800) 992-6978.
- Medicaid Recipient hotline, (800) 446-1993.
- Long-Term Care Complaints, (800) 475-1355.
- Senior Health Insurance Information Program, (800) 452- 4800.

Volunteer Programs

- Indiana Commission on Community Service and Volunteerism, Indiana Government Center South, Room E220, 302 W. Washington, Indianapolis, IN 46204, (317) 233-4273, Fax: (317) 233-5660.

Housing

Long-Term Care Facilities

In the state of Indiana, these facilities are called ***Long-Term Care/Nursing Home Facilities****.*

These facilities provide residential living and/or various levels of nursing and medical services to seniors for an extended period of time.

Types of Authorization

Licensing and/or Certification

These facilities are licensed by the Department of Health, Division of Long Term Care, and are referred to as comprehensive care facilities. These facilities provide nursing care, room, food, laun-

dry, medication administration, special diets, and rehabilitative and restorative therapy treatments under order of the attending physician. Skilled nursing facilities provide 24-hour nursing care and restorative therapies and are eligible to participate in Medicare and Medicaid programs. Nursing facilities provide basic nursing care as well as room and board for those individuals not able to live independently. Additionally, they are eligible to participate in the Medicaid program.

Memberships:

- American Association of Homes and Services for the Aging (AAHSA) represents not-for-profit organizations committed to providing high-quality health care, housing, and services to the elderly. AAHSA, 901 E St. NW, Suite 500, Washington, DC 20004-2011. Ph: (202) 783-2242. Fax: (202) 783-2285. *http://www.aahsa.org*
- Indiana Association of Homes and Services for the Aging (IAHSA) is an AAHSA Affiliated State Association. IAHSA, PO Box 68829, Indianapolis, IN 46268-0829, Ph: (317) 733-2380. Fax: (317) 733-2385, *http://www.iahsa.com/*

Accreditations:

- Continuing Care Accreditation Commission (CCAC) accredits facilities that offer seniors a contract or contracts that provide residential living and health care services for the remainder of the person's lifetime and meet CCAC's accreditation standards.
- Joint Commission on the Accreditation of Healthcare Organizations (JCAHO) is an independent, not-for-profit organization, and the nation's oldest and largest standards-setting and health care accrediting institution.

Central

Franklin United Methodist Community

1070 W. Jefferson St.
Franklin, IN 46131

Ph: (317) 736-7185 or toll free, 1-87-RETIRING
Fax: (317) 736-1150

IND: 136. RH: 128. AL: 60. HCC: 100. ALZ/MEM IMP: 48

Age 65+. Nonprofit; nondenominational; affiliated with the United Methodist Church. Apartments, lodges, condos, and private rooms. Nursing care; medical services; physical, occupational, and speech therapies; pharmacy; dental, podiatry, and optometry services; clinic; personal care; medication administration; security; emergency response system; maintenance; transportation; up to 3 daily meals; pets allowed; housekeeping and laundry services; pool; fitness center; banking and postal services; tennis court; fishing lake; access to golf course; greenhouse; hobby facilities; gated community; country store; barber/beauty shop.

APPL: $100. IND ENT: $24,000–$61,000. IND MO: Starts at $1,350. AL ENT: $24,000–$49,500. AL MO: Starts at $1,600. RH ENT: $22,000–$132,000. RH MO: $450. HCC MO: Starts at $205.

Greenwood Village South

295 Village Lane
Greenwood, IN 46143

Ph: (317) 881-2591
Fax: (317) 881-1299

IND: 207. AL: 57. HCC: 46. ALZ/MEM IMP: 60

Age 62+. Nonprofit; nondenominational; managed by Life Care Services Corp. Cottages, apartments, studios, and private and semiprivate rooms. 24-hour nursing care; physical, occupational, and

speech therapies; long- and short-term care; medical clinic, blood pressure checks; Medicare/Medicaid-approved; personal care; medication monitoring; 24-hour security; wellness program; transportation; up to 3 daily meals; housekeeping and laundry services; exercise program; nondenominational religious services; banking services; cultural and educational programs; greenhouse; woodworking shops; library; card and board games; off-site excursions; convenience store; barber/beauty shop.

IND LCF: (cottages), $86,500–$102,000; (apartments), $22,000–$87,000. IND MO: (cottages), $325–$575; (apartments), $1,200–$2,500. AL LCF: $25,000–$28,000. AL MO: $1,650–$2,300. HCC Daily: Skilled, $120; nonskilled, $115. (Rates include 10% discount to LifeCare residents.)

Hoosier Village Retirement Center, CCAC

5300 West 96
Indianapolis, IN 46268

Ph: (317) 873-3349
Fax: (317) 873-8224

IND: 75. RH/AL: 54. HCC: 80. ALZ/MEM IMP: Yes

Age 65+. Nonprofit; nondenominational. Homes, duplexes, apartments, and private rooms. 24-hour nursing care; medical services; pharmacy and lab services; physical, occupational, and speech services; personal care; medication administration; Medicare-approved; security; emergency response system; maintenance; transportation; up to 3 daily meals; pets allowed; housekeeping and laundry services; religious services; library; banking and postal services; scheduled activities; gift shop; lounge areas with fireplace; barber/beauty shop.

APPL: (no ref.) $275. DEP: (ref.) $5,500. IND ENT: $59,500–$109,000. IND MO: (with ENT), $925–$1,350; (without ENT), $1,950–$2,700. AL/RH ENT: $32,000–$72,000. AL/RH MO: (with ENT), $1,350–$2,050; (without ENT), $2,100–$3,500; AL services, $325 addl. HCC Daily: (with ENT), $130 and $150; (without ENT), $150 and $170. ENT fees are 90% refundable up to 4 years.

Kennedy Living Center

301 W. Harrison St.
Martinsville, IN 46151

Ph: (765) 342-6637
Fax (765) 342-6648

AL/RH: 39. ICF: 67. SNF: 10

Age 55+. Affiliated with the National Benevolent Association of the Christian Church. Studios and private and semiprivate rooms. Skilled and intermediate nursing care; 24-hour nursing care; restorative services; therapies; lab services; dental, optometry, and podiatry services; psychological services; hospice; occupational, physical, and speech therapies; audiological services; personal care; medication administration; home health care; Medicare/Medicaid-approved; security; emergency response system; maintenance; transportation; up to 3 daily meals; housekeeping and laundry services; religious services; resident council; activities program, library; off-site excursions; barber/beauty shop.

AL/RH MO: $1,350–$2,400. ICF Daily: Semiprivate, $115; private, $135; large private, $160. SNF Daily: Semiprivate, $180; private, $260.

Miller's Merry Manor

259 W. Harrison
Mooresville, IN 46158

Ph: (317) 831-6272
Fax: (317) 831-7662

SNF: 98

For-profit; nondenominational. Private rooms. 24-hour nursing care; medical services; on-site physician; rehabilitative therapies; dental and podiatry care; pharmacy; Medicare/Medicaid-approved; personal care; medication administration; security; emergency response system; maintenance; transportation; up to

3 daily meals; pet visits; housekeeping and laundry services; scheduled activities; barber/beauty shop.

SNF Daily: $120–$165.

Mulberry Lutheran Home

502 W. Jackson St.
Mulberry, IN 46058

Ph: (765) 299-2911
Fax: (765) 296-9116

IND: 68. RH: 28. HCC: 147

Nonprofit; nondenominational. Duplexes, apartments; private and semiprivate rooms. Intermediate and skilled nursing care; home maker and home health services provided by Lutheran Community Services; Hospice of Clinton County affiliated; medical services; therapies; pharmacy; dental and podiatry services; Medicare/Medicaid-approved; security; emergency response system; maintenance; transportation; up to 3 daily meals; housekeeping and laundry services; scheduled daily activities; off-site excursions; barber/beauty shop.

IND LEASE: $82,500. IND MO: $115.
RH Daily: Semiprivate, $70; private, $105. HCC Daily: ICF semiprivate, $115; private, $170; SNF semiprivate, $150; private, $190.

Northeast

Christian Care Retirement Community

720 E. Dustman Rd.
Bluffton, IN 46714-1234

Ph: (219) 565-3000
Fax: (219) 565-3009

IND: 29. RH: 17. AL: 17. SNF: 48. ALZ/MEM IMP: 16

About age 70+. Nonprofit. Apartments, duplexes, and private rooms. 24-hour nursing care; physical, occupational, and speech therapies; social services; personal care; medication administration; security; emergency response system; maintenance; transportation; up to 3 daily meals; housekeeping and laundry services; exercise program; religious services; library; cultural, social, and recreational programs; activities director; off-site excursions; barber/beauty shop.

IND ENT: (3 plans; 2 ref., 1 no ref.), $11,000–$38,500. IND MO: $95–$825.
RH ENT: (3 plans; 2 ref., 1 no ref.), $5,500–$38,500. RH MO: $1,100–$2,800.
SNF Daily: $120 and $130.

Lutheran Home and Concord Village

6701 S. Anthony Blvd.
Fort Wayne, IN 46816-2035

Ph: (219) 447-1591

IND: 172. AL/RH: Yes. NH: Yes. ALZ/MEM IMP: Yes

Age 55+. Nonprofit; nondenominational; affiliated with the Lutheran Church. Studios, apartments, and private and semiprivate rooms. On-site physician; 24-hour nursing care; restorative care; pain management; physical, occupational, speech, and respiratory therapies; long- and short-term care; dental, eye, and foot care; hospice; Medicare/Medicaid-approved; social services; personal care; medication administration; security; emergency response system; maintenance; transportation; up to 3 daily meals; housekeeping and laundry services; exercise program; religious services; Bible study; social and recreational activities; volunteer program; games; hobbies; arts and crafts; gardening; hair care.

DEP: $100. IND ENT: $44,000–$110,000. IND MO: $550–$1,050. RH/AL DEP: One mo. rent. RH/AL Daily: $75–$125. NH: $110–$300.

Woodcrest of Decatur, JACO

1300 Mercer Ave.
Decatur, IN 46733

Ph: (219) 724-3311
Fax: (219) 724-8696

IND: 86. AL: 32. HCC: 143. ALZ/MEM IMP: 23. ADC: Yes

Condos, apartments; duplexes, and private and semiprivate rooms. Nonprofit; nondenominational facility. Nursing care; medical services; rehabilitative therapies; pharmacy; dental and podiatry services; personal care; medication administration; emergency response system; maintenance; transportation; up to 3 daily meals; pets allowed; housekeeping and laundry services; activities.

APPL: (part. ref.), $1,100. IND ENT: (5-yr. amortization), $46,000–$67,000. IND MO: $550–$850; 2nd person, $150. AL MO: $1,900–$2,200; 2nd person, $925. HCC Daily: $110–$120.

Northwest

Chicagoland Christian Village

6685 E. 117th Ave.
Crown Point, IN 46307

Ph: (219) 662-0642
Fax: (219) 663-4260

E-mail: *ccvillag@mail.icongrp.com*

IND: 74. AL: 33. HCC: 78. ALZ/MEM IMP: 22

Age 55+ for independent living. Nonprofit; affiliated with the Independent Christian Church. Apartments and private rooms. Nursing care; medical services; Medicare/Medicaid-approved; personal care; medication administration; security; emergency response system; maintenance; transportation; up to 3 daily meals (1 daily meal included in IND MO. fee); housekeeping and laundry services.

DEP: $550. IND ENT: $57,000–$100,000. IND MO: $400–$1,100. AL MO: $2,150–$2,800. HCC Daily: $125–$150.

North

Saint Pauls Retirement Community, CCAC

3602 S. Ironwood Drive
South Bend, IN 46614-2453

Ph: (219) 291-8205
Fax: (219) 291-0858

IND/CL: Yes. RC/AL: Yes. HCC: Yes

Member of Holy Cross Care Services and Holy Cross Health System; church related; nondenominational. Apartments and private and semiprivate rooms. Skilled and intermediate nursing care; physician, dental, podiatry services; Medicare/Medicaid-approved; personal care; medication administration; wellness center; physical, occupational, and speech therapies; security; emergency response system; maintenance; transportation; up to 3 daily meals; housekeeping and laundry services; chapel and religious services; exercise program; banking services; planned activities and programs; library; arts and crafts room; workshop; lounges/multipurpose rooms; gardens; resident council; gift shop and convenience store; barber/beauty shop.

IND MO: $1,200–$2,100. CL MO: $875–$1,400. AL MO: $1,900–$3,500. HCC: Contact facility for fees.

South Central

Four Seasons, CCAC

1901 Taylor Rd.
Columbus, IN 47203

Ph: (812) 378-6184
Fax: (812) 378-6184 (res.); 379-1390 (HCC)

IND: Yes. AL: Yes. HCC: Yes

Nonprofit; nondenominational; operated by Baptist Homes of Indiana. Apartments and private and semiprivate

rooms. 24-hour nursing care; physical, occupational, and speech therapies; rehabilitative services; medical services; pain management; cardiac rehabilitation; personal care; medication administration; security; emergency response system; maintenance; transportation; up to 3 daily meals; housekeeping and laundry services; exercise program; religious services; banking services; library; crafts; book reviews; card games; choir and drama group; gift shop and bakery; barber/beauty shop.

IND ENT: (90% ref. on prorated basis for up to 48 mos.), $32,000–$135,000. IND MO: (with ENT), $1,400–$2,100; (without ENT), $2,000–$2,600. HCC ENT: (90% ref. on prorated basis for up to 48 mos.) (single), $31,500; (couple), $49,000. HCC Daily: (with ENT), $150–$250; (without ENT), $150–$200.

Southwest

Evansville Protestant Home

3701 Washington Ave.
Evansville, IN 47714-0543

Ph: (812) 476-3360

IND: Yes. AL: Yes. NH: Yes

Nonprofit; nondenominational. Apartments, studios, private and semiprivate rooms. 24-hour nursing care; therapies; personal care; medication administration; security; emergency response system; maintenance; transportation; up to 3 daily meals; housekeeping and laundry services; activities.

IND ENT: (ref. amortized up to 5 yrs.), single, $22,000; double, $27,500; studio apt., $15,500. IND MO: single, $900; double, $1,350; studio apt., $775. AL/RC ENT: $12,500. AL/RC MO: $675. (IND and AL/RC fees include up to 30 days of nursing care at no additional fee.) NH Daily: Semiprivate, $80; private, $115 and $135.

The Good Samaritan Home

601 N. Boeke Rd., PO Box 2788
Evansville, IN 47728

Ph: (812) 476-4912
Fax: (812) 474-4442

IND and AL: 18. HCC: 138. ALZ/MEM IMP: 30. ADC: to be completed June 1999.

Nonprofit; affiliated with United Church of Christ. Apartments and private and semiprivate rooms. Nursing care; therapies; dental and podiatry services; security; emergency response system; maintenance; transportation; up to 3 daily meals; housekeeping and laundry services; planned activities.

APPL: (no ref.) $50. IND and AL ENT: Plan A, $13,500–$33,500; Plan B, $5,700 (no ref.). IND and AL MO: Plan A, $950–$1,550; Plan B, $1,250–$2,300. HCC Daily: $115.

East

Swiss Village

Highway 218 West
Berne, IN 46711

Ph: (219) 589-3173
Fax: (219) 589-8369

IND: 68. RH/AL: 139. HCC: 85. ALZ/MEM IMP: 23

Age 62+. Nonprofit; nondenominational; church affiliated. Apartments and private and semiprivate rooms. 24-hour nursing care; therapies; physician and dental services; lab services; personal care; medication administration; Medicaid-approved; security; emergency response system; maintenance; transportation; up to 3 daily meals; housekeeping and laundry services; religious services; craft and recreational facilities; planned activities; off-site excursions; lakes and walking paths; barber/beauty shop.

APPL: (no ref.) $275. IND ENT: (ref. amortized up to 4 yrs.) $14,500–$37,000.

RC MO: $275–$700. AL MO: $275–$550. HCC Daily: Semiprivate/skilled, $120–$130; semiprivate/intermediate, $100–$105.

Assisted Living and Residential Care Facilities

These facilities provide room and board for ambulatory and independent adults who need minimum support.

Types of Authorization

Licensing and/or Certification

These facilities are licensed by the Department of Health, Division of Long Term Care, and are referred to as residential care facilities.

Memberships

- Assisted Living Federation of America (ALFA) is a national nonprofit membership organization whose mission is to enhance the quality of life in assisted living facilities and promote the interests of the assisted living industry. ALFA, 10300 Eaton Place, Suite 400, Fairfax, VA 22030. Ph: (703) 691-8100. Fax: (703) 691-8106. *http://www.alfa.org*

Northeast

Hubbard Hill Estates

28070 C. R. 24 W.
Elkhart, IN 46517

Ph: (219) 674-6269

IND: Yes. RC: Yes. HCC: 22

Age 62+. Nonprofit; nondenominational; sponsored by the Missionary Church. Apartments, studios, and private and semiprivate rooms. Nursing care; vital sign checks; injections; personal care; medication administration; security; emergency response system; maintenance; transportation; up to 3 daily meals; small pets allowed; housekeeping and laundry services; religious services; exercise classes; educational and recreational activities; banking and postal services; lounges; library; off-site excursions; barber/beauty shop.

DEP: Studio, $475; apt., $550. IND MO: $1,450–$2,000. RC services are additional. HCC Daily: (semiprivate), $110.

North Central

Bend in the Woods Estates

1701 Smith St.
Logansport, IN 46947

Ph: (219) 735-2088 or (800) 654-9421
Fax: (219) 722-3447

IND/RC: 48

Age 55+. Nondenominational facility. One-bedroom apartments. Personal care; medication administration; case managers; security; emergency response system; maintenance; transportation; up to 3 daily meals; pets allowed; laundry services; activities; convenient to local Senior Citizens Center.

DEP: (ref.) $150. IND/AL MO: $400.

REQ: income must be not greater than $16,000 (single) or $18,500 (double).

Central

Crown Pointe Senior Living Community, IAHSA

2727 Crown Pointe Circle
Anderson, IN 46012

Ph: (765) 641-9995
Fax: (765) 622-0340

IND: 24. AL: 56

Nonprofit; affiliated with the Church of God, Anderson. Condos and apartments. Personal care; medication administration; wellness center; security; emergency response system; maintenance; transportation; up to 3 daily meals; some

pets allowed; housekeeping and laundry services; chapel; library; recreation room; daily activities; newly constructed fishing pond with pier and gazebo; walking trails; 4-seasons room; gift shop; barber/beauty salon.

DEP: $825. IND ENT: $99,000–$127,000. IND MO: $150. RC MO: $1,500–$2,600.

Independent Living

Independent housing (primarily rentals) for seniors that may offer security features, meal service, and activities.

Central

Spruce Manor Apartments

1840 Perkins Ave.
Indianapolis, IN 46203

Ph: (317) 783-6615; TDD: (800) 948-0627
Fax: (317) 782-8446

IND: 138

Age 62+. For-profit; managed by Cornerstone Properties, Inc. Apartments. Maintenance; transportation; meal plan; social and recreational activities; bingo; barbecues.

IND MO: 30% of income; HUD-subsidized.

Adult/Resort Communities

Communities for active adults (not all are age-restricted; primarily ownership).

North

Canterbury Green Apartment Homes

2613 Abbey Drive
Fort Wayne, IN 46835

Ph: (219) 485-9687

Rental apartments. Golf course; tennis; swimming pool; racquetball; hiking/walking trails; fishing; fitness center; billiards; social clubs.

MONTHLY RENTAL: One-bedroom, from $575; two-bedroom, from $625; three-bedroom, from $825.

Rock Hollow Estates

PO Box 187
Peru, IN 46970

Ph: (765) 473-5578

Individual homes, homesites. Golf course; pro shop.

PURCHASE: Homesites, $13,500–$55,000.

Central

The Hawthorns Golf and Country Club

12255 Club Point
Fishers, IN 46038

Ph: (317) 845-9100

Individual homes, condominiums, homesites. Golf course; clubhouse; pro shop; tennis; swimming pool; hiking/biking; fitness center; dining; social clubs.

PURCHASE: Condos, from $275,000; homes, $385,000–$1.1 million+; homesites, $59,500–$330,000.

South

Eagle Pointe Golf Resort

2250 E. Pointe Rd.
Bloomington, IN 47401

Ph: (812) 824-4040 ext. 129
http://www.eaglepointe.com

Individual homes, condominiums, homesites. PGA golf course; clubhouse; pro shop; tennis; swimming pools; hiking/biking; fishing; boating; basketball; dining; social clubs.

PURCHASE: Condos, $88,000–$550,000; homes, $165,000–$550,000; homesites, $55,000–$132,000.

Iowa

http: / / www.state.ia.us

General Information

Climate

Wide range. July averages between 87° F and 64° F; January averages between 3° F and 33° F. Snow averages between 22 and 50 inches per season.

Cost of Living

Ranks 34th in the nation.

Taxes

State/Local as % of Income: 10.7%.

Property Tax Reduction: Homestead tax credit is available.

Sales: 5%.

Prescription Exemptions: Drugs and medicines sold on prescription are exempt from sales tax, as are some medical devices.

Transportation, Travel, and Tourism

General

Iowa Division of Tourism, 200 E. Grand Ave., Des Moines, IA 50309, (800) 345-IOWA.

Major Airport

- Des Moines International Airport, 5800 Fleur Drive, Suite 201, Des Moines, IA 50321, (515) 256-5100.

Railways

- Amtrak, (800) 872-7245.

Bus Tours

- Greyhound Bus, (800) 231-2222.

State Highways

- Interstate 35 runs north-south.
- Interstate 80 runs east-west.

Theater and Music

North

- Hearst Center for the Arts, 304 W. Seerley Blvd., Cedar Falls, IA 50613-4050, (319) 273-8641.
- Miss Marquette Riverboat Casino Resort, 100 Antimonopoly, Marquette, IA; Mailing Address: PO Box 460, Marquette, IA 52158, (800) 4-YOU-BET or (319) 873-3531.
- Spirit of Greene River Cruises, 2951 Greene Rd., Greene, IA (515) 823-4791.
- Okoboji Queen II Excursions, Queens Ct. and Lake St., Arnolds Park, IA (712) 332-5159.

Central

- The Donna Reed Foundation for the Performing Arts, 1305 Boardway, Denison, IA 51442, (712) 263-3334 or (800) 336-4692.
- Octagon Center for the Arts, 427 Douglas, Ames, IA 50010, (515) 232-5331.
- Prairie Meadows Racetrack and Casino, 1 Prairie Meadows Drive, Altoona, IA 50009-2100, (515) 967-1000 or (800) 325-9015.
- Story Theatre/Grand Opera House, 512 Broad St., Story City, IA 50248-1134, (515) 733-4214.

Museums, Crafts, Historical, Recreational

North

- Blanden Memorial Art Museum, 920 Third Ave. S., Fort Dodge, IA 50501-4723, (515) 573-2316.
- Iowa Great Lakes Maritime Museum, PO Box 726, Arnolds Park, IA 51331, (712) 332-5264.

- Iowa Falls Historical Museum, 320 Stevens St., Iowa Falls, IA 50126-2213, (515) 648-4603.
- Laura Ingalls Wilder Park and Museum, 3603 236th Ave., Burr Oak, IA 52131, (319) 735-5916.

South

- International Center for Rural Culture and Art, Inc., one mile east of Allerton, (515) 872-2667.
- Nelson Pioneer Farm Museum, 2294 Oxford Ave., Old Glendale Rd., Oskaloosa, IA 52577-9102, (515) 672-2989.
- Des Moines County Historical Society Museums, 1616 Dill St., Burlington, IA 52601-4008, (319) 753-2449.

Central

- Brunnier Art Museum, 290 Scheman Building, Ames, IA (515) 294-3342.
- Iowa Arboretum, Inc., 1875 Peach Ave., Madrid, IA 50156-7571 (No phone; open sunrise to sunset every day).
- Des Moines Art Center, 4700 Grand Ave., Des Moines, IA 50312-2099, (515) 277-4405.

East

- Dubuque Museum of Art, 36 E. Eighth St., Dubuque, IA 52001-7046, (319) 557-1851.
- Castaway Cruises, PO Box 1483, Dubuque, IA 52004-1483, (319) 590-2776.
- Amana Arts Guild Gallery, 1210 G. St., High Amana, IA 52203-8081, (319) 622-3678.

West

- Belle of Sioux City Riverboat Casino, 100 Larsen Park Rd., Sioux City, IA 51101-2300, (712) 255-0552 or (800) 424-0080.
- Sioux City Public Museum, 2901 Jackson St., Sioux City, IA 51104-3697, (712) 279-6174.
- Sioux City Art Center, 225 Nebraska St., Sioux City, IA 51101-1712, (712) 279-6272.
- RailsWest Railroad Museum and HO Model Railroad, 1512 S. Main St., Council Bluffs, IA 51503-6527, (712) 323-5182.
- De Soto National Wildlife Refuge, Hwy. 30 along Missouri River, Missouri Valley, (712) 642-2772.

Organizations

Advocacy Groups

- Community Services Bureau, Iowa Department of Public Health, Des Moines, (515) 281-3104.

Volunteer Programs

- Hospice of Central Iowa, The Bright Center, 401 Railroad Place, West Des Moines, IA 50265, (515) 274-3400 or (800) 806-9934.
- Ronald McDonald House of Iowa City, Children's Hospital of Iowa, (319) 356-4578.
- Retired Senior Volunteer Program (RSVP), Burlington City Hall, 400 Washington St., Burlington, IA 52601-5142, (319) 753-8155.

Housing

Long-Term Care Facilities

*In the state of Iowa, these facilities are called **Continuing Care Retirement Communities/ Nursing Home Facilities**.*

These facilities provide residential living and/or various levels of nursing and medical services to seniors for an extended period of time.

Types of Authorization

Licensing and/or Certification

These facilities are inspected by the Department of Inspections and Appeals. Nursing facilities provide regular nurs-

ing care for chronic conditions. Skilled nursing facilities provide the highest level of medical care before hospital admittance.

Memberships

- American Association of Homes and Services for the Aging (AAHSA) represents not-for-profit organizations committed to providing high-quality health care, housing, and services to the elderly. AAHSA, 901 E St. NW, Suite 500, Washington, DC 20004-2011. Ph: (202) 783-2242. Fax: (202) 783-2285. *http://www.aahsa.org*
- Iowa Association of Homes and Services for the Aging (IAHSA) is an AAHSA Affiliated State Association. IAHSA, 100 E. Grand, Suite 140, Des Moines, IA 50309-1800. Ph: (515) 283-9380. Fax: (515) 283-9382. *http://www.ageiowa.org*

Accreditations

- Continuing Care Accreditation Commission (CCAC) accredits facilities that offer seniors a contract or contracts that provide residential living and health care services for the remainder of the person's lifetime and meet CCAC's accreditation standards.
- Joint Commission on the Accreditation of Healthcare Organizations (JCAHO) is an independent, not-for-profit organization, and the nation's oldest and largest standards-setting and health care accrediting institution.
- Educational Assessment Guidelines Leading toward Excellence (EAGLE) is a voluntary self-assessment and peer review evaluation system developed by the United Methodist Association of Health and Welfare Ministries.

North Central

Lutheran Retirement Home, IAHSA

700 10th St. North
Northwood, IA 50459

Ph: (515) 324-1712
Fax: (515) 324-1716

IND: 32. NH: 84

Age 55+ for IND. Nonprofit; church affiliated. Apartments and private rooms. Nursing care; rehabilitative therapies; dental and podiatry services; pharmacy; Medicaid-approved; personal care; medication administration; security; emergency response system; maintenance; transportation; up to 3 daily meals; housekeeping and laundry services; activities.

IND MO: \$750–\$950. NH: Single, \$90; double, \$80.

South Central:

Heather Manor

600 E. Fifth St.
Des Moines, IA 50309

Ph: (515) 243-6195
Fax: (515) 243-6913

IND: 109. AL: Yes. HCC: 44

Age 62+. Nondenominational; sponsored by Iowa State Education Association; managed by Life Care Services Corp. Apartments and private and semiprivate rooms. Nursing care; rehabilitative services; home health care services; personal care; medication administration; security; emergency response system; maintenance; transportation; up to 3 daily meals; housekeeping and laundry services; exercise program; YMCA membership; chaplain services; educational, recreational, and social activities; volun-

teer opportunities; library; nearby downtown Des Moines; movies; gardening areas; barber/beauty shop.

DEP: 10% of ENT fees. IND ENT: $17,500–$172,000. IND MO: $1,300–$2,900; 2nd person, $400–$1,100. HCC Daily: Semiprivate, $100 and $115; private, $125 and $135.

Spurgeon Manor, IAHSA

1204 Linden St.
Dallas Center, IA 50063-1052

Ph: (515) 992-3735
Fax: (515) 992-3098

http://www.netins.net/showcase/spurgeonmanor

E-mail: *shelleyw@netins.net*

IND: 16. AL: 30. HCC: 29. ALZ/MEM IMP: 12

Age 65+. Nonprofit; church affiliated; Church of the Brethren. Apartments and private and semiprivate rooms. 24-hour nursing care; physical and occupational therapies; medical services; Medicaid-approved; personal care; medication administration; security; emergency response system; maintenance; transportation; up to 3 daily meals; housekeeping and laundry services; exercise programs; pet therapy; music programs; off-site activities; social and recreational activities.

APPL: (townhomes), $550. IND ENT: ($5,000 no ref.; balance ref. over 15 yrs.), $18,000–$36,000. IND MO: $800–$1,750. AL ENT: (no ref.), $3,500 and $7,000. AL MO: $1,600–$3,100. HCC Daily: $85–$105.

The Village, IAHSA

1203 North E. Street
Indianola, IA 50125

Ph: (515) 961-7458 or (800) 333-8816

IND: 101. AL: Yes. HCC: 45

Age 55+. Nonprofit; nondenominational; sponsored by Wesley Retirement Services. One-, two-, and three-bedroom apartments and townhomes. Skilled nursing care; 24-hour emergency nursing service; rehabilitative therapies; Medicare/Medicaid-approved; personal care; medication administration; security; emergency response system; maintenance; transportation; up to 3 daily meals; pets allowed; housekeeping and laundry services; fitness center; swimming pool; chapel; library; social, cultural, recreational, and spiritual activities; residents' association; lounges; solarium; pond; gazebo; gift and coffee shop; gardening; walking paths; barber/beauty shop.

APPL: (ref.) $275. IND ENT: (ref.) $44,000–$120,500. IND MO: $800–$1,200. HCC Daily: $105+.

Valley View Village, IAHSA

2571 Guthrie Ave.
Des Moines, IA 50317

Ph: (515) 265-2571

IND: 192. HCC: 79. ALZ/MEM IMP: Yes

Nonprofit; nondenominational; affiliated with the Des Moines are evangelical churches. Apartments and private and semiprivate rooms. 24-hour nursing care; rehabilitative therapies; personal care; medication administration; security; emergency response system; maintenance; transportation; up to 3 daily meals; housekeeping and laundry services; hobbies and crafts; recreational, social, and spiritual activities; lounges.

IND ENT: $10,500–$82,500. IND MO: $450–$1,250. IND fees include up to 14 days of care in HCC at no additional charge.

Wesley Acres, IAHSA, EAGLE

3520 Grand Ave.
Des Moines, IA 50312-4397

Ph: (515) 271-6505

IND: 141. AL: 39. HCC: 80. ALZ/MEM IMP: 15. ADC: Yes

Age 55+. Nonprofit; nondenominational; affiliated with the United Methodist Church. Apartments and private and semiprivate rooms. 24-hour nursing care; medical director; dental and podia-

try services; pharmacy services; blood pressure and weight monitoring; wellness clinic; personal care; medication administration; security; emergency response system; maintenance; transportation; up to 3 daily meals; housekeeping and laundry services; exercise classes; pool; chapel and religious services; library; computer center; arts and crafts; social, recreational, and cultural activities; convenience store; gift shop; gardening; within walking distance to shopping, pharmacy, restaurants, theater; barber/beauty shop.

IND ENT: (50–90% ref.) $47,000–$102,000+. IND MO: $950–$1,950. AL Daily: $100–$200. HCC Daily: $135–$150.

Central

Northcrest Retirement Community

1801 20th St.
Ames, IA 50010-5179

Ph: (515) 232-6760

IND: 116. AL: Yes. HCC: 40

Age 60+. Nondenominational; sponsored by the Mid-America Baptist Churches, American Baptist Churches. Townhomes, apartments, and private and semiprivate rooms. 24-hour nursing care; health monitoring; blood pressure checks; podiatry, ear, and eye care services; first aid treatment; personal care; medication administration; security; emergency response system; maintenance; transportation; up to 3 daily meals; housekeeping and laundry services; exercise program; library; bank services; business office (e.g., faxing, copying services); individual and group activities; off-site activities; gardens; meeting rooms; crafts; barber/beauty shop.

APPL: (no ref.) $50. DEP: $2,200. IND ENT: $63,000–$175,000. IND MO: $600–$1,300. HCC Daily: $60.

Park Centre, EAGLE

500 1st St. North
Newton, IA 50208-3112

Ph: (515) 791-5000 or (888) 877-2412

IND: Yes. HCC: Yes

Age 55+. Nonprofit; nondenominational; sponsored by Wesley Retirement Services; affiliated with the United Methodist Church. One-, two-, and three-bedroom apartments; townhomes, and private rooms. 24-hour nursing care; rehabilitative therapies; medical services; dental and podiatry services; personal care; medication administration; security; emergency response system; maintenance; transportation; up to 3 daily meals; housekeeping and laundry services; fitness center; swimming pool; exercise program; chapel; resident association; billiards room; woodworking shop; arts and crafts; activities; lounge; convenience store.

APPL: $550. IND ENT: (ref.), $55,000–$170,100. IND MO: $600–$800.

East Central

Cedar Falls Lutheran Home, IAHSA, JCAHO

7511 University Ave.
Cedar Falls, IA 50613

Ph: (319) 268-0401
Fax: (319) 268-0040

IND: 88. AL/RC: 50. ICF: 135. ALZ/MEM IMP: Yes

For-profit; nondenominational; affiliated with the Lutheran Church. Apartments and private and semiprivate rooms. Intermediate nursing care; medical services; music therapy; personal care; medication administration; security; emergency response system; maintenance; transportation; up to 3 daily meals; housekeeping and laundry services; chaplain and religious services;

volunteer opportunities; on- and off-site activities; gardening; aviary; gazebo; barber/beauty shop services.

IND LL: $49,500–$142,500. IND MO: $250–$325. AL/RC Daily: $85–$90. ICF Daily: $105–$115.

The Meth-Wick Community, ccac

1224 13th St., NW
Cedar Rapids, IA 52405

Ph: (319) 365-9171
Fax: (319) 363-5312

IND: 227. AL: 50. HCC: 65. ALZ/MEM IMP: 32. HHC: Yes

Nonprofit; nondenominational. Duplexes, apartments, private and semiprivate rooms. 24-hour nursing care; rehabilitative therapies; medical services; dental and podiatry care; pharmacy services; Medicaid-approved; personal care; medication administration; security; emergency response system; maintenance; transportation; up to 3 daily meals; pets allowed; housekeeping and laundry services; exercise classes; social and recreational activities; barber/beauty shop.

APPL: $550. DEP: 10% of ENT fee. IND ENT: (no ref.) from $25,500. IND MO: $650. AL ENT: (no ref.) from $25,500. AL MO: $675. ALZ/MEM IMP ENT: (ref.), $1,000. ALZ/MEM IMP Daily: $90. HCC Daily: $110.

Oaknoll Retirement Residence, IAHSA

701 Oaknoll Drive
Iowa City, IA 52246

Ph: (319) 351-1720

IND: 144. HCC: 48

Age 62+. Nonprofit; nondenominational. Apartments and private and semiprivate rooms. 24-hour nursing care; skilled and intermediate nursing care; medical director; physical, occupational, and speech therapies; podiatry and dental services; blood pressure monitoring; Medicare-approved; personal care; medication administration; security; emergency response system; maintenance; transportation; up to 3 daily meals; housekeeping and laundry services; fitness center; exercise classes; Bible study; worship services; continuing education classes; volunteer program; social and recreational activities; billiards; lending libraries; postal services; travel tours; lounges; barber/beauty shop.

IND ENT: $33,000–$225,000. IND MO: $1,100–$3,500.

Ridgecrest Village, IAHSA

4130 NW Blvd.
Davenport, IA 52806

Ph: (319) 391-3430
Fax: (319) 388-3287

IND: 190. HCC: 137

Age 62+. Nonprofit; nondenominational. Townhomes, apartments, and private rooms. 24-hour nursing care; rehabilitative therapies; dental and podiatry services; pharmacy; home health care services; Medicare/Medicaid-approved; personal care; medication administration; security; emergency response system; maintenance; transportation; up to 3 daily meals; pets allowed; housekeeping and laundry services; fitness center; exercise program; social and recreational activities; shopping center nearby; barber/beauty shop.

IND ENT: $35,500–$109,000. IND MO: $950–$1,900. HCC Daily: $110–$145.

Vinton Lutheran Home, IAHSA

1301 Second Ave.
Vinton, IA 52349

Ph: (319) 472-4211

IND: Yes. AL: Yes. HCC: Yes. ALZ/MEM IMP: Yes

Nonprofit; affiliated with the Lutheran Church–Missouri Synod. Townhomes, apartments, and private and semiprivate rooms. 24-hour nursing care; physical, occupational, and speech therapies; wound care; injections; monthly general health screening; licensed nurse consul-

tation; pharmacy delivery; wellness program; personal care; medication administration; security; emergency response system; maintenance; transportation; up to 3 daily meals; housekeeping and laundry services; chapel and religious services; Bible study; social and recreational activities; barber/beauty shop.

Contact facility for IND fees. AL MO: $1,600–$2,200. HCC: $95–$115.

Southeast

United Presbyterian Home

1203 E. Washington St.
Washington, IA 52353-2198

Ph: (319) 653-5473
Fax: (319) 653-5474

IND: 144+. HCC: Yes

Age 62+. Nonprofit; nondenominational; affiliated with the Presbyterian Church. Cottages, apartments, efficiencies, and private and semiprivate rooms. 24-hour nursing care; rehabilitative therapies; social worker; home health care services; personal care; medication administration; security; emergency response system; maintenance; transportation; up to 3 daily meals; housekeeping and laundry services; swimming pool; chapel; Bible study; reading groups; activity coordinator; intergenerational program; volunteer opportunities; nearby hospitals, entertainment, and shopping; gardening; barber/beauty shop.

ENDOWMENT: About $15,500–$52,000. IND MO: (with endowment), single, $425; double, $550; (no endowment), add $425–$950/mo. HCC Daily: $95 and $100. AL services vary according to level of care and type of service; can be on a monthly or daily basis.

Contact the facility for entrance fees.

West Central

Eventide Lutheran Home, IAHSA, AAHSA

114 S. 20th St.
Denison, IA 51442

Ph: (712) 263-3114

IND: Yes. AL/RC: Yes. ICF: 136. ALZ/MEM IMP: Yes

Nondenominational; affiliated with the Lutheran Church. Private and semiprivate rooms. 24-hour nursing care; intermediate nursing care; physical, occupational, and speech therapies; nutritional therapy; medical services; hospital nearby; social worker; personal care; medication administration; security; emergency response system; maintenance; transportation; up to 3 daily meals; housekeeping and laundry services; religious services; social and recreational activities.

Contact facility for fees.

Southwest

Heritage House, IAHSA, EAGLE

1200 Brookridge Circle
Atlantic, IA 50022

Ph: (712) 243-1850

IND: 31. AL: 15. HCC: 46

Nondenominational; Wesley Retirement Services. Age 55+. Apartments, studios, and private and semiprivate rooms. 24-hour nursing care; rehabilitative therapies; medical services; home health services; personal care; medication administration; security; emergency response system; maintenance; transportation; up to 3 daily meals; housekeeping and laundry services; chapel and religious services; library; social and recreational activities; resi-

dent association; gardening; gazebo; shopping, restaurants, churches, and banks nearby.

Contact facility for fees.

Risen Son Christian Village, IAHSA

3000 Risen Son Blvd.
Council Bluffs, IA 51503

Ph: (712) 366-9655

IND: 46. AL/RC: 58. NH: 102. ALZ/MEM IMP: Yes

Age 60+. Nonprofit; nondenominational; affiliated with Christian Homes, Inc. Studios, duplex and congregate apartments, and private and semiprivate rooms. 24-hour nursing care; intermediate nursing care; rehabilitative therapies; physician on staff; long- and short-term care; medical services; personal care; medication administration; security; emergency response system; maintenance; transportation; up to 3 daily meals; housekeeping and laundry services; chaplain and religious services; arts and crafts; on- and off-site activities; walking paths; barber/beauty shop.

IND ENT: (ref.) $32,500–$81,500. IND MO: $205–$305. CONG ENT: (ref.) $26,000–$88,000. CONG MO: $900–$1,850; 2nd person, $195; (plus services fees). AL/RC Daily: $45–$75. NH Daily: $100–$115.

Northeast

Hillcrest Home

915 W. First St.
Sumner, IA 50674

Ph: (319) 578-8591

IND: 10. ICF: Yes (86 residents)

Nonprofit; community-sponsored facility. 24-hour nursing care; nursing aides; physical, occupational, and speech therapies; audiologist; social worker; pharmacist; personal care; medication administration; security; emergency response system; maintenance; transportation; up to 3 daily meals; housekeeping and laundry services; chapel and religious services; activities director; planned activities.

Contact facility for fees.

Assisted Living and Residential Care Facilities

*In the state of Iowa, these facilities are called **Assisted Living/Adult Residential Care Facilities.***

These facilities provide room and board for ambulatory and independent adults who need minimum support.

Types of Authorization

Licensing and/or Certification

Facilities are certified by the Department of Elder Affairs and are inspected by the Department of Inspections and Appeals. These facilities are defined as a "safe and homelike environment for individuals of all income levels who require assistance to live independently, but who do not require health-related care on a continuous 24-hour a day basis."

Memberships

- Assisted Living Federation of America (ALFA) is a national nonprofit membership organization whose mission is to enhance the quality of life in assisted living facilities and promote the interests of the assisted living industry. ALFA, 10300 Eaton Place, Suite 400, Fairfax, VA 22030. Ph: (703) 691-8100. Fax: (703) 691-8106. *http://www.alfa.org*
- Iowa Assisted Living Association (IALA) is a state affiliate of AFLA. IALA, 9001 Hickman Rd., #2B, Des Moines, IA 50322. Ph: (515) 278-8700. Fax: (515) 278-0245.

Northeast

Rosewood Estate

1117 Maxhelen Blvd.
Waterloo, IA 50702

Ph: (319) 233-5555
Fax: (319) 232-0870

IND: Yes. AL/PC: Yes

Nondenominational. Apartments. Home health care services; 24-hour staffing; nursing care; personal care; medication administration; security; emergency response system; maintenance; transportation; up to 3 daily meals; pets allowed; housekeeping and laundry services; community room; lounges; social and recreational activities; patio; community room; sunroom with aviary; barber/beauty services.

DEP: Nonsmoker/no pets, $300; smoker/pets, $700. IND MO: $1,100–$2,450; 2nd person, $350. AL MO: $550–$1,650.

Northwest

North Park Senior Living community

2562 Pierce St.
Sioux City, IA 51104

Ph: (712) 255-1200
Fax: (712) 255-6715

E-mail: *beaumanc@mail.stlukes.org*

IND: 48. AL: 60

Age 62+. Nonprofit; nondenominational. Apartments. Personal care; medication administration; security; emergency response system; maintenance; transportation; up to 3 daily meals; housekeeping and laundry services; exercise room; library; card and game room; social and recreational activities; outdoor courtyards; barber/beauty shop.

IND ENT: $51,000–$85,000. IND MO: $1,375–$1,800. AL MO: $2,500–$2,750.

Independent Living

Independent housing (primarily rentals) for seniors that may offer security features, meal service, and activities.

North Central

The Willows

1000 N. Eisenhower
Mason City, IA 50401

Ph: (515) 422-5775
Fax: (515) 522-5212

IND: 44

Nonprofit; nondenominational; affiliated with the North Iowa Mercy Health Center. Apartments. Nursing consultation; access to health care center; security; emergency response system; maintenance; transportation; 1 daily meal; pets allowed; housekeeping and laundry services; library; lounge; craft and hobby room; card and board games; social and recreational activities; barber/beauty shop.

DEP: (ref.) $200. PET DEP: $300. IND MO: $875–$1,150.

Adult/Resort Communities

Communities for active adults (not all are age-restricted; primarily ownership).

Central

River Valley Golf Community

2267 Valley View Trail
Adel, IA 50003

Ph: (515) 993-4029

Individual homes, condominiums, homesites. Golf course; clubhouse; driving range; dining.

PURCHASE: Homes, $242,000–$440,000; homesites, $48,500–$57,750.

South

Bos Landen Golf Club

2411 Bos Landen Drive
Pella, IA 50219
Ph: (800) 916-7888 or (641) 628-4625
http://www.boslanden.com/

Individual homes, condominiums, homesites. Golf course; clubhouse; pro shop; hiking/biking; fishing; dining; fitness center; conference center.

PURCHASE: Homes, $220,000–$550,000.

Kansas

http://www.accesskansas.org/

General Information

Climate

Average annual temperature is 55° F; average January temperature is 32° F; average July temperature is 79° F. Warm summers and cold winters.

Cost of Living

Ranks 35th in the nation.

Taxes

State/Local as % of Income: 10.4%.

Property Tax Reduction: Homestead refund available for seniors age 55+ whose income is $25,000 or less.

Sales: 4.9%.

Prescription Exemptions: Prescription medication is exempt from sales tax.

Transportation, Travel, and Tourism

General

Kansas Department of Commerce and Housing, Travel and Tourism Division, (785) 296-6292.

Tour Kansas Guide, PO Box 529, Cottonwood Falls, KS 66845, (316) 273-8570.

Major Airports

- Dodge City Regional Airport, 100 Airport Road, Dodge City, KS 67801, (316) 225-8100.
- Westside Airport, 2558 South Kessler St., Wichita, KS 67217, (316) 943-5510.

Railways

- Amtrak, (800) USA-RAIL.

Bus Tours

- Greyhound Bus, (800) 231-2222.

State Highways

- Interstates 35 and 135 run north-south.
- Interstate 70 runs east-west.

Theater and Music

Northeast

- Swarthout Recital Hall, University of Kansas, Department of Music and Dance, 452 Murphy Hall, Lawrence, KS 66045, (785) 864-3436.

South

- Crown Uptown Professional Dinner Theatre, 3207 E. Douglas St., Wichita, KS 67218-1086, (316) 681-1566.
- Wichita Center for the Arts, 9112 E. Central St., Wichita, KS 67206, (316) 634-2787.

East

- Topeka Performing Arts Center, 214 SE Eighth St., Topeka, KS 66603-3948, (800) 949-8722.
- Washburn University Symphonic Band, Washburn University, 1700 SW College Ave., Topeka, KS 66621, (785) 231-1010.

Southwest

- Boot Hill Repertory Co., Homestead Theater, 210 E. Wyatt Earp Blvd., Dodge City, KS 67801-4937, (316) 225-1001.

Museums, Crafts, Historical, Recreational

Southeast

- Kansas Museum of History, 6425 SW Sixth St., Topeka, KS 66615-1099, (785) 272-8681.
- Wichita Art Museum, 619 Stackman Drive, Wichita, KS 67203-3296, (316) 268-4921.
- Manhattan Center for the Arts, 1520 Poyntz Ave., Manhattan, KS 66502-4147, (785) 537-4420.
- Botanica, 701 Amidon St., Wichita, KS 67203-3199 (316) 264-0448 (flower exhibits and shows).
- Emporia Art Center, Emporia, (316) 343-6473.

Northwest

- Prairie Museum of Art and History, 1905 Franklin, Colby, KS 67701-3710, (985) 462-4590.
- High Plains Museum, 1717 Cherry St., Goodland, KS 67735-3200, (785) 899-4595.

Organizations

Advocacy Groups

- Kansas Department on Aging, (785) 296-4986.
- Kansas for Seniors, New England Bldg., 5035 Kansas, Topeka, KS 66603-3404.
- Bureau of Health Facility Regulation, 900 SW Jackson, Suite 1001, Topeka, KS 66612, (785) 296-1240.
- Kansas Department of Health and Environment, (800) 842-0078 (to call about elderly abuse or neglect).

Volunteer Programs

- Make a Wish Foundation of Kansas, 2016 N. Amidon, Wichita, KS 67203-2113 (800) 566-WISH.

Housing

Long-Term Care Facilities

*In the state of Kansas, these facilities are called **Long-Term Care/Nursing Home Facilities**.*

These facilities provide residential living and/or various levels of nursing and medical services to seniors for an extended period of time.

Types of Authorization

Licensing and / or Certification

These facilities are licensed by the Department of Health and Environment, Division of Health Facility Regulation. Nursing facilities provide 24-hour skilled nursing care.

Memberships

- American Association of Homes and Services for the Aging (AAHSA) represents not-for-profit organizations committed to providing high-quality health care, housing, and services to the elderly. AAHSA, 901 E St. NW, Suite 500, Washington, DC 20004-2011. Ph: (202) 783-2242. Fax: (202) 783-2285. *http: / / www.aahsa.org*
- Kansas Association of Home and Services for the Aging (KAHSA) is an AAHSA Affiliated State Association. KAHSA, 700 SW Harrison St., Suite 1106, Topeka, KS 66603-3759. Ph: (785) 233-7443. Fax: (785) 233-9471. *http: / / www.kahsa.org*

Accreditation

- Continuing Care Accreditation Commission (CCAC) accredits facilities that offer seniors a contract or contracts that provide residential living and health care services for the remainder of the person's lifetime and meet CCAC's accreditation standards.
- Joint Commission on the Accreditation of Healthcare Organizations (JCAHO) is an independent, not-for-

profit organization, and the nation's oldest and largest standards-setting and health care accrediting institution.

South Central

Wesley Towers, KAHA, AAHSA

700 Monterey Place
Hutchinson, KS 67502

Ph: (316) 663-9175

IND: Yes. AL/CONG: Yes. HCC: Yes

Nonprofit; nondenominational; sponsored by the United Methodist Church. Patio homes, apartments, and private and semiprivate rooms. 24-hour nursing care; long- and short-term care; physical, occupational, and speech therapies; dental and hearing care; pharmacy; nutritional therapy; home health care; blood pressure checks; personal care; medication administration; security; emergency response system; maintenance; transportation; up to 3 daily meals; housekeeping and laundry services; exercise classes; therapeutic pool; chapel; religious services; library; residents' council; woodworking shop; lectures; concerts; movies; on- and off-site activities; gardening; barber/beauty shop.

IND ENT: (equity option plan, estate savings plan), $95,000–$148,500. IND MO: (either plan), $200–$300; (rentals), $925–$1,100. AL/CONG MO: $975–$2,300; 2nd person, $240. HCC Daily: $100–$125.

South

Cumbernauld Village

716 N. Tweed
Winfield, KS 67156

Ph: (316) 221-4141
Fax: (316) 221-4146

IND: 57. RH/AL: 29. HCC: 42

Age 55+. Nonprofit; nondenominational. Garden homes, apartments, and private and semiprivate rooms. 24-hour nursing care; rehabilitative therapies; Medicaid-approved; personal care; medication administration; security; emergency response system; maintenance; transportation; up to 3 daily meals; pets allowed for garden home residents; housekeeping and laundry services; social and recreational activities; two stocked fishing ponds; 3-hole golf course; walking trails.

IND ENT: $2,750. IND MO: $1,750–$2,400. AL ENT: $2,750 (optional). AL Daily: $80–$85. RH ENT: $2,750. RH MO: $275. HCC Daily: $105–$110.

Kidron Bethel Village, KAHSA

3001 Ivy Drive
North Newton, KS 67117

Ph: (316) 284-2900

http://www.kidronbethel.org

IND: 104. AL: Yes. HCC: 60. ADC: Yes

Age 62+. Nonprofit; nondenominational. Townhomes, apartments, and private rooms. Skilled nursing care; rehabilitative therapies; medical services; podiatry and dental care; pharmacy; wellness center; blood pressure clinic; Medicare/Medicaid-approved; personal care; medication administration; security; emergency response system; maintenance; transportation; up to 3 daily meals; housekeeping and laundry services; exercise classes; swimming pool; worship services; woodworking shop; crafts; social and recreational activities; on- and off-site activities.

Contact facility for fees.

Larksfield Place, KAHSA

7373 E. 29th St. North
Wichita, KS 67226

Ph: (888) 755-9841

IND: Yes. AL: Yes. HCC: Yes

Age 62+. Nonprofit; nondenominational; owned and operated by Wesley Retirement Communities. Villa homes, apartments, and private and semiprivate rooms. Skilled nursing care; intermediate nursing care; board-certified geriatrician medical director; physical, occupational, and speech therapies; home health services; dental and podiatry services; pharmacy; personal care; medication administration; security; emergency response system; maintenance; transportation; up to 3 daily meals; pets allowed; housekeeping and laundry services; fitness center; swimming pool; banking services; social and recreational activities; woodworking shop; crafts room; club room; auditorium; ice cream parlor; gardening; barber/beauty shop.

Contact facility for fees.

Medicalodge of Goddard

501 Easy St.
Goddard, KS 67052

Ph: (316) 794-8635
Fax: (316) 794-8635

E-mail: *MLGoddard@Feist.com*

NH: 65. AL: 25

For-profit; nondenominational. Apartments and private and semiprivate rooms. Nursing care; medical services; rehabilitative therapies; dental and podiatry care; pharmacy services; Medicare/Medicaid-approved; personal care; medication administration; security; emergency response system; maintenance; transportation; up to 3 daily meals; housekeeping and laundry services; social and recreational activities; barber/beauty shop.

AL MO: $1,350–1,500. NH MO: $2,750–3,400.

Northeast

Brewster Place Retirement Community, CCAC, KAHSA

1205 SW 29th St.
Topeka, KS 66611

Ph: (785) 267-6337

IND: Yes. AL: Yes. SNF: 60. ALZ/MEM IMP: 20

Age 62+. Nonprofit; nondenominational; affiliated with four Congregational churches. Apartments and private and semiprivate rooms. Skilled nursing care; medical director; physical, occupational, and speech therapies; wellness clinic; eye care; hearing aid evaluations; dental and podiatry services; blood pressure and weight monitoring; pharmacy; home health care services; personal care; medication administration; security; emergency response system; maintenance; transportation; up to 3 daily meals; housekeeping and laundry services; exercise rooms; library; hobby room; woodworking shop; crafts room; social, recreational, and spiritual activities; educational opportunities; gardening.

Contact facility for fees.

Claridge Court

8101 Mission Rd.
Prairie Village, KS 66208

Ph: (913) 383-2085
Fax: (913) 385-4138

http://www.claridgecourt.com/

E-mail: *info@ClaridgeCourt.com*

IND: Yes. AL: Yes. HCC: Yes

Nonprofit; nondenominational; owned by Life Care Retirement Communities; managed by Live Care Services Corp. Apartments and private and semiprivate rooms. 24-hour nursing care; short- and long-term care; rehabilitative therapies; medical services; podiatry and dental care; pharmacy; Medicare-approved; per-

sonal care; medication administration; security; emergency response system; maintenance; transportation; up to 3 daily meals; housekeeping and laundry services; exercise center; library; banking services; valet; hot tub; game room; arts and crafts; media room; social, recreational, and cultural activities; on- and off-site activities; clubhouse; soda shop; patio; barber/beauty shop.

Contact facility for fees.

The Forum at Overland Park

3501 W. 95th St.
Overland Park, KS 66206

Ph: (913) 648-4500
Fax: (913) 648-6144

IND: 113. AL: 30. SNF: 60

For-profit; nondenominational; owned by Marriott. Apartments, suites, and private and semiprivate rooms. Skilled nursing care; medical services; rehabilitative therapies; pharmacy services; wellness clinic; Medicaid-approved; personal care; medication administration; security; emergency response system; maintenance; transportation; up to 3 daily meals; pets allowed; housekeeping and laundry services; exercise room; library; social and recreational activities; movies, music, and other entertainment; resident lounges; multipurpose room; barber/beauty shop.

IND ENT: (partial ref.) $84,000–$148,000. IND MO: (with ENT fee), $2,050–$3,400; (without ENT fee), $2,700–$5,000. 2nd person fee, $725. Up to 60 days of AL/SNF care included with ENT fee.

Lakeview Village, CCAC

9100 Park St.
Lenexa, KS 66215

Ph: (913) 888-1900

IND: Yes. AL: Yes. HCC: Yes

Nonprofit; nondenominational. Cottages, apartments, studios, and private and semiprivate rooms. 24-hour nursing care; short and long-term care; medical services; rehabilitative therapies; pharmacy services; wellness program; home health services; personal care; medication administration; security; emergency response system; maintenance; transportation; up to 3 daily meals; housekeeping and laundry services; exercise room; library; chapel; social and recreational activities; volunteer opportunities; travel group; gardening; barber/beauty shop.

IND ENT: $55,000–$185,000+. IND MO: $875–$2,250. HCC fees are inclusive.

Meadowlark Hills

2121 Meadowlark Rd.
Manhattan, KS 66502

Ph: (785) 537-4610
Fax: (785) 537-3022

IND: Yes. AL: Yes. HCC: Yes

Nonprofit; nondenominational. Duplexes, apartments, and private rooms. 24-hour nursing care; medical services; rehabilitative therapies; dental and podiatry care; pharmacy services; wellness program; Medicare/Medicaid-approved; personal care; medication administration; security; emergency response system; maintenance; transportation; up to 3 daily meals; housekeeping and laundry services; exercise equipment; library; recreation room; social and recreational activities; educational and cultural programs; computer center; business services; barber/beauty shop.

APPL: $1,100/person. MEMBERSHIP: $4,400/person. LL: (partial ref.), $30,000–$143,000. IND MO: $450–$1,250.

Northwest

Atwood Good Samaritan Center, KAHSA

650 Lake Rd.
Atwood, KS 67730-1599

Ph: (785) 626-9015

http://www.good-sam.com/Kansas/gssct281.htm

IND: Yes. AL: Yes. SNF: 50. ALZ/MEM IMP: Yes. ADC: Yes

Age 62+. Nonprofit; nondenominational; affiliated with the Evangelical Lutheran Good Samaritan Society. Duplexes, townhomes, cottages, apartments, and private and semiprivate rooms. Skilled nursing care; 24-hour nursing care; subacute care; respite care; physical, occupational, and speech therapies; respiratory therapy; IV therapy; hospice care; home health care services; Medicare-approved; personal care; medication administration; security; emergency response system; maintenance; transportation; up to 3 daily meals; housekeeping and laundry services; exercise classes; religious services; library; crafts room; social and recreational activities.

Contact facility for fees. Some HUD-subsidized housing.

North Central

Sunset Home

620 Second Ave.
Concordia, KS 66901

Ph: (785) 243-2720
Fax: (785) 243-1233

IND: Yes. AL: Yes. SNF: 40

Nonprofit; nondenominational; affiliated with the American Baptist Churches. Studios, apartments, and private and semiprivate rooms. 24-hour nursing care; medical services; physical, occupational, and speech therapies; restorative care; respite care; wellness monitoring; Medicare/Medicaid-approved; personal care; medication administration; security; emergency response system; maintenance; transportation; up to 3 daily meals; housekeeping and laundry services; exercise classes; chapel and Bible study; library; discussion groups; on- and off-site activities; bingo; music and entertainment; manicures; barber/beauty shop services.

ENT: $100. IND MO: $825–$880. AL MO: $600–$1,350. SNF Daily: $75–$95.

Central

The Cedars

1021 Cedars
McPherson, KS 67460

Ph: (316) 241-0919

http://www.thecedars.org

E-mail: *cedars@midusa.net*

IND: 91. AL: Yes. HCC: 120. ALZ/MEM IMP: Yes. ADC: Yes

Nonprofit; nondenominational; affiliated with the Church of the Brethren. One- and two-bedroom apartments, and private and semiprivate rooms. Nursing care; rehabilitative therapies; dental and podiatry care; medical services; pharmacy; social worker; home health services; Medicare/Medicaid-approved; personal care; medication administration; security; emergency response system; maintenance; transportation; up to 3 daily meals; housekeeping and laundry services; chaplain; social and recreational activities; fishing; walking paths.

Contact facility for fees.

East

Ottawa Retirement Village

1100 W. 15th St.
Ottawa, KS 66067

Ph: (785) 242-9378 (Village West), 242-1127 (Village Plaza), 242-5399 (Village Manor), 242-2433 (Village Apartments)

IND: 24. AL: Yes. HCC: Yes

Nondenominational. Apartments and private and semiprivate rooms. 24-hour nursing care; skilled and intermediate nursing care; physical, occupational, and speech therapies; medical director; audiologist; podiatrist; pharmacist; home health care services; social worker; Medicare/Medicaid-approved; personal care; medication administration; security; emergency response system; maintenance; transportation; up to 3 daily meals; housekeeping and laundry services; religious services; social and recreational activities; intergenerational program; arts and crafts; on- and off-site activities; enclosed courtyard; barber/beauty shop.

Contact facility for fees.

Assisted Living and Residential Care Facilities

These facilities provide room and board for ambulatory and independent adults who need minimum support.

Types of Authorization

Licensing and/or Certification

Requires licensing by the Department of Health and Environment, Bureau of Health Facility Regulation. These facilities provide supervision, limited nursing care, personal care, and therapies to residents who are not in need of skilled nursing care, but who need some assistance to live independently.

Memberships

- Assisted Living Federation of America (ALFA) is a national nonprofit membership organization whose mission is to enhance the quality of life in assisted living facilities and promote the interests of the assisted living industry. ALFA, 10300 Eaton Place, Suite 400, Fairfax, VA 22030. Ph: (703) 691-8100. Fax: (703) 691-8106. *http://www.alfa.org*

Northeast

Atria Hearthstone East

3415 SW 6th Ave.
Topeka, KS 66606

Ph: (785) 234-6806
Fax: (785) 235-5709

Atria Hearthstone West

3515 SW 6th Ave.
Topeka, KS 66606

Ph: (785) 234-6225
Fax: (785) 234-4002

IND: Yes. AL: Yes. ALZ/MEM IMP: Yes

For profit; nondenominational; owned by Atria Communities, Inc. Studios, apartments; shared rooms. 24-hour staffing; home health services; blood-pressure checks; wellness program; daily monitoring checks; personal care; medication administration; security; emergency response system; maintenance; transportation; up to 3 daily meals; pets allowed; housekeeping and laundry services; exercise program; chapel; banking services; social and recreational activities; convenience store; barber/beauty shop.

DEP: (no ref.) $550. PETS: $330. IND MO: $1,300–$2,100; 2nd person, $330. AL MO: $1,900–$3,400; 2nd person, $825.

Sterling House, ALFA

3220 Peterson Rd.
Lawrence, KS 66062

Ph: (913) 832-9900

AL: Yes

Locally owned; Sterling House facilities are in Olathe, Lawrence, Lenexa, Leawood, and Topeka. Apartments. Home health services; 24-hour staffing; therapy whirlpool; personal care; medication administration; security; emergency response system; maintenance; transportation; up to 3 daily meals; pets

allowed; housekeeping and laundry services; exercise program; religious services; Bible study; library; social and recreational activities; crafts; movies; gardening; entertainment; resident council; courtyard with gazebo; barber/beauty shop.

AL ENT: (part. ref.) Twice the monthly rental rate. AL MO: $2,300–$5,050.

Southeast

Tara Gardens

1110 E. Carpenter
Iola, KS 66949

RH: 25

Age 60+. Private rooms. Nursing care; medical services; pharmacy delivery; security; emergency response system; maintenance; transportation; up to 3 daily meals; housekeeping and laundry services; pet visits; social and recreational activities.

DEP: (no ref.) $200. RH MO: $1,100–$1,600.

West Ridge

950 W. St. John
Girard, KS 66743

Ph: (316) 724-6760
Fax: (316) 724-6766

IND/AL: 28

Apartments. Wellness program; personal care; medication administration; security; emergency response system; maintenance; transportation; up to 3 daily meals; housekeeping and laundry services; social and recreational activities.

IND MO: $1,450–$1,925; 2nd person, $275–$360. AL MO: $350–$725 (in addition to mo. rental fee).

Independent Living

Independent housing (primarily rentals) for seniors that may offer security features, meal service, and activities.

East

The Grand Court II

1900 N. 70th
Kansas City, KS 66102

Ph: (913) 299-1166
Fax: (913) 299-9474

IND: 127

For-profit; nondenominational. Apartments. Medical services; security; emergency response system; maintenance; transportation; up to 3 daily meals; pets allowed; housekeeping and laundry services; social director; social and recreational activities.

APPL: $550. IND MO: $1,200–$1,950.

Adult/Resort Communities

Communities for active adults (not all are age-restricted; primarily ownership).

East

Cedar Creek Community

25775 W. 103rd St.
Olathe, KS 66061

Ph: (913) 829-6500

http://www.cedarcreek-kc.com

Individual homes, villas, homesites. Golf course; pro shop; clubhouse; tennis; swimming pools; hiking; fishing; boating; sailing; lake; community center; fitness center; gymnasium; dining; social clubs.

PURCHASE: Homes, $275,000–$1.65 million+.

Central

Turkey Creek

1000 Fox Run
McPherson, KS 67460
Ph: (316) 241-8530

Individual homes, homesites. Golf course; pro shop; clubhouse; biking; dining; social clubs; nearby fishing and lakes.

PURCHASE: Homes, $137,500–$385,000; homesites, $20,000–$44,000.

Kentucky

http://www.state.ky.us

General Information

Climate

For most of the state, average winter highs are in the 40s°F; lows are in the 20s°F. Average summer highs are in the 80s°F; lows are in the 60s°F.

Cost of Living

Ranks 45th in the nation.

Taxes

State/Local as % of Income: 9.4%.

Property Tax Reduction: Residents 65 or older may qualify for a homestead exemption.

Sales: 6%.

Prescription Exemptions: Prescription drugs are exempt from sales tax.

Transportation, Travel, and Tourism

General

The Kentucky Department of Travel, (502) 564-4930, or (800) 225-TRIP.

Major Airports

- Louisville International Airport, 600 Terminal Drive, Louisville, KY 40209, (502) 368-6524; Fax: (502) 368-5895.
- Blue Grass Airport, 4000 Versailles Rd., Lexington, KY 40510, (606) 425-3100.

Railways

- Amtrak, (800) USA-RAIL.

Bus Tours

- Greyhound Bus, (800) 231-2222.

State Highways

- Interstates 65 and 75 run north-south.
- Interstate 64 runs east-west.

Theater and Music

South Central

- Capitol Arts Center, 416 E. Main, Bowling Green, KY 42101-2281, (502) 782-2787 (cultural events).
- Phoenix Theater, 545 Morris Alley, Bowling Green, KY 42101-2287, (502) 782-2787 (comedies, dramas, musicals).

West

- Kentucky Opry Country Music Show, (502) 527-3869 or (888) 459-8704 (comedy/variety show with gospel, country, and bluegrass music).

North

- Kincaid Regional Theatre, Chapel Street, Falmouth, (606) 654-2636 (seasonal).
- Lexington Ballet Company and School, 161 N. Mill St., Lexington, KY 40508, (606) 233-3925.
- Lexington Philharmonic, 161 N. Mill St., Lexington, KY 40507, (606) 233-4226.
- Lexington Opera House, 201 West Short St., Lexington, KY 40507, (606) 233-4567.
- Studio Players, 601 Sayre Ave., Lexington, KY 40508, (606) 254-8905.
- Palace Theatre, 629 S. Fourth, Louisville, KY 40202, (502) 583-4555.

Museums, Crafts, Historical, Recreational

South Central

- Corvette Museum, Bowling Green, (502) 781-7983 or (800) 53-VETTE (rare and futuristic Corvettes).
- Riverview the Hobson House, Bowling Green, (502) 843-5565 (Victorian family life, 1860–90).

West

- Hardin Southern Railroad's Nostalgic Train, (502) 437-4555 (18-mile roundtrip on a century-old railroad).
- Kenlake State Resort Park, near Aurora, (502) 474-2211 (lodge, cottages, golf course, tennis, marina).
- Paxton Park, Paducah, (502) 444-9514 (golfing).

East

- Buckhorn Lake State Resort Park, near Hazard, (606) 398-7510 (hiking, fishing, lodge).
- Breathitt Country Museum, near Hazard, (606) 666-4159 (view of life in the KY mountains in the 1940s).
- Red River Historical Museum, Clay City, (606) 663-4000 (artifacts from iron, logging, and railroad industries).
- Pine Mountain State Resort Park, Pineville, (606) 337-6195 (golfing).

Central

- Berea, "Folk Arts and Crafts Capital of Kentucky," visitor center, (800) 598-5363.
- Berea College, (606) 986-9341 ext. 5018 (South's first interracial college; tours).
- Shaker Village of Pleasant Hill, Harrodsburg, KY, (606) 734-5411 (restored Shaker community).
- Kentucky Military History Museum, E. Main at Capital Ave., Frankfort, (502) 564-3265.
- Headley-Whitney Museum, 4435 Old Frankfort Pike, Lexington, KY 40510, (606) 255-6653 (fine art).
- The Kentucky Horse Park and International Museum of the Horse, Lexington, (800) 678-8813.

Organizations

Advocacy Groups

- Office of Aging Services, (502) 564-6930.
- Long Term Care, (502) 564-6930.
- Ombudsman, (800) 372-2991.

Volunteer Programs

- Kentucky Department for the Blind, Volunteer Recording Program, Paducah, (502) 575-7056 or (888) 896-0438; Lexington, (606) 257-6602 or (800) 306-3472.

Housing

Long-Term Care Facilities

*In the state of Kentucky, these facilities are called **Long Term Care/Nursing Home Facilities**.*

These facilities provide residential living and/or various levels of nursing and medical services to seniors for an extended period of time.

Types of Authorization

Licensing and/or Certification

Nursing facilities must be licensed by state to provide nursing facility services and to certify some or all of their beds for Medicare and/or Medicaid. Those nursing facilities that are not certified for Medicare and/or Medicaid are referred to as "nursing homes." All long-term care facilities are licensed by the Division of Licensing and Regulation and submit to unannounced inspections.

Memberships

- American Association of Homes and Services for the Aging (AAHSA) represents not-for-profit organizations committed to providing high-quality health care, housing, and services to the elderly. AAHSA, 901 E St. NW, Suite 500, Washington, DC 20004-2011. Ph: (202) 783-2242. Fax: (202) 783-2285. *http://www.aahsa.org*
- Kentucky Association of Homes and Services for the Aging (KAHSA) is an AAHSA Affiliated State Association. KAHSA, 1244 S. Fourth St., Louisville, KY 40203-3051. Ph: (502) 635-6468. Fax: (502) 635-9286.
- Kentucky Association of Health Care Facilities (KAHCF).
- American Health Care Association (AHCA).

Accreditation

- Continuing Care Accreditation Commission (CCAC) accredits facilities that offer seniors a contract or contracts that provide residential living and health care services for the remainder of the person's lifetime and meet CCAC's accreditation standards.
- Joint Commission on the Accreditation of Healthcare Organizations (JCAHO) is an independent, not-for-profit organization, and the nation's oldest and largest standards-setting and health care accrediting institution.

North

The Altenheim

936 Barrett Ave.
Louisville, KY 40204

Ph: (502) 584-7417

PC: Yes. ICF: Yes

Nonprofit; nondenominational facility. Apartments and private and semiprivate rooms. 24-hour nursing care; medical care; hospice; podiatry, dental, and optical care; diagnostic services (lab, X-ray, and EKG); physical and respiratory therapies; pharmacy; personal care; medication administration; security; emergency response system; maintenance; transportation; up to 3 daily meals; housekeeping and laundry services; exercise programs; chapel and religious services; arts and crafts; guest entertainers; off-site activities; movies; activities director; barber/beauty shop.

PC Daily: $65–$80. ICF Daily: $105.

Christian Church Campus of Louisville, JCAHO

960 S. Fourth St.
Louisville, KY 40203

Ph and TDD: (502) 585-5656
Fax: (502) 585-5157

IND: Yes. PC: Yes. HCC: 126. ADC: Yes

Affiliated with the Christian Church Homes of Kentucky. Apartments, and private and semiprivate rooms. 24-hour nursing care; personal, intermediate, and skilled nursing care; social services; therapies; pharmacy; health screening; health clinic; podiatry, optometry, and dental care; Medicare/Medicaid-approved; personal care; medication administration; security; emergency response system; maintenance; transportation; up to 3 daily meals; housekeeping and laundry services; exercise program; religious services and Bible study; banking services; activities room; bookmobile; craft room; resident council; gift shop; convenience shop; barber/beauty shop.

Contact facility for fees.

Masonic Homes

3701 Frankfort Ave.
Masonic Home, KY 40041

Ph: (502) 890-4907
Fax: (502) 897-8719

IND: 103. AL: 104. HCC: 123

Age 60+. Nonprofit; nondenominational. Apartments, private and semiprivate rooms. Nursing care; medical

services; rehabilitative therapies; dental and podiatry care; pharmacy services; social services; Medicare/Medicaid-approved; personal care; medication administration; security; emergency response system; maintenance; transportation; up to 3 daily meals; pets allowed; housekeeping and laundry services; religious services; social and recreational services. (Plans for adding grocery, pharmacy, and barber/beauty shop in near future.)

IND DEP: $380–$500. IND MO: $380–$500. AL DEP: $2,650. AL MO: $2,650. NH Daily: $115–$140.

Pine Tree Villa

4604 Lowe Rd.
Louisville, KY 40220

Ph: (502) 451-1401

NH: 28. PC: Yes

Efficiency apartments, and private and semiprivate rooms. Nursing care; medical services; rehabilitative therapies; pharmacy services; personal care; medication administration; security; emergency response system; maintenance; transportation; up to 3 daily meals; housekeeping and laundry services; exercise classes; religious services; social and recreational activities; bingo; bookmobile; resident council.

NH Daily: $110–$190. PC Daily: $75–$145.

Presbyterian Homes and Services of Kentucky

2116 Buechel Bank Rd.
Louisville, KY 40218

Ph: (502) 499-9383
Fax: (502) 499-3596

IND: 103. AL: 32. HCC: 31. ICF: 81

Nonprofit; nondenominational facility. Apartments and private and semiprivate rooms. Nursing care; medical services; therapies; dental and podiatry care; pharmacy; lab and X-ray services; Medicare/Medicaid-approved; personal care; medication administration; security; emergency response system; maintenance; transportation; up to 3 daily meals; pets allowed; housekeeping and laundry services; exercise programs; church services and Bible study; library; games; activities; arts and crafts; off-site activities; volunteer opportunities; walking paths; barber/beauty shop.

DEP: (ref.), 1 mo. rent. IND ENT: $24,500–$71,500. IND MO: $1,200–$3,550. PC MO: $2,250–$4,450. HCC MO: $3,700–$6,550.

Sayre Christian Village

3816 Camelot Drive
Lexington, KY 40517

Ph: (606) 273-1845
Fax: (606) 273-3852

IND: 199. NF: 109

Age 55+ (Towers living area); age 62 (Baunta living area). Nonprofit; nondenominational fellowship of Christian churches. Apartments and private and semiprivate rooms. Skilled and routine nursing care; full-time administrator; medical services; therapies; dental and podiatry services; pharmacy; social services; Medicare/Medicaid-approved; security; emergency response system; maintenance; transportation; up to 3 daily meals; pets allowed; housekeeping and laundry services; exercise programs; church services and Bible study; planned activities; bookmobile; barber/beauty shop.

DEP: $300–$500. IND MO: $660–$800. NH Daily: (semiprivate), $125–$150; (private), $140–$160. Some units HUD-subsidized.

Assisted Living and Residential Care Facilities

In the state of Kentucky, these facilities are called ***Assisted Living/Personal Care Facilities****.*

These facilities provide room and board for ambulatory and independent adults who need minimum support.

Types of Authorization

Licensing and/or Certification

Assisted living facilities are not licensed and are not required to submit to inspections or comply with regulations. There is, however, voluntary certification. Personal care homes require licensing by the state. These facilities provide supervision, health-related services, and therapies to residents who are not in need of nursing care, but who need some assistance to live independently.

Memberships:

- Assisted Living Federation of America (ALFA) is a national nonprofit membership organization whose mission is to enhance the quality of life in assisted living facilities and promote the interests of the assisted living industry. ALFA, 10300 Eaton Place, Suite 400, Fairfax, VA 22030. Ph: (703) 691-8100. Fax: (703) 691-8106. *http://www.alfa.org*
- Kentucky Assisted Living Association (KALFA) is a state affiliate of ALFA. KALFA, 2614 Shiloh Lane, Goshen, KY 40026. Ph: (502) 228-8533. Fax: (502) 228-7134.

North

Richmond Place

3051 Rio Dosa Drive
Lexington, KY 40509

Ph: (606) 269-6308
Fax: (606) 268-9095

IND: Yes. AL: Yes. ALZ/MEM IMP: Yes

For-profit; nondenominational; an American Retirement Corporation community. Apartments. Wellness nurse; home health agency; health screenings; respite care; pharmacy delivery service; personal care; medication administration; security; emergency response system; maintenance; transportation; up to 3 daily meals; housekeeping and laundry services; fitness program; pool; emotional well-being services; library; activities director; on- and off-site activities; billiards area; lounges; card room; gardens; barber/beauty shop.

MO: $1,450–$2,850; 2nd person, $425. Membership: $1,100.

Covington Ladies Home

702 Garrad St.
Covington, KY 41011-2581

Ph: (606) 431-6913

IND: Yes

Age 65+; women only. Privately owned; nonprofit; nonsectarian. Private rooms. Nursing care; respite care; personal care; medication administration; security; maintenance; transportation; up to 3 daily meals; housekeeping and laundry services; social and recreational activities; gardens; beauty shop services.

AL MO: $1,150. RSP Daily: $85. Financial assistance available.

South

Bowling Green Retirement Village

445 Middle Bridge Road W
Bowling Green, KY 42103

Ph: (502) 842-5433

IND: Yes. AL: Yes

Nondenominational. Apartments and suites. Personal care; medication administration; blood pressure monitoring; security; emergency response system; maintenance; transportation; up to 3 daily meals; pets allowed; housekeeping and laundry services; exercise classes; chapel; heated swimming pool; Jacuzzi; library; lounge; activities coordinator; off-site activities; game room; country store; barber/beauty shop.

ADM: (no ref.) $300. IND MO: $880–$1,350; 2nd person, $195–$325; pets (no ref.), $220. AL MO: $1,550; 2nd person, $330.

West

Daveco Rest Home
2526 W. 10th St.
Owensboro, KY 42301

PC: 92

Fern Terrace Lodge of Owensboro
45 Woodford Ave.
Ownesboro, KY 42301

PC: 68

Fern Terrace Lodge of Mayfield
Highway 45
Mayfield, KY 42066

PC: 140

Fern Terrace Lodge of Murray
1505 Stadium View Drive
Murray, KY 42071

PC: 103

Fern Terrace Lodge of Bowling Green
1030 Shive Lane
Bowling Green, KY 42103

PC: 114

Suites, private rooms, and semiprivate rooms. Medicaid-approved; personal care; medication administration; security; maintenance; transportation; up to 3 daily meals; housekeeping and laundry services; social and recreational activities.

PC MO: $950–$2,475.

Independent Living

Independent housing (primarily rentals) for seniors that may offer security features, meal service, and activities.

North

Ashland Terrace Retirement Home
475 S. Ashland Ave.
Lexington, KY 40502

Ph: (606) 266-2581
Fax: (606) 266-3974

IND: 22

Age 62+; women only. Nonprofit facility. Private rooms. Security; emergency response system; maintenance; transportation; up to 3 daily meals; pets allowed; housekeeping and laundry services; daily activities.

IND MO: $770.

Baptist Towers
1014 S. Second St.
Louisville, KY 40203

Ph: (502) 587-6632 TDD: (800) 247-2510
Fax: (502) 587-9113

IND: 197

Nonprofit; sponsored by Walnut Street Baptist Church. Apartments. Management team; weekly health-care clinic; security; emergency response system; maintenance; transportation; housekeeping and laundry services; community room; lounge; games; crafts; senior citizens program; off-site activities; movies; dinners.

IND MO: $275–$440 (based on income).

Southwest

Jackson Home
301 S. 9th St.
Paducah, KY 42003

(502) 442-7591 (502) 442-4318

IND: 233

Age 62+. Nonprofit; nondenominational. Apartments. Some medical services; dental and podiatry services; therapies; security; emergency response system; maintenance; transportation; optional noon meal; pets allowed; chapel; computer center; activities coordinator; grocery and gift shop; barber/beauty shop.

DEP: one mo. rent. IND MO: 30% adjusted income. HUD residence.

Adult/Resort Communities

Communities for active adults (not all are age-restricted; primarily ownership).

North

Doe Valley

1 Doe Valley Parkway
Brandenburg, KY 40108

Ph: (502) 422-2188

Individual homes, condominiums, homesites. Golf course; clubhouse; pro shop; tennis; swimming pool; fishing; boating; marina; library; dining; social clubs.

PURCHASE: Homes, from $79,500; homesites, $2,200–$27,500.

Griffin Gate

1510 Newtown Pike, Suite D
Lexington, KY 40511

Ph: (606) 281-1625

Individual homes, townhomes, homesites. Golf course; tennis; swimming pools; community center; fitness center; library; social clubs.

PURCHASE: Homes, low $132,000–$440,000; homesites, $41,000–$57,500.

Lake Forest

Middletown, KY 40245

Ph: (502) 426-4810

http://www.ntsdevelopment.com/Lake-Forest

Individual homes, homesites. Golf course; clubhouse; tennis and swim club; community lodge; jogging trails; soccer; volleyball; lakes; social clubs.

PURCHASE: New homes $220,000–$1.1 million; homesites, from $55,000.

Sutherland

Prospect, KY 40059

Ph: (502) 426-4810

Individual homes, homesites. Tennis; swimming pool; lakes; nearby marinas and riding stables.

PURCHASE: New homes, $440,000–$1.1 million; homesites, from $88,000.

Triple Crown Country Club

1 Triple Crown Blvd.
Union, KY 41091

Ph: (606) 384-1410
Fax: (606) 384-1684

http://triplecrowncc.com

Individual homes, condominiums, homesites. Golf course; clubhouse; pro shop; tennis; swimming pool; hiking trails; dining.

PURCHASE: Homes, $275,000–$3.85 million; homesites, $55,000–$192,500.

South

Eagles Nest Country Club

PO Box 553
Somerset, KY 42502

Ph: (606) 679-8341
Fax: (606) 679-8357

Individual homes, condominiums, homesites. Golf course; clubhouse; pro shop; tennis; swimming pool; dining.

PURCHASE: Homes, $154,000–$698,500; homesites, $22,000–$55,000.

Woodson Bend Resort

14 Woodson Bend
Bronston, KY 42518

Ph: (606) 561-5316 or (800) 688-5737
http://www.woodsonbendresort.com

Condominiums. Golf course; pro shop; tennis; swimming pool; hiking trails; fishing; boating; community center; library; dining; social clubs.

PURCHASE: Condos, $66,000–$275,000.

Louisiana

http://www.state.la.us

General Information

Climate

Moderate to hot: January averages 45–50° F; June averages 80° F. Humidity 60–80% year-round.

Cost of Living

Ranks 38th in the nation.

Taxes

State/Local as % of Income: 9.9%

Property Tax Reduction: No property tax on first $75,000 of market value of owner-occupied home; as of October 1998, property tax assessments were frozen on homes of citizens over 65 earning $50,000 or less.

Sales: 4%.

Prescription Exemptions: Prescriptions and medical devices are exempt from sales tax.

Transportation, Travel, and Tourism

General

Louisiana Office of Tourism, PO Box 94291, Baton Rouge, LA 70804, (504) 342-8119 or (800) 33-GUMBO.

Major Airports

- Alexandria-Ester Regional Airport, 1611 Arnold Drive, Alexandria, LA 71303, (318) 449-4642 or (800) 992-7433.
- New Orleans International Airport, 900 Airline Hwy, Kenner, LA 70062, (504) 464-0831.
- Shreveport Downtown Airport, 1550 Airport Drive Shreveport, LA 71107 (318) 673-5370.

Railways

- Amtrak, stations throughout the state, (800) USA-RAIL.

Bus Tours

- Greyhound Bus, stations throughout the state, (800) 231-2222.
- Regional Transit Authority, 6700 Plaza Drive #106, New Orleans, LA 70127, (504) 242-2600.
- West Ouachita Public Transportation, 1800 N. 7th St., West Monroe, LA 71291, (318) 324-1280.

State Highways

- Interstate 10, west-east from Orange to Baton Rouge, then southeast-northwest to New Orleans.
- Interstate 12, west-east from Baton Rouge to Mississippi.
- Interstate 20, west-east from Vicksburg to Shreveport.
- Interstate 49, northeast-southwest from Shreveport to Lafayette.
- Interstate 55, south-north from La Place to Mississippi.

Theater and Music

North

- Shreveport Little Theatre (oldest US community theater), 812 Margaret Pl., Shreveport, LA 71101-4509, (318) 424-4439.
- Red River Revel Festival (art, music, food), Waterfront, Shreveport, October, (318) 424-4000.
- Shreveport Metropolitan Ballet, Civic Theatre, 509 Marshall, Suite 1015, Shreveport, LA 71101, (318) 459-1457.

South

- Mardis Gras (parades, fireworks, costumes), throughout city, between January and March, New Orleans.
- Mandeville Seafood Festival (food, music, crafts, for Lake Pontchartrain Basin Foundation), July, Mandeville, (504) 624-9762.
- Lark in the Park, City Park Gala (restaurant fest for Friends of City Park), New Orleans, (504) 483-9376.
- Le Festival de Mardi Gras Lafayette. Cajunfield, Lafayette (music, carnival, parades), February, (318) 232-3808 or (800) 346-1958.
- Liberty Theatre (live radio show, Cajun and Zydeco bands), 200 W. Park Ave., Eunice, LA 70535, (318) 457-7389 or (318) 457-6577.

Museums, Crafts, Historical, Recreational

North

- Germantown Museum and Colony (1835 settlement), 120 Museum Rd., Minden, LA 71055, (318) 377-6061.
- Trails End Golf Course (public), PO Box 433, Arcadia, LA 71001, Hwy. 9S, (318) 263-7420.
- Huntington Park Golf Club (public), 8300 Pine Rd., Shreveport, LA 71129, (318) 948-9688.
- Querbes Park Golf Course (public), 3500 Beverly Pl., Shreveport, LA 71104, (318) 442-8746.

South

- Culinary Arts Institute of Louisiana/ Caila's Fine Cuisine (student-run restaurant, demos), 427 Lafayette St., Baton Rouge, LA 70802, (504) 343-6233, (800) 927-0839.
- African American Odyssey, (tours to historic sites), 10985 N. Harrell's Ferry Rd., Baton Rouge, LA 70816, (504) 338-6309 or (800) 385-6309.
- Steamboat Natchez (steam powered sternwheeler, dinner/jazz), Toulouse St. Wharf at JAX Brewery, New Orleans, LA 70130, (504) 586-8777 or (800) 233-2628.
- City Park Boating and Fishing (canoes, pedal boats), Dreyfous Ave., New Orleans, LA 70124, (504) 488-2896.
- Bayou Sauvage National Wildlife Refuge (fishing, hiking, canoeing), 1010 Gause Blvd., Bldg. 936, Slidell, LA 70458, (504) 646-7555.
- Audubon Zoological Gardens, 6500 Magazine St., New Orleans, LA 70118, (504) 861-2537, ext. 340.
- Chalmette Battlefield (Battle of New Orleans site, visitors center), Jean Lafitte National Historical Park, 8606 W. St. Bernard Hwy., Chalmette, LA 70085, (504) 589-4428.
- Zigler Art Museum, 411 Clara St., Jennings, LA 70546-5235 (318) 824-0114.
- Lacassine National Wildlife Refuge, HCR 63 Box 186, Lake Arthur, LA 70549, (318) 774-5923.
- Acadian Village (reconstructed 19th c. village), 200 Greenleaf Rd., Lafayette, LA 70506, (318) 981-2364 or (800) 962-9133.
- Shadows-on-the-Teche (National Trust house museum and garden), 7 E. Main St., New Iberia, LA 70560, (318) 369-6446.
- Jean Lafitte National Park Acadian Cultural Center, 501 Fisher Rd., Lafayette, LA 70508, (318) 232-0789.
- USS Kidd and Nautical Center, 305 S. River Rd., Baton Rouge, LA 70802, (504) 342-1942.
- Louisiana State Museum, PO Box 2448, New Orleans, LA 70176, (504) 568-6968, (800) 568-6968.
- Magnolia Mound Plantation, Nicholson Drive, Baton Rouge, LA 70802, (504) 343-4955.
- Bayou Oaks Golf Course (public), 1040 Filmore Ave., New Orleans, LA 70124, (504) 483-9396.
- Pine Shadows Golf Center (public), 750 N. Goodman Rd., Lake Charles, LA 70601, (504) 643-6893.
- Baton Rouge Blues Festival (blues, jazz), October, 730 North Blvd., Baton Rouge, LA 70802, (800) LA-ROUGE.

- Breaux Bridge Crawfish Festival (May; food, music), PO Box 25, Parkway Drive, Breaux Bridge, LA 70517, (318) 332-6655.

Central

- Museum of Historic Natchitoches, 840 Washington, Natchitoches, LA 71457, (318) 357-0070.
- Hodges Gardens, PO Box 900, Many, LA 71449, US 171, (318) 586-3523 or (800) 354-3523.
- Alexandria Museum of Art, PO Box 1028, Alexandria, LA 71309, (318) 443-3458.
- Kisatchie National Forest (camping, swimming, boating), 2500 Shreveport Hwy, Pineville, LA 71360, (318) 473-7160.

West

- DeQuincy Railroad Museum, PO Box 997, Lake Charles Ave., DeQuincy, LA 70633, (318) 786-7113.
- Sabine National Wildlife Refuge (visitors center, trails), 3000 Main St., Hwy. 27 S., Hackberry, LA 70645, (318) 762-3816 or (800) 456-SWLA.

Organizations

Advocacy Groups

- East Baton Rouge Council on Aging, 5790 Florida Blvd., Baton Rouge, LA 70806, (225) 923-8000.
- Governor's Office of Elderly Affairs, PO Box 80374, 412 N. 4th St., 3rd Floor, Baton Rouge, LA 70802, (504) 342-7100.

Volunteer Programs

- Greater Baton Rouge Food Bank, 5546 Choctaw Drive, Baton Rouge, LA 70821, (504) 359-9940.
- Attakapas Council–Boy Scouts of America, 1545 Jackson St., Alexandria, LA 71301, (318) 443-0482.
- Parkway Partners Program (environmental action), 2829 Gentilly Blvd., New Orleans, LA 70122, (504) 286-2282.
- NO/AIDS Task Force, 1407 Decatur St., New Orleans, LA 70116, (504) 945-4000.

Housing

Long-Term Care Facilities

In the state of Louisiana, these facilities are called ***Continuing Care/Nursing Home/Retirement Facilities****.*

These facilities provide residential living and/or various levels of nursing and medical services to seniors for an extended period of time.

Types of Authorization

Licensing and/or Certification

Facilities are regulated by the Office of Public Health. Nursing homes require the skills of a registered or a licensed practical nurse. Skills include assessment, conducting treatments, injections, and coordination of care. Related services include rehabilitative therapies, dental services, dietary consultation, lab and X-ray services, and pharmacy services.

Memberships

- American Association of Homes and Services for the Aging (AAHSA) represents not-for-profit organizations committed to providing high-quality health care, housing, and services to the elderly. AAHSA, 901 E St. NW, Suite 500, Washington, DC 20004-2011. Ph: (202) 783-2242. Fax: (202) 783-2285. *http://www.aahsa.org*
- Louisiana Association of Homes and Services for the Aging (LAHSA) is a state affiliate of AAHSA. LAHSA, PO Box 14615, Baton Rouge, LA 70815-4169, Ph: (225) 201-9933. Fax: (225) 201-9944.

Accreditations

- Continuing Care Accreditation Commission (CCAC) accredits facilities that offer seniors a contract or contracts that provide residential living and health care services for the remainder of the person's lifetime and meet CCAC's accreditation standards.
- Joint Commission on the Accreditation of Healthcare Organizations (JCAHO) is an independent, not-for-profit organization, and the nation's oldest and largest standards-setting and health care accrediting institution.

Northwest

The Glen Retirement System

403 E. Flournoy Lucas Rd.
Shreveport, LA 71115

Ph: (318) 798-3500
Fax: (318) 798-7988

IND: 162. AL: Yes. HCC: 186

Age 62+. Nonprofit; nondenominational. Efficiencies, one- and two-bedroom apartments, and private rooms. 24-hour nursing care; medical services; rehabilitative therapies; dental, podiatry, and ear care; lab and X-ray services; wellness center; pharmacy services; home health care services; Medicaid-approved; personal care; medication administration; security; emergency response system; maintenance; transportation; up to 3 daily meals; pets allowed; housekeeping and laundry services; fitness center; religious services; social and recreational activities; educational and cultural programs; community tours; volunteer opportunities; crafts; gift shop; dry cleaning services; gazebo; walking paths; fishing pier; barber/beauty shop.

IND MO: $950–$3,550.

Live Oak Retirement Community, AAHSA, LAHSA

600 E. Flournoy Lucas Rd.
Shreveport, LA 71115-3855

Ph: (318) 797-1900
Fax: (318) 797-1999
http://www.liveoakonline.com
E-mail: *liveoak@prysm.net*

IND: 120. AL: Yes. HCC: 130

Age 62+. Nonprofit; nondenominational; nonsectarian. Apartments and private and semiprivate rooms. 24-hour skilled nursing care; medical director; emergency medical care; social services; rehabilitative therapies; medical services; dental and podiatry care; eye and ear screenings; mobile lab; pharmacy services; health fairs; wellness checks; Medicaid-approved; personal care; medication administration; security; emergency response system; maintenance; transportation; up to 3 daily meals; housekeeping and laundry services; fitness center; chapel; chaplain on staff; social and recreational activities; on- and off-site activities; community-based services referral service; fishing lake; walking paths; barber/beauty shop.

APPL: Apts., $25; HCC, $35. DEP: (no ref.) $550. IND MO: IND MO: $1,300–$1,400. HCC MO: $2,400–$3,350.

North

St. Joseph's Home

2301 Sterlington Rd.
Monroe, LA 71201

Ph: HCC (318) 323-3426; AL (318) 325-9459
Fax: HCC (318) 322-6372; AL (318) 323-2527

AL: 60. HCC: 129

Age 55+. Nonprofit; affiliated with the Catholic Church. Studios, one- and two-bedroom apartments, and private rooms. 24-hour nursing care; medical services;

rehabilitative therapies; dental and podiatry care; pharmacy services; Medicare/Medicaid-approved; personal care; medication administration; security; emergency response system; maintenance; transportation; up to 3 daily meals; housekeeping and laundry services; interdenominational chapel; social and recreational activities; fishing; walking paths; barber/beauty shop.

AL MO: $1,500–$2,350. Contact facility for HCC fees.

Southeast

Chateau de Notre Dame

2820 Burdette St.
New Orleans, LA 70125

Ph: (504) 866-2741, ext. 285

IND: Yes. AL: Yes. HCC: Yes

Nondenominational. Apartments and private and semiprivate rooms. Nursing care; 24-hour staffing; physician and psychiatric services; physical, occupational, and speech therapies; X-ray and lab services; pharmacy; medical assessment; dental and podiatry care; home health care services; hospice; Medicare-approved; personal care; medication administration; security; emergency response system; maintenance; transportation; up to 3 daily meals; housekeeping and laundry services; exercise classes; library; media room; social and recreational activities; snack bar; gift shop; convenience store; barber/beauty shop.

Contact facility for fees.

Christwood Continuing Care Retirement Community, LAHSA, AAHSA

100 Christwood Blvd.
Covington, LA 70433

Ph: (504) 398-0515
Fax: (504) 898-0529

IND: 118. AL: 30. SNF: 20

Age 62+. Nonprofit; nondenominational; nonsectarian; Christ Episcopal Church affiliation. Apartments and private rooms. 24-hour skilled nursing care; rehabilitative therapies; dental and podiatry care; medical services; pharmacy; social services; Medicare-approved; personal care; medication administration; security; emergency response system; maintenance; transportation; up to 3 daily meals; pets allowed; housekeeping and laundry services; exercise room; religious services; library; banking services; social and recreational activities; on- and off-site activities; cultural and educational opportunities; pond/pier; putting green; lounges; convenience store; ice cream parlor; patios; walking paths; barber/beauty shop.

IND ENT: (partial ref.) $84,500–$181,500. IND MO: $1,250–$3,050. AL MO: Nonresident, $2,850. SFN Daily: Non- resident, $135.

Woldenberg Village

3663 Behrman Place
New Orleans, LA 70114-0906

Ph: (504) 367-7288
Fax: (504) 367-6995

IND: 60. AL: Under construction. SNF: 101

Nondenominational; nonsectarian. One- and two-bedroom apartments and private and semiprivate rooms. 24-hour nursing care; physician services; dental services; physical, occupational, and speech therapies; hospice; social services; home health services; Medicare/Medicaid-approved; personal care; medication administration; security; emergency response system; maintenance; transportation; up to 3 daily meals; housekeeping and laundry services; fitness center; religious events; chapel; library; arts and crafts; movies; music; on- and off-site activities; auditorium; snack bar; gardens; barber/beauty shop.

APPL: $250. IND MO: $1,300–$2,300. HCC Daily: $115–$135.

Assisted Living and Residential Care Facilities

These facilities provide housing, food service, and one or more personal services.

Types of Authorization

Licensing and/or Certification

Facilities are regulated by the Office of Public Health. Personal care includes help in walking, getting in and out of bed, bathing, dressing, eating, and preparing special diets. Residential services include general supervision and a protective environment, such as room and board and a planned program for the social and spiritual needs of the resident.

Memberships

- Assisted Living Federation of America (ALFA) is a national nonprofit membership organization whose mission is to enhance the quality of life in assisted living facilities and promote the interests of the assisted living industry. ALFA, 10300 Eaton Place, Suite 400, Fairfax, VA 22030. Ph: (703) 691-8100. Fax: (703) 691-8106. *http://www.alfa.org*
- Louisiana Assisted Living Association (LALA) is a state affiliate of ALFA. LALA, 5551 Corporate Blvd., Baton Rouge, LA 70808. Ph: (225) 927-4545. Fax: (225) 927-4882.

Southwest

Grand Cove Retirement Residences and Nursing Center

1525 W. McNeese St.
Lake Charles, LA 70605

Ph: (318) 474-6000
Fax: (318) 478-7522

IND: 20. RH: 88. AL: 20. HCC: 4

Age 70+. For-profit; nondenominational. Apartments and private and semiprivate rooms. 24-hour nursing care; medical services; rehabilitative therapies; dental and podiatry care; pharmacy services; Medicare-approved; personal care; medication administration; security; emergency response system; maintenance; transportation; up to 3 daily meals; housekeeping and laundry services; social and recreational activities.

DEP: (ref.), $550. IND MO: $1,450–$2,000. AL/RH MO: $2,350–$4,900. HCC MO: $2,350–$4,900.

Villa Maria Retirement Center

3905 Kingston Place
Lake Charles, LA 70605

Ph: (318) 478-4780
Fax: (318) 474-8822

AL: 62

Age 62+. Nonprofit; nondenominational; church affiliated. Apartments. Home health services; short-term care assistance; 24-hour staffing; personal care; medication administration; security; emergency response system; maintenance; transportation; up to 3 daily meals; housekeeping and laundry services; fitness center; swimming pool; chapel; religious services; intergenerational program; social and recreational activities; barber/beauty shop.

AL ENT: (ref.) $550. AL MO: $2,000–$2,700; 2nd person, $330.

Southeast

Azalea Estates

354 Robert Blvd.
Slidell, LA 70458

Ph: (504) 641-2827
Fax: (504) 645-0659

AL: Yes

For-profit; nondenominational. Suites. Wellness program; 24-hour staffing; personal care; medication administration; security; emergency response system;

maintenance; transportation; up to 3 daily meals; small pets allowed; housekeeping and laundry services; exercise classes; library; craft and hobby room; social, educational, and recreational activities; general store; garden areas; walking paths; barber/beauty shop.

Contact facility for fees.

Lakewood Quarters

8585 Summa Ave.
Baton Rouge, LA 70808

Ph: (504) 767-7877

AL: Yes. ALZ/MEM IMP: Yes

For-profit; nondenominational. Suites and one- and two-bedroom apartments. On-site health care; wellness clinic; personal care; medication administration; security; emergency response system; maintenance; transportation; up to 3 daily meals; housekeeping and laundry services; exercise classes; chapel; library; banking and postal services; business services; cultural and educational opportunities; social and recreational activities; hobby and craft room; snack shop; lounge; walking paths; patio; barber/beauty shop.

APPL: $150. DEP: 1 mo. rent. AL MO: Premier level, $2,000–$2,350; 2nd person, $330; premier plus level, $2,400–$2,800; 2nd person, $770. ALZ/MEM IMP: $2,650–$3,550; 2nd person, $1,100.

Live Oak Living Center

17010 Old Covington Hwy
Hammond, LA 70403

Ph: (504) 345-8787

AL: Yes

Nondenominational. Studios and one-bedroom apartments. Wellness program; resident assistant; personal care; medication administration; security; emergency response system; maintenance; transportation; up to 3 daily meals; housekeeping and laundry services; exercise lasses; library; social and recreational activities; postal services; media room; café; spa and garden room; courtyards; walking paths; barber/beauty shop.

DEP: (ref.), $100. COMMUNITY FEE: (no ref.), $1,100. MO: $1,950–$2,800. AL MO: $165–$500 (in addition to MO fee; based on level of care).

Pratt-Stanton Manor

1224 St. Charles Ave.
New Orleans, LA 70130

Ph: (504) 525-0895

AL: Yes

Nonprofit; nondenominational; church affiliation. Studios and one- and two-bedroom apartments. Visiting nurse service; 24-hour staffing; pharmacy services; personal care; medication administration; security; emergency response system; maintenance; transportation; up to 3 daily meals; housekeeping and laundry services; banking and postal services; social, cultural, and recreational activities; patio areas; movies; barber/beauty shop nearby.

AL MO: $1,350–$2,200.

Williamsburg Senior Living Quarters

5445 Government St.
Baton Rouge, LA 70806

Ph: (225) 929-8917
Fax: (225) 928-3284

IND: 120. AL: 43

For-profit; nondenominational. Apartments. 24-hour staffing; wellness center; personal care; medication administration; security; emergency response system; maintenance; transportation; up to 3 daily meals; pets allowed; housekeeping and laundry services; chapel; religious services; exercise classes; library; social and recreational activities; on- and off-site activities; educational and cultural programs; activities director; clubs and organizations; intergenerational program; volunteer

program; bingo; card and board games; gazebos; outdoor patios; barber/beauty shop.

DEP: 1 mo. rent. IND MO: $1,250–$2,000. AL MO: $2,050–$2,750.

The Windsor Senior Living Community

1770 N. Causeway Blvd.
Mandeville, LA 70471

Ph: (504) 624-8040
Fax: (504) 624-8822

IND: Yes. AL: Yes (total of 60 units)

Age 55+. Nondenominational. Studios and one- and two-bedroom apartments. Health center; 24-hour staffing; personal care; medication administration; security; emergency response system; maintenance; transportation; meal plan available; housekeeping and laundry services; chapel; social and recreational activities; barber/beauty shop.

IND MO: $1,300–$1,900. AL MO: Up to $660; plus IND MO.

South Central

Rosewood Retirement and Assisted Living Community, ALFAA

203 Rue Fontaine
Lafayette, LA 70508

Ph: (318) 981-0333
Fax: (318) 988-1706

IND: 20. AL: 53

Age 55+. For-profit; nondenominational. One- and two-bedroom apartments. Respite care; personal care; medication administration; security; emergency response system; maintenance; transportation; up to 3 daily meals; housekeeping and laundry services; social and recreational activities; arts and crafts; courtyard and fountain area; barber/beauty shop.

DEP: (ref.), $550. IND MO: $1,500–$1,700; 2nd person, $660. AL MO: $2,100–$2,300; 2nd person, $880.

North

The Arbor and Terrace

3702 Cypress St.
West Monroe, LA 71291

Ph: (318) 397-2220
Fax: (318) 397-4015

http://www.arborcommunity.com

IND/AL: 35. ALZ/MEM IMP: 24

Nondenominational. Cottages and apartments. Wellness program; respite care; personal care; medication administration; security; emergency response system; maintenance; transportation; up to 3 daily meals; pets allowed; housekeeping and laundry services; exercise classes; chapel; library; whirlpool; social and recreational activities; cultural and educational opportunities; courtyard; walking paths; gardening; ice cream parlor; barber/beauty shop.

PET DEP: $550. IND/AL MO: $1,550–$1,950.

Azalea Estates

4380 Old Sterling Rd.
Monroe, LA 71203

Ph: (318) 343-1626
Fax: (318) 345-4825

AL: 60

For-profit; nondenominational. Efficiency and one-bedroom apartments. Wellness program; 24-hour staffing; personal care; medication administration; security; emergency response system; maintenance; transportation; up to 3 daily meals; small pets allowed; housekeeping and laundry services; exercise classes; library; craft and hobby room; social, educational, and recreational activities; general store; garden areas; walking paths; barber/beauty shop.

Contact facility for fees.

Central

Kingsley Place at Alexandria, LALA

351 Windermere Blvd.
Alexandria, LA 71303

Ph: (318) 443-6170
Fax: (318) 443-2366

AL: 80. ALZ/MEM IMP: Yes

For-profit; nondenominational. Suites. Nursing care; personal care; medication administration; emergency response system; maintenance; transportation; up to 3 daily meals; pets allowed; housekeeping and laundry services; social and recreational activities; gift shop; barber/beauty shop.

DEP: $550. AL MO: $2,050–$4,350.

Independent Living

Independent housing (primarily rentals) for seniors that may offer security features, meal service, and activities.

Northwest Cedar Hill, AAHA

7401 St. Vincent Ave.
Shreveport, LA 71106

Ph: (318) 861-6915

IND: Yes

Nonprofit; nondenominational; Calvary Baptist Church affiliation. 24-hour staffing; security; emergency response system; maintenance; transportation; up to 3 daily meals; housekeeping and laundry services; Bible study; worship services; library; movies; quilting; choir; social and recreational activities; on- and off-site activities; crafts; bingo; walking paths; barber/beauty shop.

Contact facility for fees.

Holy Cross Villas

2140 Airline Drive
Bossier City, LA 71111

Ph: (318) 747-6497

IND: 78

Age 62+. Nonprofit; owned and sponsored by the Church of the Holy Cross, Episcopal. Apartments. Security; laundry services; pets allowed; resident clubs (includes exercise program, ceramics, quilting, cards); close to medical facilities, churches, and shopping.

Contact facility for fees.

Southeast

Annunciation Inn

1220 Spain St.
New Orleans, LA 70117

Ph: (504) 944-0512
Fax: (504) 944-0514

IND: 106

Age 62+. Church affiliated. One-bedroom apartments. Security; emergency response system; maintenance; social and cultural activities.

IND MO: 30% of income; HUD-subsidized.

Catholic-Presbyterian Apartments

655 North St.
Baton Rouge, LA 70802

Ph: (225) 383-5551

IND: 95

Age 62+. Nonprofit; nondenominational; church affiliation. Efficiencies and apartments. Security; emergency response system; maintenance; transportation; up to 3 daily meals; housekeeping and laundry services; chapel; religious services; postal services; library van; social and recreational activities; crafts; media room; lounge; restaurant; grocery store; barber/beauty shop.

IND MO: HUD-subsidized.

Lake Sherwood Village

4101 Plaza Tower Drive
Baton Rouge, LA 70816

Ph: (225) 296-0803
Fax: (225) 296-0232

IND: 120

Age 55+. For-profit; nondenominational; nonsectarian. Apartments. Some nursing care; security; emergency response system; maintenance; transportation; up to 3 daily meals; pets allowed; housekeeping and laundry services; exercise program; religious services; library; social and recreational activities; music room; porch; lake; convenience store; close to shopping and medical facilities; barber/beauty shop.

APPL: $100. IND MO: $1,300–$2,000.

Nouveau Marc

1101 Sunset Blvd.
Kenner, LA 70065

Ph: (504) 469-7988
Fax: (504) 469-7918

IND: 111

For-profit; owned by Holiday Retirement Corp. Apartments. Blood pressure checks; 24-hour staffing; emergency response system; maintenance; transportation; meal plan; housekeeping and laundry services; exercise classes; religious services; crafts; social and recreational activities; bookmobile; clubs; card and board games.

APPL: (ref.) $100. IND MO: $1,350–$2,150; 2nd person, $360

The Palms

10301 I-10 Service Road
New Orleans, LA 70127

Ph: (504) 244-6111
Fax: (504) 244-0840

IND: 286

Age 55+. Nondenominational. Efficiencies and one- and two-bedroom apartments. Some nursing care; podiatry care; maintenance; transportation; pets allowed; laundry services; swimming pool; Bible study; recreational room; social and recreational activities.

DEP: $230. IND MO: $210–$450.

St. Theresa Apartments

3620 Winbourne Ave.
Baton Rouge, LA 70805

Ph: (225) 357-0804
Fax: (225) 357-2252

IND: 88

Age 55+. Security, maintenance; pets allowed; laundry services; swimming pool.

DEP: $200. IND MO: $330–$425; HUD-subsidized.

Timber Ridge Apartments

6364 Woodlands Hwy
New Orleans, LA 70131

Ph: (504) 391-9841
Fax: (504) 391-9996

IND: 150

Nondenominational. Apartments. Maintenance; swimming pool; fitness center; tennis courts; pets allowed.

APPL: (ref.) $10. DEP: (ref.) $450. IND MO: $375–$475. HUD-subsidized.

Central

England Oaks Senior Living Community, AAHSA

1003 Norman Drive, Apt. A
Alexandria, LA 71303

Ph: (318) 445-0520 or (800) 786-6257
Fax: (318) 445-8920

E-mail: *Englandoak@aol.com*

IND: 176

Age 55+. Nonprofit; nondenominational; owned and operated by California Lutheran Homes and Community Services. Homes. Security; emergency response system; maintenance; transportation; pets allowed; weekly luncheons; exercise classes; swimming pool (under construction); Bible study; arts and crafts; card and board games; on- and off-site activities; clubs; resident advisory group.

IND ENT: (ref.) $300. IND MO: $675–$800.

South Central

Holy Trinity Villa

445 Perry Lane
Opelousas, LA 70570

Ph: (318) 948-7236

IND: Yes

Age 62+. Nonprofit; sponsored by Holy Ghost Parish, Diocese of Lafayette. Apartments. Security; community area; recreation rooms.

IND MO: 30% of income; HUD-subsidized.

Adult/Resort Communities

Communities for active adults (not all are age-restricted; primarily ownership).

South

Eastover Country Club

5690 Eastover Drive
New Orleans, LA 70128

Ph: (504) 241-4400
Fax: (504) 245-7356

http://www.eastovercc.com

Individual homes. Golf course; tennis; swimming pool.

PURCHASE: Homes, $275,000–$2.2 million; homesites, $56,000–$165,000.

English Turn Golf and Country Club

1 Clubhouse Drive
New Orleans, LA 70131

Ph: (800) 876-4299 or (504) 392-9100
Fax: (504) 391-8004

http://www.englishturn.com

Individual homes, condominiums, homesites. Golf course; tennis; swimming pool; hiking/biking; fitness center; social club.

PURCHASE: Homes, $302,500–$1.375 million; homesites, $88,000–$302,500.

Pinewood Country Club

405 Country Club Blvd.
Slidell, LA 70458

Ph: (504) 643-6892
Fax: (504) 641-6706

Individual homes. Golf course; tennis; swimming pool; social clubs.

PURCHASE: Homes, $99,000–$137,500.

Central

The Bluffs on Thompson Creek

PO Box 1220
St. Francisville, LA 70775

Ph: (225) 634-5222

http://www.thebluffs.com

Individual homes, condominiums, homesites. Golf course; tennis; swimming pool; hiking; fishing; croquet; nature trails.

PURCHASE: Homes, $209,000–$384,500.

Maine

http://www.state.me.us

General Information

Climate

Summer temperatures average 70° F and winter temperatures average 20° F.

Cost of Living

Ranks 9th in the nation.

Taxes

State/local as % of Income: About 13.3%.

Property Tax Reduction: Maine Residents Property Tax Program provides tax and rent relief to elderly residents who own or rent. Elderly tax assistance available for eligible (low income) residents 62 or older. Telephone information, (800) 321-5557 or (207) 287-1818.

Sales: 5%.

Prescription Exemptions: Low-Cost Drug Program. Residents 62 years of age or older whose total income is $10,600 or below (income for married residents or residents with dependents is $13,100 or below) may purchase certain drugs at a low cost. Telephone information, (800) 321-5557, ext. 7-1818; or (207) 287-1818.

Transportation, Travel, and Tourism

Major Airports

- Bangor International Airport, 287 Godfrey Blvd., Bangor, ME 04401, (207) 947-0384.
- Hancock County–Bar Harbor Airport, 60 State St., Ellsworth, ME 04605, (207) 667-7329.
- Portland International Jetport, 1001 Westbrook St., Portland, ME 04102, (207) 772-0690.

Railways

- Amtrak, (800) USA-RAIL.

Bus Tours

- Greyhound Bus, (800) 231-2222.

State Highways

- Interstate 95 runs north-south.
- Route 1 follows the coastline.

Ground

- Bob's Airport Livery, Portland, (207) 773-5135.

Theater and Music

Orono

- Maine Center for the Arts/Hutchins Concert Hall, University of Maine, (800) 622-8499 or (207) 581-1755. TTD-TTY, (207) 581-1888.

Portland

- Portland Symphony Orchestra, (207) 842-0800.
- University of Southern Maine, (207) 750-5555. TTY, (207) 780-5646 (music students perform classical, jazz, chamber, and string quartets).

Ogunquit

- Holy Name Theater and Booth Productions, (508) 797-9277 (summer theater at the beach).

Museums, Crafts, Historical, Recreational

Augusta

- Maine State Museum, (207) 287-5790.

Bar Harbor

- Acadia National Park Nature Center, (207) 288-3338.
- Bar Harbor Whale Museum, (207) 288-2025 or (800) 247-3794.
- Island Artisans, (207) 288-4214 (art gallery).

Boothbay

- Boothbay Railway Village, (207) 633-4727 (historical exhibits).
- Boothbay Region Art Foundation, (207) 633-2703.

Freeport

- Pettengill Farm, (207) 865-3170 (19th century rural life and natural history).
- North American Wildlife Expo, (207) 865-1449.

Kennebunkport

- Seashore Trolley Museum, (207) 967-2800.
- Port Arundel Art Gallery, (207) 967-3728.
- Goose Rocks Pottery and Tile Works, (207) 967-2105.

Orono

- Hudson Museum, (207) 581-1901.

Portland

- Maine Coastal Museum, (207) 828-0814.
- Wadsworth-Longfellow House, (207) 879-0427.
- Maine College of Art, (207) 775-3052.

Organizations

Advocacy Groups

- Long-term Care Ombudsman Program, (207) 621-1079 (Augusta) or (800) 499-0229.
- Legal Service for the Elderly, (800) 449-0229 or (207) 621-1079.
- Bureau of Elder and Adult Services, (800) 262-2232 or (207) 624-5335.
- Adult Protective Services, (800) 624-8404 or (207) 532-5000.

Volunteer Programs

- Foster Grandparent Program (volunteer to serve children with special needs), all counties except York and Cumberland, (207) 941-2830; in York and Cumberland counties, (207) 773-0202.
- Retired Senior Volunteer Program (volunteer delivering meals, provide companionship to homebound, teach in literacy programs), Aroostook, (207) 764-3396; Mid-Maine, (207) 873-1127 or 626-3430; Mid-Coast, (207) 596-0361; Southern Maine, (207) 775-6503; Eastern Maine, (207) 941-2803.
- Senior Companion Program (volunteer to work with adults with special needs), Androscoggin and Oxford counties, (207) 774-7740 or (800) 482-7412; Aroostook County, (207) 532-6548 or (800) 287-1469; Hancock County, (207) 667-8212 or (800) 287-1479; Washington County, (207) 255-3345 or (800) 287-1542.

Housing

Long-Term Care Facilities

In the state of Maine, these facilities are called ***Long-Term Care/Congregate Housing Services Program (CHSP)/Nursing Home Facilities****.*

These facilities provide residential living and/or various levels of nursing and medical services to seniors for an extended period of time.

Types of Authorization

Licensing and / or Certification

These facilities must be licensed by the Department of Human Services, Division of Licensing and Certification. CHSP is a comprehensive program of supportive

services including meals, housekeeping, case management, and other daily living assistance-type services. Four types: Type I, no personal care, medication administration, or nursing service (no licensing required); Type II, provides personal assistance; Type III, provides personal assistance and medication administration; Type IV, provides personal care, medication administration, and nursing care. Nursing facilities provide skilled nursing care and related services for persons who require medical or nursing care, rehabilitation services, or health-related care and services beyond the level of room and board. All beds are certified for both Medicare and Medicaid.

Memberships

- American Association of Homes and Services for the Aging (AAHSA) represents not-for-profit organizations committed to providing high-quality health care, housing, and services to the elderly. AAHSA, 901 E St. NW, Suite 500, Washington, DC 20004-2011. Ph: (202) 783-2242. Fax: (202) 783-2285. *http://www.aahsa.org*

Accreditations

- Continuing Care Accreditation Commission (CCAC) accredits facilities that offer seniors a contract or contracts that provide residential living and health care services for the remainder of the person's lifetime and meet CCAC's accreditation standards.
- Joint Commission on the Accreditation of Healthcare Organizations (JCAHO) is an independent, not-for-profit organization, and the nation's oldest and largest standards-setting and health care accrediting institution.
- Catholic Health Association (CHA).
- Maine Health Care Association (MHCA).
- New England Gerontological Association (NEGA).

Central

Andrews House

11 Market Square
South Paris, ME 04281

Ph: (207) 743-6979

IND: Yes. AL: Yes. HCC: Yes. ALZ/MEM IMP: Yes

Affiliated with Market Square Health Care Center and Stephens Memorial Hospital; nondenominational. Suites and private and semiprivate rooms. 24-hour nursing care; physical, occupational, speech, and respiratory therapies; lab services; respite care; personal care; medication monitoring; home health services; security; emergency call bells; maintenance; up to 3 daily meals; housekeeping and laundry services; grocery shopping; social room and whirlpool; beauty/barber shop.

IND MO: $1,450–$2,100. HCC and personal care fees are additional.

Clover Health Care

440 Minot Ave.
Auburn, ME 04210

Ph: (207) 784-3573

http://www.mainecare.com

IND: 47. RC: Yes. ALZ: 36. NH: 87

Nondenominational facility. Apartments and private and semiprivate rooms. 24-hour nursing care; personal care; medication administration; podiatry service; physical, occupational, and speech therapies; emergency pull cords; hand-held beeper for emergency; in-house home health agency; transportation to medical appointments; up to 3 daily meals (IND includes 1 daily meal with MO fee); pets allowed; housekeeping and laundry services; all utilities; recreation room; intergenerational program; library; walkways and gardens; hair care.

DEP: 1 mo. rent. IND MO: $1,850–$2,600. RC Daily: $95 and $135. ADC Daily: $70. NH Daily: (intermediate care), $155 and $170; (skilled care), $175 and $195. ALZ Daily: $110 and $170.

St. Marguerite d'Youville Pavilion

102 Campus Ave.
Lewiston, ME, 04240

Ph: (207) 777-4200
Fax: (207) 777-4255

SNF: Yes. ALZ MEM/IMP: Yes (total resident capacity: 280)

Church-related; nondenominational. Private and semiprivate rooms. 24-hour licensed nursing care; social workers; rehabilitative services; long- and short-term care; wander guard system; security system; transportation services; 3 daily meals; housekeeping and laundry services; pastoral care; chapel; schedule activities; shopping trips; off-site excursions; hairdresser.

Daily: (extended care/dementia), $140 and $150; (respite care), $160 and $170.

Southeast

St. Andre Health Care Facility, CHA, MHCA, AAHSA, NEGA

407 Pool St.
Biddeford, ME 04005

Ph: (207) 282-5171
Fax: (207) 282-5372

SNF: Yes. ICF: Yes. ALZ/MEM IMP: Yes

Nonprofit facility; nondenominational; sponsored by the Good Shepherd Sisters. Private and semiprivate rooms. 24-hour skilled nursing care; physical, occupational, speech, and respiratory therapies; wound care; IV therapies; dental, podiatry, optometry, and audiology services; social workers; security; transportation; 3 daily meals; exercise program; chapel and spiritual support; recreational activities; games; resident council; off-site trips; beauty/barber shop.

Contact facility for fees.

Southridge Rehab and Living Center

PO Box 388, 173 South St.
Biddeford, ME 04005

Ph: (207) 282-4138 (in ME) or (800) 672-4138
Fax: (207) 282-8242

SNF: Yes. RSP: Yes. REHAB: 26. ALZ/MEM IMP: Yes

For-profit; nondenominational. Owned by North Country Associates. Private and semiprivate rooms. 24-hour skilled nursing care; rehabilitative services; physical, occupational, speech, and respiratory therapies; IV therapy; wound care; restorative nursing; specialty care program; on-staff physiatrist; respite care; security; emergency response system; maintenance; transportation; 3 daily meals; housekeeping and laundry services; religious services; activities program; off-site excursions; hair care.

SNF Daily: (3-bed room), $155; (semiprivate), $160; (private), $175.

North Country Associates

PO Box 1048
179 Lisbon St.
Lewiston, ME 04243-1408

Ph: (207) 786-3554
Fax: (207) 786-8507.

Owns 13 facilities (assisted living, skilled nursing, congregate, and mental illness) in Maine and Massachusetts.

Average daily costs for facilities: (semiprivate), $151; (private), $138.

Springbrook, JCAHO

300 Spring St.
Westbrook, ME 04092

HCC: Yes. RSP: Yes. ALZ/MEM IMP: Yes. ADC: Yes

Part of Sandy River Health System; nondenominational. Private and semiprivate rooms. 24-hour registered nursing care; rehabilitative services; IV therapies; wound management; physical,

occupational, and speech therapies; personal care; medication administration; scheduled transportation; 3 daily meals; housekeeping, laundry, and linen services; pastoral care; cultural, recreational, and social activities.

Daily: (extended care), $165 and $190; (skilled unit), $205 and $225; (Alzheimer's), $165 and $190; (residential), $135 and $150.

East

Island Nursing Home and Care Center

RFD Box 1124
Deer Isle, ME 04627

Ph: (207) 348-2351
Fax: (207) 348-6154

NH: Yes. RC: Yes. REHAB: Yes. ALZ: Yes

Community supported; nonprofit care facility. Private and semiprivate rooms. 24-hour nursing care; skilled nursing care; pain management; personal care; medication administration; social work services; 3 daily meals plus snacks; housekeeping and laundry services; religious services; activities program; walkways; gazebo; memorial garden; hair care.

NH Daily: $155 and $190. ALZ Daily: $155 and $160. REHAB/SC Daily: $170 and $180. RC Daily: $105 and $115.

Maine General

40 Glenridge Drive
Augusta, ME 04330

Ph: (207) 623-2593
Fax: (207) 621-0277

IND: Yes. SNF: Yes. ICF: Yes. ALZ/MEM IMP: Yes

Community-owned and operated; nondenominational. Private and semiprivate rooms. 24-hour nursing care; medication technicians; social services; rehabilitative services; skilled and intermediate care; long- and short-term care; transportation; up to 3 daily meals; exercise program; laundry service; group and individual activities; community activities; resident council; off-site trips; gardening; baking; hair care.

IND Daily: $90 and $105. ICF: $145 and $155. SNF: $155, $165, and $190. RSP: $150. ALZ/MEM IMP Daily: (boarding), $140; (respite), $150. ADC Daily: $15.

Northeast

Gardiner Nursing Home and Assisted Living

8 Holland St.
Houlton, ME 04730

Ph: (207) 532-3323

NH: 50. RC: 10

Nondenominational facility. Private and semiprivate rooms. 24-hour nursing and skilled nursing services; social services; rehabilitation services; long- and short-term care; oxygen therapy; pharmacy; transportation; 3 daily meals; laundry; activities; day room; gazebo.

NH Daily: $115 and $130. RC Daily: $100 and $115.

Assisted Living and Residential Care Facilities

These facilities provide room and board for ambulatory and independent adults who need minimum support.

Types of Authorization

Licensing and/or Certification

Requires licensing by the Department of Human Services, Division of Licensing and Certification. Residential facilities provide assisted living services. Two levels: Level I, licensed capacity for 6 or fewer residents; Level II, licensed capacity for 7 or more residents.

Memberships

- Assisted Living Federation of America (ALFA) is a national nonprofit membership organization whose mission is to enhance the quality of life in assisted living facilities and promote the interests of the assisted living industry. ALFA, 10300 Eaton Place, Suite 400, Fairfax, VA 22030. Ph: (703) 691-8100. Fax: (703) 691-8106. *http://www.alfa.org*

Southeast

Woodford Park, JCAHO

68 Devonshire St.
Portland, ME 04103

Ph: (207) 772-2893
Fax: (207) 772-3230

AL: Yes

Private and semiprivate rooms. Registered nurse; on-call physician; personal care; medication administration; individual care plans; dental, podiatry, and ophthalmology services; emergency response system; scheduled transportation; 3 daily meals; housekeeping and laundry services; religious services; whirlpool bath; social and recreational activities; visiting authors, artists, and performers; shopping trips; gardening; hobbies; hair care.

Daily: $110.

Central

Bolster Heights

26 Bolster St.
Auburn, ME 04210

Ph: (207) 784-1364
Fax: (207) 782-2024

AL: 84 residents

Hospital-owned; nondenominational. Private and semiprivate rooms. 24-hour nursing care and supervision; personal care; medication administration; transportation; 3 daily meals; laundry services; church services; music therapy; activities program; off-site excursions; beauty shop.

RC Daily: $85 and $100.

East

Merry Gardens Estates

87 John St.
Camden, ME 07843

Ph: (207) 230-0618
Fax: (207) 230-0542

IND: 30. AL: Yes

Nonprofit; nondenominational; developed by Coastal Affordable Housing. Apartments. 24-hour nurse on call; home health services; rehabilitative therapies; personal care; medication administration; security; emergency response system; maintenance; transportation; up to 3 daily meals; pets allowed; housekeeping and laundry services; social, recreational, and educational activities; volunteer opportunities; downtown district within walking distance; barber/beauty shop services.

IND MO: $450 AL MO: about 60–70% of monthly income.

REQ: Annual income must be no more than $15,060, single; $17,220, couple.

Northeast:

Madigan Assisted Living

93 Military St.
Houlton, ME 04730

Ph: (207) 532-6593

AL: Yes

Nondenominational. Suites and apartments. Nursing services; health monitoring; therapy services; 24-hour professional staff; social service consultation; personal care; medication administration; security; emergency response system; maintenance; transportation; up to 3 daily meals; housekeeping and laundry services; recreational and social activities; barber/beauty shop.

AL MO: $1,375–$2,050

Independent Living

Independent housing (primarily rentals) for seniors that may offer security features, meal service, and activities.

East

Calais Methodist Home

10 Sunrise Circle
Calais, MA 04619

Ph: (207) 454-7196
Fax: (207) 454-2499

RH: 90

Age 62+ or disabled. Nonprofit; nondenominational. Apartments. Emergency response system; maintenance; pets allowed.

DEP: (ref.) $150. MO: 30% of adjusted income.

Adult/Resort Communities

Communities for active adults (not all are age-restricted; primarily ownership).

Central

Avalon Village

PO Box 320
239 Main Rd. North
Hampden, ME 04444

Ph: (207) 862-5100
Fax: (207) 862-6865

http://www.avalon-maine.com

Age: 60+. Cooperative cottages and apartments. 24-hour staff; gourmet meals; community rooms; guest suites; social activities; walking trails.

PURCHASE: Co-ops, from $165,000 + monthly homeowner's fee (includes maintenance, taxes, insurance, transportation, services). Rentals available.

Sugarloaf/USA

RR1 Box 5000
Kingfield, ME 04947

Ph: (207) 237-2000

http://www.sugarloaf.com

Individual homes, townhomes, condominiums. Golf club; fitness center; swimming pool; mountain biking; fishing; rafting; hiking; skiing; ice skating.

PURCHASE: Homes, $66,000–$385,000; townhomes, $135,000–$259,000; condos, $37,500–$285,000.

West

Riverbend

Sunday River Rd.
Bethel, ME

Ph: (800) 447-8020 or (207) 364-3246

http://www.bethelriverbend.com/

Condominiums. Cross-country skiing; skating; snowmobiling; hiking/biking; swimming; fishing; nearby golf and downhill skiing.

PURCHASE: Condos, $75,000–$186,000.

East

Samoset Village

220 Warrenton St.
Rockport, ME 04856

Ph: (207) 594-9153 or (800) 552-1070

Fax: (207) 594-4622
http://www.samoset.com

Townhomes. Golf course; tennis; racquetball; swimming pool; hiking trails; fishing; snow skiing; fitness center.

PURCHASE: Homes, $220,000–$440,000.

South

The Farragut

71 Portland Rd.
PO Box 613
Kennebunk, ME 04043

Ph: (877) 985-0300 or (207) 985-0300

Age: 60+. Attached garden and village homes, condominiums. Swimming pool; fitness center; walking trails; dining; recreational and spiritual programs; on-site health center; coordination of in-home services.

PURCHASE: Homes, $176,000–$220,000.

Woodlands Club

39 Woods Rd.
Falmouth, ME 04105

Ph: (207) 781-3104

Individual homes, homesites. Golf course; tennis; racquetball; swimming pool; snow skiing; fitness center; squash; social clubs.

PURCHASE: Homes, $330,000–$550,000.

Maryland

http://www.state.md.us

General Information

Climate

Moderate. Summers mild to hot; winters from moderate in the east and south to very cold in the western mountains.

Cost of Living

Ranks 23rd in the nation.

Taxes

State/Local as % of Income: About 10.2%.

Property Tax Reduction: Residents 65 or older can elect to defer the increase in their property tax bill. Administered jointly by state and local governments.

Sales: 5%.

Prescription Exemptions: Medicines are exempt from sales tax.

Transportation, Travel, and Tourism

General

Office of Tourism, (800) MD-IS-FUN.

Major Airport

- Baltimore-Washington International Airport, Baltimore, MD 21240, (800) 1-FLY-BWI.

Railways

- Amtrak, (800) USA-RAIL.

Bus Tours

- Maryland Mass Transit, (410) 539-5000.
- Greyhound Bus, (800) 231-2222.

State Highways

- Interstate 95 runs north-south.
- Interstates 68 and 70 run east-west.

Theater and Music

Baltimore

- Baltimore Opera Company, (410) 625-1600.
- Baltimore Arena, (410) 347-2020 (concerts and sporting events).
- Baltimore Center for the Performing Arts, (410) 625-4200.

Hagerstown

- Maryland Theatre, (301) 790-2000.

Museums, Crafts, Historical, Recreational

Baltimore

- Spirit of Baltimore, (410) 523-7447 (cruises of the Inner Harbor).
- Baltimore Maritime Museum, (410) 396-3453.
- Asian Arts Center–Roberts Gallery, (410) 830-2807.
- B and O Railroad Museum, (410) 752-2490.

Annapolis:

- Historic Annapolis Foundation Tours, (410) 268-5576 (self-guided audio tour of 19 historic sites).
- U.S. Naval Academy, (410) 293-2108.
- Chesapeake Bay Sport Fishing and Charter, (800) 394-4101.

Coastal Region

- Chesapeake Bay Maritime Museum, St. Michaels, (410) 745- 2916.
- St. Michaels, (410) 822-4606 (historic sites, museums, restaurants, shops, boating).
- Ocean City, (800) OC-OCEAN (beaches, family amusement).

- Ocean City Golf and Yacht Club, Berlin, (410) 641-1779 or (800) 442-3570.
- Assateague Green Gulf Center, Berlin, (410) 213-7526.

Waldorf

- Maryland Indian Cultural Center, (301) 372-1932 (Native American culture).

Organizations

Advocacy Groups

- Maryland Office on Aging, (800) AGE-DIAL. Association of Retired Persons, MD chapter, (410) 377-2905.
- Maryland Senior Action Council, (202) 624-9532.
- United Seniors of Maryland, (410) 992-9304.
- Elder Abuse Prevention Hotline, (800) 91-PREVENT.

Volunteer Programs

- Volunteer Maryland, (410) 514-7270.
- State Office on Volunteerism, (410) 767-4496 or in Maryland, (800) 321-8657.

Housing

Long-Term Care Facilities

In the state of Maryland, these facilities are called ***Continuing Care/Life Care/Nursing Home Facilities****.*

These facilities provide residential living and/or various levels of nursing and medical services to seniors for an extended period of time.

Types of Authorization

Licensing and / or Certification

These facilities must provide a secure, stimulating, and protected environment for seniors, with access to medical and nursing services. There are a range of contract agreements, terms, entrance fees, and monthly service fees that are regulated by the Department of Aging. Three types: A (all-inclusive), assisted living and nursing care fees are included in the monthly fee; B, a set number of days for assisted living and nursing care services are included in the monthly fee, and once those days are met, a daily service fee is required; C, additional fees are required for assisted living and nursing services.

Membership:

- American Association of Homes and Services for the Aging (AAHSA) represents not-for-profit organizations committed to providing high-quality health care, housing, and services to the elderly. AAHSA, 901 E St. NW, Suite 500, Washington, DC 20004-2011. Ph: (202) 783-2242. Fax: (202) 783-2285. *http://www.aahsa.org*
- Mid-Atlantic Association of Non-Profit Homes for the Aging (MANPHA) is an AAHSA Affiliated State Association. MANPHA A Senior Service Alliance, 10280 Old Columbia Rd., Suite 250, Columbia, MD 21046-1709. Ph: (410) 381-1176. Fax: (410) 381-0240. *http://www.manpha.org*

Accreditations:

- Continuing Care Accreditation Commission (CCAC) accredits facilities that offer seniors a contract or contracts that provide residential living and health care services for the remainder of the person's lifetime and meet CCAC's accreditation standards.
- Joint Commission on the Accreditation of Healthcare Organizations (JCAHO) is an independent, not-for-profit organization, and the nation's

oldest and largest standards-setting and health care accrediting institution.

South

Asbury–Solomons Island

11100 Asbury Circle
Solomons Is., MD 20688

Ph: (800) 953-3300
Fax: (301) 394-300

http://www.asbury.org/solomons.html

IND: 208. AL: 24. HCC: 42

Not-for-profit; nondenominational. Apartments, cottages, and private and semiprivate rooms. 24-hour nursing care; rehabilitative services; social services; 24-hour licensed staff availability; personal care; medication monitoring; emergency response system; maintenance; transportation; up to 3 daily meals; housekeeping and laundry services; wellness center; daily activities; bank services; library; community center; crafts; woodworking, metalworking; computer room; games; billiards; walking paths; fishing; gardens; beauty/barber salon.

IND ENT: (cottages), from $144,000; (apartments), from $66,000. IND MO: (cottages), from $910; (apartments), from $800. AL Daily: (single), $100; (double), $140. HCC Daily: (semiprivate), $155; (private), $160.

Baltimore/DC Area

Asbury Methodist Village, CCAC, EAGLE, JCAHO

201 Russell Ave.
Gaithersburg, MD 20877

IND: 650. AL: 329. HCC: 285. ALZ/MEM IMP: Yes

Age 60+. Nonprofit; nondenominational; affiliated with the United Methodist Church. Villas, apartment, and private and semiprivate rooms. 24-hour nursing care; long- and short-term care; physical, occupational, and speech therapies; medical and dental services; lab, X-ray, and pharmacy services; social services; personal care; medication administration; 24-hour security; emergency response call system; transportation; up to 3 daily meals; housekeeping and laundry services; clergy; exercise classes; resident council; educational, cultural, and recreational activities; computer room; crafts and hobbies; gardening; walking/jogging paths.

IND ENT: (ref.), $47,050–$297,500. IND MO: $625–$2,400. AL MO: $2,300–$5,775. HCC Daily: $165–$190.

Augsburg Lutheran Home of Maryland, CCAC, AAHSA

6811 Campfield Rd.
Baltimore, MD 21207

Ph: (410) 486-4573
Fax (410) 653-8744

http://www.augsburg.org/

IND: 77+. HCC: Yes. ALZ/MEM IMP: Yes

Nonprofit facility; nondenominational; affiliated with the Lutheran Church–Missouri Synod and the Evangelical Lutheran Church in America. Apartments and private and semiprivate rooms. 24-hour nursing care; rehabilitative care; on- call house physician; lab services; X-ray and EKG; pharmacy; dental and podiatry services; psychiatry; personal care; medication monitoring; 24-hour security; emergency response system; maintenance; transportation; up to 3 daily meals; exercise and fitness program; housekeeping and laundry services; library; chapel; resident association; cultural and recreational activities.

DEP: (ref.), $1,100. IND ENT: (80% ref.), $47,500–$121,000. IND MO: $925–$1200; 2nd person, $375. HCC MO:

$2,400–$4,400. AL: Additional fee dependent upon level of care.

Broadmead, CCAC

13801 York Rd.
Cockeysville, MD 21030-1899

Ph: (410) 527-1900

IND: 242. AL: Yes. ICF: Yes. HCC: Yes

Age 65+. Not-for-profit; nondenominational; Quaker association. Garden-style units and private and semiprivate rooms. Nursing care; physician on call; home health care; outpatient medical care; clinic; physical therapy; professional counseling; preventative medical program; dental, ophthalmology, and podiatry services; personal care; medication administration; security, emergency response system; maintenance; transportation; up to 3 daily meals; housekeeping and laundry services; exercise program; swimming pool; pets welcome; utilities; social and educational programs; library; crafts; country store; coffee shop; gardens; travel agent; massage therapist; nature trails; barber/beauty salon.

APPL: (single), $1,300; (couple), $1,925. IND ENT: (ref. based on a % for up to 48 mos.) $73,000–$217,000. IND MO: $1,875–$4,200. HCC and AL services are inclusive in monthly fee.

Brooke Grove

18100 Slade School Rd.
Sandy Spring, MD 20860

Ph: (301) 924-2811 or (800) 924-2811
TTY: (301) 924-1205
Fax: (301) 924-1200

IND: future plans for 300+. SNF: 148. AL: 116. ALZ/MEM IMP: 119

Nonprofit; nondenominational. Private and semiprivate rooms. 24-hour skilled nursing care; hospice; respite care; physical, occupational, and speech therapies; IV therapy; peritoneal dialysis; long- and short-term care; personal care; medication monitoring; Medicare/Medicaid-approved; maintenance; transportation; 3 daily meals; housekeeping and laundry services; social activities; scheduled off-site excursions; barber/beauty shop.

AL Daily: $95–$175. ALZ/MEM IMP Daily: $150. REHAB/SNF Daily: $160–$235.

Carroll Lutheran Village, CCAC

205 St. Mark Way
Westminster, MD 21158

Ph: (410) 848-0090 or 876-8113
Fax: (410) 848-8133

IND: Yes. AL: Yes. HCC: Yes

Age 60+. Nonprofit; nondenominational; church affiliated. Cottages, apartments, private and semiprivate rooms. 24-hour nursing care; rehabilitative therapies; social worker; personal care; medication administration; security; emergency response system; maintenance; transportation; up to 3 daily meals; housekeeping and laundry services; exercise program; religious services; planned activities; library; game rooms; workshop; resident association; volunteer programs; gardening; outdoor trails.

IND OCC: $51,000–$176,000. IND MO: $250–$900. HCC Daily: $130–$185.

Charlestown, CCAC

719 Maiden Choice Lane
Catonsville, MD 21228

Ph: (410) 737-8830 or (800) 222-9651 (DC or outlying areas)

IND: Yes. AL: Yes. SNF: Yes

Nondenominational; a Senior Campus Living development. Studios, apartments, and private and semiprivate rooms. 24-hour on-call doctor; skilled nursing care; podiatry, cardiology, eye, and dental services; rehabilitative therapies; Medicare-approved; home health care; personal care; medication administration; security; emergency response system; maintenance; transportation; up to 3 daily meals; housekeeping and laundry services; health club; chapel; banking and postal services; lounges; cultural

and educational activities; volunteer program; arts and crafts room; woodworking shop; cable TV studio; computer center; library; gift shop; convenience shop; nature trails; barber/beauty shop.

APPL: (no ref.) $150 per person. DEP: (ref.) $1,100. IND ENT: (ref.) $55,000–$366,000. IND MO: $925–$1,650. 2nd person, $500.

Collington, CCAC

10450 Lottsford Rd.
Mitchellville, MD 20721-2734

Ph: (301) 925-4610
Fax: (301) 925-7357

http: / / www.collington.com

clifecare@aol.com

IND: 300. AL: 50. HCC: 40. HHC: Yes

Age 65+. Nonprofit; nondenominational. Apartments, cottages, and private and semiprivate rooms. Skilled nursing care; therapies; pharmacy; dental and podiatry services; personal care; medication administration; Medicare-approved; security; emergency response system; maintenance; transportation; up to 3 daily meals; housekeeping and laundry services; fitness center; pool; cultural and social activities; lake; walking trails; barber/beauty shop.

APPL: $150. DEP: $1,100. IND ENT: $75,000–$338,000. IND MO: $2,000–$4,400. AL MO: $2,850–$3,500. HCC MO: $4,500–$4,850; daily, $150–$165.

Edenwald Retirement Community

800 Southerly Rd.
Baltimore, MD 21286

Ph: (410) 339-6000

IND: 240. AL: 45. HCC: Yes

For-profit facility; nondenominational. Apartments and private and semiprivate rooms. Nursing care; medical, dental, and podiatry services; personal care; medication administration; 24-hour security; maintenance; transportation; up to 3 daily meals (1 daily meal included with IND MO fee); housekeeping and laundry services; exercise classes; planned daily activities; off-site excursions; movies; speakers; educational programs; library; bank services; country store; beauty/barber salon.

IND ENT: $70,500–$238,000. MO: $1,500–$3,550. AL and HCC fees included in mo. fees.

Fairhaven, CCAC

7200 Third Ave.
Sykesville, MD 21784-5201

Ph: (410) 795-8801 or (800) 241-9997
TDD: (410) 549-5845

E-mail: *fairhaven@emaseniorcare.org*

IND: Yes. AL: Yes. HCC: 101

Nonprofit; nondenominational; a subsidiary of Episcopal Ministries of the Aging, Inc. Cottages, apartments, and private and semiprivate rooms. Nursing care; Ambulatory Care Center; eye and dental care; X-ray and lab services; physical, occupational, and speech therapies; personal care; medication monitoring; security; emergency response system; maintenance; transportation; up to 3 daily meals; housekeeping and laundry services; exercise classes; fitness center; pool; library; religious services; bank and postal services; computer room; arts and crafts; group activities; educational classes; social gatherings; nature trails; golf course; gift shop; beauty/barber salon.

IND ENT: (50-mo. or 90% ref. options), $63,000–$452,000. IND MO: $1,750–$4,550. (HCC services are inclusive.) AL ENT: $84,000–$168,000. AL MO: $2,600–$5,700.

Ginger Cove

4000 River Crescent Drive
Annapolis, MD 21401

Ph: (410) 266-7300 or (800) 299-COVE
Fax: (410) 266-6144

IND: 240. AL: Yes. HCC: 61

Age 60+. Owned and operated by Annapolis Life Care; managed by Life Care Services Corp; nonprofit; nondenominational. Apartments and private

and semi-private rooms. 24-hour nursing care; skilled nursing; personal care; medication administration; security; emergency response system; maintenance; transportation; up to 3 daily meals; housekeeping and laundry services; fitness center; pool; chapel; library; banking services; arts and crafts studio; woodworking shop; social, cultural, and recreational activities; convenience store; pier; gardening areas; barber/beauty shop.

IND ENT: (90% ref.), $167,500–$351,000. IND MO: $1,750–$2,450; 2nd person, $1,050. (AL and HCC fees included in MO fee).

Glen Meadows, JCAHO

11630 Glen Arm Rd.
Glen Arm, MD 21057

Ph: (410) 592-5310
Fax: (410) 592-6175

IND: 213. AL: 29. HCC: 31

Age 62+. Nonprofit; nondenominational; affiliated with Presbyterian Homes. Homes, apartments, and private and semiprivate rooms. Nursing care; long- and short-term care; rehabilitative services; gerontologist, dentist, audiologist, podiatrist, and therapists on staff; wellness center; personal care; medication administration: security; emergency response system; maintenance; transportation; up to 3 daily meals; housekeeping and laundry services; fitness room; banking services; activities; workshop; walking paths; country store; barber/beauty shop.

APPL: $275 (per person). DEP: 10% of ENT DEP. IND ENT: $47,500–$197,000. IND MO: $1,150–$2,200. AL ENT: $33,000–$60,500. AL MO: $3,200–$3,550. "Assisted Living Plus" services, $180 (daily). HCC Daily: $180.

The National Lutheran Home

9701 Veirs Drive
Rockville, MD 20850-8462

Ph: (301) 424-9560
Fax: (301) 9574

IND: 129. HCC: 300

Age 65+. Nondenominational; nonprofit; affiliated with the Evangelical Lutheran Church in America. Apartments. Skilled nursing and medical care; dental, podiatry, and ophthalmology care; lab services; physical therapy; security; emergency response system; maintenance; transportation; up to 3 daily meals; pets allowed.

IND ENT: (% ref. up to 10 years), $82,500–$93,500. IND MO: $200, plus property tax, about $95.

North Oaks

725 Wilson Lane
Baltimore, MD 21208-1132

Ph: (410) 486-9090

IND: 182. AL: Yes. HCC: 49

Age 65+. Affiliated with Life Care Services Corp.; nondenominational. Apartments and private and semiprivate rooms. 24-hour skilled nursing care; social services; on-call medical director; respite care; physical, occupational, and speech therapies; emergency, recuperative, and long-term care; personal care; medication administration; security; emergency call response system; maintenance; transportation; up to 3 daily meals (1 daily meal included with IND MO fee); housekeeping and laundry services; fitness center; activities director; library; banking services; planned social, cultural, and recreational activities; arts and crafts room; gardening; convenience store; barber/beauty shop.

IND ENT: (90% ref.) $109,000–$275,000; 2nd person, $5,500. IND MO: $1,900–$3,600; 2nd person, $875. HCC services are inclusive in monthly fee.

Oak Crest Village Retirement Community

8820 Walther Blvd.
Parkville, MD 21234

Ph: (410) 665-2222 or (800) 333-5693
Fax: (410) 665-2250

IND: 1,528. AL: 125. HCC: 240. ALZ/MEM IMP: Yes

Age 60+. Nondenominational; a Senior Campus Living development. Apartments and private rooms. 24-hour on-call doctor; skilled nursing care; podiatry, cardiology, eye, and dental services; rehabilitative therapies; Medicare/Medicaid-approved; home health care; personal care; medication administration; security; emergency response system; maintenance; transportation; up to 3 daily meals; housekeeping and laundry services; health club; chapel; banking and postal services; lounges; cultural and educational activities; volunteer program; arts and crafts room; woodworking shop; billiards room; computer lab; library; gift shop; convenience shop; nature trails; barber/beauty shop.

APPL: $150. DEP: (ref.), $1,100. IND ENT: (ref.) $79,500–$400,500. IND MO: $925–$1,700. AL ENT: (ref.), $89,500. AL MO: $2,500–$4,150.

HCC Daily: $175.

Presbyterian Home of Maryland

400 Georgia Ct.
Towson, MD 21204

Ph: (410) 823-4622

IND: Yes. AL: Yes. HCC: Yes (total residents, 100)

Age 65+. Nonprofit, nondenominational; church affiliated. Suites and private and semiprivate rooms. 24-hour nursing care; short- and long-term care; personal care; medication administration; security; emergency response system; maintenance; transportation; up to 3 daily meals; housekeeping and laundry services; exercise classes; religious services; Bible study; banking and postal services; volunteer opportunities; intergenerational program; holiday celebrations; daily activities; off-site excursions; barber/beauty shop.

APPL: $1,100. PROC: (no ref.) $200. IND ENT: (% ref. up to 2 yr.) $49,500 and $55,000. IND MO: $1,200–$2,400. AL MO: $2,150. HCC MO: $2,900.

Rainbow Hall, CCAC

10729 Park Heights Ave.
Owings Mills, MD 21117

Ph: (410) 484-3324
Fax: (410) 602-3697

E-mail: *baptisthome@home.com*

IND: 19. AL: 12. SNF: 23

Nonprofit; nondenominational; affiliated with Baptist Homes of Maryland/Delaware Inc. Suites and private rooms. 24-hour nursing care; physician visits; rehabilitative therapies; ophthalmology and hearing care; lab services; wellness program; personal care; medication monitoring; security; emergency response system; maintenance, transportation; up to 3 daily meals; housekeeping and laundry services; all utilities except phone and cable; chapel; solarium; scheduled activities; postal services; computer/Internet access; beauty/barber shop.

IND COMM: (no ref.) (single), $19,500; (double), $39,000. IND MO: $1,925–$2,550; 2nd person, $1,100. AL Daily: $100, $105, $110. SNF Daily: $140 and $145.

Roland Park Place, CCAC

830 W. 40th St.
Baltimore, MD 21211

Ph: (410) 243-5700
Fax: (410) 662-4906

http://www.rolandparkplace.org

E-mail: *KN@rpplace.com*

IND: 200. AL: 7 (30 under construction). HCC: 71

Age 62+. Nonprofit; affiliated with First Evangelical Lutheran Church; nondenominational. Apartments and private and semiprivate rooms. Skilled and comprehensive nursing care; medical services; physical, occupational, and speech therapies; pharmacy; dental, optometry, audiology, psychiatry, and podiatry services; personal care; medication administration; security; emergency response

system; maintenance; transportation; up to 3 daily meals; pets allowed; housekeeping and laundry services; fitness center; exercise classes; library; bank; scheduled daily activities; educational and cultural opportunities; convenience store; holiday celebrations; off-site excursions; barber/beauty shop.

IND ENT: (Traditional plan), $108,500–$220,000; (Refund plan), $157,000–$356,000. 2nd person, $16,500. IND MO: (Traditional plan), $2,250–$4,100; (Refund plan), $2,250–$4,100. 2nd person, $750. HCC fees included in ENT/MO fees. AL fees additional.

The Trellises

10910 John Hopkins Rd.
Laurel, MD 20723

Ph: (301) 604-4400 or (888) 604-4500
Fax: (301) 604-4747

IND: Yes. AL: Yes. HCC: Yes. ALZ/MEM IMP: Yes

Age 62+. Nonprofit; nondenominational; affiliated with Baptist Home of Maryland/Delaware, Inc. Apartments and private and semiprivate rooms. Nursing and medical care; therapy services; pharmacy; wellness and care management; personal care; medication monitoring; security; emergency response system; maintenance; transportation; up to 3 daily meals (1 daily meal included in IND MO fee); housekeeping and laundry services; exercise program; chapel: library/computer room; arts and crafts; educational, recreational, and cultural activities; walking paths; gardening; convenience store; cafe; barber/beauty salon.

Preconstruction prices (year 2000 completion date). IND ENT: (90% ref.), $98,500–$302,000; (no ref.), minimum ENT, $19,500. IND MO: (90% ref), $1,100–$1,750; (no ref.), $1,950–$2,850. 2nd person, $525. AL and ALZ/MEM IMP ENT: $19,500. AL MO: $3,025. ALZ/MEM IMP MO: $4,950.

Vantage House

55400 Vantage Point Rd.
Columbia, MD 21044

Ph: (410) 964-5454 or (800) 998-2682

IND: 220. AL: 26. HCC: 44

Age 62+. Nonprofit; nondenominational. Apartments and private and semiprivate rooms. Comprehensive nursing care; physician care; physical and occupational therapies; dental, podiatry, and audiology services; wellness clinic; personal care; medication administration; security; emergency response system; maintenance; transportation; up to 3 daily meals; housekeeping and laundry services; fitness and exercise room; chapel; lounges; library; auditorium; arts and crafts room; computer center; social, educational, and cultural activities; volunteer program; clubs and committees; barber/beauty shop.

DEP: 10% of ENT fee (ref.). APPL: (single), $165; (couple), $275. IND ENT: (90% ref.), $102,000–$254,000; (50 mo. declining ref.), $71,500–$178,000. IND MO: $1,800–$4,400. AL and HCC included in ENT and MO fees.

East

Heron Point

501 E. Campus Ave.
Chestertown, MD 21620-9913

Ph: (410) 778-7300 or (800) 327-9138
Fax: (410) 778-0053 TTY: (800) 735-2258

IND: 192. AL: Yes. HCC: Yes

Age 60+. Nondenominational; managed by Peninsula United Methodist Homes. Apartments, cottage homes, and private and semiprivate rooms. Skilled nursing care; long- and short-term care; therapies; rehabilitative care; personal care; medication administration; security; emergency response system; maintenance; transportation; up to 3 daily meals; pets allowed; housekeeping and

laundry services; fitness center; religious services; arts and crafts center; woodworking shop; library; computer center; volunteer opportunities; educational and cultural programs; banking services; gift shop; deli; barber/beauty shop.

Contact facility for fees.

West

Homewood at Williamsport

16505 Virginia Ave.
Williamsport, MD 21795

Ph: (301) 582-1750
Fax: (301) 582-1805

IND: 219. AL: 40. HCC: 124. ALZ/MEM IMP: Yes. ADC: Yes

Age 62+. Nonprofit; affiliated with United Church of Christ. Apartments, cottages, and private and semiprivate rooms. 24-hour nursing care; medical services; therapies; pharmacy; dental and podiatry services; personal care; medication administration; Medicare/Medicaid-approved; security; emergency response system; maintenance; transportation; up to 3 daily meals; housekeeping and laundry services; fitness center; pool; scheduled daily activities.

IND APPL: $100. IND DEP: 5% of ENT fee; 2 mos. rent. IND ENT: $40,000–$109,000. IND MO: (single), $450; (double), $500. AL MO: $2,950–$4,800. HCC Daily: $130–$150.

Central

Buckingham's Choice

30 W. Patrick St., Suite 701
Frederick, MD 21701

Ph: (301) 662-6910 or (800) 409-5491
Fax: (301) 631-5491

IND: 207. AL: 45. HCC: 41

Age 65+. Nonprofit; nondenominational facility; affiliated with the Episcopal Ministries to the Aging. Apartments, cottages, and private rooms. Skilled nursing care; outpatient and wellness care; hospice services; physical, occupational, speech, and respiratory therapies; podiatry and dental services; lab services; personal care; medication administration; security; emergency response system; maintenance; scheduled transportation; up to 3 daily meals (1 daily meal included with IND MO fee); all utilities; housekeeping and laundry services; exercise and fitness center; swimming pool; bank and postal services; woodworking shop; crafts studio; 3-hole chip-and-putt golf; game rooms; computer rooms; nature trail; library; barber/beauty shop.

IND ENT: (50-mo. declining ref.), $108,500–$320,500; (90% ref.), $162,500–$481,000; (100% ref.), $181,000–$535,500. IND MO: $1,150–$2,350. AL Daily: $135. HCC: $200.

Assisted Living and Residential Care Facilities

In the state of Maryland, these facilities are called ***Assisted Living and Group Homes****.*

These facilities provide room and board for ambulatory and independent adults who need minimum support.

Types of Authorization

Licensing and/or Certification

Senior assisted housing is for persons age 62 and older who need help with one or more daily activity. These facilities are certified by the Department of Aging.

Memberships:

- Assisted Living Federation of America (ALFA) is a national nonprofit membership organization whose mission is to enhance the quality of life in assisted living facilities and promote the interests of the assisted living industry. ALFA, 10300 Eaton

Place, Suite 400, Fairfax, VA 22030. Ph: (703) 691-8100. Fax: (703) 691-8106. *http://www.alfa.org*

- Maryland Assisted Living Association (MALA) is a state affiliate of ALFA. MALA, 10280 Old Columbia Rd. #245, Columbia, MD 21046. Ph: (410) 290-8098. Fax: (410) 381-6032. *http://www.mala-md.org*

Central

Edenton

5800 Genesis Lane
Frederick, MD 21703

Ph: (301) 694-3100
Fax: (301) 694-0308

http://www.Edenton-Retirement.com

IND: 75. AL: Yes

Nondenominational facility. Apartments. Certified nursing assistants; pharmacy delivery services; daily checks; home health care services; personal care; medication administration; security; emergency response system; maintenance; transportation; up to 3 daily meals; escort to meals; pets allowed; housekeeping and laundry services; chapel and Bible study; banking services; grocery shopping services; social, educational, and recreational activities; off-site activities; games; movies; crafts; barber/beauty shop.

IND MO: $1,100–$1,650 (includes up to $510 worth of AL services).

Kuehner House

23801 Frederick Rd.
Clarksburg, MD 20871

Ph: (301) 540-6308

AL: 5

Age 62+. County founded; managed by Victory Housing, Inc.; nondenominational. Single- and double-occupancy rooms. 24-hour support; personal care; medication administration; emergency communications; 3 daily meals; housekeeping, laundry, and linen services; deck.

AL MO: $1,900 and $2,100; subsidies are available for eligible residents.

Baltimore/DC Area

Malta House

4916-18 La Salle Rd.
Hyattsville, MD 20782

Ph: (301) 699-8600
Fax: (301) 699-1696

AL: Yes

Age 62+. Managed by Victory Housing, Inc.; nondenominational; church sponsored. Private rooms with private baths. 24-hour support; personal care; medication administration; emergency communications; 3 daily meals; housekeeping, laundry, and linen services; exercise classes; religious services; library; games; hobbies; gardening.

APP: $100. AL MO: $2,500.

South

Raphael House

1515 and 1517 Dunster Rd.
Rockville, MD 20854

Ph: (301) 217-9116
Fax: (301) 217-9119

AL: Yes

Managed by Victory Housing, Inc.; church and community sponsored. Private rooms with private baths. Personal care; medication administration; security; emergency response system; transportation; 3 daily meals; housekeeping and laundry services; handicapped equipped.

AL MO: $2,900. Sliding scale also available based on financial need.

Wildewood Retirement Village

PO Box 750
Smoke Hill and Wildewood Parkway
California, MD 20619

Ph: (301) 863-6655
Fax: (301) 863-6179

IND: 75. AL: 42. ALZ/MEM IMP: 40

Age 55+. For-profit; nondenominational; nonsectarian. Villa homes and condo apartments. Wellness clinic; medical director; home health care services; on-site physical therapist; personal care; medication administration; security; emergency response system; maintenance; transportation; up to 3 daily meals; pets allowed; housekeeping and laundry services; fitness center; exercise program; swimming pool; bank services; clubhouse; arts and crafts; social and recreational activities; restaurant; pub/lounge; deli; convenience store; barber/beauty shop.

IND PURCHASE OPTION: $148,500–$202,500. IND MO: $395–$625. AL MO: $2,550–$3,000

Independent Living

Independent housing (primarily rentals) for seniors that may offer security features, meal service, and activities.

Central

Creekside at Taskers Chance

100 Burgess Hill Way
Frederick, MD 21702

Ph: (301) 698-5700

IND: Yes

Age 62. For-profit; nondenominational. Apartments. Wellness program; security; emergency response system; 24-hour emergency maintenance; transportation; up to 3 daily meals; meal service if needed; small pets allowed; housekeeping and laundry services; exercise room; library; planned activities; gardening; shopping nearby; barber/beauty shop.

DEP: $25. APPL: $25. IND MO: (one year leases), $725–$850. Affordable housing program available for eligible persons.

Maryland Odd Fellows Home

1720 N. Market St.
Frederick, MD 21701

Ph: (301) 662-3563
Fax: (301) 662-7103

IND: 37

Nonprofit; nondenominational facility. Private and semiprivate rooms. Nursing assistants and physician on call; 24-hour custodial care; security; transportation; 3 daily meals; laundry services; exercise classes; activities director; library; sun porch; lounge; religious services; beauty/barber services.

IND MO: $1,050 and $1,100.

Baltimore/DC Area

The Gardens at Kentlands

221 Booth St.
Gaithersburg, MD 20878

Ph: (301) 926-0696 or (800) 905-1222

IND: Yes

Age 62+. Nondenominational; managed by Trammel Crow Residential Services. Apartments. Maintenance; transportation; meal plan; pets allowed; exercise room; library; media room; lounge; games and crafts; social and recreational activities; educational and cultural programs; barber/beauty shop.

APPL: $35/person. DEP: $550. PET DEP: ($150 ref.) $330. IND MO: $1,100–$1,650.

Lakeview House Apartments

10250 Westlake Drive
Bethesda, MD 20817

Ph: (301) 469-6927
Fax: (301) 469-4744

IND: 151

Age 62+ or handicapped/disabled. Nonprofit; nondenominational. Maintenance; transportation; 1 daily meal option; pets allowed; exercise room and classes; library.

DEP: 1st mo. rent; pet, $200. IND MO: 30% of gross income. HUD residence.

Adult/Resort Communities

Communities for active adults (not all are age-restricted; primarily ownership).

North

Crestwood Village

6902 Crabapple Drive
Frederick, MD 21703

Ph: (301) 662-0401

Individual homes, duplexes, quads; condominiums. Tennis; swimming pool; clubhouse; exercise room; spa; shuffleboard; game rooms; billiards.

PURCHASE: Homes, from $132,000–$187,000; condos, from $99,000.

Crofton Country Club

1691 Crofton Parkway
Crofton, MD 21114

Ph: (301) 261-6500 or (410) 721-3111

Individual homes, townhomes. Golf course; pro shop; clubhouse; tennis; swimming pool; dining.

PURCHASE: Homes, from $275,000.

Leisure World of Maryland

14901 Pennfield Circle
Silver Spring, MD 20906

Ph: (800) 398-0085 or (301) 598-2500

http://www.idigroup.com/lwmd.htm

Age 55+. Condominiums. Golf course; clubhouses; pro shop; swimming pools; lawn bowling; fitness and health spa; auditorium and theater; arts and crafts; social clubs; dining; shopping.

PURCHASE: Condos, from $143,000–$308,000.

New Colony Village

7400 New Colony Blvd.
Elkridge, MD 21075

Ph: (410) 799-9700 or (410) 750-7373

Manufactured homes, land lease community. Clubhouse; fitness center; swimming pool.

PURCHASE: Homes, $121,000–$154,000.

The Village of Cecil Woods

1801 W. Pulaski Hwy.
Elkton, MD 21921

Ph: (410) 287-0700

http://membrane.com/philanet/mckee/cecil/index.html

Age: 55+. Manufactured homes. Fishing pond; garden pavilion; five minutes from Chesapeake Bay.

PURCHASE: Homes, $55,000–$80,500.

South

Harbourside @ Heron Harbour Isle

120th St. and Bay
Ocean City, MD 21842

Ph: (410) 723-1718
Fax: (410) 723-6155

http://www.ocean-city.com/hbshome.htm

Individual homes, homesites. Recreation center; clubhouse; tennis; swimming pools; health club; community docks; wildlife sanctuary; nearby beach.

PURCHASE: Homes, $440,000–$2.2 million; homesites, $159,500–$423,500.

Harbourtowne Inn and Resort

PO Box 126
St. Michaels, MD 21663

Ph: (410) 820-9383

Individual homes, townhomes, condominiums, homesites. Golf course; clubhouse; pro shop; tennis; swimming pool; fitness center; boating; dining; social clubs.

PURCHASE: Homes, $275,000–$1.1 million; townhomes and condos, $123,500–$330,000; homesites, $55,000–$275,000.

Montego Bay Mobile Home Community

Ocean City, MD 21842

Ph: (800) 252-2223

Manufactured homes. Golf; tennis; swimming pools; walking/jogging path; fishing; pond sanctuary.

PURCHASE: Homes, $26,000–$163,000; waterfront homes, $99,000–$241,000.

Ocean Pines

239 Ocean Pkwy
Berlin, MD 21811

Ph: (410) 641-7717

http://www.ocean-city.com/land-pine.htm

Individual homes. Golf course; clubhouse; pro shop; tennis; swimming pools; marina; swim and racquet club; yacht club; beach club; community center.

PURCHASE: Homes, $55,000–$550,000.

River Run Golf Community

11605 Masters Lane
Berlin, MD 21811

Ph: (800) 733-7786 or (410) 641-7200

http://www.riverrungolf.com

Individual homes, townhomes, condominiums, homesites. Private golf course; private marina; water sports; tennis courts; Caribbean-style swimming pool; fitness center; dining.

PURCHASE: Condominiums and townhomes, from $165,000; homesites, $42,000–$88,000.

The Easton Club

7590 Oxford Rd.
Easton, MD 21601

Ph: (800) 277-9500 or (410) 820-9100

http://www.eastonclub.com

Individual homes, townhomes, homesites. Golf course; tennis; swimming pool; croquet; boating; fishing; hunting; hiking/biking; dining.

PURCHASE: Townhomes, from $143,000; homesites, from $109,000.

The Island at Hidden Harbour

125th St. on the Bay
Ocean City, MD 21842

Ph: (800) 728-7699 or (410) 250-2977

http://www.oceancitycondos.com/hiddenharbour

Condominiums. Recreation center; boat slips; fishing; boating; swimming pool; tennis.

PURCHASE: Condos, $209,000–$429,000.

Massachusetts

http://www.state.ma.us

General Information

Climate

Warm to hot summers; cold winters.

Cost of Living

Ranks 2nd in the nation.

Taxes

State/Local as % of Income: 10.2%.

Property Tax Reduction: Residents 62 or older may qualify for a homestead exemption.

Sales: 5%.

Prescription Exemptions: Prescription drugs are exempt from sales tax. The Senior Pharmacy Program (SPP) provides up to $750 annually to eligible seniors (65+) to pay for prescription drugs; (800) 953-3305.

Transportation, Travel, and Tourism

General

Senior Citizens/Transportation Access passes, (617) 222-5967.

Major Airports

- Logan International Airport, 600 Tower Rd., E. Boston, MA 02128-2904, (617) 973-5506 or (800) 23-LOGAN.
- Worcester Municipal Airport, 375 Airport Drive, Worcester, MA 01602-2294, (508) 799-1741.

Railways

- MBTA travel info., (617) 222-3200.
- Amtrak, (800) USA-RAIL.

Bus Tours:

- Greyhound Bus, (800) 231-2222.
- Bartlett Buss line, (617) 222-5175.

State Highways

- Interstate 95 runs north-south.
- Massachusetts Turnpike, Interstate 90, runs east-west; (508) 248-3907.

Theater and Music

Boston

- American Repertory Theatre, 64 Brattle St., Cambridge, MA 02138, (617) 547-8300 or 495-2668, *http://www.amrep.org*
- Boston Ballet, 19 Claredon St., Boston, MA 02116, (617) 695-6950, *http://www.bostonballet.org/*
- Boston Pops Orchestra and Symphony, Symphony Hall, 301 Massachusetts Ave., Boston, MA 02115, (617) CONCERT, *http://www.bso.org*
- Wang Center for the Performing Arts, 270 Tremont St., Boston, MA 02116, and the Shubert Theatre, 265 Tremont St., (617) 482-9393

Springfield/Pioneer Valley

- Academy of Music, 274 Main St., Northampton, MA 01060, (413) 584-8435.
- Springfield Symphony Hall, Court St., Springfield, MA 01103, (413) 787-6600, and Springfield Symphony Orchestra, (413) 733-2291.
- University of Mass. Fine Arts Center, Massachusetts Ave., Amherst, MA 01003, (413) 545-2511 or (800) 999-UMAS, *http://www.umass.edu/fac*

Cape Cod, Nantucket, Martha's Vineyard

- Cape Cod Symphony Orchestra, Mattacheese Middle School, W.

Yarmouth, MA 02673, (508) 362-1111.
- Nantucket Community Music Center, Box 1352, Nantucket, MA 02554, (508) 228-3352.
- Martha's Vineyard Chamber Music Society, Community Center Chilmark and Old Whaling Church, Edgartown, MA 02568, (508) 695-8055 *http://www.vineyard.net/org/mvcms*

Berkshires

- Berkshire Opera Company, 314 Main St., Stockbridge, MA 01262, (413) 298-5576.
- Tanglewood Music Festival, Rte. 183, Lenox, MA 01240, (413) 637-5165, or (800) 274-8499.

Central

- Worcester Foothills Theatre, Worcester Common Outlets, 100 Front St., Worcester, MA 01608, (508) 754-3314 or 4018.

Southeast

- New Bedford Festival Theatre, 99 Madison St., New Bedford, 02740, (508) 993-0772.

Museums, Crafts, Historical, Recreational

Boston

- Boston Tea Party Ship and Museum, Congress St. Bridge, Boston, MA 02210, (617) 338-1773, *http://www.historictours.com*
- Arthur M. Slacker Museum, 485 Broadway, Fogg Art Museum and Busch-Reisinger Museum, 32 Quincy St., Cambridge, MA 02138, (617) 495-9400, (part of Harvard).
- Kendall Whaling Museum, 27 Everett St., Sharon, MA 02067, (781) 784-5642, *http://www.kwm.org*
- MIT Museum, 265 Massachusetts Ave., Cambridge, MA 02139, (617) 253-4444.
- Museum of the National Center of Afro-American Artists, 300 Walnut Ave., Boston, (617) 442-8614.
- Freedom Trail, (617) 242-5642 (3-mile walking tour of 15 historic sites and structures).
- Fenway Park, 4 Yawkey Way, Boston, MA 02215, (617) 267-1700, *http://www.redsox.mlb.com*

North of Boston

- Cape Ann Historical Museum, 27 Pleasant St., Gloucester, MA 01930, (978) 283-0455.
- Long Hill, The Sedgwick Gardens, 572 Essex St., Beverly, MA 01915, (978) 921-1944.
- Mary Baker Eddy House, 23 Paradise Rd., Swampscott, MA 01913, (978) 388-1361.

Pioneer Valley

- Amherst History Museum, 67 Amity St., Amherst, MA 01002, (413) 256-0678.
- Emily Dickinson House, 280 Main St., Amherst, MA 01002, (413) 542-8161.
- Smith College Museum of Art, Elm St., Northampton, MA 01063, (413) 585-2760, *http://www.smith.edu/artmuseum*

Cape Cod

- Cape Museum of Fine Arts, Rte. 6A, Dennis, MA 02638, (508) 385-4477.
- John F. Kennedy Hyannis Museum, 397 Main St., Hyannis, MA 02601, (508) 790-3077 or 362-5230, *http://www.hyannischamber.com*

Central/Berkshires

- Old Sturbridge Village, 1 Old Sturbridge Village Rd., Rte. 20, Sturbridge, MA 01566, (508) 347-3362 or 5383, *http://www.osv.org*
- Berkshire Museum, 39 South St., Pittsfield, MA 01201, (413) 443-7171.
- Norman Rockwell Museum, Rte. 183, Stockbridge, MA 01262, (413) 298-4100.

Organizations

Advocacy Groups

- Office of Aging Affairs, (617) 727-7750 or (800) 882-2003 (MA only).
- Elder Abuse Hotline, (800) 922-2275.
- Elder Protection Unit, (508) 584-8120.
- Division of Health Care Quality, (617) 753-8000.
- Massachusetts Aging Services Association, (617) 4223-0718, *http://www.MassAging.org*

Volunteer Programs

- Worcester Area Retired and Senior Volunteer Program (RSVP), (508) 755-2216. Fax: (508)753-8061.

Housing

Long-Term Care Facilities

*In the state of Massachusettes, these facilities are called **Long-Term Care/Continuing Care/Nursing Home Facilities**.*

These facilities provide residential living and/or various levels of nursing and medical services to seniors for an extended period of time.

Types of Authorization

Licensing and/or Certification

Nursing homes provide long- and short-term care for the elderly, the disabled, and the chronically ill. They are regulated by the Department of Public Health, Division of Health Care Quality. Nursing homes are inspected about every 9 to 15 months to ensure compliance.

Continuing care retirement communities combine independent housing, assisted living, and a nursing facility, usually at one location.

All long-term care facilities must be licensed by the Department of Public Health, Division of Health Care Quality.

Memberships:

- American Association of Homes and Services for the Aging (AAHSA) represents not-for-profit organizations committed to providing high-quality health care, housing, and services to the elderly. AAHSA, 901 E St. NW, Suite 500, Washington, DC 20004-2011. Ph: (202) 783-2242. Fax: (202) 783-2285. *http://www.aahsa.org*
- Massachusetts Aging Services Association, Inc. (MASA), 45 Bromfield St., Suite 200, Boston, MA 02108-4106. Ph: (617) 423-0718. Fax: (617) 423-2109. MASA is an AAHSA-affiliated state association. *http://www.massaging.org*
- Long Term Care Federation (LTCF).

Accreditations:

- Continuing Care Accreditation Commission (CCAC) accredits facilities that offer seniors a contract or contracts that provide residential living and health care services for the remainder of the person's lifetime and meet CCAC's accreditation standards.
- Joint Commission on the Accreditation of Healthcare Organizations (JCAHO) is an independent, not-for-profit organization, and the nation's oldest and largest standards-setting and health care accrediting institution.

East/Boston Area

Brookhaven at Lexington, CCAC

1010 Waltham St.
Lexington, MA 02421

Ph: (781) 863-9660 or (800) 283-1114
Fax: (781) 863-9944

IND: 202. AL: Yes. SNF: Yes

Age 65+. Nondenominational; nonprofit facility. Patio homes, apartments, and private and semiprivate rooms. 24-hour nursing care; physicians on staff; short- and long-term care; blood pressure checks; ear and eye care; prescription consultation; rehabilitative services; personal care; medication administration; security; emergency response system; maintenance; transportation; up to 3 daily meals; housekeeping and laundry services; fitness center and program; yoga; walking groups; exercise classes; library; educational programs; social and recreational activities; biking; gardening; bridge; reading and discussion groups; barber/beauty shop.

DEP: (ref.), $2,200. PROC: (no ref.), $550. IND ENT: Single, $225,500–$475,500; double, $291,500–$497,500. IND MO: Single, $1,600–$3,600; double, $3,000–$4,400. AL and SNF fees included in IND fees.

Cadbury Commons at Cambridge

66 Sherman St.
Cambridge, MA 02140

Ph: (617) 868-0575
Fax: (617) 868-0023

http://www.CadburyCommons.com
E-mail: *Cadburyadm@AOL.com*

IND: Yes. AL: Yes. ALZ/MEM IMP: 14. RSP: Yes

Nondenominational facility. Apartments. On-site registered nurse; resident care staff; wellness program; personal care; medication administration; security; emergency response system; maintenance; transportation; up to 3 daily meals; housekeeping and laundry services; health club; fitness center; religious services; educational opportunities; computer classes; cultural and social activities; common areas; barber/beauty shop.

APPL: (ref.) $1,000. DEP: of MO fee. IND MO: $2,800–$3,400. ALZ/MEM IMP MO: Semiprivate, $3,750; private, $4,400.

The Willows at Westborough, JCAHO

One Lyman St.
Westborough, MA 01581

Ph: (508) 366-4730, in MA, (800) 464-4730
Fax: (508) 366 1930

IND: Yes. AL: Yes. HCC: Yes. ALZ/MEM IMP: Yes

Nondenominational; family owned. Apartments and private and semiprivate rooms. Skilled nursing care; physical, occupational, and speech therapies; IV therapy; wound and pain management; social and psychological counseling; short- and long-term care; resident care assessment team; Medicare/Medicaid-approved; personal care; medication administration; security; emergency response system; maintenance; transportation; up to 3 daily meals; housekeeping and laundry services; exercise program and fitness center; banking services; dry cleaning store; greenhouse; library; computer room; arts and crafts room; sewing room; social, recreational, and educational activities; summer concerts; plays; volunteer opportunities; intergenerational program; barber/beauty shop.

DEP: $2,200. IND ENT: (ref.) $121,000–$296,000. IND MO: $1,600–$2,150; 2nd person, $825. AL MO: Plan A, $2,850–$4,100; 2nd person, $1,650–$4,300; Plan B, $3,675–$4,900; 2nd person, $2,500–$3,200; Plan C, $4,350–$5,500; 2nd person, $3,150–$3,850 (plans are for type of assistance needed.)

Southeast

Bay View

4380 N. Main St.
Fall River, MA

Ph: (508) 677-0833

Fax: (508) 677-2886

IND: 47. AL: Yes. HCC: Yes

Age 55+. Nondenominational; nonprofit; owned by the Home for Aged People in Fall River, Inc. Apartments and private and semiprivate rooms. Nursing care; physical therapy; podiatry services; personal care; medication administration; security; emergency response system; maintenance; transportation; 3 daily meals; housekeeping and laundry services; fitness center; outdoor heated swimming pool; social and educational programs; personal shopping services; garden areas; walking paths; barber/beauty shop.

IND ENT: $104,500–$192,500. IND MO: $1,750; 2nd person, $675.

The Guardian Center, JCAHO, LTCF

888 North Main St.
Brockton, MA 02301

Ph: (508) 587-6556
Fax: (508) 588-1694

NH: 123. REHAB: Yes

Nonprofit; nondenominational; nonsectarian. Private and semiprivate rooms. 24-hour nursing care; skilled and intermediate nursing care; physician care; physical, occupational, and speech therapies; dental and podiatry services; hospice; wound care; respiratory services; X-ray and lab services; pharmacy; Medicare/Medicaid-approved; security; emergency response system; maintenance; transportation; 3 daily meals; housekeeping and laundry services; religious services; pet therapy; activities; music; resident council.

NH Daily: $170–$210.

Pioneer Valley

The Loomis Communities, CCAC

246 N. Main St.
South Hadley, MA 01075

Ph: (413) 532-5325
Fax: (413) 535-2349

IND: 60. AL: 37. SNF: 80

Age 62+. Nonprofit; nondenominational. Villas, apartments, and private and semiprivate rooms. 24-hour skilled nursing care; IV therapies; short- and long-term care; home health care; health record monitoring; personal care; medication administration; security; emergency response system; maintenance; transportation; up to 3 daily meals; housekeeping and laundry services; fitness program; library; woodworking area; social, cultural, and recreational activities; lounges; gardens; walking paths; cafe and convenience store; barber/beauty shop.

APPL: (ref.) $1,100/person. DEP: (no ref.) $200. IND ENT: (90% ref.), $114,000–$195,000; (declining ref.), $76,000–$131,000. IND MO: $1,150–$2,075; 2nd person, $475. AL ENT: (80% ref.), $16,500–$27,500. AL MO: (with 80% ref.), $3,800–$4,100; rental only, $3,825–$4,225; 2nd person, $1,200. SNF: 15 free days (annually).

Worcester Area

Briarwood Continuing Care Retirement Community, JCAHO

70 Briarwood Circle
Worcester, MA 01606

Ph: (508) 852-2670
Fax: (508) 856-0309

IND: 106. AL: 29. HCC: 70

Age 62+. Nonprofit; nondenominational; nonsectarian; affiliated with the First Baptist Church of Worcester and Salem Covenant Church of Worcester. Cottages, apartments, and private and semiprivate rooms. 24-hour nursing care; skilled nursing; wound care; physical, occupational, and speech therapies; IV therapy; long and short-term care; Medicare/Medicaid-approved; personal

care; medication administration; security; emergency response system; maintenance; transportation; up to 3 daily meals; housekeeping and laundry services; educational, cultural, and social activities; library; woodworking shop; resident lounges and activity rooms; barber/beauty shop.

IND ENT: $126,500–$221,500. IND MO: $1,050–$2,050. AL ENT: $71,500. AL MO: $2,550–$3,250. HCC Daily: $230.

Northwest

Sweetwood, JCAHO

1611 Cold Spring Rd.
Williamstown, MA 01267

Ph: (413) 458-8371
Fax: (413) 458-0977

IND: 70. AL: Yes. HCC: 184. ALZ/MEM IMP: Yes

Age 65+. For-profit; nondenominational; privately owned and managed. Apartments and private and semiprivate rooms. Skilled nursing care; medical director; clinical aids; social workers; physical, occupational, and speech therapies; pain management; enteral feeding; infusion therapy; health maintenance checks; wellness program; personal care; medication administration; security; emergency response system; maintenance; transportation; up to 3 daily meals; pets welcome; housekeeping and laundry services; fitness center; exercise program; educational, cultural, social, spiritual, and recreational activities; off-site activities; computer classes; crafts; billiards; lounge; convenience store; barber/beauty shop.

APPL: $1,650. IND ENT: (90% ref.), $190,000–$312,000. IND MO: $1,950–$2,500; 2nd person, $575 and $560. AL and HCC fees inclusive.

West

Kimball Farms, JHACAO

235 Walker St.
Lenox, MA 01240

Ph: (413) 637-7000 or (800) 238-0061
Fax: (413) 637-7277

http://www.kimballfarms.org

IND: 150. AL: 48. SNF: 41

Age 65+. Nondenominational. Apartments and private rooms. 24-hour nursing care; skilled nursing care; rehabilitative therapies; dental and podiatry services; medical care; pharmacy; Medicare-approved; personal care; medication administration; security; emergency response system; maintenance; transportation; up to 3 daily meals; pets allowed; housekeeping and laundry services; fitness center; membership to local resort for golfing, tennis, swimming; social and recreational activities; walking paths, barber/beauty shop.

APPL: $2,750. IND ENT: (ref.) $122,500–$229,000. IND MO: $1,700–$3,750. AL: Contact facility for fees. SNF Daily: $200.

Assisted Living and Residential Care Facilities

These facilities provide room and board for ambulatory and independent adults who need minimum support.

Types of Authorization

Licensing and/or Certification

Requires certification by the Department of Health, Office of Elder Affairs. These facilities provide apartment-like living with support services, including meals, personal care, medication monitoring, security, and social and recreational programs. They do not provide health care services.

Memberships:

- Assisted Living Federation of America (ALFA) is a national nonprofit membership organization whose mission is to enhance the quality of life in assisted living facilities and promote the interests of the assisted living industry. ALFA, 10300 Eaton Place, Suite 400, Fairfax, VA 22030. Ph: (703) 691-8100. Fax: (703) 691-8106. *http://www.alfa.org*
- Massachusetts Assisted Living Association (MASS-ALFA) is a state affiliate of ALFA. MASS-ALFA, 460 Totten Pond Rd., 6th Floor, Waltham, MA 02451. Ph: (781) 622-5999. Fax: (781) 622-5979. *http://www.massalfa.org*

Awards

- National Council on Senior Housing (NCSH).

East/Boston Area

Carmel Terrace

933 Central St.
Framingham, MA 01701-4872

Ph: (508) 788-8000
Fax: (508) 626-1603

AL: 62

Nonprofit; nondenominational; operated by the Carmelite Sisters for the Aged and Infirm. One- and two-bedroom apartments. 24-hour staffing; wellness center; personal care; medication administration; security; emergency response system; maintenance; transportation; up to 3 daily meals; housekeeping and laundry services; fitness center; chapel and multidenominational religious services; library; arts and crafts room; activities; music room; media room; club room; lounges; indoor and outdoor gardens; country store; barber/beauty shop.

AL MO: $3,100–$5,100; 2nd person, $880.

The Gables

299 Cambridge St.
Winchester, MA 01890

Ph: (781) 756-1026
Fax: (781) 756-0636

IND: 125. AL: Yes

Age 62+. Nondenominational; for-profit; a Marriott Retirement Community. Apartments. Personal care; medication administration; hospital assistance with admittance if necessary; wellness program; doctor visits; security; emergency response system; maintenance; transportation; up to 3 daily meals; housekeeping and laundry services; exercise classes; religious services; library; banking services; lounge; activities director; social and educational programs; off-site activities; lectures; nearby shopping; barber/beauty shop.

PROC: $2,200. IND MO: $3,250–$4,600; 2nd person, $550. AL Weekly: $165–$500. (AL has 2 levels of care and services/fees can be á la carte, as needed.)

Heritage at Framingham, NCSH award

747 Water St.
Framingham, MA 01701

Ph: (508) 788-6050
Fax: (508) 788-6601

http://www.heritageassistedliving.com

AL: 48. ALZ/MEM IMP: 40

Nonprofit; nondenominational. Apartments. Personal care; medication administration; wellness program; security; emergency response system; maintenance; transportation; up to 3 daily meals; pets allowed; housekeeping and laundry services; exercise classes; library; lounge; cultural and social activities; crafts; convenience store and bistro; barber/beauty shop.

APPL: $825. AL ENT: 1st and last mo. rent. AL MO: $3,025–$4,400.

River Bay Club

99 Brackett St.
Quincy, MA 02169

Ph: (617) 472-4452
Fax: (617) 472-9658

http://www.marysmith.com/projects/riverbay.html

IND: 204. AL: 80

Age 62+. For-profit; nondenominational. Studios and apartments. Rehabilitative therapies; podiatry care; pharmacy services; home health services; personal care; medication administration; security; emergency response system; maintenance; transportation; up to 3 daily meals; housekeeping and laundry services; fitness center; community-wide activities program.

All services offered on an á la carte basis. APPL: $550. DEP: 1 mo. rent. IND MO: $1,100–$2,650; 2nd person, $330. AL MO: $1,600–$3,300; 2nd person, $500 and $550. HHC MO: $675.

Northeast

Bethany Community Services

10-12 Phoenix Row
Haverhill, MA 01832

Ph: (508) 374-2162
Fax: (508) 374-2163

IND: Yes. AL: Yes

Not-for profit facility. Studios, apartments, and private rooms. Wellness health program; personal care; medication administration; security; emergency response system; maintenance; transportation; up to 3 daily meals; pets allowed; housekeeping and laundry services; within walking distance to bank and stores; activities; library; game rooms; solarium; gardening; walking paths; barber/beauty shop.

Contact facility for fees.

Brighton Gardens of the North Shore

220 Conant St.
Danvers, MA 01923

Ph: (978) 777-5717
Fax: (978) 777-1283

AL: 90. ALZ/MEM IMP: 25

For-profit; nondenominational. Apartments and private rooms. Daily nursing care; rehabilitative therapies; pharmacy services; wellness program; personal care; medication administration; security; emergency response system; maintenance; transportation; up to 3 daily meals; housekeeping and laundry services; walking club; social and recreational activities; book club; garden club.

AL MO: $3,200–$4,350.

West

Melbourne Place, MALFA

140 Melbourne Rd.
Pittsfield, MA 01201

Ph: (413) 499-1992
Fax: (413) 443-8870

AL: 90. ALZ/MEM IMP: 28

Nondenominational; operated by CMI Senior Housing and Healthcare, Inc. Apartments and studios. Licensed nurse case management; 24-hour staffing; wellness program; respite care; affiliation with local nursing and rehabilitative centers; blood pressure monitoring; podiatry services; personal care; medication administration; security; emergency response system; maintenance; transportation; 3 daily meals; small pets allowed; housekeeping and laundry services; fitness program; shopping services; banking services; dry cleaning services; social, cultural, and recreational activities; arts and crafts; game room; walking paths; barber/beauty shop.

DEP: (ref.), $1,100. AL MO: $2,100–$3,300; 2nd person, $550. ALZ/MEM IMP MO: $3,025–$4,400.

Southeast/Cape Cod

Brewster Place, MALA

855 Harwich Road
Brewster, MA 02631

Ph: (508) 896-3252 or (888) 613-2123
Fax: (508) 896-6912

AL: 68. SNF: 173

Age 62+. Operated by Epoch Senior Living, Inc.; nondenominational. Apartments and studios. Skilled nursing care; Medicare/Medicaid-approved; personal care; medication administration; security; emergency response system; maintenance; transportation; up to 3 daily meals; pets allowed; housekeeping and laundry services; fitness center; banking services; library; courtyard; garden room; music room; barber/beauty shop.

DEP: $1,100. AL MO: $3,300–$4,200. SNF Daily: $250.

Heights Crossing Assisted Living Residence

35 Christy Place
Brockton, MA 02301

Ph: (508) 580-4300
Fax: (508) 580-3433

E-mail: *Hcrossing@AOL.com*

AL: 79. ALZ/MEM IMP: 21

Nondenominational facility. Apartments. Skilled nursing care; pharmacy; dental and podiatry services; rehabilitative therapies; personal care; medication administration; security; emergency response system; maintenance; transportation; up to 3 daily meals; housekeeping and laundry services; fitness center; activities.

Contact facility for fees.

Central

Southgate at Shrewsbury

30 Julio Drive
Shrewsbury, MA 01545

Ph: (508) 842-8331 (in Massachusetts) or, (800) 492-8331
Fax: (508) 842-1354

IND: 158. AL: 75. HCC: 123

Nondenominational. Apartments. Home health care services; personal care; medication administration; security; emergency response system; maintenance; transportation; up to 3 daily meals; housekeeping and laundry services; fitness center; exercise classes; chapel; swimming pool; water aerobics; personal training; theater; art gallery; library; post office; arts and crafts; woodworking shop; billiards; card room; convenience store; bowling alley; walking paths; activities; barber/beauty shop.

IND ENT: (90% ref.) $159,500–$236,500; 2nd person, $7,700. IND MO: $1,500–$1,900; 2nd person, $715. AL ENT: (90% ref) $137,500–$220,000; 2nd person, $7,700. AL MO: $2,450–$3,025; 2nd person, $825. HCC on-site; fees separate.

Springfield Area

Glenmeadow, NCOSH

24 Tabor Crossing
Longmeadow, MA 01106

Ph: (413) 567-7800
Fax: (413) 567-7945

http://www.glenmeadow.org

E-mail: *glnmdwrc@map.com*

IND: 92. AL: 34

Age 62+. Nonprofit; nondenominational. Apartments. Nursing care; medical director; rehabilitative therapies; dental and podiatry services; home

health care services; pharmacy; priority to skilled nursing care facilities; personal care; medication administration; emergency response system; maintenance; transportation; up to 3 daily meals; small pets allowed; housekeeping and laundry services; fitness center; exercise classes; whirlpool; personal trainer; indoor swimming pool; library with Internet connection; postal and banking services; notary; educational and recreational activities; billiards room; hobby and crafts room; card and game room; woodworking shop; lounge; garden room; roof garden; conference room; shopping and churches/synagogues nearby; masseuse; walking paths; barber/beauty shop.

IND ENT: (90% ref.), $132,000–$385,000. IND MO: $1,250–$2,650. AL MO: $3,650–$4,300.

Pioneer Valley

Applewood at Amherst

One Spencer Drive
Amherst, MA 01002

Ph: (413) 253-9833
Fax: (413) 256-8423

E-mail: *info@applewood-at-amherst.com*

IND: Yes. AL: Yes. SNF: Yes

Age 62+. Nonprofit; nondenominational. 24-hour skilled nursing care; short- and long-term care; blood pressure monitoring; podiatry and auditory services; home health services; personal care; medication administration; security; emergency response system; maintenance; transportation; up to 3 daily meals; housekeeping and laundry services; fitness program; library; lounges; meeting room; educational, cultural, and recreational activities; notary services; walking paths; music appreciation; off-site activities; barber/beauty shop.

ENT: (90% ref.), $129,000–$329,000. MO: $1,200–$3,450. AL Daily: $115–$140.

Independent Living

Independent housing (primarily rentals) for seniors that may offer security features, meal service, and activities.

Central

Emanuel Village

59 Evelyn St.
Worcester, MA 01607

Ph: (508) 753-7474
Fax: (508) 753-0376

IND: 108

Age 62+ (also under 62 disabled, developmentally challenged, and handicapped). Nonprofit; affiliated with the Lutheran Social Services of New England. Apartments. Monthly blood pressure clinic; podiatry services; security; small pets allowed; tenant council association.

DEP: 30% of annual adjusted income. IND ENT and IND MO: 30% annual adjusted income. HUD-subsidized.

West

Devonshire Estates

329 Pittsfield Rd.
Lenox, MA 01240

Ph: (413) 637-1700
Fax: (413) 637-3200

IND: 128

Age 65+. Nondenominational; owned by Holiday Retirement Corp. Suites, cottages, and apartments. Wellness clinic; emergency response system; maintenance; transportation; up to 3 daily meals; housekeeping and laundry ser-

vices; resident manager; exercise equipment; library; activity room; scheduled activities; game room; billiards; media room.

DEP: (ref.), $100. IND MO: $1,250–$2,650; 2nd person, $200 and $385.

Northeast

Turtle Woods Apartments

399 Essex St.
Beverly, MA 01915

Ph: (978) 922-1256
Fax: (508) 927-9369

IND: 67

Age 62+. Nonprofit; nondenominational. Apartments. Security; emergency response system; maintenance; transportation; on-site coordinator; residents' planning committee.

IND MO: Based upon income; HUD-subsidized.

Adult/Resort Communities

Communities for active adults (not all are age-restricted; primarily ownership).

Northeast

Ipswich Country Club

4 Court Lane
Ipswich, MA 01938

Ph: (978) 356-9690
Fax: (978) 356-9803

http://www.cpberryhomes.com

Individual homes, attached homes, homesites. Golf course; tennis; swimming pool; hiking trails; snow skiing; fitness center; social clubs.

PURCHASE: Homes, $490,000–$1.1 million.

Southeast/Cape Cod

Ballymeade Country Club and Estates

PO Box 367
125 Falmouth Woods Rd.
North Falmouth, MA 02556

Ph: (508) 457-4455 or (508) 540 4005
Fax: (508) 564-6810

http://www.ballymeade.com

Individual homes, duplex townhomes, homesites. Golf course; clubhouse; pro shop; tennis; swimming pool; croquet; hiking/biking; dining.

PURCHASE: Townhomes, $407,000–$547,500; homesites, $977,000–$297,000.

The Belmont

1 Belmont Rd.
West Harwich, MA 02671

Ph: (508) 432-1160

Townhomes, condominiums. Beach; swimming pool; cabanas; tennis; dining; nearby golf, fishing, and boating.

PURCHASE: Homes, from $165,000.

Kings Way Golf Club

10 Kings Circuit
Yarmouth Port, MA 02675

Ph: (508) 362-8800
Fax: (508) 362-8666

Condominiums. Golf course; tennis; swimming pool; hiking trails; community center; fitness center; library; social clubs.

PURCHASE: Condominiums, $187,000–$319,000.

New Seabury Country Club

Shore Drive West
Mashpee, MA 02649

Ph: (508) 477-9111
Fax: (508) 477-9790

http://www.newseabury.com

Individual homes, condominiums. Golf courses; tennis; hiking/biking; fishing; hunting; boating/waterskiing; community center; fitness center; beach.

PURCHASE: Homes, $153,000–$1.65 million; homesites, $44,000–$880,000.

Round Hill

307 Smith Neck Rd.
South Dartmouth, MA 02748
Ph: (508) 992-4800
Fax: (508) 997-9607

Individual homes, condominiums, homesites. Golf course; tennis; swimming pool; hiking trails; boating/waterskiing; community center; beaches.

PURCHASE: Homes, $385,000–$770,000.

Michigan

http://www.state.mi.us

General Information

Climate

For most of the state, average winter temperatures are in the 20s°F and average summer temperatures are in the mid- to high 70s°F.

Cost of Living

Ranks 31st in the nation.

Taxes

State/Local as % of Income: 9.9%.

Property Tax Reduction: Residents 65 or older may qualify for a property tax credit of up to $1,200.

Sales: 6%.

Prescription Exemptions: Prescription drugs are exempt from sales tax, as are prescription eyeglasses. Apparatus devices, appliances, or equipment used for personal assistance when prescribed by a licensed health professional are also exempt.

Transportation, Travel, and Tourism

General

Welcome Centers: Sault Ste. Marie, (906) 632-8242; Mackinaw, (906) 249-9066; Port Huron, (810) 984-2361; New Buffalo, (906) 774-4201; Clare, (517) 386-7634; Menominee, (906) 863-6496.

Major Airports

- Ann Arbor Municipal Airport, 108 Airport Drive, Ann Arbor, MI 48108, (734) 994-2841.
- Detroit Metropolitan Wayne County Airport, Detroit, MI 48242, (734) 942-3550.
- Kalamazoo/Battle Creek International Airport, 5235 Portage Rd., Kalamazoo, MI 49002, (616) 388-3668.

Railways

- Amtrak, (800) USA-RAIL.

Bus Tours

- Greyhound Bus, (800) 231-2222.

State Highways

- Highway and Transportation Department, (517) 263-5452.
- Interstate 75 runs north-south.
- Interstates 96 and 94 run east-west.

Theater and Music

Southeast

- Pease Auditorium, 207 Welch Hall, Ypsilanti, MI 48197, (734) 487-1221 (on the campus of Eastern Mich. Univ.; provides family entertainment).
- Croswell Opera House, 129 Maumee, Adrian, MI 49221, (517) 264-7469 (Broadway musicals; plays; holiday musical).
- Purple Rose Theater, 137 Park St. Chelsea, MI 48118, (313) 475-7902 (stage shows).
- Riverside Arts Center, 76 N. Huron, Ypsilanti, MI 48197, (734) 480-ARTS (performances plus an art exhibition).

Northeast

- Temple Theatre, 203 N. Washington, Saginaw, MI 48607, (517) 793-8940 (movies and shows).

Southwest

- Battle Creek Symphony, PO Box 1319, Battle Creek, MI 49016, (616) 962-2518 (concert hall).

- Legend Theater, PO Box 652, South Haven, MI 49090, (616) 637-7829 (comedy and musical productions).

Northwest

- Old Town Playhouse, 148 E. Eighth St., PO Box 262, Traverse City, MI 49684, (616) 947-2443 (musicals/ plays).

Museums, Crafts, Historical, Recreational

South

- Capitol Tours, Capitol Ave., Lansing, (517) 373-2348 (visit House and Senate galleries).

Northeast

- Sturgeon Point Lighthouse Museum, Sturgeon Pointe Rd., Harrisville, MI 48740, (517) 724-6297.
- Dow Gardens, 1018 W. Main, Midland, MI 48640, (800) 362-4874 (100+ acres of trees, shrubs, herbaceous perennials, and flowers).

Southwest

- Alamo Township Museum, 8119 N. 6th St., Kalamazoo, MI 49009, (616) 344-2107 (early American items; memory garden).
- Gull Lake View Golf Resort, 7402 N. 38th St., Augusta, MI (800) 432-7971 (five 18-hole golf courses plus accommodations).

Northwest

- Bent Pine Golf Club, 2480 Buck Lake Rd., Whitehall, MI 49461, (616) 766-2045.

Upper Peninsula

- Michigan Iron Industry Museum, 73 Forge Rd., Negaunee, MI 49866, (906) 475-7857 (hands-on exhibits, outdoor paths).
- Tower of History, 326 E. Portage Ave., Sault Ste. Marie, MI 49783, (888) 744-7867 or (906) 632-3658 (21 stories; views; mini- museum of Native American culture).
- Shipwreck Tours, 1204 Commercial St., Munising, MI 49862-1354 (906) 387-4477 (glass bottom boat tours).
- Indian Hills Golf Course, N8881 Walnut Road, Rte. 1, Stephenson, MI 49887, (906) 753-4781.
- Ann Arbor Art Center, 117 W. Liberty, Ann Arbor, MI 48104, (734) 994-8004 (crafts, artwork, ceramics).
- Artisans Market, Between 4th, 5th, Catherine, and Kingsley, Ann Arbor, 48104, (734) 761-1078 (hand-made arts and crafts).

Statewide

- Camping: Michigan State Parks, National Parks, State and National Forests, and privately owned campgrounds, 800-44-PARKS.

Organizations

Advocacy Groups

- Area Agencies on Aging Association of Michigan, (517) 886-1029.
- Michigan Assisted Living Association, (800) 482-0118.
- Michigan Office of Services to the Aging, (517) 373-8230.

Volunteer Programs

- (Points of Light) Volunteer Centers of Michigan, E. Lansing, (517) 353-5038.
- Volunteer and Information Services, Battle Creek, (616) 965-0555. Albion Volunteer Service Center, (517) 629-5574.

Housing

Long-Term Care Facilities

*In the state of Michigan, these facilities are called **Long-Term Care/Nursing Home Facilities**.*

These facilities provide residential living and/or various levels of nursing and medical services to seniors for an extended period of time.

Types of Authorization

Licensing and / or Certification

These facilities must be licensed by the Department of Public Health. Skilled nursing facilities provide 24-hour nursing care and restorative therapies and are eligible to participate in Medicare and Medicaid programs. Nursing facilities provide basic nursing care as well as room and board for those individuals not able to live independently. Additionally, they are eligible to participate in the Medicaid program.

Memberships:

- American Association of Homes and Services for the Aging (AAHSA) represents not-for-profit organizations committed to providing high-quality health care, housing, and services to the elderly. AAHSA, 901 E St. NW, Suite 500, Washington, DC 20004-2011. Ph: (202) 783-2242. Fax: (202) 783-2285. *http: / / www.aahsa.org*
- Michigan Association of Homes and Services for the Aging (MAHSA) is an AAHSA Affiliated State Association. MAHSA, 6215 W. St. Joseph Hwy, Lansing, MI 48917-4852 Ph: (517) 886-1302. Fax: (517) 886-1670.
- Michigan Nonprofit Housing (MNPH).

Accreditations:

- Continuing Care Accreditation Commission (CCAC) accredits facilities that offer seniors a contract or contracts that provide residential living and health care services for the remainder of the person's lifetime and meet CCAC's accreditation standards.
- Joint Commission on the Accreditation of Healthcare Organizations (JCAHO) is an independent, not-for-profit organization, and the nation's oldest and largest standards-setting and health care accrediting institution.

East

Autumn Woods

29800 Hoover
Warren, MI 48093

Ph: (810) 574-3444
Fax: (810) 574-0015

SNF: 300

Nondenominational. Private and semiprivate rooms. 24-hour skilled and basic nursing care; staff physicians; physical, occupational, and speech therapies; personal care; medication administration; Medicare/Medicaid-approved; social services; maintenance; 3 daily meals plus snacks; housekeeping and laundry services; religious services; counseling; activities; volunteer program; family council; resident council; off-site excursions; snack bar; barber/beauty shop.

SNF Daily: (semiprivate), $200; (private), $220 and $230.

Bellbrook Mercy Retirement Community, JCAHO

873 W. Avon Rd.
Rochester Hills, MI 48307

Ph: (248) 656-3239
Fax: (248) 656-8160

IND: Yes. AL: Yes. SNF: Yes

Affiliated with St. Joseph Mercy Oakland; nondenominational. Apartments and private and semiprivate rooms. 24-

hour nursing care; rehabilitative services; dental and eye care; audiologists; psychological counseling and social worker services; personal care; medication administration; security; emergency response system; maintenance; transportation; up to 3 daily meals; housekeeping and laundry services; library, interdenominational worship services; some banking and mail services; arts and crafts; cultural and recreational activities; resident council; notary services; coffee shop.

IND MO: $1,250–$1,650. AL Daily: (private), $105; (semiprivate), $80; (special care), $135. SNF Daily: (private), $185; (semiprivate), $160; Medicare, $250 and $275.

Boulevard Temple Retirement, AAHSA

2567 W. Grand Blvd.
Detroit, MI 48208

Ph: (313) 895-5340

SNF: 124. AL: Yes

Nonprofit; nondenominational; Methodist affiliated. Private and semiprivate rooms. 24-hour skilled nursing care; physical, occupational, and speech therapies; visiting physician; social worker; personal care; medication administration; Medicare/Medicaid-approved; security; emergency response system; maintenance; transportation; 3 daily meals; housekeeping and laundry services; exercise program; intergenerational program; activities director; off-site excursions.

SNF Daily: (semiprivate), $125; (private), $130.

Glacier Hills Retirement Center, MAHSA

1200 Earhart Rd.
Ann Arbor, MI 48105

Ph: (313) 663-5202

IND: Yes. AL: Yes. SNF: Yes. AL/MEM IMP: 50

Age 55+. Nonprofit; nondenominational; nonsectarian. Apartments and private and semiprivate rooms. 24-hour skilled nursing care; dental and podiatry services; ophthalmology care; music therapy; on-site physician; personal care; medication monitoring; 24-hour security; wellness program; transportation; up to 3 daily meals; housekeeping and laundry services; exercise program; interdenominational religious services; cultural and educational programs; library; card and board games; off-site excursions; gardening; walking paths; barber/beauty shop.

APPL: (no ref.), $275. IND LC: (regular ent. fee), $46,000–$143,000; (ref. ENT fee), $52,000–$154,000. IND MO: $1,150–$2,400. AL LC: (regular ENT fee), $51,000–$92,200; (ref. ent. fee), $56,500–$101,200. AL MO: $2,275–$2,700. Part of entrance fee is applied toward future nursing care costs.

Green Brook Manor

481 Village Green Lane
Monroe, MI 48161

Ph: (734) 242-6282
Fax: (734) 242-6491

SNF: 103

Nondenominational. Private and semiprivate rooms. 24-hour nursing care; basic and skilled nursing care; podiatry and dental services; occupational, physical, respiratory, and speech therapies; IV fluids and medications; monitoring of vital signs; wound care; social services; Medicare/Medicaid-approved; 3 daily meals; housekeeping and laundry services; recreational activities; activities program.

SNF Daily: (semiprivate; 3 beds), $125; (semiprivate; 2 beds), $130; (private), $135.

South Central

Thornapple Manor

2700 Nashville Rd.
Hastings, MI 49058

Ph: (616) 945-2407
Fax: (616) 945-5380

NH: 138

Nonprofit; nondenominational facility. Private and semi-private rooms. 24-hour skilled nursing care; rehabilitative therapies; dental and podiatry services; pharmacy; Medicare/Medicaid-approved; personal care; medication administration; security; emergency response system; maintenance; 3 daily meals; housekeeping and laundry services.

NH Daily: $150.

Vista Grande Villa

2251 Springport Rd.
Jackson, MI 49202

Ph: (517) 787-0222, or (800) 889-8499
Fax: (517) 787-6909

IND: Yes. HCC: 60

Nonprofit; nondenominational; managed by Life Care Services Corp. Apartments and private and semiprivate rooms. 24-hour nursing care; physical, speech, and occupational therapies; pharmacy; security; emergency response system; maintenance; transportation; up to 3 daily meals; housekeeping and laundry services; exercise room and classes; arts and crafts; woodworking shop; billiards room; library; activity programs; gardening; walking paths; convenience store; barber/beauty shop.

IND ENT: (traditional plan), $51,500–$94,000; 2nd person, $12,000; MO: $1,150–$1,350; 2nd person, $600. IND ENT: (50% return of capital plan), $91,000–$165,000; 2nd person, $20,000; MO: $1,000–$1,200; 2nd person, $575. IND ENT: (75% return of capital plan), $91,000–$165,000; 2nd person, $20,000; MO: $1,150–$1,350; 2nd person, $600.

Southwest

Clark Retirement Community

1551 Franklin St. SE
Grand Rapids, MI 49506-3331

Ph: (616) 452-1568
Fax: (616) 452-0428

IND: Yes. CONG: Yes. AL: Yes. HCC: Yes. ALZ/MEM IMP: Yes

A nondenominational facility. Townhomes, lodges, duplexes, apartments, and private and semiprivate rooms. 24-hour nursing care; rehabilitative therapies; health clinic; podiatry services; pharmacy; personal care; medication administration; security; emergency response system; maintenance; transportation; up to 3 daily meals; housekeeping and laundry services; fitness center; swimming pool and hot tub; library; banking services; computer lab with Internet access; cultural, educational, and social activities; recreational areas; drama club, card club; coffee shop, convenience store, and gift shop; barber/beauty shop.

IND ENT: (ref.), $30,000–$84,000. IND RAF: $13,000–$36,000. IND MO: $325–$625. CONG RAF: $13,500–$42,000. CONG MO: $975–$2,500. AL RAF: $7,700–$20,000. AL MO: $1,925–$2,300. ALZ/MEM IMP RAF: $7,700. ALZ/MEM IMP MO: $3,050. HCC Daily:$135–$160.

Friendship Village Kalamazoo

1400 N. Drake Rd.
Kalamazoo, MI 49006

Ph: (616) 381-0560
Fax: (616) 381-5354

IND: 226. AL: Yes. HCC: Yes

Nonprofit; nondenominational; managed by Life Care Services Corporation. Apartments and private and semiprivate rooms. Nursing care; rehabilitative therapies; Medicare-approved; personal care;

medication administration; security; emergency response system; maintenance; transportation; up to 3 daily meals; pets allowed; housekeeping and laundry services; fitness center; chaplain services; bank; library; crafts; art gallery; auditorium; recreational and social activities; media room; café; convenience store; gardens and gardening; walking path; barber/beauty shop.

Michigan Christian Home, AAHSA, MNPH

1815 Boston, S.E.
Grand Rapids, MI 49506

Ph: (616) 245-9179

IND: 20. RH: 60. AL: 20. SNF: 29

Age 62+. Nonprofit; church affiliated. Apartments and private rooms. 24-hour nursing care; hospice; home health care; personal care; medication administration; security; emergency response system; maintenance; 3 daily meals; housekeeping and laundry services; activities.

Contact facility for fees.

Pilgrim Manor

2000 Leonard St. NE
Grand Rapids, MI 49505-5894

Ph: (616) 458-1133
Fax: (616) 458-8920

IND: Yes. AL: Yes. HCC: Yes

Nonprofit; affiliated with the United Church of Christ. Apartments and private and semiprivate rooms. Nursing care; rehabilitative therapies; restorative care; social services; personal care; medication administration; security; emergency response system; maintenance; transportation; up to 3 daily meals; housekeeping and laundry services; exercise program; religious services; library; social and recreational activities; off-site activities; hobbies and crafts; barber/beauty shop.

IND MO: $1,200–$2,400. AL MO: $2,050–$3,250. HCC Daily: $140–$160.

Porter Hills Presbyterian Village, JCAHO, CCAC

3600 E. Fulton St.
Grand Rapids, MI 49546-1395

Ph: (616) 949-4971
Fax: (616) 954-1795

http://www.porterhills.com

IND: 109. RH/AL: 277. HCC: 101. ALZ/MEM IMP: 16

Age 62+. Nonprofit; nondenominational. Apartments and private rooms. 24-hour nursing care; skilled nursing care; rehabilitative therapies; hospice; dental and podiatry services; medical services; home health care services; pharmacy; social services; Medicare/Medicaid-approved; personal care; medication administration; security; emergency response system; maintenance; transportation; up to 3 daily meals; housekeeping and laundry services; fitness center; exercise program; religious services; volunteer program; library; banking services; social and recreational activities; off-site activities; cafe and coffee shop; woodworking shop; convenience store; gardening; barber/beauty shop.

APPL: (no ref.), $350–$650. IND PROC: $275. IND ENT: $104,500–$155,500. IND MO: $450. RH/AL PROC: $660. AL Daily: $80, $90, $100. RH MO: $1,150–$2,250. HCC Daily: Semiprivate, $140–150; private, $170–180.

Sherwood Place

6203 Stadium Drive
Kalamazoo, MI 49009

Ph: (616) 375-1204
Fax: (616) 375-7733

SNF: 101

For-profit; nondenominational. Private and semiprivate rooms. 24-hour nursing care; rehabilitative therapies; dental and podiatry services; pharmacy; Medicare/Medicaid-approved; personal care; medication administration; security; emergency response system; maintenance;

transportation; 3 daily meals; housekeeping and laundry services; activities; park-like setting.

SNF MO: $4,500–$7,600.

Assisted Living and Residential Care Facilities

These facilities provide room and board for ambulatory and independent adults who need minimum support.

Types of Authorization

Licensing and/or Certification

Requires licensing by the Department of Health. These facilities provide supervision, limited nursing care, personal care, and therapies to residents who are not in need of skilled nursing care, but who need some assistance to live independently.

Memberships:

- Assisted Living Federation of America (ALFA) is a national nonprofit membership organization whose mission is to enhance the quality of life in assisted living facilities and promote the interests of the assisted living industry. ALFA, 10300 Eaton Place, Suite 400, Fairfax, VA 22030. Ph: (703) 691-8100. Fax: (703) 691-8106. *http://www.alfa.org*
- Michigan Assisted Living Association (MALA) is a state affiliate of ALFA. MALA, 15441 Middlebelt Rd., Livonia, MI 48154. Ph: (734) 525-0831. Fax: (734) 525-2453.

East Plymouth Inn

205 Haggerty Rd.
Plymouth, MI 48170

Ph: (734) 451-0700

AL: 50

Private and semiprivate rooms. 24-hour assistance; in-house physiotherapy services; podiatry services; personal care; medication administration; security; emergency response system; maintenance; transportation; 3 daily meals; housekeeping and laundry services; chapel; game room; activities; beauty/barber shop.

AL Daily: $80–$170.

Royal Oak I

1900 N. Washington Ave.
Royal Oak, MI 48073

Ph: (248) 585-2550
Fax: (248) 585-9085
http://www.american-house.com

IND and AL: 62

Privately owned by American House (owns 18 retirement residences in MI); nondenominational. Efficiency units. Personal care; medication administration; 24-hour staffing; security; emergency response system; maintenance; transportation; small pets welcome; 3 daily meals; housekeeping and laundry services; all utilities (except phone and cable); exercise programs; full activities program; convenience store; barber/beauty shop.

AL MO: $1,500.

Waltonwood

3250 Walton Blvd.
Rochester Hills, MI 48309

Ph: (248) 375-2500

IND: Yes. AL: Yes

A Singh Development; nondenominational. Apartments. Personal care; medication administration; daily check-in service; security; emergency response system; maintenance; transportation; up to 3 daily meals; housekeeping and laundry services; exercise and aerobics room; postal services; library; cultural and recreational activities; off-site excursions; lounge; game room; putting green; walking trails; barber/beauty shop.

IND MO: $1,650–$2,000. AL MO: $2,650–$4,550.

Woodhaven of Livonia

29667 Wentworth
Livonia, MI 48154-33256

Ph: (734) 261-9000
Fax: (734) 261-9003

AL: Yes. ADC: Yes

Church-affiliated facility. Private and semiprivate rooms. Nursing care; personal care; medication administration; appointments with physician when needed; lab and X-ray services; respite care; security; emergency response system; maintenance; transportation; 3 daily meals; housekeeping and laundry services; daily activity program; barber/beauty salon.

AL Daily: (semiprivate), $65; (private), $105; special care, $80 and $90. RSP Daily: (semiprivate), $80; (private), $105.

Independent Living

Independent housing (primarily rentals) for seniors that may offer security features, meal service, and activities.

East

Hazelcrest Place

100 Hazelcrest
Hazel, MI 48030

Ph: (248) 542-5386
Fax (248) 542-1351

IND: Yes

Age 62+. Nondenominational. Townhomes and apartments. Medical screenings and checkups; security; emergency response system; maintenance; transportation; up to 3 daily meals; library; multipurpose room; social and recreational activities; billiards; educational programs.

IND MO: 30% of income; HUD-subsidized.

Tivoli Manor

28103 Imperial Drive
Warren, MI 48093

Ph: (810) 558-9860
Fax: (810) 558-6973

IND: Yes

Age 65+. Nondenominational; managed by Wingate Management Corporation. Apartments. Medical screenings; physical checkups; security; maintenance; transportation; meal program; social and recreational activities; educational and cultural programs; located near medical and shopping facilities.

IND MO: 30% of income. HUD-subsidized; income limits, (single) $23,500; (couple), $27,000.

Adult/Resort Communities

Communities for active adults (not all are age-restricted; primarily ownership).

North

Beaver Creek Resort

5004 W. Otsego Lake Drive
Gaylord, MI 49735

Ph: (517) 732-2459

http://www.thenatural.org

Cabins. Golf course; clubhouse; pro shop; tennis; swimming pool; hiking/biking trails; fishing hunting; waterslide.

PURCHASE: Homes, from $55,000.

Crystal Mountain Resort

12500 Crystal Mountain Drive
Thompsonville, MI 49683

Ph: (800) 968-2911

http://www.crystalmtn.com

Individual homes, condominiums, homesites. Golf courses; clubhouse; pro shop; tennis; swimming pool; fitness center; hiking/biking trails; snow skiing; dining.

PURCHASE: Homes, $110,000–$550,000; condos, $93,500–$385,000; homesites, $32,000–$93,500.

Garland Resort

Garland Country Rd. 489
HCR-1, Box 364M
Lewiston, MI 49756

Ph: (800) 968-0042

http://www.garlandusa.com

Individual homes, triplexes, fourplex clusters, golf cottages, log homes, homesites. Golf courses; clubhouse; pro shop; tennis; swimming pools; basketball; volleyball; Jacuzzi; fitness center; mountain biking; nature trails; ice skating; cross-country skiing; snowmobiling; dining.

PURCHASE: Fourplexes, from $192,500; triplexes, from $296,000; golf cottages, from $190,500; homesites, $46,500–$137,500.

Grand Traverse Resort and Spa

100 Grand Traverse Village Blvd.
Acme, MI 49610

Ph: (800) 748-0303, ext. 5438; or (616) 938-5438

Individual homes, condominiums, homesites. Golf courses; clubhouse; pro shop; indoor/outdoor tennis; swimming pools; hiking/biking; boating/waterskiing; cross-country skiing; fitness center; social clubs; dining.

PURCHASE: Homes, $165,000–$440,000.

Lakes of the North

Pineview Drive
Mancelona, MI 49659

Ph: (800) 851-4653 or (616) 585-6200

Individual homes, homesites. Golf course; pro shop; clubhouse; tennis; swimming pool; hiking trails; fishing; riding stables; cross-country skiing; dining.

PURCHASE: Homes, $35,500–$264,000.

Michaywe

1535 Opal Lake Rd.
Gaylord, MI 49735

Ph: (517) 732-6777

Individual homes, condominiums, homesites. Golf course; pro shop; tennis; swimming pool; hiking trails; fishing; snow skiing; community center; social clubs.

PURCHASE: Homes, $110,000–$330,000.

Thunder Bay Resort

27800 M-32
Hillman, MI 49746

Ph: (800) 729-9375 or (517) 742-4502

http://www.thunderbaygolf.com

Individual homes, condominiums, log homes, homesites. Golf course; clubhouse; pro shop; tennis; hiking trails; fishing; hunting; cross-country skiing; community center; dining; sleigh rides.

PURCHASE: Homes, $88,000–$330,000; homesites, $17,500–$35,500.

Southeast

Heritage Hills

3837 Springwood Court
Auburn Hills, MI 48326

Ph: (248) 375-1100

Age 55+. Individual homes. Clubhouse; tennis; swimming pool; spa; walking trails; full-time social director; nearby golf.

PURCHASE: Homes, from $198,000.

Lakeview Hills Country Club and Resort

6560 E. Peck Rd.
Lexington, MI 48450

Ph: (810) 359-7333

Condominiums. Golf course; clubhouse; pro shop; racquetball; cross-country skiing; fitness center; bowling; dining.

PURCHASE: Condos, $175,000–$181,500.

Polo Fields Golf and Country Club

5200 Polo Field Drive
Ann Arbor, MI 48103

Ph: (734) 998-1555
http://www.polofields.org

Individual homes, homesites. Golf course; pro shop; clubhouse; swimming pool; fitness center; cross-country skiing; dining.

PURCHASE: Homes, $330,000–$660,000+.

Stonebridge

1759 Stonebridge Drive North
Ann Arbor, MI 48108

Ph: (734) 741-1555
Fax: (734) 741-1745

Individual homes, condominiums, patio homes, homesites. Golf course; clubhouse; pro shop; beach; swimming; fishing; volleyball; tennis; hiking trails; dining; cross-country skiing; Audubon Cooperative Sanctuary.

PURCHASE: Condos, from $296,000; homesites, $76,000–$160,000.

Minnesota

http://www.state.mn.us

General Information

Climate

In Minneapolis–St. Paul, average temperatures: January, 12° F; August, 80° F; average snowfall, 50 inches per year. In Duluth: January, 7° F; August, 78° F; average snowfall, 78 inches.

Cost of Living

Ranks 30th in the nation.

Taxes

State/Local as % of Income: 11.0%.

Property Tax Reduction: Citizens 65 years old and older with incomes $30,000 or less (plus other restrictions) may defer a portion of homestead property taxes, beginning in 1999. (This is a loan program, with 5% or lower interest, not tax forgiveness.) All state homeowners and renters received a property tax rebate in 1997 and 1998.

Sales: 6.5%.

Prescription Exemptions: Prescription drugs, as well as some medical devices, are exempt from sales tax.

Transportation, Travel, and Tourism

General

Minnesota Office of Tourism, 500 Metro Square, 121 7th Pl., St. Paul, MN 55101, (651) 296-5029 or (800) 657-3700.

Major Airports

- Duluth International Airport, 4701 Grinden Drive, Duluth, MN 55811, (218) 727-2968.
- Minneapolis–St. Paul International Airport, 6040 28th Ave. S., Minneapolis, MN 55450, (612) 726-8100.

Bus Tours

- Greyhound Bus, 1100 Hawthorne Ave., Minneapolis, MN 55403, (612) 371-3325 or (800) 231-2222.
- Minneapolis/St. Paul City Bus Metro Transit, (612) 373-3333.
- Duluth Transit Authority, Duluth, (218) 722-SAVE.

State Highways

- Interstate 35 runs north-south Duluth to Iowa.
- Interstate 90 runs east-west across south of state to LaCrosse, WI, and then to South Dakota.
- Interstate 94 runs southeast-northwest from Twin Cities to Fargo, ND.

Theater and Music

North

- Duluth Convention Center, 350 Harbor Drive, Duluth, MN 55802, (218) 722-5573.
- Myles Reif Performing Arts Center, 720 Conifer Drive, Grand Rapids, MN 55744, (218) 326-8215.
- Tenth Annual Bayfront Blues Festival, August, Duluth, (715) 394-6831 ext. 101.

South

- Fairmont Opera House, 45 Downtown Plaza, PO Box 226, Fairmont, MN 56031, (507) 238-4900.
- Rochester Orchestra and Chorale, Hamilton Music Building, 301 N. Broadway, Rochester, MN 55906, (507) 28-MUSIC (286-8742).

Twin Cities

- RiverCentre Convention Center, 175 W. Kellogg Blvd., Suite 502, St. Paul,

MN 55102, (651) 265-4900 or (800) 627-6101.

- The Ordway Music Theatre, 345 Washington St., St. Paul, MN 55102, (651) 282-3000.
- Minneapolis Institute of the Arts, 2400 3rd Ave. S., Minneapolis, MN 55404, (612) 870-3131 or (888) MIA-ARTS (642-2787).
- Fitzgerald Theater, 10 E. Exchange St., St. Paul, MN 55101, (651) 290-1221.
- Orchestra Hall, S. 11th St. at Nicollet Ave., Minneapolis, (612) 371-5656

West

- Alexandria Vikingland Band Festival, last Sunday in June, Alexandria, (800) 245-2539.

Museums, Crafts, Historical, Recreational

North

- Great Lakes Aquarium, 6008 London Rd., Duluth, MN 55804, (218) 525-2265.
- Voyageurs National Park (visitors center, snowmobiling, camping, boating), 3131 Hwy 53, International Falls, MN 56649 (218) 283-9821.
- Superior National Forest and Boundary Waters Canoe Area Wilderness (BWCAW), 8901 Grand Avenue Pl., Duluth, MN 55808, (218) 626-4302.
- Enger Park Golf Course (public), 1801 W. Skyline Blvd., Duluth, MN 55806 (218) 723-3451.
- Lake Superior Zoological Gardens, 7210 Fremont St., Duluth, MN (218) 733-3777.
- Mille Lacs Indian Museum and Trading Post, HCR 67, Box 195, MN Onamia, 56359, (320) 532-3632.
- Split Rock Lighthouse State Park, U.S. Hwy. 61, 20 miles northeast of Two Harbors, (218) 226-6372.
- St. Louis County Heritage and Arts Center at The Depot (including Chisholm Museum, Duluth Art Institute, Duluth Ballet, Duluth Playhouse, Duluth-Superior Symphony Orchestra, Lake Superior Museum of Transportation, the Matinee Musicale and St. Louis County Historical Society), 506 W. Michigan St., Duluth, MN 55802, (218) 733-7519.
- Pebble Lake Golf Club (public), County Road 82 S., Fergus Falls, MN 56537, (218) 736-7404.

South

- Ramsey Golf Club, Route 1, Austin, MN 55912, (507) 433-9098.
- Fort Ridgely, Fort Ridgely State Park, off MN Hwy 4, south of Fairfax, (507) 426-7888 or (507) 697-6321.
- Lac Qui Parle Mission, Chippewa City, Hwy. 13, off U.S. Hwy. 59, northwest of Montevideo, (320) 269-7636.
- Southeastern Minnesota Visual Artists' Gallery, 16 1st St. SW, Rochester, MN 55902 (507) 281-4920.

Twin Cities Area

- Mall of America (largest U.S. retail and entertainment complex), Bloomington, (612) 883-8800.
- Mississippi National River and Recreation Area (boating), 175 E. 5th St., Suite 418, Box 41, St. Paul, MN 55101, (651) 290-4160.
- Science Museum of Minnesota, 30 E. 10th St., St. Paul, MN 55101, (651) 221-9444.
- Museum of American Art, Landmark Center, 75 W. 5th St., St. Paul, MN 55102, (651) 292-4355.
- Columbia Golf Club (public), 3300 Central Ave. NE, Minneapolis, MN 55418, (612) 789-2627.
- Hiawatha Golf Course (public), 4553 Longfellow Ave. S., Minneapolis, MN 55407, (612) 724-7715.
- Minnesota Transportation Museum, PO Box 17240, Minneapolis, MN 55417, (651) 228-0263 or (800) 711-2591.

Organizations

Advocacy Groups

- Aging and Adult Services Division, Minnesota Department of Human Services, 444 Lafayette Rd., St. Paul, MN 55155, (651) 215-0574 or (888) 234-3703.
- Senior Linkage Line, (612) 333-2433 or (800) 333-2433.
- Adult Foster Care Consultant, (651) 297-1216 or (800) 882-6262.
- Adult Day Care Consultant, (651) 297-1216 or (800) 882-6262.

Volunteer Programs

- Minnesota State Band, 90 W. Plato Blvd, St. Paul, MN 55107, (612) 296-6187.
- Big Brothers/Big Sisters of Greater Minneapolis, 2915 Wayzata Blvd., Minneapolis, MN 55405, (612) 381-2668.
- Churches United for the Homeless, 203 6th St. S., Moorhead, MN 56560, (218) 236-0372.
- Detroit Lakes Wetland Mgmt. District, 26624 N. Tower Rd., Detroit Lakes, MN 56501, (218) 847-4431.
- Minneapolis Jewish Federation, 5901 S. Cedar Lake Rd., St. Louis Park, MN 55416, (612) 593-2600.

Housing

Long-Term Care Facilities

In the state of Minnesota, these facilities are called ***Continuing Care/Nursing Home/Retirement Facilities****.*

These facilities provide residential living and/or various levels of nursing and medical services to seniors for an extended period of time.

Types of Authorization

Licensing and/or Certification

These facilities are regulated by the Department of Health.

Memberships

- American Association of Homes and Services for the Aging (AAHSA) represents not-for-profit organizations committed to providing high-quality health care, housing, and services to the elderly. AAHSA, 901 E St. NW, Suite 500, Washington, DC 20004-2011. Ph: (202) 783-2242. Fax: (202) 783-2285. *http://www.aahsa.org*
- Minnesota Association of Homes and Services for the Aging (MAHSA), 2550 University Ave. West, Suite 350, South St. Paul, MN 55114-1900. Ph: (612) 654-4545. Fax: (612) 645-0002. MAHSA is an AAHSA Affiliated State Association.
- American Baptist Homes and Hospitals Association (ABHHA).

Accreditations

- Continuing Care Accreditation Commission (CCAC) accredits facilities that offer seniors a contract or contracts that provide residential living and health care services for the remainder of the person's lifetime and meet CCAC's accreditation standards.
- Joint Commission on the Accreditation of Healthcare Organizations (JCAHO) is an independent, not-for-profit organization, and the nation's oldest and largest standards-setting and health care accrediting institution.

South

Thorne Crest Retirement Center, AAHSA, ABHHA, MAHSA

1201 Garfield Ave.
Albert Lea, MN 56007

Ph: (507) 373-2311

IND: 93. AL: 12. HCC: 52

Age 62+. Nonprofit; nondenominational; owned and managed by American Baptist Homes of the Midwest. Apartments and private and semiprivate rooms. 24-hour skilled nursing care; physician services; rehabilitative therapies; restorative therapies; nursing supervision; dental and podiatry care; pharmacy services; Medicare/Medicaid-approved; personal care; medication administration; security; emergency response system; maintenance; transportation; up to 3 daily meals; housekeeping and laundry services; exercise room; chapel; activities; crafts; woodworking shop; gardens; lounges; common areas; barber/beauty shop.

IND LL: (ref.) $16,000–$39,000; 2nd person, $3,850. IND MO: $825–$1,950. AL Daily: Semiprivate, $75; private, $90. HCC Daily: Semiprivate, $80–$150; private, $90–$160.

East

Auburn Village

501 Oak St.
Chaska, MN 55318

Ph: (612) 361-0305
Fax: (612) 361-0333

IND: 58. AL: 55. SNF: 61

Age 62+. Nonprofit; nondenominational; Moravian Church affiliation. Apartments and private and semiprivate rooms. Skilled nursing care; medical director; respite care; rehabilitative services; medical services; social services; pharmacy services; home health services; wellness program; Medicare/Medicaid-approved; personal care; medication administration; security; emergency response system; maintenance; transportation; up to 3 daily meals; housekeeping and laundry services; exercise classes; social and recreational activities; volunteer program; parlors; snack shop; gift shop; courtyards and gardens; barber/beauty shop.

IND MO: 30% of income; HUD-subsidized. AL MO: $1,800–$3,000; 2nd person, $500. Contact facility for SNF fees.

Bethany Covenant Home

2309 Hayes St. NE
Minneapolis, MN 55418-3998

Ph: (612) 781-2691

IND: Yes. AL: Yes. SNF: Yes

Nondenominational; managed by Covenant Retirement Communities, Inc.; affiliated with the Evangelical Covenant Church. Apartments and private and semiprivate rooms. 24-hour skilled nursing care; physician services; short- and long-term care; physical, occupational, and speech therapies; IV therapy; Medicare/Medicaid-approved; personal care; medication administration; security; emergency response system; maintenance; transportation; up to 3 daily meals; housekeeping and laundry services; chaplain and religious services; library; social, cultural, recreational, and spiritual activities; courtyard; park; barber/beauty shop.

IND Daily: $60 and $65; 2nd person, $15. Contact facility for SNF fees.

Castle Ridge Care Center

625 Prairie Center Drive
Eden Prairie, MN 55344

Ph: (612) 944-8982
Fax: (612) 944-6754

AL: 21. NH: 60

Nonprofit; affiliated with the Baptist General Conference. Private and semiprivate rooms. 24-hour nursing care; physical, occupational, and speech therapies; dental and podiatry services; pharmacy services; lab and X-ray services; eye care; psychological services; Medicare/Medicaid-approved; personal care; medication administration; security; emergency response system; maintenance; transportation; up to 3 daily

meals; pets allowed; housekeeping and laundry services; exercise program; religious services; activities; barber/beauty shop.

AL MO: $2,700. NH Daily: $95–$160.

Catholic Eldercare

817 Main St., NE
Minneapolis, MN 55413

Ph: (612) 379-1370

AL: Yes. SNF: Yes. ADC: Yes. ALZ/MEM IMP: Yes

Nonprofit; nondenominational; affiliated with the Catholic Church. Apartments and private and semiprivate rooms. Skilled nursing care; physical, occupational, and speech therapies; medical services; pharmacy services; home health care; weekly health monitoring; Medicaid-approved; personal care; medication administration; security; emergency response system; maintenance; transportation; up to 3 daily meals plus snacks; housekeeping and laundry services; exercise classes; chapel and religious services; volunteer program; games; social, recreational, and spiritual activities; off-site activities.

AL MO: $1,700–$2,500. SNF Daily: About $10–$200.

Covenant Manor Retirement Community, CCAC, AAHSA

5800 St. Croix Ave.
Golden Valley, MN 55422

Ph: (612) 546-6125 or (800) 296-9114
Fax: (612) 546-8529

http://www.covenantretirement.com

IND: 129. AL: 16. HCC: 108. ALZ/MEM IMP: Yes

Age 62+. Nondenominational; managed by Covenant Retirement Communities, Inc.; affiliated with the Evangelical Covenant Church. Apartments and private and semiprivate rooms. 24-hour nursing care; rehabilitative therapies; physician clinics; podiatry care; health office; blood pressure checks; Medicare-approved; personal care; medication administration; security; emergency response system; maintenance; transportation; up to 3 daily meals; housekeeping and laundry services; exercise classes; swimming pool; Bible study and religious services; library; arts and crafts; educational and cultural activities; game room; woodworking shop; shuffleboard; horseshoes; walking paths; gardening; barber/beauty shop.

APPL: $1,500. IND ENT: $57,750–$115,500. IND MO: $1,025–$1,900. AL Daily: $110. HCC Daily: $145.

Crest View Community

4444 Reservoir Blvd. NE
Columbia Heights, MN

Ph: (612) 782-1611
Fax: (612) 782-0857

IND: 77. AL: 50. SNF: 122

Age 62+. Nonprofit; nondenominational; Lutheran Church affiliation. 24-hour skilled nursing care; medical services; rehabilitative therapies; dental and podiatry care; pharmacy services; home health care services; social services; personal care; medication administration; security; emergency response system; maintenance; transportation; up to 3 daily meals; pets allowed; housekeeping and laundry services; religious services; Bible study; library; intergenerational program; social and recreational activities; barber/beauty shop.

Contact facilities for fees.

Friendship Village, Bloomington

8100 Highwood Drive
Bloomington, MN 55438

Ph: (612) 831-7500

IND: Yes. AL: Yes. HCC: Yes

Age 62+. Nonprofit; nondenominational; owned by Life Care Retirement Communities; managed by Life Care Services. One-, two-, and three-bedroom apartments and private and semiprivate rooms. 24-hour medical assistance; nursing care; short- and long-term care; rehabilitative therapies; personal care;

medication administration; security; emergency response system; maintenance; transportation; up to 3 daily meals; housekeeping and laundry services; exercise classes; banking services; woodworking; crafts; on- and off-site activities; lectures; movies; dancing; card games; billiards; barber/beauty shop.

IND ENT: Alternative plan, $41,000–$57,750; Traditional plan, $71,000–$205,000; Return of Capital plan, $118,500–$361,500. IND MO: Alternative plan, $1,650–$1,950; 2nd person, $750; Traditional plan, $1,200–$1,800; 2nd person, $650; Return of Capital plan, $1,200–$2,000; 2nd person, $650. AL and HCC inclusive in IND fees.

Jones-Harrison Residence

3700 Cedar Lake Ave.
Minneapolis, MN 55416

Ph: (612) 920-2030
Fax: (612) 925-7101

AL: 59. NH: 163. ALZ/MEM IMP: Yes. ADC: Yes

Nonprofit; nondenominational. Apartments and private and semiprivate rooms. Nursing care; medical services; rehabilitative therapies; dental and podiatry care; pharmacy services; Medicare/Medicaid-approved; personal care; medication administration; security; emergency response system; maintenance; transportation; up to 3 daily meals; housekeeping and laundry services; fitness center; swimming pool; social and recreational activities.

APPL: (ref.), $100. DEP: $1,100. AL MO: $1,750–$2,900. HCC Daily: $100–$200.

Madonna Towers of Rochester

4001 19th Ave. NW
Rochester, MN 55901

Ph: (507) 288-3911
Fax: (507) 288-0393

IND: 96. RH/AL: 21. HCC: 62

Age 62+. Church affiliated. Apartments and private and semiprivate rooms. Skilled nursing care; medical services; rehabilitative therapies; pharmacy services; Medicare/Medicaid-approved; personal care; medication administration; security; emergency response system; maintenance; transportation; up to 3 daily meals; housekeeping and laundry services; exercise classes; chapel and religious services; library; social and recreational activities; game room; crafts; card and board games; country store; lounges.

APPL: (ref.) $50. IND ENT: Up to $93,500. IND MO: $500–$3,000. AL/RH: $3,400–$4,100. HCC Daily: $85–$165.

Mill Ridge Commons

235 N. Fern
Cambridge, MN 55008

Ph: (612) 689-4476
Fax: (612) 689-4477

Grandview Christian Home

800 Second Ave., NW
Cambridge, MN 55008

Ph: (612) 689-1474
Fax: (612) 689-4477

IND: Yes. AL: Yes. SNF: 178. ALZ/MEM IMP: Yes. ADC: Yes

Nonprofit; owned by Grandview Christian Ministries. Apartments and private and semiprivate rooms. 24-hour skilled nursing care; physical, occupational, and speech therapies; physician assistant program; social services; short- and long-term care; pharmacy services; home health care; Medicare-approved; personal care; medication administration; security; emergency response system; maintenance; transportation; up to 3 daily meals; housekeeping and laundry services; exercise room; chapel and religious services; library; social and recreational activities; game room; woodworking shop; parlor with fireplace; gardens; walking paths; patios; barber/beauty shop.

IND ENT: (ref.) $49,500. IND MO: $875–$1,250.

AL MO: $700; also hourly fees on á la carte basis. SNF Daily: $75–$150

Mount Olivet Home

5517 Lyndale Ave. S.
Minneapolis, MN 55419-1791

Ph: (612) 821-3190
Fax: (612) 821-3194

IND/AL: 92. SNF: 155. ALZ/MEM IMP: 16. ADC: Yes

Nonprofit; nondenominational; affiliated with the Mount Olivet Lutheran Church. Private and semiprivate rooms. 24-hour nursing care; skilled nursing care; physical, occupational, and speech therapies; IV and oxygen therapies; medical services; hospice services; social services; Medicare-approved; personal care; medication administration; security; emergency response system; maintenance; transportation; up to 3 daily meals; housekeeping and laundry services; exercise classes; chapel and religious services; chaplain services; pet visits; library; intergenerational program; volunteer program; social and recreational activities; gift shop; lounges and patios; barber/beauty shop.

Daily fees: $90–$170; additional $35/day for private room.

Assisted Living and Residential Care Facilities

In the state of Minnesota, these facilities are called ***Supervised Living/Residential/Assisted Living Facilities****.*

These facilities provide housing, food service, and one or more personal services.

Types of Authorization

Licensing and / or Certification

These facilities are regulated by the Department of Health. Supervised living facilities provide supervision, lodging, meals, counseling, and rehabilitative services to residents.

Memberships:

- Assisted Living Federation of America (ALFA) is a national nonprofit membership organization whose mission is to enhance the quality of life in assisted living facilities and promote the interests of the assisted living industry. ALFA, 10300 Eaton Place, Suite 400, Fairfax, VA 22030. Ph: (703) 691-8100. Fax: (703) 691-8106. *http://www.alfa.org*
- Minnesota Health and Housing Alliance (MHHA) is a state affiliate of ALFA. MHHA, 2550 University Ave. West #350S, St Paul, MN 55114. Ph: (651) 645-4545. Fax: (651) 645-0002. *http://www.mhha.com.*

South Central

Countryside Retirement Community

1100 1st Ave. South
Sleepy Eye, MN 56085

Ph: (507) 794-3200
Fax: (507) 794-5914

E-mail: *aganske@voa.org*

IND: 54. HHC: Yes

Age 55+. Nonprofit; nondenominational. Apartments. Nursing care; 24-hour home health care; personal care; medication administration; security; emergency response system; maintenance; transportation; up to 3 daily meals; housekeeping and laundry services; library; game room; social room; greenhouse.

APPL: $100. DEP: $440. IND MO: $700–$1,000.

Lake Crystal/Country Neighbors Home, ALFA, MHHA

511 W. Blue Earth St.
Lake Crystal, MN 56055

Ph: (507) 726-6537
Fax: (507) 726-6537

IND: Yes. AL: 24

Age 65+. For-profit; nondenominational; managed by the Board of Social Ministry. Private and semiprivate rooms. Registered nurse on staff; 24-hour supervision; Medicaid-approved; personal care; medication administration; security; emergency response system; maintenance; transportation; up to 3 daily meals; housekeeping and laundry services; religious services; Bible study; social and recreational activities; common areas; media room.

DEP: (ref.) $250. AL MO: $1,500–$1,650.

Southeast

Arbor Terrace

700 Second Ave. NW
Rochester, MN 55901

Ph: (507) 288-4883
Fax: (507) 289-6545

IND: 66. AL: Yes

Age 62+. Nonprofit; nondenominational; church-related; member of the Samaritan Bethany Senior Services. One- and two-bedroom apartments. Home health services; personal care; medication administration; security; emergency response system; maintenance; transportation; meal plans; housekeeping and laundry services; crafts; activities; close to public transportation and shopping.

IND MO: $1,100–$1,475.

East

Como by the Lake

901 E. Como Blvd.
St. Paul, MN 55103

Ph: (612) 489-3392

IND: 99. PC: Yes

Age 55+. Nondenominational. One- and two-bedroom apartments. Personal care; medication administration; security; emergency response system; maintenance; transportation; meal program; pets allowed; housekeeping and laundry services; social and recreational activities; arts and crafts; hobby room; community room.

APPL: $300. IND MO: $900–$1,300.

Guardian Angels Homes, MHHA, AAHSA

IND: 103. AL: Yes

Age 62+.

Angel Ridge

IND: 53. AL: Yes

Age 62+.

Evans Park

350 Evans Ave.
Elk River, MN 55330

Ph: (612) 241-4430
Fax: (612) 241-4448

E-mail: *GuardAngel1@Earthlink.Net*

IND: 36. AL: Yes

Age 55+. Nonprofit; nondenominational. Apartments. Nursing care; personal care; medication administration; security; emergency response system; maintenance; transportation; 1 daily meal; pets allowed; housekeeping and laundry services; activities; activities director; coffee shop; barber/beauty shop.

IND ENT: Evans Park only, (ref.) $825–$1,100. IND MO: 30% of income; HUD-subsidized; Evans Park, $675–$825. AL MO: $660.

Maranatha Place

5415 69th Ave., North
Minneapolis, MN 55429

Ph: (612) 569-4500
Fax: (612) 569-4576

IND: 58. AL: 7

Age 55+. Nonprofit; Baptist Church affiliation. Apartments. personal care; medication administration; security;

emergency response system; maintenance; transportation; up to 2 daily meals; housekeeping and laundry services; exercise room; social and recreational activities.

APPL: (ref.) $150. Contact facility for fees.

Rosewood Estates (3 locations)

Roseville

2750 N. Victoria St.
Roseville, MN 55113

Ph: (651) 482-1611

Maplewood

1200 Lakewood Drive
Maplewood, MN 55119

Ph: (651) 770-1111

Highland Park

750 Mississippi River Blvd.
St. Paul, MN 55116

Ph: (651) 698-1111

IND: Yes. AL: Yes. ALZ/MEM IMP: Yes

Nondenominational. Apartments. 24-hour nursing care; physical, occupational, and speech therapies; physician visits; dental and podiatry care; geriatric psychiatrist; 24-hour home health services; social services; personal care; medication administration; security; emergency response system; maintenance; transportation; up to 3 daily meals; housekeeping and laundry services; exercise classes; pet therapy; social and recreational activities; lounges; arts and crafts room; greenhouse; patio; barber/beauty shop.

IND MO: $2,150–$3,700; 2nd person, $600.

Northeast

Midtowne Manor II

2011 W. 2nd St.
Duluth, MN 55806

Ph: (218) 727-8340

King Manor

222 E. 2nd St.
Duluth, MN 55805

Ph: (218) 722-2724

AL: Yes. CONG: Yes

Nondenominational; sponsored by county Social Services Department and Housing and Redevelopment Authority of Duluth. Apartments. Nursing care; social services; health status checks; personal care; medication administration; security; emergency response system; maintenance; transportation; up to 3 daily meals; housekeeping and laundry services; social and recreational activities; on- and off-site activities; adjacent to senior center; convenience store; barber/beauty shop.

AL MO: 30% of income; HUD-subsidized.

Northwest

Lamplighter Manor

1425 Madison Ave.
Detroit Lakes, MN 56501

Ph: (218) 847-7768
Fax: (218) 847-4488

E-mail: *lamplighter@lakesnet.net*

RH: 65. ADC: Yes

Age 62+. Nonprofit; nondenominational; Lutheran Church affiliation. Apartments. Rehabilitative therapies; dental and podiatry care; volunteer checks; personal care; medication administration; security; emergency response system; maintenance; transportation; up to 3 daily meals; pets allowed; housekeeping and laundry services; social and recreational activities.

RH MO: 30% of income; HUD-subsidized.

Independent Living

Independent housing (primarily rentals) for seniors that may offer security features, meal service, and activities.

East

Parmly Lakeview Apartments

10600 282nd St.
Chisago City, MN 55013

Ph: (612) 257-0581

IND: 60

Age 62+. Nondenominational; sponsored by the Board of Social Ministry, Minnesota Synod Lutheran Church. One- and two-bedroom apartments. Security; emergency response system; maintenance; 1 daily meal; housekeeping and laundry services; close to hospital and shopping; lobby; activity and crafts room; gardens; lake views; docking on beach.

IND MO: 1 bedroom, $650; 2 bedroom, $800. Some units HUD-subsidized.

Plymouth Towne Square

15500 37th Ave., North
Plymouth, MN 55446

Ph: (612) 550-9525
Fax: (612) 551-0144

IND: 99

Age 55+. Nondenominational; owned by Plymouth Housing and Redevelopment Authority. Apartments. Security; emergency response system; maintenance; laundry services; meal plan; pets allowed; lounge; solarium; crafts; activities; barber/beauty shop.

IND MO: $165–$850; HUD-subsidized.
REQ: Resident of Plymouth; income must not exceed $30,500 (single); $35,000 (couple).

Point Pleasant Heights

28600 Fairway Lane
Chisago City, MN 55013

Ph: (651) 257-4035

IND: Yes

Age 55+. Nondenominational; sponsored by the Board of Social Ministry, Minnesota Synod Lutheran Church. One- and two-bedroom apartments. Security; emergency response system; maintenance; transportation; up to 3 daily meals; laundry services; social and recreational activities; community room; game room; putting green; walking paths; gardening; barber/beauty shop.

IND MO: About $600–$1,100.

Ridge Pointe

12600 & 12800 Marion Lane West
Minnetonka, MN 55305

Ph: (612) 540-6200
Fax: (612) 540-6244

http://www.seniorresource.com/ridge.htm

IND: 271

Age 62+. Nondenominational; managed by Pointe Management. Apartments. Wellness clinic; some medical services; security; emergency response system; maintenance; transportation; meal plans; pets allowed; housekeeping and laundry services; fitness room; whirlpools; library; woodworking shop; social, cultural, educational, and recreational activities; computer center; arts and crafts; card room; tropical atrium with art gallery; ice cream parlor; convenience store; gardens; barber/beauty shop.

DEP: $500. IND MO: $950–$2,050.

RosePointe

2555 Hamline Ave. North
Roseville, MN 55113

Ph: (651) 639-1000

IND: 148

RosePointe II (affordable housing: adjacent to RosePointe)

2545 N. Hamline Ave.
Roseville, MN 55113

IND: 42

Age 62+. Nondenominational. One- and two-bedroom apartments. Wellness clinic; security; emergency response system; maintenance; transportation; service center; up to 3 daily meals (1 meal included with IND MO fees); housekeeping and laundry services; fitness center; exercise classes; library; social, recreational, and cultural activities; educational programs; media room; billiards room; convenience store; walking paths; barber/beauty shop.

DEP: (ref.) $500. IND MO: RosePointe, $1,250–$2,000; 2nd person, $85; RosePointe II, $675–$825.

West

Brookside Manor

804 Benson Rd.
Montevideo, MN 56265

Ph: (320) 269-6506
Fax: (320) 269-6507

IND: 61

Age 62+. Nonprofit; nondenominational. Apartments. Home health services; maintenance; up to 3 daily meals; pets allowed; library; religious services; Bible study; pool table; social and recreational activities; gardening; close to hospital, clinic, and nursing home; barber/beauty shop.

IND MO: $250–$475; HUD-subsidized. Meals are extra.

Hilltop Residence

915 First Ave.
Madison, MN 56256

Ph: (320) 598-3129 or 598-7536

IND: 35

Age 62+. Nonprofit; affiliated with Madison Lutheran Home. Apartments. Home health services; pharmacy services; security; emergency response system; maintenance; transportation; "Meals on Wheels" program; housekeeping and laundry services; fitness equipment; social and recreational activities; bingo; potlucks; volunteer opportunities; game room; community room; patio and picnic area.

IND MO: $600. HUD-subsidized units available.

Adult/Resort Communities

Communities for active adults (not all are age-restricted; primarily ownership).

Central

Breezy Point Resort

HC 83 Box 1225
Breezy Point, MN 56472

Ph: (218) 562-4204

Individual homes, condominiums, cooperative units, homesites. Golf course; tennis; swimming pool; hiking/biking; fishing; hunting; riding stables; boating/waterskiing; snow skiing; community center; fitness center; social clubs.

PURCHASE: Homes, $93,500–$220,000.

Pebble Creek Country Club

14000 Club House Drive
Becker, MN 55308

Ph: (612) 261-4653

Golf course; swimming pool; snow skiing; community center; library.

PURCHASE: Homes, $137,500–$825,000.

The Pines at Grand View Lodge

134 Nokomis
Nisswa, MN 56468

Ph: (800) 432-3788 or (218) 963-2234

Individual homes, condominiums, homesites. Golf course; tennis; swimming pool; hiking/biking; fishing; hunting; boating/waterskiing; snow skiing.

PURCHASE: Homes, $203,000–$401,500.

Quadna Resort and Conference Center

100 Quadna Rd.
Hill City, MN 55748

Ph: (800) 422-6649 or (218) 697-8444

Condominiums. Golf course; tennis; swimming pool; hiking/biking; fishing; hunting; riding stables; boating/waterskiing; snow skiing; community center.

PURCHASE: Homes, $22,000–$49,500.

West Central

Minnewaska Golf Club

Golf Course Rd.
Glenwood, MN 56334

Ph: (612) 634-3680

Individual homes, condominiums, homesites. Golf course; hiking; social clubs.

PURCHASE: Homes, from $154,000.

East

Stonebrooke Golf Club

2693 S.C.R. 79
Shakopee, MN 55379

Ph: (612) 396-3171

Individual homes, homesites. Golf course; hiking; fishing; hunting; boating/waterskiing.

PURCHASE: Homes, $269,500–$550,000.

Northeast

Homestead Cooperative

Homestead Co-op Unit 100
219 11th Ave., W.
Grand Marais, MN 55604

Ph: (218) 387-1358
Fax: (218) 387-9474

http://homestead-cooperative.com

E-mail: *homecoop@boreal.org*

IND: 26

Age 55+. Nonprofit. Co-op apartments. On-site nurse; emergency response system; maintenance; transportation; pets allowed; exercise classes; crafts; community room; social and recreational activities.

PURCHASE: $90,000–$128,500. IND MO: $325–$450.

Southeast

Greystone Golf Club

8006 Rhode Island Circle
Bloomington, MN 55438

Ph: (612) 942-7380 or (612) 941-1106

Homesites. Lake; golf course and clubhouse projected for spring of 2000.

Call for property information.

St. Charles Golf Club

1920 Park Rd.
St. Charles, MN 55972

Ph: (507) 932-5444
Fax: (507) 932-5966

Individual homes. Golf course.

PURCHASE: Homes, $165,000–$220,000; homesites, from $24,500.

The Wilds

3151 Wilds Ridge
Prior Lake, MN 55372

Ph: (612) 445-3500 or (612) 421-3500

http://www.golfthewilds.com

Individual homes, townhomes, villas, homesites. Golf course; clubhouse; dining; walking paths.

PURCHASE: Homesites, $71,500–$208,000.

Staff at the Philip Lief Group, Inc.:

Editorial Director	**Maryanne Wagner**
Senior Editor	**Susan Frisch-Kowalski**
Contributing Editors	**Veronica Deisler**
	James Pomager
	Diane M. Rhodes
	Carol Gordon Carlson
	Barbara Long
Production Editor	**Marybeth Fedele**

OTHER REFERENCE TITLES BY H.W. WILSON

Facts About the Presidents, Seventh Edition
Speeches of the American Presidents, Second Edition
Facts About American Immigration
Facts About the 20th Century
Famous First Facts About American Politics
Famous First Facts About Sports
Facts About Canada, Its Provinces and Territories
Facts About China (forthcoming)
Facts About the American Wars
Facts About the British Prime Ministers
Facts About the Cities
Facts About the Congress
Facts About the States, Second Edition
Facts About the Supreme Court of the United States
Facts About the World's Languages
Facts About the World's Nations
Famous First Facts, Fifth Edition
Famous First Facts, International Edition
Famous First Facts About the Environment (forthcoming)
The Wilson Chronology of Asia and the Pacific
The Wilson Chronology of the World's Religions
The Wilson Chronology of Women's Achievements

Facts About Retiring in the United States

- A fee-for-service contract. The resident pays the full daily rate for all long-term nursing care required.

Entrance fees for CCRCs that offer extensive contracts are considerably higher than those that offer fee-for-service arrangements. During the 1990s, more and more CCRCs were opting for extensive contracts. Consumers seem to prefer the security of knowing they will be fully cared for without having to worry about additional costs.

Many CCRCs, but not all, offer to refund entrance fees if the resident leaves the community. A full refund may be available for short stays up to six months, but the refund often decreases by 1 or 2 percent each month after that. This means that after a period of a little more than four years (assuming a monthly 2 percent decrease), the resident will not be eligible for any refund at all. Of course, the more generous the refund provision, the higher the entrance fee is likely to be.

People who select a continuing care community as their place of retirement tend to be in the middle- to upper-income bracket. Many are well-educated professionals who plan ahead with deliberate care and like to be assured of their future, both financially and in terms of where they are going to live. Couples who enter a CCRC have the security of knowing they will be able to remain close to one another even if their housing needs change over time.

Most residents enter a continuing care community in their early to mid-70s. Since CCRCs usually require an individual to be capable of independent living when he or she first arrives, advance planning is vital. If you think this housing option might be for you, it is best to overcome your resistance to change—a human characteristic that is by no means confined to the elderly—and not postpone action until it is forced upon you. Suppose you are considering moving to a CCRC but want to preserve your independence in your own home for as long as you can. There is nothing wrong with such a desire, of course, but what if a fall or sudden unexpected illness puts you in need of assisted living? The chances are that the CCRC you had your eyes on will not be willing to admit you, and you will be forced into a crisis-driven move that may not entirely fit your particular needs.

How to Select a CCRC

As with any retirement community, it is essential to visit the facility, talk to staff and residents, observe as much as you can about the living conditions, and then listen to and trust your own feelings. Do not be afraid to ask questions and follow up on them until you receive straightforward answers.

One of the most important things to find out is who owns the CCRC. It may be owned by an individual or a company, and it may be a for-profit or a not-for-profit facility. If it is the latter, it will be sponsored by a tax-exempt organization, such as a church or civic association.

What is the owner's experience and background in the field of retirement housing? What are his long-term plans? What about his financial stability? You need to be assured that the services you pay for, some of which you may not need for a decade or more, will be there when you do need them. You want to avoid moving into a facility that is or may become financially troubled or poorly managed. Before signing a contract, make sure that you receive a financial disclosure statement, which should include earnings statements for the last five years and financial projections for the next five years. Many states require such disclosures. It might be advisable to hire an expert, either a lawyer or financial adviser, to examine the statement.

Ask who manages the facility on a day-to-day basis (if this is someone other than the owner) and how much experience this person has in managing housing for seniors. Look into the qualifications of the CCRC's staff and the staff turnover rate. A high turnover rate could be a sign of underlying problems with the facility.

Since CCRCs, like ALFs, offer service in exchange for a monthly fee, it is important to know exactly what services are covered in the contract and what services are available at extra cost. For example, how much health care is covered? Does coverage include dental care? Eye exams? Physical therapy? Podiatry? Can you use your own doctor or must you accept one supplied by the CCRC? Also inquire about fee increases. Is the fee likely to be raised in the future, and, if so, by what amount? It is not unusual for CCRCs to raise fees periodically, but there should not be more than one increase per year. Some contracts state that fee increases are tied to an inflation index such as the Consumer Price Index. Ask to see documentation of fee increases over the past five years and any projections for the future.

Since you may be living in a continuing care retirement community for many years, it is conceivable that some unforeseen circumstance might result in your being unable to pay the monthly fees. Ask the CCRC administrators what would happen if that situation should ever occur. Many communities have a financial assistance program, but others may expect your relatives to make up the balance of the unpaid fees. A nonprofit CCRC cannot evict a resident for nonpayment of fees without losing its nonprofit status.

Another important question to ask is, who decides when a resident moves from independent living to assisted living, and from assisted living to the skilled care facility? This area is often ill-defined in CCRC contracts. No one wants someone else telling them they must move when they do not feel the need to do so. Ideally, any decision about when to move a person to another level of care should be made by a team of evaluators, including the senior, his or her family (if appropriate), a doctor, and the CCRC staff. This team should carefully examine all relevant aspects of the resident's life and health. There should also be an appeals procedure if the resident is unhappy with the decision. Ask if the CCRC allows temporary moves between different levels of care. If a temporary health problem means you need assistance with daily activities for a while, will you be able to move back to your former independent living unit when your health improves?

Explore also the security of your tenure at the continuing care community. Can you be asked to leave? For what reasons? Do you have the right to appeal? Ideally, the CCRC must demonstrate "just cause" in order to evict a resident, and is legally required to do so in many states. Just cause might be invoked if it could be demonstrated that a resident was a danger to himself or others, had misrepresented information that the CCRC uses as criteria for admission, or had breached the signed contract.

Although you may never need the CCRC's nursing facility, it is still a good idea to gather information about it. Is the facility on the premises, or does the CCRC have an arrangement to use a nursing home nearby? What is the capacity of the facility, and what guarantee is there that a bed will be available when you need it? Are the rooms a mix of single and double occupancy? Do the rooms have private baths? Is the facility equipped to deal with patients who suffer from Alzheimer's?

You will certainly want to view the nursing facility. Look for the same things that you took note of when you inspected the assisted living facility. Does the nursing home feel like a friendly place where people are well cared for? Do the residents look well groomed? Are there planned activities and outings? Do the residents take advantage of them? How do the staff speak to the residents—with kindness, or in a brusque manner? Are the residents treated with dignity?

Check also that the CCRC is licensed for all levels of care that it provides. Some continuing care communities are also accredited.

The Question of Accreditation

CCRCs may apply for accreditation by the Continuing Care Accreditation Commission (CCAC), the only national accrediting agency for continuing care retirement communities. The CCAC's accreditation program is based on the belief that accreditation promotes quality and integrity in the continuing care and retirement industry. CCAC accredits communities that meet the agency's demanding but realistic accreditation standards and offer an older person a contract that provides residential living and various health care services for the balance of his or her life.

CCAC is not a state licensing body. State licensing authorities may apply different definitions and standards in regulating continuing care communities.

Accreditation by CCAC is important because it is widely regarded as a seal of approval for retirement communities. It is a voluntary process involving rigorous self-evaluation by the retirement community's staff, residents, and board of directors and an on-site review by CCAC evaluators. Accreditation is awarded for a period of five years, although within that period the community must submit annual progress and financial reports to demonstrate ongoing compliance with the required standards. When the five-year period expires, the retirement community must seek reaccreditation.

One of the advantages of accreditation is that it offers the retiree a standard by which to compare various retirement communities. CCAC accreditation standards seek to ensure excellence in four critical areas:

- *Resident health and wellness.* This means that the retirement community provides a variety of health programs and services designed to serve residents' changing needs and to foster their physical, mental, and emotional well-being.
- *Resident life and services.* Accreditation indicates that the community provides an environment that enhances each resident's personal dignity and protects individual independence and self-determination. Services offered encourage residents to make the most of their abilities and provide residents with opportunities for growth.
- *Financial resources and disclosure.* Accreditation indicates that the community's resources are adequate to meet its financial obligations, including debt service, resident contracts, and capital needs. It also certifies that the retirement community's disclosure statements are made available to residents, sponsors, and other appropriate parties.
- *Governance and administration.* Accreditation is granted if the community has clear statement of mission and purpose for both present and future, and if the governing board ensures that the retirement community maintains a positive, caring environment for residents, good working conditions for staff, and effective communication both within and outside the community.

In 1997 less than 20 percent of more than 1,200 continuing care communities nationwide had been accredited. Therefore, if the CCRC you are interested in is not accredited, this need not set off alarm bells. It simply may mean that the facility is new. CCRCs must be nearly 90-percent occupied for a year before applying for accreditation. Equally, if a facility is accredited, that in itself is no guarantee that the quality of care is uniformly high. As when purchasing any product or service, the onus is on the consumer to verify the quality of what is being offered and whether it suits his or her needs.

The rapid growth of CCRCs in the last decade appears to have had a positive impact on the quality of care for the elderly. A study conducted of 2,000 residents in 19 CCRCs in four states found that residents reported a high degree of satisfaction with the various services provided by their CCRC, although a significant minority said that their community was not living up to their expectations. Some frustration was apparent in that more than one-third of the residents reported that they were not able to influence the management of the CCRC. (Some state statutes allow residents to appoint a representative to the board of directors, but CCRC owners are generally unenthusiastic about such arrangements.) However, another finding of the same study was very encouraging: Recent residents reported a significant and positive change in their attitude to their own aging in the time they had been at the CCRC.

A disadvantage of CCRCs is that they are often too expensive for elderly people in the lower income levels.

Nursing Homes

First, some statistics on the use of nursing facilities. Of the over-65 population, just 4 percent (1.4 million people) lived in nursing homes in 1995. The percentage does increase with age. For people age 65 to 74, the figure is 1 percent; this rises to 5 percent for people in the 75-to-84 age bracket, and 15 percent for those over 85.

However, it is estimated that almost half of all Americans turning 65 in the late 1990s will be admitted into a nursing home at least once. This figure sounds high, but it must be remembered that many nursing home stays are temporary. Sometimes patients who are discharged from a hospital are placed in a nursing home to recuperate before returning home. In other cases seniors are admitted on a temporary basis to give overburdened caregivers at home a short break from their duties.

Nursing facilities fall into two categories. An *intermediate care facility* (ICF) is for residents who do not need specialized or intensive care. ICFs provide round-the-clock care that includes assistance with daily living, the administration of medication and preparation of special diets, and rehabilitative therapy. ICFs must be supervised by a registered nurse.

A *skilled nursing facility* (SNF) supplies more complex, intensive care for patients with a wide range of medical needs. This might include, for example, the use of feeding tubes or catheterization procedures and (in cases of Alzheimer's or dementia) constant supervision. An SNF must be under the supervision of a physician. Since SNFs are certified by Medicare but ICFs are not, the distinction is an important one.

Once you have decided on a location, there are a number of ways to locate a nursing home. Such homes are listed in the Yellow Pages, although the home that is willing and able to place the most impressive-looking advertisement may not necessarily be the best one for you. Another method would be to consult the reference book *The Inside Guide to America's Nursing Homes: Rankings & Ratings for Every Nursing Home in the U.S., 1998–1999* (see the resources list at the end of this chapter). You can also consult your state agency on aging, which can refer you to the local long-term care ombudsman. The ombudsman, although not allowed by law to recommend one nursing home over another, will have considerable information about local nursing facilities. He will be able to tell you, for example, whether there are any outstanding complaints against the facility, the nature and number of these complaints, and the outcome of any recent complaint investigations. Since ombudsmen make frequent visits to nursing facilities, they are able to provide valuable advice on what to look for when visiting the local homes.

Once you have a specific nursing home in mind, a good place to begin your fact-finding search is with the inspection report. Under state and federal government regulations, all nursing homes are

How to Select an Assisted Living Facility

Once you have located an ALF in the area in which you or your relative desires to live, review any brochures they may have sent you and talk to anyone you know who has a relative living in the facility. Local doctors or clergymen usually have some knowledge of ALFs in the community. The next step is to visit the facility yourself. Since there are many things that you need to take note of, it might be a good idea to carry a checklist so you do not leave anything out. It is important not to hurry and to make a final decision only after careful review of all the information and impressions you have accumulated. Since it is possible that an ALF is the last home that an aged parent will occupy, it is vital that the decision be a sound one.

First impressions count. As you drive into the facility, does it look well-maintained? Are the grounds neat? Are there pleasant places where residents can sit outside and enjoy the fresh air? Are the staff welcoming and friendly? Do they answer all your questions adequately?

As you walk around, observe the residents. Do they look happy? Do they seem fully engaged in their activities and responsive to their environment? Do they seem to mix a lot with each other? Or do they seem inactive and uninterested in what is going on around them?

Inquire about the food, and sample it if possible. Are the portions adequate? Are the meals nutritious and appetizing? Are beverages available all day or only at mealtimes? Is the dining room large (if it is too large it can seem impersonal), or is it divided up into smaller, homier units? Is seating assigned? Is the meal served cafeteria-style or restaurant-style? Is smoking allowed? All these factors can make a difference in whether the ALF feels like a home or like an institution.

As you inspect further, note the hallways. Are they wide and well-lit? Are there a lot of sharp corners, or is it easy to get around?

Examine to what extent the living units are "senior friendly."Are the doors wide, the shelves lower than usual, the electrical outlets higher than usual (two feet above the floor if possible)? Is there enough storage space? Are the bathrooms fitted with grab bars and nonslip surfaces?

Try to gauge the quality of life that the residents enjoy, and the extent to which the ALF attempts to enhance it. Do the residents get enough physical exercise? What programs are offered to heighten the residents' well-being in all areas of life? Do a majority of the residents take part in such activities? How much privacy do residents have? Are they treated with dignity and respect?

Medical and security issues need to be addressed. How are emergencies handled? How long does it take for an ambulance to arrive when summoned? Does a physician or nurse make regular visits to offer medical checkups? Concerning security, is the main entrance locked after dark? Is there staff coverage 24 hours a day?

Find out what services are included in the monthly fee and what services are extra. Does the service fee include any medical care?

Make sure that the facility has a current license, one issued by a governmental agency that gives the facility the legal right to operate. (In some states, licensing is referred to as "certification.") Assisted living facilities are licensed either by the Department of Health or the Department of Social Services. There is no system of accreditation for ALFs.

Involving Mom and Dad in the Decision

Finally, as you reflect, ask yourself whether the assisted living facility you have been inspecting is really, honestly, a place where you would like your mother or father to live. And even more important, would he or she like to live there? Have you asked them?

It cannot be emphasized enough that the senior citizen should be fully involved in the process of selecting an ALF. A four-year study released by Brandeis University in 1999 reported that a large number of residents of ALFs were moved there at the wishes of their children, their doctors, or their insurance companies—but the residents themselves were not consulted about the move and their wishes were not respected. The result, according to the study, is that many elderly people are living in situations that do not meet their needs. The study recommended that adult children pay more attention to what their aging parents really want, and also to preparing them to make informed choices about their future. (The reverse side of this particular coin, according to a spokesperson for the American Association of Retired Persons, is that caregivers often try to keep an elderly relative at home too long, thus placing too much strain on all the caregivers involved.)

Continuing Care Retirement Communities (CCRCs)

A continuing care retirement community (CCRC) offers retirees a continuum of care—from the time they first arrive ready to live independently to the later stages of life, when they may need some assistance with daily living or even full-time skilled care. The CCRC concept is summed up in the phrase "aging in place." Living in a CCRC means that seniors do not have to face the prospect of a physically and emotionally stressful move if their housing needs change as they grow older.

To ensure that people can age in place, continuing care communities provide three levels of housing—independent living, assisted living, and skilled care—as well as a range of social activities and amenities. Usually, a CCRC will require that residents be capable of independent living when they first enter the community. The independent living units are usually apartments but are sometimes townhouses or cottages. If and when the residents' needs change, they can then move to other housing within the same development.

CCRCs operate on the basis of a contractual agreement with their residents. Residents pay a substantial entrance fee (sometimes called a founder's fee) as well as a monthly service fee. In return, the community guarantees that the resident will have, at minimum, access to nursing care when needed, and at maximum, full coverage of all nursing home costs. The monthly service fee covers housekeeping, meals, utilities, help with the activities of daily living (dressing, bathing, etc.), recreational and social activities, and health care. The extent of health care covered by the monthly fee varies. The average monthly fee ranges from $3,100 to $4,400. Seventy-five percent of this figure covers services and medical care; 25 percent is for housing.

In many CCRCs, seniors have no equity in their residential property. The entrance fee is simply a payment made in exchange for the CCRC's guarantee that they will receive specified care and services for life. However, in some communities, residents have the option of purchasing their housing (usually a cooperative or condo).

There are three different types of contracts offered by CCRCs:

- An extensive, or all-inclusive, contract. This contract, sometimes called a life care agreement, offers unlimited long-term nursing care for little or no substantial increase in the monthly service payments.
- A modified, or limited contract. This includes a specified amount of long-term nursing care, for example, a certain number of days of care per year. Payment for any care beyond this limit is the responsibility of the resident. The CCRC may charge a full fee-for-service or offer a discount.

Facts About Retiring in the United States

Edited by

Steven S. Shagrin, J.D., CFP, CRPC, CRC

President, International Society for Retirement Planning

With contributions from

Bryan Aubrey, Ph.D.

Kate McGahan, CSW, CMC

Charles M. Sprock, Jr., Esq.

Benjamin Levine, Esq.

PricewaterhouseCoopers LLP

Helen Dennis

Produced by

The Philip Lief Group, Inc.

The H.W. Wilson Company

New York ◆ Dublin

2001

This book is intended to provide accurate and helpful information on the subjects included. The publisher is not rendering legal, financial, or other professional service, and the authors are not offering such advice in this book. If legal or other expert advice is required, seek the services of a competent professional. In addition, the publisher does not endorse any facilities, housing developments, or resources listed in this book, nor does it accept liability for any problems associated with the facilities or developments. Although information was current at the time of publication, readers should check with the facilities or developments to confirm and update specific details.

Library of Congress Cataloging-in-Publication Data

Facts about retiring in the United States / edited by Steven S. Shagrin.
p. cm.
ISBN 0-8242-0969-9 (alk. paper)
1. Retirement—United States—Planning. I. Shagrin, Steven S.

HQ1063.2.U6 F33 2000
646.7'9'0973—dc21

00-053423

Visit H.W. Wilson's Web site: www.hwwilson.com

Printed in the United States of America

Contents

Editorial Review Board

The editors also wish to gratefully acknowledge the assistance of Randall Workman, Director, Public Affairs, American Association of Retired Persons; Brian P. Duffy, PricewaterhouseCoopers LLP; Whitney J. Redding, Assisted Living Federation of America; Helen Dennis, Past President, ISRP; Donna Francisco, Managing Editor, *Senior Selections: Mature Living Choices*; Marjorie Marlin, President, National Shared Housing Resource Center; J. Daniel Pluff; Carol Glisker; Florence Peters; Mark Petitte, Esq.; Kathy Downes-McCabe, RN; Richard J. Naylor; Lori Lake, and Jennifer L.Vincent.

How to Use This Book

This book is organized to make researching information about retirement easy. In Part I, Retirement Considerations, you will find helpful facts about the general topics of housing, health care, retirement income and finances, legal concerns, and the personal side of retirement. It is an ideal reference for anyone who is planning for or in the midst of retirement, or who is helping an older person arrange for their retirement years.

Following the initial chapters, in Part II, you will find information on various retirement housing options for each state, preceded by general state information, including:

- climate;
- cost of living (ranking among the states, state/local taxes as a percentage of income, sales tax, as well as property tax reductions and prescription exemptions, if any);
- transportation, travel, and tourism (airports, bus tours, state highways, railways, theater and music, museums, historical sites, and recreational opportunities, by region where appropriate);
- relevant organizations (advocacy and volunteer groups);
- licensing and accreditation information (for facilities providing health care or personal assistance) specific to the state.

Retirement housing options within the states are grouped into the following general categories, although the terminology and descriptions of these categories may vary from state to state:

- continuing, long-term care communities;
- assisted living, personal/adult/residential care communities;
- independent and adult/resort living communities.

We have not attempted to include the broad category of nursing homes in this book, which focuses on more active retirement living.

You will find a full explanation of the state-by-state listings at the beginning of Part II. It includes a key to the abbreviations, along with a diagram of how each listing is organized so that you can easily understand the information.

Part III provides a list of organizations and resources that may be useful to you, with Internet addresses, if available. Here you'll find resources on such topics as financial planning, pensions and benefits, health care, consumer issues, housing, legal matters, women's issues, and so on.

In Part IV, you will see various worksheets, checklists, and sample forms for your retirement planning.

Introduction

Americans preparing for retirement are a diverse group of individuals with specific needs, desires, and expectations, as well as unique financial situations to consider. If you are of retirement age, you may be healthy, active, and highly independent; or you may be uncertain about your future, anxious about health problems related to aging, or worried about managing your increasing need for assistance. For some, the ideal retirement setting includes sunny weather, sports facilities, and a strong sense of community. For others, the goal may be a nice, simple home near family with an emphasis on a sense of security, or excellent medical resources nearby.

Regardless of what drives your research and planning, the process of preparing for retirement can be daunting, even to the most industrious researcher. *Facts About Retiring in the United States* is a tremendous resource, with advice for making careful, well-informed decisions about virtually every aspect of retiring and essential information about four key areas: housing, health care, retirement income and finances, and legal concerns.

Unique to this book is its presentation of housing alternatives on a state-by-state basis, along with other facts about each state's climate, cost of living, taxes, major transportation, travel and tourism, and more. The housing options are organized by categories: continuing care retirement communities (also called life care communities), residential health care facilities (also called assisted living or personal care), independent living, and residential/adult/resort communities. This section of the book can help you make a smooth transition from one living arrangement to another as your physical and emotional needs require.

The overall purpose of the book, of course, is to help you to be as prepared as possible for retirement, in whatever form it may take. However, as with any resource book, it provides only a frame of reference for the decisions you face. It is not a substitute for personalized advice from qualified, experienced, and knowledgeable professionals in the retirement planning field, nor is it by any means exhaustive. Even the state-by-state listings, for example, contain merely a fraction of the vast number of housing options available to retirees. Nevertheless, the book includes more specifics than you are likely to find elsewhere in one place. It provides an excellent current reference for rates, accommodations, services, and amenities and gives you the facts on licensing, accreditation, and more.

What Does Retirement Mean to You?

Once armed with these facts, you can begin to think more clearly about what retirement means to you. The transition from working to not working requires a great deal of personal reflection. If retirement means leaving a job you've had for years, you really do give up a lot more than a regular paycheck. You leave a whole social structure behind—people with whom you spent most of your waking hours. Without a personal agenda of what you want to do with the rest of your life, you may find yourself disoriented at first. Some people are not able to adjust to this change at all and may slip into depression because they have lost their daily routine.

Also keep in mind that your relationships with family and friends may change. Now that you are no longer away from home most of the day, you can spend more time with your family than ever before. For some families, this increased time together is a blessing, but for others it means more stress. Do not be afraid to seek competent assistance if you feel that life is more troubling than before. As we age, we become more resistant to change, and retirement causes a lot of changes, all at once. Be ready for them.

The Possibilities

Retirement planning today differs dramatically from that done by your parents. When age 65 was selected as the official retirement age back in the 1930s, normal life expectancy was not much longer. Typically, a person would retire and have to worry about providing for only a few more years of life. Now, with advances in health care, better wellness decisions, and opportunities to choose the time of retirement, a person might expect to live another 20 to 30 years or more during this stage of life.

Your retirement will be as unique to you as every other aspect of your life. It will be a time of tremendous opportunity for personal growth and development. You will have time to do the things in life you always wanted to do, and with foresight and good planning you will have the financial resources as well.

Working as a volunteer after retirement can enhance your sense of self-worth and give meaning and direction to your life, helping you make a real difference in the lives of others. Going back to school to pursue your special interests is a great way to fill a day or two a week (many colleges allow seniors to audit classes for free). Joining local hobby groups and exercising to keep fit are other good outlets for your leisure time. Even taking a part-time job unrelated to your former one gives you important social contacts and a reason to get up in the morning.

Managing Your Money

Taking financial and investment education classes to become a better manager of your portfolio is certainly another wise use of your time. Even if you have a financial adviser or a stockbroker, he or she can only make suggestions for you to consider. You ultimately make the final decision, so what better time is there to become a more educated investor?

As you gain a greater understanding of different investments, you become more proactive and more comfortable with taking on slightly higher levels of risk—exactly what you need to maximize your returns and make your money last as long as you do.

Do not forget to look to the future during your financial planning and consider how your life might change as you continue to age. As you move through your retirement years, you will most likely be more active in the first seven to ten years, slow down and stay closer to home for the next seven to ten years, and be concerned with maintaining your health and preparing for life's final transition in the last seven to ten-plus years.

Think of what a typical day, week, or month of your life might look like. What will you be doing, eating, enjoying—and where? Then consider the basic costs of the lifestyle you choose. To have a truly successful retirement, you need to project how long your money might last and then revisit your budget plan every year or so to see what has changed, and whether you are still on track. When budgeting, you should consider a number of questions, such as:

- How do you presently spend your money?
- What changes in your spending habits do you expect over time?
- How will inflation affect your particular expenses?
- What regular sources of income will you have from Social Security, monthly pensions, and so on, and do they have built-in cost of living adjustments?
- How are your investments structured with respect to income and taxation?

- What is your average tax rate now, and what might it be?
- How long do you expect to live?
- How might you take funds from your tax-deferred retirement accounts?

This type of evaluation may seem like very sophisticated fortune-telling, but a qualified financial or retirement planner can do it well—and it is vitally important to do it. Consider the consequences of postponing this type of financial projection until you have already spent a quarter or a third of your retirement savings. You do not want the surprise of running out of money before you run out of breath.

Retirement today is not simple, but your readiness for it will make all the difference in the world. Unless you get the right information and advice, plan well, and adjust to circumstances as you go, you will not enjoy retirement as much as you could. Don't shortchange yourself for what could be your most rewarding years: Get the facts and plan ahead.

Steven S. Shagrin, JD, CFP, CRPC, CRC
President, International Society for Retirement Planning

Part I: Retirement Considerations

Housing

By Bryan Aubrey, Ph.D.*

Growing older isn't such a depressing thought anymore. Americans are living longer, healthier lives than ever before. As of the year 2000 people 65 and over will represent 13 percent of the population. By 2030 they will grow to 20 percent. Life expectancy is also increasing. In 1997, people reaching the age of 65 could expect to live an additional 17.6 years (19 years for women and 15.8 years for men).

As a reflection of these changing demographics, there has been over the last decade or so an explosion of creative thinking and activity in the area of retirement housing. The present range of options for senior housing was unthinkable just a generation ago. In fact, a recent CNN report identified the boom in retirement housing as the most significant trend in the housing market today.

With all these choices, decisions about where, when, and whether a retiree should move require much careful thought and planning. And since many people may spend a quarter of their lives or more as retirees, their housing needs may change over time. Becoming familiar with all the options, and planning ahead, are essential.

In the early years of retirement, a period that may last a decade or more, many retirees pride themselves on their active and independent lifestyles. Indeed, as former president Jimmy Carter writes in his book *The Virtues of Aging*, when people first retire, they may well have more freedom than at any time in their lives since they were college students. The sudden acquisition of many hours of leisure brings with it often limitless opportunities for personal growth and the pursuit of hobbies or other interests. Recent retirees may relish the freedom to decide exactly how to spend their time, unrestricted by parental or work-related responsibilities. During this period of retirement, most seniors will choose to remain in an independent living situation.

Later, perhaps when a retiree reaches his or her early or mid-seventies, priorities may begin to change. This is often the period when health and security become primary considerations. Retirees may then look for housing that is tailored more directly to these needs, such as a continuing care retirement community (CCRC) or an assisted living facility (ALF). Such a move does not of itself mean a reduction in their level of activity or independence, or their freedom and enjoyment of life. It simply means they gain assurance that their changing needs and priorities will be met reliably in their new living situation.

Should I Sell My House?

Imagine that a retiree wakes up one Monday morning and realizes with a sigh of pleasure that he doesn't have to jump out of bed, race through his morning routine, and get to the office at some preestablished time. He is finally free of all that. In fact, now that he's retired, he doesn't have to do many of those things he spent most of a lifetime doing. Now the family home, that bastion of security and treasure trove of memories, is his to luxuriate in and enjoy. But does he

---

* Bryan Aubrey is a freelance writer who has written in the fields of current affairs, education, and health. His work has appeared in national publications.

really want to stay there? Would he be better off selling his house and moving somewhere else?

Statistically, more than 90 percent of retirees age 55 to 65 do not sell their homes. They stay exactly where they are. In fact, the elderly are less likely to change their residence than other age group. In 1997, only 5 percent of people age 65 and over had moved in the previous year, compared to 18 percent of people under 65.

There may be many good reasons to stay put. A senior citizen may have lived in the family home for many years, perhaps even his or her whole life. The house contains a wealth of happy memories. It is familiar, like the neighborhood in which it stands. The retiree may have a network of friends and relatives nearby; shopping and leisure activities are also close at hand. Why should an individual or a couple go through all the turmoil of uprooting themselves just when they finally have time to enjoy all these things?

On the other hand, other factors may combine to make a move advantageous. Perhaps the neighborhood has changed over the years and is no longer as desirable as it once was. Friends and relatives may have moved away, or may do so in the near future. Or perhaps the house that once resounded with the lively voices of children is now too large for a single person or couple. Some rooms may hardly ever be used.

There may also be design aspects of the house that are no longer suitable. Stairs, for example, may be difficult to manage in later years. Narrow doorways might become a problem if wheelchair access ever becomes an issue. Of course, modifications can be made to make a house more suitable for seniors, such as installing grab bars and nonslip flooring in the bathroom and kitchen. Wall-to-wall carpeting also reduces the risk of slipping, and handrails for all steps and stairways make them less hazardous.

Home maintenance costs are another factor to consider. Now that income has been reduced, holding on to the house may prove too expensive. Older Americans tend to own older homes, and these may require more maintenance. Statistics bear this out: Seniors pay a higher percentage of their income on housing, including maintenance and repair. (In 1995, the figure was 34 percent, compared to 27 percent for younger homeowners.) And even if the house is fully paid for—which is the situation for four out of every five senior homeowners—there are still property taxes and insurance to pay.

Deciding to Move

To Buy or Rent?

A fundamental decision to make is whether to rent or buy. After many years of owning their own home and enjoying the freedom that goes with it, many seniors may be reluctant to go back to renting. But there are advantages to such an arrangement. Renting affords more flexibility; tenants are bound only by the terms of their lease, which usually run for periods of one to two years. So if a retired couple does decide to move again, the move would be easier than if they owned a home they had to sell. Another advantage of renting is that no down payment is needed (only a security deposit—usually a month's rent), and taxes, insurance, and repairs are not the responsibility of the tenant. This can relieve a retiree of some major housing-related expenses.

On the other hand, a renter does not receive the long-term financial advantages of home ownership, and also takes a chance on whether the landlord is prompt and fair-minded in attending to any problems that may arise. Another possible disadvantage is that in many rentals pets are not allowed.

A Smaller House

If a retired couple does decide to move, and they still want and are able to maintain an independent lifestyle, they have many choices. They could move to a smaller house in the same town or the same state. In 1997, 81 percent of the seniors who had moved to another home in the previous year moved within the same state. The advantage of trading down to a smaller property is that living costs—insurance, property taxes, and maintenance—will be lower. Then the remainder of the proceeds from the sale of the original home can be invested.

Condominiums and Apartments

Another option is to move to a condominium, which is a single unit, either a smaller house or an apartment, in a multiunit development. In addition to the price of the unit itself, condominiums charge a monthly fee for the maintenance of common areas such as grounds, parking lot, lobbies, and any recreational facilities such as swimming pool or health club. Buying a condo gives the owner the tax advantages of ownership without the worries of upkeep and yard work. The availability of condos varies widely from state to state, with 37 percent of all developments in Florida and California.

Mobile Homes

Mobile homes, also known as manufactured housing, are popular with retirees, accounting for over one-third of sales. (The term *mobile home* is a misnomer, since less than 3 percent of them ever get moved.) Like condos, mobile homes are numerous in Sun Belt states such as California, Florida, and Texas. They are the cheapest form of housing available, but they are also smaller than the average house.

Although manufactured housing may be a sound choice for those on a limited budget, the disadvantage is that such homes tend to depreciate in value in most parts of the country.

Moving in with Relatives

Often seniors think about moving in with relatives, usually adult children. A blended household may not be for everyone, so all parties are advised to discuss candidly whether such an arrangement will work and what each person expects from it. Of course, every family's expectations are unique, and families differ widely in how well they express and communicate those expectations. The situation calls for tact and diplomacy, along with an open, honest expression of real feelings.

All aspects of the new living arrangement should be considered thoroughly before a decision is made. What part of the house will the parent occupy (room, basement apartment, etc.)? How separate or integrated will he or she be in the life of the household? How much privacy is expected on both sides?

Living expenses must also be discussed. Will rent be charged? If not, can the family afford the extra expense? Will the parent be expected to help with any chores? Is the son or daughter prepared for extra work around the house? If the parent will be alone for long periods during the day, is adult day care available? If health problems are an issue, is it possible to have a visiting nurse?

People live in so many different ways that lifestyle considerations are important, too. Is the lifestyle of the parent compatible with that of the child and his or her family? Does everyone eat the same kinds of food? Does everyone keep similar hours? Is the parent sociable to the same degree as the family? How much time do parent and child expect to spend together? Are those expectations compatible or likely to cause friction? Are there grandchildren living at the house, and if so, does the grandparent

Homesharing: A Cooperative Approach to Better Living

Another housing option that may suit many seniors is homesharing, which falls into two categories. In the first, sometimes known as a matchup, two unrelated adults share a house or apartment. In the second, known as shared living residences (SLRs), several older unrelated individuals live under the same roof.

The majority of those who opt for shared housing are elderly women, who are more likely than men to find themselves living alone in difficult financial circumstances. Shared housing arrangements have many advantages. Let's suppose that a recently widowed woman is now living alone in a large house that is mostly unoccupied and too expensive for her to maintain. But she doesn't wish to sell her house. Her problem may be solved if she is able to work out a shared living arrangement with another senior for whom a move is necessary. The widow will thus be able to remain in her own home and at the same time gain companionship and security. Her tenant will also find what she may have been desperately seeking, since there is a national shortage of affordable rental housing for people on a low income.

In homesharing, the house is usually divided up so that each person has a private bedroom, while other parts of the house are used in common. Homesharers work out their own agreements regarding finances and the division of household responsibilities.

In many homeshares, the tenant pays a monthly rent; in others the rent may be waived or reduced because the tenant agrees to provide services, such as housekeeping or grocery shopping. One possible arrangement is for a person who has difficulty performing some daily tasks to link up with someone who is able and willing to help that person. In exchange, the helper might receive free room and board plus a modest stipend. One possible disadvantage of the latter arrangement is that if the tenant is receiving government Supplemental Security Income (SSI), she may lose up to one-third of the monthly benefits. This is because reduced rent or food in a shared housing arrangement is considered income. If you're in this situation, check with your local Social Security office for advice.

Another government benefit that might be affected is food stamps, since the entire monthly income of the household is considered for eligibility. For more advice on this, contact your local Department of Public Social Services.

The other important fact to keep in mind is that one of the partners owns the house, so in a sense it is not an equal partnership. The tenant may, if the owner sells the house, lose her home.

Selecting a Roommate

Selecting someone with whom to share a home obviously takes careful thought. It's something that many people may not have done since their college days, and it may not be suitable for everyone. Some seniors may fear that it will reduce their independence, or they may be unwilling to share their living quarters with someone who may at first be a stranger. Some self-assessment here may be useful. Recognizing that there are pros and cons to almost every situation, the potential homesharer might ask herself these questions:

- In what ways would homesharing improve my living situation, and in what ways might it worsen it?
- Am I willing to adjust and compromise?
- Would I be able to bring problems into the open for calm discussion?
- Am I likely to be too assertive or too passive in such a situation?

Homeowners who do decide to share their home fall into two main categories. First, there are those who do it primarily as a business arrangement. They need the extra income that a tenant will provide, but they don't wish to socialize much. Some houses by their layout may be more suited to this type of self-contained arrangement than others, but in any case this type of homesharer would need to find a tenant who also desires a somewhat distant arrangement.

Others may decide to share their home as much for friendship and companionship as financial gain. In that case, the two people might wish to spend a little time together first to see if their lifestyles and personalities mesh well. Factors such as diet and allergies might be discussed, and a frank exchange about what each person hopes to gain from the arrangement would also be advisable.

Homesharers should have a written agreement on how their arrangement may be terminated if it does not prove satisfactory. A trial period should also be set for a specified number of weeks or months. After all, even if the homesharers discuss the matter extensively beforehand, it may not be possible to predict exactly how things are going to work out in practice. The end of the trial period would be an ideal opportunity to discuss how successful the arrangement has been and make any necessary adjustments. Some homesharers may also like to have a written agreement that specifies the duties and responsibilities on each side.

Shared Living Residences

Most shared living residences (SLRs) are converted from existing, privately owned housing. Some may be run by individuals, but most authorities will require the home to be run by a corporation, either a for-profit organization or a nonprofit organization affiliated with a church or temple or other institution. Nonprofits are the most common. Certain states may limit the numbers of units allowable as an SLR.

A few receive some federal subsidies, but for the large majority, costs are covered by monthly rental fees charged to residents. In almost all cases, there is an additional monthly fee for services such as food, shopping, and so on. However, residents must be independent and able to cook for themselves. Details vary widely from one SLR to the next. One great advantage in a shared residence is that everyone is equal, since none of the residents is the owner, so there is no fear of losing the home.

How to Get Information

There are about 300 programs around the country that help seniors find shared living accommodations. The National Shared Housing Resources Center (NSHRC) coordinates such programs in more than 200 communities. Their address is 5342 Tilly Mill Road, Dunwoody, GA 30338, (770) 395-2625. The American Association of Retired Persons (AAPRP) offers a number of free publications about homesharing.

Even if no homesharing program exists in your area, it may still be possible to arrange one. You might know someone suitable yourself, or you could inquire at churches, synagogues, social clubs, and senior centers, or with neighbors and relatives, to find out if anyone living locally might be interested in such an arrangement.

According to a study at the University of Kansas, 90 percent of homesharers said their lives improved after finding a roommate. There are frequent reports of people who start out with a tenant and quickly find a close friend. "My new housemate is just like a ray of sunshine," said one homesharer who found her new friend through ElderHelp of San Diego, a nonprofit social service agency. "My family no longer has to worry about me," said another client of the same agency.

get along with them? (Some grandparents have secret, or not so secret, beliefs that kids are noisy and ill-disciplined.) How will the proposed new living arrangement affect relationships among all family members?

The answers to these questions can be determined only by the family members themselves. Relationships within a family are developed over a long period of time, and each family dynamic is unique. Only the people affected can decide whether such an arrangement is going to work. Open discussion is the best way to ensure that a blended household will be a rewarding rather than a burdensome experience for everyone.

Community Living: Options for Everyone

Retirement Resort Communities

Although most retirees opt for familiarity, some may wish to join the 500,000 each year who decide to move out of their home state. Many of these adventurous folks head for traditional retirement havens in the Sun Belt: Arizona, California, Florida, Georgia, Nevada, New Mexico, North Carolina, South Carolina, and Texas. But more recently, other locations are becoming increasingly popular for retirees, including Oregon and Washington in the Pacific Northwest, northern New England, and the Rocky Mountains. Many of these migrating seniors decide to live in resort retirement communities, housing complexes that attempt to capture a resort atmosphere. The emphasis is on leisure and the enjoyment of the golden years. Such communities offer a wide range of activities, including sports, arts and crafts, and a lively social program featuring parties, fine dining, and dancing.

Some resort communities are large. Sun City in Arizona has a population of approximately 50,000, and it is not unusual for populations to number up to 20,000 people. But this does not mean that such communities have to be sprawling and impersonal. One large, well-established retirement community in central Florida, with 17,000 residents, is designed so that different village neighborhoods cluster around a central town square, thereby creating small communities within a larger community. To get an idea of what such a facility is likely to offer its residents, consider some of the amenities this community provides: The town square contains a theater, a hotel, and 16 restaurants, as well as banks, grocery stores, and other essential retail establishments and services. There are numerous fishing lakes, golf courses—professional instruction is available—tennis courts, heated swimming pools, a couple of polo fields, and a number of recreational centers. For indoor activities, residents can choose from over 200 clubs, numerous classes, and a variety of concerts and dances. About 300 different events are scheduled every week. Like many resort communities, this is the sort of place where, if a person wanted to get bored and lonely, he or she would have to work hard at it.

Most people who move into communities like these are in their 60s. They tend to be in good health and are active and sociable. Many have been successful professionals and have adequate financial resources. They feel that after working all their lives, they've earned the right to relax and enjoy themselves in a congenial atmosphere with others who share the same outlook. Such communities, with their summer camp atmosphere, will not suit everyone. If a person values solitary pursuits and tends to keep herself to herself, she might prefer another housing option. Some seniors prefer to mingle with people of all ages, not just those over a certain age. But for those who make friends easily and like to participate in group activities, such communities may be ideal.

In planning a move to a resort retirement community, one of the first things to consider is location. Many people choose a retirement community because it is close to family and friends (perhaps friends already live there), or close to places they plan to visit on a regular basis. Others make it a priority to be within easy driving distance of a large city. If cultural events, spectator sports, shopping expeditions, or other city activities are high on your list, you will probably want to get out the map and check for the nearest interstate.

Another major factor in determining where you are going to move is climate. If you have spent most of your winters shoveling snow and scraping ice off windshields, the glorious Sun Belt may beckon in your retirement dreams. Almost everyone prefers pleasant, warm, sunny weather, but are you certain that you would want it all year round? Many people like to experience all four seasons; a dose of winter can often be invigorating. However, it is a fact that as humans age, they are more comfortable in climates that do not veer between extremes. Sudden temperature changes can put stress on the physiology.

You may also want to consider humidity rates. High humidity, even at moderate temperatures, can make for unpleasant conditions and can determine the amount of rainfall and the frequency of cloudy or foggy days. Investigate whether the area is at risk for natural disasters such as earthquakes, tornadoes, hurricanes, or violent thunderstorms. (Florida has three times as many thunderstorms as any other state; California, Oregon, and Washington record the lowest number of thunderstorms.)

Many retirees become seasonal migrants, which introduces yet another factor into the climate question. If you are a "snowbird" who escapes the cold midwestern winters for, say, Arizona, you will not need to worry about whether the arid, dry heat of an Arizona summer is going to be to your liking. Similarly, those who flee Florida's hot summers for the more temperate zones of New England may have the best of both worlds.

Cost of living is another significant issue. Just as everyone enjoys warm weather, everyone likes low taxes. Some states, such as Florida, Nevada, Texas, Washington, and Wyoming, have no state income tax. But often states may make up for this with a higher sales tax. Property taxes also vary from state to state, as do housing prices. Since housing costs and taxes make up 80 percent of the difference in the cost of living from one place to another in the United States, do careful homework on these matters.

Security concerns are high on an older person's lists of priorities. Relevant questions include: What is the crime rate in the area? What type of crime is prevalent? Property crime, violent crime, or both? David Savageau, in his book *Retirement Places Rated*, rates over 180 retirement destinations for personal safety and points out that the Sun Belt tends to have a higher crime rate than other places. Florida fares worst for both violent crime and property crime. In fact, 8 of the 12 lowest-ranked cities for safety are in Florida.

The issue of personal safety may be much less worrying within a retirement community than outside it. Many communities are now gated, with access restricted to a single entrance that is guarded 24 hours a day. In high-crime areas, some retirement communities are completely enclosed by a wall or secure fence, with a guarded entrance that employs elaborate security, including closed circuit television. Even with these provisions, it would be wise to make inquiries about recent crime statistics (remembering that crime can come from within as well as from without) and make your own assessments. Are homes designed with a limited number of entrances? Are all entryways clearly visible, day and night? Are all locks on doors and windows secure?

In addition to general information about the area, prospective residents will want to find out everything they can about the resort community itself.

Most resort retirement communities offer a wide variety of housing options for independent living. Usually people buy their homes, but in some communities rentals are also available. If you plan to buy, you should assess the future salability of your house. Most people eventually move out of resort communities, and a house that is difficult to sell can be a millstone around the owner's neck. Try to find out if there is much development still going on in your community or in the neighboring area. If your house is soon to be surrounded by many newer ones, or if a neighboring community in development will boast more attractive amenities, the resale price of your own house may fall. Also, look into whether the developer places an age-related restriction on resale houses; this will reduce the potential market for your house.

It also pays to do some research into the financial stability of the developer. If he were to go bankrupt, for example, it is possible that the common areas in the community, such as golf courses and other amenities, as well as unsold houses, would pass to creditors who might sell to a buyer with very different plans for the future of the community.

As with all things, it pays to know exactly what you are buying. Resort retirement communities typically provide services, such as the maintenance of the grounds and access to recreational facilities, in exchange for a monthly fee. Make sure you know what this fee includes. Are there extra fees to use the golf course, for example? Also, check into any "escalator clauses" that allow fees to increase. Ask how any decision to increase fees is made.

One final thing to remember before making your decision—resort retirement communities offer no specialized medical care. They are designed for those who choose to live independently within a communal setting. There are rarely any facilities for assisted living, nor do such communities cater to those who need skilled nursing care. If a resident's health deteriorates and he begins to need some help with daily tasks, he will need to move out of the resort community and find alternate housing.

University-Based Retirement Communities

A growing trend during the 1990s was the establishment of retirement communities centered around colleges and universities. This phenomenon recognizes the fact that intellectual and cultural stimulation—the concept of lifelong learning—are vital elements in a person's life, especially during retirement years.

Some college towns are now earning a reputation as a mecca for retirees. A number of academic institutions, including Iowa State University, Cornell University, and Dartmouth College, have already constructed retirement facilities close to campus. Residents have access to university and university-based activities, often with no fees. Retirees who live there say the connection to the university makes life more interesting and challenging.

There are two continuing care retirement communities in Palo Alto, California, near Stanford University. At The Forest at Duke University, North Carolina, retirees can take advantage of programs not only at Duke but also at North Carolina Central University in Durham, the University of North Carolina at Chapel Hill, and North Carolina State University in Raleigh. Other universities are in the process of developing similar communities. These include the University of Michigan at Ann Arbor, and Samford University in Birmingham,

Alabama. At State College, Pennsylvania, Penn State will open a 160-acre site for people over 55 in 2002, which will include a continuing care facility. For more information about the Village at Penn State you can call (800) 238-3173.

As Leon A. Pastalan and Benyamin Schwarz state in their book *University-Linked Retirement Communities*, "Such a milieu can provide a rich and varied context for older people to be exposed to new ideas and learning, for personal growth and to discover new approaches to a meaningful life." These communities are also favored by those who do not wish to live in an age-segregated environment. Interaction between young and old in classes and other activities benefits both seniors and students, breaking down negative stereotypes on both sides.

Naturally Occurring Retirement Communities (NORCs)

The term *naturally occurring retirement communities* (NORCs) usually refers to urban apartment complexes where occupancy has remained stable over time, producing a community of residents who are growing old together. The complex may also house younger residents, but word of mouth attracts more and more retirees to these places as time passes.

NORCS can be found in many American cities; they tend to evolve spontaneously, and it is estimated that more than 1 million seniors call this type of housing home. Some examples include the Cleveland Park section in Washington, D.C.; Capitol Hill in Denver; Squirrel Hill and Shadyside in Pittsburgh; and Penn South Cooperative in New York. The term can also be used to describe any neighborhood—urban, suburban, or rural—where a majority of the population is elderly.

NORCs tend to acquire a reputation for safety and convenience to the amenities of city life. Frequently, landlords encourage the emergence of NORCs since older tenants are often perceived as highly reliable and less likely to cause excessive wear and tear on the building.

Another advantage for some is that NORCs are not considered retirement communities by the people who live there—just pleasant and enjoyable places to live. For a person who is not "clubby" and prefers to enjoy the sights and sounds of city life in an independent way, a NORC might be preferable to a more community-based living environment. And yet in an NORC, such independent-minded people also have the reassurance of knowing that when they want company of their own age, they can usually find it easily enough within the same building.

Although NORCs are for those who can live independently, some complexes will offer a limited range of services, such as the use of a van for doctor visits or other expeditions, or a room for social activities.

How do you find an NORC? Since they tend to be somewhat hidden—a NORC may not necessarily identify itself as such and there will be no listing of NORCs in the Yellow Pages—the best chance of locating one is to ask around among those in the know. Real estate agents are a good place to start, and cab companies and cab drivers can provide good leads.

Assisted Living Facilities (ALFs)

Let's assume that an elderly person living alone is finding that meal preparation and housekeeping have become burdensome. Maybe he or she just does not want the responsibility anymore after all those years. Or perhaps a person with severe arthritis cannot move around well or perform tasks with her hands that require fine motor skills, such as buttoning clothes. What if an elderly lady suffers from memory loss and sometimes forgets to switch the stove off after cooking, or is confused about whether she has paid her bills.

Such people may be able to manage adequately in most daily activities, but need assistance with some tasks. In these cases, independent living is no longer a viable option.

Some families decide to arrange for their senior to receive home help for specific tasks, and this may be an adequate solution. But home help, because it usually involves employing a number of different individuals, also requires a certain amount of organization and management. Then there are those days when a helper is unable to show up. Unless home help is supplemented with care from other family members, it does not solve the problems of isolation and loneliness that can hit a senior living alone in declining health.

Assisted living facilities (ALF) are designed to meet the needs of seniors who need help with some daily activities, such as eating, bathing, dressing, going to the toilet, walking, transferring (from bed to chair, etc.), grooming, money management, and transportation. ALFs try to preserve as much independence as possible for the resident, and offer a style of living that bridges the gap between independent living and continuous care in a nursing home.

Assisted living facilities are also known under a number of different names: board and care facilities, sheltered facilities, adult residential care homes, personal care homes, and enriched or enhanced housing. All facilities tend to be fairly small, usually with no more than 125 residents. Residents are usually local people who may even have known each other before they moved into the facility, and many may have relatives living in the area.

Over 1 million U.S. senior citizens live in assisted living facilities, and the number is growing. The average age of residents is middle-to-late 80s. Seniors tend to prefer ALFs to nursing homes because they provide more independence. They are also less expensive. The average monthly fee for an ALF is $2,600 to $3,300. Sixty-five percent of the fee covers services, including help with daily activities; 35 percent is for housing.

Facilities consist of rented apartments with kitchens and private or semiprivate rooms. In most assisted living facilities, all units are equipped with emergency call buttons. Services include three meals a day in a common dining room, personal care tailored to the needs of the individual, laundry service, escort service for doctors' appointments, and excursions to senior day care centers or to other recreational and social facilities in the wider community. Many ALFs go to considerable effort to maintain these links between their residents and the "outside" community, because such activities help older people maintain a sense of involvement with others, essential to the belief that their lives still matter.

Assisted living facilities also offer their own full program of residential activities designed to help seniors maintain good physical, mental, and emotional health. These include opportunities for socializing, such as coffee mornings, parties, dancing, or other community events. If the senior has experienced loneliness in recent years of living independently, a good residential facility is likely to banish such feelings quickly. ALF staff understand that when such social programs are well-planned and successful, residents generally need less custodial care. ALFs do not supervise medication and are not responsible for administering it. However, the staff are aware of what medications residents are taking and will encourage them to comply with their doctors' recommendations. Many ALFs have nurses on staff or available on call should a resident require special care, and many also arrange for a physician to visit the facility on a regular basis to provide medical checkups.

Mississippi

http://www.state.ms.us

General Information

Climate

Mild climate; average annual temperature of 63°F. January average low is 50° F; summer highs are in the mid-90s° F.

Cost of Living

Ranks 50th in the nation

Taxes

General: Adults age 60+ can participate in the Magnolia State Golden Age Discount Program. Through the program, seniors can purchase goods and services from participating merchants at reduced prices (about 15% below regular price). Contact Division of Aging and Adult Services, (601) 3559-4929 or (800) 948-3090.

State/Local as % of Income: 10.0%

Property Tax Reduction: Persons age 65+ are exempt from property taxes if their homes are assessed at $60,000 or less. Seniors with homes valued at $60,000+ pay taxes only on the amount above $60,000 through homestead exemption.

Sales: 7%.

Prescription Exemptions: Prescription medication is exempt from sales tax.

Transportation, Travel, and Tourism

General

Mississippi Department of Tourism, PO Box 849, Jackson, MS 39205, (601) 359-3297 or (800) WARMEST

Major Airports

- Natchez–Adams County Airport, 434 Airport Rd., Natchez, MS 39120-8943, (601) 442-5171.
- Gulfport-Biloxi Regional Airport, 14035 Airport Rd., Gulfport, MS 39503-4617, (228) 863-5951.
- Vicksburg Airport, 5855 Highway 61 S., Vicksburg, MS 39180-9359, (601) 636-4925.

Railways

- Amtrak, (800) 872-7245.

Bus Tours

- Greyhound Bus, (800) 231-2222.
- Hotard Coaches, Inc., (601) 436-0200 or (800) 565-8913 (motorcoaches and minibuses).
- Magnolia Tours and Transportation, (601) 374-7423 or (800) 642-4684 (airport transfers and sightseeing tours of the Gulf coast).

State Highways

- Interstates 20 and 10 run east-west.
- Interstate 55 runs north-south.

Theater and Music

North

- Oxford Center for the Study of Southern Culture, University of Mississippi, (601) 232-5993 (research center for southern music, folklore, and literature).
- University of Mississippi Blues Archives, Oxford, (601) 232-7753 (extensive collection of blues recordings).

East

- Grand Opera House of Mississippi, 2206 Fifth St., Meridian, MS 39302, (601) 693-5239.
- Temple Theatre, PO Box 365, Meridian, MS 39302, (601) 693-1361.

Museums, Crafts, Historical, Recreational

North

- Rowan Oak, Box 673, Oxford, MS 38655, (601) 234-4651 (home of William Faulkner).
- University of Mississippi, Oxford, (662) 915-7175, (changing exhibits; Greek and Roman antiquities).

East

- Elvis Presley Birthplace, 306 Elvis Presley Drive, Tupelo, MS 38802, (601) 841-1245.
- Tupelo Artist Guild Gallery, 211 W. Main St., Tupelo, MS 38801, (601) 844-ARTS.
- The Tupelo Museum, PO Box 1485, Tupelo, MS 38802, (800) 533-0611 or (601) 841-6438.
- Columbus Historic Homes, 402 Second Ave. North, Columbus, MS 39701, (800) 327-2686 or (601) 329-1191 (antebellum homes).
- Riverboat Julie, Columbus, MS 39701, (601) 327-2268 (sightseeing and dinner cruises; seasonal).
- Meridian Museum of Art, 628 25th St., Meridian, MS 39302, (601) 693-1501.

South

- Beauvoir Jefferson Davis Shrine, 2244 Beach Blvd., Biloxi, MS 39531, (601) 388-9074 (home of Jefferson Davis).
- Gulf Coast Aquatic Tours, 27 Joanna Lane, Gulfport, MS 39503-3836, (800) 675-9510 or (601) 832-6895 (sightseeing and shrimping tours).

West

- Greenville Writers Exhibit, 915 Washington Ave., Greenville, MS 38701, (601) 378-3141.
- Vicksburg National Military Park, 3201 Clay St., Vicksburg, MS 39180, (601) 636-0583 (1,800 acre Civil War battlefield).

Central

- Cottonlandia Museum, Highway 82 West, Greenwood, MS 38930, (601) 453-0925 (history of the Delta region).
- Florewood River Plantation State Park, Greenwood, MS 38930, (601) 455-3821 (replica of an Old South plantation).
- F. D. Hall Art Gallery, Jackson State University, Jackson, MS 39217, (601) 968-2040.
- Mississippi Museum of Art, 210 E. Pascagoula St, Jackson, MS 39201, (601) 960-1515.
- Russell C. Davis Planetarium/ Ronald McNaire Space Theater, 201 E. Pascagoula St., Jackson, MS 39201, (601) 960-1550.

Organizations

Advocacy Groups

- Mississippi Department of Human Services, (800) 346-6347.
- Division of Aging and Adult Services, 750 N. State St., Jackson, MS 39202, (601) 359-4929 or (800) 948-3090.

Volunteer Programs

- Contact the Division of Aging and Adult Services for volunteer information, 750 N. State St., Jackson, MS 39202, (601) 359-4929 or (800) 948-3090.

Housing

Long-Term Care Facilities

*In the state of Mississippi, these facilities are called **Long-Term Care/Skilled Nursing Care Facilities**.*

These facilities provide residential living and/or various levels of nursing and medical services to seniors for an extended period of time.

Types of Authorization

Licensing and / or Certification

Health care facilities are licensed and certified by the Department of Health, Division of Health Care Facilities. Skilled nursing care facilities provide facilities and health services to residents who require medical care and 24-hour nursing services.

Memberships:

- American Association of Homes and Services for the Aging (AAHSA) represents not-for-profit organizations committed to providing high-quality health care, housing, and services to the elderly. AAHSA, 901 E St. NW, Suite 500, Washington, DC 20004-2011. Ph: (202) 783-2242. Fax: (202) 783-2285. *http://www.aahsa.org*
- Mississippi Association of Homes and Services for the Aging (MAHSA) is an AAHSA Affiliated State Association. MAHSA, c/o Naval Home, 1800 Beach Drive, Gulfport, MS 39507-1597. Ph: (228) 896-3110. Fax: (228) 897-4013.

Accreditation:

- Continuing Care Accreditation Commission (CCAC) accredits facilities that offer seniors a contract or contracts that provide residential living and health care services for the remainder of the person's lifetime and meet CCAC's accreditation standards.
- Joint Commission on the Accreditation of Healthcare Organizations (JCAHO) is an independent, not-for-profit organization, and the nation's oldest and largest standards-setting and health care accrediting institution.
- Educational Assessment Guidelines Leading toward Excellence (EAGLE) is a voluntary self-assessment and peer review evaluation system developed by the United Methodist Association of Health and Welfare Ministries.

Northeast

Dungan Memorial Home, EAGLE

804 E. Main St.
West Point, MS 39773

Ph: (601) 494-3640
Fax: (601) 494-3641

http://www.umssm.org

NH: 60

Age 62+. Nonprofit; United Methodist Church affiliation. Private and semiprivate rooms. 24-hour nursing care; medical services; rehabilitative therapies; pharmacy services; Medicare-approved; personal care; medication administration; security; emergency response system; maintenance; transportation; 3 daily meals; housekeeping and laundry services; religious services; social and recreational activities.

NH Daily: Semiprivate, $75; private, $85–$90.

Traceway Retirement Community, EAGLE

2800 W. Main St.
Tupelo, MS 38801

Ph: (601) 844-1441
Fax: (601) 840-3802

http://www.umssm.org

IND: Yes. PC: Yes. HCC: Yes

Age 62+. Nondenominational; owned by the United Methodist Senior Services of Mississippi. Cottages, homes, apartments, and private and semiprivate rooms. Skilled nursing care; 24-hour staffing; rehabilitative therapies; dental and podiatry care; medical services; social services; personal care; medication administration; security; emergency response system; maintenance; transportation; up to 3 daily meals; housekeeping and laundry services; exercise classes; worship services; Bible study; postal and banking services; library; crafts and ceramics; social and recreational activities; on- and off-site activities; fishing; walking paths; barber/beauty shop.

RLUF: $55,000–$66,000. IND MO: $575–$825. AL MO: $1,450–$2,050.

Southeast

Dunbar Village

725 Dunbar Ave.
Bay Saint Louis, MS 39520

Ph: (228) 466-3099
Fax: (601) 466-3994

IND: Yes. PC: Yes. HCC: Yes

Nondenominational. Private and semiprivate rooms. 24-hour nursing care; physician services; physical, occupational, and speech therapies; respite services; pharmacy services; Medicare-approved; personal care; medication administration; security; emergency response system; maintenance; transportation; up to 3 daily meals plus snacks; housekeeping and laundry services; exercise program; social and recreational activities; barber/beauty shop.

IND MO: $950–$1,500. AL MO: $1,550–$2,000. RSP Daily: $70.

Assisted Living and Residential Care Facilities

*In the state of Mississippi, these facilities are called **Assisted Living/Personal Care Facilities**.*

These facilities provide room and board for ambulatory and independent adults who need minimum support.

Types of Authorization

Licensing and/or Certification

Personal care facilities are licensed and certified by the Department of Health, Division of Health Care Facilities. A personal care home provides residential accommodations, personal service, and social care to residents who need protective living accommodations but do not require medical or 24-hour nursing care.

Memberships

- Assisted Living Federation of America (ALFA) is a national nonprofit membership organization whose mission is to enhance the quality of life in assisted living facilities and promote the interests of the assisted living industry. ALFA, 10300 Eaton Place, Suite 400, Fairfax, VA 22030. Ph: (703) 691-8100. Fax: (703) 691-8106. *http://www.alfa.org*

Northeast

The Arrington at Plantation Pointe

234 Windsor Blvd.
Columbus, MS 39702

Ph: (601) 241-0001

AL/PC: Yes. ALZ/MEM IMP: Yes

Nondenominational. Suites and apartments. Respite care; personal care; medication administration; security; emergency response system; maintenance; transportation; 3 daily meals; housekeeping and laundry services;

social and recreational activities; services director; sitting areas; courtyard; barber/beauty shop.

RSV: (ref.) $300. DEP: $800. AL/PC MO: $1,450–$2,650; 2nd person, $880. Specialized services, $220–$330.

Chriswood Assisted Living

PO Box 542
Booneville, MS 38829

Ph: (601) 720-1121

AL: Yes

Nondenominational. Apartments. Personal care; medication administration; security; emergency response system; maintenance; transportation; up to 3 daily meals; housekeeping and laundry services; mail delivery; planned activities; off-site activities; lobby; patios; walking paths.

Contact facility for fees.

North Central

Azalea Gardens

100 Azalea Drive
Oxford, MS 38655

Ph: (601) 234-9600

IND: 62. AL: 18. ADC: Yes

Age 55+. For-profit; nondenominational. Apartments, villas, and cottages. Home health care; wellness program; personal care; medication administration; security; emergency response system; maintenance; transportation; up to 3 daily meals; pets allowed; housekeeping and laundry services; exercise room; chapel; library; game room; arts and crafts; on- and off-site activities; educational and cultural programs; barber/beauty shop.

DEP: (partial ref.) $1,100. IND MO: $1,050–$2,550. AL MO: $1,725–$2,200.

Fairfield

21 Rosemont Drive
Grenada, MS 38901

Ph: (601) 226-3363 or (800) 695-2331
Fax: (601) 226-0546

AL: 36. ADC: Yes

For-profit; nondenominational. Nursing care; LPN on-site daily; health monitoring; respite care; personal care; medication administration; security; emergency response system; maintenance; transportation; up to 3 daily meals; housekeeping and laundry services; library; activities; barber/beauty shop.

DEP: $300. AL MO: $1,725–$3,300.

East Central

Aldersgate Retirement Community, EAGLE

6600 Poplar Springs Drive
Meridian, MS 39305

Ph: (601) 482-5561
Fax: (601) 482-5567

http://www.umssm.org

IND: 120. AL: 54

Age 62+. Nonprofit; United Methodist Church affiliation. Apartments. Pharmacy delivery; personal care; medication administration; security; emergency response system; maintenance; transportation; up to 3 daily meals; pets allowed; housekeeping and laundry services; fitness center; religious services; social and recreational activities; gazebo; gardens; walking paths; barber/beauty shop.

DEP: $100. IND MO: $900–$1,200. AL MO: $1,625–$2,050.

Northwest

Flowers Manor Retirement Community, EAGLE

1251 Lee Drive
Clarksdale, MS 38614

Ph: (601) 627-2222

http://www.umssm.org

E-mail: *fmanor@clarksdale.com*

IND: 75. AL: 24

Age 62+. Nonprofit; United Methodist Church affiliation. Apartments. Personal care; medication administration; security; emergency response system; maintenance; transportation; up to 3 daily meals; housekeeping and laundry services; fitness center; pastoral care; social and recreational activities; shopping nearby.

DEP: $100–$300. IND MO: $660–$880. AL MO: $1,450–$1,550.

Wesley Meadows Retirement Community, EAGLE

1325 McIngvale Rd.
Hernando, MS 38632

Ph: (601) 429-2070
Fax: (601) 429-2496

http://www.umssm.org

IND: 80. AL: 24

Age 62+. Nonprofit; nondenominational; United Methodist Church affiliation. Apartments. Personal care; medication administration; emergency response system; maintenance; up to 3 daily meals; housekeeping and laundry services; religious services; social and recreational activities; barber/beauty shop.

DEP: $200. IND MO: $900–$1,400. AL MO: $1,750.

South

Methodist Retirement Community, EAGLE

1450 Beach Blvd.
Biloxi, MS 39530

Ph: (228) 435-3861
Fax: (228) 435-9957

http://www.umssm.org

IND: 189. AL: 50

Age 62+. Nonprofit; United Methodist Church affiliation. Efficiencies and apartments. Personal care; medication administration; security; emergency response system; maintenance; transportation; up to 3 daily meals; pets allowed; housekeeping and laundry services; religious services; social and recreational activities.

IND MO: $300–$500. AL services: $30.

Central

Riggs Manor Retirement Community, EAGLE

2300 Seven Springs Rd.
Raymond, MS 39154

Ph: (601) 857-5011
Fax: (601) 857-8131

http://www.umssm.org

E-mail: *Saraslat@aol.com*

IND: 80. AL: 24

Age 62+. Nonprofit; United Methodist Church affiliation. Apartments. Personal care; medication administration; emergency response system; maintenance; transportation; up to 3 daily meals; pets allowed; housekeeping and laundry services; religious services; social and recreational activities; two lakes; adjacent to golf course.

APPL: $500. DEP: $200. IND MO: $850–$1,375. AL MO: $1,850.

Independent Living

Independent housing (primarily rentals) for seniors that may offer security features, meal service, and activities.

Central

Magnolia Towers
809 N. State St.
Jackson, MS 39202

Ph: (601) 352-4952

IND: Yes

Studios and one- and two-bedroom apartments. Fitness center; activities; laundry facilities; convenience store; barber/beauty shop.

IND MO: $450–$600.

South Wind
260 Lowe Circle
Richland, MS 39218

Ph: (601) 664-1420

IND: Yes

Residential apartments. On-site maintenance and management; on-site courtesy officer; lake fishing.

IND MO: from $600.

East

Trinity Place Retirement Community
300 Airline Rd.
Columbus, MS 30702

Ph: (601) 327-6716
Fax: (601) 327-3039
http://www.umssm.org

IND: Yes

Nonprofit; nondenominational; United Methodist Senior Services of Mississippi. Apartments. Security; emergency response system; maintenance; transportation; meal plan; housekeeping and laundry services; exercise classes; religious services; Bible study; library; crafts; social and recreational activities; on- and off-site activities; barber/beauty shop.

IND MO: $725–$850; HUD-subsidized.

Northeast

Henry Clay Retirement Community, EAGLE
133 Commerce St.
West Point, MS 39773

Ph: (601) 494-1079
Fax: (601) 494-3978
http://www.umssm.org

IND: 27

Age 62+. Nonprofit; United Methodist Church affiliation. Apartments. Rehabilitative therapies; pharmacy services; security; emergency response system; maintenance; meal plan; housekeeping and laundry services; drugstore; coffee shop.

DEP: $200. IND MO: $350–$625.

Southeast

Saraland Manor Retirement Apartments
8010 Highway 49 North
Gulfport, MS 39501

Ph: (601) 863-7297

IND: 100

Age 62+. Nondenominational. One- and two-bedroom apartments. Security; emergency response system; maintenance; transportation; up to 3 daily meals; laundry services; religious services; educational, cultural, and social activities; lounge.

IND MO: 30% of income; HUD-subsidized.

Turner-Duvall Retirement Village, EAGLE

Highway 57 West
Leakesville, MS 39451

Ph: (601) 394-2621
Fax: (601) 394-4014

http://www.umssm.org

IND: 30

Age 62+. Nonprofit; United Methodist Church affiliation. Apartments. Emergency response system; maintenance; transportation; pets allowed.

IND MO: $575–$600.

Wesley Manor Retirement Community, EAGLE

PO Box 16298
Hattiesburg, MS 39404

Ph: (601) 264-8847
Fax: (601) 264-8976

http://www.umssm.org

IND: 100

Age 62+. Nonprofit; United Methodist Church affiliation. Apartments. Emergency response system; maintenance; transportation; meal plan; pets allowed; housekeeping services; located near medical facilities; beauty shop.

DEP: $300. IND MO: $950–$1,250. Some units HUD-subsidized.

Adult/Resort Communities

Communities for active adults (not all are age-restricted; primarily ownership).

North

Cherokee Valley

6635 Crumpler Blvd.
Olive Branch, MS 38654

Ph: (601) 893-4444

http://www.cherokeedevelopment.com

Individual homes, homesites. Golf course; pro shop; clubhouse.

PURCHASE: Homes, from $180,500.

Plantation Golf Club

9425 Plantation Rd.
Olive Branch, MS 38654

Ph: (601) 895-3530

Individual homes. Golf course; golf clubhouse; pro shop; community clubhouse; tennis; swimming pool.

PURCHASE: Homes, from $198,000.

Central

Old Waverly Golf Club

One Magnolia Drive
West Point, MS 39773

Ph: (601) 494-6463

Individual homes, condominiums, homesites. Golf course; clubhouse; pro shop; tennis; swimming pool; fishing; fitness center; dining.

PURCHASE: Homes, $220,000–$550,000.

Yoda Creek Properties, Inc.

C.R. 259
Bruce, MS 38915

Ph: (601) 983-9632

http://www.yodacreek.com

Individual homes, homesites. Golf course; pro shop; clubhouse; swimming pool; hiking/walking trails.

PURCHASE: Homes, $132,000–$550,000; homesites, $12,000–$22,000.

South

St. Andrews Golf Club

2 Golfing Green Drive
Ocean Springs, MS 39564

Ph: (228) 875-7730

Individual homes, homesites. Golf course; pro shop; clubhouse; swimming pool; dining; social clubs.

PURCHASE: Homes, from $126,500; homesites, $20,000–$38,500.

Timberton Golf Club

22 Clubhouse Drive
Hattiesburg, MS 39401
Ph: (601) 584-4653
http://www.timberton-golf.com

Individual homes, homesites. Golf course; pro shop; clubhouse; dining; fishing; driving range.

PURCHASE: Homesites, $20,000–$54,000.

Missouri

http://www.state.mo.us

General Information

Climate

Moderate. Average temperature in St. Louis: January, 30° F; August, 78° F; Kansas City: January, 26° F; August, 76° F; average snowfall about 20 inches per year.

Cost of Living

Ranks 37th in the nation.

Taxes

State/Local as % of Income: 9.6%.

Property Tax Reduction: Senior citizens and disabled veterans may receive credit for property taxes paid, or a portion of rent, through a state program in which they receive credit on their income tax, or a check from the state if they owe no income tax. Call Department of Revenue, (573) 751-3505.

Sales: 4.225% state tax; communities and counties may levy additional sales taxes.

Prescription Exemptions: Prescription drugs, as well as most medical devices, are exempt from sales tax; as of August 1998, over-the-counter medication purchased by an individual with a disability is also exempt from sales tax.

Transportation, Travel, and Tourism

General

State of Missouri, Department of Economic Development, Division of Tourism, PO Box 1055, Jefferson City, MO 65102, (573) 751-4133.

Major Airports

- Kansas City International Airport, 601 Brasilia Ave., Kansas City, MO 64153, (816) 243-3000.
- Lambert–St. Louis International Airport, 10701 Natural Bridge Rd., St. Louis, MO 63145, (314) 890-1333 or (314) 426-8000.

Railway

- Amtrak, stations through the state, (800) USA-RAIL.

Bus Tours

- Greyhound Bus, 1101 Troost, Kansas City, MO 64106, (816) 221-2835 and stations throughout the state, (800) 231-2222.
- KC Executive Coaches, 522 Locust, Kansas City, MO 64106, (816) 471-6050.
- Mid-American Coaches, 4530 Hwy. 47, PO Box 335, Washington, MO 63090; Washington: (314) 239-4700, St. Louis: (314) 316-9504 or (800) 365-8687.

State Highways

- Interstate 44 runs northeast-southwest from St. Louis to Joplin.
- Interstate 55 runs north-south from St. Louis to Arkansas.
- Interstate 70 runs east-west from St. Louis to Kansas City.
- Interstate 35 runs northeast-southwest from Iowa to Kansas City.
- Interstate 29 runs northwest-southeast from Iowa to Kansas City.

Theater and Music

South

- Showboat Branson Belle (paddlewheel, shows), Hwy. 165, Branson, (417) 336-7400.
- Lake Queen on Lake Taneycomo (stern-wheeler, meals), Branson, (417) 334-3015.
- Andy Williams Moon River Theatre, 2500 W. Hwy. 76, Branson, MO 65616, (417) 334-4500.
- Bobby Vinton Blue Velvet Theatre, 2701 W. Hwy. 76, Branson, MO 65616, (417) 334-2500.
- The Grand Palace, 2700 W. Hwy. 76, Branson, MO 65616, (417) 339-5700.
- Jim Stafford Theatre, 3440 W. Hwy. 76, Branson, MO 65616, (417) 335-8080.
- Osmond Family Theatre, 3216 W. Hwy. 76, Branson, MO 65616, (417) 336-6100.
- Roy Clark Celebrity Theatre, 3425 W. Hwy. 76, Branson, MO 65616, (417) 334-0076.
- Shepherd of the Hills Outdoor Theater, 5586 W. Hwy. 76, Branson, MO 65616, (417) 334-4191.
- Wild West Theatre, 310 Gretna Rd., Branson, MO 65616, (417) 335-2738.

East

- The Muny (oldest and largest U.S. outdoor musical theatre), Forest Park, St. Louis, (314) 361-1900.
- American Theatre, 416 N. 9th St. at St. Charles St., St. Louis, MO 63101-1405, (314) 962-4000.
- St. Louis Black Repertory Company, 3610 Grandel Sq., St. Louis, MO 63108-3626, (314) 534-3807.
- Delta Queen, Mississippi Queen, American Queen (paddlewheelers), leave from St. Louis, (800) 543-1949.

West

- Pony Express Opry (Branson-style music show), 210 N. 4th St., St. Joseph, MO 64501-1719, (816) 232-0955.

Museums, Crafts, Historical, Recreational

South

- Laura Ingalls Museum and Home (where Little House books were written), Hwy. A, Mansfield, (417) 924-3626.
- Fantastic Caverns, Springfield, (417) 833-2010.
- Ozark National Scenic Riverways (canoeing, fishing, swimming, camping), PO Box 490, Van Buren, MO 63965, (314) 323-4236.
- Bill and Payne Stewart Municipal Golf Course (public), 1825 E. Norton Rd., Springfield, MO 65803, (314) 458-3060.
- Millwood Golf and Racquet Club (public), Rte. 2, Springfield, MO 65802, (314) 939-6494.

East

- Meramec Caverns, I-44, exit 230, Stanton, (800) 676-6105.
- Washington University Gallery of Art, Steinberg Hall, St. Louis, (314) 935-4523.
- Old Cathedral (basilica built 1834), 209 Walnut St., St. Louis, MO 63102-2499, (314) 231-3250.
- Ulysses S. Grant National Historic Site, 7400 Grant Rd., St. Louis, MO 63123-1801, (314) 842 3298.
- Holocaust Museum and Learning Center, 12 Millstone Campus Drive, St. Louis, MO 63146-5776, (314) 432-0020, ext. 711.
- Lewis and Clark Center (museum), 701 Riverside Dr., St. Charles, MO (314) 947-3199.
- Scott Joplin House (restored Joplin home), 2658 Delmar, St. Louis, MO (314) 533-1003.
- Missouri Botanical Garden, 344 Shaw Blvd., South St. Louis, MO 63110, (314) 577-9400 or (800) 642-8842.
- Saint Louis Art Museum (built for 1904 World's Fair), 1 Fine Arts Drive, St. Louis, MO 63110, (314) 721-0072.

- Saint Louis Zoo, 1 Government Drive, St. Louis, MO 63110, (314) 781-0900.
- Mark Twain Boyhood Home and Museum, 208 Hill St., Hannibal, MO 63401-3316, (573) 221-9010.
- Mark Twain Birthplace and Museum, Mark Twain Park, near Perry and Paris off Rt. 107, (573) 565-3449.
- Forest Park Golf Club (public), 5591 Grand Drive, St. Louis, MO 63112, (314) 938-4653.

West

- Harry S. Truman Library and Museum, Hwy. 24 & Delaware St., Independence, (816) 833-1400 or (816) 833-1225.
- Truman Home (tours), 223 N. Main St., Independence, MO 64050, (816) 254-7199.
- Missouri Town (original 1855 village, museum), Blue Springs, (816) 795-8200, ext. 260.
- Fort Osage (reconstructed 1808 fur-trade fort), Sibley, (816) 795-8200, ext. 260.
- Jesse James Birthplace and Museum, Jesse James Farm Drive, Kearney, MO 64060, (816) 628-6065.
- National Frontier Trails Center (center for Santa Fe, Oregon, and California trails), 318 W. Pacific, Independence, MO 64050-4372, (816) 325-7575.
- The Negro Leagues Baseball Museum, 1616 E. 18th, Kansas City, MO 64108.
- George Washington Carver National Monument (birthplace, museum), off Rt. V, Diamond, (417) 325-4151.
- Minor Park Golf Course (public), 11215 Holmes Rd., Kansas City, MO 64131, (816) 263-1774.

Central

- Museum of Art and Archaeology, University of Missouri, 9th & University, Columbia, (573) 882-3591.
- Kumberland Gap Pioneer Settlement (re-created village, shop), N on Rte. TT, Warsaw, (816) 547-3899.
- Lake of the Woods Golf Course (public), 6700 E. Saint Charles Rd., Columbia, MO 65202, (314) 346-7218.
- Trout Fishing Parks: Bennett Spring, Lebanon; Montauk, Licking; Roaring River, Cassville; operated by Missouri Department of Natural Resources, Division of State Parks, PO Box 176, Jefferson City, MO 65102, (800) 334-6946.

Organizations

Advocacy Groups

- Division on Aging, Department of Social Services, PO Box 1337, 615 Howerton Ct., Jefferson City, MO 65102, (573) 751-3082.
- Division of Aging, State Office of Long-Term Care Ombudsman, PO Box 1337, Jefferson City, MO 65102, (573) 751-3082, (573) 625-0727, or (800) 309-3282.
- The Eldercare Center (state licensed care), University of Missouri–Columbia, 137 Clark Hall, Columbia, MO 65211, (573) 882-7070.

Volunteer Programs

- Therapeutic Riding of the Ozarks (horseback therapy program), 627 N. Glenstone, Springfield, MO 65802, (417) 862-3586.
- TrailWatch (trail monitoring), (417) 864-2015.
- Audrain County Crisis Intervention Services, PO Box 181, Mexico, MO 65265, (573) 581-3835.

Housing

Long-Term Care Facilities

*In the state of Missouri, these facilities are called **Continuing Care/Long-Term Care, Nursing Care Communities**.*

These facilities provide residential living and/or various levels of nursing and medical services to seniors for an extended period of time.

Types of Authorizations

Licensing and / or Certification

Regulated by the Division of Aging, Institutional Services (Department of Social Services).

Memberships:

- American Association of Homes and Services for the Aging (AAHSA) represents not-for-profit organizations committed to providing high-quality health care, housing, and services to the elderly. AAHSA, 901 E St. NW, Suite 500, Washington, DC 20004-2011. Ph: (202) 783-2242. Fax: (202) 783-2285. *http: / / www.aahsa.org*
- Missouri Association of Homes for the Aging (MAHA) is a state affiliate of the AAHSA. MAHA, 308A Monroe St., Jefferson City, MO 65101-3106. Ph: (573) 635-6244. Fax: (573) 635-6618.
- American Health Care Association (AHCA).

North

John Knox Village East

1201 W. 19th St.
Higginsville, MO 64037

Ph: (660) 584-7111 or 584-4315

IND: Yes. AL: Yes. HCC: Yes

Nonprofit; nondenominational; managed by Life Care Services Corp. Studios, efficiencies, apartments, and private and semiprivate rooms. 24-hour nursing care; physician services; rehabilitative therapies; medical services; dental and podiatry care; pharmacy services; ambulance services; wellness programs; social services; personal care; medication administration; security; emergency response system; maintenance; transportation; up to 3 daily meals; housekeeping and laundry services; exercise programs; swimming pool; worship services; Bible study; library; social and recreational activities; convenience store; shuffleboard; quilting; walking paths; barber/beauty shop.

IND ENT: $48,500–$79,000; 2nd person, $11,000. IND MO: $500–$800; 2nd person, $525 and $150.

Southwest

Lawrence County Manor and Residential Care Center

915 Carl Allen Drive
PO Box 191
Mt. Vernon, MO 65712

Ph: (417) 466-2183
Fax: (417) 466-3003

RC: 30. SNF: 90

Nondenominational. Apartments and private and semiprivate rooms. 24-hour nursing care; medical director; 24-hour certified medical technician; physical, occupational, and speech therapies; dental, podiatry, and eye care; Medicaid-approved; personal care; medication administration; security; emergency response system; maintenance; transportation; up to 3 daily meals; housekeeping and laundry services; religious services; social and recreational activities; on- and off-site activities; fishing pond; gardening; multipurpose room; crafts; barber/beauty shop.

Contact facility for fees.

The Ozarks Methodist Manor, AAHSA

205 South College
PO Box C
Marionville, MO 65705

Ph: (417) 258-2573
Fax: (417) 258-2240

IND: 57. AL: 48. HCC: 78

Age 60+. Nondenominational; managed by Life Care Services Corporation; Methodist Church affiliation. Homes, apartments, and private and semiprivate rooms. 24-hour nursing care; physician services; rehabilitative therapies; dental and podiatry care; pharmacy services; medical services; outpatient care program; clinic; Medicare/Medicaid-approved; personal care; medication administration; security; emergency response system; maintenance; transportation; up to 3 daily meals; pets allowed; housekeeping and laundry services; fitness center; chapel; religious services; library social and recreational activities; crafts; bowling; card and board games; barber/beauty shop.

IND ENT: Traditional plan, $53,000–$71,500; Return of Capital Plan, $85,000–$114,500. IND MO: About $400. AL ENT: Traditional Plan, $13,000–$27,000; Return of Capital Plan, $20,500–$43,000. AL MO: with ENT fee, $1,250–$1,400; lease, $1,500–$1,950. HCC Daily: Semiprivate, $100; private, $110.

West

Amour Memorial Home

8100 Wornall Rd.
Kansas City, MO 64114

Ph: (816) 363-5141
Fax: (816) 363-1857

IND: 24. AL: 47. SNF: 36

Nonprofit; nondenominational; affiliated with the Woman's Christian Association. Apartments and private and semiprivate rooms. 24-hour skilled nursing care; physician services; dental, podiatry, and optometry care; physical, occupational, and speech therapies; lab services; social and mental health services; Medicaid-approved; personal care; medication administration; security; emergency response system; maintenance; transportation; up to 3 daily meals; pets allowed; housekeeping and laundry services; exercise classes; religious services; chapel; library; postal services; social and recreational activities; barber/beauty shop.

IND: ENT plan; $60,500–$82,500; APPL plan, $6,050–$8,250. IND MO: ENT plan, $975–$1,150; APPL plan, $1,800–$2,350. AL MO: $1,800–$1,850; 2nd person, $330. SNF Daily: Semiprivate, $120; private, $150.

Beautiful Savior Home, MAHA, AHEA

1003 S. Cedar St.
Belton, MO 64012

Ph: (816) 331-0781
Fax: (816) 322-4975

RC: 110. SNF: 126

Age 52+. Nonprofit; nondenominational; Missouri Synod Lutheran Church affiliation. Apartments and private and semiprivate rooms. 24-hour nursing care; medical services; rehabilitative therapies; dental and podiatry care; social services; pharmacy services; Medicare/Medicaid-approved; personal care; medication administration; security; emergency response system; maintenance; transportation; up to 3 daily meals plus snacks; housekeeping and laundry services; exercise classes; religious services; social and recreational activities.

IND/AL Daily: $40–$100. HCC Daily: $105–$125.

The Groves

1515 W. White Oak
Independence, MO 64050

Ph: (816) 254-3500
Fax: (816) 521-4909

IND: 74. RH: 126. AL: 6. HCC: 300. ALZ/MEM IMP: 49

Nonprofit; nondenominational; RLDS Church affiliation. Studios, suites, one- and two-bedroom apartments, and private and semiprivate rooms. 24-hour nursing care; medical services; physician services; physical, occupational, and speech therapies; dental and podiatry services; pharmacy services; Medicare/Medicaid-approved; personal care; medication administration; security; emergency response system; maintenance; transportation; up to 3 daily meals; pets allowed; housekeeping and laundry services; exercise equipment; swimming pool; 24-hour staffing; library; arts and crafts room; woodworking shops; board and card games; social and recreational activities; atrium; barber/beauty shop.

DEP: $550; pets, $220. IND MO: $770–$1,500. AL MO: $925–$2,350; 2nd person, $550–$1,000. HCC Daily: Semiprivate, $120–$140; private, $140–$160.

John Knox Village East

1201 W. 19th St.
Higginsville, MO 64037

Ph: (660) 584-7111 or 584-4315

IND: Yes. AL: Yes. HCC: Yes

Nonprofit; nondenominational; managed by Life Care Services Corp. Studios, efficiencies, apartments, and private and semiprivate rooms. 24-hour nursing care; physician services; rehabilitative therapies; medical services; dental and podiatry care; pharmacy services; ambulance services; wellness programs; social services; personal care; medication administration; security; emergency response system; maintenance; transportation; up to 3 daily meals; housekeeping and laundry services; exercise programs; swimming pool; worship services; Bible study; library; social and recreational activities; convenience store; shuffleboard; quilting; walking paths; barber/beauty shop.

IND ENT: $48,000–$79,000; 2nd person, $11,000. IND MO: $500–$800; 2nd person, $525 and $825.

John Knox Village, CCAC, AAHSA

400 N.W. Murray Rd.
Lee's Summit, MO 64081

Ph: (816) 251-8000 or (800) 892-5669

IND: 1,500. AL: 90. HCC: 430

Nonprofit; nondenominational. Homes, garden cottages, apartments, duplexes, villas, and private and semiprivate rooms. 24-hour nursing care; physician services; rehabilitative therapies; medical services; dental and podiatry care; pharmacy services; ambulance services; wellness programs; social services; personal care; medication administration; security; emergency response system; maintenance; transportation; up to 3 daily meals; housekeeping and laundry services; exercise programs; swimming pool; worship services; Bible study; library; social, cultural, and recreational activities; intergenerational program; volunteer opportunities; computer classes; discussion groups; woodworking shop; arts and crafts; golf; bingo; concerts; movies; table tennis; tai chi classes; trips; gardening; golf; walking paths; gift shop; convenience store; barber/beauty shop.

IND ENT: (partial ref.), $27,500–$110,000+. IND MO: About $550–$1,100.

East

Beauvais Manor on the Park

3625 Magnolia Ave.
St. Louis, MO 63110-4098

Ph: (314) 771-2990
Fax: (314) 771-7960

RH: Yes. ICF: Yes. ALZ/MEM IMP: Yes

Nondenominational. Private and semiprivate rooms. 24-hour nursing care; medical director; physical, occupational, and speech therapies; dental and podiatry care; medical services; pharmacy services; hospice care; personal care; medication administration; security; emergency response system; maintenance; transportation; up to 3 daily meals; housekeeping and laundry services; exercise classes; religious services; social and recreational activities; on- and off-site activities; games and crafts; movies; music; aviaries; gardens; gift shop; barber/beauty shop.

RH Daily: $75–$130. ICF Daily: $95–$135. ALZ/MEM IMP: $100.

Brooking Park

307 S. Woods Mill Rd.
Chesterfield, MO 63017

Ph: (314) 576-5545
Fax: (314) 576-1354

AL: Yes. SNF: Yes

Nonprofit; nondenominational; operated by St. Andrew's Episcopal-Presbyterian Foundation. Apartments and private and semiprivate rooms. 24-hour skilled nursing care; physical, occupational, and speech therapies; physician services; long- and short-term care; dental and podiatry care; pharmacy services; personal care; medication administration; security; emergency response system; maintenance; transportation; up to 3 daily meals; housekeeping and laundry services; exercise classes; religious services; social, cultural, and recreational activities; educational programs; bingo; special events; courtyard; barber/beauty shop.

AL Daily: $90–$250. SNF Daily: $125–$250.

Cardinal Ritter Institute

4483 Lindell Blvd.
St. Louis, MO 63108

Ph: (314) 652-3600
Fax: (314) 652-0312

IND: 1,405. AL: 246. HCC: 230

Age 62+. Nonprofit; Catholic Church affiliation. Apartments and private and semiprivate rooms. Skilled nursing care; rehabilitative therapies; dental and podiatry care; pharmacy services; social services; home health care; Medicare/Medicaid-approved; personal care; medication administration; security; emergency response system; maintenance; transportation; up to 3 daily meals; housekeeping and laundry services; religious services; social and recreational activities; volunteer opportunities.

Contact facility for fees.

The Charless Home

4431 S. Broadway
St. Louis, MO 63111

Ph: (314) 481-4840
Fax: (314) 481-1014
http://www.thecharlesshome.org
E-mail: *TCH1853@AOL.COM*

IND: 89. AL: 26. HCC: 40

Age 55+. Nonprofit; nondenominational. Private rooms. Nursing care; medical services; rehabilitative services; dental and podiatry care; eye care; pharmacy services; personal care; medication administration; security; emergency response system; maintenance; transportation; up to 3 daily meals; housekeeping and laundry services; exercise classes; chapel and religious services; library; social and recreational activities; sunroom; patio; walking paths; barber/beauty shop.

IND ENT: $3,300. IND MO: $800–$1,475. AL ENT: $3,300. AL MO: $1,200–$1,800. HCC Daily: $95.

Friendship of South County

12503 Village Circle Drive
Sunset Hills, MO 63127

Ph: (314) 842-6840

IND: Yes. AL: Yes. SNF: 118

Age 62+. Nondenominational; managed by Life Care Services Corp. Cottages, studios, alcoves, apartments, and private and semiprivate rooms. Skilled nursing care; medical services; rehabilitative therapies; dental and podiatry care; pharmacy services; emergency services; personal care; medication administration; security; emergency response system; maintenance; transportation; up to 3 daily meals; housekeeping and laundry services; exercise classes; chaplain, interdenominational religious services; social and recreational activities; woodworking shop; arts and crafts; gardening areas; putting green; fishing pond; walking paths; barber/beauty shop.

IND ENT: Traditional plan, $42,000–$144,000; Return of Capital, $66,500–$230,000. IND MO: $975–$1,700; 2nd person, $625 and $650. AL fees extra; based on services provided.

The Gables at Breeze Park, CCAC

600 Breeze Park Drive
St. Charles, MO 63304

Ph: (314) 939-5223

IND: 144. AL: 71

Nonprofit; nondenominational; owned by Lutheran Senior Services. Ranch homes and apartments. Priority placement in Lutheran Convalescent Home; personal care; medication administration; security; emergency response system; maintenance; transportation; up to 3 daily meals; housekeeping and laundry services; exercise program; chapel; religious services; Bible study; social and recreational activities; cultural and educational programs; banking services; arts and crafts; lounges; gardens; barber/beauty shop.

IND ENT: (partial ref.), $76,500–$121,000. IND MO: with ENT fee, $900–$1,700; without ENT fee, $1,675–$2,650. 2nd person, $300. AL MO: $2,800–$3,700.

Hartnett Christian Village, AASHA, MOAHA

70 N. Hartnett
Ferguson, MO 63135

Ph: (314) 521-3915
Fax: (314) 571-1967

AL: 28. SNF: 180

Nonprofit; Church of Christ affiliation. Private and semiprivate rooms. 24-hour nursing care; medical services; rehabilitative therapies; dental, podiatry, and eye care; pharmacy services; social services; personal care; medication administration; security; emergency response system; maintenance; transportation; up to 3 daily meals; housekeeping and laundry services; chapel; chaplain services; Bible study; pet therapy; social and recreational activities; solarium.

MO: $1,650–$3,000. Some financial assistance available.

Laclede Groves, CCAC, AASHA

723 S. Laclede Station Rd.
Webster Groves, MO 63119

Ph: (314) 968-5570

IND: Yes. AL: Yes. SNF: 240. ALZ/MEM IMP: Yes

Nonprofit; nondenominational; owned by Lutheran Senior Services. Patio homes, apartments, studios, and private and shared rooms. 24-hour nursing care; skilled nursing care; rehabilitative therapies; medical services; dental and podiatry care; pharmacy services; respite care; health clinic; Medicare/Medicaid-approved; personal care; medication administration; security; emergency response system; maintenance; transportation; up to 3 daily meals; pets allowed; housekeeping and laundry services; exercise program; swimming pool; chapel; religious services; Bible study; library; banking services; educational and cultural programs; volunteer opportunities; woodworking shop; arts and crafts room; lounges; game rooms; walking trails; convenience store; barber/beauty shop.

DEP: $3,300 ($2,200 credited to move-in; $1,100 is security dep.). IND ENT: (partial ref.), $42,000–$214,500. IND MO: $425–$1,500. 2nd person, $200 and $240. AL MO: $2,350–$5,400. HCC Daily: 3/4 beds, $110–$115; semiprivate, $135–$250; private, $155–$275.

Nazareth Living Center

2 Nazareth Lane
St. Louis, MO 63129

Ph: (314) 961-5653
Fax: (314) 487-8001

IND: 150. AL: Yes. SNF: 139. AL/MEM IMP: Yes

65+. Nonprofit; nondenominational; sponsored by the Sisters of St. Joseph of Carondelet; church affiliation. Suites and private rooms. Skilled nursing care; physician services; dental and podiatry services; social services; lab and X-ray services; medical services; individualized care plans; pharmacy services; Medicare/Medicaid-approved; personal care; medication administration; security; emergency response system; maintenance; transportation; up to 3 daily meals; housekeeping and laundry services; religious services; social and recreational activities; on- and off-site activities; intergenerational program; bookmobile; resident council; common areas; barber/beauty shop.

IND/AL MO: $2,000–$2,200. HCC MO: $3,700–$4,950.

Parkside Meadows Retirement Community, JCAHO

2150 Randolph St.
St. Charles, MO 63301

Ph: (314) 946-4966
Fax: (314) 940-0214

http://www.parkside.org

IND: Yes. RC: Yes. SNF: Yes

Nonprofit; affiliated with the United Church of Christ. Apartments and private and semiprivate rooms. Skilled nursing care; medical services; rehabilitative therapies; wellness program; blood pressure checks; blood sugar screenings; Medicare-approved; personal care; medication administration; security; emergency response system; maintenance; transportation; up to 3 daily meals; housekeeping and laundry services; exercise classes; exercise equipment; religious services; Bible study; library services; volunteer program; social and recreational activities; on- and off-site activities; workshop; lounges; convenience store; card and board games; walking paths; gardens; courtyards; barber/beauty shop.

RC Daily: $55–$135. SNF Daily: $120–$150.

Central

Lenoir Retirement Community, CCAC, AAHSA

3710 S. Lenoir St.
Columbia, MO 65201

Ph: (573) 876-5800
Fax: (573) 876-5831

IND: 137. AL: 59. HCC: 75. ALZ/MEM IMP: 17

Age 60+. Nondenominational; church affiliated; Christian Church (Disciples of Christ). Homes, apartments, and private and semiprivate rooms. 24-hour nursing care; medical services; rehabilitative therapies; dental and podiatry care; pharmacy services; Medicare/Medicaid-approved; personal care; medication administration; security; emergency response system; maintenance; transportation; up to 3 daily meals; housekeeping and laundry services; fitness center; chapel; social and recreational activities; cultural and educational opportunities; library; billiards room; crafts; gift shop; convenience store; walking paths; barber/beauty shop.

APPL: $500. DEP: 20% of purchase price. IND ENT: Life Lease, $49,500–$121,000; Return of Capital, $70,500–

$171,000. IND MO: $375–$660. AL MO: $1,700–$2,150. HCC Daily: $100–$130.

Northeast

Beth Haven Nursing Home

2500 Pleasant St.
Hannibal, MO 63401

Ph: (573) 221-6000
Fax: (573) 221-6172

IND: 102. AL: 35. HCC: 75. ALZ/MEM IMP: 20

Nonprofit; Mennonite Home Association affiliation. Apartments and private and semiprivate rooms. Nursing care; medical services; rehabilitative therapies; dental and podiatry care; pharmacy services; Medicare/Medicaid-approved; personal care; medication administration; security; emergency response system; maintenance; transportation; up to 3 daily meals; pets allowed; housekeeping and laundry services; social and recreational activities.

AL Daily: $50–$55. HCC/ALZ/MEM IMP Daily: $85–$95.

Southeast

Chateau Girardeau, CCAC

3120 Independence Street
Cape Girardeau, MO 63703

Ph: (573) 335-1281

IND: Yes. AL: Yes. HCC: Yes

Age 65+. Nonprofit; nondenominational; owned by Cape Retirement Community, Inc. Homes, apartments, and private and semiprivate rooms. 24-hour skilled nursing care; physical, occupational, and speech therapies; medical services; dental and podiatry care; lab services; pharmacy services; Medicare-approved; personal care; medication administration; security; emergency response system; maintenance; transportation; up to 3 daily meals; housekeeping and laundry services; exercise program; residents council; social and recreational activities; arts and crafts; woodworking shop; lounges; walking paths; barber/beauty shop.

APPL: $200/person. IND ENT: Homes: Traditional Plan (prorated ref.), $105,500–$118,500; 25% Refundable Plan, $117,500–$132,000. Apartments: Traditional Plan (prorated ref.), $25,500–$91,500; 25% Refundable Plan, $30,000–$104,500. IND MO: Homes: $500–$550. Apartments: $875–$1,475. HCC fees inclusive.

Assisted Living and Residential Care Facilities

*In the state of Missouri, these facilities are called **Assisted Living/Residential Care**.*

These facilities offer housing with personalized support services and health care services.

Types of Authorization

Licensing and/or Certification

Regulated by the Division of Aging, Institutional Services (Department of Social Services).

Memberships:

- Assisted Living Federation of America (ALFA) is a national nonprofit membership organization whose mission is to enhance the quality of life in assisted living facilities and promote the interests of the assisted living industry. ALFA, 10300 Eaton Place, Suite 400, Fairfax, VA 22030. Ph: (703) 691-8100. Fax: (703) 691-8106. *http://www.alfa.org*
- Missouri Assisted Living Association (MALA).

Central

Kidwell Home

1000 Kidwell Drive
Versailles, MO 65084

Ph: (573) 378-5175
Fax: (573) 378-5624

AL: 44

Nonprofit; nondenominational. Private rooms. Nursing care; medical services; rehabilitative therapies; dental and podiatry services; Medicaid-approved; personal care; medication administration; security; emergency response system; maintenance; transportation; up to 3 daily meals; housekeeping and laundry services; social and recreational activities.

AL MO: Semiprivate, $1,350; private, $1,700.

East

Crystal Oakes Residential Care Center

1500 Calvary Church Rd.
PO Box 199
Crystal City, MO 63019

Ph: (314) 933-1546

IND: Yes. AL: Yes

Nondenominational. Private and semiprivate rooms. Physician services; 24-hour professional staffing; lab and X-ray services; rehabilitative therapies; dental and podiatry services; personal care; medication administration; security; emergency response system; maintenance; transportation; up to 3 daily meals; housekeeping and laundry services; intergenerational program; social and recreational activities; on- and off-site activities; gardening; nearby hospital; barber/beauty shop services.

AL MO: Semiprivate, $1,500; private; $1,850.

The Gables at Hidden Lake, ccac

11728 Hidden Lake Drive
St. Louis, MO 63138

Ph: (314) 355-8833
Fax: (314) 355-7664

IND: 116. AL: 40

Nonprofit; nondenominational; owned by Lutheran Senior Services. Ranch homes, garden apartments, and efficiency units. Priority placement at Lutheran Convalescent Home; respite care; podiatry services; personal care; medication administration; security; emergency response system; maintenance; transportation; up to 3 daily meals; housekeeping and laundry services; exercise program; chapel; religious services; Bible study; library; social and recreational activities; activities director; arts and crafts room; movies; musical programs; media room; gardens; lounges; barber/beauty shop.

DEP: $1,100. IND ENT: (partial ref.), $64,000–$103,000. IND MO: $1,500–$1,950; 2nd person, $300. AL MO: Efficiencies, $1,050–$1,600; apartments, $2,450–$3,500.

West

The Fountains at Greenbriar

2100 S. Swope Drive
Independence, MO 64057

Ph: (816) 257-5100
Fax: (816) 257-2442

http://www.thefountains.com

IND: 144. AL: 64

Age 62+. Forprofit; nondenominational; nonsectarian. Apartments. Home health care; personal care; medication administration; security; emergency response system; maintenance; transportation; up to 3 daily meals; pets allowed; housekeeping and laundry services; fitness center; whirlpool; chapel; social and recreational activities; arts and crafts; country store; walking paths; barber/beauty shop.

APPL: $330. DEP: $275. IND MO: $1,000–$1,975. AL MO: $1,050–$2,100.

Southwest

Butterfield Residential Care Center, MALA

1120 N. Butterfield Rd.
Bolivar, MO 65613

Ph: (417) 326-5200
Fax: (417) 777-5130

AL: 60

Nonprofit; nondenominational. Apartments. Nursing care; some medical services; Medicaid-approved; personal care; medication administration; security; emergency response system; maintenance; transportation; up to 3 daily meals; housekeeping and laundry services; pet visits; social and recreational activities.

AL MO: $1,650–$1,750.

Spring River Christian Village

201 S. Northpark Lane
Joplin, MO 64801

Ph: (417) 623-4313
Fax: (417) 623-5478

IND: 52. RH: 32. AL: 60

Age 60+. Nonprofit; nondenominational; sponsored by the Christian/Church of Christ. Duplexes, studios, apartments, and private rooms. Nursing care; rehabilitative therapies; podiatry care; personal care; medication administration; emergency response system; maintenance; transportation; up to 3 daily meals; housekeeping and laundry services; exercise equipment; religious services; social and recreational activities.

DEP: $550. MO: $1,100–$2,050.

Independent Living

Independent housing (primarily rentals) for seniors that may offer security features, meal service, and activities.

East

Gambrill Gardens

1 Strecker Rd.
Ellisville, MO 63011

Ph: (314) 394-2992
Fax: (314) 394-2512

IND: Yes

Age 62+. Managed by Life Care Services Corp.; affiliated with the United Methodist Church. One- and two-bedroom apartments. Security; emergency response system; maintenance; transportation; up to 3 daily meals; housekeeping and laundry services; chapel and on-site chaplain; banking services; social and recreational activities; cultural and religious programs; lounges; recreational and game rooms; convenience store; barber/beauty shop.

IND MO: $1,300–$1,550; 2nd person, $275. Some apartments are HUD-subsidized.

St. Andrew's of Jennings

9600 Halls Ferry Rd.
St. Louis, MO 63136

Ph: (314) 867-8993
Fax: (314) 867-0170

IND: 99

Age 62+. Nonprofit; affiliated with St. Andrew's Episcopal-Presbyterian Foundation. Apartments. Social services; security; emergency response system; maintenance.

DEP: 1 mo. rent. IND MO: 30% of income; HUD-subsidized.

Tower Grove Manor

2710 S. Grand Blvd.
St. Louis, MO 63118-1009

Ph: (314) 773-2800
Fax: (314) 773-1669
E-mail: *TGMLEASE@aol.com*

IND: 115

Age 55+. Nonprofit; nondenominational; a division of St. Andrew's Episcopal-Presbyterian Foundation. Studios, efficiencies, and one-bedroom apartments. Security; emergency response system; maintenance; transportation; meal plans; laundry services; exercise classes; educational opportunities; social, cultural, and recreational activities; on- and off-site activities; bookmobile; movies; close to hospitals, churches, and shopping.

IND ENT: $5,500–$16,500. IND MO: ENT plan, $1,075–$1,375; Lease plan, $1,150–$1,600. 2nd person, $200.

West

Truman Farm Villas Apartments

5300 Harry Truman Drive
Grandview, MO 64030

Ph: (816) 966-0500
Fax: (816) 966-1082

IND: Yes

Age 62+. For profit; nondenominational. Apartments. Blood pressure services; pharmacy services; security; gated property; security patrol; maintenance; transportation; pets allowed; independent home health and meal program services; fitness center; pool; social and recreational activities; on- and off-site activities; near shopping and restaurants.

APPL: $30 DEP: $220–$275. IND MO: $525–$650.

REQ: Income maximums; 1 person, $23,500; 2 persons, $27,000.

Woods Chapel Lodge

1000 NW Arlington Place
Blue Springs, MO 64015

Ph: (816) 229-7525
Fax: (816) 228-9183
E-mail: *mbmorris@ncr.org*

IND: 55

Age 62+. Nonprofit; nondenominational. Apartments. Security; emergency response system; maintenance; transportation; on- site manager; library; community room; barber/beauty shop services.

IND MO: 30% of income; HUD-subsidized.

Northwest

Country Squire

1602 Buckingham St.
St. Joseph, MO 64506

Ph: (816) 233-4200

IND: Yes

Nondenominational. Studios and one- and two-bedroom apartments. Home health services; health seminars; blood pressure checks; security; emergency response system; maintenance; transportation; up to 3 daily meals; housekeeping and laundry services; exercise classes; outdoor exercise path; religious services; bible study; library; social, recreational, and educational activities; lounges; alcoves; crafts; pool table; barber/beauty shop.

DEP: (ref) $100. IND MO: $1,100–$2,300; 2nd person, $350.

Adult/Resort Communities

Communities for active adults (not all are age-restricted; primarily ownership).

Southeast

Bent Creek Golf Club

2200 Bent Creek Drive
Jackson, MO 63755

Ph: (573) 243-6060
Fax: (573) 243-3995
http://www.bentcreek.net

Individual homes, condominiums, homesites. Golf course; library; social clubs.

PURCHASE: Homes, $165,000–$550,000.

East

Lake St. Louis Community Association

100 Cognac Ct.
Lake St. Louis, MO 63367

Ph: (314) 625-8276
Fax: (314) 561-8098

Individual homes, condominiums, homesites. Golf course; tennis; swimming pool; fishing; boating/waterskiing; community center; social clubs.

PURCHASE: Homes, $99,000–$550,000.

Terre Du Lac Country Club

1424 Rue Riviera
Bonne Terre, MO 63628

Ph: (573) 562-7528
Fax: (573) 562-1043

Individual homes; condominiums; homesites. Golf course; tennis; swimming pool; fishing; hunting; boating/waterskiing; social clubs.

PURCHASE: Homes, $88,000–$385,000.

Central

The Communities of Four Seasons

PO Box 430
Lake Ozark, MO 65049

Ph: (800) 850-5253 or (573) 365-8510
Fax: (573) 365-8505

http://www.realty.4seasonsresort.com

Individual homes; condominiums, homesites. Golf course; tennis; racquetball; swimming pool; hiking; fishing; hunting; riding stables; boating/waterskiing; community center; fitness center; social clubs.

PURCHASE: Homes, from $99,000; homesites, $11,000–$445,500.

Marriot's Tan-Tar-A

S.R. KK
Osage Beach, MO 65065

Ph: (800) 826-8272 or (573) 348-3131
http://www.estatesrealty.com

Individual homes, homesites. Golf course; tennis; racquetball; swimming pool; hiking/biking; fishing; hunting; riding stables; boating/waterskiing; fitness center; social clubs.

PURCHASE: Homes, $69,500–$385,000.

Porto Cima

PO Box 970
Lake Ozark, MO 65049

Ph: (800) 879-5687 or (573) 365-8596

In development. Individual homes, homesites. Golf courses; clubhouse; tennis; swimming pools; health facilities; boat docks; marina; yacht club; dining.

Call for property information.

South

Stonebridge Village

1600 Ledgestone Way
Reeds Spring, MO 65737

Ph: (888) 918-GOLF or (417) 332-1300
Fax: (417) 332-1332
http://www.stonebridgevillage.com

Individual homes, condominiums, homesites. Golf course; tennis; swimming pool; hiking; fishing; hunting; community center; fitness center; clubs.

PURCHASE: Condos, from $143,000; townhomes, from $150,000; homes, from $165,000; homesites, from $16,500.

Thousand Hills Resort and Golf Club

245 S. Wildwood Drive
Branson, MO 65616
Ph: (800) 864-4145 or (417) 334-4553
http://www.thousandhills.com

Condominiums. Golf course; swimming pool; fishing; hunting; boating/waterskiing; community center; fitness center.

PURCHASE: Homes, from $121,000.

Montana

http://www.state.mt.us

General Information

Climate

Cool. Average temperatures: Billings: January, 23° F; July, 73° F; Kalispell: January, 20° F; July, 63° F. Average snowfall: 48–64 inches per year.

Cost of Living

Ranks 26th in the nation.

Taxes

State/Local as % of Income: 9.5%.

Property Tax Reduction: Elderly homeowners and renters may receive credit against their state income tax for property taxes paid.

Sales: None.

Prescription Exemptions: None.

Transportation, Travel, and Tourism

Major Airports

- Helena Regional Airport, 2850 Skyway Drive, Helena, MT 59602, (406) 442-2821.
- Gallatin Field Airport, 6 Gallatin Drive, Bozeman, MT 59718, (406) 388-6632.
- Glacier Park International Airport, 4170 U.S. Hwy 2 East, Kalispell, MT 59901, (406) 257-5994.
- Missoula International Airport, 5225 Hwy 10 West, Missoula, MT 59802, (406) 728-4381.
- Great Falls International Airport, 2800 Terminal Drive, Great Falls, MT 59404, (406) 727-3404.

Railways

- Amtrak, stations throughout the state, (800) USA-RAIL.

Bus Tours

- Greyhound Bus, stations throughout the state, (800) 231-2222.
- Beach Transportation Co., 825 Mount Ave., Missoula, MT 59801, (406) 549-6121.
- Karst Stage, Inc., PO Box 1127, Bozeman, MT 59771, (406) 586-8567.
- Rocky Mountain Transportation, 1410 E. Edgewood Drive, Whitefish, MT 59937, (406) 863-1200.

State Highways

- Interstate 94 runs east-west from North Dakota to Billings.
- Interstate 90 runs south-north from Wyoming to Billings, then east-west from Billings to Idaho.
- Interstate 15 runs north-south from Canada to Idaho.

Theater and Music

South

- Alberta Bair Theater, 2722 3rd Ave. N. #400, Billings, MT 59101 (406) 256-8915.
- The Bozeman Symphony, PO Box 1174, Bozeman, MT 59771, (406) 585-9774.
- Montana Shakespeare in the Parks, MSU SUB, Rm. 354, Bozeman, MT 59717, (406) 994-5885.
- Vigilante Theatre Co., 111 S. Grand, Suite 201, Bozeman, MT 59715, (406) 586-3897.
- Intermountain Opera Association, PO Box 37, Bozeman, MT 59771, (406) 587-2889.
- Billings Studio Theatre (live theater), 1500 Rimrock Rd., Billings, MT 59102, (406) 248-1141.

West

- International Choral Festival (every 3 years, next on July 12–16, 2000; choirs from around the world), Festival 2000, PO Box 9228, Missoula, MT 59807, (406) 721-7985.

Central

- Grandstreet Theater, 325 N. Park Ave., Helena, MT 59601, (406) 442-4270.
- Myrna Loy Center (theater), 15 N. Ewing St., Helena, MT 59601, (406) 443-0287.
- Holter Museum of Art, 12 E. Lawrence St., Helena, MT 59601, (406) 442-6400.
- Helena Symphony, 340 Neill Ave., Helena, MT 59601, (406) 442-1860.

Museums, Crafts, Historical, Recreational

North

- Lewis and Clark Days (gun show, black powder shoot; last week in July every year), Cut Bank Area Chamber of Commerce, PO Box 1243, Cut Bank, MT 59427, (406) 873-4041.
- Glacier National Park (hiking, fishing, camping), PO Box 128, West Glacier, MT 59936, (406) 888-7800.

South

- Cottonwood Hills Golf Course, 8955 River Rd., Bozeman, MT 59718, (406) 587-1118.
- Bridger Creek Golf Course, 2710 McIlhattan Rd., Bozeman, MT 59715, (406) 586-2333.
- Yellowstone National Park (in Wyoming, Montana, Idaho, visitor centers, camping, fishing, hiking), PO Box 168, Yellowstone National Park, WY 82190, (307) 344-7381.
- Gallatin Pioneer Museum, 317 W. Main St., Bozeman, MT 59715, (406) 582-8122.
- Bighorn Canyon National Recreation Area, PO Box 7458, Fort Smith, MT 59035, (406) 666-2412.
- Little Bighorn Battlefield National Monument, PO Box 39, Crow Agency, MT 59022, (406) 638-2622.
- The Western Heritage Center, Parmly Billings Library (historic building), Billings, (406) 256-6809.
- Peter Yegen Jr. Golf Club (public), 3400 Grand Ave., Billings, MT 59102, (406) 883-2440.
- Lake Hills Golf Club, 1930 Clubhouse Way, Billings, MT 59105, (406) 248-3180.
- Custer National Forest, PO Box 2556, 2602 1st Ave. North, Billings, MT 59103, (406) 248-9885.
- Gallatin National Forest (camping, hiking), Bozeman Ranger District, 3710 Fallon Street, Suite C, Bozeman, MT 59718, (406) 587-6920.
- Bohart Ranch cross-country Ski Center, 16621 Bridger Canyon Rd., Bozeman, MT 59715, (406) 586-9070.
- American Computer Museum, PO Box 7190, 234 E. Babcock St. Bozeman, MT 59771, (406) 587-7545.
- Natural Exposures, Inc., Museum, 16595 Brackett Creek Rd., Bozeman, MT 59715, (406) 686-4448.
- Museum of the Rockies and Taylor Planetarium, Montana State University–Bozeman, 600 W. Kagy Blvd., Bozeman, MT 59717, (406) 994-2251.

East

- Fort Union Trading Post National Historic Site (Lewis and Clark trail, reenactments, building foundations), 24 miles north of Sidney. For information: Rte. 3, Box 71, Williston, ND 58801, (701) 572-9083.

West

- Bitterroot National Forest (hiking, riding, camping, rock climbing), 1801 N. 1st St., Hamilton, MT 59840, (406) 363-3131.
- Virginia City, Alder Gulch, and Nevada City (Gold Rush towns, original buildings, reconstructions), Virginia City Chamber of Commerce, Virginia City, MT 59755, (406) 843-5345 or (800) 829-2969.

- Bannack State Park (ghost town, ice skating, camping), Department of Fish, Wildlife & Parks, Dillon, MT 59725, (406) 834-3413.
- Museum of Fine Arts, The University of Montana, Missoula, MT 59812, (406) 243-4970.
- Beaverhead-Deerlodge National Forest and Crystal Park Mineral Collection Area (digging for crystals, camping, fishing, snow activities), 420 Barrett St., Dillon, MT 59725, (406) 683-3900.

Central

- Giant Springs State Park (freshwater spring, hiking), 4600 Giant Springs Rd., Great Falls, MT 59406, (406) 454-5840.
- Lewis and Clark National Historic Trail Interpretive Center, PO Box 2127, Great Falls, MT 59403, (406) 761-4434 or (406) 761-6129.
- Lewis and Clark National Forest (hunting, fishing, camping), 1101 15th St. N., Box 869, Great Falls, MT 59403, (406) 791-7700.
- Helena National Forest (fishing, camping, hiking, horseback riding), 2880 Skyway Drive, Helena, MT 59601, (406) 449-5201.
- Bill Roberts Golf Course (public), 205 Cole Ave., Helena, MT 59623, (406) 248-2702.
- Fox Ridge Golf Course (public), 4020 Lake Helena Drive, Helena, MT 59601, (406) 888-5471.

Organizations

Advocacy Groups

- Senior and Long Term Care Division, Department of Public Health & Human Services, PO Box 4210, 111 Sanders, Room 211, Helena, MT 59604, (406) 444-7788.
- Coalition of Montanans Concerned with Disabilities, Missoula Chapter, (406) 728-8093 or 829-9301.

Volunteer Programs

- Big Brothers and Big Sisters, 33 Neill Ave., Helena, MT 59601-3330, (406) 442-7479.
- Mai Wah Society (preserving Asian culture in the Rocky Mountain West), 17 W. Mercury St., Butte, MT 59701.
- Volunteer Montana! (join as an AmeriCorps member or individual, variety of activities), (406) 542-5061.
- Montana State Parks Volunteer Program, PO Box 200701, Helena, MT 59620, (406) 444-4701.

Housing

Long-Term Care Facilities

*In the state of Montana, these facilities are called **Continuing Care/Nursing Home/Retirement Facilities**.*

These facilities provide residential living and/or various levels of nursing and medical services to seniors for an extended period of time.

Types of Authorization

Licensing and / or Certification

Facilities are certified by the Department of Public Health and Human Services, Certification Bureau. The State Licensure Bureau is responsible for licensing and inspections.

Memberships

- American Association of Homes and Services for the Aging (AAHSA) represents not-for-profit organizations committed to providing high-quality health care, housing, and services to the elderly. AAHSA, 901 E St. NW,

Suite 500, Washington, DC 20004-2011. Ph: (202) 783-2242. Fax: (202) 783-2285. *http://www.aahsa.org*

- Montana Association of Health Care Providers, PO Box 5119, Helena, MT 59601-4657. Ph: (406) 442-1911. Fax: (406) 443-3894. MHA is an AAHSA Affiliated State Association.

Accreditations

- Continuing Care Accreditation Commission (CCAC) accredits facilities that offer seniors a contract or contracts that provide residential living and health care services for the remainder of the person's lifetime and meet CCAC's accreditation standards.
- Joint Commission on the Accreditation of Healthcare Organizations (JCAHO) is an independent, not-for-profit organization, and the nation's oldest and largest standards-setting and health care accrediting institution.

South Central

Aspen Meadows Retirement Community

3155 Avenue C
Billings, MT 59102

Ph: (406) 656-8818

NH: 90. AL: 55

Nondenominational; associated with the Deaconess Billings Clinic. Efficiencies and one- and two-bedroom apartments. 24-hour nursing care; nursing assistants; rehabilitative therapies; medical services; dental and podiatry care; pharmacy services; long- and short-term care; Medicare/Medicaid-approved; personal care; medication administration; security; emergency response system; maintenance; transportation; 3 daily meals; pets allowed; housekeeping and laundry services; exercise classes; chapel; library; pet visits; music program; social and recreational activities; on- and off-site activities; gift shop; barber/beauty shop.

DEP: (ref.) $550. NH Daily: $115–$125. AL MO: $1,475–$3,100.

St. Johns Lutheran Home

3940 Rimrock Rd.
Billings, MT 59102

Ph: (406) 655-5614
Fax: (406) 655-5656

IND: 115. HCC: Yes

Nonprofit; nondenominational; Lutheran Church affiliated. Private rooms. Nursing care; medical services; rehabilitative therapies; dental and podiatry services; pharmacy services; personal care; medication administration; security; emergency response system; maintenance; transportation; up to 3 daily meals; housekeeping services; religious services; activities director; social and recreational activities.

DEP: (ref.), $50. IND MO: $825.

Central

Valle Vista Manor Nursing and Assisted Living

402 Summit
Lewistown, MT 59457

Ph: (406) 538-8875
Fax: (406) 538-8773

AL: 34. HCC: 85. ALZ/MEM IMP: 16

For-profit; nondenominational. Apartments and private rooms. Nursing care; physical, occupational, and speech therapies; medical services; dental and podiatry care; pharmacy services; Medicare/Medicaid-approved; personal care; medication administration; security; emergency response system; maintenance; transportation; up to 3 daily meals; pets allowed; housekeeping and laundry services; exercise program; social and recreational activities; barber/beauty shop services.

DEP: $550. AL MO: $1,350–$2,300. HCC Daily: $130–$140.

West

Bitterroot Valley Living Center

63 Main St.
Stevensville, MT 59870

Ph: (406) 777-5411
Fax: (406) 777-5856

PC: Yes. HCC: Yes

Nondenominational. Private and semiprivate rooms. 24-hour nursing care; nursing aides; physician medical director; physical, occupational, and speech therapies; dental and podiatry care; eye and ear care; social services; pharmacist; Medicare/Medicaid-approved; personal care; medication administration; security; emergency response system; maintenance; transportation; up to 3 daily meals; housekeeping and laundry services; religious services; social and recreational activities; community room; barber/beauty shop.

PC Daily: $55–$95. HCC Daily: $50–$95.

The Discovery Care Center

601 10th St.
Hamilton, MT 59840

Ph: (406) 363-CARE

PC: Yes. SNF: Yes

Nondenominational. Private and semiprivate rooms. Skilled nursing care; rehabilitative therapies; medical services; dental and podiatry care; pharmacy services; personal care; medication administration; security; emergency response system; maintenance; transportation; up to 3 daily meals; housekeeping and laundry services; exercise classes; Bible studies; library; social and recreational activities; bingo; board games; shuffleboard; movies; solarium; patios; walking paths; barber/beauty shop.

PC Daily: $75–$90. SNF Daily: Semiprivate, $125; private, $140.

Evergreen Health and Rehabilitation

3018 Rattlesnake Drive
Missoula, MT 59802

Ph: (406) 549-0988
Fax: (406) 543-5606

AL: 22. SNF: 52

For-profit; nondenominational. Apartments and private and semiprivate rooms. Skilled nursing care; rehabilitative therapies; medical services; dental and podiatry care; pharmacy services; Medicare/Medicaid-approved; personal care; medication administration; security; maintenance; transportation; up to 3 daily meals; housekeeping and laundry services; social and recreational activities; on- and off-site activities.

MO: 5-bed ward, $3,250; semiprivate, $3,500; private, $3,650.

Southwest

Churchill Retirement Home

6151 Shady Rest
Manhattan, MT 59741

Ph: (406) 282-7233
Fax: (406) 282-7233

IND: 25. AL: 7. HCC: 5

For-profit; nondenominational. Apartments. Nursing care; medical services; podiatry care; personal care; medication administration; security; emergency response system; maintenance; transportation; up to 3 daily meals; housekeeping and laundry services; exercise classes; religious services; social and recreational activities.

IND MO: $525–$550. AL MO: $1,600–$1,800. HCC Daily: $1,800–$2,000.

Assisted Living and Residential Care Facilities

These facilities provide housing, food service, and one or more personal services.

Types of Authorization

Licensing and/or Certification

Facilities are certified by the Department of Public Health and Human Services, Certification Bureau. The State Licensure Bureau is responsible for licensing and inspections.

Memberships

- Assisted Living Federation of America (ALFA) is a national nonprofit membership organization whose mission is to enhance the quality of life in assisted living facilities and promote the interests of the assisted living industry. ALFA, 10300 Eaton Place, Suite 400, Fairfax, VA 22030. Ph: (703) 691-8100. Fax: (703) 691-8106. *http://www.alfa.org*
- Northwest Assisted Living Facilities Association (NOR-ALFA) is a regional affiliate of ALFA. NOR-ALFA, 34004 16th Ave. South, Suite 201, Federal Way, WA 98003. Ph: (253) 874-5211. Fax: (253) 874-5350. *http://www.noralfa.org*

West

Arron Care Home

777 Oil Well Rd.
Corvallis, MT 59828-9489

Ph: (406) 961-3458

AL: Yes

For-profit; nondenominational. Private and semiprivate rooms. Medicare-approved, personal care; medication administration; security; maintenance; transportation; 3 daily meals plus snacks; housekeeping and laundry services; daily activities.

Contact facility for fees.

The Village Senior Residence

2815 Old Fort Rd.
Missoula, MT 59804

Ph: (406) 549-1300
Fax: (406) 721-1620

IND: 102. AL: Yes

For-profit; nondenominational. Apartments. 24-hour personal care aids; blood pressure checks; personal care; medication administration; security; emergency response system; maintenance; transportation; up to 3 daily meals; small pets allowed; housekeeping and laundry services; exercise equipment; library; social, recreational, and educational activities; sunroom; lounges; bingo; movies; patios; solarium; ice cream parlor; general store; community room; barber/beauty shop.

DEP: (ref.) $475. IND MO: $1,450–$2,150. AL MO: Up to $2,250.

South

Frontier Personal Care Center

121 S. 3rd St.
Livingston, MT 59047

Ph: (406) 222-6102
Fax: (406) 222-4833

IND: Yes. AL/RH: Yes. ADC: Yes

For-profit. Private rooms. Nursing care; social services; medical services; Medicare/Medicaid-approved; personal care; medication administration; security; maintenance; transportation; up to 3 daily meals; pets allowed; housekeeping and laundry services; social and recreational activites; close to park and downtown area; barber/beauty shop.

DEP: $550. IND MO: $1,100–$2,200. AL MO: $110–$550. RH MO: $1,250–$2,200.

Grand Park Assisted Living Community

1221 28th St. W.
Billings, MT 59102

Ph: (406) 652-6989
Fax: (406) 652-4879

http://www.prestigecare.com

AL: Yes. ALZ/MEM/IMP: Yes

For-profit; nondenominational. Studios and one- and two-bedroom apartments. 24-hour personal care attendants; health monitoring; insulin injections; behavior management; medical supervision; personal care; medication administration; security; emergency response system; maintenance; transportation; up to 3 daily meals; small pets allowed; housekeeping and laundry services; exercise program; religious services; Bible study; social and recreational activities; volunteer program; intergenerational program; crafts and hobbies; guest speakers; bingo; bridge; lounge; walking paths; courtyard with patio; barber/beauty shop.

DEP: (ref.) $200. AL MO: $2,350–$3,450; 2nd person, $775. ALZ/MEM IMP MO: $3,700.

Central

Son Heaven Assisted Living

2510 Ferndale
Helena, MT 59601

Ph: (406) 449-0229
Fax: (406) 449-0231

AL: 13

For-profit; nondenominational. Private rooms with half-baths. Nursing care; personal care; medication administration; security; maintenance; transportation; 3 daily meals; pets allowed; housekeeping and laundry services; activities.

DEP: $1,000. AL MO: $2,050–$2,650.

Waterford on Saddle Drive

915 Saddle Drive
Helena, MT 59601

Ph: (406) 449-4900 or (800) 336-0716
Fax: (406) 449-4999

E-mail: *peg@his.mhs.compuserve.com*

IND: 50. AL: 51

Nondenominational; owned by Touchmark Living Centers, Inc. Cottages, apartments, and private and semiprivate rooms. Physical, occupational, and speech therapies; weekly weight and blood pressure checks; insulin injections; hearing aid maintenance; personal care; medication administration; security; emergency response system; maintenance; transportation; up to 3 daily meals; housekeeping and laundry services; exercise room; chapel; computer center; social, educational, cultural, and recreational activities; bank and postal services; library; media room; convenience store; ice cream parlor; barber/beauty shop.

AL MO: $2,200–$3,000; special care, $3,100 and $3,600.

North Central

Cambridge Court Retirement Community, ALFAA

1109 6th Ave. N.
Great Falls, MT 59401

Ph: (406) 727-7151
Fax: (406) 727-7024

AL: 108

Age 62+. For-profit; nondenominational; owned and managed by Leisure Care, Inc. Studios and one- and two-bedroom apartments. 24-hour staffing; on-site pharmacy; Medicaid waiver; personal care; medication administration; emergency response system; maintenance; transportation; up to 3 daily meals; pets allowed; housekeeping and laundry services; library; activities room; social and recreational activities; barber/ beauty shop.

DEP: (ref.) $275. AL MO: $850–$1,800; 2nd person, $325.

Cambridge Place Retirement Community, ALFAA

1104 6th Ave. N.
Great Falls, MT 59401

Ph: (406) 727-0447
Fax: (406) 727-9965

AL: Yes

Age 62+. For-profit; nondenominational; owned and managed by Leisure Care, Inc. Studios and one- and two-bedroom apartments. 24-hour staffing; on-site pharmacy; Medicaid waiver; personal care; medication administration; emergency response system; maintenance; transportation; up to 3 daily meals; pets allowed; housekeeping and laundry services; library; activities room; social and recreational activities; barber/ beauty shop.

DEP: (ref.) $275. AL MO: $1,525–$2,700; 2nd person, $325.

Horizon Lodge

701 S. Wisconsin
Conrad, MT 59425

Ph: (406) 278-3233
Fax: (406) 278-5262

IND: 84. AL: Yes

Age 62+. Nonprofit; nondenominational. Apartments. Personal care; medication administration; maintenance; up to 3 daily meals; pets allowed; housekeeping and laundry services; exercise equipment; social and recreational activities; resident council.

DEP: 1 mo. rent. IND MO: $375–$800. AL MO: $110–$880.

Rainbow Retirement Community, ALFAA

20 Third St. N.
Great Falls, MT 59401

Ph: (406) 761-6661
Fax: (406) 761-6809

IND: Yes. AL: 130

Age 62+. For-profit; nondenominational; owned and managed by Leisure Care, Inc. Studios, one- and two-bedroom apartments. 24-hour staffing; on-site pharmacy; Medicaid waiver; temporary care program, personal care; medication administration; emergency response system; maintenance; transportation; up to 3 daily meals; pets allowed; housekeeping and laundry services; library; activities room; social and recreational activities; educational program; Seniors Making Art program; barber/beauty shop.

MO: $1,050–$2,500; 2nd person, $325.

Skyline Lodge

424 7th Ave. NW
Choteau, MT 59422

Ph: (406) 466-2062
Fax: (406) 466-5523

RH: 56

Age 62+. Nonprofit; nondenominational. Home health care services; personal care; medication administration; maintenance; transportation; up to 3 daily meals; pets allowed; housekeeping and laundry services; close to hospital; social and recreational activities; card and board games; movies; music; gardening; walking paths; wildlife viewing.

RH MO: $375–$450; some apartments are subsidized.

Southwest

Springmeadows

3175 Graf St.
Bozeman, MT 59715

Ph: (406) 587-4570
Fax: (406) 582-0032

IND: Yes. AL: 76

Age 65+. For-profit; nondenominational; owned by Emeritus. Apartments. Licensed nurse on staff; Medicaid-approved; personal care; medication administration; security; emergency response system; maintenance; transportation; 3 daily meals; housekeeping and laundry services; social and recreational activities; library; clubs; cultural programs; common areas; living and TV rooms; barber/beauty shop.

IND ENT: $3,850 IND MO: $1,550–$2,100. AL ENT: $3,850. AL MO: $2,200–$3,000.

East

TLC Personal Care Home

220 N. Center
Miles City, MT 59301

Ph: (406) 232-7988

PC: 16

Nondenominational; privately owned. Private rooms. 24-hour staffing; nurse supervision; Medicaid-approved; personal care; medication administration; security; emergency response system; maintenance; transportation; up to 3 daily meals; pets allowed; housekeeping and laundry services; social and recreational activities; on- and off-site activities; entertainment.

PC MO: $1,550.

Northwest

St. John's Senior Living

308 E. 2nd St.
Libby, MT 59923

Ph: (406) 293-2607

AL: 11

Age 55+. Nonprofit; nondenominational. Private rooms. Personal care; medication administration; security; emergency response system; maintenance; transportation; up to 3 daily meals; pets allowed; housekeeping and laundry services; fitness center; social and recreational activities; walking paths, wildlife viewing.

AL MO: $1,650.

Independent Living

Independent housing (primarily rentals) for seniors that may offer security features, meal service, and activities.

North Central

Eagles Manor

1501 9th St. S.
Great Falls, MT 59405

Ph: (406) 453-6521
Fax: (406) 453-9983

IND: 141

Age 62+. Nonprofit; nondenominational. Apartments. Security; maintenance; weekly housekeeping services; up to 3 daily meals; pets allowed; exercise room.

DEP: (ref.) $50. Contact facility for fees.

Eagles Manor

20 West Third St.
Havre, MT 59501

Ph: (406) 265-5531
Fax: (406) 265-8645

IND: 100

Age 62+. Nonprofit; nondenominational. Efficiency and one-bedroom apartments. Security; maintenance; close to local transportation; meal program; housekeeping and laundry services; exercise area; religious services; mail delivery; volunteer program; clubs; card group; board games; social and recreational activities; bingo; close to banks, stores, and library.

IND MO: $475–$750; HUD-subsidized.

Cambridge Place

1104 6th Ave. N.
Great Falls, MT 59401

Ph: (406) 727-0447
Fax: (406) 727-9965

IND: 62

Age 62+. For-profit; nondenominational. Apartments. Emergency response system; maintenance; transportation; up to 2 daily meals; pets allowed; housekeeping and laundry services.

DEP: (ref.) $275. IND MO: $1,550–$2,700.

West

Missoula Manor Homes

909 W. Central
Missoula, MT 59801

Ph: (406) 728-3210 TDD: (800) 253-4091
Fax: (406) 721-7681

IND: 148

Age 62+. Nondenominational. Studios and one-bedroom apartments. Security; emergency response system; maintenance; transportation; up to 3 daily meals; pets allowed; housekeeping and laundry services; exercise area; nondenominational chapel; library; lounge with TV; social and recreational activities; arts and crafts room; convenience store; bingo; card and board games; gardens; close to shopping areas and public transportation; barber/beauty shop.

IND MO: $350–$800. HUD-subsidized; income maximum, $16,000.

Sapphire Lutheran Homes

501 N. Tenth St.
Hamilton, MT 59840

Ph: (406) 363-2800
Fax: (406) 363-3003
E-mail: *slh@bitterroot.net*

IND: 40

Age 55+. Nonprofit; affiliated with the Evangelical Lutheran Church of America. Apartments. Security; emergency response system; maintenance; transportation; up to 2 daily meals; pets allowed; housekeeping and laundry services; activities director; social and recreational activities; wildlife viewing area; barber/beauty shop.

IND ENT: (ref.), $11,000. IND MO: $1,250+.

Northwest

Buffalo Hill Terrace

40 Claremont St.
Kalispell, MT 59901

Ph: (406) 752-9624
Fax: (406) 752-9609

IND: 100

Age 59+. Nondenominational; Immanuel Lutheran Corporation. Studios and one- and two-bedroom apartments. 24-hour staffing; security; emergency response system; maintenance; transportation; up to 2 daily meals; pets allowed; housekeeping and laundry services; exercise room with hot tub; library; social and recreational activities; activities director; craft room; billiards room; woodworking shop; gift shop; greenhouse; barber/beauty shop.

DEP: (ref.) $550. IND MO: $1,650–$2,150; 2nd person, $300.

East Eagles Manor

1000 Palmer
Miles City, MT 59301

Ph: (406) 232-5320

IND: 100

Age 62+. Nonprofit; nondenominational. Studios and one-bedroom apartments. Security; maintenance; close to local transportation; meal program; laundry services; exercise area; religious services; mail delivery; volunteer program; clubs; card group; social and recreational activities; bingo; close to banks, stores, and library; barber/beauty shop.

IND MO: $325–$400; HUD-subsidized.

Central

Eagles Manor

715 N. Fee St.
Helena, MT 59601

Ph: (406) 442-0610
Fax: (406) 442-1146

IND: 120

Age 62+. Nonprofit; nondenominational. One-bedroom apartments. Home health care services; maintenance; close to local transportation; up to 3 daily meals; housekeeping and laundry services; library; social and recreational activities; community room; gardens; walking paths; barber/beauty shop.

HUD-subsidized. Contact facility for fees.

Eagles Manor

211 W. Janeaux
Lewistown, MT 59457

Ph: (406) 538-3230

IND: 146

Nonprofit; nondenominational. Studios and one-bedroom apartments. Security; maintenance; close to local transportation; meal program; housekeeping and laundry services; game room; media room; card group; social and recreational activities; bingo; close to banks and shopping; gardening; walking paths; fishing.

HUD-subsidized. Contact facility for fees.

Adult/Resort Communities

Communities for active adults (not all are age-restricted; primarily ownership).

South

Briarwood Country Club

3626 O'Shea Circle
Billings, MT 59101

Ph: (406) 248-1215
Fax: (406) 248-7856

Individual homes, condominiums, homesites. Golf course; tennis; swimming pool; hiking trails.

PURCHASE: Homesites, $14,500–$36,500.

Bridger Creek

2710 McIlhattan Rd.
Bozeman, MT 59718

Ph: (406) 587-8328 or (406) 586-1753

Individual homes, condominiums, homesites. Golf course; fishing; bicycle paths.

PURCHASE: Condos, from $154,000; homesites, from $49,500.

Fairmont Hot Springs Resort

1500 Fairmont Rd.
Fairmont, MT 59711

Ph: (800) 332-3272 or (406) 797-3241
Fax: (406) 797-3337

http://www.fairmontmontana.com

Individual homes, homesites. Golf course; tennis; swimming pool; hiking/biking; riding stables; fitness center.

PURCHASE: Homes, $137,000–$275,000.

Northwest

Cabinet View Country Club

378 Cabinet View Rd.
Libby, MT 59923

Ph: (406) 293-7332
Fax: (406) 293-7332

Individual homes, homesites. Golf course; fishing; hunting; snow skiing, snowmobiling; fitness center.

PURCHASE: Homes, $154,000–$275,000.

Meadow Lake Golf Resort

100 St. Andrews Drive
Columbia Falls, MT 59912

Ph: (800) 321-4653 or (406) 892-7601
Fax: (406) 892-1825

http://www.vacation@meadowlake.com

Individual homes, condominiums, homesites. Golf course; tennis; swimming pool; hiking/biking; fishing; snow skiing; community center; fitness center.

PURCHASE: Homes, $165,000–$660,000.

Mission Bay

100 Crescent Landing
PO Box 129
Polson, MT 59860

Ph: (800) 375-0487 or (406) 883-1730
Fax: (406) 883-1731

http://www.missionbayhome.com

Individual homes, golf course homes, homesites. Golf course; clubhouse; lake; beach; sailing; fishing; trails; nearby ski resort.

PURCHASE: Homes, from $242,000; golf homes, from $183,000; homesites, $44,000–$154,000.

Trestle Creek Golf Course

1 Trestle Creek Drive
St. Regis, MT 59866

Ph: (406) 649-2680

Individual homes, homesites. Golf course; hiking trails; fishing; hunting.

PURCHASE: Homes, $93,500–$220,000.

Village Greens

500 Palmer Drive
Kalispell, MT 59901

Ph: (406) 752-5666
Fax: (406) 752-4670

http://www.montanagolf.com

Individual homes, townhomes, homesites. Golf course; hiking trails; walking paths; fishing.

PURCHASE: Homes, $110,000–$187,000.

Nebraska

http://www.state.ne.us

General Information

Climate

Varied. The average low January temperature is -9° F and the average high July temperature is 102° F.

Cost of Living

Ranks 33rd in the nation.

Taxes

General: Nebraska Department of Revenue, Lincoln, (402) 471-2971. Taxpayer Assistance, (800) 742-7474.

State/Local as % of Income: About 11.3%.

Property Tax Exemptions: Homestead exemption for persons 65+.

Sales: 5%.

Prescription Exemptions: Prescription medicines are exempt from Nebraska sales tax.

Transportation, Travel, and Tourism

Major Airports

- Airport Authority, Lincoln Municipal Airport, Lincoln, NE 68524, (402) 474-2700.
- Omaha Airport Authority, Eppley Airfield, Omaha, NE 68119, (402) 422-6817.
- Hastings Airport Authority, Hastings Municipal Airport, Hastings, NE 68901, (402) 462-6422.
- North Platte Airport Authority, Lee Bird Field, North Platte, NE 69103, (308) 532-1900.

Railways

- Amtrak: Hastings, (402) 462-5703; Lincoln, (402) 476-1295; Omaha, (402) 342-1501.

Bus Tours

- Greyhound Bus Lines, Omaha, (402) 341-1906.
- Wade Bus Lines, Ogallala, (308) 284-4233.

State Highways

- Nebraska Department of Roads (NDOR) Transportation Services Bureau, Lincoln, (402) 471-2897.
- Interste 80 runs east-west across the state from Omaha to the Wyoming border.

Theater and Music

East

- Lied Center for the Performing Arts, Lincoln, (402) 472-4700.
- Omaha Magic Theater, Omaha, (402) 346-1227.
- Fremont Dinner Train, Fremont, (800) 942-7245.

South

- Theatre of the American West, Republican City, (308) 799-2113.
- Edgerton Explorit Center, Aurora, (402) 694-4032.

Museums, Crafts, Historical, Recreational

Northwest

- Carhenge, Alliance, (308) 762-1520.
- Crawford Museum, Crawford, (308) 665-2275.
- Dawes County Historical Museum, Crawford, (308) 432-4999.
- Fort Robinson Museum, Crawford, (308) 665-2919.
- Knight Museum of the High Plains Heritage, Alliance, (308) 762-2384.

- Museum of the Fur Trade, Chadron, (308) 432-3843.
- Pine Canyon Museum and Rock Shop, Crawford, (308) 666-1604.
- Sheridan County Historical Museum, Rushville, (308) 327-2917.
- Trailside Museum, Crawford, (308) 665-2929 or (402) 472-2639.

West

- Banner County Museum, Harrisburg, (308) 436-7228.
- Chimney Rock National Historic Site and Visitors Center, Bayard, (308) 586-2581.
- Fort Sidney Museum and Post Commander's Home, Sidney, (308) 254-2150.
- Garden County Museum, Oshkosh, (308) 772-3115.
- North Platte Valley Museum, Gering, (308) 436-5411.
- Pioneer Trail Museum, Bridgeport, (308) 262-0108.
- Western Nebraska Mexican American Historical Museum, Scottsbluff, (308) 635-1044.
- Wildlife World at the Wyo-Braska Natural History Museum, Gering, (308) 436-7104.

North and Central

- Cherry County Historical Society Museum, Valentine, (402) 376-2015.
- Coleman House, Ainsworth, (402) 387-2740.
- Custer County Historical Museum, Broken Bow, (308) 872-2203.
- Keya Paha County Historical Society, Springview, (402) 497-2526.
- Sandhills Museum, Valentine, (402) 376-3293.
- Stuart White Horse Museum, Stuart, (402) 924-3168.
- Great Platte River Road
- Aksarben Aquarium, Gretna, (402) 332-3901.
- Bellevue's Historical Places, Bellevue, (402) 293-3080 or (800) 467-2779.
- Black Americana Museum, Omaha, (402) 341-6908.
- Chevyland U.S.A. Auto Museum, Elm Creek, (308) 856-4208.
- Dawson County Historical Museum, Lexington, (308) 324-5340.
- Durham Western Heritage Museum, Omaha, (402) 444-5071.
- El Museo Latino, Omaha, (402) 731-1137.
- Father Flanagan's Boys Town, Omaha, (402) 498-1140.
- Fort Kearney Museum, Kearney, (308) 234-5200.
- Freedom Park, USS Hazard/USS Marlin, Omaha, (402) 345-1959.
- Front Street/Cowboy Museum, Ogallala, (308) 284-6000.
- Great Plains Art Collection, Lincoln, (402) 472-6220.
- Great Plains Black History Museum, Omaha, (402) 345-2212.
- Hyde Observatory, Lincoln, (402) 441-7895.
- Joslyn Art Museum, Omaha, (402) 342-3300.
- Lincoln County Historical Museum and Western Heritage Village, North Platte, (308) 534-5640.
- Malcolm X Birthsite, Omaha, (402) 444-5955.
- Museum of Nebraska Art, Kearney, (308) 865-8559.
- Museum of Nebraska History, Lincoln, (402) 471-4754.
- Petrified Wood Gallery, Ogallala, (308) 284-4488 or (308) 284-2945.
- Pony Express Station, Gothenburg, (308) 537-2143.
- Robert Henri Museum and Historical Walkway, Cozad, (308) 784-4154, (308) 784-3930.
- State Museum of Natural History and Mueller Planetarium, Lincoln, (402) 472-2642.
- Strategic Air Command (SAC) Museum, Ashland, (800) 358-5029.
- Trails and Rails Museum, Kearney, (308) 234-3041.
- Willow Point Gallery and Museum, Ashland, (402) 944-3613.

Northeast/East Central

- Ashfall Fossil Beds State Historical Park, Royal, (402) 893-2000.

- Genoa Historical Museum, Genoa, (402) 993-2330 or (402) 993-2349.
- Louis E. May Historical Museum, Fremont, (402) 721-4515.
- Norfolk Arts Center, Norfolk, (402) 371-7199.
- Omaha Indian Reservation, Macy, (402) 837-5391.
- Pierce Historical Society Museum, Pierce, (402) 329-4576.
- Platte County Historical Society Museum, Columbus, (402) 564-7960.
- Swedish Heritage Center, Oakland, (402) 685-6161.
- Winnebago Indian Reservation, Winnebago, (402) 878-2272.

South

- Cambridge Museum, Cambridge, (308) 697-4385.
- Harlan County Museum, Orleans, (308) 473-3725.
- Harold Warp Pioneer Village, Minden, (308) 832-1181 or (800) 445-4447.
- Hastings Museum/Lied IMAX Theatre and J. M. McDonald Planetarium, Hastings, (402) 461-4629, (800) 508-4629.
- Museum of the High Plains, McCook, (308) 345-3661.
- Phelps County Historical Museum, Holdrege, (308) 995-5015, (308) 995-8297.
- Willa Cather State Historic Site, Red Cloud, (402) 746-2653.

Southeast

- Arbor Lodge State Historical Park and Arboretum, Nebraska City, (402) 873-7222.
- Butler County Museum, David City, (402) 367-4643.
- Carson Home, Brownville, (402) 825-4101.
- Cass County Historical Society Museum, Plattsmouth, (402) 296-4770.
- Homestead National Monument of America, Beatrice, (402) 223-3514.
- Nuckolls County Museum, Superior, (402) 879-4144 or (402) 879-3394.
- Pawnee City Historical Society Museum, Pawnee City, (402) 852-3131.
- Thayer County Museum, Belvidere, (402) 768-6845.

Organizations

Advocacy Groups

- Area Agencies on Aging:
- Blue Rivers Area, (402) 223-1352 or (800) 659-3978.
- Eastern Nebraska, Omaha, (402) 444-6444 or (402) 721-7770 (Washington/Dodge counties).
- Lincoln Area, Lincoln, (402) 441-7022.
- Midland Area, Hastings, (402) 463-4565.
- Northeast Nebraska, Norfolk, (402) 370-3454 or (800) 672-8368.
- South Central Nebraska, Kearney, (308) 234-1851 or (800) 658-4320.
- West Central Nebraska, North Platte, (308) 535-8195 or (800) 662-2961.
- Western Nebraska, Scottsbluff, (308) 635-0851 or (800) 682-5140.
- Division of Aging Services, Lincoln, (402) 471-2307 or (800) 942-7830.

Volunteer Groups

- Foster Grandparents Program:
- Beatrice, (402) 223-6036.
- Gering, (308) 635-3089.
- Grand Island, (308) 385-5323.
- Lincoln, (402) 441-7026.
- Omaha, (402) 444-6558.

- Retired Senior Volunteer Program:
- Alliance, (308) 762-1293.
- Chadron, (308) 432-4200.
- Crawford, (308) 665-2350.
- Falls City, (402) 245-3778.
- Grand Island, (308) 385-5328.
- Lincoln, (402) 441-7026.
- North Platte, (308) 535-6777.
- Ogalla, (308) 284-6464.
- Omaha, (402) 444-6558.
- Rushville, (308) 327-2959.
- Winnebago, (402) 878-2242.

- Senior Companion Program:
- Lincoln, (402) 441-7086.

- Omaha, (402) 444-6558.
- Special Olympics:
- Omaha, (402) 331-5545.

Housing

Long-Term Care Facilities

*In the state of Nebraska, these facilities are called **Continuing Care/Intermediate Care/ Skilled Nursing Facilities**.*

These facilities provide residential living and/or various levels of nursing and medical services to seniors for an extended period of time.

Types of Authorization

Licensing and / or Certification

These facilities are licensed and regulated by the Department of Regulation and Licensure (part of the Health and Human Services system). Intermediate care facilities provide room, board, and nursing care (other than skilled nursing care) for an extended period of time. Skilled nursing care facilities provide for the care of the sick or infirm requiring skilled nursing or skilled rehabilitative services or both.

Memberships

- American Association of Homes and Services for the Aging (AAHSA) represents not-for-profit organizations committed to providing high-quality health care, housing, and services to the elderly. AAHSA, 901 E St. NW, Suite 500, Washington, DC 20004-2011. Ph: (202) 783-2242. Fax: (202) 783-2285. *http: / / www.aahsa.org*
- Nebraska Association of Homes and Services for the Aging (NAHSA) is an AAHSA Affiliated State Association. NAHSA, 1701 K St., Suite B, Lincoln, NE 68508-2699. Ph: (402) 436-2165. Fax: (402) 436-2169.

Accreditations

- Continuing Care Accreditation Commission (CCAC) accredits facilities that offer seniors a contract or contracts that provide residential living and health care services for the remainder of the person's lifetime and meet CCAC's accreditation standards.
- Joint Commission on the Accreditation of Healthcare Organizations (JCAHO) is an independent, not-for-profit organization, and the nation's oldest and largest standards-setting and health care accrediting institution.

Southeast

Eastmont Towers

6315 O St.
Lincoln, NE 68510

Ph: (402) 489-6591
Fax: (402) 486-2331

IND: 203. AL: 60. SNF: 50. ADC: Yes. HSP: Yes

Age: 62+. Nonprofit; affiliated with Christian Retirement Homes, Inc. Apartments. Nursing care; medical services; Medicare-approved; personal care; medication administration; 24-hour security system; 24-hour emergency response system; maintenance; transportation; up to 3 daily meals; housekeeping and laundry services; social and recreational activities.

IND ENT: $35,500–$110,000. IND MO: $925–$2,250. AL Daily: $85. SNF Daily: $150.

Gateway Manor

225 N. 56th St.
Lincoln, NE 68504

Ph: (402) 464-6371
Fax: (402) 467-0299

IND: Yes. HHC: Yes

Age: 62+. Apartments and duplexes. Nursing care; medical services; 24-hour security system; emergency response system; maintenance; scheduled transportation; up to 3 daily meals, housekeeping and laundry services; exercise equipment; religious services; library; social and recreational activities; billiards area; penthouse for private parties and meetings; garden plots; sun deck/ patio on rooftop; hobby room; barber/ beauty shop.

DEP: (non-ref. apartment), $1,100. PURCHASE: (duplex), $110,000–$115,500. IND ENT: (apartment), $30,250–$95,500. IND MO: Duplex, $1,900; apartment: $875–$1,850; 2nd person: $2,200.

Gold Crest Retirement Center

PO Box 79
200 Levi Lane
Adams, NE 68301

Ph: (402) 988-7115
Fax: (402) 988-2111

E-mail: *gr02404@navix.net*

IND: 8. AL: 20. SNF: 52. ADC: Yes

Age: 55+. Nonprofit; nondenominational. Apartments. Nursing care; medical services; Medicare/Medicaid-approved; personal care; medication administration; maintenance; transportation; 3 daily meals, extra charge in duplex; pets allowed (duplex only); housekeeping and laundry services; social and recreational activities.

DEP: $600. IND MO: $600. AL Daily: $60–$70. SNF Daily: $90–$150.

Immanuel Village

6803 N. 68th Plaza
Omaha, NE 68152

Ph: (402) 572-2333
Fax: (402) 572-3223

E-mail: *KShafeer@IHSI.org*

IND: 96. AL: 36. SNF: 200. ALZ/IMP: 23

Age: 65+. Nonprofit; affiliated with the Evangelical Lutheran Church of America. Apartments located on a medical campus. Nursing and emergency care; Medicare-approved; 24-hour security system; 24-hour emergency response system; maintenance; scheduled transportation; up to 3 daily meals; housekeeping and laundry services; planned social and recreational activities.

IND ENT: $33,000–$134,000. IND MO: $925–$950. AL MO: $2,650. SNF Daily: $100–$150.

Maple Crest Care Center

2824 N. 66th Ave.
Omaha, NE 68104-3996

Ph: (402) 551-2110
Fax: (402) 551-4636

IND: 175. SNF: 175. ALZ/IMP: Yes

Nonprofit. Private and semiprivate rooms. Nursing care; medical services; physical, occupational, and speech therapies; respiratory therapy; in-house optometrist; dental and podiatry care; in-house psychiatric care; in-house evaluations and hearing aid service; Medicare/Medicaid-approved; security; maintenance; 3 daily meals; mascot pets: housekeeping and laundry services; exercise; Nautilus equipment; group and individual activities for religious growth; social and recreational activities.

SNF MO: $3,350–$5,150. Private rooms daily, $140–$170; semiprivate rooms daily, $120–$150.

The Oaks (Meadowlark Estates; The Hearthstone; The Place; The Court; Duplexes)

2319 Lincoln Ave.
York, NE 68467

Ph: (402) 362-4333
Fax: (402) 362-4891

E-mail: *hs34805@navix.net*

IND: 66. SNF: 146. ALZ/IMP: 18. ADC: Yes. HPS: Yes. RSP: Yes

Age 55+. Nonprofit. Private and semiprivate rooms. 24-hour nursing care; medical services; physical, occupational, and speech-language-swallow therapy; on-site pharmacy; Medicare/Medicaid-approved; personal care; medication administration; security system; emergency response system; maintenance; transportation; up to 3 daily meals; pets allowed; housekeeping and linen services; religious services; full-time activity director; social services; gift shop; beauty shop.

IND MO: based on income. SNF Daily: private, $90; semiprivate, $85.

Southwest

Sarah Ann Hester Memorial Home

407 Dakota
PO Box 646
Benkelman, NE 69021-0646

Ph: (308) 423-2179
Fax: (308) 423-2177

AL: 18. SNF: 48. ALZ/IMP: 10

Nonprofit. Apartments and private rooms. Nursing care; medical services; Medicare-approved; personal care; nursing care; medication administration; 24-hour security system; 24-hour emergency response system; transportation; 3 daily meals; housekeeping and laundry services; fitness center; family visiting room; whirlpool baths; craft rooms.

SNF Daily: $75. AL MO: $1,500; 2nd person, $825.

West

Northfield Villa

2550 21st St.
Gering, NE 69341

Ph: (308) 436-3101
Fax: (308) 436-3493

IND: 131. AL: 10. SNF: 48

Age: 62+. Nonprofit; nondenominational. Apartments. 24-hour skilled nursing care; physician on staff; medical services; rehabilitative therapies; personal care; medication administration; Medicare/Medicaid-approved; 24-hour security system; 24-hour emergency response system; maintenance; scheduled transportation; up to 3 daily meals; housekeeping and laundry services; exercise room; nondenominational religious services; Bible study; social and recreational activities; barber/beauty shop.

DEP: (ref.), $2,200. IND ENT: $52,000–$89,500. IND MO: $825–$1,000. AL MO: $440–$660. SNF MO: same as AL MO, plus supplies and 2 meals.

The Residency

2100 Circle Drive
Scottsbluff, NE 69361

Ph: (308) 632-4342
Fax: (308) 630-8190

IND: 94. SNF: 21

Age: 62+. Nonprofit. Apartments. Skilled nursing care; medical services; rehabilitative therapies; 24-hour security system; 24-hour emergency response system; maintenance; transportation; up to 3 daily meals; pets allowed; housekeeping and laundry services; social and recreational activities.

DEP: (ref.), $2,200. IND ENT: $80,500–$135,500. IND MO: $880–$1,350. SNF MO: same as IND MO, plus supplies and 2 meals.

The Village at Regional West

320 E. 42 St.
Scottsbluff, NE 69361

Ph: (308) 630-2010

IND: 57. AL: 18. HCC: 276

Age 55+. For-profit; nondenominational. One- and two-bedroom apartments and private and semiprivate rooms. Nursing care; physician services; medical services; rehabilitative therapies; pharmacy; semiannual health screening clinics; blood pressure checks; personal care; medication administration; security; emergency response system; maintenance; transportation; up to

3 daily meals; pets allowed; housekeeping and laundry services; fitness program; whirlpool; religious services; library; social and recreational activities; on- and off-site activities; arts and crafts; educational programs; card and board games; lounges; putting green; pond; walking paths; gardens; barber/beauty shop.

IND MO: $1,000–$1,300. AL MO: $1,600–$3,500. HCC services are extra.

Northeast

The Oaks Retirement Community

1500 Vintage Hill Drive
Wayne, NE 68787-1240

Ph: (402) 375-1500
Fax: (402) 375-3579

E-mail: *the oaks@midlands.net*

IND: 27. AL: 24. HHC: Yes. RSP: Yes

Age: 50+. Nondenominational. Apartments. 24-hour licensed/certified staff; personal care; medication administration; security; 24-hour emergency response system; maintenance; scheduled transportation; 3 daily meals; housekeeping and laundry services; social and recreational activities; lobby with fireplace; ice cream parlor.

Contact facility for fees.

South Central

Cambridge Court

4107 Central Ave.
Kearney, NE 68847

Ph: (308) 237-3773
Fax: (308) 234-9832

AL: 41. HHC: Yes. RSP: Yes

Profit; nondenominational. Apartments. Nursing care; medical services; Medicaid-approved; personal care; medication administration; security system; emergency response system; maintenance; scheduled transportation; 3 daily meals; housekeeping and laundry services; self-operated elevator; snack bar; social and recreational activities.

Contact facility for fees.

Chrisoma West Christian Homes Retirement Community

Rte. 2, Box 24
Holdrege, NE 68949-9603

Ph: (308) 995-4493

AL: Yes. SNF: Yes. ALZ/IMP: Yes. ADC: Yes

Apartments. 24-hour nursing staff; personal care; medication administration; 24-hour emergency response system; maintenance; scheduled transportation; 3 daily meals; housekeeping and laundry services; chaplain; social and recreational activities; private dining room; activity room; ice cream parlor; barber/beauty shop.

Contact facility for fees.

Southeast

Paddock Kensington

105 N. 6th
Beatrice, NE 68310

Ph: (402) 228-2000
Fax: (402) 228-3287

http://www.agemark.com

E-mail: *Kensington@navix.net*

AL: 65. HCC: Yes. ADC: Yes

Age 50+ (preferred). For-profit. Apartments and private rooms. Personal care; nursing care; medication administration; 24-hour security; 24-hour emergency response system; maintenance; transportation; up to 3 daily meals; pets allowed; housekeeping and laundry services; kitchenettes on each floor; storage units;

chapel; social and recreational activities; within walking distance of stores, banks, theaters; barber/beauty shop.

DEP: (ref.), $385. AL MO: (apartments), $1,750–$2,000; (private rooms), $1,100–$1,600.

Assisted Living and Residential Care Facilities

*In the state of Nebraska, these facilities are called **Assisted Living Facilities**.*

These facilities provide housing, food service, and one or more personal services.

Types of Authorization

Licensing and / or Certification

These facilities are licensed and regulated by the Department of Regulation and Licensure (part of the Health and Human Services system). Assisted lving fcilities provide room, board, and an array of services for assistance with or provision of personal care, activities of daily living, health maintenance activities, or other supportive services.

Memberships

- Assisted Living Federation of America (ALFA) is a national nonprofit membership organization whose mission is to enhance the quality of life in assisted living facilities and promote the interests of the assisted living industry. ALFA, 10300 Eaton Place, Suite 400, Fairfax, VA 22030. Ph: (703) 691-8100. Fax: (703) 691-8106. *http: / / www.alfa.org*

East

St. Joseph's Retirement Community

320 E. Decatur
West Point, NE 68788

Ph: (402) 372-3477
Fax: (402) 372-6600

AL: 70. ALZ/IMP: 20

Nonprofit; affiliated with the Catholic Church. Apartments. Nursing care; medical services; Medicaid-approved; personal care; medication administration; 24-hour security system; 24-hour emergency response system; maintenance; transportation; 3 daily meals; housekeeping and laundry services; exercise program; swimming pool; chapel; library; planned social and recreational activities; outdoor courtyard with gazebo; walking path; whirlpool bath; game room; sewing room; aviary; barber/ beauty shop.

IND MO: $1,200–$1,950; 2nd person, $550. AL MO: depends on services.

Saunders House

1313 Hackberry St.
Wahoo, NE 68066

Ph: (402) 443-3333
Fax: (402) 443-5578

AL: Yes

Apartments. 24-hour staffing; health monitoring; Medicare/Medicaid-approved; personal care; medication administration; 24-hour security system; maintenance; 3 daily meals; pets allowed; social and recreational activities; fireplace and enclosed courtyard with covered patio; barber/beauty shop.

APPL: $200. DEP: $550. AL MO: Level I: $1,750–$2,050; 2nd person: $660, Level II: $1,925–$2,275; 2nd person, $770; Level III: $2,150–$2,475; 2nd person, $880.

Central

Chancellor Place at Aspen Park

3700 W. Philip Ave.
North Platte, NE 69101

Ph: (308) 534-8808
Fax: (308) 534-8818
http: / / www.chancellorhealthcare.com

E-mail: *debh@chancellorhealthcare.com* or *bobbik@chancellorhealthcare.com*

IND: 12. AL: 51. ALZ/IMP: 21

For-profit; nondenominational. Apartments. Medical services; Medicaid-approved; personal care; medication administration; 24-hour emergency response system; maintenance; transportation; 3 daily meals; pets allowed; housekeeping and laundry services; library; activities room; social parlor; social and recreational activities; barber/beauty shop.

DEP: (ref.), $100. IND ENT: (ref.), $550. IND MO: $1,800. AL ENT: (non-ref.), $550. AL MO: $1,650–$2,550.

Park Avenue Estates

1811 Ridgeway
Lexington, NE 68850

Ph: (308) 324-5490

AL: Yes

Age: 50+. Nondenominational. Apartments. 24-hour licensed staff on duty; personal care; medication administration; 24-hour emergency response system; maintenance; scheduled transportation; 3 daily meal; pets allowed; housekeeping and laundry services; fitness center; exercise programs; planned social and recreational activities; lobby; dining room; activity/craft room; billiards room; ice cream parlor; barber/beauty shop.

IND ENT: (ref.), 1 mo. rent. IND Daily: $45–$60, depending on level of care. AL ENT: (ref.), 1 mo. rent. AL Daily: $60–$90, depending on level of care.

Southeast

Clark Jeary Home

1313 Eldon Drive
Lincoln, NE 68510

Ph: (402) 489-0331
Fax; (402) 489-0462

AL: 108

Age: 60+. Nonprofit. Apartments. Nursing care; 24-hour professional health care staff; personal care; medication administration; emergency response system; transportation; 3 daily meals; housekeeping and laundry services; exercise programs; sun/sitting rooms; chapel; recreation room; social and recreational activities.

IND ENT: (optional), $4,000. IND MO: $1,000–$1,800. AL: services are billed.

Hickory Villa

7315 Hickory St.
Omaha, NE 68124

Ph: (402) 392-0767
Fax (402) 392-2371

IND: Yes. AL: Yes

Apartments and semiprivate rooms. Licensed nurse supervision; on-site rehabilitative therapies; 24-hour medication aides; medication administration; secure environment; 24-hour emergency call system; maintenance; scheduled transportation; up to 3 daily meals plus snacks; housekeeping and laundry services; social and recreational activities.

IND MO: $2,350–$2,450. 2nd person: $725. AL MO: semiprivate room: $1,550.

Immanuel Lakeside Village

17475 Frances St.
Omaha, NE 68130-2341

Ph: (402) 932-9506

E-mail: *KBonniwe@IHSI.org*

IND: 90. AL: 40

Age: 65+. Nonprofit; affiliated with the Evangelical Lutheran Church of America. Apartments. Personal care; medication administration; 24-hour security; 24-hour emergency response system; maintenance; scheduled transportation; 1 daily meal; pets allowed; housekeeping and laundry services; fitness center; planned social and recreational activities.

IND ENT: $53,000–$154,000. IND MO: $1,450–$2,350; 2nd person, $450. AL MO: $2,750–$2,900.

The Legacy Retirement Community

5600 Pioneers Blvd.
Lincoln, NE 68506

Ph: (402) 436-3000
Fax: (402) 436-3013

IND: 135. AL: 38

Age: 55+. For-profit. Apartments. Nursing care; podiatry; hearing test; eyeglass repair; hearing aid repair; security system; 24-hour emergency system; maintenance; van and car transportation; 3 daily meals (AL), 2 daily meals (IND); pets allowed; weekly housekeeping and linen services; laundry facilities; garden and pond with Mallard ducks and goldfish; outdoor brick sculpture with waterfall; library; sunroom; fireside room; Main Street USA with bank, general store, livery stable, saloon, and ice cream parlor; barber/beauty shop.

IND MO: $1,100. AL MO: $1,100.

New Cassel Retirement Center

900 N. 90th St.
Omaha, NE 68114

Ph: (402) 393-2277
Fax: (402) 393-3784

RH: 157. ADC: Yes

Nonprofit; affiliated with the School Sisters of St. Francis. Apartments. Personal care; nursing care; medication administration; RN 18 hours; CAN overnight shift; wellness center; 24-hour security system; 24-hour emergency response system; maintenance; scheduled transportation; 3 daily meals; weekly housekeeping and linen services; daily activity programs; computer lab; ceramic/woodworking room; sewing room; daily Catholic Mass; interfaith services; beauty shop.

IND ENT: (optional), $5,500. IND MO: studio: $700–$2,000; 1 bedroom: $1,475; 2 bedroom: $1,850. No entrance fee: studio: $800–$1,350; 1-bedroom: $1,650; 2-bedroom, $2,000.

Orchard Park Retirement Community

3110 S. 48th St.
PO Box 6146
Lincoln, NE 68506-3353

Ph: (402) 488-8191
Fax: (402) 483-2931
E-mail: *virgilcarner@juno.com*

AL: 58. RSP: Yes

Age: 55+. For-profit; nondenominational. Private and semiprivate rooms. Nursing care; medical services; Medicaid-approved; personal care; medication administration; 24-hour security system; 24-hour emergency response system; maintenance; scheduled transportation; 3 daily meals; housekeeping and laundry services; exercise programs; devotional and worship services; planned social and recreational activities; barber/beauty shop.

DEP: $150. AL MO: $50–$300. Private room: $925–$1,700; semiprivate room: $1,250.

Remington Heights

12606 W. Dodge Rd.
Omaha, NE 68154

Ph: (402) 493-5807
Fax: (402) 493-3967

IND: 88. AL: 58

For-profit. Apartments. Personal care; medication administration; 24-hour staffing; 24-hour security system; emergency response system; maintenance; scheduled transportation; housekeeping and laundry services; 3 daily meals; social and recreational activities; barber/beauty shop.

DEP: (ref.), $550. IND MO: $1,400–$2,600. 2nd person: $330. AL MO: Level I care: $1,800–$2,450; 2nd person, $550; Level II care: $2,000–$2,650; 2nd person, $770; Level III care: $2,550–$3,200; 2nd person, $1,350.

Silvercrest Miracle Hills

11909 Miracle Hills Drive
Omaha, NE 68154

Ph: (402) 431-0011
Fax: (402) 431-9257

IND: Yes. AL: Yes

Studios and one- and two-bedroom apartments. 24-hour certified staffing; registered nurse on staff; health monitoring; personal care; medication administration; 24-hour emergency response system; maintenance; scheduled transportation; 3 daily meals; housekeeping and laundry services; chapel; library; resident activities coordinator; social and recreational activities; private dining room for special occasions; country store; barber/beauty shop.

DEP: (ref.), $550. IND MO: $2,000–$2,550; 2nd person, $550. AL MO: Level I: $325; Level II: $425; Level III: $550.

The Paxton

1403 Farnam St.
Omaha, NE 68102

Ph: (402) 346-3330
Fax: (402) 221-8285

AL: 311

Age: 25+. Nonprofit. Apartments and private rooms. Nursing care; medical services; on-site podiatrist, physical therapist, and hearing specialist; personal care; Medicaid-approved; medication administration; 24-hour emergency response system; 3 daily meals; housekeeping and laundry services; social and recreational activities; cafe; thrift store; barber/beauty shop.

IND MO: $1,200. AL MO: $875–$1,400, depending on level of care.

South

St. Luke's Countryside Villa

2300 E. 32nd Place
Kearney, NE 68847

Ph: (308) 236-9395
Fax: (308) 237-3799

IND: 9. AL: 12

Age: 62+. Nonprofit; affiliated with the Evangelical Lutheran Church. Low-income apartments. Weekly nurses' visits; Medicaid-approved; personal care; medication administration; 24-hour security system; 24-hour emergency response system; maintenance; 3 daily meals; pets allowed; weekly housekeeping and laundry services; social and recreational activities.

DEP: (ref.), 1 mo. rent. IND MO: 30% of adjusted gross income. AL MO: 30% of adjusted gross income, plus service fee adjusted to ability to pay.

Northeast

The Meadows

500 S. 18th St.
Norfolk, NE 68701

Ph: (402) 371-1730
Fax: (402) 644-4702

IND: 78. AL: 42

Age: 62+. Profit. Apartments and private rooms. Medicaid-approved (AL only); personal care; medication administration; 24-hour security system; 24-hour emergency response system; maintenance; transportation; 3 daily meals; pets allowed; housekeeping and laundry services; social and recreational activities; lobby areas; ice cream parlor.

APP: $100. DEP: $100. IND MO: $875–$2,050. AL MO: $1,650–$2,250.

Independent Living

Independent housing (primarily rentals) for seniors that may offer security features, meal service, and activities.

Southeast

Brentwood Estates

1111 S. 70th St.
Lincoln, NE 68510

Ph: (402) 489-1112
Fax: (402) 489-1264

IND: 103. RH: 103

For-profit. Apartments. 24-hour security; 24-hour emergency response system; maintenance; transportation; 3 daily meals; pets allowed; housekeeping and laundry services.

DEP: 1 mo. rent. IND MO: $1,150–$2,475.

Carriage Glen

7005 Shamrock Rd.
Lincoln, NE 68506

Ph: (402) 484-5113
Fax: (402) 484-5113

IND: 51

Age: 62+. Nonprofit; sponsored by the Madonna Rehabilitation Hospital. Apartments. 24-hour security system; 24-hour emergency response system; maintenance; transportation; 1 daily meal; library; guest room; community room; workshop; card room; home theater; country store.

DEP: $200. IND ENT: (ref.) $28,500–$110,500. IND MO: $625–$1,450.

Cotner Center Condominium Association

1540 N. Cotner Blvd.
Lincoln, NE 68505

Ph: (402) 466-2509
Fax: (402) 466-2860

IND: 101

Age: 55+. Nonprofit. Condominiums. Medical services; security entrance system; biweekly transportation to grocery store; meal program; fitness center; library; pool room; craft room; small meeting room; auditorium with stage; greenhouse.

PURCHASE: $44,000–$79,500. IND MO: 1-bedroom: $135; 2-bedroom: $135, plus $15 for each additional person.

Crown Pointe

2820 S. 80th St.
Omaha, NE 68124

Ph: (402) 391-7555
Fax: (402) 391-8203
E-mail: *SulaGrace@webtv.net*

IND: 135

For-profit; nondenominational; studios and one- and two-bedroom apartments. 24-hour on-site management; emergency response system; scheduled transportation; housekeeping and laundry services; 3 daily meals; exercise room and equipment; all-faiths chapel; library; social and recreational activities; atrium; gift shop.

PROC: (non-ref.), $330. IND MO: $1,400–$2,400; 2nd person, $330.

Pacific Springs

17330 Pacific St.
Omaha, NE 68118

Ph: (402) 691-8434
Fax: (402) 691-8839

IND: Yes

Affiliated with the Lutheran Home Foundation. Apartments, homes. Screening and wellness programs; 24-hour security; 24-hour emergency response system; maintenance; scheduled transportation; optional dining plan; optional housekeeping; indoor swimming pool; exercise area; library; walking paths; fishing lake; access to golf; public and private dining rooms; woodworking shop; craft room; general store and cafe; card room; pub; theater; community room; barber/beauty shop.

Accommodation fee: (ref.), $74,250–$164,500, varies depending on model selected. IND MO: $950–$2,700.

Pioneer Manor at Geneva, Inc.

123 S. 11th St.
Geneva, NE 68361

Ph: (402) 759-3818
Fax: (402) 759-3818

IND: 20. HHC: Yes

Age: 62+. Nonprofit; sponsored by the Congregational United Church of Christ. Apartments. 24-hour security system; 24-hour emergency response system; maintenance; senior citizen bus service; pets allowed; laundry facilities; community room; social events.

IND MO: based on 30% of adjusted income.

Adult/Resort Communities

Communities for active adults (not all are age-restricted; primarily ownership).

East

Indian Creek

3903 N. 195th St.
Elkhorn, NE 68022

Ph: (402) 289-1560

http://www.indcrk.com

Individual homes, villas, homesites. Golf course; clubhouse; pro shop.

PURCHASE: Estate homesites, from $87,500; villa homesites, from $66,000; landing homesites, from $33,000.

Northridge Country Club and Estates

Tekamah, NE 68061

Ph: (402) 426-5008

http://www.northridgeestates.com

Individual homes, townhomes, homesites. Golf course; clubhouse; nearby parks, lake, fishing, swimming, boating, hiking/biking, skiing, hunting.

PURCHASE: Homesites, $22,000–$44,000.

Nevada

http: / / www.state.nv.us

General Information

Climate

Moderate. Climate varies between desert and mountain regions. In Ely, the average low January temperature is 9° F and the average high July temperature is 86° F. In Las Vegas, the average low January temperature is 31° F and the average high July temperature is 105° F.

Cost of Living

Ranks 16th in the nation.

Taxes

General: Nevada Department of Revenue, Reno, (705) 328-9553.

State/Local as % of Income: About 10.0%.

Property Tax Exemptions: The Senior Citizens Property Tax Assistance Act is a statewide program that refunds a portion of the property tax paid by those 62+ on their residence.

Sales: 6.5%.

Prescription Exemptions: Prescription medications are exempt from sales tax.

Transportation, Travel, and Tourism

Major Airports

- McCarran International Airport, Las Vegas, (775) 261-5211.
- Reno-Tahoe International Airport, Reno, (775) 328-6400.

Railways

- Amtrak, Reno, (775) 329-8638.
- Black Mountain Travel, Henderson, (775) 565-4000.

Bus Tours

- A-1-Western Tours, (774) 644-7191, (877) 219-3783.
- Adventure Charters & Tours, Las Vegas, (775) 383-0500.
- Gorham's Charters & Tours Inc., Las Vegas, (775) 633-4900.
- Grey Line, Las Vegas, (775) 384-1234.
- Las Vegas Adventure Tours, Las Vegas, (775) 564-5452.
- Regents Tours Company, Las Vegas, (775) 247-1300.
- Valen Transportation, (800) 487-2252.

State Highways

- Nevada Department of Transportation (NDOT), Caston City. (775) 888-7000. Fax: (775) 888-7115. E-mail: *info@nevadadot.com*

Theater and Music:

Central

- Eureka Opera House, Eureka, (775) 237-6006.

Reno-Tahoe Area

- Brewery Arts Center, Carson City, (775) 883-1976.
- National Bowling Stadium and Theatre, Reno, (775) 334-2600.
- Piper's Opera House, Virginia City, (775) 847-0433.
- Wingfield Park Amphitheater, Reno, (775) 334-2417.

Museums, Crafts, Historical, Recreational

North

- Barrick Goldstrike Mine Tour, Elko, (775) 778-8681.

- Buckaroo Hall of Fame, Winnemucca, (775) 623-2225.
- Elko Custom Carriage Tours, Elko, (775) 778-6969.
- Humboldt Museum, Winnemucca, (775) 623-2912.
- Northeastern Nevada Museum, Elko, (775) 738-3418.
- Pershing County Courthouse, Lovelock, (775) 273-7144.
- Pershing County Marzen House Museum, Lovelock, (775) 273-2115.
- Trail of the 49ers Interpretive Center, Battle Mountain, (775) 635-5720.
- Western Folklife Center, Elko, (775), 738-7508.

Las Vegas Area

- Bonnie Springs Old Nevada, Old Nevada, (775) 875-4191.
- Boulder City Historic District, Boulder City, (775) 293-2034.
- Boulder City/Hoover Dam Museum, Boulder City, (775) 294-1988.
- Bruno's Indian and Turquoise Museum, Boulder City, (775) 293-4865.
- Clark County Heritage Museum, Henderson, (775) 455-7955.
- Classic Auto Exhibition Hall, Laughlin, (775) 298-2535.
- Desert Valley Museum, Mesquite, (775) 346-5705.
- Donna Beam Fine Art Gallery, Las Vegas, (775) 895-3893.
- Guinness World of Records Museum, Las Vegas, (775) 792-3766.
- Hoover Dam, Boulder City, (775) 294-3585.
- King Tut's Tomb and Museum, Las Vegas, (775) 262-4500.
- Las Vegas Art Museum, Las Vegas, (775) 360-8000.
- Las Vegas Natural History Museum, Las Vegas, (775) 384-3466.
- Liberace Museum, Las Vegas, (775) 798-5595.
- Lost City Museum, Overton, (775) 397-2193.
- Magic and Movie Hall of Fame, Las Vegas, (775) 737-1343.
- Marjorie Barrick Museum of Natural History, Las Vegas (775) 895-3381.
- Nevada State Museum and Historical Society, Las Vegas, (775) 486-5205.
- Ogorek Auto Gallery, Boulder City, (775) 294-7172.
- Old Las Vegas Mormon Fort Historic Park, Las Vegas, (775) 486-3511.
- Ron Lee's World of Clowns, Henderson, (775) 434-1700.
- Searchlight Historic Museum and Historic Mining Park, Searchlight, (775) 297-1642.
- Treasure of Russia, Las Vegas, (775) 889-2441.

Central/East

- Belmont Courthouse State Historic Site, Belmont, (775) 867-3001.
- Berlin-Ichthyosaur State Park, Gabbs, (775) 964-2440.
- BHP Mining Tours, Ruth, (775) 289-7000.
- Caliente Railroad Depot, Caliente, (775) 726-3129.
- Churchill County Museum and Archives, Fallon, (775) 423-3677.
- Central Nevada Museum, Tonopah, (775) 482-9676.
- East Ely Railroad Depot Museum, Ely, (775) 289-1663.
- Eureka County Courthouse, Eureka, (775) 237-5484.
- Eureka Sentinel Museum, Eureka, (775) 237-5010.
- Goldfield Historic Equipment Park, Goldfield, (775) 485-6365.
- Lincoln County Historical Museum, Pioche, (775) 962-5207.
- McGill Drugstore, McGill, (775) 235-7082.
- Million Dollar Courthouse, Pioche, (775) 962-5182.
- Mineral County Historical Museum, Hawthorne, (775) 945-5142.
- Nevada Northern Railway Museum, Ely, (775) 289-2085.
- The Parsonage, Goldfield, (775) 485-3560.
- Rhyolite Historic Site, Beatty, (775) 553-2424.

- Tonopah Mining Park, Tonopah, (775) 482-9676.
- Ward Charcoal Ovens Tate Historic Site, Ely, (775) 728-4660.
- White Pine Public Museum, Ely, (775) 289-4710.

Reno-Tahoe Area

- Bowers Mansion, Washoe Valley, (775) 849-0201.
- Brewery Arts Center, Carson City, (775) 883-1976.
- (Julia C.) Bullette Red Light Museum, Virginia City, (775) 847-9394.
- Carson Valley Museum and Cultural Center, Gardnerville, (775) 782-2555.
- Comstock Firemen's Museum, Virginia City, (775) 847-0717.
- Fleischmann Planetarium, Reno, (775) 784-4811.
- Fourth Ward School Cultural Center, Virginia City, (775) 847-0975.
- Genoa Courthouse Museum, Genoa, (775) 782-4325.
- (W. M.) Keck Museum, Reno, (775) 784-4528.
- Lyon County Museum, Yerington, (775) 463-2245.
- Mackay Mansion Museum, Virginia City, (775) 847-0173.
- (Wilbur D.) May Museum, Reno, (775) 785-5961.
- National Automobile Museum (The Harrah's Collection), Reno, (775) 333-9300.
- Nevada Historical Society Museum, Reno, (775) 688-1190.
- Nevada Gambling Museum, Virginia City, (775) 847-9022.
- Nevada Museum of Art, Reno, (775) 329-3333.
- Nevada State Library and Archives, Carson City, (775) 687-5160.
- Nevada State Museum, Carson City, (775) 687-4810.
- Nevada State Railroad Museum, Carson City, (775) 687-6953l
- Sharkey's Memorabilia Collection, Gardnerville, (775) 782-3133.
- Sheppard Fine Art Gallery, Reno, (775) 784-6658.
- Sparks Heritage Museum, Sparks, (775) 355-1144.
- Virginia & Truckee (V) Railroad, Virginia City, (775) 847-0380.
- Warren Engine Co. No. 1 Historic Fire Museum, Carson City, (775) 887-2210.
- Way It Was Museum, Virginia City, (775) 847-0766.
- Wellington Station Museum, Wellington, (775) 465-2304.
- Wigwam Restaurant Museum, Fernley, (775) 575-2573.
- Wild West Museum, Virginia City, (775) 847-0400.

Organizations

Advocacy Groups

- AARP Senior Employment Services, Reno, (775) 323-2243.
- Adult Care Consultants, (800) 822-2523.
- Nevada Division of Aging Services:
- Carson City, (775) 687-4210.
- Elko, (775) 738-1966.
- Las Vegas, (775) 486-3545.
- Reno, (775) 688-2964.

Volunteer Programs

- Foster Grandparents Program:
- Las Vegas, (775) 647-1515
- Sparks, (775) 358-2768.
- Retired Senior Volunteer Program:
- Caliente, (775) 726-3126.
- Carson City, (775) 687-4680.
- Fallon, (775) 423-8046.
- Overton, (775) 397-8408.
- Reno, (775) 784-1807.
- Senior Companion Program:
- Las Vegas, (775) 382-0721.
- Sparks, (775) 358-2322.
- Special Olympics Nevada (emerging program), Whittier, CA, (562) 945-5828.
- United Way of Southern Nevada, Las Vegas, (775) 734-8504.

Housing

Long-Term Care Facilities

In the state of Nevada, these facilities are called ***Continuing Care/Nursing Home/Retirement Facilities****.*

These facilities provide residential living and/or various levels of nursing and medical services to seniors for an extended period of time.

Types of Authorization

Licensing and / or Certification

Facilities are regulated by the Department of Health, Bureau of Licensure and Certification.

Memberships

- American Association of Homes and Services for the Aging (AAHSA) represents not-for-profit organizations committed to providing high-quality health care, housing, and services to the elderly. AAHSA, 901 E St. NW, Suite 500, Washington, DC 20004-2011. Ph: (202) 783-2242. Fax: (202) 783-2285. *http: / / www.aahsa.org*

Accreditation

- Continuing Care Accreditation Commission (CCAC) accredits facilities that offer seniors a contract or contracts that provide residential living and health care services for the remainder of the person's lifetime and meet CCAC's accreditation standards.
- Joint Commission on the Accreditation of Healthcare Organizations (JCAHO) is an independent, not-for-profit organization, and the nation's oldest and largest standards-setting and health care accrediting institution.

Las Vegas Area

Boulder City Care Center

601 Adams Blvd.
Boulder City, NV 89005

Ph: (775) 293-5151
Fax: (775) 293-2800

SNF: 87

No age requirement. For-profit. Semi-private rooms. 24-hour skilled nursing care; full rehabilitation services; physical, occupational, and speech therapy; restorative program; Medicare/Medicaid-approved; 24-hour security system; 24-hour emergency system; maintenance; transportation; up to 3 daily meals, housekeeping and laundry services.

Daily: $130.

Assisted Living and Residential Care Facilities

In the state of Nevada, these facilities are called ***Assisted Living/Residential Care/Group Home Facilities****.*

These facilities provide housing, food service, and one or more personal services.

Types of Authorization

Licensing and / or Certification

Facilities are regulated by the Department of Health, Bureau of Licensure and Certification.

Memberships

- Assisted Living Federation of America (ALFA) is a national nonprofit membership organization whose mission is to enhance the quality of life in assisted living facilities and promote the interests of the assisted living industry. ALFA, 10300 Eaton Place, Suite 400, Fairfax, VA 22030.

Ph: (703) 691-8100. Fax: (703) 691-8106. *http://www.alfa.org*

Las Vegas Area

AmeriPark at Spencer

4255 Spencer St.
Las Vegas, NV 89119

Ph: (775) 732-0652
Fax: (775) 732-9520

IND: 80. AL: 40

For-profit. Medical services; personal care; medication administration; security; emergency response system; maintenance; transportation; up to 3 daily meals; housekeeping and laundry services; social and recreational activities.

DEP: (ref.), $100. ENT: $385 IND/AL MO: $1,100–$1,650.

The Charleston Retirement and Assisted Living

2121 W. Charleston Blvd.
Las Vegas, NV 89102

Ph: (775) 387-7746
Fax: (775) 382-8407
E-mail: *mpmcconnell@earthlink.net*

IND: 129. RH: 129. AL: 129

Age 18+. Family owned; nondenominational. Personal care; medication administration; security; emergency response system; maintenance; transportation; up to 3 daily meals; housekeeping and laundry services; planned activities; pool; courtyard; barber/beauty shop.

DEP: $220–$550. ENT: $220-$550. MO: Semiprivate, $900 (with state assistance); $1,050–$1,350 (without state assistance); private, $1,800–$2,200.

Loving Care Alzheimer Facility

155 Emden Drive and 723 Skipjack Drive
Henderson, NV 89015

Ph: (775) 565-2285
Fax: (775) 565-7427

RH: Yes. ALZ/IMP: 12

Age: 18+ and diagnosed with Alzheimer's/dementia. For-profit. Private and semiprivate rooms. Personal care; medication administration; 24-hour security system; up to 3 daily meals; housekeeping and laundry service; 2 small family-style living rooms; fenced yard; covered patio.

RH ENT: 1 mo. rent. RH MO: $3,000+.

Regent at Mira Loma

2520 Wigwam Parkway
Henderson, NV 89104

Ph: (775) 260-8400

AL: 98. ALZ/MEM IMP: 30

Health services staff; personal care; medication administration; security; emergency response system; maintenance; transportation; up to 3 daily meals; housekeeping and laundry services; social and recreational activities.

DEP: (ref.) $100. ENT: $1,550. AL MO: $1,975–$4,400.

Sunlake Terrace

3250 S. Fort Apache Rd.
Las Vegas, NV 89117-0740

Ph: (775) 256-6500
Fax: (775) 256-6736

AL: 121

Nondenominational. Studio and one-bedroom apartments. 24-hour professional and responsive staff; wellness program; personal care; medication administration; security; emergency response system; maintenance; transportation; up to 3 daily meals; housekeeping and laundry services; social and recreational activities; country store; courtyard; personal care; medication administration; security; emergency response system; maintenance; transportation; barber/beauty shop.

AL MO: $2,000–$2,650; 2nd person, starting at $425.

Sutton Terrace

3185 E. Flamingo Rd.
Las Vegas, NV 89121-4303

Ph: (775) 436-9000
Fax (775) 436-9050

http://www.arval.com

IND: Yes. AL: Yes

Nondenominational. Studios and one-bedroom apartments. 24-hour staffing; wellness program; personal care; medication administration; security; emergency response system; maintenance; transportation; up to 3 daily meals; housekeeping and laundry services; social and recreational activities.

IND MO: $1,850–$2,450. AL MO: $2,300–$2,850.

Village Oaks

3025 E. Russell Rd.
Las Vegas, NV 89120

Ph: (775) 451-7896
Fax: (775) 450-2252

AL: 105

For-profit; nondenominational. Private rooms. Personal care; medication administration; security; emergency response system; maintenance; transportation; up to 3 daily meals; housekeeping and laundry services; social and recreational activities.

APPL: $300. DEP: $550. AL MO: $1,650–$2,550.

Northwest/Reno Area

Carson Valley Residential Care Center

1189 Kimmerling Rd.
PO Box 1737
Gardnerville, NV 89410

Ph: (775) 265-1400

AL: Yes

For-profit; nondenominational. Suites and private and semiprivate rooms. Health and wellness programs; personal care; medication administration; security; emergency response system; maintenance; transportation; up to 3 daily meals; housekeeping and laundry services; social and recreational activities; crafts center; barber/beauty shop.

Contact facility for fees.

Classic Residence by Hyatt

3201 Plumas St.
Reno, NV 89509

Ph: (775) 825-1105
Fax: (775) 829-1052

AL: Yes

For-profit; nondenominational. Private studios and one- and two-bedroom apartments. 24-hour supervision; prescription delivery service; 24-hour concierge assistance; personal care; medication administration; security; emergency response system; maintenance; transportation; up to 3 daily meals; housekeeping and laundry services; social and recreational activities.

Contact facility for fees.

Dayton Parkview Adult Residence

3 Flowery Ave.
Dayton, NV 89403

Ph: (775) 246-5339
Fax: (775) 246-4250

AL: 54. RH: Yes

For-profit; nondenominational. Private and semiprivate rooms. personal care; medication administration; security; emergency response system; maintenance; transportation; up to 3 daily meals; housekeeping and laundry services; religious services; social and recreational activities.

DEP: $100 AL MO: $1,250–$1,550.

Eagle Valley Care Centre

1807 E. Long St.
Carson City, NV 89706

Ph: (775) 883-4449

AL: 38

Nondenominational. Private and semi-private rooms. Personal care; medication administration; security; emergency response system; maintenance; transportation; up to 3 daily meals; housekeeping and laundry services; social and recreational activities.

AL MO: $1,450–$2,000.

Nevada Cares A Family Home for Seniors

2907 N. Mountain St.
Carson City, NV 89703

Ph: (775) 885-9223
Fax: (775) 885-8593

IND: 40. RH: 32. AL: 40

For-profit; nondenominational. Three independently run houses with over 60 private rooms and three levels of care. Visiting nurse services; medical services; personal care; medication administration; security; emergency response system; maintenance; transportation; up to 3 daily meals; housekeeping and laundry services; social and recreational activities.

MO: $1,650–$2,450+.

Silver Rose Manor

1490 Grimes St.
Fallon, NV 89406

Ph: (775) 423-4137
Fax: (775) 423-1266
E-mail: *manor@oasisol.com*

AL: 38

For-profit; nondenominational. Private rooms. Nursing care; personal care; medication administration; security; emergency response system; maintenance; transportation; up to 3 daily meals; housekeeping and laundry services; social and recreational activities.

AL MO: $2,200–$2,650.

Independent Living

Independent housing (primarily rentals) for seniors that may offer security features, meal service, and activities.

Las Vegas Area

Country Club at Valley View

1400 S. Valley View Blvd.
South of Charleston
Las Vegas, NV 89102

Ph: (775) 878-6266 or (800) 407-9020
http://www.bes.com

IND: Yes

Age 55+. On-site shuttle bus; activity community center; full-time activity director; pets allowed; heated pool; spa; fitness center; shuffleboard; aerobics; putting green; horseshoes; dancing; live entertainment; happy hours; daily casino pickup; barber/beauty shop.

MO: $625–$850. Pet fees extra.

Flamingo West

8122 West Flamingo Rd.
Las Vegas, NV 89147

Ph: (775) 364-0320
Fax: (775) 364-2173

IND: Yes

Age 55+. Clubhouse facilities; community pool; spa; sauna; laundry; tennis court; shuffleboard; horseshoe pit; barbecue area; car wash area.

IND MO: $550.

Montara Meadows

3150 E. Tropicana Ave.
Las Vegas, NV 89121

Ph: (775) 435-3150
Fax: (775) 435-7185

IND: 172

Age: 55+. For-profit. Apartments with managers on premises. Emergency response system; scheduled transportation (bus and Lincoln Town Car); up to 3 daily meals; weekly housekeeping and linen services; laundry room; heated swimming pool; Jacuzzi; sauna; social and religious activities; dining room; card room; billiards room; TV lounge; exercise room; beauty salon.

DEP: (ref.), $100. IND MO: $1,375–$2,200; 2nd person, $375.

Paradise Cove Retirement

4330 Eastern Ave.
Las Vegas, NV 89119

Ph: (775) 369-1552
Fax: (775) 794-2481

IND: Yes

Studios and apartments. Security; emergency response system; maintenance; transportation; up to 2 daily meals; pets allowed; housekeeping and laundry services; clubhouse; swimming pool/whirlpool; full-time activities director; library; TV lounge area; dancing; beauty/barber salon.

Contact facility for fees.

Reno Area

Manor at Lakeside

855 Brinkly Ave.
Reno, NV 89509

Ph: (775) 827-3606
Fax: (775) 827-3608

IND: 91

Age 55+. Up to 3 daily meals; pets allowed; housekeeping and laundry services; fitness center; chapel; scheduled activities; bingo; games; parties.

ENT: 1st month plus deposit. IND MO: $1,250–$1,450.

Reno Camlu

1920 Harvard Way
Reno, NV 89502

Ph: (775) 825-2044
Fax: (775) 875-2045

IND: 68

Emergency response system; maintenance; transportation; up to 3 daily meals; pets allowed; housekeeping and laundry services.

DEP: (ref.) 1st mo. rent. IND MO: $1,275–$1,550.

Adult/Resort Communities

Communities for active adults (not all are age-restricted; primarily ownership).

Southwest/Last Vegas Area

Canyon Gate Country Club

2001 Canyon Gate Drive
Las Vegas, NV 89117

Ph: (702) 363-0303

Individual homes. Golf course; tennis; swimming pool; hiking; fitness center; social clubs.

PURCHASE: Homes, from $440,000.

Southshore Golf Club at Lake Las Vegas

1605 Lake Las Vegas Parkway
Henderson, NV 89011

Ph: (702) 558-0022

Individual homes, condominiums, homesites. Golf course; tennis; hiking/biking; fishing; boating/waterskiing; social clubs.

PURCHASE: Homes, from $385,000; homesites: $269,500–$1.32 million.

Spanish Trail Country Club

5050 Spanish Trail Lane
Las Vegas, NV 89113

Ph: (702) 364-5050

Individual homes, condominiums. Golf course; tennis; swimming pool; hiking/biking; fitness center.

PURCHASE: Homes, $165,000–$6.6 million.

Sun City Macdonald Ranch

2000 W. Horizon Ridge Pkwy
Henderson, NV 89012

Ph: (800) 764-9322 or (702) 269-4300

55+. Individual homes. Golf course; tennis; swimming pool; community center; fitness center; social clubs.

PURCHASE: Homes, $99,000–$185,000.

Sun City Summerlin

10351 Sun City Blvd.
Las Vegas, NV 89134

Ph: (800) 843-4848 or (702) 363-5454

55+. Individual homes. Golf course; tennis; racquetball; swimming pool; hiking; community center; fitness center; social clubs.

PURCHASE: Homes, $105,000–$299,000.

Northwest/Reno-Tahoe Area

Dayton Valley Country Club

51 Palmer Drive
Dayton, NV 89403

Ph: (800) 644-3822

Individual homes, homesites. Golf course; tennis; social clubs.

PURCHASE: Homes, $132,000–$605,000.

The Golf Club at Genoa Lakes

1 Genoa Lakes Drive
Genoa, NV 89411

Ph: (775) 782-4653

Individual homes. Golf course; fishing; hunting; bicycle paths; boating/waterskiing; snow skiing; fitness center; social clubs.

PURCHASE: Homes, $547,000–$1.072 million.

Southeast

Mesquite Vistas

PO Box 267
Mesquite, NV 89024

Ph: (800) 346-7990

Individual homes, condominiums, townhomes, homesites. Golf course; tennis; swimming pool; sports center; clubhouse.

PURCHASE: Homes, $88,000–$440,000+.

Palms Golf Resort

1137 W. Mesquite Blvd.
Mesquite, NV 89024

Ph: (800) 621-0187 or (702) 346-5232

Condominiums. Golf course; tennis; swimming pool; fitness center; gun club.

PURCHASE: Homes, $93,500–$550,000.

New Hampshire

http://www.state.nh.us

General Information

Climate

Cool summers and cold winters. Average temperature in Concord in July is 70° F; average temperature in January is 21° F.

Cost of Living

Ranks 8th in the nation.

Taxes

State/Local as % of Income: 8.5%.

Property Tax Reduction: Residents whose property taxes are more than 10% of the household income may apply for property tax relief if their income does not exceed $40,000.

Sales: None.

Prescription Exemptions: None.

Transportation, Travel, and Tourism

Major Airports

- Manchester Municiapl Airport, One Airport Rd., Manchester, NH 03103, (603) 624-6539.
- Keene Dillant-Hopkins Airport, 80 Airport Rd., Keene, NH 03431, (800) 272-5488.

Railways

- Amtrak, (800) 872-7245.

Bus Tours

- Greyhound Bus, (800) 231-2222.
- C and J Transportation, (603) 742-5111.
- Concord Trailways, (800) 639-1656.

State Highways

- Interstates 89, 93, and 95 run north-south.

Theater and Music

Dartmouth–Lake Sunapee Region

- New London Playhouse, 209 Main St., New London, NH 03755, (603) 526-4631.
- Newport Opera House Assoc., Main St., Box 35120, Newport, NH 03773-0351, (603) 863-2412.

North Country Region

- Weathervane Theatre Players, Rte. 3N, Box 127, Whitefield, NH 03598, (603) 837-9010.

Lakes Region

- Lakes Region Symphony Orchestra, PO Box 1072, Laconia, NH 03246, (603) 279-3324.
- New Hampshire Music Festival, 88 Belknap Mountain Rd., Gilford, NH 03246, (603) 524-1000.
- Village Players, Lehner St., PO Box 770, Wolfeboro, NH 03894, (603) 569-9656.

Merrimack Valley Region

- Adams Memorial Opera House, 29 W. Broadway, Derry, NH 03038, (603) 437-0505.
- Nashua Symphony Orchestra, 120 Main St., Nashua, NH 03060, (603) 880-7538.
- NH Symphony Orchestra, 81 N. Hanover St., PO Box 1298, Manchester, NH 03110-1298, (603) 669-3559.
- Stage One Productions, 132 Bridge St., Manchester, NH 03104, (603) 669-5511.

Monadnock Region (Southwest)

- Apple Hill Center for Chamber Music, Apple Hill Rd., PO Box 217,

East Sullivan, NH 03445, (603) 847-3371.
- Monadnock Chorus and Orchestra, Peterborough, NH 03458, (603) 242-6467.
- Andy's Summer Playhouse, Old Wilton Centre, Wilton, NH 03086, (603) 654-2613.

Seacoast Region

- Leddy Center for the Performing Arts, 131–133 Main St., Epping, NH 03042, (603) 679-2781.
- NH Theater Project, 133 Islington St., Portsmouth, NH 03801, (603) 432-7272.

White Mountains Region

- NCAA/Papermill Theatre, The Mill at Loon Mountain, PO Box 1060, Lincoln, NH 03251, (603) 745-2141.

Museums, Crafts, Historical, Recreational

Dartmouth–Lake Sunapee Region:

- Fort at No. 4 Living History Museum, Rte. 11, 267 Springfield Rd., Charlestown, NH 03603, (603) 826-5700 or (888) FORTAT 4.
- Enfield Shaker Museum and Dana Robes Wood Craftsmen, Rte. 4A, Enfield, NH 03748, (603) 632-4346.

North Country Region

- Christies' Maple Farm, Rte. 2, Lancaster, NH 03584, (800) 788-2118, (working sugarhouse; educational tours).

Lakes Region/White Mountains

- HOBO & Winnipesaukee Scenic Railroads, Box 9, Lincoln, NH 03251, (603) 745-2135.
- Sugar Hill Historical Museum, Main St., Sugar Hill, NH 03585, (603) 823-5336.
- NH Homecraft Cooperative Shop, Rte. 3, West Campton, NH 03223, (603) 726-8626.
- The Original Golden Pond Tour, Holderness, (603) 279-4405 (boat tour).
- Museum of Childhood of Wakefield, off Rte. 16, (603) 522-8073.
- Stonedam Island Natural Area, Meredith, (603) 279-7278.

Merrimack Valley Region

- Christa McAuliffe Planetarium, 3 Institute Drive Concord, NH 03301, (603) 271-STAR.
- Rockingham Park, Rockingham Park Blvd., Salem, NH 03079, (603) 898-2311 (horse racing).
- Museum of New Hampshire History, Eagle Sq., Concord, NH 03301, (603) 226-3189, Fax: (603) 228-6308, E-mail: *nhhsmus@aol.com*

Monadnock Region (Southwest)

- Franklin Pierce Homestead, PO Box 869, Hillsborough, NH 03244, (603) 478-3165.
- Thorne-Sagendorph Art Gallery, Keene State College, (603) 358-2720.

Seacoast Region

- Hampton Beach Casino, Rte. 1, Hampton, NH 03843, (603) 926-4541.
- Portsmouth Harbor Cruises, (603) 436-8084 or (800) 776-0915.
- Port of Portsmouth Maritime Museum and Albacore Park, 600 Market St., Portsmouth, NH 03801, (603) 436-3680.
- Portsmouth Harbor Trail, Portsmouth, (603) 436-3988.

Organizations

Advocacy Groups

- Office of the Ombudsman, Department of Health and Human Services, 6 Hazen Drive, Concord, NH 03301-6505, (603) 271-6941 or (800) 852-3345, ext. 6941, TDD, (800) 735-2964.

Volunteer Programs

- Special Olympics, New Hampshire, (800) 639-2608 (outside of Manchester), (603) 624-1250.

- RSVP of the Upper Valley and White Mountains, (603) 444-1612 (White Mtns.), (603) 787-6971 (Haverhill), (603) 448-3906 (Upper Valley). E-mail: *RSVP@valley.net*

Housing

Long-Term Care Facilities

In the state of New Hampshire, these facilities are called ***Continuing Care/Retirement Communities/Nursing Home Facilities****.*

These facilities provide residential living and/or various levels of nursing and medical services to seniors for an extended period of time.

Types of Authorization

Licensing and / or Certification

These facilities are regulated by the Department of Health and Human Services. CCRCs are required to present a contractual arrangement for a period longer than one year, which provides the rights and obligations of each party to the contract and which guarantees the resident nursing home care and other services for the duration of residence, in exchange for an entrance or other fee. Skilled nursing facilities must provide health care services on a daily basis.

Memberships

- American Association of Homes and Services for the Aging (AAHSA) represents not-for-profit organizations committed to providing high-quality health care, housing, and services to the elderly. AAHSA, 901 E St. NW, Suite 500, Washington, DC 20004-2011. Ph: (202) 783-2242. Fax: (202) 783-2285. *http: / / www.aahsa.org*
- New Hampshire Association of Homes and Services for the Aging (NHAHSA) is an AAHSA Affiliated State Association. NHAHSA, 345 Edward J. Roy Drive, Suite 201, Manchester, NH 03104-4149. Ph: (603) 626-3479. Fax: (603) 626-3763.

Accreditation

- Continuing Care Accreditation Commission (CCAC) accredits facilities that offer seniors a contract or contracts that provide residential living and health care services for the remainder of the person's lifetime and meet CCAC's accreditation standards.
- Joint Commission on the Accreditation of Healthcare Organizations (JCAHO) is an independent, not-for-profit organization and the nation's oldest and largest standards-setting and health care accrediting institution.

South

Bishop Primeau Apartments and St. Teresa's Manor, JCAHO

519 Bridge St.
Manchester, NH 03104

Ph: (603) 668-2373
Fax: (603) 668-0059

IND: Yes. SNF: 51. ICF: Yes

Nondenominational; owned and operated by the New Hampshire Catholic Charities. Apartments and private and semiprivate rooms. 24-hour nursing care and staffing; rehabilitative therapies; dental, vision, and hearing services; podiatry care; pharmacy services; Medicare/Medicaid-certified; personal care; medication administration; security; emergency response system; maintenance; transportation; up to 3 daily meals; housekeeping and laundry services; exercise classes; religious services; educational program; social and recreational activities; discussion groups; barber/beauty shop.

IND: $850–$1,050. Contact facility for SNF/ICF fees.

Mount Carmel, JCAHO

235 Myrtle St.
Manchester, NH 03041

Ph: (603) 627-3811
Fax: (603) 626-4696

NH: 120. ALZ/MEM IMP: 41

Nonprofit; nondenominational. Private and semiprivate rooms. Nursing care; rehabilitative therapies; medical services; dental and podiatry care; pharmacy services; Medicare/Medicaid-approved; personal care; medication administration; security; emergency response system; maintenance; transportation; up to 3 daily meals; housekeeping and laundry services; social and recreational activities.

NH Daily: $175.

New Hampshire Odd Fellows Home

200 Pleasant St.
Concord, NH 03301-2599

Ph: (603) 225-6644
Fax: (603) 228-7150

AL: 78. NH: Yes

Nondenominational; nonprofit. Apartments, suites, and private and semiprivate rooms. 24-hour nursing care; skilled nursing care; physical, occupational, and speech therapies; short- and long-term care; monthly health checks; podiatry care; personal care; medication administration; security; emergency response system; maintenance; transportation; 3 daily meals; small pets allowed; housekeeping and laundry services; exercise room and spa; social and recreational activities; chapel and religious services; media room; concerts and lectures; gift shop; gardening room; barber/beauty shop.

AL MO: $1,800–$4,300; 2nd person, $50. NH Daily: $200–$220.

Pleasant View Retirement

227 Pleasant St.
Concord, NH 03301

Ph: (603) 225-3970 or (800) 340-0311 (NH only)
Fax: (603) 325-8781

IND: 73. AL: Yes. HCC: Yes

For-profit facility; Genesis ElderCare. Apartments. Nursing care; home health care services; 24-hour staffing; short- and long-term care; blood pressure clinic; security; emergency response system; maintenance; transportation; up to 3 daily meals; pets allowed; housekeeping and laundry services; fitness center; swimming pool; Bible study; library; media room; hobby studio; activities room; social and recreational activities; off-site activities; lectures; movies; solarium; lounges; convenience and gift shop; golfing, archery range, and shuffleboard; barber/beauty shop.

DEP: $600. MO: $1,750–$3,550; 2nd person, $600.

Central

Bishop Bradley Apartments and St. Francis Home, JCAHO

406 Court St.
Laconia, NH 03246

Ph: (603) 524-0466

IND: Yes NH: 51

Nondenominational; owned and operated by the New Hampshire Catholic Charities. Apartments and private and semiprivate rooms. 24-hour nursing care and staffing; rehabilitative therapies; dental, vision, and hearing services; podiatry care; pharmacy services; Medicare/Medicaid-certified; personal care; medication administration; security; emergency response system; maintenance; transportation; up to 3 daily meals; housekeeping and laundry services; exercise classes; religious services; educational program; social and recreational activities; discussion groups; barber/beauty shop.

IND MO: $925–$1,150. NH Daily: Semi-private, $170; private, $175.

Southeast

River Woods at Exeter

7 River Woods Drive
Exeter, NH 03833

Ph: (603) 772-4700 or (800) 688-9663
Fax: (603) 778-9623

http://www.riverwoods-exeter.org

IND: 200. AL: Yes. HCC: 60

Nonprofit; nondenominational. Apartments and private and semiprivate rooms. Skilled nursing care; medical services; rehabilitative therapies; dental and podiatry care; pharmacy services; personal care; medication administration; security; emergency response system; maintenance; transportation; up to 3 daily meals; housekeeping and laundry services; health club; swimming pool; library; auditorium; social and recreational activities; music room; woodworking shop; art studios; caf; country store; walking paths; gardens; barber/beauty shop.

IND ENT: (90% ref.), $126,500–$355,500. IND MO: $1,250–$3,150. AL and HCC fees inclusive.

Webster at Rye

795 Washington Rd.
PO Box 530
Rye, NH 03870

Ph: (603) 964-8144
Fax: (603) 964-1483

IND: 29. AL: Yes. NH: 37

Nonprofit; nondenominational. One- and two-bedroom apartments and private and semiprivate rooms. 24-hour nursing care; medical services; physical, occupational, and speech therapies; dental and podiatry care; lab and oxygen services; hospice care; psychiatric and social services; pharmacy services; personal care; medication administration; security; emergency response system; maintenance; transportation; up to 3 daily meals; housekeeping and laundry services; religious services; social, recreational, cultural, and spiritual activities; discussion groups; knitting; bingo; bridge; walking paths; courtyard; beach nearby; patios with grills; barber/beauty shop.

IND MO: $1,825–$2,100. NH Daily: Semi-private, $165–$175; private, $200–$225.

Assisted Living and Residential Care Facilities

In the state of New Hampshire, these facilities are called ***Assisted Living/Residential Care/Personal Care Facilities****.*

These facilities provide room and board for ambulatory and independent adults who need minimum support.

Types of Authorization

Licensing and/or Certification

These facilities are regulated by the Department of Public Health and Human Services.

Memberships

- Assisted Living Federation of America (ALFA) is a national nonprofit membership organization whose mission is to enhance the quality of life in assisted living facilities and promote the interests of the assisted living industry. ALFA, 10300 Eaton Place, Suite 400, Fairfax, VA 22030. Ph: (703) 691-8100. Fax: (703) 691-8106. *http://www.alfa.org*
- New Hampshire Association for Residential Care Homes (NHARCH) is a state affiliate of ALFA. NHARCH, 6 Dixon Ave., Concord, NH 03301. Ph: (603) 225-7397. Fax: (603) 225-3790.

Central

Mountain Crest

29 Baldwin St.
Franklin, NH 03235

Ph: (603) 934-6742
Fax: (603) 934-6743

AL: Yes

For profit; nondenominational; owned by Genesis ElderCare Network. Studios, one-, two-, and three bedroom apartments. Skilled nursing and rehabilitative care (HCC adjacent to facility); 24-hour personal care; medication administration; pharmacy; security; emergency response system; maintenance; transportation; up to 3 daily meals; housekeeping and laundry services; exercise classes; Bible study; lounges and activity rooms; social and community activity programs; crafts; bingo; movies; barber/beauty shop.

AL MO: $1,650–$2,950.

Taylor Community

435 Union Ave.
Laconia, NH 03246

Ph and Fax: (603) 524-5600
E-mail: *Taylor@worldpath.net*

IND: Yes. AL: Yes. ICF: Yes

Age 62+. Nonprofit; nondenominational. Duplexes, townhomes, apartments, and private rooms. 24-hour nursing care; medical services; medical director; rehabilitative therapies; pharmacy services; personal care; medication administration; security; emergency response system; maintenance; transportation; up to 3 daily meals; pets allowed; housekeeping and laundry services; fitness center; nondenominational chapel; library; media center; social and recreational activities; resident associations; conference room.

DEP: $1,100. IND ENT: (80% ref.) $117,000–$180,000. IND MO: $550–$2,550.

South

Hunt Community, CCAC

10 Allds St.
Nashua, NH 03060

Ph: (603) 882-6511 or (888) 258-4868
Fax: (603) 598-1431

IND: Yes. AL: Yes. HCC: 40

Nonprofit; nondenominational. Apartments and private rooms. 24-hour nursing care; medical services; rehabilitative therapies; health and wellness programs; dental and podiatry care; pharmacy services; personal care; medication administration; security; emergency response system; maintenance; transportation; up to 3 daily meals; housekeeping and laundry services; exercise program; library; social and recreational activities; educational programs; intergenerational programs; crafts; woodworking shop; putting green; horseshoe pit; lounge; barber/beauty shop.

Contact facility for fees.

Pillsbury Home

95 High St.
Milford, NH 03055

Ph: (603) 672-1231

RH: Yes

Nonprofit; nondenominational. Rooms. Visiting nurse services; respite care; personal care; medication administration; security system; maintenance; 3 daily meals; housekeeping and laundry services; religious services; social and recreational activities; near town center and area hospitals.

RH Daily: $45.

West

Harvest Hill

121 Mascoma St.
Lebanon, NH 03766

Ph: (603) 448-7474
Fax: (603) 448-4263

IND: Yes. AL: Yes

Age 62+. Nonprofit; nondenominational. Apartments. Nursing care; personal care; medication administration; security; emergency response system; maintenance; transportation; 3 daily meals; pets allowed; housekeeping and laundry services; activities.

RSV DEP: (ref.), $1,650. DEP: (no ref.), $4,950. ENT: $76,000–$125,500. MO: $2,250–$3,950.

Prospect Place

361 Court St.
Keene, NH 03431

Ph: (603) 352-6051

RCH: Yes

Nonprofit; nondenominational. Private rooms. 24-hour staffing; nursing care; monitoring of weight, blood pressure, and other vital signs; personal care; medication administration; security; emergency response system; maintenance; transportation; up to 3 daily meals plus snacks; monthly religious services; housekeeping and laundry services; exercise program; library services; social and recreational activities; on- and off-site activities; bingo; gift shop; screened porch; walking paths; gardens; barber/beauty shop services.

RCH MO: $1,450–$2,300.

Independent Living

Independent housing (primarily rentals) for seniors that may offer security features, meal service, and activities.

West

Atria/The Greens

5342 Lyme Rd.
Hanover, NH 03755

Ph: (603) 643-5512
Fax: (603) 643-3725

IND: 28

Age 55+. For-profit facility; owned by Hillhaven Corp. Apartments. Wellness clinic; priority admittance to healthcare facility; some personal care services; security; emergency response system; maintenance; transportation; up to 3 daily meals; small pets allowed; housekeeping and laundry services; activities; hospital and college nearby.

DEP: $1,100. IND ENT: (90% ref.), $78,500–$96,000. IND MO: $1,725–$1,950; 2nd person, $475.

South

Briston Manor West

37 Ridgewood Rd.
Bedford, NH 03110

Ph: (603) 622-8844

IND: Yes

One- and two-bedroom apartments. Blood pressure screening; foot clinic; security; emergency response system; maintenance; transportation; 1 daily meal; housekeeping and laundry services; religious services; shopping, restaurants, and physician services nearby; social and recreational activities; community room; arts and crafts; hobbies; bingo; screened gazebo; courtyard.

IND MO: $1,150–$1,200; 2nd person, $165.

Adult/Resort Communities

Communities for active adults (not all are age-restricted; primarily ownership).

West

Eastman Community Association
PO Box 53
Grantham, NH 03753
Ph: (603) 863-4240
Fax: (603) 863-3889
http://www.eastman-lake.com

Individual homes, condominiums, homesites. Golf course; tennis; swimming pool; hiking trails; fishing; canoeing; sailing; snow skiing; community center; social clubs.

PURCHASE: Homes, $110,000–$550,000; homesites, $4,400–$55,000.

Lakes Region

Highland Links Colony
RFD 3, Box 213
Plymouth, NH 03264
Ph: (603) 536-3452

Individual homes, duplexes, triplexes, condominiums. Golf course; tennis; swimming pool; hiking trails; boating/waterskiing.

PURCHASE: Homes, $98,000–$181,500.

Perry Hollow Country Club
PO Box 250
Wolfeboro Falls, NH 03896
Ph: (603) 569-3055
Fax: (603) 569-5720

Individual homes, homesites. Golf course; clubhouse; hiking/biking; hunting; snow skiing.

PURCHASE: Homesites, from $71,500.

White Mountains

Wentworth Golf Club
Rte. 16A P.O. Box 578
Jackson Village, NH 03846
Ph: (603) 383-9641 or (603) 383-4407
http://www.wentworthgolf.com

Condominiums. Golf course; tennis; hiking/biking; fishing; snow skiing.

PURCHASE: Homes, $165,000–$253,000.

South

Crestwood
59 Manchester St.
Concord, NH 03301
Ph: (603) 224-4464
http://www.jensencommunities.com

Manufactured homes. Clubhouse; social activities; nearby athletic club with swimming pool, tennis, fitness center.

PURCHASE: Homes, $14,500–$99,000+.

River Pines
0 River Pines Blvd.
Nashua, NH 03062
Ph: (603) 882-7271
http://www.jensencommunities.com

Manufactured homes. Clubhouse; swimming pool; tennis; basketball; boating; social clubs and activities.

PURCHASE: Homes, $33,000–$99,000+.

New Jersey

http://www.state.nj.us

General Information

Climate

Moderate. Average January temperatures, 26° F to 34° F; average July temperatures, 70° F to 76° F.

Cost of Living

Ranks 3rd in the nation.

Taxes

General: New Jersey Division of Taxation Technical Services TSB/OCE, PO Box 281, Trenton, NJ 08646-0281. Tax Hotline: (609) 588-2200. Fax: (609) 588-4500 *http://www.state.nj.us/treasury/taxation*

State/Local as % of Income: About 10.8%.

Property Tax Exemptions: Homeowners 65+ may qualify for annual deductions of up to $250 from real estate taxes.

Sales: 6%. Items exempt from sales tax for seniors: food, clothing, disposable household paper products, all utilities except telephone, and professional/personal services such as doctors, dentists, and hairdressers.

Prescription Exemptions: Prescription medications, some over-the-counter medicines/medical equipment.

Transportation, Travel, and Tourism

Major Airports

- Newark International Airport, Newark, (973) 961-6000.
- Atlantic City International Airport, Atlantic City, (609) 645-7895.

Railways

- Amtrak, (800) USA-RAIL.
- New Jersey Transit, North, (800) 772-2222/(800) 626-RIDE; New Jersey Transit, South, (800) 582-5946.

Bus Tours

- Academy Bus Tours, Hoboken, (201) 420-7000.
- Community Coach & Tours, Passaic, (800) 522-4514.
- Starr Tours, Trenton, (609) 587-0626.

State Highways

- NJ Turnpike Authority, (732) 247-0900.
- Garden State Parkway, (732) 442-8600.
- Atlantic City Expressway, (609) 965-6060.

Theater and Music

North

- New Jersey Ballet, West Orange, (973) 736-5940.
- New Jersey Performing Arts Center, Newark, (888) GO-NJPAC.
- Paper Mill Playhouse, Millburn, (973) 376-4343.
- Newark Jazz Festival, Newark, (201) 733-7758.

Central

- George Street Playhouse, New Brunswick, (732) 246-7717.
- McCarter Theatre, Princeton, (732) 683-8000.
- PNC Bank Arts Center, Holmdel, (732) 442-9200.
- Count Basie Theater, Red Bank, (732) 842-9000.

South

- Garden State Philharmonic Chorus, Orchestra, and Youth Orchestra, Toms River, (732) 349-6277.
- Point Pleasant Beach, Point Pleasant, (908) 899-2424.
- Atlantic City Conventions Hall, (609) 348-7100.
- The Performing Arts Center of Middle Township, Cape May Courthouse, (609) 463-1924.

Museums, Crafts, Historical, Recreational

North

- The Jersey City Museum, Jersey City, (201) 547-4379.
- The Liberty Science Center, Jersey City, (201) 200-1000.
- The Newark Museum, Newark, (800) 7-MUSEUM or (973) 596-6550.

Central

- The New Jersey State Museum and Planetarium, Trenton, (609) 292-6464/6308.
- The Art Museum of Princeton University, Princeton, (609) 258-3787/3788.
- The New Jersey State Aquarium, Camden, (609) 365-3300.

South

- Abescon Lighthouse, Atlantic City, (609) 927-5218.
- The Noyes Museum, Oceanville, (609) 652-8848.
- Towne of Historic Smithville and The Village Green, Smithville, (609) 652-4040.

Organizations

Advocacy Groups

- Office of the Ombudsman, (800) 792-8820.
- Elder Abuse and Neglect Prevention Project, (609) 421-0903.
- The N.J. Department of Health and Senior Services, (800) 792-8820 (NJ EASE [New Jersey Easy Access, Single Entry]).
- Office of Area Agency on Aging Administration, (609) 588-3450.

Volunteer Programs

- Special Olympics (609) 734-8400 or 1-800-336-NJSO, *http://www.njso.org/*
- Foster Grandparent Programs in New Jersey, (908) 968-5531.

Housing

Long-Term Care Facilities

*In the state of New Jersey, these facilities are called **Continuing Care/Retirement Communities (CCRCs)/Life Care Communities**.*

These facilities provide residential living and/or various levels of nursing and medical services to seniors for an extended period of time.

Types of Authorization

Licensing and/or Certification

Certificate of Authority by the Department of Community Affairs. Continuing care facilities are required to register with the state and make public their services, financial stability, fees, and other contract terms. To operate a CCRC a facility must meet these regulations:

- offer housing and health care through an agreement in a contractual form;
- offer a continuum of care to seniors for a period longer than one year, or for the lifetime of the individual;

- enter into a contractual agreement for services rather than a contract to purchase or lease real estate;
- provide a continuum of care that combines independent living with provisions for health care and social services, as well as access to assisted and long term care;
- offer this care in return for an entrance fee and a monthly service fee where the entrance fee is not less than 12 times the monthly service fee.

Licensing is required by the Department of Health for facilities that offer assisted living and nursing care services.

Memberships:

- American Association of Homes and Services for the Aging (AAHSA) represents not-for-profit organizations committed to providing high- quality health care, housing, and services to the elderly. AAHSA, 901 E St. NW, Suite 500, Washington, DC 20004-2011. Ph: (202) 783-2242. Fax: (202) 783-2285. *http://www.aahsa.org*
- The New Jersey Association of Non-Profit Homes for the Aging (NJANPHA) is an AAHSA Affiliated State Association. NJANPHA, 13 Roszel Rd. Suite B 113, Princeton, NJ 08540-6211. Ph: (609) 452-1161. Fax: (609) 452-2907.
- Friends Services for the Aging is an association of Quaker organizations that provide services to older adults in Maryland, New Jersey, and Pennsylvania.

Accreditations:

- Continuing Care Accreditation Commission (CCAC) accredits facilities that offer seniors a contract or contracts that provide residential living and health care services for the remainder of the person's lifetime and meet CCAC's accreditation standards.
- Joint Commission on the Accreditation of Healthcare Organizations (JCAHO) is an independent, not-for-profit organization and the nation's oldest and largest standards-setting and health care accrediting institution.

North

The Fritz Reuter Altenheim

3161 Kennedy Blvd.
North Bergen, NJ 07047

Ph: (201) 867-3585
Fax: (201) 867-5533

http://www.germancorner.com/Fritz-Reuter/

IND: 60. RHC: 96. SNF: 60

Age 60+. Nonprofit, nondenominational. Studios, apartments, and rooms. Skilled nursing care; security; emergency call system; maintenance; transportation; up to 3 meals daily; laundry and housekeeping; physical therapy room with exercise equipment; banking; arts and crafts center; library; chapel; community room; off-site activities; barber/beauty shop.

ENT: (part. ref.) $60,500–$319,000. MO: $725–$2,750.

Lifecare Mews

36 Lifecare Drive
Lafayette, NJ 07848

Ph: (973) 300-4773 or (888) 308-8778
Fax: (973) 300-1403

IND: 40. SNF: Yes

Age 62+. New facility; nondenominational, nonsectarian. Studios, cottages, apartments, and rooms. Health screenings and medical consultations; prescription medicines and social services; security; emergency response system; maintenance; transportation; up to 3 daily meals; housekeeping and laundry services; health club; social, cultural, educational, spiritual, and recreational activities; bank and mailroom services; residents' association: coffee, gift, and convenience shops.

APP: $550 (no ref.) IND ENT: Declining ref., $104,500–$180,500; 50% min. ref., $130,500–$227,000. 2nd person, $11,000–$16,000. IND MO: $1,600–$2,400; 2nd person, $750.

Central

Arbor Glen

100 Monroe St.
Bridgewater, NJ 08807

Ph: (908) 722-4888
Fax: (908) 595-6515

IND: 210. AL: 35. RH: 12. SNF: 20. SA: 10

Older adults. Project of Friends Retirement Concepts, Inc.; not-for profit; nonsectarian; Quaker. Studios, villas, apartments, and rooms. 24-hour nursing care; rehabilitation services; nutritional management; occupational training; therapeutic, social and recreational services; personal care; medication administration; security; emergency response system; maintenance; transportation; up to 3 daily meals; housekeeping and laundry services; home repairs; library; fitness room; postal and banking services; planned activities; gift shop; barber/beauty shop.

IND ENT: (90% ref.): $104,000–$333,500; 2nd person, $23,500. IND MO: $1,550–$2,900; 2nd person, $1,075. AL Daily: $110–$175. RH Daily: $190. LTC Daily: $225–$250. SA Daily: $425.

CentraState Healthcare System

Applewood Estates
1 Applewood Drive
Freehold, NJ 07728

Ph: (732) 431-2000
Fax: (732) 303-1240
http://www.centrastate.com
E-mail: *clink@centrastate.com*

IND: 240. RH: 30. SNF: 60

First community of its kind affiliated with a medical center in New Jersey. Studios, apartments, and rooms. Skilled nursing care; safety checks; security; emergency response system; maintenance; transportation; up to 3 daily meals; housekeeping and laundry services; indoor pool and whirlpool; exercise room; community rooms; arts and crafts; library; game room; bank; barber/beauty shop.

ENT: $74,000–$368,000; MO: $1,425–$3,375.

Crestwood Manor

50 Lacey Rd.
Whiting, NJ 08759-2951

Ph: (908) 849-4900 or (800) 526-1665
Fax: (908) 849-4342

IND: 348. AL: 32. SNF: 60

Age 62+. Presbyterian Homes and Services, Inc.; nonprofit; nondenominational. Apartments and rooms. 24-hour nursing care; visiting physicians; physical, occupational, and speech therapies; social services; personal care; medication administration; Medicare/Medicaid-approved; security; emergency response system; maintenance; transportation; up to 3 daily meals; pets allowed; housekeeping and laundry services; fitness center; escort to dining; grocery shopping; companionship; concierge; chapel; recreational activities; gardens; nature trail; volunteer programs; barber/beauty shop.

IND ENT: (traditional; amortized ref.): $76,000–$107,500; 2nd person, $5,500. IND MO: $1,700–$2,400/single; $2,400–$3,100/double. AL ENT: (ref.): $103,000–$145,000; $3,275 2nd person. AL MO: $1,700–$2,400/single; $2,400–$3,100/double.

REQ: Medicare and supplemental insurance policy.

Meadow Lakes, ccac

PO Box 70
Hightstown, NJ 08520-0070

Ph: (609) 426-6801 or (800) 564-5705

http://www.phsnet.org/

IND: 276. AIP: Yes

Age 62+. Presbyterian Homes and Services, Inc.; nondenominational; nonprofit. Studios, apartments, cottages, and rooms. On-site physician offices; telephone reassurance; rehabilitative therapies; personal care; medication administration; security; emergency response system; maintenance; transportation; up to 3 daily meals; small pets allowed; housekeeping and laundry services; chaplain; pet sitting; heated pool; woodworking shop; putting green; library; resident council; arts and craft center; barber/beauty shop.

PROC: $275/person (non-ref.) DEP: $1,100 (ref.) IND ENT: $55,000–$302,500. IND MO: $1,950–$6,700. LTC: MO fee changes to current MO nursing fee, plus ENT amortized at 3% per month.

Monroe Village, CCAC

One David Brainerd Drive
Jamesburg, NJ 08831

Ph: (732) 521-6400 or (800) 833-4447
Fax: (732) 521-6741

IND: 300. AL: Yes. HCC: 60

Nonprofit; nondenominational; owned by Presbyterian Homes and Services, Inc. Studios, apartments, and private and semiprivate rooms. 24-hour nursing care; physical, occupational, and speech therapies; physician on staff; wellness center; pharmacy; X-ray and lab services; blood pressure checks and glucose and weight monitoring; EKG services; social services; Medicare/Medicaid-approved; personal care; medication administration; security; emergency response system; maintenance; transportation; up to 3 daily meals; housekeeping and laundry services; exercise program; fitness center; library; concierge services; arts and crafts room; educational programs; resident association; volunteer opportunities; on- and off-site activities; activities director; game room; convenience store; barber/beauty shop.

IND ENT: Refundable plan, $60,000–$188,500; Traditional plan, $42,500–$132,500. IND MO: Refundable plan, $1,550–$3,500; Traditional plan, $1,550–$3,500. HCC MO: Temporary stays are included in MO fee; long-term care, $3,050.

The Navesink House, CCAC

40 Riverside Ave. (Rte. 35)
Red Bank, NJ 07701

Ph: (800) 842-2480 or (732) 842-3400
Fax: (732) 842-4934

http://www.navesinkhouse.org/

E-mail: *retire@navesinkhouse.org*

IND: 151. RH: 19. SNF: 43

Age 62+. Nonprofit; nonsectarian; nondenominational. Studios, apartments and rooms. 24-hour licensed nurse on duty; certified geriatric nursing aides; registered dietitian; nursing supervision; health monitoring; pharmacy and pharmacist; physical and occupational therapy; dental, podiatry, and dermatology services; 24-hour personal care; medication administration; security; emergency response system; maintenance; transportation; 1 meal with mo. fee; breakfast and lunch additional; housekeeping and laundry services; church services; planned daily activities.

IND ENT: $47,000–$141,000; $7,700 2nd person. IND MO: $1,375–$2,300; 2nd person, $770. RH ENT: $54,000/person; 2nd person, $15,500. RH MO: $2,700/person; 2nd person, $1,550. Life care contract includes unlimited days of long-term nursing care, no additional monthly service fee.

South

Cadbury Continuing Care Retirement Community and Health Care Center, CCAC; NJANPH; Friends Services for the Aging

2150 Route 38
Cherry Hill, NJ 08002

Ph: (609) 667-4550, ext. 4155, or (800) 422-3287
Fax: (609) 482-1150

IND: Yes. SNF: 120

Age 65+. Nonprofit; Quaker sponsorship. Studios, apartments, and private and semiprivate rooms. Nursing care; physical, occupational, speech, and aqua therapies; dental consultation; podiatry and ophthalmology services; security; emergency response system; maintenance; transportation; up to 3 daily meals; housekeeping and laundry services; library; Bible study; vespers; bingo; thrift shop; gardening areas; woodworking shop; craft studio; banking; residential health clinic; community committees; barber/beauty shop.

APPL: $275/person (no ref.); DEP: $1,100 (ref.) IND ENT: (ref. within 90 days) single, $58,500–$140,000; double, $97,000–$156,500. IND MO: single, $1,500–$2,950; double, $2,850–$3,750.

REQ: Medical assessment by facility physician plus confidential financial disclosure.

Harvest Village

114 Hayes Mill Rd.
Atco, NJ 08004

Ph: (609) 753-2000 or (800) 833-4442
Fax: (609) 753-2016

IND: 252. SNF: 60

Age 62+. For-profit; nondenominational; managed by Fountains Retirement Communities. Studios, apartments, and rooms. Nursing care; rehabilitation therapies; long-term care; 24-hour staffing; security; Medicare/Medicaid-approved; emergency response system; maintenance; transportation; up to 3 daily meals; housekeeping and laundry services; all utilities; exercise center; chapel; social educational, cultural, and recreational programs; library; country store; lounges; garden; arts and crafts; woodworking shop; bank; residents' association.

IND ENT: (ref.), $70,100–$162,000; traditional, $44,000–$103,000. IND MO: $1,300–$2,550; 2nd person, $500.

Holiday Manor

Route 37 West
Toms River, NJ 08757

Ph: (732) 341-0880 or (800) 743-5880
Fax: (732) 341-3506

IND: Yes. AL: 110. SNF: 120

For-profit; nondenominational; owned by H. Hovnanian Industries. Apartments and private and semiprivate rooms. 24-hour nursing care; 24-hour on-call physician; long- and short-term care; physical, occupational, and speech therapies; hospice; home health care; personal care; medication administration; security; emergency response system; maintenance; transportation; up to 3 daily meals; housekeeping and laundry services; indoor pool; religious services; pet therapy; social, cultural, and recreational activities; off-site activities; walking paths; barber/beauty shop.

AL MO: $3,000–$3,500.

Medford Leas, CCAC

Route 70
Medford, NJ 08055

Ph: (609) 654-3009
Fax: (609) 654-7894

http://www.medfordleas.org

E-mail: *medleas@cyberenet.net*

IND: 461 (includes all options). AL: Yes

Age 55+ for homes. Age 65+ (spouse may be 60+) for other units. Nonprofit; nondenominational; Quaker-related corporation. Homes, studios, apartments, and rooms. Residence and care agreement; lifelong health care; nursing services; personal care; medication administration; all utilities; security; emergency response system; maintenance; transportation; up to 3 daily meals; housekeeping and laundry services; community building; library; greenhouses; woodshop; vesper services; guest accommodations.

DEP: (ref.) $1,100/person. PROC: (no ref.) $275. ENT Full Serv.: (ref. up to 90 days minus fees incurred), $31,100–$191,000; MO: $1,700–$3,625. ENT Partial Serv.: $89,500–$250,000; MO: $1,050–$2,300. ENT Membership Units: $142,000–$269,500; MO: $600–$2,350.

REQ: Medicare and A and B insurance, or equivalent, and personal liabilities.

Seacrest Village, JCAHO

1001 Center St.
PO Box 1480
Little Egg Harbor, NJ 08087

Ph: (609) 296-9222
Fax: (609) 296-0508

E-mail: *Seacrest@cybercomm.net*

NH: 120. ALZ/MEM IMP: Yes

For-profit; nondenominational. Nursing care; physical, occupational, and speech therapies; IV therapy; wound management; respiratory services; long- and short-term care; personal care; medication administration; security; emergency response system; maintenance; transportation; 3 daily meals; housekeeping and laundry services; individualized and group activities; off-site activities; intergenerational program; pet therapy.

NH Daily: $165–$225.

Assisted Living and Residential Care Facilities

*In the state of New Jersey, these facilities are called **Assisted Living/Personal Care Facilities**.*

These facilities provide room and board for ambulatory and independent adults who need minimum support.

Types of Authorization

Licensing and / or Certification

These facilities are licensed by the New Jersey Department of Health and Senior Services.

Memberships:

- Assisted Living Federation of America (ALFA) is a national nonprofit membership organization whose mission is to enhance the quality of life in assisted living facilities and promote the interests of the assisted living industry. ALFA, 10300 Eaton Place, Suite 400, Fairfax, VA 22030. Ph: (703) 691-8100. Fax: (703) 691-8106. *http: / / www.alfa.org*
- New Jersey Assisted Living Association (NJALA) is a state affiliate of ALFA. NJALA, c/o Anthony Geonnotti, Alternative Living Services, 115 Floral Vale Blvd., Suite A, Yardley, PA 19067. Ph: (215) 504-2858. Fax: (215) 504-2865.

North

Daughters of Israel

1155 Pleasant Valley Way
West Orange, NJ 07052

Ph: (973) 731-5100, ext. 204

E-mail: *gkruger@cybernex-im.net*

AL: 24

Age 62+. HAREL Senior Housing Lifestyle. Studio apartments. Nursing services available at sister facility, Daughters of Israel Geriatric Center; health monitoring; 24-hour supervision;

social services; personal care; medication administration; housekeeping and laundry services; 3 kosher daily meals; Jewish cultural and lifestyle programs.

AL MO: $2,000.

REQ: Residents must be ambulatory.

Father Hudson House

111 DeHart Place
Elizabeth, NJ 07202

Ph: (908) 353-6060

http://home1.gte.net/cfhh/

E-mail: *cfhh@gte.net*

RH: 25

Residency for the terminally ill. First assisted living facility in New Jersey. Rooms. Supervised care provided around the clock; 3 daily meals; nondenominational chapel; atrium.

Open admission based upon bed availability. Center for Hope Hospice (owners of Father Hudson House) receives reimbursement from Medicare, Medicaid, commercial insurances, and HMOs. No one is denied services. If payment is impossible, care is provided on a sliding scale following the residents' financial assessment. State and county grants, memorials, donations, and fund raising supplement costs.

Green Hill A Retirement Community for Women

103 Pleasant Valley Way
West Orange, NJ 07052

Ph: (973) 731-2300
Fax: (973) 731-5185

AL: 81. SNF: 100

Senior women. Private, nonprofit; nondenominational facility. Private suites. Personal care; medication reminders; security; emergency response system; maintenance; transportation; up to 3 daily meals; housekeeping and laundry services; social events; library; activities center; library; walking path; beauty shop.

APPL: $220. AL ENT: $20,000. AL MO: $3,650–$5,500. LTC Daily: $200–$275. Some services require additional fees.

Heath Village

Schooley's Mountain Rd., Rte. 24
Hackettstown, NJ 07840

Ph: (908) 852-4801
Fax: (908) 852-3748

IND: 298. RHC: 40. HCC: 90

Episcopal Diocese of Newark; nonprofit; nondenominational. Apartments, studios, and rooms. Nursing care; Medicare-approved; 24-hour emergency call system; transportation; up to 3 daily meals; pets allowed; housekeeping and laundry services; activities department; investment group; volunteer groups; committees; men's club; chapel; post office; nature trails; on-site intergenerational day care.

APP: (no ref.) $275/person; $385/couple. IND ENT: $14,500–$26,500. IND MO: $1,200–$2,400. Studios and suites (single occupancy only) ENT: $26,400. MO: (includes 3 daily meals) $2,250–$3,700. RH ENT: $28,000. RH MO: $2,350–$3,500. HCC Daily: $180–$260.

REQ: Approval of medical and financial status and proof of insurance.

Job Haines Home

250 Bloomfield Ave.
Bloomfield, NJ 07003

Ph: (973) 743-0792 or (888) 743-0794
Fax: (973) 743-1882

http://www.rde-ssg.com/seniors/special/

RH: 63 (addl. units being built).

Built in 1902, one of the nation's first facilities designed specifically for senior living. Apartments. Medical services suite; 24-hour staffing; personal care; medication administration; emergency response system; up to 3 daily meals, on-site convenience store; some banking and mail services; barber/beauty shop.

DEP: (ref.) $3,300 security deposit. RH Daily: 1-bedroom apartment, $105; large studio, $95; small studio, $85.

Marriott Brighton Gardens

1350 Route 22 West
Mountainside, NJ 07092

Ph: (908) 654-4460
Fax: (908) 654-4467

AL: 98

Marriott Senior Living Service community; nondenominational; nonsectarian. Rooms with private kitchenettes and baths. Licensed nurse on staff; reality orientation and other behavioral therapies; daily safety checks; regular health and wellness assessments; personal care; medication administration; security; emergency response system; maintenance; transportation; 3 daily meals; housekeeping and laundry services; resident activities director; library; activities and crafts studio; large common areas; barber/beauty shop.

AL MO: $2,850–$4,200; 2nd person, $825. Additional care levels priced incrementally at $385/mo.

Central

Blythe House of Tinton Falls

One Hartford Drive
Red Bank, NJ 07701

Ph: (732) 933-4700
Fax: (732) 933-0999

IND: 60. ALZ/MEM IMP: 12

Owned and operated by HDS Associates. Apartments and rooms. Personal care; medication administration; wellness program; emergency call system, maintenance; transportation; 3 daily meals; housekeeping and laundry services; community parlors; walking paths; piano; scheduled daily activities; country store; barber/beauty shop.

IND ENT: $7,900. IND MO: $4,650–$9,250.

Brandywine Assisted Living

515 Jack Martin
Brick, NJ 08724

Ph: (732) 836-1400
Fax: (732) 836-9600
http://www.BrandyCare.com

AL: 79

Brandywine Senior Care, Inc. Apartments. 24-hour licensed nurse; personal care; medication administration; customized care when necessary; security; emergency response system; maintenance; transportation; up to 3 daily meals; housekeeping and laundry services; exercise programs; social and recreational activities.

AL MO: $3,000–$3,350.

Masonic Home of New Jersey

902 Jacksonville Rd.
Burlington, NJ 08016

Ph: (609) 239-3900
Fax: (609) 386-1199

IND: 188. HCC: 339

Provides long-term care to Masonic families. Private rooms with bath and semiprivate rooms. Physical therapy; dentistry, podiatry, ophthalmology, optometry, and radiology services; Medicare/Medicaid-approved; security; emergency response system; maintenance; transportation; up to 3 daily meals; housekeeping and laundry services; chapel; game room; arts and crafts; woodworking shop; library; musical programs; barber/beauty shop.

IND Daily: $105. HCC Daily: Skilled, $160; skilled Medicare, $195.

REQ: Must be a Mason, or related to a Mason and physically and mentally stable.

Morris Hall/St. Mary Residence/St. Joseph Nursing, Commission on Accreditation of Rehabilitation Facilities and JCAHO

1 Bishops Drive, Box 6498
Lawrenceville, NJ 08648

Ph: (609) 896-0006
Fax: (609) 896-8037

IND: 35. AL: 70. SNF: 120. REHAB: 116

Nonprofit, nondenominational org. of the Roman Catholic Diocese of Trenton. Apartments, suites, private and semiprivate rooms. Nursing care; physical, occupational, and speech therapies; respite care; personal care (5 levels); medication administration; Medicare/Medicaid-approved; security; emergency response system; maintenance; transportation; up to 3 daily meals; housekeeping and laundry services; all utilities; pastoral care; chapel; library; workshops; planned activities; gift shop; barber/beauty shop.

IND Daily: $80–$160; personal assistance fee, $7–$15. AL Daily: $10–$18; Levels of assistance fees, $7–$55 per day. SNF Daily: $175 or $195.

South

Arden Courts Manorcare Health

2700 Chapel Ave.
Cherry Hill, NJ 08002

Ph: (609) 667-6543
Fax: (609) 667-9676

ALZ AL: Yes

Alzheimer's Assisted Living Facility. All levels of Alzheimer's. Operated by ManorCare Health Services. Single or double bedrooms. 24-hour nursing care; structured programs; respite care; 5 levels of care dependent upon need; health, behavioral, personal care; security; maintenance; 3 daily meals plus snacks; housekeeping and laundry services; furnishings; religious services; fitness walks; Alzheimer's caregiver support group; laundry; all utilities except phone and cable TV; pet visits; art; music; cooking; woodworking; poetry; games; dances; bingo.

ALZ AL MO: $3,200–$4,850. RSP Daily: $150.

Brandell Estates

432 Central Ave.
Linwood, NJ 08221

Ph: (609) 926-4663

AL: 85

Owned and operated by Blue Star Health Care Services. Apartments. Special program for memory impaired residents; personal care; medication administration; security; emergency call system; transportation; up to 3 daily meals; housekeeping and laundry services; all utilities except for phone; varied social, cultural, educational, spiritual, and recreational interests; barber/beauty salon.

AL ENT: $5,500. AL MO: $2,900–$4,400.

Cardinal Retirement Village and Wellington Manor Assisted Living

455 Hurffville-Crosskeys Rd.
Sewell, NJ 08080

Ph: (609) 582-5292 or (800) 742-5292
http://www.cardinalvillage.com
E-mail: *crdnlvlg@bellatlantic.net*

IND: Yes. AL: Yes

Nondenominational facility. Apartments and studios. 24-hour staffing; dementia care; licensed nurse; personal care; medication administration; security; emergency response system; maintenance; transportation; up to 3 daily meals; housekeeping and laundry services; exercise room; chapel; community rooms; social activities; village store; barber/beauty shop.

IND APP: $385. IND MO: $1,500–$1,850; $110 2nd person. AL APP: $385. AL MO: $2,600–$5,475. Basic service options and security deposit requires additional fees.

The Cinnaminson Home

1410 Riverton Rd.
Cinnaminson, NJ 08077

Ph: (609) 829-0745

AL: 32

Ambulatory men and women on a boarding basis. Founded in 1890; nonprofit organization; nondenominational; independent living with some assistance. Single occupancy rooms; some with private baths. Weekly nurse visit; personal care; medication administration; security; emergency response system; maintenance; transportation; up to 3 daily meals; housekeeping and laundry services; all utilities; religious services; exercise classes; in-house movies; local community programs; special luncheons; games; tea socials; barber/beauty shop.

AL MO: $1,050–$1,650.

The Fountains

7999 N. Rte. 130
Pennsauken, NJ 08110

Ph: (609) 488-5557
Fax: (609) 488-9523

AL: Yes. PCC: Yes

Age 55+. Must be ambulatory. Operated by SeniorCare Group, Ltd.; nondenominational; nonsectarian. Private and semiprivate suites. Wellness center; home care services; personal care; medication administration; security; emergency response system; maintenance; transportation; up to 3 daily meals plus snacks; housekeeping and laundry services; planned activities; off-site trips; library; chapel; exercise classes; bingo; card games; arts and crafts; movies.

PCC MO: Semiprivate, $1,900–$2,100; private, $2,550–$3,000. AL MO: Semiprivate, $2,200–$2,350; private, $2,900–$3,075-day contract; one month's rent plus security, plus $330 application fee.

Independent Living

Independent housing (primarily rentals) for seniors that may offer security features, meal service, and activities.

Yardley Commons

209 Laurel Rd.
Voorhees, NJ 08043

Ph: (609) 772-1313
Fax: (609) 772-9401

IND: Yes

For-profit; nondenominational; Holiday Retirement Corporation. Studios and one- and two-bedroom apartments. 24-hour management staffing; security; emergency response system; maintenance; transportation; up to 3 daily meals; housekeeping and laundry services; exercise equipment; library; arts and crafts; group activity and classes; lounges; billiards room; shopping mall nearby; barber/beauty shop.

DEP: (ref.), $100. IND MO: $1,775–$3,000; 2nd person, $435.

Adult/Resort Communities

Communities for active adults (not all are age-restricted; primarily ownership).

Types of Authorization

Registrations

Townhomes, condominiums, cooperations, or any planned unit development must be registered with the Planned Real Estate Development Section within the Department of Community Affairs.

Central

Deep Run, Not registered; existed before registration act was passed

PO Box 205
Cream Ridge, NJ 08514

Ph: (609) 758-7180

http://www.JensenCommunities.com

Age 55+. Land leasing arrangement. Low-maintenance, ranch-style homes; small pets allowed; clubhouse; lake fishing; organized activities.

PURCHASE: Homes, $99,000–$132,000. MO fee covers leasing the home site; trash removal; maintenance; land taxes.

The Fairways at Lake Ridge

2 Augusta Blvd.
Lakewood, NJ 08701

Ph: (732) 901-4900

http://www1.lakeridge.com/lakeridge/fairways/default.html

Age 48+. 539 units. 12 home designs from 1,300 to 2,700 sq. ft; regulation 18-hole golf course; indoor and outdoor pools; whirlpool and spa; fully equipped exercise center; billiards; library; and computer room.

PURCHASE: Single-family detached homes, about $148,500–$253,000; single-family attached homes, about $132,000 to $143,000.

Four Seasons at Mapleton

22 Garfield Court
Columbus, NJ 08022

Ph: (800) 871-9888 or (609) 324-1800

http://www.khov.com/homes/nj/4seamans/mansmain.htm

Age 55+. Individual homes. Clubhouse; fitness center; swimming pools; tennis; bocce; horseshoes; walking paths; billiards; putting green; library; theater; ballroom.

PURCHASE: Homes, from $165,000.

Four Seasons Spa and Country Club

1600 Spring Meadow Drive
Lakewood, NJ 08701

Ph: (800) 393-0098 or (732) 477-7200

Age 55+. Individual homes, villas. Clubhouse; tennis; 9-hole golf course; fitness center; swimming pool; spa; bocce; shuffleboard; croquet.

PURCHASE: Homes, from $165,000.

Greenbriar at Whittingham

100 Whittingham Drive
Jamesburg, NJ 08831

Ph: (800) 209-0550

Age 55+. Individual homes, villas. Clubhouse; 9-hole golf course; pro shop; swimming pools; tennis; shuffleboard; bocce; fitness center; jogging; dining.

PURCHASE: Homes, from $253,000; villas, from $198,000.

Leisure Village East

1 Dunbarton Drive
Lakewood, NJ 08701

Ph: (908) 477-7900

Retirees only. Golf course; swimming pool; fishing; community center; library; social club.

PURCHASE: Homes, $38,500–$110,000.

Leisure Village West Association

959 Buckingham Drive
Lakehurst, NJ 08733

Ph: (908) 657-8612

Retirees only. Condominiums. Golf course; tennis; swimming pool; fishing; community center; fitness center; social clubs.

PURCHASE: Homes, $27,500–$165,000.

Pine Ridge South

38 Pine Ridge Blvd.
Whiting, NJ 08759

Ph: (800) 635-8965 or (732) 849-4600

http://www.pineridgesouth.com

Manufactured homes. Clubhouse; swimming pool; fitness center; shuffleboard; bocce; billiards; craft room; activities; social clubs.

PURCHASE: Homes, $77,000–$110,000.

Renaissance

3130 Ridgeway Rd.
Lakehurst, NJ 08733

Ph: (888) 55-ADULT (552-3858)
Fax: (732) 657-0189

IND: Yes

At least one member of household must be 55+. 2,100 units. Clubhouse; heated indoor/outdoor pool; tennis courts; wellness center; library and computer center; business center; health and fitness center; arts and crafts room; 18-hole golf course.

PURCHASE: Single-family homes, $163,000–$258,000. Option prices, $1,700–$25,500. Homeowners Association maintenance MO: $110

Rossmoor Golf Club

10 Club House Rd.
Jamesburg, NJ 08831

Ph: (609) 655-1000

55+. Condominiums, cooperative units. Golf course; swimming pool; community center; fitness center; library; social clubs.

PURCHASE: Homes, $44,000–$330,000

Shadow Lake Village

1 Lock Arbor Way
Middletown, NJ 07748

Ph: (908) 842-9580

55+. Condominiums. Golf course; tennis; swimming pool; hiking/biking; fishing; boating/waterskiing; community center; fitness center; library; social clubs.

PURCHASE: Homes, $88,000–$192,500.

North

Crystal Springs Golf Club

123 Crystal Springs Rd.
Hamburg, NJ 07419

Ph: (201) 827-1444

Individual homes, condominiums, homesites. Golf course; tennis; swimming pool; hiking trails; snow skiing.

PURCHASE: Homes, $220,000–$440,000.

Jacob's Ferry

174 Price Court
West New York, NJ 07093

Ph: (201) 553-0766

Townhomes, condominiums. Waterfront promenade; parks; swimming pools; cabanas; view of Manhattan; private shuttle bus to ferry.

PURCHASE: Homes, from $517,000.

South

Greenbriar at Westlake

32 Medinah Court
Jackson, NJ 08527

Ph: (877) WESTLAKE

Age 55+. Individual homes. Clubhouse; golf course; swimming pools; fitness center; tennis; bocce; gardening; walking trails; billiards; woodworking; computer rooms.

PURCHASE: Homes, from $154,000.

Harbor Pines Golf Club Estates

1 Pebble Beach Drive
Egg Harbor Township, NJ 08234

Ph: (609) 926-4900
Fax: (609) 926-7300

http://www.golflink.net/harborpines

Individual homesites, individual homes, homesites. Golf course; hiking/biking; fishing; clubhouse.

PURCHASE: Homes, $252,000–$415,000.

The Fairways at Mays Landing

1801 Cates Rd.
Mays Landing, NJ 08330

Ph: (877) 394-GOLF or (609) 677-9070

http://www.retirenet.com/fairways

Age 55+. Individual homes. Golf course; clubhouse; swimming pool; fitness room; billiards; library; arts and crafts; banquet hall; planned social activities.

PURCHASE: Homes, from $92,500.

The Village of Blue Heron Pines

Cologne, NJ 08213

Ph: (800) 947-6557 or (609) 652-3800

http://www.khov.com

Indvidual homes, homesites. Golf course; clubhouse; pro shop; dining.

PURCHASE: Homes, $156,000–$275,000+.

New Mexico

http://www.state.nm.us

General Information

Climate

Mild and sunny. Higher elevations tend to be cooler throughout the year.

Cost of Living

Ranks 22nd in the nation.

Taxes

State/Local as % of Income: 10.8%.

Property Tax Reduction: Residents 65+ may be eligible for a property tax rebate.

Sales: 5%.

Prescription Exemptions: Residents may be eligible for a credit equal to 3% of their purchases of prescription drugs.

Transportation, Travel, and Tourism

General

New Mexico Department of Tourism, 491 Old Santa Fe Trail, PO Box 20001, Santa Fe, NM 87501, (800) SEE-NEW-MEX.

Major Airports

- ABQ International Sunport, 2200 Sunport Blvd. SE, Albuquerque, NM 87106, (505) 842-4366.
- Santa Fe County Municipal Airport, 4434 Airport Rd., Santa Fe, NM 87501-7755, (505) 473-7243.
- Los Alamos Airport, 1040 Airport Rd., Los Alamos, NM 87544-3307, (505) 662-8420.

Railways

- Amtrak, (800) USA-RAIL.

Bus Tours

- Greyhound Bus, (800) 231-2222.
- Custom Tours by Clarice, (505) 438-7116.

State Highways

- Interstate 25 runs north-south.
- Interstate 40 runs east-west.

Theater and Music

North

- Los Alamos Little Theater, 1670 Nectar St., Los Alamos, NM 87544-3029, (505) 662-5493.
- New Mexico Symphony Orchestra, PO Box 30208, Albuquerque, NM 87190-0208, (505) 881-8999.
- Albuquerque Civic Light Opera, 4201 Ellison St NE, Albuquerque, NM 87109-4503, (505) 345-4324.
- Santa Fe Desert Chorale, (800) 905-3315.
- Santa Fe Chamber Music Festival, (505) 983-2075.
- Santa Fe Opera, (505) 986-5900 or (800) 280-4654.

Southeast

- Roswell Symphony Orchestra, PO Box 2425, Roswell, NM 88202, (800) 457-0302 or (505) 623-5882/7477.

Museums, Crafts, Historical, Recreational

North Central

- Indian Pueblo Cultural Center, 2401 12th St. NW, Albuquerque, NM 87192, (505) 843-7270 or (800) 766-4405.
- New Mexico Museum of Natural History and Science, 1801 Mountain Rd.

NW, Albuquerque, NM 87104-1375, (505) 841-2800.

- Georgia O'Keeffe Museum, 217 Johnson St., Santa Fe, NM 87501, (505) 995-0785, ext. 12.
- Petroglyph National Monument, 6001 Unser Blvd. NW, Albuquerque, NM 87120, (505) 899-0205 (prehistoric, Native American, and Hispanic petroglyphs and rock art carvings).
- Albuquerque International Balloon Fiesta, 8309 Washington Place NE, Albuquerque NM 87113, (505) 821-1000 or (888) 422-7277.
- Cochiti Lake Golf Course, PO Box 125, Santa Fe, NM 87041, (505) 465-2239.
- Rio Rancho Country Club, 500 Country Club Drive, Rio Rancho, NM 87124, (505) 892-8440 (golfing).

Northeast

- Millicent Rogers Museum, PO Box A, Taos, NM 87571, (505) 758-5751 (contemporary and traditional Hispanic and Native American art forms).

Southeast

- Carlsbad Caverns National Park, 3225 National Parks Highway, Carlsbad NM 88220, (505) 785-2232 (subterranean chambers and formations).
- Riverside Country Club, PO Box 549, Carlsbad, NM 88220, (505) 885-4253 (golfing).

Organizations

Advocacy Groups

- Department of Health, Licensing and Certification Bureau, (505) 881-4379 (Albuquerque); (505) 827-4200 (Santa Fe); (505) 528-5079 (Las Cruces); (505) 347-2465 (Roswell).
- Human Services Department, PO Box 2348, Santa Fe, NM 87504, (800) 432-6217 or (505) 827-7750.

Volunteer Programs

- Challenge New Mexico, (505) 988-7621 (helping people with disabilities).
- Albuquerque Animal Rescue, PO Box 21280, Albuquerque, NM 87154-1280, (505) 255-0544.

Housing

Long-Term Care Facilities

In the state of New Mexico, these facilities are called ***Long-Term Care/Nursing Home Facilities****.*

These facilities provide residential living and/or various levels of nursing and medical services to seniors for an extended period of time.

Types of Authorization

Licensing and / or Certification

These facilities must be licensed by the Department of Public Health, Licensure and Certification Bureau. The bureau ensures that facilities meet the established standards for health and safety.

Memberships

- American Association of Homes and Services for the Aging (AAHSA) represents not-for-profit organizations committed to providing high-quality health care, housing, and services to the elderly. AAHSA, 901 E St. NW, Suite 500, Washington, DC 20004-2011. Ph: (202) 783-2242. Fax: (202) 783-2285. *http: / / www.aahsa.org*

Accreditations

- Continuing Care Accreditation Commission (CCAC) accredits facilities that offer seniors a contract or contracts that provide residential living and health care services for the remainder of the person's lifetime and meet CCAC's accreditation standards.

- Joint Commission on the Accreditation of Healthcare Organizations (JCAHO) is an independent, not-for-profit organization and the nation's oldest and largest standards-setting and health care accrediting institution.

North Central

Albuquerque Grand

1501 Tijeras NE
Albuquerque, NM 87106

Ph: (505) 842-1972
Fax: (505) 842-1655

IND: 100. AL: 50. HHC: July 1999

Age 60+. For-profit; nondenominational. Apartments and private rooms. Nursing care; medical services; rehabilitative therapies; pharmacy services; emergency response system; maintenance; transportation; low-impact aerobics; 3 daily meals; pets allowed; housekeeping and laundry services; social and recreational activities; barber/beauty shop.

DEP: $550, $500 refundable. IND MO: $875–$1,550. AL MO: $1,600–$1,850.

La Vida Llena LifeCare RetirementCommunity

10501 Lagrima de Oro NE
Albuquerque, NM 87111

Ph: (505) 293-4001
Fax: (505) 291-3199

IND: 296. AL: 45. SNF: 44. ALZ/MEM IMP: 13

Age 62+. Nonprofit; nonsectarian. Condominiums, townhouses, and apartments. Skilled nursing care; medical services; rehabilitative therapies; pharmacy services; Medicare/Medicaid-approved; 24-hour security system; 24-hour emergency response system; maintenance; scheduled transportation; 3 daily meals; pets allowed; housekeeping and laundry services; pool; Jacuzzi; fitness center; library; chapel; activity room; social and recreational activities.

IND ENT: $40,000. IND MO: $1,100. AL Daily: $105. SNF Daily: $115.

Northeast

Taos Living Center

1340 Maestas Rd.
Taos, NM 87571

Ph: (505) 758-2300
Fax: (505) 758-3081

NH: Yes. AL: Yes

Nondenominational. Rooms. 24-hour skilled and intermediate nursing care; specialized Alzheimer programs; in- and outpatient rehabilitation center; physical, speech, and occupational therapies; respiratory therapy; restorative nursing; subacute care for medically complex patients; hospice and spiritual programs; social services and discharge planning; therapeutic activity programs; personal care; medication administration; maintenance; 3 daily meals and snacks; housekeeping and laundry services; social and recreational activities; barber/beauty shop.

Daily: double occupancy, $135; single occupancy, $150.

Southeast

Lakeview Christian Home of the Southwest, Inc.

1300 N. Canal St.
Carlsbad, NM 88220

Ph: (505) 887-0551
Fax: (505) 885-3876

IND: 66. AL: 75. NC: 224. SNF: 8

Homes and apartments. 24-hour skilled nursing care; posthospital nursing services; 24-hour home health care; restorative care; physical, occupational, and speech therapies; personal care; medication administration; on-duty hostess; emergency response system; maintenance; transportation; 3 daily meals; laundry and housekeeping services; social and recreational activities; barber/beauty shop.

NH Daily: $105–$330; private room $15/day extra. AL MO: $1,050–$1,800.

Landsun Homes Retirement Community

2002 Westridge
Carlsbad, NM 88220

Ph: (505) 887-2894 or (800) 274-9966

IND: Yes. AL: Yes. HCC: 87. ALZ/MEM IMP: Yes

Nonprofit; nondenominational; owned and operated by the New Mexico Conference of the United Methodist Church. Homes, apartments, and private and semiprivate rooms. 24-hour nursing care; intermediate nursing care; physical, occupational, and speech therapies; restorative care; long term care; health clinic; home health care; personal care; medication administration; security; emergency response system; maintenance; transportation; up to 3 daily meals; pets allowed; housekeeping and laundry services; exercise program; chapel and religious services; banking and postal services; business and financial services; social and recreational activities; woodworking shop; arts and crafts; media room; lounges; gift shop; barber/beauty shop.

IND ENT: (partial ref.) $44,000–$110,000. IND MO: $475. AL MO: $1,300–$3,050. HCC Daily: Semiprivate, $125; private, $150.

Assisted Living and Residential Care Facilities

*In the state of New Mexico, these facilities are called **Adult Residential Care Facilities**.*

These facilities provide room and board for ambulatory and independent adults who need minimum support.

Types of Authorization

Licensing and/or Certification

These facilities must be licensed by the Department of Public Health, Licensure and Certification Bureau.

Memberships

- Assisted Living Federation of America (ALFA) is a national nonprofit membership organization whose mission is to enhance the quality of life in assisted living facilities and promote the interests of the assisted living industry. ALFA, 10300 Eaton Place, Suite 400, Fairfax, VA 22030. Ph: (703) 691-8100. Fax: (703) 691-8106. *http://www.alfa.org*

Southwest

Willow Manor Adult Residential Care Home

815 Adobe Drive
Deming, NM 88030

Ph: (505) 546-0546
Fax: (505) 546-6024

AL: 57

Age 18+. For-profit. Private and semiprivate rooms. Medical services; personal care; medication administration; emergency response system; transportation; 3 daily meals; pets allowed; housekeeping and laundry services; social and recreational activities.

AL MO: $1,650–$3,100.

North Central

Camlu Retirement Apartments

12101 Lomas Blvd. NE
Albuquerque, NM 87112

Ph: (505) 298-9976
Fax: (505) 298-0641

IND: Yes. AL: Yes

Apartments. 24-hour attendant on duty; personal care; medication administration; 24-hour emergency response system; transportation; 3 daily meals; housekeeping and laundry services; social and recreational activities; beauty/barber shop.

DEP: $100 refundable for nonsmoker; $300 nonrefundable for smoker. MO: Studio, $1,050 (single) and $1,250 (double); apartment, $1,375 (single) and $1,600 (double); 2nd person, $275. Additional care, $440.

Regent at Sandia Springs

1000 Riverview Drive SE
Rio Rancho, NM 87124

Ph: (505) 892-8400
Fax: (505) 896-1655

IND: Yes. AL: Yes. ALZ/MEM IMP: Yes

Apartments with 3 levels of care. 24-hour licensed medical staff; personal care; medication administration and monitoring; physicians' clinical room for appointments; pet therapy; on-site clinic; security; emergency response system; maintenance; scheduled transportation; up to 3 daily meals; housekeeping and laundry services; private dining room (for family celebrations); planned activities; recreational room; TV room; library; social and recreational activities; barber/beauty shop.

IND MO: $1,500–$1,800; 2nd person: $440. AL MO: $1,975–$4,175; 2nd person, $725–$1,600. ALZ/MEM IMP MO: $3,975–$5,200. RSP Daily: $135–$160.

The Villages at Alameda

8810 Horizon Blvd. NE
Albuquerque, NM 87113

Ph: (505) 857-7000
Fax: (505) 857-9210

AL: 72

Age 50+. Apartments; Hallmark/Premier Community. Medical services; 24-hour emergency system; maintenance; transportation; up to 3 daily meals; pets allowed, daily and weekly housekeeping services; pool; fitness center.

AL MO: $1,925–$3,025. DEP: (ref.), $100. IND MO (ref.), $100. AL MO: (ref.), $100.

Karrington Assisted Living

4910 Tramway Ridge NE
Albuquerque, NM 87111

Ph: (505) 271-9600
Fax: (505) 271-9966

AL: 60. ALZ/MEM IMP: 28

Private rooms. Nursing care; personal care; medication administration; 24-hour security system; 24-hour emergency response system; transportation; 3 daily meals; pets allowed; laundry and housekeeping services; social and recreational activities.

AL MO: $1,325–$3,850.

Vista Del Rio

1620 Indian School Rd. NE
Albuquerque, NM 87102-1678

Ph: (505) 242-3370
Fax: (505) 242-3931

IND: Yes. AL: 148. ALZ/MEM IMP: 18

Retirement age. For-profit. Apartments. Personal care; medication administration; maintenance; transportation; 3 daily meals; pets allowed; housekeeping and laundry services; library; social and recreational activities; billiard room; theater; country store; ice cream parlor; chapel; activity room; barber/beauty shop.

DEP: $275. IND MO: $1,650–$1,975. AL MO: based on point system.

Westland House Assisted Living

6600 Los Volcanes NW
Albuquerque, NM 87121

Ph: (505) 831-0002
Fax: (505) 831-2027

E-mail: *SenCareInc@aol.com*

AL: 40

Apartments. Personal care; bowel and bladder programs; dietary intake monitoring; 24-hour staff; medication management; security; 24-hour emergency call system; maintenance; transportation to clinical appointments; up to 3 daily meals; daily and weekly housekeeping and laundry services; activity program.

AL MO: studio, $2,050–$2,450; 1-bedroom, $2,550–$2,850.

South

The Aristocrat

252 Robert H. Bradley Drive
Alamogordo, NM 88310

Ph: (505) 437-3020

ALZ/IMP: Yes

Apartments with 3 levels of care. Personal care; 24-hour trained staff; licensed nurse on duty 5 days a week; medication administration; wellness program; security; emergency response system; maintenance; scheduled transportation; up to 3 daily meals; housekeeping and laundry services; whirlpool; planned activities; barber/beauty shop.

AL Daily: Studio, $60–$70; 1-bedroom, $75–$90. ALZ/IMP Daily: $70–$80. ADC hourly: $5. RSP Daily: $70.

Cottonbloom Retirement and Assisted Living Center

5525 Cottonbloom Court
Las Cruces, NM 88005

Ph: (505) 523-0300
Fax: (505) 523-8687

http://www.zianet.com/cottonbloom

IND: 45. AL: Yes

Nondenominational. Apartments. Nurse on staff and on call 24 hours; 24-hour professional staff; certified nurse assistants; daily wellness checks; ambulation; consulting pharmacist; respite room personal care; medication administration; transportation; up to 3 daily meals; weekly housekeeping and laundry services; full-time activities coordinator; social and recreational activities; whirlpool bath; fireside living area and TV lounge; elegant dining room; private room for entertaining guests.

IND MO: studio, $1,650; 1-bedroom, $2,200; 2nd person, $660.

Independent Living

Independent housing (primarily rentals) for seniors that may offer security features, meal service, and activities.

North Central

La Resolana Apartments

1025 Chelwood Park NE
Albuquerque, NM 87112

Ph: (505) 296-1425
Fax: (505) 332-0272

IND: 167

Age 62+. Nonprofit. Apartments. Security; emergency response system; maintenance; laundry services; pets allowed; swimming pool; social and recreational activities; garden; barber/beauty shop.

Contact facility for fees.

Adult/Resort Communities

Communities for active adults (not all are age-restricted; primarily ownership).

North

Las Campanas

218 Camino La Tierra
Santa Fe, NM 87501

Ph: (888) 499-9019 or (505) 992-6420
Fax: (505) 989-8577

http://www.lascampanas.com

Individual homes, homesites. Golf course; pro shop; clubhouse; spa and tennis center; swimming pools; fitness rooms; hiking trails; equestrian center; dining.

PURCHASE: Homes, from $792,000; homesites, from $247,500.

Pendaries Village

PO Box 820
Rociada, NM 87742

Ph: (505) 425-3561

Individual homes, homesites. Golf course; pro shop; lodge; tennis; hiking trails; fishing; conference center; dining; social activities.

PURCHASE: Homes, from $181,500.

Central

Sunrise Bluffs

1000 Sunrise Bluffs
Belen, NM 87002

Ph: (877) 725-8337
Fax: (505) 864-0833

http://www.sunrisebluffs.com

Age 55+. Individual homes. Clubhouse; swimming pool; chipping green; nearby golf.

PURCHASE: Homes, from $70,000.

South

Santa Fe Style Country Club Estates

2901 Country Club Rd.
Deming, NM 88030

Ph: (800) 368-9058 or (505) 544-4254
Fax: (505) 546-1465

Age 55+. Individual homes. Planned clubhouse facilities; nearby golf course, full service senior center, and municipal swimming complex.

PURCHASE: Homes, from $93,500.

New York

http://www.state.ny.us

General Information

Climate

Humid continental. Winters are mild to cold depending on the elevation; summers are cool in the higher elevations to hot in the lower portions of the state.

Cost of Living

Ranks 4th in the nation.

Taxes

State/Local as % of Income: About 13.1%

Property Tax Exemptions: Real Property Tax Credit provides credits or cash rebates to homeowners who pay a disproportionate amount of property tax in relation to their household income. NY State tax form IT-214. Property Tax Exemption for residents 65 and older. Each locality establishes its own standards. Contact local assessor.

Sales: 4%.

Prescription Exemptions: EPIC, a state sponsored prescription plan for seniors, (800) 332-3742.

Transportation, Travel, and Tourism

Major Airports

- John F. Kennedy International Airport, New York, NY (718) 244-4444.
- Albany County Airport, (518) 242-2200.
- Westchester County Airport, (607) 257-0456.
- La Guardia Airport, New York, NY, (718) 533-3400.
- Tompkins County Airport, Ithaca, (914) 285-4860.

Railways

- Amtrak, (800) USA-RAIL.
- Long Island Railroad, (718) 330-3322

Bus Tours

- Greyhound, 800-231-2222.

State Highways

- Interstates 87 and 81 run north-south.
- Interstates 90 and 88 run east-west.

Theater and Music

East

- Albany Symphony Orchestra, 19 Clinton Ave., Albany, NY 12207, (518) 465-4663.

Southeast

- Apollo Theater, 253 West 125 St., New York City, 10027, (212) 531-5337 (historic Harlem theater).
- Broadway, (212) 563-2929 for On- and Off-Broadway information in New York City.
- Caramoor Concerts (jazz, classical), PO Box 816, Katonah, NY 10536, (914) 232-1252.
- Carnegie Hall, 154 West 57th St., New York City, 10019, (212) 247-7800.
- Lincoln Center for the Performing Arts, New York City, (212) LINCOLN.
- Radio City Music Hall, 1260 Avenue of the Americas, New York City, NY 10020, (212) 632-4041, *http://www.radiocity.com*.
- U.S. Military Academy Band's Concert, West Point, (914) 983-2617.

Museums, Crafts, Historical, Recreational

West

- Genesee Country Village and Museum, PO Box 310, Mumford, NY 14511, (716) 538-6822.
- Niagara Falls Sightseeing Tours: Over the Falls Tour, (716) 283-8900.
- Niagara Historic Walking Tours, (716) 285-2132.
- Boat 'n' Bus Tours, Niagara, (716) 852-5201.
- George Eastman House International Museum of Photography and File, 900 East Ave., Rochester, NY 14607, (716) 271-3361.
- Corning Museum of Glass, Corning, NY 14830, (800) 732-6845 or (607) 974-8271.

East

- Saratoga Springs Chamber of Commerce, 28 Clinton St., Saratoga Springs, NY 12866, (518) 584-3255.
- Fort William Henry Museum and Resort, 50 Canada St., Lake George Valley, NY 12845, (800) 234-0267.
- Lake George Steamboat Company Cruises, Steel Pier, Lake George, NY 12845, (800)-553-BOAT.

Northwest

- Theodore Roosevelt Inaugural National Historic Site, 641 Delaware Avenue, Buffalo, NY 14202-1079, (716) 884-0095.

Central

- Baseball Hall of Fame and Museum, PO Box 590, 25 Main St., Cooperstown, NY 13326, (888) 425-5633 or (607) 547-7200.

Southeast

- Statue of Liberty–Ellis Island National Monument, (212) 363-3200.
- Hudson River Cruises, Kingston, (914) 255-6515.
- Fire Island National Seashore, 120 Laurel Street, Patchogue, NY 11772, (516) 289-4810.
- Museum of Natural History, Central Park West and 79th St, New York, NY 10024, (212) 769-5200.
- Metropolitan Museum of Art, 1000 Fifth Avenue at 82nd St., New York, NY 10028, (212) 535-7710.
- NY Botanical Garden, 200th St. and Kazimiroff Blvd., Bronx, NY 10458, (718) 817-8700.
- Gateway National Recreation Area, (718) 338-3338.

Organizations

Advocacy Groups

- Senior Citizens' Hotline, (800) 342-9871.
- NY Department of the Aging HIICAP Helpline (health insurance assistance), (212) 333-5511.
- Department of Insurance (Medicare Supplement information), (800) 342-3736.
- Partnership for Long Term Care Insurance, (888) NYS-PLTC.
- Medicare Hotline, (800) 638-6833, (800) 820-1202 TTY-TTD.
- IPRO Medicare Patient Rights, (800) 331-7767
- NY State Office for the Aging Long Term Care Ombudsman, (800) 342-9871.
- Coalition of Institutionalized, Aged and Disabled, (212) 481-4348.

Volunteer Programs

- Senior Companion Program. Volunteers provide supportive services to developmentally disabled adults.
- Long-Term Care Ombudsman Program. Volunteer advocacy program.

Housing

Long-Term Care Facilities

*In the state of New York, these facilities are called **Long-Term Care/Nursing Home Facilities**.*

These facilities provide residential living and/or various levels of nursing and medical services to seniors for an extended period of time. Seniors wishing to become residents of a long-term care facility are required to submit a Patient Review Instrument (PRI) and Screen. These are assessment tools used to determine level of care required.

Types of Authorization

Licensing and / or Certification

These facilities must be licensed by the Department of Health. Regulations require: a definition of the admissions agreement or entrance contract (includes costs, services, and legal responsibilities of the resident); the basic daily rate to cover room, meals, housekeeping, linen, general nursing care, medical records and services, and recreation and personal care; that a security deposit (if requested) be no more than three months' prepayment and must be deposited into an interest-bearing account; and that, upon a resident's leaving or death, any amount paid over the cost of services already provided must be refunded.

Memberships

- The Healthcare Association of NY State (HANYS) is a nonprofit organization that serves as an advocate for voluntary and public health systems, acute and long-term, home, and community health care providers. *http://www.hanys.org/*
- American Association of Homes and Services for the Aging (AAHSA) represents not-for-profit organizations committed to providing high-quality health care, housing, and services to the elderly. AAHSA, 901 E St. NW, Suite 500, Washington, DC 20004-2011. Ph: (202) 783-2242. Fax: (202) 783-2285. *http://www.aahsa.org*
- The New York State Association of Homes and Services for the Aging (NYAHSA) is an AAHSA Affiliated State Association. NYAHSA, 150 State St., Suite B 113, NY Albany, 12207-1698. Ph: (518) 449-2707. Fax: (518) 455-8908. *http://www.nyahsa.org*

Northwest

The Episcopal Church Home

505 Mount Hope Ave.
Rochester, NY 14620

Ph: (716) 546-8400
Fax: (716) 325-6553

E-mail: *ech@frontiernet.net*

SNF: Yes. ALZ: Yes

Nonprofit; nondenominational; nonsectarian. Private and semiprivate rooms. Individual health and personal care plan; 3 levels of care; 24-hour nursing staff; nurse practitioners; physicians; social workers; physical, occupational, and speech therapies, dental and podiatry services; rehabilitative services and hospice; 3 daily meals; gift shop; common areas; chapel; social activities; off-site activities; beauty/barber shop.

SNF Daily: Private, $200 (with assessment, $210); semiprivate, $195 (with assessment, $205).

Mount St. Mary's Nursing Home

2600 Main St.
Niagara Falls, NY 14305

Ph: (716) 285-9155

RHC: 131. HSP: Yes

Nonprofit; Catholic; owned by Mount St. Mary's Hospital and Sisters of St. Francis of the Third Order Regular of

Williamsville. Private and semiprivate rooms. Medical, nursing, and pastoral care; dental and podiatry services; rehabilitative therapy; 24-hour supervised nursing care; Medicare/Medicaid-approved; 3 daily meals; housekeeping services; volunteer programming; daily activities providing social interaction and educational and spiritual opportunities.

RHC Daily: Private pay, semiprivate, $170; private, $180.

REQ: Financial statement and health care coverage.

Central

Kendal at Ithaca, AAHSA and NYSAHSA

2330 N. Triphammer Rd.
Ithaca, NY 14850

Ph: (607) 266-5300, (800) 253-6325

http: / / www.kendal.org

E-mail: *Admissions@Kal.Kendal.Org*

IND: 212. AH: 12. SNF: 35

Nonprofit; nondenominational community. Cottages, apartments, and rooms. Skilled nursing care; wellness center; security; emergency response system; maintenance; transportation; up to 3 daily meals; housekeeping and laundry services; fitness center; pool; library; darkroom; craft room; wood shop; tennis courts; computer lab; resident councils; gardens; walking paths.

IND ENT: $93,500–$308,000. IND MO: $1,850–$4,250. SNF MO: $3,250–$5,700.

REQ: Medicare A and B, or the equivalent, plus a supplemental insurance policy.

Presbyterian Home for Central New York, Inc., AAHA and NYAHSA member

Middle Settlement Rd., PO Box 144
New Hartford, NY 13413

Ph: (315) 797-7500

IND: 149. AC: 72. AL: 24. ALZ/MEM IMP: Yes. ADC: Yes. SNF: 242

Nonprofit; affiliated with Presbyterian Church. Apartments and private and semiprivate rooms. 24-hour supervision; physical, occupational, speech therapies; dental and podiatry services; personal care; medication administration; individual case management; respite care; hospice care; social worker; Medicare/Medicaid-approved; security; emergency response system; maintenance; transportation; up to 3 daily meals plus snacks; housekeeping and laundry services; pastoral care; chapel; lounge; library; gift shop; barber/beauty shop.

AC Daily: $70–$80. AL Daily: $120–$130. SNF Daily: $170–$185. Payment options: private pay, SSI, Medicaid.

East

The Baptist Home at Brookmeade

198 State Route 308
Rhinebeck, NY 12572

SNF: 116

Nonprofit organization; nondenominational; nonsectarian. Private and semiprivate rooms. 24-hour nursing; rehabilitation; short-term care; physical and occupational therapies; personal care; medication administration; security; emergency response system; maintenance; transportation; up to 3 daily meals; housekeeping and laundry services; religious services in all faiths; planned activities.

Daily: (private pay), $240.

Our Lady of Mercy Life Center

2 Mercycare Lane
Guilderland, NY 12084

Ph: (518) 464-8100

SNF: Yes (4 units of 40 residents each)

Age 16+. Nondenominational facility established by the Religious Sisters of Mercy. Private and semiprivate rooms. 24-hour nursing care; social services; individualized programs of care and rehabilitation; pastoral care; 3 daily meals; planned social activities; dancing; singing; discussion groups; arts and crafts.

SNF Daily: Semiprivate, $250; private, $375.

West

Lake Shore Health Care Center, HANYS

845 Routes 5 & 20
Irving, NY 14081

Ph: (716) 934-2654

SNF: 160

Nonprofit; nondenominational. Private and semiprivate rooms. Physical, occupational, and speech therapies; 24-hour nursing services; pharmacy; nutritional plans; dental; foot care; psychiatric consultation; acute care; outpatient services; acute mental health unit; social work; personal care; medication administration; Medicaid-approved; security; emergency response system; maintenance; transportation; up to 3 daily meals; housekeeping and laundry services; games; discussion groups; crafts; music; movies; intergenerational program; garden; barber/beauty shop.

SNF Daily: Semiprivate, $165 and $175; private, $175 to $190. Therapy treatment fees additional to daily fee.

Southeast/Long Island

Bishop Jonathan G. Sherman Episcopal Nursing Home, HANYS

52 Route 25A
Smithtown, NY 11787

Ph: (516) 862-3900

NH: 240. ALZ/MEM IMP: Yes

Nonprofit; nondenominational. Medical supervision; 24-hour nursing care; acute care and short-term care; hospice care; special dietary plans; physical, occupational, and therapeutic therapies; 3 daily meals; pastoral care and social services.

NH Daily: Semiprivate, $325; private, $350.

Brandywine Adult and Nursing Home, JCAHO

620 Sleepy Hollow Rd.
Briarcliff Manor, NY 10510

Ph: (914) 941-5100
Fax: 914-941-4752
http://www.brandywinecare.com

SNF: 131. AH: 31

Privately owned and operated; nondenominational. Private rooms with baths. 24-hour skilled nursing care; subacute care; long- and short-term rehabilitative therapies; personal care; medication administration; 3 daily meals; recreational activities; music; arts and crafts; films; bridge; gardening; beauty/barber shop.

AH Daily: $110 and $140. NH Daily: (semiprivate), $250; (private), $275.

Howe Avenue Nursing Home

16 Guion Place
New Rochelle, NY 10802

Ph: (914) 632-5000, ext. 3800
Fax: (914) 637-1203

NH: 150. REHB: Yes

Nonprofit; nondenominational facility. Restorative services for those in need of short-term care; physical, speech, and occupational therapies; podiatry; ophthalmology; X-ray; pharmacy; 24-hour nursing care; 3 daily meals; social activities; bingo; movies; concerts; off-site outings.

NH Daily: Private, $350; semiprivate, $310.

Isabella Geriatric Center, JCAHO, HCANY

515 Audubon Ave.
New York, NY 10040

Ph: (212) 342-9200

IND: 70. NH: 785. HHC: Yes

Age 62+. Nonprofit; nondenominational; nonsectarian. Apartments and private and semiprivate rooms. Physicians on 24-hour call; 24-hour nursing care; social workers; in-house pharmacy; X-ray services; labs; short-term rehabilitation; physical, occupational, and speech therapies; home health care program; security; emergency response system; maintenance; transportation; optional meal plan; housekeeping and laundry services; religious services; coffee and gift shops; music; shopping trips; library; intergenerational and volunteer programs; barber/beauty shop.

IND MO: $495–$700 plus MO service $725 (includes 2 meals/day; social services, utilities, emergency call system, etc.). NH Daily: $275.

IND REQ: Must be ambulatory; maintain personal care, financially secure.

Mount Alverno Center and Schervier Pavilion, HANYS

20 Grand St.
Warwick, NY 10990

Ph: (914) 986-2267 or 5750

AL: Yes. AH: Yes. SNF: 120

Franciscan Health System of Warwick, Inc. Private, semiprivate, and one-bedroom suites. 24-hour nursing care; therapeutic and restorative programs; emotional and spiritual support; individualized care plans; personal care; medication administration; Medicaid-approved; security; emergency response system; maintenance; transportation; up to 3 daily meals; housekeeping and laundry services; religious services; scheduled activities; banking and post office; walking trails; barber/beauty shop.

AH Daily: $70–$105. AL Daily: $85–$130. SNF Daily: $210–$240.

Financial assistance available for qualified residents.

The Osborn

101 Theall Rd.
Rye, NY 10580

Ph: (914) 921-2200

IND: Yes. AL: Yes. SNF: 84. HC: Yes. ALZ: Yes

Age 65+. The Miriam Osborn Memorial Home Association, a charitable, nonprofit organization. Apartments and private and semiprivate rooms. Short-term rehab.; hospice care; social services; nursing care; health and wellness program; personal care; medication administration; Medicare-approved; security; emergency response system; maintenance; transportation; up to 3 daily meals (1 meal included in MO fee for IND); housekeeping and laundry services; all utilities (except telephone); music; dance; reminiscence groups; planned activities; utilities (except cable and telephone); libraries; convenience store; banking and business center; barber/beauty shop.

IND ENT: (New construction 100% ref.) $263,000–$579,000. MO: $2,200–$3,000. 2nd person, $600.

Renovated apts., no ENT; MO: $4,050–$5,300. 2nd person, $575. Meal options: 2 daily meals, $225/person; 3 meals, $350/person. AL MO: $5,400–$6,850.

Skilled Nursing Facility at Central Suffolk Hospital

1300 Roanoke Ave.
Riverhead, NY 11901

Ph: (516) 548-6266

SNF: 60

Not-for-profit facility. Private and semiprivate rooms. Long- term and rehabilitative medical and physical care; subacute care program; 3 daily meals;

religious services; recreational activities; scheduled trips off-site; residents council; barber/beauty shop.

SNF Daily: Semiprivate, $265; private, $275. Therapies are additional.

Victoria Home

25 N. Malcolm St.
Ossining, NY 10562

Ph: (914) 941-2962
Fax: (914) 941-2962
http://www.victoriahome.org

SNF: 49. ALZ/MEM IMP: Yes

Age 16+. Nonprofit, nondenominational; founded by the Daughters of the British Empire. Medical and dental services; 24-hour nursing care; physical, occupational, and speech therapies; social and psychotherapy services; special care unit for cognitive impaired; personal care; 3 daily meals; housekeeping and laundry services; religious services; libraries; gardens; banking; shopping service; on- and off-site activities; social gatherings; barber/beauty shop.

SNF Daily: $265.

The Wartburg Adult Care Community, JCAHO

Wartburg Place
Mount Vernon, NY 10552

Ph: (914) 699-0800

IND: 31. AL: Yes. HCC: 240. ALZ/MEM IMP: Yes

Nondenominational; Lutheran Church affiliation. Townhomes, apartments, and private and semiprivate rooms. 24-hour nursing care; certified nursing assistants, geriatric- trained physicians; physical, occupational, and speech therapies; psychological therapists; hydrotherapy, pain management; dysphasia evaluation; home health care services; hospice; Medicare/Medicaid-approved; personal care; medication administration; security; emergency response system; maintenance; transportation; up to 3 daily meals; housekeeping and laundry services; exercise program; religious services; social and recreational activities; volunteer opportunities.

IND ENT: $165,000. IND MO: $425. AL/RH MO: $3,300. HCC MO: $9,075; daily, $325.

Assisted Living and Residential Care Facilities

In the state of New York, these facilities are called ***Adult Home/ Adult Care/Assisted Living Facilities****.*

These facilities provide room and board for ambulatory and independent adults who need minimum support.

Types of Authorization

Licensing and/or Certification

Requires licensing by the Department of Health. Provide short- or long-term residential care, room, board, housekeeping, personal care, and supervision to five or more adults. Adult homes (or facilities labeled adult care) are not licensed to provide any nursing or medical care.

Memberships:

- Empire State Association of Adult Homes (ESAAH).
- Presbyterian Association of Homes for the Aging (PAHA).
- Assisted Living Federation of America (ALFA) is a national nonprofit membership organization whose mission is to enhance the quality of life in assisted living facilities and promote the interests of the assisted living industry. ALFA, 10300 Eaton Place, Suite 400, Fairfax, VA 22030. Ph: (703) 691-8100. Fax: (703) 691-8106. *http://www.alfa.org*
- Empire State Association of Adult Homes and Assisted Living Facilities (ESA) is a state affiliate of ALFA. ESA, 99 Pine St., 4th Floor, Albany, NY 12207. Ph: (518) 462-5481. Fax: (518) 426-9271. *http://www.ny-assisted-living.org*

Central

Ideal Senior Living Center

508 High Ave.
Endicott, NY 13760

Ph: (607) 786-7425

IND: 33. ACH: 62. SNF: 150

Age 62+. United Health Services development Apartments, private and semiprivate rooms. 24-hour nursing care; social services; medical assistance; case management; wellness center; personal care; medication administration; insurance counseling; security; emergency response system; maintenance; transportation; up to 3 daily meals; housekeeping and laundry services; church services; outdoor gardens; convenience store; activities; barber/beauty shop.

IND MO: $1,250–$2,175. Low-income residents' monthly fee determined by income. ACH Daily: $75–$100. (SSI recipients, $875/mo.). SNF MO: $5,450–$5,650. SNF Daily: $185–$195. RSP Daily: $195.

Sedgwick Heights

1100 James St.
Syracuse, NY 13203

Ph: (315) 234-1100
Fax: (315) 234-1105

AH: 6. AL: 90

Nonprofit; nondenominational. Private and semiprivate rooms. On-site home care services; medication administration; 24-hour nursing care; personalized care program; Medicaid-approved; short-term care; motivational activities; 3 daily meals; housekeeping and laundry services; intergenerational programs; exercise programs; games; soda shoppe; barber/beauty shop.

AH MO: Semiprivate, $1,045 and $875; private, $1,500. AL MO: Semiprivate, $875.

North

Keene Valley Neighborhood House

PO Box 46
Keene Valley, NY 12943

Ph: (518) 576-4474
Fax: (518) 576-2021

www.kvnh.org

E-mail: *kvnh@kvvi.net*

AL: Yes (up to 50 residents)

Nonprofit. Voluntary adult home operated by the Keene Valley Neighborhood House Services, Inc. Rooms. 24-hour supervisor; medical and mental health case management; therapy services; medical transportation; podiatry services; personal care; medication administration; 3 daily meals; exercise classes; church services; painting; gardening; pet therapy; scheduled off-site activities; barber/beauty shop.

AL MO: $1,400–$2,200. SSI accepted.

East

Albany Guardian Society Home

553 Clinton Ave.
Albany, NY 12214

Ph: (518) 465-6395
Fax: (518) 465-6544

AL: 44

Not-for-profit adult home. Private rooms, some with shared bath. Personal care; medication administration; security; emergency response system; maintenance; transportation; up to 3 daily meals plus snacks; housekeeping and laundry services; activities coordinator; planned daily activities; games; social events; off-site trips; gardens; barber/beauty shop.

AL MO: Private room with shared bath, $1,275; private room with private bath,

$1,350; private suite, $1,375. RSP Daily: $85. RSP Weekly: $475.

West

Bassett Manor Adult Care Residence

245 Bassett Rd.
Williamsville, NY 14221

Ph: (716) 688-4011

AL: 105

Owned and managed by Emeritus Assisted Living. Apartments. Nurse/physician office; personal care; medication administration; security; emergency response system; maintenance; transportation; up to 3 daily meals; housekeeping and laundry services; exercise classes; religious services; gift shop; lounge; bingo; crafts; intergeneration programs; daily activities; barber/beauty shop.

AL MO: $2,050–$3,250.

Southeast/Long Island

Cabrini-on-Hudson

Route 9W
West Park, NY 12493

Ph: (914) 384-6720

RC: 60. RSP: Yes

Nonprofit; nondenominational. Missionary Sisters of the Sacred Heart. Private rooms. Medical supervision; respite care; podiatry; optometry; X-ray services; 24-hour care; security; emergency response system; maintenance; transportation; up to 3 daily meals; housekeeping and laundry services; religious activities; chapel; scheduled trips; activity calendar; library visits; coffee/snack lounge; sundecks; activity room; barber/beauty service.

RC Daily: $60. RSP Daily: $85–$110

The Fountains at Millbrook

560 Flint Rd.
Millbrook, NY 12545

Ph: (914) 677-8550
Fax: (914) 677-8630

http://www.thefountains.com

E-mail: *jankmiller@thefountains.com*

IND: 135. AL: 5

Age 62+. For-profit; nondenominational; owned and operated by The Fountains. Apartments and cottages. Wellness program; regular screenings; health fairs; home health services; personal care; medication administration; security; emergency response system; maintenance; transportation; up to 3 daily meals; housekeeping and laundry services; exercise programs; yoga and massage; walking groups; water aerobics; Bible study and nondenominational services; library; computer center; banking services; financial planning workshops; educational programs; woodworking shop; music therapy; writers' workshops; theater performances; off-site activities; clubs and organizations; arts and crafts; baking; country store; barber/beauty shop.

DEP: $1,100. IND MO: $2,200–$5,500. AL MO: $3,550–$4,175.

King David Manor

80 W. Broadway
Long Beach, NY 11561

Ph: (516) 889-1300
Fax: (516) 889-2138

AH: Yes

Suites with private baths. Security; emergency response system; maintenance; transportation; 3 daily kosher meals; housekeeping and laundry services; synagogue; planned social and recreational activities.

AH MO: $1,650–$3,450.

Scharome Manor

631 Foster Ave.
Brooklyn, NY 11230

Ph: (718) 859-2400 or (888) SCHAROM
Fax: (718) 859-7911

AL: Yes

Private and semiprivate rooms. On-site medical visits; on-site nursing services; personal care; medication administration; security; emergency response system; maintenance; transportation; up to 3 daily meals; housekeeping and laundry services; synagogue; exercise; crafts; board games; choir; concert; movies; special occasion celebrations; off-site trips.

AL MO: Double, $1,925; single, $3,075.

Senior Quarters

168 Schoolhouse Rd.
Chestnut Ridge, NY 10977

Ph: (914) 620-0606
Fax: (914) 620-9056

AL/AH: Yes. HCC: Yes. ALZ/MEM IMP: Yes

Kapson Senior Quarters Corp.; nondenominational. Private and shared suites with private baths. 24-hour care by trained staff; pharmacy services; medical examining room; visiting physicians, podiatrists, physical therapists and other health care personnel; physical, occupational, and speech therapies, health care coordinator; personal care; medication administration; security; emergency response system; maintenance; transportation; up to 3 daily meals; housekeeping and laundry services; exercise classes; movies; games; library; barber/beauty shop.

AL/AH MO: from $1,725.

Northwest

Rochester Presbyterian Home (AAHA, PAHA, NYAHSA, Empire State Association of Adult Homes, National Council on the Aging, Coalition of Resident Councils)

256 Thurston Rd.
Rochester, NY 14619

Ph: (716) 235-9100
Fax: (716) 235-1315
http://www.rahsa.com/rph

AH/AL: Yes. ALZ/MEM IMP: Yes

Age 62+. Nonsectarian, nondenominational; nonprofit residence. Private rooms with private and shared bath options. Physician visits twice a week; physicians assistant on site 5 days a week; 24-hour nursing staff; respite care; social worker; personal care; medication administration; security; emergency response system; maintenance; transportation; up to 3 daily meals; housekeeping and laundry services; church services; activities; movies; library; talking book service; volunteer program; ceramics; painting; off-site activities.

AH/AL MO: Standard rate, $2,325. RSP Daily: $80 and $100.

West Side Manor

1404 Long Pond Rd.
Rochester, NY 14626

Ph: (716) 225-7210

AL: 72

Privately owned and managed by Emeritus Assisted Living. Visiting podiatrist and staff RN; doctor's office; personal care; medication administration; security; emergency response system; maintenance; transportation; up to 3 daily meals; housekeeping and laundry services; exercise classes; religious services; game room; post office; off-site outings; residence association; crafts; cultural programs; barber/beauty shop.

AL MO: About $2,050.

Independent Living

Independent housing (primarily rentals) for seniors that may offer security features, meal service, and activities.

Northwest

The Woods at Blairville Apartments

830 Oriole Lane
Lewiston, NY 14092

Ph: (716) 754-7866.
Fax: (716) 754-7825.

IND: Yes

Landmark America LLC, Developer. Apartments. Walking paths; heated pool; community building; pets allowed.

DEP: (ref.) $275. MO: About $800.

East

Doubleday Woods

91 Church Ave.
Ballston Spa, NY 12020

Ph: (518) 885-1900
Fax: (518) 884-2701

IND: Yes

Nonprofit; nondenominational; affiliated with the Presbyterian Church. Apartments. Monthly podiatry and clinic services; services coordinator on-site; security; emergency response system; maintenance; 1 daily meal, Monday–Friday; library; community room; close to hospitals, shopping, cultural activities; senior center, and local transportation; barber/beauty shop services.

IND MO: 30% of adjusted income.

Shenendehowa Village

300 Solomon Ave.
Clifton Park, NY 12065

Ph: (518) 373-1900
Fax: (518) 373-1998

IND: 49

Van Schoonhoven Square

1 Van Schoonhoven Square
Waterford, NY 12188

Ph: (518) 235-0514
Fax: (518) 237-8925

IND: 40

Age 62+. Nonprofit; affiliated with National Church Residences. Apartments. Emergency response system; maintenance; transportation; pets allowed; service coordinator; social, recreational, and religious activities; shopping; crafts.

HUD-sponsored. IND MO: 30% adjusted income.

REQ: 1 person, maximum income $17,400; 2 persons, maximum income $19,900.

Central

Sidney Senior Village

200 Fox St.
Sidney, NY 13838

Ph: (607) 563-8000

IND: Yes

Age 62+. Nonprofit; nondenominational; an affiliate of National Church Residences. Apartments. Home health care assistance; security; emergency response system; maintenance; transportation; meals provided by local senior center; laundry services; some housekeeping; library; on-site office; social, educational, and religious activities.

HUD-subsidized; income limits: one person, $13,750; two persons, $15,700.

Adult/Resort Communities

Communities for active adults (not all are age-restricted; primarily ownership).

Northeast

Parkview at Ticonderoga

PO Box 110
Ticonderoga, NY 12883

Ph: (800) 795-PARK(7275)

www.parkviewticonderoga.com

Age 55+. Attached homes. Nearby golf; country club; tennis; lakes; boating; walking paths.

PURCHASE: Homes, from $131,000.

Whiteface Club

Whiteface Inn Rd.
Lake Placid, NY 12946

Ph: (800) 422-6757 or (518) 523-2551
Fax: (518)523-1329

http://www.whitefaceclub.com

Individual homes, condominiums, homesites. Golf course; tennis; hiking/biking; fishing; boating/waterskiing; snow skiing; marina; beach; certified Audubon Wildlife Sanctuary.

PURCHASE: Homes, $275,000–$660,000.

West

Bristol Harbour Village

5400 Seneca Point Rd.
Canandaigua, NY 14424

Ph: (800) 288-8248 or (716) 396-2200
Fax: (716) 394-9254

Individual homes, condominiums, homesites. Golf course; tennis; hiking; fishing; hunting; boating/waterskiing; snow skiing; community center.

PURCHASE: Homes, $209,000–$440,000.

Holiday Valley Resort

PO Box 730
Ellicottville, NY 14731

Ph: (716) 699-2345

Individual homes, townhomes, manufactured homes. Golf course; swimming pool; hiking/biking; snow skiing.

PURCHASE: Homes, $66,000–$434,500+; townhomes, $49,500–$245,500; manufactured homes, $22,000–$54,000. Rentals available.

South

Beechwoods Estate/Villa Roma Resort

340 Villa Roma Rd.
Callicoon, NY 12723

Ph: (914) 887-4880
Fax: (914) 887-6400

http://www.villaroma.com

Condominiums. Golf course; tennis; racquetball; swimming pool; snow skiing; fitness center; bowling.

PURCHASE: Homes, $115,000–$165,000.

Emerald Green

Rock Hill, NY

Ph: (914) 796-2410

Individual homes, townhomes. 3 lakes; swimming pool; tennis; fishing; boating; sailing; shuffleboard.

PURCHASE: Homes, $98,000–$770,000+; townhomes, from $87,000.

Heritage Hills

Rte. 202, PO Box 304
Somers, NY 10589

Ph: (800) 243-7482 or (914) 276-3000
Fax: (914) 276-2944

http://www.heritagehills.com

Individual homes, condominiums. Golf courses; tennis; swimming pool; hiking; fishing; community center; fitness center; dining; social clubs; minibus.

PURCHASE: Homes, $165,000–$525,000.

Hidden Ridge

Monticello, NY 12701

Ph: (914) 794-6000

Individual homes. Golf course; tennis; racquetball; swimming pool; hiking/biking; fishing; boating/waterskiing; snow skiing; fitness center; social clubs.

Call for property information.

The Woodlands at Tuxedo

168 Woodlands Drive
Tuxedo, NY 10987

Ph: (914) 753-5560

http://www.khov.com/homes/ny/tuxedo/woodmain.htm

Individual homes, townhomes. Clubhouse; tennis; swimming pool; baseball field; fitness center.

PURCHASE: Homes, from $330,000; townhomes, from low $220,000.

Long Island

Greenwood Village

370 Chapman Blvd.
Manorville, NY 11949

Ph: (516) 878-4200

http://www.retirenet.com/greenwood-village

Individual homes, manufactured homes. Clubhouse; tennis; swimming pool; shuffleboard; exercise room; billiards; bocce; ceramics; woodworking; library; bus service.

PURCHASE: Homes, from $110,000; manufactured homes, $49,500–$88,000.

The Hamlet Golf and Country Club

1 Clubhouse Drive
Commack, NY 11725

Ph: (516) 499-5200

Individual homes, condominiums. Golf course; tennis; racquetball; community center; fitness center; beauty parlor.

PURCHASE: Homes, $434,500–$605,000.

North Carolina

http://www.state.nc.us

General Information

Climate

Mountains: Appalachian mountain chain; cool summers/cold winters. Heartland: Average winter temperature about 42° F; summer, 77° F. Coast: Average annual temperature is 63° F.

Cost of Living

Ranks 43rd in the nation.

Taxes

General: NC Department of Revenue, (919) 733-4684.

State/Local as % of Income: 10.3%.

Property Tax Reduction: Qualified owners 65 or older may receive homestead exemption.

Sales: 4%.

Prescription Exemptions: None. Some communities have local prescription assistance programs for low-income elderly adults who do not qualify for Medicaid.

Transportation, Travel, and Tourism

General

North Carolina Travel and Tourism, (919) 733-4171 or (800) VISIT NC.

Retirement magazines (N.C. Retirement, Retirement Lifestyles in North Carolina, and Destination North Carolina) available through Division of Aging, (919) 733-3983.

Major Airports

- Charlotte-Douglas International Airport, (704) 359-4000.
- Raleigh-Durham International Airport, (919) 840-2111.

Railways

- Amtrak, (800) USA-RAIL.
- North Carolina DOT Rail Division, PO Box 25201, Raleigh, NC 27611.

Bus Tours

- Greyhound Bus, (800) 231-2222.

Waterways

- Ferry Division, (919) 726-6446 or (800) BY FERRY.

State Highways

- Department of Transportation, (919) 733-2520.
- Blue Ridge Parkway, (828) 298-0398 (scenic drive linking Shenandoah and Smoky Mountain national parks).

Theater and Music

Central

- North Carolina Symphony, 2 E. South St., Raleigh, NC 27601, (919) 733-2750, Fax (919) 733-9920.
- Green Hill Center for North Carolina Art, 200 N. Davie St., Greensboro, NC, (336) 333-7460, Fax (336) 275-2787.

Southwest

- Brevard Music Center, 1000 Probart St., Brevard, NC 28712, (704) 884-2011, Fax (704) 884-2036.

Museums, Crafts, Historical, Recreational

Mountain Region

- Folk Art Center, Blue Ridge Pkway., MP 382, Asheville, NC, (704) 298-7928, Fax (704) 298-7962.

- The Hot Springs–Natural Hot Mineral Baths, 1 Bridge St., Hot Springs, NC, (704) 622-7676 or (800) 462-0933, Fax (704) 622-7615.
- Appalachian National Scenic Trail, 160A Zillicoa, Asheville, NC 28801, (704) 254-3708, Fax (704) 254-3754.

Heartland Region

- North Carolina Botanical Garden, Old Mason Farm Rd., Chapel Hill, (919) 962-0522, Fax (919) 962-3531.
- Tanglewood Park, Hwy. 158 W., Winston Salem, (336) 778-6300, Fax (336) 778-6322 (recreational park with two 18-hole championship golf courses, tennis courts, picnic areas, gardens).
- Martin Luther King Memorial Gardens, 1500 Martin Luther King Jr. Blvd., Raleigh, (919) 834-6264, Fax (919) 833-0723.
- North Carolina Museum of Art, Raleigh, (919) 839-6262.

Coastal Region

- Cape Hatteras National Seashore, (919) 995-4474, Fax (919) 995-5924.
- Wright Brothers National Memorial, Hwy. 158 Bypass, Kill Devil Hills, (252) 441-7430, Fax: (252) 441-7720.

Organizations

Advocacy Groups

- Division of Aging, (919) 733-3983
- Friends of Residents in Long Term Care, (919) 782-1530.
- North Carolina Senior Citizens Association, (919) 358-7856 or (800) 323-6525.

Volunteer Programs

- North Carolina Vista, (919) 856-4731 (helps people of low income).
- Senior Corps of Retired Executives (SCORE), (704) 344-6576 (counsels and trains owners of small businesses).

Housing

Long-Term Care Facilities

*In the state of North Carolina, these facilities are called **Continuing Care/Retirement Communities/Nursing Home Facilities**.*

These facilities provide residential living and/or various levels of nursing and medical services to seniors for an extended period of time.

Types of Authorization

Licensing and / or Certification

Continuing care facilities are regulated by the Department of Insurance and are licensed by the state Division of Facility Services for the adult care home or nursing home level of care they provide. A typical facility provides independent living accommodations, community dining, social and recreational areas, plus a range of services and amenities. There is usually an entrance fee in addition to a monthly service fee. There are four types of contracts: life care (individual living and health-related services usually at no additional fees when moving from one level of service to another), modified (health-related services provided for subsidized fee), fee-for-service (health-related services provided at per diem rate), and equity (involves purchase of real estate).

Nursing homes provide nursing or convalescent care. The care maybe long- or short-term. All nursing homes must be licensed and are regulated by the Division of Facility Services.

Memberships:

- American Association of Homes and Services for the Aging (AAHSA) represents not-for-profit organizations committed to providing high-quality health care, housing, and services to the elderly. AAHSA, 901 E St. NW, Suite 500, Washington, DC 20004-2011. Ph: (202) 783-2242. Fax: (202) 783-2285. *http://www.aahsa.org*

- The North Carolina Association of Non-Profit Homes for the Aging (NCANPHA) is an AAHSA Affiliated State Association. NCANPHA, 3700 National Drive, Suite 218, Raleigh, NC 27612-4842. Ph: (919) 571-8333. Fax: (919) 571-1297. *http://www.neanpha.org*

Accreditations:

- Continuing Care Accreditation Commission (CCAC) accredits facilities that offer seniors a contract or contracts that provide residential living and health care services for the remainder of the person's lifetime and meet CCAC's accreditation standards.
- Joint Commission on the Accreditation of Healthcare Organizations (JCAHO) is an independent, not-for-profit organization and the nation's oldest and largest standards-setting and health care accrediting institution.
- Educational Assessment Guidelines Leading toward Excellence (EAGLE) is a voluntary self-assessment and peer review evaluation system developed by the United Methodist Association of Health and Welfare Ministries.

Central

Belle Meade

95 Aviemore Drive
Pinehurst, NC 28374

Ph: (910) 215-4535 or (800) 343-7463
Fax: (910) 295-4741

IND: 224. AL: Yes. SNF: Yes. ALZ/MEM IMP: 20. ADC: Yes

Designed for active seniors; opening in 1999. Nonprofit, nondenominational; church-related; sponsored by St. Joseph of the Pines, Inc. Homes, cottages, duplexes, apartments, rooms. Licensed nursing care; physical, occupational, respiratory, and rehabilitation therapies; wellness center; personal care; medication administration; security; emergency response system; maintenance; transportation; up to 3 daily meals (for IND, 30 dining credits included in MO fee, plus daily continental breakfast); housekeeping and laundry services; health and exercise programs; chapel; intergenerational programs; game room; indoor pool and spa; putting green; garden and greenhouse; walking paths; bank; gift shop; tennis courts.

RSV AGR: (ref.) $1,100. DEP: (ref. within 30 days) 10% of entrance fee, less the RSV AGR. IND ENT (50% ref. and 90% ref. options available): About $103,500–$277,500; 2nd person, $18,000. IND MO: About $1,550–$2,400; 2nd person, $725. Ancillary medical and ALZ care are additional.

REQ: Must live independently at time of entrance.

Carol Woods Retirement Community, CCAC

750 Weaver Dairy Rd.
Chapel Hill, NC 27514

Ph: (800) 518-9333
Fax: (919) 918-3349

IND: 280. AL: 35. HCC: 60

Nonprofit; nondenominational; nonsectarian. Apartments, cottages, and private and semiprivate rooms. Skilled nursing care; physical, speech, and occupational services; physician services; outpatient clinic; Medicare-approved; personal care; medication administration; security; emergency response system; maintenance; transportation; up to 3 daily meals; pets allowed; housekeeping and laundry services; fitness center; swimming pool; library and computer room; social, educational, cultural, and recreational activities; banking services; residents association; photo lab; woodworking shop; billiards; croquet court; crafts and textile room; gardening; walking paths; barber/beauty shop.

IND ENT: $57,000–$233,750. IND MO: $1,850–$3,900. AL Daily: $15–$35; 2nd person, $20. HCC Daily: $40–$70.

Penick Village

E. Rhode Island Ave. Extension
PO Box 2001
Southern Pines, NC 28388

Ph: (910) 692-0300

IND: Yes. AL/PC: Yes. NC: Yes. ADC: Yes

(Total units/beds, 213)

Age 60+. Ministry of the Episcopal Church; nonprofit; nondenominational. Cottages, duplexes, apartments, and rooms. 24-hour nursing care; personal care; medication administration; security; emergency response system; maintenance; transportation; up to 3 daily meals; housekeeping and laundry; services all utilities (except long-distance phone); social, educational, cultural, and spiritual activities and programs.

APPL: (ref.) $1,100. IND ENT: (ref. option), $31,000–$199,000; (no ref. option), $28,500–$166,500. IND MO: Single, $1,400–$3,600; double, $2,950–$4,750. PC Daily: $105–$120. NC Daily: $150.

Sharon Village

PO Box 220130
4009 Craig Ave.
Charlotte, NC 28222

Ph: (704) 365-2620

IND: 34. SNF: Yes

Studios, apartments, private and semiprivate rooms. Nursing care; security; emergency response system; maintenance; transportation; up to 3 daily meals; housekeeping and laundry services; planned activities; library; gardening; mailroom, community area; barber/beauty shop.

IND ENT: (ref.) $13,750–$27,500. IND MO: (with ENT), $650–$1,150; (without ENT), $850–$1,600. SNF Daily: Semiprivate; $135 private, $140. ICF Daily: Semiprivate, $130; private, $140. Medicare Daily: Semiprivate, $265; private, $275.

The United Methodist Retirement Community, EAGLE

2616 Erwin Rd.
Durham, NC 27705-3899

Ph: (919) 383-2567
Fax: (919) 383-9208

IND: Yes. AL: Yes. HCC: 125. ALZ/MEM IMP: Yes

Nonprofit; nondenominational facility. Duplexes, apartments, suites, and rooms with private bath, and private and semiprivate rooms. Short-term, intermediate, and long-term care; 24-hour nursing care; physical, speech, and occupational therapies; clinic; personal care; medication administration; security; emergency response system; maintenance; transportation; up to 3 daily meals; housekeeping and laundry services; exercise; chaplain; chapel; social and recreational activities; intergenerational program; gardening and pet therapies; crafts; bookmobile; classes; clubs; library; postal service; nature trails; barber/beauty salon.

APPL: $220/single; $330/couple. IND ENT: (equity diminishes 2%/mo. for 50 mos. excluding $7,700 not ref.), $7,700–$112,000. IND MO: $1,600–$1,650. AL ENT: $7,700–$15,500. AL MO: $2,600–$5,150. HCC Daily: Intermediate care: semiprivate, $140; private, $145–$155. Skilled care: semiprivate, $155; private, $160–$170.

REQ: Health history; financial statement; pre-entrance exam.

East

Plantation Village

1200 Porters Neck Rd.
Wilmington, NC 28405

Ph: (910) 686-7181 or (800 334-0240 (NC) or (800) 334-0035 (out of state)

IND: Yes. HCC: Yes

Managed by Life Care Services Corp; nondenominational; nonsectarian. Apartments including villas, and duplexes. Emergency health care; nursing care; security; emergency response system; maintenance; transportation; special diets/tray service; up to 3 daily meals; housekeeping and laundry; activities director; library; crafts room; banking service; woodworking shop; community activities area; gardens; pool; barber/beauty shop.

IND ENT: (part. ref./return-of capital plan), $107,000–$265,000. IND MO: $1,350–$2,425; 2nd person, $725.

Northwest

Arbor Acres, CCAC, AAHSA

1240 Arbor Rd.
Winston-Salem, NC 27104-1197

Ph: (336) 724-7921
Fax: (336) 721-0271

IND: Yes. AL: 29. HHC: 122. ALZ/MEM IMP: 22 (total residency, approx. 400)

Age 65+ (spouse 60+). Nonprofit; nondenominational; affiliated with Western North Carolina Conference of the United Methodist Church. Homes, cottages, and studio and efficiency apartments. Emergency assistance; 24-hour nursing care; individual nurse consultation; short-term care; therapies; dental and podiatry services; personal care; medication administration; security; emergency response system; maintenance; transportation; up to 3 daily meals; housekeeping and laundry services; exercise programs; daily phone check; Bible study; chaplain; gardening; off-site activities; volunteer programs; lectures; painting; ceramics.

APP: (no. ref.) $100/person. (Entrance fees refundable less $2,750, plus less 2% a mo. for the 1st 50 mos.). IND ENT: (includes meals), $24,500–$48,500. IND MO: Single, $1,450–$1,850; double, $3,250 and $2,175. IND Apt/Duplex ENT: $55,000–$214,500. IND Apt/ Duplex MO: Single, $1,000–$1,150; double, $1,100–$1,250. Apt/Duplex with 3 daily meals MO: Single, $600; double, $1,200. AL ENT with 3 daily meals: $24,500. AL MO: Single, $2,650. HCC ENT with meals: $2,750. HCC Daily: Private, $155; semiprivate, $140. ALZ/ MEM IMP Daily: Semiprivate, $145; private, $160.

Brookridge Retirement Community

1199 Hayes Forest Drive
Winston-Salem, NC 27106

Ph: (336) 759-1044
Fax: (336) 759-7389

http://www.brh.org

IND and IND AL: Yes. AL: Yes. SNF: Yes. ALZ: Yes. HC: Yes

Age 62+. Owned and operated by Baptist Retirement Homes of North Carolina, Inc. Garden homes, studios, apartments, private and semiprivate rooms. 24-hour nursing care; clinic and emergency services; prescription drug service; physical, speech, and occupational therapies; IV administration; insurance and billing assistance; respite care; personal care; medication administration; security; emergency response system; maintenance; transportation; up to 3 daily meals (for IND, 1 daily meal included in MO fee); social, recreational, educational, cultural, and inspirational programs; chapel; convenience store; barber/beauty shop.

APPL: (no ref.) $150. IND ENT: $35,500–$145,750. IND MO: $825–$2,125. AL MO: (resident) $2,300; (nonresident) $2,725. SNF Daily: Skilled: semiprivate, $150; private, $165; Intermediate: semiprivate, $140; private, $165.

REQ: applicants under age 70 must secure long-term care insurance.

West

Deerfield

1617 Hendersonville Rd.
Asheville, NC 28803

Ph: (828) 274-1816 or (800) 284-1531
http://www.main.nc.us/deerfield
E-mail: *deerfield@main.nc.us*

IND: 224. AL: 40. SNF: 48. ALZ MEM/IMP: Yes

Age 62+. Nonprofit; nondenominational; affiliated with the Episcopal Diocese of Western North Carolina. Cottage homes, suites, apartments, and private and semiprivate rooms. 24-hour nursing care; physical, occupational, speech, and hydro therapies; clinic; personal care; medication administration; security; emergency response system; maintenance; transportation; up to 3 daily meals; pets allowed, housekeeping and laundry services; chaplain; lounge; computer lab; aerobics and exercise room; postal and banking services; country store; pool; woodworking shop; auditorium; crafts studio; computer lab; barber/beauty shop.

DEP: $1,100. IND ENT: (50% [ENT multiplied by 1.33] and 90% [ENT multiplied by 1.77] ref. options) $104,500–$268,500. IND MO: $1,675–$3,275.

Highland Farms Retirement Community

200 Tabernacle Rd.
Black Mountain, NC 28711

Ph: (704) 669-6473
Fax: (828) 669-6493

IND: 155. AL/RH: 113. HCC: 60

Age 55+. For profit; nondenominational; privately owned. Cluster homes, condos, garden apartments, and private and semiprivate rooms. Skilled nursing care; physician on-site; certified nursing assistants; blood pressure and weight monitoring; well visits; clinic; home health care services; pharmacy services; social services; Medicare/Medicaid-approved; personal care; medication administration; security; emergency response system; maintenance; transportation; up to 3 daily meals; housekeeping and laundry services; nondenominational religious services; library; whirlpool; woodworking shop; arts and crafts room; activities; convenience store; croquet court; horseshoe pits; putting green; gardens; greenhouse; barber/beauty shop.

IND ENT: Homes (ref. up to 76%), $200,500–$307,000; condo/cluster homes (ref. up to 76%), $77,000–$181,500; garden apartments (traditional plan), $31,000–$99,000. IND MO: Homes, $975–$1,025; condo/cluster homes, $500–$750; garden apartments (traditional and refundable plan), $1,250–$2,750; garden apartments (no ENT fee), $2,000–$3,100 (includes nonrefundable ADMN fee of $2,750). AL/RH ENT: (ref. up to 50%), $30,000–$62,000. AL/RH MO: (with ENT fee), $1,550–$1,850; (without ENT fee), $2,150–$3,050 (includes nonrefundable ADM fee). HCC Daily: $95–$150.

Lake Pointe Landing

420 Thompson St.
Hendersonville, NC 28792

Ph: (704) 693-7800 or (800) 683-7801

IND: Yes. AL: under construction. HCC: Yes

Nondenominational; owned by Life Care Centers of America. Homes, apartments, private and semiprivate rooms. Intermediate and skilled nursing care; short- and long-term care; rehabilitative services; personal care; medication administration; security; emergency response system; maintenance; transportation; up to 3 daily meals; pets allowed; housekeeping and laundry services; exercise room; pool; nondenominational chapel; woodworking shop; gardening; activities program; library; arts and crafts; general store; clubhouse; lake with recreation area; barber/beauty shop.

IND HOMES: $180,500–$203,500. APT APPL: $1,100 (no ref.). APT MO: $1,175–$2,975; 2nd person, $550; pets, $1,100 (no ref.); smokers, $1,100 (no ref.). AL MO: under construction; fees not yet available. HCC: Intermediate semiprivate, $110; private, $120; skilled, $155.

The Summit

100 Riceville Rd.
Asheville, NC 28805

Ph: (704) 299-1110
Fax: (704) 299-4077

IND: 22. AL: 39. SNF: 60

Nonprofit; nondenominational facility. Apartments and private and semiprivate rooms. Skilled nursing care; intermediate nursing care; dental and podiatry care; pharmacy; respite care; rehabilitative therapies; medical services; Medicare/Medicaid-approved; personal care; medication administration; security; emergency response system; maintenance; transportation; up to 3 daily meals; housekeeping and laundry services; planned activities.

IND MO: $1,350–$1,800; 2nd person, $385 and $475. AL MO: semiprivate, $1,900; private, $2,575; 2nd person, $1,175. SNF Daily: $125–$150.

North

Friends Homes at Guildford

925 New Garden Rd.
Greensboro, NC 27410

Ph: (336) 292-8187
Fax: (336) 854-9137

Friends Homes West

6100 W. Friendly Ave.
Greensboro, NC 27410

Ph: (336) 292-0129
Fax: (336) 294-0129

FH Guildford: IND: 178. AL: 52. SNF: 69

FH West: IND: 171. AL: 40. SNF: 40

Age 60+ for IND. Nondenominational; nonsectarian; nonprofit; Quaker affiliated. Cottages, studios, apartments, private and semiprivate rooms. Intermediate and skilled care; 24-hour health care; personal care; medication administration; up to 3 daily meals (1 to 2 meals with MO fee); educational and cultural activities; activities director; off-site activities; gardening; walking paths.

Guilford: IND ENT: (2 options; rental with loan plus ent. [loans paid at 6 1/4%]; rental with no. ref. ent.): $1,100–$41,250. IND MO: $950–$2,175. AL MO: Semiprivate, $1,775; private, $1,925–$2,350; handicap, $2,125. SFN Daily: Semiprivate, $120; private, $125–$130.

FH West: IND ENT: (ref.) $82,500–$126,500. IND MO: $1,450–$2,350. AL ENT: $49,500. AL MO: $2,700. SNF Daily: $150.

Masonic and Eastern Star Home of NC

700 S. Holden Rd.
Greensboro, NC 27407

Ph: (910) 299-0031
Fax: (910) 547-2999
E-mail: *jrose@grandlodge-nc.org*

IND: Yes. AL: Yes. HCC: Yes

Nonprofit; nondenominational; for Mason or Eastern Star families. Cottages, apartments, private and semiprivate rooms. Physicians; skilled nursing care; dental services; pharmacy; physical, occupational, and restorative therapies; personal care; medication administration; transportation; up to 3 daily meals; housekeeping and laundry services; exercise classes; nondenominational religious services; cultural, recreational, educational, and spiritual programs; off-site activities; library.

IND ENT: $71,500 and $82,500. IND MO: $600–$1,100.

Well Spring

4100 Well Spring Drive
Greensboro, NC 27410

Ph: (910) 545-5350 or (800) 547-5387

IND: Yes. AL: Yes. SNF: Yes

Nondenominational life care community. Garden homes, villas, apartments, and private and semiprivate rooms. 24-hour skilled nursing care; rehabilitative services; wellness clinic; short- and long-term care; personal care; medication administration; emergency call system; up to 3 daily meals; housekeeping and laundry services; exercise room; chapel; gardening area; exercise room; bank; lounges; tennis, walking paths; woodworking shop; convenience store; barber/beauty shop.

IND ENT: $115,500–$312,500. IND MO: $1,550–$3,650.

Assisted Living and Residential Care Facilities

In the state of North Carolina, these facilities are called ***Assisted Living/Residential Living and Adult Homes.***

These facilities provide room and board for ambulatory and independent adults who need minimum support.

Types of Authorization

Licensing and/or Certification

Requires licensing by the Division of Facility Services. Assisted living facilities must provide, at a minimum, housing, one daily meal, and personal care. Adult homes provide room and board, personal care, and some limited supervision.

Memberships

- Assisted Living Federation of America (ALFA) is a national non-profit membership organization whose mission is to enhance the quality of life in assisted living facilities and promote the interests of the assisted living industry. ALFA, 10300 Eaton Place, Suite 400, Fairfax, VA 22030. Ph: (703) 691-8100. Fax: (703) 691-8106. *http://www.alfa.org*
- North Carolina Assisted Living Association (NCALA) is a state affiliate of ALFA. NCALA, 1240 SE Maynard Rd. #203, Cary, NC 27511. Ph: (919) 467-2486. Fax: (919) 467-5132.

Central

Concord Place, ALFA, NCALFA

2452 Rock Hill Church Rd. NW
Concord, NC 28027

Ph: (704) 782-7594

AL: Yes. RC: Yes

Nondenominational; Hunt Assist Living Facility; Private and semiprivate rooms; 24-hour professionally trained staffing; nurse on staff; respite care program; wellness care program; personal care; medication administration; up to 3 daily meals with snacks; housekeeping and linen service; social, educational, cultural, and recreational activities; worship services; Residents' council.

MO: $1,375–$2,975.

The Little Flower, ALFAA

8700 Lawyers Rd.
Charlotte, NC 28227

Ph: (704) 545-7005

AL: Yes (about 45 residents)

Nondenominational; nonsectarian; privately owned; Catholic-oriented. Wellness program; routine health checks; personal care; medication administration; 24-hour emergency call system;

transportation; 3 daily meals and snacks; housekeeping and laundry services; activities; exercise programs.

AL MO: $1,550–$2,350.

Pittsboro Christian Village, AAHA

1825 East St.
Pittsboro, NC 27312

Ph: (919) 542-3151
Fax: (919) 542-5919

IND: Yes. PC: Yes. AL: Yes

Age 62+. Pittsboro Christian Village, Inc.; Christian affiliation; nonprofit; nondenominational. Apartments and rooms. Therapies; personal care; medication administration; 3 daily meals; laundry and housekeeping services; exercise classes; regular chapel services; singing groups; crafts; swimming; fishing; boating; library; missionary classes; shopping trips; off-site activities.

APP: (no ref.) $275. Two payment options: Plan A ENT (ref.) plus MO with mo. credit reduction. Plan B ENT (no ref.) with MO. ENT: (ref.) $4,400–$77,000; (no. ref.) $1,100. IND MO: (both plans) $950–$1,500. MO Care Unit: Semiprivate, $1,750; private, $1,875. MO AL: Semiprivate, $1,450; private, $1,600.

REQ: Of Christian faith; good health; financial statement.

Royal Oaks

1107 Carthage St.
Sanford, NC 27330

Ph: (919) 774-8989
Fax: (919) 708-5809

Magnolia House Retirement Center

1115 Carthage St.
Sanford, NC 27330

Ph: (919) 774-3774

AL: Yes

Family-owned and -operated; nondenominational. Private and semiprivate rooms. 24-hour supervision; wellness program; personal care; medication administration; security; emergency call system; maintenance; transportation; 3 daily meals plus snacks; housekeeping and laundry services; activities coordinator; individual and group activities; whirlpool bath; religious services; walking paths; library; barber/beauty shop.

Refundable security deposit.

RO: AL MO: Semiprivate, $2,100; private, $2,450; couple, $4,300.

MH: AL MO: Semiprivate, $1,825; privatc, $2,050; couple, $3,750.

Union Park, ALFA, NCALA

1316 Patterson Ave.
Monroe, NC 28112

Ph: (704) 282-0530

AL: Yes. RC: Yes

Nondenominational; Hunt Assist Living Facility; Private and semiprivate rooms; 24-hour professionally trained staffing; nurse on staff; respite care program; wellness care program; personal care; medication administration; up to 3 daily meals with snacks; housekeeping and laundry services; worship services; social, educational, cultural, and recreational activities; residents' council.

AL MO: Semiprivate, $1,875–$1,750; private, $1,875–$2,600; couples, $2,650–$2,825.

North

Brighton Gardens

1208 New Garden Rd.
Greensboro, NC 27410

Ph: (336) 297-4700
Fax (336) 297-1244

AL: Yes. ALZ/MEM IMP: Yes

A Marriott assisted living residence. Suites. Individual wellness plans; 4 levels of care; daily reassurance checks; licensed nurse on staff; health and wellness assessment; personal care; medication administration; emergency call system; transportation; 3 daily meals; housekeeping and laundry services; planned activities; barber/beauty shop.

AL MO: $2,175–$3,400; 2nd person, $550; additional levels of care, $350 (incrementally).

Highgrove Longterm Care Center

2135 S. Scales St.
Reidsville, NC 27320

Ph: (910) 342-4112

IND: 40. AL: Yes

Private and semiprivate rooms. Personal care; medication administration; transportation; 3 daily meals plus snacks; housekeeping and laundry services; activities director.

MO: Semiprivate, $1,375; private, $1,600–$1,900.

REQ: Must be ambulatory. Accepts private pay and state-assisted residents.

Homestead Hills

2101 Homestead Hills Drive
Winston-Salem, NC 27103

Ph: (910) 659-0708 or (888) 781-7866
Fax: (910) 659-8506

AL: Yes. ALZ/MEM IMP: Yes

Owned by Homestead Hill Retirement Limited Partnership; nondenominational. Private rooms, suites, studios, shared living, and two-room suites. Personal care; medication administration; 24-hour emergency care; transportation; 3 daily meals plus snacks; housekeeping and laundry; library; social, cultural, and spiritual activities; game rooms; barber/beauty shop.

APP: (no ref.) $330+ the 1st mo. rental. AL MO: Shared living, $2,050–$2,100; private, $2,475–$2,525; studio suite, $3,100–$3,150; two-room suite, $4,075. 2nd person, $500. PC MO: $165–$330.

The Oaks

1670 Westbrook Ave.
Burlington, NC 27215

Ph: (336) 584-3070
Fax: (336) 584-3458

AL: Yes

A HHHunt community. Private and semiprivate rooms. Licensed nurse and certified staff; personal wellness plans; personal care; medication administration; transportation; 3 daily meals; housekeeping and laundry services; exercise; activity programs; volunteer programs; barber/beauty services.

AL MO: Semiprivate, $1,875; private, $2,400.

East

Diversicare/Christian Care of New Bern

104 Efird Blvd., PO Box 12383
New Bern, NC 28561

Ph: (252) 633-3455.
Fax: (252) 633-3898

AL: Yes

Rooms. Services for those with special disabilities; scheduled medical appointments; physical and speech therapies; personal care; medication administration; 3 daily meals; housekeeping and laundry services; crafts; table games; movies; bingo; shopping trips.

AL MO: $1,375.

McDaniel Adult Care Home

2915 Brunswick Ave.
New Bern, NC 28562

Ph: (919) 638-4680.
Fax: (919) 683-4640

AL: Yes. RC: Yes

Managed by ConstantCare Services, Inc.; nondenominational. Rooms and suites. Quarterly medication review; individual care plan, 24-hour trained caregivers; personal care; medication administration; transportation; 3 daily meals plus snacks; housekeeping and laundry services; banking and postal services; activities program; social programs; barber/beauty shop.

AL MO: Semiprivate, $1,600; private, $1,725–$1,925. RC Daily: $70.

West

Chestnut Hill of Highlands

PO Box 40
Highlands, NC 28741

Ph: (828) 526-5251 or (800) 473-5093

IND: Yes. AL: Yes

Nondenominational retirement community. Cottages, apartments, and suites. Personal care; medication administration; health care facility nearby; security; emergency response system; maintenance; transportation; up to 3 daily meals; pets allowed; housekeeping and laundry services; exercise program; recreational, cultural, and social activities; clubhouse; barber/beauty shop.

IND ENT: $181,500–$285,000, plus service plan. AL MO: $2,550–$2,750.

Crescent View

2533 Hendersonville Rd.
Arden, NC 28704

Ph: (828) 687-0068
Fax: (828) 684-8929

IND: 7. AL: 24

Age 55+. Nonprofit; nondenominational. Lutheran Church affiliation. One- and two-bedroom apartments and private and semiprivate rooms. Physician referral services; health clinic services; pharmacy services; dental care; personal care; medication administration; 24-hour staff and security; emergency response system; maintenance; transportation; up to 3 daily meals plus snacks; housekeeping and laundry services; fitness center; exercise program; postal services; social, recreational, and spiritual activities; arts and crafts; residents association; walking paths; barber/beauty shop.

DEP: $1,925. IND MO: $1,250–$2,200; 2nd person, $425. AL MO: $2,350–$3,050.

Heritage Hills/Lodge

3200 Heritage Circle
Hendersonville, NC 28791

Ph: (828) 693-8510
Fax: (828) 642-6349

IND: 100. AL: 24

Age 55+. For profit; nondenominational facility. Homes, apartments, and private and semiprivate rooms. 24-hour nursing care; skilled and intermediate nursing care; podiatry and dental services; rehabilitative services; personal care; medication administration; security; emergency response system; maintenance; transportation; up to 3 daily meals; pets allowed; housekeeping and laundry services; clubhouse; community room; activities.

APPL: $550. IND PURCHASE: $76,000–$143,000. IND MO: $1,650–$2,650. AL MO: $2,100–$2,650.

Independent Living

Independent housing (primarily rentals) for seniors that may offer security features, meal service, and activities.

South Central

Carmel Place

5512 Carmel Rd.
Charlotte, NC 28226

Ph: (704) 541-8012

IND: Yes

For-profit; nondenominational. Apartments. Wellness clinic; podiatry care; home health services; on-site management; security; emergency response system; maintenance; transportation; up to

3 daily meals; housekeeping and laundry services; exercise classes; chapel; library; social and recreational activities; crafts; media room; barber/beauty shop.

IND MO: $1,475–$2,175; 2nd person, $385.

Adult/Resort Communities

Communities for active adults (not all are age-restricted; primarily ownership).

East

Albemarle Plantation

One Plantation Drive
Hertford, NC 27944

Ph: (800) 523-5958 or (252) 426-4653

http://www.albemarle.net

Individual homes, patio homes, condominiums, homesites. Golf course; clubhouse; pro shop; tennis; swim and fitness complex; marina; dining.

PURCHASE: Homes, from $247,500; condos, from $88,000; homesites: $43,500–$302,500.

The Currituck Club

PO Box 229
Kitty Hawk, NC 27949

Ph: (800) 465-3972 or (252) 261-2131
Fax: (252) 261-3083

http://www.thecurrituckclub.com

Patio homes, villas, homesites. Golf course; tennis; swimming pools; bike/jogging trail; recreational facilities; beach.

PURCHASE: Homes and villas, $275,000; homesites, from $103,500.

Landfall

1801 Eastwood Rd.
Wilmington, NC 28405

Ph: (800) 227-8208 or (910) 256-6111

http://www.landfallrealty.com

Individual homes, patio homes, homesites. Golf courses; clubhouses; pro shop; sports center; tennis; swimming pools; fitness facility; dining.

PURCHASE: Homes, $367,500–$3.3 million; patio homes, $252,000–$660,000; homesites; $63,000–$1.32 million.

Lockwood Folly

309 Club House Drive SW
Supply, NC 28462

Ph: (800) 443-7891 or (800) 537-9043 (in NC)

http://www.lockwoodfolly.com

Individual homes, homesites. Golf course; clubhouse; tennis; swimming pool; Jacuzzi.

PURCHASE: Homesites, from $44,000.

Magnolia Greens Golf Plantation

9049 Ocean Hwy.
US 17 South
Leland, NC 28451

Ph: (800) 677-7524 or (910) 383-0990

http://www.navi-gator.com/magnolia-greens

Individual homes, homesites. Golf course; pro shop; clubhouse; tennis and swim facility; sports field; lakes.

PURCHASE: Homes, from $134,500; homesites, from $41,000.

Ocean Ridge Plantation

6877 Highway 17W
Department WTR
Sunset Beach, NC 28469

Ph: (800) 556-6570 or (910) 287-1800

http://www.oceanridge.com

Individual homes, homesites. Golf courses; clubhouse; tennis; swimming pools; fitness center; walking/biking; nature trails; community gardens.

PURCHASE: Custom homes, from $209,000; homesites; from $44,000.

Porters Neck Plantation

1202 Porters Neck Rd.
Wilmington, NC 28406

Ph: (800) 423-5695 or (910) 686-7400
http://www.porters-neck.com

Village homes, villa homes, club homes, fairway homes, homesites. Golf course; clubhouse; pro shop; sports complex; tennis; swimming pools; fitness center; aerobics studio; dining.

PURCHASE: Village homes, $250,550+ (incl. homesite); villa homes, $209,000+; club homes, $231,000+; fairway homes, $240,000+; homesites, $54,000+.

St. James Plantation

4006 St. James Drive
Department WSJ99G
Southport, NC 28461

Ph: (800) 245-3871
http://www.stjamesplantation.com

Custom homes, patio homes, condominiums and townhomes. Private beach club; golf courses; waterway park; tennis; Olympic swimming pool.

PURCHASE: Homes, $156,500–$825,000+; homesites, from $49,500.

WatersEdge

PO Box 229
Kitty Hawk, NC 27949

Ph: (800) 488-0738
Fax: (252) 261-3083

Individual homes, homesites. Private boating community; swimming pool; marina; boat docks.

PURCHASE: Homes, from $142,000; homesites, from $43,000.

Winding River Plantation

PO Box 11367
Southport, NC 28461

Ph: (800) 711-5263
Fax: (910) 755-5108
http://winding-river.com

Individual homes, condominiums, homesites. Private beach club; golf course; boat docking; tennis; swimming pool; exercise center; walking/biking trail.

PURCHASE: Homesites, $35,500–$358,500.

Central

Bermuda Village

142 Bermuda Village Drive
Advance, NC 27006

Ph: (800) 843-5433 or (336) 998-6535

Age: 55+. Villas, condominiums. Golf courses; clubhouse; tennis; swimming pools; health spa; dining; social clubs; chapel; healthcare center.

PURCHASE: Condos, $132,000+; MO service fee, $1,650. Villas, $252,000+; MO service fee, $1,700.

Heritage Pines

Cary, NC 27513

Ph: (919) 469-5534

Age: 55+. Individual homes, villas. Clubhouse; tennis; swimming pool; spa; shuffleboard; computer center; social director; social clubs.

PURCHASE: Homes, from $187,000; villas, from $44,000.

Olde Beau

PO Box 32
Roaring Gap, NC 28668

Ph: (800) 752-1634 or (336) 363-3333
http://www.oldebeau.net

Individual homes, cottages, villas, homesites. Golf course; clubhouse; pro shop; tennis; swimming pools; fitness center; dining.

PURCHASE: Homes, $275,000–$440,000; cottages and villas, $148,000–$247,500; homesites, $49,500–$165,000.

Sherwood Forest

50 Forest Drive
Cameron, NC 28326

Ph: (877) 257-9282 or (919) 499-2424
Fax: (919) 499-9142
http://www.sherwoodforesthomes.com

Factory contracted homes. Private swim club; greenacres area; nature trail; nearby golf and lakes for fishing, boating, and swimming.

PURCHASE: Homes, from $88,000.

Treyburn

1214 Rocky Point Lane
Durham, NC 27712

Ph: (800) 368-8331 or (919) 620-0002

http://www.treyburn.com

Individual homes, homesites. Golf course; clubhouse; tennis complex; swimming pools; dining.

PURCHASE: Homes, from $214,500; homesites, from $43,500.

Whispering Pines

One Clubhouse Blvd.
Whispering Pines, NC 28327

Ph: (800) 742-3378 or (910) 949-2261
Fax: (910) 949-3204

Individual homes, homesites. Golf course; clubhouse; tennis; swimming; lakes; fishing; boating.

PURCHASE: Homes, $131,000–$428,000; homesites, $20,500–$82,500.

Woodlake Country Club

PO Box 648
150 Woodlake Blvd.
Vass, NC 28394

Ph: (888) THE LAKE or (800) 334-1126

http://www.woodlakecc.com/

Individual homes, townhomes, homesites. Private lake; golf courses; health and fitness center.

PURCHASE: Homes, $141,000–$478,500; townhomes, $77,000–$225,000; homesites, $16,500–$137,500.

West

Ballantyne Country Club

10933 Ballantyne Crossing Ave.
Charlotte, NC 28277

Ph: (704) 544-0201
Fax: (704) 544-1845

http://www.ballantynecc.com

Individual homes, homesites. Golf course; pro shops; clubhouse; swim and tennis center; fitness room; dining.

PURCHASE: Homes, low $462,000–$2.2 million; homesites, $71,500–$220,000.

Champion Hills

1000 Indian Cave Rd.
Hendersonville, NC 28739

Ph: (800) 633-5122 or (828) 693-0072
Fax: (828) 693-9533

http://www.championhills.com

Individual homes, villas, homesites. Golf course; clubhouse; pro shop; tennis; swimming pool, fitness center.

PURCHASE: Custom homes and villas, $247,500+; homesites, $55,000+.

Cullasaja Club

1371 Cullasaja Club Drive
Highway 64
East Highland, NC 28741

Ph: (800) 354-1859 or (828) 526-4104
Fax: (828) 526-4127

Individual homes, homesites. Golf course; clubhouse; tennis; swimming pool; canoeing; fishing; hiking/biking; dining.

PURCHASE: Homes, $506,000–$764,500; homesites, $71,500–$550,000.

Mountain Air Country Club

PO Box 1037
Burnsville, NC 28714

Ph: (800) 247-7791 or (704) 682-3600

http://www.mountainaircc.com

Individual homes, villas, homesites. Golf course; clubhouse; tennis; swimming pool; fitness center; mountain market; airplane runway.

PURCHASE: Homes and villas, $219,000–550,000+; homesites, $93,500–$440,000+.

The Point

1913 Brawley School Rd.
Mooresville, NC 28117

Ph: (704) 663-3030
Fax: (704) 663-3041

http://www.crescent-resources.com/communit

Individual homes, homesites. Nantucket-style village; golf course; pro shop; tennis; swimming pools; fitness center; boating; fishing; dining; tavern; meeting house.

PURCHASE: Homes, $440,000–$1million+; homesites, from $77,000.

Qualla Village

2 Unoga Ct.
Brevard, NC 28712

Ph: (828) 885-2651

http://www.quallavillage.com

Paired condominiums. Golf course; clubhouse; tennis; swimming; hiking trails; lakes; boating; fishing; dining; waterfalls and trout ponds.

PURCHASE: Condos, $165,000–$275,000.

Riverwind

100 Riverwind Drive
Hendersonville, NC 28739

Ph: (800) 452-3058 or (828) 891-2010
Fax: (828) 891-2360

Custom designed manufactured homes. Clubhouse; swimming pool; spa; scheduled social events.

PURCHASE: Homes, from $88,000.

Stoney Creek

911 Golf House Rd. E.
Stoney Creek, NC 27377

Ph: (336) 449-7880

http://www.golflink.net/stoney

Individual homes, golf villas. Golf course; nature trails; swim and tennis club; nearby lake for boating and fishing; shopping village.

PURCHASE: Homes, from $242,000; villas, from $198,000.

Straus Park

1175 Asheville Hwy.
Brevard, NC 28712-3056

Ph: (888) 640-2525 or (828) 885-2525

http://www.strauspark.com

Individual homes, townhomes, condominiums, homesites. Lake; hiking trails; meadow parks.

PURCHASE: Homes and townhomes, from $352,000; homes, condos, $209,000+; homesites, $77,000–$220,000.

North Dakota

http://www.state.nd.us

General Information

Climate

Average annual temperature is 70° F in the summer, 7° F in the winter.

Cost of Living

Ranks 36th in the nation.

Taxes

General: Office of State Tax Commissioner, State Capitol, 600 E. Boulevard Ave., Bismarck, ND 58505-0599. Ph: (701) 328-3700.

State/Local as % of Income: 9.5%.

Property Tax Reduction: Homeowners 65 years or older may qualify for the homestead credit property tax relief program. Applicant's income, plus the income of a spouse and any dependents, may not exceed $13,500.

Sales: 5%.

Prescription Exemptions: Prescription drugs are exempt from sales tax.

Transportation, Travel, and Tourism

General

North Dakota travel information, 1-800-HELLO-ND.

North Dakota Tourism, 604 E. Boulevard, Bismarck, ND 58505, (701) 328-2525 or (800) 435-5663.

Statewide information centers (open from May to October):

Bottineau Tourist Center, City Park, Highway 5E, Bottineau, (701) 228-3849.

Devils Lake Tourist Center, Highway 2E, Devils Lake, (800) 233-8048 or (701) 662-4903.

Dunseith Tourist Center, Log House Junction, Highways 3 and 5, Dunseith, (701) 244-5860.

Minot Tourist Center, 1020 S. Broadway, Minot, (701) 852-6000.

Rugby Tourist Center, Junction of Highways 2 and 3 Rugby, (701) 776-5846.

Major Airports

- Bismarck Municipal Airport, (701) 222-6504.
- Grand Forks International Airport, (701) 795-6981.
- Minot International Airport, (701) 857-4724.

Bus Tours:

- Greyhound Bus, (800) 231-2222.

State Highways

- Minot Highway Patrol District Office, US 2, Bypass East, Minot, (701) 857-7637.
- Law Enforcement Center, 22 West Walnut, Devils Lake, (701) 662-2527.
- Interstate 94 runs east-west across the state.

Theater and Music

West

- Medora Musical Burning Hills Amphitheater, Medora, (800) 633-6721 (season runs June through September; Broadway-style song and dance).

Museums, Crafts, Historical, Recreational:

Central

- State Museum North Dakota Heritage Center, 162 E. Boulevard Ave, Capitol Grounds, Bismarck, ND 58505, (701) 328-2666 (state

museum, state archives, research library, auditorium).
- 4 Bears Casino and Lodge, (800) 294-5454.
- Prairie Knights Casino and Lodge, (800) 425-8277.
- Knife River Indian Villages National Historic Site, Stanton, (701) 745-3309 (visitor center, trails, hiking paths, skiing).
- National Wildlife Refuges: U.S. Fish and Wildlife Service, Bismarck, (701) 250-4418.
- International Peace Garden, (701) 263-4390 (gardens, campgrounds, state park, lodging).
- Beaver Lake State Park, near Burnstad, (701) 452-2752.

East:

- Pembina State Museum, PO Box 456, Pembina, ND 58271-0456, (701) 825-6840.
- Fort Ransom State Park, Fort Ransom, (701) 973-4331.

Organizations

Advocacy Groups:

- North Dakota Department of Health, 600 E. Boulevard Ave., Bismarck, ND 58505, (701) 328-2372, Fax: (701) 328-4727.
- North Dakota Senior Information, (800) 451-8693. Aging Services, (701) 224-2310.
- North Dakota Long Term Care Association, *http://www.ndltca.org*

Volunteer Programs

- North Dakota Heritage Volunteer Program.

Housing

Long-Term Care Facilities

*In the state of North Dakota, these facilities are called **Long-Term Care/Nursing Facilities**.*

These facilities provide nursing supervised health care to elderly adults that do not require hospital care.

Types of Authorization

Licensing and/or Certification

Nursing facilities must be licensed by the state. The facility must provide health care under the supervision of a licensed health care practitioner and continuous nursing care on a 24-hour basis. In addition, the facility will provide for each resident a personal assessment and care plan; dietary services; pharmaceutical services; social, activity, and rehabilitative services; and housekeeping and maintenance services.

Memberships:

- American Association of Homes and Services for the Aging (AAHSA) represents not-for-profit organizations committed to providing high-quality health care, housing, and services to the elderly. AAHSA, 901 E St. NW, Suite 500, Washington, DC 20004-2011. Ph: (202) 783-2242. Fax: (202) 783-2285. *http://www.aahsa.org*
- North Dakota Long Term Care Association (NDLTCA) is a professional and advocacy organization representing basic care and nursing facilities in ND. It is an affiliate of the American Health Care Association, which represents not-for-profit and proprietary facilities. Memberships require that all nursing facility beds are Medicare/Medicaid-certified; that all basic care beds are licensed by the state; and that all facilities offer physical, speech, and occupational therapy.

North

Mountrail Bethel Home, NDLTCA

615 6th St. SE
Stanley, ND 58763

Ph: (701) 628-2442

IND: 12. SNF: 57

Nonprofit, church-owned corporation. Apartments with shared areas and private and semiprivate rooms. Registered and licensed nursing; doctor visits; physical therapy; up to 3 daily meals; housekeeping and laundry services; chapel; dayroom; planned daily activities; bingo; arts and crafts; movies; sing-alongs; one-on-one visiting; gardening; coffee hour; scheduled trips; barber/beauty shop.

Daily fees: $95–$165.

Souris Valley Care Center, NDLTCA

Highway 41 S.
Velva, ND 58790

Ph: 701-338-2072

SNF: Yes (50 residents)

Nonprofit facility; managed by the Evangelical Lutheran Good Samaritan Society; nondenominational. 24-hour a day nursing care; rehabilitative and social services; 3 daily meals plus snacks; planned daily activities; off-site trips; Bible study.

Fees set by the State Department of Human Services; determined by the amount of care needed. Private payment and Medicare/Medicaid.

Wedgewood Manor, NDLTCA

804 Main St. W.
Cavalier, ND 58220

Ph: (701) 265-8453
Fax: (701) 265-8752

SNF: 60

Operated by Lutheran Hospitals and Homes Society; nonprofit. Rooms. Primary care nursing; individual resident aide for each person; physical therapist and rehabilitation aides; Medicare/Medicaid-approved; registered dietitian; transportation; 3 daily meals; community and outdoor activities; social interaction; barber/beauty shop services.

SNF Daily fees: $90–$150.

South

Beverly Anne Assisted Living, NDLTCA

400 Jackson Ave. E.
Lisbon, ND 58054

Ph: (701) 683-4092

AL: 24. SNF: Yes

Apartments. 24-hour staffing; personal care; medication administration; emergency response system; transportation; up to 3 daily meals plus snacks; housekeeping and laundry services; recreation room; exercise equipment; transportation; social and wellness programs; barber/beauty shop.

AL MO: One-bedroom, $990; two-bedroom, $1,175. Second related person, $330. Additional monthly rates for special services.

Elm Crest Manor, NDLTCA

100 Elm Ave.
New Salem, ND 58563

Ph: (701) 843-7526

SNF: 61

Church-related, nondenominational facility. Private and semiprivate rooms. 24-hour nursing care; Medicare/Medicaid-approved; 3 daily meals; housekeeping and laundry services; daily activities include exercise, devotions, bingo, movies, videos, and sing-alongs.

Daily fees: $85–$145.

Golden Manor Inc., NDLTCA

215 4th St. NW
Steele, ND 58482

Ph: (701) 475-2251

SNF: 50

A not-for-profit, nondenominational facility. Rooms. 24-hour nursing care; personal care; medication administration; 3 daily meals plus snacks; housekeeping and laundry services; exercise; devotion; scheduled daily activities; games; music.

Daily fees: 16 levels of care, $85–$135. Private pay.

East

Luther Memorial Home/Sun Center Apartments, NDLTCA, certified by the Evangelical Lutheran Church of America

750 Main St. E.
Mayville, ND 58257

Ph: (701) 786-3401

IND: Yes. SNF: Yes

Not-for-profit; nondenominational facility. Apartments. 24-hour nurse staffing; emergency response system; up to 3 daily meals; housekeeping and laundry services; pool; postal and newspaper service; library; resident council.

IND MO: One bedroom (includes one noon meal), $775; two bedrooms, $925; efficiency, $475 (does not include meals).

Valley Memorial/Tufte Manor, NDLTCA

3300 Cherry St.
Grand Forks, ND 58201

Ph: (701) 775-2581
Fax: (701) 775-2259

SNF: Yes

Christian, nonprofit organization; nondenominational. Single rooms and suites with and without kitchenettes. 24-hour home care staff; personal care; medication administration; emergency response system; 3 daily meals plus snacks; all utilities; physical, intellectual, social, and recreational programs; barber/beauty shop.

SNF MO: $1,025–$1,600.

Central

Knife River Care Center, NDLTCA

106 4th St. NW
Beulah, ND 58523

Ph: (701) 873-4322

SNF: 85

No restrictions on admission. Nondenominational; nonsectarian. Private and semiprivate rooms. 24-hour nursing service; maintenance; 3 daily meals plus snacks; housekeeping and laundry services; daily activities include exercise and games.

Daily fees: $95–$145.

Assisted Living and Residential Care Facilities

*In the state of North Dakota, these facilities are called **Basic Care**.*

These facilities offer room and board, and include daily personal assistance based on an individual's level of need.

Types of Authorization

Licensing and/or Certification

These facilities must be licensed by the Department of Health and are mandated to provide room and board, health, social, and personal care. Services are provided on a 24-hour basis, either directly or through contract, and include daily living assistance, recreational and therapeutic activities, dietary needs, and medication supervision.

Memberships:

- North Dakota Long Term Care Association (NDLTCA) is a professional and advocacy organization representing basic care and nursing facilities in North Dakota. It is an affiliate of the American Health Care Association, which represents not-for-profit and proprietary facilities in North Dakota. Memberships require that all nursing facility beds are Medicare/Medicaid-certified; that all basic care beds are licensed by the state; and that all facilities offer physical, speech, and occupational therapy.

- Assisted Living Federation of America (ALFA) is a national nonprofit membership organization whose mission is to enhance the quality of life in assisted living facilities and promote the interests of the assisted living industry. ALFA, 10300 Eaton Place, Suite 400, Fairfax, VA 22030. Ph: (703) 691-8100. Fax: (703) 691-8106. *http://www.alfa.org*

North

Edgewood Vista, NDLTCA

800 16th Ave. SE
Minot, ND 58701

Ph: (701) 852-1399
Fax: (701) 852-1414

http://www.edgewoodvista.com

BC: Yes. ALZ/MEM IMP: 14

Nondenominational; nonsectarian facility. Studios and apartments. Nursing services; monitoring blood sugar, blood pressure, and weight; 24-hour personal care; medication administration; housekeeping and laundry services; 3 daily meals; monthly candlelight dinner; exercise room; chapel; library; aviary and social rooms; entertainment; trips; barber/beauty shop.

BC MO: (1 person), $1,500–$1,775; (2 persons), $1,850–$2,050. Additional costs depending upon type of care and service.

Haaland Home, NDLTCA

1025 3rd Ave. SE
Rugby, ND 58368

Ph: (701) 776-5203

BC: 80

Age 60+. Owned and operated by Good Samaritan Hospital Association; nonprofit; nondenominational. Private and semiprivate rooms. Personal care; in-town transportation for medical appointments; social services; 3 daily meals; chapel; basic cable; planned daily activities; card games; dances; movies; gardening; gift shop; library; volunteer projects; resident council; barber/beauty shop.

Daily fees: (semiprivate with half bath), $38; (single with shared bath), $40; (private with half bath), $42; (private), $45.

Odd Fellows Home, NDLTCA

1124 2nd Street S.
Devils Lake, ND 58301

Ph: (701) 662-3330
Fax: (701) 662-6672

BC: Yes (43 residents)

Open to Odd Fellows and Rebekahs and nonmembers. Nondenominational facility owned by the Grand Lodge of North Dakota, Independent Order of Odd Fellows. Private and semiprivate rooms and suites. 24-hour staff; LPN nurse; registered nurse consultant; personal care; medication administration; transportation; 3 daily meals; housekeeping and laundry services; chapel; library; activities director; barber/beauty shop.

BC MO: members: (private), $1,000; (semiprivate), $975. Nonmembers: (private), $1,075; (semiprivate), $1,025.

West

Evergreen Retirement Inn, NDLTCA

2143 6th Ave. W.
Dickinson, ND 58601

Ph: (701) 225-6606

Fax: (701) 225-6721

IND: Yes. RC: Yes

Independent living rooms with attached bath and guest suites. 24-hour professional care; nursing services when needed; respite care; security; emergency response system; maintenance; transportation; 3 daily meals plus snacks; housekeeping and laundry services; kitchenette area; activities.

IND MO: $1,250–$1,475. No endowment fees. State funding available, monthly leases, veterans' benefits, long-term care insurance.

East

St. Anne's Guest Home, NDLTCA

524 N. 17th St.
Grand Forks, ND 58203

Ph: (701) 746-9401

BC: 86 (includes some low-income rentals)

Age 62+ and/or handicapped. Owned by St. Anne's Building Corp.; managed by the Sisters of St. Francis; nondenominational. Efficiency rooms. 24-hour staff service; up to 3 daily meals; housekeeping and laundry services; fitness programs; religious services; activities and recreational programs; volunteer and community programs; crafts; barber/beauty shop.

Daily fee: $50. Moderate rentals based on a percentage of monthly income and provided via HUD.

REQ: Must be ambulatory; financial and income verification.

South

The Chateau for Senior Citizens, NDLTCA

1120 S. 3rd St.
Bismarck, ND 58504

Ph: (701) 223-9223

BC: 32

A division of TTAD, Inc. Private and shared rooms. Blood pressure checked; ear and nail clinic; personal care; medication administration; 3 daily meals plus snacks; church services; group games; volunteer programs; special and monthly events; barber/beauty shop.

Daily fee: Shared room (2 beds); $45; semiprivate room, $50; private room, $55. Medicaid accepted.

REQ: Recipient liability (monthly income minus $50 for their own use); medical and family history information.

Gackle Care Center, NDLTCA

304 1st Ave. W.
Gackle, ND 58442

Ph: (701) 485-3395

BC: 41

Nonsectarian; nondenominational facility. Double rooms except for two. 24-hour care; Medicaid-approved; personal care; medication administration; transportation; 3 daily meals; chapel services; planned on- and off-site activities; barber/beauty shop.

BC Daily fees: State, $47; private, $50.

Manor St. Joseph, NDLTCA

404 4th Ave.
Edgeley, ND 58433

Ph: (701) 493-2477
Fax: (same as phone)

BC: 40

No age restrictions. Nondenominational; nonsectarian facility. Rooms. Personal care; medication administration; 3 daily meals; housekeeping and laundry services; exercise; daily activities; crafts.

BC Daily fee: $40.

The Terrace, NDLTCA

901 E. Bowen Ave.
Bismarck, ND 58504

Ph: (701) 258-1980

BC: 40

New facility; nondenominational. Private rooms and several rooms designed to accommodate residents with physical disabilities. 24-hour supervision; personal care; health monitoring; 3 daily meals; daily housekeeping; laundry; social and recreational activity programs.

BC MO: $2,100. Financial assistance available for those who meet specific income and resource guidelines.

REQ: Must be able to self-transfer; current physical and preadmission evaluation needed.

Independent Living

Independent housing (primarily rentals) for seniors that may offer security features, meal service, and activities.

West

Golden Valley Manor

260 5th St. SW
Beach, ND 58621

Ph: (701) 872-4282

IND: Yes

Nonprofit organization; A HUD facility. Efficiency and one-bedroom units. 24-hour security; laundry facilities; mail delivery; small pets allowed; optional meal plan; bingo; devotion; hobby room; exercises; pedicures; community activities; barber/beauty shop.

MO: Efficiencies, $300; 1-bedroom, $375.

Ohio

http://www.state.oh.us

General Information

Climate

Continental, with a wide range of temperatures. Average yearly temperatures range from 49° F in the northeast to 57° F in the south.

Cost of Living

Ranks 21st in the nation.

Taxes

State/Local as % of Income: 11%.

Property Tax Reduction: Homestead exemptions for eligible residents age 65 and older.

Sales: 5%.

Prescription Exemptions: Prescription drugs and other health-related products are exempt from sales tax.

Transportation, Travel, and Tourism

General

Department of Transportation, road conditions: (800) 264-7263.

Ohio Travel and Tourism, (800) BUCKEYE.

Major Airports

- Cleveland-Hopkins International Airport, (216) 265-6030.
- Port Columbus International Airport, (614) 239-4083.
- Cincinnati–Northern Kentucky International Airport, (606) 767-3151.

Railways

- Regional Transit Authority, (216) 621-9500.

Bus Tours

- Greyhound, (800) 231-2222.

State Highways

- Turnpike information: (800) 876-7453.

Theater and Music

Northeast

- Cleveland Public Theatre, 6415 Detroit Ave., Cleveland, OH 44102, (216) 631-2727, Fax (216) 631-2575.
- Cleveland San Jose Ballet, 3615 Euclid Ave., Suite 1A, Cleveland, OH 44115, (216) 426-2500, Fax (216) 426-2524.
- The Western Reserve Playhouse, 3316 Everett Road, Bath, OH 44286, (330) 659-6444 (community theater located in Ohio's Cuyahoga Valley National Park).

Northwest

- Toledo Opera, 406 Adams St., Toledo, OH 43604, (419) 255-7464, Fax (419) 255-6344.

Central

- Columbus Symphony Orchestra, (614) 228-8600, Fax (614) 224-7273.
- Columbus Association for the Performing Arts, 55 State St., Columbus, OH 43215, (614) 469-1045.

Southeast

- Athenian Players Theatre, PO Box 283, Athens, OH 45701.
- Stuart's Opera House, 34 Public Square, Nelsonville, OH 45764-1133, (740) 753-1924.

Museums, Crafts, Historical, Recreational

West

- National Road/Zane Grey Museum, 8850 East Pike, Norwich, OH 43767, (614) 872-3143 or (800) 752-2602 (land link between the East Coast and western frontier in the early 19th century; materials relating to Zane Grey, famous author of Westerns; also Ohio art pottery).
- Neil Armstrong Air and Space Museum, 500 South Apollo Drive, Wapakoneta, OH 45895, (419) 738-8811.
- United States Air Force Museum, 1100 Spaatz St., Wright-Patterson AFB, Dayton, OH 45433, (937) 255-3284. Oldest and largest military aviation museum in the world.

Northeast

- The Cleveland Museum of Art, 11150 East Blvd., Cleveland, OH 44106, (216) 421-7350 or (888) CMA-0033, *http://www.clemusart.com*
- The Health Museum of Cleveland, 8911 Euclid Ave., Cleveland, OH 44106, (216) 231-5010, Fax (216) 231-5129.
- Akron Art Museum, 70 East Market St., Akron, OH 44308, (330) 376-9185.

Central

- Columbus Museum of Art, 480 E. Broad St., Columbus, OH 43215, (614) 221-4848.
- Ohio Village, 1982 Velma Ave., Columbus, OH 43211, (614) 297-2300 (village representing life in Ohio in the 19th century).
- Mohican Country Convention and Visitors Bureau, Loudonville, (800) 722-7588. Near Amish Country.

Southeast

- Athens County Historical Society and Museum, 65 N. Court St., Athens, OH 45701, (614) 592-2280.

Southwest

- Cincinnati Zoo and Botanical Garden, (513) 281-4700 or (800) 94-HIPPO.

Organizations

Advocacy Groups

- Department of Aging: Golden Buckeye Card (to receive discounts on meals, merchandise, services), (800) 422-1976.
- Ombudsman/Elder Rights Unit: (800) 282-1206.
- Department of Health Hotline: (800) 342-0553.
- Home Community Based Services: (800) 686-6108.
- Ohio Senior Health Insurance Information Program: (800) 686-1578.

Volunteer Programs

- Seniors Teaching and Reaching Students (STARS), (614) 466-4966 (seniors volunteer in selected Ohio elementary schools as tutors and mentors).

Housing

Long-Term Care Facilities

*In the state of Ohio, these facilities are called **Long-Term Care/Nursing Home Facilities.***

These facilities provide residential living and/or various levels of nursing and medical services to seniors for an extended period of time.

Types of Authorization

Licensing and/or Certification

Facilities that provide skilled nursing and intermediate care must be licensed by the Department of Health. In addition, all long-term care facilities that participate in Medicare/Medicaid programs must be licensed by the Department of Health. Skilled nursing facilities (SNF) provide skilled nursing care and related services for individuals who require medical/nursing care or rehabilitative services. Intermediate care facilities (ICF) provide assistance to individuals including activities of daily living, medication administration, and supervision of physical, intellectual, and social needs.

Memberships:

- American Association of Homes and Services for the Aging (AAHSA) represents not-for-profit organizations committed to providing high-quality health care, housing, and services to the elderly. AAHSA, 901 E St. NW, Suite 500, Washington, DC 20004-2011. Ph: (202) 783-2242. Fax: (202) 783-2285. *http://www.aahsa.org*
- Association of Ohio Philanthropic Homes and Housing for the Aging (AOPHA), 855 S. Wall St., Columbus, OH 43206-1921. Ph: (614) 444-2882. Fax: (614) 444-2974.
- United Methodist Association (UMA).
- Ohio Health Care Association (OHCA).

Accreditations:

- Continuing Care Accreditation Commission (CCAC) accredits facilities that offer seniors a contract or contracts that provide residential living and health care services for the remainder of the person's lifetime and meet CCAC's accreditation standards.
- Joint Commission on the Accreditation of Healthcare Organizations (JCAHO) is an independent, not-for-profit organization and the nation's oldest and largest standards-setting and health care accrediting institution.
- Educational Assessment Guidelines Leading toward Excellence (EAGLE) is a voluntary self-assessment and peer review evaluation system developed by the United Methodist Association of Health and Welfare Ministries.

North

Altenheim

18627 Shurmer Rd.
Strongsville, OH 44136

Ph: (440) 238-3361
Fax: (440) 238-3205

SNF: 150

Nonprofit facility. Private and semiprivate rooms. Skilled nursing care; physical, occupational, and speech therapies; dental, ophthalmology, and podiatry services; Medicare/Medicaid-approved; 3 daily meals; housekeeping and laundry services; planned activities; special events; barber/beauty services.

SNF Daily: (basic) semiprivate, $145; private, $155.

Breckenridge Village, CCAC, OPRC

36500 Euclid Ave.
Willoughby, OH 44094

Ph: (440) 942-4342

IND: Yes. AL: 18. SNF: Yes. ALZ: 17

Age 60+ for independent living. Nondenominational; nonprofit; Ohio Presbyterian Retirement Communities. Ranch homes, private and semiprivate rooms. Skilled nursing care; 24-hour on-site staff; health education; personal care; medication administration; security; emergency response system; maintenance; transportation; up to 3 daily meals; housekeeping and laundry services; off-site scheduled trips; community room, and lounges; barber/beauty shop.

APPL: (no ref.) $330. IND ENT: (ref. up to 50 mo.) $115,500–$160,500. IND MO: Single, $625; double, $775. AL Daily: $110. ALZ Daily: $150. SNF ENT:

$20,000–$23,500. SNF Daily: (with ENT), $140–$220; (without ENT), $155–$235.

Countryside Continuing Care Center, OHCA

1865 Countryside Drive
Fremont, OH 43420

Ph: (419) 334-2602

NH: Yes. ALZ/MEM IMP: Yes

Owned and operated by Sandusky County. Rooms. Rehabilitative services; physical, occupational, and speech therapies; dental and podiatry services; psychologist and psychiatrist services; pharmacy; 3 daily meals; activities program; off-site field trips.

NH Daily: Semiprivate, $115. ALZ/MEM IMP Daily: $130.

Elyria United Methodist Village, CCAC, EAGLE

807 West Ave.
Elyria, OH 44035

Ph: (440) 284-9594 or (888) 818-1896

IND: Yes. AL: Yes. SNF: Yes. ALZ/MEM IMP: Yes

Nonprofit; nondenominational. Age 55+ for IND. Apartments, suites, and rooms. Nursing care; physical, occupational, and speech therapies; dental office; lab; wellness clinic; personal care; medication administration; maintenance; transportation; up to 3 daily meals; meal delivery; housekeeping and laundry services; fitness center; spiritual programs; insurance counseling; social and recreational activities; pool; community and resident programs; banking services; woodworking shop; technology learning center; library; pastry shop; barber/beauty shop.

IND RLUF: (.75% of RLUF offsets MO fee), $105,500–$147,000; (1% of RLUF offsets MO fee), $28,500–$128,500. IND MO: (with offset), $750–$3,075. AL MO: $2,450–$3,275; 2nd person, $1,300.

Good Shepherd Home

725 Columbus Ave.
Fostoria, OH 44830

Ph: (419) 435-1801
Fax: (419) 435-0136

AL: 43. NH: 100

Affiliated with the Churches of the Brethren. Private and semiprivate rooms. 24-hour nursing services; rehabilitative services; physical, occupational, and speech therapies; psychological services; IV therapy; personal care; medication administration; 3 daily meals; quality assurance program; chapel and religious services; barber/beauty shop.

ENT: $1,650–$2,750. MO: $55–65. SNF Daily: $110–$130.

Kendal at Oberlin, CCAC

600 Kendal Drive
Oberlin, OH 44074-1900

Ph: (440) 775-0094

IND: Yes. AL: 24. HCC: 42 (260 total residents)

Kendal Corp.; nonprofit; nondenominational; nonsectarian. Apartments and private and semiprivate rooms. 24-hour nursing care; wellness center; personal care; medication administration; emergency response system; maintenance; up to 3 daily meals; housekeeping and linen services; fitness center; pool; library; gardens; walking paths; darkroom; craft room; wood shop; tennis courts; computer lab; resident councils.

ENT: $63,500–$261,500. IND MO: $1,750–$4,200. HCC AL Daily: $110–$150. HCC Nursing Daily: $185–$200.

Laurel Lake, AOPHA, CCAC

200 Laurel Lake Drive
Hudson, OH 44236

Ph: (330) 650-2100 or 656-2090
Fax: (330) 650-0576
E-mail: *AnnetteHenry@HMIS.ORG*

IND: Yes. AL: Yes. HCC: Yes (total community: 400+ residents)

Nonprofit; Humility of Mary Health Care System. Studios, apartments, and private and semiprivate rooms. 24-hour skilled nursing care; intermediate care; dental and medical service; personal care; medication administration; up to 3 daily meals; tray service; housekeeping and laundry services; pool; chapel; woodworking shop; gardening; volunteer opportunities; library; banking services; intergenerational program; scheduled activities; barber/beauty shop.

LC ENT: $72,500–$241,000; 2nd person, $30,000. IND MO: $1,400–$2,375; 2nd person, $800.

McGregor Retirement Community

14900 Private Drive
East Cleveland, OH 44112

Ph: (216) 851-8200
Fax: (216) 851-6634

AL: Yes. HCC: Yes. ALZ/MEM IMP: Yes (16 residents)

Nonprofit; nondenominational facility. Private and semiprivate rooms. Nursing care; personal care; medication administration; Medicare-approved; security; emergency response system; maintenance; transportation; up to 3 daily meals; housekeeping and laundry services; social and cultural activities; volunteer opportunities; resident council.

AL Daily: $100. ALZ/MEM IMP Daily: $150. SNF: $150–$160. ICF Daily: $150.

Rockynol, CCAC

1150 W. Market St.
Akron, OH 44313-7178

Ph: (216) 867-2150
Fax: (216) 867-1642

IND: Yes. AL: Yes. HCC: Yes. ALZ: Yes. ADC: Yes

Nondenominational; nonsectarian; nonprofit; Ohio Presbyterian Retirement Communities. Apartments and private and semiprivate rooms. 24-hour nursing care; physical, occupational, and speech therapies; IV therapy; wound care; dialysis; psychological services; social workers; health monitoring program; personal care; medication administration; emergency response system; maintenance; transportation; up to 3 daily meals; housekeeping and laundry services; exercise room; chapel; library; bank services; volunteer program.

IND MO: $1,500–$2,850; 2nd person, $375. AL ENT: $32,500–$60,500. AL MO: $1,975–$4,450; 2nd person, $575. HCC: (with ENT) $150 and $180; (without ENT) $165 and $195.

West

Bethany Lutheran Village, CCAC

6451 Far Hills
Dayton, OH 45459

Ph: (937) 436-6850
Fax: (937) 436-7542

IND: 350+. AL: 60+. HCC: 250. ALZ: Yes

Nondenominational, nonprofit ministry of Lutheran Social Services of the Miami Valley. Chronic and subacute care; resident care technicians; social workers; attending physicians; rehabilitation center; therapies; dental and podiatry services; internal medicine, ophthalmology, plastic surgery, and orthopedics specialties; personal care; medication administration; security; emergency response system; maintenance; transportation; up to 3 daily meals; housekeeping and laundry services; fitness center; postal and banking services; social, educational, and recreational activities; intergenerational programs; pet therapy; music therapy; gift shops; nature trails; barber/beauty shop.

IND ENT: (Life Lease Financial Plan), $22,000–$140,500; 2nd or 3rd person, $5,575. IND MO: $475–$2,500. AL Daily: $95–$120. REHAB Daily: $225 (private pay); LTC Daily: $160 and $165. ALZ Daily: $185, $195, and $200.

Dorothy Love Retirement Community, CCAC

330 W. Cisco Rd.
Sidney, OH 45365

Ph: (937) 497-6542 or (937) 498-2391
Fax: (937) 498-1198

IND: Yes. AL: Yes. HCC: Yes. ADC: Yes

Nonprofit; nondenominational; Ohio Presbyterian Retirement Community. Homes, apartments, private and semiprivate rooms. 24-hour nursing care; licensed professionals; rehabilitative therapies; social worker; respite care; clinic; home health care; personal care; medication administration; Medicare-approved; security; emergency response system; maintenance; transportation; up to 3 daily meals; housekeeping and laundry services; pets allowed; educational and recreational activities.

IND ENT: (50% and 90% ref. ENT fees available), $93,500–$117,000. IND MO: $650; 2nd person, $45. AL ENT: $25,500–$42,000. AL MO: (with ENT), $3,000–$3,500; (without ENT), $2,200–$3,800. ALZ MEM/IMP ENT: $25,500–$42,000. ALZ/MEM IMP MO: (with ENT), $3,500–$3,850; (without ENT), $4,000–$4,550. RSP Daily: (with ENT), $105; (without ENT), $115.

Hamilton County O.E.S. Home

1630 N. Bend Rd.
Cincinnati, OH 45224

Ph: (513) 542-6464
Fax: (513) 853-664

E-mail: *star@easternstar.com*

RES: Yes. NH: Yes

Older adults. Nonprofit, private home; Order of the Eastern Star Hospital Circle. Resident care evaluation; 24-hour nursing care; therapies; vision, podiatry, dental, and psychiatric consultation services; social worker; transportation; 3 daily meals plus snacks; housekeeping and laundry services; clergy and Bible study; activities director; off-site activities.

RC Daily: $70–$155. RSP Daily: $70–$165.

Judson Village Retirement Community, CCAC

2373 Harrison Ave.
Cincinnati, OH 45211

Ph: (513) 662-5880
Fax: (513) 389-7840

IND: 20. AL: 80. HCC: 50

Nonprofit facility; nondenominational; affiliated with American Baptist Church. Apartments and private and semiprivate rooms. 24-hour nursing care; medical director; dental and podiatry services; pharmacy; physical, occupational, and speech therapies; personal care; medication administration; Medicare/Medicaid-approved; security; emergency response system; maintenance; transportation; up to 3 daily meals; housekeeping and laundry services; religious services; exercise program; resident council; daily activities; off-site excursions; greenhouse; walking paths; barber/beauty shop.

DEP: (ref.) 1st mo. rent. IND MO: $925–$1,100. AL MO: $1,375–$1,700. HCC Daily: Semiprivate, $165; private, $1170.

Llanfair Retirement Community, CCAC, JACHO

1701 Llanfair Ave.
Cincinnati, OH 45224

Ph: (513) 681-4230
Fax: (513) 681-0417

E-mail: *Kgoetzel@Llanfair.OPRS.ORG*

IND: Yes. AL: Yes. SNF: 75. ALZ: Yes

Nonprofit; nondenominational; Ohio Presbyterian Retirement Services. Homes, apartments, studios, and suites. Skilled nursing care; staff medical director on call 24 hours; dentist, podiatrist, and optician on-site; licensed social worker; physical, speech, and occupational therapies; respite care; restorative/rehabilitative services; personal care; medication administration; Medicare/Medicaid-approved; security; transportation; up to 3 daily meals;

housekeeping and laundry services; in-home care; security; postal and banking services; residence councils and committees; barber/beauty shop.

IND ENT: $13,500–$112,500. IND MO: $800–$1,950; (no ENT option), $1,625–$2,650. AL ENT: $9,350–$33,500. AL MO: $2,250–$3,850; (no AL ENT option), $2,450–$4,550. SNF ENT: $9,050. SNF Daily: $165, $190, $205; (no ENT option), $180, $205, $220. ALZ ENT: $9,300. ALZ/MEM IMP Daily: $170 and $185; (no ENT option), $185, $195, and $210.

Mount Pleasant Retirement Village, CCAC

225 Britton Lane
Monroe, OH 45050

Ph: (513) 539-7760 or (888) 539-7760

IND: Yes. AL: Yes. HCC: Yes. ALZ/MEM IMP: Yes

Nonprofit; nondenominational; Ohio Presbyterian Retirement Community. Homes, apartments, private and semiprivate rooms. 24-hour nursing care; physical, occupational, and speech therapies; social services; restorative care; personal care; medication administration; security; emergency response system; maintenance; transportation; up to 3 daily meals; housekeeping and laundry services; library; programs and activities; library; social, educational, and cultural activities.

APPL: (no ref.), $100. DEP: 10% of ENT fee; $5,500 2nd person. IND ENT: $20,000–$187,000. IND MO: $465–$1,950. AL ENT: $20,500. AL IND MO: $2,100–$3,300. ALZ/MEM IMP Daily: $155–$190. HCC Daily: $150–$180.

Otterbein-Lebanon Retirement Community, EAGLE, CCAC, AAHSA, AOPHA, UMA

585 N. State Rte. 741
Lebanon, OH 45036

Ph: (513) 932-2020
Fax: (513) 932-4722

IND: Yes. AL: 48. SNF: Yes. ALZ: Yes

Age 55+ for independent living; RLUF minimum, age 65. Nondenominational; nonprofit; Otterbein Homes Senior Ministry. Homes, apartments, private and semiprivate rooms. Long- and short-term care; attending physician on call; personal care; medication administration; adult day care; up to 3 daily meals; housekeeping and laundry services; social director; activities director; greenhouses; activities center; fishing pond; guest speakers; off-site trips; educational, recreational, and spiritual programs.

PROC: (no. ref.) $100/person. IND RLUF: Apt., $10,500–$111,500; Homes, $27,500–$148,500. IND MO: Apt., $750–$2,175; Homes, $1,350–$2,350.

Scarlet Oaks Retirement Community

440 Lafayette Ave
Cincinnati, OH 45220

Ph: (513) 861-0400
Fax: (513) 475-4382

IND: 84. AL: 9. IND/PC: 74. SNF: 85

Owned and managed by Deaconess Long Term Care of Ohio; nondenominational. Apartments and private and semiprivate rooms. Professional nursing coverage; certified technicians; 24-hour medical care; physicians; podiatry and dental services; lab and pharmacy; respite care; registered nursing care; personal care; medication administration; emergency call system; up to 3 daily meals; laundry and housekeeping services; health club; sauna and whirlpool; chapel services; social activities; mini store and gift shop; barber/beauty shop.

IND MO: $1,350–$3,600. AL MO: $2,150–$3,025. HCC Daily: $140, $160, and $200. RSP Daily: $65, $95, $97, and $125.

Central

The Helen Purcell Home

1854 Norwood Blvd.
Zanesville, OH 43701

Ph: (740) 453-1745
Fax: (740) 453-6674

AL: Yes (74 residents). NH: Yes

Age 75+ senior women. Christian, nondenominational retirement home. Private rooms. 24-hour nursing care; scheduled physical checks; personal care; medication administration; respite care; private-duty nursing; pharmacy services; pets welcome; transportation; 3 daily meals; social activities; hair care.

LTC: $22,000–$34,000, or 1 mo. rent with higher mo. payments. AL MO: $1,650–$4,250. RSP Daily: $55–$135.

Wesley Glen, CCAC, EAGLE

5155 N. High St.
Columbus, OH 43214

Ph: (614) 888-7492
Fax: (614) 436-6012

IND: 181. AL: 52. HCC: 83. ALZ/MEM IMP: 20

Nonprofit; nondenominational; affiliated with Methodist ElderCare Services. Homes, apartments, and private and semiprivate rooms. 24-hour nursing care; nursing assistants; social workers; licensed dietitian; physical, occupational, and speech therapies; dental, optometrist, and podiatry services; lab services; personal care; medication administration; security; emergency response system; maintenance; transportation; up to 3 daily meals; housekeeping and laundry services; exercise room; religious services; chaplain; library; gardening; crafts workshop; educational and recreational activities; convenience store; barber/beauty shop.

APPL: $220. IND ENT: $19,000–$121,000. IND MO: $1,100–$3,350. 2nd person fee: $440 (homes), $525 (apt.).

Westminster-Thurber Community, CCAC

717 Neil Ave.
Columbus OH 43215

Ph: (614) 228-8888
Fax: (614) 228-8898

IND: 190. AL: 45. HCC: Yes. ALZ/MEM IMP: Yes. ADC: Yes

Nonprofit; nondenominational; nonsectarian; Ohio Presbyterian Retirement Services. Apartments and private and semiprivate rooms. 24-hour nursing care; physical, occupational, and speech therapies; pharmacy services; podiatry services; health monitoring program; personal care; medication administration; Medicare/Medicaid-approved; security; emergency response system; maintenance; transportation; up to 3 daily meals; housekeeping and laundry services; exercise classes; pastoral care; arts and crafts; volunteer opportunities; resident association; educational programs; special activities.

IND ENT: $31,500–$130,000. IND MO: $525–$3,300. AL ENT: $33,000–$66,000. AL MO: $2,300–$4,850. ALZ/MEM IMP ENT: $33,000. ALZ/MEM IMP Daily: $110–$200. HCC ENT: $33,000. HCC Daily: $155–$195.

Rentals (no ENT fees) are available.

East

Park Vista Retirement Community, CCAC

1216 Fifth Ave.
Youngstown, OH 44504

Ph: (330) 746-2944
Fax: (330) 746-3427

IND: Yes. AL: Yes. HCC: Yes. ALZ MEM/IMP: Yes. ADC: Yes

Nonprofit; nondenominational; nonsectarian; Ohio Presbyterian Retirement Services. Apartments and private and semiprivate rooms. Licensed nursing care; physical, occupational, and speech therapies; personal care; medication administration; Medicare/Medicaid-approved; security; emergency response system; maintenance; transportation; up to 3 daily meals; housekeeping and laundry services; health monitoring program; exercise classes; craft and hobby area; gathering room; pool; gardening.

IND ENT: $29,000–$55,500. IND MO: $550–$3,200. AL ENT: $29,000–$52,000. AL MO: $2,200–$4,600. ALZ/MEM IMP ENT: $29,000. ALZ/MEM IMP MO: $2,850–$3,700. HCC ENT: $27,500. SNF Daily: $135–$170.

All ENT fees refundable on a prorated basis within 50 mos. Rentals (no ENT fees) are available.

South

Hill View Retirement Center

1610 28th St.
Portsmouth, OH 45662

Ph: (614) 354-3135 or (800) 400-2756
Fax: (614) 353-5511

IND: Yes. AL: Yes. HCC: Yes

Age 65+. Affiliated with Methodist Church. Apartments, studios, cottages, and private and semiprivate rooms. Long- and short-term nursing care; 24-hour medical care; monthly health screening; personal care; medication administration; security; emergency response system; maintenance; transportation; up to 3 daily meals; housekeeping and laundry services; all utilities (except cable and phone); exercise room; Bible study; art class; chorus, educational programs; games; speakers; community events; travel; country store; banking services; barber/beauty shop.

ENT: $20,000–$91,500 (2nd person, $11,000). MO: $1,025–$1,350. MO fee includes any health care fees.

Assisted Living and Residential Care Facilities

*In the state of Ohio, these facilities are called **Assisted Living/ Residential Care/Personal Care Facilities**.*

These facilities provide room and board for ambulatory and independent adults who need minimum support.

Types of Authorization

Licensing and / or Certification

These facilities are licensed by the Department of Health. Residential care facilities provides supervision and personal care services for individuals who are dependent on the services of others by reason of age or physical or mental impairment.

Memberships:

- Assisted Living Federation of America (ALFA) is a national nonprofit membership organization whose mission is to enhance the quality of life in assisted living facilities and promote the interests of the assisted living industry. ALFA, 10300 Eaton Place, Suite 400, Fairfax, VA 22030. Ph: (703) 691-8100. Fax: (703) 691-8106. *http: / / www.alfa.org*
- Ohio Assisted Living Association (OALA) is a state affiliate of ALFA. OALA, 1335 Dublin Rd., Suite 211B, Columbus, OH 43215. Ph: (614) 481-1950. Fax: (614) 481-1954.

North

Hilltop Village

25900 Euclid Ave.
Euclid, OH 44132

Ph: (216) 361-8383
Fax: (216) 261-6816

http: / / www.hilltopvillage.com / index.html

IND: Yes. AL: Yes

Privately owned; nondenominational; nonsectarian. Garden apartments. Personal care; medication administration; security; emergency response system; maintenance; transportation; up to 3 daily meals; housekeeping and laundry services; daily reassurance check; social activities.

IND MO: To $1,450. Home health care services are available from an outside source for additional fees.

Light of Hearts Villa

283 Union St.
Bedford, OH 44146

Ph: (216) 232-1991

IND: Yes. AL: Yes

Age 60+. Nonprofit; nondenominational; Vincentian Sisters of Charity. Efficiencies and suites. Personal care; medication administration; pharmacy delivery; security; emergency response system; maintenance; transportation; up to 3 daily meals; housekeeping and laundry services; religious services; scheduled activities; gardening; game room; reading areas; barber/beauty shop.

APPL: $100. DEP: $440. IND MO: (level I), $1,400–$2,350; (level II), $1,775–$2,700; (level III), $2,250–$3,175. 2nd person, $825, $1,175, and $1,675.

Southwest

The Lodge of Montgomery

12050 Montgomery Rd.
Cincinnati, OH 45249

Ph: (513) 683-9966
Fax: (513) 683-3709

IND: 216. AL: Yes

Nondenominational; an ARV community. Studios, apartments, and cottages. Wellness program; personal care; medication administration; 24-hour staffing; security; emergency response system; maintenance; transportation; up to 3 daily meals; housekeeping and laundry services; exercise room; chapel; lounges; game and billiards room; social and recreational activities; store; courtyard; scheduled entertainment; barber/beauty shop.

Contact facility for fees.

Independent Living

Independent housing (primarily rentals) for seniors that may offer security features, meal service, and activities.

West

Mercy Siena Springs

6215 N. Main St.
Dayton, OH 45415

Ph: (937) 274-4790
Fax: (937) 274-9812

IND: 45

Age 62+. Nonprofit; affiliated with the Sisters of Mercy. Apartments. Security; emergency response system; maintenance; transportation; pets allowed.

IND MO: 30% of income. HUD-subsidized.

Central

Richwood Community Apartments

235 Grove St.
Richwood, OH 43344

Ph: (740) 943-2332

IND: Yes

Nondenominational. Apartments. Security; maintenance, transportation; weekly meal program; laundry services; physical fitness area; library; weekly activities; barber/beauty shop.

Contact facility for fees.

North

Valley Road Villa

4146 Valley Rd.
Cleveland, OH 44109

Ph: (216) 398-4430

IND: 90

Age 62+. For-profit; nondenominational. Apartments. Security, maintenance; pets allowed; library; social activities; ceramics room; party and game room; gift shop; barber/beauty shop services.

DEP: 1 mo. rent. IND MO: $375 and $450. Some apartments are HUD-subsidized.

Adult/Resort Communities

Communities for active adults (not all are age-restricted; primarily ownership).

North

Barrington Golf Club and Estates

220 Southwick Lane
Aurora, OH 44202

Ph: (330) 562-6000
Fax: (330) 562-1691

http://www.barringtonlifestyle.com

Individual homes, condominiums, homesites. Golf course; tennis; swimming pool; fitness center; clubs.

PURCHASE: Homes, $329,000–$2.2 million; condos, $313,500–$522,500; homesites, $115,000–$385,000.

Greenbriar River Valley

10317 River Run Lane
North Royalton, OH 44133

Ph: (440) 230-0675

http://www.en.com/users/greenb1

Age 55+. Individual homes. Clubhouse; tennis; swimming pool; fitness center; walking trails.

PURCHASE: Homes, from $176,000

Raintree Country Club Estates

4340 Mayfair Rd.
Uniontown, OH

Ph: (330) 699-3232

Individual homes. Golf course; clubhouse.

PURCHASE: Homes, $291,500–$495,000.

Royal Village

7519 Dorr St.
Toledo, OH 43617

Ph: (419) 865-8162

http://www.retirenet.com/royalvillage

Manufactured homes. Clubhouse; swimming pool; storage area.

PURCHASE: Call the facility for price information.

Sawmill Creek Resort

400 Sawmill Creek
Huron, OH 44839

Ph: (800) GO-TO-LAKE or (419) 433-2376

http://www.sawmillcreek.com

Condominiums. Golf course; lake; fishing; sailing; marina; swimming pool; tennis; yacht club; dining.

PURCHASE: Condos (resales), $330,000–$825,000; new condos (in construction), $220,000–$825,000.

South

Heritage Club

6690 Heritage Club Drive
Mason, OH 45040

Ph: (513) 459-7711

http://www.HeritageClub.com

Individual homes, homesites. Golf course; pro shop; clubhouse; tennis; swimming pool; dining.

PURCHASE: Homes, $440,000–$1.1 million+.

Oklahoma

http://www.state.ok.us

General Information

Climate

Average annual rainfall ranges from less than 15 inches in the western Panhandle to more than 50 inches in the Ouachita Mountains. In the higher, more arid, western part of the state, yearly temperatures range from -10° F in January to above 100° F in July. In the low, humid, subtropical southeast, temperatures vary from about 32° F in winter to 90° F in July.

Cost of Living

Ranks 42nd in the nation.

Taxes

State/Local as % of Income: 9.8%.

Property Tax Reduction: Residents over the age of 65 with an income less than $12,000 are eligible for a rebate (Form 538-H).

Sales: 4.5%.

Prescription Exemptions: Prescription medications are exempt from sales tax.

Transportation, Travel and Tourism

General

Oklahoma Tourism and Recreation Department, (405) 521-2406.

Major Airports

- Will Rogers World Airport, Oklahoma City, (405) 680-3200.
- Tulsa International Airport, Tulsa, (918) 838-5046.

Railways

- Amtrak service from Oklahoma City to Ft. Worth, TX, begins May 1999.

Bus Tours

- Wild West Tours, (800) 700-3928

State Highways

- Interstate 40 runs east-west.
- Interstate 35 runs north-south.
- Interstate 44 runs northeast-southeast.

Theater and Music

Northeast

- Discoveryland! & "Oklahoma!" 5529 So. Lewis Ave. Tulsa, OK 74105, (918) 245-6552.
- MidAmerica Expo Center, 69A and Sanders Mitchell St., Prior, OK 74361, (888) 627-3500.
- Tulsa Performing Arts Center, 110 E. 2nd St., Tulsa, OK 74135, (800) 364-7111.

South Central

- Ardmore Tourism Authority, Ardmore, (580) 223-5118.

Central

- Arts Council of Oklahoma City, (405) 270-4848.

Southwest

- The Opera House, Marlowe, OK (580) 658-2209.

Northwest

- Chisholm Trail Expo Center, (580) 237-0238.

Museums, Crafts, Historical, Recreational

Northeast

- Cherokee Heritage Center, Tahlequah, (918) 456-6007.
- Native American Art Gallery, Tulsa, (918) 584-5792.
- Tulsa Air and Space Center, (918)-834-9900.
- Tulsa Convention Center and Visitor's Bureau, (800) 678-7177.
- Tulsa Zoo and Living Museum, (918) 669-6600.

Southeast

- Arrowhead State Park, Canadian, (918) 339-2204.

South Central

- Gene Autry Oklahoma Museum, Gene Autry, (580) 294-3047.
- Lifestyle Center of America, Sulphur, (580) 993-2327.
- McGee Creek State Park, Ferris, (580) 889-5822.

Central

- Frontier Country Regional Tourism Organization, Oklahoma City, (405) 842-3232.
- Native American Cultural Authority, (405) 815-5129.

Southwest

- National Route 66 Museum, Elk City, (580) 225-6266.
- Oklahoma Indian Arts and Crafts Cooperative, Anadarko, (405) 247-3486.
- Senior Citizens Center of Lone Wolf, Lone Wolf, (580) 846-9163.

Northwest

- Black Mesa State Park, Kenton, (580) 261-7447.
- Plains Indian and Pioneer Museum and Art Center, Woodbird, (580) 256-6136.
- Red Carpet Country Tourism Office, (580) 327-0200.

Organizations

Advocacy Groups

- AARP Southwest Regional Office, (214) 265-4060.

Volunteer Programs

- Retired and Senior Volunteer Programs:
- Southwest Oklahoma RSVP, (405) 482-4141.
- Enid & N. Central Oklahoma RSVP, (405) 233-5914.
- Tulsa Inc. RSVP, (918) 742-7747.
- Seven Counties RSVP, (580) 623-7283.

- Foster Grandparent Programs:
- Southeast Area Health Center Inc. FGP, (405) 632-6688.
- Area I FGP, (580) 237-0995.
- Area II FGP, (918) 560-5859.
- Area III FGP, (405) 238-9367.

Housing

Long-Term Care Facilities

*In the state of Oklahoma, these facilities are called **Continuum of Care/Nursing Home Facilities**.*

These facilities provide residential living and/or various levels of nursing and medical services to seniors for an extended period of time.

Types of Authorization

Licensing and / or Certification

These facilities are licensed by the Department of Health. Continuum of care facilities provide nursing care and assisted living and/or adult day care services.

Memberships

- American Association of Homes and Services for the Aging (AAHSA) represents not-for-profit organizations committed to providing high-quality health care, housing, and services to the elderly. AAHSA, 901 E St. NW, Suite 500, Washington, DC 20004-2011. Ph: (202) 783-2242. Fax: (202) 783-2285. *http://www.aahsa.org*
- The Oklahoma Association of Homes and Services for the Aging (OAHSA) is a state affiliate of AAHSA. OAHSA, PO Box 1383, El Reno, OK 73036-5699. Ph: (405) 640-8040. Fax: (405) 262-5252

Accreditations

- Continuing Care Accreditation Commission (CCAC) accredits facilities that offer seniors a contract or contracts that provide residential living and health care services for the remainder of the person's lifetime and meet CCAC's accreditation standards.
- Joint Commission on the Accreditation of Healthcare Organizations (JCAHO) is an independent, not-for-profit organization, and the nation's oldest and largest standards-setting and health care accrediting institution.

Northeast

Forest Hills Assisted Living and Healthcare

4300 W. Houston Ave.
Broken Arrow, OK 74012

Ph: (918) 254-5000
Fax: (918) 250-2538

AL: 20. HCC: 160

Nondenominational. Apartments and private and semiprivate rooms. Nursing care; medical services; rehabilitative therapies; personal care; medication administration; 24-hour emergency response system; maintenance; transportation; up to 3 daily meals; pets allowed; housekeeping and laundry services; social and recreational activities.

AL MO: $1,925. NH Daily: $85–$125.

The Gardens Assisted Living and Healthcare

1165 S. Brenner Rd.
Sapulpa, OK 74066

Ph: (918) 224-0600
Fax: (918) 224-6287

AL: 32. HCC: 88. NH: Yes

Nondenominational. Apartments and private and semiprivate rooms. Nursing care; medical services; rehabilitative therapies; personal care; medication administration; 24-hour security; 24-hour emergency response system; maintenance; transportation; up to 3 daily meals; housekeeping and laundry services; social and recreational activities.

AL MO: $2,075. NH DAILY: $55–$115.

Go Ye Village Apartments

1201 W. Fourth
Tahlequah, OK 74464

Ph: (888) 456-2853

IND: Yes. NH: Yes

Age 62+, ambulatory (55+ for garden apartments and patio homes). Apartments, garden apartments, patio homes; private and semiprivate rooms. Nursing care; medical services; rehabilitative therapies; personal care; medication administration; maintenance; up to 3 daily meals; chapel; library; hobby room; social and recreational activities; village store; lounges; recreational areas; barber/beauty shop.

MO: $1,175–$3,125.

Green Country Care Center

3601 N. Columbia
Tulsa, OK 74110

Ph: (918) 428-3600
Fax: (918) 428-0504

NH: Yes. AZH/MEM IMP: 110

Nondenominational. Private and semiprivate rooms. Nursing care; medical services; rehabilitative therapies; Medicaid-approved; personal care; medication administration; medical services; 24-hour security; 24-hour emergency response system; maintenance; up to 3 daily meals; housekeeping and laundry services; social and recreational activities.

NH Daily: $100–$130.

Leisure Village Health Care Community

2154 S. 85th E. Ave.
Tulsa, OK 74129

Ph: (918) 622-4747

HCC: 117

Nondenominational. Private and semiprivate rooms. Nursing care; medical services; rehabilitative therapies; personal care; medication administration; 24-hour security; 24-hour emergency response system; transportation; up to 3 daily meals; laundry service; religious services; social and recreational activities; lounges; enclosed courtyard; canteen services; barber/beauty shop.

Daily: Private room, $105–$130; semiprivate room, $75–$80. Heavy care: additional $3 per day.

Oklahoma Methodist Manor

4134 E. 31st St.
Tulsa, OK 74135-1599

Ph: (918) 743-2565
Fax: (918) 743-1782

IND: 186. CONG: Yes. HCC: 100

Age 60+. Nonprofit; nondenominational, affiliated with the Oklahoma Conference of the United Methodist Church. Garden apartments, homes, cottages, studios; private and semiprivate rooms. Nursing care; medical services; rehabilitative therapies; personal care; medication administration; security transportation; up to 3 daily meals; housekeeping and laundry services; exercise program; swimming pool; chapel; religious services; postal and banking services; musical, educational, and cultural programs; gardening; games; arts and crafts; library; gift shop; barber/beauty shop.

IND APPL: $1,100. IND ENT: $44,000–$165,000+. CONG APPL: $550. HCC ENT: (non-ref.), $110. HCC MO: $2,600–$3,525.

Saint Simeon's

3701 N. Cincinnati
Tulsa, OK 74106-1599

Ph: (918) 425-3583
Fax: (918) 425-6368

IND: Yes. AL: Yes. ALZ/MEM IMP: 54. HCC: 55

Age 62+. Nonprofit; nondenominational. Apartments, duplexes, studios, suites. Nursing care; medical services; rehabilitative therapies; personal care; medication administration; security; 24-hour emergency response system; maintenance; transportation; up to 3 daily meals; housekeeping and laundry services; chapel; pastoral care; social and recreational activities; barber/beauty shop.

ENT: (non-ref.), $550. IND MO: $1,550–$1,850. AL Daily: $90–$110. ALZ/MEM IMP Daily: $110–$150. HCC Daily: $95–$130.

Southern Hills Rehabilitation Center

5170 S. Vandalia
Tulsa, OK 74135

Ph: (918) 496-3963
Fax: (918) 496-0774

IND: 9. AL: 52. ALZ/MEM IMP: Yes. LTC: Yes. SNF: 118

Nondenominational. Apartments, private rooms. Nursing care; medical services; rehabilitative therapies; Caregivers Respite Program; eye doctor visits monthly; Medicare/Medicaid-approved; personal care; medication administration; 24-hour security; 24-hour emergency response system; maintenance; transportation; up to 3 daily meals; pets allowed; housekeeping and laundry services; swimming pool; social and recreational activities; barber/ beauty shop.

IND DEP: $275. IND MO: $1,350–$2,125. AL Daily: $90–$140.

Tulsa Nursing Center

10912 E. 14th St.
Tulsa, OK 74128

Ph: (918) 438-2440
Fax: (918) 438-4124

HCC: 204

Nondenominational. Private and semiprivate rooms. Nursing care; medical services; rehabilitative therapies; Medicaid-approved; personal care; medication administration; 24-hour security; 24-hour emergency response system; maintenance; transportation; up to 3 daily meals; housekeeping and laundry services; social and recreational activities.

MO: $3,100.

University Village

8555 S. Lewis
Tulsa, OK 74137

Ph: (918) 299-2661
Fax: (918) 298-3671
http://www.hillcrest.com

IND: 210. AL: 60. HCC: 69

Age 65+. Nonprofit; nonsectarian. Apartments, cottages, private rooms. Nursing care; medical services; rehabilitative therapies; Medicaid approval in process; personal care; medication administration; 24-hour security; 24-hour emergency response system; maintenance; scheduled transportation; up to 3 daily meals; pets allowed (cottages only); housekeeping and laundry services; fitness center; library; social and recreational activities.

DEP: (non-ref.), $550–$950. IND ENT: $275. IND MO: $1,250–$2,300. AL ENT: $275. AL MO: $1,725. HCC Daily: $80 semiprivate.

Westminster Village Retirement Community

1601 Academy Rd.
Ponca City, OK 74604

Ph: (580) 762-0927
Fax: (580) 762-5807

IND: 69. AL: Yes. HCC: 58 Yes. RC: Yes

Age 55+. Nonprofit; nondenominational; affiliated with the Catholic Church. Apartments, villas. Nursing care; medical services; rehabilitative therapies; Medicaid-approved; personal care; medication administration; 24-hour emergency response system; maintenance; transportation; up to 3 daily meals; pets allowed; housekeeping services; fitness center; social and recreational activities; billiards room.

MO: $1,600–$2,350. NH Daily: $110+, depending on level of care.

Central

Baptist Retirement Center

9700 Mashburn Blvd.
Oklahoma City, OK 73162

Ph: (405) 721-2466
Fax: (405) 721-0668

IND: 257. AL: 35. ALZ/MEM IMP: 32. HCC: 88. NH: Yes

Age 55+. Nonprofit; affiliated with the Baptist General Convention of Oklahoma. Apartments, condominiums, homes. Nursing care; medical services; rehabilitative therapies; Medicaid-approved; personal care; medication administration; 24-hour security; emergency response system; maintenance; transportation; up to 3 daily meals (included in AL fees); pets allowed; housekeeping and laundry services; exercise room; chapel; religious services; social and recreational services; library; computer lab; gift shop; two enclosed patios; picnic pavilion; barber/beauty shop.

DEP: (ref.), $100. IND MO: $325–$825. AL MO: $1,775–$2,200. NH MO: $2,550–$2,700.

Epworth Villa

14901 N. Pennsylvania Ave.
Oklahoma City, OK 73134

Ph: (405) 752-1200
Fax: (405) 755-4813

http://www.epworthvilla.com

IND: 230. AL: 30. HCC: 60

Age 62+. Nondenominational. Apartments and private and semiprivate rooms. Nursing care; medical services; rehabilitative therapies; personal care; medication administration; security; emergency response system; maintenance; transportation; up to 3 daily meals; housekeeping and laundry services; fitness center; pool; religious services; Sunday school, Bible study; library; social and recreational activities; crafts room; card room; woodworking shop; walking paths; lake with gazebo; garden plots; living room; convenience store; barber/beauty shop.

ENT: $49,000–$165,500. MO: $1,050–$2,450.

The Fountains at Centerbury

1404 NW 122nd
Oklahoma City, OK 73114

Ph: (405) 751-3600
Fax: (405) 751-6511

http://www.thefountains.com

IND: 80. ADC: Yes. AL: 60. ALZ/MEM IMP: 34. HCC: 119

Age 62+. Nondenominational. Apartments, duplex-like cottages, and private and semiprivate rooms. Nursing care; medical services; rehabilitative therapies; Medicare/Medicaid-approved; personal care; medication administration; security; 24-hour emergency response system; maintenance; transportation; up to 3 daily meals; pets allowed; housekeeping and laundry services; fitness center; swimming pool; library; computer room; social and recreational activities; convenience store; massage therapy.

IND MO: $1,725–$2,175. AL MO: $2,700–$3,275. ALZ/MEM IMP: $3,075–$5,150. SNF Daily: $105–$210.

Oklahoma Christian Home, CCAC

906 N. Boulevard
Edmond, OK 73034

Ph: (405) 341-0810
Fax: (405) 341-0976

IND: Yes. AL: Yes. HCC: Yes. ALZ/MEM IMP: Yes

Nonprofit; affiliated with the Christian Church (Disciples of Christ). Cottage homes, apartments, and private and semiprivate rooms. Nursing care; 24-hour emergency health care; rehabilitative therapies; medical services; Medicaid-approved; personal care; medication administration; security; emergency response system; maintenance; transportation; up to 3 daily meals; housekeeping and laundry services; exercise classes; religious services; social and recreational activities; resident association.

PROC: (no ref.) $50. IND ENT: $71,500–$126,500. IND MO: $605–$635; plus mo. maintenance fee, $375. HCC Daily: $85–$125.

Spanish Cove Retirement Village

1401 S. Cornwell Drive
Yukon, OK 73099

Ph: (405) 354-1901

http://www.spanishcove.com/sc

IND: 191. AL: 15. LTC: 69

Age 62+. Nonprofit. Apartments, studios. Nursing care; medical services; rehabilitative therapies; personal care; medication administration; 24-hour security; 24-hour emergency response system; maintenance; transportation; meal plan; housekeeping and laundry services; exercise/recreation room; enclosed/heated pool with atrium and patio; social and recreational activities; arts and crafts center; club room; library; computer room; barber/beauty shop.

ENT: $65,500–$92,000. MO: $1,075–$1,250. 2nd person: $575.

Assisted Living and Residential Care Facilities

In the state of Oklahoma, these facilities are called ***Assisted Living Facilities****.*

These facilities provide housing, food service, and one or more personal services.

Types of Authorization

Licensing and/or Certification

These facilities are licensed by the Department of Health. Assisted living centers offer a level of services between nursing facilities and residential care homes.

Memberships

- Assisted Living Federation of America (ALFA) is a national nonprofit membership organization whose mission is to enhance the quality of life in assisted living facilities and promote the interests of the assisted living industry. ALFA, 10300 Eaton Place, Suite 400, Fairfax, VA 22030. Ph: (703) 691-8100. Fax: (703) 691-8106. *http://www.alfa.org*
- Oklahoma Assisted Living Association (OKALA) is a state affiliate of ALFA. OKALA, 122 NW 22nd St., Oklahoma City, OK 73103. Ph: (405) 521-1430. Fax: (405) 521-0446.

Northeast

Country Club of Woodland Hills

6333 S. 91st E. Ave.
Tulsa, OK 74133

Ph: (918) 252-5451
Fax: (918) 254-5136

IND: 175. AL: 27

Age 55+. Apartments, cottages. Medical services; personal care; medication administration; 24-hour security; 24-hour emergency response system; maintenance; transportation; up to 3 daily meals; pets allowed; housekeeping and laundry services; fitness center; swimming pool; social and recreational activities.

DEP: $550. IND MO: $1,550–$2,050. AL MO: $2,275–$2,750.

Green Country Village

1025 Swan Drive
Bartlesville, OK 74006

Ph: (918) 335-2086
Fax: (918) 335-3254

IND: 100. AL: 50. ALZ/MEM IMP: 28

Age 55+. Nonprofit. Apartments. Nursing care; personal care; medication administration; 24-hour security; 24-hour emergency response system; maintenance; transportation; up to 3 daily meals; housekeeping and laundry services; social and recreational activities; private lake.

APPL: $1,100. DEP: $330. IND MO: $1,225–$2,750. AL MO: $1,700–$3,325. ALZ/MEM IMP: $2,850–$4,200.

Heartworth House Senior Living Community

821 N. Foreman
Vinita, OK 74301

Ph: (918) 256-7856
Fax: (918) 256-7857

http://www.vinita.net/heartsworth

E-mail: *heartsworth@junct.com*

IND: 50. AL: 25

Age 55+. Nonprofit. Apartments. On-campus hospital and doctor's clinic; personal care; medication administration; 24-hour security; 24-hour emergency response system; maintenance; transportation; up to 3 daily meals; housekeeping; social and recreational activities.

DEP: (ref.), $275. AL MO: $1,700+. IND MO: $850–$2,000.

Heatheridge Assisted Living Center

2130 S. 85th E. Ave.
Tulsa, OK 74129

Ph: (918) 622-9191

AL: 90

Apartments. Personal care; medication administration; 24-hour security; scheduled transportation; up to 3 daily meals; housekeeping and laundry services; fitness room; social and recreational activities; central living room with fireplace; activity room; barber/beauty shop.

AL MO: $1,900–$2,750. 2nd person: $440–$770.

South Central

Ardmore Village

1550 Knox Rd.
Ardmore, OK 73401

Ph: (580) 223-4174
Fax: (580) 223-4180

E-mail: *ardville@brightok.net*

IND: 92. ADC: Yes. AL: 50 (opening in May 2000)

Age 62+. Nonprofit; affiliated with Episcopal Diocese of Oklahoma. Apartments, cottages, homes. Nursing care; medical services (for AL); personal care; medication administration; 24-hour security; 24-hour emergency response system; maintenance; transportation; up to 3 daily meals; pets allowed; housekeeping and laundry services; exercise classes; Bible study; activity center; social and recreational activities; Club Active (arts and crafts, team sports, health checkups, socials, book club, volunteer opportunities).

IND MO: Section 8 HUD. AL ENT: $1,100. AL MO: $1,725. RH ENT: $1,100. RH MO: $575–$725.

REQ: Gross annual income under $12,000 for cottages/apartments; no income cap for townhouses or assisted living residence.

Central

Brighton Gardens by Marriott

12928 N. May Ave.
Oklahoma City, OK 73120

Ph: (405) 748-6464
Fax: (405) 748-6551

AL: Yes. ADL: Yes. AIP: Yes. ALZ/MEM IMP: Yes

Suites. Wellness program; personal care; medication administration; security; 24-hour emergency response system; maintenance; transportation; up to 3 daily meals; housekeeping and laundry services; organized social, cultural, and educational activities and events; library; arts and crafts studio; barber/beauty shop.

AL MO: $2,500–$3,100.

Emerald Square Assisted Living Center

701 N. Council Rd.
Oklahoma City, OK 73127

Ph: (405) 787-4466
Fax: (405) 789-8101

E-mail: *emerald@ionet.net*

ADL: Yes. AL: 60. CONG: Yes

Age 55+, ambulatory, continent (or totally capable of self-care). Private rooms. Personal care, medication administration; 24-hour security; 24-hour emergency response system; maintenance; transportation; up to 3 daily meals; housekeeping and laundry services; exercise class; whirlpool; social and recreational activities; arts and crafts room; dining room; living room; barber/beauty shop.

ENT: (ref.), $275. MO: $1,300–$1,550.

The Gardens at Rivermont

800 Canadian Trails Drive
Norman, OK 73072

Ph: (405) 360-0606
Fax: (405) 360-5091

IND: 132. AL: 50. ALZ/MEM IMP: 20

Age 62+. Nonprofit. Apartments, studios, private rooms. Nursing care; personal care; medication administration; 24-hour security; 24-hour emergency response system; maintenance; transportation; up to 3 daily meals; housekeeping and laundry services; health and fitness room; Jacuzzi; social and recreational activities; walking paths; gardening; library; lounge with fireplace; entertainment center; activity rooms; country store; atrium; 1.5 miles from University of Oklahoma; barber/beauty shop.

DEP: (ref.), $825. IND MO: apartment, $1,250–$2,300. AL MO: private room, $2,475–$3,650.

Legacy Square by Sterling House

800 Gartrell Place
Weatherford, OK 73096

Ph: (580) 772-6600

ADL: Yes

Apartments. Personal care; medication assistance; emergency response system; maintenance; transportation; up to 3 daily meals; pets allowed; housekeeping and laundry services; social and recreational activities; enclosed courtyard; patio; library; living room; TV room; crafts room.

DEP: (non-ref.), $550. MO: $1,625–$2,975. A $550 smoking deposit and/or a $275 pet deposit may be required where applicable.

Santa Fe Village by Sterling House

1500 N. Santa Fe
Edmond, OK 73003

Ph: (405) 330-6600
Fax: (405) 330-8343
E-mail: *mobley@assisted.com*

AL: 29

Apartments. Personal care; medication administration; 24-hour security; 24-hour emergency response system; maintenance; transportation; up to 3 daily meals; pets allowed; housekeeping and laundry services; organized activities and events; whirlpool; secured courtyard; small, home-like environment.

ENT: $550. MO: $1,650–$2,700.

Independent Living

Independent housing (primarily rentals) for seniors that may offer security features, meal service, and activities.

Northeast

Burroughs Manor

111 S. Thompson
Vinita, OK 74301

Ph: (918) 256-8601

IND: 50

Age 62+. Owned by the Pilgrim Presbyterian Church of Vinita. Apartments and studios. Security; 24-hour emergency response system; community kitchen and lobby area; near public transportation; organized activities and events; library; craft room; within easy walking distance of downtown amenities; barber/beauty shop.

IND MO: 30% of resident's income; HUD-subsidized. Income must be $12,500 or less (average monthly rent is $200).

Woodland Terrace Retirement Residence

952 and E. 71st St.
Tulsa, OK 74133

Ph: (918) 250-3631
Fax: (918) 254-9049

IND: 150

Age 65+. For-profit. Apartments. Nursing care (separate contract); personal care; medication administration; 24-hour security; 24-hour response system; maintenance; transportation; up to 2 daily meals; housekeeping and laundry services; social and recreation activities.

IND ENT: (ref.), last month's rent. IND MO: $1,375–$2,000.

Central

The Gardens at Reding

3708 S. Douglas Ave.
Oklahoma City, OK 73109

IND: 157

Age 55+. Apartments. Security; emergency response system; maintenance; transportation, and close to public transportation; pets allowed; organized activities and events; clubhouse with fireplace; fitness center; hot tub; swimming pool; spa; library/game room; activity room; shuffleboard court; barbecue grills; downtown amenities within walking distance; barber/beauty shop.

APPL: (non-ref.), $30. DEP: (ref.), $175. Pet Fee: (non-ref.), $110. IND MO: $380–$550.

Oklahoma Christian Apartments

325 Enz Drive
Edmond, OK 73034-4439

Ph: (405) 340-0311
Fax: (405) 340-1340

IND: Yes

Age 62+ . Nonprofit; managed by the National Benevolent Association of the Christian Church. Apartments. Quiet neighborhood adjacent to Oklahoma Christian Home campus; nearby shopping, entertainment, medical facilities, Edmond Senior Center; emergency response system; transportation; weekly noon meal; social and recreational activities; community building with indoor walking track, exercise room, meeting rooms, wellness programs; religious services; library; community room; bingo; piano, organ; pool table; on-line computer; patio with barbecue grill; laundry rooms; barber/beauty shop.

REQ: Must meet HUD eligibility requirements

Rivermont at the Trails

800 Canadian Trails Drive
Norman, OK 73072

Ph: (405) 360-0606

IND: Yes

Age 62+. Affiliated with Baptist Senior Life Ministries. Apartments and studios. 24-hour security; 24-hour emergency response system; maintenance; transportation; up to 3 daily meals; housekeeping and laundry services; organized activities and events; dining area; atrium; health and fitness room; Jacuzzi; library; craft room; barber/beauty shop.

DEP: $825. IND MO: $1,250–$1,900.

Senior Cottages of Norman

2901 Oak Tree
Norman, OK 73072-8065

Ph: (405) 292-7714
Fax: (405) 292-6927

IND: 84

Age 62+. Income restrictions. Apartments. Gated entry; maintenance; pets allowed; games; organized activities.

APPL: $25. DEP: $100. Contact facility for fees.

Adult/Resort Communities

Communities for active adults (not all are age-restricted; primarily ownership).

Northeast

Shangri-La Resort Communities

57401 E. Highway 125
Afton, OK 74331

Ph: (800) 331-4060 or (877) 257-4204

Individual homes, condominiums, high-rise complex, homesites, rental units. Golf course; tennis; racquetball; swimming pool; hiking; fishing; hunting; bowling; boating/waterskiing; fitness center; beach.

PURCHASE: Homes, $93,500–$1.1 million.

Central

Cedar Valley Golf Club

210 Par Ave.
Guthrie, OK 73044

Ph: (405) 282-4800
Fax: (405) 282-0080

Individual homes, homesites. Golf course; dining.

PURCHASE: Homesites: $16,500–$27,500.

Cimarron National Golf Club

500 Duffy's Way
Guthrie, OK 73044

Ph: (405) 282-7888
Fax: (405) 282-0080

Individual homes, homesites. Golf course; fishing; dining.

PURCHASE: Homesites, $16,500–$27,500.

Cimarron Trails

1400 Lovers Lane
Perkins, OK 74059

Ph: (405) 547-5701
Fax: (405) 547-2211

http://www.provalue.net/project_perkins/webstreet/ctrails.htm

Individual homes, homesites. Golf course.

PURCHASE: Homes, $110,000–$242,000; homesites, $20,000–$38,500.

Oak Tree Country Club

700 N. Country Club Drive
PO Box 1189
Edmond, OK 73003-1089

Ph: (800) 642-1804 or (405) 330-9593

Individual homes, condominiums, estates. 1,500 acres of lakes, streams, and creeks; golf courses; walking/jogging paths; tennis; sports facility; clubhouse; Olympic swimming pool.

PURCHASE: Homes, $181,500–$550,000.

South

Falconhead Resort and Country Club

605 Falconhead Drive
Burneyville, OK 73430

Ph: (405) 276-9284

Individual homes, condominiums, homesites. Golf course; tennis; swimming pool; hiking; fishing; riding stables; community center; fitness center; library; social clubs.

PURCHASE: Homes, $44,000–$110,000; homesites, $1,100–$5,500.

Oregon

http://www.state.or.us

General Information

Climate

Average winter lows of 30° F; average summer highs of 80° F to 90° F. Average annual rainfall around 13 inches (19 inches in southern Oregon; 49 inches in the Willamette Valley).

Cost of Living

Ranks 20th in the nation.

Taxes

State/Local as % of Income: 9.3%.

Property Tax Reduction: Residents over the age of 65 with an income of less than $24,000 are eligible for a Senior Citizens Property Tax Deferral (more information is available from the county of residence).

Sales: None, other than itemized deductions.

Prescription Exemptions: None.

Transportation, Travel, and Tourism

General

Oregon Tourism Commission, (800) 547-7842.

Major Airports

- Eugene Airport, (541) 682-5430.
- Klamath Falls International Airport (Kingsley Field), (541) 883-5372.
- Rogue Valley International–Medford Airport, (541) 776-7222.
- Portland International Airport, (503) 460-4234.

Railways

- Amtrak, (800) USA-RAIL.

Bus Tours

- Eco Tours, (503) 245-1428.
- Gray Line Tours, (800) 422-7042.
- The Old Oregon Trail, (503) 226-1611.

State Highways

- Interstate 5 runs north-south in the western part of the state.
- Interstate 84 runs west-east along the northern border of the state and continues southeast.

Theater and Music

Portland

- Portland Center for the Performing Arts, (503) 248-4345.
- Portland Tourism, (877) 678-5263.

Oregon Coast

- Newport Performing Arts Center, Newport, (541) 265-2787.
- Florence Performing Arts Center, (541) 997-1994.

Willamette Valley

- Holt Center for the Performing Arts, (541) 682-5000.

Museums, Crafts, Historical, Recreational

Portland ("The City of Parks," "The City of Roses," fishing, boating, hiking, biking, horseback trails, skiing, windsurfing, award-winning golf courses, restaurants, coffeehouses, microbreweries, historic Old Town District)

- Contemporary Crafts Gallery, (503) 223-2654.
- Cowboy Museum, (503) 731-3333.

- OMSI Oregon Museum of Science, (503) 797-4538.
- Oregon Maritime Center and Museum, (503) 224-7724.
- Portland Art Museum, (503) 226-2811.
- Shades of Color Ethnic Art, (503) 288-3779.

Oregon Coast (Oregon Dunes National Recreation Area, camping, fishing [deep-sea and salmon] whale-watching, seafood festivals)

- Central Oregon Coast Tourist Association, (888) 628-2101.
- Oregon Coast Aquarium, Southbeach, (541) 867-3474.

Mt. Hood/Columbia Gorge Area (Historic Columbia River Highway, skiing, hiking, biking, camping, fishing)

- Mt. Hood Information Center, (503) 622-3017.

Willamette Valley (McKenzie Pass Scenic Byway, Silver Falls State Park [home to 10 waterfalls], over 50 covered bridges, rafting, kayaking, fishing, hiking, cultural festivals, Hoodoo Ski Area)

- Convention and Visitors' Information Center of Lane County, (800) 547-5445.

Southern Oregon (Crater Lake National Park, Oregon Caves National Monument, bird sanctuaries, wineries, Oregon Shakespeare Festival, Britt Festivals, Heritage Days, Dixieland Jazz Festival)

- Southern Oregon Visitors Association, (800) 448-4856.

Central Oregon (Newberry National Volcanic Monument, Dee Wright Observatory, fishing, camping, rock climbing, golfing, skiing, rock hounding, music festivals, The Sisters Rodeo, skiing)

- Central Oregon Visitors Association, (541) 382-8334.
- High Desert Museum, near Bend, (541) 382-4754.

Eastern Oregon (Hells Canyon National Recreation Area, Painted Hills, John Day Fossil Beds National Monument, horseback riding, llama trekking, rafting, hang gliding, Hart Mountain National Antelope Refuge, Pendleton Round-up Rodeo, skiing)

- Eastern Oregon Visitors Association, (800) 332-1843.

Organizations

Advocacy Groups

- AARP Oregon State Office, (503) 652-8855.

Volunteer Programs

Retired and Senior Volunteer Programs:

- Deschutes County RSVP, (541) 388-7746.
- Coos County RSVP, (541) 888-7332.
- Lane County RSVP, (541) 342-1881.
- Curry County RSVP, (541) 247-2422.
- Washington County RSVP, (503) 639-5620.
- Clackamas County RSVP, (503) 655-8862.
- Eastern Oregon RSVP, (541) 276-1926.
- Multnomah County Volunteer Center & RSVP, (503) 413-7787.
- Foster Grandparent Programs:
- FGP Southern Oregon, (541) 779-5257.
- Tri-County Area FGP, (503) 331-5924.

Housing

Long-Term Care Facilities

*In the state of Oregon, these facilities are called **Continuing Care/Nursing Home/Residential Facilities**.*

These facilities provide residential living and/or various levels of nursing and medical services to seniors for an extended period of time.

Types of Authorization

Licensing and/or Certification

These facilities are regulated by the Department of Human Resources, Health Division. The Health Care Licensure and Certification section is responsible for enforcing the rules and regulations set by the state.

Memberships:

- American Association of Homes and Services for the Aging (AAHSA) represents not-for-profit organizations committed to providing high-quality health care, housing, and services to the elderly. AAHSA, 901 E St. NW, Suite 500, Washington, DC 20004-2011. Ph: (202) 783-2242. Fax: (202) 783-2285. *http://www.aahsa.org*
- Oregon Alliance of Senior and Health Services (OASHA) is a state affiliate of AAHSA. OASHA, 7360 SW Hunziker St., Suite 207, Tigard, OR 97223-8288. Ph: (503) 684-3788. Fax: (503) 624-0870 *http://www.oashs.org*

Accreditations:

- Continuing Care Accreditation Commission (CCAC) accredits facilities that offer seniors a contract or contracts that provide residential living and health care services for the remainder of the person's lifetime and meet CCAC's accreditation standards.
- Joint Commission on the Accreditation of Healthcare Organizations (JCAHO) is an independent, not-for-profit organization, and the nation's oldest and largest standards-setting and health care accrediting institution.

Southwest

Crystal Terrace, OASHA

1000 Town Center Drive
Klamath Falls, OR 97601

Ph: (541) 885-7250

IND: Yes. AL: Yes. HCC: 100. ALZ MEM/IMP: Yes

Age 55+. Nonprofit; nondenominational; owned by Merle West Medical Center. Cottages, suites, apartments, and private and semiprivate rooms. Skilled nursing care; intermediate nursing care; medical services; physical, occupational, and speech therapies; subacute care; lab services; pharmacy services; social services; personal care; medication administration; security; emergency response system; maintenance; transportation; up to 3 daily meals; pets allowed; housekeeping and laundry services; exercise program; swimming pool; religious services; library; card and board game room; social and recreational activities; crafts; golfing; outdoor terraces; rose gardens.

Refundable ENT fees. Contact facility for fees.

Rogue Valley Manor, CCAC

1200 Mira Mar Ave.
Medford, OR 97504

Ph: (503) 857-7777

IND: 406. AL: 35. HCC: 93

Nonprofit; nondenominational; sponsored by United Methodist, Presbyterian, and Episcopal Churches. Studios, one- and two-bedroom apartments, and private and semiprivate rooms. Nursing care; medical services; rehabilitative therapies; personal care; medication administration; security; emergency response system; maintenance; transportation; up to 3 daily meals; pets allowed; housekeeping and laundry services; exercise program; swimming pool; religious services; social and recreational activities; barber/beauty shop.

IND ENT: $27,500–$218,000. IND MO: $975–$2,250.

West Central

Washington Abbey, AAHSA

494 W. 10th Ave.
Eugene, OR 97401

Ph: (503) 342-6077

IND: 48. HCC: 154

Nonprofit; Evangelical Lutheran Good Samaritan Society affiliation. Apartments and private and semiprivate rooms. Nursing care; medical services; rehabilitative therapies; dental and podiatry care; pharmacy services; Medicare/Medicaid-approved; security; emergency response system; maintenance; transportation; up to 3 daily meals; pets allowed; housekeeping and laundry services; exercise program; religious services; social and recreational activities.

IND ENT: $35,500–$113,000. IND MO: $675–$1,350.

Northwest

Baptist Manor

OASHA 900 NE 81st Ave.
Portland, OR 97213

Ph: (503) 255-0860

E-mail: *info@baptistmanor.org*

IND: Yes. NH: Yes

Nonprofit; Nondenominational. Apartments and private and semiprivate rooms. Nursing care; medical services; rehabilitative therapies; Medicaid-approved; personal care; medication administration; security; emergency response system; maintenance; transportation; up to 3 daily meals; housekeeping and laundry services; exercise program; religious services; social and recreational activities; pet therapy; intergenerational program.

IND MO: About $925. NH MO: About $3,300.

Assisted Living and Residential Care Facilities

These facilities provide housing, food service, and one or more personal services.

Types of Authorization

Licensing and / or Certification

These facilities are regulated by the Department of Human Resources, Health Division. The Health Care Licensure and Certification section is responsible for enforcing the rules and regulations set by the state.

Memberships:

- Assisted Living Federation of America (ALFA) is a national nonprofit membership organization whose mission is to enhance the quality of life in assisted living facilities and promote the interests of the assisted living industry. ALFA, 10300 Eaton Place, Suite 400, Fairfax, VA 22030. Ph: (703) 691-8100. Fax: (703) 691-8106. *http: / / www.alfa.org*
- Oregon Assisted Living Facilities Association (OALFA) is a state affiliate of ALFA. OALFA, 69006 Elk Mountain Rd. Enterprise, OR 97828. Ph: (541) 426-8404. Fax: (541) 426-3545.

Northwest

Kilchis House

4212 Marolf Place
Tillamook, OR 97141

Ph: (503) 842-2204

AL: Yes

Apartments with 3 levels of care. Personal care; nursing services; medication assistance; 24-hour trained staff; 24-hour security services; emergency response system; maintenance; transportation coordination; up to 3 daily meals; pets allowed; resident laundry; whirlpool bath; planned activities; fireplace and enclosed courtyard with covered patio; beauty shop.

AL MO: Level I care: studio, $1,525; 1-bedroom, $1,875; 2nd person, $550. Level II care: studio, $1,800; 1-bedroom, $2,125; 2nd person, $660. Level III care: studio, $2,025; 1-bedroom, $2,350; 2nd person, $770.

Nehalem Bay House

35385 Tohl Ave.
Nehalem, OR 97131

Ph: (503) 368-6445
Fax: (503) 368-6468

AL: Yes

Apartments with 3 levels of care. Nursing care; 24-hour staffing; personal care; medication administration; 24-hour security services; emergency response system; maintenance; transportation coordination; up to 3 daily meals; pets allowed; resident laundry; whirlpool bath; planned activities; fireplace and enclosed courtyard with covered patio; barber/beauty shop.

AL MO: Level I care, studio, $1,700; 1-bedroom, $1,975; 2nd person, $625. Level II care: studio, $1,900; 1-bedroom, $2,175; 2nd person, $725. Level III care: studio, $2,150; 1-bedroom, $2,400; 2nd person, $825.

Regent Assisted Living, Inc.

121 SW Morrison, Suite 1000
Portland, OR 97204

Ph: (503) 227-4000 or (888) 853-7468
Fax: (503) 274-4685

http://www.rgnt.com

E-mail: *info@rgnt.com*

AL: Yes. ALZ/MEM IMP: Yes

Age 55+. For-profit; operates 2,810 units in 9 western states. Apartments and some cottages. Wellness program; personal care; medication administration; security system; maintenance; transportation; up to 3 daily meals; pets allowed; housekeeping and laundry services; social and recreational activities; exercise program.

Contact facility for fees.

Independent Living

Independent housing (primarily rentals) for seniors that may offer security features, meal service, and activities.

Northwest

Columbia Hills Retirement Center

36050 Pittsburg Rd.
St. Helens, OR 97051

Ph: (503) 397-6131

IND: 33

Age: 62+. Nonprofit. HUD apartments in country setting. Security system; 24-hour emergency response system; maintenance; transportation; 1 daily meal; pets allowed; tenant- hired housekeeping.

DEP: security. IND MO: based on 30% of adjusted monthly income with some medical deductions.

Homewoods on the Willamette

17971 SE River Rd.
Milwaukie, OR 97267

Ph: (503) 659-3600

Fax: (503) 659-8813

IND: 113

Age: 55+. Nonprofit; affiliated with Pacific Conference of the Evangelical Church. Apartments. Monthly podiatry services; emergency response system; maintenance; transportation; up to 3 daily meals; pets allowed; housekeeping and laundry services; exercise room; library; full-time activity director; activity room; meditation room; social and recreational activities; on- and off-site activities; store; two fireside lounges; conversation areas, barber/beauty shop.

DEP: $220. IND MO: $950–$1,450.

South

Rogue Valley Manor Community Housing

1025 Ellendale Drive
Medford, OR 97504

Ph: (541) 857-7255 or (800) 714-9177
Fax: (541) 772-9995

IND: Yes

Age 62+. Private corporation; owns 562 units in 13 communities. Apartments. Security; emergency response system; maintenance; pets allowed (must meet facilities' pet policy).

IND MO: 30% of adjusted gross income.

REQ: must meet HUD income guidelines.

Adult/Resort Communities

Communities for active adults (not all are age-restricted; primarily ownership).

Northwest

The Highlands at Vista Ridge

9 SW Mt. Jefferson Terrace
Lake Oswego, OR 970335

Ph: (800) 578-7271
Fax: (503) 635-2052

http://www.easystreet.com/highlandassoc

Age 55+. Manufactured homes. Clubhouse; swimming pool; sauna; Jacuzzi; weight and exercise rooms; hiking trails; library.

PURCHASE: Homes, from $137,500.

Meadowlawn

3898 Meadowlawn Loop SE
Salem, OR 97301

Ph: (503) 363-7391

Condominiums. Golf course; clubhouse; pro shop; tennis; swimming pool; hiking trails; recreation center; spa; sauna.

MONTHLY RENTALS: from $440; some purchases available.

McNary Estates and Golf Club

155 McNary Estates Drive N.
Keizer, OR 97303

Ph: (503) 393-8401

Individual homes, condominiums, homesites. Golf course; clubhouse; pro shop; dining; social clubs; nearby fitness center.

PURCHASE: Homes, from $192,500; condos, from $165,000; homesites, $49,500–$82,500.

Persimmon Country Club

500 SE Butler Blvd.
Gresham, OR 97080

Ph: (503) 674-2555
Fax: (503) 674-2558

http://www.PersimmonGolf.com

Individual homes, golf villas, homesites. Golf course; clubhouse; pro shop; dining; swim and tennis center.

PURCHASE: Golf villas, $300,500–$377,500; homesites, $66,000–$198,000.

Senior Estates Golf and Country Club

1776 Country Club Rd.
Woodburn, OR 97071

Ph: (503) 981-0189

Age 55+. Individual homes. Golf course; clubhouse; pro shop; swimming pool; fitness center; dining; social clubs.

PURCHASE: Homes, $55,000–$192,500.

Tualatin Greens

8720 SW Tualatin Rd.
Tualatin, OR 97062

Ph: (503) 691-7861

Condominiums. Swimming pool; spa; nearby golf course, nature park and senior center.

PURCHASE: Condos, $100,000–$131,000.

Central

Awbrey Glen

2500 NW Awbrey Glen Drive
Bend, OR 97701

Ph: (541) 388-8526

http://www.ohwy.com/or/a/awbrglgc.htm

Individual homes, homesites. Golf course; pro shop; clubhouse; tennis; swimming pool; hiking/biking trails; fishing; snow skiing; dining; social clubs; nearby lakes and river.

PURCHASE: Homes $275,000–$770,000+.

Black Butte Ranch

PO Box 8000
Black Butte Ranch, OR 97759

Ph: (541) 595-1250 or (541) 549-6000

http://www.blackbutteranch.com

Individual homes, condominiums, homesites. Golf courses; clubhouses; pro shops; tennis; swimming pools; 19 miles of hiking trails; riding stables; biking; dining; social clubs.

PURCHASE: Homes, from $330,000.

Broken Top

61999 Broken Top Drive
Bend, OR 97702

Ph: (800) 382-7690 or (541) 383-7600

http://www.brokentop.com

Individual homes, townhomes, homesites. Golf course; clubhouse; pro shop; tennis; swimming pool; walking/biking; fitness room; dining; social clubs; nearby hunting and snow skiing.

PURCHASE: Homes, $330,000–$1.1 million+; townhomes, $275,000–$429,000; homesites, $70,500–$605,000.

Sunriver Resort/Crosswater

PO Box 3650
Sunriver, OR 97707

Ph: (800) 547-3920

http://www.sunriver-resort.com

Individual homes, condominiums, homesites. Golf course; clubhouse; pro shop; tennis; swimming pool; racquetball; hiking/biking trails; fishing; fitness center; riding stables; fishing; boating/waterskiing; snow skiing; dining; social clubs; nearby hunting.

PURCHASE: Homes, $165,000–$1.1 million; condos, $110,000–$330,000; homesites, $66,000–$220,000.

Widgi Creek

18707 Century Drive
Bend, OR 97702

Ph: (800) 327-5102 or (541) 317-5000

http://www.widgi.com

Individual homes, townhomes, homesites. Golf course; clubhouses; tennis; swimming pool; fishing; hiking/biking trails; fitness center; dining; social clubs; nearby hunting, snow skiing, and riding stables.

PURCHASE: Homes, $328,000–$715,000; townhomes, $247,500–$329,000; homesites, $93,500–$148,500.

Pennsylvania

http://www.state.pa.us

General Information

Climate

Temperature ranges from the high 20s° F to the mid-30s° F in the winter to the mid- to high 80s° F in the summer.

Cost of Living

Ranks 10th in the nation.

Taxes

General: Taxpayer Service, (717) 787-8201. TDD number, (800) 447-3020.

State/Local as % of Income: 10.2%.

Property Tax Reduction: Rebate for people 65 years or older. Household income limit is $15,000; maximum rebate is $500.

Claim information: (888) PATAXES (728-2937).

Sales: 6%.

Prescription Exemptions: Prescription drugs and related items, e.g., eyeglasses, contact lenses, are not subject to sales tax.

Transportation, Travel, and Tourism

General

Pennsylvania Department of Transportation, Bureau of Public Transportation, 555 Walnut St., 8th Floor, Harrisburg, PA 17101, (717) 787-7540.

Major Airports

- Philadelphia International Airport, (800) PHL-GATE.
- Pittsburgh International Airport, Pittsburgh, PA 15231, (412) 350-5313.
- Wilkes-Barre Scranton International Airport, 100 Terminal Rd., #221, Avoca, PA 18641-2224, (717) 457-7371.

Railways

- Amtrak (800) USA-RAIL.

Bus Tours

- Greyhound, (800) 231-2222.
- Capitol Bus Company, (717) 233-7673.

State Highways

- Pennsylvania Turnpike (I-76).
- Interstate 78.
- Interstate 80 runs east-west.
- Interstates 79, 99, and 81 run north-south.

Theater and Music

Southeast

- Philadelphia Orchestra, (215) 893-1900.
- Philadelphia Chamber Music Society, (215) 569-8587.

Southwest

- Pittsburgh Chamber Music Society, (412) 624-4129.

Northwest

- Erie Chamber Orchestra, (814) 871-7755.

East Central

- Schuylkill Symphony Orchestra, 91 S. Progress Ave., Pottsville, PA 17901.

Museums, Crafts, Historical, Recreational

Southeast

- Philadelphia Museum of Art, 26th St. and the Ben Franklin Parkway, Philadelphia, PA 19130, (215) 763-8100.
- Pennsylvania Academy of the Fine Arts, Broad and Cherry Sts., Philadelphia, PA 19102, (215) 972-7600.
- Liberty Bell, Liberty Bell Pavilion, Market St., Philadelphia, (215) 597-8974.
- Lancaster/Pennsylvania Dutch Country, (800) PA-DUTCH (Amish, shopping; folk art; crafts).
- Longwood Gardens, Rte. 1, Kennett Sq., PA 19348, (610) 388-1000 (gardens; DuPont estate).

Southwest

- Senator John Heinz Pittsburgh Regional History Center, 1212 Smallman St., Pittsburgh, PA 15222, (412) 454-6000 (museum and research facility devoted to the history and heritage of Western Pennsylvania).
- Carnegie Science Center, Pittsburgh, (412) 237-3400.
- Carnegie Museum of Art, 4400 Forbes Ave., Pittsburgh, PA 15213, (412) 622-3131.
- Carnegie Museum of Natural History, 4400 Forbes Ave., Pittsburgh, PA 15213, (412) 622-3131.

West

- Meadowcroft Museum of Rural Life, Washington County, (412) 587-3412 (living museum).
- Pennsylvania State Parks: (888) PA-PARKS (116 state parks in 8 regions).

Organizations

Advocacy Groups

- Department of Aging, Barto Building, 231 State St., Harrisburg, PA 17101, (717) 783-1550.
- Pennsylvania Department of Health, Nursing Home Complaint Hotline, (800)-254-5164. Consumer Grievance and Complaint Hotline, (800) 254-5164.
- Pennsylvania Association of Non-Profit Homes for the Aging, (717) 763-5724.

Volunteer Programs

- Retired and Senior Volunteer Program of Delaware County, (610) 565-5563.
- Volunteer Programs and Needs, Philadelphia, (215) 707-3579.

Housing

Long-Term Care Facilities

*In the state of Pennsylvania, these facilities are called **Continuing Care/Long-Term Care Communities**.*

These facilities provide residential living and/or various levels of nursing and medical services to seniors for an extended period of time.

Types of Authorization

Licensing and / or Certification

Continuing care communities are required to be licensed by the Department of Insurance. These facilities must provide independent living accommodations, nursing services, medical services or other health-related services, full central dining areas, and educational, recreational, and social activities. The agreement is effective for the life of the individual or for a period in excess of one year including mutually terminable contracts and in consideration of the payment of an entrance fee with or without other periodic charges.

Nursing care is required to be licensed by the Department of Health, Nursing Care Facilities, and must provide nursing care and related medical and other health services on a 24-hour basis to a person not in need of hospitalization.

Personal care services are required to be licensed by the Department of Welfare and provide assistance in daily personal activities for a person not in need of hospitalization or skilled nursing care.

Memberships

- American Association of Homes and Services for the Aging (AAHSA) represents not-for-profit organizations committed to providing high-quality health care, housing, and services to the elderly. AAHSA, 901 E St. NW, Suite 500, Washington, DC 20004-2011. Ph: (202) 783-2242. Fax: (202) 783-2285. *http://www.aahsa.org*
- The Pennsylvania Association of Non-Profit Homes for the Aging (PANPHA) is an AAHSA Affiliated State Association. PANPHA, Executive Park West, Suite 409, 4720 Old Gettysburg Rd., Mechanicsburg, PA 17055-8419. Ph: (717) 763-5724. Fax: (717) 763-1057 *http://www.panpha.org*
- Friends Services for the Aging (FSA) is an association of Quaker organizations that provide services to older adults in Maryland, New Jersey, and Pennsylvania.
- United Methodist Association of Health and Welfare Ministries promotes excellence in Christian ministry in health and welfare organizations.

Accreditations

- Continuing Care Accreditation Commission (CCAC) accredits facilities that offer seniors a contract or contracts that provide residential living and health care services for the remainder of the person's lifetime and meet CCAC's accreditation standards.
- Joint Commission on the Accreditation of Healthcare Organizations (JCAHO) is an independent, not-for-profit organization, and the nation's oldest and largest standards-setting and health care accrediting institution.
- Educational Assessment Guidelines Leading toward Excellence (EAGLE) is a voluntary self-assessment and peer review evaluation system developed by the United Methodist Association of Health and Welfare Ministries.

Certifications

- The Association of Retirement Resorts International (ARRI) is a senior advocacy organization that identifies outstanding retirement communities and certifies them as Retirement Resorts to be featured in their World Book.

Central

Morrisons Cove Home, AAHSA, PANPHA, and Association of Brethren Caregivers/Fellowship of Brethren Homes

429 S. Market St.
Martinsburg, PA, 16662

Ph: (814) 793-2104

http://www.mchome.org/

E-mail: *webmaster@intelinet.com*

IND: 63. AL: 26. SNF: 110

Nondenominational facility affiliated with the Pennsylvania District Church of the Brethren. Cottages, apartments, private and semiprivate rooms. 24-hour nursing supervision; medical management; physical, occupational, and speech therapies; personal care; medication administration; Medicare/Medicaid-approved; 24-hour security; emergency response system; transportation; up to 3 daily meals; housekeeping and laundry services, recreation center; spiritual services; social services and activities; walking areas; gift/snack shop; barber/beauty shop.

IND LL: $66,000–$125,500. IND MO: $500–$800. AL Daily: $80. SNF Daily: $145–$170152.

South Central

Calvary Fellowship Homes, PANPHA

502 Elizabeth Drive
Lancaster, PA 17601

Ph: (717) 393-0711
Fax: (717) 393-0998

IND: 100+. RC/PC: 22. HCC: 45

Age 62+. Nonprofit, nondenominational home for the aging. Cottages, apartments; private and semiprivate rooms. Long- and short-term care; 24-hour skilled nursing care; therapies; personal care; medication administration; up to 3 daily meals; exercise program; chapel; activities; gardens, gift shop; planned recreational activities; devotional services; game room; shuffleboard; barber/beauty shop.

APP: $25. IND ENT: $25,500–$129,000. IND MO: $500–$1,100; 2nd person fee, $975–$1,075. PC MO: $1,950 (semiprivate) and $2,250 (private). HCC Daily: $165.

Menno Haven, Inc.: Menno Haven Village and Menno Haven Penn Hall, AAHSA, PANPHA, Mennonites Health Services, Association of Brethren and Mennonite Older Adults Ministries, CCAC

1427 Philadelphia Ave.
Chambersburg, PA 17201

Ph: (717) 263-8545 (Village), Ph: (717) 261-4154 (Hall)

http://www.mennohaven.org/

E-mail: *info@mennohaven.org*

IND: 350. RH: 100+. AL: Yes. SNF: 233. AL/MEM IMP: Yes. ADC and HHC

Not-for-profit organization; associated with the Mennonite Churches of Franklin County. Cottages, townhomes, apartments, and private and semiprivate rooms. Social and therapeutic services; skilled nursing care; personal care; medication administration; Medicare/Medicaid-approved; security; emergency response system; maintenance; transportation; up to 3 daily meals; housekeeping and laundry services; chapels; banking services; volunteer programs; resident councils; educational programs; gift and coffee shop; pools; exercise room; library; activities; barber/beauty shop.

IND ENT: $95,500–$111,000. IND MO: $250.

RES ENT: $38,500–$82,500. RES MO: $900–$1,250. AL ENT: $2,200–$5,500. Level 1 daily fee: $80 (single); $125 (double). Level 2 daily fee: $90 (single); $140 (double). SNF Daily: (semiprivate), $140; (private), $150. Nonresident admission fee: $475. AL/MEM IMP: (semiprivate), $130 and $135; (private), $140.

Messiah Village, CCAC, PANPHA, Evangelical Council for Financial Accountability

100 Mt. Allen Drive, PO Box 2015
Mechanicsburg, PA 17055

Ph: (717) 697-4666

http://www.messiahvillage.com

E-mail: *life@messiahvillage.com*

IND: Yes. AL: Yes. ALZ/MEM IMP: Yes. SNF: Yes

Age 65+. Owned and operated by the Brethren in Christ Church; nonprofit, nondenominational. Cottages, apartments, private and semiprivate rooms. Skilled and intermediate care; social programming; daily structured programming; appointment assistance; social and rehabilitative services; personal care; medication administration; Medicare/Medicaid-approved; security; emergency response system; maintenance;

transportation; up to 3 daily meals; housekeeping and laundry services; crafts; swimming; computers; games; off-site excursions; pastoral care; volunteer programs; bank; pharmacy; country store; beauty/barber shop.

APPL: (no ref.) $1,650. IND ACQ: (part. ref.; amortized at a rate of % per month for the 1st 100 mo; unamortized portion ref. with 6 mos. of vacancy or resale): $52,000–$156,500. IND MO: $350–$650. AL/PC/ALZ/MEM IMP/SNF RSVF: $550 (non-ref. for all nonresident admissions). AL Daily: $55–$90 and $90–$130. ALZ/MEM IMP Daily: $110–$150. SNF Daily: (semiprivate), $150; (private), $200.

West

Asbury Heights

700 Bower Hill Rd.
Pittsburgh, PA 15243

Ph: (412) 571-5165
Fax: (412) 571-5111

IND: Yes. AL: Yes. HCC: Yes. ALZ/MEM IMP: Yes

A nonprofit facility operated by the United Methodist Services for the Aging. Townhomes, suites, apartments, and private and semiprivate rooms. Short- and long-term care; certified nurses; physical, occupational, and speech therapies; ALZ care for those with early- to middle-stage Alzheimer's and other memory disorders; health monitoring program; personal care; medication administration; Medicare/Medicaid-approved; security; emergency response system; maintenance; transportation; up to 3 daily meals; housekeeping and laundry services; walking paths; shuffleboard; crafts; social activities; bank and postal services; resident council.

IND ENT: (Option I non-ref.), $33,000; (90% ref.), $108,000–$248,000. IND MO: (includes 3 meals), $1,325–$2,175; (Option II, no ENT with 3 meals): $3,000–$3,850; (no meals), $1,575–$1,800; (one meal), $1,550–$2,100; (3 meals), $1,575–$2,950. PC Daily: $15.

Friendship Village of South Hills

1290 Boyce Rd.
Upper St. Clair, PA 15241

Ph: (412) 941-3100

IND: Yes. HCC: Yes

Owned and operated by Life Care Retirement Communities. Apartments and private and semiprivate rooms. Short- and long-term restorative and ongoing skilled nursing; personal care; medication administration; security; emergency response system; maintenance; transportation; up to 3 daily meals system (1 meal included in mo. fee); housekeeping and laundry services; chaplain; all utilities; lawn and grounds care; game room; 9-hole golf course nearby; walking paths; arts and crafts room; woodworking shop; art studio; library; auditorium; scheduled daily activities.

IND ENT: (90% return of capital plan) $72,000–$412,500. IND MO: $1,150–$2,900 (2nd person fee, $775).

Longwood at Oakmont, ARRI

500 Rte. 909
Verona, PA 15147

Ph: (800) 828-8841 or (412) 826-5800
Fax: (412) 826-5750

http://www.longwoodatoakmont.com

E-mail: *longwood@worldnet.att.net*

IND: 187 (75 additional under construction). AL: (39 under construction). SNF: 59. ALZ/MEM IMP: Yes

Age 62+. Presbyterian SeniorCare Network; nonprofit facility. Country homes, garden and condo apartments, and private and semiprivate rooms. Rehabilitation program; physical, occupational, and speech therapies; nursing care; security; emergency response system; maintenance; transportation; up to 3 daily meals; pets allowed; housekeeping and laundry services; exercise classes; pool; library; crafts; card and board games; movies; volunteer programs; vespers; Bible study; gardens; walking paths; woodshop; barber/beauty shop.

IND ENT: $96,000–$250,000+. IND MO: $1,700–$2,500+.

Southeast

Bair Healthcare Pavilion, PANPHA

8301 Roosevelt Blvd.
Philadelphia, PA 19152

Ph: (215) 332-4040
Fax: (215) 624-7020

http://baptisthome.org

E-mail: *apeters@baptisthome.org*

RL: Yes. AL/PC: Yes. NC: 206 (37 units SNF)

Nondenominational facility. Studios, apartments, and private and semiprivate rooms. Subacute and rehabilitative care; specialty beds; IV treatments; medical services; physical, occupational, and speech therapies; 24-hour skilled nursing care; personal care; medication administration; Medicare/Medicaid-approved; security; emergency call system; maintenance; transportation; up to 3 daily meals; housekeeping and laundry services; exercise program; clergy visits; scheduled daily activities; committee meetings; musical and entertainment programs.

$3,850 (one month advance) required. SNF Daily: $150 (semiprivate); $160 (private). ICF Daily: $145 (semiprivate); $165 (private). SA/REHAB Daily: (semiprivate), $155; (private), $165.

Cathedral Village, CCAC, ARRI

600 E. Cathedral Rd.
Philadelphia, PA 19128

Ph: (215) 487-1300

http://www.retirementresorts.com/index.html

IND: 277. AL: 50. SNF: 148

Age 65+. Nonprofit, nondenominational facility. Apartments, studios, and private and semiprivate rooms. 24-hour professional nursing care; community nursing and comprehensive health services; personal care; medication administration; security; emergency response system; maintenance; transportation; up to 3 daily meals; housekeeping and laundry services; indoor pool; health club; planned social activities.

PROC: (no ref.) $165/person. DEP: (ref.) $1,100. IND ENT: $52,000–$224,500. IND MO: $1,750–$5,100. MO fee includes unlimited nursing care.

Chandler Hall, FSA

99 Barclay St.
Newtown, PA 18940

Ph: (215) 860-4000

IND/PC: Yes. NH: Yes

Nonprofit, nondenominational organization associated with the Society of Friends. Private and semiprivate rooms. Nursing care; wellness care; social, recreational, and rehabilitative programs; personal care; medication administration; 3 daily meals; therapeutic recreation; seminars; social events.

APPL: (non-ref.), $100. IND Daily: $75–$140.

NH Daily: $180–$285. HSP Inpatient Daily: $300–$550.

Christ's Home Retirement Community

1220 W. Street Rd.
Warminster, PA 18974

Ph: (215) 956-2270
Fax: (215) 957-5178

IND: Yes. AL: Yes. HCC: Yes

Christian-based organization; nondenominational. Apartments and private and semiprivate rooms. 24-hour skilled nursing care; personal care; medication administration; transportation; 3 daily meals; laundry and housekeeping services; activity programs; exercise; Bible study; arts and crafts; movies, concerts, and plays.

APPL: $200 (non-ref.). IND ENT: (ref. up to one year) $56,500–$71,500. IND MO: $625 and $700.

AL ENT: $16,500–$33,000. MO: $880–$1,375. HCC Daily: (single), $165; (double), $185.

Dock Woods Community, Inc.

275 Dock Drive
Lansdale, PA, 19446

Ph: (215) 368-4438
Fax: (215) 362-2682

IND: 324. PC: Yes. SNF: 72

Age 62+. Not-for-profit corporation sponsored by Franconia Mennonite Conference; nondenominational. Cottages, apartments, and private and semiprivate rooms. Medical services; nursing care; therapeutic diets; personal care; medication administration; security; emergency call system; transportation; 3 daily meals; laundry and housekeeping services; exercise room; some subsidized housing; pastoral care; crafts; activities; woodshop; pool; banking office; recreational rooms; gift and coffee shops; barber/beauty shop.

APPL: $1,375. ENT (option 1): (50% ref. at termination, plus portion not earned by facility [facility earns 2% per month with a minimum of $5,000 for a term of occupancy]), $20,000–$53,000. ADMN (option 2): (non-ref.), $5,500–$8,250. MO: $1,800 (entrance fee plan); $2,475–$2,650 (admission fee, plan). 2nd person fee, $950 (both options). PC Daily: $2 to $10 (laundry service is a weekly fee).

Evangelical Manor, CCAC, PANPHA, Eastern Pennsylvania Conference of the United Methodist Church, United Methodist Association of Health and Welfare Ministries.

8401 Roosevelt Blvd.
Philadelphia, PA 19152

Ph: (215) 624-5800

IND: 144. PL: 50. HCC: 120

Age 65+. Affiliated with the Eastern Pennsylvania Conference of the United Methodist Church; not-for-profit; nondenominational. Studios, apartments, and private and semiprivate rooms. Nursing care; physical therapy; medical staff; on-site X-ray equipment; routine laboratory procedures; personal care; medication administration; Medicare/Medicaid-approved; security; emergency response system; maintenance; transportation; up to 3 daily meals; housekeeping and laundry services; all utilities except telephone; chapel; library; gift shop; bank; barber/beauty shop.

Studio ENT: $22,550–$31,500. Studio Daily: $40 (single), $55 (double). Apt. ENT: $45,000–$77,000. Apt. Daily: $50 (single), $65 (double).

Foulkeways at Gwynedd, CCAC, FSA

1120 Meetinghouse Rd.
Gwynedd, PA 19436

Ph: 215-643-2200

IND: Yes. AL: 32. SNF: 68

Founded by the Religious Society of Friends (Quakers) as the first continuing care community in Pennsylvania. Apartments, studios, cottages, and private and semiprivate rooms. Primary care by staff physicians and nurse practitioner; 24-hour nursing care; nutritional program; special programs for residents with cognitive impairments; hospice care; 24-hour emergency care by health center; preventive health care services; pharmacist; short- term and long-term stays; licensed social worker; physical, occupational and speech therapies; personal care; medication administration; security; emergency response system; maintenance; transportation; up to 3 daily meals; housekeeping and laundry services; scheduled activities; entertainment programs; pet therapy; crafts; intergenerational program; indoor pool; walking paths.

Priority List Agreement: $1,350 ($1,100 priority fee plus $250 processing fee [nonrefundable]). IND ENT: (single), $41,000–$225,000; (double), $110,000–$253,000. IND MO: $1,650–$3,700 (single); $3,300–$4,550 (double).

Kendal at Longwood-Crosslands, CCAC, FSA

PO Box 100
Kennett Square, PA 19348

Ph: (610) 388-7001

http://www.kendal.org

E-mail: *admissions@kcc.kendal.org*

RL: 475. HCC: 177

Kendal Corporation; nondenominational; Longwood and Crosslands are on separate sites but share a central building containing the health center, dining area, and activities. Cottages, apartments, and private and semiprivate rooms. 24-hour professional care; physical, speech, occupational, and recreational therapies; unlimited long-term care; security; emergency response system; maintenance; transportation; up to 3 daily meals (1 meal included in mo. fee); pets allowed; fitness center; all utilities except phone; meal tray delivery; library; auditorium; art studios; crafts; pool; walking paths; barber/beauty shop.

IND ENT: $57,000–$188,000. IND MO: $1,650–$3,600. HCC MO: $5,850.

REQ: Residents must carry Medicare A and B and a Medigap insurance policy.

Paul's Run

9896 Bustleton Ave.
Philadelphia, PA 19115

Ph: (215) 934-3000

E-mail: *paulsrun@libertynet.org*

IND: Yes. RC: Yes. AL: Yes. HCC: Yes

Affiliated with the Evangelical Lutheran Church in America. Studios, apartments, private and semiprivate rooms. Rehabilitative, short- or long-term care; nursing care; therapeutic and recreational activities; personal care; medication administration; Medicare/Medicaid-approved; security; emergency response system; maintenance; transportation; up to 3 daily meals; housekeeping and laundry services; social and religious services; utilities; shopping/delivery service; lounge; auditorium; library; thrift shop; general store; crafts and hobby activities; barber/beauty shop.

PROC: $330 (single); $495 (couple). Optional Priority Waiting List: $165 (no ref. but applied to PRO fee). IND MO: $1,450–$2,800; 2nd person $525. RES MO: $1,450–$2,800 plus assistance fees, up to $450 per month depending on level of care. PC Daily: $30–$145. HCC Daily: $160–$185.

Pennswood Village, ccac, fsa

1382 Newtown-Langhorne
Newtown, PA 18940

Ph: (888) 454-1122

http://www.pennswood.org

IND: 252. HCC: 91

Age 65+. Quaker directed; not for profit; open to all faiths. Apartments and rooms. 24-hour skilled nursing care; pharmacy; personal care; medication administration; security; emergency response system; maintenance; transportation; up to 3 daily meals; pets allowed; housekeeping and laundry services; fitness center and trainer; residents association; various committees; intergenerational program; gift shop; greenhouse; postal services; barber/beauty shop.

PROC: (no ref.) $200. APPL: (ref.) $1,350/person; $1,900/couple. IND ENT: $66,500–$196,500. IND MO: $1,875–$4,100 (MO fee remains stable if resident has nonpermanent illness and requires temporary stay at Health Care Center.)

Simpson House, CCAC

2101 Belmont Ave.
Philadelphia, PA 19131

Ph: (215) 878-6701
Fax: (215) 878-3600

http://www.simpsonhouse.org/
E-mail: *Info@SimpsonHouse.org*

IND: Yes. RL/AL: Yes. HCC: Yes

Oldest existing retirement community affiliated with the United Methodist Church. Studios, apartments, and private and semiprivate rooms. Physical, occupational, and speech-language therapies; neurological, orthopedic, functional/deconditioning, and wound care services; nursing care; respite care; in-house medical clinic; personal care; medication administration; security; emergency response system; maintenance; transportation; up to 3 daily meals; housekeeping and laundry services; arts and crafts; music; nature trails; concerts; movies; bank services; scheduled off-site trips; barber/beauty shop.

IND ENT: (ref. for a limited time), $9,900–$66,000. IND MO: $1,000–$1,925 (2nd person $500). AL ENT: (ref. for a limited time), $9,900–$11,000. AL Daily: $70–$100.

White Horse Village

535 Gradyville Rd.
Newtown Square, PA 19073

Ph: (610) 558-5000
http://www.white-horse.com/

IND: Yes. AL: Yes. SNF: Yes

Age 65+. A nonprofit, nondenominational community. Villas, studios, apartments, and private and semiprivate rooms. 24-hour skilled nursing care; medical treatment; physical, occupational, and speech therapies; wellness program; personal care; medication administration; security; emergency response system; maintenance; transportation; up to 3 daily meals (1 meal included in IND MO fee); housekeeping and laundry services; social and recreational programs; pool; exercise room; library; lounge; bank; gift shop; arts and crafts; educational programs; scheduled events; barber/beauty shop.

APPL: $1,350 (single), $1,450 (couple). IND ENT: (80% ref.), $102,000–$323,000; (ref. less 2% per month), $68,500–$220,500. IND MO: $1,575–$3,650.

William Hood Care Center, CCAC, PANPHA (formally Dunwoody Village)

3500 West Chester Pike
Newtown Square, PA 19073

Ph: (610) 359-4400

IND: 257. AL/PC: Yes. HCC: Yes

Not-for-profit, nondenominational facility. Homes, studios, apartments, and private and semiprivate rooms. Wellness programs; skilled nursing care; physical therapy; personal care; medication administration; security; emergency response system; maintenance; transportation; up to 3 daily meals; housekeeping and laundry services; fitness center; pool; post office; woodshop; arts and crafts; library; garden; putting green; planned activities.

IND ENT: (50% ref. option open to qualified applicants under 80 years of age), $97,000–$318,000; (no ref.), $66,000–$217,000. IND MO: (with ref.), $1,700–$5,125; (without ref.), $1,700–$5,125.

South Central

The Brethren Home Community, CCAC AAHSA, PANPHA

2990 Carlisle Pike
PO Box 128
New Oxford, PA 17350

Ph: (888) 624-8242 or (717) 624-5232
Fax: (717) 624-5252

IND: 340. PC: Yes. HCC: Yes. ALZ/MEM IMP: Yes

Age 62+; second person must be at least 55 years old. A nonprofit facility. Cottages, apartments, private rooms with bath, and private and semiprivate rooms. Subacute care; nursing care; home health care; medication administration; security; emergency response system; maintenance; transportation; up to 3 daily meals; housekeeping and laundry services; social activities; greenhouse; social room; shopping trips; craft room; gift shop; bank; clergy; volunteer programs; library.

Entrance fees listed for persons 65+. For those under 65, an age premium of 4% for each year under 65 is added to the entrance fee. Entrance fee is amortized at about .83%/mo. until a minimum balance of 25% of the health care account is reached. When reached, the amortization ends.

Cottage ENT: $32,000–$185,000. Cottage MO: (includes service fee plus taxes, liability insurance, and utilities), about $375–$625; 2nd person, $45. IND ENT Plan A: (a decreasing credit reserve account is amortized at about .83%/mo. until a minimum balance of 25% is reached), $77,000–$141,000; Plan B: (guaranteed refund of at least 25% to resident or estate), $88,500–$163,000. IND MO: $650–$1,000 (2nd person, $330). PC Daily: $55–$105, plus level of care fee, $15–$50 (2nd person additional). LTC Daily: $135–170. SC Daily: $155–$175. SA Daily: $205–$315.

Chapel Pointe at Carlisle

770 S. Hanover St.
Carlisle, PA 17013

Ph: (717) 249-1363
Fax: (717) 249-9511

IND: Yes. PC: Yes. HCC: Yes

Christian retirement community. Nondenominational facility. Efficiencies, apartments, and private and semiprivate rooms. 24-hour skilled nursing service for short-term rehabilitative care; physical, occupational, and speech therapies; health monitoring program; personal care; medication administration; Medicare/Medicaid-approved; security; emergency response system; maintenance; transportation; up to 3 daily meals; housekeeping and laundry services; fitness center; utilities (except telephone); social activities; chaplain; activities room; intergenerational program; library; sewing room; greenhouse; barber/beauty shop.

IND ENT: $29,000–$74,000. IND MO: $625 (single), $750 (double). PC Daily: $60–$80. HCC Daily: $140–$170, plus $165 admission fee.

Church of God Home, PANPHA, AAHSA

801 N. Hanover St.
Carlisle, PA 17013

Ph: (717) 249-5322
Fax: (717) 249-8622

IND: Yes. PC: 22. SNF: 109

Sponsored by the East Pennsylvania Conference of the Churches of God; nondenominational facility. Apartments, efficiencies, and private and semiprivate rooms. 24-hour nurse on call; skilled nursing care; blood pressure tests; medical visits; access to on-site health care center; X-rays, lab, podiatry, and counseling services; restorative and rehabilitation care; routine physician visits; personal care; medication administration; Medicare/Medicaid-approved; security; emergency response system; maintenance; transportation; up to 3 daily meals; housekeeping and laundry services; chapel; most utilities; gift shop; activities; outings; barber/beauty shop.

IND ENT: (part. ref.), $60,500–$85,500. IND MO: (with ENT fee); $550–$800; (rentals), $1,025–$1,650. HCC Daily: (semiprivate), $130; (private), $140. PC Daily: (semiprivate), $65; (private), $75.

Cornwall Manor, CCAC, AAHS, United Methodist Association of Health and Welfare Ministries

PO Box 125
Cornwall Manor, PA 17016

Ph: (800) 222-2476 or (717) 273-2647
http://www.cornwallmanor.org/

IND: Yes. AL/PC: Yes. HCC: 135 (total residents, 535)

Church-related, nonprofit facility; nondenominational. Duplex homes, apartments, and private and semiprivate rooms. Nursing care; occupational and speech therapies; dental clinic; hospice program; Medicare/Medicaid-approved; wellness center; security; emergency response system; maintenance; transportation; up to 3 daily meals; housekeeping and laundry services; fitness center; pool and spa; social and clergy services; all utilities except for cable TV and phone; daily activities; clubs; intergenerational and volunteer programs.

2 ENT plans: Traditional Plan provides for amortization of full entrance fee at 2%/mo. for 50 mos. Asset Preservation Plan provides permanent 50% refund/ credit of entrance fee when unit is vacated; balance of fee amortizes at 2% for 50 months. IND ENT: $19,000–$210,500. IND MO: $925–$1,850. Health Care fees additional.

Cumberland Crossings, PANPHA

1 Longsdorf Way
Carlisle, PA 17013

Ph: (717) 245-5951

IND: Yes. PC: SNF: 59

Nonprofit, community-based charitable organization. Cottages, studios, and private and semiprivate rooms. 24-hour emergency nurse call; rehabilitative, skilled, and intermediate care; personal care; medication administration; Medicare/Medicaid-approved; security; emergency response system; maintenance; transportation; up to 3 daily meals; pets allowed; housekeeping and laundry services; indoor recreational center; indoor pool; fitness area; library; lounge; activities director and planned activities; snack shop; wood and crafts center; gift shop; volunteer programs; social activities; barber/beauty shop.

IND Residency fee: (declining ref.), $115,500–$148,500; (90% ref.), $170,500–$203,500. IND MO: (declining ref.), $850–$950; (90% ref.), $1,075–$1,175. 2nd person, $95 (all plans). PC Daily: $95–$170. SNF Daily: $140 and $175.

Assisted Living and Residential Care Facilities

In the state of Pennsylvania, these facilities are called ***Assisted Living/Personal Care/Skilled Nursing Facilities.***

These facilities offer housing with personalized support services and health care services.

Types of Authorization

Licensing and / or Certification

Nursing care facilities are required to be licensed by the Department of Health, Nursing Care Facilities, and must provide nursing care and related medical and other health services on a 24-hour basis to a person not in need of hospitalization. Personal care services are required to be licensed by the Department of Welfare and provide assistance in daily personal activities for a person not in need of hospitalization or skilled nursing care.

Memberships

- Assisted Living Federation of America (ALFA) is a national nonprofit membership organization whose mission is to enhance the quality of life in assisted living facilities and promote the interests of the assisted living industry. ALFA, 10300 Eaton Place, Suite 400, Fairfax, VA 22030. Ph: (703) 691-8100. Fax: (703) 691-8106. *http: / / www.alfa.org*
- Pennsylvania Assisted Living Association (PALA) is a state affiliate of ALFAA. PALA, 536 Edella Rd., Clarks Summit, PA 19046. Ph: (717) 586-4292. Fax: (717) 586-4024.

Southwest

The Woodwell

306 Penn Ave.
Pittsburgh, PA 15221

Ph: (412) 242-3606 TDD: (412) 826 6135
Fax: (412) 242-9471

PC: 30. ICF: Yes. SNF: 70

Owned by the United Presbyterian Women's Association of North America; nondenominational. Private and semi-private rooms. Health care services on a regular basis; respite care; supervised nursing care; personal care; medication administration; 3 daily meals; housekeeping and laundry services; exercise room; clergy; library; planned activities; recreation room; barber/beauty shop.

ENT: About $71,500–$88,000 depending on the type of unit and level of care.

Southeast

Ashton Terrace

2109 Red Lion Rd.
Philadelphia, PA 19115

Ph: (215) 673-7000

AL: 89. ALZ/MEM IMP: Yes

Nondenominational. Private and semi-private rooms. Respite care; personal care; medication administration; security; emergency response system; maintenance; transportation; up to 3 daily meals; housekeeping and laundry services; social and recreational activities.

AL MO: $1,650–$2,300.

Bala Presbyterian Home

4700 City Line Ave.
Philadelphia, PA 19131-1599

Ph: (212) 624-7575

AL: 99

Nondenominational; Presbyterian Church affiliation. Apartments. Social services; respite care; personal care; medication administration; security; emergency response system; maintenance; transportation; up to 3 daily meals; housekeeping and laundry services; exercise room; religious services; social and recreational services.

AL MO: $1,400–$1,600.

Bethesda Ct. Assisted Living Residence

6200 Ardleigh St.
Philadelphia, PA 19135-1521

Ph: (215) 844-1889

AL: 108

Nondenominational. Private and semi-private rooms. Wellness visits; personal care; medication administration; security; emergency response system; maintenance; transportation; up to 3 daily meals; housekeeping and laundry services; religious services; social and recreational activities; educational and cultural programs; bistro; lounges.

AL MO: $880–$2,650.

Calvary Fellowship Homes

502 Elizabeth Drive
Lancaster, PA 17601-4499

Ph: (717) 393-0711

AL: 30. ALZ/MEM IMP: Yes

Cottages, apartments, and rooms. Nursing care; respite care; personal care; medication administration; security; emergency response system; maintenance; transportation; up to 3 daily meals; housekeeping and laundry services; exercise room; library; educational programs; social and recreational activities; barber/beauty shop.

AL MO: $1,925–$2,250.

Independent Living

Independent housing for seniors that may offer security features, meal service, and activities.

Southwest

Bethel Park Retirement Living

2960 Bethel Church Rd.
Bethel Park, PA 15102

Ph: (412) 833-3220
Fax: (412) 833-3997

IND: 116

For-profit; nondenominational; nonsectarian; owned by Holiday Retirement Corp. Apartments. Security; emergency response system; maintenance; transportation; up to 3 daily meals; pets allowed; housekeeping and laundry services; exercise equipment; library; arts and crafts; group activities; barber/beauty shop.

IND MO: $1,325–$2,700; 2nd person, $385.

East

Little Lehigh Manor

824 Jackson St.
Allentown, PA 18102

Ph: (610) 432-1710

IND: Yes

Age 62+. For-profit; nondenominational. Apartments. Security; emergency response system; maintenance; pets allowed.

IND MO: 30% of income; HUD-subsidized.

Adult/Resort Communities

Communities for active adults (not all are age-restricted).

Northeast

Country Club of the Poconos

Rte. 209 N.
Marshalls Creek, PA 18335

Ph: (800) 962-2006 or (570) 223-1200

Individual homes, condominiums, townhomes, cluster villages, homesites. Golf course; tennis; swimming pool; fitness center; hiking; fishing; Jacuzzi; sauna; social clubs.

PURCHASE: Condos, from $121,000; townhomes, $110,000–$126,500; cluster homes, $165,000–$220,000; homesites, $44,000–$99,000.

The Glen at Tamiment Resort

Bushkill Falls Rd.
Tamiment, PA 18371

Ph: (570) 588-3440 or (800) 252-4568 (tri-state)

Individual homes, homesites. Golf course; tennis; racquetball; swimming pool; hiking; fishing; riding stables; boating/waterskiing; snow skiing; fitness center.

PURCHASE: Homes, $98,000–$220,000; homesites, $16,500–$33,000.

Pinecrest Lake Golf and Country Club

PO Box 760
Pocono Pines, PA 18350

Ph: (800) 724-3956 or (570) 646-2452

Individual homes, villas. Golf course; clubhouse; tennis; swimming pool; hiking/biking; lake; sailing; dining; social clubs; nearby skiing.

PURCHASE: Homes, from $214,500; villas, from $154,000.

Woodloch Springs

#2 Woodloch Springs
Hawley, PA 18428

Ph: (800) 272-9428 or (570) 685-2100
Fax: (570) 685-4799

http:www.woodloch.com

Individual homes, homesites. Golf course; tennis; swimming pool; hiking/biking; fishing; community center; fitness center; indoor sports center; library; social clubs.

PURCHASE: Homes, from $192,500; townhomes, from $154,000.

Central

Deer Creek at Toftrees

Toftrees Ave.
State College, PA 16803

Ph: (814) 861-3337

http://www.toftrees.com

62+. Individual homes, condominiums. Golf course; tennis swimming pool; community center; fitness center; hiking/biking; hunting; library; social clubs; computer lab; woodworking; arts and crafts.

PURCHASE: Homes, $175,000–$440,000+.

South Central

Majestic Ridge Golf Club and Community

2437 Adin Lane
Chambersburg, PA 17201

Ph: (717) 267-3444

Individual homes, townhomes, homesites. Golf course; clubhouse; pro shop; driving range; dining.

PURCHASE: Homes, $209,000–$605,000.

Penn National Golf Club and Community

3720 Clubhouse Drive
Fayetteville, PA 17222

Ph: (800) 221-7366 or (717) 352-3000

http://www.pennhomes.com

Individual homes, condominiums, homesites. Golf courses; clubhouse; tennis; swimming pool; hiking; basketball; miniature golf; social clubs.

PURCHASE: Homes, from $132,000; homesites, from $44,000.

Southwest

Chestnut Ridge Golf Club

1762 Old William Penn Hwy.
Blairsville, PA 15717

Ph: (724) 459-5907

Individual homes, condominiums. Golf courses; clubhouse; fishing; dining.

PURCHASE: Homes, from $252,000.

Diamond Run Golf Club and Resort Community

132 Laurel Oak Drive
Sewickley, PA 15143

Ph: (412) 741-3001

http://www.diamondrun.com

Individual homes, cluster homes, homesites. Golf course, clubhouse, pro shop, dining, social clubs.

PURCHASE: Homes, $412,500–$660,000; cluster homes, $308,000–$594,000; homesites, from $101,500.

Hidden Valley Resort

1 Craighead Drive
Hidden Valley, PA 15502

Ph: (800) 228-2270 or (814) 444-8756

http://www.hiddenvalleyresort.com

Individual homes, condominiums, townhomes, homesites. Golf course; tennis; swimming pool; racquetball; hiking/biking; fishing; hunting; snow skiing; community center; fitness center.

PURCHASE: Homes, $165,000–$539,000; condos, $60,500–$252,000; townhomes, $88,000–$230,000; homesites, $60,500–$115,000.

Sand Springs Golf Community

1 Sand Springs Drive
Butler Township, PA 18222

Ph: (570) 788-5845 or (570) 788-4104

Individual homes, homesites, proposed townhome and patio home villages. Golf course; clubhouse; pro shop; hiking/biking; dining.

PURCHASE: Homesites, $31,000–$60,500.

Seven Springs Mountain Resort

RD 1
Champion, PA 15622

Ph: (814) 352-7704

http://www.7springs.com

Individual homes, condominiums. Golf course; tennis; racquetball; swimming pool; hiking/biking; fishing; riding stables; snow skiing; fitness center; indoor mini golf; bowling; alpine slide.

PURCHASE: Homes, $71,500–$385,000.

Southeast

Four Seasons at Hershey's Mill

1347 Troon Lane
West Chester, PA 19380

Ph: (610) 918-0400

http://www.khov.com/homes/pa/hershey/hersdire.htm

Age 55+. Individual homes. Golf course; tennis; swimming pool; woodworking; classes; wooded preserve.

PURCHASE: Homes, from $242,000.

Four Seasons at Saucon Valley

1842 Caryn Drive
Hellertown, PA 18055

Ph: (610) 838-1300

http://www.khov.com/homes/pa/4sealwr/lwrtown.htm

Age 55+. Garden villas. Recreation area and complex; fitness center; swimming pool; billiards; ballroom; putting green; tennis; shuffleboard; bocce; card room; walking path.

PURCHASE: Villas, from $165,000.

Fox Hill Farm

851 Smithbridge Rd.
Glen Mills, PA 19342

Ph: (610) 459-3800

http://www.membrane.com/philanet/mckee/foxhill

Age 55+. Individual homes, carriage homes. No maintenance; clubhouse; swimming pools; exercise facilities; tennis; shuffleboard; bocce; arts and crafts; library; game room; fitness and bicycle trails.

PURCHASE: Homes, from $187,000.

The Villas at Golf View

1309 Palmer Drive
Springfield, PA 19064

Ph: (610) 690-4653

http://www.membrane.com/philanet/mckee/golf

Age 55+. Townhomes. No maintenance; next to golf club and healthplex with swimming pools, racquetball, tennis squash, fitness center, personal trainers, aerobics classes.

PURCHASE: Homes, from $154,000.

Rhode Island

http://www.state.ri.us

General Information

Climate

Average winter temperatures are in the mid- to high 30s°F and average summer temperatures are in the mid- to high 70s°F.

Cost of Living

Ranks 7th in the nation.

Taxes

State/Local as % of Income: 11.5%.

Property Tax Reduction: Residents 65+ who are eligible may receive tax relief credit. Maximum credit allowed is $250.

Sales: 7%.

Prescription Exemptions: Drugs and medicines sold on prescription are exempt from sales tax.

Transportation, Travel, and Tourism

General

RI Tourism Division, 7 Jackson Walkway, Providence, RI 02903, (401) 277-2601 or (800) 556-2484.

Welcome Center, (401) 539-3031.

Major Airport

- T. F. Green Airport, Providence, (401) 737-8222 (in-state); (888) 268-7222 (out of state).

Railways

- Amtrak, Providence Station, 1000 Gaspee St. (800) 872-7265.

Bus Tours

- Bonanza Bus Lines, (888) 751-8800, or (401) 751-8800.

State Highways

- Interstate 95 runs north-south.

Ground Transportation

- Airport Taxi & Limousine, (401) 942-5990.
- Newport Shuttle, (401) 846-2500.

Theater and Music

North

- Blackstone River Theater, 549 Broad St., Cumberland, RI 02864, (401) 729-1880.
- City Nights Dinner Theater, 27 Exchange St., Pawtucket, RI 02860, (401) 72306060.
- Pawtucket Community Players, 31 Felsmere St., Pawtucket, RI 02861, (401) 724-7735.
- Temple Theatre, 203 N. Washington, Saginaw, RI 48607, (517) 793-8940 (movies and shows).

South

- Colonial Theatre, 3 Granite St., Westerly, RI 02891, (401) 596-0810.
- The University of Rhode Island Music Dept., Fine Arts Building, Kingston, RI 02881, (401) 792-2431 (classical and jazz).
- Theatre-by-the-Sea, 364 Cards Pond Rd., Wakefield, RI 02879-6998, (401) 782-3644 (summer theater by the water).

East

- Providence Performing Arts Center, 220 Weybossett St., Providence, RI 02903, (401) 421-ARTS.

Museums, Crafts, Historical, Recreational

South

- South County Museum, Route 1A, Narragansett, (401) 783-5400 (seasonal; RI life in the 18th–early 20th centuries).
- Smith's Castle, near North Kingstown, (401) 294-3521 (seasonal; 18th century garden; trading post).
- Hera Gallery/Educational Foundation, 327 Main St., Wakefield, RI 02880, (401)789-1488 (art exhibitions).
- Wickford Place, 1340 Tower Hill Rd., North Kingston, RI 02852-6624, (401) 294-4177 (crafter's gallery).

East

- Newport Art Museum, 76 Bellevue Ave., Newport, (401) 848-8200.
- Newport Mansions (Preservation Society of Newport County), 424 Bellevue Ave., Newport RI 02840, (401) 847-1000.
- Museum of Newport History, 82 Touro St., Newport, RI 02840, (401) 846-0813.
- Goddard Memorial State Park, Ives Road, Warwick, RI 02818, (401) 884-2010 (lawns, fields, saltwater beach, golfing).

North

- Slater Mill Historic Site, Roosevelt Ave., Pawtucket, RI 02860, (401) 725-8638 (birthplace of American industry).
- Lincoln Woods State Park, 2 Manchester Print Works Rd., Lincoln, RI 02865, (401) 723-7892 (swimming, fishing, hiking).

Organizations

Advocacy Groups

- Elder Affairs, 160 Pine St., Providence, RI 02903, (401) 277-2858.
- Nursing Home Ombudsmen, (401) 277-2880 or (in-state) (800) 322-2880.
- Alliance for Better Long Term Care, (401) 785-3340.
- The Gray Panthers of Rhode Island, (401) 725-1122.

Volunteer Programs

- (Points of Light) Volunteers in Action, (401) 847-4447.
- Literacy Volunteers of America–Rhode Island, 260 W. Exchange St., Suite 201/2, Providence, RI 02903. (401) 861-0815, Fax (401) 861-0863.

Housing

Long-Term Care Facilities

In the state of Rhode Island, these facilities are called ***Long-Term Care/Nursing Home Facilities****.*

These facilities provide residential living and/or various levels of nursing and medical services to seniors for an extended period of time.

Types of Authorization

Licensing and/or Certification

These facilities must be licensed by the Department of Health, Division of Facilities Regulation. Nursing homes are required to provide for resident's well-being; ensure safety of resident's funds; provide documented policies and procedures; ensure qualified and trained nursing staff; provide activities to meet resident's needs and interests; provide healthful and tasty food, housekeeping and laundry services, and emergency call systems; maintain a safe environment.

Memberships:

- American Association of Homes and Services for the Aging (AAHSA) represents not-for-profit organizations committed to providing high-quality health care, housing, and services to the elderly. AAHSA, 901 E St. NW, Suite 500, Washington, DC 20004-2011. Ph: (202) 783-2242. Fax: (202) 783-2285. *http://www.aahsa.org*
- Rhode Island Association of Facilities and Services for the Aging (RIAFSA) is an AAHSA Affiliated State Association. RIAFSA, 210 Cahir St., Providence, RI 02903-4039. Ph: (401) 453-0040. Fax: (401) 453-1160
- National Association of Senior Living Industries (NASLI).
- Alzheimer's Association (AA).
- Rhode Island Health Care Association (RIHCA).
- American Health Care Association (AHCA).

Accreditations

- Continuing Care Accreditation Commission (CCAC) accredits facilities that offer seniors a contract or contracts that provide residential living and health care services for the remainder of the person's lifetime and meet CCAC's accreditation standards.
- Joint Commission on the Accreditation of Healthcare Organizations (JCAHO) is an independent, not-for-profit organization, and the nation's oldest and largest standards-setting and health care accrediting institution.

Northeast

Beechwood at Laurelmead

353 Blackstone Blvd.
Providence, RI 02906

Ph: (401) 273-6565
Fax: (401) 273-6568

AL: Yes. SNF: Yes. ALZ/MEM IMP: Yes

Nondenominational; for-profit; locally owned; affiliated with Care New England. Apartments and private and semiprivate rooms. 24-hour nursing care; skilled nursing care; physical, occupational, speech, and respiratory therapies; wound and pain care management; hospice; IV services; X-ray services; wellness program; Medicare-approved; personal care; medication administration; security; emergency response system; maintenance; transportation; up to 3 daily meals; housekeeping and laundry services; fitness center; exercise program; swimming pool; social, educational, and recreational activities; library; game room; shopping and medical centers nearby; gardens; walking paths; barber/beauty shop.

AL Services: $2,750–$3,850. AL MO: $2,900–$5,300; 2nd person 15% discount in mo. rent. ALZ/MEM IMP MO: $3,850–$4,650. SNF Daily: $195–$215.

Cedar Crest Nursing Center, JCAHO

125 Scituate Ave.
Cranston, RI 02921

Ph: (401) 944-8600
Fax: (401) 944-5162

SNF: 45. HSP: 22. LTC: 40

Age 18+. For-profit; nondenominational. Private and semiprivate rooms. Skilled nursing care; therapy room; pharmacy; dental and podiatry services; Medicare/Medicaid-approved; security; emergency response system; maintenance; transportation; 3 daily meals; pets allowed; housekeeping and laundry services; hair care.

SNF Daily: $155–250.

Cortland Place

20 Austin Ave.
Greenville, RI 02828

Ph: (401) 949-3880 (NH), 949-3882 (AL)
Fax: (401) 949-4170

IND: Yes. AL: Yes. SNF: Yes. ALZ/MEM IMP: Yes (total residents: 160+)

For-profit; nondenominational. Studios and apartments. 24-hour skilled nursing care; respite care; physical, occupational, and speech therapies; respiratory therapy; full medical service; wellness programs; personal care; medication administration; security; emergency response system; maintenance; transportation; up to 3 daily meals; housekeeping and laundry services; exercise room; chapel; library; activities program; gift shop; walking paths; beauty/barber shop.

Contact facility for fees.

Hattie Ide Chaffee Home

200 Wampanoag Trail
East Providence, RI 02915

Ph: (401) 434-1520

NH: 56

Nonprofit; nondenominational. Private and semiprivate rooms. 24-hour nursing care; staff physician; physical, occupational, and speech therapies; IV and respiratory therapies; security; nurse call systems; up to 3 daily meals; housekeeping and laundry services; entertainment and recreational activities; beauty/barber shop.

NH Daily: $180 and $200.

Medway Place

229 Medway St.
Providence, RI 02906

Ph: (401) 751-3582

IND: 30

Bethany Home, AAHSA

111 S. Angell St.
Providence, RI 02906

Ph: (401) 831-2870

SNF: 31

Voluntary; not-for-profit; nondenominational. IND and SNF on same property. Two-bedroom condos, and private rooms (except for one) with private showers. 24-hour skilled nursing care; long and short-term care; emergency call response system; medical transportation; up to 3 daily meals; housekeeping, laundry, and linen services; library; activities director; residence council; social and recreational activities; beauty/barber services.

IND Assoc Fee: $3,850. IND ENT: $192,500. IND MO: $900. NH Daily: (semiprivate), $190; (private), $200.

St. Elizabeth Home, JCAHO

109 Melrose Place
Providence, RI 02907

Metacom Manor Health Center

One Dawn Hill
Bristol, RI 02809

Ph: (401) 941-0200
Fax: (401) 254-1919

NH: 109. SNF: 132. AL/MEM IMP: 43

Nonprofit; nondenominational; nonsectarian. Mini-suites, private and semiprivate rooms. Skilled nursing care; rehabilitation program; long- and short-term care; hospice; management of chronic illnesses; dental office; regular visits by optometrists and podiatrists; pharmacy; 3 daily meals; fitness classes; activity director and recreational therapist; laundry services; chapel; intergenerational program; bingo; Bible study; lounges; greenhouse; hair care

SNF Daily: $170; $190; $200. NH Daily: $160; $180; $190. ALZ/MEM IMP: $165; $185; $195.

Scandinavian Home, AAHSA, RIAFSA

1811 Broad St.
Cranston, RI 02905

Ph: (401) 461-1433

NH: 70

Nonprofit facility; nondenominational. Private and semiprivate rooms. 24-hour nursing care; registered and licensed nurses; certified nursing assistants; physical, occupational, and speech therapies; dental and vision care; social worker; maintenance; 3 daily meals; housekeeping and laundry services; social and recreational activities; chaplain; resident council; crafts; off-site excursions.

NH Daily: $165; $170; $175.

United Methodist Retirement Center

40 Irving Ave.
East Providence, RI 02914

Ph: (401) 438-4456

IND: 117. AL: 25. HCC: 84

Age 62+. Nonprofit; nondenominational. Apartments, studios, private and semiprivate rooms. Skilled nursing and rehabilitative care; 24-hour nursing care; medical director; Medicare/Medicaid-approved; podiatry, dental, and eye care; lab and X-ray services; pharmacy; hospice; social services; long- and short-term care; physical, occupational, and speech therapies; personal care; medication administration; security; emergency response system; maintenance; transportation; up to 3 daily meals; housekeeping and laundry services; exercise classes; multidenominational chapel and services; resident council; scheduled activities; off-site excursions; country store; barber/beauty shop.

Residents must have annual income less than $26,250 (single); $30,000 (couple). IND MO: $350–$550. AL: $18/hour (max of 3.5 hours/week). HCC Daily: $160–$225.

Waterview Villa Nursing and Rehabilitation Center, RIHCA, AHCA

1275 S. Broadway
East Providence, RI 02914

Ph: (401) 438) 7020
Fax: (401) 438-0013

http://www.rihca.com/waterviewvilla

E-mail: *lynnw@ids.net*

SNF: 88. ALZ/MEM IMP: 44

For-profit. Semiprivate rooms. Skilled nursing care; IV therapy, wound care; trachea care, lab, and X-ray services; dental and podiatry services; pharmacy; Medicare/Medicaid-approved; security; emergency response system; maintenance; transportation for medical appointments; up to 3 daily meals; housekeeping and laundry services; monthly restaurant night; activities program; weekly cocktail hour with entertainment; fish tank in lobby; barber/beauty shop.

SNF Daily: $155.

South

Village Retirement Community, ALFA, AA, NASLI

75 Minnesota Ave.
Warwick, RI 02888

Ph: (401) 737-7222

http://www.villageretirement.com

IND: Yes. AL: Yes. HCC: Yes. ALZ/MEM IMP: Yes

For-profit; nondenominational. Private rooms. Respite care; home health services; wellness program; on-site physician; registered nursing care; 24-hour medical care; podiatry and dental care; lab services; therapeutic activities; personal care; medication administration; 24-hour security; emergency pull cords; maintenance; transportation; up to 3 daily meals; housekeeping services; exercise programs; banking services; club rooms; computer center; greenhouse; fishing; gardens; activities director; boating; entertainment; off-site excursions.

East

John Clarke Retirement and Nursing Center

600 Valley Rd.
Middletown, RI 02842

Ph: (401) 846-0743
Fax: (401) 848-5890

E-mail: *jcrcretire@aol.com*

RC: 50. HCC: 60

Nonprofit; nonsectarian; nondenominational. Apartments, and private and semi-private rooms. Skilled nursing care; physical, occupational, and speech therapies; respite care; security; emergency call system; maintenance; transportation; up to 3 daily meals; housekeeping and laundry services; exercise room; chaplain; craft room; activities director and program; weekly sightseeing trips; resident council; hair care.

DEP: One mo. rent. RC MO: $800 and $850. HCC Daily: $150; $155; $160.

Silver Creek Manor, RIHCA, AHCA

7 Creek Lane
Bristol, RI 02809-2499

Ph: (401) 253-3000
Fax: (401) 254-1289

SFN: Yes (total residents, 128). REHAB: Yes. RSP: Yes. ALZ/MEM IMP: Yes

Private and semiprivate rooms. 24-hour nursing care; visiting physicians; X-rays, EKGs and ultrasounds performed in-house; physical, occupational, and speech therapies; Medicare/Medicaid-approved; security; emergency response system; transportation; 3 daily meals; housekeeping and laundry services; scheduled activities; religious program; intergenerational program; pet therapy; music and art programs.

SNF: (semiprivate), $140; (private), $145.

Assisted Living and Residential Care Facilities

These facilities provide room and board for ambulatory and independent adults who need minimum support.

Types of Authorization

Licensing and/or Certification

Requires licensing by the Department of Health, Division of Facilities Regulation. These facilities must provide housing, meals, 24-hour supervision, some personal care assistance, medication management, and housekeeping and other related services.

Memberships

- Assisted Living Federation of America (ALFA) is a national nonprofit membership organization whose mission is to enhance the quality of life in assisted living facilities and promote the interests of the assisted living industry. ALFA, 10300 Eaton Place, Suite 400, Fairfax, VA 22030. Ph: (703) 691-8100. Fax: (703) 691-8106. *http://www.alfa.org*
- The Rhode Island Assisted Living Association (RIALA) is a state affiliate of ALFA. RIALA, 239 New Meadow Rd., Barrington, RI 02806. Ph: (800) 309-9093 or (401) 247-2796. Fax: (401) 245-9630.

Northeast Pocasset Lodge

12 Old Pocasset Lane
Johnston, RI 02919

Ph: (401) 421-6610

AL: Yes

Retirement community owned and managed by Holiday Retirement Corp; for profit; nondenominational. Apartments. Medication monitoring; emergency call system; transportation; 3 daily meals; laundry and housekeeping services; exercise room; wellness clinic; religious services; utilities; all purpose room; library; lounge; activities director; movies; seminars/classes; games; concerts; bridge; arts and crafts; walking paths; hair care.

AL MO: $1,250–$2,525; 2nd person, $375.

St. Joseph Living Center

153 Dean St.
Providence, RI 02903

Ph: (401) 272-3335

IND: Yes. AL: Yes. RSP: Yes

Affiliate of St. Hospital; nondenominational. Private and semiprivate rooms. Scheduled physician and podiatrist visits; 24-hour staffing; blood pressure monitoring; personal care; medication administration; security; emergency response system; maintenance; transportation; up to 3 daily meals; housekeeping and laundry services; religious services; social and educational programs; activities director; entertainment; beauty/barber salon.

IND: $1,150–$1,875. AL: $2,000–$3,575. RSP Daily: $95 and $110.

Village Retirement Communities, ALFA, CALA

715 Putnam Pike
Greenville, RI 02828

Ph: (401) 949-4901
Fax: (401) 934-2955

http://www.villageretirement.com

E-mail: *info@villageretirement.com*

IND: Yes. AL: Yes. ALZ/MEM/IMP: Yes

Age 65+; must be ambulatory. For-profit; nondenominational. Apartments and condos. Nursing care; medical services; personal care; medication administration; pharmacy services; security; emergency response system; maintenance; transportation; up to 3 daily meals; housekeeping and laundry services; exercise area; activities director; scheduled activities; clubrooms; library; computer center; putting green; gazebo; convenience store; barber/beauty salon.

DEP: $500 ($450 ref.). IND MO: from $1,750. AL MO: from $3,000.

Southeast

Blenheim-Newport

303 Valley Rd.
Middletown, RI 02842

Ph: (401) 849-0031
Fax: (401) 849-0199

IND: 61. AL: 42

For-profit facility; nondenominational. Apartments and private rooms. Personal care; medication monitoring; security; emergency call system; maintenance; transportation; up to 3 daily meals (2 daily meals included with IND MO fee); fitness center; housekeeping, laundry, and linen services; library; social and recreational activities; walking trails; gardening; country store.

IND APPL: $500. IND DEP: 1 mo. rent. IND MO: $1,950 and $2,450. AL MO: $3,000–$3,300.

Southwest

The Elms Assisted Retirement Living Facility, ALFA

22 Elm St.
Westerly, RI 02891

Ph: (401) 596-4630
Fax: (401) 348-0113

AL: 75

No age restriction. For-profit facility. Private rooms. Nurse assessment; personal care; medication administration; wellness center; security system; emergency response system; maintenance; transportation; 3 daily meals; pets allowed; housekeeping and laundry services; fitness center; recreational and social activities; library and reading room; gardening areas; walking paths; beauty/barber salon.

DEP: one mo. rent. AL MO: $1,200–$2,750.

Independent Living

Age-restricted communities that offer activities for active adults.

Northeast

Westminster Place, AAHSA, RIAFSA

700 Westminster St.
Providence, RI 02903

Ph: (401) 273-1090 TDD: (401) 769-8027

IND: 149

Age 62+. Nonprofit; nondenominational. One- and two-bedroom apartments. Health clinic; supportive services; eye, ear, and foot care; security; emergency response system; maintenance; transportation; meals on wheels program; pets allowed; housekeeping and laundry services; resident services coordinator; postal services; library; social and recreational activities; activities room; convenience store; coffee shop.

Contact facility for fees (HUD-subsidized).

East

Shalom/Shalom II

One Shalom/Two Shalom Drive
Warwick, RI 02886

Ph: (401) 738-4414
Fax: (401) 738-2490

E-mail: *Shalom@Brainiac.com*

IND: 100 (Shalom), 53 (Shalom II)

Age 62+. Nonprofit. Apartments. Visiting nurse services; security; emergency response system; maintenance; transportation; meal program; pets allowed; housekeeping and laundry services; social and recreational activities; resident services coordinator; tenant association; crafts; convenience store; barber/beauty shop.

IND MO: 30% of income; HUD-subsidized. Income limits: $19,000–$34,000.

South Carolina

http://www.myscgov.com/

General Information

Climate

Temperate. Average winter temperature ranges from the mid-30s°F in the mountains to about 50° F in the south. Summer average temperatures range from the low 70s°F to about 80° F.

Cost of Living

Ranks 41st in the nation.

Taxes

General: Income Tax Assistance, (800) 763-1295. Taxpayer Advocate, (803) 898-5444.

State/Local as % of Income: 9.6%.

Property Tax Reduction: $20,000 Homestead Exemption is available for residents 65 years of age.

Sales: 5%. Sales to those 85 years or older are excluded from 1% of the sales tax.

Prescription Exemptions: Medicines and prosthetic devices sold by prescription and dental prosthetic devices are exempt from a sales tax.

Transportation, Travel, and Tourism

General

Hospitality Association of SC, (803) 765-9000.

Major Airports

- Hilton Head Airport, (803) 525-7154.
- Charleston International Airport, (803) 767-7000.
- Columbia Metro Airport, (803) 822-5000.
- Greenville-Spartanburg Airport, (864) 877-7426.

Railways

- Amtrak, (800) USA-RAIL

Bus Tours

- Greyhound Bus, (800) 231-2222.

State Highways

- Road information and maps, (803) 737-1130.
- Interstates 26 and 95 run north-south.
- Interstate 20 runs east-west.

Theater and Music

Myrtle Beach

- Broadway at the Beach, (843) 444-3200 or (800) 386-4662 (live theaters, restaurants, shops).
- House of Blues, (843) 913-3740 (live music).

Hilton Head

- Self Family Arts Center, (843) 842-ARTS (playhouse theater).

Charleston

- Dock Street Theatre, (843) 720-3968.
- The Charleston Music Hall, (843) 853-2000 or (800) 746-9845 (music variety shows).

Museums, Crafts, Historical, Recreational

Southwest

- Dupont Planetarium, Aiken, (803) 648-6851, ext. 3313.
- Thoroughbred Hall of Fame, Aiken, (803) 642-7630.
- Hopeland Gardens, Aiken (803) 642-7630.

- Houndslake Country Club Azalea Golf, Aiken, (803) 648-3333.

Southeast

- African-American National Heritage Museum, Charleston, (843) 723-1623.
- Gibbes Museum of Art, Charleston, (843) 722-2706.

Low Country/Southeast

- Edisto Beach State Park, Edisto Beach, (843) 869-2156.
- Pinckney Is. Nat'l Wildlife Refuge, US 278, « mile west of Hilton Head, (912) 652-4415.

Old 96 District/West

- Greenwood Museum, Greenwood, (864) 229-7093.
- Poliakoff Collection of Western Art, Abberville, (864) 459-4009.

Olde English District/North Central

- Regent Park (golfing), Fort Mill, (803) 547-1300.

Capital and Lake Murray Area/ Central

- Mann-Simons Cottage (Museum of African American Culture), Columbia, (803) 252-1770.
- SC State Museum, Columbia, (803) 898-4921.
- Northwoods Golf Club, Columbia, (803) 786-9242.

Organizations

Advocacy Groups

- SCSIS (information services for seniors), (800) 922-1107.
- SC Division on Aging, (803) 737-7500.
- Center for Carolina Living (retirement), (803) 782-7466.
- Division of Health and Human Services, (803) 734-0467.

Volunteer Programs

- Points of Light Foundation, Volunteer Center, Charleston, (803) 744-3920; Greenville, (864) 467-3400; Hilton Head, (803) 681-7821.

Housing

Long-Term Care Facilities

In the state of South Carolina, these facilities are called ***Long-Term Care/Nursing Home Facilities.***

These facilities provide residential living and/or various levels of nursing and medical services to seniors for an extended period of time.

Types of Authorization

Licensing and / or Certification

These facilities must be licensed by the Department of Health and Environmental Control. Nursing facilities are defined as facilities with organized nursing care that accommodate two or more unrelated persons over a period of 24-hours and is operated either in connection with a hospital or as freestanding facilities for the express purpose of providing nursing care for persons who are not in need of hospital care. These facilities also provide room, board, and daily activities.

Memberships

- American Association of Homes and Services for the Aging (AAHSA) represents not-for-profit organizations committed to providing high-quality health care, housing, and services to the elderly. AAHSA, 901 E St. NW, Suite 500, Washington, DC 20004-2011. Ph: (202) 783-2242. Fax: (202) 783-2285. *http: / / www.aahsa.org*
- South Carolina Association of Non-Profit Homes and Services for the Aging (SCANPHA) is an AAHSA Affiliated State Association. SCAN-

PHA, PO Box 2708, Myrtle Beach, SC 29578-2708. Ph: (843) 497-3506. Fax: (843) 497-5362.

Accreditations

- Continuing Care Accreditation Commission (CCAC) accredits facilities that offer seniors a contract or contracts that provide residential living and health care services for the remainder of the person's lifetime and meet CCAC's accreditation standards.
- Joint Commission on the Accreditation of Healthcare Organizations (JCAHO) is an independent, not-for-profit organization, and the nation's oldest and largest standards-setting and health care accrediting institution.

Northwest

Martha Franks Baptist Retirement Center, CCAC

1 Martha Franks Drive
Laurens, SC 29360-1799

Ph: (864) 984-4541 or (800) 849-3307
Fax: (864) 984-8074

IND: 55+. AL: 82. HCC: 88. ALZ/MEM IMP: Yes

Sponsored and owned by South Carolina Baptist Ministries for the Aging, Inc.; nonprofit; nondenominational. Cottages, patio homes, apartments, and private and semiprivate rooms. 24-hour skilled nursing care; rehabilitative services; wound care; personal care; medication monitoring; campus security; emergency call system; maintenance; local transportation; up to 3 daily meals (1 daily meal included in IND MO fee); housekeeping, laundry, and linen services; chapel; walking trail; library; resident activities; on-site banking services; beauty/barber shop.

DEP: $1,000. Cottage ENT (ref.): $153,000–$164,000; MO: Single, $1,350; double, $1,775. PATIO HOME ENT: $77,000–$159,500; MO: Single, $1,350–$1,700; double, $1,800–$2,125. Apt. ENT: (apt.), $33,000–$66,000; MO: Single, $1,050–$1,100; double, $1,350–$1,375. AL MO: $1,850, $2,575, and $3,700. HCC Daily: $115–$170.

Presbyterian Home

801 Musgrove St.
Clinton, SC 29325

IND: Yes. RC: Yes. AL: Yes. HCC: Yes

Affiliated with the five presbyteries of the PCUSA in South Carolina; church-related. Cottages, apartments; single rooms with private baths; and semiprivate rooms. Skilled nursing care; short and long-term care; social workers; pharmacy; personal care; medication monitoring; security; emergency call system; maintenance; transportation to local appointments; up to 3 daily meals; all utilities; exercise program; vespers; library; postal services; social activities; activities director; barber/beauty salon.

APPL: (church members), $150/person; (nonmembers), $300/person. RES MO: $1,325–$2,950. IND MO: $1,325–$2,950. AL MO: $2,025 and $2,300. AL RSP Daily: $75. HCC MO: Semiprivate, $3,050 and $3,300; private, $3,375–$3,650. HCC RSP Daily: $130.

REQ: Medical report; church forms; interview.

White Oak Estates

400 Webber Rd.
Spartanburg, SC 29307-3033

Ph: (864) 579-7009
Fax: (864) 579-7714

NH: 88

Private and semiprivate rooms. Intermediate and skilled nursing care; physician services; doctor on call 24 hours; pharmacy; visiting podiatrist; dental services; physical, speech, and hearing therapies; X-ray and lab services; social services; maintenance; 3 daily meals;

housekeeping and laundry services; social and spiritual activities; volunteer program; beauty/barber services.

NH Daily: Semiprivate, $125; private, $140.

North Central

Westminster Towers, CCAC

1330 India Hook Rd.
Rock Hill, SC 29732

Ph: (803) 328-5120
Fax: (803) 328-5140

IND: Yes. AL: Yes. HCC: Yes

Age 62+. Nonprofit; nondenominational; affiliated with the Presbyterian Church. Apartments and private and semiprivate rooms. 24-hour emergency nursing services; nurse consultation; rehabilitative therapies; medical services; dental and podiatry care; pharmacy; personal care; medication administration; security; emergency response system; maintenance; transportation; up to 3 daily meals; housekeeping and laundry services; exercise room; swimming pool; Bible study; library; arts and crafts room; woodworking shop; billiards and game room; on- and off-site activities; convenience store; shuffleboard; horseshoes; picnic areas; gardening; barber/beauty shop.

IND ENT: (ref.) $48,500–$96,000. IND MO: $1,025–$1,750. AL ENT: $22,000. AL Daily: $80. 2nd person ENT, $3,850; MO, $600.

West Central

Wesley Commons

1110 Marshall Rd.
Greenwood, SC 29646-4299

Ph: (864) 227-7140 or (888) 298-6222
Fax: (864) 227-7161

E-mail: *wesleycommons@emeraldis.com*

IND: Yes. AL: Yes. HCC: 102. ALZ/MEM IMP: Yes

Nonprofit; nondenominational; affiliated with United Methodist Church. Villas, apartments, and private rooms. Skilled and intermediate nursing care; emergency care; medical services; short and long-term care; preventative care services; rehabilitative therapies; wellness clinic; health screenings; Medicare/ Medicaid-approved; personal care; medication administration; security; emergency response system; maintenance; transportation; up to 3 daily meals; housekeeping and laundry services; exercise program; library; chapel and religious services; business center; educational and cultural programs; social and recreational activities; residents' council; arts and crafts; card and board games; convenience store; barber/beauty shop.

DEP: $1,000. IND ENT: (50% ref), $99,000–$163,000; (90% ref.), $132,000–$217,000. IND MO: $1,425–$2,050; 2nd person, $525.

South Central

The Methodist Oaks

PO Drawer 327
Orangeburg, SC 29116-0327

Ph: (803) 534-1212
Fax: (803) 535-1540

IND: 156. AL: 42. HCC: 176. ALZ/MEM IMP: Yes

Affiliated with the South Carolina Methodist Conference; nonprofit; nondenominational. Cottages, duplexes, apartments, and private and semiprivate rooms. Intermediate and skilled nursing care; physical, occupational, speech, and respiratory therapy; hospice; on-site pharmacy; social workers; personal care; medication administration; reminders; meal escort; 24-hour clinic; emergency call system; maintenance; up to 3 daily meals; housekeeping and laundry services; chaplain services; library; planned activities; postal and banking services; hobbies and crafts; picnic area; beauty/barber shop.

Pre-ADMN: (no ref.) $100. APPL: $1,000. IND RLUF: (% ref.) $66,000–$110,000. IND MO: (RLUF) $425–$1,200; (rental), $1,100–$2,075. AL MO: $2,050 and $3,575. HCC Daily: (skilled), $135 and $145; (intermediate) $125 and $135.

Trinity Lutheran Home

213 Laurens St.
Aiken, SC 29801

Ph: (803) 643-4200

IND: Yes. AL: 55. HCC: Yes. ALZ/MEM IMP: Yes

Nonprofit; nondenominational; affiliated with Lutheran Homes of South Carolina, Inc., and South Carolina Synod of the Evangelical Lutheran Church in America. Apartments and private and semiprivate rooms. Nursing care; physical, occupational, and speech therapies; wellness care; incontinent care; Medicare-approved; personal care; medication administration; security; emergency response system; maintenance; transportation; up to 3 daily meals; housekeeping and laundry services; fitness room; exercise program; religious services; postal services; reading room; resident lounge; social and recreational activities; gift shop; outdoor courtyard; barber/beauty shop.

IND APPL: (no ref.), $275. IND ENT: (no ref.), $3,300. IND MO: $1,725–$2,200; 2nd person, $330. AL MO: Semiprivate, $60; private, $80. ALZ/MEM IMP: Semiprivate, $75; private, $90.

Southeast

The Cypress of Hilton Head

20 Lady Slipper Lane
Hilton Head, SC 29926

Ph: (843) 689-7000 or (800) 458-8585
Fax: (843) 689-2315

IND: 305. AL: 22. HCC: 44. ALZ/MEM IMP: 11

Age 62+. Nonprofit; nondenominational; managed by Life Care Services Corporation. Homes, apartments, and private and semiprivate rooms. 24-hour nursing care; rehabilitative therapies; pharmacy; dental and podiatry care; wellness program; daily reassurance checks; Medicare/Medicaid-approved; personal care; medication administration; security; emergency response system; maintenance; transportation; up to 3 daily meals; pets allowed; housekeeping and laundry services; fitness center; swimming pool; community hall; on- and off-site activities; hobby and woodworking shops; pet walking; golf course and putting green; croquet course; natural wildlife preserve; lagoons and lakes; picnic areas; barber/beauty shop.

IND ENT: $170,500–$880,000. IND MO: $1,225–$2,450; 2nd person, $725. AL Daily: Nonmember, $140; member, $70. HCC Daily: Nonmember, $140; member, $70.

Life Care Center of Hilton Head

120 Lamotte Drive
Hilton Head Island, SC 29926

Ph: (843) 681-6006
Fax: (843) 681-2853

SNF: Yes. ALZ/MEM IMP: Yes

For profit facility; nondenominational. Private and semiprivate rooms. 24-hour skilled nursing care; personal care; dental, lab, optometry, podiatry, and X-ray services; physical, occupational, speech, and respiratory therapies; hospice; long-

and short-term care; security; nurse call light system; 3 daily meals; housekeeping and laundry services; exercise programs scheduled activities; off-site excursions; barber/beauty shop.

SNF Daily: Semiprivate, $125; private, $150.

The Seabrook

300 Woodhaven Drive
Hilton Head Island, SC 299928

Ph: (843) 842-3747
Fax: (843) 842-7483

IND: 210. HCC: 44

Age 60+. Nonprofit; nondenominational. Condos, apartments, and private and semiprivate rooms. Skilled nursing care; rehabilitative therapies; dental and podiatry care; pharmacy; dermatologist; audiologist; home health services; security; emergency response system; maintenance; transportation; 1 daily meal; pets allowed; housekeeping and laundry services; fitness center; swimming pool; library; social and cultural activities; educational opportunities; group travel; putting green; common rooms; outdoor decks; barber/beauty shop.

Membership: (ref.) $11,000. Purchase: $66,000–$275,000. IND MO: $725–$1,750. HCC Daily: $105–$145.

Central

The Benzie T. Rice Home

100 Finley Rd.
Columbia, SC 29233

Ph: (803) 786-7872

IND: 28. AL: 27. SNF: 20

Nonprofit; nondenominational; affiliated with Lutheran Homes of South Carolina, Inc., and South Carolina Synod of the Evangelical Lutheran Church in America. One- and two-bedroom apartments and private and semiprivate rooms. 24-hour skilled nursing care; long- and short-term care; physical, occupational, and speech therapies; physician services; dental, eye, and podiatry care; weekly health clinic; Medicare-certified; personal care; medication administration; security; emergency response system; maintenance; transportation; up to 3 daily meals; housekeeping and laundry services; exercise room; religious services; therapy room; postal services; library; lounge; social, recreational, and cultural activities; golf course nearby; barber/beauty shop.

IND ENT: (no ref.), $3,300. IND MO: $1,900–$2,925. AL Daily: $95. ALZ/MEM IMP: $100 and $105. SNF Daily: $140.

Covenant Place of Sumter

2825 Carter Rd.
Sumter, SC 29150

Ph: (803) 469-7007 or (888) 297-1212
Fax: (803) 469-7008

IND: 91. AL: 44. HCC: 44. ALZ/MEM IMP: 12

Church affiliated with 8 local congregations; 6 different denominations. Apartments and private and semiprivate rooms. Nursing care; rehabilitative therapies; dental and podiatry care; pharmacy; personal care; medication administration; security; emergency response system; maintenance; transportation; up to 3 daily meals; housekeeping and laundry services; activities.

IND ENT: 1 mo. rent. IND MO: $1,350–$2,400. AL ENT: 1 mo. rent. AL MO: $1,950–$2,100. HCC Daily: $105–$120.

Laurel Crest

100 Joseph Walker Drive
West Columbia, SC 29169

Ph: (803) 796-0370
Fax: (803) 791-1557

IND: 86. AL: 16. SNF: 12

Age 60+. Nonprofit; affiliated with the Associate Reformed Presbyterian Church. Apartments, cottages, and private and semiprivate rooms. Skilled nursing care; rehabilitative therapies; dental and podiatry services; pharmacy services; blood-pressure monitoring; personal care; medication administration; security; emergency response system; maintenance; transportation; up to 3 daily meals; pets allowed; housekeeping and laundry services; exercise equipment; religious services; library; on- and off-site activities; barber/beauty shop.

APPL: (no ref.), $300. ENT: Declining fee, $45,000–$223,500; 50% ref., $106,000–$292,500. MO: Declining fee, $950–$1,825; 50% ref., $1,125–$1,825; 2nd person, $800.

The Lowman Home

2001 Dutch Fork Rd.
PO Box 444
White Rock, SC 29177

Ph: (803) 732-8718

IND: Yes. AL: Yes. SNF: 176

Nonprofit; nondenominational; affiliated with Lutheran Homes of South Carolina, Inc., and South Carolina Synod of the Evangelical Lutheran Church in America. Homes, duplexes, apartments, and private and semiprivate rooms. 24-hour skilled nursing care; physical, occupational, and speech therapies; optometry, podiatry, and dental services; outpatient care; medical director; respiratory therapy; Medicare/Medicaid-approved; personal care; medication administration; security; emergency response system; maintenance; transportation; up to 3 daily meals; housekeeping and laundry services; exercise program; religious services; chapel; postal services; educational classes; intergenerational programs; pet therapy; art therapy; library; arts and crafts room; music; sewing; off-site activities; quilting; gardening; barber/beauty shop.

APPL: (no ref.) $250. IND Cottage ENT: $8,800; IND Cottage $86,000–$137,500; IND Cottage MO: $275. IND Apt. ENT: $3,300; IND Apt. MO: $1,300–$2,150; 2nd person, $330. AL Daily: about $60–$90. SNF Daily: $140–$180.

South Carolina Episcopal Home

PO Box 2959
West Columbia, SC 29171

Ph: (803) 796-6490

IND: 48. AL: 47. ALZ/MEM IMP: 46.
ADC: Yes. HCC: 44

Age 55+. Nonprofit; church-affiliated; nondenominational. Cottages, apartments, and private and semiprivate rooms. Skilled nursing care; physical, occupational, and speech therapies; short- and long-term care; inoculations and blood work; routine health checks; podiatry services; security; emergency response system; maintenance; transportation; up to 3 daily meals; housekeeping and laundry services; chapel and religious services; Bible study; exercise program; activities director; recreational and educational programs; off-site excursions; crafts; movies; gift shop; barber/beauty shop.

APPL: $250/person; $350/couple. ADMN: $7,700/person. IND Cottage ENT: $91,500 (average). IND Cottage MO: $825 and $1,000. IND Apt. ENT: $71,500–$88,000. IND Apt. MO: $1,175–$1,850. AL MO: $1,600–$2,525. HCC Daily: $110 and $115. ALZ/MEM IMP: $3,450. ADC Daily: $25–$35.

Assisted Living and Residential Care Facilities

These facilities provide room and board for ambulatory and independent adults who need minimum support.

Types of Authorization

Licensing and/or Certification

Requires licensing by the Department of Health and Environmental Control.

Memberships

- Assisted Living Federation of America (ALFA) is a national nonprofit membership organization whose mission is to enhance the quality of life in assisted living facilities and promote the interests of the assisted living industry. ALFA, 10300 Eaton Place, Suite 400, Fairfax, VA 22030. Ph: (703) 691-8100. Fax: (703) 691-8106. *http://www.alfa.org*

- South Carolina Association of Residential Care Homes (SCARCH) is a state affiliate of ALFA. SCARCH, 1300 Sumter St., Suite 206, Columbia, SC 29201. Ph: (803) 933-0921. Fax: (803) 933-0923.

Northwest

The Calhoun

402 N. Main
Anderson, SC 29621

Ph: (864) 226-4407
Fax: (864) 231-9661

AL/PC: Yes. ALZ/MEM IMP: Yes. RSP: Yes

Managed by American Housing Lifestyle Communities, Inc.; nondenominational. Private and shared suites. Personal care; medication administration; 24-hour staffing; wellness program; escorts; all utilities (except for phone); security; emergency response system; scheduled transportation; 3 daily meals; housekeeping and laundry services; religious services; activity rooms; lounge; planned daily activities; library; ballroom; lobby and common areas; sun deck; beauty/barber shop.

APPL: $275. AL/PC MO: $1,150–$2,300. ALZ/MEM IMP MO: Semiprivate, $2,050; private, $2,575. RSP Daily: $50–$95.

Fountainside An Eldercare Inn

709 Quillen Ave., PO Box 805
Fountain Inn, SC 29644

Ph: (864) 862-6010

AL/PC: Yes. ALZ/MEM IMP: Yes

Private and shared suites. Personal care; medication monitoring; wellness program; social workers; 24-hour staff supervision; group, pet, and gardening therapies; emergency medical access; emergency call system; maintenance; transportation; 3 daily meals; housekeeping, linen, and laundry services; daily activities; off-site excursions; religious services; shopping and banking services; walking paths; hair care.

AL MO: $1,550–$3,075. PC MO: $1,650–$3,300. (Personal care offers a slightly higher level of care).

Greenville Care Assisted Living

2100 N. Pleasantburg Drive
Greenville, SC 29609

Ph: (803) 322-6212

AL: Yes. RSP: Yes. ALZ/MEM IMP: Yes

Greenville Care, Inc.; a community of independent and active seniors. Private and semiprivate rooms; all with private baths. Personal care; medication administration; nursing care for Alzheimer's unit; physical therapy; 24-hour security; emergency response system; scheduled transportation for medical appointments, community events, and shopping; 3 daily meals plus snacks; housekeeping, linen, and laundry services; library; social and recreational programs; chapel; hair care.

AL MO: Semiprivate, $1,800; private, $2,825. ALZ/MEM IMP MO: Semiprivate, $2,650; private, $3,000. RSP Daily: $95.

Greenville Retirement Center

663 Rutherford Rd.
Greenville, SC 29609

Ph: (864) 233-2672
Fax: (864) 271-8737

AL: 76

A nonprofit facility; nondenominational. Private and semiprivate rooms. 24-hour nursing personnel; medical director; Medicaid certified; therapies; lab and X-ray services; podiatry service;

hospice; personal care; medication administration; call monitoring system; 3 daily meals; housekeeping and laundry services; scheduled activities; holiday events; recreation rooms; hair care.

AL MO: $850–$2,275.

North Central:

Colony House at Fort Mill, ALFA

1036 Maxwell Mill Rd.
Fort Mill, SC 29717

Ph: (803) 548-6680
Fax: (803) 548-6635

AL: Yes. RSP: Yes

Owned and managed by Manorhouse Retirement Centers, Inc. Private and semiprivate rooms with baths. Personal care; 24-hour nursing assistance; medication monitoring; health oversight; respite care; emergency nurse call system; security system; maintenance service; transportation; 3 daily meals; tray service; maid and linen services; laundry service; activities director; exercise rooms; recreational and social programs; beauty/barber shop.

ADMN: $500. MO: $1,825–$3,500. RSP Daily: $75, $95, and $110.

Southeast

Ashley Terrace

1900 Ashley Crossing Drive
Charleston, SC 29414

Ph: (803) 852-0505

AL: Yes. RSP: Yes. ALZ/MEM IMP: Yes

Managed by ServiceMaster Senior Living Services; nondenominational. Suites and apartments. Licensed nurses; personal care; medication administration; 24-hour supervision; reminder service; emergency response system; maintenance; scheduled transportation; 3 daily meals; weekly laundry and linen services; housekeeping; exercise room; intergenerational and volunteer programs; activity rooms; ice cream parlor; lounges; hair care.

RSVF: (ref.) $300. DEP: $800. AL MO: $2,475 and $2,850; 2nd person, $440 and $880. ALZ/MEM IMP MO: $3,075 and $3,450. Additional care MO: $220 and $330. RSP Daily: $110.

The Franke Home at Seaside

1885 Rifle Range Rd.
Mt. Pleasant, SC 29464

Ph: (843) 856-4700
Fax: (843) 856-4730

IND: 50. AL: 86. ALZ/MEM IMP: Yes

Nonprofit; nondenominational; affiliated with Lutheran Homes of South Carolina, Inc, and South Carolina Synod of the Evangelical Lutheran Church in America. Apartments, studios, and private and semiprivate rooms. Outpatient rehabilitation clinic; physical, occupational, and speech therapies; personal care; medication administration; security; emergency response system; maintenance; transportation; up to 3 daily meals; housekeeping and laundry services; fitness center; religious services; chapel/multipurpose room; postal services; arts and crafts room; social and recreational activities; gift shop; courtyard with patio; barber/beauty shop.

APPL: (no ref.), $250. IND ENT: (no ref.), $3,000. IND MO: $1,375–$2,550. AL Daily: $65 and $80. ALZ/MEM IMP Daily: $75 and $85.

East

Myrtle Beach Manor

9547 Hwy. 17 N.
Myrtle Beach, SC 29572

Ph: (843) 449-5283
Fax: (843) 497-0880.

AL: Yes. HCC: 104. ALZ/MEM IMP: Yes. RSP: Yes

A Marriott Senior Living Services community; nondenominational. Studios, apartments, and private and semiprivate rooms. Intermediate and skilled health care; rehabilitation services; onsite doctor; 24-hour nursing care; Medicare/Medicaid certified; pharmacy services; personal care; medication monitoring; wellness clinic; emergency call system; maintenance; transportation for medical appointments, shopping, or entertainment; 3 daily meals; meal trays if required; housekeeping and linen services; all utilities; social and educational programs; religious services; hair care.

AL MO: $2,050–$2,900. HCC Daily: $110–$130.

West Central

Generations

111 Generations Blvd.
Batesburg-Leesville, SC 29006

Ph: (803) 532-8428

AL: Yes

Generations of Batesburg, Inc.; nondenominational. Private and semiprivate rooms with private or hall baths. 24-hour supervision; personal care; medication monitoring; home health care; hospice; security; emergency call system; maintenance; transportation; 3 daily meals; housekeeping, laundry, and linen services; exercise program; religious services; gardening; walking areas; movies; holiday events; special occasion celebrations; multipurpose rooms; lounges; hair care.

AL MO: $1,100–$2,000.

Independent Living

Independent housing (primarily rentals) for seniors that may offer security features, meal service, and activities.

Central

Finlay House/Episcopal Housing Corp.

2100 Blossom St.
Columbia, SC 29205

Ph: (803) 799-6524
Fax: (803) 799-8538

http://finlayhouse.home.mindspring.com

IND: 204

Age 62+. Nonprofit; nondenominational. High rise apartments. 24-hour security; emergency response system; maintenance; transportation; 1 daily meal, Monday–Friday; pets allowed; library; exercise program; volunteer program; resident services director; social, spiritual, physical, and recreational activities; close to University of South Carolina, shopping, and restaurants.

HUD-subsidized; contact facility for fees.

Southeast

Dorchester Village

651 SW Railroad Ave.
St. George, SC 29477

Ph: (843) 563-2915
Fax: (843) 563-4472

IND: 24

Age 62+. Nonprofit; nondenominational. Apartments. Pets allowed; maintenance; parties; luncheons; bingo.

DEP: 1 mo. rent. MO: Sliding scale; HUD-sponsored.

Adult/Resort Communities

Communities for active adults (not all are age-restricted; primarily ownership).

North

The Cliffs

18 Dunmore Lane
Travelers Rest, SC 29690

Ph: (800) 884-2958 or (864) 836-2227

http://www.cliffsgolf.com

Mountain, valley, and lakefront communities. Individual homes, homesites. Golf courses; clubhouse; tennis; swimming pool; fitness center; hiking trails.

PURCHASE: Custom homes, from $385,000; homesites, $55,000–$440,000.

Cross Creek Plantation

PO Box 1378
Seneca, SC 29670

Ph: (800) 858-8465 or (864) 882-0200

http://www.crosscreekplantation.com

Individual homes, homesites. Golf course; clubhouse; tennis; swimming pool; dining; social clubs.

PURCHASE: Homes, from $242,000; homesites, $33,000–$110,000+.

Keowee Key

1390 Stamp Creek Rd.
Salem, SC 29676

Ph: (800) 537-5253

http://www.keoweekey.com

Individual homes, townhomes, condominiums, homesites. Golf course; clubhouse; tennis; swimming pool; fitness center; jogging; lake; boating; fishing; nature trails.

PURCHASE: Homes, $132,000–$1.1 million+; condos, $49,500–$198,000; townhomes, $92,000–$192,500; homesites, $11,000–$324,500.

Central

Cedar Creek

2213 Club Drive, Department WTR
Aiken, SC 29803

Ph: (800) 937-5362 or (803) 642-6087

http://www.cedarcreek.net

Individual custom homes, homesites. Golf course; 1,150 acres of woods and wildlife sanctuaries; nature trails; tennis; swimming; all-sports field.

PURCHASE: Homes, from $143,000; homesites, from $38,500.

Chapel Creek Plantation

PO Box 507
Santee, SC 29142

Ph: (800) 849-9944

Patio homes, villas, homesites. Golf course; hunting; fishing; boating.

PURCHASE: Patio homes, from $132,000; villas, from $88,000; homesites, from $26,000.

Woodcreek Farms

5217 Trenholm Rd.
Columbia, SC 29206

Ph: (803) 865-FARM
Fax: (803) 865-7290

http://www.woodcreekgolf.com

Individual homes, homesites. Golf course; clubhouses; tennis; swimming pools; riding stables; lakes.

PURCHASE: Homes, $220,000–$1.1 million+; homesites, $44,000–$330,000.

Woodside Plantation

1419 Silver Bluff Rd.
Aiken, SC 29803

Ph: (800) 648-3052

http://www.woodsideplantation.com

Golf courses; pro shops; clubhouse; tennis; swimming complex; nature trails; riding stables; dining.

PURCHASE: Homes, from $165,000.

Wyboo Plantation

317 Plantation Drive
Manning, SC 29102

Ph: (800) 951-2605 or (803) 478-7888

http://www.wybooplantation.com

Individual homes, homesites. Golf course; clubhouse; tennis; swimming pool; fishing; hunting; accessible by private plane.

PURCHASE: Homes, from $99,000; golf homesites, from $27,500; lakefront homesites, from $44,000.

East

Debordieu Colony

129 Luvan Blvd.
Georgetown, SC 29440

Ph: (800) 753-5597 or (843) 546-4176

http://www.debordieu.com/

Individual homes, villas, homesites. Golf course; clubhouse; tennis complex; oceanfront beach club; swimming pools; hiking; boating; fishing; dining.

PURCHASE: Homes, $373,000–$902,000+; villas, $296,000–$1.034 million; homesites, $65,000–$660,000.

Tidewater Golf Club and Plantation

4901 Little River Neck Rd.
North Myrtle Beach, SC 29582

Ph: (800) 843-3234 or (803) 249-1403

http://www.tide-water.com

Individual homes, condominiums, homesites. Golf course; clubhouse; swim and racquet club; boating; fishing; oceanfront cabana; social clubs.

PURCHASE: Homes, $140,000
$385,000+; condos, $132,000–$220,000; homesites, $33,000–$220,000+.

West

Savannah Lakes Village

PO Box 1409
McCormick, SC 29835

Ph: (800) 442-2829 or (864) 391-4115

Individual homes, townhomes, homesites. Golf course; activity center; tennis; swimming pool; fitness center; hiking trails; fishing; hunting; bowling; bocce; dining; social clubs.

PURCHASE: Homes, from $143,000; townhomes, from $108,000; homesites, $8,800–$275,000.

Stoney Point on Lake Greenwood

709 Swing About Rd.
PO Drawer 609
Greenwood, SC 29648

Ph: (800) 948-4064 or (864) 942-0108

http://www.stoneypointsc.com

Individual homes, homesites. Golf course; clubhouse; tennis; swimming pool; marina; boating; fishing.

PURCHASE: Homes, from $164,000; homesites, $27,500–$93,500.

South/Southeast

Calawassie Island

PO Drawer 2297
Callawassie Island, SC 29910

Ph: (800) 221-8431 or (843) 987-2100
Fax: (843) 987-2121

http://www.registryone.com/callawassieIsland

Individual homes, club cottages, townhomes, homesites. Golf course; clubhouse; pro shops; tennis; swimming pool; exercise room; billiards; dining; river club; boat dock.

PURCHASE: Homes, $198,000–$770,000; homesites, $49,500–$396,000.

Daniel Island

1183 Daniel Island Drive
Charleston, SC 29492

Ph: (843) 971-7100
Fax: (843) 971-0710
http://www.danielisland.com

Individual homes, homesites. Projected: waterfront parks; docks; town center; recreation areas.

PURCHASE: Homes, from $176,000; homesites, from $49,500.

Dataw Island

PO Box 819
Beaufort, SC 29901

Ph: (800) 848-3838 or (803) 838-3838
http://www.datawislandrealty.com

Individual homes, golf villas, homesites. Golf course; clubhouse; pro shop; tennis; swimming pool; deep water marina; docks; dining.

PURCHASE: Homes (with homesite), $220,000–$550,000+; golf villas, from $148,500; homesites, from $55,000.

Haig Point

PO Drawer 7319
Hilton Head, SC 29928

Ph: (800) 992-3635 or (843) 686-9200

Individual homes, townhomes, homesites. Golf course; clubhouse; pro shop; beach club; swimming pool; tennis and fitness center; equestrian center; dining; general store.

PURCHASE: Custom homes and townhomes, $385,000–$1.1 million+; plantation homes, $253,000–$352,000; homesites, $60,500–$1.045 million.

Indigo Run

PO Box 21307
Hilton Head Island, SC 29925

Ph: (800) 487-2645 or (843) 681-3300
http://www.indigo-run.com

Individual homes, club homes, homesites. Golf course; clubhouses; swim and tennis center; trails.

PURCHASE: Homes, $346,500–$703,000; club homes, from $532,500; homesites, from $159,500.

Spring Island

42 Mobley Oaks Lane
Spring Island, SC 29910

Ph: (800) 242-8175 or (843) 987-2000
http://www.RegistryOne.com/SpringIsland

Individual homes, homesites. Golf course; pro shop; recreation area; tennis; swimming; fitness; sports field; equestrian club; skeet and sporting clays; hunt club; fishing; naturalist program.

PURCHASE: Homes, from $1,635,000; homesites, $275,000–$1.1 million+.

Sun City Hilton Head

127 Sun City Lane
Bluffton, SC 29910

Ph: (800) 978-9781 or (803) 757-8555
http://www.suncity.com/sun/sch/schilthp.htm

Age: 55+. Individual homes, cottages, attached villas. Golf courses; pro shop; village center; tennis club; bocce; bowling; crafts center; computer lab; fitness complex; swimming pools; trails; lake; fishing.

PURCHASE: Homes, $139,000–$310,500; cottages, from $119,000; villas, from $139,000.

Wild Dunes

5757 Palm Blvd.
Isle of Palms, SC 29451

Ph: (800) 562-9453
http://www.navi-gator.com/wilddunes

Individual homes, condominiums, homesites. Golf courses; pro shop; tennis center; swimming pools; fitness club; recreation program; jogging; bike paths; beach; dining; yacht harbor; marina; fishing.

PURCHASE: Homes, $385,000–$2.2 million; condos, $192,500–$880,000; homesites, $165,000–$1.1 million.

South Dakota

http://www.state.sd.us

General Information

Climate

Summer lows around 60° F, highs around 85° F. Winter lows around 10° F, highs around 30° F. Snowfalls of around 6 inches. Spring is rainy, with snow possible through early May.

Cost of Living

Ranks 44th in the nation.

Taxes

State/Local as % of Income: 9.1%

Property Tax Reduction: Must be 65 or older and meet certain income requirements; amount of reduction varies. Call (800) 829-9188 for more information.

Sales: 4%.

Prescription Exemptions: Any prescription authorized by a physician is exempt from sales tax.

Transportation, Travel, and Tourism

General

Department of Tourism, (605) 773-3301.

Major Airports

- Rapid City Regional Airport, (605) 393-9924.
- Sioux Falls Regional Airport, (605) 336-0762.

Railways

- Amtrak, (800) USA-RAIL.

Bus Tours

- Stage Coach West, (888) 343-3113.

State Highways

- Interstate 90 runs east-west.
- Interstate 29 runs north-south.

Theater and Music

- Rapid City Civic Center, (605) 367-7097.
- South Dakota Arts Council, (605) 773-3131.
- Washington Pavilion, Sioux Falls, (605) 367-7397.

Museums, Crafts, Historical, Recreational

Southeast

- Civic Fine Arts Center, Sioux Falls, (605) 336-1167.
- Dakota Territorial Museum, Yankton, (605) 665-3898.
- Jim Savage Western Art Gallery and Museum, Sioux Falls, (605) 332-7551.
- Oscar Howe Art Center, Mitchell, (605) 996-4111.
- Siouxland Heritage Museums, Sioux Falls, (605) 367-4210.

East/Northeast

- Dacotah Prairie Museum, Aberdeen, (605) 626-7117.
- Dakotaland Museum, near Huron, (605) 352-4626.
- Prayer Rock Museum, Ipswich, (605) 448-5625.
- South Dakota Art Museum, Brookings, (605) 688-5423.
- Tekakwitha Fine Arts Center, Sisseton, (605) 698-7058.

Central

- Akta Lakota Museum, Chamberlain, (800) 798-3452.

- South Dakota Cultural Heritage Center, Pierre, (605) 773-3458.
- Lakota Visitors Center at St. Joseph's Indian School, Chamberlain, (605) 734-6021.
- South Dakota Discovery Center and Aquarium, Pierre, (605) 224-8295.

Black Hills, Badlands Area

- Black Hills Visitor Information, Rapid City, (605) 355-3700.
- Crazy Horse Memorial (includes Indian Museum of North America), north of Custer, (605) 673-4681.
- Dahl Fine Arts Center, Rapid City, (605) 394-4101.
- Heritage Center, Red Cloud Indian School, Pine Ridge, (605) 867-5491.
- The Journey Museum, Rapid City, (605) 394-6923.
- Mammoth Site, Hot Springs, (605) 745-6017.
- Mount Rushmore National Memorial Visitor Center, near Keystone, (605) 574-2523.
- Museum of Geology, Rapid City, (605) 394-2467.
- Ruddell Gallery, Black Hills State University, Spearfish (605) 642-6852.
- White River Visitor Center Museum, Badlands National Park, (605) 455-2878.

Organizations

Advocacy Groups

- AARP Midwest Regional Office, (773) 714-9800.
- Senior Info-Line, (800) 211-2116.

Volunteer Programs

- Retired and Senior Volunteer Programs:
- Aberdeen Area RSVP, (605) 225-0082.
- Huron Area Senior Center RSVP, (605) 352-6805.
- Rapid City RSVP, (605) 394-2507.
- Minnehaha County RSVP, (605) 367-7274.

- Foster Grandparent Programs:
- Brown County Commission FGP, (605) 229-1313.

Housing

Long-Term Care Facilities

*In the state of South Dakota, these facilities are called **Continuing Care/Nursing Home Facilities**.*

These facilities provide residential living and/or various levels of nursing and medical services to seniors for an extended period of time.

Types of Authorization

Licensing and/or Certification

These facilities are licensed by the Office of Health Facilities Licensure and Certification, a Division of Health Services. Nursing facilities may be certified by Medicare and/or Medicaid and provide services to those who require nursing care by licensed nurses.

Memberships

- American Association of Homes and Services for the Aging (AAHSA) represents not-for-profit organizations committed to providing high-quality health care, housing, and services to the elderly. AAHSA, 901 E St. NW, Suite 500, Washington, DC 20004-2011. Ph: (202) 783-2242. Fax: (202) 783-2285. *http://www.aahsa.org*

Accreditations

- Continuing Care Accreditation Commission (CCAC) accredits facilities that offer seniors a contract or contracts that provide residential living and health care services for the remainder of the person's lifetime and meet CCAC's accreditation standards.

- Joint Commission on the Accreditation of Health Care Organizations (JCAHCO) is an independent, not-for-profit organization, and the nation's oldest and largest standards-setting and health care accrediting institution.

West

Westhills Village

255 Texas St.
Rapid City, SD 57701

Ph: (605) 342-0255
Fax: (605) 394-3605

http://www.westhillsvillage.com

IND: 202. AL: 31. HCC: 44

Age 62+. Nonprofit; nondenominational. Apartments and private and semiprivate rooms. 24-hour nursing care; skilled nursing care; medical services; rehabilitative therapies; hospice care; respite services; pharmacy services; social services; Medicare-approved; personal care; medication administration; security; emergency response system; maintenance; transportation; up to 3 daily meals; pets allowed; housekeeping and laundry services; religious services; Bible study; fitness center; banking and postal services; library; social and recreational activities; cultural and educational programs; volunteer opportunities; arts and crafts; woodworking shop; bingo; concerts; picnics; walking paths; barber/beauty shop.

IND ENT: (partial refund) $54,500–$153,000. IND MO: $750–$1,600; 2nd person, $325 and $400. AL MO: $2,200.

East Central

Bethel Community

1101 S. Egan Ave.
Madison, SD 57042

Ph: (605) 256-4936 or (888) 256-4539

http://www.bethelcommunity.com

IND: Yes. AL: Yes. HCC: 59. ADC: Yes

Nonprofit; nondenominational; Lutheran Church affiliation. Apartments, suites, and private rooms. Skilled nursing care; medical services; rehabilitative therapies; dental and podiatry care; pharmacy services; personal care; medication administration; security; emergency response system; maintenance; transportation; up to 3 daily meals; housekeeping and laundry services; exercise classes; religious services; Bible study; social and recreational activities; bingo; card games.

Contact facility for fees.

De Smet Good Samaritan Center

411 Calumet Ave.
De Smet, SD 57231

Ph: (605) 854-3327
Fax: (605) 854-3143

http://www.good-sam.com

AL: 12. HCC: 59. ALZ/MEM IMP: 14

Nonprofit. Private and semiprivate rooms. 24-hour nursing care; medical services; rehabilitative therapies; dental and podiatry care; pharmacy services; Medicare/Medicaid-approved; personal care; medication administration; security; emergency response system; maintenance; transportation; up to 3 daily meals; housekeeping and laundry services; social and recreational activities.

AL MO: $1,500–$1,650. HCC Daily: $100–$120.

United Retirement Center

40 S. 1st Ave.
Brookings, SD 57006-1898

Ph: (605) 692-5351
Fax: (605) 692-5982

http://www.brookings.net/~urcpp

RH: 22. AL: 28. HCC: 81. ADC: Yes

Age 65+. Nonprofit; nondenominational. Apartments and private rooms. 24-hour nursing care; skilled nursing care; respite care; medical services; rehabilitative therapies; IV therapy; dental and podiatry care; pharmacy services; home health care services; Medicare/Medicaid-approved; personal care; medication administration; security; emergency response system; maintenance; transportation; up to 3 daily meals; housekeeping and laundry services; fitness center; religious services; library; social and recreational activities; crafts; barber/beauty shop.

RH MO: $1,075. AL MO: $1,800–$3,100. HCC Daily: $100.

Southeast

Pioneer Memorial Hospital and Health Services, JCAHO

315 N. Washington St.
Viborg, SD 57070

Ph: (605) 326-5461
Fax: (605) 326-5734

IND: 20. AL: 10. HCC: 52. ALZ/MEM IMP: 8. ADC: Yes

Age 62+. Apartments and private and semiprivate rooms. Nonprofit; nondenominational; nonsectarian. 24-hour nursing care; medical services; rehabilitative therapies; dental and optometrist clinic; Medicaid-approved; personal care; medication administration; security; emergency response system; maintenance; transportation; up to 3 daily meals; housekeeping and laundry services; pharmacy services; fitness center; social and recreational activities.

IND MO: $875–$1,250. AL MO: $1,800–$2,250 HCC Daily: $100–$110.

Prince of Peace Retirement Community, JCAHO

4500 Prince of Peace Place
Sioux Falls, SD 57103

Ph: (605) 371-0700
Fax: (605) 371-1244

IND: Yes. AL: Yes. SNF: 90

Nonprofit; nondenominational; sponsored by the Presentation Sisters. Apartments and private and semiprivate rooms. 24-hour skilled nursing care; physical, speech, and occupational therapies; long- and short-term care; dementia care; hospice services; outreach screening clinics; home health care services; lab services; Medicare-approved; personal care; medication administration; security; emergency response system; maintenance; transportation; up to 3 daily meals; housekeeping and laundry services; exercise room; religious services; chapel; banking services; social and recreational activities; lounge; gift shop; barber/beauty shop.

IND MO: $800–$1,650; 2nd person, $100. AL MO: $2,075; 2nd person, $660. SNF Daily: $110–$185.

Sioux Falls Good Samaritan Village

3901 S. Marion Rd.
Sioux Falls, SD 57106

Ph: (605) 361-3311

IND: Yes. AL: 26. HCC: Yes. ALZ/MEM IMP: Yes

Nonprofit; nondenominational. Duplexes, apartments, and private and semiprivate rooms. 24-hour nursing care; physical, occupational, and speech therapies; music therapy; skin and wound care; pain management; respiratory therapy; medical services; dental and podiatry care; pharmacy services; Medicare/Medicaid-approved; personal care; medication administration; security; emergency response system; maintenance; transportation; up to 3 daily meals; housekeeping and laundry services; exercise program; religious services; Bible study; social and recreational services; ceramics; resident council support groups; intergenerational program; volunteer opportunities; convenience store; bingo; barber/beauty shop.

DEP: $200. IND MO: $650–$925; 2nd person, $18. AL MO: $1,250–$1,925; 2nd person, $330. HCC Daily: $110–$130.

Assisted Living and Residential Care Facilities

*In the state of South Dakota, these facilities are called **Assisted Living/Congregate housing/Residential Care Facilities**.*

These facilities provide housing, food service, and one or more personal services.

Types of Authorization

Licensing and / or Certification

These facilities are licensed by the Office of Health Facilities Licensure and Certification, a Division of Health Services. Assisted living facilities provide personal care and assistance of daily living to persons who does not require more than intermittent nursing care by a licensed nurse. Congregate housing provides assisted independent living services to persons who may be functionally impaired or socially deprived, but in good health. Residential living centers are not licensed but are required to register with the state to provide services for the elderly who do not require more than meals, room, and daily living services.

Memberships

- Assisted Living Federation of America (ALFA) is a national nonprofit membership organization whose mission is to enhance the quality of life in assisted living facilities and promote the interests of the assisted living industry. ALFA, 10300 Eaton Place, Suite 400, Fairfax, VA 22030. Ph: (703) 691-8100. Fax: (703) 691-8106. *http: / / www.alfa.org*
- Assisted Living Association of South Dakota (ALASD) is a state affiliate of ALFA. ALASD, 520 11th Ave. SE, Watertown, SD 57201. Ph: (605) 882-2045. Fax: (605) 882-0132.

Northeast

Clear View Assisted Living

225 14th Ave. NE
Watertown, SD 57201-1216

Ph: (605) 882-8419
Fax: (605) 882-4961

AL: 16

Nondenominational; owned by Jenkins Living Center, Inc. Private and semiprivate rooms. 24-hour staffing; personal care; medication administration; security; emergency response system; maintenance; transportation; up to 3 daily meals; housekeeping and laundry services; social and recreational activities; whirlpool; barber/beauty shop.

AL MO: $1,800–$2,050.

Evergreen Assisted Living

90 28th Ave. SE
Watertown, SD 57201

Ph: (605) 882-8555
Fax: (605) 882-8556

AL: 10

Non-profit. Private rooms. Nursing care; blood pressure, pulse, and weight monitoring; personal care; medication administration; security; emergency response system; maintenance; transportation; up to 3 daily meals plus snacks; housekeeping and laundry services; exercise program; religious services; social and recreational activities; walking paths; barber/beauty shop.

AL MO: $2,050.

Fay Wookey Memorial Assisted Living Center

700 N. Smith
Clark, SD 57225

Ph: (605) 532-5799
Fax: (605) 532-1320

IND: 6. AL: 32

For-profit. Private rooms. Nurse on call 24-hours; Medicaid-approved; rehabilitative therapies; pharmacy services; personal care; medication administration; security; emergency response system; maintenance; transportation; up to 3 daily meals; pets allowed; housekeeping and laundry services; social and recreational activities; barber/beauty shop.

DEP: $450. ENT: $450. IND MO: $880–$990. AL MO: $1,500–$1,800.

Southeast

The Inn on Westport

4000 S. Westport Ave.
Sioux Falls, SD 57106

Ph: (605) 362-1210
Fax: (605) 361-8866

IND/AL: 133

Age 62+. Nonprofit; nondenominational. Apartments. Nursing care; respite care; wellness program; personal care; medication administration; security; emergency response system; maintenance; transportation; up to 3 daily meals; pets allowed; housekeeping and laundry services; exercise classes; spa; chapel; library; banking services; social and recreational activities; educational and cultural programs; ceramics; koi ponds; sunroom; atrium; sunroom; billiards room; barber/beauty shop.

ENT: $550. IND/AL MO: $1,750–$2,650.

Salem Mennonite Home, ALFAA

106 W. 7th St.
Freeman, SD 57029

Ph: (605) 925-4994
Fax: (605) 925-4764

IND: 4. AL. 50

Age 60+. Nonprofit; Mennonite Church affiliation. Apartments and private rooms. On-call nursing care; 24-hour staffing; personal care; medication administration; security; emergency response system; maintenance; transportation; up to 3 daily meals; housekeeping and laundry services; chapel services; social and recreational activities.

MO: $385–$1,650.

Trail Ridge Retirement Community

3408 W. Ralph Rogers Rd.
Sioux Falls, SD 57108

Ph: (605) 339-9123
Fax: (605) 373-0088

IND: 112. AL: 28

Age 62+. Nonprofit; nondenominational; owned by American Baptist Homes of the Midwest. Studios and one- and two-bedroom apartments. Personal care; medication administration; security; emergency response system; maintenance; transportation; up to 3 daily meals; pets allowed; housekeeping and laundry services; fitness center; religious services; chapel; library; social and recreational activities; hobby and craft center; lounges; courtyards; walking paths; barber/beauty shop.

APPL: (ref.), $1,000. DEP: 10% of ENT fee. IND ENT: $66,550–$135,500. IND MO: $925–$1,750; 2nd person, $450. AL MO: $1,900+.

South Central

Golden Prairie Manor

1145 Prairie Drive, Box 400
Winner, SD 57580

Ph/Fax: (605) 842-0508

IND: 16. AL: 16

Age 55+. For-profit. Apartments and private and semiprivate rooms. Personal care; medication administration; security; emergency response system; maintenance; transportation; up to 3 daily meals; pets allowed; housekeeping and laundry services; library; social and recreational activities; music room; community room; lobby; patio areas.

DEP: $1,000. IND MO: $1,100–$1,600. AL MO: $1,275–$1,600.

Haisch Haus Assisted Living

PO Box 257, 211 N. Garrison
Bonesteel, SD 57317

Ph: (605) 654-9045

AL: 16. ALZ/MEM IMP: Yes

Age 65+. For-profit; nondenominational. Private rooms. Medical services; rehabilitative services; Medicaid-approved; personal care; medication administration; security; emergency response system; maintenance; transportation; up to 3 daily meals; pets allowed; housekeeping and laundry services; exercise program; social and recreational activities.

AL ENT: $100. AL MO: $1,350–$1,500.

West Central

Garden Hills Assisted Living Residence

905 S. 34th St.
Spearfish, SD 57783

Ph: (605) 642-0404

AL: 31

For-profit. Nondenominational. Suites and private rooms. 24-hour staffing; personal care; medication administration; security; emergency response system; maintenance; transportation; up to 3 daily meals; housekeeping and laundry services; exercise room; activity areas; social and recreational activities.

AL MO: $1,725–$2,200

Linkwood Manor

HC73 Box 208
Deadwood, SD 57732

Ph: (605) 578-2058
Fax: (605) 578-7789

AL: 15

Age 60+. For-profit; nondenominational. Semiprivate rooms. Medicare-approved; personal care; medication administration; security; maintenance; transportation; up to 3 daily meals; pets allowed; housekeeping and laundry services; social and recreational activities.

AL MO: $1,650–$2,750.

Sandstone Manor Assisted Living

2010 Windmill Drive
Spearfish, SD 57783

Ph: (605) 642-4910
Fax: (605) 642-4819

AL: 16

Age 55+. For-profit; nondenominational. Private rooms and suites. 24-hour staffing; weight monitoring and vital signs checked; Medicare-approved; personal care; medication administration; security; emergency response system; maintenance; transportation; up to 3 daily meals; housekeeping and laundry services; exercise program; social and recreational program; media room; courtyard; gardening; walking paths; barber/beauty shop.

DEP: 1 mo. rent. AL MO: $1,750–$2,075.

East Central

Greenleaf Assisted Living

201 5 8th St. S.
Brookings, SD 57006

Ph: (605) 692-6311
Fax: (605) 692-6311

AL: 34

Nondenominational. Private rooms. Oxygen supplementation; personal care; medication administration; security; emergency response system; maintenance; transportation; up to 3 daily meals; housekeeping and laundry services; social and recreational activities; community interaction; barber/beauty shop services.

AL DEP: $550. AL MO: $1,625–$2,350.

Lakeside Assisted Living

1010 5th St. W.
Redfield, SD 57469

Ph: (605) 472-2191
Fax: (605) 472-2194

E-mail: *homestead@basec.net*

AL: 22

For-profit; nondenominational. Private room. Medical service; rehabilitative therapies; Medicaid-approved; personal care; medication administration; security; emergency response system; maintenance; transportation; up to 3 daily meals; pet allowed; housekeeping and laundry services; library; social and recreational activities; billiards.

DEP: (partial ref.), $400. AL MO: $1,450–$2,050.

Madison Retirement House

516 N. Highland
Madison, SD 57042

Ph: (605) 256-9049
Fax: (605) 256-3812

RH: 16

For-profit; nondenominational. Private rooms. 24-hour staffing; personal care; medication administration; security; emergency response system; maintenance; transportation; up to 3 daily meals; housekeeping and laundry services; social and recreational activities; adult day care services.

RES MO: $1,350–$1,650.

Independent Living

Independent housing (primarily rentals) for seniors that may offer security features, meal service, and activities.

Southeast

Sunnycrest Village

3900 S. Terry Ave.
Sioux Falls, SD 57106

Ph: (605) 361-1422
Fax: (605) 361-6931

IND: 111

Age 62+. Nonprofit; United Methodist affiliation. Apartments. Security; maintenance; transportation; pets allowed; lounge.

DEP: $110–$275. IND MO: $375–$725.

West

Juniper Court

1121 Tenth St.
Spearfish, SD 57783

Ph: (605) 642-4744
Fax: (605) 642-0620

IND: 14

Age 62+. Nonprofit; nondenominational. Apartments. Maintenance; transportation; pets allowed; social and recreational activities.

DEP: $200. IND MO: $650–$700.

Hickory House

430 Oriah Drive
Spearfish, SD 57783

Ph: (605) 642-4744
Fax: (605) 642-0620

IND/CONG: 86

Age 62+. Nonprofit; nondenominational. Apartments. 24-hour emergency response system; maintenance; transportation; meal program; pets allowed; social and recreational activities; barber/beauty shop.

DEP: $300. IND/CONG MO: $330–$625.

Tennessee

http://www.state.tn.us

General Information

Climate

For most of the state, average winter temperatures are in the 30s°F and average summer temperatures are in the 80s°F.

Cost of Living

Ranks 39th in the nation.

Taxes

State/Local as % of Income: 8.5%.

Property Tax Reduction: Residents 65 or older whose yearly income is $11,130 or less may qualify for property tax relief. The relief amount varies depending upon property assessment and county/city tax rate.

Sales: 6%.

Prescription Exemptions: Prescription drugs are exempt from sales tax.

Transportation, Travel, and Tourism

General

Department of Tourism, (800) 491-TENN.

Major Airports

- Memphis International Airport, (901) 922-8000.
- Nashville International Airport, (615) 275-IFLY (4359).
- Metropolitan Knoxville Airport Authority, (423) 970-2773.

Railways

- Amtrak, (800) USA-RAIL.

Bus Tours

- Greyhound Bus, (800) 231-2222.

State Highways

- Interstates 65 and 24 run north-south.
- Interstate 40 runs east-west.

Theater and Music

East

- Bessie Smith Hall, Chattanooga, (423) 757-0020 (performance hall and research library).
- Chattanooga Theater Center, Chattanooga, (423) 267-8534 (community theater).

Central

- Country Music Hall of Fame, Nashville, (615) 256-1639 or (800) 816-7652 (tours of Music Row).
- Tennessee Performing Arts Center, Nashville, (615) 782-4000 (home to Nashville Symphony, Ballet, and Orchestra).
- Chaffins Barn Dinner Theater, Nashville, (615) 646-9977 or (800) 565-3292 (Nashville's oldest professional theater in the round).
- Grand Ole Opry, Nashville, (615) 889-6611 (live weekly radio show).

West

- Circuit Playhouse, Memphis, (901) 726-4656 (community theater).
- Theater Memphis, (901) 682-8601 or 8383.
- Memphis Blues City Cultural Center, (901) 942-7707 (plays and concerts that present African-American perspectives).

Museums, Crafts, Historical, Recreational

East

- Audubon Acres, Chattanooga, (423) 892-1499 (130-acre natural and cultural history education center).
- Chattanooga Choo Choo, Chattanooga, (423-266-5000 or (800) 872-2529 (30-acre vacation complex with 1900s train station, gardens, pools, restaurants).
- Hunter Museum of Art, Chattanooga, (423) 267-0968.

Central

- Nashville Zoo, (615) 370-3333.
- Radnor Lake State Natural Area, near Nashville, (615) 373-3467 (walking trails, bird watching).
- Springhouse Golf Club at Opryland USA, Nashville, (615-871-7759.
- Aaron Douglas Gallery, Nashville, (615) 329-8720 (African Art collection).
- Belle Meade Plantation, Nashville, (800) 270-3991 (19th century Thoroughbred stud farm, antebellum mansion).
- Bicentennial Mall State Park, Nashville, (888) TN-PARKS.

West

- Memphis Botanical Gardens, (901) 685-1566 (96 acres of outside gardens).
- Graceland, Memphis, (901) 332-3322 (Elvis's mansion).
- Memphis Carriage Tours, (901) 527-7542 (horse-drawn carriages through Beale Street and downtown).
- Chucalissa Archaeological Museum, Memphis, (901) 785-3160 (Native Indian artifacts.)
- Memphis Queen Riverboats, (901) 527-5694 or (800) 221-6197 (sightseeing, sunset dinners).
- Memphis Brooks Museum of Art, (901) 722-3500.

Organizations

Advocacy Groups

- Qualified Medicare Beneficiary Hotline, (800) 624-5547.
- Adult Protective Services Hotline, (888) APS-TENN.
- Department of Human Services, (615) 313-4700.

Volunteer Programs

- Tennessee Aquarium, Chattanooga, (423) 785-3057 (volunteers help visitors at aquarium).
- East Tennessee Historical Society Volunteers, Knoxville, (423) 544-5732 (volunteers assist with guided tours, exhibits, collection, and research).

Housing

Long-Term Care Facilities

*In the state of Tennessee, these facilities are called **Long-Term Care/Nursing Home Facilities**.*

These facilities provide residential living and/or various levels of nursing and medical services to seniors for an extended period of time.

Types of Authorization

Licensing and/or Certification

These facilities must be licensed by the Division of Health Care Facilities.

Memberships

- American Association of Homes and Services for the Aging (AAHSA) represents not-for-profit organizations committed to providing high-quality health care, housing, and services to the elderly. AAHSA, 901 E St. NW,

Suite 500, Washington, DC 20004-2011. Ph: (202) 783-2242. Fax: (202) 783-2285. *http://www.aahsa.org*

- Tennessee Association of Homes and Services for the Aging (TAHSA) is an AAHSA Affiliated State Association. TAHSA, 500 Interstate Blvd. S., Nashville, TN 37210-4634. Ph: (615) 256-1800. Fax: (615) 726-3082.

Accreditations

- Continuing Care Accreditation Commission (CCAC) accredits facilities that offer seniors a contract or contracts that provide residential living and health care services for the remainder of the person's lifetime and meet CCAC's accreditation standards.
- Joint Commission on the Accreditation of Healthcare Organizations (JCAHO) is an independent, not-for-profit organization, and the nation's oldest and largest standards-setting and health care accrediting institution.
- Educational Assessment Guidelines Leading toward Excellence (EAGLE) is a voluntary self-assessment and peer review evaluation system developed by the United Methodist Association of Health and Welfare Ministries.

Central

Adams Place

1925 Memorial Blvd.
Murfreesboro, TN 37129

Ph: (615) 904-7100
Fax: (615) 904-7333

IND: 90. AL: 84. HCC: Yes

Age 55+. Owned and operated by National HealthCare, L.P.; nondenominational; nonsectarian. Apartments, studios, and private and semiprivate rooms. Skilled nursing care; long- and short-term care; physical, speech, occupational, and respiratory therapies; 24-hour nursing care; personal care; medication monitoring; security; emergency call system; up to 3 daily meals (1 meal included with IND MO fee); housekeeping and laundry services; indoor pool; library; lounge area; billiards room; banking services; investment center; arts and crafts room; walking paths; hair care.

IND ENT: (90% ref.) $139,000–$304,000; 2nd person, $11,000. IND MO: $1,175–$2,525; 2nd person, $440. AL Daily: Studios, $65–$95; apts., $105–$145. HCC Daily: Semiprivate, $110; private, $135; skilled/rehab, $375.

Lakeshore, The Meadows

8044 Coley Davis Rd.
Nashville, TN 37221

Ph: (615) 646-4466

IND: Yes. AL: Yes. SNF: Yes. ALZ: Yes

Nonprofit; nondenominational; Christian community. Homes and private and semiprivate rooms. 24-hour nursing care; physical, occupational, and speech therapies; social worker; medical director; IV therapy; dental and podiatry services; personal care; pharmacy services; medication administration; vital signs monitoring; up to 3 daily meals; housekeeping and laundry services; chapel services; planned daily activities; library; clubhouse; hair care.

Homes: from $88,000; MO Maintenance: $100. SNF Daily: $100, $115, and $140.

McKendree Village, EAGLE, JCAHO

4343-47 Lebanon Rd.
Hermitage, TN 37076

Ph: (615) 871-8297
Fax: (615) 871-8697

IND: Yes. AL: Yes. HCC: Yes. AL/MEM IMP: 50

Age 55+. Nonprofit; nondenominational; affiliated with the United Methodist Church. Apartments, cottages, and private and semiprivate rooms. Gerontological professional staff; skilled nursing care; intermediate care; rehabilitation program; special care unit; long- and short-term care; aquatic therapy; social worker; orthopedic, stroke, and cardiac recovery; home health services; dental and podiatry services; personal care; medication monitoring; 24-hour security; wellness program; transportation; up to 3 daily meals; housekeeping and laundry services; recreational, social, and spiritual programs; volunteer program; beauty/barber shop.

APPL: (non-ref.), $1,000. DEP: $550. Cottage ENT: from $88,000 plus MO fees. Apt ENT: (1-time payment refundable use fee [RUF]), $48,500–$119,500; MO: $700–$1,850. Apt. Lease MO: $1,150–$3,100. RUF applies credit to HCC fees; monthly leasing does not. HCC MO: $3,025–$4,675. RSP Daily: $215, $225–$230.

East

Briarcliff Health Care Center

100 Elmhurst Drive
Oak Ridge, TN 37830

Ph: (423) 481-3367

SNF: Yes

Long-term nursing care facility. Private and semiprivate rooms. 24-hour care; registered nurses, LPNs, and certified nurse technicians; physical, occupational, and speech therapies; IV treatment; wound care; respiratory therapy; enteral therapy; pharmacy, dental, optometry, podiatry, and psychiatric services; nurse call system; social services; 3 daily meals; laundry services; spiritual services; special occasion events; exercise programs; arts and crafts; music; resident and family councils; community activities; hair care.

SNF Daily: Semiprivate, $110; private, $115.

Oak Ridge Retirement Community

360 Laboratory Rd.
Oak Ridge, TN 37830

Ph: (615) 546-2263

IND: Yes. AL: Yes. SNF: Yes. ALZ/MEM IMP: Yes

A continuing care community. Apartments and private and semiprivate rooms. 24-hour nursing care; registered and licensed practical nurses; music therapy; therapeutic recreation specialist; social worker; personal care; medication administration; companionship services; vital signs monitoring; escort to meals/activities; 24-hour security; emergency call system; up to 3 daily meals; laundry and housekeeping services; hot tub; exercise program; library; gift shop; walking areas; educational, social, and cultural programs; volunteer programs; clubs and organizations; hair care.

Maintenance fee: (50% ref. up to 3 mos.), $1,850–$14,575. IND MO: $1,175–$2,475. AL MO: $1,500–$2,825.

North

The Windsor House

3425 Knight Rd.
Whites Creek, TN 37189

Ph: (615) 876-2754
Fax: (615) 876-9499

SNF: 127. ICF: Yes

For seniors needing short-term skilled care or long-term intermediate care. For-profit nursing home; nondenominational. Semiprivate rooms. 24-hour nursing care; physical, occupational, and speech therapies; personal care; medication administration; security system; emergency call system; maintenance; transportation; 3 daily meals; housekeeping and laundry services; social, religious, recreational, and educational activities.

ICF Daily: $105. SNF and REHAB Daily: $185.

Northeast

Appalachian Christian Village

Sherwood
2012 Sherwood Drive, Johnson City, TN 37601

Ph: (423) 928-3168
Fax: (423) 232-8240

Pine Oaks

213 University Parkway, Johnson City, TN 37604

Ph: (423) 232-5500
Fax: (423) 232-5505

IND: 188. AL: 80. ALZ/MEM IMP: Yes. ICF: 103

Age 62+. A Christian not for profit facility; nondenominational. Townhomes, cottages, studios, apartments, and private and semiprivate rooms. 24-hour nursing care; rehabilitative therapies; personal care; medication reminders; respite care; dental clinic; social workers; weekly health checks; security; 24-hour emergency assistance; maintenance; transportation; up to 3 daily meals; housekeeping and laundry services; exercise program; social, educational, cultural, recreational, and spiritual activities; library; chapel; bank and postal services; clubs; volunteer program; hobby room; beauty/barber salon.

IND ENT: (% ref.), $8,250–$39,500. IND MO: (with entry fee), $600–$1,025; (without entry fee), $800–$1,250. AL MO: $1,375–$2,600; assistance levels 1–3, $330 or $660 or $990 additional per mo. RSP Daily: $85. ICF Daily: $100 and $115.

Life Care Center

1610 Hwy. 19E
Elizabethton, TN 37643

Ph: (423) 542-4133
Fax: (423) 542-3874

SNF: Yes. ICF: Yes. REHAB: Yes

Nondenominational. Private and semiprivate rooms. 24-hour skilled nursing care; personal care; medication administration; dental, lab, optometry, podiatry, and X-ray services; physical, occupational, speech and hearing, and respiratory therapies; security; nurse call light system; 3 daily meals; exercise classes; religious services; social and recreational activities; crafts; lounges; beauty/barber salon.

SNF Daily: $160. ICF Daily: $95 and $105.

South

Alexian Village of Tennessee, CCAC

100 James Blvd.
Signal Mountain, TN 37377

IND: 277. AL: 33. SNF: 114. ALZ/MEM IMP: 42. ADC: 20

Age 62+. Nonprofit; Catholic Church sponsored; nondenominational. Apartments, suites, and private and semiprivate rooms. 24-hour nursing care; personal care; medication administration; social services; health assessment; recreational therapies; Medicare/Medicaid-approved; security; emergency response system; maintenance; transportation; up to 3 daily meals (1 meal included in IND MO fee); pets allowed; housekeeping and laundry services; chapel and religious services; banking services; health club; pool; game room; auditorium and meeting room, arts and crafts; pottery and ceramics; woodwork shop; cafe and convenience store; beauty/barbershop.

APPL: $2,200. IND RLUF: (% ref. for 10 yrs.) $57,500–$192,500. IND MO: $1,000–$2,325. AL MO: $2,050–$2,550. ALZ/MEM IMP: $2,650. SNF Daily: $115–$195. ADC Daily: $35.

St. Barnabas Nursing Home and Apartments

W. Sixth at Pine St.
Chattanooga, TN 37402

Ph: (615) 267-5320

IND: Yes. NH: Yes

Episcopal owned; nonprofit; nondenominational. Efficiency apartments and private and semiprivate rooms. 24-hour skilled and intermediate nursing care; long- and short-term care; Medicare-certified; physical, speech, and occupational therapies; individualized resident care planning; pain management; behavior management; psychological and social services; emergency call system; security; up to 3 daily meals; housekeeping and laundry services; library; volunteer committee; family and resident councils; planned activities; Bible study; bingo; sing-alongs; movies; off-site activities; walking paths; hair care.

IND DEP: $475 and $600. IND MO: $475 and $800. NH Daily: Skilled care, $130 and $160; intermediate care, $105 and $135.

Southwest

Trezevant Episcopal Home

177 N. Highland
Memphis, TN 38111

Ph: (901) 325-4000
Fax: (901) 324-5039

IND: 200+. AL: 25. HCC: 104

Nonprofit; nondenominational facility. Cottages (opening summer 1999), studios, apartments, and private and semiprivate rooms. 24-hour emergency nursing service; physician on call; HCC services; personal care; medication administration; physical therapy; podiatry and dental services; clinic; security; maintenance; scheduled transportation; up to 3 daily meals (1 daily meal included in IND MO fee); housekeeping and laundry services; exercise program; chapel; library; banking services; social, cultural, spiritual, and recreational activities; country store; beauty/barber salon.

DEP: Single, $1,100; couple, $1,650. IND ENT: (traditional), $52,000–$233,500; (50% ref.), $70,000–$315,000; (90% ref.), $90,500–$408,500. IND MO: $875–$1,825; 2nd person, $625. NH Daily: (without lifecare), $115 and $150. AL Daily: (without lifecare), $85. Home health care also available for additional fee.

Assisted Living and Residential Care Facilities

In the state of Tennessee, these facilities are called ***Assisted Living/Homes for the Aged****.*

These facilities provide room and board for ambulatory and independent adults who need minimum support.

Types of Authorization

Licensing and / or Certification

Requires licensing by the Department of Health. Must provide long-term residential care, room, board, housekeeping, personal care, and supervision. Homes for the aged, or any adult care facilities, are not licensed to provide any nursing or medical care.

Memberships

- Assisted Living Federation of America (ALFA) is a national nonprofit membership organization whose mission is to enhance the quality of life in assisted living facilities and promote the interests of the assisted living industry. ALFA, 10300 Eaton Place, Suite 400, Fairfax, VA 22030. Ph: (703) 691-8100. Fax: (703) 691-8106. *http://www.alfa.org*

East Markhill Village

700 Markhill Drive
Sevierville, TN 37862

Ph: (423) 428-2445

IND: Yes. AL: Yes. RSP: Yes. ADC: Yes. ALZ/MEM IMP: Yes

Retirement community. Apartments and private rooms. Personal care; medication monitoring; emergency health attention; blood pressure and weight monitoring; licensed nurse on staff; special diets; 24-hour emergency call system; up to 3 daily meals; escort to meals if needed; laundry and housekeeping services; all utilities; fitness and exercise equipment; library and card room; activities; beauty/barber shop.

IND ENT: (50% ref. up to 6 mos.) $7,700–$12,500; MO: $1,175–$2,400. AL DEP: 1st and last mos. rent; MO: $1,825–$2,700. RSP Daily: (room) $85; (apt.) $50 and $55; 2nd person, $15.

Wellington Place

1869 Crest Rd.
Maryville, TN 37804-4304

Ph: (423) 984-3030

AL: Yes. ALZ/MEM IMP: Yes

Wellington Group; nondenominational; nonsectarian. Private and semiprivate rooms. 24-hour assistance; occupational, physical, and speech therapies; personal care; medication monitoring; transportation; 3 daily meals; laundry and housekeeping services; social and recreational activities; health spa and whirlpool; offsite activities; arts and crafts; hair care.

AL MO: $1,650 and $1,850, plus levels of care. ALZ/MEM IMP: $2,450 and $2,750, plus levels of care.

Southeast

The Grand Court

825 Runyan Drive
Chattanooga, TN 337407

Ph: (423) 875-6723
Fax: (423) 875-6882.

IND: Yes. AL: Yes

Privately owned; nondenominational. Suites and apartments. Personal care; medication administration; home health agency referral; 24-hour staff; security; scheduled transportation; up to 3 daily meals; laundry and housekeeping services; planned activities; activities.

IND MO: $750–$1,525. AL MO: $1,500.

Northwest

Park Terrace Village

712 Broadway
South Fulton, TN 38257

Ph: (901) 479-1321

AL: 32

Age 55+. Community owned; managed by Stanley Jones Properties. Private and semiprivate suites. Personal care; medication monitoring; 24-hour supervision; respite care; security; 24-hour emergency call system; health care and wellness plan; transportation; 3 daily meals plus snacks; laundry and housekeeping services; religious services; pool; exercise classes; planned activities; library; lakes; walking paths; games; clubhouse; barber/beauty shop.

AL MO: Semiprivate, $1,100; private, $1,650.

South

Hewitt House

322 E. Washington St.
Pulaski, TN 38478

Ph: (931) 363-2222
Fax: (931) 363-3022
E-mail: *hewitths@usit.net*

AL: Yes. ADC: Yes

Suites, private and semiprivate rooms. Personal care; medication administration; 24-hour supervision; 24-hour security; emergency call system; scheduled transportation; 3 daily meals; housekeeping and laundry services; all utilities; activities director; special events; devotionals; recreational activities.

MO: $1,100–$1,700. ADC: Daily, $45; overnight, $55.

Central

Hearthside at Castle Heights, A Christian Retirement Community

215 Castle Heights Ave. N.
Lebanon, TN 37087

Ph: (615) 443-1994

IND: Yes. AL: Yes

Nonprofit; nondenominational. Private and semiprivate rooms. Personal care; medication administration; security; emergency response system; maintenance; transportation; up to 3 daily meals; housekeeping and laundry services; exercise classes; religious services; Bible study; social and recreational activities; educational program; on- and off-site activities; local senior citizens center nearby; barber/beauty shop.

RSV: (no ref.), $275. AL MO: Semiprivate, $1,650; private, $2,300; couple, $3,300.

Stones River Manor

205 Haynes Drive
Murfreesboro, TN 37129

Ph: (615) 893-5617
Fax: (615) 895-0711

IND: 9. AL: 100. ALZ/MEM IMP: 20. ADC: Yes

Age 65+. Nonprofit; sponsored by the Churches of Christ. Private and semiprivate rooms. Nursing supervision; personal care; medication administration; security; emergency call system; maintenance; transportation; 3 daily meals plus snacks; housekeeping and laundry services; religious services; activities program; community social functions; crafts; off-site excursions; hair care.

IND ENT: $660. IND MO: $1,150 and $1,375. AL ENT: $440. AL MO: $1,425–$3,200. ALZ/MEM IMP MO: $2,425.

Southwest

Heritage Place

29990 Hickory Hill Rd.
Memphis, TN 38115

Ph: (901) 794-8857
Fax: (901) 794-0162

IND: Yes. AL: Yes

Nondenominational; Holiday Retirement Corp. Studios and one- and two-bedroom apartments. Some personal care services; security; emergency response system; maintenance; transportation; up to 3 daily meals; housekeeping and laundry services; on-site manager; exercise room; chapel; library; craft room; social and recreational activities; game room; barber/beauty shop.

DEP: (ref.) $100. IND MO: $1,100–$1,875; 2nd person, $330.

Independent Living

Independent housing (primarily rentals) for seniors that may offer security features, meal service, and activities.

East

CandleRidge Plaza Apartments

3405 Harrow Gate Lane
Powell, TN 37849

Ph: (423) 938-3394

IND: 100

Age 62+. Nonprofit; nondenominational. Apartments. Personal care; medication administration; security;

emergency response system; maintenance; transportation; 1 daily meal; pets allowed; laundry services; library; craft room; media room; pool table; patios; outside grills; close to banks, medical facilities, churches, and shopping.

IND MO: 30% of income; HUD-subsidized.

Southwest

Maple Wood Village Apartments

400 Meadow Lane
Somerville, TN 38068

Ph: (901) 465-9711
Fax: (901) 465-1703

IND: Yes

Nondenominational; managed by Hallmark Management, Inc. Apartments. Blood pressure screening; security; maintenance; transportation; 1 meal on weekdays; exercise program; religious services; Bible study; social and recreational activities; nearby health care facilities, restaurants, and shopping.

Contact facility for fees.

Northwest

Cumberland View Towers

1201 Cheyenne Blvd.
Madison, TN 37115

Ph: (615) 868-8653
Fax: (615) 868-9942

IND: 151

Age 62+. Nonprofit; nondenominational; church affiliated. Rehabilitative clinic; emergency response system; maintenance; transportation; pets allowed; gardening.

DEP: (ref.), $165. IND MO: 30% of income. HUD-subsidized.

Adult/Resort Communities

Communities for active adults (not all are age-restricted; primarily ownership).

East

Baneberry Golf and Resort

704 Harrison Ferry Rd.
Baneberry, TN 37890

Ph: (800) 951-4653 or (423) 674-2500

http://www.baneberrygolf.com

Individual homes, condominiums, homesites. Golf course; tennis; swimming pool; fishing; boating; dining; social clubs.

PURCHASE: Homes, $77,000–$275,000; condos, $87,000–$98,000; homesites, $22,000–$121,000.

Deer Creek

1055 Deer Creek Drive
Crossville, TN 38557

Ph: (931) 456-4658

Individual homes, homesites. Golf course; pro shop; clubhouse; tennis; swimming pool; dining; lake.

PURCHASE: Homes, $143,000–$275,000; homesites, $22,000–$41,000.

Fairfield Glade

PO Box 1500
Fairfield Glade, TN 38558

Ph: (931) 484-3725

Individual homes, condominiums, homesites. Golf course; tennis; swimming pool; trails; biking; fishing; boating; hunting; riding stables; community center; fitness center; lakes; dining; social clubs.

PURCHASE: Homes, $137,500–$275,000; condos, $132,000–$198,000; homesites, $33,000–$66,000.

Old Island

535 Island Rd.
Kingsport, TN 37664

Ph: (423) 279-1700
Fax: (423) 279-1702

http://www.oldisland.com

Individual homes, homesites; projected patio homes and condominiums. Golf course; clubhouse; dining; projected tennis center and swimming pool.

PURCHASE: Homes, from $307,000; homesites; from $54,000.

Rarity Bay

150 Rarity Bay Parkway
Vonore, TN 37885

Ph: (888) 727-4892 or (423) 884-3000
Fax: (423) 884-3001

http://www.raritybay.com

Individual home, homesites. French Country architecture; 10 miles of natural shoreline; golf course; clubhouse; boating; swimming; tennis; trails; equestrian center; community center.

PURCHASE: Homes, $142,000–$549,000; homesites, $40,000–$275,000.

Royal Oaks

PO Box 4729
Maryville, TN 37802

Ph: (888) 681-0194 or (423) 984-9789

http://www.smokymtnmall.com/mall/royaloak.html

Individual homes, golf villas, homesites. Golf courses; clubhouse; pro shop; tennis; swimming pool; conference center; boating; fishing; hiking.

PURCHASE: Homes, $198,000–$275,000+; villas, $137,000–$198,000+; homesites, $33,000–$66,000+.

Tellico Village

100 Chota Center
Loudon, TN 37774

Ph: (800) 646-LAKE or (423) 458-6822

Individual homes, townhomes, homesites. Golf course; recreation center; tennis; racquetball; basketball; swimming pool; fitness facility; fishing; yacht and country club; dining; social clubs.

PURCHASE: Homes, $110,000–$2.75 million+; townhomes, $110,000–$715,000; homesites, $8,800–$412,500.

White Plains Plantation

4000 Plantation Drive
Cookeville, TN 38506

Ph: (931) 537-3953

Individual homes, homesites. Golf course; pro shop; clubhouse; tennis; swimming pool.

PURCHASE: Homes, $165,000–$385,000.

West

Shiloh Falls

PO Box 11
Pickwick Dam, TN 38365

Ph: (901) 689-5288 or (901) 689-5050

Individual homes, homesites. Golf course; tennis; swimming pool; fishing; boating; hunting.

PURCHASE: Homes, $143,000–$1.1 million; homesites, $16,500–$275,000.

Tennessee River Golf Club

384 Riverview Drive
Decaturville, TN 38329

Ph: (901) 852-2583 or (901) 847-3425

Individual homes, homesites. Golf course; pro shop; clubhouse; fishing; hunting; bicycle paths; boating; marinas.

PURCHASE: Homes, $110,000–$330,000; homesites: $27,500–$55,000.

Texas

http://www.state.tx.us

General Information

Climate

Moderate, but widely varied. Average temperatures—Amarillo: January, 35° F; July, 79° F; Dallas–Ft. Worth: January, 43° F; July, 85° F; San Antonio, January, 49° F; July 85° F.

Cost of Living

Ranks 48th in the nation.

Taxes

State/Local as % of Income: 9.0 %.

Property Tax Reduction: Homeowners over 65 may qualify for a $10,000 homestead exemption on the home's value to reduce property taxes; they also qualify for a school tax ceiling to keep school taxes from increasing; they may defer actions to collect delinquent taxes on homesteads (interest is added); and they may pay property taxes in four installments without penalty or interest.

Sales: 6.25%; some localities charge additional tax.

Prescription Exemptions: Prescription medicines and medical equipment are exempt from sales tax.

Transportation, Travel, and Tourism

Major Airports

- Dallas–Fort Worth International Airport, 3200 E. Airfield Drive, Dallas, TX 75261, (972) 574-8888.
- George Bush Intercontinental Airport, 2800 N. Terminal Rd., Houston, TX 77032, (281) 230-3000.
- Fort Worth Mescham International Airport, 4201 N. Main St., Fort. Worth, TX 76106, (817) 871-5400.
- Amarillo International Airport, 10801 Airport Blvd., Amarillo, TX 79111, (806) 335-1671.
- Dallas Love Field, Mainter Building # LB16, Dallas, TX 75235, (214) 670-6073.
- El Paso International Airport, 6701 Convair Drive, El Paso, 79925, TX (915) 772-4271.
- Rio Grande Valley International Airport, Airport Terminal Building, Harlingen, TX 78550, (956) 430-8600.
- William P. Hobby Airport, 7800 Airport Blvd., Houston, TX 77061, (713) 643-4597.

Railways

- Amtrak, stations throughout the state, (800) USA-RAIL.

Bus Tours

- Greyhound Bus, stations throughout the state, (800) 231-2222.
- Durham Transportation, Inc., 9011 Mountain Ridge Drive, #200, Austin, TX 78759, (512) 343-6292.
- El Paso–Los Angeles Limo Express, Inc., 720 S. Oregon St., El Paso, TX 79901, (915) 532-4061.
- Vaught Bus Charters, 5033 Mosson Rd., Fort Worth, TX 76119, (817) 572-2297.
- Texas Bus Lines, 2222 Cleburne St., Houston, TX 77004, (713) 523-8888.
- Bluebonnet Coaches, 8620 Jones Maltsberger, San Antonio, TX 78216, (210) 340-8267.

State Highways

- East-west routes: Interstate 10 from Louisiana through Houston and San Antonio to El Paso; Interstate 20 from Shreveport, LA, to west of Pecos; Interstate 30 from Texarkana

to Ft. Worth; Interstate 40 from Sayre, OK, through Amarillo to New Mexico.
- North-south routes: Interstate 45 from Galveston to Dallas, joining Interstate 35 at Dallas, which runs from Laredo to Oklahoma; Interstate 37 from Corpus Christi to San Antonio; Interstate 27 from Amarillo to Lubbock.

Theater and Music

North

- Amarillo Little Theatre, 2019 Civic Cir., Amarillo, TX 79109, (806) 355-9991.
- Texas Musical Drama, 1514 5th Ave., Canyon, TX 79015, (806) 655-2181.

South

- San Antonio Symphony, 222 East Houston St., #200, San Antonio, TX 78205, (210) 554-1000, box office, (210) 554-1010.
- Paddle Wheeler Flagship (jazz summer weekends, cruises), Peoples Street "T" Head, Corpus Christi, (512) 884-1693.
- Houston International Festival (music, events, food, crafts), every April, 1221 Lamar, Suite 715, Houston, TX 77010, (800) 541-2099.

East

- Fort Worth Early Music, performing in St. Andrew's Episcopal Church, PO Box 101902, Fort Worth, TX 76185, (817) 923-2789.
- Ballet Dallas, 309 S. Pearl, Dallas, TX 75201, (214) 931-8433.
- Dallas Opera, 3102 Oak Lawn Ave., #450, Dallas, TX 75219, (214) 443-1000.
- Dallas Theater Center, 3636 Turtle Creek, Dallas, TX 75219-5598, (214) 526-8210.
- Garland Civic Theatre, 1721 Reserve, Garland, TX 75042-7621, (214) 349-1331.
- Plano Repertory Theatre, PO Box 861859, Plano, TX 75086-1859, (972) 422-7460.
- Brazos Nights summer concert series, June and July, on the Brazos River, Waco, (254) 750-5871.
- Arbor Daze (music, carnival, food), every April, 201 N. Ector, Euless, TX 76039, (817) 685-1821.

West

- Union Dinner Theatre, 302 Union E Bldg., El Paso, TX 79968, (915) 747-6060.
- Shakespeare On-the-Rocks, 3 McKelligon Canyon Rd., El Paso, TX 79930, (915) 565-6900.
- Abilene Community Theatre, 801 S. Mockingbird Ln., Abilene, TX 79605, (915) 673-6271.
- Way Off-Broadway Players, 113 SW Main, Eldorado, TX 76936, (915) 853-2062.

Central

- JAZZ Austin Club, 214 E. 6th St., Austin, TX 78701-3626, (512) 479-0474.
- Austin Symphonic Band, PO Box 49731, Austin, TX 78765, (512) 345-7420.
- The Capital City Men's Chorus, PO Box 50082, Austin, TX 78763, (512) 477-SING (7464).
- La Follia Austin Baroque, performing in First English Lutheran Church, 3001 Whitis Ave., Austin, TX 78705-2997, (512) 892-1326.

Museums, Crafts, Historical, Recreational

North

- Kell House Museum, 900 Bluff St., Wichita Falls, TX 76301, (940) 723-0623.
- Amarillo Museum of Art, 2200 S. Van Buren, Amarillo, TX 79178, (806) 371-5050.
- Panhandle-Plains Historical Museum, WTAMU, Box 60967, Canyon, TX 79016, (806) 651-2244.

South

- Corpus Christi Botanical Gardens, 8545 S. Staples St., Corpus Christi, TX 78413-5900, (512) 852-2100.
- Oso Beach Municipal Golf Course (public), 5601 S. Alameda St., Corpus Christi, TX 78412, (915) 392-2520.
- Big Bend National Park (visitors center, museum, camping hiking, riding), PO Box 129, Big Bend National Park, TX 79834, (915) 477-2251.
- Brazoria County Historical Museum, 100 E. Cedar, Courthouse Square, Angleton, TX 77515; (409) 864-1208.
- San Antonio Missions National Historical Park, 2202 Roosevelt Ave., San Antonio, TX 78210, (210) 534-8833.
- San Antonio Zoo & Aquarium, 3903 N. St. Mary's St., San Antonio, TX 78212, (210) 734-7184.
- The Alamo (historical complex), PO Box 2599, San Antonio, TX 78299, (210) 225-1391.
- Galveston County Historical Museum, 2219 Market, Galveston, TX 77550-1503, (409) 766-2340.
- Texas Seaport Museum and 1877 Tall Ship Elissa, Galveston, (409) 763-1877.
- San Antonio Museum of Art, 200 W. Jones Ave., San Antonio, TX 78215, (210) 978-8100.
- Cedar Creek Municipal Golf Course (public), 8250 Vista Colina, San Antonio, TX 78255, (903) 498-8419.
- The Institute of Texan Cultures and Folklife Festival, every August (music, contests, crafts), 801 S. Bowie St., San Antonio, TX 78205, (210) 458-2390.
- Mission Del Lago Municipal Golf Club (public), 1250 Mission Grande, San Antonio, TX 78214, (210) 381-0964.
- Riverside Municipal Golf Course (public), 203 McDonald, San Antonio, TX 78210, (817) 641-7818.

East

- Cedar Crest Park Golf Course (public), Dallas, TX 75203, (512) 385-4653.
- Sam Houston Memorial Museum, corner of 19th St. and Avenue N, Huntsville, TX 77320, (409) 294-1832.
- White Settlement Historical Museum, 8320 Hanon Drive, White Settlement, TX 76108, (817) 246-9719.
- The Dallas Museum of Natural History, 3535 Grand Ave., Dallas, TX 75210-1006, (214) 421-3466.
- Stevens Park Golf Course (public), 1005 N. Montclair Ave., Dallas, TX 75208, (214) 625-8916.
- Chisholm Trail Round-up/Chief Quanah Parker Comanche Pow Wow, every June, Fort Worth, (817) 625-7005.
- Amon Carter Museum, 3501 Camp Bowie Blvd., Fort Worth, TX 76107, (817) 738-1933.
- Art Museum of Southeast Texas, Main St., Beaumont, TX 77701, (409) 832-3432.
- The Menil Collection, 1509 Sul Ross, Houston, TX 77025, (713) 525-9400.
- Contemporary Arts Museum, 5216 Montrose Blvd., Houston TX 77006, (713) 284-8250.
- Dallas Museum of Art, 1717 N. Harwood, Dallas, TX 75201, (214) 922-1200.
- Strecker Museum (oldest continuously operating museum in Texas), Sid Richardson Science Building, Baylor University, Waco, TX 76798, (254) 710-1110.
- Pioneer Days, every September, Stockyards National Historic District, Ft. Worth, (800) 433-5747.
- Ft. Worth Botanical Garden, 3220 Botanic Garden Drive, Ft. Worth, TX 76107, (817) 871-7686.
- State Fair of Texas, end of September every year, Dallas, (214) 565-9931.

- Log Cabin Village, 2100 Log Cabin Village Rd., Fort Worth, TX 76109, (817) 926-5881.

West

- Guadalupe Mountains National Park (visitors center, camping, hiking, riding), HC 60 Box 400, Salt Flat, TX 79847, (915) 828-3251.
- American Airpower Heritage Museum of the Confederate Air Force, 9600 Wright Drive, Midland, TX 79711, (915) 563-1000.
- The Texas Cowboy Reunion (largest amateur rodeo; dancing, food), every July, Stamford, (915) 773-2411.
- Buffalo Gap Historic Village, Box 818, Buffalo Gap, TX 79508, (915) 572-3365.

Central

- Sammons Golf Course (public), 2220 W. Ave. D, Temple, TX 76504, (915) 651-7395.
- Texas Memorial Museum, University of Texas–Austin campus, 2400 Trinity, Austin, TX 78705-5786, (512) 232-4278.
- Barton Creek Golf (Fazio Course) (public), 8212 Barton Club Drive, Austin, TX 78735, (512) 329-4000.
- Lions Municipal Golf Course (public), 2901 Enfield Rd., Austin, TX 78703, (713) 821-0220.
- Founders Day Festival, every May, Fredericksburg, (830) 997-2283.
- Annual Folkfest (food, crafts), every May, New Braunfels, (830) 629-2943.
- Jack S. Blanton Museum of Art, University of Texas at Austin, (512) 471-7324.

Organizations

Advocacy Groups

- Texas Department on Aging, 4900 N. Lamar, 4th Floor, Austin, TX 78751, (512) 424-6840 or (800) 252-9240.
- Attorney General's Office of Fraud Against Seniors, Elder Law and Public Health Division, (512) 936-1317 or (800) 337-3928.
- Governor's Ombudsman, (512) 463-1782 or (800) 252-9600.
- Texas Department of Health, Home Health Care Complaints, (800) 228-1570; Medical Transportation, (800) 252-8263; Medicaid Hotline (512) 458-7263.
- Texas Department of Human Services, (512) 438-3280; Nursing Home Complaints, (512) 438-2629 or (800) 458-9858; Services for the Aged and Disabled, (512) 438-3280.

Volunteer Programs

- Art Museum of Southeast Texas (volunteer docents), Main St., Beaumont, (409) 832-3432.
- Family Eldercare, 3710 Cedar St., Box 9, Austin, TX 78705, (512) 450-0844.
- La Follia Austin Baroque (ticket takers, other volunteering), performing in First English Lutheran Church, 3001 Whitis Avenue, Austin, call Volunteer Coordinator, (512) 323-0418.
- Legal Hotline for Older Texans, 815 Brazos, Suite 1100, Austin, TX 78701, (512) 477-3977.
- Court Appointed Special Advocate (CASA), PO Box 2885, Denton, TX 76202, (940) 243-2272.
- Volunteer Center of Tarrant County, 2610 Cullen St., Fort Worth, TX 76107, (817) 810-9111.

Housing

Long-Term Care Facilities

In the state of Texas, these facilities are called ***Continuing Care/Nursing Home/Retirement Facilities.***

These facilities provide residential living and/or various levels of nursing and medical services to seniors for an extended period of time.

Types of Authorization

Licensing and/or Certification

The Long-Term Care Regulatory (LTC-R) section (a division of the Department of Human Services) is responsible for the licensure and complaint investigation of all long-term care facilities in Texas, and certification of long-term care facilities for federal Medicaid funding.

Nursing facilities provide food, shelter, and nursing care to persons who need services beyond the basic provisions of food, shelter, or laundry.

Memberships

- American Association of Homes and Services for the Aging (AAHSA) represents not-for-profit organizations committed to providing high-quality health care, housing, and services to the elderly. AAHSA, 901 E St. NW, Suite 500, Washington, DC 20004-2011. Ph: (202) 783-2242. Fax: (202) 783-2285. *http://www.aahsa.org*
- Texas Association of Homes and Services for the Aging (TAHSA) is a state affiliate of AAHSA. TAHSA, 2205 Hancock Drive, Austin, TX 78756-2508, Ph: (512) 467-2242. Fax: (512) 467-2275.

Accreditations

- Continuing Care Accreditation Commission (CCAC) accredits facilities that offer seniors a contract or contracts that provide residential living and health care services for the remainder of the person's lifetime and meet CCAC's accreditation standards.
- Joint Commission on the Accreditation of Health Care Organizations (JCAHCO) is an independent, not-for-profit organization, and the nation's oldest and largest standards-setting and health care accrediting institution.

East

Bayou Manor

4141 S. Braeswood
Houston, TX 77025

Ph: (713) 666-2651
Fax: (713) 660-5048

IND: Yes. AL: Yes. HCC: Yes

Age 65+. Nonprofit; nondenominational; owned by Brazos Presbyterian Homes, Inc. Studios, apartments, and private and semiprivate rooms. 24-hour nursing care; skilled and intermediate nursing care; medical services; rehabilitative therapies; dental and podiatry care; pharmacy services; wellness clinic; personal care; medication administration; security; emergency response system; maintenance; transportation; up to 3 daily meals; housekeeping and laundry services; exercise room; swimming pool; library; social and recreational activities; ceramics; arts and crafts; entertainment groups; movies; bingo; gardening; barber/beauty shop.

IND ENT: (all plans partial ref.), Plan A, $32,500–$128,500; Plan B, $55,500–$218,000; Plan C, $6,500–$11,500. IND MO: Plans A and B, $1,100–$2,200; Plan C, $1,825–$2,325. 2nd person, $770–$1,550.

Buckner Villas, TAHSA, AAHSA

11110 Tom Adams Drive
Austin, TX 78753

Ph: (512) 491-5434

Fax: (512) 836-1951
E-mail: *ahillman@buckner.org*

IND: Yes. AL: Yes. HCC: Yes. ALZ/MEM IMP: Yes

Nondenominational; Christian affiliation. Garden homes, apartments, and private and semiprivate rooms. 24-hour nursing care; on-site physicians; physical, occupational, and speech therapies; restorative care; dental and podiatry care; pharmacy services; social services; hospice services; respite care; personal care; medication administration; security; emergency response system; maintenance; transportation; up to 3 daily meals; housekeeping and laundry services; exercise classes; chapel services; social and recreational activities; community room; aviary; patio area.

DEP: (no ref.), one mo. rent. IND MO: $1,225–$1,275. AL Daily: $80–$130. HCC Daily: $110–$130. ALZ/MEM IMP Daily: $110.

Crestview Retirement Community

2505 Villa Maria Rd.
Bryan, TX 77802

Ph: (409) 776-4778
Fax: (409) 774-7579

IND: Yes. AL: Yes. HCC: Yes

Age 62+. Nonprofit; nondenominational; affiliated with the United Methodist Church. Apartments and private and semiprivate rooms. Intermediate nursing care; 24-hour nursing care; medical services; rehabilitative therapies; dental and podiatry care; pharmacy services; personal care; medication administration; security; emergency response system; maintenance; transportation; up to 3 daily meals; housekeeping and laundry services; exercise classes; religious services; Bible study; pet therapy; social and recreational activities; movies; arts and crafts; gift shop; gardening; barber/beauty shop.

IND MO: $1,275–$2,225. AL Daily: $60–$70. HCC: $90–$115.

The Hallmark, CCAC

4718 Hallmark Drive
Houston, TX 77056

Ph: (713) 622-6633
Fax: (713)622-5020

IND: 134. AL: 12. HCC: 42

Age 65+. Nonprofit; nondenominational; owned by Brazos Presbyterian Homes, Inc. Apartments and private and semiprivate rooms. 24-hour nursing care; medical services; rehabilitative therapies; dental, podiatry, and ear care; home health services; wellness clinic; pharmacy services; personal care; medication administration; security; emergency response system; maintenance; transportation; up to 3 daily meals; housekeeping and laundry services; fitness center; swimming pool; religious services; social and recreational activities; educational and cultural programs; library; computer center and Internet connection; notary-public service; banking services; residents association; billiards; walking paths; barber/beauty shop.

APPL: $1,100. IND ENT: $51,000–$170,500. IND MO: $1,325–$3,100. AL MO: $2,650. HCC MO: Semiprivate, $2,650; private, $3,200.

Marriott Brighton Gardens of Tanglewood

1600 Augusta Drive
Houston, TX 77057

Ph: (713) 784-6664
Fax: (713) 784-6742

AL: 90. HCC: 43. ALZ/MEM IMP: 25

For-profit; nondenominational. Apartments and private and semiprivate rooms. 24-hour nursing care; on-site doctor's clinic; medical services; rehabilitative therapies; dental and podiatry care; pharmacy services; wellness program; respite care; social services; Medicare-approved; personal care; medication administration; security; emergency response system; maintenance; transportation; up to 3 daily meals; housekeeping and laundry services; social and recreational activities; barber/beauty shop.

AL ENT: $550. AL MO: $2,875+. HCC Daily: Semiprivate, $125; private, $180.

The Temple Meridian Retirement Community

4312 S. 31st St.
Temple, TX 76502

Ph: (254) 771-1226
Fax: (254) 774-7472

http://www.meridians.com

IND: 149. AL: 19. HCC: 60

Age 70+. For-profit; nondenominational. Cottages, studios, apartments, and private and semiprivate rooms. 24-hour nursing care; medical services; rehabilitative therapies; dental and podiatry care; pharmacy services; short- and long-term care; health and wellness program; personal care; medication administration; security; emergency response system; maintenance; transportation; up to 3 daily meals; housekeeping and laundry services; exercise program; swimming pool; library; social and recreational activities; volunteer opportunities; game and billiards room; lounges; arts and crafts; ceramics; garden areas; walking paths; greenhouse; barber/beauty shop.

DEP: (ref.) $2,200. ENT: $2,200. IND MO: $1,575–$2,275; 2nd person, $330. AL MO: $2,625–$3,175; 2nd person, $1,075. HCC Daily: Semiprivate, $115–$120; private, $175.

Westminster Manor

4100 Jackson Ave.
Austin, TX 78731

Ph: (512) 454-4643
Fax: (512) 371-7308

IND: 269. AL: Yes. SNF: 90

Age 62+. Nonprofit; nondenominational; managed by Life Care Services. Suites, efficiencies, one- and two-bedroom apartments, and private and semiprivate rooms. 24-hour skilled nursing care; physician services; rehabilitative services; medical services; dental and podiatry care; pharmacy services; on-site health clinic; home health care services; personal care; medication administration; security; emergency response system; maintenance; transportation; up to 3 daily meals; housekeeping and laundry services; exercise classes; nondenominational religious services; library; social and recreational activities; cultural programs; media room; clubs; game and billiards room; general store; barber/beauty shop.

DEP: $4,500; $7,500; $9,000. IND ENT: Standard Plan (partial ref.), $46,500–$170,000; Return of Capital Plan (partial ref.), $79,000–$288,500; 2nd person, $5,500 additional to ENT fee. IND MO: $1,225–$2,700. Most AL and SNF fees are inclusive.

North

Presbyterian Manor

4600 Taft Blvd.
Wichita Falls, TX 76308

Ph: (817) 691-1710

IND: Yes. AL: Yes. HCC: Yes

Age 65+. Nonprofit; nondenominational; Presbyterian Church sponsored. Cottages, apartments, efficiencies, and private and semiprivate rooms. 24-hour nursing care; medical services; rehabilitative therapies; dental and podiatry care; pharmacy services; short- and long-term care; personal care; medication administration; security; emergency response system; maintenance; transportation; up to 3 daily meals; housekeeping and laundry services; religious services; social and recreational activities; educational and cultural programs; hobby room; sewing room; lounges; walking paths.

IND ENT: $10,500– $30,250. IND MO: $725–$1,450. MO fees include up to 10 HCC days per year.

Dallas/Forth Worth Area

C. C. Young

4829 W. Lawther Drive
Dallas, TX 75214

Ph: (214) 827-8080

IND: 254. AL: Yes. HCC: Yes. ADC: Yes

Nonprofit; nondenominational; sponsored by the United Methodist Church. Studios, efficiencies, apartments, and private and semiprivate rooms. Skilled nursing care; physician services; medical services; rehabilitative therapies; injections; glucose and blood pressure checks; dental, podiatry, and eye care; pharmacy services; social services; wound care; X-ray and lab services; Medicare/Medicaid-approved; personal care; medication administration; security; emergency response system; maintenance; transportation; up to 3 daily meals; housekeeping and laundry services; religious services; social and recreational activities; arts and crafts; intergenerational program; barber/beauty shop.

IND ENT: $23,500–$38,000. IND MO: $1,000–$1,925. AL MO: $1,500–$2,800. HCC Daily: Semiprivate, $95; private, $120. ADC Daily: $35–$45.

Christian Care Center

1000 Wiggins Parkway
Mesquite, TX 75150-9974

Ph: (972) 686-3000
Fax: (972) 686-3744

IND: 149. AL: 61. HCC: 180

Nonprofit; Church of Christ affiliation. Apartments and private and semiprivate rooms. 24-hour nursing care; medical services; rehabilitative therapies; dental and podiatry care; pharmacy services; X-ray and lab services; social services; home health care services; hospice services; Medicare/Medicaid-approved; personal care; medication administration; security; emergency response system; maintenance; transportation; up to 3 daily meals; housekeeping and laundry services; exercise classes; chapel; religious services; social and recreational activities; arts and crafts; on-and off-site activities; resident councils; volunteer program; walking paths; barber/beauty shop.

APPL: (no ref.), $25. DEP: (no ref.), $300. IND MO: $424–$1,045; 2nd person, $50. AL MO: $1,875–$2,700; 2nd person, $440.

Lakewood Village Retirement Community

5100 Randol Mill Rd.
Ft. Worth, TX 76112-1553

Ph: (817) 451-8001
Fax: (817) 654-1219

http://www.cccinc.net

IND: 160. AL: 38. HCC: Yes

Age 62+. Nonprofit; Church of Christ affiliation. 24-hour nursing care; medical services; rehabilitative therapies; dental and podiatry care; pharmacy services; Medicare-approved; home health care services; personal care; medication administration; security; emergency response system; maintenance; transportation; up to 3 daily meals; housekeeping and laundry services; fitness center; religious services; library; billiards room; social and recreational activities; home association; crafts; barber/beauty shop.

DEP: $550. IND ENT: $27,500–$108,000. IND MO: $700–$1,500. AL MO: $2,050–$2,500. HCC Daily: $115.

Trinity Terrace

1600 Texas St.
Ft. Worth, TX 76102-3434

Ph: (817) 338-2426 or (800) 841-0561
Fax: (817) 335-2733

E-mail: *janer@retirement.org*

IND: 292. AL: Yes. HCC: Yes

Age 62+. Nonprofit; nondenominational; managed by The Cumperland Rest, Inc. Studios, one- and two-bedroom apartments, and private and semiprivate rooms. Skilled nursing care; medical services; rehabilitative therapies; dental and podiatry care; pharmacy services; social services; personal care; medication administration; security; emergency response system; maintenance; transportation; up to 3 daily meals; housekeeping and laundry services; exercise equipment; chapel; library; social and recreational activities; pool tables and game room; lobby; country store; gardening; barber/beauty shop.

IND ENT: (partial ref.), $44,000–$170,500. IND MO: $1,125–$3,400. Temporary stays at HCC are inclusive.

Southeast

Edgewater Retirement Community, TAHSA

2228 Seawall Blvd.
Galveston, TX 77553-1750

Ph: (409) 621-3310
Fax: (409) 765-6551

IND: 88. AL: 60. HCC: 104

Age 62+. Nonprofit; nondenominational; affiliated with Methodist Retirement Communities. Studios, one- and two-bedroom apartments and private and semiprivate rooms. 24-hour nursing care; medical services; physical, occupational, and speech therapies; dental clinic; social services; pharmacy services; Medicaid-approved; personal care; medication administration; security; emergency response system; maintenance; transportation; up to 3 daily meals; housekeeping and laundry services; exercise classes; religious services; social and recreational activities; educational and cultural program; notary public services; resident council; arts and crafts; gift shop; barber/beauty shop.

IND MO: $1,300–$2,750. AL Daily: $70–$85. HCC Daily: $105–$145.

South

Air Force Village I, CCAC

4917 Ravenswood Drive
San Antonio, TX 78227

Ph: (210) 673-2761
Fax: (210) 673-1441

http://www.airforcevillages.com
E-mail: *AFVFMKTG@airforcevillages.com*

IND: 370. HCC: 112. ALZ/MEM IMP: 27

Age 62+. Nonprofit; nondenominational. Homes, apartments, and private and semiprivate rooms. Nursing care; medical services; physician visits; rehabilitative therapies; dental and podiatry care; pharmacy services; short- and long-term care; counseling services; personal care; medication administration; security; emergency response system; maintenance; transportation; up to 3 daily meals; pets allowed; housekeeping and laundry services; fitness center; swimming pool; chapel; religious services; library; music room; social and recreational activities; arts and crafts; game and card room; barber/beauty shop.

DEP: Single, $550; couple, $825. IND ENT: (partial ref.) $39,500–$106,000. IND MO: $550–$1,450.

REQ: Retired officers of all uniformed services and their family.

Air Force Village II, CCAC

5100 John D. Ryan Blvd.
San Antonio, TX 78245

Ph: (210) 677-8666 or (800) 762-1122
Fax: (210) 677-8551

http://www.airforcevillages.com
E-mail: *AFVFMKTG@airforcevillages.com*

IND: 403. HCC: 68. ALZ/MEM IMP: 27

Age 62+. Nonprofit; nondenominational. Homes, apartments, and private and semiprivate rooms. Nursing care; medical services; physician visits; rehabilitative therapies; dental and podiatry care; pharmacy services; short- and long-term care; counseling services; personal care; medication administration; security; emergency response system; maintenance; transportation; up to 3 daily meals; pets allowed; housekeeping and laundry services; fitness center; swimming pool; chapel; religious services; library; music room; social and recreational activities; arts and crafts; game and card room; barber/beauty shop.

DEP: Single, $550; couple, $825. IND ENT: (partial ref.) $75,000–$198,500. IND MO: $900–$2,300.

REQ: For retired officers of all uniformed services and their family.

The Army Residence Community, CCAC

7400 Crestway
San Antonio, TX 78239-3098

Ph: (210) 646-5316 or (800) 725-0083, TDD: (210) 646-5670 or (888) 646-5670
Fax: (210) 646-5313

http://www.arcsatx.com

E-mail: *arcmktg@txdirect.net*

IND: 388. AL: 30. HCC: 101

Age 62+. Nonprofit; nondenominational. Cottages, studios, apartments, and private and semiprivate rooms. Skilled nursing care; intermediate nursing care; emergency treatment; medical services; rehabilitative therapies; dental and podiatry care; pharmacy services; personal care; medication administration; security; emergency response system; maintenance; transportation; up to 3 daily meals; housekeeping and laundry services; exercise room; swimming pool; chapel; library; postal services; social and recreational activities; resident council; pet visits; crafts; woodworking shop; auditorium; lounge; walking paths; tennis court; gardening; pond; barber/beauty shop.

DEP: Single, $1,100; couple, $1,650. IND ENT: (All plans offer partial ref.) Plan O, $88,000–$134,000; Plan 50, $70,500–$215,000; Plan 95, $91,500–$279,000. IND MO: Plan O, $1,050–$2,100; Plan 50, $2,300–$2,550; Plan 95, $1,900–$2,250. AL Daily: $60. HCC Daily: $55–$85.

REQ: For retired career military officers and family.

Golden Palms Retirement and Health Center

2101 Treasure Hills Blvd.
Harlingen, TX 78550

Ph: (956) 389-4653
Fax: (956) 389-4008

IND: 108. AL: 30. SNF: 60

Age 62+. Nonprofit; nondenominational. Studios, efficiencies, apartments, and private and semiprivate rooms. 24-hour nursing care; physician services; medical services; rehabilitative services; dental and podiatry care; pharmacy services; Medicare-approved; personal care; medication administration; security; emergency response system; maintenance; transportation; up to 3 daily meals; housekeeping and laundry services; exercise room; swimming pool; chaplain services; library; game room; woodworking shop; social and recreational activities; educational and cultural programs; craft and hobby room; gardening; snack and ice cream parlor; shuffleboard; courtyard; barber/beauty shop.

IND ENT: (90% ref.) $55,000–$121,000. IND MO: $1,275–$3,400. AL MO: $2,150–$4,275. HCC Daily: $115.

Central

Wesleyan Home

1105 Church St.
Georgetown, TX 78626

Ph: (512) 863-2528

Fax: (512) 869-2687
http://www.wesleyanhomes.org
E-mail: *wesleyan@realtime.net*

IND: 90. HCC: 184. ALZ/MEM IMP: 40

Age 62+. Nonprofit; United Methodist Church affiliation. Apartments and private and semiprivate rooms. 24-hour nursing care; medical services; rehabilitative therapies; pharmacy services; blood pressure checks and wellness classes; Medicare/Medicaid-approved; personal care; medication administration; 24-hour staffing; security; emergency response system; maintenance; transportation; up to 3 daily meals; housekeeping and laundry services; exercise program; nondenominational chapel; library; social and recreational activities; educational and cultural programs; lounges; barber/beauty shop.

DEP: $550. IND MO: $1,200–$1,925; 2nd person, $385. HCC Daily: $100–$125.

West

Manor Park, Macbee Health Care Center, and Younger Center

2208 N. Loop, 250 West
Midland, TX 79707

Ph: (915) 689-9898 or (800) 523-9898

IND: Yes. HCC: Yes. ALZ/MEM IMP: Yes

Age 62+. Nonprofit; nondenominational. Garden homes, townhomes, apartments, and private and semiprivate rooms. 24-hour nursing care; medical services; rehabilitative therapies; IV therapies; dental and podiatry care; pharmacy services; respite services; wellness program; personal care; medication administration; security; emergency response system; maintenance; transportation; up to 3 daily meals; housekeeping and laundry services; exercise program; chapel; social and recreational activities; arts and crafts; gift shop; barber/beauty shop.

Contact facility for fees.

The Monte Vista at Coronado

1575 Belvidere
El Paso, TX 79912

Ph: (915) 833-2229
Fax: (915) 581-6168

IND: 121. AL: 15. HCC: 124

For-profit; nondenominational; a Marriott Senior Living Community. Apartments and private and semiprivate rooms. Nursing care; medical services; rehabilitative therapies; dental and podiatry care; pharmacy services; wellness program; personal care; medication administration; security; emergency response system; maintenance; transportation; up to 3 daily meals; housekeeping and laundry services; exercise classes; religious services; library; banking services; social and recreational activities; educational and cultural programs; crafts; board and card games; group tours; convenience store; greenhouse.

IND MO: $2,225–$4,225. AL MO: $610 (in addition to the mo. rental fee). HCC fees are extra.

Northwest

Craig Methodist Retirement Community

5500 W. 9th Ave.
Amarillo, TX 79106

Ph: (806) 352-7244
Fax: (806) 467-7493
http://www.sears-methodist.com

IND: 108. RH: 48. AL: 40. HCC: 60. ALZ/MEM IMP: 60

Age 62+. Nonprofit; United Methodist Church affiliation. Apartments, condos, and private and semiprivate rooms. Nursing care; medical services; rehabilitative therapies; dental and podiatry care; pharmacy services; Medicaid-approved; personal care; medication administration; security; emergency response system; maintenance; transportation; up to 3 daily meals; pets allowed; housekeeping and laundry services; fitness center; exercise classes; religious services; banking services; library; social and recreational activities; activities director; country store; walking paths; barber/beauty shop.

DEP: (ref.) $1,100. IND ENT: (90% ref.), $105,500–$121,000. IND MO: $1,175–$1,225. AL MO: $2,275–$2,625. HCC Daily: $100

Assisted Living and Residential Care Facilities

*In the state of Texas, these facilities are called **Assisted Living/ Personal Care Facilities**.*

These facilities provide housing, food service, and one or more personal services.

Types of Authorization

Licensing and/or Certification

These facilities are regulated by the Long-Term Care Regulatory (LTC-R) section (a division of the Department of Human Services). Personal care facilities provide food, shelter, and assistance in daily living.

Memberships

- Assisted Living Federation of America (ALFA) is a national nonprofit membership organization whose mission is to enhance the quality of life in assisted living facilities and promote the interests of the assisted living industry. ALFA, 10300 Eaton Place, Suite 400, Fairfax, VA 22030. Ph: (703) 691-8100. Fax: (703) 691-8106. *http://www.alfa.org*
- Texas Assisted Living Association (TALA) is a state affiliate of ALFA. TALA, 5100 Bee Caves Rd., Austin, TX 78746. Ph: (512) 328-8252. Fax: (512) 328-8258.

East

The Forum at The Woodlands

5055 W. Panther Creek Drive
The Woodlands, TX 77381

Ph: (281) 367-3170

IND: 240. AL: 100. ALZ/MEM IMP: 16

Age 62+. For-profit; nondenominational; a Marriott Retirement Community. One- and two-bedroom apartments. Pharmacy services; podiatry care; medical services; wellness program; home health services; personal care; medication administration; security; emergency response system; maintenance; transportation; up to 3 daily meals; pets allowed; housekeeping and laundry services; exercise center; swimming pool; religious services; Bible study; library; postal services; social and recreational activities; educational and cultural programs; arts and crafts; billiards room; game room; sunroom; lobby; pond; walking paths; barber/beauty shop.

IND MO: $2,075–$3,350. AL MO: $2,850; 2nd person, $550.

North

Wesley Village

2800 Loy Lake Rd.
Denison, TX 75020

Ph: (903) 465-6463
Fax: (903) 465-6498

IND: 38. AL: 25

Age 62+. Nonprofit; nondenominational; United Methodist Church affiliation. Apartments and private rooms. Wellness program; personal care; medication administration; security; emergency response system; maintenance; transportation; up to 3 daily meals; housekeeping and laundry services; exercise classes; chapel; religious services; library; social and recreational activities; movies; bingo; board and card games; barber/beauty shop.

APPL: $100. DEP: (ref.), $200. IND MO: $1,200–$2,450. AL MO: $2,250–$2,550.

South Central

Amber Oaks

4415 Rio D'Oro
San Antonio, TX 78233

Ph: (210) 653-3132

IND: Yes. AL: Yes

Nondenominational. Studios and one- and two-bedroom apartments. 24-hour nursing care; home health services; rehabilitative therapies; pharmacy services; wellness center; personal care; medication administration; security; emergency response system; maintenance; transportation; up to 3 daily meals; housekeeping and laundry services; exercise classes; social, recreational, and cultural activities; clubs.

DEP: (ref.) $550. IND MO: $1,800–$3,025; 2nd person, $440. AL MO: (in addition to mo. fee), $440–$1,175.

Dallas/Fort Worth Area

Hearthstone Assisted Living

4101 W. Arkansas Lane
Arlington, TX 76016

Ph: (817) 469-7671
Fax: (817) 469-7671

AL: 119

Nondenominational. Apartments and shared suites. Respite services; day care services; wellness program; home health services; personal care; medication administration; security; emergency response system; maintenance; transportation; up to 3 daily meals; pets allowed; housekeeping and laundry services; social and recreational activities; educational and cultural programs; hobbies and crafts; sightseeing; entertainment; walking paths.

DEP: $550. AL MO: $1,700–$2,800. Additional level of care services, $275 and $550 plus rent.

Northwest

Atria Cottage Village

110 N. Frankford Ave.
Lubbock, TX 79416

Ph: (806) 799-4225
Fax: (806) 799-4597

IND: Yes. AL: Yes

Nondenominational. Apartments. Home health care services; wellness program; personal care; medication administration; security; emergency response system; maintenance; transportation; up to 3 daily meals; housekeeping and laundry services; exercise program; social and recreational activities; educational and cultural program; library; activities center.

RSV: $550. IND ENT: $425. IND MO: $1,650–$1,825; 2nd person, $360. AL ENT: $825. AL MO: $1,900–$2,675; 2nd person, $825.

West Central

Trinity Towers

2800 W. Illinois
Midland, TX 79701

Ph: (915) 694-1691 or (800) 697-8412

IND: Yes. AL: Yes

Nonprofit; nondenominational. Apartments. 24-hour nursing care; respite care; personal care; medication administration; security; emergency response system; maintenance; transportation; up to 3 daily meals; housekeeping and laundry services; exercise classes; crafts; social and recreational activities; gift shop; barber/beauty shop.

Contact facility for fees.

Southeast

The Esplanade

5813 Esplanade Drive
Corpus Christi, TX 78414

Ph: (361) 991-9600 Fax: (361) 980-8989

IND: Yes. AL: 51

Age 60+. For-profit; nondenominational. Apartments and studio suites. Rehabilitative therapies; podiatry care; personal care; medication administration; security; emergency response system; maintenance; transportation; up to 3 daily meals; pets allowed; housekeeping and laundry services; exercise classes; library; activities room; social and recreational activities; atrium; garden courtyard; barber/beauty shop.

DEP: $220. IND/AL MO: From $950.

Independent Living

Independent housing (primarily rentals) for seniors that may offer security features, meal service, and activities.

West

Polo Park Estates

2100 Castleford Rd.
Midland, TX 79705

Ph: (915) 682-5772

IND: 116

For-profit; nondenominational. Studios, cottages, and apartments. 24-hour staffing; security; emergency response system; maintenance; transportation; up to 3 daily meals; pets allowed; housekeeping and laundry services; exercise classes; chapel; library; social and recreational activities; billiards room; board game and card room; lounge; barber/beauty shop.

IND MO: $1,025–$2,125; 2nd person, $165 and $330.

East

Collier Park Retirement Community

2650 Collier St.
Beaumont, TX 77706

Ph: (409) 899-4800
Fax: (409) 899-3030

IND: 93. AL: 66

Age 55+. For-profit; nondenominational. Apartments. Nursing care; personal care; medication administration; security; emergency response system; maintenance; transportation; up to 3 daily meals; pets allowed; housekeeping and laundry services; fitness center; swimming pool; chapel; social and recreational activities; billiards room; game room; courtyards; gazebo; outdoor fireplace; barbecue grills; barber/beauty shop.

DEP: $550. ENT: $770. MO: $1,475–$2,800.

Eastman Estates

2920 Eastman Rd.
Longview, TX 75605

Ph: (903)757-6022
Fax: (903) 757-2491

http: / / www.emeritus.com

E-mail: *eastman@emeritus.com*

IND/AL: 70

For-profit; nondenominational. Apartments. Nursing care; respite care; respiratory care; wound management; personal care; medication administration; security; emergency response system; maintenance; transportation; up to

3 daily meals; pets allowed; housekeeping and laundry services; fitness center; social and recreational activities; clubs.

DEP: $385. IND MO: $1,850–$3,775. AL: fees extra.

Northwest

The Canyons Retirement Community

2200 W. 7th Ave.
Amarillo, TX 79106

Ph: (806) 374-6504
Fax: (806) 373-9023

E-mail: *JJHenry@Sears.Methodist.com*

IND: 109

Age 62+. Nonprofit; sponsored and managed by the Craig Methodist Retirement System. Apartments. Home health services; security; emergency response system; maintenance; transportation; meal program; housekeeping services; fitness center; social and recreational activities.

IND MO: $440–$990; HUD-subsidized.

Dallas/Fort Worth Area

Fowler Christian Apartments

105 Juliette Fowler St.
Dallas, TX 75214

Ph: (214) 821-4061
Fax: (214) 818-0345

IND: 144

Age 62+. Nonprofit. Apartments. Medical services; security; emergency response system; maintenance; transportation; meal program; pets allowed; swimming pool; social and recreational activities.

IND MO: HUD-subsidized.

Adult/Resort Communities

Communities for active adults (not all are age-restricted; primarily ownership).

North

Bridlewood

4000 W. Windsor Drive
Flower Mound, TX 75028

Ph: (972) 355-3795
Fax: (972) 355-3797

http://www.bridlewoodev.com

Individual homes in 7 neighborhoods. Golf course; pro shop; clubhouse; tennis; swimming pools; jogging trails; fitness and recreation center; outdoor pavilion; equestrian center; dining.

PURCHASE: Homes, $209,000–$770,000.

De Cordova Bend Estates

5301 Country Club Drive
Granbury, TX 76049

Ph: (817)-326-2381 or (817) 326-4505

Individual homes, condominiums, homesites. Golf course; clubhouse; pro shop; tennis; swimming pool; fishing; boating; fitness center; dining; social clubs.

PURCHASE: Homes, $88,000–$440,000.

Mill Creek

PO Box 67
Salado, TX 76571

Ph: (800) 736-3441 or (254) 947-5580

http://www.millcreekgolfresort.com

Individual homes, condominiums, homesites. Golf course; clubhouse; tennis; swimming pool; dining.

PURCHASE: Homes, $110,000–$880,000; homesites, from $33,000.

East

Bay Oaks

14545 Bay Oaks Blvd.
Houston, TX 77059

Ph: (281) 488-7888

Individual homes. Golf course; clubhouse; tennis; swimming pool; dining; social clubs.

PURCHASE: Homes, $300,000–$1 million+.

Bentwater Country Club

100 Bentwater Drive
Montgomery, TX 77356

Ph: (800) 313-7529
Fax: (409) 597-5797

http://www.bentwater.com

Individual homes, homesites. Golf courses; pro shop; tennis; swimming pool; fitness center; marina; yacht club; 22,000 acre lake.

PURCHASE: Homes, $198,000–$1.1 million+; homesites, $27,500–$440,000+.

Country Place

3123 Flower Field Lane
Pearland, TX 77584

Ph: (713) 436-1533

Age: 55+. Individual homes, condominiums. Golf course; clubhouse; tennis; swimming pool; fishing; fitness center; dining; library; social clubs.

PURCHASE: Homes, $99,000–$209,000; condos, $66,000–$88,000.

Hilltop Lakes

PO Box 1242
Hilltop Lakes, TX 77871

Ph: (409) 855-2100

Individual homes, homesites. Golf course; clubhouse; pro shop; tennis; swimming pool; fishing; riding stables; boating; dining; library; social clubs.

PURCHASE: Homes, $55,000–$198,000; homesites, $1,100–$11,000.

Hollytree Country Club

6700 Hollytree Drive
Tyler, TX 75703

Ph: (903) 581-7723 or (903) 581-4952

Individual homes, garden homes, courtyard homes. Golf course; clubhouse; tennis; swimming pool; hiking trails; fishing; fitness center; dining; social clubs.

PURCHASE: Homes, $275,000–$1.32 million.

Longwood Village

Cypress, TX 77429

Ph: (281) 373-0777 or (281) 379-6951

Individual homes. Golf course; recreation centers; tennis; swimming pools; hiking/biking trails.

PURCHASE: Homes, $143,000–$880,000.

Tanglewood Resort

Rte. 120 N.
Pottsboro, TX 75076

Ph: (903) 786-9004

http://www.tanglewoodresort.com/

Individual homes, condominiums, cooperatives, homesites. Golf course; clubhouse; tennis; swimming pool; hiking trails; fishing; boating; riding stables; dining; social clubs.

PURCHASE: Homes, $99,000–$346,500; condos, from $55,000.

Central

Balcones Country Club

8600 Balcones Club Drive
Austin, TX 78750

Ph: (512) 258-1621 or (512) 219-5855

http://www.balconescountryclub.com/

Individual homes. Golf courses; clubhouse; tennis; swimming pools; dining; social clubs.

PURCHASE: Homes, $198,000–$440,000.

Berry Creek

30444 Berry Creek Drive
Georgetown, TX 78628

Ph: (512) 930-9995

Individual homes. Golf course; clubhouse; racquet club; tennis; swimming pool; exercise facility; lakes.

PURCHASE: Homes, $154,000–$550,000.

Flying L Guest Ranch

PO Box 1959
Bandera, TX 78003

Ph: (800) 646-5407 or (210) 796-8466

http://www.flyingl.com

Individual homes. Golf course; tennis; swimming pool; hiking trails; riding stables; dining.

PURCHASE: Homes, $82,500–$154,000.

Heritage Hill Country

203 Heritage Hills Drive
Fredericksburg, TX 78624

Ph: (800) 505-0533 or (830) 997-9743

Age: 55+. Individual homes. Clubhouse; fitness center; swimming pool; spa.

PURCHASE: Homes, from $132,000.

Northern Hills Country Club

13202 Scarsdale
San Antonio, TX 78217

Ph: (210) 655-4148

Individual homes, condominiums. Golf course; clubhouse; tennis; swimming pool; dining; social clubs.

PURCHASE: Homes, $88,000–$143,000.

Sun City Georgetown

One Texas Drive
Georgetown, TX 78628

Ph: (800) 833-5636 or (512) 931-6900

http://www.suncity.com/sun/scgt/scgeorhp.htm

Individual homes. Golf course; recreation center; tennis; swimming pool; bocce; arts and crafts; walking/biking trails; fitness center; social clubs.

PURCHASE: Homes, $137,500–$330,000.

The Dominion

10 Dominion Drive
San Antonio, TX 78257

Ph: (210) 698-3100
Fax: (210) 698-0236

http://www.the-dominion.com

Individual homes, garden homes, homesites. Golf course; pro shop; clubhouse; tennis; swim center; jogging trail; lakes; dining; social clubs.

PURCHASE: Homes, $242,000–$3.3 million+; homesites, from $33,000.

The Island on Lake Travis

3404 American Drive
Lago Vista, TX 78645

Ph: (800) 422-ISLE or (512) 267-7107

http://www.retirenet.com/theisland

Rental apartments. Swimming pools; spa; tennis; fitness rooms; billiards; boating; fishing; private marina; arts and crafts; dining; wellness center.

MO rental: from $1,750.

South

River Bend Resort

Hwy. 281
Brownsville, TX 78520

Ph: (956) 548-0192 or (956) 548-0194

Individual homes, homesites. Golf course; clubhouse; tennis; swimming pool; fishing; library; social clubs.

PURCHASE: Homes, $87,000–$119,000.

Stuart Place
1111 Stuart Place Rd.
Harlingen, TX 78552
Ph: (956) 428-1000

Age: 55+. Individual homes. Golf course; clubhouse; swimming pool; social clubs.

PURCHASE: Homes, $88,000–$165,000.

Utah

http://www.state.ut.us

General Information

Climate

Average lows from 19° F to 64° F; highs from 69° F to 92° F.

Cost of Living

Ranks 18th in the nation.

Taxes

State/Local as % of Income: 12%.

Property Tax Reduction: A property tax credit is available to residents who are at least 65 years of age (or surviving spouses) and whose income is less than $21,644.

Sales: About 4.75%.

Prescription Exemptions: None, other than itemized deductions.

Transportation, Travel, and Tourism

General

Utah Travel Council, Council Hall, Capitol Hill, Salt Lake City, UT 84114, (801) 538-1030.

Major Airport

- Salt Lake City International Airport, (801) 575-2400.

Railways

- Amtrak, (800) USA-RAIL.

Bus Tours

- Nava-Hopi Bus Tours, (602) 970-0979.
- Gray Line Motor Tours, (800) 309-2352.
- American National Park Tours, (888) 652-9960.
- Utah Trails Resort & Tours, (888) 874-8687.

State Highways

- Interstate 80, east-west (northern).
- Interstate 15, north-south (western).
- Interstate 70, east-west (central).
- U.S. 40, east-west (northern).

Theater and Music

North

- Utah Symphony, Abravanel Hall, 123 W. S. Temple, Salt Lake City, UT 84101-1496, (801) 533-5626.
- Brigham Young University Harris Fine Arts Center, Provo, (801) 378-4322.

Museums, Crafts, Historical, Recreational

Great Basin Area (Pony Express Trail, Little Sahara Recreation Area, Territorial Statehouse, Parowan Gap Petroglyphs, state parks, camping, hiking, bicycling, hunting, fishing)

- Bureau of Land Management, Salt Lake District, 2370 South 2300 West, Salt Lake City, UT 84110, (801) 977-4300.
- Cedar City District, 176 E. D. L. Sargent Drive, Cedar City, UT 84720, (435) 586-2401.
- Golden Spike National Historic Site, PO Box 897, Brigham City, UT 84302, (435) 471-2209.
- Antelope Island State Park, 4528 West 1700 South, Syracuse, UT 84075, (801) 773-2941.
- Fishlake National Forest, 115 E. 900 N., Richfield UT 84701, (435) 896-9233.
- Golden Spike National Historic Site, PO Box 897, Brigham City, UT 84302, (435) 471-2209.

Wasatch Front Area (Old Desert Village, Mormon Pioneer National Historic Trail, Lagoon Amusement and Water Park, Farmington Bay Bird Refuge, Great Salt Lake, Temple Square, Seven Peaks, Sundance Resort, state and national parks, camping, hiking, biking, skiing, sporting events, horseback riding, water sports)

- Salt Lake Convention and Visitors Bureau, 90 South West Temple, Salt Lake City, UT 84101-1406, (801) 521-2822.
- This Is the Place State Park, 2601 Sunnyside Ave., Salt Lake City, UT 84108-1453, (801) 584-8391.
- Timpanogos Cave National Monument, near American Fork, (801) 756-5238.
- Uinta National Forest, (801) 377-5780.
- Springville Museum of Art, Springville, (801) 489-2727.

Rocky Mountain Area (Logan Canyon Scenic Byway, Willow Park Zoo, Wasatch-Cache National Forest, Uinta National Forest, Ashley National Forest, Pariette Wetlands, state parks, reservoirs, camping, skiing, watersports, biking, fishing, hiking, horseback riding)

- Park City Chamber of Commerce, (800) 453-1360.
- Bear Lake State Park, PO Box 184, Garden City, UT 84028-0184, (435) 946-3343.
- Flaming Gorge National Recreation Area, PO Box 279, Manila, UT 84046, (435) 784-3445.
- Brown's Park on the Green River Historic Site, (435) 885-3307.
- Dinosaur National Monument, PO Box 210, Dinosaur, CO 81610, (303) 374-2216 (partly in Utah).

Red Rock Area: (State parks, national forests, camping, rafting, golf, outdoor activities)

- Arches National Park, Box 907, Moab, UT 84532, (435) 259-8161.
- Bryce Canyon National Park, Bryce Canyon, UT 84717, (435-834-5322).
- Anasazi Village, PO Box 1429, Boulder, UT 84716-1429, (435) 335-7308.
- Hovenweep National Monument, near Aneth, (970) 749-0510.
- Canyonlands National Park, 2282 S. West Resource Blvd., Moab, UT 84532, (435) 259-7164.
- Capital Reef National Park, HC70, Box 15, Torrey, UT 84775, (801) 425-3791.
- Rainbow Bridge National Monument, PO Box 1507, Page, AZ 86040, (520) 608-6404.
- Natural Bridges National Monument, PO Box 1, Lake Powell, UT, 84533, (435) 692-1234.
- Zion National Park, Superintendent, Springdale, UT 84767, (435) 772-3256.
- Cedar Breaks National Monument, 2390 West Highway 56, Suite #11, Cedar City, UT 84720-4151, (435) 586-9451.

Organizations

Advocacy Groups

- AARP, Utah State Office, 6975 Union Park Center, #320, Midvale, UT 84047, (801) 561-1037.

Volunteer Programs

- Foster Grandparents Program Salt Lake County, 2001 S. State St., #S-1500, Salt Lake City, UT 84190, (801) 468-2775.
- Salt Lake County Retired and Senior Volunteer Programs, 2001 S. State Street, Suite S-1500, Salt Lake City, UT 84190, (801) 468-2472.

Housing

Long-Term Care Facilities

*In the state of Utah, these facilities are called **Continuing Care/Nursing Care Facilities (Intermediate and Skilled).***

These facilities provide residential living and/or various levels of nursing and medical services to seniors for an extended period of time.

Types of Authorization

Licensing and / or Certification

These facilities are licensed by the Bureau of Health Facility Licensure. Intermediate care facilities provide 24-hour inpatient care to residents who require licensed nursing and supportive care, but who do not need continuous nursing care. Skilled nursing care facilities maintain and operate 24-hour licensed nursing services. Nursing care facilities provide licensed nursing care and related services to residents who need continuous health care and supervision.

Memberships

- American Association of Homes and Services for the Aging (AAHSA) represents not-for-profit organizations committed to providing high-quality health care, housing, and services to the elderly. AAHSA, 901 E St. NW, Suite 500, Washington, DC 20004-2011. Ph: (202) 783-2242. Fax: (202) 783-2285. *http://www.aahsa.org*

Accreditations

- Continuing Care Accreditation Commission (CCAC) accredits facilities that offer seniors a contract or contracts that provide residential living and health care services for the remainder of the person's lifetime and meet CCAC's accreditation standards.
- Joint Commission on the Accreditation of Healthcare Organizations (JCAHO) is an independent, not-for-profit organization, and the nation's oldest and largest standards-setting and health care accrediting institution.

North

Country Pines Retirement Community

1748 West 1800 North
Clinton, UT 84015

Ph: (801) 773-1649
Fax: (801) 773-1632

IND: Yes. AL: Yes. HHC: Yes

Nondenominational. Apartments and private and semiprivate rooms. Nursing care; medical services; rehabilitative therapies; dental and podiatry care; personal care; medication administration; located next to Westside Medical Clinic; scheduled transportation; 2 daily meals; housekeeping service and laundry service; multipurpose room; activity program; private miniature golf putting course; walking exercise areas.

DEP: (ref.), $50. IND MO: $1,450–$1,650; 2nd person, $220.

Golden Living, Taylorsville

2011 West 4700 South
Taylorsville, UT 84118

Ph: (801) 966-4286
Fax: (801) 966-1405

http://www.rlg.net

E-mail: *golden@rlg.net*

AL: 120. HCC: Yes

Nondenominational. Apartments and private rooms. Nursing care; medical services; rehabilitative therapies; podiatry care; pharmacy; personal care; medication administration; 24-hour security; 24-hour emergency response system; maintenance; transportation; up to 3 daily meals (included in fees); pets allowed; housekeeping and laundry services; social and recreational activities; walking paths; activity areas.

APPL: (non-ref.), $50. DEP: (ref.), $330–$550. AL MO: $1,025–$3,300. Apartments, $1,725–$3,300; private rooms, $1,025–$1,825.

Heritage Care Center

350 East 300 North
American Fork, UT 84004

Ph: (801) 756-5293
Fax: (801) 756-4144

NH: 106. AL: 15

For-profit. Private and semiprivate rooms. Skilled nursing care; medical services; physical, occupational, and speech therapies; dental and podiatry care; pharmacy services; personal care; medication administration; personal care; medication administration; security; emergency response system; maintenance; transportation; up to 3 daily meals; pets allowed; housekeeping and laundry services; social and recreational activities.

AL MO: $1,325–$1,500. NH Daily: Semiprivate, $100–$105; private, $110–$115.

St. Joseph Villa

451 Bishop Federal Lane
Salt Lake City, UT 84115

Ph: (801) 487-7557
Fax: (801) 487-1112

IND: Yes. AL: Yes. SNF: Yes. ALZ/MEM IMP: Yes. ADC: Yes

Apartments and private and semiprivate rooms. 24-hour licensed nursing services; medical clinic personal care services; 24-hour staff; physical, occupational, and recreational therapy; music and pet therapy; podiatry services; audiology services; pharmacy; personal care; medication administration; 24-hour security; emergency response system; maintenance; up to 3 daily meals; housekeeping and laundry services; exercise room; chapel; library; social and recreational activities; dining services; gift shop, barber/beauty shop.

PROC: (non-ref.), $200. Cleaning fee: (non-ref.), $200. DEP: one month's rent. IND MO: $750–$1,375. AL Daily: $70–$75. LTC Daily: $115–$150. SNF Daily: $160–$205. ALZ/MEM IMP Daily: $140. ADC Daily: $40–$45, depending on care; transportation fee: $7.

Assisted Living and Residential Care Facilities

These facilities provide housing, food service, and one or more personal services.

Types of Authorization

Licensing and / or Certification

These facilities are licensed by the Bureau of Health Facility Licensure. There are two types: Type I, or residential facilities, are for people who need some help with daily living activities but do not require nursing care. These facilities provide housing, 24-hour protective oversight, and assistance with such daily activities as dressing, meals, bathing, and medication reminders. Type II, or assisted living facilities, are for people who need assistance with daily living activities, intermittent nursing care, administration of medication, and support services to promote independence and self-sufficiency. These facilities provide housing, 24-hour protective oversight, and assistance with such daily activities as dressing, meals, and bathing. Assisted living facilities are intended to allow elderly residents to age in place. Both types of facilities can be small residential homes, large apartment-like facilities, or part of a senior retirement community or nursing home.

Memberships

- Assisted Living Federation of America (ALFA) is a national nonprofit membership organization whose mission is to enhance the quality of life in assisted living facilities and promote the interests of the assisted living industry. ALFA, 10300 Eaton Place, Suite 400, Fairfax, VA 22030. Ph: (703) 691-8100. Fax: (703) 691-8106. *http://www.alfa.org*

- Utah Assisted Living Association (UALA) is a state affiliate of ALFA. UALA, 565 N. 300 W. Kaysville, UT 84037. Ph: (801) 546-5600. Fax: (801) 546-5605.

Southwest

The Meadows

950 South 400 East
St. George, UT 84770

Ph: (435) 628-0090
Fax: (435) 628-7092

AL: 56. RH: 61

Age 62+. For-profit; nondenominational. Apartments. Personal care; medication administration; 24-hour security system; 24-hour emergency response system; maintenance; transportation; 1 daily meal; pets allowed; housekeeping and laundry services; social and recreational activities.

DEP: $385. AL MO: $1,450–$2,450.

North

Atria Crosslands

10970 South 700 East
Sandy, UT 84070

Ph: (801) 572-4456
Fax: (801) 571-7640

IND: Yes. AL: Yes

Nondenominational. Apartments. 24-hour professional staff; physical, occupational, and speech therapies; wellness program; daily well-being checks; personal care; medication administration; 24-hour response system; maintenance; scheduled transportation; up to 3 daily meals; housekeeping and laundry services; catering service for special events; social and recreational activities; barber/beauty shop.

IND MO: $1,675–$2,300; 2nd person, $440. AL MO: $2,275–$3,825, depending on level of care; 2nd person, $660.

Canterbury Place, UALA

198 South 1300 East
Springville, UT 84663

Ph: (801) 491-9866

AL: Yes

Privately owned. Private rooms. Respite care; podiatry services; massage therapist; personal care; medication administration; emergency response system; maintenance; transportation; up to 3 daily meals; housekeeping and laundry services; social and recreational activities; deck; fireplace; walking paths; close to community park; barber/beauty shop services.

Contact facility for fees.

Chancellor Gardens of Clearfield

1425 South 1500 East
Clearfield, UT 84015

Ph: (801) 779-0798 or (888) 860-6916
Fax: (801) 779-2798

http://www.carematrix.com

AL: 66. ALZ/MEM IMP: 15

Nondenominational. Apartments. Medical services; personal care; medication administration; security system; emergency response system; maintenance; transportation; up to 3 daily meals (included in fees); pets allowed; weekly housekeeping and laundry services; social and recreational activities; library; computer room; ice cream parlor and sundries shop; on campus of Narus Hospital; barber/beauty shop.

DEP: (ref.), $550. AL MO: $1,825–$3,075. ALZ/MEM IMP MO: $3,150. Contact facility for specific information.

Chateau Brickyard

3080 South 1300 East
Salt Lake City, UT 84106

Ph: (801) 466-9999
Fax: (801) 466-7650

http://www.rlg.net

E-mail: *Chateau@rig.net*

IND: 106. AL: 20

For-profit; nondenominational. Apartments. Wellness clinic; personal care; medication administration; emergency response system; maintenance; transportation; up to 3 daily meals; pets allowed; weekly housekeeping and laundry services; social and recreational activities; private dining room; billiards room; spa; TV lounge; reading areas; card room; outdoor garden area; barber/beauty shop.

DEP: 1 mo. rent. IND MO: $1,475–$2,050. AL MO: $1,825–$2,525.

Cottonwood Creek

1245 E. Murray Holladay Rd.
Salt Lake City, UT 84117

Ph: (801) 263-0999
Fax: (801) 262-4770

IND: 103. AL: 50

Age 62+. Nondenominational. Apartments. Nursing care; medical services; personal care; medication administration; 24-hour security; 24-hour emergency response system; maintenance; transportation; up to 3 daily meals (2 meals included in fees); pets allowed; weekly housekeeping and laundry services; fitness center; spas; library; social and recreational activities; billiards room; theater; activities room; guest and private dining room; barber/beauty shop.

APPL: (non-ref.; goes toward $300 cleaning fee if applicant moves in) $200. DEP: (ret.; goes toward $300 cleaning fee if applicant moves in) $100. MO: $1,600–$2,200. AL MO: based on point system.

Curtis Residential Home, UALA

189 E. Center St.
Glenwood, UT 84750 84730

Ph: (435) 896-9359
Fax: (435) 896-9359

E-mail: *Curtis@desertonline.com*

AL: 16

Age 18+. Nondenominational. Private rooms. Personal care; medication administration; security system; emergency response system; maintenance; transportation; up to 3 daily meals; housekeeping and laundry services; social and recreational activities.

DEP: $100. AL ENT: $1,450. AL MO: $1,450–$2,100.

Friendship Manor

380 East 240 North
Orem, UT 84058

Ph: (801) 226-8338

E-mail: *friendship@rlg.net*

AL: 26. RH: 25

Nondenominational; apartments and private rooms. Personal care; medication administration; 24-hour security; 24-hour emergency response system; maintenance; transportation; up to 3 meals daily; pets allowed; weekly housekeeping and laundry services; social and recreational activities.

DEP: one month's rent. RH MO: apartment, $425–$2,200 (plus service); private room, $475–$2,650 (plus service).

Golden Living, Orem, ALFA

960 S. Geneva Rd.
Orem, UT 84058

Ph: (801) 225-6559
Fax: (801) 225-0372

http://www.rlg.net

E-mail: *glo@rlg.net*

AL: 72

Nondenominational. Apartments and private rooms with two levels of care. Medical services; personal care; medication administration; security system;

emergency response system; maintenance transportation; up to 3 daily meals; weekly housekeeping and laundry services; religious services; social and recreational activities; educational and cultural programs; crafts; bingo; sing-alongs; lounges; barber/beauty shop services.

DEP: (part ref.), $200. AL MO: apartments, $1,375–$1,550; private rooms, $1,500–$1,600.

Heritage Place

1150 S. Main St.
Bountiful, UT 84010

Ph: (801) 298-3241
Fax: (801) 298-3265

http://www.rlg.net

E-mail: *heritage@rlg.net*

IND: Yes. AL: 130. RH: Yes. ALZ/MEM IMP: 18

Age 21+. For-profit; nondenominational. Apartments and private rooms. Medical services; physical therapist; podiatry care; pharmacy; personal care; medication administration; 24-hour security; 24-hour emergency response system; maintenance; transportation; up to 3 daily meals; pets allowed (limited); housekeeping and laundry services; fitness center; swimming pool; library; social and recreational activities.

APPL: $50. DEP: (ref. with 30-day notice), $550. IND MO: $1,175–$3,550. AL MO: $1,500–$3,550.

Millcreek Retirement Residence

777 East 3900 South
Salt Lake City, UT 84107

Ph: (801) 288-0700
Fax: (801) 288-2777

IND: 48. AL: 28. ALZ/MEM IMP: No

Age 62+. For-profit; nondenominational. Apartments. Medical services; personal care; medication administration; 24-hour security; 24-hour emergency response system; maintenance; transportation; up to 3 daily meals; housekeeping and laundry services; exercise equipment; social and recreational activities.

DEP: (ref.), $660. IND MO: $1,750–$2,400. AL MO: $380.

Parklane Senior Apartments

680 East 100 South
Salt Lake City, UT 84102-3404

Ph: (801) 537-1100
Fax: (801) 537-1101

E-mail: *Parklane1@worldnet.att.net*

RH: 100

Nondenominational. Apartments. 24-hour staffing; podiatry care; health care clinic located in wellness center; incontinence management program; rehabilitation services; personal care; medication administration; 24-hour security; 24-hour emergency response system; maintenance; scheduled transportation; up to 3 daily meals; pets allowed; housekeeping and laundry services; personal laundry service; fitness center; wellness and exercise programs; church services; social and recreational activities; atrium; close to theaters, symphony, opera, ballet, other downtown amenities; on-site barber/beauty shop.

DEP: (non-ref.), $385. IND MO: $1,975–$2,800.

Prestige Assisted Living Courtyard at Jamestown

3352 North 100 East
Provo, UT 84604

Ph: (801) 377-3730
Fax: (801) 375-0808

E-mail: *prestige@inet-1.com* or *khardman@prestigecare.com*

AL: 105. ALZ/MEM IMP: 27

Age 60+. For-profit; nondenominational; nonsectarian. Apartments. Nursing care; health monitoring; incontinence management; insulin injections; medical appointment scheduling; ambulation assistance; 24-hour personal care; medication administration; 24-hour security; 24-hour emergency response system;

maintenance; scheduled transportation; up to 3 daily meals; pets allowed; weekly housekeeping and laundry services; social and recreational activities; hydrotherapy bath; private dining room; lounge; activity room; aviary; landscaped grounds with walking paths and pond; pet exercise area; barber/beauty shop.

DEP: $200. IND MO: $1,950–$2,825. AL MO: varies according to apartment type and size.

Providence Assisted Living

233 N. Main
Providence, UT 84332-9622

Ph: (435) 792-4770

http://www.rlg.net

E-mail: *providence@rlg.net*

AL: 60

For-profit; nondenominational. Private rooms. Nursing care; medical services; rehabilitative therapies; podiatry services; pharmacy; personal care; medication administration; security system; emergency response system; maintenance; transportation; up to 3 daily meals; pets allowed; housekeeping and laundry services; some exercise equipment; social and recreational activities.

DEP: $550. AL MO: $2,050–$2,450.

Salt Lake Home

112 West 200 North
Salt Lake City, UT 84103

Ph: (801) 328-0251
Fax: (801) 328-9424

http://www.rlg.net

E-mail: *slhome@rlg.net*

AL: 93

Private rooms. Nursing care; incontinence care; podiatry care; pharmacy services; personal care; medication administration; security; 24-hour emergency response system; maintenance; transportation; up to 3 daily meals; pets allowed; weekly housekeeping and laundry services; planned activities; barber/beauty shop.

DEP: (ref.), $495. AL MO: $1,350–$2,550.

Sarah Daft Home

737 South 1300 East
Salt Lake City, UT 84102

Ph: (801) 582-5104
Fax: (801) 582-8808

IND: 18. AL: 21. RH: Yes

Age 55+. Nonprofit, nondenominational. Private rooms. Medical services; health care clinics; podiatry care; 24-hour staffing; personal care; medication administration; 24-hour security; 24-hour emergency response system; maintenance; transportation; up to 3 daily meals; housekeeping and laundry services; exercise room; Sunday church service; social and recreational activities; crafts room; barber/beauty shop.

IND ENT: (non-ref.), $250. IND MO: $1,075. AL ENT: (non-ref.), $495. AL MO: $1,600–$1,950. Private room: $1,075–$1,600.

Stonewood Manor

430 S. Main St.
Orem, UT 84058

Ph: (801) 226-4343
Fax: (801) 426-5670

E-mail: *stonewood@i-net.com*

IND: Yes. AL: Yes

Private rooms. 24-hour staffing; personal care; medication administration; emergency response system; up to 3 daily meals; social and recreational activities.

Contact facility for fees.

Williamsburg Retirement Community

132 West 300 North
Logan, UT 84321

Ph: (435) 753-5502

IND: Yes. RC: Yes

Studios and one- and two-bedroom apartments. 24-hour staffing; personal care; medication administration; security; emergency response system; maintenance; transportation; up to 3 daily meals; housekeeping and laundry services; exercise classes; religious services; social and recreational activities; common areas; bingo; on and off-site activities.

DEP: $495. IND MO: $1,025–$1,450; 2nd person, $385. RC MO: $1,425–$2,425.

Independent Living

Independent housing (primarily rentals) for seniors that may offer security features, meal service, and activities.

Southwest

Rosecrest Manor

48 West 700 South
St. George, UT 84770

Ph: (801) 673-7398

IND: Yes

Private rooms. 24-hour staffing; medication administration; emergency response system; up to 3 daily meals; housekeeping and laundry services; onsite church services; social and recreational activities; flower garden.

Contact facility for fees.

North

Harrison Regent

4481 Harrison Blvd.
Ogden, UT 84403

Ph: (801) 479-1653
Fax: (801) 479-7484

IND: 90

No age requirements, but must be retired. Nondenominational. Apartments. 24-hour staff; 24-hour security; 24-hour emergency response system; resident managers; maintenance; transportation; up to 3 daily meals; pets allowed; housekeeping and laundry services; fitness room, exercise class and equipment; swimming pool; library; private dining area; social and recreational activities; three fireside lounges; barber/beauty shop.

DEP: (ref.), one month's rent. IND MO: about $1,275–$2,050.

Housing Authority of Salt Lake City

1776 South West Temple
Salt Lake City, UT 84115

Ph: (801) 487-2161
Fax: (801) 487-3641

IND: 336

Age 55+. Nonprofit. Low-income apartments. 24-hour security; 24-hour emergency response system; maintenance; pets allowed.

IND MO: 30% of gross income.

Lakeside Village

1580 West 3940 South
West Valley City, UT 84123

Ph: (801) 972-9999

http://www.rlg.net

E-mail: *lakeside@rlg.net*

IND: 144

Age: 80% of residents are 55+. Forprofit. Apartments. Maintenance; swimming pool.

DEP: $275. MO: $625–$800.

Legacy Retirement Residence

1617 W. Temple Lane (10200 South)
South Jordan, UT 84095

Ph: (801) 253-4556
Fax: (801) 253-9905

http://www.westernstateslodging.com/legacy/legacy.htm

IND: 168

Age 55+. Nondenominational. Apartments. 24-hour security; 24-hour emergency response system; maintenance; transportation; up to 2 daily meals; pets allowed; housekeeping and laundry services; fitness center; library; social and recreational activities; arts and crafts center; country store/gift shop; within walking distance of grocery store, drugstore, public library, and senior center; located next to LDS Temple; barber/beauty shop.

DEP: (ref.), one month's rent. IND MO: $375–$3,000.

The Seville

325 W. Center St.
Orem, UT 84057

Ph: (801) 224-8044
Fax: (801) 224-1280

IND: Yes

Apartments. Security; emergency response system; transportation; up to 3 daily meals; housekeeping and laundry services; exercise programs; Sunday church service; Bible study; social and recreational activities.

IND MO: studio, $1,250–$1,525; 1-bedroom, $1,525–$1,900; 2-bedroom, $2,125; 2nd person, $350.

Union Gardens

468 Third St.
Ogden, UT 84404

Ph: (801) 392-7230 TDD: (801) 565-0700

IND: Yes

Age 62+. Managed by Danville Development Corp. Apartments. Wellness program; blood pressure and blood sugar checks; oxygen saturation testing; podiatry care; health education classes; on-site service coordinator; security; maintenance; transportation; meal program; small pets allowed; laundry services; social and recreational activities; crafts; resident council; landscaped grounds.

HUD-subsidized housing.

Adult/Resort Communities

Communities for active adults (not all are age-restricted; primarily ownership).

Southeast

Kayenta

800 N. Kayenta Parkway
Ivins/Kayenta, UT 84738

Ph: (435) 628-7234

http://www.kayentautah.com

Individual homes, homesites. Tennis; swimming pool; hiking; social clubs; nearby golf, state and national parks.

PURCHASE: Homes, $220,000–$1.1 million+; homesites, $49,500–$170,500.

Sky Mountain Golf Course

1030 N. 2600 W.
Hurricane, UT 84737

Ph: (435) 635-4653

Individual homes, condominiums, homesites. Golf course; clubhouse; fitness center; swimming pool; dining facility.

PURCHASE: Homes, $129,000–$550,000+.

SunRiver St. George

1580 W. Poppy Hills Circle
St. George, UT 84790

Ph: (888) 688-6556 or (435) 688-1000

http://www.sunriver-stgeorge.com

Age 55+. Individual homes. Golf course; clubhouse; pro shop; community center; swimming pools; tennis; fitness center; crafts; ballroom; billiards; computer center; trails; dining.

PURCHASE: Homes, $124,500–$601,500.

Vermont

http://www.state.vt.us

General Information

Climate

Cold winters; warm summers. Summer day temperatures can reach into the 90s°F, but nights are cool.

Cost of Living

Ranks 12th in the nation.

Taxes

State/Local as % of Income: 11.8%.

Property Tax Reduction: Homeowner or Renter Rebate Program is available (not age-restricted).

Sales: 5%.

Prescription Exemptions: Prescription medicines are exempt from sales tax.

Transportation, Travel, and Tourism

General

Vermont Department of Tourism and Marketing, 6 Baldwin St., Drawer 33, Montpelier, VT 05633, (800) VERMONT. E-mail: *tourwebmaster@gate.dca.state.vt.us*

Major Airport

- Burlington International Airport, Airport Drive, Burlington, (802) 863-2874.

Railways

- Amtrak, (800) USA-RAIL

Bus Tours

- Greyhound Bus, (800) 231-2222.

State Highways

- Interstate 91 runs north and south
- Interstate 89 runs southeast-northwest.

Theater and Music

South

- Bennington Center for the Arts, Route 9, Bennington, (802) 442-7158.
- Brattleboro Music Center, Walnut St., Brattleboro, (802) 257-4523.
- Dorset Theatre Festival, Dorset, (802) 867-2223 or 5777.
- Southern Vermont Art Center, Manchester, (802) 362-1956.
- Stratton Mountain Resort, (802) 297-2200 (summer music festival).
- Weston Playhouse, Village Green, Weston, (802) 824-8167, (summer theater).
- Weston Priory, Rte. 155, Weston, (802) 824-5409 (Benedictine monastery, friars' music).

Central

- Barre Opera House, City Hall, Montpelier, (802) 476-8188.
- Hopkins Center for the Arts, Dartmouth College, Hanover, NH (near Norwich, VT), (603) 646-2808 (year-round concerts, plays, films).
- Middlebury College Center for the Arts, Middlebury, (802) 388-3711.
- Town Hall Theater, Rte. 4, Woodstock, (802) 457-3981.

Museums, Crafts, Historical, Recreational

North

- Old Stone House Museum, Rte. 2, Browington, (802) 754-2022 (18th- and 19th-century collections).

- Shores Memorial Museum, Main St., Lyndon Center, (802) 626-5742, (Victorian collection).
- Vermont Wildflower Farm, Rte. 7, Shelburne, (802) 425-3500.
- Furchgott Sourdiffe, 3 Falls Rd., Shelburne, VT 05482, (802) 985-3848 (art gallery).
- Robert Hull Fleming Museum, UVM Campus, Burlington, (802) 656-0750 (art, natural history, geology, archaeology).
- Rhombus, 186 College St., Burlington, (802) 652-1103 (art gallery, poetry, performances, music).

South

- American Museum of Fly Fishing, Rte. 7A, Manchester Village, (802) 362-3300.
- Belle of Brattleboro, Brattleboro Marina, Brattleboro, (802) 254-1263 (tour boat).
- Bennington Museum, Rte. 9, Bennington, (802) 447-7531.
- Historic Hildene, Rte. 7A, Manchester Village, (802) 362-1788 (Robert Todd Lincoln estate).
- Norman Rockwell Exhibition, Rte. 7A, Arlington, (802) 375-6423.
- Black River Academy Museum, Ludlow (802) 228-5050 (railroading, mining, and farming exhibits).

Central

- Justin Morrill Homestead, Strafford, (802) 828-3226 (Victorian house).
- Lake Champlain Maritime Museum, Off Panton Rd., Basin Harbor, (802) 475-2022 (history of Lake Champlain).
- New England Maple Museum, Rte. 7, Pittsford, (802) 483-9414 (history exhibits, tours, tastings).

Organizations

Advocacy Groups

- Department of Aging and Disabilities, Division of Licensing and Protection, (802) 241-2345.

Volunteer Programs

- Vermont State Parks, Volunteer Coordinator, Department of Forests, Parks and Recreation, 103 S. Main St., Waterbury, VT 05671-0603, (802) 241-3655, Fax (802) 244-1481. Develop or assist in special programs to educate visitors; administrative duties; research opportunities.
- Habitat for Humanity, PO Box 1038, White River Jct., VT 05001, (802) 295-1854.
- RSVP of the Upper Valley and White Mountains, Woodstock, (802) 295-3635.
- Brooks Memorial Library, 224 Main St., Brattleboro, VT 05301, (802) 254-5290. Volunteers needed.

Housing

Long-Term Care Facilities

*In the state of Vermont, these facilities are called **Long-Term Care/Nursing Home Facilities**.*

These facilities provide residential living and/or various levels of nursing and medical services to seniors for an extended period of time.

Types of Authorization

Licensing and / or Certification

These facilities are licensed by the Department of Aging and Disabilities; Division of Licensing and Protection. Nursing homes provide 24-hour nursing care and personal care, supervision, hospice care, and rehabilitative care.

Memberships

- American Association of Homes and Services for the Aging (AAHSA) represents not-for-profit organizations committed to providing high-quality health care, housing, and services to the elderly. AAHSA, 901 E St. NW, Suite 500, Washington, DC 20004-2011. Ph: (202) 783-2242. Fax: (202) 783-2285. *http://www.aahsa.org*
- Vermont Health Care Association (VHCA).
- The American Health Care Association (AHCA).

Accreditation:

- Continuing Care Accreditation Commission (CCAC) accredits facilities that offer seniors a contract or contracts that provide residential living and health care services for the remainder of the person's lifetime and meet CCAC's accreditation standards.
- Joint Commission on the Accreditation of Healthcare Organizations (JCAHO) is an independent, not-for-profit organization, and the nation's oldest and largest standards-setting and health care accrediting institution.

Central

Brookside Nursing Home, VHCA, AHCA

RR1 Box 2250
Bradford, VT 05033

Ph: (802) 222-5201

NH: 80

Privately owned; nondenominational. Private and semiprivate rooms. Skilled nursing care; respite care; physician on call; intermediate care; physical, occupational, and speech therapies; medical services; pharmacy services; Medicare/Medicaid-approved; personal care; medication administration; security; emergency response system; maintenance; transportation; up to 3 daily meals; housekeeping and laundry services; exercise class; religious programs; social and recreational activities; resident council; card and board games; movies; music; dining out; barber/beauty shop.

NH Daily: Semiprivate, $145; private, $155–$260.

Helen Porter Nursing Home

Porter Drive
Middlebury, VT 05753

Ph: (802) 388-4001

SNF: 118

Nondenominational facility. Private and semiprivate rooms. 24-hour skilled nursing care; medical director; physical, occupational, and speech therapies; social services; inpatient care; outpatient diagnostic testing; long- and short-term care; Medicare/Medicaid-approved; adjacent to medical center; personal care; medication administration; security; emergency response system; maintenance; transportation; 3 daily meals; housekeeping and laundry services; exercise classes; individual and group activities programs; games; arts and crafts; music; walking paths; gardening.

Contact facility for fees.

Northwest

Birchwood Terrace Health Care Center

43 Starr Farm Rd.
Burlington, VT 05401

Ph: (802) 863-6384
Fax: (802) 865-4516

NH: 110. ALZ/MEM IMP: 50

For-profit; nondenominational. Private and semiprivate rooms. 24-hour nursing care; medical director; subacute care; respiratory and rehabilitative therapies; hospice; pharmacy; assurance programs;

Medicare/Medicaid-approved; personal care; medication administration; security; emergency response system; maintenance; transportation; 3 daily meals; housekeeping and laundry services; exercise classes; religious services; pet therapy; arts and crafts; hobbies; activities director; off site activities; recreational and social activities; barber/beauty shop.

SNF Daily: $190–$300.

Burlington Health and Rehabilitation Center, JCAHO

300 Pearl St.
Burlington, VT 05401

Ph: (802) 658-4200
Fax: (802) 863-8016

NH: 168

For-profit; nondenominational. Private and semiprivate rooms. 24-hour nursing care; skilled nursing care; physical, occupational, and speech therapies; dental and podiatry services; pharmacy; short and long-term care; Medicare/Medicaid-approved; personal care; medication administration; emergency response system; maintenance; transportation; 3 daily meals; housekeeping and laundry services; activities.

NH Daily: $200.

Green Mountain Nursing Home

1102 Ethan Allen Ave.
Colchester, VT 05446

Ph: (802) 655-1025
Fax: (802) 655-3025

SNF: 73

Locally owned and operated; nondenominational. Private and semiprivate rooms. 24-hour skilled nursing care; podiatry and dental services; rehabilitative and restorative therapies; social services; Medicare/Medicaid-approved; security; emergency response system; maintenance; 3 daily meals; housekeeping and laundry services; individual and group activities; gardens; picnics.

DEP: $5,025. SNF MO: $5,025.

Southwest

Bennington Health and Rehab Center, JCAHO

360 Dewey St.
Bennington, VT 05201

Ph: (802) 442-8525
Fax: (802) 442-7225

SNF: 100

Nondenominational facility. 24-hour skilled nursing care; medical director; individualized treatment program; physical, occupational, and speech therapies; recreational therapy; psychology services; social services; pharmacy; Medicare/Medicaid-approved; security; emergency response system; maintenance; transportation; 3 daily meals; housekeeping and laundry services; exercise program; religious services; banking services; pet therapy; cooking workshops; bingo; board and card games; volunteer program; gardening; barber/beauty shop.

Contact facility for fees.

Assisted Living and Residential Care Facilities

These facilities provide room and board for ambulatory and independent adults who need minimum support.

Types of Authorization

Licensing and / or Certification

Requires licensing by the Department of Health. These facilities provide supervision, limited nursing care, personal care, and therapies to residents who are not in need of skilled nursing care, but who need some assistance to live independently.

Memberships

- Assisted Living Federation of America (ALFA) is a national nonprofit membership organization whose mission is to enhance the quality of life in assisted living facilities and promote the interests of the assisted living industry. ALFA, 10300 Eaton Place, Suite 400, Fairfax, VA 22030. Ph: (703) 691-8100. Fax: (703) 691-8106. *http://www.alfa.org*

Northwest

Canterbury Inn

46 Cherry Street
St. Johnsbury, VT 05819

Ph: (802) 748-5556

AL: 42

For-profit; nondenominational. Private rooms with baths, private rooms with shared bath, and semiprivate rooms. Registered nurse on call 24 hours; nursing attendant on call 24 hours; personal care; medication administration; Medicare/Medicaid-approved; security; security; emergency response system; maintenance; transportation; 3 daily meals plus snacks; resident cat; housekeeping and laundry services; social and recreation activities.

AL Daily: Contact facility for fees.

Central

Heaton Woods

10 Heaton St.
Montpelier, VT 05602

Ph: (802) 223-1127
Fax: (802) 229-2286

E-mail: *Hwoods2@juno.com*

AL: 43

Nonprofit; nondenominational. Private rooms with baths. Nursing care; respite care; personal care; medication administration; security; emergency response system; maintenance; transportation; 3 daily meals plus snacks; pets allowed; housekeeping and laundry services; activities director; social and recreational activities.

AL Daily: $30–$80 (sliding scale based upon total income and assets).

Independent Living

Independent housing (primarily rentals) for seniors that may offer security features, meal service, and activities.

Northwest

The Courtyard

120 E. Spring St.
Winooski, VT 05404

Ph: (802) 655-9320
Fax: (802) 655-6809

E-mail: *Courtyard@Accessvt.com*

IND: 100

For-profit; nondenominational. One- and two-bedroom apartments. Emergency response system; maintenance; meals on wheels available; pets allowed; laundry services; library; community room; media room; bingo; activities; shuffleboard and pool table; patio.

IND MO: $30–$1,000.

Heineberg Senior Housing

72 Heineberg Rd.
Burlington, VT 05401

Ph: (802) 658-6091

E-mail: *patgabe@together.net*

IND: 82

Age 55+. For-profit; nondenominational. Apartments. Nursing care; security; emergency response system; maintenance; transportation; up to 3 daily meals; pets allowed.

Contact facility for fees.

Holy Cross Senior Housing

47 Church Rd.
Colchester, VT 05446

Ph: (802) 868-0121
Fax: (802) 863-4117

E-mail: *patgehe@together.net*

IND: 40

Age 55+. For-profit; nondenominational. Apartments. Nursing care; security; emergency response system; maintenance; transportation; up to 3 daily meals; pets allowed.

Contact facility for fees.

Richmond Terrace

72 Thompson Rd.
Richmond, VT 05477

Ph: (802) 878-0997
Fax: (802) 879-9659

E-mail: *nancykid@together.net*

IND: 15

Age 62+. Nonprofit; nondenominational. Apartments. Security; emergency response system; maintenance; transportation; pets allowed.

Contact facility for fees.

Three Cathedral Square

3 Cathedral Square
Burlington, VT 05401

Ph: (802) 863-3868
Fax: (802) 863-0385

E-mail: *csc@together.net*

IND: 100

Age 62+. Nonprofit; nondenominational. Apartments. Nursing care; security; emergency response system; maintenance; transportation; up to 3 daily meals; pets allowed.

Contact facility for fees.

Whitney Hill Homestead

45 Whitney Hill Rd.
Williston, VT 05495

Ph: (802) 878-0007
Fax: (802) 879-9659

IND: 44

Age 55+. For-profit; nondenominational. Apartments. Security; emergency response system; maintenance; transportation; pets allowed.

Contact facility for fees.

South Central

Maple Village for National Church Residences

72 Pine St.
Rutland, VT 05701

Ph: (802) 775-1265
Fax: (802) 775-0677

IND: 35

Age 62+. Nonprofit; nondenominational. Apartments. Home health care services; security; emergency response system; maintenance; close to public transportation; meal program; pets allowed; laundry services; on-duty manager; community room; service coordinator.

DEP: 1 mo. rent. IND MO: 30% of income; HUD-subsidized.

Village Manor for National Church Residences

758 Arch St.
Pittsford, VT 05763

Ph: (802) 483-9312
Fax: (802) 483-2161

IND: 30

Age 62+. Nonprofit; nondenominational. Apartments. Security; emergency response system; maintenance; meals on wheels program; pets allowed; laundry services; on-duty manager; community room; service coordinator.

DEP: 1 mo. rent. IND MO: 30% of income; HUD-subsidized.

North Central:

North Barre Manor

455 N. Main St.
Barre, VT 05641

Ph: (802) 476-3185
Fax: (802) 476-3113

E-mail: *barrehousi@aol.com*

IND: 120

Age 62+. Nondenominational. Apartments. Security; maintenance; congregate meals; laundry services; community rooms and activities.

Income eligibility: Maximum income, 1 person, $16,500; 2 persons, $19,000.

Stimson and Graves

14 Stowe St.
Waterbury, VT 05767

Ph: (802) 878-0997
Fax: (802) 879-9659

E-mail: *nancykid@together.net*

IND: 14

Age 55. Nonprofit; nondenominational. Apartments. Security; emergency response system; maintenance; pets allowed.

Contact facility for fees.

Adult/Resort Communities

Communities for active adults (not all are age-restricted; primarily ownership).

North

Copley Woodlands

125 Thomas Lane
Stowe, VT 05672

Ph: (802) 253-4203

http://www.copleywoodlands.com

Condominiums. Exercise classes; pottery; art gallery; social clubs; trips; transportation.

PURCHASE: Condos, $169,000–$203,000. Monthly service fee (includes utilities, activities, insurance, security, maintenance): $1,100; 2nd adult, $330.

Central

The Quechee Club

25 River Rd.
Quechee, VT 05059

Ph: (800) 262-3186

http://www.quecheeproperties.com

Individual homes, condominiums, homesites. Golf courses; tennis; racquetball; swimming pool; fitness center; hiking/biking; boating/waterskiing; snow skiing; skating; community center; social clubs; polo team; dining; Dartmouth hospital nearby.

PURCHASE: Homes, $110,000–$440,000; condos, $82,500–$330,000; homesites, $27,500–$110,000.

Virginia

http://www.state.va.us

General Information

Climate

A mild to humid climate. Average January temperature is 36° F; average July temperature is 75° F.

Cost of Living

Ranks 27th in the nation.

Taxes

General: Department of Taxation, PO Box 115, Richmond, VA 23218.

State/local as % of Income: About 10%. Seniors age 62 and older may receive income tax benefits known as "age deduction." Those 65 and older may claim a personal exemption of $800 on their income tax return.

Property Tax Reduction: Most cities and counties offer tax relief for those 65 and older.

Sales: 4.5%.

Prescription Exemptions: Prescription medications are exempt from sales tax.

Transportation, Travel, and Tourism

General

Department of Tourism, E-mail: *vainfo@vedp.state.va.us*

Major Airports

- Newport News–Williamsburg International Airport, (757) 877-0221.
- Richmond International Airport (Byrd Field), (804) 226-3052.
- Norfolk Airport Shuttle, (757) 857-1231.
- Washington Dulles International Airport, (703) 572-2700.
- Ronald Reagan Washington National Airport, Washington, D.C. 20001, (703) 417-8000.

Railways

- Amtrak, (800) USA-RAIL.

Bus Tours

- Abbott Bus Lines, (540) 343-1133.
- Fun Tours, (757) 853-2990 (specializes in working with senior citizen groups).
- Greyhound Bus, (800) 231-2222.

State Highways

- Interstate 95 runs north-south.
- Interstate 64 runs east-west.

Theater and Music

East

- Chrysler Hall, 415 St. Pauls Blvd., Norfolk, VA 23510, (757) 664-6464 (home to Virginia Symphony).
- Tidewater Performing Arts Society, (757) 627-2314 (dance and music performances at Harrison Opera House and Virginia Beach Pavilion Theater).
- The Virginia Opera, 160 E. Virginia Beach Blvd., Norfolk, VA 23510, (757) 627-9545, Fax: (757) 622-0058.
- Virginia Beach Center for the Arts, 2200 Parks Ave., Virgimia Beach, VA 23451-4062, (757) 425-0000 (concerts, theater).
- Richmond's Landmark Theater, 6 N. Laurel St., Richmond, VA 23220-4704, (804) 780-4213 (theater, concerts, lectures).
- Richmond Symphony, 300 W. Franklin St., Richmond, VA 23220, (804) 788-4717.

- Byrd Theater, 2908 W. Cary St., Richmond, VA 23221-3516, (804) 353-9911 (films, national landmark).
- Ashland Stage Company, 500 S. Center St., Ashland, VA, (804) 798-2728.

Middle

- Lynchburg Fine Arts Center, 1815 Thompson Drive, Lynchburg, VA 24501-1051, (804) 846-8451, Fax: (804) 846-2806 (music, dance, theater).

West

- Opera Roanoke, 541 Luck Ave., Roanoke, VA 24016-5047, (540) 982-2742, Fax: (540) 982-3601.

North

- Fairfax Band, Fairfax, (703) 757-0220 (symphonic wind ensemble).
- Opera Theater of Northern Virginia, 2700 South Lang St., Arlington, VA 22206, (703) 549-5039.

Museums, Crafts, Historical, Recreational

East

- Berkeley Plantation, 12602 Harrision Landing, Charles City, VA 23030, (804) 829-6018 (on the banks of the James River).
- Colonial Williamsburg, (804) 229-1000 or (800) HISTORY (restored 18th-Century community).
- 1708 Gallery, 103 E. Broad St., Richmond, VA 23219-1733, (804) 643-7829.
- Virginia Museum of Fine Arts, 2800 Grove Ave., Richmond, VA 23221-2472, (804) 367-0844, Fax (804) 367-9393.

Central

- Charlottesville Historic District, PO Box 178, Charlottesville, VA 22902-0178, (804) 977-1783 (historic area, theater, shopping, dining).

West

- Shenandoah National Park, 3655 US Hwy 211c E., Luray, VA 22835-4702, (540) 999-3500 (hiking, park guides, camping, tours).
- Art Museum of Western Virginia, One Market Sq., Center in the Sq., Roanoke, VA 24011, (540) 342-5760 or 5798.
- Blue Ridge Parkway, Bedford, (540) 586-4357 (scenic drive).

North

- Black History Resource Center, 638 N. Alfred St., Alexandria, VA 22314-1823, (703) 838-4356 (exhibitions, lectures and special events).
- Manassas National Battlefield Park, 12521 Lee Hwy, Manassas, VA 20109, (703) 361-1339.

Southwest

- Southwest Virginia Museum, Big Stone Gap, (540) 523-1322.

Organizations

Advocacy Groups

- Long-Term Care Ombudsman, 530 E. Main St., Suite 428, Richmond, VA 23219, (804) 644-2923.

Volunteer Programs

- Volunteerism at VA State Parks, (804) 371-2675 (visitor services, office/desk, resource management).

Housing

Long-Term Care Facilities

*In the state of Virginia, these facilities are called **Long-Term Care/Nursing Home Facilities**.*

These facilities provide residential living and/or various levels of nursing and medical services to seniors for an extended period of time.

Types of Authorization

Licensing and/or Certification

Long-term care can be any system of programs that provide social, health, and related supportive services to individuals who are limited in their ability to care for themselves over an extended period of time. Nursing facilities must be licensed by the Department of Health. Services include: skilled nursing care and related services; rehabilitation services; health-related care; personal care; medication administration; personal assessment for each resident; social services; activities that aid mental, physical, and social development; rehabilitative services.

Memberships

- American Association of Homes and Services for the Aging (AAHSA) represents not-for-profit organizations committed to providing high-quality health care, housing, and services to the elderly. AAHSA, 901 E St. NW, Suite 500, Washington, DC 20004-2011. Ph: (202) 783-2242. Fax: (202) 783-2285. *http://www.aahsa.org*

Accreditations

- Continuing Care Accreditation Commission (CCAC) accredits facilities that offer seniors a contract or contracts that provide residential living and health care services for the remainder of the person's lifetime and meet CCAC's accreditation standards.
- Joint Commission on the Accreditation of Healthcare Organizations (JCAHO) is an independent, not-for-profit organization, and the nation's oldest and largest standards-setting and health care accrediting institution.
- Virginia Association of Non-profit Homes for the Aging (VANHA), Innslake Place Building, 4401 Dominion Blvd., Suite 200, Glen Allen, VA 23060-3322. Ph: (804) 965-5500. Fax: (804) 965-9089.
- Educational Assessment Guidelines Leading toward Excellence (EAGLE) is a voluntary self-assessment and peer review evaluation system developed by the United Methodist Association of Health and Welfare Ministries.

Northeast

The Jefferson

900 N. Taylor St.
Arlington, VA 22203

Ph: (703) 351-0011
Fax: (703) 516-9459

IND: Yes. AL: Yes. ALZ/MEM IMP: Yes. HCC: Yes

A Marriott-owned facility. Condos, and private and semiprivate rooms. 24-hour nursing care; postoperative care; podiatry, ophthalmology, and dentistry services; physical, occupational, and speech therapies, audiology; personal care; medication administration; Medicare-approved; supplemental services; security; up to 3 daily meals; exercise room; swimming pool and Jacuzzi; library and reading room; activity center; game room.

IND ENT: $159,500–$396,000. IND MO: $1,325–$2,475, 2nd person, $550. ASSOC: $100–$225. AL MO: (semiprivate), $2,350–$3,175; (private), $3,125–

$4,225; additional care Level II, $325, additional care Level III, $675. ALZ/MEM IMP MO: (semiprivate), $4,025; (private), $4,725–$5,600; additional care Level II, $350; additional care Level III, $725. HCC MO: (semiprivate), $5,125–$5,775; (private), $6,725. HCC Daily: $170-$225.

Manor Care Nursing and Rehabilitation

550 S. Carlin Spgs. Rd.
Arlington, VA 22204

Ph: (703) 578-5599

SNF: Yes. ALZ/MEM IMP: Yes. RSP: Yes

Nondenominational; nonsectarian. Private and semiprivate rooms. Short- and long-term care; physical, occupational, speech, and recreational therapies; skilled nursing care; social services; dental, physician, and podiatry services; lab and pharmaceutical services; personal care; medication administration; emergency response system; 3 daily meals; housekeeping and laundry services; activities program; religious services; lounges; barber/beauty shop.

Daily: $160–$225.

Vinson Hall

6251 Old Dominion Drive
McLean, VA 22101

Ph: (703) 536-4344 or (800) 451-5121
Fax: (703) 536-0340

http://www.vinsonhall.org

IND: Yes. AL: Yes. HCC: Yes. ALZ/MEM IMP: Yes

Nonprofit; serving former/retired military officers and families. Apartments and private and semiprivate rooms. Short- and long-term care; doctor on site 3 days/week; skilled nursing care; personal care; medication administration; security; emergency response system; maintenance; transportation; up to 3 daily meals; housekeeping and laundry services; exercise room; chapel; off-site cultural and recreational activities; banking services; library; crafts; hobby shop; gardens.

DEP: (ref.) 10% of ENT fee. IND ENT: (non-ref.) $32,000–$93,500; (90% ref.), $87,000–$187,000. IND MO: $975–$2,550.

The Washington House, CCAC, VANHA, AAHSA

5100 Fillmore Ave.
Alexandria, VA 22311

Ph: (703) 845-5100
Fax: (703) 671-0468

http://www.washingtonhouse.com

IND: 137. AL: 23. HCC: 68

Nonprofit; nondenominational; affiliated with the Arlington Health Foundation. Apartments, and private and semiprivate rooms. 24-hour nursing care; short- and long-term care; physical therapy; dental services; podiatrist, ophthalmologist, dermatologist, and psychologist services; on-staff medical director; personal care; medication administration; Medicare-approved; security; emergency response system; maintenance; transportation; up to 3 daily meals; housekeeping and laundry services; exercise classes; chapel; game room; country store; barber/beauty shop.

ENT: (Life Care Plan; AL and HCC unlimited use at no additional cost) $52,000–$221,500 (single); MO: $1,300–$3,125 (single). Rental: (no ENT; may convert to LCP) $2,025–$3,400/mo. (single).

Southwest

Richfield Retirement Community

3615 W. Main St., PO Box 3240
Salem, VA 24153

Ph: (540) 380-2986
Fax: (540) 380-4719

http://www.richfield-retirement.com

E-mail: *richfield@richfield-retirement.com*

IND: 193. AL: 172. HCC: 327. AL/MEM IMP: 84

Age 55+. Privately owned; nondenominational. Cottages, apartments, and private and semiprivate rooms. Skilled and intermediate nursing care; 24-hour nursing care; occupational, speech, and physical therapies; pharmacy services; personal care; medication administration; Medicare/Medicaid-approved; security; emergency response system; maintenance; transportation; up to 3 daily meals; housekeeping and laundry services; chapel; social, educational, and recreational activities; off-site activities.

RSV: $1,375. PROC: (no ref.) $165. IND LL: (% ref. up to 9 yrs.), $31,500–$170,500. IND LL MO: (with LL), $250–$575; (rental), $550–$2,225. AL MO: $1,850–$2,550; (daily) $70+. ALZ/MEM IMP MO: $3,850; (daily) $140.

Roanoke United Methodist Home, LTCA, CCAC, EAGLE

1009 Old Country Club Rd., NW
Roanoke, VA 24017

Ph: (540) 344-6248
Fax: (540) 344-8919

IND: Yes. AL: Yes. HCC: Yes

Age 65+. Nondenominational; nonsectarian. Apartments and private and semiprivate rooms. 24-hour licensed medical care; personal care; medication administration; emergency response system; 3 daily meals; housekeeping and laundry services; chapel; library; planned activities; meeting rooms; educational opportunities; crafts; greenhouse; outdoor activities.

IND ENT: $52,000–$108,000. IND MO: $475–$1,425. AL ENT: $48,500 and $54,000. AL MO: $1,950 and $2,650. HCC ENT: $55,000. HCC MO: $3,150. ENT covers 30 days in HCC (annually).

Central

The Hermitage

1600 Westwood Ave
Richmond, VA 23227

Ph: (804) 355-5721
Fax: (804) 358-0854
http://www.hermitage-vumh.com

IND: Yes. AL: Yes. HCC: 115. ALZ/MEM IMP: Yes

Age 65+. Nonprofit; Virginia Methodist Homes; nondenominational; nonsectarian facility. Studios, apartments, private and semiprivate rooms. Patient care team; speech and occupational therapies; podiatry and dental services; 24-hour nursing care; nurse call system; physical and recreational therapies; pharmacy; hearing aid checks; wellness program; personal care; medication administration; transportation; up to 3 daily meals; housekeeping and linen service; chapel; garden areas; personal shopping; crafts/workshop; library; music programs; volunteer services; resident services; computer workstations; off-site activities.

IND LC ENT: (ref./prorated 1st 30 days) $62,000–$131,000. IND MO: (single), $1,400–$2,050; (double), $1,400–$1,550/per person. AL LIFE CARE ENT: $62,000–$92,500. AL MO: $1,850–$3,000. HCC LC ENT: $31,000–$62,000. HCC MO: $3,250–$3,725. Life Care contracts include 30 days of health care/year. IND MO LEASE: (single), $1,975–$2,875; (double), $1,975–$2,175/person. AL MO LEASE: $2,575–$4,025. HCC Daily: $130/person; $175. MO: $4,050. Mo.-lease residents charged for HCC visits.

Lakewood Manor

1900 Lauderdale Drive
Richmond, VA 23233

Ph: (804) 740-2900
Fax: (804) 740-3774

IND: 265. AL: Yes. HCC: Yes

Virginia Baptist Homes; nondenominational; nonsectarian; nonprofit. Apartments and private and semiprivate rooms. 24-hour nursing care; medical director; wellness clinic; clinic and pharmacy services; respite care; physical, speech, and occupational therapies; podiatry services; personal care; medication administration; security; emergency response system; maintenance; transportation; up to 3 daily meals (1 daily meal included /in MO fee); housekeeping and laundry services; chapel; planned activities; gardens; woodworking shop; library.

PROC: (no ref.) $50. DEP: (ref.) $1,000. IND ENT: (single), $69,000–$116,000; (double), $121,000–$162,000. IND MO: (single), $1,575–$2,200; (double), $2,600–$3,075. Use of HCC and AL services no additional charges.

Our Lady of Peace

751 Hillsdale Drive
Charlottesville, VA 22901

Ph: (804) 973-1155
Fax: (804) 973-3397

IND: Yes. AL: Yes. HCC: Yes

Nonprofit; nondenominational; Catholic Diocese of Richmond. Apartments, studios, and private and semiprivate rooms. 24-hour nursing care; wellness program; personal care; medication administration; security; emergency call system; transportation; up to 3 daily meals; housekeeping and laundry services; social, recreational, and religious activities; library; patio; barber/beauty shop.

DEP: One mo. rent. IND MO: $1,500–$2,175; 2nd person, $500. AL MO: $2,700–$3,450; 2nd person, $750–$1,475.

Westminster Canterbury

250 Pantops Mountain Rd.
Charlottesville, VA 22911

Ph: (804) 980-9100
Fax: (804) 980-9173

IND: Yes. AL: Yes. HCC: Yes

Nondenominational; nonsectarian; nonprofit. Cottages, apartments, and private and semiprivate rooms. 24-hour nursing care; short- and long-term care; resident clinic with doctor's office hours; physical, occupational, and speech therapies; personal care; medication administration; security; emergency response system; maintenance; transportation; up to 3 daily meals; housekeeping and laundry services; meal delivery; social and educational activities; church programs; library; gardens; bank; gift shop; barber/beauty shop.

APPL: (no ref.) $100/single; $175/couple. DEP: (ref.) $1,100. Entrance fee options 1–3 are partially refundable. IND ENT: (option 1), $181,500–$401,500; (option 2), $170,500–$379,500; (option 3), $214,500–$456,500; (180 day cap; no ref.), $62,000–$176,000; (1 yr. ded.; no ref.), $99,000–$242,500. IND MO: $1,325–$4,150.

Westminster Canterbury, CCAC

501 V.E.S. Rd.
Lynchburg, VA 24503

Ph: (804) 386-3404 or (800) 962-3520
Fax: (804) 386-3535

E-mail: *ahamilton@wclynchburg.org*

IND: 189. AL: Yes. HCC: Yes

Nonprofit; nondenominational; church sponsored. Apartments, cottages, studios, and private and semiprivate rooms. Skilled and intermediate nursing care; therapies; wellness program, rehabilitative services; pharmacy services; 24-hour nursing care; on-call physician; podiatry and dental services; respite care; hospice care; home health care; personal care; medication administration; security; emergency response system; maintenance; transportation; up to 3 daily meals; housekeeping and laundry services; chapel; gardening; arts and crafts; hobby rooms; library; scheduled activities; cafe; barber/beauty shop.

IND ENT: Apt: Basic: (365 day health care), $43,500–$142,000; 2nd person, $6,850; (unlimited health care), $84,500–$204,000; 2nd person, $33,000; Extended ref.: (365 day health care), $50,500–$174,000; 2nd person, $20,000; (unlimited health care),$98,500–$239,000; 2nd person, $34,500. Cottage: Basic: $196,500–$264,000; 50% min ref.: $273,000–$397,000. IND MO: Apt: $1,400–$2,650; Cottage: $2,175–$3,300.

North Central

The Southerlands

600 Mt. View St.
Front Royal, VA 22630

Ph: (540) 636-2800 or (800) 286-6005
Fax: (540) 636-8585

IND: 42. AL: Yes. HCC: 11

Age 60+ for IND; age 65+ for residential. Studios, apartments, and private and semiprivate rooms. Personal care; medication administration; security; emergency response system; maintenance; transportation; up to 3 daily meals; housekeeping and laundry services; activity center and exercise room; chapel; library; social and recreational activities.

IND ENT: (single) $33,000–$82,500; (double) $41,250–$90,750. IND MO: (single) $1,425–$2,600; (double) $2,175–$3,400. AL ENT: $1,100 and $2,200. AL MO: $1,900 and $3,650. ENT part. refundable.

East

Hermitage on the Eastern Shore, VANHA, AAHSA

23610 North St.
Onancock, VA 23417

Ph: (757) 787-4343 or (888) 437-8864

IND: Yes. AL: Yes. SNF: 35

Age 65+. Nonprofit; nondenominational; Virginia United Methodist Home, Inc. Apartments, and private and semiprivate rooms. Comprehensive 24-hour nursing care; pharmaceutical services; personal care; medication administration; security; maintenance; transportation; 3 daily meals; housekeeping and laundry services; various community activities; game rooms; barber/beauty shop.

IND ENT: (Traditional Plan; minus 10% the 1st mo., less 3%/mo. for 30 mos.), $52,000–$97,000; (Refundable Plan; based on age), $85,000–$158,000. IND MO: $1,325–$2,500. AL MO: $2,675–$2,275. SNF: $2,675–$2,975.

Patriots Colony at Williamsburg

6000 Patriots Colony Drive
Williamsburg, VA 2318801396

Ph: (757) 220-9000 or (800) 716-9000
Fax: (757) 220-1681

IND: Yes. AL: Yes. HCC: Yes. ALZ/MEM IMP: Yes

Age 60+. Nonprofit community for retired officers, spouses, and retired senior executives of the federal government. Apartments and private and semiprivate rooms. 24-hour nursing care; necessary medical equipment; dental and podiatrist services; physical, occupational, and speech therapies; 24-hour supervision; wellness center; health screenings; personal care; medication administration; emergency call system; security; transportation; up to 3 daily meals; housekeeping and laundry services; lounges; pool; libraries.

DEP: $1,100 or $1,650. IND ENT: (declining ref.) $98,750–$242,500; (50% ref.), $133,500–$327,500; (95% ref.), $172,500–$424,500. IND MO: $1,450–$2,950. AL MO: $2,150–$3,225. AL Daily: $70–$105. HCC Daily: Semiprivate, $140; private, $150.

Warwick Forest

866 Denbigh Blvd.
Newport News, VA 23608

Ph: (757) 886-2000
Fax: (757) 886-2109

http://www.riverside-online.com/wforest

IND: Yes. AL: Yes. HCC: 385. ALZ/MEM IMP: 20

Virginia United Methodist Homes. Cottages, apartments, and private and semiprivate rooms. 24-hour nursing care; physical, occupational, and speech therapies; lab tests; podiatrist and dental services; recreational therapies; social services; adult day care; respite care; wellness center; personal care; medication administration; security; emergency response system; maintenance; transportation; up to 3 daily meals; housekeeping and laundry services; fitness center; exercise classes; swimming; indoor track; educational programs; social, recreational, and intellectual programs; library; activities; lounges; barber/beauty shop.

IND APPL: (no ref.) $25/person. IND CC ENT: $61,500–$113,000. IND MO: $1,000–$2,225. IND RENTAL MO: (with option to convert to CC): $1,150–$3,100. AL MO: (includes all levels of care) $2,050–$3,875; 2nd person, $1,400–$2,725. ALZ/MEM IMP MO: $3,450. HCC Daily: $130–$375 (some are additional).

Williamsburg Landing

5700 Williamsburg Landing Drive
Williamsburg, VA 23185

Ph: (800) 554-5517

IND: 239. AL: Yes. HCC: 58. ALZ/MEM IMP: Yes

Nonprofit; nondenominational. Cluster homes, apartments, and private and semiprivate rooms. 24-hour nursing care; skilled nursing care; physical, occupational, and speech therapies; long- and short-term care; medical services; dental and podiatry care; pharmacy services; home health care; medical director; wellness program; personal care; medication administration; security; emergency response system; maintenance; transportation; up to 3 daily meals; pets allowed; housekeeping and laundry services; exercise program; fitness center; swimming pool; banking services; library; computer room; social and recreational activities; educational programs; resident committees; woodworking shop; arts and crafts room; Ping-Pong table; tennis courts; walking paths; barber/beauty shop.

IND ENT: (90% ref.), $116,750–$361,500; 2nd person (no ref.), $11,000. IND MO: $2,300–$3,100. AL ENT: $71,750–$97,500. AL MO: $2,800–$4,050. ALZ/MEM IMP ENT: $71,750. ALZ/MEM IMP MO: $3,800–$4,275. HCC ENT: $115,750. HCC Daily: resident, $135 and $165; nonresident, $160 and $185.

Assisted Living and Residential Care Facilities

In the state of Virginia, these facilities are called ***Assisted Living and Adult/Residential Care Facilities****.*

These facilities provide room and board for ambulatory and independent adults who need minimum or moderate support.

Types of Authorization

Licensing and/or Certification

Requires licensing by the Department of Social Services. Two level of care: residential and assisted. Residential facilities are required to provide only minimal personal assistance. Assisted living facilities are required to provide a moderate level of personal assistance.

Memberships

- Assisted Living Federation of America (ALFA) is a national nonprofit membership organization whose mission is to enhance the quality of life in assisted living facilities and promote the interests of the assisted living industry. ALFA, 10300 Eaton Place, Suite 400, Fairfax, VA 22030. Ph: (703) 691-8100. Fax: (703) 691-8106. *http://www.alfa.org*

- Virginia Assisted Living Association (VALA) is a state affiliate of ALFA. VALA, PO Box 28477, Richmond, VA 23228. Ph: (804) 320-1412. Fax: (804) 320-5132.

Southwest

Our Lady of the Valley

650 N. Jefferson St.
Roanoke, VA 24016

AL: Yes. NH: 30

Nonprofit; nondenominational; sponsored by Catholic Diocese of Richmond. Private rooms and suites. 24-hour nurse's aide; full-time registered nurse; wellness program; personal care; medication administration; emergency response system; 3 daily meals plus snack; housekeeping and laundry services; library; gardens; solariums; outdoor grill.

ADM: (ref.) $100. DEP: Equal to 1 mo. rent. AL MO: $1,900–$2,650; Level II, add $375; 2nd person, $575.

Ridgewood Gardens

2001 Ridgewood Drive
Salem, VA 24153

Ph: (540) 387-4945
Fax: (540) 387-4947

AL: Yes. ALZ/MEM IMP: Yes (total units, 74)

Private suites. Respite care; wellness program; supportive nursing services; physical, occupational, and speech therapies; personal care; medication administration; security; emergency response system; maintenance; transportation; up to 3 daily meals; housekeeping and laundry services; bistro; fireplace lounge; library; arts and crafts room; gardening.

Community fee: (ref. on prorated basis up to 90 days) $2,200. AL MO: $2,325–$3,075; 2nd person, $1,925–$2,100. ALZ/MEM IMP MO: $2,975–$3,300; 2nd person, $2,475–$2,575.

Warm Hearth Village

Showalter Center
1060 Showalter Drive
Blacksburg, VA 24060

Ph: (540) 552-1498

AL: Yes

Nonprofit; nondenominational; managed by Warm Hearth, Inc. Apartments. 24-hour nursing; personal care; medication administration; security; emergency response system; maintenance; transportation; up to 3 daily meals; housekeeping and laundry services; church services; activities director; bookmobile; resident council; games; dancing; movies.

AL MO: $1,150–$2,875. Additional Care Daily: $85 and $170. RSP Daily: $75.

East

Chambrel at Williamsburg

3800 Treyburn
Williamsburg, VA 23185

Ph: (757) 220-1839 or (800) 868-4654
Fax: (757) 229-9367

IND: Yes. AL: Yes

Oxford Senior Living Community; nondenominational; nonsectarian. Cottages and apartments. Two levels of AL care; registered nurse on staff; 24-hour nursing care; wellness/fitness programs; personal care; medication administration; security; emergency response system; maintenance; transportation; up to 3 daily meals; housekeeping and laundry services; banking services; activities.

AL MO: Single, $1,800–$2,750; double, $2,175–$3,150.

The Chesterfield at Brandermill Woods, AAHA, VAHC, AHCA

Brandermill Parkway
Midlothian, VA 23112

Ph: (804) 379-7100
Fax: (804) 379-3726

AL: Yes. HCC: Yes. ALZ/ MEM IMP: Yes

Nondenominational; nonsectarian facility. Studios, apartments, private and semiprivate rooms. 24-hour nursing care; rehabilitative services; physical and occupational therapies; speech-language pathology services; personal care; medication administration; security; emergency response system; maintenance; transportation; up to 3 daily meals; housekeeping and laundry services; social and recreational programs.

AL Daily: $90–$115.

Manorhouse at Bellgrade

2800 Polo Parkway
Midlothian, VA 23113

Ph: (804) 379-2800
Fax: (804) 378-0174

http: / / www.manorhouse.com

AL: Yes. ALZ/MEM IMP: Yes

Owned and managed by Manorhouse Retirement Centers, Inc. Studios and suites with private baths. 24-hour nursing assistance; health oversight; respite care; personal care; medication administration; security; emergency response system; maintenance; transportation; up to 3 daily meals; housekeeping and laundry services; exercise rooms; activities director; recreational and social programs; barber/beauty shop.

ADMN: (ref./prorated) $1,075. AL MO: $1,875–$3,300. ALZ/MEM IMP: basic room rate plus $825.

Sentara Village at Virginia Beach

3751 Sentara Way
Virginia Beach, VA 23452

Ph: (757) 463-0200
Fax: (757) 431-8752

AL: Yes

Sentara Voluntary Hospitals of America, Inc. Suites, and private and semiprivate rooms. 24-hour nursing care; physician on call; access to Sentara Nursing Centers; personal care; medication administration; security; emergency response system; maintenance; transportation; up to 3 daily meals; housekeeping and laundry services; scheduled daily activities; library; walking course; barber/beauty salon.

AL MO: $1,325–$3,100.

West

Westhaven Retirement Living

860 Wolf Creek Trail, NW
Abingdon, VA 24210

Ph: (703) 628-1621

AL: Yes (up to 80 residents)

Private and semiprivate rooms with baths. 24-hour care; ambulatory and nonambulatory residents; personal care; medication administration; Medicaid-approved; 3 daily meals and snacks; housekeeping and laundry services; planned activities; lounge; barber/beauty shop.

AL MO: Semiprivate, $1,350; private, $1,825.

Central

Manorhouse at University Village

491 Crestwood Drive
Charlottesville, VA 22903

Ph: (804) 971-8889
Fax: (804) 971-7889

http: / / www.manor-house.com

AL: Yes. ALZ/MEM IMP: Yes

Owned and managed by Manorhouse Retirement Centers, Inc. Rooms with private baths. 24-hour nursing assistance; health oversight; respite care; personal care; medication administration; security; emergency response system; maintenance; transportation; up to 3 daily meals; housekeeping and laundry services; exercise rooms; activities director; recreational and social programs; barber/beauty shop.

ADMN: (ref./prorated) $1,075. AL MO: $1,875–$3,300. ALZ/MEM IMP: Basic room rate plus $825.

Outlook Pointe

2101 Deyerle Ave.
Harrisonburg, VA 22801

Ph: (540) 574-2982 ext. 5004
Fax: (540) 574-2985

http://www.balancedcare.com

AL: Yes

A Balanced Care Community. Apartments. 24-hour staffing; health screening; physical, occupational, speech, and respiratory therapies; lab services; personal care; medication administration; security; up to 3 daily meals; housekeeping and laundry services; exercise; religious services; arts and crafts; off-site activities; lectures; movies; library with computer center; lounge; walking paths.

AL Daily: $70–$85. Additional care services Daily: $15–$25.

North

Inova Assisted Living Center

4313 Chain Bridge Rd.
Fairfax, VA 22030

Ph: (703) 934-5069

AL: Yes. ALZ:MEM IMP: Yes

Nonprofit; nondenominational; managed by Sunrise Assisted Living, Inc. Shared and private suites. 24-hour nursing staff; 24-hour emergency care; physical, speech, and occupational therapies; wellness program; personal care; medication administration; 3 daily meals; laundry and housekeeping services; exercise; religious services; activities program; gift shop; barber/beauty shop.

AL MO: $55–$150. AL Daily: $20 and $35.

Independent Living

Independent housing (primarily rentals) for seniors that may offer security features, meal service, and activities.

Northeast

The Fairmont

9852 Fairmont Ave.
Manassas, VA 20109

Ph: (703) 257-7111
Fax: (703) 330-2475

IND: Yes

Nondenominational. Studios and one- and two-bedroom apartments. Security; on-site managers; emergency response system; maintenance; transportation; up to 3 daily meals; housekeeping and laundry services; exercise program; chapel; library; social, religious, and recreational activities; media room; bingo; barber/beauty shop.

DEP: (ref), $100. IND MO: $1,425–$2,700; 2nd person, $425.

East

The Virginian

300 Twinridge Lane
Richmond, VA 23235

Ph: (804) 330-4242

IND: Yes

For-profit; nondenominational; owned by Holiday Retirement Corporation. Studios and apartments. Security; emergency response system; maintenance; transportation; up to 3 daily meals; housekeeping and laundry services; exercise program; chapel; Bible study; library; on-and off-site activities; social, recreational, and cultural activities; card and board games; craft and activity room; billiard room; media room; gardening; walking paths; barber/beauty shop.

IND MO: $1,200–$2,150; 2nd person, $180 and $360.

West

Elm Park Estates

4230 Elm View Rd.
Roanoke, VA 24014

Ph: (540) 989-2010

IND: Yes

For-profit; nondenominational; owned by Holiday Retirement Corporation. Studios and apartments. Security; emergency response system; maintenance; transportation; up to 3 daily meals; housekeeping and laundry services; exercise program; chapel; Bible study; library; on-and off-site activities; social, recreational, and cultural activities; card and board games; craft and activity room; billiards room; media room; gardening; walking paths; barber/beauty shop.

IND MO: $1,200–$2,275; 2nd person, $360.

Adult/Resort Communities

Communities for active adults (not all are age-restricted; primarily ownership).

North

Heritage Hunt

6920 Netherstone Ct.
Gainesville, VA 20155

Ph: (888) 424-4868 or (703) 753-9535

Age: 55+. Individual homes, villas. Golf course; pro shop; clubhouse; community center; fitness complex; tennis; swimming pools; hiking/biking trails.

PURCHASE: Homes, from $242,000; villas, from $165,000.

Leisure World of Virginia

19400 Leisure World Blvd.
Lansdowne, VA 20176

Ph: (703) 581-1711

http://www.idigroup.com/virginia.html

Age: 55+. Condominiums. Golf course; pro shop; swimming center; health spa; billiards; bowling; auditorium and theater; arts and crafts; woodwork; computer room; walking/biking paths; beauty salon; shuttle bus.

PURCHASE: Condos, $143,000–$308,000.

Regency Lakes

101 Mulligan Lane
Winchester, VA 22603

Ph: (800) 606-6646 or (540) 662-1999

Manufactured homes. Clubhouse; tennis; swimming pool; fishing lakes; exercise facility; basketball; sports fields.

PURCHASE: Homes, $33,000–$77,000.

East

Brandermill Country Club

3700 Brandermill Parkway
Midlothian, VA 23112

Ph: (804) 744-1185 or (804) 744-1035

Individual homes, condominiums, homesites. Golf course; tennis swimming pool; hiking/biking trails; fishing; boating; dining; social clubs.

PURCHASE: Homes, $88,000–330,000+.

Ford's Colony

One Ford's Colony Drive
Williamsburg, VA 23188-9912

Ph: (800) 334-6033 or (757) 258-4072

http://www.fordscolony.com

Custom homes, courtyard homes, townhomes, homesites. Golf courses; clubhouse; tennis; swimming; fitness room; dining; social clubs; lake; recreational activities.

PURCHASE: Townhomes and courtyard homes, $192,500–$412,500; custom homes, $302,500–$1.65 million; homesites, $77,000–$660,000.

Glenmore

1318 Piper Way
Keswick, VA 22947

Ph: (800) 776-5111 or (804) 977-8865
Fax: (804) 977-8940

http://www.glenmore.com

Individual homes, cottages, homesites. Golf course; swimming and tennis complex; clubhouse, equestrian center; walking and jogging trails.

PURCHASE: Homes, $385,000–$1.1 million+; homesites, $131,000–$330,000+.

Governor's Land at Two Rivers

2700 Two Rivers Rd.
Williamsburg, VA 23185

Ph: (800) 633-5965 or (757) 258-4653

http://www.govland.com

Individual homes, homesites. Golf course; clubhouse; tennis; swimming pools; walking trails; beach; marina; boating; lakes; fitness center; dining; island nature sanctuary.

PURCHASE: Homes, $434,500–$990,000+; homesites, $104,500–$440,000+.

Kiln Creek

1405C Kiln Creek Parkway
Newport News, VA 23602

Ph: (757) 877-9835

Individual homes, townhomes, condominiums. Golf course; tennis swimming pool; hiking/biking trails; community center; fitness center; dining.

PURCHASE: Homes, $137,000–$440,000; townhomes and condos, $66,000–$192,500.

Kingsmill on the James

100 Kingsmill Rd.
Williamsburg, VA 23185

Ph: (800) 392-0026 or (757) 253-3393

http://www.kingsmill.com

Individual homes, patio homes, townhomes, condominiums, homesites. Golf courses; clubhouse; tennis club; sports club; swimming pool; fitness center; racquetball; spa; marina; fishing; canoeing; hiking/biking trails.

PURCHASE: Homes, $220,000–$2.2 million; patio homes, townhomes, condos, $137,500–$935,000; homesites, from $137,000.

Wintergreen

Rte. 151, PO Box 747
Wintergreen, VA 22958

Ph: (800) 325-2200 or (804) 325-2500

http://www.wintergreenrealestate.com

Individual homes, condominiums, homesites. Golf courses; pro shop; clubhouses; tennis; swimming pools; hiking/biking trails; fishing; riding stables; snow skiing; community center; dining; fitness centers; social clubs; lakes.

PURCHASE: Homes, $137,000–$2.75 million; condos, $54,000–$440,000; homesites, $33,000–$440,000.

West

Blacksburg Country Club

1064 Club House Rd.
Blacksburg, VA 24060

Ph: (540) 552-9165 or (540) 552-5221

Individual homes. Golf course; clubhouse; pro shop; tennis; swimming pool; dining; social clubs.

PURCHASE: Homes, $165,000–$440,000; homesites, $52,000.

Lake of the Woods

HC 75 Box 1
Locust Grove, VA 22508

Ph: (540) 972-2237

http://www.lowa.org

Individual homes, homesites. Golf course; clubhouse; swimming pools; hiking trails; boating; fishing; riding stables; community center; dining; bowling; social clubs.

PURCHASE: Homes, $88,000–$440,000.

The Virginian Golf Club

22512 Clubhouse Ridge
Bristol, VA 24202

Ph: (800) 452-8065 or (540) 645-7050
Fax: (540) 645-7055

http://www.thevirginian.com

Individual homes, homesites. Golf course; swim and racquet club; tennis; nearby fishing lakes and trails.

PURCHASE: Homes, from $220,000; homesites, from $55,000.

Washington, D.C.

http://www.ci.washington.dc.us

General Information

Climate

Moderate. Average temperature in January, 32.6° F; in July, 77° F.

Cost of Living

Unranked.

Taxes

State/Local as % of Income: 14.4%.

Property Tax Reduction: The Senior Citizen Tax Relief Program is for citizens 65 or older who own property and meet certain income requirements. For information, call the Assessment Services Division and ask about the Homestead and Senior Citizens Tax Relief section, (202) 727-4TAX.

Sales: 5.75%.

Prescription Exemptions: Prescription medications are exempt from sales tax.

Transportation, Travel, and Tourism

Major Airports

- Washington Dulles International Airport, (703) 572-2700.
- Ronald Reagan Washington National Airport, (703) 661-2700.
- Baltimore-Washington International Airport, (301) 261-1000 or (800) FLY-BWI.

Railways

- Metro (The Washington Metropolitan Area Transit Authority), 83 stations throughout the city, (202) 637-7000.
- Amtrak, (800) USA-RAIL.
- Virginia Railway Express, 1500 King St., Suite 202, Alexandria, VA 22314, (703) 684-0400 or (800) RIDE-VRE

Bus Tours

- Greyhound Bus, stations throughout the state, (800) 231-2222.
- Williams Bus Tours, 5512 5th St. NE, Washington, DC 20011, (202) 269-0945.
- Henderson Bus Service, 3765 J St. NE, Washington, DC 20019, (202) 399-5280.
- McMillian Charter Service, 5228 Illinois Ave., NW, Washington, DC 20011, (202) 829-8744.

Main Highways

- Interstate 95 runs north-south through the city and breaks into a bypass around the city.
- Interstate 66, running east-west, junctions with the city bypass.

Theater and Music

- The John F. Kennedy Center for the Performing Arts, 22700 F St. NW, Washington, DC 20566, tickets: (202) 467-4600 or (800) 444-1324, tours: (202) 416-8340.
- Arena Stage, 6th & Maine Ave. SW, Washington, DC 20024, (202) 488-4377.
- Ford's Theater (site of Lincoln assassination), 511 10th St. NW, Washington, DC 20004-1499, (202) 347-4833.
- National Theatre, 1321 Pennsylvania Ave. NW, Washington, DC 20004-1799, (202) 628-6161.
- Shakespeare Theatre, 450 7th St. NW, Washington, DC 20004-2207, (202) 393-2700.

- Washington Stage Guild, 924 G St. NW, Washington, DC 20001-4532, (202) 529-2084.
- The Washington Opera, 2600 Virginia Ave. NW, Suite 104, Washington, DC 20037, (202) 295-2400 or (800) 876-7372.
- DAR Constitution Hall, 1776 D St. NW, Washington, DC 20006, (202) 628-4780.
- Lincoln Theatre, 1215 U St. NW, Washington, DC 20009, (202) 328-9177.

Museums, Crafts, Historical, Recreational

- East Potomac Public Golf Club (public), Ohio Drive SW, Washington, DC 20006, (202) 397-8638.
- Langston Golf Course & Driving Range (public), 2600 Benning Rd. NE, Washington, DC 20002, (202) 882-7332.
- Rock Creek Public Golf Course, 1600 Rittenhouse St. NW, Washington, DC 20011, (302) 655-3336.
- Smithsonian Information Center for information on all Smithsonian Museums, (202) 357-2700.
- Smithsonian Institution Building (The Castle), 1000 Jefferson Drive SW, Washington, DC 20560-0009, (202) 357-2700.
- Anacostia Museum and Center for African American History and Culture, 1901 Fort Pl. SE, Washington, DC 20020-3298, (202) 357-2700.
- Arthur M. Sackler Gallery, 1050 Independence Ave. SW, Washington, DC 20560.
- National Museum of Arts & Industries, 900 Jefferson Drive SW, Washington, DC 20560-0004.
- Freer Gallery of Art, Jefferson Drive at 12th St. SW, Washington, DC 20560, (202) 357-4880.
- Hirshhorn Museum and Sculpture Garden, Independence Ave. and 7th St. SW, Washington, DC 20560-0350.
- National Air and Space Museum, Independence Ave. and 7th St. SW, (202) 357-1400.
- National Museum of African Art, 950 Independence Ave. SW, Washington, DC 20560-0006, (202) 357-4600.
- National Museum of American Art, 8th and G St. NW, (202) 633-8998.
- National Museum of American History, 14th St. and Constitution Ave. NW.
- National Museum of History & Technology, 12th St. & Constitution Ave. NW.
- National Museum of Natural History, 10th St. and Constitution Ave. NW, Washington, DC 20560.
- National Collection of Fine Arts, 8th St. & G St. NW.
- National Portrait Gallery, 8th and F St. NW, (202) 357-2920.
- National Zoological Park, 3000 Block of Connecticut Ave. NW, Washington, DC 20008, (202) 673-4717.
- The White House, 1600 Pennsylvania Ave. NW, Visitors Office, Washington, DC 20502, (202) 456-7041.
- Library of Congress, 101 Independence Ave. SE, Washington DC, 20540, (202) 707-5000.
- Washington Botanical Gardens, 1st St. and Maryland Ave. SW, (202) 225-8333.
- Bureau of Engraving and Printing, 14th St. and Maryland Ave. SW, (202) 874-3019.
- The National Capitol (daily tours), Capitol Hill, (202) 224-3121.
- Federal Bureau of Investigation (tours), 9th St. and Pennsylvania Ave. NW, (202) 324-3447.
- Folger (Shakespeare) Library, 201 E. Capitol St., Washington, DC 20003-1094, (202) 324-3447.
- Jefferson Memorial, South Bank of the Tidal Basin.
- Lincoln Memorial, West Potomac Park at the foot of 23rd St. NW, (202) 426-6895.
- Marine Corps Memorial, Rte. 50 across from Arlington Memorial Bridge.

- National Archives, 7th St. and Constitution Ave. NW, (202) 501-5000.
- Pentagon (tours), (703) 695-1776.
- Supreme Court (tours, lectures), 1st St. and Maryland Ave. NE, (202) 479-3395.
- Treasury Department (tours), Pennsylvania Ave. and 15th St. NW, (202) 622-0896.
- U.S. Naval Observatory (official residence of vice president on the grounds), 34th St. and Massachusetts Ave. NW, (202) 653-1507.
- Vietnam Veterans' Memorial, Henry Bacon Drive and Constitution Ave. NW.
- Washington National Cathedral, Wisconsin and Massachusetts Ave. NW.
- Washington Monument, on the Mall at 15th St. NW, (202) 426-6839.
- National Museum of Women in the Arts, 1250 New York Ave. NW, Washington, DC 20005, (202) 783-5000.
- United States Holocaust Memorial Museum, 100 Raoul Wallenberg Place SW, Washington, DC 20024, (202) 488-0419 or (202) 488-0455.

Organizations

Advocacy Groups

- District of Columbia Office on Aging, One Judiciary Square, 9th Floor, 441 4th St. NW, Washington, DC 20001, (202) 724-5622.
- District of Columbia Department of Health, 800 9th St. SW, 3rd Floor, Washington, DC 20024, (202) 645-5556.
- Board of Real Property Assessments and Appeals, 441 4th St. NW, Suite 430, Washington, DC 20001, (202) 727-6860.

Volunteer Programs

- Friends of the Kennedy Center, John F. Kennedy Center for the Performing Arts, Washington, DC 20566, (202) 416-8301.
- National Zoological Park (many volunteer activities), 3000 Block of Connecticut Ave. NW, (202) 673-4717.
- The National Museum of Natural History (many volunteer activities), 10th St. and Constitution Ave. NW, (202) 357-3045 or (202) 357-2623.
- Freer and Sackler Museums (many volunteer activities), (202) 357-4880, ext. 393, ext. 245

Housing

Long-Term Care Facilities

In Washington D.C., these facilities are called ***Continuing Care/Nursing Home/Retirement Facilities.***

These facilities provide various levels of nursing and medical services to seniors for an extended period of time.

Types of Authorization

Licensing and / or Certification

These facilities are regulated by the Department of Health.

Memberships

- American Association of Homes and Services for the Aging (AAHSA) represents not-for-profit organizations committed to providing high-quality health care, housing and services to the elderly. AAHSA, 901 E St. NW, Suite 500, Washington, DC 20004-2011. Ph: (202) 783-2242. Fax: (202) 783-2285. *http: / / www.aahsa.org*

Accreditations

- Continuing Care Accreditation Commission (CCAC) accredits facilities that offer seniors a contract or contracts that provide residential living and health care services for the remainder of the person's lifetime and meet CCAC's accreditation standards.

- Joint Commission on the Accreditation of Health Care Organizations (JCAHCO) is an independent, not-for-profit organization, and the nation's oldest and largest standards-setting and health care accrediting institution.

Ingleside at Rock Creek (formerly The Presbyterian Home)

3050 Military Rd. NW
Washington, DC 20015

Ph: (202) 363-8310
Fax: (202) 363-0950

IND: 85 (102 under construction). AL: 28. SNF: 60. ALZ/MEM IMP: Yes

Age 65+. Nonprofit; affiliated with the Presbyterian Church. Apartments and private rooms. Skilled nursing care; medical services; rehabilitative therapies; dental and podiatry services; pharmacy services; Medicare/Medicaid-approved; personal care; medication administration; 24-hour security system; 24-hour response system; maintenance; transportation; up to 3 daily meals; housekeeping and laundry services; swimming pool (under construction); social and recreational activities; convenient to shops, restaurants, and cultural attractions.

APPL: (ref.), $1,100. DEP: (ref.), 10% to reserve new unit. IND ENT: $31,500–$66,000+. IND MO: About $1,600–$3,300. AL MO: About $2,700–$3,850. SNF Daily: (resident rate), $135; (direct admittance rate), $190.

Knollwood

6200 Oregon Ave. NW
Washington, DC 20015

Ph: (202) 541-0149 or (800) 541-4255
Fax: (202) 364-2856

E-mail: *adfine@aol.com*

IND: 168. RH: 50. AL: 38. SNF: 50

Nonprofit. Apartments. Medicare/Medicaid-approved (SNF). 24-hour skilled nursing care; medical services; rehabilitative therapies; dental and podiatry services; pharmacy services; wellness center; personal care; medication administration; 24-hour security; 24-hour emergency response system; maintenance; transportation; up to 3 daily meals; pets allowed; housekeeping and laundry services; pool; fitness center; 1920s Tudor mansion for parties and social and recreational activities; putting green.

APPL: $1,100. DEP: (ref., until move in), $3,300. IND ENT: $62,000–$143,000. IND MO: $1,050–$2,725. AL ENT: (optional), $30,500. AL MO: $3,125. SNF MO: $4,400. SNF Daily: $150.

The Methodist Home

4901 Connecticut Ave. NW
Washington, DC 20008

Ph: (202) 966-7623
Fax: (202) 362-6917

IND/AL: 46. SNF: 26

Nonprofit; nondenominational. Apartments and private rooms. 24-hour nursing care; skilled nursing care; medical services; wellness clinic; personal care; medication administration; 24-hour security; maintenance; scheduled transportation; up to 3 daily meals; housekeeping and laundry services; social and recreational activities.

IND ENT: $19,000–$55,000. IND MO: (with ENT fee), $1,350–$3,025; (without ENT fee), $1,900–$4,775. AL ENT: $19,000–$55,000. AL MO: (with ENT fee), $2,000–$3,675; (without ENT fee), $2,550–$5,425. SNF MO: (with Founder's Fee of $17,000), $3,200; (without Founder's Fee), $4,050.

Thomas House Continuing Care Retirement Community

1330 Massachusetts Ave. NW
Washington, DC 20005

Ph: (202) 347-3983
Fax: (202) 638-0649

IND: 180. SNF: 53

Age 62+. Nonprofit; nondenominational; nonsectarian. Apartment. Skilled nursing care; medical services; rehabilitative therapies; dental and podiatry care; pharmacy services; Medicare/Medicaid-approved; personal care; medication administration; 24-hour security system; 24-hour emergency response system; maintenance; transportation; up to 3 daily meals; pets allowed (no dogs); housekeeping and laundry services; fitness center/health club; swimming pool; social and recreational activities; convenience store; gift shop; downtown location convenient to Kennedy Center, art galleries, theaters, stores, amenities; barber/beauty shop.

APPL: $100. DEP: 10% of entrance fee. IND ENT: $38,000–$134,500. IND MO: from $1,300. SNF Daily: from $205.

U.S. Soldiers' and Airmen's Home

3700 N. Capitol St. NW
Washington, DC 20317

Ph: (800) 422-9988
Fax: (202) 722-3492

http://www.AFRH.com

E-mail: *ussah11@erols.com*

IND: 1,000. AL: 30. SNF: 220. ALZ/MEM IMP: 30

Age 60+. Government-run residency for military retirees and certain veterans. Private rooms. Skilled nursing care; medical services; rehabilitative therapies; personal care; medication administration; 24-hour security; emergency response system; maintenance; transportation; up to 3 daily meals; laundry services; fitness center/health club; social and recreational activities; bowling alley; golf course; fishing lake; garden plots.

IND MO: 35% of income. AL MO: 35% of income. SNF MO: 65% of income.

REQ: Must be military retiree or veteran.

Assisted Living and Residential Care Facilities

These facilities provide housing, food service, and one or more personal services.

Types of Authorization

Licensing and/or Certification

These facilities are regulated by the Department of Health.

Memberships

- Assisted Living Federation of America (ALFA) is a national nonprofit membership organization whose mission is to enhance the quality of life in assisted living facilities and promote the interests of the assisted living industry. ALFA, 10300 Eaton Place, Suite 400, Fairfax, VA 22030. Ph: (703) 691-8100. Fax: (703) 691-8106. *http://www.alfa.org*

Chevy Chase House

5420 Connecticut Ave. NW
Washington, DC 20015

Ph: (202) 686-5504
Fax: (202) 537-0037

AL: Yes. RSP: Yes

For-profit; owned by The Medallion Group. Studios and apartments. Trial stay available. 24-hour nursing care services; physical, occupational, speech, and dietary therapies; diabetic and pacemaker monitoring; personal care; medication administration; security; emergency response system; maintenance; up to 3 daily meals, with room service on request; housekeeping and laundry services; exercise program; social and recreational activities; cultural, educational, and spiritual programs; banking and postal services; personal shopping services; chauffeur service; barber/beauty shop.

AL DAILY: $130–$185.

Independent Living

Independent housing (primarily rentals) for seniors that may offer security features, meal service, and activities.

Friendship Terrace Retirement Community

4201 Butterworth Place NW
Washington, DC 20016

Ph: (202) 244-7400
Fax: (202) 362-2587

http://www.esm.org
E-mail: *esmfriend@aol.com*

IND: 200

Age 62+. Nonprofit; nonsectarian. Apartments. Wellness programs; 24-hour security system; 24-hour emergency response system; maintenance; transportation; 1 daily meal (lunch optional for $55); pets allowed; library; social and recreational activities; educational forums; barber/beauty shop.

APPL: $50. DEP: one month's rent. IND MO: $725–$825.

REQ: minimum monthly income limit $385 above rental rate.

NCCBA Estates

2801 14th St. NW
Washington, DC 20009

Ph: (202) 387-4022
Fax: (202) 462-8403
E-mail: *ncbahsng@aol.com*

IND: 174

Age 60+. Nonprofit, affiliated with the National Caucus and Center on Black Aged, Inc. Apartments. 24-hour security; maintenance.

IND MO: 30% of gross income.

REQ: must meet income eligibility standards.

Saint Mary's Court

725 24th St. NW
Washington, DC 20037

Ph: (202 223-5712
Fax: (202) 223-6191

http://www.stmaryscourt.org
E-mail: *smchdc@aol.com*

CONG: Yes. IND: 140

Age 62+. Nonprofit; nondenominational; affiliated with the Episcopal Diocese. Apartments. Medical services; emergency response system; 1 daily meal; laundry facilities; social and recreational activities; art, yoga, and other classes; recreation area; pool table; lounge; library; computer classes.

DEP: one month's rent. Contact facility for fees.

REQ: must meet HUD eligibility requirements.

Sarah's Circle

2551 17th St. NW, Apt. 103
Washington, DC 20009

Ph: (202) 332-1400
Fax: (202) 667-9529

IND: 34

Age 65+. Nonprofit; nondenominational; nonsectarian. Apartments. Health and nutrition programs; 24-hour security system; maintenance; transportation; 1 daily meal (free during week only); senior center.

DEP: one month's rent. IND MO: $250–$725.

REQ: Must meet HUD eligibility requirements.

Adult/Resort Communities

Communities for active adults (not all are age-restricted; primarily ownership).

The Consulate

2950 Van Ness St. NW
Washington, DC 20008

Ph: (202) 362-6870

High rise rental apartments. Swimming pool; tennis; fitness center; laundry room; storage; parking; pets allowed; nearby park, zoo, shopping, dining, and entertainment.

DEP: $100. MO: 1-bedroom, $1,175–$1,275; 2-bedroom, $1,725–$1,800. Lease terms, 6–12 mos.

Ellicott House

4849 Connecticut Ave. NW
Washington, DC 20008

Ph: (202) 244-7724

High-rise rental apartments. Swimming pool; tennis; spa; fitness center; party room; laundry room; storage; parking; paid utilities; pets allowed; nearby park, zoo, shopping, dining, and entertainment.

MO: Studio, $700–$775; 1-bedroom, $925–$1,000; 2-bedroom, $1,375–$1,550. Deposit, $330. Lease terms vary.

The Lansburgh

425 8th St. NW
Washington, DC 20004

Ph: (202) 393-1800

High-rise rental apartments. Swimming pool; spa; exercise and aerobics rooms; full service health club; entertainment room; 500-seat performing arts theater; dining; storage; parking; pets allowed; nearby shopping.

MO: 1 bedroom, $1,525–$2,150; 2-bedroom, $1,925–$2,500. Lease terms, MTM/3/6/12 mos.

Park Plaza

1629 Columbia Rd. NW
Washington, DC 20009

Ph: (202) 265-2549 or (800) 948-3835

High-rise rental apartments. Swimming pool; fitness center; laundry room; storage; parking; paid utilities; pets allowed; nearby zoo, shopping, and dining.

MO: Studio, $700–$775; 1 bedroom, $925–$1,000; 2-bedroom, $1,375–$1,550. Deposit, $275. Lease terms vary.

Washington

http://www.state.wa.us

General Information

Climate

Average lows from 21° F to 56° F; average highs from 33° F to 87° F.

Cost of Living

Ranks 11th in the nation.

Taxes

State/Local as % of Income: 10.6%.

Property Tax Reduction: Retired persons age 61+ may, based on income, qualify for property tax exemptions.

Sales: 6.5%

Prescription Exemptions: Prescription drugs are exempt from sales tax.

Transportation, Travel, and Tourism

Major Airports

- Bellingham International Airport, (360) 676-2500.
- Olympia Municipal Airport, (360) 586-6164.
- Sea-Tac International Airport, (800) 544-1965.
- Spokane International Airport, (509) 455-6455.
- William R. Fairchild International Airport, (360) 417-3433.

Railways

- Amtrak, (800) USA-RAIL.

Bus Tours

- Gray Line of Seattle, (800) 426-7505.
- Greyhound Lines, Inc., (800) 231-2222.
- Scenic Bound Tours, (206) 433-6907.
- Weathervane Tours, (206) 780-5003.

State Highways

- Interstate 90, east-west (central).
- Interstate 82, east-west (central).
- Interstate 5, north-south (western).
- U.S. 101, north-south (western).
- U.S. 97, north-south (central).
- U.S. 395, north-south (eastern).

Theater and Music

Coastal Region

- Washington Center for the Performing Arts, Olympia, (360) 753-8586.

Puget Sound Region

- Seattle Center Opera House, (206) 389-7676.
- Paramount Theater, 911 Pine St., Seattle, WA 98101, (206) 682-1414.
- Seattle Symphony at Benaroya Hall, 200 University St., Seattle, WA 98101, (206) 215-4700.

East Region

- The Cutter Theatre, 302 Park Ave., Metaline Falls, WA 99153, (509) 446-4108.
- Spokane Civic Theatre, PO Box 5222, Spokane, WA 99205, (509) 325-1413.

Museums, Crafts, Historical, Recreational

Coastal Region (State Capitol complex, outdoor activities, wildlife refuges, camping, golf)

- Olympia/Thurston Chamber of Commerce, 521 Legion Way, PO Box 1427, Olympia, WA 98507, (360) 357-3362.
- Olympic National Park, 600 East Park Ave., Port Angeles, WA 98362-6798, (360) 452-4501.

- Washington State Capitol, Olympia, WA, (360) 586-TOUR.

Northwest Region (whale watching, outdoor activities, skiing, boat trips to San Juan Island)

- Mount Baker Ski Area, (360) 734-6771.
- Emerald Tours, 1178 Sunset Ave., Bellingham, WA 98226, (360) 647-7060.
- San Juan Island Shuttle Express, 355 Harris Ave. 105, Bellingham, WA 98225, (888) 373-8522.

Puget Sound Region (Seattle Aquarium, Woodland Park Zoo, Space Needle, Snoqualmie Falls, wildlife refuges, ferry tours of Puget Sound, sporting events)

- Greater Seattle Chamber of Commerce, (206) 389-7200.
- Mount Rainier National Park, Ashford, WA 98304, (360) 569-2211.
- Port Townsend and the Keystone Ferry, (360) 678-7771.
- Boeing Hangars, (206) 342-4801.

Southern Region (Yakima Indian Reservation, Yakima Rim Skyline Trail, Grandview Historical Museum, state parks, golf, wineries, outdoor activities)

- Mount St. Helens National Volcanic Monument, 3029 Spirit Lake Highway, Castle Rock, WA 98611, (360) 274-2100.

Central Region: (river rafting, fishing, camping, outdoor activities, skiing, golf)

- Grand Coulee Dam, (800) COULEE-2.
- Lake Chelan, (800) 4-CHELAN.
- North Cascades National Park, 2105 State Route 20, Sedro-Woolley, WA 98284, (360) 856-5700.

North East (casinos, wineries, golf, wildlife refuges, skiing, sporting events, outdoor activities)

- Spokane Chamber of Commerce, 801 West Riverside Ave., Spokane, WA 99201, (509) 624-1393.
- Hells Canyon Tours, 1451 Bridge St., Clarkston, WA 99403, (800) 522-6966.
- Riverfront Park, 507 N. Howard, Spokane, WA 99201, (509) 625-6600.

Organizations

Advocacy Groups

- AARP, Washington State Office, 9750 Third Ave., NE, #102, Seattle, WA 98115, (206) 517-9348.

Volunteer Programs

- Washington State Foster Grandparents Program, PO Box 45600, Olympia, WA 98504, (360) 493-2549.
- Clark County Foster Grandparents Program, PO Box 1995, Vancouver, WA 98668, (360) 696-8221.
- King County Retired and Senior Volunteer Programs, 215 W. Harrison, Seattle, WA 98103, (206) 273-9114.
- Spokane County Retired and Senior Volunteer Programs, 507 N. Howard, Spokane, WA 99201, (509) 838-3577.
- Lewis/Mason/Thurston Retired and Senior Volunteer Programs, 222 N. Columbia, Olympia, WA 98501, (360) 586-7787.

Housing

Long-Term Care Facilities

In the state of Washington, facilities are called ***Continuing Care/Nursing Home Facilities.***

These facilities provide residential living and/or various levels of nursing and medical services to seniors for an extended period of time.

Types of Authorization

Licensing and/or Certification

These facilities are regulated by the Department of Health, Division of Health Systems Quality Assurance.

Memberships

- American Association of Homes and Services for the Aging (AAHSA) represents not-for-profit organizations committed to providing high-quality health care, housing, and services to the elderly. AAHSA, 901 E St. NW, Suite 500, Washington, DC 20004-2011. Ph: (202) 783-2242. Fax: (202) 783-2285. *http://www.aahsa.org*

Accreditations

- Continuing Care Accreditation Commission (CCAC) accredits facilities that offer seniors a contract or contracts that provide residential living and health care services for the remainder of the person's lifetime and meet CCAC's accreditation standards.
- Joint Commission on the Accreditation of Healthcare Organizations (JCAHO) is an independent, not-for-profit organization, and the nation's oldest and largest standards-setting and health care accrediting institution.

Coastal Region/Puget Sound

Bethany of the Northwest

3322 Broadway
Everett, WA 98201

Ph: (425) 259-5508
Fax: 425-258-5656

http://www.fp.premier1.net/bethany/

E-mail: *bethany@premier1.net*

IND: 146. AL: 22. SNF: 243. ALZ/IMP: 30

Age: 60+ or AL/SNF needs. Nonprofit; affiliated with the Evangelical Lutheran Church in America. Apartments. Nursing care; medical services; rehabilitative therapies; pharmacy services; Medicare/Medicaid-approved; personal care; medication administration; security system; emergency response system; maintenance; van and wheelchair van transportation; 3 daily meals; pets allowed (apartments only); housekeeping and laundry services; social and recreational activities.

DEP: (ref.), $200. Pet DEP: $275. IND MO: $575–$750. AL MO: $1,100–$2,025. SNF Daily: $165–$225 (depending on level of care).

Christa Shores

1600 NW Christa Shores Lane
Silverdale, WA 98383

Ph: (360) 613-3502
Fax: (360) 613-3529

IND: 110. AL: 30. SNF: 31

Apartments and private and semiprivate rooms. Nurse care; medical services; rehabilitative therapies; pharmacy services; personal care; medication administration; 24-hour security; maintenance; transportation; up to 3 daily meals; chaplain services; social and recreational activities.

IND ENT: decreasing and increasing refund plans. IND MO: 1-bedroom, 1 bath: $925–$1,050; 2-bedroom, 1 bath: $1,325; 2-bedroom, 1 bath: $1,625.

Covenant Shores Retirement Community

9150 N. Mercer Way
Mercer Island, WA 98040

Ph: (206) 268-3000
Fax: (206) 236-1438

RH: 191. AL: 22. SNF: 43

Age: 62+. Nonprofit; affiliated with the Evangelical Covenant Church. Apartments and private rooms with 3 levels of care. Nursing care; medical services; rehabilitative therapies; pharmacy services; wellness clinic; Medicare/Medicaid-approved; personal care; medication administration; security system; emergency response system; maintenance; bus and private car transportation; up to 3 daily meals; housekeeping and laundry services; social and recreational activities; library; game room; Jacuzzi; woodshop; arts and crafts room; private marina.

APP: $385. DEP: $1,000. IND ENT: $63,000–$290,000. IND MO: $925–$2,450. AL ENT: $22,000. AL MO: $2,450–$2,650. SNF MO: $6,000. SNF Daily: $190–$220.

Crista Senior Community

19303 Fremont Ave. N.
Seattle, WA 98133

Ph: (206) 546-7502
Fax: (206) 546-7447

http://www.crista.org

E-mail: *KRT@crista.org*

IND: 278. AL: 81. SNF: 176. ALZ/MEM IMP: 30

Age 65+. Nonprofit; nondenominational. Apartments. Nursing care; medical services; Medicare/Medicaid-approved; personal care; medication administration; 24-hour security; maintenance; transportation; up to 3 daily meals; housekeeping and laundry services; exercise program; swimming pool; library; lounges; greenhouse; social and recreational activities.

APPL: $150–$550. IND ENT: $32,000–$200,500. IND MO: $575–$1,775. AL MO: $1,975–$3500. SNF MO: $3,300–$5,500. SNF Daily: $160–$275.

Emerald Heights

10901 176th Circle NE
Redmond, WA 98052

Ph: (425) 556-8100
Fax: (425) 556-8128

http://www.emeraldheights.com

RH: 280. AL: 30. SNF: 41. ALZ/IMP: 15

Age: 62+. Nonprofit; nondenominational. Apartments and cottages. Nursing care; medical services; rehabilitative therapies; pharmacy services; residential clinic; Medicare-approved; personal care; medication administration; security; emergency response system; maintenance; transportation; up to 3 daily meals; housekeeping and laundry services; game room; craft room; lawn bowling; 2 nature trails; putting green; country store; coffee shop; barber/beauty shop.

Wait list: $1,000. DEP: 10% of IND ENT at time apartment is offered. IND ENT: $62,000–$371,000. IND MO: $1,250–$3,300. AL and SNF included in IND ENT.

Exeter House

720 Seneca St.
Seattle, WA 98101

Ph: (206) 627-1300
Fax: (206) 622-1920

http://www.pminc.org

E-mail: *–exeter@seanet.com*

IND: 87. AL: 25. SNF: 32

Age: 62+. Nonprofit; affiliated with the Presbyterian Church. Apartments. Nursing care; medical services; prescription medication delivery; Medicare/Medicaid-approved; personal care; medication administration; security; emergency response system; maintenance; transportation; up to 3 daily meals; housekeeping and laundry services; fitness center; social and recreational activities; library; pool table; patio with outdoor dining; country store.

DEP: $1,000. IND ENT: $27,500–$187,000. IND MO: $1,075–$3,200. AL MO: $2,750–$4,200. SNF daily: $160–$300.

Franke Tobey Jones

5340 N. Bristol
Tacoma, WA 98407

Ph: (253) 752-6621
Fax (253) 756-1862

IND: (approx.) 50. RH: (approx.) 8. AL: (approx.) 60. SNF: 43. ALZ/IMP: 10

Age: 62+. Nonprofit. Apartments, condominiums, and private rooms. Nursing care; medical services; rehabilitative therapies; pharmacy services; wellness program; security system; emergency response system; maintenance; transportation; up to 3 daily meals; pets allowed (limited); housekeeping and laundry services; fitness center; spa; social and recreational activities.

APPL: $2,750. IND/AL ENT: $2,750. Apartment MO: $1,500–$3,975. Condominium MO: $1,700–$2,750. Private rooms daily: $160–$185. SNF daily: $145–$185.

The Fountain at Pacific Regent

919 109th Ave. NE
Bellevue, WA 98004

Ph: (425) 688-1460
Fax: (425) 453-1361

http://www.thefountains.com

IND: 114. SNF: 54

Age: 62+. Profit. Condominiums. Nursing care; medical services; rehabilitative therapies; pharmacy services; Medicare-approved; health and wellness clinic; personal care; medication administration; security system; emergency response system; maintenance; transportation; 2 daily meals; pets allowed; exercise equipment; pool; Jacuzzi; library; social and recreational activities; rose garden.

DEP: $1,000. IND ENT: $110,000–$440,000. SNF daily: private room, $210–$225; semiprivate room, $165–$195.

The Hearthstone

6720 E. Green Lake Way N.
Seattle, WA 98103

Ph: (206) 525-9666
Fax: (206) 522-0190

http://www.hearthstone.org

E-mail: *jims@hearthstone.org*

IND: 189. AL: 30. SNF: 44

Age: 62+. Nonprofit; affiliated with the Lutheran Church. Apartments. Nursing care; medical services; rehabilitative therapies; pharmacy services; Medicare/Medicaid-approved; personal care; medication administration; security; emergency response system; maintenance; transportation; up to 3 daily meals; housekeeping and laundry services; social and recreational activities.

DEP: $1,000. IND ENT: $36,500–$85,000. IND MO: $1,075–$1,575 2nd person: $6,125. AL MO: $1,500–$2,550. SNF daily: $170–$195.

Judson Park Retirement Community

23600 Marine View Drive S.
Des Moines, WA 98198

Ph: (206) 824-4000
Fax: (206) 878-6404

E-mail: *JudsonPark@aol.com*

IND: 134. AL: 36. SNF: 116

Age: 62+. Nonprofit; affiliated with the American Baptist Homes of the West. Apartments. Nursing care; 24-hour assistance; medical services; rehabilitative therapies; pharmacy services; Medicare/Medicaid-approved; personal care; medication administration; security; emergency response system; maintenance; transportation; up to 3 daily meals; housekeeping and laundry services; hot tub; exercise rooms; chapel; library; social and recreational activities; hobby rooms; woodworking shop; solarium, barber/beauty shop.

DEP: (ref.), $1,000–$3,000. IND ENT: $32,500–$137,000. IND MO: $1,325–$2,650. AL ENT: $22,000 or rental. AL MO: $2,825–$5,825 (dependent on fee structure). SNF MO: $6,000–$6,175. SNF daily: $195–$205.

Masonic Retirement Center of Washington

23660 Marine View Drive S.
Des Moines, WA 98198-7394

Ph: (206) 878-8434
Fax: (206) 878-9116

IND: (150 under construction). AL: Yes. HCC: Yes

Nonprofit. Private and semiprivate rooms (apartments under construction). Nursing care; emergency care; rehabilitative therapies; medical services; social services; personal care; medication administration; security; emergency response system; maintenance; transportation; up to 3 daily meals; housekeeping and laundry services; exercise groups; swimming spa/pool; religious services; social and recreational activities; educational and spiritual programs; crafts; bingo; on- and off-site activities; general store; gift store; gardening areas; walking paths; barber/beauty shop.

ENT: $5,500–$8,250. IND Daily: $30–$50. AL Daily: $40–$85. HCC Daily: $155–$160.

The Kenney Presbyterian Retirement Community

7125 Pauntleroy Way SW
Seattle, WA 98136

Ph: (206) 937-2800
Fax: (206) 933-2795

http: / / www.thekenney.org

E-mail: *–thekenney@thekenney.org*

IND: 36. RH: 62. AL: 30. SNF: 20. HCC: Yes

Age: 60+. Nonprofit. Nursing care; medical services; rehabilitative therapies; pharmacy services; Medicare-approved; personal care; medication administration; security; emergency response system; maintenance; transportation; up to 3 daily meals; housekeeping and laundry services; social and recreational activities.

APPL: $275. DEP: $1,000. IND ENT: (60% ref.), $44,500–$132,500. IND MO: $350–$375. RH ENT: $15,000–$85,500. RH MO: $1,225–$1,525. SNF daily: $140, $165, $190.

Panorama City

1751 Circle Lane SE
Lacey, WA 98503-2570

Ph: (360) 456-0111 or (800) 999-9807
Fax: (360) 438-5901

http: / / www.panoramacity.org

E-mail: *retire@panoramacity.org*

IND: 839. RH: Yes. AL: 14. SNF: 155

Age: 62+. Nonprofit. Homes, condominiums, apartments, and private rooms. Nursing care; medical services; rehabilitative therapies; pharmacy services; Medicare/Medicaid-approved; personal care; medication administration; 24-hour security system; 24-hour emergency response system; maintenance; transportation; up to 3 daily meals; pets allowed; housekeeping and laundry services; social and recreational activities.

APP: (ref. up to 5 years), $2,750. IND ENT: $36,500–$275,000. IND MO: $550–$1,450. AL MO: $2,900–$3,300. SNF daily: $145–$165. Apartment: $64,000-$108,000. Condominium: $131,000–$247,500. Homes: $198,000–$275,000.

East

Riverview Retirement Community

801 E. Upriver Drive
Spokane, WA 99207

Ph: (509) 483-6683

Fax: (509) 482-8444
E-mail: *pbickley@riverview-retirement.org*

IND: 116. RH: 110. AL: 34. SNF: 75. ALZ/IMP: 37

Age: 60+. Nonprofit; affiliated with the Lutheran Church. Apartments. Nursing care; medical services; rehabilitative therapies; pharmacy services; Medicare/ Medicaid-approved; personal care; medication administration; 24-hour security system; 24-hour emergency response system; maintenance; transportation; up to 3 daily meals; pets allowed; housekeeping and laundry services; pool; fitness center; social and recreational activities.

DEP: $550. IND ENT: $137,000–$174,000. IND MO: $310. AL ENT: $3,300. AL MO: $2,000–$2,625. SNF Daily: $150–$170.

Rockwood Retirement Community

2903 E. 25th Ave.
Spokane, WA 99223

Ph: (509) 536-6650 or (800) 727-6650

IND: 152 (Rockwood Manor); 91 (Rockwood Forest Estates). HCC: Yes

Nonprofit; affiliated with United Methodist Church. Apartments. Nursing care; wellness program; health center; personal care; medication administration; transportation; 24-hour security system; 3 daily meals; housekeeping and laundry services; maintenance; swimming; water aerobics; Jacuzzi; exercise rooms; gardening and greenhouse; chaplain and religious services; meeting rooms; on-site catering; library; woodworking shop; artists' studio and gallery; full-time activity director; social and recreational activities.

IND ENT: Rockwood Manor, $35,000–$65,500; Forest Estates, $153,000–$220,000+. IND MO: Rockwood Manor, $1,300–$2,500; Forest Estates, $575 (single); $600 (couple).

Assisted Living and Residential Care Facilities

In the state of Washington, these facilities are called ***Assisted Living/Adult Family Homes/Personal Care****.*

These facilities provide housing, food service, and one or more personal services.

Types of Authorization

Licensing and/or Certification

These facilities are regulated by the Department of Health, Division of Health Systems Quality Assurance. Adult family homes provide personal care, special care, room, and board to more than one but not more than six adults.

Membership

- Assisted Living Federation of America (ALFA) is a national non-profit membership organization whose mission is to enhance the quality of life in assisted living facilities and promote the interests of the assisted living industry. ALFA, 10300 Eaton Place, Suite 400, Fairfax, VA 22030. Ph: (703) 691-8100. Fax: (703) 691-8106. *http://www.alfa.org*
- Northwest Assisted Living Facilities Association (NOR-ALFA) is a regional affiliate of ALFA. NOR-ALFA, 34004 16th Ave. S., Suite 201, Federal Way, WA 98003. Ph: (253) 874-5211. Fax: (253) 874-5350. *http://www.noralfa.org*

East

Brighton Court Assisted Living

1308 N. Vercler Rd.
Spokane, WA 99216

Ph: (509) 926-4533
Fax: (509) 926-9091
http://www.brightoncourt.com

E-mail: *brightCourt@aol.com*

AL: 55. RH: 51

Age: 55+. For-profit. Apartments. 24-hour security; 24-hour emergency response system; Medicaid-approved; maintenance; transportation; up to 3 daily meals; pets allowed; housekeeping and laundry services; library; social and recreational activities; resident lounge; solarium; library; gift shop; barber/beauty shop.

AL ENT: $200–$300. AL MO: $1,775–$2,350.

Mission Ridge Assisted Living

12903 E. Mission Ave.
Spokane, WA 94216

Ph: (509) 927-7148
Fax: (509) 927-7176

AL: 56

Age: 65+. Profit; nondenominational. Apartments. Nursing care; physical, occupational, and speech therapies; wellness screenings; personal care; medication administration; fitness programs; security system; 24-hour professionally trained support staff; 24-hour emergency system; maintenance; transportation; up to 3 daily meals; pets allowed; housekeeping and laundry services; social and recreational activities; lounge with TV and VCR; private areas for family meetings; barber/beauty shop.

APP: $300. DEP: $300. AL MO: $1,900–$3,025.

Park Place Retirement Community

601 S. Park Rd. (Assisted Living) or S. 511 Park Rd. (Independent)
Spokane, WA 99212

Ph: (509) 922-7224
Fax: (509) 992-4378

IND: 113. AL: 63. ALZ/MEM IMP: 32

Age: 62+. For-profit. Apartments. Personal care; medication administration; 24-hour security system; 24-hour emergency response system; maintenance; transportation; up to 3 daily meals; pets allowed; housekeeping and laundry facilities; fitness center; social and recreational activities; located in a park setting that adjoins to wildlife natural area.

DEP: $200. IND ENT: $200. IND MO: $950–$2,000. AL ENT: $220. AL MO: $2,000–$2,700. ALZ/MEM IMP ENT: $220. ALZ/MEM IMP MO: $3,125–$3,900.

Northwest

Orchard Park Assisted Living

844 W. Orchard Drive
Bellingham, WA 98225

Ph: (360) 647-3709
Fax: (360) 647-7908

AL: 82

For-profit. Apartments. Nursing care; medical services; Medicaid-approved; personal care; medication administration; security; emergency response system; maintenance; transportation; up to 3 daily meals; housekeeping and laundry services; social and recreational activities.

DEP: (ref.), $800. AL ENT: $450. AL MO: $1,825–$2,925. 2nd person: $550.

Puget Sound Region

Cascade Plaza Retirement–Assisted Living Center

7950 Willows Rd. NE
Redmond, WA 98052-3896

Ph: (425) 885-4157
Fax: (425) 882-3308

IND: Yes. AL: Yes

Rooms. 24-hour staffing; personal care; medication administration; security; emergency response system; maintenance; transportation; up to 3 daily meals; housekeeping and laundry services; social and recreational activities.

DEP: (cleaning), $550. IND MO: $1,375–$1,425. 2nd person: $550.

The Norse Home

5311 Phinney Ave. N.
Seattle, WA 98103

Ph: (206) 781-7400
Fax: (206) 781-7575
http://www.vikingnorse.com

IND: (approx.), 90. AL: 30–40

Age: 65+. Non-profit. Apartments. Nursing care; medical service; Medicare-approved; personal care; medication administration; 24-hour security; emergency system; maintenance; transportation to activities only; weekly shopping trips; 3 daily meals; housekeeping and laundry services; 6-week exercise/balance program; lounges; libraries; social and recreational activities; barber/beauty shop.

APPL: $25. DEP: $1,000. IND MO: $1,450–$3,025. AL Daily: $80, $90, $100.

Washington Court, ALFA

900 124th Ave. NE
Bellevue, WA 98005

Ph: (425) 455-4333

IND: Yes. AL: Yes

Nondenominational; owned by Leisure Care, Inc. Studios and one-bedroom apartments. Respite care; blood pressure checks; personal care; medication administration; security; emergency response system; maintenance; transportation; up to 3 daily meals; housekeeping and laundry services; exercise program; religious services; social and recreational activities; library; banking services; board and card games; crafts; barber/beauty shop.

AL MO: $1,425–$2,050; 2nd person, $275.

Southwest

Kamlu Assisted Living

7514 NE 13th Ave.
Vancouver, WA 98665

Ph: (360) 693-2402

AL: 71

Age 60+. For-profit; nondenominational. Apartments. 24-hour nursing care; medical services; personal care; medication administration; 24-hour security; 24-hour emergency response system; maintenance; transportation; 3 daily meals; pets allowed (on main floor); housekeeping and laundry services; exercise program; social and recreational activities.

APPL: (ref.), $100. DEP: $550. AL ENT: $1,975–$2,325. AL MO: $1,975–$2,325; 2nd person: $330, plus AL fees.

Independent Living

Independent housing (primarily rentals) for seniors that may offer security features, meal service, and activities.

Southwest

The Bedford

13303 SE McGillivray Blvd.
Vancouver, WA 98683

Ph: (360) 891-6898
Fax: (360) 254-0016

IND: 107

Apartments. Nighttime safety patrol; security; transportation; meal plan; housekeeping and laundry services; enclosed lap pool; Jacuzzi; business center available for fax and photocopying; formal dining room with fireplace, stage, and dance floor; game billiards room with fireplace; library with fireplace; exercise room; multipurpose/party room with full kitchen and large-screen TV; putting green; smoking lounge; computer room; barber/beauty shop.

IND MO: studio, from $1,425; 1-bedroom, from $1,625; 2-bedroom, from $2,525.

Puget Sound Region

Canterbury Manor

703 Callahan Drive
Bremerton, WA 98310

Ph: (360) 377-0113
Fax (360) 377-2655

http://www.episcopalretirement.org

IND: 76

Age 62+. Nonprofit; nondenominational; affiliated with the Episcopal Diocese of Olympia. Apartments. Medical services; routine health screens; 24-hour security system; 24-hour emergency response system; maintenance; transportation; 1 daily meal; pets allowed; monthly housekeeping services.

DEP: (ref.), $3,300–$5,450. IND MO: $950–$2,050.

Cristwood Retirement Center

350 N. 190th St.
Seattle, WA 98133

Ph: (206) 546-7563
Fax: (206) 546-7236

E-mail: *KAD@crista.org*

IND: Yes

Apartments. Registered nurse visitation; 24-hour security; transportation; 1 daily meal; special diet meals; housekeeping and laundry services; enclosed swimming pool; whirlpool; exercise room; chapel; chaplain services; library; social and recreational activities; wood shop; walking paths; guest apartment.

IND MO: $575–$825.

The Firs Retirement Community

426 Lilly Rd. NE
Olympia, WA 98506

Ph: (360) 456-3477
Fax: (360) 438-0558

IND: 141

For-profit. Apartments. 24-hour security; 24-hour emergency system; maintenance; transportation; up to 3 daily meals; pets allowed; weekly housekeeping services; fitness center; library; lounges; activity room; walking trail,

AL MO: $1,125–$2,650.

Harbor View Manor

919 S. Fawcett
Tacoma, WA 98402

Ph: (253) 272-5552
Fax: (253) 572-6159

IND: 169

Age: 62+ with income limits (single person: $26,500 annually; couple: $30,250 annually). Nonprofit. Apartments. 24-hour security system; 24-hour emergency response system; 2 daily meals (meal program $129.50 per month); pets allowed.

DEP: $100; with pets, $200. IND MO: $250–$575.

Kawabe Memorial House

221 18th Ave. S.
Seattle, WA 98144

Ph: (206) 322-4550
Fax: (206) 329-3330

E-mail: *kmhs@concentric.net*

IND: 156

Age: 62+. Low income/permanently disabled. Nonprofit. Apartments. 24-hour security system; 24-hour emergency response system; maintenance; transportation for grocery shopping and recreational outings; 1 daily meal; pets allowed; planned activities; Japanese/Korean language capabilities; close to downtown and Seattle's international airport.

DEP: $300. IND MO: $350–$725.

Kloshe Illahee Mobile Home Community

2500 S. 370th St.
Federal Way, WA 98003

Ph: (253) 838-3344
Fax: (253) 83-7446

IND: 258

Age: 55+. Mobile homes. Clubhouse; heated pool; indoor Jacuzzi; tennis court; billiard tables; planned activities.

APPL: $25. PURCHASE: $49,500–$88,000. IND MO: (lots), $475–$525.

Life Manor Retirement Community

1601 S. Union St.
Tacoma, WA 98405

Ph: (253) 383-3363
Fax: (253) 596-0407

IND: 157

Apartments. 24-hour nursing staff; pharmacy consultation service; emergency call system; scheduled transportation; up to 3 daily meals; weekly housekeeping and linen services; laundry facilities.

APP: $500. IND MO: studio, $1,825–$1,925; 1-bedroom: $2,325; 2-bedroom, $2,650. 2nd person, $440.

Marymount Manor

317 152nd St. E.
Tacoma, WA 98445-1298

Ph: (253) 537-8910
Fax: (253) 537-8910

IND: 39

Age 62+. Nonprofit; affiliated with the Dominican Sisters. Apartments. 24-hour security system; 24-hour emergency response system; maintenance; small pets allowed; large community room; landscaped yard.

IND ENT: security deposit. IND MO: 30% of gross income, minus allowable medical expenses and elderly allowance.

REQ: must meet income eligibility standards.

Sno Ridge Apartments

401 Stow
North Bend, WA 98045

Ph: (425) 888-2793
Fax: (425) 831-7050

IND: 40

Age: 62+. Nonprofit. Low-income apartments. Pets allowed.

Contact facility for fees.

The Theodora

6559 35th Ave. NE
Seattle, WA 98115

Ph: (206) 523-3565

IND: Yes

Age: 62+. Affiliated with the Volunteers of America. Private and semiprivate rooms. Medication monitoring; on-site health care; 24-hour staff; part-time staff nurse; personal care; medication administration; personal intercoms; transportation; laundry services; up to 3 daily meals; dining room; social and recreational activities; lounge; atrium.

Contact facility for fees.

Central

Briarwood Common Apartments

1001 S. Chestnut St.
Ellensburg, WA 98926

Ph: (509) 933-1888
Fax: (509) 933-1891
E-mail: *–briarwd@kvally.com*

IND: 174

Age: 55+ (or disability under 55). Tax credit program. Apartments. Wellness clinic; 24-hour security system; maintenance; transportation; pets allowed (20 lbs. or less and 1 per household); pool; planned activities; exercise program.

APPL: $25. DEP: $175. IND MO: $200–$450.

Garden Terrace/Garden Terrace West

500 N. Emerson Ave.
Wenatchee, WA 98801

Ph: (509) 663-2154
Fax: (509) 663-1440

E-mail: *gardenterr@aol.com*

IND: 148

Age 62+. Nonprofit; affiliated with the Wenatchee Brethren Baptist Church. Apartments. 24-hour security system; maintenance; 1 daily meal; pets allowed (under 25 lbs.); laundry facilities.

DEP: (ref.), $250–$500; with pet, additional, $165. IND MO: $250–$500.

East

Holman Gardens

12912 E. 12th St.
Spokane, WA 99216

Ph: (509) 927-2300 or (509) 924-5616
Fax: (509) 927-3402

E-mail: *hlmngrdn@triax.com*

IND: 96

Nonprofit. Apartments. Wellness nurse program; blood pressure checks; medications monitored; resident bus transportation; city bus stops nearby; exercise facilities; indoor walking track; handyman's workshop; outdoor shuffleboard and horseshoe courts; barbecue and community garden area; planned activities.

Contact facility for fees.

Northwest

Hamilton Place

4625 Cordata Parkway
Bellingham, WA 98226

Ph: (360) 715-0871
Fax: (360) 715-0972

IND: 94

Age 55+. For-profit; nondenominational. Apartments. Security system; pets allowed; maintenance; transportation; access to shopping; laundry facilities; planned activities; community rooms; exercise room; billiard table; library; barber/beauty shop.

APPL: $385. DEP: $275. IND MO: $525–$625.

Merrill Gardens

4415 Columbine Drive
Bellingham, WA 98226

Ph: (360) 715-8822
Fax: (360) 715-8818

http://www.merrillgardens.com

IND: Yes

Apartments. Personal care; AL services available; 24-hour licensed staff; emergency call system; scheduled transportation; up to 3 daily meals; private dining room; library; chapel; large-screen TV lounge; barber/beauty shop.

IND MO: studio, $1,625–$1,675; studio alcove, $1,800–$1,825; 1 bedroom, $2,000–$2,175; 2-bedroom, $2,750–$2,775. 2nd person: $330.

Rosecreek Apartments

625 S. Stillaguamish
Arlington, WA 98223

Ph: (877) 715-2787 (toll-free)

http://www.rentnet.com

IND: 100

Age: 55+ with income guidelines. Apartments. Controlled access building; maintenance; van transportation; small pets allowed; laundry rooms on each floor; covered portico; elevator.

APP: $35. DEP: ($125 non-ref.), $275. IND MO: $575–$725.

Twin Ponds

8510 212th St. NE
Arlington, WA 98223

Ph: (877) 715-2787 (toll-free)

Apartments. Close to shopping; small pets (under 25 lbs.) allowed; planned activities; clubhouse with large-screen TV.

IND MO: 1-bedroom, $575–$595; 2 bedroom, $700–$725.

South

Sun Tower

6 N. 6th St.
Yakima, WA 98901

Ph: (509) 248-3191

IND: 152

Age: 62+. Apartments. Laundry facilities; activity and exercise room; craft room; meeting room with serving kitchen; lounge; dining room; solarium; guest room for visiting family members; doctors and nurses room; barber/beauty shop.

DEP: (security and cleaning), 1 mo. rent; (key), $3. IND MO: $275–$450.

Adult/Resort Communities

Communities for active adults (not all are age-restricted; primarily ownership).

Northwest

Homestead Golf and Country Club

PO Box 409
Lynden, WA 98264

Ph: (360) 354-8188

http:americanbuilders.com/Homestead

Fieldstone Place, age 55+. Individual homes, condominiums, homesites. Golf course; clubhouse; pro shop; tennis; swimming pool; walking/biking trails; fitness center; dining.

PURCHASE: Homes, $165,000–$275,000; condos, $93,500–$109,000; homesites, $55,000–$110,000.

Port Ludlow

40 Teal Lake Rd.
Port Ludlow, WA 98365

Ph: (800) 872-1323

http://www.ptludlow.com

Individual homes, condominiums, homesites. Golf course; recreation center; tennis; swimming pool; sailing; kayaking; hiking/biking; marina; beaches; nearby snow skiing and wildlife refuge.

PURCHASE: Homes, $176,000–$660,000+; homesites, $44,000–$220,000.

Sudden Valley Community Association

2145 Lake Whatcom Blvd.
Bellingham, WA 98226

Ph: (360) 734-6430

http://www.suddenvalley.com

Individual homes, homesites. Golf course; pro shop; clubhouse; tennis; swimming pool; fitness center; hiking trails; fishing; boating; snow skiing; dining; social clubs.

PURCHASE: Homes, $99,000–$715,000; homesites, $13,500–$165,000.

Puget Sound/Central

Belmor Park Golf and Country Club

2101 S. 324th St.
Federal Way, WA 98003

Ph: (253) 838-0517

Age 55+. Mobile homes. Golf course; clubhouse; walking paths; fitness center; spas; saunas; billiards; bingo; library; dining; social clubs.

PURCHASE: Mobile homes, $11,750–$53,000.

Canterwood Golf and Country Club

12606 54th Ave. NW
Gig Harbor, WA 98332

Ph: (800) 874-7967 or (253) 851-9199

http://www.canterwood.com

Individual homes, townhomes, club homes, homesites. Golf course; clubhouse; pro shop; tennis; swimming pool; fitness center; hiking trails; riding stables; dining; social clubs.

PURCHASE: Homes, $252,000–$880,000+.

Crescent Bar Resort

8894 Crescent Bar Rd. NW
Quincy, WA 98848

Ph: (509) 787-1511 or (800) 824-7090 (in WA)

Condominiums, RV homes. Golf course; clubhouse; pro shop; tennis; swimming pool; fishing; boating; hunting; dining; nearby snow skiing.

PURCHASE: Condos, $66,000–$198,000; RV homes, from $38,500 (land lease arrangement).

Lake Chelan

1501 Golf Course Drive
Chelan, WA 98816

Ph: (800) 246-5361 or (509) 682-8026

Individual homes. Golf course; clubhouse; pro shop; dining.

PURCHASE: Homes, $110,000–$275,000.

Lake Limerick Country Club

E. 811 St. Andrews Drive
Shelton, WA 98584

Ph: (360) 426-6290

Individual homes, homesites. Golf course; pro shop; clubhouse; tennis; lake; swimming; fishing; boating; hiking trails; dining; social clubs.

PURCHASE: Homes, $93,500–$220,000; homesites, $8,250–$110,000.

McCormick Woods

5200 McCormick Woods Drive SW
Port Orchard, WA 98367

Ph: (800) 375-DEER or (360) 895-DEER
Fax: (360) 895-0156

http://www.mccormickwoods.com

Individual homes, condominiums, homesites. Golf course; clubhouse; pro shop; tennis; basketball; soccer; baseball; walking trails; dining; member of Audubon Cooperative Sanctuary System.

PURCHASE: Homes, $209,000–$418,000.

Meadowmeer Golf and Country Club

8530 Renny Lane NE
Bainbridge Island, WA 98110

Ph: (206) 842-2218

Individual homes, homesites. Golf course; pro shop; clubhouse; dining; nearby tennis club.

PURCHASE: Homes, $220,000–$770,000.

Meridian Campus Golf Communities

9340 Lewis Drive NE
Lacey, WA 98516

Ph: (360) 456-7336

Individual homes, homesites, proposed townhomes and condominiums. Golf courses; clubhouse; pro shop; nature trails; dining.

PURCHASE: Homes, $176,000–$440,000.

West Virginia

http://www.state.wv.us

General Information

Climate

Moderate. Minimum winter temperatures average about 25° F and maximum summer temperatures average over 85° F.

Cost of Living

Ranked 49th in the nation.

Taxes

General: West Virginia State Tax Department, Charleston, WV 25305, (304) 558-3333, (800) 982-8297, *http://www.state.wv.us/taxrev/*

State: 10.6% of income.

Property Tax Exemptions: Residents 65 and older as well as those totally and permanently disabled may be eligible for a $20,000 homestead exemption against the total assessed value of the property.

Sales: 6%.

Prescription Exemptions: Sales of drugs dispensed upon prescription and sales of insulin to consumers for medical purposes are exempt from sales tax.

Transportation, Travel, and Tourism

Major Airports

- Benedum Airport, Clarksburg/Bridgeport, (304) 842-3400.
- Cumberland Regional Airport, Keyser, WV/Ridgeley, MD, (304) 738-0022.
- Greenbrier Valley Airport, Lewisburg, (304) 645-3961.
- Morgantown Municipal Airport/Hart Field, Morgantown, (304) 291-7461.
- Raleigh County Memorial Airport, Beckley, (304) 255-476.
- Tri-State Airport (Walker Long Field) Huntington, (304) 453-6165.
- Wood County Airport, Parkersburg, (304) 464-5113.
- Yeager Airport, Charleston, (304) 345-0661.

Railways

- Amtrak, (800) USA-RAIL.
- MARC rail commuter system, (800) 325-7245.

Bus Tours

- Greyhound Bus Lines, 300 Reynolds St., Charleston, WV 25301-2014, (304) 357-0056.
- Cross Country Express, 2817 Pike St., Parkersburg, WV 26101-8607, (304) 489-1986.

State Highways

- Division of Highways, Charleston, (304) 558-0191.
- West Virginia Parkways Economic Development and Tourism Authority, Charleston, (304) 926-1909.

Theater and Music

New River/Greenbrier Valley (South)

- Bluefield Area Arts and Science Center, Bluefield, (304) 325-8000.
- Carnegie Hall, Lewisburg, (304) 645-7917.
- Camp Washington-Carver, Clifftop, (304) 438-3005.
- Greenbrier Valley Theatre, Lewisburg, (304) 645-3838.
- Historic Fayetteville Theatre, Fayetteville, (304) 574-4840.

- Outdoor Dramas at Grandview, Beckley, (304) 256-6800.

Potomac Highlands (East Central)

- Augusta Heritage Arts Workshops, Elkins, (304) 637-1209.
- Country Store Opry, Petersburg, (304) 257-1743.
- McCoy-McMechen Theatre, Moorefield, (304) 538-6685.

Eastern Panhandle

- Apollo Civic Theater, Martinsburg, (304) 263-6766.
- Contemporary American Theatre Festival, Shepherdstown, (304) 876-3473, (800) 999-CATF.
- Ice House Art Center, Berkeley Springs, (304) 258-2300.
- Old Opera House, Charles Town, (888) 900-SHOW.

North

- Sagebrush Round-Up, Fairmont, (304) 363-6366.
- West Virginia Public Theater, Morgantown, (304) 598-0144.

Metro Valley (Central/West)

- The Aracoma Story, Logan, (304) 752-0253.
- The Cultural Center, Charleston, (304) 558-0220.
- Marshall Artists Series, Huntington, (304) 696-6656.
- Mountaineer Opry House, Milton, (304) 733-2721.
- Mountain Stage, Charleston, (304) 733-2721.

Mid-Ohio Valley (Northwest)

- Actor's Guild, Parkersburg, (304) 485-1300.
- Smoot Theatre, Parkersburg, (304) 422-PLAY.

Museums, Crafts, Historical, Recreational

New River/Greenbrier Valley (South)

- Bluestone Museum, Hinton, (304) 466-3596.
- Cooper Gallery, Lewisburg, (304) 645-6439.
- Court Street Gallery, Fayetteville, (304) 574-9010.
- Hawks Nest State Park Museum, Ansted, (304) 658-5212.
- Science Center of West Virginia, Bluefield, (304) 325-8855.
- Wildwood House Museum, Beckley, (304) 256-1747.

Potomac Highlands (East Central)

- The Art Company, Davis, (304) 259-4218.
- August Heritage Arts Workshops, Elkins, (304) 637-1209.
- Cheat Summit Fort, north of Durbin, (304) 456-3335, (800) 336-7009.
- Day-Vandevander Mill, Harman, (304) 227-4466.
- Fort Ashby, Fort Ashby, (304) 298-3319.
- Lost River General Store, Lost River, (304) 897-6169.
- Pearl S. Buck Birthplace Museum, Hillsboro, (304) 653-4430.
- Pocahontas County Historical Museum, Marlinton, (304) 799-6659, (800) 336-7009.
- Randolph County Historical Museum, Beverly, (304) 637-7424.

Eastern Panhandle

- Berkeley Castle, Berkeley Springs, (304) 258-3274, (800) 896-4001.
- Boarman House Art Center, Martinsburg, (304) 263-0224.
- Bunker Hill Mill, Bunker Hill, (304) 229-8707.
- Ice House Art Center, Berkeley Springs, (304) 258-2300.
- James Rumsey Steamboat Museum, Shepherdstown, (304) 876-6907.
- Jefferson County Museum, Charles Town, (304) 725-8628.

- Morgan Cabin, Bunker Hill, (304) 229-8946, (304) 229-2742.
- Berkeley Springs, (304) 258-3743.

North

- American Museum, Terra Alta, (304) 789-2361.
- Creative Arts Center, West Virginia University, Morgantown, (304) 293-4841.
- Marion County Museum, Fairmont, (304) 367-5398.
- Monongalia Arts Center, Morgantown, (304) 292-3325.
- West Augusta Historical Society Museum, Mannington, (304) 986-2636, (304) 986-1089.
- West Virginia Northern Railroad, Kingwood, (800) 253-1065.

Metro Valley (Central/West)

- The Cultural Center, Charleston, (304) 558-0220.
- Huntington Museum of Art, Huntington, (304) 529-2701.
- Hurricane=s Historic Homes, Hurricane, (304) 562-5896.
- Jenkins Plantation Museum, Greenbottom, (304) 762-1059.
- Museum of Radio and Technology, Huntington, (304) 525-8890.
- West Virginia State Farm Museum, Point Pleasant, (304) 675-5737.
- West Virginia State Museum, Charleston, (304) 558-0220.

Mid-Ohio Valley (Northwest)

- Cedar Lakes Crafts Center, Ripley, (304) 372-7860.
- Parkersburg Art Center, Parkersburg, (304) 485-3895, (304) 485-3850.
- Beauchamp-Newman Museum, Elizabeth, (304) 275-6534.

Organizations

Advocacy Groups

- Aging Institute, (304) 766-4106.
- Altenheim Resource and Referral Center, Wheeling, (304) 243-0996
- Appalachian Area on Aging, Princeton, (304) 425-1147.
- Central West Virginia Aging Services, Inc., Buckhannon, (304) 472-0395, (800) 296-0069.
- Northwestern Area Agency on Aging, Wheeling, (304) 242-1800, (800) 294-0088.
- Upper Potomac Area Agency on Aging, Petersburg, (304) 257-1221
- West Virginia State College–Metro Area Agency on Aging Institute, (304) 766-4106.
- West Virginia University Center on Aging, Morgantown, (304) 293-2968, (888) 982-4464.
- Wyoming County Council on Aging, Inc., Itmann, (304) 294-8800.

Volunteer Programs

- Foster Grandparents in West Virginia, (800) 424-8867.
- Intergenerate, Morgantown, (304) 293-3905, *http://www.wvu.edu/~intergen*
- Ohio Valley Chapter of American Red Cross, Wheeling, (304) 232-0711.
- Retired Senior Volunteer Program (RSVP):
- Boone County, (304) 949-3673, (304) 949-0451.
- Kanawha County, (304) 340-3507.
- Putnam County, (304) 757-2656.
- West Virginia Jaycees, Madison, (304) 369-663, (304) 369-7388.

Housing

Long-Term Care Facilities

*In the state of West Virginia, these facilities are called **Long-Term Care/Nursing Home Facilities**.*

These facilities provide residential living and/or various levels of nursing and medical services to seniors for an extended period of time.

Types of Authorization

Licensing and/or Certification

The West Virginia Bureau for Public Health (a division of Department of Health and Human Resources), Office of Health Facility Licensure and Certification, oversees licensing and compliance of long term care and nursing home facilities.

Memberships

- American Association of Homes and Services for the Aging (AAHSA) represents not-for-profit organizations committed to providing high-quality health care, housing, and services to the elderly. AAHSA, 901 E St. NW, Suite 500, Washington, DC 20004-2011. Ph: (202) 783-2242. Fax: (202) 783-2285. *http://www.aahsa.org*
- West Virginia Hospital Association is a state affiliate of AAHSA. WVHA, 100 Association Drive, Charleston, WV 25311-1571. Ph: (304) 344-9744. Fax: 304-344-9745. *http://www@wvha.com*

Accreditations

- Continuing Care Accreditation Commission (CCAC) accredits facilities that offer seniors a contract or contracts that provide residential living and health care services for the remainder of the person's lifetime and meet CCAC's accreditation standards.
- Joint Commission on the Accreditation of Healthcare Organizations (JCAHO) is an independent, not-for-profit organization, and the nation's oldest and largest standards-setting and health care accrediting institution.

North

Cortland Acres

PO Box 98
Thomas, WV 26292

Ph: (304) 463-4181
Fax: (304) 463-4140

IND: 24. HCC: 99. ALZ/MEM IMP: 28

Age 62+. Nondenominational. Homes, apartments, and private rooms. Nursing care; medical services; rehabilitative therapies; dental and podiatry care; pharmacy services; Medicare/Medicaid-approved; personal care; medication administration; emergency response system, maintenance; transportation; up to 3 daily meals; laundry and housekeeping services; social and recreational activities.

IND MO: HUD-subsidized. HCC Daily: $125.

Grand County Nursing Home

27 Early Ave.
Petersburg, WV 26847

Ph: (304) 257-4233

IND: 4. PC: 10. SNF/ICF: 110

Homes, and private and semiprivate rooms. Nondenominational; sponsored by the county. Skilled and intermediate nursing care; rehabilitative therapies; medical services; dental and podiatry care; pharmacy services; social services; Medicare/Medicaid-approved; personal care; medication administration; security; emergency response system; maintenance; transportation; up to 3 daily meals; housekeeping and laundry services; chapel; religious services; social and recreational activities; lounges and parlors; barber/beauty shop services.

Contact facility for fees.

The Madison, JCAHO

445 Van Voorhis Rd. or 161 Bakers Ridge Rd.
Morgantown, WV 26505

Ph (304) 598-2900
Fax: (304) 598-2903

IND: 28. AL: 30. HCC: 62. ALZ/MEM IMP: 14

Nondenominational; a part of the Genesis ElderCare Network. Apartments and private rooms. 24-hour nursing care; rehabilitative therapies; medical services; dental and podiatry care; pharmacy services; Medicare/Medicaid-approved; personal care; medication administration; security; emergency response system; maintenance; transportation; up to 3 daily meals; housekeeping and laundry services; gym; exercise equipment; social and recreational activities.

DEP: $100. IND MO: $1,100–$1,650. AL MO: $2,550–$3,225. HCC Daily: $125–$150.

Wishing Well Manor, Inc.

1543 Country Club Rd.
Fairmont, WV 26554

Ph: (304) 363-2273

AL: Yes. SNF: Yes

Privately owned; nondenominational. Suites and private and semiprivate rooms. Skilled and intermediate nursing care; on-call physician care; physical, occupational, and speech therapies; dental and podiatry care; social services; long- and short-term care; pharmacy services; personal care; medication administration; security; emergency response system; maintenance; transportation; up to 3 daily meals; housekeeping and laundry services; exercise classes; religious services; social and recreational activities; crafts; bingo; movies; on- and off-site activities; solarium; outdoor courtyard; barber/beauty shop services.

AL/PC Daily: $60–$105. SNF Daily: $110–$130.

Central

Edgewood Summit

300 Baker Lane
Charleston, WV 25302

Ph: (304) 346-2323

Fax: (304) 346-2352

IND: 90. AL: Yes

Nonprofit; nondenominational; managed by Greystone Communities, Inc. Alcoves, suites, and one- and two-bedroom apartments. 24-hour nursing care; personal care; medication administration; security; emergency response system; maintenance; transportation; up to 3 daily meals; housekeeping and laundry services; exercise room; library; social and recreational activities; activities director; speakers; arts and crafts room; multipurpose rooms; convenience store; lounges; barber/beauty shop.

IND ENT: (ref.), $54,000–$138,000. IND MO: $1,275–$2,250; 2nd person, $675. AL ENT: $1,325 and $1,450. AL MO: $2,625–$3,775.

Assisted Living and Residential Care Facilities

In the state of West Virginia, these facilities are called ***Assisted Living/Personal Care/Facilities/Residential Board and Care Homes.***

These facilities provide housing, food service, and one or more personal services.

Types of Authorization

Licensing and/or Certification

The West Virginia Bureau for Public Health (a division of the Department of Health and Human Resources), Office of Health Facility Licensure and Certification, oversees licensing and compliance of personal care facilities.

Memberships

- Assisted Living Federation of America (ALFA) is a national nonprofit membership organization whose mission is to enhance the quality of life in assisted living facilities and promote the interests of the assisted living industry. ALFA, 10300 Eaton Place, Suite 400, Fairfax, VA 22030.

Ph: (703) 691-8100. Fax: (703) 691-8106. *http://www.alfa.org*

West

Chateau Grove Personal Care

3410 Rte. 60 E.
Barboursville, WV 25504

Ph: (304) 736-3445
Fax: (304)738-3444

IND: Yes. AL: 105

Privately owned; nondenominational. Apartments and private rooms. Nursing care; rehabilitative therapies; medical services; physician services adjacent to facility (includes X-ray and lab services and pharmacy); home health services; personal care; medication administration; security; emergency response system; maintenance; transportation; up to 3 daily meals; housekeeping and laundry services; social and recreational activities.

IND MO: $2,150. AL MO: $1,725–$1,925.

Central

SweetBriar

505 Caldwell Lane
Dunbar, WV 25064

Ph: (304) 744-7400

AL: 78

Nondenominational. Private and semiprivate rooms. Personal care; medication administration; security; emergency response system; maintenance; transportation; up to 3 daily meals; housekeeping and laundry services; exercise classes; Bible study; library; social and recreational activities; whirlpool; lounge; crafts; cards; bingo; courtyard with gazebo; barber/beauty shop.

AL MO: Semiprivate, $1,650; private, $2,225.

Sheltering Arms PCH

Box 37 122 2nd Ave.
Fayetteville, WV 25840

Ph: 574-0540
Fax: 574-0481

RH: 33

For-profit; nondenominational. Apartments and private rooms. Some nursing care; personal care; medication administration; emergency response system; maintenance; transportation; up to 3 daily meals; housekeeping and laundry services; social and recreational activities.

RH Daily: $45–$65.

Independent Living

Independent housing (primarily rentals) for seniors that may offer security features, meal service, and activities.

Central

Agsten Manor

715 Randolph St.
Charleston, WV 25302-1845

Ph: (304) 344-0994

IND: 102

Age 62+. Nondenominational. Security; emergency response system; maintenance; transportation; laundry services; close to churches, medical facilities, and businesses.

IND MO: 30% of income; HUD-subsidized.

Edgewood Village

40 Ridgewood Ave.
Richwood, WV 26261

Ph: (304) 846-2250
Fax: (304) 846-6558

IND: 34

Age 60+. Nonprofit; nondenominational. Apartments. Security; emergency response system; maintenance; pets allowed.

IND MO: Based on income.

Elk Riverview Terrace Apartments

#1 S. Main St.
Webster Springs, WV 26288

Ph: (614) 451-2151 (National Church Residences)

IND: Yes

Nonprofit; nondenominational; nonsectarian; part of National Church Residences. Studio and one-bedroom apartments. Home health care services; security; emergency response system; maintenance; transportation; meal program; homemaker services; laundry services; library; community room; close to churches, medical facilities, shopping, and senior center.

Contact facility for fees.

Rivermont Presbyterian Homes

60 Fourth Ave.
Montgomery, WV 25136

Ph: (304) 442-4767
Fax: (304) 442-8586

IND: 90

Age 62+. Nonprofit; nondenominational; Presbyterian Church affiliation. Apartments. Security; emergency response system; maintenance; pets allowed; social and recreational activities.

DEP: 1 mo. rent. IND MO: $750–$825.

South

Twin Oaks Plaza

201 Oak Hill Ave.
Oak Hill, WV 25901

Ph: (304) 469-9938
Fax: (304) 465-1742
E-mail: *twinoaks@citynet.net*

IND: 59

Age 62+. Nonprofit; nondenominational. Apartments. Security; emergency response system; maintenance; pets allowed.

IND MO: $575–$675.

North

Elmhurst, The House of Friendship, Inc.

1228 National Rd.
Wheeling, WV 26003

Ph: (304) 242-0248
Fax: (304) 242-0587

AL: 35

Nonprofit; nondenominational. Apartments. Personal care; medication administration; security; emergency response system; maintenance; transportation; up to 3 daily meals; housekeeping and laundry services; social and recreational activities.

AL MO: $950–$1,300.

Serra Manor

100 Serra Drive
Weirton, WV 26062

Ph: (304) 723-5363

AL: 22

Nonprofit; nondenominational. Private rooms. 24-hour nurses aid services; personal care; medication administration; security; emergency response system; maintenance; transportation; up to 3 daily meals; housekeeping and laundry services; exercise program; social and recreational activities; dry cleaning services; outdoor patio.

AL Daily: $60 (base rate).

Adult/Resort Communities

Communities for active adults (not all are age-restricted; primarily ownership).

North

Alpine Lake Resort

700 West Alpine Drive
Terra Alta, WV 26764

Ph: (800) 752-7179 or (304) 789-2481

http://www.alpinelake.com

Individual homes, homesites. Golf course; pro shop; clubhouse; swimming pool; hiking/biking; fishing; boating; snow skiing; dining.

PURCHASE: Homes $44,000–$220,000; homesites, $1,100–$33,000.

Northeast

Cress Creek Golf and Country Club

100 Cress Creek Drive
Shepherdstown, WV 25443

Ph: (304) 876-1260

http://www.cresscreek.com

Individual homes, villas, homesites. Golf course; pro shop; clubhouse; tennis; swimming pool; social clubs.

PURCHASE: Homes, from $198,000; homesites, from $66,000.

Snowshoe Mountain Resort

1 Snowshoe Rd.
Snowshoe, WV 26209

Ph: (304) 572-1000

http://www.snowshoemtn.com

Individual homes, townhomes, condominiums, homesites. Mountain golf course; clubhouse; pro shop; tennis; swimming pool; hiking/biking; fishing; riding stables; fitness center; winter sports; dining; nearby hunting.

PURCHASE: New homes, $121,000–$385,000; resale homes, $33,000–$330,000+; homesites, $44,000–$71,500.

Stonebridge Golf Community

PO Box 2454
Martinsburg, WV 25401

Ph: (304) 262-4514

http://www.danryanbuilders.com

Individual homes. Golf course; clubhouse; pro shop; tennis; swimming pool; hiking trails; dining; nearby river stocked with trout.

PURCHASE: Homes, from $123,500.

The Woods Resort

Mountain Lake Rd.
Hedgesville, WV 25427

Ph: (800) 248-2222 or (304) 754-3358

http://www.thewoodsresort.com

Individual homes, homesites. Golf courses; pro shop; clubhouse; recreation center; tennis; swimming pools; racquetball; hiking trails; fishing; hunting; fitness center; dining; social clubs; nearby riding stables.

PURCHASE: Homes, $131,000–$440,000+.

West

Fairway Estates

Lynn Oak Drive, PO Box 477
Lavalette, WV 25535

Ph: (304) 525-7405

Individual homes, homesites. Golf course; pro shop; clubhouse; driving range; dining.

PURCHASE: Homesites, $24,500–$38,500.

South

Glade Springs Resort

200 Lake Drive
Daniels, WV 25832

Ph: (800) 634-5233 or (304) 763-5000
http://www.gladesprings.com

Individual homes, condominiums, homesites. Golf course; clubhouse; pro shop; tennis; swimming pool; hiking/biking; fishing; riding stables; snow skiing; fitness center; dining.

PURCHASE: Condos, $44,000–$153,000; homes, $175,000–$660,000+; homesites, $32,000–$110,000.

Wisconsin

http://www.wisconsin.gov/state/home

General Information

Climate

Continental with some modification by Lakes Michigan and Superior; cold, snowy winters and warm summers. The average annual temperature varies from 39°F in the north to about 50°F in the south. During more than one-half of the winters, temperatures fall to minus 40°F or lower, and almost every winter temperatures of minus 30°F or colder are reported from northern stations. Summer temperatures above 90°F average 2 to 4 days in northern counties and about 14 days in southern districts.

Cost of Living

Ranked 28th in the nation.

Taxes

General: Wisconsin Department of Revenue, Division of Administrative Services, 125 S. Webster St., PO Box 8933, Madison, WI 53708-8933. Ph: (608) 266-8651 Fax (608) 261-6245.

State/Local as % of Income: 12.2%.

Property Tax Exemptions: Residents age 65+ with an income of $19,154 or less are eligible for a homestead tax credit.

Sales: 5%.

Prescription Exemptions: Exemptions include drugs prescribed for treatment or dispensed by a pharmacist.

Transportation, Travel, and Tourism

Major Airports

- Dane County Regional Airport, Madison, (608) 246-3380.
- General Mitchell International Airport, Milwaukee, (414) 747-5300.

Railways

- Amtrak, (800) USA-RAIL.
- Midwest Rail (plans to implement in 2005).
- Osceola and St. Croix Railway (seasonal), Osceola, (612) 228-0263, (800) 711-2591.

Bus Tours

- Metro Plus Elderly & Disabled, 1101 E. Washington Ave., Madison, WI 53703, (608) 267-8787.
- Anderson Leisure Lines, 5305 Verona Rd, Madison, WI 53711-4420, (608) 271-3811.
- Greyhound Bus Lines, 606 N. 7th St., James Level, Milwaukee, WI 53206, (414) 272-3464.

State Highways

- Wisconsin Department of Transportation, Madison, (608) 246-3265.

Theater and Music

Great Lakes

- American Folklore Theatre, Fish Creek, (920) 868-9999.
- Golden Rondell Theater, Racine, (414) 260-2154.
- The John Michael Kohler Arts Center, Sheboygan, (920) 458-6144.
- Lake Superior Big Top Chautauqua, Washburn, (888) 244-8368.
- Peninsula Players, Fish Creek, (920) 868-3287.

Northern

- Indian Bowl Powwows, Lac du Flambeau, (715) 588-3333.

- Northern Lights Playhouse, Hazelhurst, (715) 356-7173.
- Pinewood Dinner Theater, Harshaw, (715) 282-5500, (800) 746-3963.
- Red Barn Theater, Rice Lake, (715) 234-8301, (800) 523-6318.
- Scheers Lumberjack Shows, Hayward, (715) 634-5010.

Central

- Fanny Hill Inn and Dinner Theatre, Eau Claire, (800) 292-8026.
- The Grand Opera House, Oshkosh, (920) 424-2355, (920) 424-2350.
- Grand Theater, Wausau, (715) 842-0988.
- Center for Visual Arts, Wausau, (715) 842-4545.

Southern

- Eddie Cash Show at Belfry Music Theater, Williams Bay, (414) 245-0123, (800) 786-0700.
- Fireside Restaurant and Playhouse at Fort Atkinson, (800) 477-9505.
- American Players' Theater, Spring Green, (608) 588-2361.
- Shakespeare Box Office, Platteville, (608) 342-1298.

Museums, Crafts, Historical, Recreational

Great Lakes

- Chambers Island Lighthouse, Fish Creek, (920) 868-3100.
- Door County Maritime Museum, Sturgeon Bay, (920) 743-5958.
- Green Bay Packer Hall of Fame, Green Bay, (920) 499-4281.
- Heritage Hill Living History Museum, Green Bay, (920) 448-5150, (800) 721-5150.
- The Miller Art Center, Sturgeon Bay, (920) 746-0707.
- National Railroad Museum, Green Bay, (920) 437-7623.
- Oneida Nation Museum, Oneida, (920) 869-2768.
- Pinecrest Historical Village, Manitowoc, (920) 684-4445.
- Pioneer Village, Saukville, (414) 377-4510.
- S.S. Meteor Museum, Superior, (715) 392-5742.
- Washburn Historical Museum and Cultural Center, Washburn, (715) 373-5591.
- Wisconsin Maritime Museum, Manitowoc, (920) 684-0218.

Northern

- Carl's Wood Art Museum, Eagle River, (715) 479-1883.
- Fred Smith House and Countryside Artists' Gallery, 1 mile south of Phillips, (715) 339-6479.
- George W. Brown, Jr., Ojibwe Museum and Cultural Center, Lac du Flambeau, (715) 588-3333.
- Harley-Davidson Plant Tours, Tomahawk, (715) 453-2191.
- Logging Museum Complex, Rhinelander, (715) 362-2193.
- National Fresh Water Fishing Hall of Fame, Hayward, (715) 634-4440.
- Pioneer Village Museum, Cameron, (715) 458-2841, (715) 458-2080.
- Railroad Memories Museum, Spooner, (715) 635-3325, (715) 635-2752.

Central

- Charles A. Grignon Mansion, Kaukauna, (920) 766-3122.
- Dell Mill Museum, Augusta, (715) 286-2714.
- Fond du Lac Lighthouse, Fond du Lac, (800) 937-9123.
- Houdini Historical Center/Outagamie Museum, Appleton, (920) 735-9370.
- Lehigh Yawkey Woodson Art Museum, Wausau, (715) 845-7010.
- Menominee Logging Museum, Keshena, (715) 799-3757.
- New Visions Gallery, Marshfield, (715) 387-5562.
- Oshkosh Public Museum, Oshkosh, (920) 424-4730.

Southern

- The Angel Museum, Beloit, (608) 362-9099.

- Cedarburg Cultural Center, Cedarburg, (414) 375-3676.
- Fennimore Doll and Toy Museum, Fennimore, (608) 822-4100.
- Geneva Lake Area Museum of History, Lake Geneva, (414) 248-6060.
- Logan Museum of Anthropology, Beloit College, Beloit, (608) 363-2677.
- Mid-Continent Railway Museum, North Freedom, (608) 522-4261.
- Mining Museum–Rollo Jamison Museum, Platteville, (608) 398-3301.
- Ripley's Believe It or Not! Museum, Wisconsin Dells, (608) 253-7556.

Mississippi River

- Laura Ingalls Wilder Wayside and Cabin, north of Pepin, (715) 442-3161.
- Prairie du Chien Museum at Fort Crawford, Prairie du Chien, (608) 326-6960.
- Stonefield Village and State Farm Museum, Cassville, (608) 725-5210.

Metro Cities

- America's Black Holocaust Museum, Milwaukee, (414) 264-2500.
- Milwaukee Art Museum, Milwaukee, (414) 277-9094.
- Discovery World: James Lovell Museum of Science, Economics and Technology, Milwaukee, (414) 765-9966.
- Madison Art Center, Madison, (608) 257-0158.
- Milwaukee Public Museum, Milwaukee, 9414) 278-2700.
- State Historical Museum, Madison, (608) 264-6555.
- Wisconsin Veterans' Museum, Madison, (608) 264-6086.

Organizations

Advocacy Groups

- Ageadvantage, Madison and Eau Claire offices, (608) 243-2450.
- Alzheimer's Family and Caregiver Support Program, Madison, (608) 267-9583.
- Bay Area Agency on Aging, Green Bay, (920) 469-8858.
- Milwaukee Area Agency on Aging, Milwaukee, (414) 289-5950.
- Northern Area Agency on Aging, Rhinelander, (715) 365-2525.
- Southeastern Area Agency on Aging, Brookfield, (414) 821-4444.
- Wisconsin Bureau of Aging and Long Term Care Resources, Madison, (608) 266-2536. Fax (608) 267-3203.

Volunteer Programs

- Foster Grandparent Program:
- Antigo School District, Antigo, (715) 627-4355.
- Great Lakes Inter-Tribal Council, Lac du Flambeau, (715) 588-3324
- Southwest Community Action Program, Dodgeville, (608) 935-2326

- The Retired Senior Volunteer Program (RSVP):
- Department of Health and Family Services, Madison, (608) 266-1865.

Housing

Long-Term Care Facilities

In the state of Wisconsin, these facilities are called ***Continuing Care/Nursing Home/Retirement Facilities****.*

These facilities provide residential living and/or various levels of nursing and medical services to seniors for an extended period of time.

Types of Authorization

Licensing and/or Certification

Facilities are regulated by the Department of Health and Family Services. Long-term care is defined as any service or support that a person needs because a disability or chronic illness limits his or her ability to do everyday personal care tasks. Community-based residential facilities (CBRF) provide assisted living including some nursing care.

Memberships:

- American Association of Homes and Services for the Aging (AAHSA) represents not-for-profit organizations committed to providing high-quality health care, housing, and services to the elderly. AAHSA, 901 E St. NW, Suite 500, Washington, DC 20004-2011. Ph: (202) 783-2242. Fax: (202) 783-2285. *http://www.aahsa.org*
- Wisconsin Association of Homes and Services for the Aging is a state affiliate of AAHSA; 204 S. Hamilton St., Madison, WI 53703-3212. Ph: (608) 255-7060. Fax: (608) 255-7064. *http://www.wahsa.org*

Accreditations:

- Continuing Care Accreditation Commission (CCAC) accredits facilities that offer seniors a contract or contracts that provide residential living and health care services for the remainder of the person's lifetime and meet CCAC's accreditation standards.
- Joint Commission on the Accreditation of Health Care Organizations (JCAHCO) is an independent, not-for-profit organization, and the nation's oldest and largest standards-setting and health care accrediting institution.
- Educational Assessment Guidelines Leading toward Excellence (EAGLE) is a voluntary self-assessment and peer review evaluation system developed by the United Methodist Association of Health and Welfare Ministries.

Northeast

Scandia Village Good Samaritan

290 Smith Drive
Sister Bay, WI 54234

Ph: (920) 854-2317
Fax: (920) 854-9529

http://www.good-sam.com

IND: 58. RH: 4 (more villas under construction). AL: 20. HCC: 60

Age 62+. Nonprofit; nondemoninational; Evangelical Lutheran Good Samaritan Society affiliation. Apartments, villas, and private and semiprivate rooms. 24-hour nursing care; skilled nursing care; physician services; physical, occupational, and speech therapies; outpatient therapy; hospice services; respite care; podiatry and eye care; social services; respite care; health screening; Medicare/Medicaid-approved; personal care; medication administration; security; emergency response system; maintenance; transportation; up to 3 daily meals; pets allowed; housekeeping and laundry services; exercise room; chapel; religious services; library; social and recreational activities; crafts; volunteer opportunities; walking paths; barber/beauty shop.

IND MO: $700–$1,250. AL Daily: $65–$75. HCC Daily: Semiprivate, $130-$150; private, $140–$165.

South

Attic Angel Place, CCAC

602 N. Segoe Rd.
Madison, WI 53705-3113

Ph: (608) 238-8282
Fax: (608) 231-5908

E-mail: *aangel@atticangel.org*

IND: 74. AL: 36. HCC: 44

Age 62+. Nonprofit; nondenominational. Apartments and private and semiprivate rooms. 24-hour nursing care; medical services; physical, occupational, and speech therapies; dental and podiatry care; pharmacy services; social services; Medicare-approved; personal care; medication administration; security; emergency response system; maintenance; transportation; up to 3 daily meals; housekeeping and laundry services; fitness center; chapel; library; business center; social and recreational activities; educational and cultural programs; convenience store; cafe; greenhouse; barber/beauty shop.

APPL: $1,000. IND ENT: $28,500–$39,500. IND MO: $1,500–$2,150. AL ENT: $5,500. AL MO: $3,100. HCC Daily: $135–$170.

Evergreen Retirement Community, EAGLE

1130 N. Westfield St.
PO Box 1720
Oshkosh, WI 54903-1720

Ph: (920) 233-2340
Fax: (920) 233-4347

IND: 66. AL: 82. HCC: 108. ALZ/MEM IMP: 20

Age 55+. Nonprofit; nondenominational; United Methodist Church affiliation. Homes, apartments, studios, and private and semiprivate rooms. Skilled nursing care; 24-hour nursing care; medical services; rehabilitative therapies; pharmacy services; podiatry care; social workers; Medicare-approved; personal care; medication administration; security; emergency response system; maintenance; transportation; up to 3 daily meals; housekeeping and laundry services; exercise program; chaplain; religious services; social and recreational activities; volunteer opportunities; arts and crafts; woodworking studio; greenhouse; convenience store; barber/beauty shop.

Contact facility for fees.

Meriter Retirement Center, CCAC

110 S. Henry St.
Madison, WI 53703

Ph: (608) 283-2000
Fax: (608) 283-2028

IND: 193. AL: 44. SNF: 120

Age 55+. Nonprofit; nondenominational. Apartments and private and semiprivate rooms. 24-hour skilled nursing care; geriatric nursing; physician services; rehabilitative therapies; medical services; dental and podiatry care; lab and X-ray services; pharmacy services; social services; wellness program; Medicare/Medicaid-approved; personal care; medication administration; security; emergency response system; maintenance; transportation; up to 3 daily meals; pets allowed; housekeeping and laundry services; exercise classes; interdenominational chapel; pastoral care; social and recreational activities; educational and cultural programs; volunteer opportunities; lounges; auditorium; ice cream parlor; snack shop; convenience store; aviary; patio and gardening areas; barber/beauty shop .

APPL: $25. IND ENT: $15,500–$33,000. IND MO: $1,000–$1,900. AL ENT: up to $5,500. AL MO: $3,100–$3,300. SNF Daily: $150–$160.

Oakwood Lutheran Homes, Inc., AAHSA, ALFAA, WAHSA, WALA

6201-09 Mineral Point Rd.
Madison, WI 53705

Ph: (608) 231-3451
Fax: (608) 231-1504

IND: 209. AL: 60. HCC: 137. ALZ/MEM IMP: 40 (under construction)

Nonprofit; nondenominational; Evangelical Lutheran Church in America and Lutheran Church–Missouri Synod. Studios, one- and two-bedroom and deluxe apartments, and private and semiprivate rooms. 24-hour nursing care; medical services; rehabilitative therapies; dental and podiatry care; pharmacy services; geriatric clinic; Medicare/Medicaid-approved; personal care; medication administration; security; emergency response system; maintenance; transportation; up to 3 daily meals; pets allowed; housekeeping and laundry services; cultural and educational opportunities; exercise room; swimming pool; religious services; library; social and recreational activities; game and party room; lounges; auditorium; grocery store; coffee shop; gift shop; gardening; barber/beauty shop.

DEP: $500– $1,000. IND ENT: Up to $34,500. IND MO: $600–$1,950. AL ENT: $5,500. AL Daily: $105–$120. HCC Daily: $150–$210.

Schmitt Woodland Hills Retirement Community

1400 W. Seminary St.
Richland Center, WI 53581

Ph: (608) 647-8931

IND: 38. AL: 30. SNF: 25

Age 60+. Nonprofit; nondenominational; affiliated with the Wisconsin Conference of the United Methodist Church. Apartments and private and semiprivate rooms. 24-hour nursing care; skilled nursing care; rehabilitative therapies; medical services; dental and podiatry services; pharmacy services; social services; personal care; medication administration; security; emergency response system; maintenance; transportation; up to 3 daily meals; housekeeping and laundry services; exercise program; chapel; religious services; library; educational programs; social and recreational activities; discussion groups; lounge; woodworking shop; painting; greenhouse; gardening.

DEP: $500. IND ENT: (partial ref.), $4,125–$66,000. IND MO: $775–$1,800. AL ENT: $2,750. AL Daily: $85–$120. SNF Daily: $135–$175.

Southeast

Alexian Village, CCAC

9301 N. 16th St.
Milwaukee, WI 53223

Ph: (414) 355-9300
Fax: (414) 357-5106

E-mail: *market@alexianvillage.org*

IND: 310. AL: 82. HCC: 108

Age 62+. Nonprofit; nondenominational; sponsored by Alexian Brothers. Studios, alcoves, one- and two-bedroom apartments, and private and semiprivate rooms. 24-hour nursing care; skilled nursing care; rehabilitative therapies; medical services; dental, podiatry, and eye care; pharmacy services; psychiatric services; Medicare/Medicaid-approved; personal care; medication administration; security; emergency response system; maintenance; transportation; up to 3 daily meals; pets allowed; housekeeping and laundry services; exercise room; whirlpool; chapel; religious services; library; banking services; social and recreational activities; educational program; store; woodshop; crafts; solarium; patios; gardening; barber/beauty shop.

DEP: $500. IND ENT: $56,500–$181,500. IND MO: $1,025–$2,350.

Cedar Lake Campus, Cedar Crossings, Cedar Bay, AAHSA, WAHSA

5595 Hwy Z
West Bend, WI 53095

Ph: (414) 334-9487

IND: 85. AL: 109. SNF: 415. ALZ/MEM IMP: Yes

Age 62+. Nonprofit; nondenominational; United Church of Christ affiliation. Homes; apartments, and private and semiprivate rooms. Skilled nursing care; physical, occupational, and speech therapies; respite care; dental and eye care; pharmacy; lab services; social services; Medicare/Medicaid-approved; personal care; medication administration; security; emergency response system; maintenance; transportation; up to 3 daily meals; housekeeping and laundry services; exercise program; religious services; social and recreational activities; educational and cultural programs; intergenerational programs; volunteer opportunities; library; lounge; resident council; walking paths; coffee shop; crafts; barber/beauty shop.

IND ENT: (ref.) $53,000–$90,000. IND MO: $550. AL ENT: $5,500. AL MO: $2,000–$2,575. HCC Daily: $165–$220.

Fairhaven

435 Starin Rd.
Whitewater, WI 53190-1125

Ph: (414) 473-2140
Fax: (414) 473-5468

IND: 160. AL: Yes. SNF: 84

Age 65+. Nonprofit; nondenominational; Wisconsin Conference of the United Church of Christ affiliation. Efficiencies, alcoves, one- and two-bedroom apartments, and private and semiprivate rooms. 24-hour nursing care; skilled and intermediate nursing care; physical, occupational, and speech therapies; medical services; dental and podiatry care; pharmacy services; Medicare/Medicaid-approved; personal care; medication administration; security; emergency response system; maintenance; transportation; up to 3 daily meals; housekeeping and laundry services; exercise room; religious services; social and recreational activities; library; workshop; indoor garden; barber/beauty shop.

IND LL: (partial ref.), $15,000–$32,000. IND MO: $525–$1,150. AL LL: $15,000–$24,000. AL Daily: $90–$170. ALZ/MEM IMP Daily: $115. SNF Daily: $135–$170.

Freedom Village and Friendship Village, CCAC

7300 W. Dean Rd.
Milwaukee, WI 53223

Ph: (414) 3554-3700

IND: Yes. AL: Yes. HCC: Yes

Nonprofit; nondenominational; Aurora Health Care. Townhomes, apartments, and private and semiprivate rooms. 24-hour skilled nursing care; physician services; rehabilitative therapies; medical services; dental, podiatry, eye, and ear care; lab and X-ray services; pharmacy services; personal care; medication administration; security; emergency response system; maintenance; transportation; up to 3 daily meals; housekeeping and laundry services; exercise program; swimming pool; weekly chapel services; library; banking services; social and recreational activities; card and game room; educational and cultural programs; woodworking shop; arts and crafts; aviary; country store; garden area; barber/beauty shop.

Contact facility for fees.

Lincoln Village Convalescent Center

1700 C. A. Becker Drive
Racine, WI 53406

Ph: (414) 637-9751
Fax: (414) 637-9329

SNF: 122. ALZ/MEM IMP: Yes

Becker-Shoop Center

6101 16th St.
Racine, WI 53406

Ph: (414) 637-7486
fax: (414) 637-7851

SNF/ICF: 110. ALZ/MEM IMP: Yes

Lincoln Lutheran Care Center

1600 Ohio St.
Racine, WI 53406

Ph: (414) 637-7491
Fax: (414) 637-6780

NH: 256. ALZ/MEM IMP: Yes

Lincoln Lutheran Home

2015 Prospect St.
Racine, WI 53406

Ph: (414) 637-6531
Fax: (414) 637-5765

SNF/ICF: 211. ALZ/MEM IMP: Yes

Nonprofit; nondenominational; owned and sponsored by Lincoln Lutheran. Private and semiprivate rooms. 24-hour nursing; physical, occupational, and speech therapies; dental, podiatry and eye care; pharmacy; medical services; social services; respite care; Medicare/Medicaid-approved; personal care; medication administration; security; emergency response system; maintenance; transportation; up to 3 daily meals; housekeeping and laundry services; chaplain services; social and recreational activities; barber/beauty shop.

Contact facilities for fees.

LindenGrove–Mukwonago Campus

841 County Rd. NE
Mukwonago, WI 53149

Ph: (414) 363-6830
Fax: (614) 363-6834

http: / / www.lindengrove.org

AL: 50. HCC: 56. ALZ/MEM IMP: 20

Age 62+. Nonprofit; nondenominational. Apartments and private and semiprivate rooms. Nursing care; rehabilitative therapies; medical services; dental and podiatry care; subacute care; pharmacy services; Medicare/Medicaid-approved; personal care; medication administration; security; emergency response system; maintenance; transportation; up to 3 daily meals; pets allowed; housekeeping and laundry services; banking services; social and recreational activities; crafts; activity rooms; barber/beauty shop.

AL MO: $2,075–$3,550. HCC Daily: $155–$175.

LindenGrove–Waukesha Campus

425 N. University Drive
Waukesha, WI 53188

Ph: (414) 524-6400
Fax: (614) 524-9233

http: / / www.lindengrove.org

NH: 135. AL: 55

Age 62+. Nonprofit; nondenominational. Apartments and private and semiprivate rooms. Nursing care; rehabilitative therapies; medical services; dental and podiatry care; subacute care; pharmacy services; Medicare/Medicaid-approved; personal care; medication administration; security; emergency response system; maintenance; transportation; up to 3 daily meals; pets allowed; housekeeping and laundry services; banking services; social and recreational activities; crafts; activity rooms; barber/beauty shop.

AL MO: $2,050–$2,350. HCC Daily: $175–$200.

Luther Manor

4545 N. 92nd St.
Milwaukee, WI 53225

Ph: (414) 464-3880

IND: 425. AL: 164. HCC: 245. ADC: Yes

Nonprofit; nondenominational; a ministry of the United Lutheran Program for the Aging, Inc. Apartments and private and semiprivate rooms. Skilled nursing care; physical, occupational, and speech therapies; hospice care; medical services; dental and podiatry care; eye and ear care; pharmacy services; wellness clinic; Medicare/Medicaid-approved; personal care; medication administration; security; emergency response system; maintenance; transportation; up to 3 daily meals; housekeeping and laundry services; exercise program; religious services; banking and postal services; library; educational programs; social and recreational activities; intergenerational program; woodworking shop; crafts; gift shop; convenience store; barber/beauty shop.

IND ENT: No refund, $15,500–85,500; refund, $32,500–$178,000. IND MO: $650 $2,250. AL ENT: $7,150. AL Daily: with ENT, $70 and $90; without ENT, $85; $100; $105. HCC Daily: $155–$195. ADC Daily: $50–$165.

Milwaukee Catholic Home

2462 N. Prospect Ave.
Milwaukee, WI 53211

Ph: (414) 224-9700
Fax: (414) 224-1666

http://www.milwaukeecatholichome.org

E-mail: *info@milwaukeecatholichome.org*

IND: 145. AL: 29. HCC: 93. ALZ/MEM IMP: 29. ADC: Yes

Age 62+. Nondenominational. Apartments and private rooms. 24-hour nursing care; medical services; rehabilitative therapies; dental and podiatry care; pharmacy services; Medicare/Medicaid-approved; personal care; medication administration; security; emergency response system; maintenance; transportation; up to 3 daily meals; pets allowed; housekeeping and laundry services; religious services; social and recreational activities.

IND ENT: Up to $129,000. IND MO: $1,000–$3,525. AL ENT: $5,500. AL MO: $2,675–$2,900. HCC Daily: $185–$200.

Milwaukee Protestant Home

2559 N. Downer Ave.
Milwaukee, WI 53211

Ph: (414) 332-8610

IND: 123. SNF: Yes

Nonprofit; Protestant Church affiliation. Apartments and private and semiprivate rooms. Skilled nursing care; medical services; rehabilitative therapies; social services; dental and podiatry care; pharmacy; personal care; medication administration; security; emergency response system; maintenance; transportation; up to 3 daily meals; housekeeping and laundry services; banking services; library; social and recreational activities; craft shop; coffee shop; general store; outdoor patios; barber/beauty shop.

IND ENT: $31,000–$108,000. IND MO: with ENT, $1,075–$2,250; without ENT, $1,500–$3,175. SNF Daily: with ENT, $145–$180; without ENT, $170–$200.

Sheboygan Retirement Home and Beach Health Care Center

930 N. 6 St.
Sheboygan, WI 53081

Ph: (920) 458-2137
Fax: (920) 458-5922

AL: 70. HCC: 84

Age 55+. Nondenominational; United Methodist Church affiliation. Apartments and private and semiprivate rooms. 24-hour nursing care; rehabilitative therapies; dental and podiatry care; pharmacy services; Medicare/Medicaid-approved; personal care; medication administration; security; emergency response system; maintenance; transportation; up to 3 daily meals; housekeeping and laundry services; social and recreational activities.

AL MO: $1,450–$1,925. HCC Daily: Semiprivate, $135; private, $145.

Shorehaven Apartments, Towers, Health Center

1306 W. Wisconsin Ave.
PO Box 208
Oconomowoc, WI 53066-0208

Ph: (414) 567-8341
Fax: (414) 567-0273

IND: 94. AL: 100. HCC: 240. ADC: Yes

Age 62+. Nonprofit; nondenominational; Lutheran Church affiliation. Apartments and private and semiprivate rooms. 24-hour nursing care; skilled nursing care; rehabilitative therapies; medical services; dental and podiatry care; pharmacy services; wellness program; Medicare-approved; personal care; medication administration; security; emergency response system; maintenance; transportation; up to 3 daily meals; housekeeping and laundry services; religious services; exercise room; library; social and recreational activities; billiards; game room; crafts; woodworking shop; skywalk; general store; barber/beauty shop.

RSV: (ref.), $2,750. IND ENT: $53,500–$109,000. IND MO: $625–$1,025. AL MO: $1,650–$2,650; 2nd person, $600. HCC: $155–$195.

Tudor Oaks

S77 W12929 McShane Drive
PO Box 901
Hales Corners, WI 53130-0901

Ph: (414) 529-0100

IND: 185. AL: 12. HCC: 62

Age 62+. Nonprofit; nondenominational; American Baptist Homes of the Midwest. Studios, alcoves; one- and two-bedrooms, and private and semiprivate rooms. 24-hour skilled nursing care; physical, occupational, and speech therapies; physician care; medical services; podiatry care; pharmacy services; wellness clinic; Medicare/Medicaid-approved; personal care; medication administration; security; emergency response system; maintenance; transportation; up to 3 daily meals; housekeeping and laundry services; exercise room; chapel; religious services; banking services; crafts; woodworking shop; social and recreational activities; educational and cultural programs; lounges; country store; greenhouse; barber/beauty shop.

IND LC: $43,500–$141,000. IND MO: (with LC), $1,075–$2,325; (without LC), $1,600–$2,700. AL and HCC services inclusive in LC.

Northwest

Christian Community Home and Services

1320 Wisconsin St.
Hudson, WI 54016

Ph: (715) 386-9303
Fax: (715) 381-4200

IND: 83. AL: 33. HCC: 81

Nonprofit; Methodist Church affiliation. Apartments and private rooms. 24-hour nursing care; medical services; rehabilitative therapies; dental and podiatry care; pharmacy services; Medicare/Medicaid-approved; personal care; medication administration; security; emergency response system; maintenance; transportation; up to 3 daily meals; pets allowed; housekeeping and laundry services; fitness center; religious services; social and recreational activities; walking paths; barber/beauty shop.

IND ENT: (ref.) $6,600–$11,000. IND MO: $700–$1,375. AL ENT: $1,100. AL Daily: $75–$95. HCC Daily: $125–$150.

Assisted Living and Residential Care Facilities

In the state of Wisconsin, these facilities are called ***Assisted Living/Community-Based Residential Facilities.***

These facilities provide housing, food service, and one or more personal services.

Types of Authorization

Licensing and/or Certification

Facilities are regulated by the Department of Health and Family Services and include assisted living facilities, community based residential facilities (CBRF), and adult family homes. CBRFs provide assisted living, including some nursing care.

Memberships

- Assisted Living Federation of America (ALFA) is a national nonprofit membership organization whose mission is to enhance the quality of life in assisted living facilities and promote the interests of the assisted living industry. ALFA, 10300 Eaton Place, Suite 400, Fairfax, VA 22030. Ph: (703) 691-8100. Fax: (703) 691-0100. http://www.alfa.org
- Wisconsin Assisted Living Association (WALA) is a state affiliate of ALFA. WALA, 2875 Fish Hatchery Rd., Madison, WI 53713. Ph: (608) 288-0246. Fax: (608) 228-0734.

Southeast

Lake Terrace

5761 S. 68th St.
Franklin, WI 53132

Ph: (414) 525-0290
Fax: (414) 525-0294

AL: 20. ALZ/MEM IMP: 20

Age 50+. For-profit; nondenominational; owned by Senior Miniums; Catholic Church affiliation. Private rooms. 24-hour nursing care; medical services; rehabilitative therapies; dental, podiatry, and audiology services; pharmacy services; 24-hour staffing; personal care; medication administration; security; emergency response system; maintenance; transportation; up to 3 daily meals; housekeeping and laundry services; exercise room; religious services; library; social and recreational activities.

MO: $3,200.

Lincoln Center

3710 Douglas Ave.
Racine, WI 53581

Ph: (414) 639-1375
Fax: (414) 639-5789

Schmidt Memorial Home

10441 S. Nicholson Rd.
Oak Creek, WI 53154-6421

Ph: (414) 762-5118
Fax: (414) 762-5223

Pennoyer Home

6305 7th Ave.
Kenosha, WI 53143

Ph: (414) 552-7008
Fax: (414) 652-8243

AL: Yes

Nonprofit; nondenominational; owned and sponsored by Lincoln Lutheran. Apartments. Wellness nurse; respite care; 24-hour staffing; personal care; medication administration; security; emergency response system; maintenance; transportation; up to 3 daily meals; housekeeping and laundry services; chaplain services; social and recreational activities; barber/beauty shop.

Contact facility for fees.

National Regency Retirement Community

13750 W. National Ave.
New Berlin, WI 53151

Ph: (414) 789-1699
Fax: (414) 789-1806

IND: 70. AL: 88. AC: 10

Age 62+. Nonprofit; nondenominational. Apartments. Nursing care; rehabilitative therapies; medical services; personal care; medication administration; security; emergency response system; maintenance; transportation; up to 3 daily meals; housekeeping and laundry services; fitness center; whirlpool; social and recreational activities.

DEP: 2 mos. rent. IND MO: $1,100–$1,400. AL/AC MO: $1,450–$3,300.

Villa Saint Anna

5737 Erie St.
Racine, WI 53402

Ph: (414) 639-9757

AL: 71

Age 62+. Nonprofit; nondenominational; sponsored by Wheaton Franciscans and Racine Dominicans. Private suites. Nursing care; wellness care; monthly health screenings; outpatient therapy lab; personal care; medication administration; security; emergency response system; maintenance; transportation; up to 3 daily meals; housekeeping and laundry services; religious services; social and recreational activities; card and board games; store; sunrooms; barber/beauty shop.

AL MO: Basic, $1,475–$4,650; level 2, add $140 to the basic fee; level 3, add $275 to the basic fee.

Some financial assistance may be possible.

West

Bethany on Cass

1315 Cass Street
La Crosse, WI 54601

Ph: (608) 784-6656

IND: 48. AL: 7

Age 62+. Nonprofit; nondenominational; affiliated with the Lutheran Church. Apartments. Personal care; medication administration; security; emergency response system; maintenance; up to 3 daily meals; housekeeping and laundry services; fitness center; exercise program; religious services; social and recreational activities; walking paths.

MO: $1,825–$2,150.

East Avenue Terrace

3900 East Ave. S.
La Crosse, WI 54601

Ph: (608) 788-5700

AL: Yes

Nondenominational; Bethany–St. Joseph Corporation. Private and semiprivate rooms. Personal care; medication administration; security; emergency response system; maintenance; transportation; up to 3 daily meals; housekeeping and laundry services; social and recreational services.

AL Daily: Semiprivate, $50; private, $60.

Woven Hearts

733 W. Hamilton
Eau Claire, WI 54701

Ph: (715) 832-3970
Fax: (715) 832-4193

AL: Yes

Nondenominational; Owned by Alternative Living Servcies. Private and semiprivate rooms. 24-hour nursing care; holistic care; personal care; medication administration; security; emergency response system; maintenance; transportation; up to 3 daily meals; housekeeping and laundry services; social and recreational activities; on- and off-site activities; patios; gardening; walking paths.

Contact facility for fees.

Central

Bell Tower

1500 O'Day St.
Merrill, WI 54452-3497

Ph: (715) 536-5575

AL: Yes

Nonprofit; nondenominational; sponsored by the Sisters of Mercy of the Holy Cross. Private studios and one-bedroom apartments. Nurse on staff weekly and on call; 24-hour staffing; nursing assistants; personal care; medication administration; security; emergency response system; maintenance; transportation; up to 3 daily meals; housekeeping and laundry services; chapel and church services; social and recreational activities; hobby groups; flower and vegetable gardens; walking paths; access to public golf course; near medical facilities; barber/beauty shop.

AL MO: $950–$1,400.

Forest Park Village

2901 N. 7th St.
Wausau, WI 54403

Ph: (715) 845-1214

E-mail: *forestpv@dwave.net*

IND: 80. AL: 27+

Age 55+. Nonprofit; nondenominational; sponsored by 47 Lutheran congregations in central Wisconsin. Apartments. 24-hour staffing; therapeutic programs; blood pressure screenings; wellness program; nurse consultation; personal care; medication administration; security; emergency response system; maintenance; transportation; up to 3 daily meals; pets allowed; housekeeping and laundry services; exercise classes; religious services; chapel; Bible study; banking and postal services; library; social and recreational activities; intergenerational program; crafts; woodworking shop; activities center; barbecue areas; horseshoe courts; gardens; barber/beauty shop.

IND MO: $1,725–$2,025. AL MO: $1,600.

South

Wywood of Madison

1601 Wheeler Rd.
Madison, WI 53704

Ph: (608) 249-5558
Fax: (608) 249-1776

AL: 62

For-profit; nondenominational; owned by Alternative Living Services. Apartments and private and semiprivate rooms. 24-hour staffing; nursing services; home health care services; hospice care; personal care; medication administration; security; emergency response system; maintenance; transportation; up to 3 daily meals; housekeeping and laundry services; exercise classes; library; music therapy; pet visits; social and recreational activities; bingo; movies; outdoor patios; gardens; walking paths; barber/beauty shop.

DEP: $275. Move in: $2,750. AL MO: $2,825–$3,425; 2nd person, $1,100 and $1,650.

Independent Living

Independent housing (primarily rentals) for seniors that may offer security features, meal service, and activities.

Southeast

The Atrium Retirement Community

3900 N. Main St.
Racine, WI 53402

Ph: (414) 639-1100

IND: Yes

Nonprofit; nondenominational; owned and sponsored by Lincoln Lutheran. One-, two-, and three-bedroom apartments. Wellness nurse; priority placement at Lincoln Lutheran facilities if needed; 24-hour staffing; home health services; emergency response system; maintenance; transportation; on-site nutrition program; laundry services; exercise room; chaplain services; library; craft room.

Flexible financing options; contact facility for fees.

Cedar Ridge Retirement Campus

113 Cedar Ridge Drive
West Bend, WI 53095

Ph: (414) 334-9487

IND: 312

Nonprofit; nondenominational; United Church of Christ affiliation. Apartments. Wellness nurse; security; emergency response system; maintenance; transportation; up to 3 daily meals; housekeeping and laundry services; exercise room; swimming pool; country store; religious services; library; social and recreational activities; educational and cultural programs; clubs; hobbies; woodworking shop; crafts; lapidary shop; gardens; greenhouse; barber/beauty shop.

IND ENT: $36,500–$93,500. IND MO: $475–$700.

Lincoln Manor

5801 16th St.
Racine, WI 53406

Ph: (414) 632-8036

Lincoln Villas

5820 Lincoln Village Drive
Racine, WI 53406

Ph: (414) 637-7877

Lincoln Villas North

3919 Ruby Ave.
Racine, WI 53402

Ph: (414) 639-1166

Trinity Terrace

2132 Center St.
Racine, WI 53403

Ph: (414) 634-1426

IND: Yes

Nonprofit; nondenominational; owned and sponsored by Lincoln Lutheran. Apartments. Wellness nurse; priority placement at Lincoln Lutheran facilities if needed; 24-hour staffing; home health services; emergency response system; maintenance; transportation; on-site nutrition program; laundry services; chaplain services; resident council; barber/beauty shop.

IND MO: HUD-subsidized.

East

Round House Manor

300 Bicentennial Ct.
Kaukauna, WI 54130

Ph: (920) 766-2233
Fax: (920) 766-2233

IND: 50

Age 62+. Nonprofit; affiliated with the United Church of Christ Assemblies of God, Methodist. Apartments. Emergency response system; maintenance; transportation; pets allowed.

IND MO: 30% of income; HUD-subsidized.

St. Clare Terrace

31 Everett St.
Fond du Lac, WI 54935

Ph: (920) 923-7996
Fax: (920) 923-7995

IND: Yes

Nonprofit; sponsored by the Congregation of St. Agnes (CSA). Apartments. Security; emergency response system; maintenance; transportation; up to 3 daily meals; housekeeping and laundry services; chapel; library; postal service; social and recreational activities; lobby; hobbies and crafts; walking paths; gardening; barber/beauty shop.

DEP: $400. IND ENT: $32,500–$60,500; 2nd person, $2,750. IND MO: $650–$1,100; 2nd person, $85.

South

Colonial View Apartments

601 Thomas Drive
Sun Prairie, WI 53590

Ph: (608) 837-3174
Fax: (608) 837-9302

IND: 94

Age 62+. Nonprofit; nondenominational. Apartments. Emergency response system; maintenance; pets allowed; exercise area; library; senior center; convenience store; sunroom; patios; barber/beauty shop.

IND MO: Based on income; HUD-subsidized.

West

Shelby Terrace

2525 & 2527 Shelby Rd.
La Crosse, WI 54601

Ph: (608) 788-5700

IND: 36

Nondenominational; Bethany–St. Joseph Corporation. Apartments. Emergency response system; maintenance; transportation; up to 3 daily meals; laundry services; lounges.

IND MO: $575–$625.

Adult/Resort Communities

Communities for active adults (not all are age-restricted; primarily ownership).

North

Lakeland Village

11070 Bellwood Drive
Minocqua, WI 54548

Ph: (715) 356-6368
Fax: (715) 358-2848

http://www.lakelandvillage.com

IND: 107

Age 55+. Manufactured homes. Lodge with recreation room; clubhouse; laundromat; lake; fishing pier; boat launch; boat and trailer storage; lawn maintenance; swimming pool.

PURCHASE: Homes, $22,000–$165,000.
Lot MO: $300.

Strawberry Creek Estates

1500 Tacoma Beach Rd.
Sturgeon Bay, WI 54235

Ph: (920) 743-4478

Individual homes, condominiums, homesites. Tennis; clubhouse; swimming pool; boating; marina.

PURCHASE: Condos, $220,000–$330,000; homesites, $77,000–$242,000.

South

Abbey Springs

1 Country Club Drive
Fontana, WI 53125

Ph: (414) 275-6113

http://www.abbeysprings.com

Individual homes, condominiums. Golf course; pro shop; clubhouse; tennis; swimming pool; racquetball; recreation center; fitness center; hiking trails; fishing; boating; dining; nearby biking and snow skiing.

PURCHASE: Homes, $302,500–$550,000+.

Geneva National

1221 Geneva National Ave. S.
Lake Geneva, WI 53147

Ph: (800) 248-4642 or (414) 245-8000

Individual homes, condominiums, homesites. Golf courses; clubhouse; pro shop; racquet and swim club; hunt club; hiking trails; dining; social clubs; nearby fishing.

PURCHASE: Homes, from $362,000.

Mequon Country Club

12400 North Ville du Parc Drive
Mequon, WI 53092

Ph: (800) 465-3881

Condominiums. Golf course; clubhouse; pro shop; tennis; swimming pool; hiking trails; fishing; boating; dining; social clubs.

PURCHASE: $187,000–$550,000.

Muskego Lakes Country Club Villages

S. 100 W. 14020 Loomis Rd.
Muskego, WI 53150

Ph: (414)425-6500 or (414) 529-1661

http://www.mlcc@muskegolakes.com

Individual homes, condominiums, duplexes, homesites. Golf course; clubhouse; pro shop; dining.

PURCHASE: Homes $214,500–$357,500; homesites, $44,000–$77,000.

Wyoming

http://www.state.wy.us

General Information

Climate

Average lows from 9° F to 54° F; average highs from 33° F to 87° F.

Cost of Living

Ranks 25th in the nation.

Taxes

State/Local as % of Income: 9.1%.

Property Tax Reduction: Property Tax Relief Program available to qualified persons. For more information, call (307) 777-7961.

Sales: About 4%.

Prescription Exemptions: Prescription drugs and related items, such as wheelchairs, eyeglasses, hearing aids, and prosthetic devices, are exempt from sales tax.

Transportation, Travel, and Tourism

Major Airport

- Jackson Hole Airport, (307) 733-7682.

Railways

- Amtrak, (800) USA-RAIL.

Bus Tours

- LeBus Tours, (800) 366-0288.

State Highways

- Interstate 80, east-west (southern).
- Interstate 90, east-west (northern).
- Interstate 25, north-south.

Theater and Music

Casper Area

- Wyoming Symphony Orchestra, PO Box 667, Casper, WY 82602, (307) 266-1478.

Grand Teton Area

- Grand Teton Music Festival, PO Box 490, Teton Village, WY 83025, (307) 733-1128.

Museums, Crafts, Historical, Recreational

Yellowstone Area (Yellowstone National Park, Mammoth Hot Springs, Old Faithful, skiing, outdoor activities)

- Yellowstone National Park, PO Box 168, Yellowstone, WY 82190, (307) 344-7381.

Grand Teton Area (Grand Teton National Park, National Elk Refuge, Teton Village, Old Menor Cabin and Ferry, Chapel of the Transfiguration, national fish hatchery, skiing, outdoor activities)

- Grand Teton National Park, Moose, WY 83012-0170, (307) 739-3399.
- Teton Valley Chamber of Commerce, Box 250, Driggs, ID 83422, (208) 354-2500.

Jackson Hole/Western Region (Fossil Butte National Monument, J. C. Penney Co. Mother Store,

national forests, museums, wildlife refuge, golf, campgrounds, skiing, outdoor activities)

- Jackson Chamber of Commerce, Box E, 555 E. Broadway, Jackson, WY 83001, (307) 733-3316.
- Kemmerer Chamber of Commerce, 800 Pine, Kemmerer, WY 83101, (307) 877-9761.
- Pinedale Chamber of Commerce, Box 176, Pinedale, WY 82941, (307) 367-2242.
- Fossil Butte National Monument, Box 592, Kemmerer, WY 83101, (307) 877-4455.

Northern Region (Devils Tower National Monument, Bighorn Canyon National Recreation Area, Old Trail Town, Wild Horse Range, national forests, state parks, historic sites, camping, rodeos, golf, outdoor activities)

- Cody Chamber of Commerce, Box 2777, 836 Sheridan, Cody, WY 82414 (307) 587-2777.
- Sheridan Chamber of Commerce, Box 7155, 5th and I-90, Sheridan, WY 82801, (307) 672-2485.
- Gillette Chamber of Commerce, 810 S. Douglas Hwy. #A, Gillette, WY 82718, (307) 686-0040.
- Devils Tower National Monument, Box 10, Devils Tower, WY 82714, (307) 467-5283.
- Bighorn Canyon National Recreation Area, PO Box 487, Lovell, WY 82431, (307) 548-2251.

Central/East Regions (Wind River Reservation, Hells Half Acre, Natural Bridge, Fort Laramie, Shoshone National Forest, golf, wildlife centers, state parks)

- Casper Chamber of Commerce, CVB Box 399, 500 N. Center, Casper, WY 82602, (307) 234-5311.
- Douglas Chamber of Commerce, 121 Brownfield Rd., Douglas, WY 82633, (307) 358-2950.
- Riverton Chamber of Commerce, 1st & Main, Riverton, WY 82501, (307) 856-4801.
- Lander Chamber of Commerce, 160 N. 1st St., Lander, WY 82520, (307) 332-3892.
- Shoshone National Forest, PO Box 2140, Cody, WY 82414, (307) 527-6241.

Medicine Bow–Flaming Gorge Area (South) (Flaming Gorge National Recreational Area, Wyoming State Capitol, Killpecker Sand Dunes, Medicine Bow National Forest, museums, wildlife refuges, state parks, historical sites, camping, golf, outdoor activities)

- Rock Springs Chamber of Commerce, Box 398, 1897 Dewar Drive., Rock Springs, WY 82902, (307) 362-3771.
- Evanston Chamber of Commerce, Box 365, 36 10th St., Evanston, WY 82931, (307) 789-2757.
- Laramie Chamber of Commerce, 800 S. 3rd St., Laramie, WY 82070, (307) 745-7339.
- Cheyenne Chamber of Commerce, CVB Box 765, 309 W. Lincolnway, Cheyenne, WY 82003.
- Medicine Bow National Forest, 2468 Jackson St., Laramie, WY 82070-6535, (307) 745-2300.
- Flaming Gorge National Recreation Area, PO Box 278, Manila, UT 84046, (801) 784-3445.

Organizations

Advocacy Groups

- AARP West Regional Office, 9750 Third Ave., NE, Suite 400, Seattle, WA 98115, (206) 526-7918.

Volunteer Programs

- Cheyenne/Southeast Wyoming Foster Grandparents Program, PO Box 1005, Cheyenne, WY 82003, (307) 634-1265.

- Foster Grandparents program Northern Wyoming, 319 S. 6th St., Thermopolis, WY 82443, (307) 864-5544.
- Central Wyoming Retired and Senior Volunteer Programs, 136 W. 8th St., Casper, WY 82601, (307) 265-4678.
- Southeastern Wyoming Retired and Senior Volunteer Programs, 3304 Sheridan Ave., Cheyenne, WY 82009, (307) 634-7787.

Housing

Long-Term Care Facilities

*In the state of Wyoming, these facilities are called **Continuing Care/Nursing Home/Retirement Facilities**.*

These facilities provide various levels of nursing and medical services to seniors for an extended period of time.

Types of Authorization

Licensing and / or Certification

These facilities are licensed by the Department of Health, Office of Health Quality.

Memberships

- American Association of Homes and Services for the Aging (AAHSA) represents not-for-profit organizations committed to providing high-quality health care, housing, and services to the elderly. AAHSA, 901 E St. NW, Suite 500, Washington, DC 20004-2011. Ph: (202) 783-2242. Fax: (202) 783-2285. *http://www.aahsa.org*

Accreditations:

- Continuing Care Accreditation Commission (CCAC) accredits facilities that offer seniors a contract or contracts that provide residential living and health care services for the remainder of the person's lifetime and meet CCAC's accreditation standards.
- Joint Commission on the Accreditation of Health Care Organizations (JCAHCO) is an independent, not-for-profit organization, and the nation's oldest and largest standards-setting and health care accrediting institution.

Southwest

Castle Rock Convalescent Center and The Villa

1400 and 1445 Uinta Drive
Green River, WY 82935

Ph: (307) 875-4030 or (307) 875-3844

IND: 27. AL: Yes. HCC: Yes

Nonprofit; nondenominational; owned by the Castle Rock Special Hospital District. Private and semiprivate rooms. 24-hour nursing care; physical, occupational, and speech therapies; medical services; dental and podiatry care; pharmacy services; social services; Medicare/Medicaid-approved; personal care; medication administration; security; emergency response system; maintenance; transportation; up to 3 daily meals; housekeeping and laundry services; church services; social and recreational activities; activity areas; community room; patios and walking paths; barber/beauty shop.

IND MO: $1,125–$1,475. AL MO: $1,125–$1,475.

Central

Poplar Living Center, JCAHO

4305 S. Poplar St.
Casper WY 82601

Ph: (307) 237-2561
Fax: (307) 234-9937

NH: Yes. ALZ/MEM IMP: Yes

For-profit; nondenominational; Living Centers of America, Inc. Private and semiprivate rooms. 24-hour nursing care; physician services; long- and short-term care; physical, occupational, and speech therapies; respiratory therapy; medical services; dental and podiatry care; pharmacy services; Medicare/Medicaid-approved; personal care; medication administration; security; emergency response system; maintenance; transportation; up to 3 daily meals; housekeeping and laundry services; exercise classes; religious services; pet therapy; social and recreational activities; courtyard; ice cream parlor; barber/beauty shop.

NH Daily: Semiprivate, $120; private, $130. ALZ/MEM IMP: Semiprivate, $125; private, $140.

Assisted Living and Residential Care Facilities

These facilities provide housing, food service, and one or more personal services.

Types of Authorization

Licensing and/or Certification

These facilities are licensed by the Department of Health, Office of Health Quality.

Memberships

- Assisted Living Federation of America (ALFA) is a national nonprofit membership organization whose mission is to enhance the quality of life in assisted living facilities and promote the interests of the assisted living industry. ALFA, 10300 Eaton Place, Suite 400, Fairfax, VA 22030. Ph: (703) 691-8100. Fax: (703) 691-8106. *http://www.alfa.org*

Central

Garden Square of Casper Assisted Living

1950 S. Beverly
Casper, WY 82601

Ph: (307) 472-1153

AL: 48

For-profit; nondenominational. Private rooms. Nursing care; personal care; medication administration; emergency response system; maintenance; transportation; up to 3 daily meals; pets allowed; housekeeping and laundry services; social and recreational activities.

Contact facility for fees.

Maurice Griffith Manor

77 Gardenia
Casper, WY 82604

Ph: (307) 234-0572

PC: 23

Nondenominational. Suites and private rooms. Personal care; medication administration; maintenance; transportation; up to 3 daily meals; housekeeping and laundry services; social and recreational activities.

MO: $1,075–$1,575. AL services are separately charged, $20–$60.

Park Place Retirement Village

1930 E. 12th St
Casper, WY 82604

Ph: (307) 265-2273
Fax: (307) 265-5384

AL: 61

For-profit; nondenominational. Nursing care; personal care; medication administration; security; emergency response system; maintenance; transportation; up to 3 daily meals; pets allowed; housekeeping and laundry services; social and recreational activities.

DEP: $300. ENT: $300. IND MO: $1,450–$2,550. AL MO: $1,900–$3,100.

Wyoming Pioneer Home

141 Pioneer Home
Thermopolis, WY 82443

Ph: (307) 864-3151
Fax: (307) 864-2934

IND: 38. AL: 46

Age 55+

Contact facility for fees.

Southeast

Aspen Wind Assisted Living Community

4010 N. College Drive
Cheyenne, WY 82001

Ph: (307) 778-9511
Fax: (307) 772-0977

AL: 77

Age 65+. For-profit; nondenominational; managed by Regent Assisted Living. Studios, alcoves, and one-bedroom apartments. Nursing care; personal care; medication administration; security; emergency response system; maintenance; transportation; up to 3 daily meals; pets allowed; housekeeping and laundry services; whirlpool spa; social and recreational activities; gardens and courtyards; barber/beauty shop.

AL ENT: (ref.) $100–$500. AL MO: $1,775–$2,650. RSP Daily: $90.

Pointe Frontier Retirement Community

1406 Prairie Ave.
Cheyenne, WY 82009-4855

Ph: (307) 635-6953

IND: 113. AL: 47

Nonprofit; nondenominational. Studios and apartments. Nursing care; rehabilitative therapies; personal care; medication administration; security; emergency response system; maintenance; transportation; up to 3 daily meals (tray services available); pets allowed; housekeeping and laundry services; exercise room; library; banking services; card room; billiards room; social and recreational programs; gift shop; convenience store; barber/beauty shop.

IND DEP: (no ref.) $100. IND MO: $660–$880; 2nd person, $550. AL DEP: $440. AL ENT: $100. AL MO: $1,550–$3,425; 2nd person, $550–$1,450.

Northeast

Sugarland Ridge

Sugarland Drive
Sheridan, WY 82801

Ph: (307) 674-5575
Fax: (307) 674-8070

E-mail: *ridge@cyberhighway.net*

IND: 12. AL: 55

Age 55+ for IND; 65+ for AL. For-profit; nondenominational. Condos and apartments. Nursing care; 24-hour staffing; personal care; medication administration; security; emergency response system; maintenance; transportation; up to 3 daily meals; pets allowed; housekeeping and laundry services; social and recreational activities; barber/beauty shop.

APPL: $500 (includes $200 waiting list fee). MO: $1,825–$2,625; 2nd person, $425.

Veterans' Home of Wyoming

700 Veterans' Lane
Buffalo, WY 82834-9402

Ph: (307) 684-5511; TTY: (307) 684-5511
Fax: (307) 684-7636

E-mail: *jtartc@mjssc.state.wy.us*

AL: 120

Nondenominational. Suites and private rooms. 24-hour nursing care; doctor visits; personal care; medication administration; security; emergency response system; maintenance; transportation; up to 3 daily meals; housekeeping and laundry services; exercise groups; exercise equipment; social and recreational activities; music groups; card and board games; fishing; bowling; bingo; hobbies; movies; gardening.

MO: up to $1,275.

REQ: For veterans and their spouses who have served in the U.S. armed forces. Limited space available for nonveterans.

West Central

Homestead Living Center

950 Homestead Ave.
Riverton, WY 82501

Ph: (307) 856-5789
Fax: (307) 856-0381

AL: 43

Nonprofit; nondenominational. Apartments. Medical services; 24-hour staffing; personal care; medication administration; security; emergency response system; maintenance; transportation; up to 3 daily meals; pets allowed; housekeeping and laundry services; exercise room; social and recreational activities; game room; pool table.

DEP: $300. AL MO: $1,450–$4,600.

Showboat Retirement Center

150 Wyoming St.
Lander, WY 82520

Ph: (307) 332-6788 or (800) 531-5989

AL: 28. ADC: Yes

For-profit; nondenominational. Apartments. Nursing care; respite care; home health care services; personal care; medication administration; security; emergency response system; maintenance; transportation; up to 3 daily meals; pets allowed; housekeeping and laundry services; social and recreational activities; outdoor walking paths.

AL MO: $1,300–$1,800.

Independent Living

Independent housing (primarily rentals) for seniors that may offer security features, meal service, and activities.

Southeast

Evergreen Court

2110 E. F St.
Torrington, WY 82240

Ph: (307) 532-7330

IND: 26

Nondenominational; Lutheran Health Systems affiliation. Single and double suites and apartments. 24-hour staffing; maintenance; transportation; up to 3 daily meals plus snacks; housekeeping and laundry services; social and recreational activities; resident council; barber/beauty shop services.

IND MO: $1,225–$2,000.

Holy Trinity Manor

2516 E. 18th St.
Cheyenne, WY 82001

Ph: (307) 778-8850

IND: 30

Age 62+. Nonprofit; nondenominational; managed by Housing Management Services. One-bedroom apartments. Security; emergency response systems; maintenance; pets allowed; laundry services; exercise classes; nearby shopping and medical facilities.

IND MO: 30% of income; HUD-subsidized.

Regency Retirement Residence of Laramie

2021 E. Sheridan St.
Laramie, WY 82070

Ph: (307) 742-6366
Fax: (307) 742-6366

IND: 24

Age 62+. Nonprofit. Apartments. Security; emergency response system; maintenance; transportation; meal program; pets allowed; fitness center; library; woodworking shop; social and recreational activities; community room.

DEP: (ref.) $200. IND ENT: (ref.) $24,500–$71,500. IND MO: $625–$1,100.

West Central

Pioneer Homestead Apartments

300 S. Rancher
Jackson, WY 83001

Ph/Fax: (307) 733-9787

IND: 52

Age 62+. Nonprofit; nondenominational; nonsectarian. Apartments and private rooms. Security; emergency response system; maintenance; transportation; meal program; pets allowed; fitness center.

APPL: $25. DEP: $200. IND MO: $375–$750; HUD-subsidized.

Sempiternal Society

524 N. 6th E.
Riverton, WY 82501

Ph: (307) 856-7117
Fax: (307) 856-5298

IND: 32

Nonprofit; nondenominational. Apartments. Security; pets allowed.

IND MO: $625.

Sertoma Senior Citizens Housing, Inc.

524 N. 6th St. E.
Riverton, WY 82501

Ph: (307) 856-7117
Fax: (307) 856-5298

IND: 60

Age 62+. Nonprofit; nondenominational. Apartments. 24-hour staffing; security; emergency response system; maintenance; transportation; up to 3 daily meals; housekeeping and laundry services; social and recreational activities; entertainment.

IND MO: HUD-subsidized.

Teton Sertoma

101 N. 3rd E.
Riverton, WY 82501

Ph: (307) 856-6969
Fax: (307) 856-5298

IND: 27

Nonprofit; nondenominational. Apartments. Security; 24-hour staffing; meal program; laundry services; library; educational program; hobby room; recreational room; pool table; meeting room; senior citizens center.

IND MO: $220–$450.

Central

St. Anthony Manor

211 E. 6th St.
Casper, WY 82601

Ph: (307) 237-0843
Fax: (307) 237-3516

IND: 64

Age 62+. Nonprofit; nondenominational. Apartments. Security; emergency response system; maintenance; transportation for groceries; pets allowed; library; social and recreational activities; board and card games; potluck dinners.

IND MO: 30% of income; HUD-subsidized.

Adult/Resort Communities

Communities for active adults (not all are age-restricted; primarily ownership).

Central West

Sertoma West Adult Residential Community

PO Box 846
101 N. 3rd E.
Riverton, WY 82501

Ph: (307) 856-4782
Fax: (307) 856-5298

RH: Yes

Age 55+. Nonprofit; nondenominational. Homes. Maintenance; pets allowed.

PURCHASE: Homes, $93,500–$110,000.

North

The Powder Horn

161 Hwy 335
Sheridan, WY 82801

Ph: (800) 329-0598 or (307) 674-9545

http://www.thepowderhorn.com

Individual homes, patio homes, homesites. Golf course; clubhouse; pro shop; jogging/hiking/biking trails; dining; proposed pool area; trout-stocked lake; Audubon Signature Sanctuary Program participant.

PURCHASE: Custom homes, from $247,500; patio homes, from $202,450; homesites, from $49,500.

Part III: Organizations and Resources

Advocacy Groups

Aging with Dignity

PO Box 11180
Tallahassee, FL 32302-3180

Ph: (850) 681-2010
Fax: (850) 681-2481

http://www.agingwithdignity.org

Aging with Dignity, founded in 1996 by Jim Towey, is a privately funded, non-profit organization that advocates for the needs of elders and their caregivers, with a particular emphasis on improving care for those at the end of life. Their Five Wishes living will is available by phone or through their Web site.

Alliance for Aging Research

2021 K Street NW
Washington, DC 20006

Ph: (202) 293-2856
Fax: (202) 785-8574

http://www.agingresearch.org

Promotes scientific research in human aging. Publications about health issues available. Web site offers newsletter, *Living Longer and Loving It.*

American Association for Retired Persons (AARP)

601 E. St. NW
Washington, DC 20049

Ph: (202) 434-2277
Toll-free information: (800) 424-3410

http://www.aarp.org

Provides information and education; community service; legislative, judicial, and consumer advocacy; and member services. Offers a mail-order discount pharmacy service; group health insurance; auto, life, and home insurance; and programs for investments and annuities. Members receive a monthly bulletin and *Modern Maturity*, a bimonthly magazine featuring health, consumer, and financial news as well as travel and entertainment updates. Web site contains information on senior issues as well as a guide to Internet resources related to aging. Free publications on health and fitness, finances and retirement planning, housing, and more. Membership open to anyone age 50 or older.

Choice in Dying

1035 30th St. NW
Washington, DC 20007

Ph: (202) 338-9790
Fax: (202) 338-0242

http://www.choices.org

Choice in Dying, the inventor of living wills in 1967, is dedicated to fostering communication about complex end-of-life decisions. Provides educational information on end-of-life issues and state-specific advance directive forms. To receive an advance directive package in the mail, use the order form on their Web site or call (800) 989-WILL (9455). Fee of $5.00 ($5.41 for New York State residents and $5.29 for Washington, DC, residents) for documents distributed by mail.

Gray Panthers

733 15th St. NW, Suite 437
Washington, DC 20005

Ph: (202) 737-6637
Information: (800) 280-5362
Fax: (202) 737-1160

http://www.graypanthers.org

Local chapters organize groups of all ages to address issues of health care, social security, housing, sustainable environment, education, and peace. Publications available.

Japanese American Citizens League

1765 Sutter St.
San Francisco, CA 94115

Ph: (415) 921-5225
Fax: (415) 931-4671

http://www.jacl.org

Sponsors and participates in local community service programs that assist older and retired members of the Japanese-American community.

National Alliance of Senior Citizens

2525 Wilson Blvd.
Arlington, VA 22201

Local branches provide seniors with ideas and opportunities to expand their network.

National Asian Pacific Center on Aging

Melbourne Tower
1511 3rd Ave., Suite 914
Seattle, WA 98101-1626

Ph: (206) 624-1221

Advocacy for senior Asian Pacific Americans. Maintains national network of service agencies. Administers the Senior Community Service Employment Program for older people.

Melbourne Tower

1511 3rd Ave., Suite 914
Seattle, WA 98101-1626

Ph: (206) 624-1221

Advocacy for senior Asian Pacific Americans. Maintains national network of service agencies. Administers the Senior Community Service Employment Program for older people.

National Association for Hispanic Elderly

1452 W. Temple St., Suite 100
Los Angeles, CA 90026-1724

Ph: (213) 202-5900

Advocates for the concerns of older Hispanic citizens. Administers the Senior Community Service Employment Program to employ low-income people 55 years of age and older in 10 states. English- and Spanish-language publications are available on Social Security, Medicare, and health-related topics.

National Caucus and Center on Black Aged, Inc. (NCBA)

1424 K St. NW, Suite 500
Washington, DC 20005

Ph: (202) 637-8400
Fax: (202) 347-0895
http://www.ncba-blackaged.org

Advocates for the concerns of African Americans. Operates the Senior Community Service Employment Program,which provides part-time employment in community service agencies for low-income persons age 55 and older. Manages the Senior Environmental Employment Program, which uses persons age 55 and older to provide technical assistance to environmental agencies for pollution prevention and control. NCBA Housing Management Corporation provides health and social services in its 12 housing projects for low-income elderly. Offers various wellness promotion and disease prevention programs.

National Center on Elder Abuse (NCEA)

1225 I St. NW, Suite 725
Washington, DC 20005

Ph: (202) 898-2586
Fax: (202) 898-2583

Publications include *Elder Abuse: Questions and Answers—An Information Guide for Professionals and Concerned Citizens.*

National Citizens' Coalition for Nursing Home Reform

1424 16th St. NW, Suite 202
Washington, DC 20036-2211

Ph: (202) 332-2275
Fax: (202) 332-2949
http://www.nccnhr.org

Offers publications on nursing home issues. Web site provides a directory of long-term-care ombudsmen for each state.

National Committee to Preserve Social Security and Medicare

10 G St. NE, Suite 600
Washington, DC 20003

Ph: (202) 216-0420
Senior Flash Hotline: (800) 966-1935
Fax: (202) 216- 0451

http://www.ncpssm.org

Publishes a bimonthly member magazine, *Secure Retirement, the Newsmagazine for Mature Americans.* Distributes free brochures on Social Security disability, advance directives, nursing homes, and related topics. Web site provides links to helpful sites for seniors.

National Urban League

120 Wall St., 8th Floor
New York, NY 10005

Ph: (212) 558-5300
Fax: (212) 344-5332

http://www.nul.org

Offers nutrition, health, housing, and intergenerational services to African-American seniors. Seniors in Community Service Program provides training and part-time employment to low-income people 55 and older. Publishes *Health Alert*, a quarterly bulletin of health tips for older African Americans, and *Mature Worker*, a quarterly newsletter.

Books and Publications

Housing

Dickinson, Peter. *Sunbelt Retirement.* Regnery Gateway, 1992.

Fox, Richard L., ed. *America's Best Places to Retire.* Vacation Publications Inc., 1996.

Gollattscheck, James. *Choose Florida for Retirement.* Globe Pequot Press, 1999.

Greenwald, Robert. *50 Fabulous Planned Retirement Communities for Active Adults: A Comprehensive Directory of Outstanding Master-Planned Residential Developments.* Career Press, 1998.

Hayward, J. Keesey. *The ARRI Retirement Resorts Worldbook: Directory of the World's Finest Retirement Communities.* Association of Retirement Resorts International, 1998.

Howells, John. *Choose the South.* Gateway, 1997.

Howells, John. *Choose the Southwest for Retirement: Retirement Discoveries for Every Budget.* 2nd ed. Globe Pequot Press, 1999.

Howells, John. *Where to Retire.* Gateway Books, 1991.

Howells, John, and Richard Harris. *Choose the Northwest.* Gateway, 1996.

Howells, John, Don Merwin, and Joseph Lubow. *Choose California for Retirement.* Globe Pequot Press, 1998.

Lee, Alice, and Fred Lee. *The 50 Best Retirement Communities in America.* St. Martin's Press, 1994.

Martin, Don, and Betty Martin, eds. *Arizona in Your Future: The Complete Relocation Guide for Job-Seekers, Retirees, and Snowbirds.* Pine Cone Press, 1998.

McGarry, Betty. *Practical Guide to Florida Retirement.* Pineapple Press, 1998.

Morse, Sarah, Donna Quinn Robbins, and Sally Quinn. *Moving Mom and Dad: Why, Where, How and When to Help Your Parents Relocate.* Lanier Publishing International, 1998.

Savageau, David. *Retirement Places Rated.* 5th ed. Frommer, 1999.

Sherwood, Sylvia ed., Hirsch S. Ruchlin, Clarence C. Sherwood, and Shirley A. Morris.*Continuing Care Retirement Communities.* Johns Hopkins University Press, 1997.

Stern, Ken. *50 Fabulous Places to Retire in America.* 2nd ed. Career Press, 1996.

Legal Concerns

Holden, Ronald. *Estate Planning—A Family Affair Workbook.* Family Estate Planning Institute, 1986.

Sabatino, Charles, American Bar Association, and Nancy M. Coleman. *The American Bar Association Legal Guide for Older Americans: The Law Every American over Fifty Needs to Know.* Times Books, 1998.

Personal/Life Planning

Arnold, Suzanne, Jean Brock and Henry Richards. *Ready or Not; Your Retirement Guide.* Manpower Education Institute, 1997.

Ballard, Jack, and Phoebe Ballard. *Beating the Age Game: Redefining Retirement.* MasterMedia, 1993.

Bennett, Robert, and Catherine Bennett. *Retirement Handbook: A Complete Guide to Living Your Dreams.* Melrose Plantation Press, 1998.

Biracree, Tom, and Nancy Biracree. *Over Fifty: Resource Book for the Better Half of Your Life.* Harper Collins, 1991.

Blum, Laurie. *Free Money and Services for Seniors and Their Families.* John Wiley & Sons, Inc., 1995.

Brown, Duane. *How to Find Your New Career Upon Retirement.* Vgm Career Horizons, 1994.

Brown, Paul. *From Here to Retirement.* Word Books, 1988.

Coleman, Ellen Schneid. *The Lump Sum Advisor.* Prentice Hall, 1999.

Downs, Hugh. *Fifty to Forever.* Thomas Nelson Publishers, 1994.

Downs, Hugh, and Richard Roll. *The Best Years Book.* Delacorte Press, 1981.

Drilling, Vern. *Closing Doors, Opening Worlds: Looking Beyond the Retirement Horizon.* Fairview Press, 1993.

Driskill, J. Lawrence. *Adventures in Senior Living: Learning How to Make Retirement Meaningful and Enjoyable.* Haworth Press, 1997.

Fetridge, Guild. *The Adventure of Retirement: It's About More Than Just Money.*Prometheus Books, 1994.

French, Virginia Robinson, and James C. French. *Avoiding the Retirement Trap.* Acta Publications, 1995.

Fromme, Alan. *Life After Work: Planning It, Living It, Loving It.* Scott, Foresman; AARP Books, 1987.

Goodman, Gloria Bledsoe. *Keys to Living with a Retired Husband.* Barrons, 1991.

Hansen, Leonard. *Life Begins at Fifty: A Handbook for Creative Retirement Planning.* Barrons Education Series, 1989

Hawley, George. *Dynamic Retirement: A Guidebook for the Golden Years.* Leathers Publications, 1999.

Haynes, Marion. *From Work to Retirement.* Crisp Publications, 1993.

Henderson, Carter. *Funny, I Don't Feel Old!: How to Flourish After 50.* Institute for Contemporary Studies, 1997.

Howells, John. *Retirement on a Shoestring.* Gateway, 1995.

Karpel, Craig. *The Retirement Myth.* HarperCollins, 1995.

Kerschner, Helen K., and John E. Hansan, eds. *365 . . . Retirees' Resource Guide for Productive Lifestyles.* Greenwood Publishing Group, 1996.

Kessler, Regina. *Who Says Retirement Has to Be Boring?* Pharos Books, 1991.

Kimeldorf, Martin. *Serious Play: A Leisure Wellness Guidebook.* 1994.

Lee, Alice, and Fred Lee. *A Field Guide to Retirement: 14 Lifestyle Opportunities and Options for Successful Retirement.* Doubleday, 1991.

Lesko, Matthew, Mary Ann Martello, and Andrew Naprawa, ed. *Free Stuff for Seniors.* InfoUSA, Inc., 1995.

Levitin, Nancy. *Retirement Rights: The Benefits of Growing Older.* Avon Books, 1994.

Mesrobian, Armen Z. *Prepare and Enjoy Creative Retirement.* Excel Publishing Services, 1993.

Murphy, John. *The Joy of Old: A Guide to Successful Elderhood.* Geode Press, 1995.

Parmley, Mary T. *New Work Styles for Your Retirement Career.* National Council on the Aging, 1997.

Redd, Robert. *Achievers Never Quit.* Thornapple Pub. Co., 1989.

Salend, Elyse, Anna Nolen Rahman, David Harris, Soloman and Marie Bolduc Liston. *A Consumer's Guide to Aging.* Johns Hopkins University Press, 1992.

Schrader, Constance. *1001 Things Everyone Over 55 Should Know.* Doubleday,1999.

Shelton, Phyllis R. *Long Term Care Planning Guide.* Shelton Marketing Services, Inc., 1998.

Silverstone, Barbara, and Helen Kandel Hyman. *Growing Older Together: A Couple's Guide to Understanding and Coping with the Challenges of Later Life.* [large print] Thorndike Press, 1998.

A Single Person's Guide to Retirement Planning. AARP, 1995.

Smith, Joseph. *Holidays in Retirement: A Guide to Trips Around Europe.* Foulsham, 1996.

Smith, Mary Helen. *The Retirement Sourcebook.* Roxbury Park, 1999.

Wagner, Tricia, and Barbara Day. *How to Enjoy Your Retirement: Activities from A to Z.* VanderWyk & Burnham, 1998.

Warner, Diane. *How to Have a Great Retirement on a Limited Budget.* Writers Digest Books, 1992.

Willing, Jules. *The Reality of Retirement.* Morrow, 1989.

Retirement/Financial Planning

AARP. *Planning Your Retirement.* 1995.

AARP. *Think of Your Future.* HarperCollins, 1995.

Allen, Klosowski. *Personal Financial Fitness.* Crisp Publications, 1987.

Bancroft, Daniel. *The Paradox of the Gold Watch—Planning Twenty Years Before Retirement.* Retirement Income Associates, 1988.

Battersby, Mark. *10 Minute Guide to Long-Term Retirement Planning.* Macmillan, 1996.

Battersby, Mark. *10 Minute Guide to Short-Term Retirement Planning.* Macmillan, 1996.

Baxter, Ralph. *The Arthur Young Preretirement Planning Book.* John Wiley & Sons, 1985.

Beardstown Ladies. *Stitch-in-Time Guide to Growing Your Nest Egg: Step-by-Step Planning for a Comfortable Financial Future.* Hyperion, 1996. Also available in audiocassette.

Bennett, Jarratt. *Making the Money Last: Financial Clarity for the Surviving Spouse.* Kendall/Hunt Publishing Company, 1995.

Berger, Lisa. *Feathering Your Nest: The Retirement Planner (The IDS Financial Library).* Workman Publishing Company, 1993.

Bledsoe, John D. *Roth to Riches: The Ordinary to Roth IRA Handbook.* Legacy Press, 1998.

Bogosian, Wayne G., and Dee Lee. *The Complete Idiot's Guide to 401(k) Plans.* Macmillan, 1998.

Boroson, Warren. *Keys to Investing in Your 401(k).* Barrons, 1994.

Boroson, Warren. *Keys to Retirement Planning.* Barrons, 1995.

Brenner, George. *Plan Smart, Retire Rich: The Book Designed to Help You Reach Your Retirement Dreams.* McGraw-Hill, 1999.

Brown, Carolann. *100 Questions Every Working American Must Ask.* Dearborn Trade, 1995.

Chapman, Elwood, and Marion Haynes. *Comfort Zones: Planning Your Future.* 4th ed. Crisp Publications, 1997.

Cleary, David and Virginia Cleary. *Retire Smart*. Allworth Press, 1993.

Coyle, Joseph S. *How to Retire Young and Rich*. Warner Books, 1996.

Cunningham, Timothy W., and Clay B. Mansfield. *Pay Yourself First: A Commonsense Guide to Life-Cycle Retirement Investing*. John Wiley & Sons, 1996.

Daryanani Gobind. *Roth IRA Book: An Investor's Guide*. Digiqual, 1999.

Dickens, Thomas, and D. Larry Crumbley. *Keys to Understanding Social Security Benefits*. Barrons, 1992.

Dickinson, Peter. *The Complete Retirement Planning Book*. E. P. Dutton, 1984.

Dickman, Barry, Trudy Lieberman, and Elias M. Zuckerman. *How to Plan for a Secure Retirement*. Consumer Reports Books, 1998.

Downing, Neil. *Maximize Your IRA*. Dearborn Trade, 1998.

Editors at Beam, and Editors at Morin. *Healthy, Wealthy, & Wise*. Jist Works, 1997.

Ferguson, Karen and Kate Blackwell. *The Pension Book: What You Need to Know to Prepare for Retirement*. Arcade Publishing, 1996.

Gallea, Anthony. *The Lump Sum Handbook: Investment and Tax Strategies for a Secure Retirement*. Prentice Hall Trade, 1993.

Garner, Robert J., et. *Ernst and Young's Retirement Planning Guide: Take Care of Your Finances Now . . . And They'll Take Care of You Later*. John Wiley, 1997.

Godin, Seth. *If You're Clueless About Retirement Planning and Want to Know More*. Dearborn Trade, 1997.

Goldberg, Seymour. *J. K. Lasser's How to Pay Less Tax on Your Retirement Savings*. Macmillan, 1997.

Hallman, G. Victor. *Financial Planning for Retirement*. McGraw-Hill, 1992.

Hallman, V., and J. Rosenbloom. *Personal Financial Planning*. McGraw-Hill, 1987.

Hannon, Kerry. *10 Minute Guide to Retirement for Women*. Macmillan, 1996.

Haynes, Marion, ed. *The Best of Retirement Planning*. Crisp, 1997.

Hinrichs, Paul R. *Estate and Retirement Planning: Making Your Money Work Harder*.Now Books, 1996.

Hoffman, Ellen. *Bankroll Your Future: How to Get the Most from Uncle Sam for Your Retirement Years—Social Security, Medicare, and Much More*. Newmarket Press, 1999.

Holzer, Bambi, Elaine Floyd and Mary Farrell. *Retire Rich: The Baby Boomer's Guide to a Secure Future*. John Wiley, 1998.

Hutchison, Anna Marie. *IRA Investing Made Easy*. Globe Pequot Press, 1996.

Iwaszko, Knute, and Brian O'Connell. *The 401(k) Millionaire*. Villard Books, 1999.

Johnson, Richard, and Warren Jensen. *The Fifteen Factors of Retirement Success*. Kendall/Hunt Pub. Co., 1989.

Jorgensen, James A., James. *It's Never Too Late to Get Rich: The Secrets of Building a Nest Egg at Any Age*. Dearborn Financial Publishing., 1994.

Katzeff, Paul. *10 Minute Guide to 401(k) Plans*. Macmillan, 1996.

Kehrer, Daniel. *Kiplinger's 12 Steps to a Worry-Free Retirement*. Kiplinger Books, 1995.

Keithley, M. C. *Retire Early Retire Well: The No Nonsense Guide to Million Dollar Wealth Building Alternatives*. Bookmasters, 1996.

Krane, J. *Can I Afford to Retire?* New Leaf Communication, 1993.

Lee, Barbara. *The Financially Independent Woman: a Step-by-Step Guide to Successful Investing*. Citadel Press, 1998.

Leedy, Jack, and James Wynbrandt. *Executive Retirement Management: A Manager's Guide to the Planning and Implementation of a Successful Retirement.* Facts on File, 1988.

Littauer, Stephen L. *Financial Independence the Smart Way: Investing for Growth, Income, and Retirement.* Dearborn Trade, 1999.

Malaspina, Margaret A. *Don't Die Broke: How to Turn Your Retirement Savings into Lasting Income.* Bloomberg Press, 1999.

Martin, Deirdre. *The 21st Century Investor: Investing for Retirement.* Avon Books, 1998.

McAleese, Tama. *Money Power for* Retirement. Chelsea House Pub, 1997.

Merritt, Steve. *All About the New IRA: How to Cash in on the New Tax Law Changes.* Halyard Press, 1998.

Merritt, Steve. *How to Build Wealth with Your 401(k): Everything You Need to Know to Become More Than a Millionaire over the Course of Your Working Lifetime.* Halyard Press Inc., 1997.

Michaels, Joe. *Prime of Your Life.* Facts on File, Inc., 1981.

Morris, Virginia B., Kenneth M. Morris and Virginia Morris. *Creating Retirement Income.* McGraw-Hill, 1999.

Orman, Suze. *You've Earned It, Don't Lose It: Mistakes You Can't Afford.* Newmarket Press, 1997.

O'Shaughnessy, James. *How to Retire Rich: Time-Tested Strategies to Beat the Market and Retire in Style.* Broadway Books, 1997.

Parrot, William, and John Parrot. *You Can Afford to Retire.* Prentice Hall, 1992.

Petras, Kathryn, and Ross Petras. *The Only Retirement Guide You'll Ever Need.* Poseidon Press, 1991.

Phillips, Lee, and Kristy Phillips. *Protecting Your Financial Future.* Lega-Lees, 1997.

Powers, Jacqueline K., Michael D. Powers and Stephen Pollan eds. *How to Start a Retirement Business.* Avon Books, 1996.

Price Waterhouse Retirement Planning Advisor. Pocket Books, 1990.

Price Waterhouse LLP, and Roger Hindman, ed. *Secure Your Future.* Irwin Professional Publishing, 1996.

Quinn, Jane Bryant. *Making the Most of Your Money: Smart Ways to Create Wealth and Plan Your Finances in the '90s.* Simon & Schuster, 1991.

Robinson, Marc. *Managing Your 401(k).* Time-Life, 1997.

Rosenberg, Stephen. *Last Minute Retirement Planning.* Career Press, 1998.

Rowland, Mary. *A Commonsense Guide to Your 401(k).* Bloomberg Press, 1997.

Salwen, Judy. *Solo Retirement.* Dodd, Mead & Co., 1983.

Schurenberg, Eric. *401(k): Take Charge of Your Future.* Warner Books, 1996.

Shirley, Kay R., and Anita Sharpe. *The Baby Boomer Financial Wake-Up Call: It's Not Too Late to Be Financially Secure!* Dearborn Trade, 1999.

Silver, Don. *Baby Boomer Retirement: 65 Simple Ways to Protect Your Future.* Adams Hall Publications, 1998.

Slesnick, Twila, and John C. Suttle. *IRAs, 401(k)s, and Other Retirement Plans: Taking Your Money Out.* Nolo Press, 1998.

Smith, James. *The Path to a Successful Retirement.* Sligo Publishing Co., 1995.

Spare, Anthony. *Last Chance Financial Planning Guide: It's Not Too Late to Plan for Your Retirement if You Start Now.* Prima Publishing, 1997.

Staff of Kiplinger's Personal Finance Magazine. *Kiplinger's Retire Worry-Free.* Kiplinger Books, 1998.

Stein, Michael K. *The Prosperous Retirement: Guide to New Reality.* Emstco Press, 1998.

Trock, Gary R. *The Roth IRA Made Simple.* Conquest Publishing, 1998.

Vernon, Steve. *Don't Work Forever! Simple Steps Baby Boomers Must Take to Ever Retire.* J. Wiley, 1994.

Waitley, Denis, and Eudora Seyfer. *How to Be Happily Retired.* Celestial Arts, 1995.

Warner, Ralph E. *Get a Life: You Don't Need a Million to Retire Well.* Nolo Press, 1998.

Wasik, John F. *The Late-Start Investor: The Better-Late-Than-Never Guide to Realizing Your Retirement Income.* Owl Books, 1999.

Weltman, Barbara, and Art Linkletter. *The Complete Idiot's Guide to Making Money After You Retire.* Alpha Books, 1998.

Williamson, Gordon K. *Making the Most of Your 401(k).* Adams Media Corporation, 1997.

Zimmerman, Elaine. *How to Retire with a Million Dollars.* HarperCollins, 1998.

American Association of Retired Persons Publications

AARP Publications

601 E. St. NW
Washington, DC 20049

Ph: (202) 434-2277
Toll-free information: (800) 424-3410
http://www.aarp.org

To order a free AARP Publications Catalog which lists the organization's most frequently requested printed materials, call (800) 424-3410. Individual documents can be ordered at no charge via the toll-free information line or by mail using the order form included with the catalog. Here's a sampling of what is available through AARP:

Advance Directives

Medical Treatment: Decide in Advance, (D15632)

Planning for Incapacity: A Self-Help Guide, (D14821)

Shape Your Health Care Future with Health Care Advance Directives, (D15803)

Americans with Disabilities Act

Accessibility: It's Yours for the Asking!, (D15520)

Assisted Living Facilities

Assisted Living: Reconceptualizing Regulation to Meet Consumers' Needs & Preferences, (D16261)

A Home Away from Home: A Consumer Guide to Board and Care Homes and Assisted Living Facilities, (D12446)

Consumer Fraud

AARP Connections for Independent Living—Fraud, (D16234)

Senior Consumer Alert—Are Your Donations Hitting Their Target?: Charity Scams and Deceptive Fundraising Tactics, (D16616)

Unfair and Deceptive Acts and Practices: Survey of State Laws, (D16027)

Consumer Protection

Consumer Rights, (D15891)

Consumer Rights: Do You Know What Your Consumer Rights Are?, (D15890)

A Guide to Deregulation and Competition in the Electric and Telecommunications Industries, (D13936)

Unfair and Deceptive Acts and Practices: Survey of State Laws, (D16027)

Durable Medical Equipment

Product Report—Electric Scooters, (D15979)

Product Report—Walkers, (D14390)

Product Report—Wheel Chairs, (D14049)

What You Need to Know About Durable Medical Equipment Fraud, (D16774)

Early Retirement Incentives

Look Before You Leap: A Guide to Early Retirement Incentive Programs, (D13390)

Employment

The First Step: Getting Started in Starting Your Own Business, (D15084)

Using the Experience of a Lifetime—Update, (D13353)

Working Options, (D12403)

Estate Planning

Life Transitions, (D15870)

Financial Planning

AARP Connections for Independent Living—Financial Security, (D16235)

Facts About Financial Planners, (D14050)

Grandparenting

AARP Grandparent Information Center, (D15212)

AARP Grandparent Information Center (Spanish version), (D16513)

Grandparents Raising Their Grandchildren, (D15272)

Parenting Grandchildren: A Voice for Grandparents, (D15536)

Tips for Grandparents: Raising Healthy Grandchildren, (D15514)

Tips for Grandparents: Starting a Support Group, (D16022)

Tips for Grandparents: Starting a Support Group (Spanish version), (D16725)

Tips for Grandparents: Welfare Reform and Your Family, (D16472)

Health Insurance

Health Care Delivery and Insurance, (D15868)

Reforming the Health Care System: State Profiles, 1998, (D16828)

Health Maintenance Organizations

An Assessment of Medicare Beneficiaries' Understanding of the Differences Between the Traditional Medicare Program and HMOs, (D16726)

Hearing Impairment

Resource Guide for Persons Who Are Deaf or Hard of Hearing, (D14925)

Housing Options

Expanding Housing Choices for Older People, (D15819)

Facts About Older Women: Housing and Living Arrangements—Fact Sheet, (D12880)

Housing, (D 15561)

Independent Living

How to Help Older Adults in Your Community Live Independently, (D16431)

Information Distribution, (D16429)

Neighbor to Neighbor, (D16430)

Information and Referral Services

Directory of Toll-Free Numbers, (C1172)

Investments

Investor Tips on Understanding Broker Compensation Practices, (D16711)

What Every Investor Needs to Know: How to Prevent and Resolve Problems with Investment Professionals, (D15863)

Legal Problems

Legal Q & A, (D15947)

Living Trusts

Product Report—Wills & Living Trusts, (D14535)

Long-Term Care Insurance

Before You Buy: A Guide to Long-Term Care Insurance, (D12893)

Managed Care

AARP Bulletin Special Report on Managed Care, (D16348)

Checkpoints for Managed Care: How to Choose a Health Plan, (D16342)

Consumer Protections in Managed Care, (D16240)

Making Medicare Choices, (D16747)

Managed Care: An AARP Guide for Medicare Beneficiaries, (D15595)

Nine Ways to Get the Most from Your Managed Health Care Plan, (D16615)

Medicaid

Do You Need Help Paying for Your Health Care Bills?, (D16615)

Medicaid Estate Recovery for Long-Term Care Under OBRA '93, (D16443)

Medicare

Medicare Basics, (D16812)

Medicare Fraud Kit, (D16881)

What You Need to Know About Durable Medical Equipment Fraud, (D16774)

What You Need to Know About Medicare Fraud, (D16773)

Your Three-Step Plan to Fight Medicare Fraud, (D16660)

Your Three-Step Plan to Fight Medicare Fraud (Spanish version), (D16661)

Medigap

Payment Record for Health Insurance Policies, (D13561)

Selecting Medicare Supplemental Insurance, (D16813)

Mental Health

I Wonder Who Else Can Help, (D13832)

I Wonder Who Else Can Help (Spanish version), (D14946)

If Only I Knew What To Say or Do . . . Ideas for Helping a Friend in Crisis, (D13830)

Pensions

Fighting Inflation: How Does Your Cola Compare?, (D16444)

Woman's Guide to Pension Rights, (D12258)

Your Pension Plan: A Guide to Getting Through the Maze, (D13533)

Your 401(k) Plan: Building Toward Your Retirement Security, (D15975)

Personal Finances

Choosing Mutual Funds, (D16359)

Finance, (D15809)

Living Better on Less, (D14944)

A Primer on Personal Money Management for Midlife and Older Women, (D13183)

Public Assistance

AARP Reach Fact Sheet, (D16882)

Barriers to Getting Public Benefits, (D15738)

Many Older People Can Get Extra Income But Aren't Getting It. Could You Be One?, (D16850)

Public Benefits—Who Gets Them and Who Still Needs Them?, (D15739)

Safety

AARP Connections for Independent Living—Burglary Prevention, (D16233)

Falls and Older People, (D14195)

Fire Safety Checklist for Older Consumers, (D16487)

Home Safe Home: How to Prevent Falls in the Home, (D16598)

Shared Housing

A Consumer's Guide to Homesharing, (D12774)

Social Security

Facts About the Notch: Information from AARP, (D13509)

Social Security and Supplemental Security Income Programs for People with Disabilities: How They Compare—PPI Fact Sheet, (D15433)

Social Security Q & A—Earnings Limit, (D13761)

Social Security Q & A—Earnings Limit (Spanish version), (D13834)

Social Security Q & A—Public Pension Offset, (D14613)

The Social Security Book: What Every Woman Absolutely Needs to Know, (D14117)

Supplemental Security Income

Persons Who Are Disabled or Over 65—You May Be Eligible for Additional Cash Benefits from SSI!, (D14755)

Social Security and Supplemental Security Income, (D15433)

Telemarketing Fraud

AARP Bulletin Special Report on Fighting Phone Fraud, (D16604)

Consumer Fraud: Telemarketing, (D15385)

Consumer Fraud: Telemarketing (Spanish version), (D16343)

Findings from a Baseline Omnibus Survey on Telemarketing Solicitations, (D16361)

Telemarketing Fraud, (D16540)

Telemarketing Fraud (Spanish version), (D16541)

Telemarketing Fraud Victimization of Older Americans: An AARP Survey, (D16055)

Vision Disorders

Resource Guide for Persons Who Are Blind or Visually Impaired, (D14926)

Volunteer Opportunities

AARP Volunteer Talent Bank—Fact Sheet, (D15049)

Bringing Lifetimes of Experience: A Guide for Involving Older Volunteers, (D15539)

Ever Thought About Volunteering But Didn't Know Where to Begin?, (D12329)

To Serve, Not to Be Served: A Manual of Opportunity and a Challenge, (D12028)

Volunteer Talent Bank Guidelines for Participation, (D12560)

Women's Issues

Women's Issues, (D15889)

Social Security Administration

Office of Public Inquiries

6401 Security Blvd.
Baltimore, MD 21235

Ph: (410) 965-7700
Information: (800) 772-1213
Fax: (410) 965-0695

http://www.ssa.gov

Free Social Security publications are available by calling the toll-free information line or by downloading them from the Social Security Administration Web site. Or, use the SSA's FAX Catalog. Call the toll-free number, (888) 475-700, from a touch-tone phone and a voice menu will guide you through the steps necessary to receive your documents. You must have the telephone number of the fax machine to which you want the documents sent.

Social Security Program—General

The Future of Social Security, 2/99, (05-10055)

Schedule of Social Security Benefit Payments 1999 & 2000, 1/99, (05-10031)

Social Security Update 1999, 1/99, (05-10003)

Social Security: 24-Hour Telephone Service, 3/99, (05-10082)

Social Security: How You Earn Credits, 1/99, (05-10072)

Social Security: Basic Facts, 3/98, (05-10080)

Social Security: An Employer's Investment, 1/97, (05-10059)

Social Security: Facts and Figures, 4/98, (05-10011)

Social Security: Getting in Touch, 12/97, (05-10048)

Social Security: How It's Financed, 5/98, (05-10094)

Social Security: Report to Our Customers, 9/96, (05-10617)

Social Security: A "Snapshot," 3/98, (05-10006)

Social Security: Understanding the Benefits, 1/99, (05-10024)

Social Security: What Every Woman Should Know, 9/98, (05-10127)

Social Security: When You'll Get Your Benefit, 5/97, (05-10031)

*Social Security: Your Taxes . . . What They Are Paying for and Where the Money Goes,*1/99, (05-10010)

The Appeals Process

Appeals, 4/99, (05-10041)

How to File an Unfair Treatment Complaint, 5/93, (05-10071)

Your Right to Representation, 3/98, (05-10075)

Disability Benefits

Disability, 5/96, (05-10029)

Disability Based on Drug Addiction oOr Alcoholism, 5/96, (05-10047)

A Guide to Social Security and SSI Disability Benefits for People with HIV Infection, 5/97, (05-10020)

How Social Security Can Help with Vocational Rehabilitation, 6/97, (05-10050)

How We Decide If You Are Still Disabled, 4/96, (05-10053)

How Worker's Compensation and Other Disability Payments May Affect Your Benefits, 6/97, (05-10018)

Project ABLE: Able Beneficiaries' Link to Employers, 12/97, (05-10056)

Reviewing Your Disability, 6/97, (05-10068)

Social Security: Benefits for Children with Disabilities, 04/96, (05-10026)

Social Security: If You Are Blind How We Can Help, 6/96, (05-10052)

Social Security: What You Need to Know When You Get Disability Benefits, 6/98, (05-10153)

Social Security Benefits for People Living with HIV/AIDS, 05/95, (05-10019)

Social Security Disability Programs Can Help, 9/95 (05-10057)

Receive Your Benefits by Direct Deposit, 1/99, (05-10123)

Working While Disabled . . . How We Can Help, 2/98, (05-10095)

Retirement Benefits

Retirement Benefits, 2/99, (05-10035)

Government Pension Offset, 1/99, (05-10007)

How Work Affects Your Benefits, 1/97, (05-10069)

How Your Retirement Benefit Is Figured, 3/99, (05-10070)

Medicare, 6/96, (05-10043)

A Pension from Work Not Covered by Social Security, 1/99, (05-10045)

Receiving Your Benefits by Direct Deposit, 1/99, (05-10123)

Social Security: What You Need to Know When You Get Retirement or Survivors Benefits, 1/99, (05-10077)

Special Payments After Retirement, 3/99, (05-10063)

Social Security Number

Changing Your Name?, 4/95, (05-10642)

Lawfully Admitted Aliens—When You Need a Social Security Number and When You Don't, 4/97, (05-10096)

Social Security: Numbers for Newborns, 7/96, (05-10023)

Social Security: Your Number, 2/98, (05-10002)

When Someone Misuses Your Social Security Number, 3/98, (05-10064)

Supplemental Security Income Program (SSI)

A Desktop Guide to SSI Eligibility Requirements, 1/99, (05-11001)

Food Stamps and Other Nutrition Programs, 3/98, (05-10100)

Food Stamp Facts, 3/98, (05-10101)

A Guide to Social Security and SSI Disability Benefits for People with HIV Infection, 5/97, (05-10020)

How Worker's Compensation and Other Disability Payments May Affect Your Benefits, 6/97, (05-10018)

The Definition of Disability for Children, 7/97, (05-11053)

Receiving Your Benefits by Direct Deposit, 1/99, (05-10123)

Reviewing Your Disability, 6/97, (05-10068)

Social Security: What You Need to Know When You Get SSI, 1/99, (05-11011)

Social Security: Working While Disabled . . . A Guide to Plans for Achieving Self-Support, 1/97, (05-11017)

Social Security: You May Be Able to Get SSI, 1/99, (05-11069)

Supplemental Security Income, 1/97, (05-11000) *Supplemental Security Income for Noncitizens*, 11/97, (05-11051)

Survivors Benefits

Government Pension Offset, 1/99, (05-10007)

Social Security: What You Need to Know When You Get Retirement or Survivors Benefits, 1/99, (05-10077)

Survivors, 10/96, (05-10084)

Work and Earnings

Coverage for State and Local Government Employees, 8/97, (05-10051)

Government Pension Offset, 1/99, (05-10007)

A Guide for Farmers, Growers, and Crew Leaders, 5/97, (05-10025)

Household Workers, 1/99, (05-10021)

How International Agreements Can Help You, 9/98, (05-10180)

How Work Affects Your Benefits, 2/99, (05-10069)

If You Are Self-Employed, 1/99, (05-10022)

If You Work for a Nonprofit Organization, 1/99, (05-10027)

Military Service, 1/99, (05-10017)

A Pension from Work Not Covered by Social Security, 1/99, (05-10045)

Social Security: How You Earn Credits, 1/99, (05-10072)

Social Security Update 1999, 1/99 (05-10003)

Social Security: Working While Disabled . . . A Guide to Plans for Achieving Self-Support, 3/99, (05-11017)

Social Security: Your Taxes . . . What They Are Paying for And Where the Money Goes, 1/99, (05-10010)

When You Retire from Your Own Business: What Social Security Needs to Know, 1/99 (05-10038)

Subjects of Special Interest—Miscellaneous

A Factsheet for Volunteer and Nonprofit Agencies, 1/93, (05-10102)

Government Pension Offset, 1/99, (05-10007)

How International Agreements Can Help You, 9/98, (05-10180)

Misleading Advertising, 7/96 (05-10005)

Social Security: A Guide for Representative Payees, 4/97, (05-10076)

Social Security Benefits for Children, 06/97, (05-10085)

Social Security: Your Payments While You Are Outside the United States, 6/97, (05-10137)

Employment and Training

Green Thumb, Inc.

2000 N. 14th St., Suite 800
Arlington, VA 22201

Ph: (703) 522-7272

http://www.greenthumb.org

Operates the Senior Community Service Employment Program, which provides training and employment opportunities to low income adults age 55 and older who reside in primarily rural areas.

MaturityWorks

http://www.maturityworks.org

Nationwide program that matches mature workers to jobs with participating organizations.

Financial/Retirement Planning

Investment Planning

Organizations

American Association of Individual Investors (AAII)

625 N. Michigan Ave.
Chicago, IL 60611

Ph: (800) 428-2244 or (312) 280-0170

Fax: (312) 280-9883

http://www.aaii.org

Assists individual members in managing their own assets, through education, information, and research. Web site has information on investing basics, mutual funds, stocks, brokers, portfolio management, as well as publications. Call or see Web site for member services.

American Savings Education Council (ASEC)

2121 K St. NW, Suite 600
Washington, DC 20037-1896

Ph: (202) 659-0670
Fax: (202) 775-6360

http://www.asec.org

An *EBRI* program. Web site has information on the "Choose to Save Campaign", which offers savings tools such as *Top 10 Ways to Prepare for Retirement;Ballpark Estimate,* a retirement planning worksheet; and *The Power to Choose*, advice on saving for retirement. Brochures and worksheet can also be ordered by mail.

Financial Planning Association

Suite B-300
5775 Glenridge Drive NE
Atlanta, GA 30328

Ph: (800) 282-7526 or (404) 845-0011

http://www.fpanet.org

Publishes *Avoiding Investment and Financial Scams: Seeking Full Disclosure Is the Key*. Web site offers a Planner Search that connects individuals with CFP licensees who can help with financial planning.

Financial Literacy Center

15 Corporate Circle
Albany, NY 12203

Ph:(866) 352-1234

http://www.flconline.com

Offers financial education products for purchase. Online education center provides various types of savings calculators.

Good Money, Inc.

Attn. Peter Lowry
370A Granite Rd.
Ossipee, NH 03864

Ph: (603) 539-3852

http://www.goodmoney.com

Social, ethical, and environmental investing. Web site includes how-to guides, company profiles, and information on socially responsible investing. Publications available.

International Society for Retirement Planning

2121 Arlington Ave. #5
Upper Arlington, OH 43221

Ph: (614) 485-9650

http://www.isrplan.org

A professional association dedicated to comprehensive retirement and life planning. Web site provides an extensive bibliography of books, software, Web sites, and films aimed to improve the quality of life of mature adults.

Investment Company Institute

1401 H St. NW
Washington, DC 20005

http://www.ici.org

Represents its members and their shareholders in matters of legislation, registration, public information, taxation, and more. Web site offers information on mutual funds. Includes a section about retirement security issues.

National Association of Investors Corporation (NAIC)

PO Box 220
Royal Oak, MI 48068

Ph: (248) 583-6242
Toll-free: (877) 275-6242

http://www.better-investing.org

Offers products, services, and professional support to help members become informed investors. Publishes *Better Investing*, a monthly magazine with the latest investment information. *NAIC Online* offers investment advice and ideas, investment club information, and an online store.

National Association of Personal Financial Advisors (NAPFA)

355 W. Dundee Rd., Suite 200
Buffalo Grove, IL 60089

Ph: (888) FEE-ONLY

http://www.napfa.org

Information about fee-only financial advisers. Call or use search form on Web site to locate a nearby fee-only financial adviser.

U.S. Securities and Exchange Commission Headquarters (SEC)

450 Fifth St. NW
Washington, DC 20549

Ph: (202) 942-7040

http://www.sec.gov

Regulates firms engaged in the purchase or sale of securities, people who provide investment advice, and investment companies. Manages the Office of Investor Education and Assistance. Publications available. Web site provides directory of regional offices, information on saving and investing, a mutual fund cost calculator, as well as links to investor education sites.

The Vanguard Group

Vanguard Financial Center
PO Box 2600
Valley Forge, PA 19482

Ph: (800) 662-7447

http://www.vanguard.com

Offers a broad range of mutual funds and auxiliary financial services to meet the needs of individual investors. Web site offers a retirement planning center. Also see online library for *Investing with Simplicity.*

Financial Planning

Internet

About.Com Guide to Retirement Living: U.S.

http://retireplan.about.com

Links to information about annuities, calculators, estate planning, 401(k)s, IRAs, investment strategies, mutual funds, Social Security, tax planning, retirement living and many other topics.

Alliance for Investor Education

http://www.investoreducation.org

Information on financial planning, estate planning, stocks, bonds, mutual funds, investing basics, fraud, and selecting an investment adviser or broker, as well as links to member organizations.

American Express

http://www.americanexpress.com/401k

This site details seven financial-planning subjects, including the "cost of waiting," which relates to the hazards of procrastination.

American Savings Education Council

http://www.asec.org

Information about the programs of the ASEC to promote savings.

http://www.asec.org/toolshm.htm

Balance Worksheet—a worksheet designed to help individuals quickly identify approximately how much savings they will need to live comfortably in retirement.

Center for Financial Well-Being

http://www.healthy.net/wellness/healthycash/center

Explores link between personal finance and wellness.

Centura

http://www.centura.com/formulas/whatif.html

Easy-to-use calculators that help determine how much you can borrow, or how much you should invest for particular financial goals. Includes personal loans, auto loans, home loans, investment/savings. The investment/savings calculator is especially useful for planning how to reach retirement savings goals.

Deloitte & Touche LLP

http://www.dtonline.com/prptoc/prptoc.htm

A financial counseling service helps users to understand and develop their own retirement plans.

Fidelity

http://www400.fidelity.com:80

Provides information on asset allocation and the effect of inflation on retirement, the pros and cons of converting to a Roth IRA, and the benefits of cutting back on discretionary expenses, such as eating out. Assists users to develop long-range savings strategies by helping to address retirement income, how much you'll need to support your lifestyle after you've left the workforce, and how much you need to start saving now. Online retirement calculator.

Financial Calc

http://www.fincalc.com

Offers personalized financial plans such as retirement, college funding, insurance needs, mortgage refinance, credit card payoff, etc. Many features require downloading of free plug-in program from the links provided.

***Financial Planning* Magazine Online**

http://www.fponline.com

Industry reports on fee services providers, qualified plan providers, and long-term care providers, as well as related links and articles.

GreenMoney Online Guide

http://www.greenmoney.com

Promotes socially responsible investing. Offers a resource guide and information on socially responsible investments and mutual funds. Publishes *The GreenMoney Journal*, which can also be ordered by phone at (800) 318-5725, or by mail at GMJ, West 608 Glass Ave., Spokane, WA 99205.

International Society for Retirement Planning

http://www.isrplan.org

Links to financial planning and investment resources.

Investor Guide

http://www.investorguide.com

Guide to investing on the Internet. Retirement section includes information on 401(k)s, IRAs, Social Security, and estate planning.

John Hancock

http://www.jhancock.com

The site provides extensive information on many financial-planning topics and takes into account drains on your finances while trying to save, together with potential income from the sale of your house or part-time work.

Kiplinger

http://www.kiplinger.com

Retirement information and calculators. Offers *Kiplinger's Retirement Report* online.

Legg Mason

http://www.leggmason.com

A simple calculator program for determining retirement investment needs.

Metropolitan Life Insurance

http://www.lifeadvice.com

Web site offered by Metropolitan Life Insurance Company. Offers information about finances, health, insurance, and other issues of interest to seniors.

Money Magazine

http://www.pathfinder.com/money/depts/retirement

Money magazine's online financial strategy center for retirement.

Mutual Fund Investors Center

http://www.mfea.com

Web site of the Mutual Fund Education Alliance. Offers a Retirement Center with information on retirement planning, calculators and worksheets; IRAs and 401(k) plans; laws and taxes; and building a retirement portfolio.

NASD Office of Individual Investor Services

http://www.investor.nasd.com

Information about investor training and protection; *The Basics of Saving and Investing*, a teaching guide; publications including *All About Nasdaq;* Nasdaq quotes; financial calculators; and a section on working with a broker.

PricewaterhouseCoopers

http://www.pwcfps.com

A variety of PricewaterhouseCoopers planning tools—just click on *Retail Catalog* on this Web site.

Quicken

http://www.quicken.com/retirement

Topics include IRAs, 401(k)s, annuities, social security, pension plans, mutual funds, and stocks. Provides an online retirement planner.

Securities Fraud and Investor Protection

http://www.securitieslaw.com

Information on the nature of securities fraud, investor rights, broker duties, how to know if you've been defrauded, and what you can do about it.

***Smart Money* Magazine**

http://www.smartmoney.com

Smart Money Magazine's online retirement strategy; covers all aspects of investment planning.

T.Rowe Price

http://www.troweprice.com/retirement

Offers a worksheet that tells you the percentage of your salary that you need to save. It will also estimate how much your current taxable and tax-deferred investments will grow and how much you'll need altogether.

TIAA-CREF

http://www.tiaa-cref.org

Nationwide retirement and financial services system for people who work at colleges, universities, independent schools, and other nonproft education and research institutions. Joint effort of the Teachers Insurance and Annuity Association and the College Retirement Equities Fund. Information on retirement plans, SRAs, personal annuities, IRAs, mutual funds, and insurance. Offers contact information for regional offices, help-line phone numbers, and individual counseling.

Time Value Software

http://www.timevalue.com

Allows the user to calculate how much money to put away tax deferred to get a certain amount of money in the future and how much one could expect to draw out of that money.

Pensions and Benefits

Organizations

Employee Benefit Research Institute (EBRI)

2121 St. NW, Suite 600
Washington, DC 20037-1896

Ph: (202) 659-0670
Fax: (202) 775-6360

http://www.ebri.org

Undertakes a set of research and education programs on health, retirement, and Social Security issues. Web site offers information on programs and publications.

Pension and Welfare Benefits Administration

U.S. Department of Labor
200 Constitution Ave. NW
Washington, DC 20210

Publication Hotline: (800) 998-7542
Technical Assistance and Inquiries:
(202) 219-8776

http://www.dol.gov/dol/pwba

Assists the public with technical questions relating to pension, health, or other employee benefits. Web site offers consumer information on pension and health benefit plans, as well as the Retirement Savings Education Campaign.

Pension Benefit Guaranty Corporation

1200 K St. NW
Washington, DC 20005-4026

Ph: (800) 400-7242

http://www.pbgc.gov

Protects retirement income of over one third of American workers. Web site offers Department of Labor publications on health benefits and pensions.

Pension Rights Center

1140 19th St., Suite 602
Washington, DC 20036

Ph: (202) 296-3776
Fax: (202) 833-2472

Protects the rights of workers, retirees, and their families. Offers a self-help manual, *Where to Look for Help with a Pension Problem;* a pension handbook, *A Guide to Understanding Your Pension Plan;* and a divorce book, *Your Pension Rights at Divorce.*

Social Security Administration

Office of Public Inquiries
6401 Security Blvd.
Baltimore, MD 21235

Ph: (410) 965-7700
Toll-free Information: (800) 772-1213
Fax: (410) 965-0695

http://www.ssa.gov

Responsible for Social Security retirement, survivors benefits, disability insurance, and the Supplemental Security Income (SSI) program.

Free publications available by phone and online.

Internet

BenefitsLink

http://www.benefitslink.com

Nationwide link to information about employee benefits, including health and retirement planning.

Pension Research Council

http://prc.wharton.upenn.edu/prc/prc.html

Web site provides research about private pension and Social Security programs and related benefit plans. Publications available for purchase.

Health Care Financing and Insurance

Organizations

American Association of Health Plans

1129 20th St. NW, Suite 600
Washington, DC 20036-3421

Ph: (202) 778-3200
Fax: (202) 331-7487

http://www.aahp.org

Web site offers consumer information on how to choose a health plan, as well as on health plan definitions.

Health Care Financing Administration

7500 Security Blvd.
Baltimore, MD 21244-1850

Ph: (410) 786-2165
Toll-free Medicare Hotline: (800) 638-6833

http://www.hcfa.gov

The *Medicare Handbook* and *Guide to Health Insurance for People on Medicare Financing Review,* published yearly.

Health Insurance Association of America

1201 F St. NW, Suite 500
Washington, DC 20004

Ph: (202) 824-1600
Toll-free Information: (800) 879-4422

Fax: (202) 824-1722
http://www.hiaa.org

Provides information about health insurance issues, including group health benefits, major medical, Medicare supplements, and long-term care insurance. Publications: *Guide to Long- term Care Insurance; Guide to Disability Insurance;* and *Consumer's Guide to Health Insurance.*

Hill-Burton Program

Health Resources and Services Administration
5600 Fishers Lane, Rm. 10C16
Rockville, MD 20857

Ph: (301) 443-5656
Toll-free Hotline: (800) 638-0742
http://www.hrsa.dhhs.gov/osp/dfcr

Hotline provides information about health facilities that are required to provide services at no or reduced cost to eligible persons. Publications available.

Internet

Health-Line.org

http://www.life-line.org/health

From the Life and Health Insurance Foundation for Education. Describes basic forms of health coverage, a checklist to compare plans, and a glossary of terms.

Medicare

http://www.medicare.gov

Official U.S. government site for Medicare information.

National Committee for Quality Assurance

http://www.ncqa.org

Offers a brochure on choosing a health plan. Provides a list of health plans with accreditation summary reports.

Consumer Issues

National Institute for Consumer Education (NICE)

G 12 Boone Hall
Eastern Michigan University
Ypsilanti, MI 48197

Ph: (734) 487-2292
Fax: (734) 487-7153
http://www.emich.edu/public/coe/nice

Promotes consumer, economic, and personal finance education. Web site offers consumer fact sheets and mini-lessons on credit, fraud, and financial management, including *Plan Now for a Comfortable Retirement.*

Other

The Internal Revenue Service Online

http://www.irs.gov

Income tax information, forms and publications, and taxpaper help and education.

The National Committee on Retirement Policy (NCRP)

The CSIS Press
1800 K St. NW
Washington, DC 20006

Ph: (202) 887-0200
Fax: (202) 775-3199
http://www.csis.org/retire

Order the 21st Century Retirement Security Plan by mail, phone, fax, or download it from the Web site. Also offers *Can America Afford to Retire?* and a retirement fact sheet.

National Endowment for Financial Education (NEFE)

5299 DTC Blvd., Suite 1300
Englewood, CO 80111

Ph: (303) 741-6333
http://www.nefe.org

Order a free Wealth Care Kit and a 401(k) brochure for the general public by mail. Address for Wealth Care Kit is: NEFE, 4695 S. Monace St., Denver, CO 80237.

Special Committee on Aging

G-31 Senate Dirksen Office Building
Washington, DC 20510

(202) 224-5364

Offers a free publication designed to help older adults pay fewer taxes, *Protecting Older Americans Against Overpayment of Income Taxes.* Details legitimate income tax deductions, exemptions, and tax credits. It's written in easy-to-understand language, with many examples and checklists.

General Resources

Organizations

Administration on Aging

330 Independence Ave. SW
Washington, DC 20201

Ph: (202) 619-0724
Fax: (202) 260-1012

http://www.aoa.gov

Works closely with state and area agencies on aging to offer supportive services to older persons. Web site provides an aging information center, links to Web sites of interest to seniors, and a resource directory of organizations for older people.

Center for Universal Design

North Carolina State University
Box 8613
219 Oberlin Rd.
Raleigh, NC 27695-8613

(919) 515-3082

Provides "accessible products" that can make life easier as we age.

Consumer Information Center

Rm. G-142 (XC)
1800 F St. NW
Washington, DC 20405

Ph: (202) 501-1794

http://www.pueblo.gsa.gov

Webpage offers full text versions of hundreds of federal publications of interest to consumers.

Enrichments for Better Living Catalog

145 Tower Dr.
Box 579
Hillsdale, IL 60521

(800) 323-5547

Offers a catalog of items that make the lives of seniors easier and safer.

Maxi-Aids

42 Executive Blvd.
Farmingdale, NY 11735

(631) 752-0521

http://www.maxiaids.com

Sells cleverly designed household products that can make life more comfortable as we age.

National Association of Area Agencies on Aging

927 15th St. NW, Sixth Floor
Washington, DC 20005

Ph: (202) 296-8130
Toll-free Eldercare Locator: (800) 677-1116
Fax: (202) 296-8134

http://www.n4a.org

Provides the Eldercare Locator, a nationwide, directory assistance service designed to help older persons and caregivers locate local support and housing resources.

National Consumers League

1701 K St. NW, Suite 1201
Washington, DC 20006

Ph: (202) 835-3323
National Fraud Information Center: (800) 876-7060
Fax: (202) 835-0747

http://www.natlconsumersleague.org

Publishes brochures on medications and consumer guides on hospice care, home health care, and life-care/continuing care communities. Web site provides information about fraud and the elderly.

The National Council on the Aging, Inc.

409 3rd St. SW, Suite 200
Washington, DC 20024

Ph: (202) 479-1200
Consumer Information Network: (877) 390-7828
Fax: (202) 479-0735

http://www.ncoa.org

Web site offers state by state directory of Adult Day Service Centers, as well as financial and health information.

National Rehabilitation Information Center

1010 Wayne Ave., Suite 800
Silver Spring, MD 20910

(800) 346-2742

Provides information on safety items for seniors such as handrails, stools for baths, and grippers that make opening jars easier.

Yes I Can, Inc.

35-325 Date Palm Drive
Suite 131
Cathedral City, CA 92234

(800) 366-4226

Provides products to make life easier for seniors.

Internet

Access America for Seniors

http://www.seniors.gov

Delivers online services from government agencies and organizations to seniors. Topics include benefits, health and nutrition, consumer protection, taxes, employment and volunteer activities, travel and leisure, education and training. Also provides links to federal agencies.

AOA ElderPage: Information for Older Persons and Families

http://www.aoa.dhhs.gov/elderpage.html

Information and links for topics of interest to seniors.

AOA The Resource Directory for Older People

http://www.aoa.gov/aoa/resource.html

Contains contact data for organizations that provide information and resources relevant to the needs of older persons.

AOA's National Aging Information Center (NAIC)

http://www.aoa.gov/naic

Allows users to search its bibliographic and statistical databases. Provides online copies of fact sheets on various topics of interest to seniors.

Eldernet

http://www.eldernet.com

Senior guide to health, housing, legal issues, financial planning, retirement benefits, lifestyles, and entertainment.

National Network for Family Resiliency

http://www.nnfr.org/igen

Provides information on intergenerational and grandparenting issues.

SeniorCom

http://www1.senior.com

General information on travel, entertainment, money matters, health, employment, and housing. Offers a nationwide directory of doctors and a link to the Senior Alternatives guide to housing.

Sixty-Five Plus in the United States

http://www.census.gov/ftp/pub/socdemo/www/agebrief.html

A statistical brief of the U.S. Census Bureau's study on individuals 65 and older.

The Spry Foundation

http://www.spry.org

Provides online managed care resource guide and links to health and financial resources for seniors. Publications available for purchase.

ThirdAge

http://www.thirdage.com

Web site for older adults that focuses on family, health, living, money, romance, shopping, and work.

Health

Alzheimer's Disease

Organizations

Alzheimer's Association

919 N. Michigan Ave.
Chicago, IL 60611

Ph: (312) 335-8700
Toll-free information: (800) 272-3900
Fax: (312) 335-1110

http://www.alz.org

A 24-hour toll-free hotline provides information about Alzheimer's disease and links families with local chapters.

Alzheimer's Disease Education & Referral Center

PO Box 8250
Silver Spring, MD 20907-8250

Ph: (301) 495-3311
Toll-free information: (800) 438-4380
Fax: (301) 495-3334

http://www.alzheimers.org/

Responds to inquiries from the public and provides information about diagnosis, treatment, research, and services available for Alzheimer's disease.

American Health Assistance Foundation

15825 Shady Grove Rd., Suite 140
Rockville, MD 20850

Ph: (301) 948-3244
Toll-free information: (800) 437-2423
Fax: (301) 258-9454

http://www.ahaf.org

The Alzheimer's Family Relief Program offers emergency grants of up to $500 to Alzheimer's patients and their caregivers in need. Free publications available on Alzheimer's disease, glaucoma, heart disease, and stroke.

Heart, Lung, and Blood

Organizations

American Heart Association

7272 Greenville Ave.
Dallas, TX 75231

Ph: (214) 373-6300
Affiliate office: (800) 242-8721
Toll-free Stroke Connection (800) 553-6321

http://www.amhrt.org

The Stroke Connection maintains a listing of nationwide groups for referral to stroke survivors and their families. It also publishes *Stroke Connection*, a forum for sharing information about coping with stroke.

National Heart, Lung, and Blood Institute (NHLBI)

Education Programs Information Center
31 Center Dr., MSC 2480
Rm. 4A21
Bethesda, MD 20892-2480

Ph: (301) 592-8573

http://www.nhlbi.nih.gov/index.htm

Provides consumer materials on cholesterol, smoking, high blood pressure, asthma, chronic cough, heart disease, exercise, stroke, and blood resources.

National Stroke Association

9707 E. Easter Lane
Englewood, CO 80112

Ph: (303) 649-9299
Fax: (303) 649-1328

http://www.stroke.org

Provides information about stroke to the general public and offers supportive services to stroke survivors and their families. Brochures available.

Mental Health

Organizations

National Institute of Mental Health

Information Resources and Inquiries Branch
6001 Executive Blvd., Room 8184
MSC9663
Bethesda, MD 20892-9663

Ph: (301) 443-4513
Fax: (301) 443-4279

http://www.nimh.nih.gov

Free publications include *Alzheimer's Disease; Plain Talk About Aging; Plain Talk About Handling Stress;* and *If You're Over 65 and Feeling Depressed: Treatment Brings New Hope.*

National Mental Health Association

1021 Prince St.
Alexandria, VA 22314-2971

Ph: (703) 684-7722
Information Center: (800) 969-6642
Fax: (703) 684-5968

http://www.nmha.org/index.cfm

The Information Center provides written materials on mental health topics and referrals to callers requesting information on mental health service organizations. Publications include two quarterly newsletters, *NMHA Prevention Update* and *The BELL.*

Orthopedics

Organizations

American Academy of Orthopaedic Surgeons

6300 N. River Rd.
Rosemont, IL 60018-4262

Ph: (847) 823-7186
Toll-free information: (800) 346-2267

http://www.aaos.org/

Information available about arthritis, osteoporosis, artificial joints, and prevention of hip fractures.

Arthritis Foundation

1330 W. Peachtree St.
Atlanta, GA 30309

Ph: (404) 872-7100
Toll-free information: (800) 283-7800

http://www.arthritis.org/

Offers nationwide health education programs in local communities, including arthritis self-help courses, aquatic and exercise programs, support groups and public forums.

National Institute of Arthritis and Musculoskeletal and Skin Diseases

Information Office
1 Ams Circle
Bethesda, MD 20892-3676

Ph: (301) 496-8188

http://www.nih.gov/niams

Offers brochures and information on arthritis, rheumatic diseases, and osteoporosis.

National Osteoporosis Foundation

1232 22nd St. NW
Washington, DC 20037-1292

Ph: (202) 223-2226
Fax: (202) 223-2237

http://www.nof.org

Publishes *Osteoporosis: A Woman's Guide* and *An Older Person's Guide to Osteoporosis.* Web site has information on prevention and available medications.

Sight and Hearing

Organizations

American Academy of Ophthalmology

PO Box 7424
San Francisco, CA 94142-7424

Ph: (415) 561-8500

Http://www.eyenet.org

Toll-free National Eye Care Project Helpline for people age 65 or older to put them in touch with local ophthalmologists who volunteer to provide medical eye care at no out-of-pocket expense.

Better Hearing Institute

POB 1840
Washington, DC 20013

Ph: (703) 642-0580
Toll-free Hearing Helpline: (800) 327-9355

http://www.advancedhearing.com/bhi.htm

Hearing Helpline provides information on hearing loss.

Better Vision Institute

1700 Diagonal Rd., Suite 500
Alexandria, VA 22314

Ph: (703) 548-4650
Toll-free publications service: (877) 642-3253
Fax: (703)548-4580

http://www.visionsite.org

Provides information about the prevention, detection, and treatment of eye diseases.

The Glaucoma Research Foundation

200 Pine St., Suite 200
San Francisco, CA 94104

Ph: (415) 986-3162
Toll-free Support Network: (800) 826-6693
Fax: (415) 986-3763

http://www.glaucoma.org

National peer support network for glaucoma patients and their families. Free glaucoma patient guide.

International Hearing Society

16880 Middlebelt Rd., Suite #4
Livonia, MI 47154

Ph: (734) 522-7200
Toll-free Hearing Aid Helpline: (800) 521-5247
Fax: (734) 522-0200

http://www.hearingihs.org

Hearing Aid Helpline offers information on hearing loss, hearing aids, and locating a qualified hearing aid specialist, as well as handling consumer complaints about hearing aids.

National Association of the Deaf

814 Thayer Ave., Suite 250
Silver Spring, MD 20910-4500

Ph: (301) 587-1788
Fax: (301) 587-1791

http://www.nad.org

Responds to written and telephone requests from the public for information about hearing.

National Center for Vision and Aging

The Lighthouse, Inc.
111 E. 59th St.
New York, NY 10022

Ph: (212) 821-9200
Information/Resource Service: (800) 829-0500
Fax: (212) 821-9705

http://www.lighthouse.org

Provides information on vision rehabilitation agencies, low-vision centers, support groups, eye conditions, assistive devices, and free literature on eye diseases. Distributes the *Lighthouse Consumer Catalog*, a mail-order catalog of products for persons with impaired vision.

National Eye Institute

Information Office
2020 Vision Place
Bethesda, MD 20892-3655

Ph: (301) 496-5248
Fax: (301) 402-1065

http://www.nei.nih.gov

Free brochures on cataracts, glaucoma, age-related macular degeneration, and diabetic retinopathy.

Prevent Blindness America

500 E. Remington Rd.
Schaumburg, IL 60173

Ph: (847) 843-2020
Information: (800) 331-2020
Fax: (847) 843-8458

http://www.preventblindness.org

Issues pamphlets on eye safety, glaucoma, and eye exams. Local chapters offer community services such as eye exams and self-help groups for people with glaucoma.

Nutrition and Fitness

Organizations

American Dietetic Association

216 W. Jackson Blvd.
Chicago, IL 60606-6995

Ph: (312) 899-0040
Publications Service: (800) 745-0775
Nutrition Hotline: (800) 366-1655
Fax: (312) 899-1757

http://www.eatright.org

Consumer publications on nutrition and fitness for families, women, and older adults, as well as information on nutrition legislation and a hotline for locating a nearby registered dietician.

International Food Information Council (IFIC)

1100 Connecticut Ave. NW, Suite 430
Washington, DC 20036

http://www.ific.com

Publishes bimonthly issues of *Food Insight*. Web site section on food safety and nutrition information has data on adult nutrition, health, and physical activity, including elderly nutrition.

National Association for Human Development

1424 16th St. NW, Suite 102
Washington, DC 20036

Ph: (202) 328-2191
Toll-free Information: (800) 424-5153

Published print and audiovisual materials on health and physical fitness for older adults.

President's Council on Physical Fitness and Sports

200 Independence Ave. SW, Suite 738-H
Washington, DC 20201-0004

Ph: (202) 690-9000
Fax: (202) 690-5211

http://www.fitness.gov

Distributes information about health-related benefits of regular exercise. Publications include *Pep Up Your Life,* a fitness book for older people, and *The Nolan Ryan Fitness Guide* for adults 40 and over.

Internet

The American Council on Exercise Fit Facts

http://www.acefitness.org/fitfacts

Fit facts, such as *Exercising with a Health Challenge* and *Exercise and Arthritis*.

Nutrition Navigator

http://www.navigator.tufts.edu

Tufts University's guide to nutrition Web sites includes focus on senior health and fitness.

Physical Activity and Health for Older Persons

http://www.cdc.gov/nccdphp/sgr/olderad.htm

Summary of the Surgeon General's Report online.

A Senior's Guide to Good Nutrition

http://www.vrg.org/nutrition/seniors.htm

The Vegetarian Resource Group provides this useful Web page, including sample meal plans and recipes.

Hospice and Home Care

Organizations

Choice in Dying

1035 30th St. NW
Washington, DC 20007

Ph: (202) 338-9790
Counseling Line: (800) 989-9455
Fax: (202) 338-0242

http://www.choices.org

Invented living wills. Counsels patients and families on making decisions about end-of-life medical care. Offers publications and services, including information about advance directives.

National Association for Home Care

228 7th St. SE
Washington, DC 20003

Ph: (202) 547-7424
Fax: (202) 547-3540

http://www.nahc.org

Information on how to select a home care agency.

National Hospice Organization

1901 N. Moore St., Suite 901
Arlington, VA 22209

Ph: (703) 243-5900
Hospice Referral Line: (800) 658-8898

http://www.nho.org

Offers toll-free hospice referral line and publishes the *Guide to the Nation's Hospices* every year.

Other Health Resources

Organizations

American Diabetes Association

Customer Service
1701 Beauregard St.
Alexandria, VA 22311

Ph: (703) 549-1500
Information: (800) 342-2383

http://www.diabetes.org

Offers general information about diabetes and its management. Web site includes recipes for diabetics, research updates, and a list of recognized providers.

National Association of Community Health Centers

1330 New Hampshire Ave. NW, Suite 122
Washington, DC 20036

Ph: (202) 659-8008
Fax: (202) 659-8519

http://www.nachc.com

Offers *Affordable Healthcare for Seniors—A Guide to Federally Qualified Health Centers,* which contains a directory of state primary care associations.

National Cancer Institute

Office of Cancer Communications
Building 31, Room 10A07
31 Center Drive MSC 2580
Bethesda, MD 20892-2580

Cancer Information Service (CIS): (800) 422-6237

http://www.nci.nih.gov

Information about cancer-related resources and publications on cancer prevention, early detection, diagnosis, treatment, and survivorship.

National Institute on Aging

Public Information Office
Building 331, Room 5C27
31 Center Drive MSC 2292
Bethesda, MD 20892-2292

Ph: (301) 496-1752

Information: (800) 222-2225
Fax: (301) 496-1072
http://www.nih.gov/nia

Offers free brochures and fact sheets on nutrition, medications, safety, exercise, diseases, and health promotion.

National Library of Medicine

8600 Rockville Pike
Bethesda, MD 20894

Ph: (888) FIND-NLM or (301) 594-5983
http://www.nlm.nih.gov

Web site provides links to resources that will help research health questions.

Prostate Health Council

The American Foundation for Urologic Disease, Inc.
1128 North Charles St.
Baltimore, MD 21201

Offers general information about the health of your prostate.

Senior Action in a Gay Environment (SAGE)

305 7th Ave., 16th Floor
New York, NY 10001

Provides HIV/AIDS information and referrals for people 50 and over.

Internet

Diabetes.Com

http://www.diabetes.com

Health Library provides information that encourages educated self-care.

Health Answers

http://www.healthanswers.com

General health information. Has a section dedicated to senior health topics.

HealthFinder

http://www.healthfinder.gov

General information on health topics. Section on seniors has links to primarily government resources on health, Social Security, and pensions.

Housing

Organizations

AARP Fulfillment

1909 K St. NW
Washington, DC 20049

(800) 424-3410

Ask for *Housing Options for Older Americans* (D12063).

American Association of Homes and Services for the Aging (AAHSA)

2519 Connecticut Ave. NW
Washington, DC 20008-1520

Ph: (202) 783-2242
To order publications: (800) 508-9442
Fax: (202) 783-2255
http://www.aahsa.org

Represents over 5,000 nonprofit organizations that provide health care, housing, and services to the elderly. Home of the Continuing Care Accreditation Commission. Webpage offers tips on choosing suitable housing and services, and provides a searchable directory of nursing homes, continuing care retirement communities, assisted living residences, senior housing facilities, and community service organizations. Also offers links to affiliated state associations and information on understanding Medicare managed care.

American Health Care Association

1201 L St. NW
Washington, DC 20005

Ph: (202) 842-4444
Fax: (202) 842-3860
http://www.ahca.org

Publications on choosing a nursing home or assisted living facility, financing long-term care, understanding advance directives, as well as *A Family Guide: Making the Transition to Nursing Facility Life.*

American Retirement Corporation

111 Westwood Pl., Suite 402
Brentwood, TN 37027

Ph: (615) 221-2250
Fax: (615) 221-2269

http://www.arclp.com

Owns or provides services for 36 residential care, assisted living, and nursing care communities in 15 states. Currently building a number of assisted living facilities that provide memory-impaired services.

ARV Assisted Living

Corporate Office
245 Fischer Ave., D-1
POB 5046
Costa Mesa, CA 92626

Ph: (714) 751-7400 or (800) 624-0236

http://www.arvi.com

Nationwide company with facilities in 14 states. See Web site for listings.

Assisted Living Federation of America (ALFA)

11200 Waples Mill Rd.
Suite 150
Fairfax, VA 22030

Ph: (703) 691-8100
Fax: (703) 691-8106

http://www.alfa,org

E-mail: *info@alfa.org*

The Assisted Living Federation of America (ALFA) is the only trade association exclusively devoted to the assisted living industry and the population it serves. Members include assisted living providers, as well as a diverse range of industry partners and supportive organizations. This nonprofit organization has been developing state affiliates to work with regulators and legislators on the state level.

Atria Inc. (formerly Senior Quarters)

501 S. 4th Ave.
Suite 140
Louisville, KY 40202

Ph: (502) 719-1600 or (888) 287-4201
Fax: (502) 719-1699

Assisted living facilities in 26 states. Web site provides listings.

Del Webb's Sun Cities

The Del Webb Corporation
Corporate Headquarters
6001 N. 24th St.
Phoenix, AZ 85016

Ph: (602) 808-8000

http://www.delwebb.com

Planned adult communities in Arizona, California, Illinois, Nevada, South Carolina, and Texas. Web site offers information on individual communities.

Sunrise Assisted Living, Inc.

National Office
7902 Westpark Dr.
MacLean, VA 22102

Ph: (703) 273-7500 or (888) 434-4648
Fax: (703) 744-1601

http://www.sunrise-al.com

Nationwide company with assisted living facilities, including some Alzheimer's, in 22 states. Web site provides individual listings.

Internet

Assisted Living Info

http://www.assistedlivinginfo.com

Search by state and map for assisted living facilities. Also offers tips on selecting a facility.

Assisted Living On-Line

http://www.assistedlivingonline.com

An online directory of assisted living and retirement centers by region and state.

Association of Retirement Resorts International

http://www.RetirementResorts.com

A listing of senior living resort communities that provide on-site supportive services, such as assisted living and/or nursing care. Includes 11 states and 2 international sites.

CareGuide.com

http://www.careguide.com

Search by state for elder care, including nursing homes, assisted living, home care, hospice, and care managers. Also a resource center for health care information and a bookstore with publications about elder care and retirement planning.

Continuing Care Accreditation Commission

http://www.ccaconline.org

Provides a list of accredited communities as well as links to possible sources of information on aging and senior services.

Guide to Retirement Living Online

http://www.retirement-living.com

Listing of CCRCs, assisted living and nursing facilities, and independent living communities. Information on home health care, rehabilitation, and remodeling for the disabled.

NorALFA Online

http://www.noralfa.org

Offers links to retirement facilities in the Northwest.

Private Communities Registry

http://www.registryone.com

Private, gated, or master-planned retirement communities in 11 states. See Web site for listings.

The Retirement Net

http://www.retirenet.com

Search for retirement communities. Includes active living, independent and assisted living, nursing care, and RV/resort.

Senior Alternatives for Living

http://www.springstreet.com/seniors

Search by state for long-term care and senior communities, Alzheimer's care, home health care, hospice care, and adult day care.

Senior Living Online Network

http://www.livon.com

Search for senior housing and services by location and cost. Includes independent and assisted living, nursing care, and life care. Sometimes payment is requested.

Senior Selections: Mature Living Choices

http://www.seniorselections.com

Regional listings of retirement locations. Printed color booklets available through Network Communications, 2305 Newpoint Parkway, Lawrenceville, GA 30043, (770) 962-7220.

Senior Sites

http://www.seniorsites.com

Source of nonprofit housing and services for seniors. Over 5,000 communities listed.

Summerville Health Care Group

http://www.summervillehg.com

Provides a listing of its senior living facilities in eight states, including assisted living and continuing care retirement communities.

Legal Concerns

General

Hotlines

Arizona Legal Hotline for the Elderly

(800) 231-5441

California Senior Legal Hotline

(800) 222-1753

Florida Hotline for Older Floridians

(800) 252-5997

Maine Legal Services for the Elderly

(800) 750-5353

Michigan Senior Alliance Inc.

(800) 347-5297

New Mexico Lawyer Referral Services for the Elderly

(800) 876-6657

Ohio Pro Senior Inc.

(800) 488-6070

Pennsylvania Legal Hotline for Older Americans

(800) 262-5297

Texas Legal Hotline for Older Texans

(800) 622-2520

Free hotlines to help older Americans with legal advice on Social Security and Medicare. Services vary. Some will refer you to lawyers who offer assistance on a sliding fee scale, while some offer help at no charge

Organizations

Better Business Bureau Wise Giving Alliance

4200 Wilson Blvd., Suite 800
Arlington, VA 22203

Ph: (703) 276-0100

Provides information about charitable giving and avoiding charitable fraud.

Council of Better Business Bureaus, Inc.

Publications Department
4200 Wilson Blvd., Suite 800
Arlington, VA 22203

Offers information about protecting yourself while traveling, charitable giving, and avoiding charitable fraud.

Federal Trade Commission

6th & Pennsylvania Ave. NW
Washington, DC 20044

Ph: (202)326-2222

Offers a free pamphlet, *Telemarketing Travel Fraud.*

National Academy of Elder Law Attorneys (NAELA)

1604 N. Country Club Rd.
Tucson, AZ 85716

Ph: (520) 881-4005
Fax: (520) 325-7925

http://www.naela.org

Web site provides an online consumer directory to elder law attorneys. Search by name, location, or experience.

National Consumers League

1701 K St. NW, Suite 1201
Washington, DC 20006

Ph: (202) 835-3323
National Fraud Information Hotline: (800) 876-7060
Fax: (202) 835-0747

Provides information on crime prevention.

National Charities Information Bureau

19 Union Square West
New York, NY 10003

Ph: (212) 929-6300

Offers information about charitable giving and avoiding charitable fraud.

National Crime Prevention Council

1000 Connecticut Ave., 13th floor NW
Washington, DC 20036

Ph: (202) 466-6272

Offers a free crime prevention packet covering home security and assault prevention.

National Legal Support for Elderly People with Mental Disabilities

Bazelon Center for Mental Health Law
1101 15th St. NW, Suite 1212
Washington, DC 20005-5002

Ph: (202) 467-5730
Fax: (202) 223-0409

http://www.bazelon.org

Legal advocacy for the civil rights of older people with mental disabilities. Publications include *Elders Assert Their Rights,* a guide for residents, family members, and advocates to legal rights of elderly people with mental disabilities in nursing homes. Learn about the Older Mental Health Consumer *Network*, an advocacy group that will allow older mental health consumers a voice in public policy.

National Organization of Social Security Claimants' Representatives

6 Prospect St.
Midland Park, NJ 07432

Referral Service: (800) 431-2804

http://www.nosscr.org

Offers assistance in locating representation for Social Security cases. Web site answers FAQs about Social Security disability benefits.

National Senior Citizens Law Center (NSCLC)

1101 14th St. NW, Suite 400
Washington, DC 20005

Ph: (202) 289-6976
Fax: (202) 289-7224

http://www.nsclc.org

Serves Legal Aid Offices and private lawyers who offer legal assistance to low-income people. NSCLC will refer eligible individuals to legal service providers in their area. Those ineligible should refer to the NAELA consumer directory.

Internet

Consumer Law Page

http://www.consumerlawpage.com

Offers articles of interest, free consumer information brochures, and a resource page with links to other useful sites. Published by the Alexander Law Firm.

Senior Alternatives for Living

http://www.springstreet.com/seniors

Listing by state of elder law attorneys. Information on living wills.

SeniorLaw

http://www.seniorlaw.com

Access information about elder law, Medicare, Medicaid, estate planning, trusts, and the rights of the elderly and disabled. National list of elder law attorneys on the Web.

Estate Planning

Organizations

American Association of Retired Persons

Consumer Affairs Section
Program Coordination & Development Department
601 E St. NW
Washington, DC 20049

Offers a pamphlet called *A Consumer's Guide to Probate.*

Legal Counsel for the Elderly

601 E St. NW
Washington, DC 20049

Ph: (202) 434-2120

Provides information about wills and probate.

Nolo Press

950 Parker St.
Berkeley, CA 94710

Ph: (510) 549-1976

Publishes how-to books designed to help people avoid legal fees, including a workbook on preparing a will yourself.

Internet

Crash Course in Wills and Trusts

http://www.mtpalermo.com

Also includes information on powers of attorney, advance medical directives, life insurance, and long-term care insurance.

ICLE Online

http://www.icle.org/practice/probate.htm

The Institute of Continuing Legal Education in Michigan offers numerous weblinks for probate and estate planning.

Leisure

AARP Travel Services

601 E. St. NW
Washington, DC 20049

Ph: (800) 424-3410

Offers approximately 250 tours for members and their families.

Elderhostel

11 Avenue de Lafayette
Boston, MA 02110-1746

Ph: (617) 426-7788
Toll-free: (877) 426-8056
http://www.elderhostel.org

Offers programs at educational and cultural institutions around the world to adults age 55 and over. Course areas include intergenerational, crafts, performance arts, and active/outdoor.

Interhostel

University of New Hampshire
6 Garrison Ave.
Durham, NH 03824

(800) 733-9753

Offers an educational and travel adventure with an enhanced awareness of other cultures. Most of its 50 programs are international and last for two weeks. Excursions to historic and cultural sites enhance the classroom experience.

National Senior Golf Association

83 Princeton Ave.
Hopewell, NJ 08525

Ph: (609) 466-0022
Information: (800) 282-6772 or (800) 752-9718
Fax: (609) 466-9366
http://www.amgolftour.com

A membership organization for men and women over 50 who enjoy travel and golf. Holds monthly golf tournaments for amateurs at premier golf resorts. Publishes *Senior Sports News* monthly.

President's Council on Physical Fitness and Sports

200 Independence Ave. SW
Washington, DC 20201-0004

Ph: (202) 690-9000

Produces a pamphlet called *The Fitness Challenge in the Later Years.*

SeniorNet

121 Second St., 7th floor
San Francisco, CA 94105

Ph: (415) 495-4990
Fax: (415) 495-3999
http://www.seniornet.org

Educates seniors (50+) in the use of computers and the Internet at over 140 learning centers nationwide. Web site provides online discussions as well as locations of learning centers.

Senior Partners in Education

Family Literacy Center
Indiana University
Smith Research Center, Suite 140
Bloomington, IN 47408-2698

Ph: (800) 759-4723
Fax: (812) 856-5512

http://www.indiana.edu/~eric_rec/seniors/intro.html

Pen pal program that matches seniors with students from kindergarten through teen years.

Superintendent of Documents

PO Box 371954
Pittsburgh, PA 15250-7954

Ph: (202) 512-1800

Offers booklets dealing with foreign travel, such as: *Your Trip Abroad: Customs, Shots, Insurance; A Safe Trip Abroad; Travel Tips for Older Americans;* and *Foreign Entry Requirements.*

Services

Organizations

Aging Network Services

4400 East-West Hwy., Suite 907
Bethesda, MD 20814

Ph: (301) 657-4329

http://www.agingnets.com

Geriatric social workers who serve as care managers for aging parents.

American Red Cross

430 17th St. NW
Washington, DC 20006

Ph: (202) 737-8300

http://www.redcross.org

Local chapters offer programs such as retirement planning, crime prevention instruction, safety courses, shopper/chore programs, telephone reassurance, health screening clinics, visitation, and home nursing care instruction.

B'nai B'rith

1640 Rhode Island Ave. NW
Washington, DC 20036

Ph: (202) 857-6600
The CaringNetwork: (800) 222-1188
Travel/Volunteer Programs: (800) 500-6533
Fax: (202) 857-1099

http://bnaibrith.org

Builds and maintains federally subsidized apartment houses for older adults. Also provides travel and travel/volunteer programs for seniors and their families. The CaringNetwork is a fee-for-service program that offers information, referrals, and advice.

Catholic Charities USA

1731 King St., Suite 200
Alexandria, VA 22314

Ph: (703) 549-1390
Fax: (703) 549-1656

http://www.catholiccharitiesusa.org

Provides services to older people, including counseling, homemaker services, foster family programs, group homes and institutional care, public access programs, caregiver services, and emergency assistance and shelter.

Catholic Golden Age

RD # 2, Box 161
Olyphant, PA 18447

Toll-free Information: (800) 836-5699
Fax: (570) 586-7721

Helps older people meet their social, physical, economic, intellectual, and spiritual needs. Offers various group insurance plans, as well as discounts on eyeglasses, prescription drugs, and travel.

Children of Aging Parents

1609 Woodbourne Rd., Suite 302-A
Levittown, PA 19057

Ph: (215) 945-6900
Toll-free Information and Referral: (800) 227-7294
Fax (215) 945-8720

http://www.caps4caregivers.org

Provides information, local resources, and emotional support to caregivers of older people. Members receive *The Capsule*, a bimonthly newsletter. Web site offers a state-by-state eldercare search.

Family Caregiver Alliance

690 Market St., Suite 600
San Francisco, CA 94104

Ph: (415) 434-3388
Fax: (415) 434-3508

http://www.caregiver.org

Supports and assists caregivers of brain-impaired adults through education, research, services,and advocacy.

U S Customs Service

1301 Constitution Ave.
PO Box 7404
Washington, DC 20044

Produces a free booklet, *Know Before You Go,* for foreign travel.

Volunteers of America (VOA)

1660 Duke St.
Alexandria, VA 22314

Ph: (703) 341-5000
Information Service: (800) 899-0089

http://www.voa.org

Provides affordable senior housing, assisted living and nursing facilities; nutrition services and Meals on Wheels; home health care and home repair services; senior citizen centers and adult day care; congregate meals; transportation; and senior volunteer programs.

Call local affiliate for a list of services offered.

Volunteering

Organizations

Corporation for National and Community Service

1201 New York Ave. NW
Washington, DC 20525

Ph: (202) 606-5000
Toll-free Information: (800) 424-8867
Fax: (202) 565-2794

http://www.nationalservice.org or
http://www.seniorcorps.org

The National Senior Service Corps (Senior Corps) helps people age 55 and older find service opportunities in their home communities. In the Foster Grandparent Program, older people serve as mentors and tutors to children with special needs. Retired and Senior Volunteers Program (RSVP) participants offer their services to education, service, and other community organizations. *Senior* Companion Programvolunteers provide supportive services to older adults. AmericaCorps VISTA, a program not only for seniors, places volunteers for a full year in disadvantaged communities in order to help local public agencies and non-profit groups address community needs. Web site provides listings of each volunteer program by state.

Elder Craftsmen

610 Lexington Ave.
New York, NY 10022

Ph: (212) 319-8128
Fax: (202) 319-8141

http://www.eldercraftsmen.org

The Elder Crafters Helping Others program enlists former craftsmen to make and contribute items for sick, homeless, or otherwise needy children.

Environmental Alliance for Senior Involvement (EASI)

8733 Old Dumfries Rd.
POB 750
Catlett, VA 20119

Ph: (540) 788-3274
Fax: (540) 788-9301

http://www.easi.org

Recruits and trains seniors for environmental projects.

International Executive Service Corps (IESC)

333 Ludlow St.
POB 10005
Stamford, CT 06902

Ph: (800) 243-4372 or (203) 967-6000
Fax: (203) 324-2531

http://www.iesc.org

Volunteers provide technical and managerial expertise to developing countries and emerging democracies. Most projects last from one to three months. Web site provides list of volunteer openings in the United States and overseas.

Literacy Volunteers of America

635 James St.
Syracuse, NY 13203-2214

Ph: (315) 472-0001
Fax: (315) 472-0002

http://www.literacyvolunteers.org

National program that trains volunteer tutors to teach basic literacy and English for speakers of other languages. See Web site for a list of local affiliates.

Meals on Wheels Association of America (MOWAA)

1414 Prince St., Suite 302
Alexandria, VA 22314

Ph: (703) 548-5558
Fax: (703) 548-8024

http://www.projectmeal.org

Provides home-delivered meal services to people in need.

National Court Appointed Special Advocate Association (CASA)

100 W. Harrison St.
North Tower, Suite 500
Seattle, WA 98119-4123

(800) 628-3233

Volunteers support children caught in the foster care system by reviewing case records, interviewing adults involved, and speaking for children at court hearings.

National Executive Service Corps

120 Wall St.
New York, NY 10005

(212) 269-1234

Advises nonprofit organizations, especially in the areas of health care, social services, education, culture, and religion.

National Health Information Center

PO Box 1133
Washington, DC 20013-1133

(800) 336-4797

Lists organizations and self-help and support groups for getting involved in helping to care for the sick.

National Park Service

1849 C St. NW
Washington, DC 20240

Ph: (202) 208-6843

http://www.nps.gov/volunteer

Volunteers in Parks *(VIP)* program. Volunteers may work part-time, seasonally, or full-time in almost every park in the National Park System. Web site provides nationwide list of volunteer opportunities, as well as contact information for regional offices and local parks.

Points of Light Foundation

1400 I St. NW, Suite 800
Washington, DC 20005

Ph: (202) 729-8000
Information: (800) VOLUNTEER
Fax: (202) 729-8100

http://www.pointsoflight.org

Connect Americaprogram joins forces with other organizations to encourage volunteers to engage in all kinds of community service in order to help solve serious social problems. Web site offers list of local volunteer centers to contact.

SERVEnet

1101 15th St., Suite 200
Washington, DC 20005

Ph: (202) 296-2992

http://www.servenet.org

Matches volunteers with opportunities.

Service Corps of Retired Executives (SCORE)

409 3rd St. SW, 6th Floor
Washington, DC 20024

Ph: (800) 634-0245

http://www.score.org

Retired executives help train and mentor small-business owners and operators.

Shepherd's Centers of America

One W. Armour Blvd., Suite 201
Kansas City, MO 64111

Ph: (816) 960-2022
Fax: (816) 960-1083

http://www.shepherdcenters.org

Coordinates over 100 centers in 26 states that help older adults through in-home and community services. Volunteers, who are older adults themselves, deliver meals, repair houses, and give caregivers respite. Web site provides updated list of centers, as well as information on how to start a center.

United Way of America

701 N. Fairfax St.
Alexandria, VA 22314-2045

Ph: (703) 836-7100
Information: (800) 411-8929
Fax: (703) 683-7813

http://www.unitedway.org

A national system of volunteers, contributors, and charities that support local community programs. Locate nearest local United Way in phone book or call toll-free information number. Web site offers links to local United Way Web sites.

USDA Forest Service

201 14th St. SW at Independence Ave.
Washington, DC 20250

http://www.fs.fed.us/people/programs/volunteer

Offers information on three volunteer programs, Volunteers in the National Forests, Council on International Educational Exchange, and Volunteers for Peace. Write or call the nearest Forest Service office for more information. Look in phone book under "U.S. Government" and "Department of Agriculture, Forest Service." Web site also provides a Forest Service directory.

Volunteer Talent Bank

AARP
601 E St. NW
Washington, DC 20049

Ph: (202) 434-3219
Fax: (800) 424-3410, ext. 3219

A referral service that matches the skills and interests of people over 50 with the needs of AARP projects, and with other national organizations such as Special Olympics International, the U.S. Forest Service, Habitat for Humanity, and Big Brothers/Big Sisters of America.

Volunteers for Peace (VFP)

1034 Tiffany Rd.
Belmont, VT 05730-0202

Ph: (802) 259-2759
Fax: (802) 259-2922

http://www.vfp.org

Offers over 1,500 short-term International Workcamps for volunteer service projects. Web site has a workcamp directory updated weekly.

Volunteers of America (VOA)

National Office
1660 Duke St.
Alexandria, VA 22314

Ph: (800) 899-0089 or (703) 341-5000

http://www.voa.org

Service areas include youth, families, the elderly, the homeless, and corrections. Sponsors Meals on Wheels and RSVP programs for volunteers over 55. Contact nearest affiliate for services offered. Web site provides links to local affiliates.

Internet

AARP Tax Aide Program

http://www.aarp.org/taxaide

Free, volunteer-run tax preparation service for middle-and low-income taxpayers, especially for those 60 and older.

Impact Online

http://www.impactonline.org

Provides *Volunteer Match*, an online matching service for volunteers and organizations; Virtual Volunteering, which allows anyone to volunteer services from their home or office; and advice on finding the right volunteer opportunity.

Volunteer Opportunities for Older Americans

http://www.aoa.dhhs.gov/aoa/eldractn/voluntr.html

Information on volunteering opportunities for federal programs.

Women

Organizations

AARP Women's Initiative

601 E., St. NW
Washington, DC 20049

Ph: (202) 434-2400

http://www.aarp.org/programs/women

Call for information on specific topics. Web site provides an overview of women's issues with a contact list of resources.

National Black Women's Health Project

600 Pennsylvania Ave. SE, Suite 310
Washington, DC 20003

Ph: (202) 543-9311
Fax: (202) 543-9743

http://www.nbwhp.org

Provides wellness education and services, self-help group development, health information, and advocacy to black women. Members receive newsletters and educational data.

National Center on Women and Aging

Heller Graduate School
MS 035
Brandeis University
Waltham, MA 02454-9110

Ph: (781) 736-3866
Information Services: (800) 929-1995
Fax: (781) 736-3865

http://www.brandeis.edu/heller/national/ind.html

Promotes the security, health, and dignity of older women. Publishes *The Women and Aging Letter,* a bimonthly newsletter that provides information on health, pensions, living options, caregiving, financial planning, and other topics. Consumer booklets on memory enhancement and estrogen replacement available for a small fee.

National Coalition Against Domestic Violence

PO Box 18749
Denver, CO 80218-0749

Ph: (303) 839-1852
National Domestic Violence Hotline: (800) 799-7233
Fax: (303) 831-9251

http://www.ncadv.org

Call hotline or locate a state coalition office at the Web site to learn about the nearest shelter or support. Web site also offers guidelines for getting help.

National Women's Health Network

514 10th St. NW, Suite 400
Washington, DC 20004

Ph: (202) 347-1140
Fax: (202) 347-1168

http://www.womenshealthnetwork.org

Clearinghouse of information on women's health issues. Publishes bimonthly newsletter about women's health topics, including lobbying efforts of the Network.

National Women's Health Resource Center

120 Albany St., Suite 820
New Brunswick, NJ 08901

Ph: (732) 828-8575
Information: (877) 986-9472
Fax: (732) 249-4671

http://www.healthywomen.org

A national clearinghouse for women's health information. Publishes *The National Women's Health Report,* a bimonthly newsletter with information about preventive care. NSHRC staff will perform topic-specific research on personal health concerns, free of charge for members. Maintains a database of health resources. Web site offers links to health resources for women.

Older Women's League (OWL)

666 11th St. NW, Suite 700
Washington, DC 20001

Ph: (202) 783-6686
OWL PowerLine: (202) 783-6689
Information: (800) 825-3695

Advocacy group that addresses the concerns of midlife and older women. Publishes *OWL Observer* and *The Field Advocate,* which informs members of public policy issues.

Women Work!

National Network for Women's Employment
1625 K St. NW, Suite 300
Washington, DC 20006

Ph: (202) 467-6346
Information and Referral: (800) 235-2732

http://www.womenwork.org

Provides education, training, and employment programs for women. Web site has contact list of state affiliates.

Women's Bureau Clearinghouse

U.S. Department of Labor
200 Constitution Ave. NW, Rm. S-3002
Washington, DC 20210-0002

Ph: (202) 693-6710
Information: (800) 827-5335
Fax: (202) 693-6725

http://www.dol.gov/dol/wb

Focuses on rights of women in the workplace. Offers free *Resource Kit* of information on work and family; *Don't Work in the Dark: Know-Your-Rights,* information about women's rights in the workplace, as well as other brochures.

The Women's Connection

5030 38 Ave.
Moline, IL 61265

Ph: (309) 762-3940 or (866) 762-3940
Fax: (309) 762-3940

http://www.womensconnectionqc.com

Sponsors events in the Iowa/Illinois area that focus on health or finance issues from a woman's point of view. Web site offers *WomeNews* on similar topics and free online *CyberConnections.*

Women's Institute for a Secure Retirement (WISER)

1201 Pennsylvania Ave. NW, Suite 619
Washington, DC 20004

http://www.wiser.heinz.org

Publishes a quarterly newsletter, *WISERWoman*

Web site has information on pensions, social security, savings and assets, long-term care insurance, divorce, and widowhood.

Internet

MoneyMinded: What Every Woman Needs to Know About Money and Retirement

http://www.moneyminded.com/security/retir/48bklt11.htm

Good Housekeeping booklet. Subjects include IRAs, calculating your nest egg, retirement myths about Social Security and savings, survivors' pension and 401(k) benefits, and protecting retirement after divorce, as well as links to information on insurance and health care, estate planning, and finding a financial planner.

Women and Pensions

http://www.asec.org/wopens.htm

American Savings Education Council Web site provides information and sources about women and retirement.

WomenCONNECT.com

http://www.womenconnect.com/LocLink/MONC/RETIRE

Information for women on retirement planning.

Part IV: Retirement Planning Tools and Forms

Estimating an Annual Retirement Budget

How do you make sure you'll have enough income to live on in retirement? The answer starts with careful planning. This worksheet should help you see where you stand now.

Instructions:

1. List your current income and expenses as completely as possible.
2. Adjust for inflation. Multiply your current annual expenses by the inflation factor for the number of years until you retire. (Inflation rates of 4% and 5%, compounded annually, are represented here. This rate may vary from year to year. If you want to be more conservative, figure inflation at 5%.)

Income

Salary	$________
Bonuses	$________
Pension	$________
Social Security	$________
Other income/ Annuities	$________
Profit-sharing plan	$________
Dividends/ Capital gains	$________
Interest	$________
Rents	$________
Bank/Credit union accts.	$________
Certificates of deposit	$________
Other investments/ income	$________
Total Annual Income	**$________**

Expenses

Rent/mortgage	$
Insurance:	$
Health	$
Homeowner's	$
Auto	$
Taxes:	$
Federal	$
State	$
Local	$
Loan payments	$
Credit card/installment payments	$
Food	$
Clothes	$
Medications/other medical expenses	$
Home maintenance	$
Auto maintenance	$
Other transportation costs (commuting, gas, etc.)	$
Utilities	$
Telephone	$
Major purchases	$
Entertainment	$
Vacations	$
Charitable contributions	$
Emergency fund	$
Misc. expenses	$
Current Annual Expenses	$

Expenses

Inflation Adjustment (Inflation factor below based on no. of yrs to retirement)	X
Inflation-adjusted annual expenses at retirement*	$

* Note: You may have fewer expenses during retirement. Many retirement calculators estimate 60% to 80% of your current expenses.

Inflation Factor at 4% and 5%

Years to retirement	4% Inflation factor	5% Inflation factor
1	1.04	1.05
2	1.08	1.10
3	1.12	1.16
4	1.17	1.22
5	1.22	1.28
6	1.27	1.34
7	1.32	1.40
8	1.37	1.48
9	1.42	1.55
10	1.48	1.63
11	1.54	1.71
12	1.60	1.80
13	1.67	1.89
14	1.73	1.98
15	1.80	2.08
16	1.87	2.18
17	1.95	2.29
18	2.03	2.40
19	2.11	2.52
20	2.19	2.65

Net Worth Statement

Assets

Cash on hand	$
Checking accounts	$
Savings accounts	$
Savings bonds	$
Credit union accounts	$
Money market accounts	$
Certificates of deposit	$
Mutual funds	$
Stocks/Bonds	$
Life insurance (cash value)	$
IRA, SEP, or 401(k) accounts.	$
Annuities	$
Business interests	$
Residence	$
Vacation home	$
Other real estate	$
Furnishings (value)	$
Automobiles	$
Jewelry/Art	$
Other property	$
Total Assets	**$**

Liabilities

Mortgages (principal)	$
Auto loans	$
Other loans	$
Charge/Credit card balances	$
Other debts/ Contractual obligations	$
Taxes owed:	
Federal	$
State	$
Local	$
Total Liabilities	**$**

Total Net Worth

Total Assets – Total Liabilities	$

Organizing Your Important Documents

As you begin your estate planning, be sure to gather all the important documents you'll need, keep them in a safe place, and let your family know where that is.

Personal

Birth certificates
Adoption documents
Marriage license, prenuptial agreement
Divorce decree

Estate documents

Life insurance policies
Wills
Living wills

Trust documents

Insurance
Personal property/liability
Health
Homeowner's
Disability
Long-term care

Financial

Social Security cards
Property deeds or leases
Net worth statement
Recent income tax returns (3–5 years)
Pension statements
List of investments
Stock/bond certificates
Contracts

Five Wishes[*]

How to get copies of *Five Wishes*™

If you would like a copy of *Five Wishes*™ for yourself, family, or friends, please send $4 per copy. Individuals and organizations making bulk requests (10 copies or more) are asked to send $1 per copy. Check or money orders may be made payable to Aging with Dignity. Send requests to: Aging with Dignity, P.O. Box 1661, Tallahassee, FL 32302-1661. *Five Wishes*™ is also available in Spanish.

AGING with Dignity

FIVE WISHES™

FOR

Print Your Name

Print Your Birth Date

My Wish For:

1. The Person I Want To Make Care Decisions For Me When I Can't
2. The Kind of Medical Treatment I Want or Don't Want
3. How Comfortable I Want To Be
4. How I Want People To Treat Me
5. What I Want My Loved Ones To Know

Five Wishes makes it easier for you to let your doctor, family, and friends know how you want to be treated if you become seriously ill and cannot tell them. *Five Wishes* is a gift to your family members and friends so that they won't have to guess what you want. *Five Wishes* is easy to understand and simple to use.

FIVE WISHES

has captured the hearts and minds of people in Florida from the day it was introduced. Hundreds of thousands of Floridians are using *Five Wishes*, including Florida's Governor, Supreme Court Chief Justice, and thousands of others.

Because *Five Wishes* was so successful in Florida, it was featured on the NBC Today Show. Aging with Dignity wanted to see if it could be used in other states. We consulted experts who reviewed the laws of all fifty states. We found out that *Five Wishes* could be written in a way that made it valid under the health care statutes in most states.

With the help of the American Bar Association Commission on Legal Problems of the Elderly, we came up with this new version of *Five Wishes*. We are confident that *Five Wishes* meets the legal requirements under the health decisions statutes of 33 states and the District of Columbia.

FIVE WISHES STATES

If you live in the District of Columbia or one of the 33 states listed below, you can use *Five Wishes* and have the peace of mind to know that it meets your state's requirements under the law:

Arizona	Idaho	Mississippi	Pennsylvania
Arkansas	Illinois	Missouri	Rhode Island
Colorado	Iowa	Montana	South Dakota
Connecticut	Louisiana	Nebraska	Tennessee
Delaware	Maine	New Jersey	Virginia
District of Columbia	Maryland	New Mexico	Washington
Florida	Massachusetts	New York	Wyoming
Georgia	Michigan	North Carolina	
Hawaii	Minnesota	North Dakota	

Unfortunately, if your state is not one of the 33 states listed above, *Five Wishes* does **not** meet the technical requirements in the statutes of your state, and some doctors in your state may be reluctant to honor *Five Wishes*. However, you can still use *Five Wishes* to put your wishes in writing. This will be a helpful guide to your care providers. Most doctors and health care professionals understand that they have a duty to listen to your wishes no matter how you express them.

Talk to your doctor during your next office visit. Give your doctor a copy of *Five Wishes* and ask to have a talk about it. Make sure your doctor understands your wishes and will honor them. Ask him or her to urge other doctors treating you to honor them.

You have a legal and moral right to decide what kind of medical treatment you want or don't want when you are seriously ill and your death is expected. You also have a right to choose a person to make health care decisions for you when you are no longer able to speak or think clearly. *Five Wishes* helps you exercise these rights. But remember, your doctor needs to know, and be willing to follow, your wishes.

PART A

1 The Person I Want To Make Health Care Decisions For Me When I Can't Make Them For Myself

If I am no longer able to make my own health care decisions, this form names the person I choose to make these choices for me. This person will be my Health Care Agent (or other term that may be used in my state, such as proxy, representative, or surrogate).

This person will make my health care choices if both of these things happen:

1) My attending or treating doctor finds that I am no longer able to make health care choices,

AND

2) Another health care professional agrees that this is true.

PICKING THE RIGHT PERSON TO BE YOUR HEALTH CARE AGENT

Choose someone who knows you very well and cares about you, and who can make difficult decisions. Sometimes a spouse or family member is not the best choice because they are too emotionally involved with you. Sometimes they are the best choice. You know best. Make sure you choose someone who is able to stand up for you so that your wishes are followed. Also, choose someone who is likely to be nearby so that they are ready to help you when you need them.

Whether you choose your spouse, family member or friend to be your Health Care Agent, make sure you talk about your wishes with this person and that he or she agrees to respect and follow them.

Your Health Care Agent should be at least **18 years or older** (in Colorado, 21 years or older) and should not be:

- your health care provider, including owner or operator of a health or residential or community care facility serving you.
- an employee of your health care provider.
- serving as an agent or proxy for 10 or more people unless he or she is your spouse or close relative.

The person I choose as my Health Care Agent is:

____
NAME

____
PHONE NUMBER

____
ADDRESS

____
CITY/STATE/ZIP

If this person

- Is not able or willing to make these choices for me,
- Is divorced or legally separated from me,

  OR
- This person has died,

Then these people are my next choices:

____
SECOND CHOICE NAME

____
PHONE NUMBER

____
ADDRESS

____
CITY/STATE/ZIP

____
THIRD CHOICE NAME

____
PHONE NUMBER

____
ADDRESS

____
CITY/STATE/ZIP

I understand that my Health Care Agent can make health care decisions for me. I want my Agent to be able to do the following **(Please cross out anything you don't want your Agent to do that is listed below):**

- Make choices for me about my medical care or services, like tests, medicine, or surgery. This care or service could be to find out what my health problem is, or how to treat it. It can also include care to keep me alive. If the treatment or care has already started, my Health Care Agent can keep it going or have it stopped.
- Interpret any instructions I have given in this form or given in other discussions, according to my Health Care Agent's understanding of my wishes and values.
- Arrange for admission to a hospital, hospice, or nursing home for me. My Health Care Agent can hire any kind of health care worker I may need to help me or take care of me. My Agent may also fire a health care worker, if needed.
- Make the decision to request, take away or not give medical treatments, including artificially-provided food and water, and any other treatments to keep me alive.
- See and approve release of my medical records and personal files. If I need to sign my name to get any of these files, my Health Care Agent can sign for me.
- Move me to another state, to carry out my wishes. My Health Care Agent can also move me to another state for other reasons.
- Take any legal action needed to carry out my wishes.
- Apply for Medicare, Medicaid, or other programs or insurance benefits for me. My Health Care Agent can see my personal files, like bank records, to find out what is needed to fill out these forms.
- Listed below are any changes, additions, or other limitations on my Health Care Agent's powers:

____
____
____
____
____
____
____
____

If I change my mind about having a Health Care Agent, I will:

- Destroy all copies of this Part of the Five Wishes form, OR
- Write the word "Revoked" in large letters across the name of each agent whose authority I want to cancel and signing my name on that page, OR
- Tell someone, such as my doctor or family, that I want to cancel or change my Health Care Agent.

2 My Wish For The Kind Of Medical Treatment I Want Or Don't Want

I believe that my life is precious and I deserve to be treated with dignity. When the time comes that I am very sick and am not able to speak for myself, I want the following wishes, and any other instructions I have given to my Health Care Agent, to be respected and followed.

The instructions that I am including in this section are to let my family, my doctors and other health care providers, my friends and all others know the kind of medical treatment that I want or don't want.

A. General Instructions

- I do not want to be in pain. I want my doctor to give me enough medicine to relieve my pain, even if that means that I will be drowsy or sleep more than I would otherwise.
- I do not want anything done or omitted by my doctors or nurses *with the intention of taking my life.*
- I want to be offered food and fluids by mouth, and kept clean and warm.

B. Meaning of "Life-Support Treatment"

Life-support treatment means any medical procedure, device or medication to keep me alive. Life-support treatment includes: medical devices put in me to help me breathe; food and water supplied artificially by medical device (tube feeding); cardiopulmonary resuscitation (CPR); major surgery; blood transfusions; dialysis; and antibiotics.

If I wish to limit the meaning of life-support treatment, I write this limitation in the space below :

____

____

____

____

____

____

____

____

____

____

____

____

____

____

____

____

C. If I am close to death:

If my doctor and another health care professional both decide that I am likely to die within a short period of time, and life-support treatment would only postpone the moment of my death **(choose *one* of the following):**

☐ I want to have life-support treatment.

☐ I want to have life-support treatment if my doctor believes it could help, but I want my doctor to stop giving me life-support treatment if it is not helping my health condition or symptoms.

☐ I do not want life-support treatment. If it has been started, I want it stopped.

D. If I am in a coma and I am not expected to wake up or recover:
If my doctor and another health care professional both decide that I am in a coma from which I am not expected to wake up or recover, and I have brain damage, and life-support treatment would only postpone the moment of my death **(choose *one* of the following):**

- ☐ I want to have life-support treatment.
- ☐ I want to have life-support treatment if my doctor believes it could be helpful, but I want my doctor to stop giving me life-support treatment if it is not helping my health condition or symptoms.
- ☐ I do not want life-support treatment. If it has been started, I want it stopped.

E. If I have permanent and severe brain damage and I am not expected to recover:
If my doctor and another health care professional both decide that I have permanent and severe brain damage, (for example, I can open my eyes, I can not speak or understand) and I am not expected to recover, and life-support treatment would only postpone the moment of my death **(choose *one* of the following):**

- ☐ I want to have life-support treatment.
- ☐ I want to have life-support treatment if my doctor believes it could help, but I want my doctor to stop giving me life-support treatment if it is not helping my health condition or symptoms.
- ☐ I do not want life-support treatment. If it has been started, I want it stopped.

F. If I am in another condition under which I do not wish to be kept alive:
If there is another condition under which I do not wish to have life-support treatment, I describe it below. In this condition, I believe that the costs and burdens of life-support treatment are too much and not worth the benefits to me. Therefore, in this condition, I do not want life-support treatment. (Please write the condition or conditions in the space below, or leave the space blank if you have none):

____
____
____
____
____
____
____
____
____
____
____
____
____
____
____

When you talk with your family, doctor, Health Care Agent, and priest, minister or rabbi about what you have chosen, you may feel that the above instructions do not express all of your wishes, or your own religious beliefs. Please use the space below to make very clear what you want, and under what conditions.

____
____
____
____

Part B

I want to be treated with dignity near the end of my life as Part A of Five Wishes is followed. To be treated with dignity means that I would like people to do the things written in Part B when it can be done.

I understand that my family, my doctors and other health care providers, my friends, and others may not be able to do the things, or are not required by law to do the things written in Part B.

I do not expect my wishes in Part B to place new or added legal duties on my doctors or other health care providers. I also do not expect these wishes in Part B to excuse my doctor or other health care providers from giving me the proper care asked for by law.

3 My Wish For How Comfortable I Want To Be

(Please cross out anything that you ***don't*** *agree with)*

- I do not want to be in pain. I want my doctor to give me enough medicine to relieve my pain, even if that means that I will be drowsy or sleep more than I would otherwise.
- If I show signs of depression, nausea, shortness of breath, or hallucinations, I want my caregivers to do whatever they can to help me.
- I wish to have a cool moist cloth put on my head if I have a fever.
- I want my lips and mouth kept moist to stop dryness.
- I wish to have warm baths often. I wish to be kept fresh and clean at all times.
- I wish to be massaged with warm oils as often as I can be.
- I wish to have my favorite music played when possible until my time of death.
- I wish to have personal care like shaving, nail clipping, hair brushing, and teeth brushing, as long as they do not cause me pain or discomfort.
- I wish to have religious readings and well loved poems read aloud when I am near death.

4 My Wish For How I Want People To Treat Me

(Please cross out anything that you ***don't*** *agree with)*

- I wish to have people with me when possible. I want someone to be with me when it seems that death may come at any time.
- I wish to have my hand held and to be talked to when possible, even if I don't seem to respond to the voice or touch of others.
- I wish to have others by my side praying for me when possible.
- I wish to have the members of my church or synagogue told that I am sick and asked to pray for me and visit me.
- I wish to be cared for with kindness and cheerfulness, and not sadness.
- I wish to have pictures of my loved ones in my room, near my bed.
- If I am not able to control my bowel or bladder functions, I wish for my clothes and bed linens to be kept clean, and for them to be changed as soon as they can be if they have been soiled.
- I want to die in my home, if that can be done.

5 My Wish For What I Want My Loved Ones To Know

(Please cross out anything that you ***don't*** *agree with)*

- I wish to have my family members and loved ones know that I love them.
- I wish to be forgiven for the times I have hurt my family, friends, and others.
- I wish to have my family members and friends know that I forgive them for what they may have done to me in my life.
- I wish for my family members and loved ones to know that because of the faith I have, I do not fear death itself. I think it is not the end, but a new beginning for me.
- I wish for all of my family members to make peace with each other before my death, if they can.
- I wish for my family and friends to think about what I was like before I had a terminal illness. I want them to remember me in this way after my death.
- I wish for my family and friends to look at my dying as a time of personal growth for everyone, including me. This will help me live a meaningful life in my final days.
- I wish for my family and friends to get counseling if they have trouble with my death. I want memories of my life to give them joy and not sorrow.

If anyone asks how I want to be remembered, please say the following about me:

____

____

____

____

The following person knows my funeral wishes: ________________________

If there is to be a memorial service for me, I wish for this service to include the following *(list music, songs, readings or other specific requests that you have)*:

____

____

____

____

Add other wishes here *(such as your wishes about donating any or all parts of your body when you die)*:

____

____

____

____

____

____

Residents of Institutions in Connecticut, Delaware, Georgia, New York, and North Dakota Must Follow Special Witnessing Rules

If you live in certain institutions (a nursing home or other licensed long term care facility, a home for the mentally retarded or developmentally disabled, or a mental health institution) in the states of Connecticut, Delaware, Georgia, New York or North Dakota, you may have to follow special "witnessing requirements" for your *Five Wishes* to be valid. For further information on what you need to do if you live in an institution in one of these five states and want to fill out *Five Wishes*, please contact a social worker or patient advocate at your institution.

If you live in Connecticut, Delaware, Georgia, New York or North Dakota, and you do not live in an institution, then you can fill out the *Five Wishes* form just the way it is.

Signing the Five Wishes Form

Please make sure you sign your Five Wishes form in the presence of the two witnesses. Make sure they sign their names in your presence. You do not need to have this form notarized unless you live in Hawaii, Missouri or North Carolina (see below).

I, ______________________ (Print Your Name), ask that my family, my doctors and other health care providers, my friends, and all others, follow my wishes as communicated by my Health Care Agent (if I have one and he or she is available), or as otherwise expressed in this form. If any part of this form cannot be legally followed, I ask that all other parts of this form be followed.

Signature: ______________________________

Address: ______________________________

____

Phone #: ______________________ Date: ____________

Signatures Should Be Notarized in Hawaii, Missouri and North Carolina

If you live in Hawaii or North Carolina, you should have your signature, and the signatures of your witnesses, notarized on page 8. If you live in Missouri, only your signature should be notarized.

Five Wishes is meant to be a helpful resource for you as you talk with your doctor, family and others about how you want to be treated when you are seriously ill. *Five Wishes* does not try to answer all questions about all situations you may come up against. And remember, while the information in this booklet is up-to-date as of the date it was published, laws can change quickly! So if you have a specific question or problem, you should talk to a professional for medical or legal advice.

WITNESS STATEMENT (2 witnesses needed):

I declare that the person who signed or acknowledged this form (hereafter "person") is personally known to me, that he/she signed or acknowledged this [Health Care Agent and/or Living Will form(s)] in my presence, and that he/she appears to be of sound mind and under no duress, fraud, or undue influence.

I also declare that **I am over 19 years of age and am NOT**:

- the individual appointed as (agent/proxy/surrogate/ patient advocate) by this document,
- the person's health care provider, including owner or operator of a health, long-term care, or other residential or community care facility serving the person,
- an employee of the person's health care provider,
- financially responsible for the person's health care,
- an employee of a life or health insurance provider for the person,
- related to the person by blood, marriage, or adoption, and,
- to the best of my knowledge, a creditor of the person or entitled to any part of his/her estate under a will or codicil, by operation of law.

Signature of Witness (1) ______________________________

Print Name of Witness ______________________________

Address ______________________________

____

Phone Number(s) ______________________________

Signature of Witness (2) ______________________________

Print Name of Witness ______________________________

Address ______________________________

____

Phone Number(s) ______________________________

If you are a resident of Hawaii, Missouri, or North Carolina, you should have the following completed. If you live in any other state, you do not need to have the following completed.

NOTARIZATION

STATE OF ______________________)
)ss.
COUNTY OF______________________)

On this _____ day of ______________, 19/20____ , the said __________________ ______________________________, and ________________________, known to me (or satisfactorily proven) to be the person named in the foregoing instrument and witnesses, respectively, personally appeared before me, a Notary Public, within and for the State and County aforesaid, and acknowledged that they freely and voluntarily executed the same for the purposes stated therein.

My Commission Expires:

____
NOTARY PUBLIC

The Commission on Aging with Dignity is a private, non-profit organization founded in 1996 to affirm and safeguard human dignity, and to promote better care of the dying. Living in Mother Teresa's home for the dying in Washington, DC as a full-time volunteer inspired Aging with Dignity's founder, Jim Towey, to develop *Five Wishes*. If you would like more information on Aging with Dignity, visit our website at *www.agingwithdignity.org*. Or you can write us at P.O. Box 1661, Tallahassee, Florida 32302.

"Jim Towey has been a friend to me for 11 years and has founded* Aging with Dignity *to bring God's love and compassion."

Mother Teresa of Calcutta

Aging with Dignity wishes to thank *Oregon Health Decisions*, an organization which contributed to the drafting of wish number two.

Help Us Help Others...

We are happy to send you *Five Wishes* free of charge. If you can, please send Aging with Dignity a check or money order in the amount of four dollars. It will help us to reduce our mailing and handling costs.

TO ENSURE YOU OR YOUR DOCTORS HAVE ACCESS TO YOUR *FIVE WISHES,* LIFELINE® Healthcare Directives™ IS A SERVICE AVAILABLE TO YOU. FOR MORE INFORMATION ON THIS SERVICE CALL 1-800-562-1931.

Important Notice to Medical Personnel:

I have a Five Wishes™ Living Will

SIGNATURE

Please consult this document and/or my Health Care Agent in case of an emergency. My Health Care Agent is:

NAME

ADDRESS

PHONE

Listed on back of card are locations of copies of my document

My primary care physician is:

NAME

ADDRESS

PHONE

My document is located at:

CUT OUT CARD, FOLD AND LAMINATE FOR SAFEKEEPING

AGING with Dignity

FIVE WISHES™

AGING WITH DIGNITY
P.O. Box 1661
Tallahassee, Florida 32302-1661
www.agingwithdignity.org

The *Five Wishes* project is supported by a generous grant from
The Robert Wood Johnson Foundation
Princeton, New Jersey

Checklist for Choosing an Assisted Living Community

The following is a consumer checklist of important services, amenities, and accommodations in assisted living communities. Every community is unique. Be sure to make several visits, at various times of day, to each residence you are considering.

Ask for written material. The Assisted Living Federation of America (ALFA) recommends that all providers have a written statement or copies of their resident agreement outlining, at a minimum, services, prices, extra charges, admission and discharge criteria, staffing, and house rules. For examples of "model" forms, visit www.alfa.org. A disclosure statement may also be available discussing ownership and the financial solvency of the provider.

As you start your search, assess your needs as they are now and ask each provider how they might accommodate any changes over time. It is also important to examine your finances and ask about costs. Monthly rates and fee structures vary.

If you are seeking a residence for someone who cannot visit the residence personally, respect their needs and wishes by including them in the process as much as possible. To help, many homes now offer videotapes or "virtual tours."

Consider the following as you visit and assess an assisted living residence:

Atmosphere

- Good location and outward appearance.
- Attractive and homelike decor.
- Residents socialize with each other and appear happy and comfortable.
- Residents seem to be appropriate housemates for you or your loved one.
- Staff are appropriately dressed, personable, and outgoing.
- Staff members treat each other in a professional manner.
- Visits with the resident are welcome at any time.

Physical Features

- Community is well designed for resident's needs.
- The floor plan is easy to follow.
- Doorways, hallways, and rooms are accommodating to wheelchairs and walkers.
- Elevators are available for those unable to use stairways.
- Hand rails are available to aid in walking.
- Cupboards and shelves are easy to reach.
- Floors are of a nonskid material and carpets are firm to ease walking.
- Has good natural and artificial lighting.
- Is clean, free of odors, and appropriately heated/cooled.
- Meets local and/or state licensing requirements.
- Has sprinklers and clearly marked exits.
- Has a means of security if a resident wanders.

Needs Assessments, Contracts, Costs, and Finances

- A contractual agreement is available that discloses health-care and supportive services, all fees, and admission and discharge criteria.
- There is a written plan for the care of each resident.
- Residence has a process for assessing a potential resident's need for services and for ensuring that those needs are addressed periodically.
- The process includes the resident, his or her family, and facility staff, along with the potential resident's physician.

- Staff is available to meet scheduled and unscheduled needs.
- Billing, payment, and credit policies seem fair and reasonable.

Answer these questions about contracts, payments, and policies:

- When may a contract be terminated and what are the refund and transfer policies?
- Are there any government, private, or corporate programs available to help cover the cost of services to the resident?
- Are additional services available if the resident's needs change? If so, is there a procedure to pay for additional services like nursing care when the services are needed on a temporary basis?
- Are there different costs for various levels or categories of services?
- Are residents required to purchase renters' insurance for personal property in their units?
- Can residents handle their own finances with staff assistance if able, or should a family member or outside party be designated to do so?
- Is there an appeals process for dissatisfied residents?

Medication and Health Care

- Residence has specific policies regarding storage of medication, assistance with medications, training and supervision of staff, and record keeping.
- Is self-administration of medication allowed?
- A staff person is available to coordinate home care visits from a nurse, physical therapist, occupational therapist, etc., if needed.
- Staff is available to assist residents who experience memory, orientation, or judgment losses.
- A physician or nurse visits the resident regularly to provide medical checkups.
- Residence has a clearly stated procedure for responding to a resident's medical emergency.
- To what extent are medical services available and how are they provided?

Services

- A list of available services is provided.
- Staff is available to provide 24-hour assistance with activities of daily living (ADLs) if needed. ADLs include:
- Dressing
- Eating
- Mobility
- Hygiene and grooming
- Bathing, toileting, and incontinence
- Using the telephone
- Shopping
- Laundry
- Residence provides housekeeping services in residents' units.
- Residence provides transportation to doctors' offices, the hairdresser, shopping, and other activities desired by residents.
- Are pharmacy, barber/beautician and/or physical therapy services offered on site?
- Can residents arrange for transportation on fairly short notice?

Individual Unit Features

- Different sizes and types of units are available.
- Are units for single and double occupancy available?
- Do residents have their own lockable doors?
- A 24-hour emergency response system is accessible from the unit.
- Bathrooms are private with accommodations for wheelchairs and walkers.
- Residents can bring their own furnishings for their unit. What may they bring?
- Do all units have a telephone and cable TV? How is billing for those services handled?
- Is a kitchen area/unit provided with a refrigerator, sink, and cooking element?
- May residents keep food in their units?

- May residents smoke in their units? In public spaces?
- May residents decorate their own units?

Social and Recreational Activities

- There is evidence of an organized activities program, such as posted daily schedule, events in progress, reading materials, visitors, etc.
- Do residents participate in activities outside of the residence in the neighboring community?
- Do volunteers, including family members, come into the residence to help with or conduct programs?
- Does the residence create a sense of community by requiring residents to participate in certain activities or perform simple chores for the group as a whole?
- Are residents' pets allowed in the residence? Who is responsible for their care?
- Does the residence have its own pets?

Food Service

- Do dining room menus vary from day to day and meal to meal?
- Three nutritionally balanced meals are provided each day, seven days a week.
- Are snacks available?
- May a resident request special foods?
- Are common dining areas available?
- May residents eat meals in their units?
- May meals be provided at the time a resident would like or are there set times for meals?

In addition to this checklist, look for a general philosophy of care based on 10 principles that make assisted living residents the top priority:

- Offering cost-effective quality care personalized to the individual's needs
- Fostering independence for each resident
- Treating each resident with dignity and respect
- Promoting the individuality of each resident
- Allowing each resident choice of care and lifestyle
- Protecting each resident's right to privacy
- Nurturing the spirit of each resident
- Involving family and friends in care planning and implementation
- Providing a safe, residential environment
- Making the assisted living residence a valuable community asset.

Source: Assisted Living Federation of America (Fairfax, VA). Reprinted by permission. To obtain a free copy of ALFA's consumer guide and checklist brochure, call (703) 691-8100. Visit ALFA's Web site (*www.alfa.org*) for more information.

Index